The Bhagavad Gita

for Daily Living

VOLUME I: THE END OF SORROW

SECOND EDITION

रागद्वेषवियुक्तैस्तु विषयानिन्द्रियैश्चरन् । आत्मवश्यैर्विधेयात्मा प्रसादमधिगच्छति ॥२-६४।
प्रसादे सर्वदुःखानां हानिरस्योपजायते । प्रसन्नचेतसो ह्याशु बुद्धिः पर्यवतिष्ठते ॥२-६५॥

But when you move amidst the world free from attachment and aversion alike, there comes the peace in which all sorrows end, and you live in the wisdom of the Self.

–BHAGAVAD GITA 2:64–65

The Bhagavad Gita

for Daily Living

VOLUME I: THE END OF SORROW

SECOND EDITION

EKNATH EASWARAN

JAICO PUBLISHING HOUSE
Ahmedabad Bangalore Chennai
Delhi Hyderabad Kolkata Mumbai

Published by Jaico Publishing House
A-2 Jash Chambers, 7-A Sir Phirozshah Mehta Road
Fort, Mumbai - 400 001
jaicopub@jaicobooks.com
www.jaicobooks.com

Published in arrangement with
Nilgiri Press
P.O. Box 256, Tomales, California 94971
www.easwaran.org

To be sold only in India, Bangladesh, Bhutan,
Pakistan, Nepal, Sri Lanka and the Maldives.

THE BHAGAVAD GITA FOR DAILY LIVING
Volume I:
The End of Sorrow
ISBN 978-93-91019-83-9
(Set of 3 Volumes)

First Jaico Impression: 1997
First Jaico Impression (Second Edition): 2021
Third Jaico Impression: 2025

Printed by
Nutech Print Services - India, New Delhi

To my Teacher

EKNATH CHIPPU KUNCHI AMMAL

my Grandmother & my Playmate

Table of Contents

FOREWORD TO THE FIRST EDITION

A Living Tree

This practical commentary on the Bhagavad Gita, one of the greatest scriptures of the world, has grown out of the weekly talks given by Sri Eknath Easwaran[1] to a group of his devoted students and friends in Berkeley. The talks, beginning in May 1968, have been carefully recorded and transcribed weekly with the help of many members of Easwaran's āshram, or spiritual family. The transcribed lectures were then compiled and edited under Easwaran's close supervision.

The Gita class, like all of Easwaran's classes, is primarily a preparation and inspiration for the practice of meditation as well as a commentary on a particular scripture. Group meditation follows the hour-long talk, in which Easwaran usually covers one or two verses from the Gita. In these impromptu talks, he may apply the verse to the biggest challenges facing the world today or direct his comments to solving the personal problem of a friend in the audience. But whether talking about local incidents in Berkeley or international issues, his unchanging purpose is to inspire his listeners to practice the Gita in their daily life and to make the Gita a driving force in their consciousness. The purpose of this book is to enable Easwaran's readers, also, to translate the timeless values of the Gita into their daily living through the practice of meditation.

Easwaran began studying Sanskrit, the language of the ancient Hindu scriptures, at the age of ten in his village school in Kerala state, India. He

1. *Easwaran* is the given name by which he is known among his friends; *Eknath* is the name of his ancestral family. *Sri* is used in India as a respectful form of address.

also studied Sanskrit at his ancestral Shiva temple under a priest from a community which is well known in India for its pure Sanskrit tradition. Thoroughly familiar with the Gita in the original Sanskrit, Easwaran is also perfectly at home in English, though Malayalam is his mother tongue. In interpreting the scriptures, however, he relies on neither his Sanskrit nor his English scholarship, but on his experience in meditation and his personal practice of the spiritual life. He grew up in a large joint family in the matrilineal tradition of Kerala, and he considers his mother's mother, the flower of the Eknath family, his spiritual teacher.

It is said that every spiritual teacher has a particular context in which he or she flourishes best. Easwaran is an educator. Formerly, he would say, it was education for scholarship, education for degrees; now it is education for living. Before he came to the United States he was chairman of the Department of English at the University of Nagpur and was devoted to his students and the literature he taught them. After coming to this country on the Fulbright exchange program in 1959, Easwaran began giving talks on meditation and the spiritual life, and the response was so great that in 1961 he established the Blue Mountain Center of Meditation in Berkeley to carry on his work of teaching meditation. Since that time, except for one return to India, he has been giving ongoing classes each week on the practice of meditation and commenting on the writings of the great mystics of all religions, including the *Yoga Sūtras* of Patanjali, the *Little Flowers* of St. Francis, the writings of Meister Eckhart, the Upanishads, the *Bhaktisūtras* of Nārada, the Dhammapada of the Buddha, the Sermon on the Mount, Thomas a Kempis's *Of the Imitation of Christ*, and the Bhagavad Gita. He also teaches courses on meditation and on Mahatma Gandhi for the University of California Extension, Berkeley. In Nagpur, he likes to tell us laughingly, he had a reputation for always dragging Sri Ramakrishna into his lectures on Shakespeare and Shaw. Now, in these talks on the Gita, it is Shakespeare who illustrates the teachings of Sri Ramakrishna and St. Francis. The content has changed, but the context in which Easwaran flourishes cannot be very different: a small but extremely devoted group, perhaps eighty to a hundred, mostly young people of the sort who gravitate to a university town, gathered around in a semicircle to drink in the words of a man who is talking not about something he has read or something he has thought out, but about something he has experienced in his own life.

So this is a very special kind of book. Easwaran likes to say that it has grown like a tree because it issues directly from his life, which is so completely rooted in the Gita that every day he gains a deeper understanding of its teachings during even the most commonplace experiences: sharing ice cream with the āshram children in Santa Rosa, walking with friends down Telegraph Avenue in Berkeley, watching a mime with his wife in San Francisco's Union Square. Every Tuesday night in class this tree would flower, and we would hear these incidents retold as precise, profound illustrations of the Gita's applicability to our modern world. You can follow these incidents in this book, week by week, and at the same time you can trace the growth of the Blue Mountain Center of Meditation itself: the long months of looking for an āshram site, the building and remodeling when Ramagiri Ashram was acquired, the arrival of Easwaran's mother and nieces from India. The result is a living document which, as Easwaran says, is still growing even now, and which will continue to grow as it is read and absorbed by others into their own lives.

Easwaran has chosen to comment on the eighteen chapters of the Gita in three volumes, each volume covering six chapters. It is said that these three parts of the Gita illustrate the profound truth of the Upanishads, *Tat tvam asi:* "That thou art." The first six chapters are an exposition of *tvam,* 'thou,' the Ātman, and reveal the nature of our real, eternal Self. The second six chapters concern *Tat,* 'That': Brahman, the supreme Reality underlying all creation. The last six chapters explain *asi,* 'is,' the relationship between *tvam* and *Tat:* the identity of the Self within and the supreme Reality, which unites all existence into one whole. The Gita develops this truth, "That thou art," in practical terms: by discovering our real Self, we realize the indivisible unity of life and become united with the Divine Ground of existence.

Easwaran would like to convey his appreciation to everyone who has helped with this book, including those who have attended the Gita talks with sustained enthusiasm over the years. He wishes to express his deep love to all the members of his spiritual family who have assisted in translating, recording, transcribing, editing, and printing this commentary on the Gita.

In turn we, the editors, speaking for everyone who has helped, feel that working on this book has been a great privilege. Nachiketa, the student in the Katha Upanishad, tells Yama, "A teacher of this, another like you, is not to be found. No other boon is equal to this at all." The combination of enlightenment and practical, effective teaching in these pages is rare indeed, difficult to find in the modern world.

THE EDITORS

This second edition (2020) incorporates revisions made across all three volumes following the author's final instructions.

INTRODUCTION

The Bhagavad Gita for Daily Living

There is no significant problem in life which cannot be referred to the Bhagavad Gita for a perfect solution. The Gita is one of the most powerful of the Sanskrit scriptures of ancient India, but in my eyes it is neither philosophy nor theology, metaphysics nor poetry. It is a practical manual for daily living in any age, in any religious tradition, and my commentary is an attempt to apply its teachings specifically to the problems facing us in modern life.

Today there is an urgent need for such a manual. We see this reflected in our newspapers, magazines, books, movies, and television programs, but most of all in our daily living. Life has never seemed more futile. In spite of all our technological advances and material prosperity, we have no peace of mind and live in fear and anger in the midst of increasing violence. We are caught in the lurid dream that the pursuit of pleasure will lead us to joy, the pursuit of profit will lead us to security, and most of us have no other purpose in life than this driving urge to bring about our own private fulfillment even if it is at the expense of other persons, races, or countries.

The Bhagavad Gita shows us how we can awaken from this dream. In Sanskrit, the language of the Gita, the underlying Reality of life is called by a simple but very powerful name: *advaita*, 'not two.' In the words of a lovable mystic of modern India, Meher Baba, "You and I are not 'we'; you and I are One." There is no division, no fragmentation in life at all; no matter how much we may appear to differ on the surface, the welfare of each one of us is inseparable from the welfare of all others.

Even on the level of the body, we know that in cancer the whole organism is eventually destroyed when even a single cell begins to pursue its own course independently of the rest. Similarly, the Bhagavad Gita tells us, you and I cannot fulfill ourselves by going our own way. We can find lasting fulfillment only by contributing to the joy and fulfillment of others, in which our own joy and fulfillment are included. This is not a philosophical platitude, but a practical principle which we must learn to live by if our civilization is to survive.

Every mystic will interpret the scriptures in accordance with the urgent needs of the times. Though the Bhagavad Gita is timeless, it too must be interpreted in accordance with the needs of the times – the *yugadharma* in Sanskrit, the 'special law of the age.' In commenting on the Gita, I always stress the indivisible unity of life because this is the need of our time. I do not stop with the human family, but extend this unity to all life and to the environment as well. It is the urgent need of our time to recognize the unity of all forms of life, and the intimate relationship between water, earth, air, plants, and all creatures. I am a vegetarian not only because my ancestors were, but also because I perceive this unity. Ecologists have begun to tell us that there is an interpenetrating relationship among all things which we can violate only at our peril. Jacques Cousteau, who has devoted his life to studying the oceans of the earth, tells us: "We forget that all life-cycles are one. Environment is one too. There is no such thing as an environment of a single species, of man for example." Spiritual living and sound ecological practice go together. A vegetarian diet respects this partnership among all forms of life and meets our nutritional needs with a minimum demand on the earth's resources.

Salvation, Self-realization, *nirvāna*, *moksha* – these are just different words for the same discovery of the unity of all life. This is what we have come into life to accomplish, and until we have accomplished this, we have not attained fulfillment. Even one person attaining this goal elevates the entire consciousness of humanity. As Philo of Alexandria said: "Households, cities, countries, and nations have enjoyed great happiness when a single individual has taken heed of the Good and Beautiful. Such people not only liberate themselves; they fill those they meet with a free mind." In the Hindu spiritual tradition there is an unbroken continuity of illumined men and women who have verified the supreme goal in their lives. There is always someone with us in India to embody the ideals of spiritual living, and through their personal life such people are able to inspire those around them to follow the supreme goal. When they write a commentary on the scriptures, it is in the light of their own experience and enables us to practice their teachings in our daily life.

My own approach to the spiritual life appeals to many men and women today, partly because I have not retired from the world – I live very much as a family man, a good husband, son, and friend – but also because I have tried to combine the best of West and East. I live together with forty friends at our ashram, or spiritual community, and though I have heavy responsibilities in guiding our work, I take time for recreation. I go with friends to the theater; I am fond of Western and Indian classical music; I like to take the children to the ice cream parlor and the dogs to the beach for a run. But perhaps what appeals most deeply is that I understand the difficulties of living in the modern world. Before taking to meditation, in my ignorance of the unity of life, I too committed most of the mistakes that even sensitive people commit today. As a result, I understand how easy it is to make those mistakes, and I know how to guide and support those who are trying to learn a wiser way of living.

I am a believer in ordinary people and do not look to governments and corporations to set the world right. In India, the tropical sun dries up almost all vegetation during the hot season, and a shade tree is a precious shelter from the deadening heat. The leaves of the tamarind tree are very small, but they are packed so closely together that they give better shade than the large leaves of the banana tree. My grandmother, my spiritual teacher, used to point to the tamarind tree and remind me that a large number of little people, working together closely, can accomplish much more than a few big people. The Lord within, whether we call him Krishna, Christ, the Buddha, or Allah, is the source of all power, and when we live for others in accordance with the unity of all life this power flows into our hands, enabling us to take on the biggest problems facing the modern world. In Hindu mythology, Ganesha, the elephant god, is the symbol of the Lord's power. The elephant is a huge, strong creature, but very gentle. Often he does not know his own strength. His eyes are so small that in India we say he thinks he is only a small creature, not capable of much. He never knows his own size. My Gita commentary is aimed at ordinary men and women who think they are small, who do not realize their real stature.

Even if it takes us a whole lifetime to learn to practice the teachings of the Gita, we shall have made a valuable contribution in life. You and I can make a contribution to the spiritual evolution of humanity by learning to resolve the terrible civil war described vividly in the Gita. This war is continually raging within every one of us, and the two armies in conflict are all that is selfish in us pitted against all that is selfless in us. It is a lifelong struggle between the demonic and the divine.

The Bhagavad Gita, which is found in the Hindu epic the *Mahābhārata*, is the most influential scripture to come down the ages in India. It is the quintessence of the Upanishads, giving us their perennial wisdom in a manner that can be systematically practiced. The Upanishads, which come at the end of the Vedas and are among the oldest, most revered Hindu scriptures, contain flashing insights into the nature of life and death. The Gita gives order to the insights of the Upanishads and tells us how to undertake spiritual disciplines to become aware of the supreme Reality always.

My surmise is that the Gita was originally an Upanishad which has been inserted into the *Mahābhārata*, its first chapter serving as a bridge between the epic story and the upanishadic teaching in chapters two through eighteen. Perhaps this interpretation cannot be substantiated by scholarship, but in the traditional invocation to the Gita we find this verse:

Sarvo 'panishado gāvo
dogdhā gopālanandanah
Pārtho vatsah sudhīr bhoktā
dugdham gītāmritam mahat

All the Upanishads are cows
milked by Krishna, the cowherd boy,
and Arjuna is the calf.
Those who are wise and pure drink the milk,
the supreme, immortal nectar of the Gita.

The Gita also uses the dialogue form of the Upanishads and is especially similar to the Katha Upanishad, where Yama, the King of Death, teaches the teenager Nachiketa how to attain immortality through Self-realization. In the Gita, the dialogue is between Sri Krishna (a full incarnation of Vishnu, the Preserver in the Hindu Trinity) and Arjuna, a young prince who represents you and me. Arjuna is a man of action, living in the midst of society and confronting essentially the same problems that challenge us today. His friend and spiritual teacher, Sri Krishna, is the Lord of Love who dwells in the depths of our consciousness. He is the Ātman, our real Self.

To practice the teachings of the Bhagavad Gita no amount of intellectual study can be of much help, because intellectual knowledge, by its very nature, has little power to transform character, conduct, and consciousness. Meditation is the mighty instrument which enables us to bring the timeless teachings of the Gita into our life, day by day, step by step.

In the Hindu scriptures meditation is called *Brahmavidyā*, the supreme science, in which all human desires are completely fulfilled. If we practice meditation sincerely, systematically, and with sustained enthusiasm, our physical and emotional problems find their solution, all of our artistic and creative capacities come to full maturity, and we are able to contribute to the welfare of our family and community. We live in the world as integral members of our society, and by transforming ourselves, we transform those with whom we live. This is joyful living; it is not running away from problems but facing problems with a quiet confidence and unfailing insight that come to us day by day in the practice of meditation.

In order to bring the teachings of the Gita into our daily lives and to practice meditation, we must observe the simple rules of right living.

On the strength of my own small spiritual experience, let me indicate here the eight-point program which I have found extremely useful in my own life. This body of disciplines, which can enable us to fulfill the supreme goal of life, Self-realization, can be followed by every person capable of some resolution, some endurance, and some sense of dedication.

THE EIGHT-POINT PROGRAM

1. *Meditation on a Passage.* The heart of this program is meditation: half an hour every morning, as early as is convenient. Do not increase this period; if you want to meditate more, have half an hour in the evening also, preferably at the very end of the day.

Set aside a room in your home to be used only for meditation and spiritual reading. After a while that room will become associated with meditation in your mind, so that simply entering it will have a calming effect. If you cannot spare a room, have a particular corner. Whichever you choose, keep your meditation place clean, well ventilated, and reasonably austere.

Sit in a straight-backed chair or on the floor and gently close your eyes. If you sit on the floor, you may need to support your back lightly against a wall. You should be comfortable enough to forget your body, but not so comfortable that you become drowsy.

Whatever position you choose, be sure to keep your head, neck, and spinal column erect in a straight line. As concentration deepens, the nervous system relaxes and you may begin to fall asleep. It is important to resist this tendency right from the beginning, by drawing yourself up and away from your back support until the wave of sleep has passed.

Once you have closed your eyes, begin to go *slowly,* in your mind, through one of the passages from the scriptures or the great mystics which I recommend for use in meditation. I usually recommend learning first the Prayer of St. Francis of Assisi:

Lord, make me an instrument of thy peace.
Where there is hatred, let me sow love;
Where there is injury, pardon;

Where there is doubt, faith;
Where there is despair, hope;
Where there is darkness, light;
Where there is sadness, joy.

O Divine Master, grant that I may not so much seek
To be consoled as to console,
To be understood as to understand,
To be loved as to love;
For it is in giving that we receive,
It is in pardoning that we are pardoned,
It is in dying [to self] that we are born to eternal life.

Do not follow any association of ideas or try to think about the passage. If you are giving your attention to each word, the meaning cannot help sinking in. When distractions come, do not resist them, but give more attention to the words of the passage. If your mind strays from the passage entirely, bring it back gently to the beginning and start again.

When you reach the end of the passage, you may use it again as necessary to complete your period of meditation until you have memorized others. It is helpful to have a wide variety of passages for meditation, drawn from the world's major traditions. Each passage should be positive and practical, drawn from a major scripture or from a mystic of the highest stature. Passages from the Gita which are perfect for meditation will be found at the end of each volume of this commentary. In addition, I heartily recommend the Lord's Prayer, the Twenty-third Psalm, the Beatitudes, St. Paul's *Epistle on Love* (1 Corinthians 13), and the first and last chapters of the Dhammapada of the Buddha. These and many other beautiful passages can be found in my collection *God Makes the Rivers to Flow.*

The secret of meditation is simple: we become what we meditate on. When you use the Prayer of St. Francis every day in meditation, you are driving the words deep into your consciousness. Eventually they become an integral part of your personality, which means they will find constant expression in what you do, what you say, and what you think.

2. *Repetition of a Mantram.* A mantram is a powerful spiritual formula which, when repeated silently in the mind, has the capacity to transform consciousness. There is nothing magical about this. It is simply a matter of practice, as all of us can verify for ourselves.

Every religious tradition has a mantram, often more than one. For Christians the name of Jesus itself is a powerful mantram; Catholics also use *Hail Mary* or *Ave Maria*. Jews may use *Barukh attah Adonai,* 'Blessed art thou, O Lord,' or the Hasidic formula *Ribono shel olam,* 'Lord of the universe.' Muslims repeat the name of Allah or *Allahu akbar,* 'God is great.' Probably the oldest Buddhist mantram is *Om mani padme hum,* referring to the 'jewel in the lotus of the heart.' In Hinduism, among many choices, I recommend *Rāma, Rāma, Rāma,* which was Mahatma Gandhi's mantram, or the longer mantram I received from my own spiritual teacher, my grandmother:

Hare Rāma Hare Rāma
Rāma Rāma Hare Hare
Hare Krishna Hare Krishna
Krishna Krishna Hare Hare

Select a mantram that appeals to you deeply. In many traditions, it is customary to take the mantram used by your spiritual teacher. Then, once you have chosen, do not change your mantram. Otherwise, as Sri Ramakrishna puts it, you will be like a person digging shallow holes in many places; you will never go deep enough to find water.

Repeat your mantram silently whenever you get the chance: while walking, while waiting, while doing mechanical chores like washing dishes, and especially when you are falling asleep. You will find that this is not mindless repetition; the mantram will help to keep you relaxed and alert. Whenever you are angry or afraid, nervous or worried or resentful, repeat the mantram until the agitation subsides. The mantram works to steady the mind, and all these emotions are power running against you which the mantram can harness and put to work.

3. *Slowing Down.* Hurry makes for tension, insecurity, inefficiency, and superficial living. To guard against hurrying through the day, start the day early and simplify your life so that you do not try to fill your time with more than you can do. When you find yourself beginning to speed up, repeat your mantram to help you slow down.

It is important here not to confuse slowness with sloth, which breeds carelessness, procrastination, and general inefficiency. In slowing down we should attend meticulously to details, giving our very best even to the smallest undertaking.

4. *One-Pointed Attention.* Doing more than one thing at a time divides attention and fragments consciousness. When we read and eat at the same time, for example, part of our mind is on what we are reading and part on what we are eating; we are not getting the most from either activity. Similarly, when talking with someone, give him or her your full attention. These are little things, but all together they help to unify consciousness and deepen concentration.

Everything we do should be worthy of our full attention. When the mind is one-pointed it will be secure, free from tension, and capable of the concentration that is the mark of genius in any field.

5. *Training the Senses.* In the food we eat, the books and magazines we read, the movies we see, all of us are subject to the dictatorship of rigid likes and dislikes. To free ourselves from this conditioning, we need to learn to change our likes and dislikes freely when it is in the best interests of those around us or ourselves. We should choose what we eat by what our body needs, for example, rather than by what the taste buds demand. Similarly, the mind eats too, through the senses. In this age of mass media, we need to be very discriminating in what we read and what we go to see for entertainment; for we become in part what our senses take in.

6. *Putting Others First*. Dwelling on ourselves builds a wall between ourselves and others. Those who keep thinking about *their* needs, *their* wants, *their* plans, *their* ideas cannot help becoming lonely and insecure. The simple but effective technique I recommend is to learn to put other people first – beginning within the circle of your family and friends, where there is already a basis of love on which to build. When husband and wife try to put each other first, for example, they are not only moving closer to each other, they are also removing the barriers of their ego-prison, which deepens their relationships with everyone else as well.

7. *Spiritual Fellowship*. The Sanskrit word for this is *satsang*, 'association with those who are spiritually oriented.' When we are trying to change our life, we need the support of others with the same goal. If you have friends who are meditating along the lines suggested here, you can get together regularly to share a meal, meditate, and perhaps read and discuss this commentary on the Gita. Share your times of entertainment too; relaxation is an important part of spiritual living. Who has ever seen a mystic with a sour face?

8. *Spiritual Reading*. We are so immersed these days in what the mass media offer that it is very helpful to give half an hour or so each day to reading the scriptures and the writings of the great mystics of all religions. Just before bedtime, after evening meditation, is a particularly good time, because the thoughts you fall asleep in will be with you throughout the night.

If we want to make the discovery that will fulfill all our desires and establish us in abiding joy, bringing to our life limitless love, wisdom, and beauty, then the mystics have described the path for us to follow. By following these simple rules of right living and practicing meditation regularly, we can learn to fulfill the supreme goal of life, which is to discover experientially that all life is one.

The Bhagavad Gita for Daily Living, Volume 1

CHAPTER ONE

The War Within

धृतराष्ट्र उवाच ।
धर्मक्षेत्रे कुरुक्षेत्रे समवेता युयुत्सवः ।
मामकाः पाण्डवाश्चैव किमकुर्वत संजय ॥ १-१ ॥

DHRITARASHTRA:[1]

1. O Sanjaya, tell me what happened at Kurukshetra, on the field of dharma, where my family and the Pāndavas gathered to fight.

"The Gita," says Mahatma Gandhi, "is not a historical discourse. A physical illustration is often needed to drive home a spiritual truth. It is the description not of war between cousins, but between two natures in us – the Good and the Evil." Volumes have been written about the battle which is said to have taken place on the field of Kurukshetra, located north of Delhi, but for the spiritual aspirant, the battle described in the Bhagavad Gita is not limited to a particular historical setting. Sri Krishna's message is as valid today as it was centuries ago, and it will continue to be so tomorrow, for it describes the eternal truth of life that the fiercest battle we must wage is against all that is selfish, self-willed, and separate in us. Today when the world is being torn asunder by war, when violence stalks our streets and invades our homes, when anger disrupts our relationships and separateness pervades our consciousness, Sri Krishna's immortal words, given to us in the Gita, are of urgent practical value. The violence we see about us is a reflection of the anger

1. Dhritarāshtra, a blind king, is the father of the forces of darkness. His name means "he who has usurped the kingdom."

and self-will burning deep within us. Most of us carry a conflagration around with us in the depths of our consciousness, and many of us are skilled tacticians in guerilla warfare right in our own homes. The war the mystics of all the world's great religions talk about is not the one erupting in the Middle East or in Southeast Asia that makes newspaper headlines; it is the one erupting from the fierce self-will afflicting all of us, estranging individuals, families, communities, races, and nations.

Once I was on a train going from Delhi to Simla, high on the Himālayas, and on the way we passed through Kurukshetra, the historical battlefield of the Bhagavad Gita. My fellow passengers were talking about the tremendous battle which took place there, and when we arrived at the scene, they eagerly climbed out to have a look. To me there was no need to disembark, because I already had an inkling that the real battlefield in the Gita was right inside each passenger on the train. The language of battle is often found in the scriptures, for it conveys the strenuous, long-drawn-out campaign we must wage to free ourselves from the tyranny of the ego, the cause of all our suffering and sorrow. By setting before us the inspiring ideal of the victorious man or woman as one who has conquered himself or herself, the mystics urge us on to fight this battle and eradicate all that is selfish in us.

How can we ordinary men and women, living in the midst of our family and society, achieve such a victory? In the Gita Sri Krishna gives us the precious jewel of spiritual wisdom, of immediate practical value to everyone's life. He tells us how we can learn to fight the battle against self-will and separateness through the practice of meditation and its allied disciplines, and he shows us how in our own daily lives we can gain the will and the wisdom to transform anger into compassion, fear into courage, and greed into tireless striving for the welfare of others.

संजय उवाच ।
दृष्ट्वा तु पाण्डवानीकं व्यूढं दुर्योधनस्तदा ।
आचार्यमुपसंगम्य राजा वचनमब्रवीत् ॥ १-२ ॥

पश्यैतां पाण्डुपुत्राणामाचार्य महतीं चमूम् ।
व्यूढां द्रुपदपुत्रेण तव शिष्येण धीमता ॥ १-३ ॥

अत्र शूरा महेष्वासा भीमार्जुनसमा युधि ।
युयुधानो विराटश्च द्रुपदश्च महारथः ॥ १-४ ॥

धृष्टकेतुश्चेकितानः काशिराजश्च वीर्यवान् ।
पुरुजित्कुन्तिभोजश्च शैब्यश्च नरपुंगवः ॥ १-५ ॥

युधामन्युश्च विक्रान्त उत्तमौजाश्च वीर्यवान् ।
सौभद्रो द्रौपदेयाश्च सर्व एव महारथाः ॥ १-६ ॥

अस्माकं तु विशिष्टा ये तान्निबोध द्विजोत्तम ।
नायका मम सैन्यस्य संज्ञार्थं तान्ब्रवीमि ते ॥ १-७ ॥

भवान्भीष्मश्च कर्णश्च कृपश्च समितिंजयः ।
अश्वत्थामा विकर्णश्च सौमदत्तिस्तथैव च ॥ १-८ ॥

अन्ये च बहवः शूरा मदर्थे त्यक्तजीविताः ।
नानाशस्त्रप्रहरणाः सर्वे युद्धविशारदाः ॥ १-९ ॥

अपर्याप्तं तदस्माकं बलं भीष्माभिरक्षितम् ।
पर्याप्तं त्विदमेतेषां बलं भीमाभिरक्षितम ॥ १-१० ॥

अयनेषु च सर्वेषु यथाभागमवस्थिताः ।
भीष्ममेवाभिरक्षन्तु भवन्तः सर्व एव हि ॥ १-११ ॥

SANJAYA:[2]

2. Having surveyed the forces of the Pāndavas arrayed for battle, Duryodhana,[3] the prince, approached his teacher and spoke.

2. The entire dialogue of the Bhagavad Gita is reported to us by Sanjaya, who sees what is taking place on the battlefield within through his power of divine vision.
3. Duryodhana, eldest son of Dhritarāshtra, is the leader of the forces of darkness.

3. "O my teacher, look at this mighty army of the Pāndavas; it has been assembled by your gifted disciple, the son of Drupada.
4–6. "There are heroic warriors and great archers who are the equals of Bhīma and Arjuna: Yuyudhāna, the mighty Virāta, Drupada, Dhrishtaketu, Cekitāna, the valiant king of Kāshī, Purujit, Kuntibhoja, the great leader Shaibya, the powerful Yudhāmanyu, the valiant Uttamaujas, the son of Subhadrā, and the sons of Draupadī; all these command mighty chariots.
7–8. "You who are the best of the brahmins, listen to the names of those who are distinguished among us: Bhīshma, Karna, and the victorious Kripa; Ashvatthāma, Vikarna, and the son of Somadatta.
9. "There are many others, too, heroes giving up their lives for my sake. They are all proficient in war and armed with a variety of weapons.
10. "Our army is unlimited and commanded by Bhīshma; theirs is small and commanded by Bhīma.
11. "Let everyone take his proper place and stand firm supporting Bhīshma."

Religion is realization of the unity of life; this is the supreme purpose for which we have come into the human context. Our intellectual orientation, useful though it is in helping us solve some of our problems, tends to make us forget that the scriptures of the great religions are meant to be personally experienced in daily life. I appreciate the scholarly editions of the Gita, the Bible, or the Dhammapada that abound in footnotes and appendices, but I always ask myself: will this approach show me how to translate the teachings of Sri Krishna, Jesus the Christ, or the Compassionate Buddha into my own life? Will it prepare me to undertake the long, exhausting war I have come into this world to win?

Sri Krishna insists we do the actual fighting in this battle ourselves, but with his infinite mercy, he outlines the battle plan and gives us the maps, weapons, and strategies necessary to win. The first tip the Gita gives us is on the nature of the contesting armies, the Kauravas and the Pāndavas. The Kauravas are usually identified with the forces of darkness that bring about death and despair, and the Pāndavas with the forces of light which bring abiding joy and unshakable security. The ancient Sanskrit scriptures throw a flood of light on this dichotomy by describing it as a choice between *preya* and *shreya*. *Preya,* the passing pleasure that seems pleasing to the senses but soon fades into its opposite, is what we choose when we indulge in injurious physical habits or retaliate against others. *Shreya*, the good that leads to lasting welfare for the whole, is what we choose by cultivating healthy habits, by bringing conflicting parties together, and by putting the happiness of those around us first. These two conflicting forces are very much in evidence in the world today: on the one hand we have made great strides towards eliminating poverty and disease, but on the other hand, we have stockpiled sufficient arms to kill every man, woman, and child on the face of the earth several times over. We seek peace and freedom for all, but we are letting the selfish pursuit of personal profit and pleasure destroy our families, our communities, and even our society. As Sri Ramakrishna, the great saint who lived in India in the last century, was fond of saying, "If you want to go east, don't walk towards the west." Such is the confusion of our lives that we have forgotten there is this choice to be made at all, and in fact we no longer know whether we are running east or west.

Another set of beautiful Sanskrit terms for describing the perennial opposition between the forces that elevate us and those that bring about our downfall is *nitya* and *anitya*. *Nitya* refers to that which is eternal and unchanging, and this is what we seek by forgiving those who harm us and supporting those who differ from us. *Anitya* is that which fades away and brings suffering in its wake, and this is what we seek when we give in to an angry impulse or do what leads to self-aggrandizement at the expense of our family, community, and society. When we fight others, whether physically or in the mind, we harm them and ourselves, but when we fight all that is base and self-willed in us, we bring lasting joy to everyone. This is a central theme in all the great scriptures. We can all learn to conquer hatred through love by drawing on the power released through the practice of meditation to throw all our weight, all our energy, and all our will on the side of what is patient, forgiving, and selfless in ourselves and others.

तस्य संजनयन्हर्षं कुरुवृद्धः पितामहः ।
सिंहनादं विनद्योच्चैः शङ्खं दध्मौ प्रतापवान् ॥ १-१२ ॥
ततः शङ्खाश्च भेर्यश्च पणवानकगोमुखाः ।
सहसैवाभ्यहन्यन्त स शब्दस्तुमुलो ऽभवत् ॥ १-१३ ॥
ततः श्वेतैर्हयैर्युक्ते महति स्यन्दने स्थितौ ।
माधवः पाण्डवश्चैव दिव्यौ शङ्खौ प्रदध्मतुः ॥ १-१४ ॥

12. Then the powerful Bhīshma, the grandsire, oldest of all the Kurus, in order to cheer Duryodhana, roared like a lion and blew his conch horn.
13. And after Bhīshma there was a tremendous noise of conchs and cowhorns and pounding on drums.
14. Then Sri Krishna and Arjuna, who were standing in a mighty chariot yoked with white horses, blew their divine conchs.

In this greatest of all battles between the forces of good and evil, Arjuna represents you and me, and Sri Krishna, the Lord of Love enshrined in the heart of every creature, is his best friend, his dearest companion, and above all, his beloved teacher and guide. Sri Krishna is not someone outside us, swinging between Neptune and Uranus; he is closer to us than our body, nearer to us, as the Sufi mystics put it, than our jugular vein. The word *Krishna* comes from the Sanskrit root *krish*, 'to draw'; Krishna is the one inside us who is drawing us to himself all the time. The title *Sri* means 'Lord.' Sri Krishna is eternal and omnipresent; he is our real Self. Whether we call him the Christ, the Buddha, or Allah, he is the supreme Reality underlying consciousness and uniting all creation.

पाञ्चजन्यं हृषीकेशो देवदत्तं धनंजयः ।
पौण्ड्रं दध्मौ महाशङ्खं भीमकर्मा वृकोदरः ॥१-१५॥
अनन्तविजयं राजा कुन्तीपुत्रो युधिष्ठिरः ।
नकुलः सहदेवश्च सुघोषमणिपुष्पकौ ॥१-१६॥
काश्यश्च परमेष्वासः शिखण्डी च महारथः ।
धृष्टद्युम्नो विराटश्च सात्यकिश्चापराजितः ॥१-१७॥
द्रुपदो द्रौपदेयाश्च सर्वशः पृथिवीपते ।
सौभद्रश्च महाबाहुः शङ्खान्दध्मुः पृथक्पृथक् ॥१-१८॥
स घोषो धार्तराष्ट्राणां हृदयानि व्यदारयत् ।
नभश्च पृथिवीं चैव तुमुलो व्यनुनादयन् ॥१-१९॥

15. Sri Krishna blew the conch named Pāncajanya,
and Arjuna blew that called Devadatta. The
mighty Bhīma blew the huge conch Paundra.
16. Yudhishthira, the king, the son of Kuntī,
blew the conch Anantavijaya; Nakula and
Sahadeva blew their conchs as well.[4]
17–18. The king of Kashī, the leading bowman,
the great warrior Shikhundī, Dhrishtadyumna,
Virāta, the invincible Sātyaki, Drupada, all
the sons of Draupadī, and the son of Subhadrā
with the mighty arms all blew their conchs.
19. And the noise tore through the heart of
Duryodhana's army. Indeed, the sound was
tumultuous, echoing throughout heaven and earth.

The tumult and confusion of warfare are the same no matter what the times or circumstances, no matter who the contestants or what the issues involved. In ancient India it was the mighty bowman and the strong elephant, today it is the missile and the tank, but the dreadful disruption of life which results is the same in both cases. As the

4. Yudhisthira, Bhīma, Nakula, and Sahadeva are Arjuna's brothers.

Compassionate Buddha said more than two thousand years ago, "Hatred will never cease by hatred at any time. Hatred ceases only through love. This is an eternal law." We can never bring an end to violence by using violent means; far from resolving conflicts, hostility and retaliation drive people further apart and make havoc of life.

The tragedy of self-will is that it leads to increasing insecurity, ill health, loneliness, and despair. This cannot but be the discouraging prognosis for those who pursue personal profit, power, prestige, and pleasure at the expense of the welfare of their family and community. In the beautiful words of St. Francis of Assisi, "It is in giving that we receive; it is in pardoning that we are pardoned." Most of us suffer from the mistaken belief that it is in grabbing that we receive, it is in venting anger that we improve our relationships, and it is in having our own way that we find fulfillment. Unfortunately happiness escapes us the more we clutch at it by manipulating those around us and accumulating more material possessions. Security is not found in a stockpile of weapons but in mutual trust and respect among individuals, races, and nations; peace is not found in asserting our rights over others but in assuring the lasting welfare of our extended circle of family and friends. This is the great insight that comes in meditation: on the spiritual path there is no possibility of defeat, for the Lord – called Sri Krishna by some and the Christ by others – is in the depths of our consciousness to support us, guide us, and help us win the war against our self-will.

One of the glorious names for Sri Krishna, used here and elsewhere throughout the Gita to remind us of the complete, unending joy lying within us, is Hrishīkesha, 'he whose hair stands on end with joy.' The name used here for Arjuna should also inspire us: Dhananjaya, 'conqueror of wealth.' This is the perfect epithet for the person who meditates, for he discovers that real wealth comes from giving freely of himself to others. We do not learn to do this overnight; we do not go to sleep selfish one evening and wake up the next morning with every trace of self-will gone. The battle against the ego is a long, agonizing affair that may take our entire lifetime. When we accept this challenge, all the boredom goes out of life; every day brings new tests of our endurance, strength, and desire to win the battle. All our angry, aggressive instincts are harnessed to the effort; instead of anger using us, we control it and use it as a source of tremendous power. We can take heart from the great mystics who have successfully met this challenge. As the Buddha declared twenty-five hundred years ago: "One person may conquer in battle a thousand times a thousand others; but the true heroes are those who conquer themselves." It is only the mystics who can understand what struggle is required to extinguish self-will, to gain the patience that will not be exhausted by any attack and the forgiveness that will bear even with those who slander them.

अथ व्यवस्थितान्दृष्ट्वा धार्तराष्ट्रान्कपिध्वजः ।
प्रवृत्ते शस्त्रसंपाते धनुरुद्यम्य पाण्डवः ॥ १-२० ॥
हृषीकेशं तदा वाक्यमिदमाह महीपते ।
अर्जुन उवाच ।
सेनयोरुभयोर्मध्ये रथं स्थापय मे ऽच्युत ॥ १-२१ ॥
यावदेतान्निरीक्षे ऽहं योद्धुकामानवस्थितान् ।
कैर्मया सह योद्धव्यमस्मिन्रणसमुद्यमे ॥ १-२२ ॥
योत्स्यमानानवेक्षे ऽहं य एते ऽत्र समागताः ।
धार्तराष्ट्रस्य दुर्बुद्धेर्युद्धे प्रियचिकीर्षवः ॥ १-२३ ॥
संजय उवाच ।
एवमुक्तो हृषीकेशो गुडाकेशेन भारत ।
सेनयोरुभयोर्मध्ये स्थापयित्वा रथोत्तमम् ॥ १-२४ ॥
भीष्मद्रोणप्रमुखतः सर्वेषां च महीक्षिताम् ।
उवाच पार्थ पश्यैतान्समवेतान्कुरूनिति ॥ १-२५ ॥
तत्रापश्यत्स्थितान्पार्थः पितॄनथ पितामहान् ।
आचार्यान्मातुलान्भ्रातॄन्पुत्रान्पौत्रान्सखींस्तथा ॥ १-२६ ॥
श्वशुरान्सुहृदश्चैव सेनयोरुभयोरपि ।
तान्समीक्ष्य स कौन्तेयः सर्वान्बन्धूनवस्थितान् ॥ १-२७ ॥
कृपया परयाविष्टो विषीदन्निदमब्रवीत् ।

अर्जुन उवाच ।
दृष्ट्वेमान्स्वजनान्कृष्ण युयुत्सून्समवस्थितान् ॥ १-२८
सीदन्ति मम गात्राणि मुखं च परिशुष्यति ।
वेपथुश्च शरीरे मे रोमहर्षश्च जायते ॥ १-२९ ॥

20. Then, O Dhritarāshtra, lord of the earth, having seen your son's forces set in their places and the fighting about to begin, Arjuna spoke these words to Sri Krishna.

ARJUNA:

21–22. O Krishna, drive my chariot between the two armies. I want to see those who desire to fight with me. With whom will this battle be fought?

23. I wish to see those assembled to fight for Duryodhana, those who desire to please the evil-minded son of Dhritarāshtra by engaging in war.

SANJAYA:

24–25. Thus Arjuna spoke, and Sri Krishna, driving his splendid chariot between the two armies, facing Bhīshma and Drona and all the kings of the earth, said: "Arjuna, behold all the Kurus gathered together."

26–29. And Arjuna, as he stood between the two armies, saw fathers and grandfathers, teachers, uncles, and brothers, sons and grandsons, in-laws and friends. Seeing his kinsmen established in opposition, Arjuna fell into confusion and mournfully spoke these words:

ARJUNA:

O Krishna, I see my own relations here with the desire to fight, and my limbs are weak; my mouth is dry, my body is shaking, and my hair is standing on end.

One of the best definitions of confusion is doing what is unnecessary and failing to do what is necessary. This is our condition in life when we clash with our family and friends and fail to fight our worst enemy, our own self-will and separateness. Arjuna is beginning to realize that the battle he must wage is against what he has always considered to be a part of himself. Faced with the task of ridding his consciousness of every trace of selfish desire, Arjuna, like you and me, moans and groans to Sri Krishna: "How can I possibly fight these people, my best pals, with whom I have painted Hastināpura red?"

We have been so conditioned to search for happiness in sense-pleasure that defying these urges appears to be a denial of life itself. Actually the opposite is true. As we progress on the spiritual path, our vision begins to clear and our passions begin to come under our control, and we discover that we have been pursuing agitation instead of joy and accumulation instead of security. The curious thing is that we are convinced we can isolate pleasure as our own private possession, although it has escaped our grasp time and again. We may have failed in the past, but the next time we think we will succeed for sure, and we go on trying. The other day, while going for a walk, we saw two Alsatians that reminded me of our flair for chasing pleasure and profit. These two dogs were trying to catch a rainbow over a water sprinkler so they could take it home to their doghouse. One after the other they would come, jump into the spray, and snap at the rainbow hovering there. As soon as one had finished his jump, the other one would follow right on his heels as if to say, "You don't know how to do it. Let me show you," over and over again. This is what you and I do when we try to catch the rainbow that is personal pleasure, power, profit, and prestige. Even though we go through the experience many times, we do not seem able to learn from it. The Gita very compassionately says that the sooner we learn this lesson in life, the better it will be.

It is not surprising that we follow passing pleasure instead of abiding joy when we consider the extensive influence of the mass media and the widespread use of advertising. From childhood onwards we are conditioned to believe that we are our body, senses, and mind, and that happiness lies in satisfying their whims and desires. We have become so accustomed to telling Mr. Ego "You say, I do" that the very idea of questioning his authority by training the senses and changing our attitudes makes us tremble in anxiety. In meditation we begin to suspect that the ego is really a tyrant who has usurped the throne from our real Self, called the Ātman in Sanskrit, which is the source of all wisdom and beauty in life. Once this suspicion arises, the days of the ego's tyranny are numbered, and the cloud of confusion which has blinded us begins to be dispelled.

गाण्डीवं स्रंसते हस्तात्त्वक्चैव परिदह्यते ।
न च शक्नोम्यवस्थातुं भ्रमतीव च मे मनः ॥१-३०॥

निमित्तानि च पश्यामि विपरीतानि केशव ।
न च श्रेयो ऽनुपश्यामि हत्वा स्वजनमाहवे ॥१-३१॥

न काङ्क्षे विजयं कृष्ण न च राज्यं सुखानि च ।
किं नो राज्येन गोविन्द किं भोगैर्जीवितेन वा ॥१-३२॥

30. My skin is burning, and the bow Gāndīva has slipped from my hand. I am unable to stand, and my mind seems to be whirling.
31. The signs are evil for us. I do not see that any good can come from killing our relations in battle.
32. O Krishna, I do not desire victory, or a kingdom, or pleasures. Of what use is a kingdom, O Govinda,[5] or pleasure, or even life?

Arjuna is suffering from a very contemporary malady, paralysis of the will. This is the crux of many of our problems. We say we want to put an end to war, yet we go on making missiles, guns, tanks, and bombs, and arming other countries in the name of peace. We are alarmed about violence, yet we let our children watch hour after hour of violent television programs. We are concerned about pollution, but we pour pollutants by the ton into our rivers and oceans; we make the air unfit to breathe and strip the earth of irreplaceable resources. Even when we can clearly see the urgency of stopping pollution and putting an end to

5. *Govinda*, a popular name for Sri Krishna, means 'leader of the cowherds'. As a young man Sri Krishna lived in a village of cowherds called Vrindāvana, and many legends are told of his pranks and exploits there.

violence, we lack the will and the wisdom to translate our desire into effective action.

Though Arjuna deplores this state of inertia and self-pity, he is unable to shake it off. This is often our problem too; we can diagnose our shortcomings and even give a brilliant synopsis of the world's woes, but as long as our knowledge is limited to intellectual analysis, we will not have the capacity to make the world more peaceful; we will not be able to prevent pollution or even bring together estranged families and friends. It is the deeper will and wisdom which come through meditation that enable us to tap the creative resources and untiring energy lying latent in our consciousness.

Looking at the opposing army, Arjuna is plunged into confusion. His special bow, Gāndīva, slips from his grasp, and his mind reels at the prospect of fighting. This confrontation comes to all of us who are in earnest about putting an end to the cause of our sorrow and suffering, our petty little personality driven by self-will. Success on the spiritual path requires the highest kind of courage we can muster, for every ounce of our strength and resolution will be tested. It was my spiritual teacher, my mother's mother, who showed me through the example of her own life that it is the nonviolent person who cannot be frightened; the violent person can always be threatened with greater violence. If you want to see real bravery, look at the person who is patient under attack, who will not retaliate, who will suffer rather than inflict suffering on others. This is the heroic ideal Jesus the Christ gives us to follow: "Love your enemies, bless them that curse you, do good to them that hate you, and pray for them which despitefully use you, and persecute you, that ye may be the children of your Father which is in heaven." Sri Krishna, in his infinite grace, helps Arjuna find this source of strength within himself, just as he enables us, when we turn to him, to become patient when attacked, forbearing when provoked, and loving when hated. This is the way we grow fearless and strong enough to grapple with the grave problems that threaten our world.

येषामर्थे काङ्क्षितं नो राज्यं भोगाः सुखानि च ।
त इमे ऽवस्थिता युद्धे प्राणांस्त्यक्त्वा धनानि च ॥ १-३३ ॥

आचार्याः पितरः पुत्रास्तथैव च पितामहाः ।
मातुलाः श्वशुराः पौत्राः स्यालाः संबन्धिनस्तथा ॥ १-३४ ॥

एतान्न हन्तुमिच्छामि घ्नतो ऽपि मधुसूदन ।
अपि त्रैलोक्यराज्यस्य हेतोः किं नु महीकृते ॥ १-३५ ॥

निहत्य धार्तराष्ट्रान्नः का प्रीतिः स्याज्जनार्दन ।
पापमेवाश्रयेदस्मान्हत्वैतानाततायिनः ॥ १-३६ ॥

तस्मान्नार्हा वयं हन्तुं धार्तराष्ट्रान्सबान्धवान् ।
स्वजनं हि कथं हत्वा सुखिनः स्याम माधव ॥ १-३७ ॥

यद्यप्येते न पश्यन्ति लोभोपहतचेतसः ।
कुलक्षयकृतं दोषं मित्रद्रोहे च पातकम् ॥ १-३८ ॥

कथं न ज्ञेयमस्माभिः पापादस्मान्निवर्तितुम् ।
कुलक्षयकृतं दोषं प्रपश्यद्भिर्जनार्दन ॥ १-३९ ॥

कुलक्षये प्रणश्यन्ति कुलधर्माः सनातनाः ।
धर्मे नष्टे कुलं कृत्स्नमधर्मो ऽभिभवत्युत ॥ १-४० ॥

अधर्माभिभवात्कृष्ण प्रदुष्यन्ति कुलस्त्रियः ।
स्त्रीषु दुष्टासु वार्ष्णेय जायते वर्णसंकरः ॥ १-४१ ॥

33–34. Those for whose sake we would desire a kingdom, or pleasures, or happiness – teachers, fathers, sons, even grandfathers, uncles, in-laws, grandsons, and others with family ties – they are engaging in this battle, renouncing their wealth and their lives.
35. Even if they were to kill me, O Krishna, I would not want to kill them, not even to become ruler of the three worlds. How much less for the earth alone?
36. O Krishna, what satisfaction could we find in killing Dhritarāshtra's sons? We would become

sinners by slaying these men, even though evil.
37. The sons of Dhritarāshtra are related
to us; therefore, we should not kill them,
O Mādhava. How can we gain happiness
by killing members of our own family?
38–39. Though they are overpowered by greed
and do not see evil in the decay of the family
or the sin in injuring friends, we see the evil
which comes from the destruction of the family.
Why shouldn't we turn away from this sin?
40. When a family declines, ancient traditions are
destroyed. With them are lost the spiritual foundations
for life, and the entire family loses its sense of unity.
41. O Krishna, where there is no sense of
unity the women of the family become
corrupt. With the corruption of the women,
O Vārshneya, society is plunged into chaos.

To realize the unity underlying all life and live in harmony with this awareness, we do not have to quit our jobs, leave our family, drop out of school, or turn our back on society. Living in the midst of our extended circle of family and friends provides the perfect context for learning to see the Lord in everyone, everywhere, every minute, for in these deep personal relationships we can easily forget ourselves, our comforts, and our conveniences in ensuring the joy of others. This is a straightforward way of reducing our self-will, which is the only obstacle standing between the Lord and us.

In these verses Arjuna has addressed Sri Krishna very appropriately by using two of his family names: Mādhava, 'son of the Madhu clan'; and Vārshneya, 'he who belongs to the family of the Vrishnis.' The family has always been a symbol of unity and selfless love in spite of the serious problems that have afflicted it from time to time. Arjuna's confusion over his family responsibility is ours as well, for we have let competition and self-interest tear our families apart. Husband and wife compete against each other, parents and children compete, sister and brother compete; even the grandparents are trying to get into the act. This competitive tendency has spread from the home to the school and campus, to organizations, and of course to international relationships. It breeds distrust, suspicion, and jealousy wherever it goes. As our security increases through meditation, we find we do not need to compete, for the source of joy and wisdom is right within us. Competition has so distorted our vision that we are defensive towards even our dear ones, but as our meditation deepens, we see what lasting joy there is in trying to complete one another rather than compete against one another.

If just one person in a family takes to the spiritual life, he or she can slowly transform the home from a battleground into a citadel of strength for family and friends alike. This is particularly true when the woman takes to meditation, for she is in an advantageous position to support and inspire others with her selfless love, patience, and forbearance. Over a period of time, her quiet example will enable her partner, parents, children, and friends to grow strong and secure. My grandmother used to tell the girls in my ancestral family that it was their privilege to light up the home with their generosity and forgiveness; she showed them in her own personal life how everyone cannot but respond to such a woman, and how family and friends eagerly return to such a home. We should bear in mind that this concept of family loyalty and unity is not limited just to parents and children; those who deeply care for each other's welfare are a family in the best sense of the word, and it is by extending our capacity to love and support to a widening circle of friends that we transform our life into a permanent force for good in the world. Anandamayi Ma, the great woman saint of modern India whom my wife, Christine, and I have had the blessing of meeting, expresses this awareness of unity when she says: "The different organs of the human body fulfill different functions; some more noble certainly than others, but for the good of the body they must all be cared for. In the same way, try to treat with equal love all the people with whom you have relations. Make a habit of this and soon you will perceive that all humankind is as your family. Thus the abyss between 'myself' and 'yourself' will be filled in, which is the goal of all religious worship."

संकरो नरकायैव कुलघ्नानां कुलस्य च ।
पतन्ति पितरो ह्येषां लुप्तपिण्डोदकक्रियाः ॥ १-४२ ॥

42. Social chaos is hell for the family, and for those who have destroyed the family as well. It disrupts the process of spiritual evolution begun by our ancestors.

The perennial truth expressed in the scriptures, which we can realize in our own lives, is that all creation is evolving towards the unitive state. Any sensitive person can appreciate the grandeur of this process; just observe a hive of bees at work, or walk through a forest, or live with a selfless person, and you cannot but be profoundly moved by the way every aspect of creation can work with all the rest as a unit in perfect harmony. This truth has far-reaching application in our daily life. On the one hand, every time we violate the unity of life by venting our anger on those around us, or by harming our fellow creatures, we work against this evolution; on the other hand, every time we forgive others, do what benefits them, or alleviate the distress of any creature, we contribute towards this evolution. By striving to live in accord with this unity we bring about the fulfillment of all creation, which of course includes our own, but by going our separate ways, we obstruct the evolution of consciousness towards the unitive state.

The unity underlying life is so complete and pervasive that when we inflict suffering on the smallest creature, we injure the whole. When we refrain from habits that harm others, when we take up jobs that relieve suffering, when we work to put an end to anger and separateness, we strengthen the whole. John Donne reminds us of this when he says, "No man is an island entire of itself; every man is a piece of the continent, a part of the main; if a clod be washed away by the sea, Europe is the less, as well as if a promontory were, as well as if a manor of thy friends or of thine own were; any man's death diminishes me, because I am involved in mankind; and therefore never send to know for whom the bell tolls, it tolls for thee."

There is nothing more important in life than learning to express this unity in all our relationships: with our family and friends, with our colleagues and fellow workers, with other communities and countries, with other races and religious groups, and with other creatures. This is the way we come to see the presence of the Lord.

दोषैरेतैः कुलघ्नानां वर्णसंकरकारकैः ।
उत्साद्यन्ते जातिधर्माः कुलधर्माश्च शाश्वताः ॥ १-४३ ॥
उत्सन्नकुलधर्माणां मनुष्याणां जनार्दन ।
नरके नियतं वासो भवतीत्यनुशुश्रुम ॥ १-४४ ॥

43. The timeless spiritual foundations of the family and society are destroyed by these terrible deeds which violate the unity of life.

44. It is said that those who have lost sight of this unity dwell in hell.

Arjuna is beginning to see the terrible consequences of disunity. We have a tendency to think of heaven and hell as physical domains located on some celestial map, when really they describe our state of being right here on earth. This is the practical meaning of unity and separateness in our daily living; we have a taste of heaven every time we forget ourselves in ensuring the joy of others, and we have a bitter dose of the other place when we think or behave unkindly.

Violence, war, pollution, estrangement, and insensitivity to our fellow creatures are external manifestations of the disunity seething in our consciousness. Because we live on the surface level of life we are often unaware of the anger and fear burning deep within us. It is only after practicing meditation for some years that we learn to descend into the depths of our consciousness where we can observe these negative forces at work and put an end to their disruptive activity. Right from the first days of our *sādhana*, the spiritual disciplines we practice begin, however slowly, to transform our character, conduct, and consciousness. When the divisiveness which has been agitating us and making life difficult begins to mend, we get immediate evidence in our daily life: our health improves, long-standing personal conflicts subside, our mind becomes clear and our intellect lucid; an unshakable sense of security and well-being follows us wherever we go, and whatever challenges loom before us, we know we have the will and the wisdom to meet them effectively.

Unification of consciousness can turn the most ordinary of us into a spiritual force; this is the power of the unitive state that we enter in the climax of meditation, called *samādhi* in Sanskrit, when our heart, mind, and spirit come to rest in the Lord. Swami Ramdas, a delightful saint whom we met in his āshram in South India, summarizes this in simple, clear words: "All sādhanas are done with a view to still the mind. The perfectly still mind is universal spirit."

अहो बत महत्पापं कर्तुं व्यवसिता वयम् ।
यद्राज्यसुखलोभेन हन्तुं स्वजनमुद्यताः ॥ १-४५ ॥

45. This is a great sin! We are prepared to kill our own relations out of greed for the pleasures of a kingdom.

It is easy to see why Arjuna represents you and me so well, for with a few well-chosen words he is able to point right to the cause of our disrupted relationships and increasing insecurity. With dismay he tells Sri Krishna how he fears the devastating consequences of not keeping in mind the unity underlying all life. For personal pleasure and profit we are willing to sacrifice the welfare of our family and friends, our society and environment. In Arjuna's time, it was greed for a kingdom; in ours it is greed for a higher salary, a prestigious home, and a partner who will always agree with our opinions. As long as we seek to be lord and master over our petty personal kingdom, we bar the door to the Lord of Love within us, and confusion and chaos reign. This is the inevitable consequence of violating the unity of life by attempting to go our own separate way.

The Bible tells us we cannot love both God and Mammon at the same time, and in the spiritual tradition of India, great sages like Sri Ramakrishna will remind us that for Rāma – the source of abiding joy – to come into our lives, Kāma – the craving to satisfy our personal desires – must go. Our capacity for joy is so great that going after passing pleasure is like throwing a peanut in an elephant's mouth and expecting him to be full. We are so trapped in our self-willed existence that we do not realize how clouded our judgment is and how tragically we waste the gift of life trying to acquire another car, which will pollute our environment, or enjoy an extra gourmet meal, which will add to our weight and injure our health.

The English mystic William Law describes how most of us go through life under the illusion that satisfying selfish desires can bring happiness: "A life devoted to the interests and enjoyments of this world, spent and wasted in the slavery of earthly desires, may be truly called a dream, as having all the shortness, vanity, and delusion of a dream; only with this great difference, that when a dream is over nothing is lost but fictions and fancies; but when the dream of life is ended only by death, all that eternity is lost, for which we were brought into being." As long as we have not seen someone who has conquered all that is self-willed in himself, we will find it hard to believe that we can cast off this spell of separateness and awake to the unity of life. But in the world's great religions, we have mystic after mystic showing us that this is possible if we are willing to change the direction of our lives through the practice of meditation. In our own time we have the inspiring example of Mahatma Gandhi, who attained the unitive state and helped many others undertake the struggle against all that is selfish and separate. His real name was Mohandas K. Gandhi, but in India we prefer to call him by the title Mahātmā, 'the great soul,' because by reducing himself to zero he was able to identify himself with the four hundred million suffering people of India and bring about not only their political emancipation but a spiritual renewal as well. Sometimes he is known as Gandhiji, the *ji* being added to his name as a sign of affection and respect. Such was Gandhiji's spiritual stature that he could transform little people made of clay into heroes and heroines. During India's struggle for independence, we had a leader from the North-West Frontier Province whose people were very brave and enduring, but also rather violent. Gandhi had the daring to go into their midst and tell them that if they really were brave they would throw away their guns and learn to fight nonviolently. Their leader, Khan Abdul Ghaffar Khan, responded to Gandhi's challenge and transformed himself into such an invincible combination of courage and gentleness that he became known as the Frontier Gandhi.

Even one person standing against violence, whether it is in the home, in the community, or between nations, can become a source of inspiration for everyone who comes in contact with him. The words from the Sermon on the Mount are not just to be illuminated in manuscripts; the Dhammapada is not just to be inscribed on *stūpas;* the Bhagavad Gita is not just to be etched on palmyra strips and carried in our hip pocket as a talisman. The man or woman who practices the teachings of these great scriptures will become aware of the unity of life, and this awareness will give constant strength and inspiration to those who seek to turn anger into compassion, fear into courage, and selfishness into self-forgetfulness in the joy of the whole.

यदि मामप्रतीकारमशस्त्रं शस्त्रपाणयः ।
धार्तराष्ट्रा रणे हन्युस्तन्मे क्षेमतरं भवेत् ॥ १-४६ ॥

46. If the sons of Dhritarāshtra, weapons in hand,
attack me in battle, and if they kill me unarmed
and unresisting, that would be better for me.

My spiritual teacher, my grandmother, did not know how to read or write, but she knew Sri Krishna, and she gave me the message of the Gita in language that all of us can remember. All life is a battlefield, she used to tell me; whether we like it or not, we are born to fight. We have no choice in this, but we do have the choice of our opponent and our weapon. If we fight other people, often our dear ones, we cannot but lose, but if we choose to fight all that is selfish and violent in us, we cannot but win. There is no such thing as defeat on the spiritual path once we join Sri Krishna, but if we try to fight against him, we shall never know victory.

When we fight others, we are harming everyone; when we fight all that is base and self-willed in us, we are benefiting everyone. This is the constant theme of the great scriptures. We need not be impressed by anyone who recites the scriptures or observes all the outer rituals of religion, but we cannot help being impressed by those who can forgive, who can forget harm done to them or turn their backs on their own personal profit and prestige for the welfare of all. From the Old

Testament we have these words: "He that is slow to anger is better than the mighty; and he that ruleth his spirit, than he that taketh a city." It is the same theme as in the Hindu and Buddhist scriptures. Conversely, those who are quick to anger are the weakest, most pathetic, and most harmful of human beings.

Unfortunately, in our day anger is considered to be part of expressing oneself, a vital means of communication. We have anger groups, called by other names, and we have anger seminars, called by other names, in which people agitate one another and send each other out as harmful influences into their homes and society. We have anger books, anger plays, and even films glorifying the angry man or woman. After attending a violent movie like this, people may come to us with virulent words and fling these words at us like lances. But if we can sit secure and patient and, after they have exhausted themselves, comfort them by our patience, win them over by our love, we are practicing the words of the Bible: "Blessed are the peacemakers, for they shall be called the children of God."

The capacity to be patient, to bear with others through thick and thin, is within the reach of all those who will practice meditation and put the welfare of those around them before their own. We do not realize what tremendous energy for selfless living we have lying dormant within us. Because we see the world through eyes of separateness, we think of ourselves as frail, fragmented creatures, with hardly any strength to stand up in life and make our contribution. But when we take to the spiritual path and start putting into practice the wise, compassionate counsel Sri Krishna gives us in the Gita, we shall discover our real stature and be able to contribute in good measure to life.

संजय उवाच ।
एवमुक्त्वार्जुनः संख्ये रथोपस्थ उपाविशत् ।
विसृज्य सशरं चापं शोकसंविग्नमानसः ॥ १-४७ ॥

SANJAYA:

47. Overwhelmed by sorrow, Arjuna spoke these words. And casting away his bow and his arrows, he sat down in his chariot in the middle of the battlefield.

Arjuna, like you and me, wants to contribute to his family's happiness and his country's welfare, but he falls despondent at Sri Krishna's feet because he does not know how to make this contribution. Sri Krishna has not yet opened his divine lips to reveal himself to Arjuna as the supreme Teacher, but he will soon do so in the second chapter, giving Arjuna the practical instruction and guidance he needs to shake off this depression and inertia.

My ancestral family used to render a community service by staging a performance of Kathakali, the traditional dance drama of Kerala, in the open courtyard of our home under the warm evening sky of spring. Everyone was welcome, and hundreds of people would come from the village and surrounding neighborhood to see these stories from India's spiritual tradition enacted, to refresh their memory of the scriptures and deepen their devotion to the Lord who is always present in our consciousness. During the opening scenes the children would fall asleep on their mothers' or grandmothers' laps, but as soon as Sri Krishna is about to come on stage the mothers awaken them and they sit up with eyes wide open. Everyone gets ready: people who were nodding become alert, and those who were talking become silent. We concentrate the moment we hear Sri Krishna is coming, because he is our real Self. So for me, the real Gita begins with the second chapter where the Lord begins to teach. When we see Sri Krishna, it is a reminder that beneath all our surface deficiencies and seeming drawbacks, there is always present in our hearts the source of all joy and security who is the Lord.

To discover the Lord within is the supreme purpose of life, worthy of all our time, energy, resources, and dedication. For most of us, pain and suffering are necessary to make us grow up. Like little children learning to walk without support, we have to learn to walk without clutching at pleasure or profit. Watch a child learning to walk; it can be a pathetic sight to watch the little one get up only to fall down again and again. It is tempting to say out of sympathy, "Alfred, don't bother to get up. Just lie there and we'll bring everything to you." But this would permanently stunt poor Alfred's capacity for living.

It is reassuring to remember that many before us have learned to stand up to life's challenges; the mystics of both East and West tell us in inspiring words how all boredom and drabness go out of life in this greatest of all adventures. We must learn to be vigilant constantly; we cannot lapse into lack of watchfulness for one minute. Swami Ramdas describes the joy of rising to this challenge: "There is no greater victory in the life of a human being than victory over the mind. He who has controlled the gusts of passion that arise within him and the violent actions that proceed therefrom is the real hero. All the disturbances in the physical plane are due to chaos and confusion existing in the mind. Therefore to conquer the mind through the awareness of the great Truth that pervades all existence is the key to real success and the consequent harmony and peace in the individual and in the world.... The true soldier is he who fights not the external but the internal foes."

All the capacity for fighting, all the aggressive capacity we waste in conflict with others, can be harnessed through the practice of meditation to fight against our own self-will and separateness. This is a twenty-four-hour fight, because even in our dreams we can learn to dispel fear and anger. But it will take many, many years of valiant and unceasing resistance to win the peace that passeth all understanding.

When we meditate every morning we are putting on armor for the day's battle against our own impatience, inadequacy, resentment, and hostility. Of course, it is going to be extremely painful and distressing when we have to put all around us first and ourselves last, but at night when we go to bed there is such a fierce joy in the knowledge that we have contributed in some measure to the joy and growth of our family and community, even though we have suffered deeply ourselves. Often, however, when we have to choose to suffer ourselves rather than bring suffering to others, we do exactly what Arjuna does at the end of this chapter: we moan that we will not, cannot fight.

Without the grace and guidance of the Lord none of us can win this battle. In inspiring words, Sri Krishna will rouse us to action by reminding us that our real Self is pure, perfect, and untainted, no matter what our past errors. It does not matter what mistakes we may have committed or what trouble we may have brought on ourselves and others out of our ignorance; if we surrender ourselves completely to the Lord of Love who is always present in the depths of our consciousness, we will discover that these mistakes never touched us. We can throw away the ugly ego mask at last if we will turn our face to the Lord, take to meditation, and do everything possible to bring peace and security to our world.

अर्जुनविषादयोगो नाम प्रथमोऽध्यायः ॥ १ ॥

CHAPTER TWO

Self-Realization

संजय उवाच ।
तं तथा कृपयाविष्टमश्रुपूर्णाकुलेक्षणम् ।
विषीदन्तमिदं वाक्यमुवाच मधुसूदनः ॥२-१॥

SANJAYA:

1. These are the words that Sri Krishna spoke to Arjuna, whose eyes were burning with tears of self-pity and confusion.

Right from the beginning of the second chapter Sri Krishna reveals himself as the perfect spiritual teacher, striking a strong note intended to shock Arjuna out of his despondency. When Sri Krishna, silent until now, opens the dialogue, there are no soft words, no honeyed phrases. He pours withering contempt upon Arjuna, who has been weeping and protesting that he cannot fight against his senses, passions, and self-will. No spiritual teacher fails to resort to this method of shocking and strengthening us with strong words when occasion demands – and of course, when opportunity calls for it, supporting us with tender, compassionate, and loving words also.

Once I went to my spiritual teacher, my grandmother, complained to her that I was in great sorrow, and asked her why people should cause me suffering. You should not picture my granny as a sweet old lady seated in a rocking chair, knitting. There were times when she would take me to task and use language that would hurt and yet strengthen me. She could be very harsh, particularly to those who were close to her. This was the mark of her love. And on this occasion, she pricked my bubble with ease by pointing out that I was not suffering from sorrow, but from self-pity. When I grieve for others, that is sorrow, which is ennobling and strengthening. But when I grieve for myself, it is not really sorrow; it is the debilitating emotion called self-pity.

Immediately, like a true friend, Lord Krishna tells Arjuna to stop behaving like a water buffalo, which if it sees a pool of mud will go and roll in it over and over again until it is completely covered with mud. In order to live like a human being, to lead the spiritual life, Sri Krishna insists, Arjuna must stop wallowing in self-pity. To apply this to ourselves, we have only to look into our minds to see how much of our time we spend in dwelling upon what our father did to us, what our mother did to us, or what our partner said five years ago on a certain rainy morning. This is what goes on in the witches' caldron seething in our consciousness.

Arjuna has beautiful eyes, but he has been sulking like a little child, and shedding so many tears of self-pity that he cannot see anything clearly. Our eyes, when full of self-pity, see even those who are dear to us as very cruel, as persecutors – not because they are like that, but because the tears of self-pity have clouded our vision. As the Buddha puts it: "'He abused me, he beat me, he defeated me, he robbed me,' in those who harbor such thoughts hatred will not cease. 'He abused me, he beat me, he defeated me, he robbed me,' in those who do not harbor such thoughts hatred will cease." In the next verse Lord Krishna will tell Arjuna to silence this "she did this to me, he did this to me" refrain in his consciousness so that he can hear the Lord. Sri Krishna has to shock. He has to be severe to get Arjuna out of this morass. This is the way he shows his love.

श्रीभगवानुवाच ।
कुतस्त्वा कश्मलमिदं विषमे समुपस्थितम् ।
अनार्यजुष्टमस्वर्ग्यमकीर्तिकरमर्जुन ॥ २-२ ॥

SRI KRISHNA:

2. This despair and self-pity in a time of crisis is mean and unworthy of you, Arjuna. How have you fallen into a state so far from the path to liberation?

Sri Krishna looks with severity at Arjuna, who is overwhelmed by the horror and agony of self-naughting, and says, "Where does this depression, despair, and self-pity come from, Arjuna? Get rid of these things. They have no place where I live in your heart of hearts."

The Lord uses the word *anārya*, which means 'unworthy,' to refer to Arjuna, whose conduct has not been fully worthy of himself as a human being. You and I, by coming into the human context, have evolved beyond the animal stage. What distinguishes us from the animal level is our capacity to forget our own petty, personal satisfactions in bringing about the happiness of all those around us.

On one occasion when I was in college, a group of college friends and I were discussing the usual topics that young men talk about when my spiritual teacher overheard a few key words, mostly about personal pleasure, profit, and prestige. She was just coming from the cow shed, which she cleaned with her own holy hands every morning. The cows provided us with milk, butter, and yogurt, and therefore she considered it a necessary part of hospitality to make the home of the cows clean, to give them proper food, and to guard them against sickness. So, just as she was coming out of the cattle shed, she heard us all talking in this vein. She never wasted time on many words. She caught hold of one of my cousins, who was the ringleader, and told him, "You get in the cow shed. That is where you belong. We will give you plenty of hay, cotton seeds, and rice water." Because of her great love for us, she could shock us with these strong words without hurting us at all.

It is not enough if we walk on two legs, part our hair, and go about in a new suit. That does not make us a human being. The capacity to forget our own personal pleasures, and to bless those who curse us – these are what mark a human being.

Arjuna cowers now because there is lightning darting out of the eyes of the Lord when he says *asvargya:* "You have locked the door of the kingdom of heaven within by refusing to eliminate your ego, by failing to turn your back upon self-will and separateness." The Lord shocks Arjuna out of his torpor by using these strong words, and when he has been pulled out of his despondency and despair, Sri Krishna continues in the third verse:

क्लैब्यं मा स्म गमः पार्थ नैतत्त्वय्युपपद्यते ।
क्षुद्रं हृदयदौर्बल्यं त्यक्त्वोत्तिष्ठ परंतप ॥२-३॥

3. It does not become you to yield to this weakness.
Arise with a brave heart, and destroy the enemy.

Sri Krishna asks Arjuna to come out of this whirlpool in which he has been caught, saying, "It is unworthy of you. You are a blessed human being now and you cannot say that these challenges are too great to face."

When the senses are driving us, we cannot make the excuse that we are unable to resist. We cannot say that just because there is food nearby we must eat. We cannot say that everybody smokes, therefore we must smoke; everybody drinks, therefore we must drink. However difficult circumstances may be, however formidable the challenges may be, we can be certain that because the Lord is within us we have the infinite resources of his love and wisdom to meet the challenge. When our dear ones are agitating us, we cannot complain that we cannot live with them, because the Lord will answer: "Why can't you? I am in you. Draw upon me to return love for hatred, goodwill for ill will."

Having thus made short work of Arjuna's ego, Sri Krishna now tells him to get up, to rise to his full stature, to straighten his head until it reaches the stars with the whole sky as a crown. He says, "Arjuna, you have such valor in you because I live in you; all you need do is to draw upon me and you can destroy the enemy completely." He ends the verse by addressing Arjuna as *parantapa*, 'destroyer of the foe,' which is the ego.

अर्जुन उवाच ।
कथं भीष्ममहं संख्ये द्रोणं च मधुसूदन ।
इषुभिः प्रतियोत्स्यामि पूजार्हावरिसूदन ॥२-४॥
गुरूनहत्वा हि महानुभावान्
श्रेयो भोक्तुं भैक्ष्यमपीह लोके ।
हत्वार्थकामांस्तु गुरूनिहैव
भुञ्जीय भोगान्रुधिरप्रदिग्धान् ॥२-५॥

ARJUNA:

4. How can I ever bring myself to fight against Bhīshma and Drona, who are worthy of reverence? How can I, Krishna?
5. Certainly it would be better to spend my life begging than to kill these great and worthy souls; if I killed them, every pleasure I found would be tainted.

Even though Sri Krishna has been taking Arjuna to task for bemoaning his helplessness and his inability to conquer his own sense cravings and selfish urges, Arjuna still feels that the senses are his friends. He turns to Sri Krishna and says, "What kind of counsel are you giving me? These senses are good, steady friends of mine. I should receive them with hospitality and give them everything they ask for. I am shocked that you should use such unspiritual language and ask me to defy the clamor of my senses."

In our own daily life we can see how much conflict we have where the senses are concerned. When the eyes want to see something agitating, we feel we must show them all kinds of violent sights. When the ears want to hear raucous music that will agitate the mind and damage our hearing, we tell the Lord, "You don't expect us to say no, do you?" Since we do not want to be cruel to our ears, we take them to all kinds of parties where the din is so great it lifts the roof. Then food – what the palate demands *must* be good for the body. Highly spiced, deep-fried, overrefined – this is the stuff the palate enjoys; so we conclude that it is very good for the body.

In the early part of our spiritual development this conflict is likely to come to all of us because we have given license to our senses most of the time. Similarly, we have never consciously tried to go against our self-will, and therefore even the discipline of putting our family and friends first is going to take a long time to master. We are likely to complain to the Lord that by asking us to put other people first all the time, he is making our path too difficult. "Why should I inflict violence on my self-will?" we moan. "This agitates my mind, making meditation difficult."

न चैतद्विद्मः कतरन्नो गरीयो
यद्वा जयेम यदि वा नो जयेयुः ।
यानेव हत्वा न जिजीविषामस्
तेऽवस्थिताः प्रमुखे धार्तराष्ट्राः ॥ २-६ ॥

6. I don't even know which would be better, for
us to conquer them or for them to conquer us.
The sons of Dhritarāshtra have confronted us;
but why would we care to live if we kill them?

Arjuna now raises a question which many of us may be tempted to ask when we are having difficulties on the spiritual path. He says, "After all, even if I conquer the senses, how do I know that I will be able to control my mind? And even if I control my mind, how do I know that I will be able to eliminate the ego? This is all speculation. I am not convinced that all this is so carefully connected. It appears too logical. What does it matter if I conquer my senses or my senses conquer me? What is the use of rising to the summit of human consciousness and conquering the world if I am not there to enjoy it – if my senses are detached, my mind cannot get excited, and there are no more likes and dislikes?"

It seems to Arjuna that he is being asked to throw himself into an even more painful, agitating state. He is completely bewildered, and now breaks down and asks for spiritual guidance from Sri Krishna, the Lord of Love, who has been listening quietly and compassionately all the while.

कार्पण्यदोषोपहतस्वभावः
पृच्छामि त्वां धर्मसंमूढचेताः ।
यच्छ्रेयः स्यान्निश्चितं ब्रूहि तन्मे
शिष्यस्तेऽहं शाधि मां त्वां प्रपन्नम् ॥२-७॥

7. My will is paralyzed, and I am utterly confused. Tell me which is the better path for me. Let me be your disciple. I have fallen at your feet; give me instruction.

Arjuna tells Sri Krishna, "I am your disciple. Now be my teacher and instruct me." In the orthodox Hindu tradition, until we ask a spiritual teacher to be our guru, showing our readiness to receive guidance on the path of meditation, the teacher does not offer to do this for us. It is a great moment in the Gita when for the first time Arjuna declares himself the devoted disciple of Sri Krishna and asks him to be his beloved teacher. The word *guru* means 'one who is heavy,' so deeply established within himself or herself that no force on earth can affect the complete love the guru feels for everyone. If you curse him, he will bless you; if you harm her, she will serve you; and if you exploit him, he will become your benefactor. It is good for us to remember that the guru, the spiritual teacher, is in every one of us. All that another person can do is to make us aware of the teacher within ourselves. The outer teacher makes us aware of the teacher within, and to the extent we can be loyal to the outer teacher, we are being loyal to ourselves, to our Ātman. We are told in the scriptures to select a teacher very carefully. We should not get carried away by personal appearance – because we like their hairstyle or saffron robe. We have to listen carefully, judge carefully, and then make our own decision. Once we make a decision and select an outer teacher who is suited to our spiritual needs, we must be completely loyal.

If I may refer to my own small example, I have committed the innumerable mistakes that most of us commit in our modern civilization, but in giving all my love to my grandmother, I was able to attain some spiritual awareness. When the disciples love the guru, it is this love that unifies their consciousness. At the time when we are ready for it, the spiritual teacher will step aside to show us that all the love we have been giving to our teacher has been directed to our own Ātman. The guru, who has become complete in himself, does not need anyone's love to make him secure; it is in order to unify the consciousness of the disciple that the relationship exists.

If you are prepared to undertake the long journey, the teacher will give you the map and all necessary instructions, but you have got to do the traveling yourself. That the teacher cannot provide. The purpose of visiting a spiritual teacher is to be reminded that there is a destination, there is a supreme goal in life, and we all have the innate capacity to undertake the journey. When people used to sit in the presence of Sri Ramana Maharshi and praise him, he would just smile as if to say, "There is no Sri Ramana Maharshi. I am just a little keyhole through which, when you fix your eye with complete concentration, you can see the beckoning, irresistible vision of the Lord."

The Lord is most eager to meet us. He is much more eager than we are. He has been waiting and waiting for millennia, and we are standing him up. Every minute he is looking to see whether there is anybody coming home at last, and finally, after millions of years of evolution, when all our toys are broken, we decide reluctantly to turn back. When we go back like this after millions of years of separation, the Lord tells us out of his infinite love, "What good boys and girls to have come on your own." In this verse Arjuna begins to turn to the Lord, by asking him to lead him forward on the path to Self-realization.

न हि प्रपश्यामि ममापनुद्याद्
यच्छोकमुच्छोषणमिन्द्रियाणाम् ।
अवाप्य भूमावसपत्नमृद्धं
राज्यं सुराणामपि चाधिपत्यम् ॥२-८॥

संजय उवाच ।
एवमुक्त्वा हृषीकेशं गुडाकेशः परंतप ।
न योत्स्य इति गोविन्दमुक्त्वा तूष्णीं बभूव ह ॥२-९॥

8. What can overcome a sorrow that saps all my vitality? Even power over men and gods or the wealth of an empire seems empty.

SANJAYA:

9. This is how Arjuna, the great warrior, spoke to Sri Krishna. With the words, "O Govinda, I will not fight," he became silent.

Arjuna, taking his bow and arrows and putting them away, looks silently at the ground. His actions tell the Lord, "I am not going to fight because I do not have the strength, the will, or the wisdom to turn all my endeavor toward the conquest of myself." It is impossible for any of us to take on the ego, which is really a formidable foe, without undergoing tremendous spiritual disciplines. When, in the early stage of their meditation, people complain to me about difficulties in controlling the palate, or giving up smoking or drinking, the Job's consolation that I give them is that these are just preliminaries. The fight has not begun yet; you are just clearing the arena. The real fight begins only when the ego, huge and ferocious, comes onto the field.

Yesterday I was listening to a reading from the Bible about the combat between David and Goliath, which I took as a firsthand description of the spiritual life. Goliath comes and tells the armies of Israel to send their best man; if their man wins, then Goliath and his followers will serve the Israelites, but if Goliath wins, then the Israelites will become the servants of their enemy. The description of Goliath is impressive and terrifying. His armor is invulnerable. He stands on the field like a giant. When David comes up with his five little stones and his puny sling, Goliath gets furious and says, "What are you trying to do, catch a dog?" David takes a little pebble and hits Goliath with a fatal blow right on the center of his forehead. I interpret such stories spiritually. One of the Shiva mantrams is called *pancākshara*, the 'five-lettered' mantram, and for me the five pebbles that David was carrying were a five-lettered mantram with which he was able to defeat his own ego.

The ego's size can be gauged by our anger, and the further we get into the depths of our consciousness, the more we shall see what anger surges in us when our self-will is violated. To defeat this colossal ego will take a long, long period of struggle with many reverses. But finally, the Gita and the scriptures of all religions assure us, through the grace of the Lord we will be able to eliminate our ego and extinguish our self-will, which is the only barrier between us and the Lord.

तमुवाच हृषीकेशः प्रहसन्निव भारत ।
सेनयोरुभयोर्मध्ये विषीदन्तमिदं वचः ॥२-१०॥

10. As they stood between the two armies
Sri Krishna spoke with a smile to Arjuna,
who had fallen into despair.

The Lord, Sri Krishna, does not get angry or agitated while listening to Arjuna's many objections, but smiling with great affection for his disciple and friend, he now begins to teach.

श्रीभगवानुवाच ।
अशोच्यानन्वशोचस्त्वं प्रज्ञावादांश्च भाषसे ।
गतासूनगतासूंश्च नानुशोचन्ति पण्डिताः ॥२-११॥

SRI KRISHNA:

11. You speak sincerely, but your sorrow has no cause;
the wise grieve neither for the living nor for the dead.

It is a marvelous line where the Lord implies: "You speak very wise words, but your action is just the opposite of wise. You say you want joy, but the direction in which you are going is towards sorrow. You say you want fulfillment, but what you are going after every day is frustration." Sri Krishna is now implying all this to Arjuna by pointing out that the way he uses words is one thing, but the way he lives is another.

Do we want joy, security, and fulfillment? This is the question you and I have to ask ourselves first, and then we must move towards these goals. We all say we want peace. There is no individual that says he does not want peace, no nation that says it does not want peace. But if we want peace, we must do the things that make for peace. If we do the things that make for war, only war will come. Bismarck, the Iron Chancellor of Germany, used to say, "I do not want war; I only want victory." On the individual level, too, we are tempted to say, "I don't want to fight with my parents, but I want to have my way. I don't want to have any conflict with my partner, but I want to have my way." In answer to statements like these, Sri Ramakrishna would say, in a childlike outburst, "If you want to go east, you mustn't go west." It is not enough if we talk about peace; we must work for it. Even today, after more than two thousand years of recorded history scarred by frequent wars, all the countries on the face of the earth say they long for peace but keep producing armaments, keep suspecting other countries. The Lord of Love therefore asks you and me through Arjuna, "If you want peace, why don't you work for peace?"

In the second line the Lord, in strong words, gives us the secret of our nature. Arjuna has been talking about death, saying that he does not want to be killed, that he does not want to kill, but Sri Krishna reminds him that it is only the body which is born and which dies. You and I were never born, nor will we ever die, because our real Self is not limited by our physical body. We are spirit, eternal, infinite, and immutable. This is the great discovery we make in the climax of meditation, that we are not the body, senses, mind, or intellect, but supreme spirit.

When Sri Ramana Maharshi's body was about to be resolved back into the five elements at the time of his death in 1950, all India wept for him, saying, "You are leaving us; you are going away." His simple reply was, "Where can I go? I am everywhere. How can I leave you?" This is the supreme experience of unity that comes to us in samādhi. No adventure in the external world, however great, can ever be compared to the experience of Sri Ramana Maharshi seated on his little bamboo cot, going beyond time, place, and circumstance and seeing the cosmos as one, all creation as one in the Lord.

न त्वेवाहं जातु नासं न त्वं नेमे जनाधिपाः ।
न चैव न भविष्यामः सर्वे वयमतः परम् ॥२-१२॥

12. There has never been a time when you and I and the kings gathered here have not existed, nor will there be a time when we will cease to exist.

We are now getting into one of the central themes of the Gita. Looking at Arjuna compassionately, the Lord tells him, "You have always been; you will always be." This is the realization we have to make in life – that we are immortal, that we have everlasting life. Jesus in the Christian scriptures often says, "I have come to bring you everlasting life." It is into this experiential discovery that we shall move in the course of our meditation. As our meditation deepens, we shall find we are delivered from time into the Eternal Now.

One of the ways to test our progress on the spiritual path is to see how much we are able to free ourselves from the oppressive pressure of time. The clock is the most eloquent symbol of the tyranny of time. I sometimes speculate that before long we may be wearing watches with only one hand, showing a second divided into sixty subseconds. When we make an appointment we will say, "Come at two seconds and thirty-nine subseconds after two thirty." This is the direction in which we are moving as we become more and more conscious of time. I notice that if at a traffic signal the automobile in front delays ten seconds, immediately the other drivers begin using the horn. I always ask, "What is the harm if that person repeats the mantram for ten seconds and gives us all a chance to slow down?"

The constant craze for going faster, faster, faster throws us more and more into consciousness of time; and curiously enough, when we are oppressed by time, we make many mistakes. It is possible to do our work and attend to our duties without in any way being oppressed by time, and when we work free from the bondage of time we do not make mistakes, we do not get tense, and the quality of our living improves.

One of the easiest ways to free yourself from the tyranny of time is to get up early in the morning. When we used to go for our walks in Oakland in the morning, I would invariably see a few people – usually the same people – making a dash to catch the bus as if they were participating in the Olympics. Often they would be too late, and I always wanted to ask, "Why do you want to run to miss the bus? You might as well walk slowly and miss it." This is the irony. You run and you still miss the bus, and in addition, the expression you direct at the bus driver is far from loving. You think that he has been doing it on purpose – just waiting until he saw you coming, then stepping on the gas.

This simple step of starting the day early in the morning gives you an opportunity to get up leisurely, take a short walk, and then have your meditation. In meditation, also, do not be aware of time. The moment you become aware of time in meditation, there is an unfavorable factor introduced. When we were having our large class of four or five hundred people on campus, the first night in meditation a few people kept looking at their watches, which I did not object to. But I did begin to protest when they started listening to see if the watches were still ticking. Once you start meditating, forget about time. There is no need to check the clock; you can learn to time the length of the meditation fairly well by the length of the passage you are using.

In order to regain our birthright of eternal life we have to rise gradually above the physical level. Any habit that ties us to the body through a sensory bond eventually has to be thrown away. Right at the outset of the spiritual life we must begin to rid ourselves of physical habits, such as smoking, drinking, and overeating, which will impede our progress. This is not at all a moral or ethical problem; it is a question of spiritual engineering. As long as we tie ourselves to the body by stimulating the senses, and especially by building relationships on the physical level, we cannot realize this legacy of everlasting life.

देहिनो ऽस्मिन्यथा देहे कौमारं यौवनं जरा ।
तथा देहान्तरप्राप्तिर्धीरस्तत्र न मुह्यति ॥२-१३॥

13. As the same person inhabits the body through childhood, youth, and old age, so too at the time of death he attains another body. The man of wisdom is not deluded by these changes.

Just as the body, with which all of us identify ourselves, changes from childhood to youth to old age, similarly, Sri Krishna says against the background of reincarnation, we acquire a new body when we pass from one life into another after the last great change called death. There is no need to subscribe to the theory of reincarnation to lead the spiritual life, but it cannot be easily dismissed with a shrug of the shoulders as a feverish product of the tropical imagination. There is a wealth of evidence based upon scientific research available to those who want to understand this subject before pronouncing a verdict on it. Somerset Maugham, who came to India in the late thirties and had the glorious opportunity of meeting Sri Ramana Maharshi, from whom he drew the saint in his novel *The Razor's Edge,* says that even for a nonbeliever it is very difficult to attack the philosophical structure on which reincarnation is based.

One of the common questions about the theory of reincarnation that people ask is, "How is it we do not remember anything of our previous lives?" Sri Krishna is now implying that just as it is very difficult to remember even our childhood in this life, it is impossible for most of us to remember our past lives. If the Lord were to ask us what we were doing on our birthday when we were one year old, we would say that we do not remember. If he said, "Then you didn't exist," we would object to his teasing and say, "Of course we existed. We received presents and great love from our parents on that day."

Sri Krishna now hints to Arjuna, "Just take your thoughts back to your childhood and look at yourself as a child." If we go back as far as we can to our childhood and picture ourselves as we were then, what our needs, ambitions, hopes, and desires were, we just cannot believe that it is the same person. Today what makes us happy is money, and to a child money means nothing, gold means nothing. One of my cousins, when she was going to the elementary school in our village, had a beautiful gold necklace made by our village goldsmith. One day when she was about eight she came home at noon for lunch, and her mother was alarmed to see that the necklace was not around her neck. "Have you lost your gold necklace, our family treasure?" she asked. And the little girl smiled and said, "No, mommy, I haven't lost it. I traded it for a mango." Somebody had offered her a mango, which was much more important, much more enjoyable, and she had just given the necklace away.

In these verses we are being led gradually to the question of death. I think it is Dr. Carl Jung who tells us that in the deep consciousness of most people there is a great fear of death, even among those who say they want to die. One of the most beneficial effects of meditation is that as our meditation deepens, we gradually lose our fear of death. This is the proof that we are rising above physical consciousness. If we talk about death to a great mystic like Sri Ramana Maharshi, who attained illumination at age seventeen, he will just chuckle quietly and say, "I died when I was seventeen." When at the time of samādhi we lose our 'I,' our separate ego, that *is* death. This is the experience of St. Paul when he says, *Not I, not I, but Christ liveth in me*. Even intellectually we can ask ourselves the question: when our 'I' is wiped out, who is there to die? As we keep putting the happiness of others first all the time, our little 'I' is erased, and with the elimination of the little finite 'I,' the Immortal 'I,' which is the Lord of Love, is revealed in our consciousness.

मात्रास्पर्शास्तु कौन्तेय शीतोष्णसुखदुःखदाः ।
आगमापायिनोऽनित्यास्तांस्तितिक्षस्व भारत ॥२-१४॥

14. When the senses contact sense objects,
Kaunteya,[1] *we experience cold or heat,*
pleasure or pain. These are fleeting; they come
and go. Bear them patiently, Arjuna.

Sri Krishna is now telling Arjuna the nature of the stimulus and response relationship that our body, senses, and mind have with the finite world. When the material object that is the body comes in contact with other material objects, such as the dollar, then there is some kind of relationship established with which we have nothing to do at all. Sri Krishna, as I imagine him, now almost seems surprised and asks Arjuna, "Why should you get elated or depressed if one material object has its physical reaction with another material object?"

Depression has become one of the scourges of the modern world. Here the Gita can give immediate advice: when you are getting excited, when good things are happening to you, when fortune is smiling on you and you want to go on talking, telling everyone about how happy you are, that is the time not to get elated. On such occasions of elation – when your play is on Broadway, when your novel is on the best-seller list, when people are wanting your autograph – I am usually a bit of a wet blanket and say, "Now is the time not to jump up. Don't pick up the telephone. Don't call people. Just keep repeating the mantram." When the mind is getting agitated, when the waves of elation are starting to rise, do not give them a chance.

Elation expresses itself in many ways in many people. We have some friends for whom the danger signal is the tendency to talk constantly; for others it is grandiose visions of the future. Apparently modest, apparently humble people can have such grand visions of the future that it is difficult to remind them how ordinary most of us are in the present. People with a talent for writing, drama, music, or painting,

1. Here Sri Krishna addresses Arjuna by the familiar name Kaunteya, 'the son of Kuntī.' Kuntī is Arjuna's mother.

however mediocre, may get caught on such occasions in the visualization of scenes of great grandeur. They see audiences looking adoringly at them, fighting for their autograph, and in their elation they actually believe that these things can come true. The Gita suggests that when we conjure up elated visions of grandeur, we should guard ourselves against this kind of excitement. If we keep our equilibrium when good things happen, then when fortune frowns, as she surely will because that is her nature, we can sit back with fortitude and forbearance and remain secure.

When you are in a depression, do not withdraw into yourself. There are people with the best intentions who say, "We don't want to come and force our depression on others." This is another trick of the mind, which tells you, "Since you're in a depression now, why not confine yourself to your little cell?" This is likely to make you more and more depressed. When despondency comes, I would suggest a smile. Even if it does not look quite like a real smile, it does such good for everyone, because even a smile comes from a deeper level of consciousness. If you can at least repeat the mantram and smile, the great process of relaxation begins.

Not allowing ourselves to get elated is neither callousness nor passivity; it leads us into a deeper level of awareness where we find we are completely secure and joyful. Anything that tends to make us elated is inevitably going to throw us into depression, and one of my grievances against psychedelic drugs is the very deceptive state of euphoria into which they lead us. In order to guard ourselves against elation and the following state of deprivation, we cannot allow our senses to be stimulated unduly.

In the language of the Gita, not only elation and depression, not only pleasure and pain, but everything in life is a duality; and in order to attain samādhi, one of the magnificent disciplines taught by Sri Krishna is evenness of mind. He will say, *Samatvam yoga ucyate:* "Yoga is evenness of mind."

यं हि न व्यथयन्त्येते पुरुषं पुरुषर्षभ ।
समदुःखसुखं धीरं सो ऽमृतत्वाय कल्पते ॥२-१५॥

15. The person who is unaffected by these,
who is the same in pleasure and pain, is
truly wise and fit for immortality. Assert
your strength to realize this, Arjuna.

The Lord of Love begins to tell us how we can prepare ourselves for reclaiming our birthright of everlasting life. In the scriptures of all religions this promise of eternal life is given, but people usually understand it only as a very inspiring metaphor, not to be taken with scientific gravity. The mystics say that it is time that is an illusion; eternity is the reality.

How is it that you and I see people, very often our own dear ones, dying around us, and yet never ask ourselves the question: "Is this one day going to happen to me, too? Is there no way by which I can transcend death?" In my beautiful village in Kerala state, whenever a death took place, which is not infrequent in a poor country like India, my grandmother would always insist that I accompany her to the scene of sorrow, even when I was still an impressionable and sensitive child. As I sat by the side of dying people while my grandmother held their hand, it used to torture me. Even in my dreams, I long remembered the sight of all this agony I witnessed during the days when I was growing up at my granny's feet.

Later on, when through her blessing I began to turn inwards, I realized why she had taken me to those scenes of great bereavement. It was to make me ask if there were any way to transcend death. Her grace enabled me to know that in the midst of life I am in death, and it made me want above everything else to go beyond death, to attain immortality in this very life. As my meditation deepened, I was able to harness even the fear of death, turning it into power to help me to overcome death.

As I began to recall the words of my spiritual teacher, it began to dawn upon me for the first time that we are not mortal. When Einstein was asked how he discovered the law of relativity, he said that it was by questioning an axiom accepted by all the world, and the scriptures say the stage will come in your meditation when you will begin to question whether death is inevitable. This is not an intellectual question at all, but an experience in which some lurking suspicion comes into your consciousness and whispers that you are not mortal. Once you hear that, there is great hope, and a great desire to turn your back upon all lesser desires so that you can use all your capacity to make the supreme discovery that you are eternal.

In every religion, the great founders will promise us everlasting life. In the Bhagavad Gita it is enunciated in very clear terms. The Gita says that as long as we identify ourselves obsessively with our body, we will keep falling into the jaws of death. In meditation we can very skillfully minimize this obsessive identification with the body. On many levels, in many ways, we can practice the spiritual disciplines which will gradually lift us above physical consciousness, giving us a continuing sense of freedom and a continuing sense of progress on the spiritual path.

नासतो विद्यते भावो नाभावो विद्यते सतः ।
उभयोरपि दृष्टो ऽन्तस्त्वनयोस्तत्त्वदर्शिभिः ॥२-१६॥

16. The impermanent has no reality; reality lies in the eternal. Those who have seen the boundary between these two have attained the end of all knowledge.

The main difficulty with Arjuna, as with all of us, is that he looks upon himself as the body, as the biochemical mechanism with which all of us identify ourselves. Sri Krishna is trying to help Arjuna break through this wrong identification to remind him that he is not the perishable body, which is only the house in which he dwells. He is the imperishable Ātman.

In this verse Lord Krishna distinguishes between what is real and what is unreal. With the far-reaching spiritual penetration of the Sanskrit scriptures, the Gita says that whatever perishes is not real. Whatever exists in reality, exists always. That which comes into being today and passes away a hundred years from now cannot truly be said to exist. In this sense the body, which is conditioned by time, is unreal.

Mahatma Gandhi, who studied Sanskrit while in jail, pointed out that the Sanskrit word *sat* has two meanings: the first is 'truth,' and the second is 'that which is.' When asked for a definition of God, Gandhi said, "Truth is God. God alone is and nothing else exists." During the campaign to free India of British domination, he told the oppressed millions of India that evil has no existence in itself; we support evil, therefore it exists, but if we withdraw our support, it ceases to exist. In the example of his own life, Gandhi applied this truth on the practical level in his campaigns of nonviolent resistance against British exploitation.

Those who see the supreme Truth, the Lord, in their own consciousness, says Sri Krishna, know that that which is not real has no existence, and that which is real has no nonexistence. Arjuna just gets confused. He looks at his body, he looks at Sri Krishna's body, he looks at Sri Krishna's peacock feather, and he just cannot believe that all this is an optical illusion. This is why the Lord limits the vision of the unreality of the passing phenomenal world only to the great mystics, who have realized that beneath the apparent, impermanent world, the world of separate fragments, there lies the changeless Reality called God. But this vision does not apply to the vast majority of human beings. As long as we believe we are a separate fragment, as long as we identify ourselves with our body, we have to deal with the phenomenal world which is very real to us. I am real. Every one of us is real. Even after we realize the truth that all life is one, we can continue the activities of the workaday world, establishing personal relationships with loving artistry. We learn to show our love to each individual in the way that is most correct for that special relationship, though never forgetting the underlying unity of all.

अविनाशि तु तद्विद्धि येन सर्वमिदं ततम् ।
विनाशमव्ययस्यास्य न कश्चित्कर्तुमर्हति ॥२-१७॥

17. Realize That which pervades the universe
and is indestructible; no power can affect
this unchanging, imperishable Reality.

Sri Krishna is driving into Arjuna's consciousness the great truth that he is neither the perishable body, nor the changing senses, nor the unsteady mind, nor the wavering intellect, but the Ātman, as immutable and infinite as Brahman itself. The Lord of Love tells Arjuna the nature of that which pervades the cosmos. All that we see in life is pervaded by the immortal, immutable, infinite Reality we call God.

अन्तवन्त इमे देहा नित्यस्योक्ताः शरीरिणः ।
अनाशिनो ऽप्रमेयस्य तस्माद्युध्यस्व भारत ॥२-१८॥

18. The body is mortal, but he who dwells in the
body is said to be immortal and immeasurable.
Therefore, O Bhārata,[2] *fight in this battle.*

This body of ours will come to an end, but we, the Ātman, are eternal. Here again there is the reminder that we have no end, and therefore never should confuse ourselves with the perishable body. The body is changing from moment to moment, and even in the few minutes you have been reading these words, the body has already moved closer to the great change called death. The mind is subject to even more rapid changes. We have only to look at our desires and moods to see how much the mind is subject to change. In Sanskrit the word for the phenomenal world is *samsāra,* 'that which is moving intensely' – being born, dying, being born again, dying again.

Whenever we cling to anything that is continually changing, we will become more and more insecure with the passage of time. When we

2. Bharata was the first universal emperor of ancient India. By addressing Arjuna as Bhārata, 'descendant of Bharata,' Sri Krishna is reminding him of his nobility and his Indian citizenship.

identify ourselves obsessively with the body, every morning begins to pose a threat as we get older and move into the latter half of life. Every morning we look in the mirror to see if there are new wrinkles on the face, bags under the eyes, or grey showing in our hair. Even if, with the advance of modern surgery, these bags and wrinkles can be removed, after ten or twenty years the same fate will come to us. Such is the paradox of life: when we cling to the body, it loses its beauty, but when we do not cling to it, and use the body as an instrument given to us to serve others, even on the physical level it glows with health and beauty, as we can see from the lives of many great mystics. When Sri Ramakrishna walked along the streets of Calcutta, legends say people were dazzled by his beauty. His spiritual radiance was so great that it would shine through the body. Ramakrishna did not like drawing the attention of people, so with his childlike simplicity he got an old blanket and covered his body when going out. When our consciousness becomes pure, even the body begins to reflect its light.

The body is the temple of the Lord and must be looked after with care. Even at the age of seventy-seven, my grandmother had a beautiful, healthy body because she was always aware that this temple had to be kept in good order, swept with the mantram broom, and purified through the daily practice of meditation and discriminating restraint of the senses. We show respect for the Lord within by keeping the body healthy, clean, and beautiful. Any attempt to misuse the body, or to indulge the senses at the expense of the body, is a violation of the divine presence. Where books, movies, television, and our eating habits are concerned, we must be vigilant to see we are not indulging the senses at the cost of the health of our body or mind. Even with those who are making progress on the spiritual path, the senses can play havoc if vigilance is relaxed. In order to transform our belief that we are the changing body to identification with the Ātman, we begin by governing the senses very carefully for many years. This is not done in an ascetic spirit, or for the purpose of mortification, but to see that every day we give the body what is needed to sustain it as a spiritual instrument.

Just as we purify the physical body, called *sthūlasharīra* in Sanskrit, with vigilant care of the senses, healthy physical exercise, and repetition of the mantram, we purify the subtle body, *sūkshmasharīra,* by cultivating healthy thoughts. Thoughts are the food of the subtle body of *samskāras,* our mental and emotional conditioning.[3] We are eating this food all the time, and every time a thought rises in the mind we have added either to the nutrition of the subtle body or to its malnutrition. The unhealthy effect on the mind of anger, resentment, and hostility is so great that it can cause far-reaching damage even on the physical level. To keep the subtle body pure and healthy we must first and foremost cultivate the virtue of forgiveness.

य एनं वेत्ति हन्तारं यश्चैनं मन्यते हतम् ।
उभौ तौ न विजानीतो नायं हन्ति न हन्यते ॥२-१९॥
न जायते म्रियते वा कदा चिन्
नायं भूत्वा भविता वा न भूयः ।
अजो नित्यः शाश्वतोऽयं पुराणो
न हन्यते हन्यमाने शरीरे ॥२-२०॥

19. One person believes he is the slayer, another believes he is the slain. Both these are ignorant; there is neither slayer nor slain.
20. We were never born, we will never die; we have never undergone change, we can never undergo change. Unborn, eternal, immutable, immemorial, we do not die when the body dies.

Sri Krishna continues to explain our real nature in this verse, which is a favorite of mystics in India. *Na jāyate,* we were never born; *na mriyate vā,* therefore we will never die; *nā 'yam bhūtvā bhavitā vā na bhūyah,* we have never undergone any change, and we will never undergo any change. *Aja,* never born; *nitya,* eternal; *shāshvata,* immutable. And

3. A samskāra is a latency or a tendency in our personality, conditioned by experiences in this and former lives. It is almost always a negative term, implying rigidity and lack of freedom. A very strong samskāra might be called an obsession. *Samskāra* comes from the root *kri,* 'to do' or 'make,' plus the prefix *sam,* 'fully', 'completely'; therefore the word implies that something is fully formed, elaborated, or rigid.

finally, in a flash of subtle humor, the Lord adds *purāna*, 'the ancient one': compared to us the Himālayas are like a newborn baby. When the world was not, when the galaxies were not, we were already greybeards faltering with a staff.

The play of the Lord, in which he assumes a body and seems to pass through childhood, youth, and old age, is beautifully portrayed in Kerala in the Guruvayur Temple, dedicated to Lord Krishna. Sri Krishna is worshipped there in three different forms during the three periods of the day. In the morning if you go to the temple you will see a little baby Krishna in a cradle being fed, bathed, and sung to sleep. Most children like to go for the morning service. They see that the Lord is even younger than they, and they have such compassion for him, and feel so protective, that they do not want any harm to come to the little one. This protective feeling towards the Lord as a little boy is very good discipline for spiritual awareness. At noon Sri Krishna is a young man straight as a palm tree, outgoing and very vigorous. You see Lord Krishna as the embodiment of physical fitness at its best. You find the peacock feather, the garland of wildflowers, the yellow silk dhoti, and the bamboo flute. Young people like to visit the temple at noon, when it is easy for them to identify with the Lord. In the evening, when the sun is about to set and tropical India is at its artistic best, the old people like to go and see the Lord, who, hardly able to stand up with a staff, is ready to shed the body. The different images serve to remind you that these are all changes which affect only the body, and that you should learn to rise above the physical level so that you do not get caught in the cycle of change.

वेदाविनाशिनं नित्यं य एनमजमव्ययम् ।
कथं स पुरुषः पार्थ कं घातयति हन्ति कम् ॥२-२१॥

वासांसि जीर्णानि यथा विहाय
नवानि गृह्णाति नरो ऽपराणि ।
तथा शरीराणि विहाय जीर्णान्य्
अन्यानि संयाति नवानि देही ॥२-२२॥

21. Realizing That which is indestructible,
eternal, unborn, and unchanging, how
can we slay or cause another to slay?
22. As we abandon worn-out clothes and acquire
new ones, so when the body is worn out a new
one is acquired by the Self, who lives within.

In this homely verse, Sri Krishna says that just as when our clothes become old and tattered we throw them away to put on new ones, similarly, when this body has become unfit for serving others, it is time to throw it away. We should not cling to it. When Sri Ramana Maharshi's body was about to fall away and thousands of his disciples begged him to continue on, he said, "No, this body is no longer able to serve you. As long as it can serve you, I will retain it, but when the time comes when it can no longer serve you, I am going to lay it aside."

One of the facts about my granny's life that I do not usually refer to is her attitude towards death. For her, death was not a painful topic because she believed so firmly that our real Self cannot die. In other words, even though we cannot but grieve when our dear ones pass away, the mystics tell us that underneath this grief we should always remember that death is only a change of rooms. They are speaking mostly against the background of transmigration, or reincarnation. We should all be aware, though, that the spiritual life does not depend on our acceptance of reincarnation, nor does meditation require that we subscribe to the theory of transmigration of souls. Whether we believe in one life or in a million lives, the supreme goal is valid; the basis of meditation remains valid for all. I would strongly discourage trying to speculate about previous or future lives; this life is headache enough. Let us confine our attention to this life and try as far as our capacity goes to learn to love the Lord here and now.

नैनं छिन्दन्ति शस्त्राणि नैनं दहति पावकः ।
न चैनं क्लेदयन्त्यापो न शोषयति मारुतः ॥२-२३॥
अच्छेद्यो ऽयमदाह्यो ऽयमक्लेद्यो ऽशोष्य एव च ।
नित्यः सर्वगतः स्थाणुरचलो ऽयं सनातनः ॥२-२४॥
अव्यक्तो ऽयमचिन्त्यो ऽयमविकार्यो ऽयमुच्यते ।
तस्मादेवं विदित्वैनं नानुशोचितुमर्हसि ॥२-२५॥

23. The Self cannot be pierced by weapons or burned by fire; water cannot wet it, nor can the wind dry it.
24. The Self cannot be pierced or burned, made wet or dry; it is everlasting and infinite, standing on the motionless foundations of eternity.
25. The Self is unmanifested, beyond all thought and beyond all change; knowing this, you should not grieve.

Arjuna still does not grasp what Sri Krishna means by "our real Self, our Ātman." In this particular verse, the Lord is trying to awaken Arjuna, and all of us, to the truth of our existence. In referring to our real personality, which is divine, he uses three words beginning with *a*, which means 'not': *avyakto 'yam, acintyo 'yam, avikāryo 'yam. Avyakta* means 'that which is not expressed,' 'that which remains concealed.' Our real personality is not revealed at all; it is very cunningly concealed. It is *acintya*, or unthinkable, because it is beyond the dualities of conceptual thinking. It is *avikārya*, beyond all change. Our real personality never grows because it is ever perfect. It is never enriched because it is always full. If we try to understand the applicability of these three terms to our own personality, we may begin to suspect that it lies beyond the fleeting body, beyond the turbulent senses, beyond the restless mind, beyond the clouded intellect.

Avyakta comes from the word *vyakta,* which means 'completely expressed,' 'manifested.' We all look upon ourselves as only our apparent personality, the body-mind complex, never realizing our real personality, which is the infinite, immortal, immutable Ātman. If someone were to ask us what we consider our personality, we would be likely to say that our height is six foot three, our weight two hundred twenty pounds. To this a sage like Sri Ramana Maharshi would say, "I did not ask you the dimensions of your house; I want you to tell me what your real personality is." If we tell him that we have two million in the bank, the illumined man will say, "You haven't answered my question." If we add that we have won the Nobel prize, he would still say, "Don't beat about the bush."

Meister Eckhart summarizes the truth of the Ātman beautifully when he points out that the seed of God is latent in all of us. In Sanskrit it is called the Ātman; Meister Eckhart prefers to use the homely expression "the seed of God." He says that just as apple seeds grow into apple trees and pear seeds into pear trees, God seeds grow into God trees. The word *avyakta* implies that our only purpose in life is to reveal the divine personality that is concealed in all of us. The seed has to be helped to germinate, the weeds have to be removed regularly, and then the plant becomes a God tree.

The question then arises as to how we can reveal this hidden divinity in our everyday life. To see what noxious weeds keep the seed of our true divinity from growing, we have only to look at people who are insecure, who dwell upon themselves. Such people look at everything, everyone, through their own personal needs; these are the people who say they are very, very sensitive. In my early days in Berkeley, one of the expressions that I heard often when I visited Telegraph Avenue was "I'm so sensitive." According to this interpretation, "insensitive" refers to anybody who treads on my corns, although when I tread on another's corns, I don't even know it. In the language of the mystic, being sensitive means being sensitive to the needs of others. You will find that the more you attend to the needs of others, in your own family for example, the less you will get hurt, agitated, or hostile over seemingly trivial things.

In a movie my wife and I saw recently, one that had been highly praised by critics, the daughter could not sleep one night just because her mother had repeated one question twice: "Have you forgotten my candy?" The daughter thought that her insomnia that night was a result of utter sensitiveness. Now, my mother often repeats herself half a dozen times – repetition runs in our family. And I don't say she is casting aspersions on my integrity. I just say she knows I am an absentminded professor, and I am likely to forget things. As long as we are deeply convinced that our parents want only our happiness, that our partner or our children want only to add to our joy, things are not likely to upset us. My mother uses curt language at times, but under no circumstances would it occur to me to think that she is trying to vent some pent-up hostility or to take it out on me, say, because the milkman diluted the milk more than he is permitted to. Wherever there is not this deep faith in those around us, I think that no attempt at courtesy, no attempt to repeat the right words and phrases, will bring about clear communication. Whenever we get agitated or apprehensive in daily relationships, because of some remark, some act of omission or commission from those around us, the very best thing we can do is use the mantram.

All of us are trying to build our personality on the short span of time in which we thrash about in the sensory world. During the Anglo-Saxon period, a few Christian emissaries came to England to preach the gospel of Christ. One of the Anglo-Saxon kings, Edwin, took counsel with his advisors over the new faith. It must have been a bitter winter evening, with snow outside and torches lighting up the hall, for the answer Edwin received is as evocative as it is thoughtful. "My lord," one man replied, "it has often seemed to me that we live like a swallow that suddenly darts through this hall at dinnertime and passes out again through a far window. It comes from the darkness and returns to darkness; for only a short while is it warm and safe from the winter weather. That is how I regard our life. I don't know where I have come from; all I know is a little span of light, until I pass again into the darkness beyond. If this new faith can tell us truly what lies before and after, I think it most worthy of being followed."

The Gita says that outside of this life we come from infinity and go again into infinity. This short spell in between, called *vyakta,* the finite, the mortal, the physical spell, has hypnotized us so that we say, "My personality lives only for one hundred years, from the time my body was born until the time it will die." But in the first word of this verse, *avyakta,* we are reminded that our life is infinite. Jesus constantly reminds the people not only of ancient Judea but of the whole modern world that we can have everlasting life by rising above the physical level of consciousness. This is a great challenge that can set our imagination on fire if we can understand that it is possible to rise so high above physical consciousness and fragmentation that we can see not only what goes on in the lighted hall, but also what is outside in the infinite darkness beyond death.

The second word is *acintya.* Because our real Self, our divine personality, is beyond all the dualities of conceptual thinking, it can only be revealed when the turbulent factory of the mind has become completely still. For most of us, the mind factory keeps working twenty-four hours, day in and day out, without a holiday, and without any strikes either. There is only overtime. All of us must have experienced moments when we have begged, "If only I could stop thinking. If only I could close down, put up a little note, 'Don't enter here. It's a misdemeanor.'" If we could, we would find ourselves beginning to reveal our true identity. One of the unfortunate trends of our modern civilization is described by that learned phrase, *Cogito ergo sum:* "I think, therefore I am." The mystic says, "I have stopped thinking; therefore I am." You can see the diametrical contrast. We are all under the impression that if we go beyond thinking, we are nowhere. If the mind is closed down, we fear we will be out of a job: "What will I do? How will I spend my time? What will I dream about in my sleep?" The answer is: why do you want to dream? Why do you want to go after personal profit and personal pleasure? It is in forgetting yourself, and in serving others, that you really come to life.

One of the constant reproaches that used to be flung at me in my early days of meditation was, "You have such a fascinating personality.

Why do you want to throw it away? Look at your intellect, razor sharp; why do you want to blunt it? Look at your mind, so active, so productive; why do you want to still it?" It is not even possible for most of us to suspect that at present we have no personality. Most of us cannot reveal even one ray of the magnificence within us. This is why Sri Ramana Maharshi and other mystics will not take us seriously when we say we live. The mystics tell us that if we can only succeed in throwing away this mask which has become part of our face, the physical-psychical mask that we now call our personality, then all our magnificent capacity for loving, acting, and serving will come into our lives.

अथ चैनं नित्यजातं नित्यं वा मन्यसे मृतम् ।
तथापि त्वं महाबाहो नैनं शोचितुमर्हसि ॥२-२६॥

जातस्य हि ध्रुवो मृत्युर्ध्रुवं जन्म मृतस्य च ।
तस्मादपरिहार्येऽर्थे न त्वं शोचितुमर्हसि ॥२-२७॥

अव्यक्तादीनि भूतानि व्यक्तमध्यानि भारत ।
अव्यक्तनिधनान्येव तत्र का परिदेवना ॥२-२८॥

26. O mighty Arjuna, even if you believe the Self to be subject to birth and death, you should not grieve.
27. Death is inevitable for the living; birth is inevitable for the dead. Since these are unavoidable, you should not grieve.
28. Every creature is unmanifested at first, and then attains a manifestation, O Bhārata. When its end has come, it once again becomes unmanifested. What is there to lament in this?

In spite of all the Lord's assurances about the immortality of the Self, there still lurks in Arjuna's consciousness the thought: "I am the body; when the body dies, I die." This is one of the occasions in the Gita when Sri Krishna teases Arjuna, telling him that even if he believes he is the body, even then he should not be afraid of death, because death is the natural consummation of the body's span of life. The Lord is forcing Arjuna to break through his wrong identification with the body, which is only the house in which he dwells.

Through the practice of meditation, we will acquire the delightful incapacity to associate people very much with their physical appearance. If someone asks me, "How tall is Jeff?" I have to take time to try to picture him, then use a mental tape and try to remember his height. This is a healthy sign. Particularly when someone asks me how old a person is, it takes a certain amount of time for me to recall. When we do not associate people with their physical appearance, with their age, we are beginning to associate them with the Ātman. The more we dwell upon the physical appearance and age of others, the more we are conscious of our own appearance and age. The mystics tell us we should be concerned less about these details of packaging and concerned more with the contents. When I look at people, I like to look at their eyes. These are the windows into the contents, which is the Lord. Gradually, as we become more and more conscious of the Ātman, we will be looking straight at people through their eyes and deep into the Lord of Love who is within.

आश्चर्यवत्पश्यति कश्चिदेनम्
आश्चर्यवद्वदति तथैव चान्यः ।
आश्चर्यवच्चैनमन्यः शृणोति
श्रुत्वाप्येनं वेद न चैव कश्चित् ॥ २-२९ ॥

29. The glory of the Self is beheld by a few, and a few speak of its glory; a few hear about this glory, but there are many who listen without understanding.

Sri Krishna passes on to a verse for which there is a close parallel in the parables of Jesus. Sri Krishna says that people in their response to the spiritual life seem to fall into various categories. Similarly, Jesus tells this parable: "Hearken; Behold, there went out a sower to sow: And it came to pass, as he sowed, some fell by the wayside, and the fowls of the air came and devoured it up. And some fell on stony ground, where it had not much earth; and immediately it sprang up, because it had no depth of earth. But when the sun was up, it was scorched; and because it had no root, it withered away. And some fell among thorns, and the thorns grew up, and choked it, and it yielded no fruit. And other fell on good ground, and did yield fruit that sprang up and increased; and brought forth, some thirty, and some sixty, and some an hundred." (Mark 4:3-8)

It is a beautiful presentation. "And it came to pass, as he sowed, some fell by the wayside, and the fowls of the air came and devoured it up." Unless there is a window open in our consciousness, some entry into the deeper state of consciousness, we will be unmoved by even the most eloquent presentation of the spiritual life. Somewhere in our consciousness there must be the suspicion that the passing toys of the world can never satisfy us. Even intelligent, educated, successful people, after listening to a talk on the spiritual life and meditation, may turn to their friends and ask, "What is he talking about?" In such people there is no window open; they are skimming, however successfully, on the surface of life. Very often they may ask, "Why do we need meditation?" Or, after I have waxed eloquent on what meditation can do in transforming all that is ugly into all that is beautiful in our consciousness, some good people have come up and said, "We don't need meditation because we *are* beautiful. You folks need this transformation; evidently you have quite a lot to transform." Still others of this tribe will say, "We are always happy. We get up happy; we go to bed happy; even in our dreams we are happy." One of our friends on the Blue Mountain used to tell me to call such people "smiling cabbages." When Jesus talks about the seeds falling by the wayside and the fowls devouring them, he is talking mostly about people in whom the words go in one ear and out the other.

In order to grow, you need sorrow; in order to become loving, you very often need distress, and turmoil is often required to release your deeper resources. Unless you have suffered yourself, it is not easy for you to understand those who are suffering acutely. Unless you have gone through some of the distressing vicissitudes of life, you cannot easily sympathize with others. Many people, even when they have gone through a good deal, suffer from a convenient amnesia with the passage of time. Older people have a tendency to forget some of the things they did when they were young. That is why they condemn the failings of the younger generation too readily. Their own past sufferings should enable them to understand, sympathize, and help.

"And some fell on stony ground, where it had not much earth; and immediately it sprang up, because it had no depth of earth." This is the second category. In Sanskrit there is a word – *ārambhashūra,* 'those who are heroes at the beginning' – which applies to many of us. The first time we hear a good talk on meditation, we really catch fire. On one occasion a young fellow came up at the end of my talk and said, "This is what I've been looking for all my life." I am still looking for him. Others, on the way home, get a deerskin, a Patanjali pillow, Mysore incense, and Ravi Shankar records, all in preparation for meditation. But after this upsurge of enthusiasm has exhausted itself in shopping, meditation is forgotten. It is not enough if we content ourselves with the preliminaries; we have to see that it is not a temporary infatuation, which passes away within a few days. Jesus must have met quite a number of this type in ancient Jerusalem, because he goes into greater detail: "But when the sun was up, it was scorched; and because it had no root, it withered away."

"And some fell among thorns, and the thorns grew up, and choked it, and it yielded no fruit." This is the third type. When we were in Berkeley twelve years ago, we tried to have a vegetable garden at the back of our house. We had tomatoes, corn, and pumpkins. My agricultural advisor was a young British friend who knew even less about gardening than I did; his main advice to me was, "Give the weeds a chance." I listened to him carefully, and between us we got one ear of corn, a few tomatoes, and pumpkins which I was told would not be edible at all. The weeds had really prospered; they choked out the corn, the tomatoes, and the pumpkins. In meditation, even though we meditate regularly in the morning, if we do not take care to pull out the weeds that are rampant in the garden of the mind, spiritual seeds are not likely to thrive. On Lee Street, where we reside, we have one of the best lawns, thanks to our friend Sumner. The dandelions which used to form the majority on the lawn are now disappearing. The dandelions are rather attractive, and they also have a place in the scheme of existence, but on our street they are not looked upon with favor. In the early days, our neighbors must have found it a little disquieting when these dandelions came up so quickly. We would come and pull up the weeds, and as soon as we walked away the dandelions would say, "Have they gone? Let's come up." We didn't know about their habits, so we had just been pulling off the flowers and throwing them away. Later Sumner explained that their roots go deep, and unless something drastic is done at the root, it is not possible to prevent the dandelions from coming up.

"And other fell on good ground, and did yield fruit that sprang up and increased; and brought forth, some thirty, and some sixty, and some an hundred." There is sometimes a suspicion that the spiritual life is rather selfish. In the early days, when we try to make meditation the basis of our life and retire from some of our former activities and former cronies, it is not unlikely that we will be branded as unsociable. On such occasions we can strengthen ourselves by remembering that the practice of meditation is not going to benefit us alone. We may not be able to reach thousands, as does a great mystic like Sri Ramakrishna; but each of us, as our spiritual awareness deepens, can help a few members of our family and a few friends to find their center of gravity within.

देही नित्यमवध्यो ऽयं देहे सर्वस्य भारत ।
तस्मात्सर्वाणि भूतानि न त्वं शोचितुमर्हसि ॥२-३०॥

30. The Self of all beings, living within the body, is eternal and cannot be harmed. Therefore, you should not grieve.

In my village, where death was not uncommon, most people on their death bed would send for my grandmother just to have her sit by their side. They would hold her hand or look into her eyes, which said, "There is no death." For her, the dissolution of the body was not death at all. At the time of samādhi, this is the realization the lovers of God attain. When they become united with the Lord in their hearts, they go beyond identification with the body. The physical nexus is cut once and for all, and afterwards, though they look after the body very carefully, they know that it is just an instrument to be used to convey the truth of immortality to all those ready to receive it.

The body is not me; it is only the jacket which I wear. When this jacket is torn and tattered, the time has come for me to throw it away and put on a new jacket. Sri Krishna asks, "What is there to grieve about? What is so tragic about putting on a new jacket? Do you want to keep an old jacket that lets in cold air, makes you uncomfortable, and can no longer be used to serve others?"

When you are able to go deep into meditation and rise above physical consciousness, it will seem as though you can just take off the body as you would take off a jacket and leave it on the hanger until you finish meditating. If sometime in meditation you go very deep into your consciousness, after going home you may even find that you have left your jacket at the āshram. Mystics in India have been victims of this divine phenomenon at the most inopportune times. Once, while walking on the streets of Calcutta, Sri Ramakrishna heard a song about the Divine Mother, or saw someone seated in meditation with eyes closed, and had such a sudden transformation of consciousness that he dropped his dhoti. The dhoti is wrapped very gently around the hips. It is not meant for sudden attacks of higher states of consciousness; it is meant for the secular way of life. I can imagine Ramakrishna's embarrassed disciples gathering around him and asking, "Blessed One, where is your dhoti?" and he, in sublime simplicity, answering, "You ask me where is my dhoti? I ask you where is my body!"

Body consciousness is the obstacle to divine awareness, and every day we must ask ourselves what is likely to decrease our identification with the body. Whatever increases physical consciousness cannot be an aid to the spiritual life. Overeating, for example, intensifies body consciousness. Every time we are tempted to eat something because of an advertisement or an old samskāra, we should ask ourselves if the body needs it or if it will merely stimulate the palate. Once we start retraining our sense of taste, which is in the mind, we can enjoy green salad and fruits as the greatest of delicacies. Skipping a meal, especially when we have eaten a little more than is necessary at the previous meal, is another way of lessening body consciousness. Other aids for lessening physical consciousness are giving up harmful habits such as smoking, drinking, the use of drugs, and overindulgence of any kind. The Gita does not ask you to do this for puritanical reasons; it says that if you want to rise above physical consciousness, these are the things you have to throw away. Once this obsessive physical identification has been broken through, you feel so good, so high, all the time that you cannot imagine using any artificial aid to be a few inches high when you are now almost the height of the cosmos.

स्वधर्ममपि चावेक्ष्य न विकम्पितुमर्हसि ।
धर्म्याद्धि युद्धाच्छ्रेयो ऽन्यत्क्षत्रियस्य न विद्यते ॥२-३१॥
यदृच्छया चोपपन्नं स्वर्गद्वारमपावृतम् ।
सुखिनः क्षत्रियाः पार्थ लभन्ते युद्धमीदृशम् ॥२-३२॥
अथ चेत्त्वमिमं धर्म्यं संग्रामं न करिष्यसि ।
ततः स्वधर्मं कीर्तिं च हित्वा पापमवाप्स्यसि ॥२-३३॥
अकीर्तिं चापि भूतानि कथयिष्यन्ति ते ऽव्ययाम् ।
संभावितस्य चाकीर्तिर्मरणादतिरिच्यते ॥२-३४॥

भयाद्रणादुपरतं मंस्यन्ते त्वां महारथाः ।
येषां च त्वं बहुमतो भूत्वा यास्यसि लाघवम् ॥२-३५॥
अवाच्यवादांश्च बहून्वदिष्यन्ति तवाहिताः ।
निन्दन्तस्तव सामर्थ्यं ततो दुःखतरं नु किम् ॥२-३६॥
हतो वा प्राप्स्यसि स्वर्गं जित्वा वा भोक्ष्यसे महीम् ।
तस्मादुत्तिष्ठ कौन्तेय युद्धाय कृतनिश्चयः ॥२-३७॥

31. Considering your dharma, you should
not vacillate. For a warrior there is nothing
higher than a war against evil.
32. O Arjuna, the warrior who is confronted
with such a war should be pleased, for it has
come of itself as an open gate to heaven.
33. But if you do not participate in this battle
against evil, you will be violating your dharma
and your honor, and you will incur sin.
34. The story of your dishonor will be
repeated by people endlessly; and for a man
of honor, dishonor is worse than death.
35. These brave charioteers will think you have
withdrawn from battle out of fear; those who formerly
esteemed you will treat you with disrespect.
36. Your enemies will ridicule your strength
and say things that should not be said.
What could be more painful than this?
37. Death means the attainment of heaven; conquest
means the enjoyment of the earth. Therefore rise
up, Kaunteya, with the resolution to fight.

Now Sri Krishna begins giving specific instruction to Arjuna, a very practical man who is a little impatient with all the philosophical touches the Lord has been adding. He looks ready for the supreme teaching, and Lord Krishna, who knows when the time is right, plunges into the great verse:

सुखदुःखे समे कृत्वा लाभालाभौ जयाजयौ ।
ततो युद्धाय युज्यस्व नैवं पापमवाप्स्यसि ॥२-३८॥

38. Having made yourself alike in pain and pleasure, profit and loss, victory and defeat, engage in this great war and you will be freed from sin.

Tato yuddhāya yujyasva. Yuddhāya means 'for battle,' for the great war. We are all born to fight the ego, to do battle against the three phalanxes of the ego's formidable army: fear, which is the infantry; anger, which is the cavalry; and lust, most powerful of all, which is the elephantry. The language of the Gita is really appropriate when it describes this as a long, drawn-out war. If we talk in terms of one life, then all our life this war will rage; if we talk in terms of a million lives, against the background of evolution, this war has been going on all the time. The war is between what is selfish in me and what is selfless in me: what is impure in me pitted against what is pure in me, and what is imperfect against what is perfect.

Sukhaduhkhe same kritvā. Here is the way to embark upon this war against all that is death in yourself so that you may have immortal life. *Sukha* is pleasure; *duhkha* is pain. Make yourself alike in pleasure and pain. Here is one of the central themes of the Bhagavad Gita. Even if you fight with all your might, the ego will always win, you will always die again, the cycle of birth and death will go on and on, unless you succeed in being alike in pain and pleasure. When I used to hear this from my grandmother, I would always make the same practical objection: "I don't know how to do this. I like pleasure, and I don't like pain." In answer, her smile seemed to say, "How original of you!" This is everybody's problem; it is the human condition to be pleased by pleasure, and to be displeased by pain. This is why Sri Krishna says, *Sukhaduhkhe same kritvā:* transform your mental state into perfect equanimity if you do not want to die. When you get the firm resolve not to die, when there is no price you are not prepared to pay in order to transcend death, then you have the unfailing motivation for carrying out this great discipline of being alike in pleasure and pain.

When pleasant things happen to us, the mind immediately gets agitated, and we say, "I am pleased; I am happy." We wrongly identify ourselves with this passing wave of mental agitation called pleasure, and because we identify with the wave of pleasure, we cannot help identifying with the passing wave of pain also. When something is a little more pleasant, the mind gets a little more agitated and becomes excited. If we repeatedly get caught up in the same experiences of pleasure and excitement, they become samskāras; the mind becomes more turbulent, and we get caught more and more in the cycle of birth and death.

Suppose someone praises us, "Look at your hair: gleaming like molten gold. Look at your eyes: Mediterranean blue. Look at your lips: ruby from the mines of Golconda." When somebody praises our appearance, almost all of us respond in the same way; immediately our mind becomes agitated. The point Sri Krishna makes is not that we have to tell people, "Don't praise me; I am trying to make my mind calm." What Sri Krishna says is to be grateful if someone declares that you are irresistible, but do not depend for your security on that; do not allow your mind to be affected. The way to remain calm when good things are happening to you, when people are praising you, is to repeat the mantram. As soon as someone looks appreciatively at your appearance, start repeating *Rāma, Rāma, Rāma*. I know it is dampening, but as long as you are vulnerable to praise, you will be vulnerable to condemnation also.

Most of us do not realize how much we depend upon other people's approval for our security. The time may come on the spiritual path, as it came many times in the life of Gandhi, when people withdraw their appreciation and their support because we are not going the way they want us to go. When we are established within ourselves, criticism, even condemnation, will not shake our security, will not make us hostile. We can function beautifully alone, against the whole world if necessary. If criticism is destructive, we can ignore it; when it is constructive, we can benefit from it.

More than once the people of India refused to follow Gandhi, particularly in the early days. "You are an ascetic," they said. "You are a dreamer; you are impractical. We cannot follow you." Gandhi would always answer, in effect, "I am not asking you to follow me. If you want me, my terms are complete nonviolence. If you are not prepared for that, look for another leader." Many times he said this, and many times the people of India said, "All right, we are going to look for another leader." But after some days they would return to him. This is what faith in oneself means: if necessary, I will go alone. What do I want when I know the Lord is within me? Whose criticism am I afraid to face?

The Lord continues to emphasize the duality of life in the word *lābhālābhau*, 'profit and loss.' Today you may get fifty percent on your investment; tomorrow you may lose fifty percent. Be alike in gain and loss, not only in terms of money, but in terms of time, energy, and effort. Personal profit agitates the mind and gets you selfishly involved. "How much is it going to bring me? If it brings me fifty percent it is a philanthropic enterprise. If it brings me loss it is not good business." Even though you may have a high code of personal conduct, the mental agitation continues when you are attached to profit. In whatever you are doing, says Sri Krishna, keep your equanimity. He uses one more word, *jayājayau*, 'victory and defeat.' Make your mind alike in victory and defeat, in gain and in loss, in pain and in pleasure; then you will go beyond death to the supreme state.

एषा ते ऽभिहिता सांख्ये बुद्धिर्योगे त्विमां शृणु ।
बुद्ध्या युक्तो यया पार्थ कर्मबन्धं प्रहास्यसि ॥ २-३९ ॥

39. *You have heard the intellectual explanation of sānkhya, O Pārtha.*[4] *Now listen to the principles of yoga; by practicing these you can break through the bonds of karma.*

Arjuna is an intelligent man who has been taught by the best teachers in ancient India, and Sri Krishna therefore tries to satisfy his intellectual needs to some extent. This kind of intellectual background to the spiritual life is called *sānkhya*, which literally means 'counting' or

4. Another matronymic for Arjuna, meaning 'son of Prithā.'

'listing.' First the spiritual teacher lists carefully the benefits of meditation and spiritual disciplines; but listening to these theories is not enough. The disciple must begin their practice. The theory is called *sānkhya;* the actual practice is *yoga.* The word *yoga* often has been misunderstood, especially in the West, as the practice of certain physical exercises. These exercises are not yoga; they are *āsanas.* Neither is music or dancing yoga. There may be musicians in India who say their music is yoga, but it is not. There may be dancers who claim their dancing is yoga, but I am afraid it is not. Yoga is the practice of meditation and the allied spiritual disciplines. When the senses are stilled, when the mind is stilled, when the intellect is stilled, when the ego is stilled, then the state of perfect yoga is reached.

Arjuna, having accepted Sri Krishna as his teacher and listened carefully to his initial instruction, is now ready to hear in detail about the actual practice of spiritual disciplines.

In this verse the Lord promises Arjuna that if he practices these disciplines – bases his life on meditation, repeats the holy name, restrains his senses intelligently, and puts the welfare of all those around him first – then he shall go beyond the law of karma. The law of karma is not a concept limited to only the Hindu and Buddhist traditions; no one has stated this law in clearer terms than Jesus the Christ: "As ye sow, so shall ye reap." If we contribute to the suffering of those around us, we cannot escape the law which will bring this suffering back to us. Similarly, if we begin to keep the welfare of others in view, and contribute to it every day, we are contributing to our own joy as well.

In the ultimate analysis, our resentments and hostilities are not against others. They are against our own alienation from our native state, which is cosmic consciousness, Krishna-consciousness, or Christ-consciousness. All the time we are being nudged by some latent force within us. Somebody is trying to remind us what our native state is, and all the time we are under this pressure from within. Our senses are turned outwards, and we are adepts at personal profit and pleasure, so we do not like to hear these little reminders; but the needling goes on. When we get tense, it is easiest to vent our frustration by making cracks at our children, our wife, or our husband – it is just a matter of geographic proximity. When we attack other people, when we become a source of trouble to others, it is not because we want to add to their trouble; we have just become an object of trouble to ourselves. Our nerves are tense; we cannot sleep properly; we cannot sit down and meditate. Our partner is close by, our parents are close by, our neighbor is next door, so why not go and get them agitated? We succeed in agitating seven people, and each of them is now prepared to agitate seven more. Agitation, particularly the form that follows the precept "Express your anger; explode your anger on society," is infectious, and this chain of retribution will eventually bring our agitation back to us. When we are agitated, when we are ready to burst our anger upon others, the immediate solution is to go for a long walk repeating the mantram.

नेहाभिक्रमनाशो ऽस्ति प्रत्यवायो न विद्यते ।
स्वल्पमप्यस्य धर्मस्य त्रायते महतो भयात् ॥२-४०॥

40. On this path effort never goes to waste, and there is no failure. Even a little effort toward spiritual awareness will yield protection from the greatest fear.

For me this is one of the most memorable verses in the Gita, and it will take a lifetime on the spiritual path to appreciate its applicability to every aspect of human life. When we meditate on the Lord within for even a short time every day, this effort is not wasted. Even if we meditate only thirty minutes every morning, and try to practice the allied spiritual disciplines to a small extent during the day, this can go a long way in guarding us against many fears, known and unknown, which lurk in our consciousness. Most of us have fears of losing what we believe gives us security. Those who go after money are doing so under the impression that this is the way to become secure. They are the victim, the toy, of the stock exchange. There are others who are afraid of losing their youth. Beauty has nothing to do with age. We can be beautiful in childhood, in youth, and in old age to the extent we are unselfish. To be secure, we must find the source of security within ourselves. The advice given by Sri Krishna in the Gita is simple and profound: if times are bad today, try to contribute the best you can to the welfare of those around you. If times are good today, also try to contribute the best you can to the welfare of those around you. You can serve others no matter if times are good or bad. This is the choice we make in order to find security within ourselves.

व्यवसायात्मिका बुद्धिरेकेह कुरुनन्दन ।
बहुशाखा ह्यनन्ताश्च बुद्धयो ऽव्यवसायिनाम् ॥ २-४१ ॥

41. Those who follow this path, Arjuna, who resolve deep within themselves to seek me alone, attain singleness of purpose. For those who lack resolution, the decisions of life are many-branched and endless.

Sri Krishna says to look at the lives of worldly people, whose minds are many-pointed, jumping like a grasshopper from one blade of grass to another. Every day they keep making decisions, most of them wrong. This is the natural pattern of worldly life when we go after personal pleasure, profit, prestige, and power. In comparison, in the spiritual life only one major decision is necessary. If, after turning to meditation, we look back upon our past, upon the innumerable wrong decisions we have made in seeking fulfillment in the world without, going down one blind alley after another, and contrast this with our present development, where everything is being subordinated to reaching the supreme goal, we see that now our consciousness is slowly being unified.

We are all granted a reasonable margin in life to make our experimentation with personal pleasure, but one day we must begin to suspect that it is not going to fulfill our deepest need, which is for Self-realization. When we begin to have this suspicion, when it is already at work deep inside, we may still resist it for a while. We are all ego-centered, and it is only natural that when our old props are being taken away we fear that we are going to lose out. None of us need have any qualms if now and then a little voice whispers, "See what you are missing." Even after taking to meditation we are likely to have a few reservations. We may have a secret hope that in one of the rooms in our consciousness some old cravings can find an occasional welcome – we can leave the key under a stone, and they can just slip in; we do not have to invite them, but if they come we need not be inhospitable. In other words, we are all human.

In order to find the freedom of being able to function everywhere, under both hostile and favorable circumstances, to be able to reach the goal of Self-realization, we have to make the decision to find the Lord, and to subordinate everything else to union with him. If we can make this decision to base our life on meditation, to repeat the mantram as often as we can, to restrain the senses vigilantly, and to put the welfare of those around us first, the Gita says we need have no doubts about the outcome. We need not be anxious about the results; this is the Lord's responsibility. Self-realization comes through the grace of the Lord, who is ever present within.

यामिमां पुष्पितां वाचं प्रवदन्त्यविपश्चितः ।
वेदवादरताः पार्थ नान्यदस्तीति वादिनः ॥ २-४२ ॥
कामात्मानः स्वर्गपरा जन्मकर्मफलप्रदाम् ।
क्रियाविशेषबहुलां भोगैश्वर्यगतिं प्रति ॥ २-४३ ॥
भोगैश्वर्यप्रसक्तानां तयापहृतचेतसाम् ।
व्यवसायात्मिका बुद्धिः समाधौ न विधीयते ॥ २-४४ ॥

42–43. There are ignorant people who speak flowery words and take delight in the letter of the law, saying that there is nothing else, O Pārtha: whose hearts are filled with selfish desires, whose idea of heaven is their own enjoyment, and who engage in myriad activities for the attainment of pleasure and power. The fruit of their actions is continual rebirth.
44. Those whose minds are swept away by the pursuit of pleasure and power are incapable of following the supreme goal and will not attain samādhi.

One of the beauties of the Bhagavad Gita is that it does not say "You should do this" or "You should not do that." Sri Krishna simply says that if you want joy, security, wisdom, then this is the path. If you want sorrow, insecurity, and despair, then that is the path. He gives both the maps in graphic detail, and tells you that it is for you to decide where you want to go.

In these strong verses Sri Krishna describes those who will not see samādhi. Those who say there is nothing other than this world, who say there is no God, no other life than eating, drinking, making merry, and dying – such people will not attain samādhi. When people say they are atheists, I usually feel a little amused, because even to say that one is an atheist requires a definite experience. In order to say that there is no one in our deeper consciousness, we have to go there, knock on the door, and find that no one is at home. Of those who tell me they are atheists, I ask, "Don't you believe in yourself?" Their answer is, "Of course." "Then," I say, "you believe in God." When the Gita uses the terms "God" or "Lord," *Īshvara* or *Bhagavān,* it is not referring to someone "out there." It is referring to someone who is inside us all the time, who is nearer to us than our body, dearer to us than our life.

When our heart is full of selfish desires and sense cravings, we cannot see the underlying principle of existence which is divine. This is the significance of the word *kāmātmānah,* 'one whose soul is clouded over by selfish desires.' Ramakrishna was fond of saying that Rāma, the principle of abiding joy, and Kāma, selfish desire, cannot live together. This is difficult for most of us to understand because we usually feel that even if Rāma has to be brought in, Kāma can be given a little closet, or some little corner with a drapery so that he isn't visible. Every mystic worth the name says it must be Rāma *or* Kāma; we cannot have both together. Here, too, we have to be prepared for a long period of development before Kāma finally packs up his belongings and leaves without any forwarding address. Let us not get agitated if, after a long time on the spiritual path, we still feel some of our old cravings. As our spiritual awareness deepens, we will come not to identify ourselves with those desires. Then a big desire may come and crawl like a rat across the stage of our consciousness, but we will just calmly sit and watch.

It is when we identify with the desire that there is trouble. For a long period, I would suggest that when old desires and urges come, when the old samskāras come into play, the very best way to deal with them is to go for a long, brisk walk repeating the mantram.

त्रैगुण्यविषया वेदा निस्त्रैगुण्यो भवार्जुन ।
निर्द्वन्द्वो नित्यसत्त्वस्थो निर्योगक्षेम आत्मवान् ॥२-४५॥

45. The scriptures describe the three gunas. But you should be free from the action of the gunas, established in eternal truth, self-controlled, without any sense of duality or the desire to acquire and keep.

It is difficult to translate the word *guna;* the English word "quality" is only a rough equivalent. According to the cosmological theory presented in the Gita, everything in the universe is a combination of the three gunas – *sattva, rajas,* and *tamas* – in varying proportions. We human beings, also, are considered to be varying combinations of sattva, 'law'; rajas, 'energy'; and tamas, 'inertia.' Evolution is from tamas to rajas to sattva. This far-reaching concept not only accounts for the way in which human beings conduct themselves in daily life, but also gives guidelines as to how we can proceed on the path of evolution by transforming tamas into rajas and rajas into sattva.

Let us first take our good old companion tamas, inertia. Tamas shows itself in not wanting to move, not wanting to act – in other words, in wanting to be a stone just lying on the road. It is all right for a stone to be inert; that is its dharma. But it is not all right for you and me to be inert, to try to avoid problems, to say, "What does it matter?" When I hear the phrase "well adjusted," I do not always take it as a favorable comment. Mahatma Gandhi has said that to be well adjusted in a wrong situation is very bad; in a wrong situation we should keep on acting to set it right. When Gandhi, at the peak of his political activity, was asked in a British court what his profession was, he said, "Resister." If he was put in a wrong situation, he just could not keep quiet; he had to resist, nonviolently but very effectively, until the situation was set right.

In order to transform tamas into rajas there is a series of simple steps we can all take in our daily life. Postponement is one of the valuable allies of tamas. One of the ways to tackle inertia and expedite its transformation into rajas is never to delay anything. "Immediately" is one of the favorite words of the mystics, who live completely in the present. Jesus often used the word "forthwith."

Concentration is perhaps the most effective way of transforming tamas into rajas. Those who have a tangible element of tamas can work only for a little while. Even if they are enthusiastic, they will begin work with gusto, but at the end of thirty minutes their morale collapses. They often complain they are bored. The answer to boredom is to give a little more attention to what we are doing; any job, the moment we attend to it completely, becomes interesting. If a job bores us, we should not yield to tamas, but should give more attention to our work and try to increase our span of concentration. This not only helps us get over tamas, but helps our meditation as well.

The transformation of rajas into sattva is not extraordinary either, for all of us have an element of sattva in us. We all have this capacity for some degree of forgiveness and friendship in our relationships. It is already there; we just have to extend it slowly to include a wider and wider circle. There is no human being who does not have an element of tamas, and there is none who does not have an element of sattva. As tamas becomes transformed into rajas, particularly as our meditation deepens, there is more and more energy available to us; there is more capacity for productivity, for action, and for service. We must harness this newly released energy in order to transform it into sattva. One reason why I emphasize that we should have plenty of physical exercise, and should work at our job or studies with concentration, is that this enables us to harness all this energy. If we meditate regularly but do not take regular exercise, do not work at a suitable job, and do not give at least some of our time to selfless service without thought of return, there is a possibility that this energy may become too much for us.

Though there is a vital need for hard work, we should take care in our fast-paced modern world to see that we do not get caught in work.

This is one of the real dangers against which we should be on guard. There are people who become victims of work, who carry their work from their office or campus into their living room, then into the dining room while they eat, and then into the bedroom to dream about in their sleep. We should do our work with concentration and yet be able to drop it with complete detachment at a minute's notice. This frees us from tension and enables us to give our very best.

The characteristics of the man or woman established in sattva are calmness, compassion, and complete fearlessness. When the mind is agitated, judgment is likely to be clouded; therefore the Gita says we should never undertake any action when angry or afraid. Such action is not likely to be correct or effective. Any time our mind is agitated, the repetition of the mantram is a great help in calming our agitation, and when the mind is calm, judgment is clear.

Another characteristic of sattva is the capacity to forgive. Most of us perhaps are not even dimly aware of how, under the surface level of consciousness, old resentments keep burning, old hostilities keep flaming up. A sudden agitation, or a sudden depression, is often caused by old resentments which we still harbor in the depths of our consciousness. We cannot learn to forgive by reading books about forgiveness. I once saw a big book entitled *The Dynamics of Forgiveness*, and I could not help wondering what the author would have done to me if I had written a strong review against it. He probably would have come to the Center and given me a piece of his mind. Writing books about forgiveness, reading about forgiveness, and talking about forgiveness do not enable us to forgive. When we rely upon our own capacities, I do not think it is easy for us to forgive, but when we repeat the mantram, the holy name, we are calling upon the Lord to help us transform all our resentments into love.

Finally Sri Krishna concludes that it is not enough if we transform tamas into rajas and rajas into sattva; we must go beyond sattva also. Going beyond the three gunas means going beyond time, space, and causality – going beyond death into eternity, immortality, and infinity, here and now.

यावानर्थ उदपाने सर्वतः संप्लुतोदके ।
तावान्सर्वेषु वेदेषु ब्राह्मणस्य विजानतः ॥२-४६॥

46. Just as a reservoir is of little use to people when the country is flooded all around, so the scriptures are of little use to the illumined man or woman, who sees the Lord everywhere.

When the whole countryside is flooded, as it is during the monsoon in my native state of Kerala, where is the need for a little reservoir to get water from? In the villages of India, during the heavy monsoon period, all the tanks, pools, rivers, and wells are filled up with water. But as the summer sets in, wells begin to dry up; tanks and pools dry up, and people in the village have to walk long distances to the river to have their baths and fetch water. In the dry season not even a bucketful of water is wasted.

As long as the living waters of spiritual awareness are not flowing all the time within, you have to get little pots of water from outside. This evening you bring a little pot here to meditation class, and take it home full. By tomorrow the pot is empty, and you have to come again in the evening to see that it is filled up once more. Now all this is necessary, but when the living fountain from within bursts forth, when the love of the Lord who is ever present within wells up, why would you want pots? Why would a person want pools who is in the midst of the limitless sea of love? At that time, you do not need to meditate; you do not need the scriptures. You do not need to repeat the mantram, because it will go on in your consciousness ceaselessly. This is the great ideal to be attained; but for the present we must be regular about our meditation, repeat the mantram regularly, restrain our senses discriminatingly, and be careful to put the welfare of others first.

कर्मण्येवाधिकारस्ते मा फलेषु कदा चन ।
मा कर्मफलहेतुर्भूर्मा ते सङ्गो ऽस्त्वकर्मणि ॥२-४७॥

47. You have the right to work, but never to the fruit of work. You should never engage in action for the sake of rewards, nor should you long for inaction.

"You have only the right to act; you have no right to the fruit thereof." This line is often quoted by people who do not want to act, who get overpowered by circumstances and say, "What is the use? Everything is going to the dogs." But Sri Krishna is really trying to tell us here, "If you throw yourself heart and soul into a selfless undertaking, using the right means, the purest means that are available to you, I'll be responsible for the outcome." We all have to use our judgment, weighing the pros and cons before we select a selfless goal, assessing our capacity thoughtfully, and then selecting the right means. According to the great mystics, wrong means can never bring about a right end and right means can never fail to bring about a right end. This is why Gandhi has said, "Full effort is full victory."

Gandhi followed the path of karma yoga or selfless service, which requires the capacity to be perfectly detached from results and undaunted by reverses. When he returned to India from South Africa in 1915, the country had been in political bondage for nearly two hundred years, and nobody believed him when he said that through the grace of the Lord he could lead us to freedom without firing a shot, without using any means of violence. Everywhere he went, he identified himself with the people. He woke them from their long stupor, and within a little more than three decades, a very short period for a nation, the country became politically independent because of the tremendous capacity of nonviolence to win respect and cooperation even in Britain.

Gandhi was subject to the severest criticism, not only in foreign countries but in India as well. Composite photographs and scandalous stories were published in the papers. It is a painful experience when those who have supported us turn against us. Very few can remain calm and considerate when the crowd is crying for their downfall. This happened many times to Gandhi, and I do not remember even one occasion when he lost confidence in himself or in the final goal. At the same time he was very firm, saying, in effect, "If you are not prepared to be nonviolent, I do not want to have anything to do with you." He was prepared to wage the fight alone, because he knew that the Lord would use him as a humble instrument if he used right means for attaining a right goal.

The second line warns us not to interpret Sri Krishna's words as a counsel for inaction. There is sometimes a dangerous tendency in the contemplative life to withdraw, to retire into our ivory tower, to ignore the tremendous need for all of us to contribute selflessly to solve the problems of the world. Every one of us has a debt to pay in life, and those who drop out of society, who turn their backs on the problems of the world, are incapable of leading the spiritual life. The Gita is a forceful call to action – but to action in which the right goal is pursued by the right means.

योगस्थः कुरु कर्माणि सङ्गं त्यक्त्वा धनंजय ।
सिद्ध्यसिद्ध्योः समो भूत्वा समत्वं योग उच्यते ॥ २-४८ ॥

48. Perform work in this world, Arjuna, as a man established within himself – without selfish attachments, and alike in success and defeat. For yoga is perfect evenness of mind.

Here Sri Krishna defines yoga in a single word, *samatvam:* 'to be equal,' to be completely serene. This is yoga. Those who are established in yoga, who are illumined, are equally loving to the person who supports them and to the person who attacks them, equally concerned about the welfare of all around them, regardless of other people's attitudes and actions. Besides my granny, the one person I have seen in life who never allowed himself to be shaken by the attacks of unfavorable circumstances was Mahatma Gandhi, who is a source of inspiration as to how you and I can free ourselves from dependence upon public applause and appreciation. Following Gandhi's example we can develop such calmness and such confidence in the Ātman that during reversals of fortune, which will inevitably come to all of us, we can maintain our equanimity and tranquility. We do not need any external support because we are complete in ourselves. We need not be downcast when people withdraw their support, or even attack us, because we can draw upon the Lord within to face any challenge.

Sri Krishna tells Arjuna, *Yogasthah kuru karmāni:* "First become established within yourself, be united with me; then begin a career of selfless service." Do not be intimidated by heavy odds, by changing winds of fortune, or by the vacillations of people. *Sangam tyaktvā:* do not worry about the results, thinking, will this come about? How long will it take? Will the results be delayed? Do not be anxious about all this because you have nothing to do with results. This is the secret of Gandhi, who embodies the ideal of karma yoga for the twentieth century. From the Gita he learned to throw himself into an undertaking for a selfless goal, to use right means, and never to be anxious about the results.

Sri Krishna says *siddhyāsiddhyoh:* be alike in victory and defeat. What does it matter if you have won temporarily, or have been defeated temporarily? When victory comes, do not get elated; do not let the ego get inflated; do not go about saying, "I have won; I have defeated my opposition." Instead, remain calm, remain considerate, and remember that the Lord has given you victory. When defeat comes, do not moan, but grit your teeth and increase your effort, using right means to attain a selfless goal. This is yoga; this is the spiritual life: being alike in pain and pleasure, victory and defeat, praise and censure.

The Gita is a call for enthusiastic, selfless action. Sri Krishna impresses upon us that by practicing meditation daily, by repeating the mantram daily, we too can learn to establish ourselves within Him and then throw ourselves into tireless service for our family, community, country, and world.

दूरेण ह्यवरं कर्म बुद्धियोगाद्धनंजय ।
बुद्धौ शरणमन्विच्छ कृपणाः फलहेतवः ॥२-४९॥

49. Seek refuge in the attitude of detachment and you will amass the wealth of spiritual awareness. The man who is motivated only by desire for the fruits of his action, and anxious about the results, is miserable indeed.

"Miserable" is the word used here to describe people who are caught in results. Such people do not have any peace of mind; they are consumed with the anxiety, "Am I going to fail? Am I going to succeed?" They begin to use unscrupulous means once they become afraid of not achieving the results they desire. Sri Krishna tells us through Arjuna: "Whatever you do, therefore, do not get caught in the result. That is for me to give; as long as you use right means and strive for a selfless goal, you can be sure that I shall give you the right results."

Even after we have selected a selfless goal and the right means, and have thrown ourselves into the endeavor, we have to free ourselves from anxiety about the results, which is the most difficult part of the discipline for all of us. If I may take an example from our own work, when I started looking for an āshram over ten years ago, I could not help being somewhat entangled in the results. Now, through long, strenuous years of detaching myself, and through the hard discipline of reminding myself that the results are not in my hands, that the world does not belong to me, that not even a leaf of the tree in the back yard belongs to me, I have been relieved of all anxiety and agitation. Today I take a great deal of interest in finding a suitable āshram – read the papers, underline the property that is likely to be of interest to us, go to these places and ask, "What is the temperature like? Do many motorcycles come this way?" I do everything possible to further our work, but I do not get at all apprehensive. I do not get at all anxious about the results because I know these are in the hands of the Lord, and it is for him, who knows our needs and our difficulties, to give us the right place at the right time. This is detachment: throwing oneself completely into selfless work, and yet knowing the results are always in the hands of the Lord.

बुद्धियुक्तो जहातीह उभे सुकृतदुष्कृते ।
तस्माद्योगाय युज्यस्व योगः कर्मसु कौशलम् ॥ २-५० ॥

50. When consciousness is unified, all vain anxiety is left behind. There is no cause for worry, whether actions proceed well or ill. Therefore, devote yourself to the disciplines of yoga, for yoga is skill in action.

"Yoga is skill in action." When we become detached from results and work hard without thought of profit or prestige, deeper resources come to us. We see our way clearly; we do not waver when difficulties come. Selfish motives hide our goal, for when we are attached to results, when we are worried about the outcome, we do not see the goal; we see only the opposition and the obstacles before us. Most of the time we just do not know what to do when caught in a wrong situation in which we should not rest content. Feeling unequal to the difficult circumstances, we become resigned. But no matter how complicated and explosive the situation may be, there is always something we can do. Many small people working together can take on even the biggest problem of our age – violence. Sri Krishna repeats over and over again, "Do not get caught in the results. I am in you; therefore keep on striving, and at the right time I shall give you victory."

कर्मजं बुद्धियुक्ता हि फलं त्यक्त्वा मनीषिणः ।
जन्मबन्धविनिर्मुक्ताः पदं गच्छन्त्यनामयम् ॥ २-५१ ॥

51. The wise, who have unified their consciousness and abandoned the attachment to the fruits of action which binds a man to continual rebirth, attain a state beyond all evil.

Sri Krishna continues to tell us the secrets of karma yoga, the path of selfless action. Whatever the situation, we can act if we do not get caught in results; karma yoga can be practiced against the heaviest odds if we do not allow the ego to get us caught in attachment to results. Prior to Gandhi, even people who had seen and grieved over the political bondage of India could not bring themselves to act because they thought the situation was impossible. They could not act because even before taking the first step they were already caught in results. We too, when faced with problems, have a tendency to think, "There is nothing we can do about it." The secret of karma yoga is never to accept a wrong situation, a situation in which you are exploited, discriminated against, or manipulated, because it is bad not only for you but for the exploiter as well. In the early days, before India's independence, I myself used to see how young British men coming to India, fair-minded and interested in doing a good job for the benefit of the people, would gradually lose their fairness and come to believe they were superior, sent to civilize the people of Asia. This is a deterioration in character that no exploiter can escape. We all know, even in our own personal life, that with selfish people if we yield an inch, they will ask for a yard. In such cases, therefore, it is necessary quietly to say no. This is the great art of nonviolent resistance, where you love and respect everyone, but you will not allow anyone to exploit you, because it is bad for that person just as it is bad for you. Wherever we find a wrong situation – in our personal life, in our country's life, or in our world's conflicts – we all have a duty to work to correct it.

In karma yoga every reverse will send you deeper into your own resources. This is one of the marvelous changes in perspective that comes over you in deepening spiritual awareness. When an obstacle is coming you say, "Come on. Let it be a big reverse, because then it will drive me deeper." You lose your fear of defeat. You learn to use defeat and disappointment to deepen your resources. Lord Krishna says, therefore, "Do not be afraid if out of my love for you I send you a few defeats. On the surface level you have no weapons, but when I send you defeat after defeat, then you will be able to draw upon your deeper awareness where my resources will be open to you."

यदा ते मोहकलिलं बुद्धिर्व्यतितरिष्यति ।
तदा गन्तासि निर्वेदं श्रोतव्यस्य श्रुतस्य च ॥२-५२॥
श्रुतिविप्रतिपन्ना ते यदा स्थास्यति निश्चला ।
समाधावचला बुद्धिस्तदा योगमवाप्स्यसि ॥२-५३॥

52. When your mind has overcome the confusion of duality, you will attain the state of holy indifference to things you hear and things you have heard.
53. When you are unmoved by the confusion of ideas, and your mind is completely united in love for the Lord of Love, you will attain the state of perfect yoga.

The Sanskrit word used here for "confusion" is *moha,* the duality of the sensory experience, beyond which lies the unitive state of samādhi. When we cease to pursue sensory pleasure in the hope of finding lasting joy, which the senses will never be able to give, we come to have what the Catholic mystics call "holy indifference." This is not a negative state, but a very positive one in which we learn to make the mind undisturbed and equal under all circumstances. When the mind is calm it is ready for samādhi.

अर्जुन उवाच ।
स्थितप्रज्ञस्य का भाषा समाधिस्थस्य केशव ।
स्थितधीः किं प्रभाषेत किमासीत व्रजेत किम् ॥२-५४॥

ARJUNA:

54. Tell me of those who live always in wisdom, ever aware of the Self, O Krishna; how do they talk, how sit, how move about?

This question of Arjuna's introduces the glorious eighteen stanzas which, as Gandhi points out, hold the key to the interpretation of the entire Bhagavad Gita. Gandhi, a devoted student of the Gita, was especially drawn to these last eighteen verses of the second chapter. I have seen him meditating on them with such intense concentration that as

I watched, I could see the great stanzas coming to life in a human being. When Gandhi said that the Gita describes the war going on within, scholars in many countries, including India, would not take him seriously. In reply, Gandhi only asked them to look at these verses and see what reference there is to the conquest of international enemies, the conquest of enemies outside. In every verse of this passage we have clear proof that the battle referred to is within, between the forces of selfishness and the forces of selflessness, between the ferocious pull of the senses and the serene tranquility of spiritual wisdom. I strongly recommend these verses to be memorized for use in meditation because they gradually can bring about the transformation of our consciousness. The secret of meditation is that we become what we meditate on, and when every day we use these verses with the utmost concentration we are capable of, gradually we will become what they describe as the God-conscious person. If I might refer to my own small spiritual endeavor, before taking to meditation I was subject, as most normal people are, to all kinds of cravings and foibles that naturally led me to make many mistakes. But due to the spiritual awareness emanating from these verses, I have been able to surmount these obstacles. It is because of this small personal experience that I recommend all of you use these verses in your meditation.

What Sri Krishna is really trying to do in the first part of the Gita is to rouse Arjuna's interest, to prepare him for receiving instruction, and to make him ask this practical question. Without this preparation it is difficult to communicate spiritual wisdom. When I give my introductory talk on meditation, sooner or later there will be someone in the audience to say, "How do you do it?" In the early days I had to restrain myself from saying "Hurray!" because this is what I had been waiting for. Arjuna now begins to ask the same kind of question, which Sri Krishna has been waiting impatiently to hear.

Here Arjuna calls the Lord by a very charming name: *Keshava,* 'he who has beautiful, infinite hair.' In the Upanishads there is a marvelous simile that describes the entire cosmos as hair growing out of the Lord's head. In order to understand the beauty of this name *Keshava,* you really have to go to India, and to Kerala more than any other state, where women have the longest, richest, blackest hair. Early morning when they go to the temple pool to have their bath, it is a gorgeous sight to see their hair cascading down their backs, sometimes reaching even to the knees. Long black hair has always been considered a great mark of beauty, and when Arjuna uses this loving term, Sri Krishna must be blushing under his deep blue complexion.[5]

Arjuna asks, *Sthitaprajnasya:* "Tell me about the person who is firmly established in himself." *Kā bhāshā:* "What kind of person is he?" *Samādhisthasya:* "Tell me a few words about his samādhi; how does he live in union with you?"

Sri Krishna wants Arjuna to be more explicit, and probably the look in the Lord's eyes makes Arjuna feel he is expected to be more precise. Arjuna gets the point and says, *Sthitadhīh kim prabhāsheta kim āsīta vrajeta kim:* "How does such a person talk? How does he sit? How does he walk, move about, and conduct himself in the everyday vicissitudes of life?" It is a marvelous question, in which Arjuna by implication is telling the Lord not to recommend the study of the scriptures, not to give him papers published on the subject, not to impart some spiritual gossip, but to give clear signs as to how he can recognize the illumined man or woman who lives in complete union with the Lord.

श्रीभगवानुवाच ।
प्रजहाति यदा कामान्सर्वान्पार्थ मनोगतान् ।
आत्मन्येवात्मना तुष्टः स्थितप्रज्ञस्तदोच्यते ॥२-५५॥

SRI KRISHNA:

55. They live in wisdom who see themselves in
all and all in them, whose love for the Lord
of Love has consumed every selfish desire
and sense craving tormenting the heart.[6]

---

5. Sri Krishna is usually depicted as blue. The scriptures say he is *meghashyāma,* 'dark like a cloud'. His color may suggest the all-encompassing sky.
6. The last eighteen verses of Chapter 2 make an ideal passage for meditation. See pages 393–394 for a translation that has been made especially for this purpose.

They are established within themselves in whose hearts every selfish desire has been completely eliminated. The word the Lord uses here is *kāma*, which I translate as 'selfish desire.' Though the dictionary gives other meanings as well, the significance of the word is selfishness, especially as it expresses itself in cravings on the sensory level. The Lord is very particular about his words in this verse: *kāmān sarvān*, 'all selfish desire.' Not a trace of any selfish desire, which agitates all human minds, may remain. Sri Krishna looks compassionately at Arjuna, whose eyes reveal his thought: "Does it mean *all*?" This is why I say that Arjuna represents you and me perfectly; we, too, feel that Sri Krishna must mean just the majority of desires, that a few must be allowed.

There is no human being, unless he or she belongs to the category of Jesus, the Buddha, Sri Ramakrishna, or Sri Ramana Maharshi, who does not have some taint of selfishness in their consciousness. Sri Ramana Maharshi will say that selfishness is I-ness. He also says that the I-thought is the mind. When in the Christian tradition St. Paul says, "Not I, not I, but Christ liveth in me," he is also showing us that if we could tirelessly endeavor to expunge the I-concept from our consciousness, purification would be complete. In Sanskrit the word used for separateness and selfishness is *ahamkāra: aham* means 'I'; *kāra* means 'maker.' This 'I-maker' shows itself in many, many ways in daily conduct and behavior, particularly in our intimate personal relationships.

Anything we can do to subordinate our profit, our pleasure, and our prestige to the welfare of all those around us naturally results in the reduction of I-consciousness. When we keep imposing our self-will on, for example, our partner – very often unwittingly and under the impression that we are defending our rights – to that extent we actually are adding to our separateness, building up a higher wall between our partner and ourself. In the early days of almost all married relationships there is this tendency to stand on our rights, and to get so agitated when our rights are violated that we naturally build a higher and higher wall under the impression that we are demolishing it. Right from the early days of marriage, or of any relationship, we must try to forget about rights and remember duties if the relationship is to last.

One of my favorite poets when I was professor of English was Milton, who has given the world a spiritual masterpiece in *Paradise Lost*. There is a moving sonnet by Milton on his blindness which concludes with the lines:

> God doth not need
> Either man's work or his own gifts. Who best
> Bear his mild yoke, they serve him best. His state
> Is kingly: thousands at his bidding speed,
> And post o'er land and ocean without rest;
> They also serve who only stand and wait.

I interpret this "standing and waiting" as inexhaustible patience, as bearing with people, particularly in close personal relationships. When everything around us is swirling, when we feel our feet are slipping, we get terrified. We fear that we are going to be swept away, and even with our very good intentions, we are not sure whether unkind words may not come out of our mouth, whether unkind actions may not come from our body. It is when everything is uncertain like this, when the whirlpool is going round and round, that we must be able to draw upon enormous patience to stay firm and steadfast. This is the significance of the word *sthitaprajna,* 'established in wisdom.' On every occasion where there is resentment, resistance, and hostility around us, let us not use it as an opportunity for making ourselves more uncertain, more unstable, and more insecure by taking it out on other people and retaliating. Let us instead forgive and help them to overcome their problems, which means we will also be helping to eliminate our separateness.

The capacity to yield is not defeatism; it is not weakness. It is immense strength whereby you are able to get over your demands, your claims, the shrill voice of your ego, to contribute even to those who oppose you, ridicule you, attack you. Without forgiveness, I do not think anyone can enjoy life. In order to enjoy life completely, it is not a bank balance or material possessions that is required, but an immense capacity to forgive those who injure you and are hostile to you. St. Francis of Assisi puts it perfectly when he says that those who have not learned to forgive have lost the greatest source of joy in life.

We can recognize those who are united with the Lord of Love, ever present in us all, because they have been enabled by the grace of the Lord to come out of the forest of selfish desires in which most of us seem to be wandering, unable to find our way. Life on the egoistic level, on the physical level, is called *samsāra,* which is from the root *sri,* 'to move.' Samsāra is that which is moving all the time, the ceaseless flux of life in which we cannot stand anywhere. Everywhere is movement; everywhere is change and flux. This is the cycle of birth and death, whether we believe in reincarnation or only in evolution.

In one of the great scriptural stories of Hinduism, the ferocity of the senses is brought out with terrible humor. A man who is very body-conscious, as we all are, was being pursued by a tiger. The man, panic-stricken, ran as fast as he could until he reached the brink of a precipice. There, just when he thought the tiger was about to pounce upon him, he saw a mango tree below him and leaped down onto it, finding shelter on one of the middle branches. The tiger was standing on top of the precipice looking down with its tongue hanging out. The man breathed a sigh of great relief and started to climb down the trunk of the tree. He looked down and there was another tiger looking up at him. This is samsāra. In this most precarious position – death above, death below – the man sees a mango. "Ha!" he says. "Just what I've been looking for." At that moment tigers, life, death, samsāra, all disappear, just for the few moments' satisfaction of a sense craving. It is a terrible story because this is what sense craving can do to us. At the particular moment when there is a fierce sensory craving, even though we are being submerged under it, it is good to remember that the nature of the mind, the nature of desire, is to change. If we can hold out and resist the temptation, we are free.

दुःखेष्वनुद्विग्नमनाः सुखेषु विगतस्पृहः ।
वीतरागभयक्रोधः स्थितधीर्मुनिरुच्यते ॥२-५६॥

56. Not agitated by grief or hankering after pleasure,
they live free from lust and fear and anger.

This second verse in the inspiring picture Sri Krishna is painting of the illumined man or woman is of extreme importance in daily life, because according to the Gita the very texture of this life is one of duality – pain and pleasure, success and defeat, birth and death. Like most of you, in my earlier days, I also held on to the hope that I would be able to isolate pleasure, take it home, keep it on my table, and throw out pain. This has been the hope of every ambitious person, but up to this day no one has succeeded. If you go after pleasure, honesty demands, you cannot complain when you come across pain. If you do not want pain, do not go after pleasure either.

When we hear this from the Gita, we immediately get frustrated because we believe, on the evidence of the intellect and senses, that we have a choice of either pain or pleasure. There is no choice. But when we do not go after pleasure, we do not have to be on intimate terms with pain; we go beyond the duality of pain and pleasure, into a state of tranquility, serenity, security, and abiding joy. Beyond pleasure and pain there is this realm of abiding joy that is called, to use Gandhiji's phrase, *Rāmarājya,* the Kingdom of Rāma. We just do not want to go there. We want to live in the border kingdom where we are haunted by pain and pleasure.

Sri Krishna does not use mystical terms here; he does not go in for exaggerated language. He asks, "Don't you want to be *sthitadhī*?" This means: aren't you tired of being a plaything of the forces of life, of being pushed by pleasure here and pulled around by pain there? Aren't you tired of being dependent upon other people's praise, afraid of other people's censure, trying to manipulate people and to return unkindness for kindness?

We all need joy, and we can all receive joy in only one way, by adding to the joy of others. This is the simple teaching of the Gita: do not complain against the Lord, and do not complain against fate; if you are miserable, it is because you have added to the misery of others. If you are very happy, it is because you have added to the happiness of others. Sri Krishna says that no matter what may have taken place in your past, here is the choice you have today; why don't you make it? Often our way of translating this into action is to write in our diary, "Today I began a life of putting other people first," and to have a sticker on the back of our car saying "Put Others First" and a button saying "I Put Myself Last." This is all very easy, but it does not add to security; it does not add to anybody's joy except that of the manufacturer of the sticker and button.

We have been dwelling upon ourselves so long, caught for so long in our own needs, urges, impulses, and conditioning, that we should be patient with ourselves while undergoing the discipline of gradually subordinating our personal profit and pleasure to the needs of those around us. This is the first and last of the spiritual disciplines, and it is not a matter of high IQ. It is a matter of high WQ, Will Quotient.

In order to strengthen the will, start early morning when you want a third piece of toast. Just push it away, and you have increased your will. From breakfast onwards this goes on, and every time you can say no to the craving of the palate you have added to the will just a little. Now just imagine: breakfast, lunch, high tea, dinner, and midnight snack; five attempts at strengthening the will every day – in one month, one hundred fifty opportunities. When you do not yield to the craving of the palate, after a long period of discipline the great day will come when you will realize that these cravings were a thorn in your flesh.

An even more effective way of increasing your will is to put the comfort and convenience of other people first in situations where you are used to putting yourself first. In many little matters every day it is very painful to make these concessions. It is not too difficult to be a hero on a great stage, but to be a hero when nobody is looking except your cat is extremely difficult. When there is an immense upsurge of self-will saying, "This is how I want it to be. Not you, not you, but me!" that is the time to give, particularly to your parents, to your husband or wife, to your children, and to your friends. That is the time to yield, and yield, and yield. You will find, beautifully enough, that when you start practicing this others start doing the same. This is the advantage of a spiritual family where everybody is putting the welfare of everybody else first – everybody is first.

I do not indulge in too much sympathy when I see someone is growing up, even though he or she groans a little. Whenever I see somebody growing up and standing on his or her own feet, it is a day of jubilation for me. Tears, sighs, and groans are a part of the process of growth; so Sri Krishna says that when suffering comes, we should remember that we can use it to increase our spiritual awareness. It is said that pain is the only teacher you and I will accept, and without this stern teacher, none of us would grow up to our full stature. When we are suffering, we may be tempted to say, "If the Lord wants me to lead the spiritual life, I would expect him to be more cordial and more hospitable, instead of hitting me and making me cry. This is no way to treat a devotee." The Lord is extremely fond of us, but he has no sense of false pity. He wants us to grow out of our selfishness and separateness to be united with him, and he knows suffering is often the only language you and I understand.

यः सर्वत्रानभिस्नेहस्तत्तत्प्राप्य शुभाशुभम् ।
नाभिनन्दति न द्वेष्टि तस्य प्रज्ञा प्रतिष्ठिता ॥२-५७॥

57. Fettered no more by selfish attachments,
they are not elated by good fortune or
depressed by bad. Such are the seers.

Sarvatrā 'nabhisneha: his wisdom is unshaken, he is deeply rooted in himself, who has no trace of selfish attachment on any level. In all the mystical teachings, we are told it is our identification with the ego, our obsessive attachment to our self-will, which is responsible for the friction, frustration, and futility in our lives. The most unfortunate part of this tragedy is that as long as we are caught in the ego trap we will always maintain we are free. With a certain degree of progress in meditation, we come to realize with great alarm how even in the most endearing of human relationships there is the tendency to impose our self-will unwittingly and unconsciously on those around us.

There is a Sanskrit saying that gives the key as to how we can remove the taint of egoism in our relations with our children. According to this Hindu saying, until the child is five we should treat the little one as a god or goddess. This does not mean that we give up our power of authority, but that we give the children all the attention and affection we can, hugging them, carrying them, and keeping them physically close to us. Such affection is essential for maintaining unity on the physical level, and children respond to it easily. These five years of intense physical intimacy and intense emotional love reassure them more than any other experience – more than any words can – and in later life they will be able to draw upon this security they received in early childhood.

Three or four days ago, while we were seated in a restaurant, we saw a couple come in with a little baby, probably a few months old. Both of them were expressing their love for the little one and smoking the whole time. It is not enough if we talk about loving our children; we have to show our love in our personal life in every way, and this can be very, very difficult. If we want to be a loving parent, we cannot afford to smoke, because it is a bad example we are setting before the child. If we want to be a loving parent, we cannot afford to drink; we cannot afford to be selfish. It is an extremely serious responsibility to be a good father or mother. Those parents who can put their children's welfare first all the time, and can teach by their personal example of vigilantly restraining the senses and adding to the welfare of others, may rest assured that their children will follow their example when they grow up.

It is good to remember the words of Jesus: "Unless you become like a little child again, you cannot enter the kingdom of heaven." As Wordsworth puts it: "Heaven lies about us in our infancy"; and when we fail to set an example before our children, we are violating their divinity.

One day when Sri Krishna was a little boy, his mother was churning curds into butter in an earthen pot, using a wooden pestle which she moved round and round by means of a rope. Little Krishna was up to mischief as usual, and when his mother tried to get him to behave like an obedient child, he was defiant. She took the rope she was using and said, "If you don't stop your mischief, I'm going to tie your arms." Little Gopāla opened his rosebud of a mouth and put out his arms. The mother came up and tried to tie his hands, but the rope would not reach. She got another rope, but it also was not long enough. Soon everybody on the street had become interested. They all brought ropes and tied them together until the rope was very, very long, yet it would not reach around the wrists of the boy because of the infinity of the Lord present in him. With his slender hands he held the whole cosmos. Consciousness of this divinity of children can enable all parents to lead lives of reasonable sense restraint and utter selflessness in order to inspire their little ones to realize the divinity ever present within them.

After five, until the age of sixteen, the Sanskrit injunction tells us to treat our child as a servant. It sounds harsh, but the more I see of life, the more I appreciate the utility of this training in obedience. In modern psychology, it is said that growing young people get puzzled when their parents cannot take a positive stand. Even though teenagers may slam the door in anger, I think they cannot help appreciating parents who can draw a line very intelligently and tenderly, showing them they must learn to discriminate in life. It is during the years five to sixteen that children are going to rebel, and it is during these years that they must learn to obey their parents so they can learn to obey the Ātman later on. In their daily life the parents have to approximate themselves to the image of the Ātman. This is why parenthood is an extremely valuable aid to meditation.

From sixteen on, the saying concludes, your children are your equal. Afterwards do not try to push them about; do not throw your weight about, but try to explain. Appeal to their sense of reason; try to make them understand your position, and make a great effort to understand theirs. It is because parents and growing young people find themselves unable to be detached from their opinions that there is conflict, and obsessive identification with opinions can be the worst kind of attachment. The parents are not their opinions, nor are the children theirs.

If we are prepared to listen with respect to opinions that are different from ours, it is not impossible that once in a way we will find the other party is right. If we can go to our parents with the attitude that we will not contradict them because they may be right, we will find our feeling of hesitation and apprehension is lost. They will appreciate this; our father may even say to our mother, "You know, the boy may be right." In most personal friction this simple discovery of "you may be right, I may be wrong" can go a long, long way to facilitate communication and bring about better understanding. One of the unmistakable signs of spiritual awareness is the cheerful capacity to say, "I was wrong"; and it will save us a lot of trouble in life if we can make that very daring statement, "I don't know."

यदा संहरते चायं कूर्मो ऽङ्गानीव सर्वशः ।
इन्द्रियाणीन्द्रियार्थेभ्यस्तस्य प्रज्ञा प्रतिष्ठिता ॥२-५८॥

58. Even as a tortoise draws in its limbs, the wise can draw in their senses at will.

Sri Krishna uses the simile of the humble tortoise. In Kerala, it is very common for children to get excited when they see a tortoise. They gather around it and playfully hit it with their bamboo sticks. So as soon as a tortoise sees children coming, he issues an order immediately to all his limbs, his head, and his tail, "Return. Get inside." When the children come, the tortoise just waits patiently inside his bamboo-proof shell until they are tired of playing. I was reminded of this simile years ago when we went to the zoo. The lions and tigers, the panthers and leopards were all in cages, but a huge tortoise was wandering around unattended. On his back was written, "Don't report me to the management – I am free." If you have developed the capacity to withdraw your senses immediately when there is danger, then you are completely free. You can go anywhere and live in the midst of any agitation. When the situation is serious you just say, "Withdraw," and the gates are closed.

As Sri Krishna says in this verse, *Tasya prajnā pratishtitā:* "That person is unshaken and firmly established in me, the Lord of Love, who can withdraw the senses at will from sensory objects."

Most of us are unaware of how mercilessly our senses are being exploited by today's mass media. It requires some progress in meditation to become aware of how much we have become tyrannized by the siren song of the mass media: "Stimulate your senses, and you will find joy." Aldous Huxley went to the extent of calling the anonymous advertisement copywriter the apostle of our modern civilization.

On the sexual level, for instance, we have been subjected to relentless conditioning. Somebody has only to bring a matchbox and we are on fire. There is no point in saying that we are a wicked generation; this is how we are conditioned – by the movies we see, by the magazines we read, by the television we watch, by the conversation we indulge in. In advertisements, sex is the motif that is played over and over again. None of us need be guilt-laden, therefore, if we find that preoccupation with sex has become extreme. The Gita says that there is only one way to dehypnotize ourselves, and that is to get some measure of control over the senses. Until this has been accomplished, it is not advisable to attend sensate movies, where old memories, slowly fading, are refreshed. This does not mean we have to give up movies altogether. What I do, when I find one of these scenes coming on where people start taking off their clothes, is to close my eyes and have a little nap. There is no point in thinking of these movies as wicked. "Silly" is a better word for the childish illusion that by taking off our clothes we can reveal our beauty, which is only revealed when we rise above physical consciousness.

It is necessary also to be very discriminating in the books and magazines we read. When I go to the store and look at magazine covers, I envy my grandmother her illiteracy. Most of the magazines that people read by the million cause more agitation, insecurity, and despair than we can imagine. I would suggest that we choose only those books that add to our self-knowledge, our self-respect, and our sense control.

If we want to be able to withdraw our senses at will, we should train them in such a way that they listen immediately to the slightest command we give them. What often obstructs this is our diffidence and agitation. We should have confidence in our capacity to train the senses. In disciplining the senses, do not get angry with them, but be courteous and say "Please" and "I beg your pardon." This is the kind of artistry I always recommend on the spiritual path. Do not do things by force, but with patience.

In training the eyes, we can begin by not staring at things in which we are likely to be caught. For most of us, the shop window may exercise a certain pull, particularly for those who have been used to buying things in order to maintain their security. The spell of attraction is broken when we realize that by buying things and giving presents we are not likely to become secure, and relationships are not likely to be repaired. The ear, also, can be trained not to listen to what is harmful, especially to gossip. The time will come when we can actually close our ears and not hear what is going on. I suggest that when there is unkind talk, unsavory gossip, we can always get up and walk out, or, even better, we can say something in praise of the person who is being attacked.

In order to understand the full import of this verse, we have to see where attachment to sense objects has brought our civilization. I am an admirer of science, and I know that the modern world needs the wise help of technology to solve many of its material problems, but the misuse of science and technology has brought us to a very serious pass. Today's paper carried a brilliant article by one of the foremost authorities in the country on the pollution of the environment. The writer traces the environmental crisis directly to our excessive attachment to objects, showing that we have produced for the sake of production, multiplied things for the sake of multiplying things, without any reference to their wise use or their necessity in our daily life. This is a serious pronouncement, and all of us should pay it more than lip service.

We are all aware of the terrible impact of the automobile on our environment. There are a number of simple ways we can help relieve this problem. The first is by walking more. Some years ago, when my wife and I were first walking around Lake Merritt, the only company we had was the seagulls and a black dog. Now we just keep bumping into people; old, middle-aged, and even little ones have started walking. A second suggestion, which is also beginning to be practiced, is to form car pools. There may be practical problems with this. We may have to wait three minutes for one person, five for another, but we can look upon these little inconveniences as part of our sādhana, as an opportunity for repeating the mantram while we wait. Third, we can all avoid travel that is unnecessary. We do not need to travel around the world when the source of all joy and all beauty is right within us.

We can be discriminating, too, in the way we furnish our homes. In Kerala, even in well-to-do homes, there is very little furniture, just a few pieces of teak or ebony. Teak is not expensive there; it grows in abundance, as does redwood here in California. The rooms are beautiful, austere, with just a few touches here and there. Once we begin to exercise our judgment in these matters, we shall see many other avenues in which we can simplify our life yet maintain all its comfort, joy, and beauty.

In a world where natural resources are limited, we should not waste a single particle of anything. When we were on the Blue Mountain, my wife and I met often with a British Quaker friend, Mary Barr, who had been close to Gandhi. She had so deeply imbibed this lesson from Gandhi that if I left two or three grains of rice on my plate, she would say, "Don't waste," and I would obediently pick up every last grain and put it in my mouth. Similarly, with regard to clothing, it is possible to be very attractively dressed with a select wardrobe, and it is possible to be very unattractively dressed with a vast wardrobe. There are many people, I am told, who have sentimental attachments to clothing with a story – this dress they wore in Acapulco in 1959, or that jacket in which they hitchhiked to New York. Give these to someone who needs clothing. Get rid of these attachments. These are the ways in which we can help relieve the state of emergency which overproduction and overconsumption have brought us to. Ultimately, you and I are responsible. If we do not buy, they cannot make; if we do not buy, they cannot sell.

By meditating and leading the spiritual life we are showing how we can make the ecological emergency disappear. Sri Krishna says: "I am the source of all the joy, all the love, all the wisdom, and all the beauty within you. You do not need these external attachments. Just have enough to keep your family in comfort, and whatever else you have, give to those who need."

विषया विनिवर्तन्ते निराहारस्य देहिनः ।
रसवर्जं रसो ऽप्यस्य परं दृष्ट्वा निवर्तते ॥ २-५९ ॥

59. Though aspirants abstain from sense pleasures, they will still crave for them. These cravings all disappear when they see the Lord of Love.

If we remember Patanjali's[7] definition of *dhārana,* the first stage in meditation, it may give us some idea of the behavior of the senses in the early years of our sādhana. Patanjali with his unfailing spiritual accuracy says that dhārana is the effort to confine the mind in a limited area. Imagine the mind to be a dog. If I take a dog to the store and chain him outside while I go in, telling him, "I'll be out in two minutes – just a few groceries and I am done," the dog will expect me to come back soon. When he does not see me coming out, he will start going round and round, howling and putting his paws on the glass, trying to see me. After a while, when I still have not come out, the dog will finally become tired of looking. After a lot of restlessness, after walking about and whining, he will turn around three times and then lie down. The mind is very much like that. It has got to run about and howl a little, then stand up and see who is inside and what is coming out. But after a while it will turn around three times and lie down.

The senses, too, are very restless. They are so turbulent, and have been indulged so long, that even when you are beginning to restrain them, by eating only when hungry and only what is nourishing, they

7. A famous teacher of meditation in ancient India, around the second century B.C. He is the author of the *Yoga Sūtras*, aphorisms teaching the practice of meditation and allied disciplines.

still may rebel. Though you may be having only a meager breakfast, a spare lunch, and a pauper's dinner, you are still thinking about what makes a sumptuous meal, and mentally you are eating a long list of items. In your external consumption of food there may be extreme restraint, but for a long, long time the old sense cravings and selfish desires are going to be there in the mind. Sri Krishna is very compassionate. When you are restraining the senses, he admires you for that, and he does not hold it against you if once in a while you are tempted to say, "If only I hadn't taken to meditation!"

What is required for a long time is our conscious effort, our sustained discipline, in restraining the senses. Gradually these noxious weeds of sense cravings will begin to wither away if we do not yield to them. Even though the desires may arise in the mind, if we subject the senses to an external discipline, the desires will gradually cease to agitate our minds through the practice of meditation.

Listening to people who are subject to compulsive habits of eating is sometimes a little like science fiction. They say they are just walking along, thinking about what passage to memorize for meditation, and all of a sudden an unseen hand pulls them inside. Before they know where they are, the door has closed on them and they are in the restaurant. For such compulsive cases, what I would say is even if you are being pulled in the doorway, try a judo twist. In this way you can actually manage to come out and start running. When you are nearing a bakery, if you are not quite sure whether you are bakery-proof, make a dash for it. It helps your physical system, you get vigorous exercise, and you conquer temptation, too. So in the case of bakeries, candy shops, and restaurants, for all those who do not mind a certain amount of curiosity on the part of passersby – *run*.

In samādhi, when we see the Lord, the source of all joy, then we do not need any other source of pleasure. When we see the source of all beauty, then we do not need any other source of beauty. When we see the source of all love, we do not need any other source of love. In samādhi, Sri Krishna says, we become complete; all the vacancies are filled, and there is no more craving.

When we consistently practice this exhilarating discipline of discriminating sense restraint, the time will come when we shall see for ourselves that the connection between our senses and the sense objects is cut. It is a glorious day that we can mark on our calendar as Deliverance Day, and celebrate every year because it brings such relief. Then we can go everywhere in freedom; there is no compulsive liking or disliking. We are free to choose.

यततो ह्यपि कौन्तेय पुरुषस्य विपश्चितः ।
इन्द्रियाणि प्रमाथीनि हरन्ति प्रसभं मनः ॥२-६०॥

60. For even of one who treads the path, the stormy senses can sweep off the mind.

Even though we are trying our best to lead the spiritual life, the senses are so fiercely turbulent that if we yield to them for a little while, and a little while more, we will be swept away. *Vipashcitah indriyāni pramāthīni:* even if we are very wise, the senses can become so powerful that they just pick us up and throw us from the path. This is a warning given to all of us, particularly on the level of sex.

We do not have to belong to the monastic order to lead the spiritual life, and sex has a beautiful place in a completely loving, loyal relationship, though even there with discrimination. But for people who indulge in sex in the wrong context, even though at the outset there may be some satisfaction, ultimately the relationship will be disrupted. If we ask any two people who have built their relationship on the physical level, they will say that in just a few months they could not bear each other. The tragedy is that after a short time they are again in the same relationship with someone else. If you ask them the same question again, they will say their new relationship also could not last even a few months. The senses are getting stronger and stronger, resistance is getting weaker and weaker, and one day such people will find that even if they want to, they will not be able to lead the spiritual life because of the turbulence of the mind. Sex is sacred; it has beauty and tenderness in a completely loving, loyal relationship, where it brings two people closer and closer to become one. But on no account is it going to help us physically, psychologically, or spiritually to indulge this impulse as the mass media are trying to make us do.

We shall find that we give our best to each other when we put each other first; and when we do not put each other first, particularly in the married relationship, sex breeds jealousy. Shakespeare does not exaggerate when he talks about the "green-eyed monster" of jealousy, which is characteristic of sex on the physical level. Even when we do not suspect a trace of jealousy in ourselves, it may be clouding our eyes. I remember one of our friends who told me he could not take his girlfriend out on Telegraph Avenue because there were so many fellows there who wanted to deprive him of her. I got permission to accompany them one day, and as far as my rather bright eyes could see, nobody was looking at them. People were all engrossed in themselves or in their dinner. In his case, he was trying to build the relationship on the physical level, and as he could not avoid admitting that, I told him that jealousy is the nature of such a relationship.

Jealousy comes in only when we try to possess something for ourselves. It is good to admire beauty, but it is neither beautiful nor good if we want to take it home, put it on the mantle, and say, "You just stay there." When we see something beautiful, we begin to want it for ourselves. It may be a beautiful house, it may be a beautiful flower, it may be a beautiful dancer we just want it. The Gita says that by wanting it, we have lost it. It is a very difficult secret to understand that when we do not want to possess another selfishly, he or she will always love us. It is when we do not want to possess, when we do not make demand after demand, that the relationship will last. Sri Krishna is giving us the secret of all relationships, not only between husband and wife, boyfriend and girlfriend, but between friend and friend, parents and children. Instead of trying to exact and demand, just give, and give more, and give still more. This is the way to keep love and respect; and it is something we have to learn the hard, hard way.

Unless we exercise vigilant control over the senses, we cannot put other people first. For example, if we let the palate run away with us, we will want to eat only what we like and may try to force others to eat what we like. If we do not restrain the senses, we may try to impose our self-will on those around us in all the little matters of daily living. I am sure that all of you will find, as I have, how delightful it can be to forget your own taste in eating what your wife, girlfriend, or mother wants you to eat. When you are not appreciating the taste very much, when it reminds you of gall and wormwood, try to smile, and you will see what real freedom means. Inside, the taste glands are conducting a funeral, but you just free yourself and smile. It begins with a half-paralyzed expression, but through repetition of the mantram the smile slowly pervades the whole face, until at last the eyes light up. We can train our senses with artistry by doing what will add to the joy of our parents, partner, children, and friends.

तानि सर्वाणि संयम्य युक्त आसीत मत्परः ।
वशे हि यस्येन्द्रियाणि तस्य प्रज्ञा प्रतिष्ठिता ॥२-६१॥

61. But they live in wisdom who subdue them,
and keep their minds ever absorbed in me.

That person is of unshakable wisdom and security who has subdued the senses and become completely absorbed in the Lord of Love, call him Krishna or Christ. The subjugation of the senses is enormously difficult when we keep telling ourselves, "I must subdue my senses; I must deny my body." On this impersonal path – the path of *neti neti,* 'not this, not this,' as the Upanishads put it – you are told you are not the body, you are not the senses, you are not the mind, you are not the intellect, you are not the ego. There are great mystics who have traveled this way to Self-realization, but it is hard to imagine ordinary people like ourselves climbing the Himālayas up such precipitous slopes.

One of the practical beauties of the Gita is that it is not negative in its presentation. The Gita approach, which I try to follow, is expressed here in the words *yukta āsīta matparah:* the Lord is in me, and I ask him, "Reveal yourself to me; unite me to yourself; make me the dust of your lotus feet." This is the positive approach, and I have seldom found it useful to keep on the negative path. Let us follow the positive way of asking the Lord to reveal himself to us in the depths of our consciousness, and of loving him in our parents, partner, children, and friends. This discipline of adding to the joy of those around us itself weakens the tyranny of the senses.

ध्यायतो विषयान्पुंसः सङ्गस्तेषूपजायते ।
सङ्गात्संजायते कामः कामात्क्रोधो ऽभिजायते ॥ २-६२ ॥
क्रोधाद्भवति संमोहः संमोहात्स्मृतिविभ्रमः ।
स्मृतिभ्रंशाद्बुद्धिनाशो बुद्धिनाशात्प्रणश्यति ॥ २-६३ ॥

62–63. When you keep thinking about sense objects, attachment comes. Attachment breeds desire, the lust of possession which, when thwarted, burns to anger. Anger clouds the judgment; you can no longer learn from past mistakes. Lost is the power to choose between the wise and the unwise, and your life is utter waste.

In his autobiography, Gandhi narrates in moving language how these two verses, which he read for the first time in London, haunted him day in and day out and began to protect him from the dangers of life on the sensory level. Many times when I, too, have been tempted to follow the call of the senses, these words have rescued me from rushing headlong into torrential waters. I would suggest these two verses be used in meditation, particularly by people who want to subdue their senses, not to negate them but to use them as faithful servants in the service of others. The purpose of these verses is not negative; their purpose is to bring under our command the resources of love, wisdom, and selfless action which lie dormant within us all.

Dhyāyato vishayān pumsah means 'dwelling on sense objects.' To apply this to the modern context, we are dwelling on sense objects when we read books, for example, that are erotically charged, which means most of the books that come hot off the press today. Whenever I go into a bookstore now, I fail to find a section where Eros has not homesteaded. There is a tendency for all of us to be drawn into this kind of reading. Partly it is our conditioning, and partly it is our deep belief that we are the body, which leads us to think that by giving in to the senses we can win love, we can give love, we can become beautiful and fulfilled. It is good to select books in which there is not undue and distasteful description of what stimulates sexual desire. As a former student of both Sanskrit and English literature, I can say the most beautiful love scenes can be conveyed without a single sensate word. Last month we had the pleasure of seeing a movie by Satyajit Ray, the distinguished producer and director from Bengal, whose movies are well attended in this country. It was a powerful love story narrated from beginning to end without a kiss, without the two people ever throwing themselves into each other's arms, all the more powerful because it was so beautifully done with great restraint. It should not be too difficult for us to understand that power can be conveyed better by restraint than by taking the lid off. This is one of the great secrets of the classical tradition, where the enormous power that is contained within is suggested rather than explicitly described.

Books are a stage through which we pass, but we should slowly outgrow the need to draw upon other people's imagination and information, and especially upon the mass media, for our entertainment. Magazines particularly must be read with discrimination. When I am in the supermarket and take a look at the covers of the magazines on the shelves, every week there seems to be some new scandal, couched in such inconsiderate, unkind language that I often wonder why people even like to look at these articles. By not reading most magazines, we are not losing out on our education, though there are one or two we can select carefully and pass on to our friends.

My wife looks upon me as a well-informed critic of the movies, but I do not mind confessing that now and then I make a faux pas. Sometimes, after looking at the reviews, I come to the conclusion that I have found a peaceful movie. I think the scenes are going to be rather restrained, but before we know where we are, pandemonium has burst loose on the screen, and people are taking off their clothes on all sides. As far as the movies are concerned, I have now almost become resigned; and for those of you who want to share my secret, whenever this kind of disrobing begins I close my eyes and take a nap. The dangers of such movies are more serious than we sometimes think. We are still beginners on the spiritual path. We are still trying to bring the senses under control. The desires are all there, just hidden in a corner, waiting for their opportunity. When we see a voluptuous scene on the screen, we may not even notice it very carefully, or be conscious when we come home that it is this scene we see in our dream, meaning that it has gone into our deeper consciousness. The advertisers and movie makers know much better than we do how these stray, seductive, highly suggestive images get into our consciousness. Movies can be harmful if we do not have some kind of resistance, and one of the easiest ways to immunize oneself against the seductive powers of the movies is to learn to laugh, not with them, but at them.

Sangas teshū 'pajāyate. If we keep on reading about something, and seeing it, and hearing about it, even in the most self-controlled among us the seed will gradually germinate; and *sangāt samjāyate kāmah:* we will come to desire to have the experience ourselves. This is all underneath the surface level of consciousness, so we are often not even aware of what is going on until we suddenly find ourselves in a situation where we can gratify the desire.

Here the Gita does not talk about morality or ethics; it says what Patanjali also says: when we have a desire for a certain thing or experience, and fulfill that desire, the happiness we feel is due to having no craving for a little while. It is not because this craving has been satisfied, but because for just a little while there is a state of no craving. The Gita is in no way deprecating love and tenderness between two people; it is merely trying to tell us that sensory desire makes us wrongly believe the object of desire can bring us satisfaction. It is our desire which gives quality to a relationship or a thing. In our own experience, where we have built a relationship on the sensory level, we must have asked the question: "Why is it that six months ago I thought I could go through ten incarnations with this person, and now I cannot go through ten weeks?" There is nothing wrong with us, nor is anything wrong with the other person. Our desire has exhausted itself. It is the nature of sensory desire to come to an end very, very soon.

In most of us our desires are not under our control; but if, as the Upanishads say, we can get hold of our desires, we will get hold of our destiny. We can then direct our desires at will. The Katha Upanishad (1:3) uses a particularly vivid image:

> Know the Self as lord of the chariot,
> The body as the chariot itself,
> The discriminating intellect as
> The charioteer, and the mind the reins.
> The senses, say the wise, are the horses;
> Selfish desires are the roads they travel.
> When the Self is confused with the body,
> Mind, and senses, they point out, it seems
> To enjoy pleasure and suffer sorrow.
> When a person lacks discrimination
> And his mind is undisciplined, his senses
> Run hither and thither like wild horses.
> But they obey the rein like trained horses
> When a person has discrimination
> And the mind is one-pointed. Those who lack
> Discrimination, with little control
> Over their thoughts and far from pure,
> Reach not the pure state of immortality
> But wander from death to death; while those
> Who have discrimination, with a still mind
> And a pure heart, reach journey's end,
> Never again to fall into the jaws of death.
> With a discriminating intellect
> As charioteer, a well-trained mind as reins,
> They attain the supreme goal of life,
> To be united with the Lord of Love.

The more we indulge the senses, the less we get out of them, and the less we get out of them, the more we indulge them. Finally, we begin to get angry. This is the anger that bursts out between two people in a physical relationship, when they begin to quarrel and drag up the past.

The physical desire has been exhausted, and now they just go on doing things which will bring the relationship to an end. When both parties become resentful, the most tragic stage in personal relationships is reached. Formerly, every little thing the other person did was so lovely that you could have gone on watching these innumerable acts of grace forever. Now the same thing begins to irk you. These were the things with which you used to be in love, about which you wrote minor poetry; why is it that now they only irritate you? When resentment begins to arise, even things not meant to be hostile are interpreted with hostility. The whole atmosphere of the home, of the relationship, becomes vitiated because the desire on the physical level has been exhausted.

When this kind of constant resentment and anger becomes established in our consciousness – it may be for any apparent reason outside – we begin to see what is not there. *Krodhād bhavati sammohah:* from anger arises delusion. We accuse people of things they have not dreamt of; we attack people for what they are not doing, and *sammohāt smritivibhramah:* we lose the capacity to learn from previous mistakes. All of us commit mistakes, and none of us need feel guilty about past errors if we have learned from them. The tragedy of this kind of anger is that the power of discrimination goes completely. Sri Krishna uses terms here which he very rarely uses, *smritibhramshād buddhināsho buddhināshāt pranashyati:* when a human being has lost all capacity to learn from the past, lost all judgment, that person's life might as well be written off as a complete waste. Such a person, whatever else he may do in life, will be bringing misery upon himself as well as on those connected with him. He will leave this life having proved to be a burden, instead of being a contributor to the welfare of others.

Arjuna is now terrified because the Lord of Love does not talk in this way very often. These verses are meant to remind you and me that we cannot play the sensory game for long, saying, "Oh, we can always run away when it gets too hot." By restraining ourselves we do not lose joy; by indulging ourselves we lose all joy. By putting other people first, we do not lose joy; by putting ourselves first, we lose all joy. Many young people are under the impression that the only way to build a relationship is on the physical level. They are not aware that there is an alternative basis for relationships, which can grow in mutual understanding, love, and respect with the passage of time. The physical relationship promises what it cannot give, while the spiritual relationship gives and continues to give an abiding sense of joy all our life.

रागद्वेषवियुक्तैस्तु विषयानिन्द्रियैश्चरन् ।
आत्मवश्यैर्विधेयात्मा प्रसादमधिगच्छति ॥२-६४॥
प्रसादे सर्वदुःखानां हानिरस्योपजायते ।
प्रसन्नचेतसो ह्याशु बुद्धिः पर्यवतिष्ठते ॥२-६५॥

64–65. But when you move amidst the world of sense, free from both attachment and aversion, there comes the peace in which all sorrows end, and you live in the wisdom of the Self.

To go beyond suffering, to live in the full confidence that our life is meant for the service of others and that the Lord has given us ample resources to perform this service whatever the obstacles, we must shed all likes and dislikes. We cannot afford to say, "I like this; I dislike that. I like him; I dislike her." To try to translate this into neurological language, our nervous system is meant for two-way traffic. It should be able to move towards pain, if necessary, as well as towards pleasure. Now in the case of most of us, our nervous system will flow only one way, towards what we like. Most forms of allergy are a screaming protest from the nervous system: "You can't do this to me! I move in one direction only." If we are forced to go towards what we do not like, we get an ulcer in our stomach, a creeping sensation under the skin, and numbness of the fingers. Finally we faint, and then ask, "Do you blame me?" In order to grow up to our full beauty and maturity, we have to learn very often to go near what we have turned away from, to go with appreciation to the person we have always avoided. There is joy in this, and there is fulfillment in this, because we can do it for the sake of others – the parent for the child, the husband for the wife, the wife for the husband, and the friend for the friend. When the nervous system has been reconditioned for serving others, we will find ourselves free to enjoy what we do not like just as much as what we like. In the monastic order, I am told, they apply this kind of discipline with artistic perfection. If there is someone who has always been fond of books, out he goes into the garden, and if there is someone who is always after the potato bugs, in he goes to the library. The principle is to free ourselves.

We all can begin this discipline in many little ways in our daily life, particularly between parents and children, and husband and wife. We can fill the hours with freshness by putting the other person first. Whenever, for example, we go to a restaurant, it is good for the wife to give the menu to her husband and ask him to choose for her, or for the husband to ask the wife. In the early days the going may be hard, but if we can repeat the mantram and persist, we will find that gradually each person will be thinking only of what pleases the other. This exercise in the reduction of self-will can be done in all the little matters of daily life – hairstyle, books, movies, attitudes, and even opinions. I am very much in the prehistoric tradition. I have been charged with living five thousand years in the past, and I wouldn't disagree with this because, after all, my life is entirely based on the spiritual values proclaimed by the illumined sages of ancient India and the great mystics of the world. These values are timeless. They were completely valid five thousand years ago; they are completely valid today; and they will be completely valid five thousand years hence. Whatever unites people permanently is spiritual and heals individuals, families, and society. On the fundamental issues of life, a man and woman cannot help but see alike if they realize the unity underlying life. This is not losing one's personality but gaining it. All of us need to work towards realizing this unity in all our relationships.

The person who has gone beyond likes and dislikes, Sri Ramakrishna will say, is like an autumn leaf floating in the wind. It floats gently here when the wind blows here, it goes there when the wind blows there, and slowly it settles to the ground. On most occasions we can be pliable and ready to bend without any disloyalty to our ideals. People who will easily bend our way under normal circumstances can stand like a rock when a great crisis comes. Sometimes good things come to us, sometimes bad. We can learn from both; we have enough resources to meet any challenge that comes. This awareness does not denude life of joy, but enables us to accept the joy that comes, and also to face the sorrow that comes, with equanimity and resourcefulness.

नास्ति बुद्धिरयुक्तस्य न चायुक्तस्य भावना ।
न चाभावयतः शान्तिरशान्तस्य कुतः सुखम् ॥ २-६६ ॥

66. The disunited mind is far from wise; how can it meditate? How be at peace? When you know no peace, how can you know joy?

Here there is no mention of religion, or of the spiritual life, or of God; Sri Krishna simply asks Arjuna what intelligence anyone has who is not united within. To bring this into a modern context, try to imagine an automobile whose four wheels want to go off in four different directions. This is actually what is happening to you and me. The senses are always running out towards stimulation; the mind runs out in the direction of agitation; the intellect goes in the direction of argumentation; and the Ātman just sits there watching and says, "We cannot do anything with this car. These people shouldn't be given their driver's license, and this particular car should be recalled." Meditation and the disciplines recommended by the great mystics of all religions are for putting the four wheels of our car back on the same road.

Nā 'sti buddhir ayuktasya na cā yuktasya bhāvanā: "If you are not united inside, with all your desires flowing towards one goal, you cannot get access to your deeper creative faculties." This is practical language. If you want to be a great painter, you do not try to be a sculptor, a financier, and a linguistic expert, saying, "Well, painting is one of the many things I am going to do." If you are going to paint, you paint. Then the Lord continues, *Na cā 'bhāvayatah shāntir:* "If there is no harmony inside, if there is no unity inside, how can you have peace?" This is something all of us can understand. If we are restless inside, if there is a war going on inside, wherever we go, no matter what abundance we live in, we will never be able to know security. Then, *Ashāntasya kutah sukham:* "When you have no peace in your heart, how can you know joy?" The purpose of meditation and spiritual disciplines is to lead us to joy. It is understandable if we are rather skeptical about this in the earlier stages. We may even be unable to associate joy with meditation. "Getting up early morning when it is more joyful to sleep? Eating less when it is more joyful to eat more? And putting other people first? Have you heard of a more ridiculous idea of joy?" These are not unnatural questions for us to ask. We may feel the discipline dull and dreary in the early years of our sādhana, but the goal of meditation is complete, abiding joy, releasing the great capacities for service which lie untouched in all of us.

Bhakti yoga, the path of devotion or selfless love, is the very best way for ordinary people like ourselves to move towards the total unification of consciousness that is the climax of meditation. People often ask me how to deepen the vein of devotion that is in all of us, and I reply that by unifying our desires and undergoing the disciplines of meditation, we can all become devoted to the Lord and aware of his presence in everyone around us.

The other day we saw a movie filmed on the Himālayas, and in one scene a group of pilgrims was crossing a deep ravine on a rope bridge. While on the bridge, which is swinging like a pendulum, they are all saying *Rāma, Rāma, Rāma, Rāma* with as much devotion as they can muster. But as soon as the first step is taken on terra firma, it is likely to be *kāma, kāma, kāma, kāma.* When there is trouble and turmoil we are very responsive to the mantram; but as soon as the current turns, when our health is good, income is steady, and pleasures are all flowing smoothly, we forget the Lord.

When trouble and turmoil come, let us remember that it is the Lord's way of saying, "Don't forget me." Let us be grateful when God sends us joy, because we all need joy. But let us also be grateful when he sends us sorrow – physical ailments, mental distress, financial breakdown – because these can enable us to turn inwards to remember him.

Sri Ramakrishna was fond of saying that our love of God should be as great as the love of a miser for his gold, the love of a mother for her child, and the love of a lover for the beloved, all combined. That is the kind of bhakti we should try to cultivate. Most of us have our infinite capacity for love dissipated into innumerable little channels, but we can all develop single-minded, concentrated devotion by putting the welfare of those around us first. Devotion in any relationship helps to unify consciousness, and in the modern world, people who find it too difficult to accept a divine incarnation with complete love and loyalty can all cultivate devotion, or selfless love, in personal relationships.

Many of us may not find it easy to choose a personal incarnation to whom we can surrender our entire devotion. My suggestion to such people is to let the personal incarnation choose them. Instead of shopping around the pantheon of incarnations, why not just say, "We are at your feet. We are pretty bad, and we are going to be an encumbrance. Now will someone who has mercy, and who doesn't mind having a stone around his neck, pick me up?" There are great mystics who say in complete self-surrender, "Will somebody please pick me up?" and that is all there is to it. Because they have so completely unified their love for the Lord, their travail is over within an instant. The Lord comes to them immediately.

In our repetition of the mantram, we are asking the Lord to come and help us out because we cannot lift ourselves up by ourselves. For those who have this simple faith, the time may come when they will receive an indication that the Lord is coming to say, "You are mine." This is grace. And when the Lord puts his mark on us, every samskāra picks up its bag and leaves. This experience of grace is not unlikely to come to most of us who are steadfast in their meditation and who, even though they have occasional lapses, are doing the very best they can.

इन्द्रियाणां हि चरतां यन्मनो ऽनुविधीयते ।
तदस्य हरति प्रज्ञां वायुर्नावमिवाम्भसि ॥२-६७॥
तस्माद्यस्य महाबाहो निगृहीतानि सर्वशः ।
इन्द्रियाणीन्द्रियार्थेभ्यस्तस्य प्रज्ञा प्रतिष्ठिता ॥२-६८॥

67. When you let your mind heed the Siren call of the senses, they will carry away your better judgment as storms drive a boat off its safe-charted course to certain doom.
68. Use all your power to set the senses free from attachment and aversion alike, and live in the full wisdom of the Self.

These two verses are a comment upon the fate our modern civilization faces if we do not correct the sensate philosophy on which it seems to be operating at present. Anyone who tries to follow the seductive call of the senses, which promise satisfaction, security, and fulfillment, is likely to meet with disaster. The Lord therefore tells us to train our senses, to turn them from turbulent masters into obedient servants. Without this period of discriminating sense restraint, all of us risk the danger of rebellion and continuous riots inside.

These two verses are of direct application every day, from morning when we go to the breakfast table until night when we finish the midnight snack. There is a close connection between letting the palate have its way and letting the mind have its way; Gandhi says that the control of the palate is a valuable aid to the control of the mind. Today the mass media subject us to so many skillful advertisements which tickle the palate that even the most vigilant among us may find themselves falling into their trap. We must consistently retrain the palate by giving the body nourishing, temperate food, rather than responding to the advertiser's slogans, which try to make us eat things that are undesirable and unnourishing. Even during the past ten years there has been an increase in concern about good nutrition. More and more dieticians and doctors are telling us how necessary it is to restrain the palate in order to be physically healthy. There is likely to be a certain initial resistance by the senses, which are used to being pampered, but we can all change our food habits gradually to anything that we approve of. Here each person is at liberty to do a certain amount of experimentation. We need not be too harsh, nor should we be too lenient, in changing our food habits. The changeover, for example, from nonvegetarian to vegetarian food can be made gradually. In most textbooks on nutrition we find statements about what foods to avoid and what foods to rely on, and often the ones to be avoided are nonvegetarian, especially in the case of heart disease. Even if they do not advocate it consistently, nutritionists seem to be slowly coming to the conclusion that the vegetarian diet is good for physical as well as mental well-being.

Vegetarianism not only helps us to maintain our health on the optimum level but also has the spiritual purpose of deepening our awareness of the unity of life. I am fortunate in being born in a Hindu family that has been vegetarian probably for over a thousand years, but I am not a vegetarian because my ancestors were; I am a vegetarian because I have come to know that I form one unity with everything around me. As our spiritual awareness deepens, we will come to have great compassion for animals and will never want to be a party to their ill-treatment. Vegetarianism affirms the unity of all life.

या निशा सर्वभूतानां तस्यां जागर्ति संयमी ।
यस्यां जाग्रति भूतानि सा निशा पश्यतो मुनेः ॥२-६९॥

69. Such a sage awakes to light in the night
of all creatures. That which the world calls
day is the night of ignorance to the wise.

What is night to the vast majority of human beings is day to the illumined man; and what we call day is night to the mystic. The world of our ego is the world of sense data, and as long as we identify ourselves with the body, we move in the sense-world of samsāra, that which is moving all the time. As long as we live in the field of the senses, as long as we live in the sea of flux, none of us can escape change, which culminates in the great change called death.

As our meditation deepens, our view of even the external world will change considerably. I do not see the world today as I used to see it twenty years ago. I do not see people as I saw them twenty years ago. Everything changes in an almost miraculous fashion. Where we looked upon someone as a threat to us, we come to regard that person as a friend; we begin to see the unity underlying all life. This change comes on so gradually that we are not even aware of it unless we stop to compare how we saw life a few years ago with how we see it today.

Most of us see life not as it is, but as we are. We look at life through our own needs and prejudices, and the ultimate narrowing of vision occurs when we look at everything as pertaining to ourself. Most people look at life through a very narrow ego-slit. We should never say we see life as it is, and never denounce the world as evil and tempestuous, because we are looking at it through one tiny slit. If we could ask Sri Ramana Maharshi or Sri Ramakrishna what they see in the world, we would be heartened to hear them say they see it whole. They do see the turbulence and violence, but for them the world is a hospital where we are all being treated and made whole. Ramana Maharshi, with his dry humor, said that the body is the biggest disease of all; and Sri Ramakrishna told his disciples that no one can be discharged from the hospital without being fully cured. The Buddha also, in the Four Noble Truths, declares that in the world we are all suffering from the same devastating disease, *tanhā*, the fierce thirst of selfish desire, and to cure this disease he gave us the regimen of the Eightfold Path.

All we need learn in life is to forget ourselves little by little by not dwelling upon the dullest, dreariest subject on earth, "I." In order to widen the ego-slit, we put first the welfare of those with whom we live as good friends or family, and realize the unity of life in that circle. Someone once asked me if it is possible to realize the unity of all life just by putting first a few people with whom he lived. I answered, "If you want to be the tennis champion of the world, do you go and play against every tennis player in the world? You just go to the central court at Wimbledon and beat the few there, and when you get the cup, you have become champion." Even in a small circle of good friends, if we can consistently try to put their welfare first, this will enable us to widen the slit until finally there is no slit at all, and we see the whole panorama. This is what nirvāna means: removing the constriction that makes me see only what conduces to my own profit and pleasure, until I see all life as it is, as one.

आपूर्यमाणमचलप्रतिष्ठं
समुद्रमापः प्रविशन्ति यद्वत् ।
तद्वत्कामा यं प्रविशन्ति सर्वे
स शान्तिमाप्नोति न कामकामी ॥ २-७० ॥

70. As the rivers flow into the ocean, but cannot make the vast ocean overflow, so flow the magic streams of the sense-world into the sea of peace that is the sage.

The first word is *āpūryamānam,* 'ever full.' This is your nature and mine. Our idea, born of ignorance, that we will become full if we can make a lot of money or enjoy a little pleasure is absurd, because we are already full. Our account is full; we cannot add to it, nor can we take away from it. Within ourselves we have the biggest bank in the cosmos, but instead of going in to claim our legitimate account, we go to little banks asking for petty loans. As long as we live on the egocentric level, we will never suspect what fullness and security lie within ourselves. We will always have an emptiness inside that only Self-realization can take away.

The Compassionate Buddha tells his disciples that the egocentric life consists of *duhkha*. On one level, the word *duhkha* means 'sorrow.' As long as we live as separate fragments in a world of separate fragments, clashing against one another, we cannot but suffer. There is also another connotation to the word: *duh* means 'bad'; *kha* means 'hole.' The Buddha says there is a fathomless hole running through our consciousness. To fill this emptiness inside, we keep running to bring pail after pail of dollars and pour them in; but at the end of the day it is still duhkha, the fathomless hole. We pour in money, material possessions, pleasure, power, prestige, and it all goes down the fathomless drain. Once we begin to realize that nothing can fill this chasm, we will understand St. Augustine's cry: "Lord, how can I ever find rest anywhere else when I am made to rest in thee?" Sri Krishna tells Arjuna, "Why waste your life going after things that pass away? You do not need them. You are already full because I am living in the depths of your consciousness. You have only to look within to realize me."

The second word is *achalapratishtham,* 'established in motionlessness.' This is the complete stillness of Brahman, the complete motionlessness of the supreme Reality. In order to be established in the changeless, immutable Reality called God, we have to still the turbulent mind completely. If you want to see what your mind is like, go stand on a high parapet overlooking a rocky seacoast when there is a storm. The only creatures who enjoy this maelstrom are the sea lions. They float along with the waves, and when a giant one comes, they all jump up to ride on it with joy. But being made in the image of the Lord, and having been brought into the human context, our glory is to play in the sea that is still. The mind is often compared in Sanskrit to the sea, ever moving, ever rolling, ever restless; but even though there are turbulent waves on the surface, in the depths of our consciousness is the divine stillness which, through the grace of the Lord, we enter as our meditation deepens. Ten years ago, when I used to talk about the still mind and transcendental wisdom, people would sometimes object: "But we are rational people. Ours is an age of reason." I agree that if we could act as rational people, there would be a good deal of satisfaction in it, but our mind is not used to rational thinking. Very few people have the capacity to concentrate completely on a given topic. In the morning, when you are brushing your teeth, try to keep your mind on the toothbrush for just two minutes; you will find the mind jumping about from one topic to another, all irrelevant, and each more disconnected than the last. Most of our tension, frustration, conflict, fatigue, and lack of will are due to the continuous working of the mind. And in people who are self-centered and capable of resentments, this constant, undisciplined activity of the mind can lead to a terrible drain on energy. When we have a resentment, *prāna,* or vital energy, is leaking out all the time, even in our dreams.

This is why some people may get up in the morning after eight hours of sleep saying, "Why is it I am so tired?" In order to stop this continuous draining of vital energy that demoralizes and debilitates us, we have to learn to keep the mind still.

Meditation in the early stages is a discipline to slow down the mind, which is now traveling at breakneck speed, weaving from lane to lane and observing no signals, no regulations. If you are practicing meditation sincerely, systematically, and with sustained enthusiasm, there will be certain times when the mind becomes concentrated. Just for ten minutes there may be complete concentration on the second chapter of the Gita, and you feel as if you are getting control over a very powerful car. You are on U.S. 101, there is very little traffic, and you are able to travel fifty-four miles per hour without even turning the wheel or stepping on the brakes. Everything is under control. You go down one lane only; there are no turns, no merging traffic. When you can concentrate on one thought, there is no tension because there is no division; there is complete security because there is complete concentration. On the other hand, most of us are like the drivers we see in San Francisco during the Christmas rush. You have only to look at the tension on their faces to see how much effort is required; they seem to be trying to lift the car and throw it forward. This is what we are doing in life – taking all our weight upon ourselves and trying to push ourselves forward, when the Lord is behind us saying, "Why don't you let me do it? I have many arms."

When we realize the complete fullness and complete stillness within us, it is an extremely satisfying experience, which, in the course of time as our meditation deepens, many of us may have. Just for a little while all the wires are disconnected, and there is no contact with the external world. The Buddha, using a negative term, calls it *shūnyatā*, the Void, where there is no friction, no disharmony, no separateness. The Hindu mystics describe this stillness as *pūrnatā*, complete fullness.

Even after we have attained deep spiritual awareness, however, occasional desires may still come into our minds. This may happen to all of us because we are encased in the body; we are corporeal beings functioning in a physically oriented world. But when we are aware spiritually, even if desires come, we will not identify ourselves with them or be upset by them. Desires will come into the mind just as rivers come into the vast sea, which remains full and established in stillness. As long as we are living on the separate level, putting ourselves first, when a canal brings in a little water there are huge waves and landslides, and banks are swept away. But when we begin to live in the depths of our being, realizing that all of us are one, however different we may appear, then even a big river like the Ganges, coming down from the Himālayas with the monsoon flood, will not disturb the sea of stillness within.

The last word of this verse is *kāmakāmī*, 'the desirer of desires.' One friend who is going to accompany us deep, deep into our meditation is kāma in the form of sexual desire. Even after many years of meditation, when we think we have at last parted from this companion, we will sit down to meditate one morning and there he will be, as friendly as ever. Kāma, which is personified in the Hindu tradition as Kāmadeva, has many names:

> *Madano manmatho mārah pradyumno mīnaketanah*
> *Kandarpo darpako 'nangah kāmah pancasharah smarah*

Manmatha is 'he who churns the mind': when Kāma comes with his cosmic churner, we cannot sit quiet; we cannot breathe; we cannot think. This is a very penetrating name, because sex is not just on the physical level. It is very much in the mind, and it is in the mind, not just the body, that we must learn to control this powerful force. *Māra* is 'the striker.' *Smara* is 'he who will not let you forget.' Once we have had a sexual experience, we just cannot forget it; such is the power of *Kāma* that no matter what we try to do, we cannot help dwelling on it. The only refuge we have at that time is Shiva – *Smarāri*, 'the enemy of Smara,' who enables us to forget and to recall our vital power. *Pancashara* is 'having five arrows.' When *Kāma* draws back his bow to the end of the world, aims at our heart, and begins to fire his arrows, we feel we are completely lost. Our refuge then is in the mantram.

When a strong desire is threatening to sweep us away, we grapple with it in morning meditation and still the mind a little. But the real challenge comes afterwards, during the rest of the day, in using the power released in meditation to meet the temptation. We still have the desire, but we turn against it. Whenever desires threaten to agitate us, we have an opportunity to remain calm and compassionate and repeat the mantram. This is the greatest challenge in life. Every time we push these desires back, we strengthen the will; and gradually we begin to realize that He who made the sea and sun, sky and moon, is within us, giving us the infinite power and immense energy to transform our desires. The control of sex is not the negation of it. Sex is closely connected with *kundalinī,* which is evolutionary energy, and when we learn to control this power instead of being controlled by it, all our creative abilities and capacities for selfless service are released.

विहाय कामान्यः सर्वान्पुमांश्चरति निःस्पृहः ।
निर्ममो निरहंकारः स शान्तिमधिगच्छति ॥२-७१॥

71. They are forever free who break away
from the ego-cage of 'I,' 'me,' and 'mine'
to be united with the Lord of Love.

In this verse the Lord gives us the secret of how to attain *shānti,* "the peace that passeth all understanding," that resolves all conflicts, fulfills all desires, and banishes all fear. In our consciousness there is a division, just a little split at first, that prevents our being completely loving and loyal. When we allow conflicts to rage within us, or disloyalty to separate us from others, the split grows wider and wider until finally it runs clear through our consciousness. Meditation is the process of healing this split so that the two parts become one indivisible unity. This is the purpose of meditation: to do away with the internal divisions of our heart and mind and to mend the external division that separates us from our family, community, and world.

If we are trying to unify our consciousness, we cannot afford to be disloyal to anyone. If we are disloyal to our parents, the same disloyalty will enter our relationship with our partner and our friends. Right in our home, in our early days, we can learn how to unify our fragmented love and loyalty. Otherwise, once we have left home and begun to deal with the problems of the world, disloyalty may begin to disrupt our relationships.

Disloyalty gave the Buddha serious problems, as it did Jesus the Christ. Peter was always promising Jesus, "I am completely loyal to you." But Jesus said, "Before the cock crows, you will deny me three times." Just as disloyalty breeds division, loyalty brings union. Every relationship is an opportunity to develop complete loyalty. When I suggest that the family context is the ideal situation in which to learn this art, I do not mean that we should all be married and have a dozen children. Where friends live together, or where people play or work together, there is a family. We all have somebody to put first, and if no friend is available, then we can always find an enemy. Someone may have said or done something harsh towards us. If we can bear with such a person, we are becoming loyal. If, instead of retaliating, we try to help him get over his problem, we are healing the division that splits his consciousness and ours too. As St. Francis reminds us, the man or woman who has not learned to forgive others has lost the greatest joy in life.

In the Hindu tradition, religious functions such as marriages and funerals always conclude with the words *Om shānti shānti shānti*, because everyone is destined for this peace which words cannot capture nor concepts convey. Every day the work you do in meditation is preparing you for shānti. You may have slept a little, digressed a little, or lost the passage at times; still your meditation is bringing you closer to the supreme fulfillment that is shānti. One day when you least expect it, your concentration will become complete. Then the mind quietly puts down a pillow and sleeps for just a few minutes. You look at the slumbering mind and say, "God bless you; may you never wake up." This is what the Buddhists call the state of no-mind. No-mind is a profound condition in which you know intuitively and directly, without the medium of the senses or the intellect. All mystics tell us this immediate knowledge far exceeds the limitations of the intellect.

It takes a long time to have even a preliminary experience of shānti. When you have this experience even for a few minutes, it is as if the factory of the mind has closed down completely. Everywhere there is a soothing stillness, a silent splendor. Only when you experience this state can you know how healing it is for the body, senses, mind, and intellect, and how bad it is for the ego. This is the only party who suffers. I have said more than once that I am not competent to perform a marriage or a funeral ceremony. But for the funeral of the ego you may call me any time, and I will come immediately. This is the job I love. When you have the ego lying on the funeral pyre, light the torch and give me the signal; I will set it on fire. Shānti is the supreme state of perfect peace and purity in which we become love itself, loving not only this or that person but all creation, for we have realized the unity underlying all life.

To be *nihspriha* is to be without sensory craving, without any desire for satisfaction from the outside. One by one, each of these desires has to be given up. This is why it takes a long, long time to attain spiritual awareness. If we had only five desires, it might take us just five weeks; but we have an almost endless number of desires, for the nature of the mind is to desire, to desire, to desire. Most of us seem to believe that if we could make a lot of money, or win prizes, or have our portrait unveiled in the city hall, we would be happy. I have even heard people insist that the day they made their first million, or the moment the curtain fell from their portrait, they were very happy. Patanjali is a wet blanket to such people when he explains what really happens on these occasions. He says we are happy because one desire has temporarily subsided, and there is not time for another desire to well up in our mind. The mind-factory is closed down for the weekend. Happiness comes when the mind is at rest. We can all attest that when one desire has been fulfilled, there is an interim period of peace before another desire rises. I do not deny that this temporary satisfaction can be very pleasant, but when we yield to one desire, the next one is usually stronger, and if we continue to give in to selfish desires, the interval between them will become shorter and shorter until there is hardly any respite at all.

A close relationship exists between the constant desire for things outside ourselves and the drain of vital energy. Window-shopping is considered an inoffensive relaxation. Maybe it does not affect our bank balance, but it does affect our vital wealth. When we look at things and want to have them, or look at people and envy them, vitality is ebbing out. To become nihspriha we must vigilantly ask, "Should I go after this?" By asking this question in every situation, we will gradually learn which things are really necessary and which are only cumbersome.

Then Sri Krishna adds *nirmamo*. Just as the sense of 'I' can be very painful and can cost us our best friendships, so can the desire for 'mine.' In politics this is particularly true. War breaks out when the concept of 'mine' becomes outrageously inflated. All of us can be caught in mass estrangement. When Jesus says, "Blessed are the peacemakers, for they shall be called the children of God," he is telling us, as does Sri Krishna, that you and I can help bring friends, communities, countries, and enemies together by the example of our own personal lives.

Nirmamo should also remind us that the Lord gives us all the resources and life of the earth to care for as trustees. Sri Krishna is the landlord and we are poor tenants. What we have done to his apartment no human landlord would tolerate. Just try to misuse the apartment you are renting – fill it with smoke, pollute the water, punch holes in the walls, smash the windows – and see how fast you are evicted. The Lord, though, keeps on putting up with us. He doesn't even collect his rent. The rent he expects from every one of us is that we live for other people, and very few will pay so much. We want to live for ourselves, and we expect him to subsidize our selfishness and our self-will. Yet nothing on earth is ours; everything is the Lord's. We have always assumed we could use as much air as we like, as much water as we like, because there would be an unending supply. Now we know our resources are limited and must be used carefully. When we abuse our environment, our water and air, it is at the cost of future generations.

Nirahamkāra means free from self-will. I have just been reading the life of St. Francis of Assisi, and I am captivated by the saint's capacity to extinguish his self-will. Jesus says that if we want to find ourselves we have first to lose ourselves, and the Sufi mystic Ansari of Herat tells us in glorious language: "Know that when you learn to lose yourself, you will reach the Beloved. There is no other secret to be learnt, and more than this is not known to me."

In order to lose myself, I have to stop thinking about that most dreary topic, 'me.' When your spiritual awareness deepens, you will find what a monotonous, infernal bore the ego is, always wanting to be the cynosure of all eyes and the center of attention. As a matter of discipline, it is good to remain in the background. Sometimes I cannot help chuckling at the ways young people here in Berkeley try to attract attention. On one occasion I saw a truck drive past the campus carrying a piano at which a young fellow was sitting and playing away as the truck moved along. Naturally, everyone stopped and looked at the pianist, and his face beamed. There is a similar purpose behind dressing in unusual clothes. This is all right for a child, Sri Krishna tells us, but you and I do not want attention from those outside; we want to draw the attention of the Lord of Love who is within. The way to draw the Lord is to repeat the mantram. Keep on calling him, *Jesus, Jesus* or *Rāma, Rāma*. When we grow more secure, we shall see there is no need to search for security outside ourselves. We are all very important because the Lord lives in us. We need not daydream, "I wish I were like him; I wish I were like her." One of the nicest things anyone has said about me is, "He is very much at home with himself." When we are at home with ourselves, we are at home everywhere in the world. When we have found peace within ourselves, peace and love follow us wherever we go.

एषा ब्राह्मी स्थितिः पार्थ नैनां प्राप्य विमुह्यति ।
स्थित्वास्यामन्तकाले ऽपि ब्रह्मनिर्वाणमृच्छति ॥२-७२॥

72. This is the supreme state. Attain to this,
and pass from death to immortality.

When the ego dies, we come into eternal life. When in the climax of meditation called samādhi we break through the wrong identification with the body, senses, mind, and intellect, learning experientially that we are the Ātman, the Christ within, the Krishna within, we go beyond death and know our immortality. This promise of immortality is given us by mystics of all religions who have attained illumination. When Sri Ramana Maharshi talked about death, he was able to convey to those who were deeply responsive and devoted to him that death need not come to all. Sri Ramana Maharshi attained complete illumination when still a high-school boy. He was not Sri Ramana Maharshi then; he was just Venkataraman, a high-school student trying to cut classes like everyone else. He had some difficult exercises to do in English grammar, and behaving as any schoolboy would, he did not go to school that day. Instead, he just lay down in his room and killed his ego. It was all done in half an hour's time. In the language of mysticism, what died during that thirty minutes was not Ramana Maharshi, but the separate, finite ego. This is nirvāna: the annihilation of the finite boundary of separateness in which we realize our true, immortal Self.

To throw a little light on this elusive spiritual phenomenon, we must look at what takes place in meditation. In meditation, over a long, long period of time, we learn to recall all our vital energy from the past and future. In samādhi the future vanishes, the past vanishes, and we live completely on the pinpoint of the moment. To live completely in the moment is to realize immortality, here and now. Mystics who have lived like this tell us that in the complete unification of consciousness we are released from time; we are delivered from time into eternity.

My spiritual teacher, my grandmother, used to go every morning for many, many years to a sacred spring near our village. This spring is considered to have been sanctified by Rāma. Legends say that when he and Sītā were wandering through South India during their period of exile, Sītā became thirsty. She told her husband, "You have great love for me, so you must be able to give me a drink of cool water." There was no water in that place, so Rāma took an arrow and, sending it deep into the earth, caused a spring of sacred Ganges water to come up. Today the spring is a place of pilgrimage. On one side, roughly hewn in black stone, are the feet of Rāma. Just the feet alone are considered to be a beautiful, respectful way of representing an incarnation, and this humble image is in the best spiritual tradition. My simple grandmother, after having her ceremonial bath, would stand looking at the rough, long, black feet in stone and repeat the mantram. She must have done this every morning for half a century, and when the time came for her to shed her body, according to my mother's own words, the last she said was, "I have caught Rāma by his feet."

This experience at the time of death is narrated of many mystics who have attained immortality. Until we experience a unification of consciousness and are released from the bondage of time, we cannot realize that it is not going to satisfy us to live a hundred or even a thousand years. Our need is to live forever.

साङ्ख्ययोगो नाम द्वितीयोऽध्यायः ॥ २ ॥

CHAPTER THREE

Selfless Service

अर्जुन उवाच ।
ज्यायसी चेत्कर्मणस्ते मता बुद्धिर्जनार्दन ।
तत्किं कर्मणि घोरे मां नियोजयसि केशव ॥३-१॥

ARJUNA:

1. O Janārdana, you have said that knowledge is greater than action; why then do you ask me to wage this terrible war?

Arjuna addresses Sri Krishna as *Janārdana,* 'he who stirs up the people,' because he is being aroused by the Lord's wisdom and love. But, like a worthy man of the world, he is not prepared to admit it. Instead he asks, "If you say that spiritual wisdom is the best path to Self realization, then why do you ask me to fight against my passions and tyrannize over my senses? Just show me the path to spiritual wisdom and stop talking about discriminating restraint of the senses. Tell me about the spirit. As for the senses, I am content to believe you when you say I am not my senses. Let's leave the matter there."

Arjuna believes the paths of knowledge and action to be separate or even inconsistent. But there is no contradiction between these two paths. St. Francis will say that our knowledge is as deep as our action. There may be no connection between intellectual knowledge and the will, but spiritual wisdom always reveals itself in our actions.

व्यामिश्रेणैव वाक्येन बुद्धिं मोहयसीव मे ।
तदेकं वद निश्चित्य येन श्रेयो ऽहमाप्नुयाम् ॥ ३-२ ॥

2. Your advice seems inconsistent, O Keshava; give me one path to follow to the supreme good.

Arjuna is trying to judge with his intellect, which believes in classification. The intellect must divide and categorize. This does not mean that we should not value the intellect, but we should realize its limitations; it can see only the parts, not the whole. This tendency of the intellect often leads to problems on the spiritual path. Many people used to ask Sri Ramakrishna, "Is God personal or impersonal?" and he would say, very wisely, that He is both personal and impersonal. Shankara[1] probably would say, on one occasion, "God is both"; on another occasion, "He is neither."

Arjuna is thinking, "I wouldn't have believed it, Krishna, if someone had told me you were not very consistent, but I see a contradiction, and in the Lord of Love this is not permissible." *Buddhim mohayasī 'va me:* "My head reels. Before I listened to those last eighteen verses, I had some idea of who I was. Now I don't know who you are or who I am." *Nishcitya:* "Think carefully. Don't try to talk in a higher state of consciousness." Then, *Ekam vada:* "Show me only one line of action. Be rigid." Arjuna wants one single line of action, no eight steps on the path, no total way of life. Otherwise, as you and I do, he complains that he will become more and more bewildered.

This confusion, which many of us face as we start the spiritual life, will be gradually overcome through the practice of meditation as we begin to develop a higher mode of knowing called *prajnā* in Sanskrit, which leaps beyond the duality of subject and object. In meditation, as we grow from day to day, many of the problems we now face will be transcended. As long as we are meditating sincerely, there may be no need even to try to understand the cause of our difficulties – to analyze them, dwell on them, or discuss them. There is no need because we

1. A mystic from Kerala, eighth century A.D. Foremost teacher of the Vedanta school.

are going to leave the slum where they live. After a few years of meditation, many of the physical and emotional problems in which we are caught will be left behind, even if at present they are so oppressive they will not let us sleep at night. As we gradually detach ourselves from the ego, those terrific conflicts of the past will seem like Gilbert and Sullivan operas.

श्रीभगवानुवाच ।
लोके ऽस्मिन्द्विविधा निष्ठा पुरा प्रोक्ता मयानघ ।
ज्ञानयोगेन सांख्यानां कर्मयोगेन योगिनाम् ॥ ३-३ ॥

SRI KRISHNA:

3. At the beginning of time I declared two paths for the pure heart, the intuitive path of spiritual wisdom and the active path of selfless service.

Long ago, when life was simple, when the environment was pure, when there was little competition, the Lord revealed two paths to Self-realization. For people whose self-will and separateness were very small, who could discriminate between the real and the unreal, who had an awareness of the unity of all life, he revealed the path of spiritual wisdom, or *jnāna*. In those times, when people identified themselves very little with the body and ego, jnāna yoga, or the way of spiritual wisdom, was feasible. Jnāna is not an intellectual but an intuitive mode of knowing, which transcends the duality of subject and object. Arjuna, however, is a very active person, and for his type Sri Krishna recommends karma yoga, the path of selfless action. In our own age, when competition is rife, when we are so conditioned by the mass media, jnāna yoga is extremely difficult except for a rare spiritual genius like Sri Ramana Maharshi. Karma yoga, too, is difficult, but when we live in the midst of so much suffering, all of us must learn to act as selflessly as possible for the amelioration of the problems which face mankind.

This verse, like almost all verses in the Gita, can be applied to our daily life in the modern world if interpreted in relation to the spiritual life. Many mystics will say that for people who are extroverted, more meditation is necessary, and for people who are introverted, more work. This is an adjustment which we shall find useful even in our daily sādhana. There are days when we just do not want to work. Meditation is the greatest thing on earth! After two and a half hours, we don't want to get up: "Let us meditate for two more hours!" On days like this you really feel that meditation is the thing, that it is what you have to do all the time. But that is the day to get outside and start digging. When you feel highly contemplative, get a shovel and start digging. The urge to meditate is a good one, but it must be under your control. When you begin to work hard, attention is slowly turned outward, as it must be for every human being who wants to be healthy, happy, selfless, and spiritual. With vigorous exercise – particularly for the young, under no pressure, with no desire for profit or prestige – tensions are released. The senses turn outward, and you just want to keep on digging. The contemplative mood is gone, and now "shoveling, more shoveling, and still more shoveling" has become your slogan.

Just as some people are contemplative, there are others who are action-oriented all of the time. If they finish all of their work during the day and have a few free hours at night, they complain, "We keep awake at night. We will come to your place and do some typing." This is not free work when we cannot keep quiet, when we cannot lie down and go to sleep peacefully at night. Such work, Sri Krishna says, should be discouraged. For people who are working all the time, who work compulsively, who cannot drop their work when necessary, more meditation is called for.

When lethargy is coming, that is the time to get after work. When tamas is descending upon us, that is the time to be rajasic, and when rajas is driving us, that is the time not to go back into tamas, but to go forward into sattva. This requires a certain amount of self-knowledge and comparative freedom from the sway of likes and dislikes.

न कर्मणामनारम्भान्नैष्कर्म्यं पुरुषो ऽश्नुते ।
न च संन्यसनादेव सिद्धिं समधिगच्छति ॥३-४॥
न हि कश्चित्क्षणमपि जातु तिष्ठत्यकर्मकृत् ।
कार्यते ह्यवशः कर्म सर्वः प्रकृतिजैर्गुणैः ॥३-५॥

4. He who shirks action does not attain freedom, nor does he gain perfection by abstaining from work.
5. Indeed, there is no one who rests for even an instant; every creature is driven to action by his own nature.

Here Sri Krishna makes a significant statement about the necessity for hard work on the spiritual path. Though we give a good deal of time every day to the practice of meditation and to the repetition of the mantram, we still cannot abstain from work and expect to attain the spiritual state. We have all come into the world to make a contribution, to pay off old debts which have accumulated during millions of years of evolution. No one among ordinary people like you and me can abstain from hard work on the spiritual path. There will come a time for all of us when work will fall away, but if I can make a prediction, this is not likely to take place during the present century; so, during this century, let us make a virtue of necessity and be cheerful about our work. This is the message of the Gita, that without work none of us is likely to go forward on the spiritual path.

An effective safeguard against erratic impulses, against uncontrolled wisps of consciousness floating in our mind, is to concentrate completely on the job we have to do. One of my simple observations has been that many of us have difficulties in dealing with work we do not like because we cannot concentrate. When we have a job to do which we dislike, most of us find our attention wandering. We become like children. Children will be looking at this glass for a moment, then at this bell; after that there is nothing to look at and they start crying. This is what often happens to us. When we get a job that we do not like, we say that we are artists, that this job is drudgery, that we require work challenging our creative talents. This is often just a very euphemistic way of saying that the job is one we don't like doing. I have seen that if we could only attend a little more to work we dislike, it would become interesting. It is not in the nature of the job to be interesting or not; it is in the nature of the attention we give to it. Anything, when we can give it our full attention, becomes interesting. And anything, when we do not give it full attention, becomes uninteresting.

We should give our full attention to whatever we are doing. This is not easy. When we try to concentrate upon a given job, even for a short time, we will often find our attention flickering. And then the question comes: "Am I concentrating, or am I not concentrating?" If we are observing ourselves like this all the time, we have introduced another distraction to divide our consciousness. The capacity to give full attention grows with effort, and if we keep giving more and more effort in everything we do, we shall benefit even in our meditation. It is not only by meditating that we deepen our meditation; it is by working hard, giving our concentrated attention, and taking into account the needs of the body for recreation and rest. In this way we make rāja yoga, the path of meditation, and karma yoga, the path of selfless action, go together. This is Sri Krishna's advice to all of us: by throwing ourselves into energetic, selfless action, we shall be deepening our meditation as well as serving the Lord.

There is a widespread notion that the spiritual life is a passive one. But Gandhiji exploded this long-held superstition by showing that when we lead the spiritual life and remove all selfishness from ourselves, we are able to contribute to life in the fullest measure. Gandhi transformed almost every phase of life in India during his lifetime, and if I can make a prediction, the twentieth century may come to be known not as the nuclear age, but as the Gandhian age, because it is only by renouncing violence and working for others without any selfish motive that we can continue to survive as the human race.

Naishkarmya, or 'the state of worklessness,' is the state attained by great mystics like Sri Ramana Maharshi, who was physically with us in India until 1950. For anyone coming into his presence, he could swiftly resolve their dilemmas. In orthodox Hindu circles he is considered an *avatāra*, a divine incarnation. He was never involved in the world. He never committed any of the mistakes that even some of the greatest mystics have committed. Like Sri Ramakrishna, he was always pure, having attained illumination around the age of seventeen. When European writers would ask him whether it wasn't possible for him to lead a productive life, he just used to sit and chuckle because his life influenced not only South India, but the entire world. By just one person attaining this stature, finding union with God, human evolution takes a step forward. And you and I, even without our knowledge, have benefited from the presence on earth of these great spiritual figures.

Naishkarmya is a glorious ideal whereby we help humanity by just sitting, and I can understand all of us being drawn by this ideal: we do not have to lift a finger; we just sit and everybody is helped. But now Lord Krishna points out that this state of worklessness, where action falls away and we become a living center of the divine spirit, is not reached by the path of inaction. It is not by abstaining from action, by refraining from work, by dropping out of society, by quitting school, by throwing up our hands in despair, that the state of *naishkarmya* is achieved.

When I say I have the softest corner in my heart for Arjuna, it is because he is so much like you and me. Now I imagine him asking just the question we would have asked. Arjuna begins, "Supposing, just for the sake of argument, hypothetically . . ."

Sri Krishna says, "Yes, you are talking about yourself. Go on."

"If I were to put on saffron robes, grow my hair very long, wear a rosary around my neck, and go from village to village singing hymns, eating where there is a meal, sleeping where there is a temple, wouldn't that also be a path to *naishkarmya*?"

Now Sri Krishna answers him, *Na ca samnyasanād eva siddhim samadhigacchati:* "Not through mere renunciation is perfection to be attained." Even if you retire to the Himālayas, find the most isolated, ice-ridden cave there, get in, put out a sign saying "There is nobody here," and live there for twelve years – even then you will not attain this state.

The Lord is emphasizing here that you and I have a debt to pay to the world. This concept of karma is personified in Sanskrit as Chitragupta, the "hidden auditor" in every cell of the human system. The moment

I think a selfish thought, every cell in my biological system has received a minus, and the moment I think a selfless thought about my parents, partner, children, friends, and even enemies, as to how I can contribute to their welfare, every cell of my being has received a plus sign. Chitragupta doesn't work an eight-hour day, but all the twenty-four hours, because even in our sleep he has to keep on, mostly giving minuses. His supply of minus signs is a big pile. Only once in a way does he have to give a plus.

When we were on the Blue Mountain, I was invited to address the local club of Indian businessmen which met in a hotel called the Ritz. When my wife and I arrived, we found the members dressed in fine British suits and carrying attaché cases. Telephones were ringing all over the place, and everyone was running about. It was a tense business atmosphere. At the dinner we said we were vegetarians, and the majority of them, being successful business people, must have thought that vegetarian food wasn't strong enough to bring in high dividends, because they were asking us, "You mean even after wandering all over the West, you still stick to okra and eggplant?" So I told them I not only continued to be a vegetarian, but all my friends in the West had become complete vegetarians. At the end of my talk there was a question and answer period, and the secretary of the club, who was an Indian Christian, got up and said, "I presume that the law of karma is only applicable to people born into the Hindu or Buddhist traditions. May I take it we Christians are all exempted from this law?" I would be happy if he could have been exempted, but Jesus states the law of karma in precise terms, "As ye sow, so shall ye reap." If we have caused suffering to other people, we are going to reap suffering. If we have added to the happiness of others, we will receive happiness more and more. And Jesus adds: "With what measure you mete, it shall be measured to you again."

It is a terrifying thought for all of us that we have the choice of joy or sorrow, happiness or misery in our hands; and nobody is justified in saying, "My parents made me like this; my partner, children, and society made me like this," because we all reap what we sow. In whatever troubled circumstances we live, in whatever country, we all have one choice: shall we go after our own profit and pleasure, or shall we forget these and add to the happiness and welfare of those around us?

कर्मेन्द्रियाणि संयम्य य आस्ते मनसा स्मरन् ।
इन्द्रियार्थान्विमूढात्मा मिथ्याचारः स उच्यते ॥ ३-६ ॥

6. Whoever abstains from action while allowing the mind to dwell on sensual pleasure cannot be called a sincere spiritual aspirant.

Last Sunday we spent an Indian day in Berkeley. We went to a classical music concert given by Ali Akbar Khan, India's greatest sarod player. Two days before the concert, I found my mind saying, "It certainly will be nice to listen to good Indian classical music." Even while I was walking on the beach my mind was trying to jump out of control, and I had to get blunt with it and tell it to keep quiet. This is controlling the mind, not letting it jump out of my grasp into the past or the future. Even when good things are likely to come, I do not anticipate them, and every time my mind jumps out to try and meet them, I bring it back by repeating the mantram in order to keep it in the present. Then, when the event takes place, my mind will be all there, completely concentrated.

Even though we refrain from eating a large pizza, even though we keep our eyes from spinning like ocular tops when we go to the beach, if we are not struggling to keep the mind from dwelling on these sense objects, then we are what Sri Krishna calls *mithyācāra*, 'hypocrites.' Particularly in the early days, the aspirant is expected to struggle as much as possible against the blandishment of the senses. It is not possible to be completely successful, but as long as we try our best to concentrate during meditation and to restrain the senses during the day, we are doing well. Of course, if we are yawning in meditation, we are not trying very hard; it is only by making a maximum effort that we develop the capacity to make greater effort.

Later on, when our meditation has been very good and we have really been concentrating, the Lord not infrequently tries to test us by placing us in a difficult situation. We get up from meditation confident that the mind has been stilled; we open the door and walk right into a booby trap. Such difficult situations enable us to verify the strength and validity of our meditation. As we can see from the life of every great mystic, it is when our capacities to govern our thoughts, to control our mind, and to unify our consciousness develop to an enormous degree that the tests, the problems we face, become more exacting. After all, a freshman is not asked to take the qualifying examination for the doctoral degree. When I was head of the department of English at my university in India, we had two examiners: the external examiner tried to see how much the students did not know, and the internal examiner, usually played by me, found out how much they did know. In meditation there will be all kinds of examinations by the external examiner, who is Kāma, but the internal examiner, the Lord of Love, is always there within us to help us show who we really are.

यस्त्विन्द्रियाणि मनसा नियम्यारभतेऽर्जुन ।
कर्मेन्द्रियैः कर्मयोगमसक्तः स विशिष्यते ॥ ३-७ ॥

7. But they excel who control their senses through their mind and use them for selfless service.

This is a perfect description of Mahatma Gandhi. When Gandhi was in London, he made the discovery that taste lies in the mind. Whenever he discovered that something was good for the body, he would smack his lips over it and enjoy it as none of us can enjoy even the most delectable ice cream. In India we have a tree, called the neem tree, with the bitterest-tasting leaves imaginable. These leaves are said to have antiseptic value, and Gandhi, in a stroke of culinary genius, decided to make them into chutney. For him any discovery was translated immediately into action. He stripped the neem tree of a bagful of leaves and got his wife, Kasturbai, to grind them into a chutney; and it is said there was an unexpected exodus from the āshram when Gandhi started serving this bitter dish. It was in the bitterness of life we call grief that he used to find joy; he was at his best when taking on suffering to save other people. The same insight is given us in this verse. When we are involved in an unfortunate episode with our parents, partner, children, or friends, it is very bitter to pocket the resentment and try to behave affectionately. But doing this will benefit us like Gandhi's neem chutney. At first it will be quite bitter, but if we swallow it, it will act as a disinfectant to remove the virus of selfishness, anger, and fear from our hearts. By acting selflessly, no matter how painful it is, there will come a time when we can enjoy not only what is pleasant but what is unpleasant as well.

नियतं कुरु कर्म त्वं कर्म ज्यायो ह्यकर्मणः ।
शरीरयात्रापि च ते न प्रसिध्येदकर्मणः ॥ ३-८ ॥

8. You are obliged to act, Arjuna, even to maintain your body. Fulfill all your duties; action is better than inaction.

Work is a necessity. Just imagine what would happen to people if they did not have the stimulus and release of daily work! That is why my granny used to say, "When God gave you a mouth, he gave you two hands with which to feed the mouth." Instead of using our hands to manipulate others, or to attack our enemies, we should use them to sustain ourselves and others.

Eating, exercising, and all activities that keep the body healthy for serving others can be considered sacraments. The implication is that bodies which are overfed, overstimulated, and underexercised are not capable of learning to act selflessly. Good health is essential if we are to lead the spiritual life.

The Lord of Love gives Arjuna an axiom now: Action is better than inaction. Eons back in our evolution, when we were rocks, it was all right for us just to sit inactively; but in the human context, inaction is a violation of the basis of our existence. The Bible tells us we must earn our bread by the sweat of our brow. Hard physical work is good for us in the early stages of our sādhana, for it keeps us from dwelling on the body, a great cause of much of our tension. Work is a particularly effective tonic when it is performed without desire for profit, prestige, or power.

In order to practice the teaching contained in this verse, let us ask ourselves how much our daily work contributes to the welfare of our family and community. We are all given the choice in this life of acting for our own personal pleasure and profit, which will lead to ill will, frustration, and insecurity, or of acting for the benefit of others, which will lead to increasing health, security, and wisdom. If we lead a selfish life, by the time the body and senses wear out the story will have come to an end. If we lead a selfless life, our contribution becomes an eternal force, released into the stream of life, that will help in however small a way to elevate the consciousness of mankind. This is why people like Gandhi never die; his body was assassinated, but his spirit lives on in everyone who tries to be nonviolent.

यज्ञार्थात्कर्मणो ऽन्यत्र लोको ऽयं कर्मबन्धनः ।
तदर्थं कर्म कौन्तेय मुक्तसङ्गः समाचर ॥३-९॥

9. The world is imprisoned in selfish action, Kaunteya;
act selflessly, without any thought of personal profit.

The Lord of Love continues in the same vein by telling Arjuna, *Loko 'yam karmabandhanah:* "The whole world is imprisoned in action." This may strike us as removed from the facts of life because we are all under the impression that when we are pursuing prestige, pleasure, and power we are really free agents. It never occurs to us that we are so driven we hardly have any liberty to lift even a finger to help somebody lying helpless by the roadside. We begin life with action that is motivated by selfish desire, for this is the stuff of which ego-centered life is made. But after a certain period of experimentation with money, material possessions, pleasure, and power, the Lord expects us to find out that these things are not the real goal of life.

This reminds me of the game of hide and seek called "Kooee" which we used to play in my village. We would scatter ourselves throughout my ancestral home in little rooms where people were not likely to look for us, and then, when everyone was well hidden, we would shout "Kooee." The person who was "it" would try to locate the call, which was very difficult because the house was large and full of echoes. "Kooee . . . kooee" – he would hear the voice from all sides and lose his sense of direction. Similarly, we hear the desire for pleasure or profit calling "kooee . . . kooee . . . kooee," and we think, "Maybe that voice is coming from under the floor." We tear up the floor, look all around under it, and discover nothing there after all. When we climb out, we hear the call again. This time we think, "Maybe it's above the ceiling," so we tear down the ceiling. We go on this way, trying to follow echoes, wasting time in endless searching until life is about to ebb out. This is applicable to almost all of us, because once we get caught in the sense game, in the profit game, in the power game, or in the prestige game, it can go on and on until it becomes an inescapable compulsion.

It is necessary for us to engage ourselves in selfless action, which we can learn to do over a long period of time. Sri Krishna refers to selfless action as *yajna*. There are many ways in which even the busiest people can serve the welfare of others. We can give our time, our money, our skill, our land. Yajna can take any form when we give to a worthy cause without expecting any return. To give in this spirit, Sri Krishna tells us, we must develop *muktasangah samācara,* the capacity not to get caught in any of our actions. When we get caught in our own job, our own interests, we lose our discrimination and forget the real purpose of life. One of the ways we get caught in our actions is by bringing our work home, from our job, our campus, or our factory. We do not have to put it in a briefcase to bring it home; we carefully store it in our minds where we can dwell on it all the time. When we can drop our work in the evening and pick it up completely the following morning, we are masters of our work. This capacity comes after a long time of striving to concentrate on the job at hand.

It is true that most of us are good at doing the jobs we like, but a necessary part of the spiritual life is to be able to do the things we do not like. Life has a subtle way of ferreting out what we do not like and sticking it right under our nose, where we cannot ignore or escape it. One of the eloquent laws of life is that when you do not dislike anything, only the things you like come your way, whereas if you dislike a job and quit, the next job will be even worse. Just as Gandhiji says taste lies in the mind, I would say the taste for work lies in the mind. When you understand that doing a particular job will enable you to function in freedom in all matters, whether you like them or not, joy will slowly begin to rise in your heart. Then you will want to verify the truth of this timeless teaching in your own life by working in whatever way you can for the welfare of others. In this connection, Gandhi is an inspiring example, showing that when you begin a life of selfless service you really become secure, established in the center of your being, which is divine.

सहयज्ञाः प्रजाः सृष्ट्वा पुरोवाच प्रजापतिः ।
अनेन प्रसविष्यध्वमेष वो ऽस्त्विष्टकामधुक् ॥३-१०॥

10. At the time of creation the Lord gave humanity the path of selfless service and said: "Through selfless service you will always be fruitful and find the fulfillment of all your desires."

In the Hindu scriptures there is a miraculous cow called *Kāmadhenu* that is said to grant all our desires. Here we have the term *kāmadhuk*, 'that which grants all our right desires.' Any boon not connected with our profit or pleasure that we ask for in order to carry out spiritual work, to add to the welfare of our society or to the peace of the world, will be given to us.

In this verse Sri Krishna says that the very principle behind our individual growth lies in forgetting ourselves in living for the welfare of all. On this basis alone will we be granted peace, joy, beauty, and wisdom. Here the Gita urges us to regard our very lives as *yajna* by trying to act selflessly in all circumstances. When we talk about war, for example, we should include the guerilla strategies that go on in our homes. In this sense we can all claim ourselves as experts on warfare, because whenever we put ourselves first we are making war. But if we can learn to live for our family, our country, and our world, then there will be peace everywhere. So far, in thousands of years, we have verified this statement only negatively. In the last two thousand years there have been innumerable wars, and some statistician once calculated that peace treaties last on average only two years. Peace treaties do not produce peace. Until we have peace in the home and on the street we cannot have peace in the world. Sri Krishna's language is thus applicable to political turmoil, to racial strife, and to domestic friction. In all of us there is a selfless motive and a selfish motive coming together in mortal combat most of the time. To establish peace in our hearts all we need to do is identify ourselves more and more each day with our selfless Self.

देवान्भावयतानेन ते देवा भावयन्तु वः ।
परस्परं भावयन्तः श्रेयः परमवाप्स्यथ ॥३-११॥

11. Honor and cherish the devas as they honor
and cherish you; through this honor and
love you will attain the supreme good.

Sri Krishna uses the significant spiritual word *deva,* 'divine being' or 'shining one.' Artists often represent the splendor of the sage and the saint by the symbol of the halo, but the selfish person has a distinguishing mark, too – a dark cloud. Just as the saint radiates light, the selfish person spreads darkness; just as the saint lights up the path of ordinary people, the selfish person makes confusion worse confounded.

In Sanskrit literature, when a man addresses a woman, he often uses the title *Devī.* This perfect form of address is used even today in orthodox communities in India. *Devī* is also an epithet for the Divine Mother. When we address a woman as Devī, she cannot afford to be angry; she has to be patient and forgiving, she has to endure and forbear, as this is the way a devī behaves. My grandmother, even in her seventies, took our breath away by the glow of her skin, the gentleness of her eyes, and the resolute set of her mouth which said, "Self-willed people, be careful when you come near me." Even some of my least spiritual uncles could not stay away from her. Everyone would gather around her because all were aware that here was beauty and femininity that time could not touch.

All of us are devas and devīs, and we reveal the divinity of our nature in the details of daily life by serving and loving one another. When a man and woman love and honor one another, the relationship will grow more beautiful with the passage of time. We can foster this type of relationship in many ways. In Kerala little girls look after their fathers, grandfathers, brothers, and uncles. It is not just make-believe; they are actually learning to forget themselves by thinking about the needs of their menfolk. If I may say so, it is not easy to be looked after; it is a great art. To receive love gracefully and gratefully is one of the most difficult jobs in the world. But by trying harder each day to be loving towards those around us, we help everyone, including ourselves, to become devas and devīs.

इष्टान्भोगान्हि वो देवा दास्यन्ते यज्ञभाविताः ।
तैर्दत्तानप्रदायैभ्यो यो भुङ्क्ते स्तेन एव सः ॥३-१२॥

12. *When you engage in selfless service, all your desires are fulfilled by the devas. But anyone who enjoys the things given by the devas without offering selfless acts in return is a thief.*

The Lord declares he has sent us into this world to serve one another, and anyone who lives for pleasure, profit, power, or prestige is *stena,* 'a thief.' The greatest motive for action we can have is the awareness that the Lord has given us life, time, and energy to contribute to the welfare of those around us. Remember the words of St. Francis, "It is in giving that we receive." It is in always trying to receive that we lose everything, but when we give to those around us, we will have more and more to give.

यज्ञशिष्टाशिनः सन्तो मुच्यन्ते सर्वकिल्बिषैः ।
भुञ्जते ते त्वघं पापा ये पचन्त्यात्मकारणात् ॥ ३-१३ ॥

13. The spiritually minded, who eat in the spirit of service, are freed from all their sins; but the selfish, who prepare food for their own satisfaction, eat sin.

To eat to satisfy the palate, to crave for gourmet foods, to go to restaurants just to taste exotic food – all this, Sri Krishna says, is wrong. Food that we eat just to titillate the palate often disagrees with us, while temperate, nourishing food, cooked and served with love and eaten to strengthen our body and mind for serving others, is considered to be part of sādhana.

Eating good food is not a sin, but we should not dwell on it; we should not let our mind wander in meditation from the words of St. Francis to the cheese omelette we hope to have for breakfast. Even too much talk about food amounts to dwelling on it. See that you are eating nourishing, healthy food, and then forget about it. As the Chinese mystic Huang Po puts it aptly: "Thus there is sensual eating and wise eating. When the body composed of the four elements suffers the pangs of hunger and accordingly you provide it with food, but without greed, that is called wise eating. On the other hand, if you gluttonously delight in purity and flavor, you are permitting the distinctions which arise from wrong thinking. Merely seeking to gratify the organ of taste without realizing when you have taken enough is called sensual eating."

What is important is what we do with the energy food gives us. As Jesus told the Pharisees: "Not what goes into the mouth defiles a man, but what comes out of the mouth, this defiles a man." Of what use is it to procure hand-cultivated, organically grown food when we act violently or use resentful language? If instead we use our vitality to help other people, to wipe away their tears, our eyes will become brighter and our life a source of strength to a deeply troubled world.

अन्नाद्भवन्ति भूतानि पर्जन्यादन्नसंभवः ।
यज्ञाद्भवति पर्जन्यो यज्ञः कर्मसमुद्भवः ॥३-१४॥

14. Living creatures are nourished by food, and food is nourished by the rain; this rain is the water of life that comes from selfless action, worship, and service.

Food is one of our ubiquitous topics. Here Sri Krishna reminds us that it is extremely important for us to eat the right kind of food, in the right amount, at the right time, and in the right company. Translated into daily life, this means eating healthy, nutritious food, in temperate quantities, that is prepared and served with love. It also implies that eating together is a great sacrament, a time not for acrimonious discussion but for a loving, peaceful atmosphere.

This verse suggests the delicate relationships existing throughout all nature. We know today from the work of ecologists that our actions can easily upset the balance of nature. In India vast forests have been cut down, and now people are worrying about the lack of rain. This reminds me of Gandhi, a skilled ecologist, who was so careful about using resources that he would clip the blank margins from newspapers and magazines for letter writing. I notice that little children in America write two words on a sheet of paper and throw it away, whereas Meera and Geetha, my two little nieces from India, have been taught to start writing way up in the left corner of a piece of paper and to fill the whole page down to the lower right comer. We should teach children the habit of using all resources correctly. By every economy we make in paper, we save a tree. In this connection, I would also say that many of the books written are only an injury to trees. Isn't it Truman Capote who makes a pointed comment to the effect that many people who write are not writers but typists? We can always save a tree by not purchasing books that are not really necessary for our education, our job, our wholesome entertainment, or our spiritual development.

Many of the steps we must take to preserve our environment require us to change our habits, to transform our lives, and this is what all of us can learn to do through the practice of meditation. The basis of ecological improvement is to turn what is selfish and violent in us into selflessness and compassion. We do not realize the power little people have. My grandmother used to say that the elephant does not know its own size at all because it looks out at the world through tiny eyes, ridiculously small for its huge bulk. We, too, are much larger than we think, for the Lord lives in us. We cannot see ourselves as we really are, but if we could, we would say, "How big, how tremendous, how invincible!" Once we see who is within us, we are not afraid of any problem in the world – pollution, violence, or war. We can solve the transportation problem with our feet; we can solve the job problem with our own industries; we can change the present political framework by transforming ourselves. We shall find that everyone around us participates in the change we are able to bring about in our own lives. So whatever challenges confront us, whatever perils threaten to swallow us up, none of us need be despondent, for the Lord who is the source of all power, all wisdom, and all beauty is waiting to act through us.

कर्म ब्रह्मोद्भवं विद्धि ब्रह्माक्षरसमुद्भवम् ।
तस्मात्सर्वगतं ब्रह्म नित्यं यज्ञे प्रतिष्ठितम् ॥३-१५॥

15. Arjuna, understand that every selfless act is born from Brahman, the eternal, infinite Godhead, and that he is present in every act of service.

In order to be a brahmin, we do not need to wear a sacred thread or to undergo purification ceremonies. Whoever tries to know Brahman, the supreme Reality embedded within us, is a brahmin. Another name for the brahmin is *dvija,* 'twice-born.' You and I are born once and we die once, but the brahmin is born twice and does not die at all. That is a very enviable state. According to the tradition of *dvija,* we are born once at the hands of the doctor or midwife. This is our physical birth. But we can be born again, to the joy of the spirit, if we put our ego to death. Now we imagine that when all our selfishness and separateness die, when all the desires that torment our heart are burnt to ashes, there will be a terrible funeral pyre. Actually it is a jubilant procession with bands in the front, people singing *Hare Rāma,* and others strewing flowers all over our path. It is a day of great celebration for the whole world, because when we put the ego to death in ourselves we have done the greatest service we can render to others. Whatever our lives have been, they now become a constant source of support and inspiration and an unending reminder that this is the supreme state we have come into the world to attain. Meister Eckhart calls the second birth "a mighty upheaval"; to bring it about requires enormous endurance, immense patience, and the resolute dedication to overcome every obstacle on the path.

The desire and the capacity to eliminate our ego come through the grace of the Lord. You and I are really modest, humble people, and for a long time we cannot accept the idea that the Lord of Love could want poor, paltry us. To illustrate from my own life, many mornings I used to get up and say, "Is there anyone less suited for this high destiny than I am?" Finally, with utter humility, I accepted this boundless gift of the Lord's grace, and since then there has been a continuing spring of joy and love for him.

एवं प्रवर्तितं चक्रं नानुवर्तयतीह यः ।
अघायुरिन्द्रियारामो मोघं पार्थ स जीवति ॥ ३-१६ ॥

16. All life turns on this law, O Pārtha; whoever violates it, indulging his senses for his own pleasure and ignoring the needs of others, has wasted his life.

The Lord, our Creator, has written the law of selflessness into every one of our cells. This law is what the Buddha called *dharma*. The dharma of the human being is to turn anger into forgiveness and hatred into love. In practical, straightforward language, the mystics tell us that those who live for themselves die, while those who live for others live completely and joyfully. It is all too easy to say, "An eye for an eye, and a tooth for a tooth." Retaliation requires very little courage, but making the mind calm and compassionate when it is seething with fury requires tremendous courage and endurance.

The more we can reduce our ego, or self-will, the more our real personality, the Ātman, can reveal all its beauty, wisdom, and love in our lives. Now we are all wearing a mask of separateness made from selfish desires for pleasure, profit, prestige, and power. To take off this mask of misery, we need only to call on the Lord and calm our mind with his holy name. By ceaselessly repeating the mantram when we feel a wave of anger or fear erupting in our consciousness, by using the power of the holy name to move closer to others when we want to go our own separate way, we will gradually pry off the ugly mask of the ego. Then we will know the boundless joy that springs from the loss of self-will.

Once when Sri Krishna was playing on his flute, Rādhā eyed it with jealous eyes and asked, "What has your flute done to enjoy the blessing of being held to your lips while you play upon it hour after hour?" In answer, Sri Krishna took the flute from his lips and turned it so Rādhā could see inside, saying, "Look, it's completely empty, so it is easy for me to fill it with the melody of my divine song." We, too, can become full of the Lord's infinite love and abiding joy when we empty ourselves of all that is selfish and separate.

यस्त्वात्मरतिरेव स्यादात्मतृप्तश्च मानवः ।
आत्मन्येव च संतुष्टस्तस्य कार्यं न विद्यते ॥३-१७॥
नैव तस्य कृतेनार्थो नाकृतेनेह कश्चन ।
न चास्य सर्वभूतेषु कश्चिदर्थव्यपाश्रयः ॥३-१८॥

17–18. But they who have found the Ātman are always satisfied. They have found the source of joy and fulfillment, and no longer seek happiness from the external world. They have nothing to gain or lose by any action; neither people nor things can affect their security.

As long as we have a hankering for personal profit or power, we cannot act freely. Gandhi is the perfect model for us to follow in this respect, for he was able to work fifteen hours a day without any trace of tension or fatigue. Imagine the responsibility he had for the lives of millions of people in his *satyāgraha* campaign, and for the state of peace or war between two countries. Yet because he had extinguished every desire for self-aggrandizement, he could always act in freedom. According to the Gita, all work motivated by selfish urges, no matter how subtle, is tainted. In order to follow in Gandhi's footsteps, we need to embark on the exhilarating discipline of putting others first without any thought of whether or not we are going to be recognized or rewarded.

As long as there is a desire for anything external to us, there is a vacuum in our consciousness. If we think we will be happy if only we can get a million dollars, we are really claiming bankruptcy. If we feel we will be happy if only we can become president of our country, we are really saying, "I am now completely vacant – an utter vacuum." Even in the daily activities of life, we cannot escape feeling we would be happy "if only . . ." But when we desire happiness conditioned by the possession of anything or anybody, we are likely to manipulate people and to work unconsciously at the expense of even our dear ones. Thus we should heed well Sri Krishna's words: if you want to act in freedom, develop a sustained spiritual campaign to remove every vestige of self-will and separateness from your consciousness.

तस्मादसक्तः सततं कार्यं कर्म समाचर ।
असक्तो ह्याचरन्कर्म परमाप्नोति पूरुषः ॥ ३-१९ ॥

19. Strive constantly to serve the welfare of the world; by devotion to selfless work a man attains the supreme goal of life.

Sri Krishna tells us, through Arjuna, to detach ourselves from our ego, to escape from the grip of our self-will so that we can act for the welfare of all around us. As we gain this freedom in action, we will begin, ever so gradually, to realize we are only an instrument of which the Lord is the operator. This truth, no matter how dimly perceived, gives tremendous motivation for removing every trace of selfishness in order to be as perfect an instrument as is within our power.

We like to think that we make big decisions and carry terrible responsibilities on our shoulders. Our shoulders are bent, our back gives us problems, and we are too tired to stand on our feet because of the weighty burdens we try to bear. Few of us realize there is somebody standing with arms outstretched, just waiting to carry our burdens for us.

In Kerala, the state in South India from which I come, there are stone parapets along the roadside at the height of a person's head. When people need to rest from carrying heavy loads of rice or fruit on their heads, they stand next to the parapet and shift their load onto it. For us the Lord is the perennial parapet, standing at exactly the right height for each one of us. For those of us who are very selfish, he stands very tall to support an awesome load; for those of us who are average in selfishness, he stands about six feet high; and for the selfless, the parapet can hardly be seen because the burden is so light that almost no support is needed. Through the practice of meditation, we can gradually learn to shift our load into the Lord's mighty arms. By developing this blessed capacity, we will be able to face the greatest of challenges, terrifying even to national leaders, with ease and equanimity.

कर्मणैव हि संसिद्धिमास्थिता जनकादयः ।
लोकसंग्रहमेवापि संपश्यन्कर्तुमर्हसि ॥३-२०॥

20. Keeping in mind the welfare of others, you should work in their service. It was by such action that Janaka attained perfection; others, too, have followed this path.

Janaka appears in the Brihadāranyaka Upanishad as a great king, and he is also renowned as the father of Sītā, wife of Rāma. Janaka attained complete illumination while reigning as king; he had a wife, a family, and a kingdom to attend to, and yet he remained an ideal lover of the Lord. We can be a perfect professor and lover of the Lord, a perfect nurse and lover of the Lord, or a perfect lawyer and lover of the Lord. But we cannot be a manufacturer of weapons and a lover of the Lord; it is not possible to work at the expense of others and progress greatly on the spiritual path.

The phrase *lokasamgraham* used in this verse is a famous one indicating the Lord sent us into the world to contribute to it. Whether we work on a large or a small scale does not matter, as long as we are doing the best within our power to make our parents, our partner, our children, our friends, and even our enemies happier. This means forgetting ourselves and reversing all the selfish inclinations we have followed. This going against what seems to be the grain of our nature is what makes the spiritual life seem so difficult. It is a hard thing to do, but by calling on the Lord, by repeating his name, it is gradually possible to extinguish our self-will. When we start living for others, we come to life. All our deeper capacities flow into our hands; our security increases and our wisdom grows, as does our creative ability to solve the problems that confront the world. Living and acting selflessly, we will be constantly aware that all life is one – that all men are brothers, as Gandhi would say – and that throughout creation there is an underlying unity binding us all together.

Today was smoggy, so we sought fresh air and freedom from the hurly-burly of city life by going to the Marina. We walked on the pier for a long distance, and from beginning to end it was a very depressing spectacle. I will describe it in some detail because it is good for us to know how our preoccupation with pleasure can blind us and make us callous, almost brutal. It is good for us to know this so that we can begin to transform these responses into the more positive ones of compassion and sensitivity to the welfare of all living creatures.

The pier was crowded with hundreds of men, women, and children, all fishing. There were chairs, sleeping bags, and transistor radios all over the place contributing to the pandemonium. A man was sleeping, but he still had his fishing rod in hand. There were little children six and seven years old, beautiful boys and girls being taught to kill fish. When one little boy caught one, his father came up to him, patted him on the back, and congratulated him saying, "Chip off the old block." A little girl came squealing, "Mommy, I've got another one." Parents were giving instructions to their children and friends to their friends. But to me the saddest sight of all was when the fish were landed. Still alive, they were dashed against the wooden plank, and the hooks torn away.

It is perhaps not fair to condemn or censure these people; we can only try to help them out of the situation by our own personal example. They were not really cruel, but insensitive. This can happen to all of us when we become preoccupied with our own pleasure and forget the unity underlying all life. When we were coming back from the end of the pier, we saw a big, broad, beautiful fish lying on the pier. As I don't know much about fish, I asked my wife about it, and she said it was a sea fish that probably doesn't often come close to shore. As I walked by, its eyes gazed at me in agony. It was almost telling me with its last breath, "Tell them about us."

We shouldn't say that we don't know about these things, or that our children don't know, for it is our duty in life to know about them. Ignorance of the law is not accepted as an excuse for crime. In the days of British rule, in an Indian court of law we couldn't say we didn't know Section XYZ of the Indian Penal Code by which we could be thrown into political prison. If we went to court and claimed we didn't know about this section, the British judge used to say, "Two months in solitary," and add some strong remarks. Similarly, when those little children fishing on the pier grow up, they cannot hide behind the shield of ignorance, for it is no shield at all. The law of karma is an impersonal, relentless force that doggedly follows everybody. The Buddha tells us, "You can try to find shelter in the skies, or in the bowels of the earth; the law of karma will come after you." Thus it is the duty of all parents to tell their children that all life is one. William Blake, who saw this unity of life, said:

> A robin red-breast in a cage
> Puts all heaven in a rage. . . .
> A dog starved at his master's gate
> Predicts the ruin of the State.

Even by putting a little robin into a cage, the cosmic order is violated; the law of karma is at work all the time in the smallest details of life.

Everything is closely interwoven, and even a little hook causing pain in the smallest fish disturbs the consciousness of the Lord.

It is our duty, particularly where children are concerned, to remind others, as my spiritual teacher, my grandmother, reminded me, that we must respect our kinship with all living creatures. This can be conveyed in simple language like my granny's. She used to tell me, "Squirrels have grannies, and if you hurt a squirrel, it'll go complain to its granny." I had never thought about animals like that, and it really opened my eyes. Likewise our children can understand the simple story that little fish have grandmas and grandpas to whom they run complaining and crying when we hurt them.

Although some biologists say that animals may not have any consciousness or emotions, we have to agree that as yet we do not know what animals do or do not feel. In fact, there may be some other mode of expressing their pain with which we are not acquainted. Two days ago, when we were coming back from Ramagiri, the conversation turned to cows. Someone who had grown up in Utah remarked, "We just leave them, even during the depths of the winter, and they thrive in the snow." I would like to hear the Utah cow's point of view. It may not know how to convey its feelings in the language with which we are accustomed, but if it could talk, I have an idea that it may not corroborate the statement that it is "thriving" in the snow. I have even come to suspect it is not advisable for children to have dogs, because even to have a pet you should have the capacity to put it first all of the time, and a little child is not capable of doing this unless guided by the parents.

In India we have had cows for five thousand years. Cows have always been an important symbol in the rural economy. People count their wealth in cows; instead of saying "We have four cars in our garage," we say "We have four cows in our cow shed." One of our cows, called Shobha, had been born in our home on the Blue Mountain, and my mother and sister brought her up from the time she was just a baby. She became a big cow and served us very well, giving us a lot of milk, curds, and butter, and then, like a human being, she became old, decrepit, and developed rheumatism. Some of our animal husbandry experts used to come and look at our cows and approve of them, but then they would tell my mother, "Why don't you sell that one? Let her go to the butcher."

My mother, who can get roused when we talk about her cows, said, "I have rheumatism just as that cow has, and do you think that I, too, should be discarded now that I am not able to serve people very well?"

We should try to practice this awareness of the unity of life in every relationship. Ten years ago, when I would go to restaurants where my eating habits caused consternation, I used to explain, "I'm a vegetarian." They would suggest fish: "You are a vegetarian; you will love fish." I used to add, "I do love fish; that's just why I don't eat them." This is the point of the Gita: you eat fish because you don't love them, and when you love something, you cannot eat it. Once we saw a French movie, which you couldn't say was influenced by the Hindu mystics, in which a little boy who had pet rabbits was served rabbit for dinner. He said, "I don't eat my buddies." This is the language of the Gita: "You don't eat your buddies." Cats, dogs, cows, and rabbits – these are all our buddies.

Another way we can look at our deep kinship with all living creatures is in terms of the long story of evolution. According to this, our friend Garry was a little orchid long, long ago; that is why he likes them so much. He loves orchids and grows them and looks after them because of this faint memory that gives him a sense of unity with the orchid. There is a similar explanation, according to the theory of reincarnation, that today on the pier I remembered in a very dim way the days when I used to splash about in the water; and I remembered the joy and the sparkle of it and identified myself with the fish as if it were really I swimming about. This is what spiritual awareness means. The pain inflicted on the fish is in me. It was not the fish out there on the pier who were suffering, as separate beings; it was I who was suffering in them. This is how spiritual awareness shows itself in us; we begin to suffer in everything that is subjected to suffering. Until we become aware of this unity underlying all life, all talk of spiritual awareness is just playing games.

यद्यदाचरति श्रेष्ठस्तत्तदेवेतरो जनः ।
स यत्प्रमाणं कुरुते लोकस्तदनुवर्तते ॥ ३-२१ ॥

21. What the outstanding person does, others will try to do. The standards such people create will be followed by the whole world.

The more gifted we are intellectually, spiritually, and even physically, the greater is our responsibility to contribute to life. Through the practice of meditation our deeper resources will come into play, and we will have to be increasingly careful about not writing or speaking a word that adds to the agitation of others or tends to separate friends, families, communities, races, or countries.

As householders we can begin to influence others beneficially right in our own home, starting with our children. Our idea of setting an example is to improvise a domestic pulpit and preach to our dear ones. I would say that all of us are preaching all the time through our actions, our words, and our thoughts. Little ones are ruthless observers. When I see a five-year-old watching me, I feel as though Sherlock Holmes is on my track. I can almost hear him saying, "Elementary, Dr. Watson. I can see the inconsistency between his word and deed quite clearly." The way to make our children patient and loving is to be that way ourselves.

There are innumerable opportunities every day to set a good example to others. I have been asking Meera and Geetha to take off their muddy shoes outside so as not to bring dirt into the house. They paid no heed to my request because they saw me walking inside wearing my shoes. So the next time we were going indoors together, I just sat on the steps, and without making any comments I took off my clean shoes and placed them near the door. They sat down next to me and followed my example. On the subject of patience, my pen disappears every day, and I used to show an unconscious trace of annoyance and ask, "Who has been taking my pen?" Today when it was missing, however, I put on my best smile, looked at Meera and Geetha, and asked, "Has anyone seen my pen?" One of them brought it to me. Whether or not the pen was returned was not so important as their knowing I am continually trying to be patient with them.

Those who have children can become masters of patience, endurance, and steadfastness, because children will test you at every turn. When we are provoked, most of us get agitated, and it is on these occasions we can repeat the mantram. By continually calling on the Lord, who is the source of strength within us, we can make our lives an inspiring example to all those who come in contact with us.

I have been reading, too, about the tragic tendency among young people to experiment with drugs and how easily it can lead to heroin addiction. Doctors are telling us that as parents we can help our children by not making them drug-conscious – by not depending on drugs to go to sleep, to change our moods, or to become more active. If we really love our children, we will give up smoking and drinking and the use of pep pills and tranquilizers. Our children will be strengthened if instead of drugs we use the most perfect tranquilizer we have, the name of the Lord.

न मे पार्थास्ति कर्तव्यं त्रिषु लोकेषु किं चन ।
नानवाप्तमवाप्तव्यं वर्त एव च कर्मणि ॥३-२२॥
यदि ह्यहं न वर्तेयं जातु कर्मण्यतन्द्रितः ।
मम वर्त्मानुवर्तन्ते मनुष्याः पार्थ सर्वशः ॥३-२३॥
उत्सीदेयुरिमे लोका न कुर्यां कर्म चेदहम् ।
संकरस्य च कर्ता स्यामुपहन्यामिमाः प्रजाः ॥३-२४॥

22. *O Pārtha, there is nothing in the three worlds for me to gain, nor is there anything I do not have. I continue to act, but am not driven by any need of my own.*
23. *If I ever refrained from this continuous work, everyone would immediately follow my example.*
24. *If I ever stopped working, I would be the cause of cosmic chaos, and finally of the destruction of this world and these people.*

In these verses Sri Krishna is telling us how he, from whom the cosmos comes, in whom the cosmos exists, and to whom it returns, works incessantly for our welfare. Yesterday we saw a big spider's web glistening in the light; it was perfectly woven and in the center sat a spider, having his siesta. The Upanishads tell us the Lord weaves the whole universe out of himself and sits in the midst of it, working hardest of all. It is difficult even to imagine the Lord's labor. In a period of decline and dissent over twenty-five hundred years ago, he came as the Compassionate Buddha to toil for our enlightenment. He shed his Buddha body and no sooner got home when a call came from the shores of Galilee: "Trouble brewing – come quickly." With hardly any rest, he went off again to look for suitable parents. He finally decided on Mary and Joseph, but there was no place in which to be born except a stable. With this humble birth the Lord came to us as Jesus and worked for us until his body was crucified. Then he went home only to hear another call of tribulation, this time from Arabia. He came again as an ordinary man who became united with Allah and gave us the Koran. Once again he returned home, but while he was recovering from the desert heat the call came for him to be born as Shankara in Kerala, then again in the nineteenth century as Sri Ramakrishna.

Our age, called *Kaliyuga* or the Age of Anger, demands a chain of incarnations, one after the other. If we really love the Lord, we should be able to say, "We do not want you to be so overworked. We'll be good; we'll meditate every day, repeat your name all the time, restrain our senses at every opportunity, and always put everybody else first." In India there is a festival called *Shivarātrī,* Shiva's Night, popular especially among devotees of Shiva. Shiva stays awake 364 nights of the year looking after us, but on this last night we tell him tenderly that we will be selfless so that he can rest in peace. If we truly love the Lord, our proof is not to cause him any problems by being self-willed. When the Lord does not have a dire need to come into the human context as an incarnation, it means that every one of us has become aware of him. Since the Lord has toiled so long for us, it is not unreasonable for us to try to follow his personal example of selfless living. When our own little tragedies are interfering with our capacity to contribute to the welfare of our family or friends, it is good to remind ourselves of how the Lord labors for everyone's benefit, no matter how distressing the context into which he is called.

Every time a great incarnation comes to us, even today, it is not to bring new truths or to establish a new religion. In fact, they do not come to teach us but to remind us of what we have forgotten – that we are neither our body nor our mind, neither our intellect nor our ego, but pure love, eternal and immutable. Any suffering inflicted on others is suffering inflicted on ourselves; any joy given to others is joy that will permeate our own consciousness.

सक्ताः कर्मण्यविद्वांसो यथा कुर्वन्ति भारत ।
कुर्याद्विद्वांस्तथासक्तश्चिकीर्षुर्लोकसंग्रहम् ॥ ३-२५ ॥

25. The ignorant work for their own profit,
O Bhārata; the wise work for the welfare of
others, without thought for themselves.

It is difficult to persuade people not to go after personal profit, pleasure, prestige, or power, because it is asking them to go against the conditioning to which they have been subjected. The word "rebel" is often misused by our modern mass media. It takes a tremendous amount of endurance and an enormous faith in the Lord within to rebel. Playing games with our appearance is not rebellion. Real rebellion is going against our selfish desires and sense cravings. One of the greatest rebels in the world, Jesus, tells us: "Love your enemies, bless them that curse you, do good to them that hate you." When the Buddha encourages us to seek nirvāna, he is raising the banner of real rebellion. He is asking us to blow out our self-will, to extinguish our limited, selfish personality. To help others understand the truth of rebellion, it is of little avail to put pressure on them. The best way of influencing others is to show by our personal example how the spiritual life adds to the unity of the family, the peace of the neighborhood, and the security of the country. Lord Krishna tells Arjuna, whom he calls *Bhārata*, the 'representative of India': "If you want to influence India, remove all that is selfish, all that is calculating, all that seeks self-aggrandizement in yourself, and you will help the whole country, from the Himālayas to Kanyakumārī."

I can testify to the incredible influence one little man, Gandhi, exercised over all of India. He lived in utter simplicity in a one-room hermitage, and yet he received everybody with the same love and respect, whether it happened to be a member of the British cabinet or a sweeper from Sevagram. When India became independent, the offices of president and prime minister were his for the asking; but he declined, saying that he wanted no reward, that he had worked for Indian independence in order to show the world how even the greatest of international problems can be solved nonviolently. On the night when all India celebrated independence, Gandhi went into prayer.

As the result of Gandhi's contribution, people are taking nonviolence seriously all over the world; fortunately, it has become an important force even on our campuses today. In our own lives, if we want to find the joy of living in peace, we have to establish peace first in our hearts and our homes. We start by cultivating perfect love between all the members of our family; then we extend this love to the members of our community, and by expanding our love ever so gradually, we finally bring the whole world into its embrace.

न बुद्धिभेदं जनयेदज्ञानां कर्मसङ्गिनाम् ।
जोषयेत्सर्वकर्माणि विद्वान्युक्तः समाचरन् ॥३-२६॥

26. By abstaining from work you will confuse
the ignorant, who are engrossed in their actions;
perform all work selflessly, guided by compassion.

This is a very simple verse, yet far-reaching in its application to our lives. Sri Krishna is telling Arjuna, "You are always influencing others, not only your dear ones but also your antagonists." On the one hand, when we hate our enemies, we are helping them hate us more; when we attack them, we are encouraging them to attack us back. On the other hand, when we forgive them, we are helping them forgive us, and when we move closer to them, we are drawing them closer to us.

Gandhi was always at his best with those who thought they were his mortal enemies. His favorite hymn, "Vaishnava Janato," reminds us in its refrain that the true lover of the Lord is the one who returns love for hatred. All we need to do to love the Lord is love those that hate us and be compassionate with those who strike out against us. When we develop the capacity to love those whom we hate, we will be united with the Lord through his grace.

प्रकृतेः क्रियमाणानि गुणैः कर्माणि सर्वशः ।
अहंकारविमूढात्मा कर्ताहमिति मन्यते ॥३-२७॥

27. All actions are performed by the gunas of prakriti; deluded by his identification with the ego, a man thinks, "I am the doer."

Prakriti is the word used for anything that changes, anything that is impermanent, anything that is born and will die one day. The entire physical universe is within the realm of prakriti. The body is prakriti, which means that just as it was born one day, it will die one day. The Buddha, in one of his very tender moments, will tell those around him in reference to his body, "This house was assembled one day, and it has to be disassembled one day; what is there in this to grieve about?"

It is because we identify ourselves obsessively with the body that the very thought of dismantling the house fills us with terror. Last week, on our way to class from our home in Oakland, we saw a gracious old home which could have served a useful purpose for many decades. When we were passing by the next day it was gone. I could not help feeling a little sense of grief, because a beautiful home had been demolished. In this way we do feel a detached sense of loss when the house in which one of our dear ones lived has been dismantled. But if we can realize that we are not the house, but the dweller within it, we will lose our terrible fear of death.

The relationship between prakriti, the body, and *Purusha,* our real Self, may be explained with the homely metaphor of old clothes (see Gita 2:22). This coat that I am wearing is still rather new, only five years old. At the end of ten years, which is its natural span of life, when I have to discard it, I quietly take it off, throw it into the give-away box, and put on a new one. When I throw away this old jacket, I am not going to say, "My heart is broken; my old jacket is gone." I will say, "Yes, it has served its useful purpose; now I will get a new one."

Another important word used in this verse is *guna,* which denotes the three ultimate constituents of prakriti. The first is sattva, or law; the second is rajas, or energy; the third is tamas, or inertia. In each of us there is a different combination of sattva, rajas, and tamas. No one is entirely free from sattva; there is no one who cannot be selfless. You will find some of the most objectionable characters suddenly becoming very selfless towards their pet parrot or raccoon. We can all suddenly reveal ourselves in innocence.

The second guna, rajas, is predominant in many of us in the modern world. It is energy, restlessness, desire. This energy and restlessness, when directed inward, can help us progress rapidly on the spiritual path.

The third factor is tamas, which is inertia or lethargy. "What does it matter? Let the world go" – this is the attitude of tamas. Such an attitude is the opposite of spiritual wisdom. Everything matters on the spiritual path; it is little things, when put together, that amount to a great change. We may feel that we are small people, but working together, we are tremendous. In the realization that each of us can make a definite contribution to the world about us, tamas disappears. Gandhi, inspired by the Gita, tells us that evil has no existence of its own. We support it; that is why it exists. His program of noncooperation was based on his conviction that evil would cease to exist if we would withdraw our support from it. This knowledge enables us to transform tamas into rajas, rajas into sattva, and finally to go beyond all three gunas.

Our real Self, the Ātman or Purusha, exists outside the realm of change and the three gunas. It is ever pure, ever free. But, deluded by self-will, we remain unaware of the Ātman and identify ourselves with the mind and body, which are subject to change. It is helpful, even when we cannot realize it completely, to remind ourselves that we are not the mind. It is the mind that is angry, it is the mind that is afraid, it is the mind that is selfish, not our real Self. That is why the Buddha says, “Take the mind and throw it out.” It is very easy to say this, but extremely difficult to do. Yesterday I saw a boy at the āshram playing with a new toy. I asked him what he was playing with, and he explained: “It’s a yo-yo. You just can’t get rid of the thing!” This is the ego; you throw it anywhere and it will come back to you. No amount of saying “I am going to throw this far away” will eliminate the ego.

The surest way of reducing self-will is to begin to put the welfare of those around us first, to love others more than we love ourselves. We must not love only those who love us; we must learn to love our enemies as well. It is good to forgive those who have offended us. As St. Francis says, those who have not learned to forgive have lost the greatest source of joy in life. If, through the practice of meditation and the repetition of the mantram, we can forgive others from the depths of our being and transform our attitude towards them into selfless love, we will immediately be able to forgive our own mistakes and drawbacks. The more we forgive others, the more the Lord, who is within, forgives us.

तत्त्ववित्तु महाबाहो गुणकर्मविभागयोः ।
गुणा गुणेषु वर्तन्त इति मत्वा न सज्जते ॥३-२८॥
प्रकृतेर्गुणसंमूढाः सज्जन्ते गुणकर्मसु ।
तानकृत्स्नविदो मन्दान्कृत्स्नविन्न विचालयेत् ॥३-२९॥

28. But the illumined man or woman understands
the domain of the gunas and is not attached.
Such people know that the gunas interact with
each other; they do not claim to be the doer.
29. Those who are deluded by the operation
of the gunas become attached to the results
of their action. Those who understand these
truths should not unsettle the ignorant.

The theory of the three gunas tells us about the nature of our desires. When we have desires which require urgent satisfaction, none of us, no matter what we try to do, can divest ourselves of the belief that we are these desires. If only we could jump out of this little circle of desires and look at any one desire, we would realize that it is not ours at all, because our real nature is ever full. Our real nature, the Ātman, can admit of no desire, and when we say "I desire this," "I cannot be happy without this," we are making statements which are metaphorical. When I first arrived here from India, I was not used to automobiles. I have some acquaintance with them now, but the phrases that people use about automobiles used to strike me as rather puzzling. When I first heard someone saying, "I am out of gas," I did not understand that he was talking about his car. Most of our statements which begin with "I desire" are in this category. This is what Sri Krishna is sending deep into Arjuna's consciousness. When we say, "I desire money, material possessions, pleasure, power," Sri Krishna says we are the victim of our own language.

The Lord tells Arjuna that when the senses and sense objects see one another, they are just drawn to each other. You and I have no part in this; we are neutral. This is such a compassionate, humorous, and factual observation, and Arjuna is so enraptured by it, that he begins to understand that we actually do not participate in any selfish desire or sensory attraction. We wrongly identify ourselves with these desires because we have been conditioned to do so in our home, by our friends, and by the mass media.

Attraction and aversion are closely related; they are the extremes of a pendulum. We are tied to what we hate; we cannot help thinking about people we hate. Naturally we think about those whom we love, but we also dwell on those we hate. As long as we believe we are our desires, we have to be a party in the quarrel of attraction and aversion, very often on the wrong side. But as our mind becomes less and less agitated through the practice of meditation, we shall see, to our great surprise, that we are just spectators. Once we understand this, we are free from the clamor of the senses, and they can no longer drag us into their quarrel of attraction and aversion.

When the senses and sense objects draw each other, do not be afraid that you will be swept away. Your desires may look towering, but through the grace of the Lord of Love within, you can learn to master even the greatest of them. In trying to release yourself from your involvement in the attraction and repulsion between the senses and sense objects, it is necessary to be very vigilant for a long time. It is by yielding to small desires that you are drawn gradually into greater desires. Today, for example, we took our nieces to the circus, and when we went in, everyone had a carton of popcorn. Someone very unsophisticated – someone, say, from a village in India – seeing that everyone has a ticket in one hand and popcorn in the other, might actually think that you couldn't be admitted without popcorn. Our nieces had some, and to keep them company, I ate a little also. Then, after eating the popcorn, I got thirsty. I hadn't expected this. But the salesboys, who *had* expected it, were right there selling cold drinks; and later, outside, the cigarette merchant was waiting too.

In the second line of this verse, Sri Krishna is reminding us, through Arjuna, that we should not disturb people by preaching at them; it is much easier to influence others through our personal example. When Gandhi was observing his day of silence, someone once asked him for a message. He just wrote, "My life is my message." This is true of us also. We are always influencing those around us by our daily life, and when we try to lead the spiritual life, putting those around us first, we cannot help but win them over in the end.

मयि सर्वाणि कर्माणि संन्यस्याध्यात्मचेतसा ।
निराशीर्निर्ममो भूत्वा युध्यस्व विगतज्वरः ॥३-३०॥

30. Completely absorbed in the Ātman, without expectations, and free from the fever of the ego, fight your self-will, performing all actions for my sake.

You may remember in the first chapter where Arjuna, like you and me, says, "Why should I govern my passions, why should I reduce my self-will?" and refuses to fight. Sri Krishna now tells him, "You are not well now; you are suffering from the fever of self-will. But when your fever has subsided, get ready to fight. Do your very best: meditate regularly, try to restrain your senses, and put the welfare of those around you first." In other words, Sri Krishna reminds us, we are all likely to make mistakes on the spiritual path, and we can be overcome by regret. But rather than regretting our mistakes, it is much more useful to forget the past and keep marching forward with renewed enthusiasm.

Sri Ramakrishna often refers to the fever of the ego from which all of us suffer to some degree. In many of us it is only a little above normal – ninety-nine degrees. We get on very well in life; we are loved and respected. But when the temperature begins to rise above one hundred, we become more and more dangerous, not only to ourselves but to the family and community in which we dwell. When we suffer from this fever, we become blind to the needs of those around us and to the unity of life.

Adhyātmacetasā means completely absorbed in the Ātman. This complete absorption can happen to all of us as our meditation deepens through the grace of the Lord. We may be enabled to go through all of the last eighteen verses of the second chapter of the Gita, for example, without our mind wandering once, without falling asleep once. This indicates that we have reached a profound state of concentration in which there is unbroken continuity of meditation. When such a state is attained, those verses have become an integral part of our consciousness, and the proof of it will be seen in our life. When suffering comes, we are not agitated, because we are equal to it. All our compassion, which has been misspent on ourselves, now goes to the person who has caused us sorrow. When desires come, we do not identify ourselves with them; we are masters of our desires. If they are selfless, we welcome them; if they are selfish, we defy them with equal joy. We have gained freedom from selfish attachments, fear, and anger.

Nirāshī means having no expectations; it is only when you have expectations that you have disappointments, get frustrated, become insecure, and try to manipulate others. Here Sri Krishna is giving Arjuna very strong counsel. He says, "Whatever I give, accept it gratefully: say yes if it is joy, say yes if it is sorrow. Then you will be free." Gradually you will find that as you detach yourself from the results of your actions and stop worrying about results, you are able to concentrate better on your work. "If you want to give your best in any selfless service," the Lord says, "choose the right goal, use right means, and don't think about results; leave them to me."

ये मे मतमिदं नित्यमनुतिष्ठन्ति मानवाः ।
श्रद्धावन्तो ऽनसूयन्तो मुच्यन्ते ते ऽपि कर्मभिः ॥३-३१॥

31. Those who live in accordance with these divine laws with an unwavering sense of purpose, firmly established in faith, are released from karma.

The teaching which Sri Krishna gives to Arjuna contains the divine laws of existence, which are inscribed deep in our consciousness, written in the very cells of every creature. It is because these laws are within us that we suffer so much when we try to break them. As someone wisely said, we cannot break God's laws; we can only break ourselves against them. Here the appeal of the Gita lies not in forcing us, saying *thou shalt* or *thou shalt not,* but in presenting us with two alternatives: one leading to abiding joy, unassailable security, and an enormous capacity for contributing to the welfare of others, and the other leading to sorrow, insecurity, and the suffering of those around us. The Lord tells Arjuna, "If you cannot shake yourself free from the fever of the ego, you will become a curse on the face of the earth. But if you can turn your back upon your own pleasure, profit, and prestige, and devote yourself to enriching your family, community, and world, you will become a great blessing to all."

Thus all of us have the choice, in whatever country we live, whatever position we occupy, to live for ourselves or to live for others. The choice is left entirely to us. If we live for others, we live in complete harmony with the laws of life, bringing joy to those around us and to ourselves. If we live only for ourselves, as most of us are conditioned to do, we will plunge ourselves and all those around us into misery.

With the words *mucyante te 'pi karmabhih,* "they also are released from karma," Sri Krishna makes a promise, a promise that has been fulfilled in the lives of many who have surrendered to the Lord. When we devote ourselves completely to the service of all, our families' needs are provided for by the Lord, who knows how to look after them better than we do. Sri Krishna tells Arjuna that if he will throw himself wholeheartedly into the service of mankind, he will be released from the responsibility of working for personal needs; these become the Lord's responsibility.

When we dedicate our whole life unreservedly to the service of humanity, the Lord will magnify all our faculties. In some amazing way, even our sleep will be given us to serve others. As our meditation deepens, we will find that we need less sleep, less food, and more opportunities for service. We will find that we must use the tremendous forces placed in our hands. A family of two or three or four will not satisfy us; we will want a whole continent for our family, as Gandhiji had. When Mrs. Gandhi was asked how many children she had, her reply was, "I have four, but my husband has four hundred million." As meditation deepens and self-will becomes less, we come to regard everyone as our own; if they have problems, it is our privilege to live for helping them to solve those problems. When at last we regard the entire world as our family, we will be enabled to draw upon the vast reservoir of love and wisdom lying unsuspected in all of us.

We should not mistakenly interpret Sri Krishna's declaration as telling us to go serve others and neglect our own at home. It is not that we learn to love our family less, but that we learn to love everyone equally well. It is a travesty of the spiritual life to think that Gandhi did not love his family because he loved everybody else. His capacity to love became so limitless that he was able to flood the whole country and the whole world with it. Not only in India are his teachings cherished; all over the world we are beginning to see what a tremendous contribution this humble man has made to the welfare of all. Gandhi loved all humanity and showed us the way to regard all countries with love, trying to understand the other person's needs exactly as we understand our own.

Here again Arjuna is very much like us; the prospect of having his resources magnified is very appealing. He would like to have his creative intelligence and capacity to love increased; he knows that they are in need of magnification. The Lord understands what is going on in his mind and tells him:

ये त्वेतदभ्यसूयन्तो नानुतिष्ठन्ति मे मतम् ।
सर्वज्ञानविमूढांस्तान्विद्धि नष्टानचेतसः ॥३-३२॥

32. Understand that those who violate these laws, criticizing and complaining about fate, are utterly deluded, and are the cause of their own suffering.

Here Sri Krishna cautions Arjuna that if he chooses not to observe the Lord's spiritual laws, but lives for his own pleasure and profit, even the small capacities that he has will be reduced still further. Instead of being maximized, they will be minimized. We have only to look at people who live only for themselves to see how constricted their consciousness is, how easily they can be upset, and how people naturally avoid them. We cannot avoid making this choice between living for ourselves and living for others. If we try to serve others without turning our back on our own self-will, we will neither be able to serve others nor to help ourselves.

Ignorance and scepticism do not exempt us from the spiritual laws governing the world. Many people question the validity of these laws, and I remind them that whether we believe in them or not they apply equally to all of us. When I was speaking at the Kaiser Center in Oakland – not before a gathering of Hindu mystics but before hard-headed Kaiser businessmen – one of my friends there came up to me one day and told me in a very affectionate manner, "We like you, and we appreciate your talks, your enthusiasm, and your humor, but this law of karma isn't applicable to us. We do not believe in it as you do in India. We live west of Suez, and the law of karma stops at Port Said."

I just said, "All right, I'm going to the roof, and I'm going to wave my arms and fly over Lake Merritt."

He got terribly upset and said, "Why do you want to try that? Don't you know it will kill you?"

"Why should it kill me?"

"The law of gravity, man!"

So I said, "The law of gravity stops at Port Said; we in the East don't subscribe to it. After all, it was not given to us by a Hindu mystic but by a British scientist."

He came close to me, put his arm on my shoulder, and said, "My dear fellow, whether you believe in it or not, the law of gravity works."

Then I put my arm around him saying, "Whether you believe it or not, the law of karma works everywhere, every day, in everyone's life."

This should remind us to start going beyond the law of karma by subordinating our personal feelings and desires to the welfare of all those around us. There are people who claim they know nothing of these laws. They will tell you, "I am completely ignorant. I always thought that by living for myself I would become secure. I always thought that by dwelling upon myself I would enhance my personality. You shouldn't hold these things against me when I didn't know." Sri Krishna's reply to this is that all of us are expected to use our common sense in observing who is secure, who is at peace, who is able to contribute to the welfare of others.

When we make the choice to lead a selfless life, we are really being practical and using our common sense. One of Gandhiji's favorite hymns in his mother tongue says, "Lord, give me piety, give me devotion, but please don't deny me common sense." On the spiritual path there seems to be the mistaken belief in some minds that the less common sense we have, the more advanced we are on the path. If there is anybody terribly practical in life, it is the mystic. If there is anybody terribly impractical in life, it is the man of the world, because worldly people spend their whole lives in the pursuit of money, trying to follow a pattern of life that only fills them with insecurity.

सदृशं चेष्टते स्वस्याः प्रकृतेर्ज्ञानवानपि ।
प्रकृतिं यान्ति भूतानि निग्रहः किं करिष्यति ॥३-३३॥

33. Even a wise man acts within the limitations of his own nature. Every creature is subject to prakriti; what is the use of repression?

Even though all of us are governed by the indivisible unity that is the divine principle of existence, on the surface level of life we are all individuals, with special samskāras. Though we are all one at the very source of life, no two of us are alike on the surface of it. This is the marvel of life – that we should be so different outwardly, yet in the deepest sense be one and indivisible.

In the Upanishads, there is a vivid description of how the one reality, the Lord, became very lonesome. The Lord, being *advaita,* 'One without a second,' had no one to play with, and just like a little boy he said, "I want boys and girls to play with, and animals and birds. But there is no one in the world but me, so whom can I ask to be my playmate?" He began to meditate, and thought, "Why don't I ask myself?" Then he divided himself into millions of creatures, and when he looked around, he was surrounded by a big football team. He said, "Now I want a big stadium to stage all these big games. Let the world be my stadium." This is the coliseum of the ego, and for the superficial observer, life is really like going to a big game. Everyone looks different – different clothes, different things to eat, different ways of cheering. But in this stadium it is the Lord himself who is playing on both teams. The home team and the visiting team are part of a conspiracy, just pretending to play against each other, to win or lose.

Once we begin to perceive the unity underlying all life, we will have nothing but love and respect for everyone around us, beginning in our home and extending to the entire world. We have only to look at the newspapers today, every page reporting violence and conflict, to see that the vast majority have forgotten this unity. Sri Krishna reminds all of us that in politics also we should never forget that there is only One; what conduces to the welfare of all is inclusive of the welfare of each one of us. There is no one in the world except the Lord disguised as many, but as long as we live for ourselves, pursuing our own private satisfaction and dwelling upon ourselves, we can never see this underlying unity. It is selfish people who see separateness everywhere because they look at life through their own selfishness, whereas selfless people see what is common to themselves and others. Spiritual awareness is seeing this basic unity.

The one Lord within, who has disguised himself as many, is the soul or Self in each of us. This *Purusha,* as it is called in Sanskrit, is what unites us all. *Prakriti* is what makes us appear separate. Our physical and mental being evolves according to the laws of prakriti. To use the language of Hindu mysticism, all of us have evolved through millions of lives to become human beings, but even among humans there are different degrees of evolution. From this point of view, those who are excited by money have come into the human context just recently. They have been wandering in the jungle as lions or tigers and have never seen money. No one uses currency in the jungle, so they have had no contact with money at all. When they come into the human situation, they are fascinated by the dollar, the pound, the rupee, and the ruble, because these are all new. According to this theory, when such people have been this way a number of times – have been to banks, bought shares, seen them going up and down, and been agitated – they slowly learn to look upon money as rather irrelevant. Then when they see it they say, "This is just metal; it has no intrinsic value at all."

The process of learning is the same in the case of pleasure. People who have been through the sensory game a number of times do not get easily drawn into sensate stimulations. The compassion of this explanation can appeal to all of us, for it does not classify us as either good or bad. It is not good to sit in judgment on those who pursue ephemeral pleasure; in a little while they will find it fails to satisfy, because there is an innate need for a supreme purpose in every human being. We cannot live without a supreme purpose, and though we may mistakenly try to fulfill this purpose by building houses or sailing boats or painting pictures, we must eventually find that nothing finite will ever satisfy us. We can go to the moon; it is a great achievement, but after a while our eyes turn beyond to Neptune. Wherever we go in space, wherever we go in time, we find limitations. Our need is for infinite joy, infinite love, infinite wisdom and infinite capacity for service, and until this need is met, we can never, never rest peacefully. But from the very day we begin meditation, supplementing it by discriminating restraint of the senses and putting the welfare of those around us first, we have started after the infinite. We will find our very endeavor gives us joy.

We begin our journey towards the supreme goal of life from where we stand. All of us begin the spiritual ascent by accepting ourselves as we are. Just as it is good to be patient with others, it is equally necessary to be patient with ourselves. After all, when the desire to lead the spiritual life and live for others comes to us, we can be haunted by our past mistakes, by the amount of time and energy we have wasted in selfish pursuits. But the Lord of Love implies here that we must accept ourselves with all our strengths and weaknesses. Without this kind of great patience with ourselves, the precipitous ascent to the summit of human awareness is fraught with great danger. There are many obstacles on the spiritual path meant to strengthen us, and these cannot be overcome unless we have infinite patience with ourselves. When we are patient with others, we cannot help being patient with ourselves. As this verse indicates, each of us is individual, with our own special samskāras and qualities. We start now, where we are, with our partial love for money, partial love for pleasure, partial love for prestige, and a little love for the Lord.

Just as we all start our sādhana from a different point, as determined by our prakriti, we also set our own pace on the path. We should each be careful to keep within our own stride. Christine and I are usually rather fast walkers, but when we go for a walk with our little nieces, Meera and Geetha, we shorten our stride, rest a little more on each foot, and make use of any excuse to look at a seagull or pick up a pebble. One of the necessities in spiritual counseling is to see that each person goes at the right pace. People who have spent their time in the pursuit of money and pleasure may sprain an ankle with a long stride and fast walk.

There are different types on the spiritual path. There are people capable of tremendous enthusiasm who suddenly turn over a new leaf. Those who slept until noon now start getting up at three in the morning for meditation. The same enthusiasm they had for money or pleasure can be redirected towards the spiritual life. People who are highly enthusiastic are already one-pointed and, because of their concentration, can easily take to the spiritual life. It is the butterfly, flitting from flower to flower, that will find it difficult to attain samādhi. Those who say, "What does it matter? Why go to school? Why take up a job?" will also question, "Why meditate? Why repeat the mantram?" People capable of throwing themselves heart and soul into any great endeavor, even though it may not be the most spiritual, will find themselves taking enthusiastically to the spiritual life when the time comes. It is good to have enthusiasm, not for many things but for one big passion, because this unifies the mind and increases concentration.

We do not have to wait until we have advanced on the path of evolution to turn our face to the Lord. There are many great sinners in the annals of mysticism who have turned to the Lord and become completely pure and perfect through his grace. In the ninth chapter there is a tremendous verse which has consoled millions of human beings who have committed many mistakes through ignorance. The Lord tells us: "People may be very selfish, may have led very reckless lives, causing suffering to others as well as to themselves, but when they turn their backs upon themselves and surrender to me, they become pure rapidly, and I lead them into the perfection which is my nature. All those who take refuge in me, whatever their past, become free and are united with me" (Gita 9:31–2).

All of us, no matter what our past has been, no matter what our present drawbacks are, can take to the spiritual life, and we will progress on the path at our own pace. It is not good to compare one person's progress with another's. This, as well as guidance in meditation, is very much a personal matter.

Last Saturday when we took my mother and nieces to Santa Rosa, we went to a big shopping center where we were able to treat the children to ice cream. The children then wanted to ride on the escalator, which they had never seen in India. My mother was very timorous about this, but I assured her that the art could be learned gradually. First Meera wanted to try. I stood by her side and told her to watch me and do as I did. We took the first step together, as I held her hand. When the time came for us to get off, I said, still holding her hand, "Now you do the same thing; take your foot off and put it on the floor, just as I do it." We came down the escalator in the same way. In this first experience she had been just doing what I was doing because she identifies herself easily with me. Even my mother was reassured. Then we made the same pilgrimage, but without holding hands. Now confident, she went up and came down by herself. This is very much the meditation experience too; for a long time we have to hold on to an experienced person.

Now, seeing Meera, who is older, doing this in three easy lessons, Geetha said, "I want to go up and down the escalator too, just like Meera." I took Geetha's hand, but as we stepped onto the escalator, it was as if I were holding her in the air. All her weight was on my arm, but she was under the impression that she was on her own.

Similarly in meditation there are a few people who have to be helped in this way without their ever becoming aware of it. A good teacher is one whose touch is so light that you can hardly feel it, whose muscles are so supple that he shows no effort at all. He just looks at you saying, "Yes, you are doing well; you are doing very well." Even those who must be helped in this way will begin to learn, but they may not learn in three easy lessons. They may require six hard lessons. We should never ask ourselves why there is this difference between people. It is good to be content with the speed at which we are able to go because it is in accordance with our dharma.

इन्द्रियस्येन्द्रियस्यार्थे रागद्वेषौ व्यवस्थितौ ।
तयोर्न वशमागच्छेत्तौ ह्यस्य परिपन्थिनौ ॥ ३-३४ ॥

34. The senses have been conditioned by attraction to the pleasant and aversion to the unpleasant. Do not be ruled by them; they are obstacles in your path.

Two of the important words used in this verse are *indriya* and *indriyārtha*. *Indriya* denotes the sense organs, and *indriyārtha* the sense objects of which the external world is composed. In the relationship between these two, there exists *rāgadvesha*, 'attraction and aversion.' All of us are governed in a large measure by this tyrannical duality of likes and dislikes. We avoid something because we do not like it; we move away from people because we dislike them. We are tied not only to what we like but also to what we dislike. To give an extreme example, when we love someone, we are always thinking about that person, wanting to serve their welfare. Unfortunately, when we hate someone, we also think about the person all the time, about how to frustrate their welfare. It is the same emotional relationship.

In my mother tongue, there is a folk song about a boy who knows a good bit about girls. He tells his girl, "Love me or hate me, I don't care; I have got you. But don't ever become indifferent to me; then I have lost you." When someone says, "I hate you," don't give up – they are as entangled emotionally with you as they can ever be. When your girlfriend says this, do not slam the door and say, "I don't want to see you again." That is the time to close the door from inside and say, "I am not going to leave you at all."

I think it was Sai Baba, one of the spectacular mystics of modern India, who put this concept of likes and dislikes into epigrammatic words when he said that if you do not do what you like, then you can do what you want. As long as we are dominated by likes and dislikes – in our job, in our studies, in our friendships, in our food, in our recreation – we are just being compelled by our nervous system to move towards what we like and away from what we dislike.

A friend of ours who is a physicist made the keen observation that most of meditation is a reconditioning of the nervous system. As long as our nervous system works only one way, enabling us to run towards the pleasant and away from the unpleasant, it is considerably damaged. It is really meant for two-way traffic, the mystics tell us, and it is only because of our long conditioning that it has come to be so constricted, able to move only towards the pleasant. When it has been reconditioned through meditation, we can live in freedom, choosing to do what is in the interests of others even though it may be painful to us, may cause us mental and physical distress.

After the nervous system has been reconditioned, we will find such joy in contributing to the welfare of others that we no longer will fear moving towards the unpleasant and doing what previously we did not like. Then we will find we have been psycho-allergic, to use a modern term, towards certain people, partly because of the distorting medium of our own prejudices and conditioning through which we view the world. This veil which we throw over others can magnify their faults and sometimes even attribute to them faults which are really ours. For example, if we believe, as many people do, that only the desire for money can motivate people deeply, we will be suspicious even of a person who works without any thought of personal profit. But when the nervous system has been reconditioned, we see life without likes and dislikes. The veil which we have thrown over others is removed, and we come to have *samadrishti,* an equal eye for all. Then we discover that all life is one – that underlying all our infinite variety there exists the indivisible unity, the divine principle of existence.

Sri Krishna is telling you and me, through Arjuna, that we should try every day to calm the mind and not become agitated by likes and dislikes. This is practical advice because very often in life we must do many things we dislike. Every day we should do a few things we do not like and try to do them with enthusiasm. Everyone begins this with a certain amount of reluctance, but by welcoming jobs we dislike, and doing them with concentration, we can learn to enjoy them. It is often just the fear of having to face an unpleasant task that makes us complain, saps our will, and finally makes us give up. The will is strengthened greatly when we welcome jobs we dislike, when we do first what we like least.

One of the most graceful ways of learning to juggle with our likes and dislikes is to do things we dislike for those we love. For example, at home, where kitchen chores are concerned, there are many things which no one likes to do. But my mother, even at the age of almost eighty, is able to take delight in preparing meals for us. Two days ago, to celebrate the harvest festival of Kerala, she spent hours preparing a delicious meal of the traditional dishes, without any feeling of being tired or under pressure, because of her desire to make a contribution to the health and happiness of all at Ramagiri.

Another way of overcoming dislikes in the matter of work is to give more attention when we are becoming bored with a particular job. I have known many students both in India and in America, and when they say something is "boring," what they usually mean is they are not interested in it. The simple cure for boredom is to give a little more attention, a little more concentration, and we will find the more concentration we give, the more interesting the subject becomes. But we are so perverse that when something bores us, we immediately begin thinking about something else. If we can only straighten ourselves up and give more concentration, we will find how good this discipline is for our intellectual development. Ultimately, we should be able to give our concentration to anything.

Today I was reading a brilliant paper by a friend of ours on biophysics. He appreciates our work and has visited us many times, so I thought it a token of my appreciation to give my complete concentration to this highly scientific essay. To my amazement, halfway I was beginning to understand it, and by the time I finished, I agreed with it. Even subjects with which we are not familiar can be understood and appreciated by giving them enough concentration.

It is only after we have freed our nervous system from the tyranny of likes and dislikes that we live in complete freedom and security. Every morning we will get up eager to continue our life of service, and every evening we will go to bed at peace in spite of the terrible problems with which the world is confronted, knowing that we have made a contribution, however small, to the solution of these problems.

श्रेयान्स्वधर्मो विगुणः परधर्मात्स्वनुष्ठितात् ।
स्वधर्मे निधनं श्रेयः परधर्मो भयावहः ॥३-३५॥

35. It is better to strive in one's own dharma than to succeed in the dharma of another: nothing is ever lost in following one's own dharma, but competition in another's dharma breeds fear and insecurity.

The word used here is *dharma,* a word common to Hinduism and Buddhism. It comes from the root *dhri,* 'to support'; dharma is what supports us, keeps us together, prevents us from flying to pieces in the face of stress. Dharma is the central law of our being, which is to extinguish our separateness and attain Self-realization, to lose ourselves and be united with the Lord. In Buddhism this transformation is called nirvāna, the extinction of self-will in union with the infinite. Ansari of Herat, a great Sufi mystic, tells us, "Know that when you learn to lose yourself, you will reach the Beloved." And in the Gita (12:8), Sri Krishna says, "Still your mind in me, still yourself in me, and without doubt you shall be united with me, Lord of Love, dwelling in your heart." This universal law is inscribed on every cell of our being, and the proof of it is that the more we live for others, the healthier our body becomes, the calmer our mind becomes, the clearer our intellect becomes, the deeper our love and wisdom become.

When *sva* is added to *dharma,* the word becomes *svadharma,* our own personal dharma. This is our present context, our present assets and liabilities. On the spiritual path, we start from where we stand by fulfilling our present responsibilities, on the campus, at the office, or in the home. This svadharma may change as our spiritual awareness deepens. Later on, as our capacities grow, our responsibilities and opportunities for service will become greater. What is the right occupation now may not be right later on, but as long as it is not at the expense of others, our job or profession can be made a part of our sādhana. We should be careful, however, to choose a career that is not at the expense of any living creature.

By using the word *svadharma* Sri Krishna is saying not to try to follow a profession because someone else is following it. It is much better for you to learn to know yourself, to know your assets and liabilities, to remember your training and follow the career which blends with your sādhana, than for you to compare yourself with others and do what they are doing. Try to exercise your own judgment instead of doing things because some movie star or baseball player does them. Why should I look like the Beatles? I look better when I am myself. Why should I drink something because some baseball player drinks it?

I would drink it if the nutritionist Jean Mayer told me to.

It is a very enjoyable thing to be oneself, to stop acting. Only after considerable progress in meditation do we discover what consummate actors we are. Early morning we get up and start acting; we go to the office or to the campus and keep acting. It is because we are always on the stage, worrying if the audience is going to applaud or if anyone is going to throw rotten tomatoes, that tension builds up. But Sri Krishna says, "Be yourself completely; accept yourself completely."

The ability to know oneself and be oneself comes through a long period of discipline. One of the mistakes young people often make is thinking, "I am going to be spontaneous. Tomorrow morning when I get up I am just going to be myself." It is only after we have unlearned many of our old habits and freed ourselves from the tyranny of likes and dislikes that we are truly spontaneous. Then we will find that when we are at home with ourselves we are at home with everyone else.

अर्जुन उवाच ।
अथ केन प्रयुक्तो ऽयं पापं चरति पूरुषः ।
अनिच्छन्नपि वार्ष्णेय बलादिव नियोजितः ॥ ३-३६ ॥

ARJUNA:

36. What is the force that binds us to selfish deeds, Vārshneya? What power moves us, despite our desire to act for the good of all?

Arjuna, like all of us, has a great desire to lead a selfless life, but has great difficulties in implementing his desire. In this question, which is so human, so personal, that it is easy to appreciate how much Arjuna represents every one of us, Arjuna addresses Sri Krishna as *Vārshneya.* Sri Krishna was born in the Vrishni community as an *avatāra,* an incarnation; and just as Sri Krishna calls Arjuna *Kaunteya,* 'son of Kuntī,' Arjuna here returns the compliment. This is the give-and-take of good friends. Arjuna is asking this question of Sri Krishna partly as his spiritual teacher and partly as his good friend, who will not be offended, who will not misunderstand, and who will not hold anything against him.

Arjuna is saying, "I want to lead the right life; I want to enter into a state of abiding joy, and I do not want to be a plaything of circumstances. I want to do what is good for every creature in the world, but what force prevents me from carrying out these high ideals? What makes me fall over and over again? What makes me go after my personal profit and personal pleasure?"

Sri Krishna will answer Arjuna in the concluding words of the third chapter. Try to imagine Sri Krishna now as I do, as looking at Arjuna and almost saying, "So you think you are the only one who has this problem?" It is in this bantering, loving, divine tone that Sri Krishna reveals what causes the great ordeal for all of us on the spiritual path.

श्रीभगवानुवाच ।
काम एष क्रोध एष रजोगुणसमुद्भवः ।
महाशनो महापाप्मा विद्ध्येनमिह वैरिणम् ॥३-३७॥

SRI KRISHNA:

37. It is selfish desire and anger, arising from the guna of rajas; these are the appetites and deeds which threaten a person in this life.

The Lord says that our greatest enemies, waiting to bring about our downfall, are *kāma* and *krodha*. Kāma is selfish desire, or self-will. It drives us to impose our will on all around us, to satisfy our selfish desires even at the expense of others, to feel that it is *our* family, *our* friends, *our* country alone that deserve consideration. Kāma shows itself in many ways: in physical cravings, greed for money, and lust for power and prestige. This drive for personal satisfaction is inevitably connected with krodha, or anger, because when we are driven in this way there is always the possibility of being frustrated by obstacles, of being challenged by others. The same urges which we have for personal satisfaction, others have too; therefore friction arises.

In my mother tongue, when someone is very angry, he will say, "Hum!" In the village you will often hear this exclamation. You can see mothers shaking their finger and saying *hum!* Sometimes even a little boy can imitate his mother and reply *hum!* in exactly the same tone. It was my grandmother who taught me that this *hum!* is very often an expression of violated self-will, and because of her teaching, when I hear *hum!* it reminds me of the Sanskrit word *aham*, which means 'I.' When I say *hum!* to you it really means, "Do you know who I am? I am I." There can still be peace if you do not challenge me, but you too are likely to reply, "*Hum!* I too am I." Just as this problem of ahamkara, or self-will, exists between individuals, it exists among nations as well. The same language of anger that is used by one nation is used by the other when national self-will is frustrated.

Even though we have good intentions, once our ego is opposed, our self-will is challenged. Once our personal desires are flouted, our mind becomes agitated, and the moment our mind is agitated, our judgment becomes clouded. With the very best intentions, we may impose our self-will on our partner. With the desire of cementing the relationship, we say, "Why don't you do what I want you to do?" Our partner, also with the very same intentions of cementing the relationship, says, "Why don't *you* do what *I* want you to?" Once this clash comes about, both minds become agitated, and both, with the desire of strengthening the partnership, do everything possible to disrupt it. At that time, even though propelled by anger, we should try not to give in to it, but to maintain our attitude of love and respect for the person who has opposed us.

This morning it was so hot that we weren't able to have our long walk in Oakland, so we went to the San Francisco beach. Looking down from Cliff House at the great array of surfers – whom I enjoy watching because they remind me so much of what takes place in meditation – we noticed many of the surfers were beginners, dhārana people. There were also a few more experienced ones, the dhyāna people. There were no samādhi people. It was very interesting to watch these two categories. The beginners would wade into the water, wait for a big wave, and when it came, they would try to stand up. Then not only would they be thrown down, but the surfboard would fly up like a toy in the air. But not even the most timid would immediately put their surfboards on their heads and go home. They just came back and got into the water again.

This is the real secret of the spiritual life. When the passions, which can tower over the tidal waves of the Pacific, come and ask us, like the waves, "Would you like to play a game with us?" we must be ready to control them and ride them just as we ride a wave. To me this surfing is a game between the waves and the surfboard. It isn't a hostile encounter; it's a very friendly game where the waves are telling the surfboard, "You bring your rider along. I'll throw you both up in the air. Why don't you try me? You can learn to ride on me, but first I am going to make both of you fly in the air like toys."

The other surfers we saw were more skillful, more resolute, more secure. They were not content with the white waters, but would go into what Ramakrishna calls the black waters, far away from the shore, where the waves were getting very high. Today we saw two or three people getting the right timing and "shooting the tube" so fast that we were amazed a person could learn such a skill. In governing our passions, it is the same story. It is a game in which the passions dare us, "Would you like to come? We are three: fear, anger, and greed. You are only one." To this the really adventurous person will say, "You are three, I am one, so this is the right game for me. I am going to fall. I am going to drink a lot of sea water. But one day I will ride on you." When we bring this determination to our sādhana, the great day will soon come when, through the grace of the Lord, we will be able to harness the power of anger, fear, and greed and use it in contributing to the welfare of others. When we are angry we are allowing power to rise against us and enslave us, but when we learn to control these tremendous sources of power, we can use them to meet the most formidable challenges of the day and to make our greatest contribution to those around us.

In daily living, even though we advance fairly well in meditation and are able to use the mantram most of the time, we will all have to face circumstances in which the senses will be strongly tempted. The Bible tells us that even Jesus was not free from these great temptations, and the Buddhist scriptures record for us the Buddha's struggle with

Māra, the tempter. When sense cravings and self-will propel us, when we find ourselves almost helpless, the example of Jesus and the Buddha inspires us to turn against these powerful drives and learn to control them. The duel with the senses can be so satisfying, so thrilling, that no victory in worldly life can compare with it. And gradually, as we free ourselves from the tyranny of these selfish desires in our actions, they will subside from the mind also.

धूमेनाव्रियते वह्निर्यथादर्शो मलेन च ।
यथोल्बेनावृतो गर्भस्तथा तेनेदमावृतम् ॥ ३-३८॥

38. Just as a fire is covered by smoke and a mirror is obscured by dust, just as the embryo rests deep within the womb, knowledge is hidden by selfish desire.

Just as a great pall of smoke obscures the fire blazing underneath, just so the pall of desire – selfish, self-willed, separate – hides the blazing fire of power, the blazing light of divinity, that shines forever in the depths of our consciousness.

Just as a mirror is covered by dust, so is knowledge of the Ātman hidden by kāma. Sri Krishna is telling Arjuna that if you try to use a mirror clouded by dust, you will not be able to see yourself at all. Just so, if you indulge your senses all of the time, exercising no discrimination in what you eat, what you read, what you say, and what you think about, you will not be able to see your real Self at all. You will see only the body, not the dweller within, only the house, not the resident. In order to see yourself as you are – as beautiful, wise, loving, universal – you must rise above physical consciousness. You can put this into practice every day by asking yourself, "In what ways can I guard myself against being trapped in body consciousness?" Once you ask this question, you see that everywhere there is a choice. Let the bakery put all kinds of cakes in the window; you will say, "I don't want to get trapped in them." Let the stores advertise the latest fashions; you will say, "I don't want to get trapped here." It is these right choices which will gradually enable you to rise above physical consciousness.

Sri Krishna goes on to use the simile of the embryo, well protected and hidden in the mother's womb. With these three similes, the Lord reminds us that the Ātman is always within us. The Lord is always present, call him Krishna, Christ, the Buddha, or Allah, but it is we who bring all kinds of covers to hide his glory. Wherever we go we bring home some cover to conceal the Lord, and it will take a lot of recycling to get rid of all these envelopes. Sri Krishna is telling Arjuna, "We don't want all of this. Instead of bringing more covers home, start removing them; instead of adding to your burden of envelopes, begin to remove them one by one." The moment we begin to restrain our senses diligently and practice other spiritual disciplines, we shall see that envelope after envelope – or as the Sufis say, veil after veil – falls away until we at last see the Beloved, who is the Lord, in the depths of our own consciousness.

आवृतं ज्ञानमेतेन ज्ञानिनो नित्यवैरिणा ।
कामरूपेण कौन्तेय दुष्पूरेणानलेन च ॥३-३९॥

39. Knowledge is hidden, Kaunteya, by
this unquenchable fire for self-satisfaction,
the inveterate enemy of the wise.

Arjuna has asked Sri Krishna a very personal question, which could be asked by any one of us when we make mistakes in spite of the fact that we know they are mistakes. "What makes me do these things? I know this is not the way to joy and security, but there seems to be some compulsion in me to make these mistakes." And Sri Krishna, who has infinite love for you and me, answers Arjuna by saying that this compulsion is kāma, the worst enemy we have on the face of the earth. If we try to look at life through this perspective, we shall see how conflicts cannot help arising when a nation, group, or individual keeps its eyes only on its own development, ignoring the needs and rights of others. The Buddha calls this compulsion by a very homely name: *tanhā,* the fierce thirst that demands to be quenched at any cost, if necessary by robbing other people of their water.

Take, for example, the question of money. The mystics do not say that money is bad; money is just metal or paper, which is amoral. It is the love of money that is bad. The Gita says that to be able to use anything wisely we must not be attached to it. Gandhiji, whose material possessions were worth only two dollars at the time of his death, handled millions and millions of rupees. Because he had no personal attachment, no selfish craving to accumulate money, he was able to use it very wisely to benefit millions of helpless people in India.

Not only in the accumulation of money, but in the accumulation of every material thing, we are likely to get caught unless we have the capacity for detachment. We know people, for example, who give much of their love to their wardrobe. I have seen one of those wardrobes – countless pairs of shoes to match the colors of the season, and numberless dresses and hats. I could not see how that lady would have any time for meditation, and when I was told she didn't meditate, I said, "No wonder." I have seen very well-dressed women, both here and in India, having a small, select wardrobe that freed them from spending hours weighing the pros and cons of particular colors and hemlines. They have a small closet where they can walk in and come out well dressed without becoming prey to the whims and fancies of some fashion expert in Europe. Even to wear clothes well, we must be detached. To keep our hair in the best condition, we have to be detached; otherwise we are likely to be caught in fads and fancies.

Arjuna must now be completely overwhelmed. I can imagine his agreeing, "Without detachment, you can't do anything in life." And here, as elsewhere, when Sri Krishna throws a flood of light on something in his life, I imagine Arjuna saying "That's right!" just as you and I would say it.

In this verse Sri Krishna uses the very strong word *kāma* which, in general, means keeping our eyes only on what will serve our personal ends, what will satisfy our needs to the exclusion of the rights and needs of others. Unfortunately, there is no human being who, once he develops this sense of 'I and mine' by dwelling upon himself, can remain sensitive to the needs of others. Once we get caught in money, everywhere we go there is a dollar sign painted on our pupils. Everywhere we see money. We see a beautiful landscape and instead of wanting to write a poem about it, or paint a picture of it, or just enjoy it, we say, "If it could only be subdivided, developed, and rented out, it would bring in millions of dollars for us." This is just what is now happening in some of the most beautiful areas of our state of California.

Sri Krishna's teaching can be translated into practice every day by remembering that everything belongs to the Lord. The basis of all ecology is the awareness that the whole world belongs to the Lord. We are just transients or, if you prefer, guests who refuse to move out. The Lord doesn't expect any rent; he doesn't expect any cleaning deposit. All that he asks is that we please don't tear up the curtains, don't cut up the carpets, don't pull away the pillars, and keep the house reasonably tidy, which is the least any landlord will ask of us.

Even this body doesn't belong to us, but has been given to us to serve others; therefore, we cannot afford to do whatever we like with it, to give it cigarettes, alcohol, drugs, or too much food. The body is really like a rented car. As we come into the cosmos, we line up and say, "I would like to have a body." We specify the color and the horsepower, and the Lord, whose models are infinite, says, "You've got it." He trusts us; we look so honest and conscientious that he doesn't take any deposit; he doesn't even ask for references. But when we return it at the end of the journey, there is no battery, there are only two wheels, there is only one windshield wiper, and the hood is missing. To understand this, one doesn't have to be very philosophical; one can be very practical. Ordinary courtesy requires that when someone has very graciously lent us a body, we should use it for a good purpose and return it in good condition.

When we talk about the use of tobacco, alcohol, and drugs, it is not just a personal matter; the owner also has a say in it. The Lord has given this body to us on trust, and we shouldn't betray his trust under any circumstances. In the early days, when our selfish desires and sense cravings may not be very strong, we may say, "We will take it out for a small detour on a rough road. After all, it is only a couple of miles. We will come back and not go there again." Once we have taken our car on a detour of a couple of miles, the next time we want to take it three miles, four miles, and finally, taking it further and further from the main road, we don't know how to get back.

In yielding to most compulsions, like drugs, this is unfortunately what happens. No one wants to be a victim; no one wants to lose his liberty. But we know from many, many incidents every day in the Bay Area alone that there comes a time when in order to maintain, for example, a heroin habit, people rob and even kill.

This is the application of the simple word *kāma*. The Lord warns Arjuna never to lose his vigilance against the blandishments of the desire for selfish satisfaction, whether it is the craving of the senses or the urge to enforce self-will on those around. Little by little, Sri Krishna says, this will become his fiercest enemy; any time he yields to a selfish desire, he is actually strengthening his enemy.

इन्द्रियाणि मनो बुद्धिरस्याधिष्ठानमुच्यते ।
एतैर्विमोहयत्येष ज्ञानमावृत्य देहिनम् ॥ ३-४० ॥

40. Selfish desire is said to be found in the senses, mind, and intellect, misleading them and burying the understanding in delusion.

Sri Krishna now tells us where Kāma lives. Just as a wealthy person may have a house in London, a manor in Yorkshire, and a villa in the south of France, similarly Kāma has three houses – *indriya, manas,* and *buddhi.* His favorite house is indriya, the five senses, where he is usually to be found. He spends most of the year in the eye, in the ear, and of course on the palate. If we want to see Kāma, we do not have to look very far at mealtime to see which is his favorite room.

Kāma's second home is manas, the mind, where he lives during the turbulent periods. Though the word *kāma* is usually applied on the sensory level, and especially to sexual desire, it can also refer to the lust for power, which is one of the most terrible urges in the human being. By the side of the lust for power, the cravings of the palate are insignificant. The control of the palate is not a serious problem. Yielding to the senses does not usually harm others. It is the lust for power that in our modern age is responsible for so much misery all over the world. In order to guard ourselves against competition and turmoil, whether in international politics or in the home, we must remember the needs of those around us and forget our personal needs for power and prestige.

Buddhi, the intellect, is Kāma's third home. Even though we usually do not associate the intellect with selfish desire, we cannot help agreeing with Sri Krishna if we examine many of the books published today. Good books are rare, and to have a really good library, a few shelves are all we need. When I was still on my campus in India, I was convinced, like many professors, that if the Lord was to be found anywhere, it was in the lower stacks of the library. But now – just as when I go into a big department store, I can say, "How many things I don't need! How many expensive suits I don't want!" – when I enter a big library I say, "What tomes I don't have to read again! What folios I will never open!" This feeling of freedom will come to all of us when we realize, in the depths of our meditation, that all wisdom lies within.

Even to use the intellect wisely, we must be detached from it. The communication gap between the older and younger generations is caused mostly by our identifying ourselves with our opinions. We all can render a great service by listening to opposing opinions without agitation, discourtesy, or violence, and by offering our opinions not as nonnegotiable demands but as calm, courteous statements. Gandhi could listen to opposing views with concentration, calmness, and respect, which would enable his opponent to ask for his views also. Gandhi showed the world that we can state our case well in simple, gentle, and respectful language. It is the person with a weak argument who tries to rely on violent or obscene language.

When most of us say "True! Absolutely right!" the translation is "Just what I think!" At my university in India, I would emphasize to my classes not to make marginal comments in library books. On one occasion I found, in delicate feminine handwriting, "How true!" As

I recognized the handwriting, I went to the girl, sat by her and said, "My dear, what do you mean by 'How true!'" Immediately she said, "This is exactly what I think."

Even though we may use courteous phrases like "apparently" or "to the best of my knowledge," underneath we are saying our statements are completely, irrevocably true. If we really mean "to the best of my knowledge" – or as I like to say, "to the best of my ignorance" – there would be no agitation. Today I read a penetrating anecdote from the meditation notebook of a student in our university extension class. She and her husband were having a heated discussion. When the situation was almost out of control, she said, "My course instructor says we are not arguing about opinions or philosophies; we are just trying to impose our self-will on each other." Even in a moment of heat, when patience is wearing thin, it is good to remind ourselves that it is not a philosophical dispute, it is not a question of principles; it is just your self-will against mine. If we can remember this, we will be more courteous, more lenient, and not condemn views different from ours or use violence to express our disapproval.

When the senses have come under our control and Kāma has been evicted from his first home, he moves with all his luggage to the mind, his second line of defense. Evict him there too, and you will find him in the intellect, where he is so strongly barricaded he can be thrown out only with great difficulty.

तस्मात्त्वमिन्द्रियाण्यादौ नियम्य भरतर्षभ ।
पाप्मानं प्रजहिह्येनं ज्ञानविज्ञाननाशनम् ॥ ३-४१ ॥

41. Fight with all your strength, O Bhārata; controlling your senses, attack your enemy directly, who is the destroyer of knowledge and realization.

We begin our conquest of Kāma by controlling the senses, especially the palate, which is very much like training a puppy. Today, as we were walking around Lake Merritt, we saw an Alsatian being trained by a lady who was tugging at his leash, giving him angry looks, and using strong language. Knowing something about the dog's point of view, I told my wife that I had easily trained my own dogs just by loving them, being patient with them, and giving them my appreciation when they obeyed. When we went to the circus some time ago, we saw a group of dogs who were really in love with their trainer, a girl. After every performance they would leap into her arms, and she hugged them and talked baby language to them. Even the really big dogs would act like little pups, playing up to her. In this way, little by little, we can train the senses if we have a deep desire to bring them under control and a sense of artistry that prevents us from being too austere or over-indulgent.

Sri Krishna tells us through Arjuna to put to death this greed for personal pleasure, profit, prestige, and power. It is our worst enemy, which prevents us from living in joy and security and attaining spiritual wisdom.

In the *Rāmāyana,* this enemy is personified as Rāvana, the ten-headed one. Rāma, the desire for selfless service, and Rāvana, the desire for selfish satisfaction, both exist within us. When Rāma faces Rāvana on the battlefield, he must sever all ten heads of his enemy at once, which is how we must slay the selfish 'I,' the only barrier between us and the Lord. In our own daily life we begin the conquest of Rāvana by keeping the happiness of those around us first and ours last.

इन्द्रियाणि पराण्याहुरिन्द्रियेभ्यः परं मनः ।
मनसस्तु परा बुद्धिर्यो बुद्धेः परतस्तु सः ॥३-४२॥

42. *The senses are said to be higher than the body, the mind higher than the senses; above the mind is the intellect, and above the intellect is the Ātman.*

Here we have a simple hierarchy of the various members composing the human individual. We not only have a family at home; each of us in ourselves is a family, whose members are the body, senses, mind, and intellect, who seldom pay any respect to the advice of the head, the Ātman. Sometimes in meditation the Ātman says, "Let's all get together and think one thought on the Lord." Immediately the body goes to sleep; that is its way of meditation. It says, "This is good for me. In this I find security," and the Ātman really doesn't know what to do. Then the palate says, "I am going out for a quick one." The mind begins to re-enact a quarrel which everyone else has forgotten, saying, "I don't want to live in the present; I want to re-enact a drama that took place five years ago in which my girlfriend gave me my hat." The intellect, supposedly the most cultured member of the group, says, "Nobody listens to my opinions." Finally the Ātman says, "I guess we'd better wait for another incarnation to get these boys together," and we just throw up our hands.

We can become united within only by training these rebels to act in harmony with the Ātman through a total discipline based on the practice of meditation. We train the body by giving it the right exercise and food. The senses are trained through discriminating restraint. The Gita will tell us that we can poison ourselves not only through our mouth, but through our eyes and ears. In this respect, we can do our children a great service by guiding them in the movies they go to, the television programs they watch, and the books they read. We should remember that children do not know what to read and what not to read. It is the duty of the parents to educate their tastes gradually by giving them the right books and then, when they are older, leaving them to make their own choice.

Just as the body and senses can be trained and made to act in harmony with the Ātman, the mind and intellect can also be trained. We train the mind by learning to transform negative emotions into positive ones, ill will into goodwill, hatred into love. To train the intellect, we must learn to be detached from our opinions. Even to have sound intellectual knowledge, we have to be, in a certain measure, detached from the intellect. In using the word "objective," a favorite term in academic circles, we should remember that we cannot be objective as long as we identify ourselves with our opinions.

It is good to respect the opinions of the opposite camp and of the older generation. One day our children are going to look upon our opinions as rather old-fogyish. When we are looking upon ourselves as the avant garde, the spearhead of radicalism and revolution, we should remember that our grandchildren one day are going to point us out with "Here comes the rear guard, bringing up reaction." Often those who are fanatically attached to their opinions come with the passage of time to be just as fanatically attached to the opposite views. One could write a comedy, if it were not so macabre, about how radicals become reactionaries in their old age. But if we can have respect for opposing opinions now, later on also, whatever time or circumstance may bring, we will have the same tolerance. Even in the evening of our life, we will be able to listen to the views of our grandchildren and say, "There is something in what you say."

No problem is insoluble if we are prepared to sit down and listen affectionately and respectfully to what the other person has to say. This is true not only in the home and on the campus but in areas of international friction as well. As Winston Churchill put it, "It is better to jaw, jaw, jaw than war, war, war." In communicating with the enemy, Gandhi was really at his best. There was a very important political figure in India who opposed every move Gandhi made. It was said that he had a problem for every solution that Gandhiji brought forth, but even with him, Gandhi was loving, respectful, yet completely clear in elucidating his own point of view.

एवं बुद्धेः परं बुद्ध्वा संस्तभ्यात्मानमात्मना ।
जहि शत्रुं महाबाहो कामरूपं दुरासदम् ॥ ३-४३ ॥

43. Thus, knowing that which is supreme, let
the Ātman rule the ego; use your mighty arms
to slay the fierce enemy that is selfish desire.

If all our faculties do not listen completely to the Ātman, there is division, conflict, and despair; there can never be joy. Meditation is a practical discipline for bringing under control these rebels who try to destroy the unity of the individual. Drawing upon the power released in meditation, we can train the body, senses, mind, and intellect to work in perfect harmony, until we finally go beyond these to realize the Ātman within.

This transformation requires enormous perseverance and, as Gandhiji would point out, the infinite patience of a person trying to empty the sea with a cup. But even here people differ, especially at the outset. There are a few rare people in every country, every age, who require only a minimum of work to make themselves selfless. These people are like our meditation hall, called Shānti, which is solid and well built. When we first moved to the āshram, it required only reroofing to make it suitable for our use. For the vast majority of us, however, the appropriate simile is the men's dormitory. There we had to rebuild the foundations completely. It required an enormous amount of work, a good deal of equipment, and a lot of thinking on the part of the authorities before they could give their approval. Most of us have to change completely the foundations of our lives, which are at present based upon the belief that by following personal profit, pleasure, and prestige we can build a personality that is beautiful and loving.

In the deeper stages of meditation, we make the salutary discovery that the ego is a crashing bore. We all know how unpleasant it can be to associate with people who dwell upon themselves. Nobody wants our selfishness, including us. Do not try to show your ego to anybody; no one wants to look at it. Do not talk about it; nobody wants to hear about it. Whatever our past may have been, if we can dissolve the ego, we shall find this is all we need to do to become radiantly beautiful, perennially wise, and tireless in our service of those around us.

The Lord concludes the third chapter with this resounding verse, in which he tells Arjuna: "Slay all that is selfish in you. Extinguish your ego completely." This is exactly what the word *nirvāna* means: *nir,* 'out'; *vāna,* 'to blow.' Blow out all that is selfish in you, extinguish all that is separate in you, and you will realize the Ātman, the indivisible unity of all life.

कर्मयोगो नाम तृतीयोऽध्यायः ॥ ३ ॥

CHAPTER FOUR

Wisdom in Action

श्रीभगवानुवाच ।
इमं विवस्वते योगं प्रोक्तवानहमव्ययम् ।
विवस्वान्मनवे प्राह मनुरिक्ष्वाकवे ऽब्रवीत् ॥४-१॥

SRI KRISHNA:

1. I told this eternal secret to Vivasvat. Vivasvat instructed Manu, and Manu instructed Ikshvāku.

This verse is very much in the traditional scriptural style, almost like the Old Testament narratives where A begat B, B begat C, C begat D. But we should not get bored; they will tell us in their own way what finally happened.

When Sri Krishna says, "I told this eternal secret to Vivasvat," he means that he inspired Vivasvat to start meditating, to restrain the senses, to put other people first, and to discover the Lord within. Vivasvat, having traveled this way, instructed Manu in meditation and the allied disciplines, and he too discovered the Lord within himself. Manu immediately ran after another man, called Ikshvāku, and instructed him to meditate and attain Self-realization also.

Almost all religions emphasize the precious truth of God's grace. In some inscrutable way, there comes a time when the grace of the Lord touches us. When this happens, as Meister Eckhart says, we thrash about like a fish caught by the fisherman's hook. The hook has entered the flesh of the fish, and though it may thrash and jump about, trying to get free, the hook only enters deeper and deeper.

We do not want to be released out of the prison we have come to love.

But even though the grace of the Lord may have touched us, we cannot expect him to do all of the work. In order to progress on the spiritual path, we must have the grace of our own mind as well. We must make the right choices. As my granny would say, "Even if the Lord grants you grace, the temple priest may still stand in your way."

Grace can come like the explosion of a bomb in our consciousness and often is followed by a period of turmoil and turbulence. Nothing seems to satisfy us. Money, material possessions, and prestige no longer satisfy us. The old palate-blandishments now taste insipid. We say that peach ice cream is not as good as it used to be; maybe the secret of making peach ice cream has been lost. So we try spumoni, but that proves to be even worse than peach.

Along with dissatisfaction comes utter restlessness. We cannot sit still; we cannot sleep in peace. This is the call from the Lord within to sit down and start meditating. Restlessness is power rising, which can be harnessed to turn us inwards to the practice of meditation.

एवं परंपराप्राप्तमिमं राजर्षयो विदुः ।
स कालेनेह महता योगो नष्टः परंतप ॥४-२॥

2. Thus, O Arjuna, eminent sages received knowledge of yoga in a continuous tradition. But through time the practice of yoga was lost in the world.

The word used here is *parampara,* which means from one person to another, from one generation to another, very often in the family line. Even today, in the Indian musical tradition, there are ancient families who, instead of bequeathing land or wealth to their children, bequeath a love for music. A few miles away from my little village in India there was a family like this. A boy from that home was in my high school. While we had our lunch under a mango tree he would sing devotional songs, and we would all stop eating to listen to him. When we would ask him, "How did you learn to sing" he would say, "You don't have to learn to sing. I was just born singing." In this tradition, the parents grant the legacy of musical consciousness to the children, and the son and daughter glory in carrying on the tradition of the parents to greater heights.

In the mystical tradition, if even one person takes to meditation and tries to lead the spiritual life, that person is establishing a parampara. After many years, someone in the family or an old friend, even someone who was sceptical in the beginning, may be inspired to meditate. Sometimes these paramparas may come to a temporary stop. The son becomes a potter, the daughter becomes a Shakespeare critic; the tradition goes down a blind alley and appears to stop there. But it is never lost for long, as we can see in the case of India, which has been blessed with an unbroken continuity of sages and saints. This spiritual tradition has sustained her civilization for more than five thousand years, even though her history is sorrowfully marred by invasion after invasion. Whenever India began to look away from her supreme goal, there has always arisen a great spiritual teacher, like Ramakrishna, Ramana Maharshi, or Mahatma Gandhi, to restore her sense of direction.

But today, if travelers go to India, it is difficult for them to see traces of this tradition. The cities are like cities everywhere – turbulent, often violent, driven by material pursuits. Some people who go to India in search of the spiritual life, idealizing the country, imagine that as soon as they board Air India and put the safety belt on, the pilot and air hostess will begin chanting the mantram. They expect, upon landing at the Madras airport, to see people seated in meditation in the lobby. Unprepared for the appalling poverty and superstition they find almost everywhere, they want to run back to the airport and get the first flight to the West. But on the way back they may find someone like Ramana Maharshi sitting quietly under a banyan tree, fully enlightened, aware that all life is one. Immediately, they tear up their round-trip ticket and decide to settle down in his āshram.

In the following verses, the Lord reassures us that even though humanity seems to lose its way now and then, a great spiritual figure will arise at the appropriate time to remind us that it is not in the accumulation of money, prestige, and power but in living for others that we discover and fulfill the supreme goal of life.

स एवायं मया ते ऽद्य योगः प्रोक्तः पुरातनः ।
भक्तो ऽसि मे सखा चेति रहस्यं ह्येतदुत्तमम् ॥४-३॥

3. The secret of these teachings is profound.
I have explained them to you today because
you are my friend and devotee.

Arjuna likes to be called Krishna's friend, as we saw recently in the excellent Kerala Kalamandalam performance of *Kirātārjunīyam*, "Arjuna and the Kirāta." In this Kathakali drama there is a scene where Arjuna is tested by Shiva, who is disguised as a rough forester. Shiva taunts him by asking the Indian equivalent of "Who do you think you are?"

Arjuna answers, "I come from a very ancient, noble family, the Pāndavas."

Shiva says, "Never heard of them." That doesn't upset Arjuna too much; he goes on talking about himself, his family, his kingdom. To everything Shiva says, "Never heard of it." Finally, Shiva says, "Can't you even tell me one little thing about yourself that might impress me?"

Arjuna, very proudly drawing himself up, says, "I have a friend. Guess who!"

"You tell me."

"Krishna!"

Arjuna expects his opponent to be completely overwhelmed, but instead Shiva just laughs and tests Arjuna by saying, "That butter-stealing, flute-playing cowherd who calls himself a divine incarnation?" Then, all of his love for Sri Krishna aroused, Arjuna pounces on Shiva, who is delighted with Arjuna's devotion.

Now Lord Krishna reassures Arjuna of his love and says, "It is true that the spiritual tradition seems to come to a stop now and then, but I am going to whisper in your ears and give you personal instruction as to how you can discover me in your consciousness. I am doing this especially for you because you love me so much." This is the same emphasis on love that we find in the words of Jesus: "Thou shalt love the Lord thy God with all thy heart, and with all thy soul, and with all thy mind, and with all thy strength." When we love those around us with all our heart by putting their welfare first, even though it is not easy for us, we are loving the Lord.

अर्जुन उवाच ।
अपरं भवतो जन्म परं जन्म विवस्वतः ।
कथमेतद्विजानीयां त्वमादौ प्रोक्तवानिति ॥४-४॥

ARJUNA:

4. You were born much after Vivasvat; he was born long ago. Why do you say that you taught this yoga in the beginning?

"Krishna," says Arjuna, "you and I are about the same age, but you are telling me that you have guided the meditation of spiritual aspirants in ancient times. I find this difficult to grasp. Perhaps my imagination is limited, but it looks to me as if you were not there. Why are you telling me of events that took place thousands of years before you were born in Mathurā?" This is not asked critically, but Arjuna is historically oriented, just as you and I are, and would like to have a rational explanation.

श्रीभगवानुवाच ।
बहूनि मे व्यतीतानि जन्मानि तव चार्जुन ।
तान्यहं वेद सर्वाणि न त्वं वेत्थ परंतप ॥४-५॥

SRI KRISHNA:

5. You and I have passed through many births, Arjuna. You have forgotten, Parantapa, but I remember them all.

Now I imagine the Lord of Love as smiling, *prahasann iva* and looking at Arjuna with great love; we should picture Sri Krishna now not as a forbidding spiritual figure, beetle-browed, with pursed lips, but as a playful, loving, and rather mischievous cowherd from Vrindāvana. He tells Arjuna, "This is going to be a bit of a shock to you, but this is not the first time you have been on earth. You have been here many times before."

It is not necessary to believe in reincarnation in order to lead the spiritual life. Whether we believe in one life or in many, we can all meditate, restrain our senses, and put others first. There is even a little danger in blindly accepting reincarnation. It may breed resignation and apathy if interpreted wrongly. The urgency of a task can be forgotten when we know we are going to come this way again. There is a story about a Hindu aspirant who was learning the headstand. He tried a few times but lost his balance and fell down. Then he gave up, saying, "I can always learn to do it the next time I come this way."

Reincarnation is something like going back to school again. The other day, one of our friends, a professor on the Berkeley campus, was taken by his wife to get "back-to-school" clothes, and I told him that all of us have back-to-school clothes already – this body of ours. Until we are able to put our parents, partner, children, friends, and enemies first, we will have to come back to school. After a long semester, one hundred years, we are asked for our progress report, and we say, "We have dropped out. We haven't taken the finals. We still love ourselves." Whoever is in charge, whether it is Jesus the Christ, the Buddha, or Sri Krishna, will say very compassionately, "You had better register for the next semester." In the Tibetan tradition, *Bardo* is the name given to the place where we wait between terms. The semester break may sometimes last a few hundred years while we wait for the right context. Someone who has dropped out this semester may come back a thousand years later and run into old classmates who ask, "What have you been doing the last nine hundred years?" "Oh, just waiting in Bardo," comes the reply. "Just couldn't get readmitted."

The purpose of life is to finish our schooling by eliminating all that is selfish and separate in us. And when the degrees are awarded at commencement, our real parent, seated right in front, sometimes looking like Sri Krishna, sometimes like the Compassionate Buddha or Jesus the Christ, will proudly say that we have really graduated at last.

While Sri Krishna explains to Arjuna that he has been here many times, Arjuna thinks to himself, "My memory is a blank. I just don't remember anything at all." He is too polite to say, "I never have been here before. Why do you try to put all of these ideas into my head?"

The Lord says, "You have just forgotten. I too have been this way before, but I remember because I have maintained the continuity of my existence which is the Ātman."

As long as we believe we are the body, we cannot escape a disruption of consciousness at the time of death. But if we can rise above physical consciousness and discover for ourselves that we are not the perishable body but the imperishable Self, there can be no break in our awareness of the infinite continuity of existence. As Jalalu'l-Din Rumi has said:

> I was a mineral, and arose a plant.
> I died as a plant, and became a beast.
> I died as a beast, and evolved into a man.
> Why should I fear that I will lose by dying?
> Once again I shall die as man to join
> The holy company of angels. But I must
> Soar above them too. "Everything must die
> Save His Face." When I have died as an angel,
> I shall be that which is beyond the mind's grasp.
> Let me die to myself, for the ego's death
> Declares, "To Him we return."

This is the unanimous testimony of the great mystics of what the practice of meditation can lead to in the supreme climax called samādhi.

अजो ऽपि सन्नव्ययात्मा भूतानामीश्वरो ऽपि सन् ।
प्रकृतिं स्वामधिष्ठाय संभवाम्यात्ममायया ॥४-६॥
यदा यदा हि धर्मस्य ग्लानिर्भवति भारत ।
अभ्युत्थानमधर्मस्य तदात्मानं सृजाम्यहम् ॥४-७॥

6. My true being is unborn and changeless.
I am the Lord who dwells in every creature.
Through the power of my own Māyā, I
manifest myself in a finite form.
7. Whenever dharma declines, O Bhārata, and
the purpose of life is forgotten, I manifest myself.

The Lord of Love, even though immortal and infinite, comes as a divine incarnation in times of great crisis to rescue mankind from disaster. The Lord, who is enthroned in all hearts, comes to life in a blessed individual in every country, every age, to bring humanity back to the spiritual path.

Dharma, the central law of our being, is to live for others, to love others more than we love ourselves. The proof of this law is that the more we dwell upon ourselves, the more insecure we become. It is only when we forget ourselves in the welfare of those around us that we can live in abiding joy and unshaken security. Jesus puts this into immortal words when he says, "Bless them that curse you; do good to them that hate you." By doing so we will help not only them, but ourselves also.

In any conflict, it is absurd to retaliate. It only adds to the chaos and makes conflict more violent. Never in the history of human relations has any problem been solved except through greater love, endurance, and forgiveness on the part of some person. Between parents and children, husband and wife, friend and friend, the central law of the relationship is putting the other person first.

Even in international relations, in order to establish peace on earth and goodwill among men, Gandhi has shown that nonviolence is the only way. At the beginning of the twentieth century, if anything looked eternal, it was the British Empire. When I was in high school, one of our geography teacher's favorite tests was to have us color the Empire with our red crayon, and a good part of the world was red. Most of us took the Empire for granted and thought all we could do was accept it and learn to live with it. But Gandhi, as ordinary as you and I, received the touch of grace.

Gandhi's school life was quite normal. He played truant and postponed projects just like you and me; and when he went to London to fulfill his family's desire that he become a little pillar of the Empire, his early days there were just as ordinary. One of the most delightful pictures that we have of Gandhiji, the future ascetic, is in his striped suit, frock coat, and top hat. He carried a silver-headed cane and wore those indescribable relics of fashion, spats. He was growing up just like any other young fellow, wanting to be the mirror of fashion. He even tried to learn to play the violin and to dance the foxtrot. But already the light was being lit inside, entirely without his knowledge. The perennial spring of grace was beginning to open up inside, and when it finally reached the surface, it produced such power that one whole nation was able to free itself from foreign domination without firing a single shot. This measures the power locked up inside our consciousness; because this divine explosion took place in the deepest consciousness of one little man in faraway India, those days of imperialism and colonialism are ended.

In the early days of mystical transformation, people may not take it very seriously. They are likely to think, "He is always playacting. This is just another role that he has assumed. He is a born actor, but he will get tired of this mystic's role soon." Gandhiji said that in the early days he was supposed to be either an imposter, a madman, or a fool. And in Sri Ramana Maharshi's village, I can imagine them saying, "At seventeen what can you expect? This is just another of his games. He thinks he is illumined, that he has attained nirvikalpa samādhi, but one of these days he will snap out of it and go back to his old crowd again." It is during this period, when we have to face criticism and scepticism, that we learn to remain patient and unperturbed, sure that the source of all security is within.

It takes a few years for ordinary people like us to come to accept that the greatest blessing has fallen upon us without our deserving it. We can never get over the amazement of it. We are so frail, so petty, so full of weaknesses, yet in spite of all this, He whose love and power know no bounds has in his infinite mercy chosen us. For a long time, we think there must have been some mistake. Only after years of observing the daily growth in security, the increasing capacity to think of others, do we come to accept that, for no reason we can give, the mystic's mantle has fallen upon us. Afterwards, this wonderment continues all the time. There was a mystic in India who used to sit on the bank of the river, look at his reflection in the flowing waters from morning to evening, and say, "How wonderful! How miraculous!" Once he was asked by the people passing by, "Whom are you describing, Blessed One?" The simple mystic became very shy and very embarrassed, but replied, "Myself." Even in our dreams, we may come to hear the voice of Sri Krishna or Jesus the Christ saying, "My beloved." And when we have reluctantly, humbly accepted this, there is no earthly circumstance that can ever affect our security. Once this mystical transformation has begun to take place, even though we may be small people, each one of us can make a significant contribution to world peace. If we can establish peace in our hearts, return love for hatred, and live for the welfare of our family and community, we have changed the world picture. In this way, many small candles can light up the night of selfishness that threatens us.

परित्राणाय साधूनां विनाशाय च दुष्कृताम् ।
धर्मसंस्थापनार्थाय संभवामि युगे युगे ॥४-८॥

8. I am born in every age to protect the good,
to destroy evil, and to re-establish dharma.

In age after age, when violence increases, there comes a time when Mother Earth says, "I cannot bear any more; I am filled with grief seeing the way my children are raising their hands against each other." To this cry, the Lord responds by coming to inspire and protect those who turn to him, who live in harmony with the law of unity, and who contribute to the joy of others. He comes to protect such people from the heavy odds ranged against them, to defeat violence, and to eliminate selfishness.

These words may be interpreted on several levels. First is the divine incarnation, called *avatāra* in Sanskrit, of which Sri Krishna, the Compassionate Buddha, and Jesus the Christ are supreme examples. These mighty spiritual figures come, in answer to Mother Earth's plea, to rescue the world from the morass of selfishness and violence in which it gets caught now and then.

There is another level also on which this incarnation can take place, as in the case of Mahatma Gandhi, who was completely transformed by the grace of the Lord. Gandhi, whose stature became like the Himālayas, changed the direction of human evolution by showing us through his life that nonviolence is the only way, that love is no longer a luxury, but a dire necessity. Hate and perish or love and prosper is the choice placed before us in the great crisis of human civilization facing the modern world. So even though spiritual giants like Mahatma Gandhi are not in the same category as Jesus or the Buddha, who were never involved in life, they do achieve great victories for the human spirit over selfishness.

On the third level, the ordinary level which I call the blessed anonymous level, every one of us has this choice: shall I prepare for the divine incarnation to take place in my consciousness by abolishing every vestige of selfishness and separateness in my heart, and thus contribute to the progress of humanity, or shall I, by foolishly running after my own profit and pleasure, handicap humanity to the extent that it is in my power?

Sri Ramakrishna, in one of his inimitable images, says that a great incarnation is like a mighty ship that takes many thousands across the sea. Avatāras like Jesus or the Buddha are like mighty liners that ply the seven seas, but you and I can be little boats, or at least canoes. In Tamil there is a word which has passed into English, *kattumaram: kattu* is 'to tie,' *maram* is 'wood,' so *catamaran* means tying a few planks together and floating on the sea. We may not have the Ātman-power to propel a big ship, but we can improvise – pick up a few pieces of driftwood, tie them together, and get into the sea. We may be able to take at least our family with us across the sea of life.

It is up to you and me to keep our doors open, to put up a little sign outside, "Ready for receiving an incarnation." But the hall inside must not be cluttered up. It must be completely empty of attachments to one's opinions and self-will. If we can empty our house and put up the little board outside, the Lord will come, pick it up, and say, "I am here."

Even ordinary people like ourselves can gradually blossom into mahātmas. *Mahā* is 'great,' and *Ātma* is 'Self.' You and I are imprisoned in our little self. We just don't like being free; we like thinking about ourselves, always on the lookout to see if others are denying us things to which we are entitled. The mahātmā is the Great Self, the person who says "You and I are one," and who lives in accordance with this oneness which is the divine principle of existence.

Even the desire to empty ourselves – to turn our back on our own pleasure and profit and to contribute to the happiness of others – is the result of divine grace. The desire to go against desires is one of the surest signs of grace. When desires come which formerly used to pick us up by the scruff of the neck and throw us from here across the Bay, we will now want to resist – not with weeping and sobbing but with a fierce joy, a sense of exultation.

But there is also the old momentum which now and then drives us to cling to some strong, secret selfish attachment. While we are progressing, resisting old desires, suddenly we see a little ego-hold. Immediately we cling to it. And this is the finest sign of grace: the Lord takes out his holy hammer and gives such a well-aimed, direct hit on the knuckles that we let go. Do not think that this happens only to you and me. Some of the greatest mystics have said, "How much you must love us, Lord! How many times you have hit us! If you had cared less, you would have given just one hit and said, 'All right, they are free to choose.'" The great mystic will even say with joy, "Every time my thoughts stray from you, hit me hard. Take your hammer back as far as you can and bring it down hard." All sorrow is lost when we can say this; everything becomes joy.

जन्म कर्म च मे दिव्यमेवं यो वेत्ति तत्त्वतः ।
त्यक्त्वा देहं पुनर्जन्म नैति मामेति सो ऽर्जुन ॥ ४-९ ॥

9. He who knows me as his own divine Self, as the Operator in him, breaks through the belief that he is the body and is not born separate again. Such a one is united with me, O Arjuna.

When you have known the divine birth of the Lord within yourself, and you know the Lord to be the operator and yourself the instrument, you will never again fall into the superstition that you are the body, neither in this life nor thereafter.

We are so enmeshed in identification with our body that it is beyond our wildest imagination even for a split second to see what we will be without our body. It is a very merciful provision of sādhana that it takes many years to get over the age-old, race-old fallacy that we are the body. If out of a playful sense of mischief the Lord were to deprive us of our body-consciousness during meditation tonight, if kundalinī were to burst into a cataclysmic explosion and send us fathoms deep into our consciousness, we would not be able even to get up from our chair. So for practical purposes, there may be some disadvantages in instant illumination. To be able to function in life after realizing the indivisible unity, Sri Ramakrishna says delightfully that we need to keep the "ripe ego," in which we still know that we have parents, partners, and children. But this selfless little ego does not get trapped in its role. It knows it is acting in a play, performing with complete artistry.

We should do everything possible to reduce identification with the body. This can be done in many ways: by not allowing the palate to dictate what we should eat, by eating what is nourishing for the body, and by getting plenty of physical exercise.

Body-identification is perhaps the greatest superstition ever to trouble the world. That the sun goes around the earth is a small superstition. That the sun sinks in the sea and has his bath in its waters, as an old poem in my mother tongue puts it, is a very small superstition that does no one any harm. But this superstition that we are the body immediately leads to disastrous consequences. When we talk about people being different, races being different, we are really referring to the body. Separateness and insecurity are at their worst in people who are excessively body-conscious.

Sometimes there is the misunderstanding that in talking about rising above physical consciousness I am striking a note of stoicism. But it is the person who is least body-conscious who feels most deeply the departure of dear friends. If I may draw upon a personal example, yesterday I received a letter from my village informing me that one of my old friends in India passed away last week. I know he cannot die. I know that he is eternal because he is the Ātman. But at the same time I so humanly remember his body, his little ways, that even in my sleep last night I was troubled. My friend's cousin, whom I also knew in India, said in his letter yesterday, "Whatever the scriptures may say, it is terrible to bear the departure of somebody who has grown up with you and lived with you." Rising above physical consciousness does not mean losing my sense of endearment and love for the Lord disguised in my own family and friends.

वीतरागभयक्रोधा मन्मया मामुपाश्रिताः ।
बहवो ज्ञानतपसा पूता मद्भावमागताः ॥४-१०॥

10. Delivered from selfish attachment, fear, and anger, filled with me, surrendering themselves to me, purified in the fire of my being, many have reached the state of unity in me.

Vītarāgabhayakrodha: "Be without selfish attachment, fear, or anger." The Lord says, "Throw these three away. They are your worst enemies, trapping you in the cycle of birth, death, sorrow, and despair. Every day, do everything possible to get over selfish attachment to people and to things. Do everything possible to get over being the victim of fear and anger. Surmount these obstacles." In this the practice of meditation can be of enormous help. In the very depths of your meditation, when you are no longer aware of the body, when concentration is complete, you can free yourself from selfish attachments to money, to material possessions, and to people, whom you may try to manipulate because of lack of detachment from your own ego.

Pain often accompanies the development of detachment. If as a child I have not been told no by my parents, then when I become an adult, I will not be able to take no from anyone at all. In relationships with children, love often expresses itself in the capacity to say no when necessary.

The other day we went to Santa Rosa to buy shoes for our little nieces, Meera and Geetha. While Christine was buying the shoes, with my mother smiling approval, I noticed a very loving mother with a girl about nine years old, who had probably been spoiled by always being allowed to have her own way. To everything that the salesgirl brought she said, "I don't want it. It looks ugly. I am not going to wear it." Within ten minutes the mother was at the end of her tether. She was a loving mother, but she had lost control of the situation.

So the application of this verse comes even in small things. We should not allow children to keep demanding what they want; we should exercise our good judgment and fill their needs but not spoil them by yielding to their likes and dislikes all the time. It is better to cross our child a little, and give him or her the shoes and clothes we think best, rather than let the child go on saying "No, no, no." It is not a matter of clothes; it is a matter of self-will. If we cannot say no to our children when necessary, we will actually be teaching them to have more self-will.

In every relationship, the cultivation of detachment is painful, because we must go against our self-will, opinions, and pleasures. Even in our most intimate personal relationships, it must be admitted that often there is this taint of trying to bend others to our will, of expecting others to conform to our image of what they should be. This is often what disrupts personal relationships between older and younger people.

I must say with infinite gratitude to my grandmother, who had never heard of educational psychology, that after I left high school she began actively to help me rebel against some of the ideas with which I had been brought up. This was marvelous spiritual psychology, because when my spiritual teacher encouraged me to rebel against constricting ideas, it was no longer rebellion.

Without detachment, it is very hard for parents to go against their own self-will, their ways and upbringing, even though they know that their children are living in a different world and are exposed to a different climate. Only when we are detached in good measure from our own ego can we encourage our children to follow their own dharma, to grow to their full stature in their own way, by saying, "We will support you as long as you turn your back on what is selfish and self-willed." Young people can respond tremendously to this capacity on the part of the older people to put their children first.

If only I can extinguish all that is selfish in me, erase every desire for personal profit, personal pleasure, personal prestige, and personal power, which is often at the expense of others, then the Lord will be free to fill me with his own love, his own wisdom, his own beauty. This is the significance of the word *manmayā*, 'filled with me.'

In the classical Krishna tradition this is expressed in a very loving manner in a story about Sri Krishna and Rādhā. Rādhā is a lovely girl who represents the human heart, longing for the Lord. Sri Krishna is always represented as playing on the flute. One of his names is *Venugopāla,* the divine flute-player, who is always playing his magic melody to rouse us from sleep, to make us come alive. Rādhā is head over heels in love with Krishna. This is just what you and I are wanting all the time, though we don't know it: to be united with him, which means to be united with our Self, to be always embracing him who is our real Self. Rādhā looks at Sri Krishna with great jealousy in her eyes, and Sri Krishna says, "Honey, what's the matter? Why are your eyes so green with jealousy?"

Rādhā answers, "Look at that flute; your lips are always resting on it. When will your lips rest on mine like that always?"

And Sri Krishna, very mischievously, takes the bamboo flute from his lips and shows it to Rādhā, saying, "See! It is empty, so I can fill it with music. You are so full of yourself, dwelling upon yourself all the time, that I cannot send in even one breath."

Mām upāshritāh: "Depend completely on the Lord within." Once when we went to the park, we saw a big circular area in which there were a number of little electrically run cars. Children would get into them, and at the appointed signal, the cars would all go around. Then the little children would call out to their parents, "Look! We are driving all by ourselves!"

All we have to do on the spiritual path is to surrender completely to the Lord within, to identify ourselves completely with him. He is the perfect driver. But instead we keep doing all sorts of things without really going anywhere at all – stepping on the brake, accelerating, and honking the horn, which we are really good at. We just keep honking, making the loudest noise possible. The Lord within says, "Why don't you let me drive the car? You just keep quiet. You can sit by my side, but don't give me instructions about where to go or what speed to use. Just trust me completely."

One of the names of the Lord is *Pārthasārathi. Pārtha* means 'son of Prithā,' which is a name for Arjuna; *sārathi* means 'he who drives the chariot.' The Lord is Arjuna's charioteer and can be ours also. He comes to us and says, "I am such a good driver, let me be your chauffeur. You don't have to give me anything; you don't have to pay my salary; you don't even have to repair your car. Just give me the keys; that's all I want. Come and sit down, be quiet, and keep repeating my name."

This does not mean that we should not take necessary precautions. Just because we are leading the spiritual life, we cannot afford to take traffic risks. We should not be under the impression that because the Lord is in us we can drive against the red light. If we were to ask Sri Krishna, "How do we show our faith in you during rush-hour traffic?" he would say, "It's very simple. Don't try to travel during rush-hour traffic. If you have to, check your car carefully and don't ask the driver questions or get him entangled in arguments." We show our respect for the Lord by taking every reasonable precaution and then saying, "I have done all that I can; now look after me."

Madbhāvam āgatāh: "He enters into my being." As you drive out the love of material things from your heart, overcome selfish attachment to people, and free yourself of fear and anger, the Lord says, "I will fill you with love for everyone, love in which there is not the slightest trace of selfish desire for pleasure or prestige. And I will release the deeper resources in you to translate that love into selfless service."

ये यथा मां प्रपद्यन्ते तांस्तथैव भजाम्यहम् ।
मम वर्त्मानुवर्तन्ते मनुष्याः पार्थ सर्वशः ॥४-११॥

11. As men approach me, so do I receive them. All paths lead to me, O Arjuna.

In medieval India there was a mystic called Kabir, who was claimed both by the Hindus and by the Muslims. Actually he was neither, because once he had experienced the unitive state, no names could confine him. One of his beautiful poems begins with the lines:

Where are you searching for me, friend?
Look! Here am I right within you.
Not in temple, nor in mosque,
Not in Kaaba, nor Kailas,
But here right within you am I.

Tragically enough, in the history of religious institutions, there sometimes has been a gradual forgetfulness of the central teaching of the founder, and an increase in emphasis on dogmas, doctrines, and rituals which are not of primary importance. This preoccupation with superficial matters makes us forget that all religions are founded upon the same mystical experience of the indivisible unity that is the Divine Ground of existence.

In this verse, one of the most marvelous in the Gita, the Lord says, with his infinite love, that it does not matter what religion you profess. Be a Christian. Be a Jew. Be a Buddhist. Be a Hindu, Muslim, or Zoroastrian. The important point is to follow faithfully what the Lord reveals through your particular scripture with all your heart and all your mind and all your strength and all your spirit, and you will become united with the Lord of Love. This verse is perhaps the most superb exposition of the reality of all religions, the reality of all divine incarnations. Here, once and for all, the equality of all religions is emphasized, and we are told that we do not have to change our cultural context or leave the country, religion, or society in which we were born to attain the supreme goal of life and become united with the Lord.

The change that the Lord wants is a change of heart in which we turn our back upon all that is self-willed and separate in us. When the time comes for us to enter the portals of heaven, we are not going to be asked to show our membership card, not even of the Blue Mountain Center. The Lord is not going to ask us to which religion we belong, which church we attended, or who is our favorite padre. What he is going to ask us is, "Do you love me in all those around you? Have you put me first in those around you?" And the only answer we have to make is that, to the extent possible for us, we have been trying our best to submerge our own petty personality in the general joy and welfare of our family, community, and world.

काङ्क्षन्तः कर्मणां सिद्धिं यजन्त इह देवताः ।
क्षिप्रं हि मानुषे लोके सिद्धिर्भवति कर्मजा ॥४-१२॥

12. *Those who desire the pleasures of this world, which are born of action, are really praying for them through their desires. For by action in the world the fulfillment of these desires is quickly obtained.*

In this verse, the Lord lets us in on a big secret: that every desire is a prayer. Those who keep on thinking "I want money," even if they may call themselves atheists or wear a button saying "I don't believe in God," are really saying to the Lord, who is within them, "Please give me money." In this sense, the stock exchange is a temple. Everyone arrives early in the morning to perform the ritual. In the āshram, we meditate only one or two hours a day, but they meditate on money from morning until night, going through all kinds of altered states of consciousness with the advance of the bulls and the bears.

One of the cogent ways of looking upon the smoker, too, is as a religious person. In many oriental religious traditions the worshipper will come stand in front of the shrine, take a sandalwood incense stick, light it, put it in place gently, and pray. And the smoker, too, performs his ritual. He takes out his little packet and ceremoniously strikes the match. He does not just take the match and strike it: there is a way of balancing it and lighting it very artistically; otherwise it is not right. It is not just lighting the cigarette and putting it between his lips. There is a traditional way, sanctified by centuries, which must be followed. The way the smoker really prays is: "Lady Nicotine, if I find favor in your eyes, give me cancer. And if I am not found worthy of that, please don't deny me emphysema."

In everything we do, whenever we desire, we are praying to ourselves, and if our desire becomes deep enough, it will give us the will and show us the way in which we can fulfill it. For example, there is the desire for fame, which Ben Jonson called the "fruit that dead men eat." How many millions of people keep praying for fame! Even among our own ordinary friends, there are likely to be a few with the innate desire for attention. Right from the time that they are three or four, children can develop this desire. Children who have learned a nursery rhyme – "Humpty Dumpty had a great fall" – must recite it in front of their grandfather, their grandmother, and anybody else who is prepared to listen. As our self-knowledge begins to improve, it is very interesting to see in what ways we try to draw attention. In innumerable little acts, from morning until evening, the main motive seems to be to draw attention, prop ourselves up, and make ourselves secure. Sri Krishna will say, "Why do you want to draw attention? You are completely secure, because I am here all the time." Even a temporary awareness that the Lord of Love is always present within us will immediately free us from this deleterious habit of doing things to draw attention.

It is very easy to become famous. But one of the paradoxes of fame is that people who have longed for fame and striven for many years to become famous, to have their picture on the cover page of weekly magazines, after achieving fame come to envy anonymous people like us. It is so good not to be known. It is so refreshing to be anonymous, to live on the blessed anonymous level. Nobody recognizes us, nobody bothers us, everybody ignores us. Well-known figures from all over the world will say how much they deplore publicity. But if I may say so, if we do not want publicity, nobody is going to give it to us. There is no difficulty in remaining obscure, which is the ideal condition for leading the spiritual life.

It is very easy to make money. It is very easy to become famous. If we can unify our desires, even for a finite goal, we can attain it; but once all of our desires are unified, we will find that nothing finite can ever satisfy us.

In the Upanishads, there is a glorious passage that is one of the central principles of mysticism. It sums up the secret of all life: "You are what your deep, driving desire is. As your deep, driving desire is, so is your will. As your will is, so is your deed. As your deed is, so is your destiny." All of us are capable of immense desires, but our capacity to desire and love is unfortunately cut up into innumerable little desires for profit, power, pleasure, and prestige. It is possible, through the dynamic discipline of meditation, to recall our innumerable detrimental desires from the wasteful channels into which they have flowed. And when we recall our desires from the restaurant, from the bank, from our wardrobe, and from all the petty little channels which consume our vital wealth, they all merge into one huge, all-consuming desire that can never be satisfied with anything finite. It is only those who live on the superficial level who can be satisfied by money, material possessions, pleasure, or fame. There is no point in blaming them. They live on the superficial level, and their mouth is very small, just a little parrot beak. Put one cherry in, and they are satisfied. But as our meditation deepens, our capacity to desire grows greater, and as a Hindi proverb says, you cannot satisfy the hunger of a camel by putting a mustard seed in its mouth.

Our capacity to desire is infinite when all of our desires are unified. Nothing finite can ever really satisfy the immense desires of a human being. St. Augustine – who used to paint Carthage red and knew what he was talking about – would say, "Lord, how can I ever find peace anywhere else when I am made to rest in thee?" This is written in every cell of our being, and paraphrasing it in applying it to modern times,

I would say, "When you and I are made to find our joy in the Lord, how can we find it in LSD, in money, in food, in clothes?"

Once when Christine and I were going for our walk, we saw a little girl playing a game I hadn't seen since we left India. She was making mud pies. I was so delighted on seeing a little girl making mud pies, just as they do in all the villages of Kerala, that I watched her for some time and, just to make conversation, asked her, "What are these?"

"Oh," she said, "mud pies" – adding, just as her mother would, "but I don't make them as well as I used to."

I said, "Will you please let me have a few to eat?"

She looked at me and said, "They're horrible! You shouldn't eat mud pies. If you're hungry, you should go home and ask your mother or wife to give you lunch."

Unfortunately, what most of us are trying to do in life is eat mud pies.

The Lord says, "Don't waste your love on money; that love is meant for me. Don't waste your love on your own petty pleasure and profit. This is misusing the capacity for love that I have given you to find me present in everyone, everywhere." The Lord has given us all a wide margin for experimenting with our desires. It requires a certain amount of juggling with the senses to find out they will not bring us abiding joy, but it becomes very tragic when we keep on juggling all our lives: first three balls, then four, then five, until finally we are the expert, juggling with sixteen balls while riding on a horse.

Over and over again, the Gita will say that this is not a moral issue at all; it is an engineering issue. Sri Krishna has given each of us a certain amount of fuel to undertake the long journey to the goal of life. The Lord is not miserly, either, so with all the responsibility of love, he gives us a few extra gallons for making a few detours. If he were an efficiency-minded fuel manager, he would say, "This is all you need, not one drop more." But he loves us so much that he says, "I know the quirks of your mind, and I have given you some extra fuel." He knows that before setting out on our transatlantic flight we will want to go to Milpitas or Walnut Creek once or twice, just to see what is going on. And as long as we make a few trips and find out that there is nothing doing in Milpitas, the Lord is satisfied, and life has served its purpose.

But tragedy strikes when we use all of our great total of fuel in just making little local flights, going around and around in the same old circle, so that when the time comes to try the flight across the Atlantic, we find we do not have any gas. This is what may happen to all of us if we postpone the spiritual search too long.

चातुर्वर्ण्यं मया सृष्टं गुणकर्मविभागशः ।
तस्य कर्तारमपि मां विद्ध्यकर्तारमव्ययम् ॥४-१३॥

13. The distinctions of caste, guna, and karma have come from me. Understanding that I am their cause, realize that I am changeless and beyond all action.

The perennial philosophy in the Hindu tradition interprets the cosmos in terms of three gunas – sattva, rajas, and tamas. *Sattva* means law, *rajas* means energy, and *tamas* means inertia. According to this theory of the gunas, there may be surface differences between all of us, even though at bottom we are one. If you look at the five fingers of your hand, Booker T. Washington used to say, they all look different. Even the names are different. The thumb will say, "Don't call me finger. I am the Thumb." And another will say, "Don't just call me finger. I am Little Finger." Another says, "I point. I am the Index Finger." The vision of people who are living on the physical level, going by physical appearance, living just for the moment, is only on the fingers. They see everything as separate. But as Booker T. Washington put it, if you look below at the palm, you will see there is only one.

It is only on the surface of life that we all look different and feel separate, only on the surface that sometimes, in order to bring about our own satisfaction, we clash with those around us. But if we can only deepen our awareness through the practice of meditation and direct our vision deep below, we shall begin to see that, as Meher Baba has said, "You and I are not 'we'; you and I are One."

The lowest guna is tamas, the state of inertia. This is a state familiar to all of us. When duties call for us to act, we feel inclined to say, "What does it matter? Why not drop out of society? Why not live in my ivory tower, the world forgetting, by the world forgotten?" One of the interesting characteristics of our time is the belief that by dropping out of society and turning our back upon the world, we can become aware of the indivisible unity of all life. But the Bhagavad Gita says emphatically that this is not the path for us to follow, and the language it uses is to the point: it is all right for a rock not to act, it is all right for a stone just to sit, but you and I as human beings have to respond to the challenges of the day and make a contribution in our own way to the solution of its problems. In one of the strong verses of the Gita (3:12), Sri Krishna says the person who refrains from action and drops out of life, when there are such terrible problems pressing upon us, is *stena,* a thief. The Gita is a call to selfless action, not action just for feathering our own nest but for contributing to the greatest extent possible to the welfare of our family, community, and world.

On the campus, the application of this verse is not to procrastinate, not to postpone last quarter's project until next quarter. This only makes the problem worse. When we try to postpone we are making tamas more established instead of transforming it into rajas. When I was a professor at my university in India, during finals time all the usual symptoms that I see in Berkeley used to break out there, too. But there was one additional thing that I used to see in the Hindu temples, particularly in the villages. Many students who had seldom been to the temple would feel a sudden spurt of devotion on the eve of the finals. They would ask the Lord for his blessing and break coconuts in front of Lord Ganesha, who is called "the remover of obstacles." The faculty used to say that when the price of coconuts has gone up, it means that finals have begun. And when the price of coconuts went down, I knew that finals were over and that students were not going to the temple any more. When she saw students going to the temple on the eve of finals, my grandmother used to remind me that not even the Lord would help those who postponed and did not study. She would say that it is good to go to the temple to show our faith in the Lord, but he expects us to study well all the same.

Whenever there is a tendency to postpone, it is good to get down to work immediately whether it is at our job, on the campus, or in the home. When there is something not very pleasant to be done, do it immediately. The pleasant things can wait a little, but the unpleasant things should be done immediately.

Here the practical hint I would give is that when you feel lethargic, unequal to the tasks that are incumbent upon you, go for a good, long walk repeating the mantram. This can change your attitude in less than an hour's time. It is the initial leap that you have to make. You just have to press hard on the arms of your chair and leap like a mustang. The initial leap should give you the momentum to go for a long, fast walk, and once the blood has started spinning in your veins, the lungs have started going strongly, and the rhythm of the mantram has started echoing in your consciousness, in an hour's time your attitudes change. There is no longer what you thought was a permanent resistance to work, no longer the diffidence in yourself. Even to prepare for the most important occasion, I would suggest a good, long walk repeating the mantram.

The body is meant for motion, but in our modern way of life, we have almost begun to forget this. In the morning we move about from the bedroom to the dining room where we sit. Then we go into the garage, get into the car, and sit until we reach our office, where we sit again at our desk. We come back in the evening and sit in front of the bridge table or television set. It is helpful to remember that the heart is not what the poets represent it to be – a delicate, brittle instrument. It is a sturdy old pump, and it has an immense capacity to keep itself well, to keep itself strong, provided we obey the simple, sensible rules of good health: eat moderately, eat only what is nourishing, eat only when hungry, keep walking whenever there is the chance, and keep repeating the name of the Lord whenever there is agitation, fear, anxiety, or conflict. If we observe these simple rules, we shall see in our own life how easy it is to be well.

The way to transform tamas into rajas is through activity. Then slowly we have to transform rajas into sattva; we must begin to direct all of our energies to the selfless service of those around us. We can harness our energy and restlessness and direct it to the supreme goal. Whenever we feel restless, that is the time not to run away, but to sit down, meditate, and sink down into the depths of our own consciousness.

The third stage, sattva, is known by its characteristics of serenity, tranquility, and detachment, which all of us need, particularly today in our troubled times. In sattva we work arduously but not for our own personal aggrandizement. Even in sattva, however, we still believe that we are the doer; therefore we are still involved in the fruits of action. It is not enough if we attain the sattvic level, because the supreme purpose of life according to the scriptures of all religions is to realize the Lord of Love who is present in everyone. Those who have become aware of the Lord are said to have gone beyond the three gunas. They have realized the unchanging reality, the indivisible unity which underlies the world of change. In every religion there are those who have gone beyond the three gunas, like Jesus the Christ, the Buddha, or, in our own times, Mahatma Gandhi, who is an inspiring example of one who transcended the limitations of space, time, and causality to become the perfect instrument of the Lord.

Applying the categories of the gunas to human evolution, the Gita says that the least evolved are the apathetic who do not act at all. Higher are those who act, even though part selfishly. Higher than they are those who act selflessly, but the highest are those who have realized the indivisible unity of all life, who have seen the Lord within all. This spiritual evolution is the original basis of what is called the caste system in India. But though in ancient times a man could move from one caste to another depending upon his personal merits, the system became rigid so that a man's caste was determined only by birth, not by merit. In modern times the caste system in India became a great source of suffering and exploitation to all of us. It was a crying evil which Mahatma Gandhi tackled with his indomitable weapon of nonviolence, so that today the system is dying out in the cruel form it had gradually acquired over the centuries.

In the early days, one of the questions that I had to face often on the platform was, "What about the caste system?" I would ask in turn, "Where?" Every country has its own caste system wherever there is exploitation or discrimination, whether because of nationality, religion, property, race, color, education, or sex. There is one kind of caste system in India, another kind in Europe, a third in America, and a fourth in Africa; everywhere there is a caste system as long as we do not treat all those around us with complete love and respect, knowing the Lord is present in everyone.

न मां कर्माणि लिम्पन्ति न मे कर्मफले स्पृहा ।
इति मां यो ऽभिजानाति कर्मभिर्न स बध्यते ॥४-१४॥

14. Actions do not cling to me because I am not attached to their results. He who understands this and practices it lives in freedom.

In this verse, Sri Krishna, the Lord of Love present in all hearts, gives us the secret of selfless action, called karma yoga. Anyone, according to Sri Krishna, who pursues personal pleasure and profit, anyone who indulges in action for money, for material possessions, power, or prestige, is a prisoner in action.

This is a marvelous concept which most of us cannot even grasp, because we live in the prison of the ego, compelled and driven into action for the sake of money, material possessions, power, and pleasure. As long as we continue to act while propelled by these personal motives of self-interest, we are not free agents but robots, automata being pushed from behind by forces out of our control. We can live selfishly, doing as much as we like and working very hard, but we know from the Gita that this action will only imprison us more and more. There may come a time, later in life, when the walls of this prison have become so high we cannot climb over them at all.

As long as we are living only for ourselves, to make a little money or to acquire a little prestige, we cannot have access to the deeper resources within us. On this point, my grandmother would sum up the message of the Gita in a few simple words. She would say that Sri Krishna gives me two ways to live. One is for myself, and when

I live for myself I wither away and die. The other is to live for those around me, no matter how painful it may be at the outset, and to widen the circle more and more until it at last embraces all creation. With this path, the more I live for others the more resources will come into my hands.

A few days ago, on the way to San Francisco, we saw the new arrangement at the tollgate of the Bay Bridge. The traffic was particularly heavy, bumper to bumper, but there was one lane marked Exact Change where you keep your change ready, throw it in the basket, and shoot through. There are some rare people who have this kind of ego. It is just little and crumpled up from living for their parents, their partner, their children, their family, their community, country, and world. They have always been thinking about others and never about themselves, so their ego is tiny like a peanut. In life they go through the Exact Change line, throw their ego into the basket, and shoot through. The others come with their egos on trucks – sometimes huge trucks with two trailers, which are so large that they have to wait for all the other trucks in front to pass through first.

On the spiritual path, we have one choice, whether we live in a rich or a poor family, whether we are ignorant or learned, whether we are healthy or ailing: shall we go after what pleases us, or shall we go after what promises to bring the increasing happiness of all those around us? When we work under the compulsion of self-will, we are preventing the Lord from using us as instruments of his work. But if we let the Lord act through us and realize that he is the operator, we go beyond the law of karma, no longer to be bound by actions.

एवं ज्ञात्वा कृतं कर्म पूर्वैरपि मुमुक्षुभिः ।
कुरु कर्मैव तस्मात्त्वं पूर्वैः पूर्वतरं कृतम् ॥४-१५॥

15. Knowing this truth and desiring liberation, the spiritual aspirants of ancient times engaged in action. Perform action in the manner of those ancient sages.

Sri Krishna now tells Arjuna about *mumukshu,* which means 'he who is very eager to have awareness of the indivisible unity of life.' It is this eagerness to know for ourselves, in our own consciousness, that parents and children are one, husband and wife are one, boyfriend and girlfriend are one, friend and friend are one, and even friend and enemy are one, that will deepen our meditation, strengthen our willpower, and enable us to turn our back upon what is petty and selfish in all of us. Whenever people have deeply desired liberation, whenever they have wanted to realize the Lord of Love who is ever present in all creatures, they have always learned to act selflessly, to live for others, and to turn their back upon whatever selfish satisfaction they may have wanted in their earlier days.

Whatever mistakes you may have committed in the past, once you turn your back upon personal profit and pleasure and set your eyes on the shining goal, then the past begins to fall away from you. Thus, Sri Krishna adds, you, too, have the latent, seldom-suspected capacity within yourself to change yourself completely, to become mumukshu. It is this divine unpredictability which is the mark of the mystic, and in everyone there is this capacity. Through the practice of meditation, one of the most delightful pastimes you develop is the capacity to change your habits at will. You can take tea and become a tea addict, like Dr. Johnson, for a few months, and when your body is beginning to clamor for tea in the morning, you can just give it a cup of coffee. There is no "Et tu, Brute?" Then you give it coffee for a number of weeks, and when the body has forgotten tea and has become addicted to coffee, you give it decaf. This is how you win the freedom of the body.

The Gita will say, in marvelous language, even good habits are ties. First you get rid of bad habits by developing good habits. You cannot get rid of bad habits by saying "Go, go, go"; you get rid of bad habits by bringing in good habits which will force them out, and you don't have to push because there won't be any room to put their sleeping bag down. And then, the giants of all religions say, even the good habits have to go, because any habit is a form of rigid conditioning; any habit keeps you from freedom.

My wife and I used to go around Lake Merritt every day when we were in Oakland. We had been used to going around clockwise, and you know the feet; they almost get automatic: you get there and they immediately turn in the same direction. So one day I just turned in the opposite direction instead. Even in little things you can experience this thrill of liberating yourself from your habits. When you want to sit in a very comfortable chair, go and sit down in a very uncomfortable one. This is how you free yourself.

A friend of ours, who is much more daring than I am, once went into an ice cream parlor and said, "What is the worst kind of ice cream you have?"

The proprietor answered, "Licorice."

"Bring a bowlful, please."

The proprietor gasped. "You're sure? One spoonful may be enough."

She said, "Please bring a bowlful of licorice ice cream, and leave it to me."

She disposed of every vestige of it, and when she asked for the bill, the proprietor looked at her with awe and said, "It's on the house."

This is one of the secrets the mystics tell us: when you free yourself from the tyranny of likes and dislikes, you can enjoy everything. With freedom from the tyranny of likes and dislikes comes freedom from allergy, which has become the bane of millions. Allergy is often a protest by the nervous system: "I have strong likes and strong dislikes; don't try to trifle with me." This is allergy. Gradually you can so free your nervous system that you can juggle with your likes and dislikes, which means you have gone beyond the law of duality where things are divided into pleasure and pain, success and defeat, birth and death. It is freedom from the tyranny of pain and pleasure, likes and dislikes, that will eventually give us the strength to realize *moksha,* or the indivisible unity of life, in our own consciousness.

किं कर्म किमकर्मेति कवयो ऽप्यत्र मोहिताः ।
तत्ते कर्म प्रवक्ष्यामि यज्ज्ञात्वा मोक्ष्यसे ऽशुभात् ॥४-१६॥

16. What is action and what is inaction? This question has confused the greatest sages. I will give you the secret of action, with which you can free yourself from bondage.

Here Sri Krishna comforts Arjuna by telling him that he needn't think badly of himself because he lacks discrimination. Even some of the great sages lacked discrimination when they started on the spiritual path. Arjuna says, "Wait! Great sages? Maybe one day I too will become a great sage!" And he is consoled by the way that Sri Krishna says that even the *kavis,* the great sages, were sometimes confused about action and inaction.

Then Sri Krishna adds, "I will give you practical hints which will enable you to cultivate this discrimination. And" – to put his advice in the modern idiom – "remember, *yaj jnātvā mokshyase 'shubhāt:* these words are not only for your diary. They are not to be put on buttons or on stickers for the back of your chariot. They are to be practiced. You have to carry them into your daily life, even though it may be unpleasant or even distressing."

कर्मणो ह्यपि बोद्धव्यं बोद्धव्यं च विकर्मणः ।
अकर्मणश्च बोद्धव्यं गहना कर्मणो गतिः ॥४-१७॥

17. You must understand what is action, what actions should be avoided, and what is inaction. For the true nature of action is difficult to grasp.

Sri Krishna, the Lord of Love present in all hearts, tells us how best we can use our life to alleviate the many woes to which the world has become subject during the course of the centuries. In understanding this secret of karma yoga, or selfless action, the word *karma* has to be understood not only as meaning deeds, but also words and thoughts.

Even words are actions, and we all know from the advertising world the power of the word. Those word wizards who coin slogans which can even come with us into our sleep are, to use Aldous Huxley's words, "the most influential of popular moralists and philosophers." Some of these advertising slogans are the surest proof of the negative power of words. Anyone who doubts the efficacy of the mantram should simply observe the power of the advertising slogan.

Even thinking is a subtle form of action. Sigmund Freud has said that thought is action in rehearsal. When we are thinking angry thoughts against somebody, we actually are throwing abstract rocks at them. Sometimes I think a rock does not hurt so much as a harsh thought. We know how long people to whom we have unfortunately shown anger can suffer because of resentment and hostility. And we, too, suffer because we are violating the fundamental law of the unity of life.

People who think selfish thoughts can really show us that, as the mystics say, thinking is action. Living in a place where people are always thinking about their selfish satisfactions is living in an atmosphere worse than smog. The worst kind of smog is ego smog, and we have only to live with very egocentric people to know how deleterious it is. When we associate with agitated people, we come home so agitated that we cannot sit and have our dinner; we cannot go to sleep in peace. We cannot understand: in the afternoon we were feeling so placid and so composed; what happened to make us so agitated? Then we suddenly see: we went out with that fellow. We can all testify to this. When we are with agitated people, if we are not fairly calm within ourselves, naturally we participate in their agitation.

Conversely, in a very beautiful manner, when we are agitated, when we want to express our agitation by agitating a few more around us, we may go by mistake to the house of a serene person. Quietly established in himself, he comes out and says, "You want to agitate me? Come in." We go right in and start agitating, recapitulating what wrongs the world has done to us, how we have always been innocent. But halfway we begin to say that maybe sometimes we do make mistakes, maybe sometimes we do provoke people. Our host is still not saying anything.

He is just looking with shining eyes of love and understanding, and by the time the interview ends, we have become calm. We come out and don't know what has happened to our agitation. "Is it the meal I had that may have corrected my agitation?" It takes a long time to understand that when we associate with people we also participate in their mental states. In Sanskrit there is a very good saying, *Samsargād doshagunam bhavati:* "By association we can become good and selfless, and by association we can become bad and selfish."

Let us remember that we cannot avoid action by staying at home. Even if we tie ourselves up in a chair and take a vow not to move for the whole day, we are acting inside, and thoughts can be action in a very subtle form. In order to be entirely free in our action, the mystics say, thought has to be controlled at its origin. The Buddha has said in the Dhammapada that all we are is the result of what we have thought. The thoughts that germinate in the depths of our consciousness slowly drive us into action. Action, therefore, begins at the level of thinking, and the purpose of meditation is to control action at the source.

Vikarma is action which is prohibited to us because it inflicts suffering on others. Vikarma is wrong action. Any action which is born of anger, fear, or greed is vikarma. The Gita will say that any action that is propelled by anger is likely to bring sorrow not only to those against whom the action is directed, but also to the doer. When we are angry, most of us are prompted to action. Immediately tamas is transformed into rajas. Even the most phlegmatic person, when roused to anger, will leap up and start acting right and left, bringing suffering on everyone around.

In order to act wisely, we have to be free from anger, free from hostility, free from resentment. Unfortunately, even in the efforts being made to banish violence from our midst, I sometimes see an element of resentment and hatred. In order to counter violence, we should not get violent at all. We can deal effectively with violence by being persuasive, courteous, and considerate, and yet very, very firm. Gentleness and friendly persuasion can be effective with all human beings. The moment I get angry, you are going to get more angry; and when you get more angry, I am going to get most angry. This is what happens when we meet anger with anger. We move further and further apart; and two people who stood only two yards apart at the outset, by the time the peace negotiations are finished, have moved two hundred yards apart. Jesus has said that it is by bearing with people who provoke us, by blessing those who curse us, by doing good to those who hate us, that we can win them over. My humble conviction is that there is no human being who lacks this capacity to love and respond to love, because the Lord lives in all of us.

Just as action born of anger leads to disaster, so do actions done out of fear and greed. When we do things out of fear, we are likely to be far off the mark. When we do things out of the third propelling force, greed, this too leads to disaster. Actions motivated by these three do not benefit anyone.

The third term used is *akarma,* 'inaction.' When we empty ourselves of all selfishness and realize that the Lord within is the operator, all action falls away. We do not act; the Lord acts through us. Whenever Gandhi was asked how he was able to free India from the political domination of the greatest empire the world has known without firing a shot, he would reply that all he did was empty himself of his selfishness and separateness to become a humble instrument in the hands of the Lord.

This is the real meaning of inaction, but we do not achieve this state by merely refusing to act. There is a tremendous need for action in all of us ordinary human beings. The choice that we have is: shall we act under the compulsion of self-will, bringing about our own downfall and the downfall of others, or shall we act as an instrument of the Lord, contributing to the welfare of our family, community, country, and world?

कर्मण्यकर्म यः पश्येदकर्मणि च कर्म यः ।
स बुद्धिमान्मनुष्येषु स युक्तः कृत्स्नकर्मकृत् ॥४-१८॥

18. They who see action where there is inaction, and inaction where there is action, live in wisdom. Their consciousness is unified, and their every act is done with complete awareness.

Here Sri Krishna says a strange thing to Arjuna: "When a person becomes united with me, when he becomes an instrument in my hands, then even though he acts, he does not act." Those who have surrendered themselves to the Lord do not act; the Lord acts through them.

This reminds me of when we held weekly meetings on the University of California campus in Berkeley. Curious things used to take place on campus in those days. One day, as I was leaving the meditation meeting, I saw a group of demonstrators being hauled away by the police. They would struggle for a while and then suddenly go limp. Then there was no struggle, no effort, and evidently no resistance at all. This was very protective, and I saw what effect it had on the people who were dragging those students away. It took away all their animosity, for what is the use of dragging a person who doesn't object to being dragged? In this verse Sri Krishna tells Arjuna, "When the ego tries to drag you away, go limp." When spiritual awareness increases, you can act from morning to night with great power and in the evening come back so fresh, so vital, and so light on your feet that you say, "Oh, I am not tired. I haven't been acting; I've just been going limp."

For me, Gandhi is the perfect example of the statement that a person filled with the love of God, practicing the presence of God, never acts at all. Once when I went to Gandhiji's āshram, as I walked about in the neighborhood of his little cottage, I saw the unending stream of political leaders from Britain and India who came to him throughout the day. I was wondering how he was able to bear the pressure of these significant interviews which would change the relations of two great countries, and in the evening, I expected to see a tired, irascible, very impatient man coming out. Instead I saw a smiling figure who looked as if he had been playing bingo with children all day. I could not believe my eyes, because I was used to the idea that if we work eight hours we should be tense and ready to be irritated by anybody who tries to be nice to us. But he was completely untouched by his action.

Every day in our work, as long as it is not at the expense of others, we can learn to avoid tension and pressure when attending to the most challenging tasks that life may bring us. For most of us, tension has become a badge of action. In fact, we usually expect those who have engaged in intense action during the day to complain about their ulcers. Tension need not accompany action; we can act free from any tension, any movement in the mind, any ripple of consciousness. Once Gandhi was asked by Western friends, "Mr. Gandhi, you have been working fifteen hours a day for fifty years for these helpless millions of India. Why don't you take a long holiday?" Gandhi replied, "I am always on holiday."

When a person has made himself an instrument in the hands of the Lord as Gandhi did, then Sri Krishna says, "He is not acting at all. I act through him." In the Gita this is called "inaction in action." Conversely there are people who say they want to drop out of society and go away from the world. Such people, even if they try to keep quiet in the midst of the woods, are still active. All of us are active everywhere, and all of us influence our environment everywhere. Parents influence their children all the time by their attitudes and by their ways. Even when we refuse to act, Sri Krishna maintains, we influence people by our apathy.

The practice of meditation demands intense action. Without energetic, intense, selfless action, the practice of meditation can become quite dangerous, and we can become caught inside. To the orthodox Hindu the working out of bad karma through good karma is an essential part of spiritual progress. As long as we have a heavy load of unfavorable karma on our back, it will not be possible for us to wake up when we plunge into the depths of the unconscious. In some of the most profound stages of meditation, when we have touched the floor of consciousness, we are like divers who have gone fathoms deep to stand on the sea bed. Similar to the tremendous pressures bearing down on the diver is the pressure that bears down on the person who reaches the unconscious in meditation. When we reach the depths of the unconscious, we naturally become completely unconscious, but we must learn to become conscious at that time. Now to give a little preview of this magnificent climax of meditation, when we are standing there with this vast sea of consciousness pressing down upon us, instead of being frightened or paralyzed, or becoming completely unconscious, we must be able to repeat the mantram in the depths of our unconscious. If we can do this, we are worthy of becoming aware of the Lord.

यस्य सर्वे समारम्भाः कामसंकल्पवर्जिताः ।
ज्ञानाग्निदग्धकर्माणं तमाहुः पण्डितं बुधाः ॥४-१९॥

19. The awakened sages call a man wise when all his undertakings are free from anxiety about results; all his selfish desires have been consumed in the fire of knowledge.

The Gita is an imperative call to action in which the Lord insists that none of us can afford to lie here inactive while the world burns in turmoil and violence. If we would all make the maximum contribution that lies within our power to conquer violence, we would see the reign of peace, of good will, and of love. It is natural for the vast majority of us, as we look around the world and see the conflagration threatening to engulf us, to throw up our hands in despair and say, "What can I do?" "But," Sri Krishna will ask, "what is it that you cannot do?"

If we realize that in the depths of our consciousness dwells the Lord of Love, who is infinite love, infinite wisdom, and infinite capacity for selfless service, none of us would ever feel despondent or defeated. The feeling of being inadequate to the call made by life upon us, the Gita says precisely, is caused by our anxiety about results. We get involved in the results. We want to say, "See what I have accomplished." We want posterity to turn the pages of history to see how many are devoted to our exploits. The secret of all action, as embodied by Mahatma Gandhi in his own masterly personal life, is to select a selfless goal – it does not matter how big or impossible – and do everything we can, in the face of challenges, difficulties, or persecution, to move towards that goal. It may not be possible for one person to achieve that goal, but the work will be continued and supplemented, becoming larger and larger until it reaches fulfillment.

The word used here is *budhāh,* 'those who are awake.' These awakened ones would not say that you and I are acting. They would say we are only chasing our tail, going round and round in ineffective action, wasting our time and energy. Only those who turn their backs upon their own self-will and dedicate all their energy, time, resources – everything – to the Lord in the service of him in everyone around, can be said to be truly wise.

If we look at the so-called great achievements of people who have made their name in history, we will find the motive often may have been ambition, or prestige, or the lust for power. The Gita says such people do not really make a lasting contribution to the world. This is particularly true of the lust for power, which is perhaps the most corrupting of all lusts. As Lord Acton once said, "Power tends to corrupt and absolute power corrupts absolutely." When we go after personal power, in the early days we might really want to make a contribution to our country and to world peace, but as power begins to intoxicate us, all these honest motives recede until finally we want power for the sake of power, for imposing our self-will on everyone around.

Sometimes after dinner at Ramagiri we talk about current issues, and the other day we were having a discussion about the concept of leadership in modern politics. I pointed out that the concept of leadership placed before us by Gandhi is that of leaders who turn their backs upon personal power, who seek not to enjoy the perquisites of office, and who think not of their image or of what posterity will read about them in history books. We all know how many times the occupants of office do things simply for ensuring victory in the next election. In India, too, it was not uncommon for us to see leaders coming on the platform to harangue us about what they were going to do for our benefit, what they were going to do for our progress, only to ensure their personal re-election. The concept that Gandhiji placed before the whole world is that the best leaders are those who are not interested in themselves but only in making their maximum contribution to the welfare of the people and the world. I give Mahatma Gandhi as an unvarying example of a great leader in politics who has worked for his people and his country without any thought of profit, prestige, or power.

People like Mahatma Gandhi, according to Sri Krishna, are those whose selfish desires, whose personal motives of profit, prestige, and power, have been consumed to ashes in the fire of knowledge. Sri Krishna, very compassionately, is saying that those who aim for office or anything else only for themselves are ignorant. They are ignorant of the most basic truth, that you and I are one.

त्यक्त्वा कर्मफलासङ्गं नित्यतृप्तो निराश्रयः ।
कर्मण्यभिप्रवृत्तो ऽपि नैव किं चित्करोति सः ॥४-२०॥

20. The wise man, ever satisfied, has abandoned all external supports. His security is unaffected by the results of his action; even while acting he is only an instrument.

When you have directed your life towards a selfless goal, then *Tyaktvā karmaphalāsangam:* "Do not get entangled in the result." In order to undertake the great work for peace that is dear to all of us, we should have an adequate sense of detachment from the results of our work. If we are going to get agitated every time there is a rebuff, every time there is a reverse, we ourselves will become violent. As we all know, sometimes even the demonstrators against violence become violent. In the words of the Compassionate Buddha: "Hatred does not cease by hatred at any time. Hatred ceases by love. This is an unalterable law." Similarly, we can say today: "Violence will not cease by violence. Violence ceases by nonviolence. This is an unalterable law." In order to win over opposition, to bring people together, we have to be serene and compassionate, whatever the vicissitudes of life may bring us. Mahatma Gandhi was at his best when seemingly defeated. He used to say it was from prison that he struck his hardest bargains. Most of us look upon defeat and reverses as weakening us; but in karma yoga, every time we are defeated we seem to go deeper into our consciousness to bring out greater resources. When we think we have been defeated, when we come home and tell our family that we have been beaten, Sri Krishna may say, "In my book I say the guy is doing well." In order to grow, in order to strengthen our muscles, we need opposition.

Defeat is found very often in the lives of selfless people as an opening into opportunity. The Gita says that when you follow the spiritual path, living for others, very often there come to you increased challenges, increased threats, to make you go deeper and deeper into your consciousness. If there were no difficulties, you would only be skimming on the surface of life. Gandhiji, in a rare statement in which he gave himself away, said, "I love storms." It is a thrill to be in the midst of a storm when you are keeping the welfare of those around you first, when the lightning is playing about your eyes, and thunder is crashing in your ears. When everything is against you, you feel so sure that the Lord is within you that you have only to put your hand out and say, "Hold me; my morale is sinking." It is not that Gandhiji was not afraid. He could get as afraid as you and I do under the pressure of circumstances, but he always knew how to say, "Please take my hand. See, it's trembling." And Sri Krishna loves trembling fingers when they are stretched towards him. He does not like those who proudly say, "Feel my hand. How steady it is!" When you surrender to him – when you say, "By myself I am so weak, so incapable of facing opposition, but with the Lord supporting me, what opposition is there that I will not face?" – then he comes to help you.

Nityatripta means 'always satisfied.' When we are engaged in a great struggle, for example against violence, one day we will gain a small victory. Then we want to celebrate, sing and dance, and get very elated. But on the following day there may come defeat, and on that evening there will be wailing and gnashing of teeth. Here Sri Krishna says,

"What kind of equanimity are you observing? When there is victory, you should go about quietly repeating my name and at night peacefully fall asleep. There is nothing to be elated about. And when there is a reverse, why gnash your teeth? It's not good for them. At that time, too, repeat my name and in the evening go to bed and fall asleep in the mantram."

Every movement in the mind is insecurity. Every movement of the mind, whether it is caused by ambition, anger, fear, lust, or any other agitation, alienates us from our real nature. This is why the Bible says, "Be still, and know that I am God." When the mind is still, we have gone beyond the mind. In meditation we try to still the mind, which is a very difficult thing to do. We may have been meditating for half an hour, and the mind is fairly calm. "Well, the mind is still," we think. "I don't have to concentrate now." We relax our vigilance and immediately pandemonium bursts loose.

At no time should we allow the mind to be agitated. Agitation of the mind prevents us from releasing our deeper resources for creative action. *Nityatripta* also conveys the idea, given elsewhere in the Gita, that in order to be united with the Lord, in order to discover the indivisible unity of life, the mind has to be serene and waveless. In the Gita (12:17) Krishna says the person who never gets excited is very dear to him. This word "exciting," that has become part and parcel of our advertising paraphernalia, is a very dangerous word, because its other side is "depressing." We usually see only the facade. But whenever we see excitement, we should say, "Turn your back. Let me see what is written on it: *d-e-p-r-e-s-s-i-o-n*." This is the lettering on the back of excitement. If we could have excitement without depression, I would recommend it for everybody, but so far no one has ever succeeded in separating the two, and according to the Gita this separation is not likely to be effected, not even by our best psychologists or technologists.

When John F. Kennedy was being installed as president, and all of us were looking forward eagerly to what he had to say, I remember a journalist going up and asking him, "Mr. President, you must be greatly excited today." It was a very mature reply, in the Gita tradition, that he gave: "Excited, no. Very interested." This is the mature attitude. After all, one is likely to be very interested when one is moving into the White House. This mature equanimity that all of us can learn to have is not lack of interest. It is the mystic who is interested in everything. There is a photograph of Gandhiji looking through a microscope, and I do not think even Louis Pasteur could have had that expression of concentration. Gandhi was interested in everything, but not excited by anything at all.

When you and I have a tendency to get excited, especially when good things happen, that is the time to go out for a walk, repeating the mantram. When your ship comes home, when you see it moving up to the pier, don't stand there clapping wildly. Get off the pier and go for a long walk repeating *Rāma, Rāma, Rāma* or *Jesus, Jesus, Jesus*. Otherwise, if you keep on saying, "My ship has come home! My ship has come home!" before you know where you are, you will not be on the pier; you will be floating about on cloud number nine. It is all right riding on cloud nine, but the next day you will be skin diving. Sri Krishna tells Arjuna, "I am not asking you to avoid excitement. But when depression comes, as it must, don't ask, 'Why did this happen to me?'"

In order to understand the powerlessness of the intellect, talk to people who are just beginning to feel depressed. If we ask people who have some self-knowledge, "Why do you look like that? Why are your eyes so glassy? Why are you so indrawn? And why can't I hear some of those old chuckles?" they will reply, "Oh, I am just feeling a bit low."

And I have often suggested, "You have a bright intellect. Say 'I am not feeling depressed,' and pull yourself out."

"It doesn't work," is their answer.

At that time, go for a tearing walk, burning up the sidewalk. Walk as fast as you can, repeating the mantram, and see what just one hour of walking repeating *Rāma, Rāma, Rāma* can do. When you come back, you may even have forgotten what you were depressed about. This is a comment on the powerlessness of the intellect as compared to the immense power of the holy name.

The next objective is even more severe: *nirāshraya*, 'without any support.' In order to be the instrument of the Lord, we must let go of all supports other than the Lord himself. Now we are prepared to let our right hand go free, provided we can hold on with our left. We all are trying to hold on to something. If it is not money, it is food, or cigarettes, or alcohol. Others try to draw support and security from prestige and power. This is the human condition. We have to hold on to something, and the Lord says, "Why don't you hold on to me? I am right inside you. You don't have to walk miles in the rain. You don't have to go searching for anything. You don't have to work hard to make money. Just hold on to me and say, 'Let me be firm.'" The Lord says to all of us through Arjuna, "Let go of all your supports. Throw yourself at my feet, and I will protect you."

Almost all of us will call to the Lord, "Hold me, help me," but at the same time we continue to hold on to external supports. My grandmother drove this home to me when we went together to see a ballet in Kathakali based on a very moving episode in the *Mahābhārata*. Draupadī, Arjuna's wife, is being stripped of her clothes in front of a large number of courtiers by a revengeful enemy of her husband. Draupadī, whose honor is being violated, cries aloud, "Krishna, Krishna, Krishna, protect me!"

Then, on another part of the stage, Sri Krishna is seen quietly seated playing on his flute. Sri Krishna's queen gets very angry at her lord and says, "What kind of god are you? Here is your devotee, a loving, beautiful woman, being stripped naked in front of a hundred jeering enemies, and you are seated here, playing on your flute. Have you no love in your heart?"

Sri Krishna takes the flute from his lips very leisurely and pointing with it says, "Look." Krishna's queen looks down from their heavenly vantage point and sees that Draupadī is holding on to her sari with one hand while she stretches the other up towards the Lord in supplication. For a while Sri Krishna and his queen both look at Draupadī, until suddenly she lets go of her sari and joins both hands in prayer. It is a very thrilling moment, and when the whole gathering of courtiers gasps with terrible suspense, Sri Krishna sends down an unending sari. My grandmother, even though she must have seen this scene enacted many times, was so thrilled that she said, "Go on! Keep pulling the sari. Let us see you exhaust it!" And the more the enemy pulled, the more sari there was.

On the spiritual path we are likely to say to the Lord, "We know you are the citadel of security, Lord, but we would prefer to keep 25 percent in shares, 25 percent in currency, and 50 percent in you." We shall find that it is this reservation, this looking backward, that keeps us from making rapid progress on the spiritual path. Never has anyone succeeded in seeing the Lord except by surrendering completely to him.

Those who are the same in victory and defeat, who are always loyal to the goal, come obstacle, come ordeal, and who do not depend upon any external support, do not act at all; the Lord acts through them. The Lord will act through us if we will only empty ourselves of all self-will, of all separateness. This is what we do when we truly love. When a husband loves his wife more than himself, or a wife loves her husband more than herself, this is what they are doing; they are emptying themselves of themselves. This can be done in every relationship, and we all have the opportunity to empty ourselves of our selfishness in our relationships with our parents, partner, and friends. Someone once asked me, "Supposing there is someone who doesn't have any of these?" I said, "How about enemies? Who is there who doesn't have enemies?" It is possible for all of us, through unremitting endeavor and the practice of meditation, to empty ourselves of all that is selfish, self-willed, and separate, so that we can make a great contribution to the amelioration of the lamentable conditions that exist in the world today.

निराशीर्यतचित्तात्मा त्यक्तसर्वपरिग्रहः ।
शारीरं केवलं कर्म कुर्वन्नाप्नोति किल्बिषम् ॥४-२१॥

21. Free from expectations and all sense of possession, with mind and body firmly controlled by the Self, such a one does not incur sin by the performance of physical action.

To be free in action, to make his greatest contribution to the welfare of society, Sri Krishna tells Arjuna *nirāshī:* he should have no expectations. It is a difficult concept for us to understand, because we think that if we do not have expectations, we will have no motive for action. But as long as we are expecting something, life can hold us hostage. Quiet reflection can bring home the profound wisdom of these words: if you want to go through life free, do not expect anything.

Sri Krishna says, "Do not go about begging of life, 'Give me this; give me that.' Then you are bound. Say instead, 'I don't want anything, Lord. If you want to give me defeat, I am not afraid. If you want to give me victory, I won't object.'" This is the stature that the human being can reach by becoming aware of the Lord of Love within. We can function with complete freedom, not dependent on what comes to us in the way of success or defeat.

We have only to examine ourselves to see what a catalog of expectations we have in life. Accordingly, "disappointed" is one of the most frequently used words in our vocabulary. Almost every day there is some disappointment because, as the Gita implies, expectation and disappointment go together. In very loving language, Sri Krishna tells us through Arjuna, "I don't want you to be beggars. You are my children, inheritors of all my wisdom, love, and beauty. There is no need for you to go about hankering for success or apprehensive of defeat." When we take up a task which contributes to at least one person's welfare – without asking, "Will this bring me promotion? Will this send my image down in history as a great man? Will this bring me that prize, or this profit?" – then we work without anxiety. To work in this way, without expectation, it is necessary to have complete faith in the Lord of Love within, who always sends us what is good for our spiritual development.

If we are to work and live in freedom, our body and mind must listen to us. When we sit down in meditation we are slowly teaching the body and mind to listen to us implicitly, to obey even our gentle hints. In the early days of meditation it is likely that the body will go to sleep. This is its idea of security. In order to train our body to keep awake in the deeper stages of meditation, every time we get sleepy we must draw away from our back support, sit up straight, and make the maximum effort possible to keep awake. For everybody at some time there is the problem of drowsiness. As concentration deepens, as the words of the inspirational passage begin to go slowly, the neuromuscular system relaxes. To see this happening during meditation we have only to look at the faces of people who have been tense; slowly they start smiling and the lips begin to open in beatitude. It pains me to say that this is the time when we should jut our chin forward and sit sternly erect.

As for the mind, for everyone the path of meditation begins with a wealth of distractions, because we have always let the mind have its own way. The Compassionate Buddha used to remark that there is nothing so disobedient as an undisciplined mind. When we do not want to think about something, the mind will say, "That's exactly what I am going to think about, and you can't do anything about it." None of us like harboring resentful thoughts, and we all have known times when hostile thoughts have kept boiling in our minds and we have tried to tell the mind, "This is not good for me." But the mind says, "It's good for *me!* It may not be good for you, but I like resentment. I like agitation, because that's what makes me come to life."

For a long, long time in meditation the main effort is in disciplining the mind, in bringing it back whenever it wanders away, in keeping it on the words of the passage in spite of all its attempts to get away from them. This is drastic and very dull discipline, but it will pay the richest dividends in the long run. Even if you sit for an hour in meditation doing nothing but bringing your mind back to the passage sixty times in sixty minutes, you have made progress on the spiritual path. Every time the mind runs out, you run after it, pick it up from the restaurant, or the bank, or the movie theater, and bring it back. Then, the moment you are not looking, the mind has run out again. You again run after it and bring it back. It is just like following a little child. For some years in meditation there is a real test of your patience. There are no thrills. There are no visions. There is no rapture. There is just plain tedium. If your desire for the Lord is great, you will put up with all this cheerfully, but if you are meditating just because, for example, the Beatles did it, your enthusiasm will not last long.

In the next word, *tyaktasarvaparigraha,* the Lord says, "You must not own anything. I am the owner. Don't try to put your tag 'mine' on anything. Don't ever say 'This is my exclusive property.'" We own nothing because the Lord is the owner. He is the landlord; we are just transients. Here the practical application is that only when we are detached from things can we use them wisely. Those who are fond of money cannot use it wisely. Often rich people unfortunately use money to their own detriment, because they do not know how to use it for their own and others' benefit. This does not mean we should give away everything. Sri Krishna is saying we should not be attached to our wealth and material possessions. It is possible for a millionaire to be completely detached in his villa in the south of France, while it is possible for a poor man to be attached to his shack with violent egoism. It is the attitude that matters here.

In the final stages of meditation, we become very eager to unify our love, to give everything to the Lord and be united with him. As Sri Ramakrishna puts it, when our boat is nearing the harbor we want to reach the harbor so soon, we are so eager to be in our home, that we start picking up everything and throwing it overboard to lighten the boat. We start throwing away all of the excess baggage that we have hoarded down the years. Then our eagerness becomes so great that we may start throwing away the anchor and the sails. This is where we have to be discriminating. The spiritual life does not require us to give up reasonable comfort and the necessities of life. If we live in poverty, without having enough food, instead of meditating on the Lord we will be meditating on food. It is luxury and the hoarding of things because of selfish attachment that we must give up.

Those who have no expectations, who are prepared for weal or woe, who have no selfish attachments to things or people, who do not even look upon their bodies as their own but as instruments given them by the Lord with which to serve humanity – such people do not act. The Lord acts through them. Sri Krishna almost implies, "Even when such a person raises his arm, it is not he who does it; it is I." When they do anything, it is from the deepest level of their consciousness, where the Lord dwells all the time. Instead of acting, on the surface level of life, they allow the Lord to act through them from the deepest level. Then there is no tension, no fatigue, no fear, and there is immense creative activity which enables them to give their very best even in the most adverse circumstances.

यदृच्छालाभसंतुष्टो द्वंद्वातीतो विमत्सरः ।
समः सिद्धावसिद्धौ च कृत्वापि न निबध्यते ॥४-२२॥

22. They live in freedom who have gone beyond
the dualities of life, and who never compete.
They are alike in success and failure and
content with whatever comes to them.

The nature of life is to bring us sunshine and shadow, pleasure and pain, success and failure, praise and censure. Wherever we live, in the West or in the East, on the campus or in the bazaar, this inescapable duality of life will always be around us. It shows our pathetic condition that almost every one of us hopes that one day we will be able to isolate pleasure from pain. This is one of the everlasting projects of humanity. It may not have been done by anybody in history, but I am going to do this one day in my lab; and when I have isolated the pleasure bacillus, I will be free. There are others who would like to isolate praise. Most of us appreciate praise, but it is disastrous to become dependent on it. If we are going to allow our security to be bolstered up by the praise, appreciation, and applause of others, we are done for. I have even heard about a well-known movie star who goes to sleep at night with an applause record playing. This is going to make him more and more insecure.

Under no circumstances should we be agitated if someone ignores us. I for one cannot find enough words for the advantages of being ignored. Nobody recognizes me – how good it is! I can walk anywhere in freedom, for nobody thinks I am anybody – how good it is! I always say that if I could write a play I would call it "A Place to Be Nobody," which means that I do not want any attention from others, I do not want any appreciation from others, I do not want any support from others, because I have the source of all appreciation, support, and security within me. In life there are occasions when we are ignored and sometimes forgotten. That is the time for us to remind ourselves, "Oh, I am forgotten, very good! Nobody attends to me – excellent! Why should I need anybody's attention?" This is the attitude of the real mystics, who are content because they are complete. We have a standing invitation from the Lord within, who says, "Any time you feel like it, you can make yourself free. Come to me. I have a banquet spread for you with ambrosia, the nectar that gives everlasting life."

These attitudes can be cultivated skillfully. When I see the kind of feats performed in the circus, I know they must have required enormous endeavor. Most of us have seen two trapeze artists swinging over and under each other across the tent to exchange trapezes in midair; you don't just go on the trapeze one day and say, "I am going to jump from one to another." It is the same kind of practice, the same kind of skill, that people develop who win tennis championships. You do not go to Wimbledon on the first day you play tennis; you keep practicing, you develop your skills, and one day you will be at Wimbledon playing on the central court. It is the same on the spiritual path. These are attitudes that all of us can develop; even those of us who are the most sensitive to praise and appreciation can learn to be so secure within ourselves that the word *rejected* can be expelled from our dictionary. The one person who will never reject us is the Lord, and that is enough to make up for all the rejections we may have to undergo at the hands of everyone else.

One of the central ideas of the Gita is that as long as you look at life through the spectacles of pain and pleasure, success and failure, praise and censure, you will never see life whole. One of the fatal flaws of the intellect is that it can thrive only in the land of duality. You take the intellect from the sea of duality and throw it on the land of unity, and it dies. It says, "You mean, I can't divide, I can't categorize, I can't classify things? I'm done for." When Sri Ramana Maharshi used to tell people to go beyond pleasure and pain, they would ask, "Do you mean be indifferent?" His answer would be, "When you go beyond pleasure and pain, you reach abiding joy."

Pleasure is something that comes and goes; joy is something that abides, and it is this state of abiding joy for which the mantram *Rāma* stands. We enter into this state when we gradually go beyond the duality of pleasure and pain, success and defeat, praise and censure.

The next word is *vimatsara:* "Do not compete." It is a strong word, and a concept which is alien to us today. We have come to believe it is only when we compete that we can give our best. I think there are other ways in which we can be inspired to give our best, and one is by reminding ourselves that when we contribute to the welfare of our family, our community, our country, and our world, we are actually serving the Lord. If we want to be aware of the Lord, if we want to be united with the Lord, we must contribute as much as we can to the happiness of those around us, turning our back upon our own petty pleasures and profit when necessary.

This word *vimatsara* also touches upon the harmful way in which most of us tend to compare ourselves with others. This, too, has become so common today that in order to esteem myself, I should always be able to say, "I am better than he, so I am good." We have a distinguished American spiritual teacher in India, nearing his hundredth year now, who took the Sanskrit name *Atulānanda*. It is a lovely name which means 'one who does not compare people.' As our spiritual awareness grows, we will know that the Lord is present in everyone and that there is a uniqueness about everyone. Truly spiritual people never try to compare themselves with others. I have never been able to understand the origin of this phrase "keeping up with the Joneses." It does not matter very much whether we keep up with Tom Jones or anybody else; what is important is for us to keep up with the Lord by serving him in everyone around us. Even here, as long, as we compete with each other and compare one with another, a certain amount of envy is inescapable. There is a girl in Kālidāsa's play *Shakuntalā* who has a very beautiful name: *Anasūyā,* 'she who is free from jealousy.' This is a very rare type, an ideal we can all try to imitate by not competing among ourselves or comparing ourselves to others around us, remembering that all of us have complete worth and value because the Lord is present in us all the time.

Samah siddhāv asiddhau ca. Siddha is success; *asiddha* is failure. Sri Krishna again repeats these important words, saying, "If you want to love me, you must remain alike in success and failure." In my humble observation it is not so very difficult to remain calm in failure. It is much more difficult to remain calm in success, which goes straight to the head. Those who have made money, who have become famous, for example, sometimes drop their old acquaintances and move out of their old area. In the spiritual tradition, it is when you become famous that you go to your old area and say to your old friends, "Now you can all bask in my success. We have grown up together, and you have taught me so many things that I owe my upbringing to you." This is the kind of reverse perspective we can all try to follow. The higher we rise the more we should remember those who are less fortunate. Whether people recognize us, or praise us, or drop us, or even denounce us, there is no need for us to lose our calmness, our security, and our awareness that the Lord is within us all the time.

गतसङ्गस्य मुक्तस्य ज्ञानावस्थितचेतसः ।
यज्ञायाचरतः कर्म समग्रं प्रविलीयते ॥४-२३॥

23. *Those without attachment to the ego are free; their minds are purified by the knowledge that all life is one. They perform all work freely, in the spirit of service.*

Here Sri Krishna gives us the word *gatasanga,* 'he who is free from attachment to his own ego.' All of us have immense resources of love, most of which swirl around our own ego. As long as we are in love with our own ego, dwelling upon ourselves, dreaming about ourselves, it will not be possible for us to love our family or our community. In meditation, we gradually release this swirling whirlpool into channels of fruitful service which flow towards others. The more we think about ourselves, the less we can love others; the less we think about ourselves, the more we are able to love others. When the great day comes when I forget that most monotonous subject in the world, myself, on that day I am free to love everybody.

We all can enter into this state of abiding love by working at it every day, particularly in our domestic relationships, where we have the greatest opportunities for forgetting ourselves. It is absurd to talk about leading the spiritual life when we do not try to put the welfare of our family first. This is the training ground, and though the training is not easy at all, it can be accomplished by all of us with the repetition of the mantram. When irritations or conflicts occur – as they are bound to occur between two people who are brought up differently, who are conditioned differently, who have been exposed to different cultural influences in their early days – do not try to move further away; do not say, "I am not going to talk to you; I don't want to see you." That is the time to say, "I am going to get closer to you, and I am going to try to put your welfare first." This is the challenge of friction; even friction can have spiritual value. The Bhagavad Gita throws a flood of light on how the unfavorable circumstances in our life can be utilized. If we do not utilize them, we are failing to take advantage of the great opportunities that come to us for removing friction, for banishing conflict, and for moving closer to the Lord in everyone around us.

The next word is one of Sri Krishna's favorites: *muktasya. Mukta* means free. Sri Krishna asks, "Don't you want to live in freedom?" When somebody is angry at you, and you are angry at that person, you are not living in freedom; you are living in bondage. You are only doing what the other person is making you do.

I used to get amazed at my granny, my spiritual teacher, when she would tell me that when I retaliate, when I move away from people, when I get estranged, I am only dancing to a tune anybody can play. I was a little puppet, she said, whose wires were being pulled by some of my high school classmates whom I disliked. If I want to be free, all that I have to do, whatever others may do, is try to stand calm, move closer, and give them greater love and greater respect. In my own small personal experience, when people get angry and cause trouble in personal relationships, I have found they are often crying out, "Help me to move closer to you." We all have such experiences. All of us can do something in our own homes, in our own lives, to apply these precious words of the Lord to enable us to live in freedom.

We should remember that "freedom" here implies not only my own freedom, but also the freedom of all around me, in which I find my freedom. According to the Gita, it is not possible to find freedom by one's own self; it is not possible for X, Y, or Z alone to become free and lead a free life. Freedom is indivisible, and in order for me to be free, I have to help others to be free. When we use the word "freedom," what we usually mean is that as long as I am free, it does not matter whether or not you are free. What does matter is that I should be free, my community should be free, my country should be free. The Gita implies that this concept is preposterous; all life is one, and it is only in this total freedom that I can enjoy freedom.

The most challenging effort of freeing ourselves by helping those around us to become free begins, as usual, in the family. I have been reading a good deal lately about the family becoming obsolete. This is the fantasy of those who do not understand the value of the family in training us to learn to find our freedom by living for the freedom of all those around us. The family is really a free university. We are now familiar with free universities; we find them in Palo Alto and Berkeley. Everywhere now people are trying to establish free universities. I would say this is carrying coal to Newcastle. We all have a free university at home, where we really get our finest education in freedom. If we do not learn that the freedom of the family is the freedom of the individual members of the family, we are likely to be misfits in life for a long, long time. I would have no hesitation in saying a good son or daughter makes a good husband or wife, a good father or mother, and a good citizen. We can all start acting on this concept of freedom right in our own family, which does not mean Papa, Mama, Junior, and Janie, but all the members, including grandparents, uncles and aunts, and country cousins. The family can include our dearest friends and those who participate closely in all our endeavors.

To begin the spiritual life, which will enable us to become free, we need not play a part on a gigantic scale. Mogul art, one of the great periods of artistic achievement in India, often is in miniature. The artist concentrated on very small areas, on little things, and worked with such tenderness and precision that only somebody who understands art will be able to see all the love and labor that has gone into it. Family living is like Mogul art, worked in miniature. The canvas is so small, and the skill required is so great, that most of us really do not evaluate the vast potentialities of family life which can enable us all to find our freedom.

My wife and I can draw a little parallel from our own life at Ramagiri with my mother and the children. We usually keep one day in the week for outings, and last Sunday, a beautiful, balmy day, we took them to Santa Rosa. On the way, I was seated with Meera on one side and Geetha on the other, and they were asking me all kinds of questions to which it is very easy to say, "Keep quiet." From an adult viewpoint, most of their questions were juvenile. But that is exactly what children are – juvenile people who are asking me juvenile questions that are just right for them. In fact, if they had asked me some adult question, I would have said, "Keep quiet." All the time I was trying to remember what most of us older people forget: that every child has a point of view. They have their outlook on the world, their way of looking at life, which makes them ask these questions, and for them, these are matters of vital importance. They wanted to know, for example, why *Texaco* and *Mexico* should be spelled differently, why *Texaco* should be spelled with an *a* and *Mexico* with an *i*. To this you just do not say, "They are not the same."

I had my arms around both of them. They had those high rainboots on, so every now and then I would get a kick from both sides, and it hurt. They are children, active and lively, and they sometimes kick. They do not intend to kick others, but my legs happened to be in the way so they got hit. In all these little details, we have to remind ourselves, "These children are not really kicking me; they are kicking their heels in the air, and my legs happen to be in the way." I had to repeat the mantram, *Rāma Rāma,* to keep smiling. It is in these little things that we learn how to be loving. In order to love, to find our freedom, we do not have to go to the Himālayas or the Sierras. We just go to Santa Rosa in one of those little VW bugs, where we are so constricted that every kick is amplified.

When we got to Santa Rosa, we had to walk slowly because my mother is nearing her eightieth year. But the children wanted to run. We were in a crowded shopping center, where it is not proper for a sedate professor to be running about. But they were saying, "Uncle, we want you to run; to run is fun." I did not say that a pompous professor like me should not be running; it would take away from my pomp. Instead I said, "I don't care what people say; I'll run with you," and I started to make a good dash for it. I thought I was going to meet with appreciation, but little Geetha came up to me and said, "You are not supposed to step on the lines." There was no "Thank you," there was no "Well done," so I had to do it all over again. This is the way you show love for children.

We usually conclude our visit to Santa Rosa by dropping in at an ice cream parlor. Little Geetha has just learned to read, and she was looking at the big board and asking, "What are all those flavors?"

I said, "There are many there."

She tried to read a few, and then she said, "What is that long word I can't read?"

I said, "Pistachio."

"That's my flavor." So she got that, double dip, and Meera got butter brickle. They wanted to nurse their ice cream cones all the way back to Ramagiri. I was in the back seat again with both of them on either side, and such is their love for each other that every now and then they would exchange licks across my lap. It was dripping all along. I do not like suits being spoiled by pistachio and butter-brickle drips, and my first impulse was to say, "Stop dripping all over me." Instead, I again tried to look at the situation from their point of view. For them it is not clothes that are important; it is their ice cream. I could see they were cone-conscious, and so I let them drip all the way home.

My mother, watching all this, was very happy that I still have not forgotten how to be tender to my own family. I learned how to be tender from my mother and from my grandmother, because they were able to show great tenderness to me. It is in this way that we find our freedom, by being tender and unselfish and putting up with innumerable discomforts for the sake of adding to the joy of the members of our family, and then gradually extending our love to include our friends, our community, our country, and our world.

Finally we come to *jnānāvasthitacetas*, 'the person whose mind has been purified by the knowledge that all life is one.' When we begin to realize the unity of life in all our personal relationships, our mind becomes purified.

ब्रह्मार्पणं ब्रह्महविर्ब्रह्माग्नौ ब्रह्मणा हुतम् ।
ब्रह्मैव तेन गन्तव्यं ब्रह्मकर्मसमाधिना ॥४-२४॥

24. The process of offering is Brahman; that which is offered is Brahman. Brahman offers the sacrifice in the fire of Brahman. Brahman is attained by the man who sees Brahman in every action.

This is an image taken from an ancient form of ritualistic worship in the orthodox Hindu tradition. In this ritual, called *yajna*, or sacrifice, the sacrificial fire is lighted and butter is poured as an oblation into the fire which represents the Lord. When we live for others in peace, in love, and in wisdom, our life becomes divine, and everything we do becomes an offering unto the Lord.

दैवमेवापरे यज्ञं योगिनः पर्युपासते ।
ब्रह्माग्नावपरे यज्ञं यज्ञेनैवोपजुह्वति ॥४-२५॥

25. Some aspirants perform sacrifices to the gods. Others offer selfless service as sacrifice in the fire of Brahman.

There are many ways in which you can make your offering unto the Lord. It is not what you give to the Lord, but the love with which you give that makes your sacrifice acceptable to him. The greatest gift you can give the Lord is yourself, and in order to do this, you must eliminate all your self-will and banish all violence from your life. Let me assure you that when you make this supreme offering to the Lord, it is not the Lord who is getting the bargain. He is not a good businessman. If at any time the Lord says he is prepared to receive you, do not make any terms. Agree on the spot, and he will never desert you.

श्रोत्रादीनीन्द्रियाण्यन्ये संयमाग्निषु जुह्वति ।
शब्दादीन्विषयानन्य इन्द्रियाग्निषु जुह्वति ॥४-२६॥

26. Some renounce all enjoyment of the senses
and sacrifice them in the fire of sense restraint.
Others partake of sense objects, offering them
in service through the fire of the senses.

Here Sri Krishna is distinguishing between two different approaches to the spiritual life. One is the ascetic way, followed by members of the monastic order, and the other is the middle path of moderation to be followed by those of us who live in the world.

We should respect members of the monastic order in all religions because they have turned their backs upon the world in order to lead the spiritual life. While we were in India, we had the privilege of knowing a Hindu monk who had been the head of a great monastery in the Himālayas for many years. He retired from this office in his later years to lead a completely contemplative life. There is nothing in the world to tempt him. His eyes are always fixed on the supreme goal, and he therefore feels no conflicts. He does not envy the man of the world's freedom to go to a movie or drop in at an ice cream parlor; in fact, he probably feels compassion for those of us who still respond to the call of these little delights. For him, these are wrong, but for those of us who live in the world, who follow the householder's path to spiritual awareness, these little pleasures are not wrong. To live the monastic life and turn our back upon the world, and, in a sense, negate our senses and the world, is only one approach to the spiritual life. This path is suitable for a very rare type of person, and we should never deprecate those who follow it. But there is another approach to the spiritual life which is just as challenging, and more suited for the vast majority of us living in the modern world. On this path we live in the world and yet are not of it. For me, this kind of spiritual life is very satisfying. We live in the bosom of our family, as integral members of our society, and yet never forget that the Lord is enthroned in the hearts of all. We live in the midst of life and find our fulfillment not by negating the senses, but by harnessing them in the selfless service of others. Instead of going on fasts, for example, I try to eat good, wholesome food in temperate quantities, not for the satisfaction of my palate, but to strengthen the body so that I can help carry the burdens of those around me. If my body is not strong, I cannot contribute to the welfare of society, and I cannot give the best account of myself in life. Instead of fasting, therefore, I suggest eating moderately. Fasting may not be as easy as feasting, but after a while it is not too different. Both are extremes. It is not hard to go the extreme way, but what is really difficult is neither to fast nor to feast, but to be moderate in everything we do. This is what the Buddha called *Madhyamārga*, the Middle Path – the ideal path for the householder. It requires great artistry and vigilance. Instead of negating the body and senses, we train them to be instruments of selfless service. We harness our physical, mental, and intellectual capacities not to make money or achieve power or fame for ourselves, but to use these faculties with great detachment to make our contribution to life.

सर्वाणीन्द्रियकर्माणि प्राणकर्माणि चापरे ।
आत्मसंयमयोगाग्नौ जुह्वति ज्ञानदीपिते ॥४-२७॥
द्रव्ययज्ञास्तपोयज्ञा योगयज्ञास्तथापरे ।
स्वाध्यायज्ञानयज्ञाश्च यतयः संशितव्रताः ॥४-२८॥

27. Some offer the workings of the senses
and the vital forces through the fire of self-
control, kindled in the path of knowledge.

28. Some offer wealth, and some offer sense restraint and suffering. Some take vows and offer knowledge and study of the scriptures; and some make the offering of meditation.

This word *yajna*, 'offering,' means that everything we do should be for the welfare of all those around us. There are different ways in which people make contributions in the Lord's service, and one is through wealth. Money is not evil; it is love of money that is evil. The scriptures always emphasize that it is the Lord alone who is to be loved; everything else is to be used.

We can look to Mahatma Gandhi to see how yajna can be applied in life. His material possessions were worth only two dollars at the time of his death, yet some of his best friends were very successful businessmen. He had a group of multimillionaires around him, and he was often criticized severely for being so close to them. But Gandhi would say that the Lord was present in them also. We should never forget that the Lord is present not only in the poor but in the wealthy too, not only in the ignorant but in the learned too.

When Gandhi was on a fast, distinguished doctors from various parts of the country would come to examine him, sometimes to get on the front page of the newspapers, and Gandhiji, who was aware of their motives, would allow himself to be examined carefully and then say, "My fee is twenty-five rupees." All his faculties, all his skills, everything was used to raise money for his work. Among the women of the villages of India, he was particularly successful. There is a saying in India that a man's best bank is his wife's neck, and most well-to-do Indian wives have a lot of jewelry, which is considered to be a good investment. Gandhi would tell these women, "Your beauty does not depend on diamonds; your beauty comes from inside. You should reveal this beauty by putting the welfare of your family, your community, and your country first." Then he would ask them all, even the little girls, to take off their gold bangles, and almost everybody present would respond immediately to his call. As long as there are poor people in the world, as long as there are people who are deprived and handicapped in the world, if we are sensitive, we will not load ourselves with unnecessary adornment. Again, this is not a plea for poverty but a plea for contented, simple living, in which all the legitimate needs of the body are satisfied. We can use our money, whether we have a lot of it or not, to contribute to selfless work that is aimed at the welfare of all.

Another way of making an offering to the Lord is *tapoyajna*. The word *tapas* has a number of related meanings: suffering, the practice of sense restraint, and heat. In deepening meditation a sense of rising heat, which is the rise of kundalinī, is not unusual. On such occasions, have as much physical exercise as you can. Hard physical labor is the very best use of this rising heat, which becomes an offering unto the Lord when it is given for selfless service.

Now comes the word *yogayajna*, 'the offering of meditation.' People who meditate for long hours in the morning and evening are not doing so for selfish ends. It is a misunderstanding to think that people who meditate are seeking only their own salvation or illumination. What they are seeking is the removal of their selfishness and separateness. Every person who meditates rightly is doing so for all of us. In a home where there is one person, say the granddaughter, meditating regularly, even if the rest of the family does not see eye-to-eye with her, they will share in the spiritual bonus, because she is going to be secure, selfless, and able to put the welfare of those around her first. All of us benefit by living with someone who does not live for himself or herself. We do not need to examine all the pros and cons; we have only to live with such people, and by some unwritten law, our hearts and our respect gradually go out to them. In an unguarded moment we may say, "I wish I could be like that."

Once a student from the University at Berkeley came to me at our meditation class and said, "I have a roommate who used to be a pain in the neck for a long time. Now I kind of like him, and I'm even beginning to wish I could be like him. I want to see what is happening here to turn him from a person I disliked into a person I want to be like." My comment was, "That's about the best description of meditation I have ever heard."

So if in your home people refer to your meditation by saying, "Oh, he is still out on that Indian trip," do not get agitated or try to defend yourself. There is no need to defend yourself; when you are meditating you have got a good defense lawyer in the Lord, who not only knows the law but wrote it. At first it is only natural that people will have misgivings about your moving away from the normal ways of life. But if you can show by your life that you are becoming less selfish, less self-willed, and increasingly able to love others, it is only a matter of time before everybody will benefit from your meditation.

In order to live the spiritual life, therefore, we can all follow this concept of *yajna,* which means we should give some of our time, our talent, our resources, our wealth, our skill, and our love to everyone around us. The more we give to those around us, the more we shall have to give. It is not the person who has much who is rich; it is the person who gives much. In other words, Sri Krishna is telling us through Arjuna that there are many, many ways in which we can worship the Lord who is in every one of us.

अपाने जुह्वति प्राणं प्राणे ऽपानं तथापरे ।
प्राणापानगती रुद्ध्वा प्राणायामपरायणाः ॥४-२९॥

29. *Some offer the forces of vitality, regulating their inhalation and exhalation, and thus gain control over these forces.*

The word used here is *prāna,* which has a number of meanings. Most generally it means vitality, or to use a colloquialism, that which makes us tick. *Prāna* can also be translated as our immense capacity to desire, which is closely related to our capacity to love.

Another meaning of the word *prāna* is breath. In certain schools of meditation breathing exercises are prescribed to control the mind. I lose no opportunity to caution everyone not to take to these breathing exercises, because they can be dangerous. This is especially the case in our modern times, as our way of life is so artificial, so divorced from the natural rhythm of life, and these exercises require pure living conditions, which are rarely found anywhere these days. Such exercises must be done under the close supervision of a teacher who is thoroughly familiar with all the turns and twists we may come across on this particular path. Some of the occult exercises are so powerful that they can split a personality in two.

The very best practice for improving the breathing rhythm is to go for a long, hard, fast walk repeating *Jesus, Jesus, Jesus* or *Rāma, Rāma, Rāma*. The rhythm of breathing, coupled with the rhythm of the footstep, will blend with the rhythm of the mantram to calm the mind. In the deeper stages of meditation, as our concentration increases, breathing can become so slow that it can drop from sixteen times per minute to eight. Do not pay any attention to this; the more attention you pay to the breathing rhythm, the more difficult it is for it to slow down. When you are meditating sincerely, the great day will come when breathing is suspended for two or three minutes. At the time, you may not be aware of it at all. But afterwards you feel such relaxation in the nervous system, such a quiet knowledge that things are going well on your spiritual path, that you will long more and more to recapture this spell when breathing has been momentarily suspended.

People who are very forgiving, who do not easily get agitated by dwelling upon themselves and can return good will for ill will, love for hatred, usually have long breathing rhythms. Those who are agitated and resentful, who are ready to take offense any time at anything, are the ones who breathe fast and irregularly. Any provocation can throw their breathing out of gear. This disruption cannot help but affect physical well-being, and in many forms of physical illness, emotional stress is very much responsible. For example, asthma and many more serious ailments are often emotional in origin. As our meditation deepens, our concentration increases, and our breathing rhythm slows down, we shall find the answer to many of our physical problems. In order to facilitate this slowing of the breathing rhythm, it is helpful to have regular walks every day repeating the mantram.

अपरे नियताहाराः प्राणान्प्राणेषु जुह्वति ।
सर्वे ऽप्येते यज्ञविदो यज्ञक्षपितकल्मषाः ॥४-३०॥

30. Some offer the forces of vitality through restraint of their senses. All these understand the meaning of service and will be cleansed of their impurities.

The purification of the body is an essential step on the spiritual path. If we want to discover our real identity, to realize that all life is one and live in harmony with this unity, we must have a body that is healthy and strong, one which will never fail in the selfless service of others. This gives us a deep motive for exercising discriminating restraint over the senses. For example, we should not eat things simply because they look or taste good. The proper function of food is to have food value, and we should take care to eat only what is nourishing. It is not good to dwell on food, either. The gourmet who is constantly looking for new ways to stimulate the palate will become more and more trapped on the physical level. After we have taken reasonable care to see that we get the right food, served with love, we should then forget about it and leave it to the digestive system to do the rest. There is no need to talk about it; there is no need to ask, "When are we going to have another meal like this?" In this way, instead of being used by the senses and wasting our vital capacity on petty sensory pleasures, we must train the senses to be obedient servants. In recalling our desires from the wasteful sensory channels into which they are now flowing, we unify our capacity to desire. Then we can direct this unified love and energy towards the supreme goal.

यज्ञशिष्टामृतभुजो यान्ति ब्रह्म सनातनम् ।
नायं लोको ऽस्त्ययज्ञस्य कुतो ऽन्यः कुरुसत्तम ॥४-३१॥

31. True sustenance is in service, and through it a man or woman reaches the eternal Brahman. But those who do not seek to serve are without a home in this world. How can they be at home in any world to come, Arjuna?

It is in making others happy that we find our happiness, and it is in serving others that we become fulfilled. If we pursue only our own private satisfaction, even in this world we are likely to be completely frustrated and insecure. In other words, even if we do not meditate, even if we do not follow the spiritual path, we cannot help finding that when we forget ourselves we are happy, and when we dwell upon ourselves we are miserable. Egocentric people are not only cut off from the mystical experience; they are also unable to enjoy the world. Selfless people enjoy life to the fullest, because they are always free.

एवं बहुविधा यज्ञा वितता ब्रह्मणो मुखे ।
कर्मजान्विद्धि तान्सर्वानेवं ज्ञात्वा विमोक्ष्यसे ॥४-३२॥
श्रेयान्द्रव्यमयाद्यज्ञाज्ज्ञानयज्ञः परंतप ।
सर्वं कर्माखिलं पार्थ ज्ञाने परिसमाप्यते ॥४-३३॥

32. These offerings are born of work, and
each guides man along a path to Brahman.
Understanding this, you will attain liberation.
33. The offering of wisdom is better than
any material offering, Arjuna. For the
goal of all work is spiritual wisdom.

The concept of *yajna* is now brought to its consummation. The Lord says that it is good to give our money, material possessions, time, and energy to a worthy cause that seeks the general welfare. It is good for us to give, if necessary by reducing our style of living to simple comfort. This does not mean that we must sacrifice minimum comforts, but most of us can work long and hard enough to be able to give part of our time and earnings to a great cause. To be able to work for others without thought of a paycheck can bring joy to everyone. As long as we have been working just for pay, calculating how much we are making per hour, we cannot realize that working for a selfless cause can give more satisfaction than the pay envelope we bring home. This does not mean that we must give up our jobs; all of us have to maintain ourselves and our families. But over and above this it is necessary for all of us, in our own interest and in the interest of the general welfare, to give part of our time, talent, and money to a selfless cause.

But even though all these offerings are very important, the Lord will not be fully content with only these gifts. The greatest sacrifice is *jnānayajna,* the offering of wisdom. The greatest gift we can give the Lord is the sharing of spiritual wisdom with others. Helping others to find the Lord of Love hidden in their own heart is the greatest yajna. The Lord says here, "I want you to be united with me, to realize that I live in every living thing, that all life is one."

All actions must eventually lead us to this knowledge of the unity of life. Even the mistakes we make will force us gradually, through increasing suffering, to go forward on the spiritual path. The Lord does not want us to suffer, but suffering is the only way he can keep us from going further and further away from him. We can all save ourselves a great deal of pain by the simple method of learning to respect other people's needs more than our own. We may ask, "How do I know other people's needs? I am not psychology-oriented. I am not a very good observer." The Buddha's answer to this is simple: "What hurts you hurts others." We do not have to read books about other people's needs. We do not have to go to the university or read Sanskrit or study Pānini's grammar. All we must do is remember that what hurts us hurts our father, what pains us pains our mother, what annoys us annoys our children, and what irritates us irritates our friends. All the psychology we need to know is contained in this: "Others and I are one." We can understand everybody's needs just by looking at our own, and we can realize the unity underlying all life by resolving: "Even if I have to inconvenience myself, even if I have to lead an uncomfortable life, may I be given the strength, wisdom, and humility never to contribute to the suffering of anyone on earth." This is the supreme yajna which the Lord asks everyone to make.

तद्विद्धि प्रणिपातेन परिप्रश्नेन सेवया ।
उपदेक्ष्यन्ति ते ज्ञानं ज्ञानिनस्तत्त्वदर्शिनः ॥४-३४॥

34. You should approach someone who has realized the purpose of life, and question him with reverence and devotion. He will instruct you in this wisdom.

In this and the following verses, Sri Krishna uses the word *jnāna* again and again. *Jnāna* means 'knowing' in the sense in which Socrates used it, that is, knowing oneself. We all have an amusing idea of knowledge. We can answer any question about Shakespeare, about Milton, or even about Beowulf, but if someone asks us who we are, we say, "How do I know?" This is the strange paradox that all the great spiritual teachers point out: what is the use of knowing everything else on earth if we don't know who the knower is? We are born, we go to school, we get married, beget children, buy and sell, and pass away without knowing who we are. It is an appalling commentary on our concept of knowledge. In knowing ourselves we fulfill the supreme purpose of life; when we know ourselves, we know all life is one, and we have the desire and the will to live in harmony with this knowledge.

Spiritual awareness is really not taught; it is caught. This is a beautiful way of saying that when we love someone who lives without any thought of his own personal satisfaction, who devotes all his energy, love, and wisdom to help those around him find wisdom, we absorb, through our deep love for him, something of his spiritual awareness. Constant association with people who are spiritually advanced supports us by a process of absorption.

In English poetry, Edmund Spenser, the author of the *Faerie Queene*, is often called the poet's poet because he has inspired so many poets. I sometimes feel tempted to call Sri Ramana Maharshi the saint's saint because he has inspired so many saints. That is the kind of saint who takes my breath away. It is said also of Mahatma Gandhi that his glory lay in transforming little people into heroes. We go into the presence of a great mystic, look at him, listen to him, open our hearts to him, and even those of us who are clay are transmuted into gold.

The small quantity of spiritual awareness that has come to me is through my deep love for my grandmother, my spiritual teacher, who, without knowing how to read or write, is the most educated person I have ever known.

When I was a student at college, every weekend some students would have a holiday by going boating; but my idea of a holiday was to make for my village, about fifty miles from the college, to be reunited with my grandmother. It became quite a standing joke on the campus; everyone would say, “He has gone to see his grandmother.” Slowly, however, they began to see, even in this simple gesture, how intensely I yearned to be with her, and how intensely I felt the deprivation of being away from her. I used to go by train to the little town close to my village. On one Saturday morning I didn't have a penny, but I had to go. I had such faith that I went to the railway station where the train was waiting. The guard of the train was watching me rather curiously because I looked so wistful. He asked me where I was going, and I said, “I want to go and see my granny.” He suppressed a smile and told the driver that there was a boy who wanted to go and see his granny. Then he asked, “Where does your granny live?”

“Near Palghat.”

“Have you got a ticket?”

“That's the problem. I don't have any money.”

Touched, he said, “Hop into my compartment. Don't tell anybody. Don't put it in your college magazine or I'll lose my job. Just jump in here.” And he told the driver, “We have to take him to see his granny.”

There was such love in my eyes and such eagerness that even a railway guard, who sometimes can be pretty tough, was prepared to go out of his way and put me into his compartment. He let me out at Palghat and said, “Now run!”

From Palghat to my village it was seven miles of beautiful road with big trees on either side, sometimes with monkeys swinging from them. I used to enjoy walking along it, but more than the monkeys, and more than the trees, and more than the brooks, what gave me joy was the knowledge that every step would bring me closer to my granny. At that time I didn't know she was my spiritual teacher; she was just my grandmother. When I arrived home, she would hold my hands and look and look at me; she didn't need words. The first question she would ask me was, "What did you learn this week?" This gave me just the opportunity I had been waiting for. I would put my hands behind my back and say, "Now, Granny, listen carefully. This week the professor who teaches me logic has taught me what a syllogism is." She used to gasp with admiration. "Syllogism!" Then, like most scholars, I would indulge in academic jargon to my heart's content. Today I use very simple language; my standard is that what I say must be completely understandable to the garbage collector as well as the graduate student. If I were to consult some of my old academic colleagues on this, they would say I have become simplistic. I really thought my granny was simplistic, though I didn't dare call her so. With the childlike simplicity of the spiritual woman, she would say, "Now, son, give me an example of this great learning that you have absorbed." So I would quote my logic professor and say, "All men are mortal. I am a man. Therefore, *ergo*, I am mortal." She just laughed and laughed and said, "I pay all this money so that you can learn this trash?" Then this unlettered, untutored woman stated the syllogism perfectly: "All men, all creatures, are immortal because the Lord lives in them. I am a creature. Therefore I am immortal."

The secret of absorbing such spiritual wisdom is to open our hearts wide and give all our love to our spiritual teacher, who symbolizes our Ātman for the present. When I would run home to see my granny, I did not know I had an Ātman. Now that I look back I see that my grandmother was my Ātman. That is why I loved her; she was my real 'me,' my perfect 'me,' my pure 'me.' I didn't know this intellectually, but deep inside, from the very depths of my heart, a little voice was saying, "That's you." This is what happens to us when we see a great saint like Sri Ramana Maharshi. People whose hearts are not open, who have the window of their consciousness bolted and barred, look and see only a dapper, brown little man in a dhoti. But those whose hearts have opened, who are searching for the answer to the riddle of life and have flung the doors of their consciousness wide open, have only to see Sri Ramana Maharshi seated quietly before them to hear that little voice within them say in its sweet tones, "That's you." Beautiful hymns have been composed to Sri Ramana Maharshi; great singers and poets have described his beauty. But he will quietly say, "There is no Ramana Maharshi here. There is nobody here. It's all empty. I am just an empty keyhole." You apply your eye closely and look through this empty keyhole, and in the dim distance, you see the immense glory of the Lord flaming up against the background of the cosmos.

It is by this process of osmosis that spiritual awareness really comes to all of us. Books can never give spiritual awareness; it is only by seeing someone who has become united with the Lord through His grace that ordinary people like you and me can learn to discover our real Self.

यज्ज्ञात्वा न पुनर्मोहमेवं यास्यसि पाण्डव ।
येन भूतान्यशेषेण द्रक्ष्यस्यात्मन्यथो मयि ॥४-३५॥

35. Arjuna, having attained this wisdom you
will never again be deluded. You will see yourself
in all creatures, and all creatures in me.

Once we wake up through the grace of the Lord from the long, lurid dream of multiplicity and separateness into the indivisible unity that pervades all life, we will never fall asleep again. Once we have awakened into this higher state of consciousness in which we see all as coming from God, subsisting in God, and returning to God, we cannot fall back again into the old dream of separateness. This is a significant verse because some people – great writers and artists, for example – have had an occasional flash in which they see the unity behind life for just a moment. Although they treasure the memory of this experience, they fall asleep again; they are caught again in the dream. Just as among dreams there are a few significant ones which strengthen us inwardly, so in this waking dream we may have an occasional insight into Reality, but we have no control over these experiences. Waking up permanently into a higher level of consciousness comes as the result of sustained sādhana. We can become established in the unitive state only through long and systematic discipline. These occasional flashes of mystical experience are only indications of a latent capacity which must be cultivated through the practice of meditation and ancillary disciplines if we are finally to wake up completely, never to fall asleep or dream again.

The word *moha,* 'delusion,' is used by Sri Krishna to tell us we are under a kind of hypnotic spell. We are all running after what we have been hypnotized to believe we want. We are told to go after money, and we start looking for money everywhere. We don't want to know who we are because we are only looking for money. Some people even seem to have a dollar sign printed on their pupils; wherever they look they see possibilities for making money. They see a beautiful landscape and say, "Ah, what a nice subdivision this would make." They go to a mountain top and see it as a good place for a motel. The same applies to pleasure. We are told to give our senses free rein by the mass media. The senses are wild horses that we can train to respond to the slightest move of our fingers. But if we do not train them, if we leave these wild horses to themselves, they will not know where to go; they will plunge headlong across moor and mountain, into morass and quagmire. We should never follow the siren call of sense-pleasures which seems to tell us, "We will give you joy; we will give you security; we will give you fulfillment." These promises are phantoms that will lead us further and further away from joy, from security, and from fulfillment.

As we progress on the spiritual path and awake from the confusion of separateness and self-will, we will begin to see the unity of life. We will begin to see the Lord in all. Even to be able to love a dog, we have to be spiritual. It is not enough if we buy a dog, get a collar, and call him Fido. The other day we saw a beautiful Newfoundland retriever in a car. He looked exactly like a small bear, occupying the whole front seat. The family who owned the dog must have been traveling throughout the night, because I could see from the bleary eyes of the dog that he hadn't slept. His eyes reminded me of a scholar who has been poring over his books through the night; if he had been a human being he might have said, "I didn't have a wink of sleep; I was up all night writing a paper on the tragedies of Shakespeare." Instead he was trying to jump out of the car. I understand dogs very well, because I love them very much. I patted him and tried to clear his eyes a little, and he almost told me, "You know, I don't like being cooped up in automobiles. One whole night I've been traveling. All I want is to jump out and run and run and run." His eyes kept saying, "Run, run, run," and in one moment he gave a leap and was out of the car. People thought he was a bear, and they were all running helter-skelter when his master, who would say he loves dogs, came and issued an order, "Get in!" He expected the dog to stand up and salute. The poor dog was trying to say, "All I want is a long, long run on the beach. Take me for a run, and then put me back in the car." But there was one little boy we saw who really loved his dog. The dog was running on the beach wherever he wanted, and the boy was telling the dog, "I will follow you wherever you want to go." The dog darted into the water, and the boy followed him into the water; then the dog jumped out of the water and onto a rock, and the boy followed him onto the rock. The boy was putting the dog first. In every relationship this is the secret of love. If I love you it means only one thing: that your happiness is more important to me than my own. This kind of love will give me the wisdom, the sensitiveness, and the will to conduct myself selflessly.

अपि चेदसि पापेभ्यः सर्वेभ्यः पापकृत्तमः ।
सर्वं ज्ञानप्लवेनैव वृजिनं संतरिष्यसि ॥४-३६॥

36. Even if you were the most sinful of all sinners, you could cross beyond all sin by the raft of spiritual wisdom.

Spiritual wisdom, or jnāna, which is developed through the practice of meditation, can do what nothing else can do; it is a boat that can take you across the stormy, treacherous sea of life. Sri Krishna says this jnāna enables you to pick up two planks, discrimination and dispassion, tie them together, sit on them, and paddle with your hands until you reach the other shore of abiding joy, peace, and love.

The Compassionate Buddha was very fond of representing himself as a boatman offering to take us to the other shore that is nirvāna. We usually tell ourselves he is misleading us; we like to be on this shore quarreling, manipulating, and being separate. The thought of going across to the other shore, where there are no quarrels, makes us wonder what we would do there.

Sri Krishna too says, in a magnificent verse in the invocation to the Bhagavad Gita, that he is *kaivartakah keshavah,* the boatman who will ferry us across the river of life to the other shore. We, however, prefer this shore. We don't want to begin the journey towards peace and security; the mind keeps us on this shore visiting different ports here and there. In almost every port we have a love: food, money, clothes, all kinds of exotic things to add to our collection. But in moving away from this coast to the other, we must throw all these attachments overboard.

The grace of the Lord is like a wind that is blowing all the time, but it is our responsibility to get rid of our excess luggage and set the sail correctly. For a long, long time in meditation we are merely bailing out the boat and throwing things overboard. We all have an antique shop right in the basement: over the years we have collected all sorts of things, this one because it was on sale, that one because we couldn't resist it. Some of the great mystics started, as you and I did, by throwing out things they had become tired of. This is how renunciation begins, by getting rid of things to which we are not very attached. If I have two sets of the Encyclopaedia Britannica, I can give you one. We shouldn't blame ourselves for beginning this way, for renunciation grows slowly with renunciation.

The second stage is harder; then we begin to throw away some of the things to which we are attached. There is a tussle, an inner conflict; to throw or not to throw is the question, but out it goes. But in the final stages, when we see the lights on the other shore, when we see Jesus walking about, the Buddha meditating, and Sri Krishna playing on the flute, all we want is to get where the action is. At that time, even selfish people like you and me, who have committed many mistakes in their ignorance, want to get there so fast that they take hold of everything – their glasses, the shirt on their back, even the sail and rudder – and start throwing it all overboard. The spiritual teacher will say at that time, "Don't throw your glasses away; you won't be able to see Sri Krishna!" In the final stages, the great difficulty is to persuade people to keep a few things, to keep their body fit and their intellect active to serve the Lord.

After reaching the other shore, to come back and take other people in your boat seems heartbreaking. When you have reached the shore of bliss and then come back, you see wars, famines, pestilence, and selfishness. You come back, as the Bible puts it, to the "valley of the shadow of death," which takes a lot of renunciation. Sri Ramakrishna uses language which no other mystic has ever used to describe this. He calls it a soccer match. India is a poor country, and many of the fellows who really want to see a soccer match do not have the money to buy a ticket. But they have acrobatic skills, so they say to their friends, "Let's stand on each other's shoulders and have the fellow on the top, who can see over the bamboo fence, describe the game kick for kick, pass for pass, goal for goal." With great effort, one of them finally gets to the top and sees the game. The whole team is playing as one; each team is putting the other one first. Who can lose? He gets so excited and so drawn in that he forgets his friends and throws himself over the fence. But a great mystic like Sri Ramakrishna, even though he sees the game and wants to jump in, thinks of all the poor people outside in life, so caught up in strife, so utterly miserable, and he denies himself the game. He jumps backwards, goes and gets us, and stands on the bottom so that we can get up on his shoulders and watch the game too. This is what Jesus is doing, what the Buddha is doing, standing and allowing anyone who wants to climb upon their shoulders and see the game. Great saints like Sri Ramakrishna, Sri Ramana Maharshi, St. Francis of Assisi, Meister Eckhart, and St. John of the Cross have come and told us what the game is like. The Gita now asks us, "Don't you too want to see this game where all become one, and to understand the game of *līlā*, the divine play called life?"

यथैधांसि समिद्धो ऽग्निर्भस्मसात्कुरुते ऽर्जुन ।
ज्ञानाग्निः सर्वकर्माणि भस्मसात्कुरुते तथा ॥४-३७॥

न हि ज्ञानेन सदृशं पवित्रमिह विद्यते ।
तत्स्वयं योगसंसिद्धः कालेनात्मनि विन्दति ॥४-३८॥

37. O Arjuna, even as the heat of a fire reduces wood to ashes, the fire of knowledge turns to ashes all selfish attachment to work.

38. Nothing in this world purifies like spiritual wisdom. It is the perfection achieved in time through the path of yoga, the path which leads to the Self within.

Sri Krishna says that even if in the past we have lived selfishly, often trying to snatch our happiness at the expense of others, jnāna or spiritual wisdom will reduce our big funeral pyre of unfavorable karma to ashes. Do not be despondent over the past. Do not let it become oppressive. All the past, with all its mistakes, will fall away from us if we turn our eyes to the Lord with a one-pointed mind and travel untiringly towards the spiritual goal. This is the Lord's promise given to us by the Gita.

In order to develop jnāna, I know of no other discipline than the practice of meditation. In all religions, meditation – sometimes called contemplation or interior prayer – is emphasized by the great mystics as the path, the ladder of love, leading to the Lord. There are many allied disciplines, too, that accompany the practice of meditation, such as the discriminating restraint of the senses and the constant attempt to put the welfare of those around us first. One of the remarkable developments in meditation is that even if we take to meditation without any desire to practice these related disciplines, after a while we will be drawn to them. I used to have a friend who was allergic to my talk on vegetarianism. In an attempt to initiate me into the delights of eating my fellow creatures, he actually took me for dinner to a number of restaurants. He was meditating regularly, but every time I would talk about not wanting to eat my friends, he would say, "This doesn't apply to me. I am going to show you that it is possible to progress in meditation without changes in diet." I didn't argue with him, which disappointed him; but after a year of meditation, he began to have a distaste for nonvegetarian food.

If we are practicing meditation regularly with sustained enthusiasm, this development is likely to take place. As meditation dispels the delusion of separateness, we become more and more conscious of a sense of fellowship with all creatures. The other day, while going to the beach, I was delighted to see the young lambs, some black-faced, some white-faced, running about on the green hills just like children. When we got to the beach, I enjoyed watching the sea gulls and those little creatures that I love so much, the sandpipers, who are like the imp Ariel in Shakespeare's *Tempest*. They go up to the very edge of the water, and when a wave rolls in, they come running back on their thin little legs. We also saw three deer, a mother and two fawns, which had come down onto the beach. The people living nearby must have been very good to these deer for them to have such confidence; they were playing about, sure that the people loved them and wouldn't harm them in any way.

As meditation deepens, our spiritual awareness should show itself in the capacity to understand the point of view of other creatures. Ecology is beginning to teach us that even in our relationships with plants and trees, we must be careful lest we exploit them thoughtlessly. Mahatma Gandhi was so aware of this relationship that he did not even like flowers to be plucked. He said a flower is most beautiful when it is on the bush. In India we have a hoary custom of garlanding people with heavy strings of flowers. Gandhi was constantly subjected to this garlanding, but when he became aware of his kinship with plants and trees, he told everyone that he would accept only garlands of homespun yarn made by the person offering the garland. This considerably reduced garlanding.

But while it is good to be friendly with trees and animals, it is most important to be friendly with human beings. It is most of all in our human relationships that we realize the unity of life. Trees don't talk back. Animals don't say, "Now you listen to me." This give-and-take is the joy of the human situation. Wherever we go and say, "Now you listen to me," the other person will say, "You first listen to me." Where we find the you-first-listen-to-me attitude, there is the opportunity for patience. If there weren't impatient people around us, how would we learn patience? I once asked my grandmother, my spiritual teacher, why there should be people to scold me, criticize me, attack me. Her reply was, "How else can you learn patience?" Left to ourselves we find it quite pleasant to say "Quiet!" and prevent others from talking. People who are not used to hearing no can become insufferable. When we purify ourselves by learning to be patient, by learning to forbear, we come at last to see the Lord hidden in our own and everyone's heart.

श्रद्धावांल्लभते ज्ञानं तत्परः संयतेन्द्रियः ।
ज्ञानं लब्ध्वा परां शान्तिमचिरेणाधिगच्छति ॥४-३९॥
अज्ञश्चाश्रद्दधानश्च संशयात्मा विनश्यति ।
नायं लोको ऽस्ति न परो न सुखं संशयात्मनः ॥४-४०॥

39. The man or woman who has spiritual wisdom as the highest goal, whose faith is deep and who restrains the senses, attains that wisdom quickly and enters into perfect peace.
40. But the ignorant, who are indecisive and without faith, waste their life. They can never be happy in this world or any other.

If I haven't come to have faith in the Lord within, who is my real Self, then how can I be secure? How can I be at peace? How can I live for others or be loved by others? Here "faith," or *shraddhā* in Sanskrit, does not mean mere blind faith, but a deep belief based on personal experience. When we lead the spiritual life, we will begin to see an inner power guiding and protecting us in even the most difficult situations.

When we experience this over and over again, we come to have a deep faith or shraddhā in the Lord within. It is not enough if we have blind faith in spiritual ideals, based on the testimony of the scriptures or sages. We must realize these truths for ourselves, in our own life and consciousness. As the Buddha was fond of saying, the spiritual teacher only points the way; we must do our own traveling. The personal experience of others may plant the seed of shraddhā in our hearts, inspiring us to lead the spiritual life, but shraddhā can develop fully only if we experience these truths for ourselves.

While in South Africa, Gandhi made many friends among the people of the Christian community. One of these acquaintances tried to convert Gandhi to Christianity by assuring him that if he only had faith in Jesus he would be saved in spite of all his sins. Gandhi replied, "I do not seek redemption from the consequences of my sin. I seek to be redeemed from sin itself, or rather from the very thought of sin."

Without using the words *religion* or *Lord*, we can comment on this verse by recalling the famous inquiry of Sri Ramana Maharshi, *Who am I?* The whole purpose of spiritual discipline is to discover who we are. In the supreme climax of meditation called samādhi, I discover that there is no separate me, no separate you, that all of us are governed by the underlying unity that is divine. On making this discovery, the rest of our life becomes an earnest endeavor to live in harmony with this unity, never inflicting suffering upon any creature but contributing to the best of our capacity to the progress of those around us.

Sri Krishna emphasizes that until and unless we come to have at least a dim awareness of the Lord within – which is what he calls shraddhā, faith in oneself, faith in the unity of life, faith that the Lord is present in all – it is not possible to live in peace. Violence, in whatever form we see it, is a negation of this central unity. Any attempt at violence can only move people further and further apart. In every home and community there are likely to be occasional differences, occasions when someone may make a mistake. But the home or community can be held together if we believe in this underlying unity and act upon it.

योगसंन्यस्तकर्माणं ज्ञानसंछिन्नसंशयम् ।
आत्मवन्तं न कर्माणि निबध्नन्ति धनंजय ॥४-४१॥

41. O Dhananjaya, the man or woman who is established in the Self, who has renounced selfish attachments in work and cut through doubts with spiritual wisdom, acts in freedom.

It is only after we have dehypnotized ourselves from the enticements of money and the blandishments of pleasure that we find how good it is to work when there is no paycheck coming. It is so soothing to work hard for the welfare of those around us without a mercenary motive that we forget all our tensions and frustrations. Some of us may contribute our time; for others it may be energy or skills. For still others it may be material possessions, or expert advice. But it is incumbent upon everyone to devote part of his or her resources to the welfare of others without any thought of personal profit or prestige.

Whatever we contribute to the welfare of others without a thought for our own profit or advancement is an offering made unto the Lord. On a poignant occasion, Jesus took his disciples to task by saying: "I was thirsty, and you gave me no drink; I was a stranger, and you took me not in; naked, and you clothed me not; sick, and in prison, and you visited me not."

And the disciples perhaps answered him, "We never saw you hungry; we never had any occasion to quench your thirst."

Then Jesus really hit hard in answer: "Inasmuch as you did it not to one of the least of these, you did it not to me."

When people agitate us, it is often their way of asking for help. Anger is often a cry for help, and when we immediately get angry in return, we are actually pushing away a person who is half paralyzed. When someone is angry, the very best help we can render him or her is to be patient. The first time we do this the other person may actually take advantage of it, thinking, "Here is somebody who is very patient. I want a suitable outlet for my anger, and here is a godsend, just waiting for me to let him have it." But we cannot improve the situation by returning anger for anger. This does not mean that we simply let angry people have their way, but that we patiently help them to see that their anger and self-will are not only harmful to others but to themselves as well.

तस्मादज्ञानसंभूतं हृत्स्थं ज्ञानासिनात्मनः ।
छित्त्वैनं संशयं योगमातिष्ठोत्तिष्ठ भारत ॥४-४२॥

42. O Bhārata, cut through this doubt
in your heart with the sword of spiritual
wisdom. Arise; take up the path of yoga!

Yoga is neither belief, nor dogma, nor metaphysics, nor philosophy. It is a method of union, a way of uniting all that is divided in our consciousness, uniting all life into the Divine Ground which is one. Yoga has very little to do with physical postures; the correct word for them is *āsana*. We find all kinds of misuses of the word *yoga* in newspapers, magazines, and books, but in the Hindu scriptures yoga refers to the method, the spiritual disciplines, used to unify our consciousness so that we can come to love the Lord within.

Sri Krishna gives us a secret useful in daily life when he says we should be free from doubts. Most of us are plagued by doubts: "Does she love me? Sometimes I think so, but maybe she doesn't." She is also thinking the same thing. My grandmother had a severe statement to make about this kind of misgiving. She would say that we doubt whether others love us because our own love is divided. Wherever we have some reservation or division within ourselves, we look at others through it and immediately say, "He isn't loving me enough." The whole secret of love is not to ask how much others love us but to keep on loving – as St. Francis would say, more than we can. The more we try to love, the more we will be able to love. The passage of time should enrich our love: the person who loves at sixteen should be able to love much more at thirty. It is possible for all of us to deepen our capacity to love by constantly trying to put the welfare of those around us first, until we are finally able to love the Lord in everyone around us.

When we begin to practice meditation, too, it is not unnatural for us to have some doubts and misgivings about the timeless truths of the spiritual life. We all accept the infallibility of physical laws, but when it comes to spiritual laws we are not quite sure. We all believe in the law of gravity, but we sometimes ignore the law of karma. The spiritual teacher does not say that physical laws do not work; he says that spiritual laws, however, are also valid. The charge of fanaticism should really be leveled at the worldly person, because that is the person who says, "Only the physical world is real. I only believe in what I see with my eyes, hear with my ears." But we have the personal testimony of those who have rebuilt their lives on these timeless truths that they are not only real, but accessible to all. Gandhi, who practiced complete nonviolence in thought, word, and deed, said, "I have not the shadow of a doubt that any man or woman can achieve what I have, if he or she would make the same effort and cultivate the same hope and faith." Gandhi, who always claimed he had no more than ordinary capacities, is proof that these spiritual laws do work, and that by obeying them we can transform our character and consciousness. Gandhi belongs to our own century and faced many of the problems we ourselves are facing today, and even though physically dead, he still continues to give new direction to our civilization.

Even when we do come to believe in the validity of spiritual laws, we may still doubt our capacity to reach the goal by following all the drastic disciplines of meditation and sādhana. It is natural that this doubt should continue to haunt us for a long time, but as we go deeper and deeper into our consciousness through the practice of meditation, this doubt also will disappear when our desires are completely unified. What is most urgent is that we start now without allowing our purpose to be weakened by doubts and misgivings, and follow with resolute enthusiasm the path recommended by the Gita.

Sri Ramakrishna used to say that if you repeat *Gita, Gita, Gita* it becomes *tagi, tagi, tagi,* which means 'one who has renounced.' The Gita does not ask us to renounce our family or the world, but to renounce our self-will and separateness, which are the only barriers between us and the Lord of Love enshrined in our hearts. The English word "renounce" strikes a cold note, but the Sanskrit word *tyāga* implies a positive, joyful act in which we find fulfillment. In the words of Jesus, we have to lose ourselves to find ourselves.

When Gandhi was asked to sum up the secret of his life in three words, he quoted the opening of the Īshā Upanishad: *Tena tyaktena bhunjīthāh,* "Renounce and enjoy." Only when we renounce all selfish attachment, he meant, can we really enjoy anything in life. I would go farther and say, "Renounce and rejoice." When we renounce our petty, finite ego in living for the welfare of all, we find infinite joy. In self-naughting we gain the joy of self-mastery and the limitless capacity to love others more than we love ourselves.

We can practice this in the midst of our own family if we try to keep the happiness of our parents, partner, children, and friends first in our consciousness, and our own happiness last. The going may be rough, but gradually we will gain the love and respect of everyone in our family and community. In time all those who come in contact with us will benefit by our sādhana and our selfless living.

ज्ञानकर्मसंन्यासयोगो नाम चतुर्थोऽध्यायः ॥ ४ ॥

CHAPTER FIVE

Renounce & Rejoice

अर्जुन उवाच ।
संन्यासं कर्मणां कृष्ण पुनर्योगं च शंससि ।
यच्छ्रेय एतयोरेकं तन्मे ब्रूहि सुनिश्चितम् ॥५-१॥

ARJUNA:

1. O Krishna, you have recommended
both the path of selfless action and also
sannyāsa, the path of renunciation of action.
Tell me definitely which is better.

In the last chapter, Sri Krishna was talking to Arjuna about *sannyāsa*, renunciation of action, and karma yoga, performance of action. In particular, he was telling Arjuna that it is by karma yoga, through hard, intense, selfless performance of action, that we reach the unitive state where by our very presence we help those around us and even influence our environment.

Arjuna now shows how representative he is of all of us in his tendency to classify everything into this or that. We can imagine Sri Krishna listening to him with a friendly smile in the same way that we listen to our little children at home when they ask questions which amuse us. For example, the other day little Geetha asked me whether she could tie the laces of my shoes. When I said yes, she asked, "Tight, loose, or medium?" For a first-grader I thought she was commanding a wealthy vocabulary. She is right in the Arjuna line of thinking, but while he talks only about two classes, she had three.

This need to categorize is a characteristic of the intellect; it must divide everything into two. One has to be either good or bad according to the intellect. However, there isn't any person who falls into such categories. Most of us are sometimes good, sometimes bad, and at other times both. Just as there is no human being who cannot show signs of utter selflessness, there is no one among the majority of us who also cannot show signs of utter selfishness.

श्रीभगवानुवाच ।
संन्यासः कर्मयोगश्च निःश्रेयसकरावुभौ ।
तयोस्तु कर्मसंन्यासात्कर्मयोगो विशिष्यते ॥५-२॥

SRI KRISHNA:

2. *Both renunciation of action and performance of action lead to the supreme goal. But the path of action is better than renunciation.*

It is difficult for us to understand those rare creatures in the history of mysticism who help people around them by their very presence. Sri Ramana Maharshi was one of these. Sometimes when people came to him for help, he would sit reading the newspaper. This is not our usual conception of action: somebody sits rustling his newspaper and helps people. But many who were sore in spirit, or insecure and resentful, having knocked on all other doors, have gone into Sri Ramana Maharshi's presence as a last resort, sat and looked at him, and come out with their burden relieved, with their heart strengthened and their spirit soaring.

A distinguished philosopher once went to Ramana Maharshi's āshram with his pocket bulging with a long series of questions. He wondered whether the sage would have time to answer all his questions in detail. With utter simplicity, not very characteristic of a distinguished philosopher, he tells us how he went in and looked at Sri Ramana Maharshi, kept on looking at him, and found that none of his questions were necessary. This is the best way to answer questions – by making them unnecessary. Remember, too, the story of Jesus; troubled people had only to touch the hem of his garment, and they would find an upsurge of security and strength within. This is an experience even you and

I can have when we go into the presence of someone who has attained the supreme state. When we are with such people, by some strange means of communication they send some of their strength, love, and wisdom into our hearts.

A Westerner once asked Sri Ramana Maharshi why he wasn't leading a productive life. Sri Ramana Maharshi just chuckled. As far as I know, he is one of the few productive figures the world has produced. Because he was always meditating on the unity of life, everyone belonging to the human species has received an unearned bonus. Gandhiji, however, gives us another ideal: that of helping through selfless action. Sri Ramana Maharshi's way of helping is as effective as Mahatma Gandhi's, and both have a legitimate, important place on the spiritual path. It is the same whether we try to help through selfless action or selfless inaction; the whole world will receive the benefit of our contribution.

Arjuna, however, is an intellectually oriented person given to action, and he doesn't understand that there is a place for both selfless action and renunciation of action. Confused, he asks Sri Krishna which path is better: "Now, think clearly, and don't be vague. Can't you put these two ways in the balance and tell me which is faster, safer, and easier? That's the only language I can understand."

Sri Krishna, so loving, so patient, begins from Arjuna's point of view. He says, "It's true. I have placed renunciation of action before you as a great ideal, and I have also placed intense selfless action before you as a great ideal. But since you have an intellectual need for comparison, and an inescapable tendency to weigh one thing against the other, I am prepared to concede that selfless action is better for you than renunciation of action." At present we are not ready to renounce action. Even if we try not to act, even if we take a vow not to act, we will be forced into action. If there is no action physically, action still continues to go on all the time in the mind. The choice, therefore, for you and me is: shall we act selflessly for the benefit of all, or shall we act selfishly for our own personal aggrandizement? Meister Eckhart advises us in glorious words: "To be right, a person must do one of two things; either learn to have God in his work and hold fast to him there, or give up work altogether. Since, however, we cannot live without activities that are both human and various, we must learn to keep God in everything we do, and whatever the job or place, keep on with him, letting nothing stand in our way."

In the practice of meditation, particularly as concentration increases, you should see to it that you engage yourself in intense, selfless action during the day. You should ask yourself if you have plenty of opportunity to be with other people. Suppose you have been meditating for a number of years alone in the forest, away from the hurly-burly of life. When you come back to the city and somebody pushes you aside on the sidewalk, not all your meditation in the forest is going to make you smile sweetly and say, "Forgive me for having been in your way." This capacity comes through regular meditation, and by walking on sidewalks where people push and are pushed about. Then you learn that if somebody pushes you, the person may be just looking in the shop window and not seeing you. It is only by being with people who are irascible, sometimes because of you, that the angles and corners of your personality are slowly smoothed out. You, of course, are never short-tempered, but you sometimes run into people who are short-tempered, who do not easily understand your point of view. The answer here is to repeat the mantram, become patient, listen respectfully to the other's point of view, and be even more persuasive in presenting your position.

The world has become so difficult, so violent, that no one today can afford to keep quiet. No one can afford to drop out of society or fail to make a contribution. Each of us can change the whole world by changing ourselves a little. When, instead of reacting violently, I renounce all violence in action, in word, in thought, and in my relationships with everybody else, I have actually changed my environment. When I can show others love instead of hatred, good will instead of ill will, respect instead of criticism, I not only change myself but also those who come in contact with me. In everything I do, every day, I am affecting my environment either favorably or unfavorably. To make this influence completely beneficial, and to enable it to reach as many people as possible, hard, intense, selfless action is a necessity.

In meditation we are going deep into ourselves, into the utter solitude that is within. As a counterbalance to this, it is necessary to be with people: to laugh with them, to sing with them, and to enjoy the healthy activities of life. It is not a luxury on the spiritual path to have hard work, or to have the company of spiritually oriented people; these are necessary for our spiritual development.

ज्ञेयः स नित्यसंन्यासी यो न द्वेष्टि न काङ्क्षति ।
निर्द्वन्द्वो हि महाबाहो सुखं बन्धात्प्रमुच्यते ॥५-३॥

3. Those who have attained perfect renunciation are free from any sense of duality; they are unaffected by likes and dislikes, Arjuna, and are free from the bondage of self-will.

Sannyāsī, 'one who has renounced,' usually refers to a monk who has retired from the world to a monastic order to seek the supreme goal of life. *Sannyāsa* is often misunderstood as renunciation of the world, but for the vast majority of ordinary people like you and me, when the Lord asks us to renounce, he is not asking us to renounce the world. He is asking us to renounce our ego, our self-will, our separateness, which is the main obstacle to spiritual development.

In a story from the spiritual lore of India, the jackfruit is used to bring out the meaning of renunciation or detachment. The jackfruit is a big, burly fruit that grows plentifully in Kerala and Bengal. If you're a guest in Kerala, when we want to know if a household is well-to-do, we ask, "Do they have a lot of jackfruit and mango trees in their back yard?" A back yard groaning with jackfruit and mangoes is the equivalent of a land flowing with milk and honey. None of the jackfruit is wasted; the thorny skin is a delicacy for the cows, the pods are a delicacy for us, and the seeds are used in curry. People in some other parts of India, however, are not usually acquainted with the jackfruit. If you're a guest in Kerala a mischievous boy may ask you to eat a piece of it, and after you have eaten the fruit and enjoyed it thoroughly, the boy starts asking you all sorts of questions: where you come from, what your name is, and where you went to school. When you try to speak you cannot articulate your words, because the jackfruit has a very thick, gluey juice, like cement, and your lips have become glued together. But in Kerala, before we eat the jackfruit, we smear our hands and lips with coconut oil. Then, if I had been the guest, I could have finished eating and started in, "To be or not to be, that is the question"; and I would have been able to continue with the whole soliloquy of Hamlet because the coconut oil would have prevented my lips from being glued together. Sri Ramakrishna in a magnificent simile says that we cannot love God, we cannot put others first or forget ourselves in the welfare of all those around us, because our heart is glued so that not a drop of love can come out of it. Love circulates inside, wanting to flow out; but there is not a pinprick of a hole that is not completely glued up by the fruit of the ego, which is much bigger than the biggest jackfruit to be seen in Kerala. If we want to release our capacity to love all those around us and find the joy of selfless living as members of our family, our community, our society, then we should apply the oil of renunciation and dispassion so that we will not get stuck in the glue of the ego.

It is most important to remember that all of us have this inborn capacity to love. We don't have to go to India or any other place to learn to love. Love is right within us; what prevents us from letting it flow outward to everyone around us, flooding our home and our community with happiness, is the glue of the ego which is so sticky that it hinders any attempt to love.

What is the evidence that we are detaching ourselves from our ego, that we are making our mind serene, that we are going beyond separateness? The word Sri Krishna uses is *nirdvandva:* 'without duality,' free from the pairs of opposites. As long as we see life divided into good and bad, right and wrong, success and defeat, birth and death, as long as we groan under the tyranny of likes and dislikes, always seeking the pleasant and avoiding the unpleasant, so long will our mind be like a sea that is agitated all the time.

Yesterday I happened to remember something my grandmother did that shows how she could change her likes and dislikes at will. Many years ago, in our village, one of my uncles wanted to marry into a family which his family did not approve of on very legitimate grounds. Seldom in our village did any marriage take place without both families agreeing, and my uncle's choice caused a good deal of agitation. My granny, who was quite fond of my uncle, told him, "This choice of yours is making all your people unhappy. Tomorrow your wife has got to come and meet them, and she is not going to be happy when they are unhappy." She tried all kinds of persuasive ways to get my uncle to choose another girl and let the girl choose another man, but it was springtime, and all of her persuasion fell on deaf ears. They married, even though everybody in his family showed their disapproval. On the very day when the marriage took place, when all the others were sulking, my grandmother dropped all her opposition and disapproval and went up to them saying, "You are both meant for each other." She had tried her level best to dissuade my uncle in the interests of the whole family, but when she saw that they wanted each other so much, she immediately dropped her opposition. This is how freedom comes, even in attitudes. There are times when we feel that we should oppose a certain course of action, but when we find there is another side to it, a better side, we should be able to drop our opposition immediately. There are few people capable of this, but through the practice of meditation, we can all develop this capacity to change our likes and dislikes at will.

How to go beyond likes and dislikes in everyday living is an immediate problem. For those of us who are living with our families and friends, and who have wide contacts, I think reducing self-will and going beyond likes and dislikes is an easy job because of the many opportunities we receive for putting others first. Arjuna has four brothers, and Sri Krishna reminds him that five brothers all living together should have ample opportunity for overcoming likes and dislikes. In our own case, therefore, it is good to put the needs of those around us first in matters like food, recreation, and of course comforts and conveniences. We can find opportunities even in little things. We want to go to one movie and our friend wants to go to another. His may be more likely to suit both of us, but we have read all about our movie: the stars are our favorites, and the music is by someone we like. There are all sorts of ways we can support our arguments, but all we have to say is, "I would very much enjoy going to this movie, but I'd rather go with you to the other movie which you will enjoy." This is an excellent spiritual discipline.

सांख्ययोगौ पृथग्बालाः प्रवदन्ति न पण्डिताः ।
एकमप्यास्थितः सम्यगुभयोर्विन्दते फलम् ॥५-४॥

4. Children say that knowledge and action are different, but the wise see them as the same. The person who is established in one path will attain the rewards of both.

Sri Krishna is making a statement here about people who think that knowledge and action are different. People who talk about wisdom but are not able to translate it into their daily life are children, says Sri Krishna. If we have spiritual wisdom, it has to show itself in our daily living. There is no condemnation in this; the Lord, very compassionately, looks upon us as not fully grown up when we talk about the spiritual life yet yield to our self-will, have difficulties in our personal relationships, and are unable to exercise reasonable government over our senses.

St. Francis of Assisi expressed this same truth when he said that our knowledge is as deep as our action. In the Upanishads, the sages make a useful distinction between two kinds of knowledge. One, called *apara,* is intellectual knowledge, which is useful for living in the world and manipulating our physical environment but is of little help in transforming our character, conduct, and consciousness. The other, called *para,* is spiritual wisdom. This spiritual wisdom is directly connected with the will, and shines radiantly through our every action.

Intellectual knowledge is unfortunately not readily transformed into everyday action. Take, for example, smoking. We have such alarming evidence of the causal connection between smoking and cancer, yet there are millions of educated people, quite aware of this connection, who still continue to smoke because they cannot give it up. Even in hospitals we see many of the patients, who have come to be cured, smoking while sitting in the waiting room. I, for one, do not understand why cigarettes are sold in hospitals. This is the contradiction between intellectual knowledge and action. Intellectual knowledge, apara, does not seep into and transform the deeper recesses of our consciousness.

Contrasted with apara is para, spiritual wisdom. As our meditation deepens, we can ask the Lord, who is our real Self, "Let this craving fall away from me," and it falls away. This is the miracle of meditation. When we have gone sufficiently deep, many old cravings fall away without any violence done to ourselves; as our desires become unified, they are withdrawn from lesser cravings.

All of us would like to be more loving, but we cannot love those around us more until we have learned to withdraw our love from material things. Victims of money, who are always thinking about money, are not capable of loving their families, their friends, or anyone else. People who are on drugs are not capable of giving their complete love and loyalty to another. Every little desire for pleasure or power diminishes our capacity to love. Desire is the raw material of love.

The mind is really an endless series of desires. To desire, to desire, to desire – this is the nature of the mind. In our attempt to recall our love from all the wasteful channels into which we have allowed it to go, and to still the continual waves of desire agitating our consciousness, the intellect is of no avail at all. Whether it is the frantic pursuit of money, material possessions, pleasure, power, or drugs, the problem is the same: we are caught in these cravings as long as we do not have access to our deeper resources. In meditation we develop the spiritual wisdom and the strength of will to recall our desires little by little. Our desires are like untrained puppies; they will run down any blind alley we pass. We may be walking down Telegraph Avenue; they see a blind alley and immediately they're off and we don't know how to call them back. In meditation, we can actually train our desires by telling them, "When we are on the Avenue, we keep on the Avenue. We don't go down side streets."

Little, little desires, thousands of them – for this dress, for that car, for this candy, for that prize – by themselves weigh only a little, but when put together, they amount to a large sum. All these little desires, every day, drain our vital capacity to love.

To quote the bank advertisement, "It all adds up": a few pennies here, a few pennies there, collected every day. While we were living on the Blue Mountain in India, we noticed that our local bank there had a very homely arrangement for collecting funds from the villagers. Poor villagers have very little to save, only a few copper pennies at most. To encourage them to deposit even these few pennies every day, the bank employed a boy who would go into the village to their homes, collect their few coppers, and enter the total in their account. In meditation it is the same: when the Lord comes, we can say, "We are no great mystic, but a few times today we have tried to be patient. A few times today we have tried to put our family first. A few times today we have resisted some little craving for personal satisfaction." And the Lord will say, "Give me your coppers." This is how most of us are going to lead the spiritual life for a long time. It's mostly in coppers. But in these innumerable little acts of selflessness lies spiritual growth, which over a long period can transform every one of us into a loving and spiritual person.

When we meditate on an inspirational passage, repeating it every day in the depths of our consciousness, we will find that it releases our inner resources of spiritual wisdom. When, for example, we meditate on the Prayer of St. Francis of Assisi, "It is in giving that we receive; it is in pardoning that we are pardoned," we find in our daily relationships that we are not getting angry any more, that we are not being resentful, that we are beginning to forgive and forget. This transformation of character, conduct, and consciousness comes naturally to us when we begin to draw upon the power released in meditation.

यत्सांख्यैः प्राप्यते स्थानं तद्योगैरपि गम्यते ।
एकं सांख्यं च योगं च यः पश्यति स पश्यति ॥५-५॥
संन्यासस्तु महाबाहो दुःखमाप्तुमयोगतः ।
योगयुक्तो मुनिर्ब्रह्म नचिरेणाधिगच्छति ॥५-६॥

5. The goal of wisdom and the goal of service are the same. If a man fails to see that knowledge and action are one, he is blind.
6. Perfect renunciation is difficult to attain without performing action. But the wise, who follow the path of selfless service, quickly reach Brahman.

The search for transcendental wisdom through negation of the world, and the path of karma yoga or a life of selfless action in the world, are both based on the practice of meditation, and both lead ultimately to the same goal. But Sri Krishna points out that the path of karma yoga is the easier of the two. Renunciation of the world, or rather of our selfish attachment to the world, is impossible for the vast majority of us without first practicing the disciplines of selfless action and meditation. Often we hear people, particularly the young, saying they want to lead the spiritual life and, therefore, have dropped out of school, quit their job, moved away from their family, and are living in the woods. They hope this will enable them to pursue their spiritual goal in peace. But the only barrier between the Lord and ourselves is our self-will, called *ahamkāra* in Sanskrit. There is no other barrier, and the whole purpose of spiritual living is somehow to break through this barrier, which can assume gigantic proportions in our modern world. To eliminate our self-will, we need the salutary context of our family, our friends, our campus, and our society. Friends and family are not always easy to be with, but they give us the much-needed opportunity for rubbing off the angles and corners of our self-will little by little, in the innumerable acts of give-and-take in everyday life.

When we were living on the Blue Mountain in India, we ran into a young fellow from the Northwest who used to come to our place now and then and had become very fond of us. He had led a very lonely life: if ever there was a lone spiritual wolf, it was he. He used to avoid people completely, staying in lonely places so as not to come in contact with them. Sometimes he would twit me affectionately for always being with people, and would invite me to go on long walks to see the trees and hills. But even though I admire a beautiful landscape, I pleaded guilty to the charge of being more fond of people than of trees: I didn't try to argue with him when he praised the virtue of solitude, but one day a suitable opportunity presented itself, and I explained my point of view.

He was fond of talking about "flower power" and about being able naturally to love everybody. One day he was working in the garden in the midst of the flowers with the gardener's son, who was given to fist power. There was some altercation between them, and the gardener's son, being a simple boy, took a spade and threatened our young friend, who retaliated by threatening him with the hoe. Someone separated them before they could do each other any harm, and our young friend came to us so agitated that his hands were trembling. His teeth were clenched and he was bursting with fury. Instead of arguing with him, I asked him to join us at dinner. It is difficult to be furious when eating, and this gave him a little time to cool down. After he had finished his dinner, I said, "What happened to all your flower language? What happened to all your love? Why didn't you show him the universal love that you are capable of?"

He didn't know what to answer. He said, "You tell me what happened."

I said, "You are not used to people. You have never had the opportunity of living together with people who provoke you. You haven't learned to grit your teeth, repeat the mantram, stand firm, and move closer to people when they provoke you. It takes a man to do this. To be angry, to take a spade and hit the other person – that is not worthy of a human being."

He said, "How do you learn to do this?"

"Oh," I said, "by living with people like you!"

Even for a deeply spiritual person, selfless action is necessary for a long, long time. Today our troubled world is clamoring for action from each of us to help resolve the dilemmas with which it is faced. The Gita must be interpreted in accordance with the times in which we live, and in our age, we all must make a contribution to the world. It is not the time for us to "do our own thing"; it is the time to make selfless action a part of our spiritual way. Those who try to drop out of life, to turn their backs upon society, are depriving the world of the contribution they can make. Without being the president of the country or the prime minister, even in our own small life, in our home, with our neighbors, on our campus, in our town, all of us can make a real contribution to peace by not being violent under any circumstances and learning to live in harmony even with those who may cause trouble to us.

Even if there is one person in the home who is really selfless, he or she – usually she – helps everyone else in becoming selfless. I never tire of pointing out that the noblest role of the woman is to be the selfless support of everyone around her, whether as a mother or wife, as a sister or niece. Through my simple eyes, any home is beautiful where there is a woman looking with love at all those around her, forgetting her own self-will and separateness in supporting those around her. Even though a home may have carpets from Bokhara, candelabra from Italy, and all the conveniences of modern civilization, if the woman is not selfless, I do not see beauty in the home.

Meditation and selfless action go hand in hand. When we try to live more for others than for ourselves, this will deepen our meditation. When we deepen our meditation, more and more energy will be released with which we can help others.

योगयुक्तो विशुद्धात्मा विजितात्मा जितेन्द्रियः ।
सर्वभूतात्मभूतात्मा कुर्वन्नपि न लिप्यते ॥५-७॥
नैव किंचित्करोमीति युक्तो मन्येत तत्त्ववित् ।
पश्यञ्शृण्वन्स्पृशञ्जिघ्रन्नश्नन्गच्छन्स्वपञ्श्वसन् ॥५-८॥
प्रलपन्विसृजन्गृह्णन्नुन्मिषन्निमिषन्नपि ।
इन्द्रियाणीन्द्रियार्थेषु वर्तन्त इति धारयन् ॥५-९॥

7. Those who follow the path of service, who have completely purified themselves and conquered the senses and self-will, who see the Self in all creatures, are untouched by any action they may perform.
8–9. The person whose consciousness is unified thinks, "I am always the instrument." He is aware of this truth even while seeing or hearing, touching or smelling; eating, moving about, or sleeping; breathing or speaking, letting go or holding on, even opening or closing the eyes. He understands that these are the movements of the senses among sense objects.

In our villages in Kerala, bags of rice, water jars, and other heavy burdens are often carried on the head. Villagers will walk long distances to market with their produce balanced on their heads. After carrying a bag of rice for many miles, when they want to rest, they find it difficult to sit down, take the burden from their heads, and then, after resting, put it back on their heads and get up again. So by the side of the rugged country roads they have constructed stone parapets, called *athāni* in my mother tongue, which are about the height of a person's head. When I have been carrying a heavy burden for a few miles, I come to a stone parapet, and all I have to do is move close to the athāni, nod my head, and the bag of rice will slide onto the wall. I can lie down and rest peacefully, and when I have refreshed myself, I can go back to the slab, give the bundle a little push, and balance it on my head again.

Vallathol Narayana Menon, a Malayali poet who was a Hindu, but who was deeply in love with Jesus as a divine incarnation, wrote a poem about Mary Magdalene in which he uses this image of the athāni. In this beautiful poem in my mother tongue, with the title "Magdalana Mariyam," Jesus tells Mary: "Why do you carry the load of your guilt, the burden of your sins on your head? I am here, like the stone parapet. Don't stand far away. Come close to me; keep your head right near me, and when you nod your head, I am ready to take your burden."

This is an experience that will come to all of us when we lead the spiritual life and are prepared to live for others around us. Sometimes our problems will be greater, sometimes the challenges will be immense, but the Lord will always say from within, "I am the stone parapet. I am your support. Shift your burden to me." My spiritual teacher, my grandmother, who had more than her share of problems – partly because she had me on her hands – was never oppressed by her burden nor trapped in action and the results of action. When she had a great problem facing her, all that she had to do was close her eyes, surrender herself to the Lord, and then come back to us with wisdom, love, and the skill to help me or the family solve the problem.

The God-filled person, who is an instrument in the hands of the Lord, doesn't get discouraged or fatigued. He is so completely identified with the Ātman, so sure that the Lord is the operator, that he does not get entangled at all in the interplay of senses and sense objects, in which all of us are caught when we live for ourselves. His every action is done with utter detachment, as an offering to the Lord. Even when such a person eats, it is not for the sake of satisfying the palate; it is for the sake of serving the Lord. When we eat nourishing food as an offering unto the Lord, it strengthens the body, the mind, and the intellect. Similarly, we can keep our body strong and healthy with exercise so that it can be used for many years in selfless service.

We have another opportunity to move closer to the Lord when we go to sleep repeating the holy name. Between the last waking moment and the first moment of sleep there is an arrow's entry into the depths of our subconscious, into which the name of the Lord, whether it is *Jesus* or *Rāma,* can enter if we keep repeating it as we go to sleep. It takes some effort and perseverance, but when we have learned to fall asleep in the mantram, throughout the night the healing process continues in our sleep, and we wake up refreshed in body, mind, and spirit.

Every activity of ours should be performed as a service to the Lord if we are to become completely united with him. No harsh word, no sarcastic crack, no resentful look should come from us. We can see how demanding the Lord is: even the opening and closing of our eyes should be done with love. In all our little acts, we should come to feel that we are an instrument of the Lord. My grandmother used to say that even in our dreams we should not have resentful thoughts or hostile attitudes toward anybody. We can come to have such mastery over our consciousness that even in our sleep we reach the state where nothing but love and the awareness of unity pervades us.

ब्रह्मण्याधाय कर्माणि सङ्गं त्यक्त्वा करोति यः ।
लिप्यते न स पापेन पद्मपत्रमिवाम्भसा ॥५-१०॥

10. Those who have surrendered all selfish attachments in work to the Lord are like the leaf of a lotus floating clean and dry in water. Sin cannot touch them.

The lotus is a favorite flower in the Sanskrit scriptures, both Hindu and Buddhist. *Pankaja*, 'born in the mud,' is one of the Sanskrit names for this flower which grows abundantly in the pools and lakes of India. Born in the mud and dirt at the bottom of the pool, the lotus grows up through the water, rises above its surface, and blossoms towards the sun. The leaf of the lotus, which floats on the surface of the water, is a large one. In the villages, it is often used as a plate because it is waterproof; you can pour water on it and the water will not soak through the leaf but will just run off. Similarly, when we surrender ourselves to the Lord and become his instruments for carrying on selfless service, even though difficulties are sure to come to us, they will not cling to us; we will be able to face challenges without fatigue, tension, or diffidence.

कायेन मनसा बुद्ध्या केवलैरिन्द्रियैरपि ।
योगिनः कर्म कुर्वन्ति सङ्गं त्यक्त्वात्मशुद्धये ॥५-११॥
युक्तः कर्मफलं त्यक्त्वा शान्तिमाप्नोति नैष्ठिकीम् ।
अयुक्तः कामकारेण फले सक्तो निबध्यते ॥५-१२॥

11. Those who follow the path of service renounce their selfish attachments, and work with body, senses, and mind for the sake of self-purification.
12. The man whose consciousness is unified abandons all attachment to the results of actions and attains supreme peace. But the man whose desires are fragmented, and who is selfishly attached to the results of his work, is bound in all he does.

All of us begin the spiritual life with mixed motives. Perhaps we perceive dimly that selfless action is a sure way of removing the barrier between ourselves and the Lord, and we want to contribute to the welfare of those around us; but at the same time, we are concerned with ensuring our own private advantage. It takes quite a while for most of us to become fully aware that our welfare is included in the welfare of all and to realize that when we are working for everybody, we are also ensuring our own well-being.

To imagine that we are going to learn the secret of selfless action in a few months, or even years, is being a little optimistic. Even sincere philanthropists, who do a lot of good for the world, are sometimes motivated by personal drives. I, for one, do not think it possible for anyone to become completely selfless in action without the practice of meditation. It is rather easy to think that we are living for others and contributing to their welfare, but very often we may not even know what the needs of others are. In order to become aware of the needs of those around us, to become sensitive to the difficulties they face, we must minimize our obsession with ourselves. This requires the discipline of meditation, which enables us gradually to reduce self-will and preoccupation with our private needs.

It is all right for a child to be very aware of its needs and unaware of the needs of others, but for grown-up people like you and me to be conscious only of our wants and blind to those of others puts us back in the nursery. Sometimes I think that whether or not we have children, the nursery is an essential component of the modern home. When we are designing our house we shouldn't forget to include a nursery, into which we can crawl whenever we lose our adulthood and maturity and begin to brood upon ourselves. On such occasions we can simply crawl into the kiddie corral and put up a little sign, "Spoil me or spank me." Even brilliant intellectuals and people who are very effective in action sometimes crawl into their kiddie corral and do not know how to come out at all. For this reason, I would question whether it is possible to lead the spiritual life without being able to draw from a deeper source of power the energy we need to reduce our self-will. Meditation is the method we can use to reach these inner resources which are hidden deep in our consciousness. It is the bridge from the individual to the universal, from the ephemeral to the eternal, from the human to the divine.

We all have to begin the spiritual life with action that is partly egoistic, partly egoless, and none of us need be discouraged when we find, in the early days of our sādhana, that there is some motive of enlightened self-interest driving us on to action. Without this motive in the beginning, action may be difficult. But even though we may act partly for selfish reasons, we must make sure our action is not at the expense of other people. Any occupation harmful to others is not right occupation. Take, for example, the field of advertising. Though advertising of cigarettes has gone off television, we can see the increased vehemence of the advertiser's campaign on all the roadsides. Not content with billboards, the companies are giving out sample cigarettes on the streets. The other evening, coming back from San Francisco, we were grieved to see young girls distributing free cigarettes. Just imagine the cupidity of the human being: when people walking by were offered attractive cartons of cigarettes by these nicely dressed girls, they would turn and go out of their way to take them. Even though these girls are not doing this with any ill will, even though it may be just a job to them, they are going to acquire a certain load of karma because they are actually tempting people to get cancer. They are selling cancer to the people around them. Every day we have to ask ourselves how much of our life and work is for the welfare of mankind. If it is to the detriment of anyone, it does not matter how much money we are making, or how much power the job is bringing us; it is much better to live and die in poverty than to continue working at such a job.

When we are driven by the motive for personal profit, continually working for money, power, and prestige, anxiety takes a heavy toll on the nervous system. It is not work that tires us, but profit-motivated work: always doing work we like and avoiding work we dislike. It is the preoccupation with results that makes us tense and deprives us of sleep. When we are enmeshed in the results, anxious whether we will fail or win, our very anxiety exhausts us. For the majority of us, uncertainty is worse than disaster. Disaster comes to us only rarely; worry depletes us often. We never know whether we are going to get a brick or a bouquet. If we knew for certain it would be a brick, there would be no anxiety. We would just say, "Throw it and be done with it." For those who have become aware of the Lord, however, it is all the same whether it is brick or bouquet, praise or censure, success or defeat. These will neither intoxicate them nor discourage them. When we can say, "Whatever disasters come, we will not be afraid because the Lord is within us," then this resoluteness and faith will enable us to work in complete security, free from tension, agitation, and fear of defeat. The person who works with this attitude is always at peace, always secure, because he is not anxious about the results of his action.

सर्वकर्माणि मनसा संन्यस्यास्ते सुखं वशी ।
नवद्वारे पुरे देही नैव कुर्वन्न कारयन् ॥५-१३॥

13. Those who are self-controlled, who through discrimination have renounced attachment in all their deeds, live content in the city of nine gates. They are not driven to act, nor do they involve others in action.

If you want to enjoy life, you have to renounce, not the world, but your ego. If you really want to have a merry time, all you need do is take out your ego and hide it where nobody will be able to find it. Unfortunately, the ego usually does not want to be thrown away; every time you try to throw it away it will come back to you.

No amount of trying to throw it away, no amount of resolving to be completely selfless from this moment on, is going to rid us of this unwanted ego-burden. Only by gradually learning to think about others, to love others more than we love ourselves and serve them rather than our own self-interest, can we finally get rid of the ego. By some strange magic, the more we love others, the wider we extend the circle of our love, the less the ego seems to like us; and one day, when we forget ourselves entirely, it disappears. Then we are free of it once and for all.

In the second line of the verse, there is the dryly humorous description of the body as the little town with nine gates. Our eyes are two wide-open gates through which sights are marching in procession. Our ears are two gates where sounds are coming through in long, long queues. Most of us are firmly convinced that we are the body; we are not aware that the body is just the little city in which we dwell. Because we identify others as well as ourselves with the body, we go through life without ever really seeing those around us. We do not even really get to know our own dear ones. Even after years of marriage, we have never seen our partner. Living with the members of our family all our life, we pass out of this world without even having seen them as they really are: as the Ātman, the pure, perfect dweller within the body.

न कर्तृत्वं न कर्माणि लोकस्य सृजति प्रभुः ।
न कर्मफलसंयोगं स्वभावस्तु प्रवर्तते ॥५-१४॥
नादत्ते कस्यचित्पापं न चैव सुकृतं विभुः ।
अज्ञानेनावृतं ज्ञानं तेन मुह्यन्ति जन्तवः ॥५-१५॥

14. Neither self-will, nor actions, nor the union of action and result comes from the Lord of this world. They arise from ignorance of our own nature.

15. The Lord does not partake in the good and evil deeds of any person. When wisdom is obscured by ignorance, a person's judgment is clouded.

Though we may have committed many mistakes in life, as most of us do in our ignorance, the Lord will never desert us. Sri Krishna is telling us with great simplicity: "I love everyone because I am in everyone. How can I hate anyone, even though he commits mistakes, when I am in that person?" We often forget in dealing with people who have gone astray that the Lord continues to dwell in them even though they have made mistake after mistake. It is a great art to be able to resist wrongdoing without withdrawing our love from the wrongdoer. To be able to love someone very deeply and yet resist firmly the wrong that person may be doing us out of ignorance is one of the most important arts we can learn in life. Such people cannot resist for long when we use the spiritual technique of embracing them with all our love while still resisting what is selfish in them. Under no circumstances should we condemn people even if they are being selfish and self-willed. It serves no purpose to attack them. The only thing to do is to love and respect them because the Lord is present in them, and to resist them nonviolently, bearing patiently whatever suffering they may be inflicting upon us in their ignorance.

Mistakes are a natural part of growing up, and there is no need to brood over the sins of the past. The purpose of making a mistake is to learn not to make that mistake again. As my grandmother used to tell the young girls in my ancestral home when they began to work in the kitchen, we can all expect to do a little spilling and burning in order to learn to cook. Even though we have a certain margin for error, the sooner we can learn from our mistakes, the less suffering we will have to undergo in life. Mistakes are inevitably followed by consequences. The consequences of a mistake may last for many years, and in making a major decision, many of us are prone to overcalculate the satisfaction we are going to get out of it and overlook the suffering involved for ourselves as well as others. We often forget that the action we are contemplating contains the seed of its result. We try to connect wrong means with right ends, which will never work. Right ends are included in right means; wrong ends are included naturally in wrong means.

ज्ञानेन तु तदज्ञानं येषां नाशितमात्मनः ।
तेषामादित्यवज्ज्ञानं प्रकाशयति तत्परम् ॥५-१६॥

तद्बुद्धयस्तदात्मानस्तन्निष्ठास्तत्परायणाः ।
गच्छन्त्यपुनरावृत्तिं ज्ञाननिर्धूतकल्मषाः ॥५-१७॥

16. But ignorance is destroyed by knowledge of the Self within. The light of this knowledge shines like the sunrise; it reveals the supreme Brahman.
17. The person who has cast off all sin through this knowledge, whose mind is absorbed in the Lord, and who is completely established in the Lord as his one goal and refuge, is never born again.

When our self-will dies completely, when our separateness is extinguished completely, then we see the splendor of the Lord.

Yesterday we had a triune celebration at Ramagiri. It was Easter, the wedding reception of our dear friends Steve and Debbie, and also the Kerala New Year. I had forgotten all about New Year, so I was a little surprised when I came out of our room after meditation on Sunday morning and found our two little nieces waiting on either side of the door. I had my red knit cap on. They said, "Close your eyes, uncle." I closed my eyes like an obedient uncle, and they pulled the wool over them. Taking my hands, they led me into their room and had me sit down. Then they asked, "Would you like to see the Lord?"

"Very much," I replied.

"Then open your eyes!"

I did, and found myself looking into a mirror all beautifully decorated with fruits and flowers. The face I saw was my own.

This is the Kerala tradition, in which all members of the family are led to a mirror and reminded that the face they see there is the Lord's. Once this tradition has seeped into our consciousness, it is enough for a woman in the home – mother, sister, wife, or niece – just to say in a very loving voice when we are getting angry: "Don't you remember where you saw the Lord on New Year's Day?" I have seen angry people breaking out in angelic smiles when they heard this. It is a beautiful thing to remind those who are getting angry that they are really trying to prevent the Lord within them from looking out through their eyes.

In order to see the Lord within we must do what the Bible commands us: "Be still and know that I am God." This supreme state is stillness of the body, mind, intellect, and, of course, the ego. In the Katha Upanishad the King of Death tells his disciple that when all these have been stilled, that is the highest state, in which he will find the Lord in his own heart and in the heart of everyone around him.

We cannot attain this state as long as we are searching for fulfillment without. It is difficult for us to understand that we are always out, always going on a trip somewhere. Today, when we were coming back from Ramagiri, we saw an unusually large number of hitchhikers with all kinds of sign boards. They have now started making changes on these little placards: formerly it was just "LA" or "SF," but today we saw one board which read, "Chicago – sister's wedding." I thought this was a personal way of getting the message across, something that touches all of us. After all, we have to give him a lift if he is going to attend his sister's wedding. Then there was a very quiet sign, "East, please." To me this also was rather personal. Another sign, probably by an Eskimo, just read "North." Now, if you ever find me with a placard by the roadside, it will read "In." This is what we do in meditation; we try to recall all our wandering energies back to the original source which is our home.

विद्याविनयसंपन्ने ब्राह्मणे गवि हस्तिनि ।
शुनि चैव श्वपाके च पण्डिताः समदर्शिनः ॥५-१८॥

18. Those who possess this wisdom have equal love for all. They see the same Self in a spiritual aspirant and an outcaste, in an elephant, a cow, and a dog.

In the one beautiful word *samadarshin* – 'looking upon all equally,' having equal love for all – the Lord tells us the mark of those who live in God. The person who lives in God will love and respect all, without ever deprecating anybody because he or she is of a different religion, country, race, culture, or sex. Once we have realized the unity of all life, we will be incapable of feeling that we are superior to another, no matter what surface differences there appear to be.

In developing the capacity to love and respect all, we must go beyond superficial gestures. We must learn to be understanding and sympathetic to all. It is easy to appear cosmopolitan, to seem well disposed to all, but deep inside there still may be a tacit sense of superiority – the feeling that our culture, our country, our religion, or our race is greater than someone else's. Some of the books, for example, that are published about different countries by respected scholars are attempts, whether conscious or unconscious, to deprecate other countries and other cultures simply because they are foreign.

One of the deep causes of agitation in India during the British regime was the quiet pervasion of all levels of society with the attitude that British culture was superior. The worst thing about foreign domination is that it can gradually undermine the self-reliance and self-respect of a nation. Because of these far-reaching consequences of long periods of foreign misrule, it is not surprising that most of the Asian and African countries which have endured colonial governments have a kind of national neurosis. Western nations which have not had the misfortune of being dominated by a foreign power must bear with these nations of Asia and Africa, remembering that because they have been mercilessly exploited, they have the constant suspicion that they are likely to be exploited again.

As Mahatma Gandhi has pointed out, imperialism damages not only the ruled, but the rulers also. Even young Englishmen – often university graduates from Oxford or Cambridge – who came to India with high ideals and the desire to serve would in the course of a decade or so slowly become arrogant and come to believe that they belonged to a superior race, culture, and country. In recalling the dark days of foreign rule, however, we should not forget that many British people tried to make amends during the freedom struggle by joining Mahatma Gandhi to help him in his work. Today there are many British people who have settled down in India as citizens and who love the country as much as they loved England.

We begin the practice of equal love and respect for all right in our home. We need not be afraid or agitated if there are people with different opinions living in the same home. What makes us afraid of opinions opposed to ours, often causing the so-called generation gap, is the tendency to identify ourselves and others with opinions. Just because you happen to be one color and I happen to be another does not mean that we are different; we are just wearing different colored jackets. Similarly with opinions: even if our opinions differ, this is no reason for us not to love and respect one another. Even though there may be differences of opinion between them, each generation can greatly enrich the life of the home. There is a contribution that older people can make with their experience of life, for which there is no substitute. Similarly, young people make a contribution to the home with their vitality and freshness. Children also can add to the life of the home with their innocence; they remind us of the words of Jesus: "Suffer the little children to come unto me, and forbid them not: for of such is the kingdom of God. Verily I say unto you, whosoever shall not receive the kingdom of God as a little child, he shall not enter therein."

In this verse Sri Krishna also refers to animals. We should show love and respect even to animals because the Lord is in them also. I need hardly say how much animals respond to a person who really loves them. Because they understand in some way that we have great love for them, that we are trying to realize the unity that makes us all one, more and more creatures are now coming to Ramagiri. I remember how nervous the jackrabbits were when we first moved to Ramagiri. As soon as we saw a jackrabbit, he would go sit behind a bush and say, "I am a bush." I used to reply, "If you believe that, all right. I won't look at you if you don't want me to." Then I would go away. They had probably been chased and were afraid. But our people at Ramagiri are extremely loving and particularly solicitous of the welfare of the creatures which live there, and one year has changed the atmosphere of the place considerably. So yesterday, when I saw a jackrabbit and immediately said, "That's a bush," he didn't try to hide. In fact, he might have heard me – jackrabbits have very long ears – because he turned around, came back close to the path, and started performing.

इहैव तैर्जितः सर्गो येषां साम्ये स्थितं मनः ।
निर्दोषं हि समं ब्रह्म तस्माद्ब्रह्मणि ते स्थिताः ॥५-१९॥

19. Such people have conquered separate existence. Their minds are even and reflect the unity and perfection of Brahman.

In order to look with an equal eye of love and respect on all, whether they conduct themselves selfishly or selflessly towards us, we must have the capacity to keep our mind even at all times. In the Gita, Sri Krishna defines the unitive state as evenness of mind (2: 48). Now what usually happens to most of us is just the opposite of even-mindedness. As soon as someone pleases us, we begin to get exhilarated; when someone does what we want, there is an automatic sense of satisfaction. On the other hand, when someone says no to us, we immediately get dejected. This constant fluctuation of the mind takes away from our capacity to deal with everyday difficulties. To deal successfully with a difficult situation, all that is usually required is that we preserve our equilibrium and not get agitated. When someone is flying into a rage, it is very easy for us to get angry in return, which can only change things for the worse. Arithmetic tells us there are now two people in a rage. The question is, how has the situation been improved by doubling the number of people in a rage?

When we are getting agitated and angry, the best thing we can do to maintain our equilibrium is to go out for a long, brisk walk repeating the mantram in our mind. In the early days, after going around the block, we will want to come back because we have thought of a sparkling repartee which in our normal state of consciousness we wouldn't have been able to think of. When we want to come back, knowing what satisfaction our ego is going to get by making one more crack, that is the time to propel ourselves onwards saying the mantram. It is painful, because we have such good things to hit with. It seems a sorry waste. But after we have kept walking for an hour and the rhythm of the footstep, mantram, and breathing has calmed the mind, we will remember some of the nice things about the other person. When we were upset, it was unmitigated evil that we saw embodied before us. But it takes only an hour's walk, with the repetition of the mantram, to know that the evil is mitigated. If we can control our anger a few times this way, we will be able to remember when people provoke us that even though they are angry now, when they come back to normal they will be good, kind, and loving.

When we are burning with anger, we often conclude that this burning is going to last forever. But if we could quench the flames of anger consuming us and remember that in a little while we will have forgotten our anger, none of us would go to the extreme of moving away from people, which we now often try to do. Moving away is the worst thing to do in case of differences. Alienation deprives both parties of becoming aware of the unity in that relationship, and it weakens both. By strengthening the other person, in contrast, we are also strengthening ourselves. Living in peace and harmony with people who are agitated is one of the greatest services we can render them. Everyone is prepared to move away from people who are troubled, who are angry or afraid, but when troubled people find that we can bear with them and support them, and at the same time guide them by our personal conduct, they respond beautifully with greater love and respect. It is the capacity to bear with people, whatever they do, which is the secret of love.

न प्रहृष्येत्प्रियं प्राप्य नोद्विजेत्प्राप्य चाप्रियम् ।
स्थिरबुद्धिरसंमूढो ब्रह्मविद्ब्रह्मणि स्थितः ॥५-२०॥

20. They are not elated by good fortune or
depressed by bad. With mind established in
Brahman, they are free from delusion.

Those rare people who are able to receive good fortune without getting excited and bad fortune without getting depressed, who are able to treat those who are good to them with love and those who are not good to them with love, will never be deluded by the seeming multiplicity of life. When the mind gets agitated, we do not see life as it is, as one. The scriptures say that it is the constant agitation going on in our mind that deludes us into believing that you and I are separate.

The question we may ask is, "If we are to have neither pleasure nor pain in life, are we not likely to become insensitive to the joy of life?" The Gita says this doubt arises from the wrong assumption that in life there is only pleasure and pain and nothing else. One of the fatal weaknesses of the intellect is that it must always cut things up into two classes – everything must be either this or that. Because of this intellectual trap, we may find it difficult to understand that the person who has gone beyond both pleasure and pain lives in abiding joy. The Gita is telling us to go beyond pleasure and pain so that we may come into our legacy, which is the state of continuous joy and security.

To enter this state of abiding joy we must be very vigilant in the early years of our sādhana and often say no to pleasure while welcoming pain with a smile. In this way the nervous system can be reconditioned. Because of the conditioning we have received through the long travail of evolution, we are always looking for what is pleasant in life and trying to run away from what is not pleasant. This is the reaction that has now become inscribed on the nervous system: to the pleasant it says "Good, good," and to the painful, "Bad, bad." The Gita does not say we should not go after pleasure. When I first heard this from my grandmother, I really took to the Gita immediately, but I wasn't expecting what she said next: "The Gita doesn't say not to go after pleasure; it says that when you go after pleasure you are also going after pain." It is not possible for most of us to accept this. There is always the distant hope in every one of us that while no other human being has ever succeeded in isolating pleasure, *we* are going to achieve this magnificent feat and live in a state of pleasure always.

For a long time, sādhana is a reconditioning of the nervous system to accept a temporary disappointment, if necessary, when it is for our permanent well-being. Sometimes on the spiritual path, when we want to eat a particular dainty that appeals to us, or when we want to eat a little more than is necessary, we can't help feeling a little tug at the heart as we walk out of the restaurant. We cannot help thinking that we could as well have stayed on at the table and had five more minutes of pleasure, forgetting that it would probably be followed by five hours of stomachache at night. The right time to get up from the meal is when we want just a little more. This is real artistry, real gourmet judgment: when we find that everything is so good that we would like to have one more helping, we get up and come out.

We should learn this art not only with food, but in all aspects of daily life. Even in personal relationships, when we call on a person or are at a party, we shouldn't linger until we reach the dregs of the cup. When the party is really bubbling and everyone is saying, "You are the life and soul of the party. Why don't you stay on?" – that is the time to leave in good dignity. If we can do this, we are living in freedom. To be able to break up the party at its zenith, before the downward curve begins, we must not get caught in it. In everything, we must have the freedom to drop what we are doing at will. We may not get the little pleasures that we have been going after, but we shall gradually find ourselves in the permanent state of joy which is indicated by the mantram *Rāma.*

बाह्यस्पर्शेष्वसक्तात्मा विन्दत्यात्मनि यत्सुखम् ।
स ब्रह्मयोगयुक्तात्मा सुखमक्षयमश्नुते ॥५-२१॥

21. Not dependent upon any external support,
they have realized the joy of spiritual awareness.
With their consciousness unified through the
practice of meditation, they live in abiding joy.

When the mind has become even, when we can retain our equanimity in pleasure and pain, friendship and enmity, treating everyone with equal love and respect, we truly have realized the Lord who is enthroned in every heart. Then our love will be given to all those around us without any expectation of return. This is the mark of true love. As the Catholic mystic St. Bernard puts it, "Love seeks no cause beyond itself and no fruit; it is its own fruit, its own enjoyment. I love because I love; I love in order that I may love." The moment we say, "I love you because I want something from you," it is no longer love; it is a contract.

When we are able to love all those around us and to live only for their welfare, we will find that all our support comes from within. It is when we are expecting something from other people in return that we are leaning on them for our support, but when we do not expect anything in return, and love with all our heart, we are free. We are not dependent upon any external support but derive our support from the Lord within. When we discover that the Lord of Love is ever within us, we have entered into the state of joy and security which Jesus calls the kingdom of heaven within.

This joy and security that knows no end can never come to a person who is dependent upon external circumstances and external stimuli for satisfaction. It is when you become dependent entirely on the Lord within, who is the source of all joy and security, that you become free; and until you have this freedom in some measure, you will not be able to use even material resources wisely. In order to use money or any material resources wisely, you must have no attachments to them. Otherwise you will get caught in them, as can happen when, for example, you start going after money. I often tease a friend who works with the media by saying that one day we hope to make a movie called Leave the Money and Run. "Take the money and run," as the real title goes, and you run into despair. Leave the money and run, and you run into fulfillment. In order to use any material possession wisely, whether it is a house, a car, or a guitar, you must not be attached to it. When you are greatly attached to a guitar, for example, the guitar will say at the time your term paper is due, "Now is the time for you to strum on me," and instead of writing your paper you will have to play your guitar.

If we are to enter into a state of unending joy, Sri Krishna says, on the one hand we should not be dependent on any external circumstances for our happiness, and on the other, we should be meditating regularly with complete concentration on the Lord who is within us. For a long time, until we break through the surface layers of consciousness, meditation is nothing but arduous discipline. But once we enter the depths of our consciousness, we shall begin to sense the deep peace that is called *shānti* in Sanskrit. When the tensions of the nervous system are relaxed, there is such profound peace inside that even the body turns over like a little cat and basks in this newfound joy.

ये हि संस्पर्शजा भोगा दुःखयोनय एव ते ।
आद्यन्तवन्तः कौन्तेय न तेषु रमते बुधः ॥५-२२॥

22. *Pleasures conceived in the world of the senses have a beginning and an end and give birth to misery, Kaunteya. The wise do not look for happiness in them.*

He or she is not wise who goes after any pleasure which has a beginning and an end. Our need is for joy that knows neither beginning nor end, for the eternal joy called *Rāma* in Sanskrit. No lasting joy, no lasting security can be ours if we pursue finite things, things that pass away.

A little pleasure will satisfy us as long as we are living on the surface level of consciousness, but when we break through to the deeper recesses of our consciousness, our capacity for joy is unlimited. If we just keep throwing little pleasures inside, they will be completely lost in that vast space that is the world within. People with access to deeper consciousness, with deeper states of awareness open to them, will not take seriously the blandishments of material possessions, because they know that these cannot satisfy them.

It takes a long time for most of us to learn that pleasure is not permanent. If we go to the beach on days when the sea is stormy, we sometimes find big footballs of foam and froth. We are tempted to pick them up and say, "Why not bring these home to play soccer with?" They look very round and inviting, but if we pick up a big foam bubble in the hope of keeping it permanently, by the time we get it home, it has vanished. This is the way pleasure slips through our fingers: when we are almost sure we have got it right here in our palm, it vanishes.

In the early years of our life, it is permissible to have the attitude that pleasure is something we can have always. But the Gita warns us to learn as quickly as we can that pleasure is impermanent. It is like the bubble that is blown away, dissolving immediately. The sooner we are able to learn this lesson in life, the less suffering we will be forced to undergo. The Gita is not talking only about the situation as it existed in India twenty-five hundred years ago, but about contemporary problems. What it says will always be found valid, because wherever we live, our fundamental need is to find within ourselves the Lord of Love who is the source of all joy and security.

The timelessness of the Gita was brought home to me today as I was reading an article about a recent convention of psychologists in San Francisco. One of the major concerns of the psychologists and medical doctors attending the conference is the increase in the use of "legal psychoactive" drugs, such as tranquilizers. Many patients who do not have an organic illness go to their doctors because of emotional problems and are given drugs which will calm them, help them sleep better, or stimulate them. As these psychologists point out, this chemical therapy is based partly on the assumption that we should all be in a state of continuous pleasure, untroubled by stress. The consequences of taking these drugs are far-reaching, and dependence upon them actually takes away from the capacity to deal with the problems of life. Also, dependence upon drugs by the older generation can influence their children to seek instant happiness through the more powerful mind-altering drugs.

शक्नोतीहैव यः सोढुं प्राक्शरीरविमोक्षणात् ।
कामक्रोधोद्भवं वेगं स युक्तः स सुखी नरः ॥५-२३॥
यो ऽन्तःसुखो ऽन्तरारामस्तथान्तर्ज्योतिरेव यः ।
स योगी ब्रह्मनिर्वाणं ब्रह्मभूतो ऽधिगच्छति ॥५-२४॥

23. Those who overcome the impulse of lust and anger which arises in the body are made whole and live in joy.
24. They find their joy, their rest, and their light completely within themselves. They live in freedom and become united with the Lord.

This is the same truth conveyed by Jesus when he tells us the kingdom of heaven is within. He is warning us not to roam the outer world looking for security. We can only find security by entering the world within, and then we shall find we can function with complete freedom in the outer world.

लभन्ते ब्रह्मनिर्वाणमृषयः क्षीणकल्मषाः ।
छिन्नद्वैधा यतात्मानः सर्वभूतहिते रताः ॥५-२५॥

25. With all their conflicts healed and all their sins removed, the holy sages work for the good of all beings, and attain the nirvāna of Brahman.

In this verse, the word *nirvāna* is used to indicate the goal towards which, according to the founders of the great religions of the world, all creation is moving. The mystics are not theorizing when they declare that the supreme goal of life is to become aware of the indivisible unity that is the Divine Ground of existence. They are drawing upon their own personal experience in which they have realized that all life is one.

The source of all sorrow lies in trying to resist our evolution towards this goal by maintaining our own separateness. It does not take much depth of observation, even for ordinary people like us, to discover that the person who does not merge his or her welfare into that of the family is usually very insecure, and so is the family in which that person lives. If, for example, husband and wife try to compete with each other and maintain their separateness, they make themselves miserable, their children miserable, and even their locality miserable. In contrast, if we look at people who are secure, loved, and respected wherever they go, we usually find that they are able to base their action on an awareness that the interests of those around them are more important than their own individual interests. When I forget myself in the joy of those around me, I am fulfilling myself. It is when I try to maintain my separateness that I become more and more insecure, because my innate need, my deep, driving need, is to realize my oneness with all life.

This concept of the unity of all life is not peculiar to the mystics. Even the progress of science has brought us today very close to discovering that the welfare of the whole world is necessary if all of us are to live in peace and goodwill. The science of ecology has its basis in the spiritual truth that all life is one. We are now beginning to discover that there is a close relationship not only between human beings and animals, but among trees, land, water, and air as well, and that we cannot try to promote our own interests at the expense of even the trees. Nirvāna, therefore, is not a concept applicable only to ancient India. It is a concept which thoughtful people all over the world are beginning to appreciate.

In Hinduism and Buddhism, where reincarnation is a working proposition and not just a philosophical theory, and the law of karma is taken to be as infallible as the law of gravity, the whole responsibility of my development is thrown on my own shoulders. I have sometimes been asked whether the law of karma makes people fatalistic. It is just the opposite. The law of karma says that no matter what context I find myself in, it is neither my parents, nor my science teacher, nor the mailman, but I alone who have brought myself into this state because of my past actions. Instead of trapping me in a fatalistic snare, this gives me freedom. Because I alone have brought myself into my present condition, I myself, by working hard and striving earnestly, can reach the supreme state which is nirvāna.

Until we reach the unitive state, however, we have to continue to come back, life after life, to this world of separateness. In the *Tibetan Book of the Dead,* there is a sensible, scientific, and dryly humorous presentation of exactly what takes place in the process of rebirth. According to this description, there is a period between two lives where we wait in a place called Bardo, which is very much like a big, crowded bus depot. Between one life and another, we have to sit and wait to get the right context for rebirth. If I have been lacking in respect to my parents, I have to be born into a situation where my children will show me the same lack of respect. This is the law. We can't blame Sri Krishna and complain, "Why have you made me the parent of children who don't respect me?" Whatever we have given with one hand we must receive with the other. I have to get a son who drops out of college, a daughter who goes to Europe and spends the rest of her life skiing, and another daughter who goes to Mexico and learns to make pottery. It is not an easy combination to get: a Mexican potter, a Swiss ski buff, and a university dropout. Not many homes have this unusual combination. India is ruled out; Africa is ruled out. We slowly come to ask, "What is that state within two hours of snow, university, and Mexico?" By elimination comes the answer, "California!"

Bardo is a kind of cosmic waiting room where, after they have shed the body, people just sit, as we sit at a bus depot. Some time ago we went to a big bus depot in Oakland. There were buses leaving for many different places, and people of all kinds seated on the benches waiting to hear their particular bus called. A disembodied voice calls out over the loudspeaker, "Reno Special leaving at Gate 9." Not everybody jumps up when the man announces the Reno bus; it is only those with the gambling samskāra who immediately jump up and tell the others, "Stick with me; I've got a system." This small group, who have bought their special Reno packet that contains fare, room, and gambling tokens, queue up and get on the bus. Similarly, in Bardo, those with anger samskāras have a special bus; they will be born into times which are propitious for bringing their samskāras into play. In the Hindu scriptures, our own age is called *Kaliyuga,* the Age of Anger. Everybody is angry about something or other, against somebody or other, and in such an age, it is not difficult to get a suitable context for the anger samskāra.

Often I remind our young people to show particular consideration for their parents' weaknesses because often the children suffer from the same weaknesses. Usually, the very defect we suffer from annoys us when we see it in another person. For this reason we should bear with older people, with our parents, and with others who suffer from our own infirmities. It is by supporting such people in moments of stress that we can use even unfavorable samskāras to make greater progress on the spiritual path.

The practice of meditation has been described marvelously as taking our evolution into our own hands. Instead of waiting for the forces of evolution to buffet us for the next million years and make us selfless, we say, "Let me try during this very life to take my destiny in my hands and, by working at my life day in and day out, remove every particle of selfishness from my consciousness so that I may become aware of the unity of life." There are rare creatures who catch fire when presented with this goal, and they will give everything they have to the pursuit of it. Patanjali says that it is this enthusiastic, hardworking person who will attain the goal. Success in meditation comes not to those whose horoscope is right or who live in the perfect place and era, but to those who grit their teeth and work at it all the time. We need not be born under Capricorn, or live in the Golden Age, to attain the supreme goal. In any age, any context, we can, through the practice of meditation, realize the unity of life and fulfill the goal of human evolution. No matter what context we find ourselves in, what samskāras we labor under, or what our horoscope may read, we can always redirect our lives to the goal, because our Ātman, or real personality, is eternal, immutable, and infinite.

कामक्रोधवियुक्तानां यतीनां यतचेतसाम् ।
अभितो ब्रह्मनिर्वाणं वर्तते विदितात्मनाम् ॥५-२६॥

26. Those who have broken out of the bondage of selfish desire and anger through constant

> *effort, who have gained complete control over their minds and realized the Self, are forever established in the nirvāna of Brahman.*

Sri Krishna uses the word *brahmanirvāna* to refer to that supreme goal which Jesus calls "the kingdom of heaven within." In order to reach this state, there are two obstacles which must be overcome. The first is selfish desire, which drives me to seek my own personal profit, prestige, and power, if necessary at the expense of those around me. The Buddha calls this *tanhā*, the fierce thirst which consumes me and drives me often to be at loggerheads with all those around me. The second obstacle is anger. Wherever there is the fierce thirst for separateness, for selfish satisfaction, there is bound to be anger. Kāma and krodha, selfish desire and anger, go together, because when I have a fierce thirst for my personal aggrandizement, and you have a fierce thirst for your personal aggrandizement, it is inevitable that we will clash.

In most estrangements, not only individual but even international, there is this question of my interests against your interests, my prosperity against your prosperity. Prosperity is one and indivisible. Peace is one and indivisible. We are being told more and more by thoughtful leaders all over the world that peace is necessary for the whole world, that it is impossible to have war in one corner of the world and maintain peace elsewhere. It is impossible, too, to have real prosperity in one country and starvation in another. If we start a fire in the kitchen, it is only a matter of time before it will spread to the bedroom and finally to the entire home. The central truth of the Gita, that all life is one, is applicable not only to ancient India; this truth is being rediscovered here and now, and if we do not act upon it, it is at our peril.

To overcome selfish desires and anger, we have to begin to be more loving in our own home. It is here that the seeds of war begin to grow. In a home where there is friction, where there is the clash of separateness, there is a little war going on. It may not be the Thirty Years War or the World War of 1914–18, but it is a war nonetheless. It breaks out at breakfast. There may be a truce at lunch, but guerilla warfare can rage quietly in the kitchen, and again battle lines are drawn at dinner.

Sometimes, even though there may not be an actual outbreak of hostility, there is a kind of cold war carried on. War is born in the mind: first it comes to our hearts, then to our homes, then to our community, and finally to our world. This is the nature of war. We have only to observe the little state of warfare in homes to see the appropriateness of the Gita's message that war rages fundamentally in the human heart, between what is selfish and what is selfless, impure and pure, demonic and divine. When the Gita talks about warfare, it is the war that rages in the human breast, and in this battle, all of us have the choice to identify ourselves either with the forces of light or with the forces of darkness. This is the choice that we all have, in whatever country, community, or context we may live.

स्पर्शान्कृत्वा बहिर्बाह्यांश्चक्षुश्चैवान्तरे भ्रुवोः ।
प्राणापानौ समौ कृत्वा नासाभ्यन्तरचारिणौ ॥५-२७॥
यतेन्द्रियमनोबुद्धिर्मुनिर्मोक्षपरायणः ।
विगतेच्छाभयक्रोधो यः सदा मुक्त एव सः ॥५-२८॥

27–28. *Having closed their eyes in meditation and focused their attention on the center of spiritual consciousness, their breathing becomes even. The wise man or woman among these, who has controlled body, senses, and mind, who is dedicated to the attainment of liberation and has gone beyond selfish desire, fear, and anger, lives in freedom.*

These two verses describe the state of samādhi insofar as it can be expressed in words. Sri Krishna uses the word *mukta*, 'free,' to describe the person who has attained the supreme state of samādhi. He or she alone lives in freedom who has reached this unitive state, in which he or she knows that all life is one and has the will and wisdom to live in harmony with it. In order to live in complete freedom, which is the goal of the spiritual life, we should not be dependent upon any external object for our security, joy, and fulfillment. This is not a plea for poverty, which can be debilitating and degrading. It is a plea for being free from selfish attachments to our environment. This is the state of complete freedom that we enter in samādhi, the climax of meditation, when the windows of the senses close completely as a result of long spiritual discipline.

There is also a reference here to what happens to the eyes in deepening meditation. As our mind becomes quieter and our security begins to increase, the eyes become still, bright, and beautiful. It is an amazing commentary on our modern civilization that if we go to almost any store we will find a special section devoted to aids for eye-beautification, with a long row of all kinds of little bottles and brushes containing things to put around the eyes. When I first came to this country I wasn't used to these things, and whenever I saw those false eyelashes, Christine had to remind me not to stare. One day when I was riding on the cable car in San Francisco, I saw sitting in front of me a very attractive girl with some bluish stuff around her eyes. When I came home, I told Christine that I had met an awfully pretty girl with some kind of eye ailment which had made her eyelids blue. Christine said, "Don't be silly. That's a beauty aid." I am told that it takes quite a long time to apply all these cosmetics. This is time that might be used for the practice of meditation.

Beauty comes into the eyes from within. We have only to look at a mother looking at her child to see how gloriously beautiful her eyes become when she loves. Or look at a husband and wife who live together in love and harmony; what beauty comes into their eyes! Even when long-lost friends meet at a class reunion, beauty leaps out from within through their eyes. All of us have beautiful eyes. But our eyes lose their beauty when we become angry, brood upon ourselves, nurse grievances, and become violent. The quiet mind, the heart full of love and forgiveness, lights up the eyes and reveals the beauty of the Lord through them.

In the practice of meditation, when we are deeply concentrated on the inspirational passage we are using, the pupils of the eyes will look a little upward. When concentration deepens, the eyes turn towards what is called the center of Christ-consciousness in the Christian tradition. This is usually referred to as the third eye in Hindu and Buddhist mysticism. Even in the early days of our meditation, when we are concentrating intensely, there is a sense of movement in this spot, which is considered the seat of spiritual awareness.

Another change which takes place in deepening meditation is the slowing down of the breathing rhythm. According to the great mystics, especially in Hinduism and Buddhism, the breathing rhythm is closely connected with the rhythm of the mind. We know, for example, that as we are getting angry, the rhythm of the mind changes; and as the mind changes, there are a number of corresponding changes that take place in the body. Usually when we are angry our breathing becomes stertorous. My advice here is not to go in for any occult breathing exercises, which are fraught with danger. The best breathing exercise is to go for a long, fast walk repeating the mantram in our mind. This is the natural, effective way of regulating the breathing rhythm.

भोक्तारं यज्ञतपसां सर्वलोकमहेश्वरम् ।
सुहृदं सर्वभूतानां ज्ञात्वा मां शान्तिमृच्छति ॥५-२९॥

29. Those who know me as the friend of all creatures, the Lord of the universe, the source and end of all paths, attain eternal peace.

With body, mind, and intellect under control, with all selfish desire, anger, and fear eliminated from consciousness, the human being attains the supreme goal of life, which is to become aware of God, from whom we come, in whom we subsist, and to whom we return. In this supreme state, we see in our own heart of hearts the Lord of Love, whether we call him Christ, Krishna, Shiva, or Buddha, and become united with him here and now in this very life.

संन्यासयोगो नाम पञ्चमोऽध्यायः ॥ ५ ॥

CHAPTER SIX

The Practice of Meditation

श्रीभगवानुवाच ।
अनाश्रितः कर्मफलं कार्यं कर्म करोति यः ।
स संन्यासी च योगी च न निरग्निर्न चाक्रियः ॥ ६-१ ॥

SRI KRISHNA:

1. Not those who lack energy or refrain from action, but those who work without expectation of reward have attained the goal of meditation and made true renunciation.

The Gita gives us three paths to illumination: karma yoga, the path of selfless action, jnāna yoga, the path of spiritual wisdom, and bhakti yoga, the path of love and devotion. All three are based upon the practice of meditation.

Karma yoga appeals easily to people who are energetic and enterprising, but energy and effort are not enough. There must be no thought of feathering our own nest or of earning profit and prestige, for the moment these thoughts come in, our action is no longer karma yoga. This is what makes karma yoga so difficult, why it takes a giant like Mahatma Gandhi to practice it to perfection. But even though we do not have the stature of Gandhi, we cannot afford to wait until we are completely selfless to act, because that day is a long way off. We can begin karma yoga now, and through the practice of meditation, over a long period of time, we can gradually eliminate all our selfish motives. So for the vast majority of us, the practice of karma yoga has to be based on meditation.

Jnāna yoga is even more difficult; it is like climbing a ninety-degree precipice. Without meditation no jnāna, or spiritual wisdom, will come to any of us. *Jnāna* does not refer to intellectual effort but to leaping beyond the duality of subject and object, going beyond the finite intellect into the intuitive mode of knowing – a capacity which is characteristic of a great spiritual genius like Meister Eckhart, and present to some degree even in a great scientific genius like Albert Einstein. For most of us, however, the path of love or bhakti is the safest, the swiftest, and the sweetest.

This word "love" is easy to read and write, but very difficult to put into practice. The basis of all loving relationships is the capacity to put each other's happiness first. Sometimes it is distressing to try to make another's happiness more important than our own; yet when we keep at it, there comes a fierce exhilaration. We can go to bed knowing that we have grown a tenth of an inch that day; and one tenth of an inch every day will make us tall by the time the year is out. Spiritual awareness grows little by little; it is sometimes easy to make a spectacular, dramatic gesture, but it is very difficult to bear incessant pinpricks patiently. Life is a permanent state of pinpricks that come in the form of likes and dislikes. Through constant patience and the practice of meditation, we learn to bear these pinpricks until finally we can overcome them joyfully, without effort.

We call our age materialistic, but I notice there is a refreshing change in the younger generation, which has a good deal of detachment from material goods and money. But if detachment is going to be complete, we also have to become detached from our self-will, which often expresses itself in our opinions. People will give away their money, clothes, and gifts, but the one thing they do not know how to give away is their opinions. If we were to stand on a busy street corner tomorrow and distribute our opinions free to anybody who would come and take them, everyone would just ignore us. Nobody wants our opinions because everyone wants to keep his own. One of our strongest drives is to impose our will on others, yet we can never understand why others should want to impose their self-will on us. In personal relationships, love expresses itself in accepting the other person's ways, particularly if they are better than our own.

To have harmonious personal relationships, the practice of meditation is necessary to keep the mind from getting agitated when someone goes against our grain. When we live together in intimate personal relationships, we have to expect a little bruising, a little spraining, and a little bumping, which are all part of life. Those who do not live together, who have not learned to accept the give-and-take of life, are forfeiting one of its fundamental joys: that of being a large family, in which we recognize the unity of life that is divine. In any home, whether with our family or with our friends, living together can multiply the joy of all, for the source of joy is in putting more and more people's welfare before our own. When we follow the path of integrated yoga, there is a place for selfless action, a place for knowledge, and a special place for love. But all these are governed by meditation, which we should practice every morning and every evening.

यं संन्यासमिति प्राहुर्योगं तं विद्धि पाण्डव ।
न ह्यसंन्यस्तसंकल्पो योगी भवति कश्चन ॥६-२॥

2. *Therefore, Arjuna, understand that renunciation and the performance of selfless service are the same. Those who cannot renounce attachment to the results of their work are far from the path.*

The expectation of getting money, prizes, prestige, or power, the idle imagination of rewards or results, is called *sankalpa* in Sanskrit. My grandmother, who was as good as Aesop, used to tell a story which conveyed to me the idea of sankalpa better than great scholars have been able to do. In her simple manner, she would describe a village girl of about ten, walking home gracefully with a pot full of milk on her head. Under the spell of sankalpa, the little girl begins to daydream: "I am going to sell all my milk for five rupees, and with the money I'll get a dancing dress and real anklets with bells." Then she dreams of how she will be able to dance; and carried away, she starts dancing. The pot falls and the milk spills. This is what we do every day, only we say, "When my novel has gone into its sixth edition, and the movie rights have been bought, I am going to buy a yacht and a villa on the Mediterranean." People are given to this kind of imagining in all kinds of terms: money, pleasure, fame, and worst of all, power.

As long as we are subject to sankalpa, we are imprisoned in our selfish ways of thinking, and have no access to the deeper capacities in our consciousness that clamor to be used. There is no more effective way to rid the mind of sankalpa than the practice of meditation. Every time we meditate we free the mind a little more by not allowing it to wander off on a trail of fancy or vague associations. I am the first to admit that bringing the mind back over and over again to the words of the Prayer of St. Francis is dull, dreary work, but over a period of time this effort will free us from the oppressive memories of past events and the expectations of future actions. One of the signs that we are coming closer to this freedom is an increase in our vitality, energy, and capacity for selfless work. The more we work for others, stretching out our arms to embrace all those around us, the stronger our arms will grow.

आरुरुक्षोर्मुनेर्योगं कर्म कारणमुच्यते ।
योगारूढस्य तस्यैव शमः कारणमुच्यते ॥६-३॥

3. For aspirants who wish to climb the mountain
of spiritual awareness, the path is selfless work.
For those who have attained the summit of union
with the Lord, the path is stillness and peace.

Now Sri Krishna uses an image from mountain climbing, a sport that requires great endurance and skill. He compares two types: one is *ārurukshu*, someone who wants to climb the mountain of spiritual awareness; the other is *yogārūdha*, the adept who has already made it to the top. In order to climb the Himālayas within us, we have to train ourselves, little by little, every day. Sir Edmund Hillary, who climbed Mount Everest for the first time, did not just stand at the bottom, take one leap, and land on top of the Himālayas. He practiced climbing mountains for a long time to learn all the required skills; and for you and me to climb the spiritual mountain, we too have to strengthen our muscles over a long, long period of time.

When those of you who lead the householder's life are asked what you are doing, you can say, "Learning to climb a mountain." You are getting your training experience in the heart of your family. In mountain climbing, you tie yourself to others with ropes so that if somebody slips you do not say, "Have you hit the ground?" or "Good riddance"; you try to prevent that person from falling by hauling him up and saving him. Similarly in living with family or friends, if somebody slips you do not say, "Aha! Serves you right," or "You've been asking for that for a long time." Instead you pull them up. Even if they have offended you, do not tell them, "Remember what you did last week? You'd better just stay there on the floor." If you do not like someone, it is good for both of you if you can pull the person up and offer support. People whom others have abandoned, who are looking at you through their own selfishness, expect you to walk away and wash your hands of them. At first they do not believe you are coming to help them, but when you support them, help them walk, and then give them something to get home with, they begin to think about what you have done; and on the way home they begin to like and finally love you.

There is no other way to deal with people who are difficult, who make mistakes. Demonstrating violently against them only makes the situation worse by making everyone blind with fury. This is where the practice of meditation is invaluable: when we are surrounded by people who cause us harm, we can help them by being patient and loving and returning good for their evil. To work like this for those whom we do not like, especially when we are involved in a tense emotional situation, is hard work. But when we work wholeheartedly in the service of others without thought of profit or prestige, we are using karma yoga every day as a mighty ladder to climb safely and steadily on the spiritual path. For a long, long time we will be aware only of the distress and the difficulty of always trying to turn our back upon ourselves; but after a period of years, when we think we have been stagnating all the time, we turn the corner and suddenly the goal is in view. We are no longer in the foothills; we are near Lhasa, the capital of Tibet, high among the clouds. We can see the Ganges flowing down, we can see views of some of the peaks, and we cannot help but thrill with exultation.

After we have reached the top of the spiritual Mount Everest, *shama*, perfect peace, becomes our ladder. This stillness of the ego means that we have become infinite love: that all our agitation has died down, all our anger, fear, greed, malice, and envy have died down, and there is a vast ocean of love flowing in our consciousness. This is what we discover after many years of assiduous effort. When our ego is completely eliminated and we have become all love, we no longer work; the Lord works through us. Our work then is to be the still center in the eye of the storm of the world which rages all about us.

यदा हि नेन्द्रियार्थेषु न कर्मस्वनुषज्जते ।
सर्वसंकल्पसंन्यासी योगारूढस्तदोच्यते ॥६-४॥

4. When a man has freed himself from attachment to the results of work, and from desires for the enjoyment of sense objects, he ascends to the unitive state.

Here we have a perfect picture of the person who has climbed to the summit of human consciousness, who sees the complete unity of all life and has the wisdom, the will, and the energy to live in harmony with it. The Buddha calls such a person one who has attained nirvāna – that is, one who has broken out of the prison of selfishness, self-will, and separateness in which most of us spend our whole life.

The person who has become established in the Lord within cannot be pushed about by selfish cravings, which can overwhelm even the most cultured and humanitarian among us if we let ourselves be drawn by prestige, fame, and power. Entirely independent of the external world for support, the person who has attained the unitive state lives in abiding joy and security. As long as we lean on anything outside ourselves for support, we are going to be insecure. Most of us try to find support by leaning on all sorts of things – gold, books, learning, sensory stimulation – and if these things are taken away, we fall over. To the extent that we are dependent on these external supports, we grow weaker and more liable to upsets and misfortune.

Our sole support is really the Lord within. In a magnificent verse at the end of the Gita (18:66) Sri Krishna tells us not to cling to anything outside ourselves, but to cast aside all other supports and embrace only the Lord of Love who is within us all. Then we shall be free. It is a strange paradox that when we surrender everything to the Lord, we receive everything: when we depend entirely on the Lord, we become independent. In meditation we slowly learn to depend more and more on the Lord by increasing our concentration on the words of the inspirational piece. When the mind tries to slip out to the movie theater or the ice cream parlor and we bring it back to the words of St. Francis or the Gita, we are gently dislodging external supports and turning our eyes to the Lord.

उद्धरेदात्मनात्मानं नात्मानमवसादयेत् ।
आत्मैव ह्यात्मनो बन्धुरात्मैव रिपुरात्मनः ॥६-५॥

5. A man should reshape himself through the power of the will. He should never let himself be degraded by self-will. The will is the only friend of the Self, and the will is the only enemy of the Self.

No one can help us grow up, no one can help us become beautiful, except ourselves. We cannot expect anyone on the face of the earth to do the work necessary for our own enlightenment. Great teachers only show the way; we have to travel it, and the first step we can take is to accept responsibility for the position in which we find ourselves today and not try to leave it at the door of our parents, our partner, our children, or our society. By accepting this responsibility we immediately gain the certainty that if we brought ourselves into this morass, then we have the power to pull ourselves out completely, reshape ourselves, and become perfect.

The seed of perfection is within all of us. Meister Eckhart, in his inimitable way, tells us that as apple seeds grow into apple trees and pear seeds into pear trees, so the God-seed within us will grow into a mighty God-tree if it is watered, weeded, and protected. In India, the price of seeds goes up during the rainy season because that is the right time for planting. Because the seeds are expensive, the foolish farmer says, "I think I'll wait until there is a fifty-percent reduction in the price of seeds. During the summer months you can pick up two packets of seed for the price of one." But at that time, when there is not a drop of water in the ground, nothing is likely to grow. Similarly, the right time for leading the spiritual life is now. When my grandmother used to ask me when I was going to do a certain good deed, I would say, "One of these days, Granny." She would immediately retort in my mother tongue, "One of these days is none of these days." Most of us have a tendency to put things off until the right moment, the auspicious day, when everything is right. There are people who throw away jobs or move to a new home just because what they have now doesn't feel right. I would suggest a little less concern with feeling right and more with doing things now. If you want to lead the spiritual life, the time to start is immediately, and not one minute later. We have a venerable Hindu friend who says, in frightening language, "Don't postpone the spiritual life until tomorrow. How do you know you will be here tomorrow?"

Whatever mistakes we have committed, whatever difficulties we have, all that we have to do is leave aside all supports and trust the Lord completely, because he is right within us. In trusting the Lord, we are trusting our real Self; in putting our life under his guidance, we are letting our life be governed by the wisest part of our consciousness. Ultimately we have only one friend in the world: the Ātman, the Lord within, who is our real Self. He is telling us all the time, "I will forgive you whatever you have done, provided you now try to remove all selfishness from your heart and your life. I'll support you despite all the mistakes of the past, if you will now start to live for your family and your community. And I will bring you into your full beauty and wisdom if you will meditate on me and remember that I am present in every creature that lives on the face of the earth."

बन्धुरात्मात्मनस्तस्य येनात्मैवात्मना जितः ।
अनात्मनस्तु शत्रुत्वे वर्तेतात्मैव शत्रुवत् ॥६-६॥

6. To those who have conquered themselves,
the will is a friend. But it is the enemy of those
who have not found the Self within them.

We all have within us that curious pair, Dr. Jekyll and Mr. Hyde. That is, we all have a pure, perfect, divine Self, side by side with a hobgoblin with cloven feet and wagging tail who tries to make us believe that he is our real Self. This hobgoblin is called by many names. When Jalalu'l-Din Rumi, the great medieval Sufi saint, would talk to his disciples about the devil, they used to retort in their sophistication: "Devil? Devil? Never heard of him! We don't believe in him." And Jalalu'l-Din Rumi replied, "You never heard of him? Just turn your ear inward and listen to some of your thoughts. 'I hate him. Drop dead.' That's the voice of the devil." We don't have to go outside ourselves if we want to meet Mr. Mephistopheles. We have only to ask for an appointment, and he will tell us to come any time – to walk right in, sit down, and make ourselves at home. This is the selfish part of us, the monstrously ugly part of us. When we hate, when we carry resentments, when we refuse to forgive or become violent in our home, on the street, or on the campus, we are telling Mephistopheles that we look upon him as our leader and will do whatever he wants.

Side by side with this hobgoblin is our pure, divine Self. One of the beautiful names for this Self in Arabic is *al-Rahīm*, 'the Merciful.' The beauty of forgiveness, compassion, and love is that they heal all the wounds within us, leaving not even a scar. Where there is no forgiveness, not only are there scars; there are festering wounds which sap our vitality. Remember the words of the Buddha in the Dhammapada: "Hatred does not cease by hatred at any time; hatred ceases by love. This is an unalterable law." He did not say it is advisable to love, or it is recommended; he said it is an unalterable law: breaking it, we break ourselves; obeying it, we fulfill ourselves.

To learn to return love for hatred, all of us have to struggle for a long,

long time. Learning any skill takes considerable effort, and we should not be surprised that learning to be selfless is the result of many, many years of difficult, exhilarating labor. Our niece Geetha has taken about a year to graduate from reading in that odd alphabet called ITA to the kind of books you and I read. When she came to us a year ago, she knew only a few words of English. Then she started going to school and saying *b-u-k* spells *book*, which really puzzled me. I would look this word up in the dictionary and say, "I don't think *buk* is English." She would say, "Uncle, it's that thing you're looking at – *buk*." "Oh," I said, "that's *b-o-o-k*." Now she too is beginning to read *book*, and there is such joy in the achievement. This morning, while Christine and I were meditating, a little slip of paper was passed underneath the door with a message written by Geetha, consisting of five words, every one of them lovingly misspelled: *Anti, ples pik ar dreses*; "Aunty, please pick our dresses." We were so overjoyed that we didn't see spelling peculiarities; we said, "How beautiful – she is able to communicate," which we often forget is the purpose of language.

In communicating with the Lord, for a long time we are going to say "ples Lord," and he is not going to consult the great mystics in heaven and say, "Poor English!" Instead he will say, "This person has turned to me and wants my help." In other words, we are not going to be perfect for a long, long time. We are going to have lapses, outbursts of temper, and difficulties, but as long as we keep trying our very best, the Lord is more than happy to receive our offering.

जितात्मनः प्रशान्तस्य परमात्मा समाहितः ।
शीतोष्णसुखदुःखेषु तथा मानावमानयोः ॥६-७॥

7. The supreme Reality stands revealed in the consciousness of those who have conquered themselves. They live in peace, alike in cold and heat, pleasure and pain, praise and blame.

To grow up we all need to learn to maintain an even mind in pain and pleasure, joy and sorrow, and we will find that keeping our balance, no matter how difficult the challenges we face, leads to security, cheerfulness, and the permanent happiness that is Rāma. In our world we are slowly forgetting that, as Meher Baba puts it, "Cheerfulness is a divine virtue." We go on a bus and see eyes that are glazed and faces that have no expression at all. It is as if some kind of arctic weather is blowing inside us all: our emotions are beginning to freeze; glaciers are forming, and icebergs are looming up everywhere. We are feeling less and less for others and less for ourselves as well. The impersonality of our modern urban society has become so frightening that people are trying to form smaller groups, smaller societies, where they can know and serve one another. It is a source of unending delight to all of us at Ramagiri to live as members of a large family, loving one another, working hard, and always being cheerful.

There are times when it is difficult to smile, but that is the perfect time to learn. When you are already happy, there is no effort in trying to smile. But when things are slowly beginning to look a little blue, when morale is sagging at the edges and people around you are beginning to irritate you, that is the time to start smiling. In the very act of smiling there seems to be some secret switch that is turned on, and somewhere inside a little fountain of joy begins to play.

Yogananda Paramahamsa has a beautiful suggestion for thawing the arctic state of our feelings; it is for all of us to become smile millionaires. This is the kind of millionaire that everyone can be, because everywhere we go we can always smile. Wherever you find someone seated alone, not knowing what to do, feeling utterly desolate, just smile. Almost everyone will thaw immediately and smile back. When you have been smiling at people in the park, at meter-maids passing by, at the mailman, and at schoolchildren, one day when you go to the mirror you will find smiling has become a habit. Your mouth has forgotten to droop at the corners; you try your best to scowl but you have lost the ability. Depression, unsociability, and lack of goodwill are beginning to get erased from your consciousness.

Every smile can be beautiful when we repeat the mantram, because gradually the mantram brings the smile into our eyes. We start smiling with our lips and end up smiling with our eyes as well. Once we have learned to do this we can never really be angry again. It is good to be with people who have smiling eyes – we do not even have to talk to them because communication is going on all the time at a deeper level.

ज्ञानविज्ञानतृप्तात्मा कूटस्थो विजितेन्द्रियः ।
युक्त इत्युच्यते योगी समलोष्टाश्मकाञ्चनः ॥६-८॥

8. They are completely fulfilled by the knowledge and wisdom of the Self. Having conquered their senses, unmoved by opposition, they have climbed to the summit of human consciousness. To such a person a clod of dirt, a stone, and gold are the same.

It is good to remember that gold is not valuable by itself; it is valuable because there is so little of it. If sand were found only in small quantities, people would treasure it in their safe-deposit boxes; they would buy sand certificates, on important occasions they would exchange a little sand, and they would have the expression "as good as sand." It shows how gullible we are and how little sense of value we have. What really gives value to anything is its usefulness in serving others. Our body draws its value from its usefulness in serving others, and our life draws its value not from the money we make, or the prizes we win, or the power we wield over others, but from the service we give every day to add a little bit more to the happiness of our family and our community. There is no better epitaph than "He lived for others," and this is all that the Lord asks us to do in order to move closer to him day by day.

The word *kūtastha*, 'established on the summit,' describes the man or woman who has learned the supreme skill of life, who has climbed the slopes of the Himālayas within to stand unshaken at the summit of human consciousness, no matter what storms rage about him or her. Not all the forces in the universe can shake one who is established in the Lord, the supreme protector. Gandhi's life is a perfect example of how one man who is established in himself can stand against all violence and yet be neither afraid nor alone.

There is a story in the *Mahābhārata* in which Duryodhana, the leader of the forces of selfishness, and Arjuna, the leader of the forces of selflessness, go to Sri Krishna to ask for help. Like a good Hindu god, Sri Krishna was having his siesta. There was one chair, a throne, near his head. Duryodhana, who always saw himself as the sun around which other planets should move, came in first and seated himself comfortably in his host's chair with the complete arrogance of the inflated ego. Sri Krishna, who was not really sleeping, opened his eyes slightly and thought, "That's where I thought you would sit." Then Arjuna came in and, seeing the lotus feet of the Lord, sat on the floor with his head at Sri Krishna's feet. When Sri Krishna opened his eyes, he naturally first saw the man sitting at his feet, and he asked Arjuna what he wanted. Arjuna, showing great love for his enemies, said, "There is somebody in the chair behind you who came before me. Give him what he wants first." Sri Krishna was greatly touched by Arjuna's putting Duryodhana first even on this special occasion, so he said, "I have two things to offer. To one of you I can give armies, navies, and any devastating weapon you want. To the other I will give myself."

Duryodhana made a note of this and said, "This is what I've been looking for. Throw in nuclear weapons as well and we'll be invincible."

Sri Krishna said, "You can have everything you want, but I won't come with it."

"Oh, that doesn't matter," Duryodhana said. "As long as we have a powerful arsenal, who can beat us?"

Then Sri Krishna asked Arjuna what he wanted, and Arjuna replied, "I don't want weapons; I want you to be with me and nothing else."

So Sri Krishna went with Arjuna, and to Duryodhana went all the forces of violence which finally destroyed him and his family. And in our lives, when we follow Arjuna's example and seek to become united with the Lord of Love within, no amount of violence can shake us.

सुहृन्मित्रार्युदासीनमध्यस्थद्वेष्यबन्धुषु ।
साधुष्वपि च पापेषु समबुद्धिर्विशिष्यते ॥ ६-९ ॥

9. They are equally kind to relative, enemy, and a friend; to someone who supports them, someone who is indifferent or neutral, and even someone hateful. Through the ability to give love and respect to all, they rise to great heights.

One of the secrets of victorious living is found in the word *samabuddhi*, 'having an equal attitude towards all,' which tells us to live in harmony with the law of life, to realize that all of us come from God, exist in God, and return to God. In the supreme climax of meditation called samādhi, we see the Lord in everyone, because we see the indivisible unity which is the divine principle of existence.

To everyone, it is necessary to behave with respect: to those who help us, to those who hinder us, to those who talk nicely to us, to those who do not talk to us at all. This is the secret of perfect human relations. Showing respect to our parents, to our friends, and to our enemies not only helps us; it helps them as well. Even if others are not entirely worthy of our respect, when we show respect to them, they begin to rise up to it. If we can keep faith in even the most self-willed people, if we can put our trust in them and expect them to grow, gradually they will try to deserve our respect. We do not have to worry about how the other person will behave towards us, and we do not need to think constantly in terms of reciprocity: "You take the first step; let me see how long it is, and then I'll take the next – not one inch shorter or longer." Here my actions are dependent on the other person, and when we act in this way, our steps get smaller and smaller until we do not move at all. In all our relationships, our primary concern should be how best to give our love and respect. When we try in this way to give every possible service without any thought of return or remuneration, others respond deeply and reveal what is divine within them also.

The code of behavior that many so-called civilized people observe is stimulus and response: you love me, I'll love you; you hate me, I'll hate you in return. But through the practice of meditation, when we begin to mold ourselves in the image of an inspiring incarnation like Sri Krishna, Jesus the Christ, or the Compassionate Buddha, we will find, to our great delight, that we are no longer dependent on how others conduct themselves towards us. This is real freedom. Now we are far from free; we are always wondering how the other person is going to react. We have all kinds of defenses – moats, drawbridges, walls, and then several trapdoors – which prevent us from acting with natural grace. But when we find the exhilarating freedom in which we are able to give our very best without getting caught up in others' reactions, others' attitudes, we find that those around us begin to benefit from our freedom. Those who come into close contact with us will start to lower their defenses, little by little, centimeter by centimeter, and slowly they too will learn to give their very best without worry or fear.

If there is just one person in the family who is self-willed and always on guard, everyone else will automatically raise their defenses a little when they are around that person. It is almost like a reflex; as soon as we see someone who is on guard we say, "That person makes me feel uncomfortable." When we become comfortable with ourselves, we make everyone else comfortable too. The way to be permanently free from these tensions in personal relationships is to put the welfare of those around us first.

At Ramagiri some of our young men have become master carpenters. One of them is making an oddly shaped table which is full of angles and corners, but all the pieces fit so well that when they are together there are no angles or corners at all. When we try to manipulate someone else to fit into our angles and corners, we are actually making the corners sharper, and the sharper they get the more difficult it is to fit the pieces of our own life together into an harmonious whole. How much happier we would be if we could think less about everyone else's angles and corners and more about how we can dovetail into their lives: if we could concentrate less on others' reactions and more on how best to conduct ourselves. Even if others are irritable, we can be more generous. This is the attitude that comes from learning to see the Lord of Love in everyone.

Yesterday when I was taking our dog Muka for a walk I saw a jackrabbit in front of us seated on the road, full of confidence that none of us at Ramagiri would harm him. But seeing Muka, he became unsure and gave a couple of leaps, getting out of our way. Muka looked up at me as if to say, "Why does he have such abnormal legs? Why are the back two so much longer than the front ones?" Muka looks upon his four legs of equal length as normal, and he measures the world from this point of view; anything not conforming to his dimensions is abnormal. The jackrabbit is no different. Looking at the world from his vantage point, he would have said, "What strange legs your dog has – all equal length. How does he manage to hop?" Of course, from our point of view the rabbit's legs are just right for a rabbit and Muka's are just right for a dog.

Similarly, most of us live with people who have different opinions than ours. We all have different dimensions, and we each walk or jump forward in our own way; yet there is a common core in all of us. Twelve years ago, when I had just arrived in America, everyone asked me, "How do you like it here?" I always replied, "Just as I liked it there." There are no differences between people, no matter whether they are in India, Africa, America, or Europe. All our greatness comes from this common humanity, and when we constantly keep our eyes fixed on it, we discover the unity of life which is divine.

योगी युञ्जीत सततमात्मानं रहसि स्थितः ।
एकाकी यतचित्तात्मा निराशीरपरिग्रहः ॥६-१०॥

10. The aspirant should constantly seek the Self within him through the practice of meditation. Controlling his body and his mind he should practice one-pointedness, free from expectations and attachments to material possessions.

Meditation is a dynamic discipline by which we learn to focus our complete concentration at will. Every spiritual aspirant should try to practice *ekāgratā*, or one-pointedness of mind, at all times. In order to become one-pointed, it is necessary to do only one thing at a time, giving full attention to the job at hand. This is a discipline which can deepen our love and loyalty to everyone around us. There is a close connection between deep concentration and loyalty, and with the practice of meditation, we can greatly increase this precious capacity to remain loving and loyal no matter what the vicissitudes or circumstances.

One-pointed attention is something we have to train our minds to achieve, and a good place to begin is with our senses. Often the agitation of the mind is reflected in the restlessness of the eyes. We have only to look at people for a little while to see how tempestuous their minds are; their eyes are like the pendulum of a clock, swinging from one side to the other. As the eyes have never been trained, however, we cannot blame them for thinking their dharma is to be a pendulum. We should train them instead to stop when they get to one side, and keep all their attention there rather than swing immediately somewhere else. Finally, when the mind becomes still, the eyes will become still also. Sri Ramana Maharshi's eyes were extremely beautiful, for they were so still that to look into them was to fall fathoms deep into infinite love.

We can begin practicing one-pointed concentration today by giving our complete attention to whatever we are doing. While eating, for example, we can give our complete attention to our food and not to the newspaper or book we have brought with us. On one occasion in San Francisco we saw a businessman eating the Wall Street Journal for lunch. He wasn't paying any attention to his food, so only a few morsels went into his mouth; but he was gorging himself on the newspaper. The same principle of training applies to all the other senses too. Personal conversations give us a splendid opportunity to train our ears. If we are listening to a friend, even if a parrot flies down and perches on his head we should not get excited, point to the parrot, and break out, "Excuse me for interrupting, but there's a parrot on your head." We should be able to concentrate so hard on what our friend is saying that we can tell this urge, "Keep quiet and don't distract me. Afterwards I'll tell him about the bird."

Finally we come to the concept of nonattachment. This is where most of us are vulnerable, for just about everyone is caught and entangled in all sorts of selfish attachments to people and material objects. As long as we are susceptible to these attachments we are not aware that they are ropes tying us down. It is good to remember the picture of Gulliver lying on the ground, tied by innumerable little ropes to innumerable little pegs by innumerable little men that seem almost like hobgoblins. We, too, are prostrate when we are tied down by countless little selfish, self-willed, and separating attachments to people and to things. It is only when we have broken loose from these ties through the practice of meditation that we find freedom.

शुचौ देशे प्रतिष्ठाप्य स्थिरमासनमात्मनः ।
नात्युच्छ्रितं नातिनीचं चैलाजिनकुशोत्तरम् ॥ ६-११ ॥

11. Establish yourself firmly in a clean spot,
neither too high nor too low, seated on a
cloth, a deerskin, and kusha grass.

Here Sri Krishna advises us to choose a clean place for practicing meditation – clean in the sense of having pure air, quietness, and austerity. Next we should find a suitable way of sitting. It should not be too high, for if we are prone to bouts of sleep we may fall and hurt ourselves. It is wise to sit on the floor, or in a chair with arms. Then Sri Krishna mentions spreading *kusha* grass and a deerskin. This is how it is done in the traditional āshrams of India, but we can sit on an Acrilan blanket or on our bed and still attain spiritual awareness. What is important is to keep our mind one-pointed. To any question of whether we should sit in the full lotus, half lotus, or quarter lotus positions, we can apply Sri Ramana Maharshi's pungent comment that we should sit in the posture in which the mind is still.

Currently we are seeing all kinds of paraphernalia advertised for meditation: special incense, shirts, pillows, and even, I am told, kits for regulating brain waves. Please do not fall for this talk about chemical or mechanical grace; there is only one form of grace: that which comes from the Lord of Love within, which leads to self-purification, strengthening of the will, and selfless service.

तत्रैकाग्रं मनः कृत्वा यतचित्तेन्द्रियक्रियः ।
उपविश्यासने युञ्ज्याद्योगमात्मविशुद्धये ॥६-१२॥

12. Having taken your seat, strive to still your thoughts. Make your mind one-pointed in the practice of meditation, and your heart will be purified.

In order to sit for meditation one has to be firm, not only in body, but in mind as well. Here firmness does not mean sitting rigid and tense as if rigor mortis had set in; it means sitting with the firm resolve to train the mind to come gradually to rest in the Lord.

No matter whether you sit in a chair or on the carpet, the proper posture for meditation is with the spinal column erect. Every time your mind wanders away from the subject of meditation, or you get drowsy or get into a deeper state of concentration, check to make sure your spinal column is straight. Many people are not aware of how their heads droop or turn in meditation, or of how their bodies sway back and forth when a deeper level of consciousness is reached; so without dwelling on it, please check your head and back position occasionally during meditation to make sure they are correct.

Again, Sri Krishna emphasizes here the need to cultivate a one-pointed mind. Our mind is like a grasshopper chirping and jumping from one blade of grass to another, and to train the mind to be one-pointed, we should do only one thing at a time. In our kitchen at Ramagiri this is one of the main principles our cooks observe; when they are cutting a vegetable, they keep their eyes completely on the knife. On one or two occasions they didn't do this, and minor first aid had to be rendered.

When our attention is wandering, we have to render first aid mentally. People whose attention wanders easily are subject to one of the greatest sources of suffering – boredom. There is nothing more disastrous in life than to be bored, and one of the effective ways to relieve boredom is to give more concentration to whatever we are doing, because it is the quality of attention we give to a job that makes it interesting. Unfortunately, most of us cannot give our attention with complete freedom. We are likely to give it only to things we like. There are people who can give their attention freely to trigonometry, but when you give them poetry they will find it impossible to concentrate. My suggestion is that there is real challenge in doing something we do not like, especially when we are overcome by lethargy, backache, and all kinds of problems that seem to prevent us from getting down to work. At first the mind says, "*You* may want to work on this project, but I'm not with you." But you tell it, "It isn't as bad as it looks, really. Let's just see what it is like. After all, there is no harm in putting our toes in the water and seeing what the temperature is like." Then, when the mind has touched the water, you go a little further and say, "Let's play about a little and see what happens." Little by little you can coax the mind to get so absorbed that it will say at last, "I'm not going to get out of the water. I like playing about."

The capacity to give our undivided attention is one of the essential ingredients of the learning process. All of us have unpleasant chores to do, and sometimes it is helpful to draw up a list of things which need to be done joyfully and without delay, including in this list the jobs we detest, the jobs we would rather delegate. By working at such jobs we gradually release ourselves from the tyranny of likes and dislikes, which means we can give our complete concentration to any task, whether it is pleasant or not.

समं कायशिरोग्रीवं धारयन्नचलं स्थिरः ।
संप्रेक्ष्य नासिकाग्रं स्वं दिशश्चानवलोकयन् ॥६-१३॥

13. *Hold your body, head, and neck firmly in a straight line, and keep your eyes from wandering.*

To sit in meditation with the back, neck, and head in a straight line is not as easy as it sounds. As long as your eyes are open, everything is straight. But once you gently close your eyes and start going through the Prayer of St. Francis slowly in the mind, word by word, you begin to concentrate, which means you begin to sink below the surface level of consciousness. As your concentration increases and the mind begins to get one-pointed, forgetting all the distractions you have been occupied with throughout the day, your nervous system starts to relax. All your knots and taut nerves begin to loosen and there is a very natural sense of how good meditation feels. But simultaneously the trunk begins to shorten, the shoulders hump, the neck disappears, and before you know it, the chin has come to rest on the chest. This is just the time, when meditation feels so nice, so relaxing, to draw yourself up, move away from the back support, and sit again with the back, neck, and head in a straight line. The mind says, "I'm alert now. You can trust me." You start the memorized passage again, but it is the same old story. You have to keep straightening your posture over and over again until at last, when a wave of sleep comes near you, your will says, "Vanish. Go back where you came from."

The problem of sleep in meditation will haunt us for some years and as meditation deepens, the will must be strengthened in order to remain awake on a plane of consciousness on which we are not at home, on which we have not learned to travel. In the final stages of meditation, when we go down like a plummet into the depths of our unconscious, there is nothing we can do if we fall asleep. So from now on in meditation, when sleep is overcoming you, draw yourself up by sheer exercise of willpower, keep your spinal column erect, and if necessary open your eyes for a moment and repeat the mantram. At such times you may find it helpful also to look at a picture of Jesus, the Buddha, or some other inspiring spiritual figure. When you have overcome the obstacle of sleep, close your eyes and go back again to the passage.

Not only in meditation can the will be strengthened, but at breakfast, too, when we are eyeing the third piece of toast or the second cup of coffee. Even more effective, when we are greatly agitated and want to go our own way because our parents, partner, friends, or children differ from us, is to make a painful turnabout and go their way instead of ours. If we can do this, the following morning in meditation the wave of sleep will take one look at our will and subside without a murmur. For anyone who wants to overcome the problem of sleep in meditation, this is one of the surest ways to go about it: to make a sudden turnabout and violate one's own self-will in order to foster the happiness of others.

Gradually this turnabout will bring a delicious satisfaction, although not unmixed with pain.

Another reason this erect posture must be maintained, according to the Hindu and Buddhist mystics, has to do with the vast mass of evolutionary energy called kundalinī that is located at the base of the spine. As meditation deepens, kundalinī rises up through the spinal column, activating the different centers of consciousness. According to this theory, keeping the spinal column erect in meditation, when accompanied by allied disciplines such as discriminating restraint of the senses and putting the welfare of others first, helps kundalinī to rise.

Sri Krishna also refers here to the position of the eyes, for this can indicate our state of mind. We can see from someone's eyes whether the person is angry, sorrowful, or restless, because in these states the pupils keep darting to and fro. Similarly, when the mind is at rest and the heart is full, the eyes become still and begin to shine. If we want the beauty of the eyes to shine forth, we have to learn to still the mind through the practice of meditation.

प्रशान्तात्मा विगतभीर्ब्रह्मचारिव्रते स्थितः ।
मनः संयम्य मच्चित्तो युक्त आसीत मत्परः ॥ ६-१४ ॥

14. When his mind has ceased to wander,
a man finds complete fulfillment in me. In
this state all fears dissolve in the peace of the
Self, and all actions proceed toward me.

As our meditation deepens, the mind will become so calm that agitated people will find rest in our presence, and angry people will be forgiving. Even without preaching to others or advising them, our conduct and our unfailing sympathy and support will have a beneficial influence on all those around us. We are all concerned about external pollution, but internal pollution is equally dangerous. One angry person, for example, can upset a whole family. For some, anger is even a feast, a way of introducing excitement into a dull, torpid existence. When people have been agitated for a long time, it is difficult for them to give up their agitation. We can help them by never indulging in violence ourselves: by never retaliating, never using harsh words, and never failing to love even those who hate us.

It is difficult to understand that most angry people are frightened. As Gandhi told us, those who carry guns are really walking about in fear for their lives. When we trust and respect others, all fear vanishes because those around us become our protector, our shield. Another fear that many have is of growing up. Many of us carry a big cradle on our backs, and wherever we go we put it down, get into it, and lie there saying, "You do what I want you to do, and if you don't I'm going to howl and howl and howl." Growing up means taking on life with all its responsibilities and facing whatever comes our way with courage, calmness, and security. We will lose all fears when we realize the Lord is in everyone, making them loving and merciful at heart.

Fear exists only when there is a division in the mind. In the mind there are deep crevices where little bugs of selfishness and separateness live, which thrive on all the minor irritations which occur day in and day out. To remove these little bugs we do not need to use pesticides; all we need to do is reduce our separateness by putting others first, by embracing in our consciousness not only those who support us, which is very easy, but also those who provoke and attack us. Meditation gradually transforms the negative capacity for resentment into a positive capacity for moving closer to our family, our friends, and finally our enemies. By overcoming the obstacles of separateness and self-will that come our way daily in all shapes and sizes, from little irritations to big storms, we eliminate all fear from our consciousness and move closer to the state of perfect peace which is union with the Lord.

युञ्जन्नेवं सदात्मानं योगी नियतमानसः ।
शान्तिं निर्वाणपरमां मत्संस्थामधिगच्छति ॥६-१५॥

15. When he constantly controls his mind and senses through the practice of meditation and seeks the Self within, he attains nirvāna, the state of abiding joy and peace in me.

Those who keep their eyes on the Lord all the time, who practice meditation regularly with sustained enthusiasm, train their senses, and discipline their minds to be obedient, at last become established in nirvāna, the state of abiding joy, in which they see that all of us are one. Nirvāna is not to be found beyond the grave; it is found right here in this life. As the Buddha teaches in the Dhammapada, worldly people who live for themselves suffer in this life and afterwards as well, while those who are established in nirvāna live in joy both in this life and in the life to come. It is possible to live in the world and find nirvāna; it is possible to live within the family and yet be established completely in oneself and see the presence of the Lord everywhere.

नात्यश्नतस्तु योगो ऽस्ति न चैकान्तमनश्नतः ।
न चातिस्वप्नशीलस्य जाग्रतो नैव चार्जुन ॥६-१६॥

16. O Arjuna, they will not succeed in the practice of meditation who eat too much or eat too little, who sleep too much or sleep too little.

We should always try to follow the middle path, which means we should strive to be temperate in all we do. We should neither indulge our senses excessively nor mortify them excessively; we should have neither too much wealth nor too much poverty, neither too much learning nor too much ignorance, neither too much work nor too much leisure. Striking this balance in all activities is an exhilarating discipline we all can learn to practice.

Most of us, for example, do not need as much food as we may think we do. One of the finer points of the art of eating is to stop just when you are about to ask for another helping: when your hand is outstretched, you should be able to get up and turn your back on the table. It can be a little distressing at the time, but afterwards you have much more appreciation of the meal. I would suggest that we eat just three times a day – a hearty breakfast after meditation, a moderate lunch, and a lighter dinner, based on the findings of modern nutrition rather than on fads or fancies.

There are all kinds of interesting ways in which we can keep the palate on the middle path. When it is craving candy or a hot fudge sundae, go for a walk repeating the mantram, and bargain for time with the mind by telling it, "In two hours when we are going home we can go to an ice cream parlor for a deluxe sundae." Interestingly enough, two hours later the mind has forgotten ice cream sundaes and is thinking about the movie it will enjoy tomorrow evening. All you need do is put just a little break of time between the palate and its desire, for you can count on the mind to change its desires. A gentler technique, whenever the mind asks for some unnutritious delicacy like a chocolate candy bar, is to try giving it raisins instead. Very soon it will stop asking for candy.

Playing these little tricks on the mind will bring no harm, but do not be violent with it. Treat it gently, patiently, and compassionately; since we have allowed it license for so many years, it is not fair to expect it to come to heel in a day or two. Occasionally, however, when there is a first-rate conflict – when you see a wave of resentment, anxiety, or frustration welling up – it is helpful to skip a meal. When this is done with discrimination, taking particular care that the body is not deprived of its energy, you will find that not only is the mind easier to control, the body benefits too.

Too much sleep, too, is bad for the body, mind, and meditation. When we sleep too much, we may be unable to face a challenge; then, instead of stretching out to meet the challenge, the will simply becomes paralyzed. Sleeping too much is like saying, "I don't like being human; I prefer to be inert like an old tree, or a rock." But too little sleep is equally an enemy of meditation. In order to live in harmony with the laws of life, we need to observe the rhythm of night and day by going to sleep as early as possible at night and getting up as early as possible in the morning. When you get into bed early, repeat the mantram until you fall asleep. Though at first you may not fall asleep easily, you will have no trouble after your body has had a little time to recondition itself. All our habits can be changed completely by using the immense learning tool we acquire through meditation. Going to sleep too early or too late, getting up too early or too late, eating too much or too little, bursting out in anger or crying in agitation – these are all just repeated patterns of thinking, speaking, and acting which can be altered through the practice of meditation.

युक्ताहारविहारस्य युक्तचेष्टस्य कर्मसु ।
युक्तस्वप्नावबोधस्य योगो भवति दुःखहा ॥६-१७॥

17. The person who has learned to be detached in all his actions through the practice of meditation, who is temperate in eating and sleeping, work and recreation, will come to the end of sorrow.

Sorrow is necessary for us only when we require it to grow to our full stature. We can think of the Lord as a physical education teacher; he looks us over carefully and selects those of us who are drooping with selfishness and self-will. To these he gives sorrow, saying, "Let me give you some special exercises to help you grow as tall and as straight as you can." When we have grown to our full height and can push ourselves out of the way to become sensitive to the needs of others, the Lord will say, "You don't require any more sorrow, any more ordeals. You have gone beyond all suffering by extinguishing your self-will and selfishness. Now you are ready to help reduce the suffering and sorrow of those around you."

If we start looking carefully at our own suffering, we shall find that it often comes to teach us to stop repeating our mistakes. In my young ignorance I committed many mistakes, and much sorrow came my way. But through my grandmother's blessing came the desire never to be separate or selfish, and with it the horror of being angry or violent towards any living creature. I was able to learn the lessons of sorrow so that it became impossible for me to commit the same mistakes again. When we have learned not to commit selfish mistakes in life, not to impose our self-will upon our dear ones, our society, and even our enemies, there is no reason why personal suffering should come to us at all.

यदा विनियतं चित्तमात्मन्येवावतिष्ठते ।
निःस्पृहः सर्वकामेभ्यो युक्त इत्युच्यते तदा ॥६-१८॥

18. Through constant effort a person learns to withdraw the mind from selfish cravings to the Self within, and thus attains union with the Lord.

In the early days of meditation we often seem to hear, as it were, two tape recorders playing in our consciousness at the same time. The first tape is the inspirational passage we are using in meditation; the second is a distraction expressing itself in words that contradict and distort the words of the passage. On such occasions all we have to do is give more and more attention to the words of the passage, which means that we are giving less and less attention to the second tape recorder. For a long, long time our meditation will be this dull, dreary discipline of bringing the mind back to the words of the passage and shunning associations and distractions. But if we persist the great day will come, through the grace of the Lord, when our mind will not wander once from the Upanishads or the Prayer of St. Francis. At that time we will not be aware of the jets roaring in the sky, or the trumpets blaring in our neighbor's apartment; we will not be aware of the body which we have always believed ourselves to be. Even if the rapture of this state lasts for only a few minutes, it is long enough for the Divine Physician to dissolve our tensions, resolve our conflicts, and give us the certitude that we can function with a new freedom no matter what problems come our way.

In this verse Sri Krishna tells Arjuna *viniyatam cittam:* "Have a completely disciplined mind; be the master of your senses and mind." The Buddha would say that most of us do not live intentionally. In fact, he would question whether most of us are actually alive; to him we are like puppets pulled by forces outside ourselves, running after what satisfies our senses and away from what violates our self-will. This is not living; this is being flotsam and jetsam on the sea of life. Only when we have brought our senses under control, when we have extinguished our self-will, can we say we live intentionally.

Just imagine what would happen if all the cars in a city were to roll out of their garages and roar out onto every road at top speed without a driver, without obeying signals or traffic rules. There would be hundreds of accidents. This is just what is happening today when people go about driven by their senses, controlled by their self-will instead of sitting in the driver's seat directing their body, senses, and mind. I admire the ease with which good drivers drive; it is almost as though they have eyes in the back of the head. In order to master the art of living we too need eyes in the back of our heads to be able to look at our behavior in the past and correct ourselves wherever we made mistakes. When we have learned in this way to respect the freedom of all, never to manipulate others and never to attack others, we have a driver's license which is valid always. This is the sign of those who are established in themselves: they do not collide with those who are angry but go about with love and respect for others no matter what the circumstances.

यथा दीपो निवातस्थो नेङ्गते सोपमा स्मृता ।
योगिनो यतचित्तस्य युञ्जतो योगमात्मनः ॥६-१९॥

19. When meditation is mastered, the
mind is unwavering like the flame of
a lamp in a sheltered place.

When I was at the University of Kansas I visited the President Truman Museum where I saw a little clay lamp from Israel, on whose pedestal were inscribed these words from Proverbs 20:27: "The spirit of man is the candle of the Lord." These clay lamps, common in ancient Jerusalem, are still used today in Kerala, where they are lit and placed in an alcove of the shrine. Since there is no wind in the protected niche, the tongue of the flame burns without a flicker.

In the depths of your meditation, when you are concentrating on an inspirational passage such as the Prayer of St. Francis, your mind should be like the tongue of a flame in a windless place, motionless and steady. At that time you will be concentrating completely on the words of the prayer, which means that you are slowly becoming like St. Francis in your daily conduct and consciousness. It requires enormous endeavor to do this, but through ceaseless effort I think every one of us can reach the state in which the mind, like the flame of the clay lamp, does not flicker or waver at all.

यत्रोपरमते चित्तं निरुद्धं योगसेवया ।
यत्र चैवात्मनात्मानं पश्यन्नात्मनि तुष्यति ॥ ६-२० ॥
सुखमात्यन्तिकं यत्तद्बुद्धिग्राह्यमतीन्द्रियम् ।
वेत्ति यत्र न चैवायं स्थितश्चलति तत्त्वतः ॥ ६-२१ ॥
यं लब्ध्वा चापरं लाभं मन्यते नाधिकं ततः ।
यस्मिन्स्थितो न दुःखेन गुरुणापि विचाल्यते ॥ ६-२२ ॥
तं विद्याद्दुःखसंयोगवियोगं योगसंज्ञितम् ।
स निश्चयेन योक्तव्यो योगो ऽनिर्विण्णचेतसा ॥ ६-२३ ॥

20. In the still mind the Self reveals itself.
From the depths of meditation a man draws
the joy and peace of complete fulfillment.
21. Having attained that abiding joy beyond the
senses, revealed in the stilled mind, he will never
swerve from the eternal truth that all life is one.
22. In this state he desires nothing else, and cannot
be shaken by the heaviest burdens of sorrow.
23. The practice of meditation frees him from all
affliction. This is the path of yoga. Follow it with
determination and sustained enthusiasm.

In these verses Sri Krishna is trying to tell us, as far as words can convey, the state we reach when our mind becomes completely one-pointed. First of all, we see ourselves as we really are. Up until this point, the one person we have never seen is ourselves. When Nureyev appeared in San Francisco not long ago there were quite a few ballet fans who, I was told, flew all the way from New York to see him. The mystics would point out how fruitless it is to go to see important people when our first priority is to see ourselves. We think we know Tom, Dick, and Harry, but we really know everyone, including ourselves, only on the surface level. If we could see our real Self coming down Āshram Street, we would wonder who this beautiful, radiant, magnificent creature could be. We would not be able to take our eyes away, we would be so full of love. Then our real Self would come to us, slowly, step by step, and enter our consciousness. All of us are full of dazzling beauty just waiting to reveal itself, and in order to let this radiance emerge all we must do is throw off the mask of the self-willed, separate ego with which we identify ourselves today.

Once we have seen our real Self in all its glory, no treasure on earth, no achievement, no pleasure is even worth mentioning. When we look at money, it is only dull metal; when we look at pleasure, it is just dull tinsel; when we look at power and prestige, they are no more than dime-store jewelry. Today we can be excited about the pursuit of little satisfactions because we lack a frame of reference in which to evaluate them meaningfully. It is only when we have made a certain amount of progress on the spiritual path through meditation that we develop a standard of comparison. When we acquire this deeper, clearer point of view, we can compare the joy of St. Francis to the joy of going into a pizza parlor, or the joy of Meister Eckhart to that of going into a beer garden. Then we realize we have been penny-wise and pound-foolish in life, going after trivia when we could as well go after the supreme goal.

In the final stages of meditation the whole burden of regret, resentment, vague longing, and restlessness falls away. This is the end of all sorrow. We become established in the Lord and see him in the heart of every creature – human, beast, bird – and in all life. With this inspiring picture of the goal of meditation, Sri Krishna appeals to Arjuna: "Make your will resolute, and throw yourself into this spiritual endeavor so that you too will go beyond sorrow to become established in the indivisible unity that is divine."

संकल्पप्रभवान्कामांस्त्यक्त्वा सर्वानशेषतः ।
मनसैवेन्द्रियग्रामं विनियम्य समन्ततः ॥६-२४॥

24. Renouncing wholeheartedly all selfish desires and expectations, use your will to control the senses.

In order to attain the supreme state of complete security and boundless joy, we have to renounce every trace of selfish desire and sweep away the last little selfish urge hiding in the cobwebs in the corner of the ego. For the vast majority of us, this takes a whole lifetime of sweeping with the broom of meditation.

Every morning my grandmother used to sweep the veranda of our house, which was constantly threatened by the dust of tropical India. If she had neglected her sweeping, the dust would have grown thick after just one morning; and if left unswept for a few weeks, the entire veranda would have been hidden under the dust. Similarly, our minds get cluttered and covered with debris when we fail to have our daily meditation. We may be tempted to meditate only once or twice a week, so that on weekdays we can devote all our time to pursuing our pleasure and profit. But when we try to clean only on the weekend, it takes all day. Even then we sometimes add further difficulties by stimulating our senses. After a few weekends like this, we begin to clean only once a month, but at that point the pile of dirt and debris is too high for even a vacuum cleaner to clear away.

The way to keep the mind clean and pure is to spend half an hour every day, no matter what other responsibilities we have, in the practice of meditation. If we do this regularly every morning, we gradually shall find that it becomes easy to keep the place clean. By practicing meditation regularly and keeping our senses under control, we can clean away the debris of sankalpa, all our selfish desires, and make room for the Lord of Love. Without the practice of meditation, it is difficult to bring the senses under control, and without sense control, it is difficult to rise above the physical body; without rising above the physical body, it is not possible to discover the indivisible unity of life. From this we can see how important it is to devote a half hour every morning – such a small amount of time – regularly and enthusiastically to the practice of meditation.

शनैः शनैरुपरमेद्बुद्ध्या धृतिगृहीतया ।
आत्मसंस्थं मनः कृत्वा न किं चिदपि चिन्तयेत् ॥६-२५॥

25. *Keep your mind from wandering. Little by*
little, through patience and repeated effort,
the mind will become stilled in the Self.

Instead of being impatient and always wondering when the Lord will come, if we throw ourselves heart and soul into the practice of meditation and the allied disciplines of sense restraint and selfless service, gradually over the years we shall become complete master of every area of consciousness. On the spiritual path we must make every effort to move forward even if it is little by little, even if every day we keep making mistakes. Sometimes we are so insensitive and preoccupied with ourselves that when we try to put others first we simply are not aware of their needs. Our mistakes begin to haunt us; but rather than sitting in a corner and crying over the day's errors, or developing a comfortable guilt complex, we should repeat the mantram and make sure that we do not repeat the same mistakes the next day.

I remember how difficult it was for me to change my food habits, especially after years of highly spiced Indian food which was sadly lacking in nutrition. In the company of friends, seated around the table, you sometimes cannot resist temptation. When they are smacking their lips over french-fried potatoes or English muffins spread thick with butter, you find yourself joining in, and before you know it you have eaten food that will not help your body, mind, or intellect. In meditation, when I used to come to the verse in the Gita where the Lord says, "Those who allow their senses to sweep them away are like little boats caught in a storm – they will never make harbor," it would stab me like a dagger. The memory of something I had eaten would try to prevent me from meditating, but I would concentrate more and more on the words of the passage as hard as I could. During the day, when I was tempted to indulge in some special sweet, all that I had to do was think of how I would have to go through all that conflict again. When the senses are trying to sweep us away from the path, when our self-will is disrupting relationships with those around us, it is good to remind ourselves that even though we may get some temporary satisfaction, we will have to go through the pain of ridding ourselves of these selfish desires all over again.

In learning to control the mind, the repetition of the holy name is an invaluable aid. When we get angry or afraid, we should not ask the mind why it is in such a state, because this gives it more attention and intensifies its anger or fear. The mind is something like a high-powered computer which sometimes goes out of order, and when it gets angry or afraid, this is just a mechanical breakdown which does not affect our real Self at all. If anger or fear is taking possession of the mind, the way to prevent a breakdown is to go for a long, brisk walk repeating the mantram, and anger will become compassion, fear will become courage, and hatred will become love.

By doing this for many years, we can correct our destructive responses and cultivate a positive, constructive state of mind. Even if our habits have been developing since we were two years old, they can be changed through the practice of meditation. In this sense meditation is the most powerful learning tool we have, and though it may take years of hard work to get hold of it, once we have acquired this immense skill nothing on earth can equal the satisfaction, the joy, and the sense of mastery it will bring. We are all subject to deep resentments going back to the early days of our childhood. Usually there is very little that we can do about these deep-seated problems, but with the learning tool of meditation we can travel into the depths of our consciousness and get rid of them once and for all.

When you are able to travel into deeper levels of consciousness, you may have an experience in your sleep in which something almost like a pistol shot goes off in your head. On the following morning, you can almost see your inhibitions lying at the foot of the bed. You get up and feel as if shackles have been taken off your feet, as if handcuffs have been removed from your hands. This will take place over and over again, because we have a list of fears to shed as big as a Sears Roebuck catalog, and it is only after we have shed all these fears and resentments that we will find ourselves in the supreme state, seeing the Lord everywhere, in everyone, all the time.

यतो यतो निश्चरति मनश्चञ्चलमस्थिरम् ।
ततस्ततो नियम्यैतदात्मन्येव वशं नयेत् ॥६-२६॥

26. It is the nature of the mind to be restless and
diffuse, always seeking satisfaction without.
Lead it within; train it to rest in the Self.

The nature of the mind is to desire, to desire, to desire, and most of us firmly believe that permanent joy can be found by satisfying our desires. The mind is such a cunning, clever customer that I have a sneaking admiration for it when it comes and says it will make us happy by giving us, say, Helen of Troy. We fall for the mind's tempting promise, but we find the Cyclopes instead. When we complain to the mind, "Hey, Desire, this is not what you promised – people with eyes in their foreheads trying to gobble us up," the mind says, "Well, that was just an experiment; here is a real offer for happiness, and if you will accept it, I'm sure you will be completely satisfied." Again we are convinced that we will not be led astray, but it is still the same story: we still haven't learned; we still go searching for joy outside ourselves. Some of the great mystics have thrown up their hands at the number of times we have to go around the world before we see that it is round, at the way we turn our back upon joy until we discover, through the grace of the Lord, that joy has been right here within us all the time.

One of the games I used to enjoy was table tennis, and with concentration I mastered all sorts of styles of gripping the paddle and returning the ball. I haven't played table tennis for many years now, but with the news of how table tennis tournaments between China and the United

States have mended international relations, I had a little yearning to play the game again. Now when two people are arguing I can always bring them together and say, "Let's play table tennis." When we were in Portland, Oregon, we visited Reed College, where we found a room with tables and paddles but not a ball in sight. I felt a little frustrated having gone that far out of my way to play table tennis and not being able to, but I repeated the mantram a few times and forgot all about the incident. Then yesterday at dinner one of our friends told us he had discovered a table complete with balls and paddles in the barn at Ramagiri. Imagine going to Oregon and looking for table tennis equipment when all the time it is lying right there in your barn! This is my illustration of Jesus' statement, "The kingdom of heaven lies within."

In order to realize this inner joy for ourselves, it is necessary to still the mind, to rid it of all selfish desires and expectations. This is what we are learning to do in meditation when we bring our mind back every time it wanders away from the words of the inspirational passage to the movie theater or the supermarket. As time goes on, the mind will wander less and less, so that after some years we may have to bring it back only two or three times. In deeper meditation the great day may come when it does not wander away at all but stays put on the words of the inspirational piece, which means the mind is so concentrated in all its power that it lights up the whole passage. In the mystical tradition this is described as the words opening their doors and taking us in. They are no longer just words we are repeating in our mind; they have become integrated into our consciousness, transforming our character and our daily lives. When we can concentrate completely on St. Francis's words, "It is in pardoning that we are pardoned," then instead of holding things against our parents, our children, or our friends, we will be able to open our arms wide to them. We will be able to stand steadfast with love and respect for those who oppose us, and our former enemy will come to us as a good friend. This steadfast love for all is abiding joy.

प्रशान्तमनसं ह्येनं योगिनं सुखमुत्तमम् ।
उपैति शान्तरजसं ब्रह्मभूतमकल्मषम् ॥६-२७॥

27. Abiding joy comes to those who still the mind and senses, who free themselves from the taint of self-will and unify their consciousness in the Lord.

Those who see the Lord present in all life have unshakable strength, for they are rooted in the Lord. Not all the dangers in the world will shake them out of their security, because nothing can agitate them: their minds are still, and their thoughts are completely under control.

Every day we have opportunities for spiritual growth when things happen to us which we do not like, which start the mind moving in all directions in agitation. There is no use getting mad at the mind, because the angrier we get at the mind, the more we will be agitated. The best thing to do is to keep the mind quiet by repeating the mantram over and over again. If you cannot repeat the mantram in your mind, write it in a book kept for this purpose. We used to have people dropping in at odd hours very agitated, and when they would start telling me what so-and-so said and how they wish they could have put him in his place, I would give them the mantram notebook and ask them to write the mantram in it two hundred times. When they had finished writing, they would leave with their minds peaceful. It is not at all helpful to exchange agitating stories, so when people start narrating their tales of resentment, ask them to write the mantram a number of times instead.

Another secret for stilling an agitated mind is to throw yourself into work with no thought of reward or remuneration. A necessary part of spiritual discipline for most young people is hard physical work, which when combined with the use of the mantram calms the mind.

When all our selfish, agitating desires have been expelled from our mind, what is left is pure joy, pure spirit, of which we have been unaware all this time. Joy is imprisoned within us, just waiting to be released from the jailer, our selfish desires. To release it, all we have to do is eliminate every selfish craving and extinguish every selfish impulse, which takes tremendous effort and inexhaustible patience.

Spiritual joy is sometimes described as a bashful girl who is just waiting to tiptoe up and put her arms about us, while all we are trying to do is keep her away. Our selfish desires and cravings tell us not to let her come near us because then they will have to go; and since we are under an hypnotic spell of ignorance, we believe that these selfish urges, which make us miserable to the point of agony, are our real friends. It is astonishing that we can be so perverse as to do just the things that will make us unhappy. Resentment and retaliation tear us apart, yet we let ourselves be driven by them. Instead, we need to learn to accept joy, who is always ready to come to us. This is what we are learning to do through the practice of meditation, to throw open our arms and welcome the joy of living that has been waiting all this time to embrace us.

युञ्जन्नेवं सदात्मानं योगी विगतकल्मषः ।
सुखेन ब्रह्मसंस्पर्शमत्यन्तं सुखमश्नुते ॥६-२८॥

28. This infinite joy of union with the Lord is easily attained by those who are free from the burden of self-will and established within themselves.

It is wise to remind ourselves that our real Self is absolutely pure; in our natural state we are untainted by any selfish desires, completely free of self-will. Anger, fear, greed, lust, malice – these are all unnatural states that we have come to accept as natural. Today we are imprisoned by our passions and cravings, but through the practice of meditation we can break off these shackles and live freely like the eagle soaring in the air.

Several days ago at Ramagiri I watched six baby swallows learn how to fly. They were seated on the telephone wires observing the mother bird, who came flying slowly in front of them, doing the easier turns and showing them the basics of flying. There was no point in telling these baby swallows to read books or attend lectures on how to fly; they have an inborn instinct for flying. They learn the skills of flight by watching their mother, who was showing her babies that there was no need to sit there quaking as if they were going to fall. Learning to fly may not be easy, but this is what birds are born to do. This was the lesson she taught her little ones.

Likewise, Sri Krishna sees us sitting on a perch made of pleasure, profit, power, or prestige, quaking with every variation in our bank account and every critical comment that comes our way, and he asks us if we would not rather forget our failings, weaknesses, and insecurities and become united with him. This is what we are born to do: to turn our back on our selfish interests and give all our love to the Lord, so that all the faculties and resources which have been hidden in us can come into our lives to the great benefit of those around us. Then we will no longer be acting; the Lord will take hold of our arms and act through us.

Today at a park in San Francisco we saw a mime show in which a young man really illustrated, to my mind, how we can be transformed when we yield ourselves to the Lord's direction. At first the mime was seated on a bench, talking and eating like everyone else; then he started his performance, and all his movements changed as if some puppeteer were standing behind him pulling the strings. There were all sorts of people passing by, and he had an uncanny knack for imitating them. I enjoyed the performance so much because it showed what all of us are like when we are ego-driven. For example, a high-powered businessman was shooting along to the financial district repeating his Dow Jones mantram. He was annoyed at the mime's clever caricature of his self-important air, but the young fellow's gestures were so eloquent that he forgot his high-powered business freeze and became a human being again and walked on smiling. The only occasion on which the young fellow lost was when a buxom, middle-aged lady came along; when he tried to imitate her, she just hugged him.

When we are ego-driven, living for ourselves, revenging the wrongs others do to us and hating those who hate us, we are like the people the mime was imitating. But if we surrender ourselves to the Lord, when he picks us up and pulls the strings behind us we can make a tremendous contribution to the welfare of all those who come in contact with us.

सर्वभूतस्थमात्मानं सर्वभूतानि चात्मनि ।
ईक्षते योगयुक्तात्मा सर्वत्र समदर्शनः ॥६-२९॥

29. They see that the Lord is enshrined in every creature, and that all creation comes from the Lord. With consciousness unified through the practice of meditation, they see the Lord everywhere.

The mark of the man or woman who has become united with the Lord is that he or she sees the Lord in all fellow beings, in every form of life. In one of the delightful anecdotes in the *Mahābhārata*, Dharmaputra, the oldest of the Pāndavas, turns up at the gates of heaven with his dog. Dvārapāla, the gatekeeper, takes down all the vital information about Dharmaputra – name, address, siblings – and then he notices the dog. "Sorry," says Dvārapāla, "we don't admit dogs. See that little sign? It says Dogs Not Allowed." Then follows an awfully confusing situation: Dharmaputra is established in the Lord and should be admitted, but what should be done about the dog? Finally Dvārapāla gives Dharmaputra a choice: to enter heaven alone, without the dog, or to go back where he came from with his dog. Without the slightest hesitation, Dharmaputra chooses to be with his dog, who is then immediately revealed as Lord Krishna in disguise.

Those who are illumined see the Lord in every creature and are incapable of exploiting any other being for their own profit or pleasure. When we were on the Blue Mountain, we once saw a little black calf, only a few months old, being led to slaughter. I looked at the calf, and it was as if tears were flowing from his eyes; he was trying to tell me in his dumb language, "See what your brother is going to do to me?" Right then I decided that at every opportunity I would put in a good word on behalf of all animals.

It is not easy to understand, when we are caught in cultural habits, that eating meat violates the indivisible unity of life. It used to be very difficult to find a restaurant that served vegetarian food. Now, however, there are good vegetarian restaurants springing up in many cities, and at every chance we get, we can recommend these restaurants to our friends. This is a simple way of showing our love and respect for the Lord, who lives in the lamb, the deer, the cow, and all other forms of life.

यो मां पश्यति सर्वत्र सर्वं च मयि पश्यति ।
तस्याहं न प्रणश्यामि स च मे न प्रणश्यति ॥६-३०॥

30. I am ever present to those who have realized me in every creature. Seeing all life as my manifestation, they are never separated from me.

Now the Lord tells us that when we see him in everyone, when we show everyone the same courtesy and consideration regardless of what they do to us, we will receive his guidance, and he will protect us against all the storms of life. We can cultivate this equal vision every day by trying to see the Lord in everyone around us.

If in spite of our best efforts we become angry, agitated, or afraid, we can bring our mind back to the state of calmness by going for a walk repeating the mantram. The rhythm of our footsteps and the rhythm of the mantram will blend and stabilize the rhythm of our breathing, which is closely connected with our state of mind. Angry people breathe irregularly; those who are calm, loving, and secure breathe like a little child, smoothly, slowly, and deeply.

Even if we turn to the Lord as a last resort, when all else fails, he is still content to receive us. When I was at the University of Minnesota I became friends with a young fellow from Kerala studying to be an engineer. He had always been a good student, but the night before his final examination he came to me afraid and anxious that he might fail. He had tried pep pills and lecture notes, but when they failed to dispel his fears he had come to see if there was anything in the Gita that could help him. I did not ask him why he had not come six years sooner; I just told him that the Lord is always glad when we come to him, always ready to help us when ruin is staring us in the face and all other paths have failed. He was so relieved to hear this that he asked me what exactly Sri Krishna had to say about engineering exams in the Gita. I told him that there was no exact reference, but in times of danger – "Oh," he broke in, "that's my final, all right. Real danger – I'll lose my scholarship and my lifelong desire to be an engineer will never be fulfilled." So I asked him to repeat the mantram while I took him for a walk from Minneapolis to Saint Paul and then back again – a distance of about twelve miles. He was so completely relaxed when we got home that he was asleep before his head touched the pillow. The breathing exercise of walking with the mantram changed his anxiety and insecurity into calm assurance that he would do well in his exam, and he did, too.

Whenever we have a difficult examination or a trying emotional situation to face, the best thing we can do is repeat the mantram. In going to sleep at night, it is simple to close our eyes and repeat the holy name until we fall asleep. No matter how difficult the problems we have to face, this simple tonic will rest and refresh us so that we will be at our best in meeting the day's challenges. I have the responsibility of guiding the meditation of hundreds of people, but when I go to bed now, after years of practice, I can just hand my responsibilities over to the Lord. The mantram takes over so that I hear it in my sleep, so that I see the Lord in my sleep; and when I wake up I am refreshed in body, mind, and spirit, able to face whatever the day brings because I have placed my burden at the feet of the Lord.

सर्वभूतस्थितं यो मां भजत्येकत्वमास्थितः ।
सर्वथा वर्तमानो ऽपि स योगी मयि वर्तते ॥६-३१॥

31. They worship me in the hearts of all, and all their actions proceed from me. Wherever they may live, they abide in me.

Outward signs of spiritual effort such as going to temple or church are no substitute for the practice of meditation, for without meditation we will not have the capacity for transforming anger into compassion, ill will into good will, and hatred into love. We may have a brilliant intellect, may have won the Nobel Prize; but when it comes to changing anger into sympathy or hostility into kindness, we will be helpless without the spiritual discipline of meditation.

You have probably seen that huge machine which demolishes old buildings by hoisting a heavy metal ball high into the air and then dropping it with a terrific crash. This is similar to what occurs in the early stages of meditation, in which we destroy old habits of acting, speaking, and thinking. This is a painful process; the joy comes when we start rebuilding. At that point we do not have to drive miles to pick up materials, cart them home, unload them, and store them until we are ready to use them. The Lord has all the materials ready, and he is waiting to hand them to us as we need them. We have only to demolish our self-will and selfishness and he will give us the materials of love, wisdom, patience, and endurance with which to build a house that can never be destroyed.

If we continue to use our old house, built with selfishness, fear, and anger, without a secure foundation, it is likely to crash and bury us in its ruins. But if we tear down the old, creaking structure and build a new one on firm foundations, with materials given by the Lord, then we will live free from anxiety and fear. With such a house, we will be able to offer shelter to more and more of those around us. This is another way of phrasing the truth that Sri Krishna never tires of repeating: "Do not depend on things outside yourself, on money, possessions, power, or fame, for they will not bring lasting joy or security; they will bring only a temporary satisfaction which will leave you weaker and weaker with the passage of time."

आत्मौपम्येन सर्वत्र समं पश्यति योऽर्जुन ।
सुखं वा यदि वा दुःखं स योगी परमो मतः ॥६-३२॥

32. When a person responds to the joys and sorrows of others as if they were his own, he has attained the highest state of spiritual union.

In this verse Sri Krishna sums up the entire art of living in one simple, practical suggestion: to understand how to behave towards others, all we have to do is understand that what gives us pain gives others pain also. Jesus uses similar language when he tells us, "All things whatsoever ye would that men should do to you, do ye even so to them."

We can apply this wise advice even to the smallest trifles of daily living. When we are waiting for a friend who is a few minutes late, for example, we look at our watch, shake it, and get more agitated as the seconds go by. But when we are half an hour late, we expect our friend to be patient and understanding. We expect others to overlook our few foibles because of our many virtues, yet at the same time we consider it our prerogative to point out everyone else's weaknesses and mistakes. To understand others, to be considerate towards others, we have only to recognize how much we appreciate consideration ourselves.

The person with real spiritual consideration will help others forget about their failings. Learning to make others comfortable, even when they have made a mistake, is another way of going beyond our petty little selves and becoming aware of everyone else's needs. The more we can forget ourselves by being sensitive and aware of everyone else, the more the Lord comes to life in us. The Compassionate Buddha was good at driving this point home to his disciples. He would tell them there was nothing to discourse or debate about in understanding other people: what offends you, offends others. It is that simple. When someone makes a sarcastic remark about us, we are not exactly delighted; therefore, we cannot afford to make sarcastic remarks to others.

Harsh thoughts, resentful thoughts, can wound others more deeply than knives. We are not used to thinking of thoughts as things; our idea of a thing is something we can put in a cup and rattle. We are unaware of the cacophony of the thoughts that rattle in our consciousness. If we could open our inner ear, we would be surprised to hear these hateful thoughts making such horrible noises in our consciousness: "I hate you, I hate you," or "Drop dead, drop dead." Such hateful thoughts injure others like a knife we throw at them over and over, and injure us too because each thought rankles and digs further into our consciousness as the days go by. Yet thoughts can be curative also. When people burst out in anger against us, if we can remain friendly, not hold their mistakes against them, and move closer to them, we will bring them continual relief from their anger. This is true of even the roughest character; everyone responds to forbearance and forgiveness, which bless not only the one who gives them and the one who receives them, but everyone who associates with the man or woman who forgives.

अर्जुन उवाच ।
यो ऽयं योगस्त्वया प्रोक्तः साम्येन मधुसूदन ।
एतस्याहं न पश्यामि चञ्चलत्वात्स्थितिं स्थिराम् ॥६-३३॥

ARJUNA:

33. O Madhusūdana, the complete stillness of union which you describe is beyond my comprehension. How can the mind, which is so restless, attain lasting peace?

Madhu is the name of a demon, the ego demon; *sūdana* refers to one who destroys. This is a beautiful name for Sri Krishna: Madhusūdana, 'the slayer of the ego.' Arjuna addresses him in this way with great respect, confessing that he sees no way of conquering his restless, turbulent mind.

We know that in meditation there are days when we come confidently out of the meditation room thinking we have performed the funeral ceremony of the ego; but then, on the following morning in meditation, we hear a titter from the mind which says, "Fooled you, didn't I?" Sometimes we feel almost ridiculous for trying to conquer this demon called the mind; yet we must not let ourselves lapse into negative thinking, for it is completely within our power to reshape our mind, our conduct, and our destiny. We do this by making intentional choices about how we act, how we speak, and how we think, day in and day out. By using inspirational passages like the Prayer of St. Francis or the second chapter of the Gita, our choices in daily living will become wiser and more in harmony with the selfless ideal we are meditating upon. In this way we begin to transform our thinking from fear, anxiety, and despair into courage, love, and wisdom.

चञ्चलं हि मनः कृष्ण प्रमाथि बलवद्दृढम् ।
तस्याहं निग्रहं मन्ये वायोरिव सुदुष्करम् ॥ ६-३४ ॥

34. O Krishna, the mind is restless, turbulent,
and violent. Trying to control the mind
is like trying to control the wind.

Now Arjuna gets down to specifics by telling the Lord, "You might as well ask me to control the wind, to ride on a storm or to master a hurricane, as to control my mind." Even the expression "I think" is more a euphemism than a statement of fact: we do not think most of our thoughts; they think us. We sit in meditation with a deep desire to meditate on the Lord, but how is it our thoughts go to the local pizza parlor, or to the movie we saw? The answer is that the mind just thinks what thoughts it likes. When we at last become aware, through meditation, of the lack of liberty in our own realm, we get the incentive to drive the usurper, our ego, from the throne. The ego is seated there scepter in hand, and since we do not know that he really isn't king, we all say, "You command, we obey." Patanjali, the great teacher of ancient India, calls meditation *rāja yoga*, the 'royal path,' the way to depose the ego and reinstate the Lord as the true ruler of our body, mind, and spirit.

Having listened to Arjuna's lamentation that the battle of the ego is too fierce for him, and heard him say he can defeat others but not his own selfish passions, Sri Krishna now smiles lovingly, puts his arm around his friend, and encourages him to take on his greatest foe, his own selfishness and separateness.

श्रीभगवानुवाच ।
असंशयं महाबाहो मनो दुर्निग्रहं चलम् ।
अभ्यासेन तु कौन्तेय वैराग्येण च गृह्यते ॥६-३५॥

SRI KRISHNA:

35. It is true that the mind is restless and difficult to control. But it can be conquered, O Mahābāho, through regular practice and detachment.

The Lord does not address Arjuna as "mister" here; he calls him *Mahābāho*, 'you whose arms extend to the heavens.' Our arms, too, can extend to the heavens if we try to reach beyond ourselves. Today we are leading selfish lives, going after what concerns us, oblivious of the needs of others, and this selfishness has crippled our arms. But the Lord of Love tells us that if we stretch our arms wide to embrace everyone, if we use them for comforting and strengthening others, we will find them growing longer and longer until finally we will be able to reach out and catch the Lord.

Stretching our arms is not easy, for it takes untiring effort and the grit to bear with others no matter how unlovingly they treat us. We start strengthening our arms right with our family, with our friends, and on our job, by doing little things for others. It is easiest to begin by establishing good relationships with our family, because they want to be loving and close as much as we do. Then, after we have brought a cease-fire to the guerilla warfare in our own home, we can gradually develop good relationships with our neighbors, then with our city council, then on to the state capital; and finally, when we have proven ourselves to be an unshakable negotiator for peace, we can work on a national and international level.

Yesterday we took the children to start their swimming lessons, and I was recalling how I learned swimming from my grandmother in just two easy lessons. First she showed me how; then she told me to get into the water and swim like her, reassuring me that she would rescue me if I needed help. I had such trust and faith in her that I plunged right in and, after swallowing some water, started swimming. In contrast, the gradual, incremental method of the modern instructor is a safe and sure way of teaching a large number of people to swim. From what I saw yesterday, they start you out in the baby pool, blowing bubbles. Then they take you on to kicking, and when this is mastered, you learn to dog paddle. Likewise, on the spiritual path the incremental approach is the logical sequence for us. We gradually make our arms long and strong by setting our lives right, first in our own homes and then in our community and society.

The instructions we need to follow to develop selflessness are very simple. Practice meditation regularly every day. Repeat the mantram at every opportunity. Restrain the senses with temperate, moderate choices, and put the welfare of all those around you first. At the swimming pool I saw an object lesson in what is meant by carrying out instructions. An excellent instructor was teaching four children to dive by showing them all the movements they should follow to do a perfect dive. Although all four were listening to everything he said, and watching him closely, each gave a different performance. The little girl did such a perfect dive that I had to hold myself back from applauding loudly. She had the capacity to translate instruction into practice. Then came the little boys: one did a belly flop, another tried to curl into a ball, and the third, overenthusiastic, landed on his back. For them, the capacity to translate instruction into practice was still in the making. Like the little girl, we should try to remember Sri Krishna's instructions exactly and follow them to the letter.

In the second line Sri Krishna tells us there are two essential aids for bringing the mind under control. One is *abhyāsa*: regular, systematic practice. Every day, no matter what problems try to interfere, we must get up as early as we can and meditate. When we do this regularly, our practice will become perfect. The other is *vairāgya*: detachment from our opinions, our actions, our ego. We are so entangled and embroiled in ourselves that we take everything personally. Once, after I had been talking about some of our human weaknesses, someone in the audience indignantly asked me why I had been talking about her that way in public. Anger, jealousy, malice – these are weaknesses we all have. Instead of giving in to them, however, we should turn our back on these petty demands for attention and go against our frustration and anger when these demands are not met. With sustained practice of meditation and sustained detachment from the ego, Sri Krishna reassures us that we will be able to reach him at last.

असंयतात्मना योगो दुष्प्राप इति मे मतिः ।
वश्यात्मना तु यतता शक्यो ऽवाप्तुमुपायतः ॥६-३६॥

36. Those who lack self-control will find it difficult to progress in meditation. But those who are earnest in the practice of meditation and self-restraint will attain the goal.

If we are prepared to base our lives on meditation and follow Sri Krishna's instructions exactly, union with the Lord is possible. But if we are lethargic or sporadic – if we start out on the spiritual path with a big bang and end up with a whimper – the unitive state is not possible. The Sanskrit word *ārambhashūra*, 'hero at the beginning,' describes this second type perfectly.

Those who succeed on the spiritual path are the pluggers, the ones who will not give up. If they cannot run, they will walk; if they cannot walk, they will crawl. They will not take no for an answer. To reach a selfless goal, they are prepared to climb over any obstacle; whatever barriers are in their way, they will pile them up into a big heap to climb over an even greater barrier. If we keep trying to make the most of these opportunities, we will discover that there is joy in overcoming what seemed to be an immovable obstacle. At first these efforts to grow are extremely painful, because they usually require us to go against our self-will. But if we keep our eyes on the supreme goal, these agonizing stabs will turn into little pinpricks and finally into just the tickling of a feather. When we have such complete, unqualified dedication to the supreme goal, we shall find what joy there is in going forward on the spiritual path.

अर्जुन उवाच ।
अयतिः श्रद्धयोपेतो योगाच्चलितमानसः ।
अप्राप्य योगसंसिद्धिं कां गतिं कृष्ण गच्छति ॥६-३७॥

ARJUNA:

37. Krishna, what happens to the man who has faith, but who wanders from the path and loses sight of the goal?

Here Arjuna is very much our representative, giving voice to the disquieting doubts that keep nibbling at little bits of our consciousness. Sounding like a skeptical modern man, Arjuna asks Sri Krishna: "Supposing that after practicing meditation for some years, a force beyond my control makes me give it up. Are all those years of hard discipline wasted?" This is a question we are all likely to ask in the early stages of meditation.

After we have been meditating for some years we will gradually begin to see some of its great rewards. By bringing the senses under control, we will come to have vibrant health; by bringing the mind under control, we will find a state of quiet joy; and by bringing the ego under control, we will develop more loving relationships with our family and friends. If, after having a glimpse of these rewards, we give up meditation for some reason, we will find there is nothing in the world to take its place. We can throw ourselves into feverish pleasure and excitement, into the driving pursuit of power, but there will always be a little voice inside us saying, "You've lost the path."

This verse is very apposite today, especially with respect to the pressing problem of drug addiction. Thousands of young people are being misled by the assertion that psychedelic drugs can bring about spiritual awareness. Even well-known people have made statements about Indian sages using drugs; but I have no hesitation in saying that no sage worth his mantram has ever taken drugs for spiritual purposes. Meher Baba, a great modern mystic, warned us that not only do drugs not bring spiritual awareness, but when taken for a long time they may damage our capacity for spiritual awareness. If we look for a chemical shortcut through drugs, there is a possibility we will reach a point where we will be unable to meditate. Meditation is such a demanding expedition into the world within that we must have a strong, resilient body, a fit nervous system, a calm mind, and a lucid intellect, all of which are likely to be impaired not just by drugs, but by any form of excessive indulgence in the senses and in self-will.

कच्चिन्नोभयविभ्रष्टश्छिन्नाभ्रमिव नश्यति ।
अप्रतिष्ठो महाबाहो विमूढो ब्रह्मणः पथि ॥६-३८॥
एतन्मे संशयं कृष्ण छेत्तुमर्हस्यशेषतः ।
त्वदन्यः संशयस्यास्य छेत्ता न ह्युपपद्यते ॥६-३९॥

38. If a man becomes deluded on the spiritual path will he lose the support of both worlds, like a cloud scattered in the sky?
39. O Krishna, you who are the dispeller of all doubts, remove this doubt which binds me.

Probably everyone has watched the wind break up a big billowy cloud into tiny pieces and scatter them all over the sky. Arjuna compares himself to such a cloud and asks Sri Krishna, "What will happen if some great calamity, some overwhelming desire, picks me up, cuts up my consciousness, and scatters my mind, my resolve, and my will in all directions, making my desire for the spiritual life disappear like a cloud? Will I have lost both the world of sense pleasure and the joy of the spiritual life?" This is a very practical question, which is likely to occur to all of us who have been used to indulging our senses and imposing our self-will on others. Having confessed his doubts, Arjuna here pleads with the Lord to give them a fatal blow. In samādhi, when the Lord of Love permeates our consciousness, all our doubts will cease, and there will come a tremendous inner certitude that will convey itself to everyone around us.

श्रीभगवानुवाच ।
पार्थ नैवेह नामुत्र विनाशस्तस्य विद्यते ।
न हि कल्याणकृत्कश्चिद्दुर्गतिं तात गच्छति ॥ ६-४० ॥

SRI KRISHNA:

40. Pārtha, my son, spiritual work will never be wasted, nor will one who does such work ever come to a bad end, either here or in the world to come.

Now we can almost see Sri Krishna coming closer to Arjuna, putting his arm about him, and saying, "Never will meditation on me be wasted, even if it has been done only for a short time. No step taken on the spiritual path is ever in vain." According to the Hindu and Buddhist scriptures, no person is ever lost, for we are all children of the Lord. We can find the most secluded place to hide and delay our reunion all we want; but whether we like it or not, one day we are going to go home to the Lord.

A beautiful aspect of the Hindu mystical tradition is that the word *damnation* never occurs. All of us, even though we are tardy and playing truant, are still children of the Lord. A good way to strengthen ourselves and ward off negative states of feeling is to remember that in spite of our outward acts and appearances we are pure, perfect, and ever divine in origin.

Many years ago I went to a church service where the minister delivered a very strong sermon. The congregation seemed to enjoy it tremendously, and I realized how, in today's world, we need someone who will occasionally shock us into the awareness that we are on the wrong path. Once in the pulpit this minister started hurling forked lightning in all directions; and when the climax of the sermon came, he started singling out members of the congregation whom he knew, telling them, "You're a sinner." I was cowering, hoping that he wouldn't call on me, because in the Hindu way I had always been told, "You're a saint." When everyone is in a conspiracy to convince us, even when it seems unjustified, that we are a saint, one day we give in and actually become one. On the other hand, when our negative behavior is emphasized, when we are told we are sinners, we develop guilt feelings. So please tell your children that they are little saints, even when they seem not to warrant it. We can help adults in this same way too by always emphasizing their bright side. Everyone has a favorable side, and when we are patient and forbearing, people will rise to our expectations.

प्राप्य पुण्यकृतांल्लोकानुषित्वा शाश्वतीः समाः ।
शुचीनां श्रीमतां गेहे योगभ्रष्टो ऽभिजायते ॥६-४१॥

41. When such people die, they go to other realms where the righteous live. They dwell there for countless years and then are reborn into a home which is pure and prosperous.

In this verse Sri Krishna tells us that if we give up meditation after some years because of overpowering sense-desires or self-will, he will carefully store our sādhana for us so we can pick it up later. The Lord is a good storekeeper, and he will keep our sādhana in a packet carefully put away on the shelf until we come and reclaim it the next time we enter the human context. When we return to the store and ask him, "Will you look for something I forgot last time? It's a packet of six years' meditation," Sri Krishna will say, "I've kept it very carefully up on this shelf. It's a pretty good packet; weighs a good bit, you know."

As proof of this he tells us we will be born next time into a family with good parents, who will help us by their personal example to be patient and forgiving and to lead the spiritual life. This is perhaps why I had the great blessing to be born as the grandchild of my grandmother. If you ask my mother how she accounts for her boy, who led such an ordinary life, becoming aware of his real Father, she will say that I have been looking for Him for many centuries, practicing meditation and calling, "Where are you, Dad?" all the time, until one day He said, "Here I am, son."

अथ वा योगिनामेव कुले भवति धीमताम् ।
एतद्धि दुर्लभतरं लोके जन्म यदीदृशम् ॥ ६-४२ ॥

42. Or they may be born into a family where meditation is practiced. To be born into such a family is extremely rare.

It is a sound law that whatever effort we put forward on the spiritual path is never wasted. In accordance with the theory of rebirth or reincarnation, Sri Krishna reassures us that if we find it too difficult to meditate and lead the spiritual life, then in our next life we may be born into a home where our parents meditate. There is no greater privilege than this, for it gives us an early start in our search for the Self.

According to the theory of reincarnation, we have chosen every one of our relationships carefully, especially our relationship with our parents. In Bardo, where according to the Tibetans we wait to come into this life, all of us have scorecards, and we tally up our samskāras to make sure we have a perfect match. Parents and children resemble each other in so many ways that it is unfair for us to criticize our mother or father, for we are so much like them. In Bardo nobody gets a lemon; there are good points about every parent and every child that we should always emphasize. Where the parents support meditation, it is especially fortunate; and where the family considers it a great boon for the son or daughter to be meditating, it is a blessing to the whole family. But even if our parents are not meditating with us, they will come to have a certain gratitude that their child is striving to lead a life that will benefit everyone around. Therefore it is good for all of us to begin or end our meditation with a prayer for the welfare of our parents and all the other members of our family.

तत्र तं बुद्धिसंयोगं लभते पौर्वदेहिकम् ।
यतते च ततो भूयः संसिद्धौ कुरुनन्दन ॥ ६-४३ ॥
पूर्वाभ्यासेन तेनैव ह्रियते ह्यवशो ऽपि सः ।
जिज्ञासुरपि योगस्य शब्दब्रह्मातिवर्तते ॥ ६-४४ ॥

43. The wisdom they have acquired in previous lives will be reawakened, Arjuna, and they will strive even harder for Self-realization.
44. Indeed, they will be driven on by the strength of their past disciplines. Even one who inquires after the practice of meditation rises above those who simply perform rituals.

For twenty or twenty-five years we may have been studying at school, going surfing, and learning all kinds of skills, but never thinking about meditation or the spiritual life because the need for it seemed far away. Then one day we go to the Tilden Meditation Room at the University of California, where someone is talking about the Bhagavad Gita. Some words and phrases get into our consciousness, and we go home dazed. We think about what he said, we ponder over it, and finally a little window in our consciousness opens and we decide to give meditation a try.

There is a certain magnetism between us and the Lord which we have been unaware of all this time. Until we come of age we are like little magnets, trying by our own efforts to find fulfillment; but when we bring ourselves close to the Lord, his immense magnetism draws us on effortlessly.

According to the Gita, desire for the spiritual life is not a sudden development. It lies within us, just waiting for us to remember it. After meditating several years there is a sudden deepening in meditation, and we start regaining the memory of what we had already learned; our values become more selfless, more noble, and more spiritual. When this occurs, we are not adding anything new to our knowledge or wisdom; we are remembering what has been within us all the time. All of us who are meditating have had some previous spiritual experience; and in certain cases this experience is rather substantial, which explains some of the differences in progress in meditation. These dissimilarities need never dishearten us, because we all can pick up and go forward as rapidly as we want from wherever we stopped before.

When the power of our spiritual efforts in past lives begins to rise up in our consciousness, it is often felt as restlessness, a condition that is characteristic of many young people today. Restlessness is really a call to meditation; and once we have regained our previous knowledge, once we have recalled our previous sādhana, all our desires, all our motivation for the spiritual life will deepen tremendously. The first three or four years of meditation require a lot of strenuous, often painful effort, but once we have regained our knowledge, much of the pain and many of our doubts fall away. Then we want to strive even harder and give all we can to the spiritual life, which is a sign that we have regained our spiritual heritage. It is as if we were vīnā players who have not played for twenty-five years. When we pick up the vīnā, it feels so strange; our fingers do not know their way. But we go on practicing day after day, day after day, and suddenly our fingers remember their skill and the song comes out in all its sonorous glory: *Hare Rāma, Hare Rāma, Rāma Rāma, Hare Hare; Hare Krishna, Hare Krishna, Krishna Krishna, Hare Hare.*

प्रयत्नाद्यतमानस्तु योगी संशुद्धकिल्बिषः ।
अनेकजन्मसंसिद्धस्ततो याति परां गतिम् ॥६-४५॥

45. Through constant effort over many lifetimes a person becomes purified of all selfish desires and attains the supreme goal of life, union with the Lord.

One day Sri Ramana Maharshi was telling those around him that they had been together for many, many centuries, and Major Chadwick, a good British disciple, said, "I don't believe it." Sri Ramana Maharshi just smiled and told his disciple, "You have simply forgotten." We, too, have forgotten our previous sādhana; but even if we try to lead a careless, sensate life, the power of our past efforts will turn all pleasure to ashes.

I have seen people plunging into the world of sense pleasure in the hopes that this would lead to joy, and I have seen these hopes turn into frustration and despair in a very short time. Sri Krishna says that these are people who are highly evolved but do not realize their true capacities, who are highly spiritual but like to think that they are very sensate. They go to every restaurant on Telegraph Avenue, but only find their palate clamoring to be controlled. Terribly bored, they ask if this is all there is to the pleasure of the senses. There are many such young people today who have forgotten their real spiritual stature, and it is a great pity that in spite of their boredom and frustration they should keep on trying to play the game of the senses, which I sometimes call the sad-go-round. Instead of criticizing such people, we should remind them of the joy which awaits them if they will only reclaim their spiritual heritage.

Sri Krishna tells us that when the power of our previous spiritual development forces us to turn to meditation as a last resort, even on these terms he will welcome us, saying: "This is one of my thousand names, the Last Resort. Far from holding it against you, I welcome you with open arms; for you have come in spite of yourself, driven by your true spiritual nature."

In order to claim our past sādhana, in order to recall our old disciplines, the family context is just right for us. Instead of trying to embrace the whole world at the outset, we should learn to love our family and then gradually extend this love more and more. We are living in a world racked with violence and agitation, and in the early days of our sādhana it is difficult to go against our self-will, say no to our senses, and put the welfare of others first. Yet we have to learn not only to swim in this sea of strife but to contribute to its calmness and peace. So Sri Krishna tells us to jump in and he will teach us to swim; and when we jump we find ourselves safe in his arms.

Yesterday at the swimming pool I played the role of instructor. Geetha, who had missed a number of swimming lessons because of a cold, made me promise to give her special instructions. First I had to get her to jump into the water, which naturally frightened her. She loves me very much, so I had only to tell her to jump into my arms and she jumped. Then, holding on to me tightly, she kicked her way across the pool. I told her that next time she should hold on to me with only one hand; then the third time, she should use both her arms and feet to swim. In this way she would soon discover she could swim, and I would be by her side all the time. Similarly, when we become completely self-reliant and depend on the Lord of Love within in order to live for those around us, we will find he is there all the time. Even if we try, we cannot be drowned.

Around the pool there were swimming instructors walking about with long poles to rescue anyone in trouble. To me, living today is like being in a swimming pool without knowing how to swim. When we hate those who hate us, when we burst out in anger against those who are angry against us, it is because we do not know how to swim. But when we try to swim – returning love for hatred and compassion for anger – even if we sink a little and gasp for air, Sri Ramana Maharshi, Sri Ramakrishna, St. Francis, and many others are there holding out a long pole to rescue us. There is no need to be afraid, for there is always some illumined person to rescue us from the sea of life called samsāra.

तपस्विभ्यो ऽधिको योगी ज्ञानिभ्यो ऽपि मतो ऽधिकः ।
कर्मिभ्यश्चाधिको योगी तस्माद्योगी भवार्जुन ॥ ६-४६ ॥

46. Meditation is superior to severe asceticism and the path of knowledge. It is also superior to selfless service. May you attain the goal of meditation, Arjuna!

Here Sri Krishna tells Arjuna that the person who meditates is superior even to those who follow ascetic disciplines. The Buddha, who once underwent such disciplines, reminds us that by starving the body or breaking the senses we cannot attain illumination, but by treating the body with wisdom, by giving it what it needs and gently denying it what it does not need, we turn the body into a true servant.

Sri Krishna also says the person who meditates is superior to those who follow the path of knowledge. Knowledge is looked upon here as a steep slope up which ordinary people like us cannot climb, but meditation enables us to acquire wisdom gradually and become wise by developing a higher mode of knowing.

Finally, the Lord tells us that the person who meditates is superior to those who are devoted to selfless action, for without meditation, self-will can enter into the most loving relationships and distort the most selfless efforts. The verse ends with the Lord's blessing, given out of such love and compassion that it should be dear to everyone who seeks the Self: "May you attain the goal of meditation." So may we all attain the goal.

योगिनामपि सर्वेषां मद्गतेनान्तरात्मना ।
श्रद्धावान्भजते यो मां स मे युक्ततमो मतः ॥६-४७॥

47. Even among those who meditate, that man or woman is dearest to me who has become completely absorbed in me, and worships me with perfect faith.

Even among meditators, Sri Krishna has a special favorite whom he loves to support, whom he wants united with him. This is the one who meditates on the Lord with a one-pointed mind, who does everything in life for the Lord's sake. Such people will ask themselves: "If I eat this, will it strengthen my body so that I can serve the Lord? If I act this way, will it strengthen my mind and my will so that I can serve the Lord?" Sri Krishna is deeply in love with such a man or woman, whose consciousness is permeated with the presence of the Lord.

Every one of us can become Sri Krishna's favorite through sustained, systematic, enthusiastic practice of meditation. In this sixth chapter, "The Practice of Meditation," the Lord has told us that without meditation it is not possible to acquire spiritual wisdom, to act selflessly, or to bring about the much-needed transformation of our character, conduct, and consciousness. When we take to meditation and persevere, no matter what the obstacles, we will find the Lord's grace coming to us in many ways; we will be blessed with vibrant health, with increasing security, and with the ability to harness our creative resources to solve even the most difficult problems. By seeking the Self through meditation, we will come to live in awareness of the unity of life expressed in everyone, everywhere, every minute.

आत्मसंयमयोगो नाम षष्ठोऽध्यायः ॥ ६ ॥

PASSAGE FOR MEDITATION

Living in Wisdom

ARJUNA:

Tell me of those who live in wisdom,
Ever aware of the Self, O Krishna;
How do they talk, how sit, how move about?

SRI KRISHNA:

They live in wisdom
Who see themselves in all and all in them,
Whose love for the Lord of Love has consumed
Every selfish desire and sense craving
Tormenting the heart. Not agitated
By grief or hankering after pleasure,
They live free from lust and fear and anger.
Fettered no more by selfish attachments,
They are not elated by good fortune
Nor depressed by bad. Such are the seers.

Even as a tortoise draws in its limbs,
The wise can draw in their senses at will.
Aspirants abstain from sense pleasures,
But they still crave for them. These cravings all
Disappear when they see the Lord of Love.
For even of those who tread the path,
The stormy senses can sweep off the mind.
But they live in wisdom who subdue them
And keep their minds ever absorbed in me.

When you keep thinking about sense objects,
Attachment comes. Attachment breeds desire,
The lust of possession which, when thwarted,
Burns to anger. Anger clouds the judgment
And robs you of the power to learn from
Past mistakes. Lost is the discriminative
Faculty, and your life is utter waste.

But when you move amidst the world of sense
From both attachment and aversion freed,
There comes the peace in which all sorrows end,
And you live in the wisdom of the Self.

The disunited mind is far from wise;
How can it meditate? How be at peace?
When you know no peace, how can you know joy?
When you let your mind follow the Siren
Call of the senses, they carry away
Your better judgment as a cyclone drives
A boat off the charted course to its doom.

Use your mighty arms to free the senses
From attachment and aversion alike
And live in the full wisdom of the Self.
Such a sage awakes to light in the night
Of all creatures. In which they are awake
Is the night of ignorance to the sage.

As the rivers flow into the ocean
But cannot make the vast ocean overflow,
So flow the magic streams of the sense world
Into the sea of peace that is the sage.
They are forever free who have broken out
Of the ego-cage of *I* and *mine*
To be united with the Lord of Love.
This is the supreme state. Attain to this
And pass from death to immortality.

Glossary & Guide to Sanskrit Pronunciation

GUIDE TO THE PRONUNCIATION OF SANSKRIT WORDS

Consonants. Consonants are generally pronounced as in English, but there are some differences. Sanskrit has many so-called aspirated consonants, that is, consonants pronounced with a slight *h* sound. For example, the consonant *ph* is pronounced as English *p* followed by an *h* as in ha*ph*azard. The *bh* is as in a*bh*or. The aspirated consonants are *kh, gh, ch, jh, th, dh, ph, bh.*

c as in *ch*urch	*g* as in *g*old
h as in *h*ome	*j* as in *J*une

The other consonants are approximately as in English.

Vowels. Every Sanskrit vowel has two forms, one short and one long. The long form is pronounced twice as long as the short. In the English transliteration the long vowels are marked with a bar ( ). The diphthongs – *e, ai, o, au* – are also pronounced twice as long as the short vowels. Thus, in the words *nīla* 'blue' and *gopa* 'cowherd,' the first syllable is held twice as long as the second.

a as in *u*p	*ri* as in w*ri*tten
ā as in f*a*ther	*e* as in th*e*y
i as in g*i*ve	*ai* as in *ai*sle
ī as in s*ee*	*o* as in g*o*
u as in p*u*t	*au* as in c*ow*
ū as in r*u*le	

SPELLING OF SANSKRIT WORDS

To simplify the spelling of Sanskrit words we have used a minimum of diacritical marks, retaining only the long mark (¯) for the long vowels and omitting the other diacritics which are sometimes used in rendering Sanskrit words into English.

abhyāsa Regular practice.

advaita ['not two'] Having no duality; the supreme Reality, which is the "One without a second." The word *advaita* is especially used in Vedānta philosophy, which stresses the unity of the Self (Ātman) and Brahman.

ahamkāra [*aham* 'I'; *kāra* 'maker'] Self-will, separateness, the fundamental barrier which prevents Self-realization and awareness of the unity of all life.

Anasūyā [*an* 'not'; asūyā 'jealous'] She who is free from jealousy, a character in the ancient Indian drama *Shakuntala*. She is a symbol for devoted friendship, free from rivalry and envy.

apara [*a* 'not'; *para* 'beyond'] That which is not transcendent, i.e. lower knowledge, intellectual knowledge.

Arjuna One of the five Pāndava brothers. He is an important figure in Indian epic and legend, and is Sri Krishna's beloved disciple and friend in the Bhagavad Gita.

āsana A posture; a system of physical exercise taught in ancient India, designed to tone up the nervous system as a preparation for meditation.

āshram [Skt. *āshrama*, from *shram* 'to exert oneself'] A spiritual community where students live with a spiritual teacher as members of his family; a retreat where meditation and spiritual disciplines are practiced.

Ātman The Self, the innermost soul in every creature which is a spark of the divine essence.

avatāra [*ava* 'down'; *tri* 'to cross'] The descent of God to earth; the incarnation of the Lord on earth; the birth of the Lord, of divine consciousness, in the heart of man.

Bardo [Tibetan *bar* 'between'; *do* 'two'] In Tibetan mysticism, the state between two lives in which the soul awaits a proper body and context for rebirth.

Bhagavad Gītā [*Bhagavat* 'Lord'; *gītā* 'song'] The Song of the Lord, the name of the important Hindu scripture which contains the instructions of Sri Krishna.

bhakti yoga The Way of Love.

Brahmā The god of creation. *Brahmā,* the Creator, *Vishnu,* the Preserver, and *Shiva,* the Dissolver, make up the Hindu Trinity. (Note: *Brahmā*, which is a word with masculine gender, should not be confused with *Brahman*, the supreme Reality, which has the neuter gender.)

Brahman The supreme Reality underlying all life; the Divine Ground of existence; the impersonal Godhead.

brahmin [Skt. *Brāhmana*] One who seeks to know Brahman; also, a member of the priestly learned caste in traditional Hindu society.

Buddha [from *budh* 'to wake up'] The Awakened One. An enlightened being; the title given to the sage Siddhārtha Gautama Shākyamuni after he obtained complete illumination. The Buddha lived and taught in North India during the sixth century B.C.

buddhi Understanding, intelligence; correct view, idea, purpose.
deva A god.
devī A goddess.
Dhammapada [*Pāli*, from Skt. *Dharmapada*] Name of an important early Buddhist scripture.
dhārana The first stage in meditation.
dharma Law, duty; the universal Law which holds all life together in a unity.
dhoti A piece of cloth – wrapped around the body, drawn between the legs, and tied at the waist – which is worn as a lower garment.
dhyāna Meditation. Specifically, in Patanjali's yoga, the second stage in meditation.
duhkha Suffering.
Duryodhana The oldest son of Dhritarāshtra and the chief enemy of the Pāndavas and Sri Krishna.
ekāgratā One-pointedness; disciplining the mind to concentrate on only one thing at a time.
Ganesha The elephant-headed god of prosperity in the Hindu pantheon, symbol of divine power. He is the son of Shiva and Pārvatī.
Gītā "The Song," a shorter title for the Bhagavad Gita.
guna Quality; specifically, the three qualities which make up the phenomenal world: sattva, law; rajas, energy; and tamas, inertia.
guru A spiritual teacher.
Hare [vocative of *Hari*] The Lord Vishnu.
Hastināpura "City of the elephants," an important city in ancient India, located about sixty miles northeast of the modern Delhi. It was the capital city of the Pāndavas and their line.
Himālaya [*hima* 'snow'; *ālaya* 'abode'] The great mountain range which stretches across the northern border of India, important in mythology as the home of Shiva and other gods.
Īshvara The Lord; the Inner Ruler who guides from within.
jnāna yoga The Way of Wisdom.
Kailāsa Name of a peak in the Himālayas, in Indian myth the home of Shiva.
kāma Selfish desire, greed; sexual desire, sometimes personified as Kāmadeva, god of desire.
karma yoga The Way of Action, the path of selfless service.
karma yogī One who does selfless work.
Kauravas The sons of Kuru, usually referring to Duryodhana and his brothers, who are the enemies of the Pāndavas.
Krishna [from *krish* 'to draw to oneself'] The Lord of Love who dwells in the hearts of all.
krodha Anger.
kundalinī "The serpent power"; spiritual energy, evolutionary energy.
Kurukshetra "The field of the Kurus," where the Mahābhārata battle takes place.

līlā Game; the divine play of the Lord disguising himself as many.
Madhyamārga The Middle Path, the way of moderation taught by the Buddha.
Mahābhārata The great epic of ancient India which contains the Bhagavad Gita.
manas The mind; the faculty which registers and stores sensory impressions.
mantram A holy name or phrase; a spiritual formula.
Māra "The Striker"; in Buddhism, the Tempter, the Evil One who tries to prevent the Buddha's enlightenment.
Māyā Illusion; appearance, as contrasted with Reality. The creative power of the Lord.
moksha Liberation, salvation, illumination.
neti, neti [*na iti, na iti*] "Not this, not this," the refrain of the Upanishads, which teach that the supreme Reality is indescribable, undefinable, beyond the dualities of this world.
nirvāna [*nir* 'out'; *vāna* 'to blow'] Complete extinction of self-will and separateness; realization of the unity of all life.
nirvikalpa samādhi A state of spiritual awareness in which there is no perception of duality, of inside or outside, of subject and object; merger in the impersonal Godhead.
Om [or *Aum*] The cosmic sound, which can be heard in deep meditation; the Holy Word, taught in the Upanishads, which signifies Brahman, the Divine Ground of existence.
Pāndavas "The sons of Pandu," a collective name for Arjuna and his four brothers: Yudhishthira, Bhima, Nakula, and Sahadeva.
para ['the beyond'] Higher knowledge; spiritual insight.
prajnā [from *jnā* 'to know'] A transcendental mode of knowing developed in deep meditation.
prakriti The basic stuff from which the mental and physical worlds take shape; nature.
prāna Breath; vital force.
preya That which is temporarily pleasing.
Purusha ['person'] The inner soul, the spiritual core of man.
Rādhā Name of the milkmaid who is Sri Krishna's beloved while he sojourns in Vrindāvana. She represents the human soul longing for the divine Beloved.
rāja yoga The Royal Path, the path of meditation taught especially by Patanjali in the *Yoga Sūtras*.
rajas Passion, energy, the second of the three qualities (gunas).
Rāma [from *ram* 'to rejoice'] The Lord of Joy, the principle of joy within.
Ramagiri "The Hills of Joy," name of the country retreat of the Blue Mountain Center of Meditation.
sādhana A body of disciplines, a way of life, which leads to the supreme goal of Self-realization.
samādhi [sam 'with'; Ādhi 'Lord'] Union with the Lord; a state of intense concentration in which consciousness is completely unified.

samsāra The world of flux; the round of birth, decay, death, and rebirth.
samskāra A personality trait conditioned over many lives or one life: a mental and behavioral pattern; a latency or tendency within the mind which will manifest itself if given the proper environment and stimulus.
sat [from *as* 'to be'] Truth, That which really is; the Good.
sattva Goodness, purity, law, the highest of the three qualities (gunas).
shānti Perfect inner peace, "the peace that passeth all understanding."
Shiva Third in the Hindu Trinity; he who destroys the ego and conquers death.
shraddhā Faith.
shreya The Good, that which is permanently beneficial.
Sītā The wife of Rāma and the ideal for womanly love and loyalty.
Srī [pronounced *Shrī*] A title of respect originally meaning 'Lord' or 'holy'; now, in modern India, simply a respectful form of address.
sthūlasharīra The gross body, the physical body.
stūpa A shrine containing a relic of the Buddha.
sukha Pleasure.
sūkshmasharīra The subtle body made up of samskāras, or mental impressions.
svadharma The duty appropriate to a particular person, one's own individual dharma.
tamas Inertia, ignorance, the lowest of the three qualities (gunas).
tanhā [Prākrit, from Skt. *trishnā* 'thirst'] The thirst for selfish satisfaction, the craving of the senses and the ego.
tapas Austerity, control of the senses; the spiritual power acquired through self-control.
Upanishads Ancient mystical documents to be found at the end of the Vedic canon.
vīnā An ancient South Indian stringed instrument used in classical music.
Vishnu Second in the Hindu Trinity; the Preserver who incarnates in age after age for the establishment of dharma and the welfare of all creatures.
yajna Sacrifice; selfless service; an offering.
yoga [from *yuj* 'to unite'] Union with the Lord, realization of the unity of all life; a path or discipline which leads to such a state of total integration or unity.

Index

END

MORE BOOKS BY EKNATH EASWARAN

The Bhagavad Gita for Daily Living:
A Verse-By-Verse Commentary

Volume 1: Chapters 1–6 The End of Sorrow

These opening chapters explore the concept of the innermost Self and source of wisdom in all of us. Easwaran explains how we can begin to transform ourselves, even as householders engaged in busy lives.

Volume 2: Chapters 7–12 Like a Thousand Suns

These chapters go beyond the individual Self to explore the Supreme Reality underlying all creation. Easwaran builds a bridge across the seeming divide between scientific knowledge and spiritual wisdom and explains how the concept of the unity of life can help us in all our relationships.

Volume 3: Chapters 13–18 To Love Is to Know Me

Global in scope, these final chapters make an urgent appeal for us to see that all of us are one – to make the connection between the Self within and the Reality underlying all creation. Easwaran shows how the Gita can guide us to make wiser choices, to heal our environment and establish peace in our world.

The Bhagavad Gita, The Upanishads, The Dhammapada

Classics of Indian Spirituality Series

These best-selling translations each include a comprehensive, accessible introduction explaining the cultural background and core concepts of the scripture.

MORE BOOKS BY EKNATH EASWARAN

Passage Meditation: A Complete Spiritual Practice

Train your mind and find a life that fulfills

This classic manual presents Easwaran's universal method of passage meditation. It is a unique source of practical support for new and experienced meditators, offering all the instruction needed to establish a vibrant meditation practice and keep it going.

Essence of the Bhagavad Gita: A Contemporary Guide to Yoga, Meditation, and Indian Philosophy

Based on talks given in the later years of Easwaran's life, this book is his in-depth exploration of the key themes of the Gita: the nature of reality, the meaning of yoga, and the unity of life. It complements Easwaran's other writings on the Gita, offering further insights into this much-loved scripture.

Essence of the Upanishads: A Key to Indian Spirituality

Easwaran shows how the Katha Upanishad, another ancient wisdom text, embraces all the key ideas of Indian mysticism and presents them in the context of a mythic quest – the story of a young hero who ventures into the land of death in search of immortality.

Gandhi the Man: How One Man Changed Himself to Change the World

Easwaran, who grew up in Gandhi's India, gives a moving account of the turning points and choices in Gandhi's life that made him not just a great political leader but also a timeless icon of nonviolence in the world today. This book includes more than 70 photographs and a chronology.

Blue Mountain Center of Meditation

The Blue Mountain Center of Meditation publishes Eknath Easwaran's books, videos, and audio recordings, and offers retreats and online programs on his eight-point program of passage meditation.

For more information and resources, please visit: www.bmcm.org

The Blue Mountain Center of Meditation
Box 256, Tomales, California 94971 USA
Telephone: +1 707 878 2369
Toll-free in the US: 800 475 2369
Email: info@bmcm.org

The Bhagavad Gita

for Daily Living

VOLUME II: LIKE A THOUSAND SUNS

SECOND EDITION

दिवि सूर्यसहस्रस्य भवेद्युगपदुत्थिता । यदि भाः सदृशी सा स्याद्भासस्तस्य महात्मनः ॥११-१२॥

If a thousand suns were to rise at the same time, the blaze of their light would resemble a little the supreme splendor of the lord.

— BHAGAVAD GITA 11:12

The Bhagavad Gita

for Daily Living

VOLUME II: LIKE A THOUSAND SUNS

SECOND EDITION

EKNATH EASWARAN

JAICO PUBLISHING HOUSE

Ahmedabad Bangalore Chennai
Delhi Hyderabad Kolkata Mumbai

Published by Jaico Publishing House
A-2 Jash Chambers, 7-A Sir Phirozshah Mehta Road
Fort, Mumbai - 400 001
jaicopub@jaicobooks.com
www.jaicobooks.com

Published in arrangement with
Nilgiri Press
P.O. Box 256, Tomales, California 94971
www.easwaran.org

To be sold only in India, Bangladesh, Bhutan,
Pakistan, Nepal, Sri Lanka and the Maldives.

THE BHAGAVAD GITA FOR DAILY LIVING
Volume II:
Like a Thousand Suns
ISBN 978-93-91019-83-9
(Set of 3 Volumes)

First Jaico Impression: 1997
First Jaico Impression (Second Edition): 2021
Third Jaico Impression: 2025

Printed by
Nutech Print Services - India, New Delhi

To my Teacher
EKNATH CHIPPU KUNCHI AMMAL
my Grandmother & my Playmate

Table of Contents

INTRODUCTION
The Unity of Life

The Bhagavad Gita is the most practical of the Hindu scriptures. Some of its poetry is so magnificent that I have seldom seen its equal in any other language, but to me, the Gita is only secondarily a great work of art. Its primary value, which cuts across all barriers of time, culture, and religious background, lies in showing us how to make a work of art out of our own lives.

It is the essence of the mystical experience to enter into the depths of consciousness and discover that none of us is separate from the rest of life. All creation is part of one infinite Reality – or, in more personal language, all of us are one. This is the theme of this volume, which presents the middle six chapters of the Gita. The Lord of Love, by whatever name – Christ or Sri Krishna, Allah or Adonai or the Divine Mother – dwells in every creature as our real Self.

In India, this realization has been part of a common spiritual heritage for thousands of years, fed by the personal experience of mystics from most of the world's major religions. Hinduism and Buddhism, of course, originated there; Islam and Zoroastrianism have contributed to its culture for several centuries. Jewish communities in South India date from before the Christian era; and Christianity arrived in Kerala state, where I was born, long before it reached most of Europe – in fact, according to Church tradition, the Gospel was brought to India by the Apostle Thomas himself in the first century A.D. Indians are used to being surrounded by many paths to God, and I don't think any people are more catholic in accepting truth in whatever religion they find it.

Against this background, there is a story about a missionary school being inspected by one of the church officials. These inspections could come at any time, and the inspector – who, of course, was usually not Indian – had the privilege of stepping unannounced into any classroom, playing the teacher, and asking whatever question he liked. In this story, an inspector steps in on an English class and says – in English – "Let me ask you three questions: One, what does God know? Two, what can he do? Three, where is he to be found?"

Most of the village children were taken by surprise: after all, it is hard enough to discuss theology in your own language, let alone in somebody else's. But there was one little fellow at the back who really knew his spiritual heritage. He stood up and said politely, "Sir, may I ask *you* three questions?"

The examiner was a good sport, so he said yes. And the boy asked: "What does God *not* know? What can he not do? Where is he not?"

It is a simple reply, but it says a great deal. To the mystic, it is absurd to say there is no God. He is our life, our very Self; how can we deny him? Only when we think that God is something outside us is it possible to say that God does not exist.

A few years ago I remember a columnist describing his family's trip to Europe. While they were driving through France, the children kept complaining, "Dad, when are we going to see Europe?" It is much like that with God. If you want to see the Lord, the mystics say, just look around you; what else is there? "Open your eyes," says Hugh of St. Victor; "the world is full of God."

The Sufis have a vivid image for this. The Lord, they say, is the Showman, but he is also the show. In Sanskrit he is *Mahāmāyī,* the Cosmic Magician, who has cast the illusion of separateness over all the universe. P.T. Barnum may have been proud of the "greatest show on earth," but the earth itself is only a small part of the vast show that is the Lord's. So the Hindu scriptures do not talk about God creating the world; they say that he *became* the world. It is not something different from him; it is a form which he has put on.

In our āshram, our spiritual community, we have three boys living with us who are under the age of four, and every day I have to ask them what they are. One day it is an elephant; the next, a fox or rabbit or raccoon. As one of them says, "When I see an animal, I *be* it." He comes over in the morning and announces, "I'm a baby elephant!" I pretend to be Uncle Elephant, twisting my trunk and wiggling my broad ears – and then he suddenly says, "Now I'm a mouse!" And everything changes; he becomes a mouse. Yet the mouse is not somebody else; it is always the same little boy.

This is how it is with the Lord. He is eternal, formless Reality, yet in his play he has put on a cosmic form, which the Buddhists call *Dharmakāya:* the universe itself. Galaxies, black holes, quasars, the very fabric of space and time – all are part of the Cosmic Magician's display. "There is nothing that exists separate from me," the Lord says in the Gita. "The entire universe is suspended from me as my necklace of jewels."

In Sanskrit, the Lord as Sri Krishna is called *Vistāra,* 'he who has expanded himself' – much in the language of modern cosmology, which describes an expanding universe. Yet in the same breath he is called *Sthāvarasthānu,* 'he who is completely still.' This is the paradox; he is both. When we look through the eyes of duality, we see a world of phenomena, of constant change – matter and energy, time and death, creation and destruction. But when we look through the eye of unity – as Jesus says, "when our eye is single" – we see that all this is only surface appearance. The restlessness, the change, the duality were in our vision; beneath that appearance there is only the changeless Reality we call God.

One of the appealing implications of this is that it pulls the rug out from the disputes between religion and science. The underlying assumption in these disputes is that God and the world are separate – that we are here and the Lord is out there. It is not only scientists who make this mistake; it is made in the name of religion too. Yet both science and religion are talking about the same thing, as I try to show abundantly in the chapters that follow. I have no particular interest in the philosophy behind these traditional disagreements. But it is a matter of utmost concern to all of us that scientific inquiry proceed hand in hand with spiritual awareness. Without this awareness, we are liable to violate the unity of life everywhere we go, in everything we do.

Scientific knowledge, in other words, is knowledge of separate parts of life. Spiritual knowledge – "wisdom" is a better word – is knowledge of the whole. Scientific knowledge means knowing facts; spiritual wisdom means knowing how to live. A man may be an excellent astronomer, but if he comes home in the evening and loses patience with his children, he is showing his ignorance of life's unity. A woman may be a first-rate physician, but if she is selfish, she has not yet realized that all of us are one. Because life is whole, everything in it is interconnected; everything we do affects the rest. If we live in harmony, everything benefits a little, from our own lives through the rest of the biosphere. But if we violate the unity of existence, everything suffers – our family, our society, and our own health and happiness.

Today, because of the impact of ecology, we are accustomed to this idea that all things in nature are connected. But to judge from our behavior, I think very few of us realize that the same unity applies to life at every level. The implications are very practical. For one, it means that I cannot find my happiness at your expense. If I try, it is not only you who will suffer, I will suffer too. If I am hostile, *I* will get asthma or peptic ulcer; if I am resentful, *I* will get high blood pressure. More than that, if I try to make money at the expense of the environment, all of us are going to suffer – I have to breathe the air and drink the water too. On the other hand, if I live for the welfare of the whole, my own individual welfare is included in that. If I am patient, everyone near me benefits – including me. I will be more relaxed, more secure, better able to weather the storm and stress that is an inescapable part of living.

The unity of life is an unalterable law, the central law of existence. We cannot break it; we can only break ourselves against it. This is our greatest source of suffering, and to me there is nothing more grievous than to see every day how this law is being flouted – by nations, by families, by individuals, everywhere. After thousands of years of evolution we should be beginning to understand the basis of living: nobody can attain fulfillment separately. For all of us, our destiny is one and indivisible.

This is why we need a commentary on the world's great scriptures that addresses itself to daily living. The Gita strikes the same note at the beginning of this volume. It is not enough to have a poetic awareness of unity. It is not enough to have *jnāna,* the direct realization that life is one. In these troubled times, it is essential that we also strive for *vijnāna* – the skillful capacity to apply spiritual understanding to bridge divisions in the home, heal wounds in the minds of individuals, bring together estranged communities, put out the flames of violence, and banish the menace of nuclear war that threatens life today.

Sometimes I hear the mistaken notion that to be spiritual we should withdraw from the world – hide ourselves in a cave and put up a sign saying, "Meditating. Do Not Disturb." The message of the Gita is just the opposite: heal the divisions within yourself and throw yourself into service of others without any thought of profit or prestige for yourself. It is not necessary to preach at others or force them to follow particular ideas. If we try to live out the unity of existence where we are – in our homes, at our jobs – the influence of our lives cannot help spreading to others in proportion to our spiritual growth.

So it should not be surprising that after all the illustrations about galaxies and quasars, the climax of this volume is the chapter entitled "The Way of Love." This is what unity means when translated into daily living. Most of us think of love as a one-to-one relationship. But the mystics tell us, "Don't ever be satisfied with just loving two or three people, with loving only now and then. Learn to make the whole world your own." As the Buddha puts it, when we realize the unity of life, we shall love and protect every creature on earth as a mother loves and protects her only child.

This is a complete transformation of consciousness. The medieval mystic Ruysbroek, when some students asked him for a motto, said, *Vos estis tam sancti sicut vultis*: you are as holy as you want to be. I would add, in the same way, we are as happy as we want to be, or as selfless, or as secure – just as, conversely, we are as hostile as we want to be, as selfish, as lonely. The choice in all this is up to us, and the tool for exercising choice is meditation.

Since "meditation" can refer to so many practices today, I think it will be helpful here to summarize the eight-point program for spiritual living which I have found effective in my own life. These steps are elaborated more fully throughout the pages that follow.

THE EIGHT-POINT PROGRAM

1. *Meditation on a Passage*. The heart of this program is meditation: half an hour every morning, as early as is convenient. Do not increase this period; if you want to meditate more, have half an hour in the evening also, preferably at the very end of the day.

Set aside a room in your home to be used only for meditation and spiritual reading. After a while that room will become associated with meditation in your mind, so that simply entering it will have a calming effect. If you cannot spare a room, have a particular corner. Whichever you choose, keep your meditation place clean, well ventilated, and reasonably austere.

Sit in a straight-backed chair or on the floor and gently close your eyes. If you sit on the floor, you may need to support your back lightly against a wall. You should be comfortable enough to forget your body, but not so comfortable that you become drowsy.

Whatever position you choose, be sure to keep your head, neck, and spinal column erect in a straight line. As concentration deepens, the nervous system relaxes and you may begin to fall asleep. It is important to resist this tendency right from the beginning, by drawing yourself up and away from your back support until the wave of sleep has passed.

Once you have closed your eyes, begin to go *slowly*, in your mind, through one of the passages from the scriptures or the great mystics which I recommend for use in meditation. I usually recommend learning first the Prayer of St. Francis of Assisi:

Lord, make me an instrument of thy peace.
Where there is hatred, let me sow love;
Where there is injury, pardon;
Where there is doubt, faith;
Where there is despair, hope;
Where there is darkness, light;
Where there is sadness, joy.

O Divine Master, grant that I may not so much seek
To be consoled as to console,
To be understood as to understand,
To be loved as to love;
For it is in giving that we receive,
It is in pardoning that we are pardoned,
It is in dying [to self] that we are born to eternal life.

Do not follow any association of ideas or try to think about the passage. If you are giving your attention to each word, the meaning cannot help sinking in. When distractions come, do not resist them, but give more attention to the words of the passage. If your mind strays from the passage entirely, bring it back gently to the beginning and start again.

When you reach the end of the passage, you may use it again as necessary to complete your period of meditation until you have memorized others. It is helpful to have a wide variety of passages for meditation, drawn from the world's major traditions. Each passage should be positive and practical, drawn from a major scripture or from a mystic of the highest stature. Passages from the Gita which are perfect for meditation will be found at the end of each volume of this commentary. In addition, I heartily recommend the Lord's Prayer, the Twenty-third Psalm, the Beatitudes, St. Paul's *Epistle on Love* (1 Corinthians 13), and the first and last chapters of the Dhammapada of the Buddha. These and many other beautiful passages can be found in my collection *God Makes the Rivers to Flow.*

The secret of meditation is simple: we become what we meditate on. When you use the Prayer of St. Francis every day in meditation, you are driving the words deep into your consciousness. Eventually they become an integral part of your personality, which means they will find constant expression in what you do, what you say, and what you think.

2. *Repetition of a Mantram.* A mantram is a powerful spiritual formula which, when repeated silently in the mind, has the capacity to transform consciousness. There is nothing magical about this. It is simply a matter of practice, as all of us can verify for ourselves.

Every religious tradition has a mantram, often more than one. For Christians the name of Jesus itself is a powerful mantram; Catholics also use *Hail Mary* or *Ave Maria*. Jews may use *Barukh attah Adonai*, 'Blessed art thou, O Lord,' or the Hasidic formula *Ribono shel olam*, 'Lord of the universe.' Muslims repeat the name of Allah or *Allahu akbar*, 'God is great.' Probably the oldest Buddhist mantram is *Om mani padme hum*, referring to the 'jewel in the lotus of the heart.' In Hinduism, among many choices, I recommend *Rāma, Rāma, Rāma*, which was Mahatma Gandhi's mantram, or the longer mantram I received from my own spiritual teacher, my grandmother:

Hare Rāma Hare Rāma
Rāma Rāma Hare Hare
Hare Krishna Hare Krishna
Krishna Krishna Hare Hare

Select a mantram that appeals to you deeply. In many traditions, it is customary to take the mantram used by your spiritual teacher. Then, once you have chosen, do not change your mantram. Otherwise, as Sri Ramakrishna puts it, you will be like a person digging shallow holes in many places; you will never go deep enough to find water.

Repeat your mantram silently whenever you get the chance: while walking, while waiting, while doing mechanical chores like washing dishes, and especially when you are falling asleep. You will find that this is not mindless repetition; the mantram will help to keep you relaxed and alert. Whenever you are angry or afraid, nervous or worried or resentful, repeat the mantram until the agitation subsides. The mantram works to steady the mind, and all these emotions are power running against you which the mantram can harness and put to work.

3. *Slowing Down*. Hurry makes for tension, insecurity, inefficiency, and superficial living. To guard against hurrying through the day, start the day early and simplify your life so that you do not try to fill your time with more than you can do. When you find yourself beginning to speed up, repeat your mantram to help you slow down.

It is important here not to confuse slowness with sloth, which breeds carelessness, procrastination, and general inefficiency. In slowing down we should attend meticulously to details, giving our very best even to the smallest undertaking.

4. *One-Pointed Attention.* Doing more than one thing at a time divides attention and fragments consciousness. When we read and eat at the same time, for example, part of our mind is on what we are reading and part on what we are eating; we are not getting the most from either activity. Similarly, when talking with someone, give him or her your full attention. These are little things, but all together they help to unify consciousness and deepen concentration.

Everything we do should be worthy of our full attention. When the mind is one-pointed it will be secure, free from tension, and capable of the concentration that is the mark of genius in any field.

5. *Training the Senses.* In the food we eat, the books and magazines we read, the movies we see, all of us are subject to the dictatorship of rigid likes and dislikes. To free ourselves from this conditioning, we need to learn to change our likes and dislikes freely when it is in the best interests of those around us or ourselves. We should choose what we eat by what our body needs, for example, rather than by what the taste buds demand. Similarly, the mind eats too, through the senses. In this age of mass media, we need to be very discriminating in what we read and what we go to see for entertainment; for we become in part what our senses take in.

6. *Putting Others First.* Dwelling on ourselves builds a wall between ourselves and others. Those who keep thinking about *their* needs, *their* wants, *their* plans, *their* ideas cannot help becoming lonely and insecure. The simple but effective technique I recommend is to learn to put other people first – beginning within the circle of your family and friends, where there is already a basis of love on which to build. When husband and wife try to put each other first, for example, they are not only moving closer to each other, they are also removing the barriers of their ego-prison, which deepens their relationships with everyone else as well.

7. *Spiritual Fellowship.* The Sanskrit word for this is *satsang,* 'association with those who are spiritually oriented.' When we are trying to change

our life, we need the support of others with the same goal. If you have friends who are meditating along the lines suggested here, you can get together regularly to share a meal, meditate, and perhaps read and discuss this commentary on the Gita. Share your times of entertainment too; relaxation is an important part of spiritual living. Who has ever seen a mystic with a sour face?

8. *Spiritual Reading.* We are so immersed these days in what the mass media offer that it is very helpful to give half an hour or so each day to reading the scriptures and the writings of the great mystics of all religions. Just before bedtime, after evening meditation, is a particularly good time, because the thoughts you fall asleep in will be with you throughout the night.

By practicing this eight-point program sincerely and systematically, as I can testify from my own small experience, it is possible for every one of us to realize the unity of life. This is the purpose for which we have been born, and though it is called by different names in different religions – *moksha, nirvāna,* illumination, entering the Promised Land or the kingdom of heaven within – it is all the same supreme discovery, nothing less than which will ever fill the void in our hearts.

There is a Sufi story which illustrates this. One day a man gave coins to four travelers he met on the road. The first, a Persian, said, "Let's spend this on *angur*." The second, an Arab, objected, "I don't want *angur;* I want *inab*." "What's *inab*?" said the Greek. "What's *angur*? What we need on a hot day like this is *stafilia*." And the fourth, a Turk, insisted, "Friends, be still; the thing to buy is *uzum*."

The man who had given them the coins laughed and interrupted their bickering. "I can understand all of you," he said. "Give me back the money and I'll get you something you'll all be happy with." He took them to the bazaar, found the fruit stall, and bought them the grapes for which they had all been asking.

The Bhagavad Gita for Daily Living, Volume 2

CHAPTER SEVEN

Wisdom from Realization

श्रीभगवानुवाच ।
मय्यासक्तमनाः पार्थ योगं युञ्जन्मदाश्रयः ।
असंशयं समग्रं मां यथा ज्ञास्यसि तच्छृणु ॥७-१॥

SRI KRISHNA:

1. With your mind intent on me, Arjuna, discipline yourself with the practice of yoga. Depend on me completely. Listen, and I will dispel all your doubts; you will come to know me fully and be united with me.

We are dropping into the middle of a long conversation between Arjuna, a prince in ancient India, and Sri Krishna, Arjuna's charioteer and spiritual teacher, who represents the Lord, present in the hearts of us all. This is not an external conversation; it is very much internal. Arjuna is every man and every woman, and in the Bhagavad Gita we have slipped into his heart to listen in on a dialogue between two levels of our own consciousness. The voice we recognize belongs to the surface level of awareness – intelligent and well-intentioned, but full of doubts about the meaning of life and how we ought to live. The other voice, so full of wisdom, is the voice of our real Self, the Lord of Love, whether we call him Sri Krishna or the Christ, Allah or the Buddha or the Divine Mother.

As long as we are living for ourselves, dwelling on our own separate needs and problems, we cannot help identifying with our apparent self. It is very much like wearing a mask too long, so long that we think we are the mask and forget who we really are. But through the practice of meditation and its allied disciplines, all of us can learn to take off this mask and discover beneath it our real Self, called the Ātman in Sanskrit, who is the source of all love, all security, all wisdom, and all joy.

In 1960, when I first began teaching meditation in the United States, these ideas were still very new. In those days, if you told someone you were interested in meditation, you had to be prepared to face a certain amount of laughter. Later, when I offered a credit course on meditation on the University of California campus in Berkeley – probably the first course of its kind to be offered by an American university – it drew about six hundred people and thirteen dogs. Now meditation is in the air, and I think the idea must be familiar to everyone in this country. Yet I think there is still no more maligned word in any language than the word *yoga,* with which Sri Krishna opens this chapter. Yoga is not exercises or physical postures; it is not a religion; it is not art or archery or music or dance. It is a body of dynamic disciplines which can be practiced by anyone, from any religious tradition or from no tradition at all, to enable us to remove this mask of separateness and learn to identify ourselves completely with our real Self.

Every spiritual tradition has its own formulation of these disciplines, but though they may differ in name and detail – the Sermon on the Mount, the Noble Eightfold Path, the Eight Limbs of Yoga – there is no difference between them when it comes to the actual practice and their effect on daily living. In my own life, I have found a set of eight points to be tremendously effective in leading the spiritual life in the modern world. I have listed these points in the Introduction, and everything I say is with an eye to how they can be applied.

The heart of this program is meditation, which Patanjali, a great spiritual teacher in ancient India, divides conveniently into three stages: *dhārana, dhyāna,* and *samādhi.* Patanjali's exposition is so precise and so free from dogma that I don't think it can ever be improved on in these qualities. But it is written in a kind of lecture note style, in the expectation that other teachers will elaborate on these notes in their own way on the basis of their experience. So instead of quoting Patanjali, let me tell you from my own experience what these three stages in meditation amount to in their impact on daily living.

In the first stage of meditation, called *dhārana,* we make an astonishing experiential discovery: we are not the body. It is not an intellectual discovery, it is an experiential discovery, and the first time we hear this statement it doesn't make sense at all. If this body is not us, what is it? This is the question I was always asked after my talks, and I have developed all sorts of ways to convey what this experience of dhārana means.

For one, this body of mine is very much like a jacket. I have a brown jacket with a Nehru collar, made in India, which has served me very well; I take good care of it, and I expect it to last me at least another five years. In just the same way, this body of mine is another brown jacket, made in South India and impeccably tailored to my requirements by a master tailor, whose label is right inside. This jacket has to last me much longer than the other, so I am very careful with it; I give it the right amounts of nutritious food and exercise and keep it clean inside as well as out. But just like my Nehru jacket, this body-jacket will someday become too worn to serve me well, and having made this discovery that I am not my body, when death comes I will be able to set it aside too, with no more tears than I would shed when I give my Nehru jacket to the Salvation Army.

In this discovery that you are not your body, you discover simultaneously that others are not their bodies either. The consequences of this are far-reaching. For one, you no longer see people as white or black, yellow or red or brown; you see people just like yourself wearing different-colored jackets. The whole question of race or skin color becomes absurd: black is beautiful, white is beautiful, and of course brown is beautiful too.

Secondly, when you no longer identify others with their bodies, you will be able to see them as people instead. It lifts an immense burden from your relationships with the opposite sex. No matter what the media try to tell us, I don't think anything is more certain to disrupt a relationship than treating the other person as a physical object. On the physical level, all of us are separate, and it is the very nature of physical attraction to change with the passage of time. On the other hand, nothing is more certain to deepen a relationship than concern for the other person's real welfare, which we can see clearly only when we cease identifying people with the body-jackets they wear.

Another way I sometimes look at my body is as a compact little car, built for service. It doesn't guzzle a lot of gas; I can park it anywhere; nobody notices it at all. But it is the car; I have to be the driver. I don't let it pick me up in the middle of the night and take me off to some casino; it has to go where I choose to drive it. As St. Francis put it, speaking of his body, "This is Brother Ass. I will wash him, I will feed him, but I am going to ride on him; he is not going to ride on me."

The practical implication is that in this stage of meditation, we gain some measure of control over problems at the physical level. Many of our problems have a physical component, even if their roots are in the mind, and in dhārana we learn to have some say in things that used to be compulsive. Overeating, for example, is not really a physical problem; it can be solved only in the mind. But if you have a problem with overeating, it is a tremendous help to be able to tell your hand what to do. I have friends with this problem who sometimes come to me and confess, "I can't believe I ate the whole thing." I can understand this kind of craving easily, but what used to puzzle me was, even if we want something terribly, why should we have to put our hand out and put it into our mouth? If we know we shouldn't eat it, we should be able to sit on our hands and that would be the end of the matter. But when I mentioned this to my friends they would just reply, "I couldn't help myself. Some unseen power took over my hand and put the whole lemon meringue pie into it." This kind of eating is compulsive, which means there is very little enjoyment in it. But in dhārana, as we begin not to identify with the body, our whole perspective on eating changes; we begin to have some say in what we put into our mouths.

The second stage of meditation is called *dhyāna,* from which the Japanese get their word for meditation, *zen.* In this stage we make an even more astonishing experiential discovery: we are not the mind either. When I used to say this in my classes on meditation on the

Berkeley campus, there would be groans from the back of the lecture hall. "First he says I'm not my body; now he tells me I'm not my mind." And they would ask, "Then what *is* the mind?" My answer is that just as the body is the external instrument we use in life, the mind is the internal instrument. If the human body is like the body of a car, the mind is very much like the engine. It is capable of tremendous power, but most of us spend so much time on the appearance of the body of the car that we don't get around to opening up the hood to see if the engine is still there. It *is* there, but in order to get it running properly, it is essential not to think that we are a part of it. And once we get this perspective in dhyāna, we can lie down on our backs on our little meditation trolleys, just as mechanics in garages do, get under the mind, and say, "Oh, yes, that old resentment; there's a little screw over there that's too tight." Then we make the necessary adjustments and the problem is gone.

In other words, emotional problems like depression and insecurity are only mechanical difficulties with our engine, the mind, which means that every one of them can be solved. The implications of this are tremendous. Most of us go through life thinking that we can never be different from what we are. We may like it, more often we may dislike it, but we cannot get rid of the liabilities with which we have been born or which we have acquired in growing up. As long as we think that we are the body and the mind, this is true. But just as in the first stage of meditation we see that it is possible to change any physical habit, in the second stage of meditation we gain the capacity to change any emotional habit, to transform insecurity into security, rigidity into flexibility, hostility into compassion, hatred into love.

The secret of this transformation is breathtakingly simple: we become what we meditate on. There is a story in ancient India about a sculptor who was so gifted that his statues almost seemed to come to life out of the stone. Once, lost in admiration over his stone elephants, one of his students asked, "How do you do this? These elephants are more real than real elephants are; you can almost hear them trumpeting." And the sculptor replied, "There's no secret to it. I just go and get a big block of stone, set it up in my studio, and study it very carefully. Then I take my hammers and chisels and slowly, over a number of years, I chip away everything that is not elephant."

When I see a person sitting quietly with eyes closed, giving all his attention to the Prayer of St. Francis, I like to think of this great sculptor, studying his big block of stone with such intense concentration that he really can see the elephant coming to life within: the trunk, and the big ears, and those keen, absurdly small eyes. *We* see only a block of stone, but for the sculptor, the elephant is already right there inside, struggling to be released. This is very much what we do in meditation, only instead of an elephant, it is the Ātman who is imprisoned within us. In meditation, each of us is in a life sculpture class in which we are both the sculptor and the rock. Billions and billions of big, shapeless rocks – no wonder we are sometimes uncomfortable with ourselves or think the world is ugly. But a mystic like St. Francis might say, "Of course, the rock *is* shapeless; no one would deny that. But look within, with intense concentration, and you can see the halo and the harp."

In meditation we give the mind a shining model and study it very carefully every morning and every evening until it is printed on our hearts. Then, throughout the rest of the day, we go along chipping away at everything that is not Self. It takes many years, but in the end, the great mystics of all religions tell us, every bit of anger, fear, and greed can be removed from our consciousness, so that our whole life becomes a flawless work of art. This is the third stage of meditation, called *samādhi*. Samādhi really is not a stage at all, but a stupendous realization in which all the barriers of separateness fall. Then there are no walls between the conscious and unconscious, no walls between you and others; your consciousness is completely integrated, from the attic to the cellar. When this happens, Patanjali says in one of the grandest understatements in mystical literature, you see yourself as you really are: the Ātman, the Self, who dwells in the hearts of us all.

Most of us cannot even glimpse how miraculous this transformation is until we try to achieve it ourselves. Then we shall see why the mystics tell us there is no greater challenge on earth than the challenge of Self-realization. The Compassionate Buddha puts it beautifully in one simple word: *patisotagāmi*, "going against the current" – the current of all our conditioning, in how we act, how we speak, and even how we think.

In my village in Kerala state, South India, when the sky was a solid wash of water and the river was swollen from the monsoon rains, we boys liked to jump into the river and swim to the other side, not with the current – anyone could do that – but against it. It wasn't just that the current was fierce; the river would be full of branches and all sorts of other debris, so that even if you had good, strong arms and a lot of stamina, there was the danger of being drowned. That was the challenge of it. It might take an hour to get across, and there were very few who could reach the other side exactly opposite the point from which they left. Most of us would end up a few hundred yards downstream. But there were one or two – we used to admire them tremendously – who were such strong swimmers that they could make it straight across. It required strong muscles, powerful lungs, a lot of endurance, and – most of all – an indomitable will.

That is just the kind of spirit you need in meditation. When a flood of anger is sweeping over you with monsoon swiftness, that's no time to let yourself be carried away. As Jesus might say, "Anyone can do that." Swim against it; that's what it means to live. You will find your arms almost breaking, your endurance stretched to the limit, but you'll find there is such satisfaction in the achievement that nothing easier will seem worthy of your effort again. That is why the spiritual life appeals so deeply to the young and adventurous. It is only when you take on this challenge and begin to understand the extent of it, the daring and the courage and the resolute, dauntless spirit it requires, that you can look at St. Teresa of Ávila or Sri Ramakrishna and see that this is someone who has climbed the Himālayas of the spirit, who has stood on Mount Everest and seen the entire cosmos aflame with the glory of God.

Can you see from this what Sri Krishna means when he says in this verse, "Depend on me completely"? No one in the world is so self-reliant as those who have realized God, just because they have put all their faith in the Lord within. When the mystics talk about God, when they refer to the Lord or the Divine Mother, they are not talking about somebody outside us, floating in space somewhere between Uranus and Neptune; they are talking about the Self, the Ātman, who is nearer to us than the body is, dearer to us than our life. In samādhi, when all the barriers between us and the Self fall, there are no more doubts about the meaning of life, no more vacillations, no more sense of inadequacy or insecurity. We become part of an infinite force of love that can never perish, and all the resources of the Lord within flow into our lives to be harnessed for the welfare of the whole.

ज्ञानं ते ऽहं सविज्ञानमिदं वक्ष्याम्यशेषतः ।
यज्ज्ञात्वा नेह भूयो ऽन्यज्ज्ञातव्यमवशिष्यते ॥७-२॥

2. I will give you both jnāna and vijnāna – spiritual wisdom and the capacity to apply it to daily living. When both these are realized, there is nothing more you need to know.

Once, while the Compassionate Buddha was camping in a shimshapā grove with his disciples, one of the more philosophical among them was asking him all kinds of abstract questions – whether or not there is a God, whether or not there is an immortal soul, whether the universe had a beginning and will have an end. In reply, the Buddha is said to have picked a few leaves from a shimshapā tree and asked, "Are there more leaves in my hand or on this tree?"

Everybody agreed, "Of course, there are many more leaves on the tree than the Blessed One has in his hand."

"Similarly," the Buddha replied, "there is much more in my consciousness than you can see, much more than you can grasp, much more than you can use. What I give you is only what you need to free yourself from the conditioning in life that is the cause of all your sorrow."

That is the sense in which Sri Krishna tells us here, "I will give you jnāna and vijnāna; that is all you need to know." It is not that there is not more to know; it is that these two together are the key to the art of living.

According to Shankara, an eighth-century Indian mystic and one of the greatest spiritual authorities of any age, jnāna is spiritual knowledge and vijnāna is spiritual experience. Spiritual knowledge is not intellectual knowledge; it is direct experiential knowledge of the unity of life. As Sri Ramakrishna, the great saint of nineteenth-century Bengal, puts it, it is knowing for oneself that God dwells in all beings, which is the discovery we make in the climax of meditation called samādhi. But what is vijnāna, "spiritual experience"? Sri Ramakrishna goes on to tell us in his inimitable way, "He who has only heard of milk is ignorant. He who has seen milk has jnāna. But he who has drunk milk and been strengthened by it has attained vijnāna."

This interpretation can be made even more practical to meet the needs of the world today. In the light of my own small experience, I would say that jnāna is spiritual wisdom and vijnāna is the capacity to apply this wisdom in daily living. Jnāna is knowledge of timeless truths; vijnāna is putting this knowledge into action – to solve problems, to deepen personal relationships, and to show those around us how to wake up from this dream of separateness in which virtually everyone is caught today. Vijnāna, in other words, is "inside" knowledge. Once you have realized the unity of life and begin to live it out, you begin to see into the heart of life. It's very much like being taken into a family; you're on such close terms with the head of the house that everything is opened to you. Here you are on such intimate terms with the source of life that all you have to do is knock at the door of a problem and it will open, so that you know both its cause and its cure.

There is nothing mysterious about this capacity; it is simply a matter of wisdom and will. When, after many years of meditation, you attain the realization that all life is one, you will find it impossible to think or act like a separate creature again. You will not be able to exploit anyone, or discriminate against anyone, or do anything that is at the expense of life; and you will never forget that the welfare of each of us can only be found in the welfare of all. But to solve the grave problems that are making life impossible today – violence in the streets, environmental pollution, loneliness, the breakdown of the family and of personal relationships – it is not enough just to live in constant awareness of this unity. For that you need vijnāna, the skillful capacity to apply this awareness of unity to heal the deep divisions in people's hearts and minds and to bring them together in trust and harmony.

You don't get this skill overnight; it comes with the overwhelming desire to help. When, after many years, you have succeeded in freeing yourself from all the things that people suffer from, you will not be able to sit by and let others go on suffering; you will have to come up with solutions that are of immediate value to everyone. Not only that, it must all be very skillfully and attractively done. You can't just say, "Here, now, stop competing with each other; don't you know that husband and wife are one?" You have to offer a more desirable alternative, and package it attractively in your own life so that people can look at you and say, "Oh, yes, *now* I see; that's what it means for two people to complete each other. I want to be like that too." With some of these problems this may take years. But you won't take no for an answer; you just will not rest until all these problems are solved. Your desire, your concentration, is so intense that it can penetrate into the heart of the matter. You will be able to see below symptoms to the underlying cause and come up with a creative solution.

In other words, this is a skill that flows naturally from the intimate realization that all of us are one. Once this realization comes, with your eyes you will still see people around you as different – different names, different faces, different hair styles, different ways of thinking and acting – but in your heart you will never forget for an instant that there is no real separation between you and others at all. When you talk to your friend Jessica, you will *be* Jessica. You will be able to put yourself in her shoes and see the world through her eyes, which means that you will understand her completely. You will be incapable of judging her, because you will see how any problems she has have evolved. But you *will* be able to help her, because you will not be caught in her perspective; you will have the vantage point of your own experience from which to extend a hand.

Once you reach this state, there is no possibility of misunderstanding in personal relationships. I'm not saying there will not be differences of opinion, there will be. But in my experience it is not differences of opinion that disrupt relationships; it is lack of faith, lack of love. When you have jnāna, you will trust Jessica completely. You will know that she is incapable of doing anything that can harm you, and that her deepest need is to love and be loved. And when you have vijnāna, you will find all kinds of little ways to express your trust and draw your friend Jessica to you, no matter how different your views might be on inflation or French novels or the causes of the First World War. That is why I said that vijnāna is "inside" knowledge. You don't stand around outside a problem the way you do when you meet someone at church on Sunday; you get right inside, into the kitchen, and see it as it is at home.

This doesn't apply just to your own relationships; it applies to every human problem. If you have vijnāna, wherever you go you will be a peacemaker – as Jesus puts it, "a child of God." Wherever there are differences of opinion, no matter how serious, you will be able to slip behind the lines on each side and see things through their eyes, probably better than they can see for themselves. From your perspective you *will* see the problems, but you will also see the underlying unity in which the welfare of both sides is included. Both sides can come to see the other's point of view, and when this happens, though it may take a lot of work, it is only a matter of time before you can find a point of view that is common to all.

I can give you a small example of this from my own experience. It's not something that happened after I had become established in meditation, either; it took place at the very beginning of my teaching career in India, when relations between Hindus and Muslims were particularly strained. Even in the college where I was teaching, where tempers were not yet so inflamed, Hindu and Muslim students had begun to isolate themselves in groups on opposite sides of the room and refuse to speak to each other. All this used to hurt me deeply. As I said, I still had a long way to go in my meditation, but from my association with my grandmother I already had some awareness of the unity of life, and it grieved me deeply to think that our campus might become divided into warring camps.

Now, it happened that one of my closest friends on the faculty was a Muslim, and a devout Muslim at that. He and I had gone to graduate school together, where we were inseparable, and it had never occurred to us that there was anything in our two backgrounds that put us in opposite camps.

After we graduated we went separate ways, and we lost track of each other. Then, after a few years, I was posted to a beautiful campus in central India. On the long train journey from Kerala I was wondering where I was going to stay, because suitable rooms are not readily available in small college towns in India. But when I got down from the tonga, the horse-drawn carriage, my Muslim friend just walked up from nowhere with a big grin on his face. "Come on," he said. "You're coming home with me. What are you looking so dumbfounded about?" That was the kind of bond we had; it wasn't something that could be broken by communal quarrels that had nothing to do with religion at all.

So when Hindu-Muslim antagonism began to disrupt our classrooms, instead of criticizing one community or the other, my friend and I quietly went to share the home of a Muslim aristocrat who had gone on pilgrimage to Mecca. It wasn't a deliberate effort; it just came about naturally, without planning, out of the depth of our concern. At first our students couldn't believe that we could live peacefully under the same roof. People kept telling us, "It's an extremely dangerous situation; both of you will be hurt." Neither of us were very brave. But we put our heads together and said, "If we are going to get hurt, we might as well get hurt together."

What was important was that we hadn't done this as some political gesture. Everyone knew we were the very best of friends, and yet both very deeply in love with the heritage of our different faiths. So though people criticized us sharply, they were watching us very closely to see how we held up. And gradually, as our friendship only deepened, our students began to feel a little ashamed. One by one, some of our bolder students began sitting next to each other again. Then they began to talk to each other, and finally they were laughing and working together just as they had before. It opened our eyes to how just two little people trying to practice the unity of life can change the direction of a whole community. That is vijnāna, and there is no art more essential to daily living today.

In later chapters, Sri Krishna will show how this art can be developed through the practice of meditation. First, however, he will tell Arjuna more about the unity of life.

मनुष्याणां सहस्रेषु कश्चिद्यतति सिद्धये ।
यततामपि सिद्धानां कश्चिन्मां वेत्ति तत्त्वतः ॥७-३॥

3. One person in many thousands may seek perfection, yet of these only a few reach the goal and come to realize me.

Many years ago, before the Blue Mountain Center of Meditation was even founded, I gave a series of talks on the Upanishads and the Bhagavad Gita in a little bookstore in San Francisco. In those days very few people had heard of meditation, and if you told them they were not the body, they might just call the police. So I used to introduce topics like this very gradually, and in a public lecture I never gave instruction in meditation at all. But this particular audience was quite responsive. Many of them were from the "beat generation," and when I told them they were never born and would never die they wouldn't even bat an eye. I began to get the idea that they could take to meditation, and finally, toward the end of the series, I gave them the instructions you will find summarized in the Introduction and suggested that we all close our eyes and give it a try for just ten minutes. When I opened my eyes, there were only three people in that room: me, my wife, and the store owner.

Many people have read about mysticism, many have attended lectures on meditation, but few have the daring to lead the spiritual life. The majority will admit, "We concede the validity of spiritual living, but we are not prepared to pay the price."

Meditation is dull, hard work; I would be the first to admit it. To continue to practice meditation day in and day out requires real depth of desire and commitment. This should not be surprising; after all, to attain excellence in anything we have to work at it morning, noon, and night. The outstanding tennis player thinks tennis, eats tennis, and dreams tennis. The members of his family never worry about him, because they always know where to find him – on the tennis court. An Olympic swimming champion doesn't go for her workout to the Richmond Plunge once a week on a Sunday afternoon; she swims for hours every day. Whether it is in swimming or tennis or meditation, mastery does not come from dabbling.

Today it is a rare person who can give himself or herself completely to a great purpose. Granted, there are many who are prepared to give themselves to a not-so-worthy cause. But even these are to be preferred to people who sit on the fence until, as some wit said, the wood finally enters their soul. Those who vacillate achieve nothing in life. They go out by the same door they came in, and the Hindu and Buddhist scriptures add that such people keep coming in and going out again and again, until the door falls off its hinges. It is good to have consuming enthusiasm, especially sustained enthusiasm that motivates you to give your best; but it is better still to have it for the right purpose. Look at our films, our folk art festivals and rock concerts, and see what talent is lavished on an embroidered shirt or on a guitar or a piece of pottery. Some of these people have tremendous potential and the capacity to subordinate everything in life to a single purpose. When they take to meditation, they can go far.

In spite of our best efforts, however, there will be times in meditation when we find ourselves in a difficult predicament – times when the senses defy us, when self-will goes on a rampage. Then it is that an experienced, skillful spiritual teacher can come to our rescue. The spiritual journey is long and full of peril. It is fortunate that we are not able to enter the depths of consciousness in meditation until we have already gone some distance towards our goal. The seabed of consciousness is a vast, uncharted domain, full of mountains and canyons where selfish passions roam like monsters in the darkness. If we do not have a map of this world showing what to avoid and how to make the return trip, we can become completely lost. This is why it is essential to have the guidance of someone who has made the journey before us and who knows how to avoid the pitfalls we can encounter on the way.

Once, on a drive in the country, my wife and I somehow managed to back our car into a particularly awkward position with the axle over a rock, so that we could go neither forward nor backward. Three strong young fellows who happened to be walking by stopped and tried to help, but they only succeeded in getting the car more completely wedged in. Finally a friend called a nearby service station to bring a tow truck, and in less than fifteen minutes we were able to drive away. That is the kind of service a spiritual teacher performs. A good spiritual teacher is like a tow truck driver who is on call twenty-four hours a day, and one of the hooks in his vast assortment is just the right size for us. When we get ourselves stuck in meditation and find we can't go forward or back, he pulls us forward just enough to get us free. Then, the moment we can move again, he removes the tow chain and lets us go forward again on our own.

भूमिरापो ऽनलो वायुः खं मनो बुद्धिरेव च ।
अहंकार इतीयं मे भिन्ना प्रकृतिरष्टधा ॥७-४॥

4. Earth, water, fire, air, ether, mind, intellect, and ego – these are the eight divisions of my prakriti.

Now, as he promised, the Lord begins to reveal to Arjuna his real nature.

This verse always makes me think of a market scene in village India. When you want to buy curry powder, you go to the marketplace and find a stall which has all the basic spices in separate pots. The merchant takes a large banana leaf and puts the spices on it as they are selected: a bit of turmeric, a pinch of chili powder, some cardamom, pepper, and coriander, and maybe a little garlic. Then the merchant puts them all together, wraps up the packet, and ties a strand of fiber from the banana leaf around it so you can carry it home.

This is very much like what the Lord does with *prakriti*, which is the basic stuff of which the universe is created. I like to imagine Sri Krishna going to his cosmic marketplace and picking out just the right pair of brown eyes, the right ears, mouth, and other organs, even the right mind, with just the right weakness for classical literature – wrapping them all up in a beautiful brown skin for protection from the tropical sun of India, and calling it this body. Even to the biologist, that is all the body really is: a compact package of chemical components, which when I was going to school used to be worth less than two dollars. By now, because of inflation, that two dollars may be more like five, but that has nothing to do with the value of you or me. We are not this packet of chemicals; the body is only a house for our real Self.

In this verse and the one which follows, Sri Krishna is explaining the vital distinction between what the Sanskrit scriptures call *prakriti* and *Purusha*. Purusha is eternal spirit, the Ātman or Self, beyond all change and limitation. Everything else, everything that is subject to change, belongs to the realm of prakriti, the world of birth, decay, and death. The body, of course, is part of prakriti; made up of the five elements, it was assembled in the process called birth and will one day be resolved back into its constituents in the change called death. We like to think of the body as relatively stable, but this is because our vision is so limited. If we could see more deeply, we would see that every cell of the body is in a state of constant change. It is just the same with the mind. If we could perceive our thoughts more clearly – as we gradually learn to do through the practice of meditation – we would see that our interior world, too, is in a constant state of change. So prakriti includes not only the material world of matter and energy, but emotion, thought, and ego as well. All these came together when our body was born, and all will go their separate ways again at the time of death.

The Katha Upanishad describes prakriti in terms of a chariot drawn by horses straining at the bit:

Know the Self as lord of the chariot,
The body as the chariot itself,
The discriminating intellect as
The charioteer, and the mind as the reins.
The senses, say the wise, are the horses;
Selfish desires are the roads they travel.
When the Self is confused with the body,
Mind, and senses, they point out, it seems
To enjoy pleasure and suffer sorrow.

To use more contemporary language, I sometimes describe this body of mine as a rented car, which I leased at birth and which I would like to return with as few dents, rattles, and broken parts as possible when the lease is up. Discrimination – *buddhi,* the discriminating intellect – is the driver of this car. He has special instructions from the Boss not to exceed the speed limit or grind the gears, to make sure it gets regular checkups, and to use the best gasoline and oil so that the engine will last a long time. But he is only the chauffeur; it is I who decide where to go.

Unfortunately, however, most of us do not realize that this car needs a careful driver, and we let it take us wherever it likes – to the bar, or Reno, or one of these "disaster" films, or wherever the senses tell us that joy is being given away to all. This, of course, takes quite a lot of gas, and with all these side trips we slowly use up our supply of fuel until finally we run out completely. Soon it is time for us to return the car to the rental agency without even having realized there is a destination to reach. It is only when we no longer let our energy and vitality leak out in activities which take us nowhere that we will be able to reach the journey's end.

The day we take to meditation, we begin the long process of breaking through our obsessive identification with the body. At first this may produce a cry of protest. The senses will complain that they are being starved; the body will tell us that all the fun has gone out of life; the mind will complain that it's restless and doesn't want to quiet down. It is like trying to train a dog when you have always let him chase cars, sleep on the couch, and run about freely all night. Just the other day, for example, someone was telling me how he had managed for a week to keep to three nutritious meals a day until he happened to walk by a Danish bakery and got sucked in by some mysterious power. So we shouldn't get angry with the palate for not knowing about vitamins and trace elements and amino acids; we haven't educated it along these lines. If we could have a private talk about nutrition with the palate, it would say, "Nutrition? Never heard of it. George Briggs? Jean Mayer? Never heard of them. Ask me about Marco Polo, without whom we wouldn't have ice cream; I can tell you about him."

In the spiritual life, it is especially important to eat fresh, nutritious food, have daily physical exercise, and get the right amount of sleep every night. If we set ourselves up as stoics, eating only soy grits and sleeping on the bare floor, we will only ruin our health and deprive ourselves of the strength we need for serving others. Instead we need to train the senses by making wise choices. One of the most noticeable benefits of meditation is the growing capacity to turn a deaf ear to the clamor of the senses when they demand wrong food, cigarettes, alcohol, or other things to which they have become addicted. When we have a great purpose that we are eager to achieve and the powerful tool of meditation with which to achieve it, it is only a matter of time before even the most tenacious addiction will lose its power over us. Hundreds of people who have been meditating with me have given up smoking, drinking, and drugging. I don't criticize them when they come to me, and I don't insist that they change their ways in order to start meditating. I know that once they take to meditation these old habits will get up and leave of their own accord, because in meditation we gradually lose our obsessive identification with the body, senses, and mind.

Actually, training the senses is not a physical problem; it is a mental problem. When I first began to speak in this country about the world within the mind, scientists used to tell me, "We don't understand all this talk about a 'world within.' Our instruments can't measure it." To talk about a world without and a world within, as if these were two places we could identify in an atlas of the universe, is to create an artificial division. What we call external and internal are part of one continuous whole. Health, for example, is not maintained just by following certain physical rules; there are also mental and spiritual rules which we must follow. Illness is not only caused by harmful bacteria and viruses, but by destructive passions and negative states of mind. If we cannot control our competitiveness, it may lead to ulcers; if we cannot control deep-seated resentments, we may end up victims of severe breathing disorders like asthma.

Hindu and Buddhist spiritual psychology accounts for this by pointing out that the mind is no less a part of prakriti than matter is. Thoughts are things, even though we cannot hold them in our hands or see them with our eyes. This is very different from our usual view. Usually we consider thoughts as immaterial, so we are not aware of how a fleeting thought can affect us. If I throw a beach ball at you, it won't hurt much; in five minutes you will have forgotten about it. But if I say something harsh to you, you will not be able to forget that thought; you will take it home in your mind, have nightmares about it, and wake up oppressed the next morning. We all know from personal experience how a harsh comment from a parent or a friend can rankle in our consciousness for years. This is the immense power of thoughts.

The intellect is also classified as an aspect of prakriti, for intellectual knowledge too is subject to change. When I was a boy, I used to run home after school every day to tell my grandmother and mother what I had learned. Once, I remember, I told my mother they had taught us something quite astonishing – that the earth is round. She laughed until tears came to her eyes. Even years later she was still telling her friends with great amusement, "He's a professor of English; he writes for the newspapers; he gives talks over All India Radio – but he still believes the earth is round." When I was a boy, of course, I tried to convince her that those who know about geography would say that her idea of a flat earth was a dinosaur. But it is not impossible that in the next century some geophysicist may discover that the earth is not spherical either, but is constantly changing in shape. This is the nature of intellectual knowledge; it is always subject to revision because it describes a relative, changing world that is limited by space, time, and circumstance.

Lastly, the ego itself is classed as prakriti, because it has no more permanence than the thoughts or emotions it claims to own. The implications of this are tremendous. If our thoughts and emotions are constantly changing, what we call our personality must be constantly changing too. We like to think of ourselves as always the same person, yet as Somerset Maugham points out, most of us are a bundle of endless contradictions, behaving differently to different people innumerable times every day. Yet through all these inconsistencies, there is something deep within us whispering that we are the same person from day to day. The Gita would say, very reassuringly, "Yes, you *are* the same. The problem is that this fickle collection of thoughts and desires is not you; it is just a mask with which you've come to identify. Underneath that mask is your real Self, which is beyond all change."

अपरेयमितस्त्वन्यां प्रकृतिं विद्धि मे पराम् ।
जीवभूतां महाबाहो ययेदं धार्यते जगत् ॥७-५॥

5. Beyond this prakriti I have another, higher nature, Arjuna; it supports the whole universe and is the source of life in all beings.

When I first came to this country and was still growing used to American English, I remember being driven to some engagement or other by a young woman who suddenly turned to me and exclaimed, "I'm out of water!" I was really alarmed; I thought perhaps she had some rare disease in which all the vital fluids dry up. But instead of going to a hospital, she pulled into a gas station. Only then did I realize that she didn't mean herself; she meant her car.

When we are asked to identify ourselves, most of us pull out our driver's license and list our vital statistics or launch into a discussion of our personality. It is very much like thinking we are the car we drive. This is not our real identity; this is the limited, egocentric, ever-changing mask which lies within the realm of prakriti. Our real personality, called Purusha in the Sanskrit scriptures, is infinite, immortal, and immutable.

Shankara, the great spiritual teacher of ancient India, has given us a profound principle called *adhyāropa* to explain why we make the colossal mistake of identifying ourselves with what is subject to change and death. Scholars usually translate *adhyāropa* as the "theory of superimposition," which sounds rather forbidding until we realize how it applies in our own lives. According to this principle, each of us confuses his or her limited, mortal ego and the real, immortal Self. This is what we do when we say "I am five foot seven" or "I like to ski"; we are looking at prakriti – the body and mind – and imagining we see Purusha instead. As long as this confusion clouds our minds, we can never see life as it is; we have to look at everything through this narrow little ego-slit we think is us: Sagittarius, thirty-five years old, slightly more open-minded than most of the people we know, with a weakness for spinach crepes and a slight tendency to begrudge opinions different from our own.

Of course, we are not just confused about our own identity, we are also confused about the identity of everyone else. Each of us has certain needs and expectations which we tend to project, or "superimpose," onto those around us. It's as if we had taken our own needs and expectations and shaped them into plastic molds with eyes, ears, a nose, and a mouth. We carry these molds around with us and try to put them on our parents, our partner, our children, our friends, everybody. Then, of course, we expect people to behave exactly like the mold we have imposed on them. In India we have a beautiful marriage ceremony in which bride and groom each place a garland of flowers around the other's neck. It signifies marriage so deeply that in my mother tongue you have only to say "So-and-so was garlanded the other day"; everyone will understand you mean a wedding. Actually, in most marriages all over the world, what really happens is that in place of garlands, the bride and groom use their adhyāropa molds. They stand facing one another, raise their molds, and pull them down over their partners, folding over an ear and pushing the nose to one side until each is squeezed into the other's image of what he or she should be like. Most of us, in fact, carry around an extensive collection of molds like this that we have accumulated over the years, and when we meet someone we hurry to our private collection, select a mold, and mentally cram him into it. When our unsuspecting friend goes on acting the way he is used to, we become outraged because he is ruining our mold. Then we wonder why our relationship is falling apart. Shankara would answer that the estrangement has nothing to do with our friend; the problem is what we have imposed on him.

To repair our relationships, we have to stop playing this game of adhyāropa and put a padlock on the mold-room door. There is only one way to do this, and that is to break out of the mold we have imposed on ourselves. This is not at all a pleasant task. The prospect of pulling apart someone else's mold isn't too distressing; what we find heartrending is breaking open our own mold, which we are absolutely convinced is just right. It may take years, but if we can even get a glimpse of ourselves as we really are, not separate from anyone but a part of the whole, the mold will crack. When we have learned to translate this insight into our daily living, the mold will be in a hundred pieces at our feet, and with it all the molds we once imposed on others. Then we will see ourselves, and others as well, as we really are: the Ātman or Purusha, who is pure, perfect, and immortal.

एतद्योनीनि भूतानि सर्वाणीत्युपधारय ।
अहं कृत्स्नस्य जगतः प्रभवः प्रलयस्तथा ॥७-६॥
मत्तः परतरं नान्यत्किंचिदस्ति धनंजय ।
मयि सर्वमिदं प्रोतं सूत्रे मणिगणा इव ॥७-७॥

6. In these two aspects of my nature is the womb of all creation. The birth and dissolution of the entire universe take place in me.
7. There is nothing which exists separate from me, Arjuna. The entire universe is suspended from me as my necklace of jewels.

In India when you go to see a film they usually fill out the program by showing a trailer, in which the highlights of the coming films are all run together so that you have something to which you can look forward. These next few verses are like that; they are a kind of preview of what is to come in the following chapters. Sri Krishna is stirring up Arjuna's love for him until finally, in chapters eleven and twelve, Arjuna will beg to see the Lord's real nature and be united with him forever.

Here the Lord begins by giving us a glimpse of the vastness of his glory. Everything in the cosmos, he tells Arjuna, takes its rise from him, and one day it will be dissolved back into him again. This is not a matter of the Lord standing *here* and creating something *over there;* Sri Krishna is trying to explain in these verses that the everchanging world of time and space, matter and energy called prakriti, and the changeless Reality which underlies that world, are simply two aspects of his divine nature. Spinoza, the seventeenth-century Dutch mystic, calls this the finite world resting on the bosom of the Infinite, as if the universe were just the restless surface of the infinite, motionless expanse of God. Ramdas, the delightful mystic of South India whom my wife and I had the blessing of meeting some years ago, puts it simply when he says, "The world *is* God." This is the great truth that will be developed throughout this volume of the Gita: the Lord is everywhere, in everything, for those who open their eyes to see. In the next few chapters Sri Krishna will go into the mysteries of his real nature, how he creates, pervades, supports, and dissolves the cosmos. Now, to whet Arjuna's enthusiasm, he just mentions casually that this whole vast universe, with all its galaxies and forms of life, is no more than a necklace adorning his dark neck.

Recently I have been looking into a few books on astronomy to see the backdrop against which these insights of the Bhagavad Gita are set. The sweep and majesty of it can take our breath away. Now, for example, we take space travel for granted, and every schoolchild probably knows that it takes a ray of light just one second to reach us from the moon. It makes me feel very comfortable; I can look up at the moon and think, "Just one second! You might as well live next door." If we could ride a beam of light, we could get here from the moon before we even had a chance to say where we were going; that's how fast light travels. Yet even at that rate it would take us eight minutes to get from here to the sun, ninety-three million miles away. It should make us pause to think. Ninety-three million miles isn't exactly next door – until we back up a little. Even at the speed of light – about 5,878 billion miles a year – we would be riding that light beam for four whole years before we came to the nearest star. That gives us the units our sun must be thinking in; for him, "next door" means four light-years, which is already more than we can comprehend. For the sun, a long voyage is something like crossing the Milky Way, a vast galaxy of stars and incandescent gases one hundred thousand light-years across, where Mr. Sun is tucked away in a little corner towards the outside edge. It isn't possible even to imagine a distance like that. Yet the Milky Way is just one of the countless galaxies our modern instruments have detected in the starry sky. If we could back up still further, we would see these vast galaxies sprinkled by the millions across incomprehensible stretches of empty space, each just a single jewel in the necklace of the Lord.

Astronomers have become quite humble about all this. They no longer talk about the universe as it is; they say, "This is what we know about the *observable* universe; what's beyond that we just can't say." They tell us there are stellar objects billions of times brighter than our sun and "black holes" into which billions of tons of matter disappear without a trace; and when we ask how all this can be, even the most hard-boiled of astronomers will just shrug and answer, "We don't know." And Sri Krishna smiles mischievously as if to say, "Keep on going. Even if you could travel till the end of time, you would never find a place where I am not, or reach the limit of my creation."

I read about these things and I am not lost in wonder, I am *found* in wonder. One of the books I have been reading is by Sir Fred Hoyle, a brilliant British astronomer whom I like very much. Sir Fred seems to have been working recently with an Indian astronomer, because when I read one of these astounding statements and then look down at the footnote I see it is attributed to Sir Fred Hoyle and Jayant Vishnu Narlikar. It always makes me smile, because Vishnu is one of Sri Krishna's names. He is the Author of all these wonders, and whenever I run into that little footnote I glance up at the picture of him above my bed. His body is a deep blue like the monsoon sky or a stormy night, above his forehead he wears a peacock feather, shimmering with all the colors of the universe, and in place of the traditional necklace I see bright galaxies and quasars and black holes like dark, lustrous gems strung in garlands about his neck. I look at him and think, "Is it true? You really did all this?" And he just smiles as if to say, "Read on; that's only the beginning."

रसोऽहमप्सु कौन्तेय प्रभास्मि शशिसूर्ययोः ।
प्रणवः सर्ववेदेषु शब्दः खे पौरुषं नृषु ॥७-८॥

8. Arjuna, I am the taste of pure water and the radiance of the sun and moon. I am the sacred word and the sound heard in air, and the courage of human beings.

Now Sri Krishna startles us: he is not only the infinitely vast; he is the essence in every created thing. In India, where the sun can get terribly hot and the monsoon rains literally make the difference between life and death for millions of living creatures, water is precious every day of the year. In summer, one of the services my ancestral family used to perform was to keep huge earthen pots of water in the outer courtyard so that travelers in the hot sun could quench their thirst without anyone ever asking who or why. In this kind of heat school begins early in the morning so as to let out early in the afternoon, and when I was a boy, as soon as school was out, we all used to run back to the village to play soccer together for hours. After even a little of this, running constantly in the heat of an Indian afternoon, every pore of your body is crying out for water; and when it was time to go home we would throw ourselves on those huge pots and drink them almost dry. Nothing could have tasted better to us than that water did after hours of playing soccer in the sun, and if Sri Krishna could have got my ear then he would have whispered, "Do you know what's so satisfying in that water? It's *me*."

The Compassionate Buddha must have had a village like ours in mind when he called the ego's fierce cravings for personal satisfaction *tanhā,* the kind of burning thirst that will not let us rest until it has been satisfied. No earthly waters can satisfy this thirst. Our need for fulfillment is infinite, and as long as we think we are the body and try to find satisfaction in things that come and go, we are only going to get more and more parched. That is the point of the story of Jesus and the woman of Samaria, whom Jesus asks for a drink of water. When she questions him because he is a Jew, he replies: "Whoever drinks of this water shall thirst again, but whoever drinks of the water I give him shall never thirst; the water that I give him shall be in him a well of water springing up into everlasting life."

Then Sri Krishna adds, a bit playfully, "When you were quenching your thirst on those hot days, I wasn't just in the water you drank; I was also the blazing radiance of the sun." It is not just beautiful poetry; it's a simple statement of fact, though one which is very difficult to comprehend. The Sanskrit scriptures tell us that just as the moon reflects the light of the sun, the sun only reflects the light of the Self, from which all forms of energy come. If our vision were not so drastically limited, physicists tell us, we could look beneath the illusion of solid forms to see the whole of creation as a dance of light, from which elements and substances emerge and to which they return. This pure energy is the light which is the source of all the light we see. The Katha Upanishad says:

> There shines not the sun, neither moon nor star,
> Nor flash of lightning, nor fire lit on earth.
> The Self is the light reflected by all.
> He shining, everything shines after him.

Similarly, just as the Lord is the Light in all forms of light, he is the Sound that underlies all sounds. In the Hindu scriptures this sound is said to be approximated by the sacred syllable *Om* – or, as it is sometimes pronounced, *Aum*. This is not a physical sound, so it cannot be heard by the ear. But after many years of meditation, when your concentration is so deep that you are no longer aware of the cars on the road or the birds outside your window, this sound may sometimes be heard reverberating throughout consciousness.

In the Hindu and Buddhist traditions, *Om* is often repeated as part of a mantram or spiritual formula. But the use of such formulas is not confined to Hinduism and Buddhism; it plays an important part in all the world's great mystical traditions, usually in connection with the holy name. In Christianity, for example, the name of Jesus is one of the most powerful of mantrams. In Jewish mysticism, we have similar formulas in *Barukh attah Adonai* and the Shema – "Hear, O Israel; the Lord thy God, the Lord is one." Muslim mystics repeat the name of *Allah* or a formula like the *Bismillāh:* "In the name of God, the Merciful, the Compassionate." One of the oldest Buddhist mantrams is *Om mani padme hum,* referring to the Self as the "jewel in the lotus of the heart." And the most common Hindu mantram is simply *Rāma, Rāma,* calling on the Lord within us as the source of all joy. In all these traditions, we are urged to choose one mantram and then repeat it over and over again whenever we have an opportunity. It sounds simple, but these formulas carry tremendous power. Over a period of years, they can transform everything negative in our consciousness into what is positive: anger into sympathy, impatience into patience, hostility into love.

After many years of mantram repetition, or *japam* in Sanskrit, the mantram becomes an integral part of consciousness. In Sanskrit this is called *ajapajapam,* 'japam without japam.' The person who becomes established in this state carries the Lord with him wherever he goes. Sri Ramakrishna says that such people are like office workers who retire on their pension after many years of working with the company: they don't have to work any more, but they still receive their check every month in the mail for all the years of work they have done before. Similarly, after many years of making an effort to repeat the mantram, it becomes as much a part of you as your breathing or the beat of your heart. Then you don't have to work at it; you don't have to think about it; it will go on unceasingly of itself.

पुण्यो गन्धः पृथिव्यां च तेजश्चास्मि विभावसौ ।
जीवनं सर्वभूतेषु तपश्चास्मि तपस्विषु ॥७-९॥

9. I am the sweet fragrance in the earth and the heat in fire; I am the life in every creature, and the effort of the spiritual aspirant.

To appreciate this verse fully you have to experience the onset of the monsoon season in a tropical country like India, when the ground has been parched for months by the burning sun. It isn't just the villager with his little rice field that waits almost breathlessly for rain; the food supply of the whole Indian subcontinent depends on the monsoon. Everybody waits for the dark clouds to gather on the horizon, and as the day gets close, no matter what you are doing, you always have one ear open for the first sweet clap of thunder proclaiming the advent of rain. You can almost hear the earth panting for water. Then, the great Sanskrit poets say, there is no fragrance so satisfying as Mother Earth's when the rain clouds finally break and pour heavy rain on her dried, burnt soil; it delights the senses and soothes the mind and spirit. Sri Krishna says, "As the earth gives a deep sigh of joy and gratitude when the monsoon waters slake her thirst, so the longings of all those who have been parched for lasting joy and unshakable security are fulfilled by union with me."

Calling our little planet Mother Earth is a beautiful way of expressing the unity of life, for every aspect of life on earth is part of an interrelated whole. Not only can we not raze a rain forest in the Amazon basin without affecting the lives of the millions of creatures who live there; that rain forest in Brazil influences long-range climatic patterns as far away as India. And when the monsoon rains of India fall into the ocean instead of on the continent, leaving the croplands barren – as they are now beginning to do, through just such pillage – it means suffering to Mother Earth and all her children, not only in India but in Russia and America, too.

That is why I say it is not enough simply to have jnāna, the knowledge of life's unity; we have to learn to apply this knowledge to the problems of daily living. In the case of the environment, this means learning to be trustees for all the earth's resources. We would never dream of throwing old beer cans into our bathtub, yet many people do not think twice about tossing their cans into a river or dumping tons of garbage into the ocean. If our house has faulty plumbing or a leaking roof, we can always call the repairman or figure out a way of solving the problem ourselves. But the poor creatures of the earth have no say in the condition of their home. All they can do is suffer in silence until you and I, their trustees, realize what we are doing and clean up the mess we have created.

In clear, simple language the Lord is telling us that all life is sacred: *jīvanam sarvabhūteshu,* 'I am the life in every creature.' It's not just a philosophical statement. When I go out in the morning and see all these quail scurrying around outside our meditation hall, I do see them as quail, but only with my eyes, with my intellect. With the little spiritual awareness that has come to me from my grandmother, I see that the power that makes them scurry and peck is the power of the Lord; their very life is the divine energy that moves us all. That is why we should not kill. This is the way to show respect for life – by not injuring any being, because the Lord is present in every creature on the face of the earth. When I walk down the lane to our home there are usually cows and calves grazing on both sides of the road, and on summer evenings the calves frolic about playing games that look very much like those our boys and girls play. The mother cows mutter among themselves while their little ones romp, and to my ears their *maa, maa* becomes *ammama,* which in my mother tongue means uncle. They are telling their children, "Hey, there goes your uncle, who is helping to save your life."

The other two key words here are *tapas* and *tejas,* 'heat' and 'brilliance' – not just of an external fire but also of the fire within. This is an image you see often in the annals of mysticism all over the world, and probably no one has used it more beautifully than St. John of the Cross:

O fire that burns to purify,
O wound that brings love of the Lord,
Whose soft hand and tender caress
Reveals new life, cancels all debts,
And, slaying, grants eternal life.

This inner fire is not a figure of speech; it is associated with the rise of an immense source of energy called *kundalinī* in Sanskrit. Kundalinī is the power behind the process of evolution. By virtue of our being human, each of us has a vast amount of this energy, but very few ever learn to harness it. As long as we are living for ourselves we have no access to kundalinī, though we can get a glimpse of its power in the tremendous drive of sex. But when, through the practice of meditation, we begin to harness our personal desires for the sake of a higher goal, kundalinī slowly gets released into daily living. We find ourselves more patient and more cheerful; things that used to rankle in our consciousness for weeks now no longer bother us; we have more energy for giving to others, and a greater ability to understand the problems around us and come up with a lasting solution. And when some old attachment comes and wants us to dance to its tune – to smoke this, or sniff that, or buy this, or nibble at that – we can turn our backs on it. All these are signs of kundalinī rising, and when this power is completely harnessed, as in great mystics like Mahatma Gandhi or St. Francis, it can transform every negative factor in the personality into a positive force. This is why the Hindu mystics say that in meditation you can take your evolution into your own hands: by getting hold of kundalinī, you can learn to go beyond all biological conditioning.

Of course, it isn't at all easy to turn your back on a strong desire; often it is quite painful. It's very much like learning to use a stiff arm again. When your arm has been cramped and twisted into a rigid position, even the slightest little movement becomes painful. Yet you have to learn to move it in order to regain the use of your arm. There *is* suffering in this, as there so often is in any kind of growth. This suffering, this painful effort, is tapas, and it should be a source of great consolation to remember that whenever you choose to go against some self-centered desire for the sake of spiritual growth, the Lord says here, "I am your effort; I am your suffering; I come to life in your will."

बीजं मां सर्वभूतानां विद्धि पार्थ सनातनम् ।
बुद्धिर्बुद्धिमतामस्मि तेजस्तेजस्विनामहम् ॥७-१०॥

10. O Partha, my eternal seed is to be found in every creature. I am the power of discrimination in those who are intelligent, and the glory of the heroic.

The Lord is the seed of creativity in every being. Meister Eckhart uses the same image when he says that the seed of God is in everyone. Just as pear seeds grow into pear trees and apple seeds grow into apple trees, so this God-seed within us will grow into a God-tree of love and service if we nourish it and protect it from weeds.

These days, I am glad to say, more and more people seem to be growing their own vegetables. I'm told there are even office buildings that offer little plots to their workers to make a cooperative garden. This is a very encouraging movement, but though it is good to know how to raise your own food in your backyard, it is much more important to know how to cultivate the God-seed in your heart. If you want to grow tomatoes, you buy some seeds and plant them in your garden. But what would you think of someone who looks out the window the next morning, can't see a single tomato, and phones the store to complain that their merchandise is bad? It would require a great deal of patience on the part of the storekeeper to explain that tomato seeds don't produce tomatoes overnight, and that the seeds need just the right conditions before they will germinate and grow. It is very much the same with the God-seed; we need to nurture it carefully if we want it to grow and bear fruit.

Fortunately, however, this seed is indestructible. It does not need to be planted on a particular calendar date, for it is already within us. In the depths of the Dakota winter, at ten degrees below zero, the God-seed can thrive; in the heat of Death Valley it can still flourish. No matter what our past has been, no matter how many mistakes we have made, the God-seed is still intact. When at last we begin to search for it we discover it is covered with weeds – weeds of fear and anger and giant thistles of greed that try to choke out everything else. But once we take to meditation and start making all the little choices that strengthen it every day, the weeds begin to wither and droop, and finally they fall to enrich the soil where the God-seed has begun to grow.

In Sanskrit, all the little choices we make in weeding out this inner garden are ascribed to buddhi, 'discrimination' or 'intelligence.' Buddhi is the precious capacity to discriminate between what is pleasant for the moment and what is fulfilling always. In the chariot image from the Katha Upanishad a few verses earlier, buddhi is the charioteer; when it takes its directions from the Ātman or Self, it can guide us intelligently down even the most dangerous road. Today, surrounded by a bewildering array of attitudes and lifestyles and models of behavior, most of which promise just the opposite of what they deliver, we need this capacity to make wise choices every moment just to keep from being swept away.

Buddhi and the will – the capacity to see clearly what is wise and the capacity to translate that insight into action – go hand in hand. So this verse is very much like the last; Sri Krishna says, "Whenever you make an intelligent decision, even if it is unpleasant at the time, I am the wisdom in your choice." Once you begin to taste the freedom of this, you will find a certain fierce joy in choosing something of lasting benefit over what you crave right now. But for a long, long time, these choices are never easy, for they go against the very grain of our conditioning. It takes real courage and endurance to go on making such choices day in and day out, and that is why even climbing the Himālayas or venturing into space would seem tame to a great mystic like Gandhiji or St. Teresa. So the Lord returns to this word *tejas* again: "If you have the courage to take to this challenge, *I* will be your courage."

Do you see the insight these verses give us into the nature of God? It's not as if the Lord were something outside us, in a given place at a given time; he is right within, in our will, in our determination, whenever we are giving our very best to achieve the goal of life. As a Sufi mystic puts it, God is the life of our life, nearer to us than our body is; throughout creation he is the principle of creativity itself. One astronomer I have been reading recently calls it cowardly to conclude that God created the universe just because we cannot comprehend the conditions of its creation. He is still thinking of someone outside, holding court beyond the Andromeda galaxy; he hasn't glimpsed that all this *is* God, and wherever there is light, or beauty, or excellence in anything, we are seeing a little more of God's glory.

बलं बलवतां चाहं कामरागविवर्जितम् ।
धर्माविरुद्धो भूतेषु कामो ऽस्मि भरतर्षभ ॥७-११॥

11. In those who are strong, I am strength, free from passion and selfish attachment. I am desire itself, if that desire is in harmony with the purpose of life.

Often over the years I have met people who amazed me with some of their physical exploits. They could run very fast, or jump very far, or lift immense weights, or dive from great heights into shallow pools in the river that runs by our village in Kerala. It always used to surprise me to see how many of these people, endowed with uncommon physical capacities, would just go to pieces when faced with some emotional crisis. Gradually, as I began to observe my granny, I came to understand that real strength has nothing to do with developing a set of muscles that is the envy of Muscle Beach. Strength is endurance, resilience, stamina, the capacity to face everything life sends you squarely and turn it into an opportunity.

This kind of strength can only come from self-control. During the struggle for Indian independence Gandhiji used to ask us over and over again, "What kind of strength does it take to retaliate, to lash back at others?" Retaliation simply means that the person is out of control, and if you watch someone who gets angry easily, you will see that he or she is vulnerable to any little impulse that comes along. But when you can rein in your passions and hold them in check, you have enormous power at your fingertips to harness for the welfare of all.

When I was learning English in my little village school, we used to encounter the phrase "a bull in a china shop." It didn't mean much to us, since we had never even seen china, much less a china shop. We used to eat off fresh banana leaves, which make perfect plates for curry dishes; and after a meal, instead of washing the dishes, we would feed them all to the cows, to whom banana leaves are like ice cream. So our English teacher, who was my uncle, would explain it in terms of a mad elephant. *That* we understood. An elephant is one of the most powerful of creatures; no animal except perhaps a tiger would even dream of attacking an elephant, and even the tiger has to resort to a sneak attack by lying in wait on the branch of a tree and jumping on the elephant's head. Usually this giant of a creature is, as the Bible puts it, "slow to wrath." But there is a peculiar condition called *must* – fortunately rare – in which the elephant will suddenly go into a rage and run amuck, tearing up everything that gets in its way. It is a terrible sight, and the moment they hear cries of "mad elephant!" everyone in the village will run for cover. Anger is like that; it is immense power that is running amuck and striking out at anyone who gets in its way. But when that same power, instead of running amuck, is doing something constructive, it is no longer anger; it is immense strength. It is much the same with other nearly uncontrollable emotions, too. Fear, for example, is as great a source of power as anger; and an obsessive desire, especially for pleasure or power, is a real Niagara. It takes a lot of endurance to turn your back on a powerful emotion or an obsessive, self-centered desire, but when you can do this, Sri Krishna says, "that endurance, that strength, is me."

Then, as if reading the look in Arjuna's eyes, the Lord adds: "But if that desire is *not* self-centered, I am that desire too." This is the real artistry of the Gita. You don't have to give up all desires to be strong; you just have to give up all selfish desires. For example, when you have food that strengthens the body, especially when it is cooked and served with love and eaten in the company of family or friends, you don't need to pass it up just because you like the taste of it. The Lord would say, "Dig in; I am in that desire too."

I am very much like my grandmother in this respect. When there was a feast coming I don't think she ever thought about the food before or after; but while she was eating I have never seen anyone enjoy a meal more. At our āshram, whenever there is a special occasion, whether it be Jewish or Christian, Hindu or Muslim, we really have a feast. And when someone comes in and puts a steaming platter of blintzes on the table, we don't turn our eyes away and say, "We can't eat blintzes; they're not mentioned in the scriptures." We sit down, repeat the mantram, and polish them off.

On the other hand, you can't expect Sri Krishna to be present in, say, Puerto Rican rum, which you drink when you can't solve a problem. There the way to celebrate is to ignore the rum and solve the problem; then, if you still want to celebrate, ask for another problem and solve that one too.

The question in all these matters is, are you doing this for yourself or for others? You can't go to a wedding and have lentil soup and ice water when everyone around you is having quiche and champagne; it makes people feel a little sour. So when I go to the wedding of one of our friends, I have champagne too. Once in a way I have two glasses, one for the bride and one for the groom, and if afterwards a little poetry comes out, a speech from Shakespeare or a few lines by Shelley, I don't mind at all; it's part of the occasion. Once I went to a wedding where sparkling cider was served instead of champagne, and nothing came out but prose.

It is much the same with the other legitimate pleasures of life; they all can have a place in spiritual living. Though I lead a very busy life, I still find time to go swimming with my wife and friends, or follow championship tennis, or attend a concert of South Indian devotional music or a movie of Satyajit Ray's. In fact, I go to our local repertory theater so regularly that when we went to see *Hamlet* the other day I couldn't help nudging Christine and whispering, "That's not Hamlet; that's last month's Bluntschli in *Arms and the Man*." In other words, we don't need to turn our backs on the innocent delights of life to be spiritual. We can participate fully in life as long as we are trying our best to put those around us first.

ये चैव सात्त्विका भावा राजसास्तामसाश्च ये ।
मत्त एवेति तान्विद्धि न त्वहं तेषु ते मयि ॥७-१२॥
त्रिभिर्गुणमयैर्भावैरेभिः सर्वमिदं जगत् ।
मोहितं नाभिजानाति मामेभ्यः परमव्ययम् ॥७-१३॥

12. The states of sattva, rajas, and tamas come from me. They are in me, but I am not in them.
13. These three gunas deceive the world, so people fail to look beyond them to me, supreme and imperishable.

According to the Sanskrit scriptures, the universe evolved out of a state of undifferentiated consciousness, in which there was not a trace of separate existence. The world was a thought lying unexpressed in the consciousness of the Lord, as the impressions of our waking and dreaming states lie latent in the mind when we rest in dreamless sleep. In their usual vivid way, some of these scriptures picture this unimaginable state as the Lord – Vishnu, 'he who pervades everything,' of whom our own Sri Krishna is an incarnation lying fast asleep on his favorite bed, the endless serpent Ananta, in the cosmic sea. There is very little to disturb the scene. Not only is there no light, there is nothing else: the sea is Vishnu, Ananta is Vishnu, everything is Vishnu. Then, it is said, the Lord begins to dream. The dream is our own world, called Māyā in Sanskrit, and the substance of this dream is the three qualities called *gunas: sattva, rajas,* and *tamas,* which may be roughly translated as law, energy, and inertia. At the time of creation the gunas begin to interact with each other, and out of this interaction, step by step, the world of prakriti evolves.

We can see these three forces at work in our own evolution as human beings, too. Although each of us has some measure of sattva, rajas, and tamas, usually there is one of the three which dominates our character. Those who are overcome by inertia and lethargy, who procrastinate and give up easily, are under the sway of tamas. They may as well be statues; you could put them on a pedestal and come back after a month to find they had not moved a hair's breadth. But it is more positive to look on tamas as frozen power, latent drive which has been kept in a deep freeze of disuse for so long that it has turned into a block of ice. Through the practice of meditation, this glacier inside begins to melt, releasing tremendous energy for overcoming old habits of lethargy and apathy.

It is a very different story with those in whom rajas predominates. They have left tamas behind them, often for the sake of achieving great success in the eyes of the world. Rajasic people are certainly more evolved than those governed by tamas, but unfortunately they are frequently the victims of tempestuous passions. They are the movie idols, the empire builders, and the marathon walkers who make newspaper headlines. They enjoy competing and breaking records; if there is a pie-eating competition, the rajasic man or woman will walk away with the prize. Such people may have great enterprise and remarkable digestion, but they often have little sense of direction. For them the greatest danger lies in getting caught in things that are enjoyable but meaningless.

It amazes me to see the extent to which rajas is running wild in the world today. It is rajas that drives individuals and nations to manipulate others for their own ends. It is rajas that drives us to pollute the earth for profit. And it is rajas that drives us to keep adding to our own convenience and comfort, even if it brings harm to our fellow creatures. One example is "junk food" – food that is produced essentially for profit rather than for nutrition. Years ago I read that we pay some thirty billion dollars on medical bills for ailments related to poor nutrition. Since that time the Surgeon General, the American Heart Association, the American Cancer Society, and other expert bodies have linked poor diet to a much larger percentage of health problems, many of which are the result of eating things because they look lavish, fill a craving for calories, or have a catchy theme song. More and more of the items I see on the so-called food shelves of today's supermarkets have only "empty calories": sugar and fat, but very little nutrition. We Americans consume on the average about *one-third pound* of sweetener per person per day: in terms of calories, nothing else every fourth day. Imagine giving your child a bowl of white sugar for breakfast, some lunch, and a glass of honey for dinner! And when I first heard about additives in food, I naturally thought they were to preserve our health. Then I learned that we eat dangerous quantities of chemical additives whose purpose is to prolong not our lives but the shelf-life of processed foods, so that a real banana can sit for weeks without changing much more than a plastic banana would.

Another sign of rajas is restlessness, which is endemic in our modern civilization. Whenever you see someone who is restless, who travels around the world once a year or takes up one job after another, this may be a sign that he or she has real potential for meditation. In this connection I remember a story about Paramahamsa Yogananda, the distinguished spiritual teacher from India who established the Self-Realization Fellowship in Los Angeles. One of Yogananda's students, James J. Lynn, was an oil magnate who had begun to see that money could not bring the security and lasting satisfaction he sought. When Yogananda asked Mr. Lynn in his simple, sweet manner if he would like to learn to meditate, Lynn replied, like many of us, that his desires made him too terribly restless; he had to keep on drilling for more and more oil. Beneath the restless surface of consciousness, however, Yogananda recognized a deep spiritual longing. He told Mr. Lynn to turn all his drilling desires inwards in meditation until he hit the deep strata of unitive awareness, where he would find an endless source of joy, security, and wisdom. Lynn responded with all the energy and enthusiasm that had gone into drilling for oil. First, through meditation and its allied disciplines, he learned to transform rajas into sattva, bringing every aspect of his life into balance. Then, through Yogananda's close guidance, he learned to go beyond the conditioning of the gunas altogether and attain the abiding joy of Self-realization. It is a perfect example of how the restless energy of rajas can be harnessed to reach the supreme goal of life.

Through meditation and its allied disciplines, all of us can learn like this to transform the self-directed energy of rajas into the selfless power that is characteristic of the third stage of consciousness, called sattva. Then instead of becoming angry, we will find it natural to forgive;

instead of becoming irritated, we will find it easy to be patient; instead of grabbing all we can, we will work to fulfill the needs of others. People in whom sattva predominates appear serene, but we should never make the mistake of thinking they lack energy. Instead of scattering their energy over a lot of restless activity, they make effective use of it when it will do some good and conserve it when it will not. This sense of discrimination gives them an evenness of mind and constancy of action that make them a blessing wherever they go.

दैवी ह्येषा गुणमयी मम माया दुरत्यया ।
मामेव ये प्रपद्यन्ते मायामेतां तरन्ति ते ॥७-१४॥
न मां दुष्कृतिनो मूढाः प्रपद्यन्ते नराधमाः ।
माययापहृतज्ञाना आसुरं भावमाश्रिताः ॥७-१५॥

14. These three gunas make up my divine
Māyā, difficult to overcome. But they cross
over this Māyā who are devoted to me.
15. Others are deluded by Māyā; performing
evil deeds, they have no devotion for
me. Having lost all discrimination, they
follow the way of their lower nature.

Years ago I spent a week as a guest in an hospitable retreat not far from San Diego, where I had a magnificent view of the Pacific Ocean. I used to take long walks along the beach there and watch the surf, which makes me think of the restless sea of the mind and the "sea of birth and death" that we call everyday life. But what fascinated me was the surfers. I had never seen surfing in India, and I really enjoyed the ease with which these young people had learned to ride the waves.

One day I was surprised to see among the surfers a young woman with Indian features. Sure enough, she had a good Sanskrit name, Māyā, and when she found out I was from India she invited me to her home for dinner just as my students used to do in India. Her parents were from the Punjab, a part of India noted for its hospitality, and in keeping with their tradition, I was given a real Indian feast. Then, after dinner, the daughter asked me if I could tell her the meaning of her name. I can still remember telling her that if I could explain this Sanskrit word *Māyā,* I would have given her the secret of life.

Māyā cannot be explained because it permeates everything; it conditions all our thinking and perceiving. Māyā is the hypnotic spell of separateness that is the source of all our confusion. It is very much like a kind of hypnotic trance, or a vivid but frustrating dream in which everything appears to be just the opposite of what it is. We see people as separate when we are all one; that is Māyā. We think that pleasure, or power, or material possessions will make us happy, that it is absurd to say "it is in giving that we receive." Yet the more we go after the things that please us, the less they seem to satisfy; the more we look for excitement, the more everything in life seems stale; the more we try to manipulate people, the more insecure we become. This is Māyā, which hides the source of joy from us and then drives us to look for joy everywhere but where it is.

In the Sanskrit scriptures, these two aspects of Māyā, the powers of concealing and diverting, are ascribed to the gunas of tamas and rajas. The gunas are the very substance of Māyā. Tamas, inertia, keeps us wrapped up in ourselves, always thinking we are the body and separate from everyone else. Then rajas comes along, restless energy, and whips up an endless series of desires for selfish satisfaction that sends us racing after mirage after mirage, always thinking that what we are after is just around the corner. We may have been down a particular blind alley a thousand times before, but with rajas at the wheel it doesn't matter; we're always surprised when we see the same old brick wall at the end. Sometimes there is a little twinge of memory: "Oh, yes, haven't I seen this wall before? . . . Why do I ever listen to you?" But rajas just says, "I say, old fellow, look over there; why don't we back up and try that alley across the way?" And before we have time to think, we've forgotten our suspicions and are off towards another dead end.

It is this bewildering razzle-dazzle of what we desire for ourselves that keeps us from seeing life whole. As long as we go after happiness just for us, as long as we see everything in terms of what we want for ourselves only, there will always be this wall of separateness between ourselves and others. And one of Māyā's cruelest tricks is that as we begin to get more frustrated, more lonely, more alienated behind our wall, we try to grab more fiercely at what we want and end up building the wall even higher.

Even before I took to meditation, I had a great love for natural beauty and a deep interest in people. I had a rather keen eye for human nature and could sympathize easily, and nothing could have convinced me that I was not seeing the world clearly. But all this was nothing like the way I see life today. Earlier, when I saw a mountain or a river or looked at the stars in the autumn sky, the response to beauty was deep and immediate, but it was still just an aesthetic response. Now, if I may try to put it into words, it's like seeing the beauty of the hills and the stream and the starry night and the faces of those around me and knowing that all this is one. That is what happens when the veil of Māyā falls. Afterwards, though you are back in the world of separateness and know how real it is for everyone still caught in it, you will never forget that all the bewildering array of differences in the world around you – different faces, different habits, different races, different beliefs – is just window dressing; beneath all this there is no one but the Lord.

When I came to this country on the Fulbright exchange program, all the talk was about how different everything was going to be; you'd have thought I was going to Mars. Some of the orientation programs I went to must have been intended to *dis*orient us, because the emphasis was never on what Indians and Americans had in common but always on how we differed. To me it was absurd, because all these little differences are only on the surface; they are no more significant than differences in food or dress. The mystic doesn't deny these differences; all he or she says is, "So what?" When our ship pulled into New York harbor we all stood at the rail and watched the skyline. I don't think I had ever seen a building more than three or four stories high, and here were buildings a hundred stories high. A British lady by my side looked at me and said, "Aren't you *overwhelmed?*" I just asked, "By what?" People don't get overwhelmed by more bricks piled on top of each other or more wire strung together; they get overwhelmed when they see someone whose patience is inexhaustible. So that night, when my colleagues wanted to take in Times Square, they all stood around looking up at the tall buildings and the neon lights, but I was looking at the people. That gave me more delight than anything else: seeing how different they all looked and how alike they all were inside. It really makes you appreciate the magic of Māyā to see Times Square and realize that there is no one there except the Lord.

The explanation for all this is that it is not our eyes with which we see; it is our mind. And the mind can operate only in a world of differences. It has to have separate people and different things to like and dislike; otherwise there isn't any mind. Where there is no anger, no fear, no greed, no separateness, the mind just goes to sleep; it cannot operate at all. There is nothing to get excited about, nothing to take notice of; there is only pure joy, which is something the mind simply can't experience. This is what the Buddhists call the state of no-mind, and it gives us the clue to going beyond Māyā. The more you can still the mind, which is the whole purpose of meditation, the more you will be able to see beneath the surface level of life and remember its unity. Everything that quietens the mind helps to weaken the spell of Māyā, just as everything that agitates the mind works to strengthen the spell of Māyā. That's why I say over and over again not to think about yourself but to think always of others; give yourself freely, be patient always, slow down, and don't ever dwell on your problems or your resentments, because these are the things that inflame self-will and fan the fires of separateness. The agitation of the mind *is* Māyā, and if you can remember that you are seeing everything and everyone through the medium of the mind, that will provide motivation for keeping it calm and clear always.

चतुर्विधा भजन्ते मां जनाः सुकृतिनोऽर्जुन ।
आर्तो जिज्ञासुरर्थार्थी ज्ञानी च भरतर्षभ ॥७-१६॥

16. Good people come to worship me for different reasons. Some come to the spiritual life because of suffering, some in order to understand life; some come through a desire to serve humanity, and some come seeking self-knowledge.

People come to the spiritual life for all sorts of different reasons. First, and by far the most numerous, are those who come because of suffering, either physical, emotional, or spiritual. Like most people, before I began meditating I did not understand the lesson suffering has to teach us. Only when I had some deeper awareness of life did I realize the truth of my grandmother's words, that the grace of God often comes in the form of sorrow. If we are not prepared to realize the unity of life, the Lord in his infinite love will let us suffer until we are forced to change our ways.

Probably the most acute kind of suffering is the spiritual anguish that comes from an intense sense of deprivation, of being alienated from ourselves. When, suffering from this anguish, we turn inwards in meditation, we find that the Lord has been waiting for years to console us, support us, and inspire us. We may wonder how he who is the embodiment of love can let us suffer so, until we realize that his sole purpose is to bring us closer to him. The purpose of suffering is to take us beyond all suffering. It is the driving force to be separate that is the cause of all our estrangement, and the person who extinguishes his or her self-will has no more need of sorrow.

The second category Krishna mentions is *jijnāsu,* 'those who desire to know.' It is quite an interesting group. These are people with a restless curiosity. They have tried all sorts of things in their search for fulfillment: different restaurants, different nightclubs, different countries, different drugs. But finally, after trying these things for a while, they will conclude: "Going to restaurants only makes you fat; taking drugs only leaves you addicted. There has to be more to life than this."

This kind of restlessness is what drives people to seek out anything they haven't yet seen. If there is a veil over an empty box, they *must* peek under the veil to see what's hidden inside. Mention a big hole you saw by the roadside and they won't be satisfied until they go there and see this hole for themselves. Curiosity like this is the beginning of inquiry, which is the basis of knowledge in any field. The person who is curious about the nature of the universe, for example, asks all kinds of questions that don't usually trouble the rest of us: "Where does matter go when it passes into a black hole in space? Does it fall over the edge of the universe?" This same capacity for asking questions can be transformed into asking about the meaning of life.

There is another group of people in this category, too, who have shown up often in our classes in Berkeley: those who are artistic. With a half-humorous, half-serious tone, they will confide to me, "We know we have something inside, but we just can't get it out. There's a stoppage somewhere; the flow just doesn't come." I tell them, "Why not try meditation?" Meditation can unlock the reservoir of creativity inside every one of us. Near my village in Kerala there used to live a simple, uneducated man who had received deep inspiration from one of the greatest of Indian sages, Sri Ramana Maharshi. A friend of mine told me, "This man has written some poetry. You're a professor of literature; why don't you look at his work and evaluate it?" This is a job that every professor of English has to do at times, and having been steeped in the university tradition, I took it for granted that this man's efforts couldn't amount to much. After all, what could he know about meter, or scansion, or rhetorical devices? I wasn't prepared to take him seriously, but I accepted a manuscript in what looked like a child's handwriting and read a little. I was amazed. Here was living poetry from the depths of the heart. I hadn't seen anything like it, from my colleagues or my graduate students or in any literary magazines. Since then I have tried to warn people taking to meditation, "Watch out; you may become a poet."

This leads to the fourth group, those who take to meditation because they want to know what the purpose of life is and how to fulfill it. They have discovered that making money is not living, owning an elegant home is not living, indulging the senses is not living, acquiring a position of power is not living. Now they ask, "How can we find lasting joy?" Eventually, everyone who is meditating sincerely and systematically will come to ask this question, even if they had some other purpose in mind when they began. In time, many of those who came with a particular emotional or physical problem will become interested in tapping their deeper resources, and finally they will join the ranks of those who want to know how to live in permanent peace and abiding joy.

तेषां ज्ञानी नित्ययुक्त एकभक्तिर्विशिष्यते ।
प्रियो हि ज्ञानिनो ऽत्यर्थमहं स च मम प्रियः ॥७-१७॥
उदाराः सर्व एवैते ज्ञानी त्वात्मैव मे मतम् ।
आस्थितः स हि युक्तात्मा मामेवानुत्तमां गतिम् ॥७-१८॥

17. Unwavering in devotion, always united with me, the man or woman of wisdom surpasses all the others. For such a person I am the highest goal, and he or she is very dear to me.
18. All those who follow the spiritual life are blessed. But they who are always established in union with me, for whom there is no higher goal than me, they may be regarded as my very Self.

The key word here is *nityayukta*, 'always united with me.' Such a person fills Sri Krishna's heart with joy, for with such people he can lift the hearts and relieve the suffering of many, many others.

To inspire us, Sri Krishna goes on to say in the next verse: "Whenever you see a person like that, you are seeing me." Jesus uses almost identical words when he tells his disciple Philip, "He that hath seen me hath seen the Father." It is a magnificent tribute to the many men and women over the centuries from both East and West who have devoted their lives to the Lord. Moses, Meister Eckhart, St. Teresa of Ávila, St. Francis of Assisi, John Woolman, Jalalu'l-Din Rumi, Sri Ramakrishna, Mahatma

Gandhi – all these and many others of all religions were born as we were born, suffered more than we have suffered, and yet realized the divine unity underlying life by meditating and practicing selfless living until they were united with the Lord of Love. So when we see someone seated in a corner with closed eyes, completely absorbed in meditation, it is wise to remember that he or she is not just a friend or relative, but someone through whom the Lord is beginning to do his work.

बहूनां जन्मनामन्ते ज्ञानवान्मां प्रपद्यते ।
वासुदेवः सर्वमिति स महात्मा सुदुर्लभः ॥७-१९॥

19. After many births the wise learn to meditate on me, seeing me everywhere and in everything. Such great souls are very rare.

One of the names for Sri Krishna in Sanskrit is Hari, 'the thief.' The Lord is a divine pickpocket who has stolen our heart and then sent us out into the world to search for him. People who ski on precipitous slopes or go skindiving in exotic waters are really looking for the Lord. Others are looking for him in a safe-deposit vault or on the floor of the stock exchange. Scholars think they hear him calling from the library; the expression on their faces as they enter the stacks would make you think the Lord was curled up in a rare book. But no matter what we think we are looking for, all of us suffer ultimately from a gnawing sense of deprivation at being separated from our real Self.

In this verse, the Gita is using the traditional language of reincarnation to explain why some of us take a long, long time to understand that exploits like these can never fill the vacuum within us. In this view, selfless men and women are said to be highly evolved; they have learned to see through the games we all play. It is those who have had little experience of life who are fascinated with these games. Often, for example, it is the person born into a wealthy family who is detached from money and knows how to use it wisely. He or she has enough experience with it to know its true value. For those who have only recently acquired wealth – whom my grandmother used to call "today's mushrooms after last night's rain" – everything about money is still new; everything money can buy is still exciting. Most of us have to play with material possessions a bit in order to discover that they are just toys. That is the advantage of living in an abundant economy. In a poor country, where the products of technology are expensive and hard to come by, people set a high value on material things. Take the craze for television. Our friend Sultana, who was born in Greece, tells me that when television first became available there everyone wanted to watch it, even though all the programs were in other languages which most people couldn't understand. In the United States, where there is television all around us, it shouldn't take much imagination to see that no amount of watching television can ever make us happy. The same is true for everything else in the material world. Happiness has nothing to do with having two cars in the garage, or a terraced swimming pool, or the latest dress from Paris. Happiness lies within us, and the more desires we have for this and that, the less happy we are going to be. Nothing we can buy, nothing we can own can ever fill the aching void within us, and the restlessness of modern living is really a signal from the Lord that it is time to turn inwards and find the source of all joy, wisdom, and security in our own hearts.

When we finally attain this source of joy, we shall see that there is no one in the universe but the Lord. It is not an intellectual concept; everything we see will be whole, and everything will be full of God. The beautiful expression in this verse might easily be the refrain of this volume: *Vāsudevah sarvam,* 'The Lord is everything'; there is no place where he is not found. St. Angela of Foligno uses much the same language to describe her own experience of God:

> The eyes of my soul were opened and I beheld the fullness and perfection of God, in which were comprehended the whole world, both here and beyond the sea, and the abyss and ocean of all things. In all this I saw nothing but the power of God, in a way that is beyond the power of words to explain; so that the soul, through excess of marveling, cried out with a loud voice, saying, *This whole world is full of God.*

कामैस्तैस्तैर्हृतज्ञानाः प्रपद्यन्ते ऽन्यदेवताः ।
तं तं नियममास्थाय प्रकृत्या नियताः स्वया ॥७-२०॥

20. There are others whose discrimination is misled by many desires. Following their lower nature, they worship the gods of the sense-world in their actions.

In the Hindu tradition, many of the forces which motivate our behavior are represented as gods and goddesses. There is a great deal of practical wisdom to this, because these personifications give us a vivid picture of these forces which all of us can understand. For example, people who build their lives on the pursuit of money are called devotees of Kubera, the god of wealth, who lives in a temple of twenty-four karat gold studded with sapphires, diamonds, and rubies. Each time we play the stock market or switch jobs for better pay, we are paying homage to Kubera in hopes that he will grant our desire for wealth. Kubera's devotees see opportunities for making money everywhere, and people can become so driven by this desire that they will find ways of increasing their bank account even if it means that someone else has to suffer.

Pleasure-seekers too have their god in the Hindu pantheon: Kāma, the god of selfish desire, who is portrayed as an archer with five arrows tipped with flowers – one for every sense organ – which he shoots at the hearts of his devotees. It is a comment on our times that a man's (or woman's) fancy for Kāma is no longer limited to spring; worship is continuous throughout the year.

These two desires, for money and for pleasure, are the source of most of our confusion in the modern world. This constant clamor of *I want this, I want that* makes buddhi's job impossible. Buddhi is supposed to be listening to the Ātman and making intelligent choices, but all it can hear is Kubera and Kāma trying to get it to go in a hundred different directions at once. After some time of this, we can't even imagine that there is a guiding principle in our lives at all, and we wonder why there is so little purpose in what we do.

In the West it is often the mass media that create and perform daily worship of these gods of money and sex. Now a third god is being added to the altar – the god of violence. Violence on television and in films is more than just a temporary form of excitement; these scenes of murder and assault get deep into our consciousness. Pleasure is glamorized, but instead of bringing joy, the drive for pleasure is leading to assault and molestation. Money is made the goal of life, but instead of bringing fulfillment, the craving for money and material possessions is spreading disregard for people, property, and resources. Gradually, we have become accustomed to living in a climate of fear. "Stop-thief" fashions such as handbags that sound an alarm and coats with purses sewn into their seams are featured in the stores. Homeowners and apartment dwellers are investing in elaborate, expensive alarms, closed circuit television, ultrasonic sensors, and computer-operated locks. These are advertised as security systems, but they should really be called *in*security systems because they only increase the fear of those who use them.

Those of us who have grown up under the influence of the mass media deserve sympathy and help, for it is very rare to have someone around to give us a higher alternative in life. This cannot be done by books or workshops or lectures. It has to be communicated through personal example, which is what *vijnāna* means. We cannot just settle for the intellectual approach, which is to analyze the problem and then go home; we have to show in our own lives that these spiritual ideals work. That is what Gandhi did. His whole life was a showcase for his experiments with nonviolence, not just in politics but in education and economics and many other areas too, and it had such an impact that in the long run I think historians will refer to our times not as the nuclear age but as the age of Gandhi. After all, the discovery of nuclear power only marks another revolution in technology. Gandhi's life marks a revolution of an entirely different order, for it showed that the problems we have been trying to deal with by manipulating atoms and manipulating nations can be solved for good by transforming ourselves.

Once, when a foreign correspondent asked Gandhi for a message he could take back to his paper, Gandhi wrote on a scrap of paper: "My life is my message." In this sense all of us are teachers in the example we give others, though often not in a particularly positive way. People who live for profit are a full-scale advertisement for making money the goal of life. They talk constantly about diversified investments, they vacation in Monte Carlo and Las Vegas, they dream about the Dow Jones index; everything they do advertises their way of life. Their lives are an open book for anyone who cares to observe it, and those who observe carefully will see how the lust for money robs such people of their capacity to love. On the other hand, the man or woman who lives for others is a constant reminder of the love and wisdom that come from selfless living. People like this do not need to preach or attract attention to themselves; we cannot help being drawn to them and drawing inspiration from their life.

यो यो यां यां तनुं भक्तः श्रद्धयार्चितुमिच्छति ।
तस्य तस्याचलां श्रद्धां तामेव विदधाम्यहम् ॥७-२१॥
स तया श्रद्धया युक्तस्तस्या राधनमीहते ।
लभते च ततः कामान्मयैव विहितान्हि तान् ॥७-२२॥

21. When a man is devoted to something with complete faith, I unify his faith in that.
22. Then, when his faith is completely unified, one gains the object of his devotion. In this way, every desire is fulfilled by me.

There is a haunting verse in the Brihadāranyaka Upanishad which says:

You are what your deep, driving desire is.
As your deep, driving desire is, so is your will;
As your will is, so is your deed;
As your deed is, so is your destiny.

The key word here is one of the most important terms in the Gita: *shraddhā*. *Shraddhā* has a wealth of meanings; it may be a deep desire, or strong conditioning, or the underlying assumptions which shape our thoughts and actions. The basic meaning is faith – not just intellectual adherence to something, but what we believe in, what we trust in, in our heart of hearts. Shraddhā is the key to life. It is our shraddhā, our conditioned assumptions, that shapes our thoughts and actions, and it is our shraddhā, our faith, that shapes our will and our destiny. We become what our shraddhā is, because all of us live out what we believe and desire in the deepest recesses of our consciousness.

The ancient Greek story about Midas is a story of shraddhā. Midas was obsessed with gold. He may have thought he was a man of many interests – music, horticulture, Olympian wines – but in the depths of his consciousness, his deepest belief was that wealth is the source of all joy. He found himself thinking about gold, dreaming about gold, wanting gold more and more as time went on. Gradually, without realizing it, he was thinking about nothing else. He wanted everything he touched to be turned to gold, just as there are people who want everything they do to make them a profit or bring them a little power or pleasure. And – so the story goes – the gods granted his desire. Midas got up one morning, picked up his toothbrush, and in an instant it turned to gold. Midas was ecstatic. In delight he hopped around touching everything in his palace and watching it turn to gold.

After a while, however, the novelty wore off, and Midas sat down to have some breakfast. He tried some grapes, but they turned to gold. So did his toast, and his egg, and even his Greek coffee. Midas was a little irritated; he was hungry, and he had enough imagination to suspect that there might not be much future in eating now that he had this golden touch. It raised some questions which he didn't feel like thinking about before breakfast. A little subdued, he went out to his garden to take his mind off his stomach. It was a beautiful Mediterranean morning. The roses he had been cultivating so carefully were still filled with the first liquid rays of the sun. Their beauty took him by surprise, and he bent over to pick one for his table. But in an instant the lovely petals turned into harsh, cold metal.

Midas was beginning to get the picture. He threw the gold rose into the bushes and muttered some bad Greek. Then, suddenly, he looked up and saw his little daughter running to greet him. Her smile was so bright that he forgot all about his golden toast and his golden rose, and he reached down joyfully to take her into his arms. The instant he touched her, she too turned into gold, leaving only a lifeless statue for him to love. At last Midas understood. Weeping, he fell to the ground and begged the gods to take away his curse.

Most of us, fortunately, are not as obsessed as Midas was. But his fate is not as fanciful as it might seem. Midas's shraddhā was in gold; for others it might be property, or power, or personal pleasure, but the result is very much the same. When we get caught in these things, we begin to mold our lives around them. All our capacity to love is trapped in getting what we desire, and without really wanting to, we begin to treat those around us as only figures in a game. Seen through our shraddhā, they are scarcely real at all, and there are people who spend their whole lives together without ever really seeing each other, just because of their preoccupation with themselves.

There is no point in blaming people like this; to some extent, this is the conditioning of our times, and all of us have been affected by it. But all of us have the capacity to change our shraddhā. Through the practice of meditation, we can learn to withdraw our trust from the things that separate us from others – wealth and pleasure, power and prestige – and place it more and more in what contributes to the welfare of us all.

अन्तवत्तु फलं तेषां तद्भवत्यल्पमेधसाम् ।
देवान्देवयजो यान्ति मद्भक्ता यान्ति मामपि ॥७-२३॥

23. Those whose understanding is small attain only transient satisfaction. Those who worship the gods of the sense-world go to the gods of the sense-world, but my devotees come to me.

Every deep desire is a prayer. In the deepest levels of our consciousness all of us are praying constantly, and when the prayer is intense enough and consistent enough, we will live out our lives in such a way that that prayer is answered. The difference is in what we pray for. If we worship the gods of the sense-world – wealth, power, pleasure, status – we will get more and more caught up in the world of change. Every day we will play that old game with the mirror: "Mirror, mirror on the wall, how am I doing?" And more and more often the mirror will reply, "Not so hot." But if we try to give all our love to the Lord of Love, Sri Krishna reminds us, we will gradually become unaffected by any change, even the great change called death.

Here again, the key to understanding this is shraddhā. Shraddhā supports our whole outlook on life. Everyone has faith in something; we cannot live without faith. When I get into our Volvo I have faith in the people who make Volvos. I take it for granted that there is still an engine there, that the wheels won't fall off, that the steering wheel is connected to something; that is shraddhā. When I take my friends out for ice cream in Berkeley and pay for it with little green pieces of paper, that is shraddhā which the storekeeper and I and everyone else in the country all share. If we didn't have this common shraddhā, the entire economy would collapse. Without shraddhā, we would be questioning everything; there would be time for nothing but worry.

It's very much like this at a deeper level, too. Just as we all share this belief in money, without which this whole game of buying and selling would collapse, so we all share the deep conviction that we are separate, that we are the body, that our nature and behavior are conditioned by our genes. In this verse, Sri Krishna is reminding us that the more we identify with the world of prakriti, the physical world of change, the more we will be subject to the ravages of time and eventually death. But by placing our shraddhā in the Lord, who is our real Self, we gradually come to remember our real nature, and the passage of time affects us less and less. Finally, when our faith in God is unshakable, we are united with him completely. Then, when the time comes to shed this body, there is no rupture in consciousness, any more than there is when we pass from one room to another.

This is the promise Sri Krishna is giving us in this verse. Faith in this promise is the highest kind of shraddhā. It is not blind faith; it is the trust in spiritual values, the confidence in their applicability, that comes as our experience deepens. We don't just go to bed one night and wake up with perfect faith; as the lives of all the great mystics show us, shraddhā grows over a long period of time, as we try these timeless values out in our own lives. All that the mystics ask at the beginning is that we trust them enough to give what they say a try.

This is much the way a scientist works. A scientist like Sir Isaac Newton doesn't build theories out of faith; his faith is in the method. He says, "Well, there is some reason to think that the fall of this apple and the motion of the moon *are* related; let's see if that proves true." He doesn't say they are related; he says, "Let's see." He has enough shraddhā in the idea to try it out; and gradually, after many experiments, his faith in a uniform force of gravity is unshakable.

Most of us, after this, never repeat these experiments, but we *do* trust the conclusion. At the most, I might go to the top of the campanile tower at our campus and drop a marble and a bowling ball at the same time, and when they landed at the same time, I would just say "Good, it *does* act equally on unequal masses" and be done with it. A great mystic like St. Francis of Assisi or Sri Ramakrishna would ask us gently, "Don't you at least trust us as much as Galileo or Sir Isaac Newton? We're not telling you about things we've read about or things we've heard from others; we're telling you what we know, from a lifetime of personal experience."

There is a story much like this in the Buddhist tradition. The Compassionate Buddha was once speaking to a large number of villagers about nirvāna and the way it can be attained. After he had finished, one of them asked: "Blessed One, everything you have told us about nirvāna is wonderful. All of us would like to go beyond sorrow and death. But this Eightfold Path of yours isn't easy, and if it doesn't work we would have thrown our lives away in looking for the impossible. How do we know there *is* a nirvāna that people like us can attain?"

The Buddha smiled. "Are there any mountains to the north of here?" he asked.

"Of course," the villager answered; "the Himālayas."

"How do you know? Have you been to see these 'Himālayas'?"

"No," the man admitted, "but everybody says they're there. My father has told me all about them; they're the source of the Ganges and it has to come from somewhere."

"Has your father seen these mountains?"

"No, but he heard all about them from *his* father, whose uncle went there on pilgrimage many years ago."

"Perhaps this uncle had a vivid imagination."

"Oh, no, he wouldn't have misled us like that! Everyone remembers him as a very honest man."

"My friend," said the Compassionate Buddha gently, "if you have such faith in the words of someone whom you know of only by hearsay, don't you think you can have faith in someone who has seen nirvāna and who stands in the flesh before you?"

अव्यक्तं व्यक्तिमापन्नं मन्यन्ते मामबुद्धयः ।
परं भावमजानन्तो ममाव्ययमनुत्तमम् ॥७-२४॥

24. Through lack of understanding, people believe that I, the Unmanifest, have been born as a person. They fail to realize my true nature, which transcends birth and death.

Shankara, the great saint from Kerala state in India, has a profoundly inspiring invocation which begins, "O Thou from whom all words recoil." This is the supreme, unmanifested Reality, called Brahman in the Sanskrit scriptures. Brahman cannot be described, for It has no attributes. As a youth, Shankara wanted to have the famous seer Gaudapāda teach him how to realize Brahman. After an extensive search, he finally found Gaudapāda on the banks of the river Narmadā. But when Shankara asked him to be his teacher, the sage refused. He had resolved to remain absorbed in union with the total Godhead, in which state there is no teacher and no one to teach. So he directed Shankara to his foremost disciple, the sage Govindapāda, who had realized the personal form of God.

In the ancient Hindu scriptures, union with the impersonal Godhead is called *nirvikalpa samādhi*. This is a state of pure, undifferentiated consciousness, and it is attained by very few. The more devotional form of union with God is called *savikalpa samādhi,* or union with the personal God. Devotees are absorbed in meditation on the Lord, but they still have one foot in the world of dualism. There is still a difference between subject and object for them, and they remain devotees who are in communion with the Lord.

For the vast majority of us, limited as we are by our human condition, it is not possible to love the impersonal Godhead. We may feel intellectually attracted to the concept, but intellectual attraction is not enough. In order to undergo the tremendous transformation of personality that the spiritual life demands, we need a personal form of God that we can love, an embodied ideal that can draw us with all our heart. So Sri Ramakrishna says that God is with form and without form: the formless Godhead seems to take on form through the powerful lens of the devotee's love.

In an earlier verse in the Gita, Sri Krishna explains that whenever the human condition becomes heartbreaking, the Lord of Love is born on earth in the form of a human being, to rekindle our love for God. In Sanskrit this is called an *avatāra* or divine incarnation: someone like Jesus the Christ, or Sri Krishna, or the Compassionate Buddha. Laughing like us, talking like us, weeping like us, the incarnation of God seems to pass like us through all the changes of birth and death. But though the Lord allows himself to appear limited in this way, he is really beyond all limitation. Later, in chapter eleven, Sri Krishna will lift the veil of his Māyā for an instant to remove his disguise and reveal to Arjuna his cosmic form as Lord of the universe, who transcends all space and time.

I sometimes amuse my friends by imagining how our dogs and cats must think of God. It is a very helpful shift in perspective. Our dog Muka would tell his friend Hebbles, "What's all this talk about God as a human incarnation? God has four legs and a tail, and his barking resounds throughout the universe." And the cats would be saying, "Those dogs have no sense; *bow-wow* is all they know. God must be a cosmic Cat, filling the universe with an endless *meow*." It's easy to laugh at this sort of talk from dogs and cats, but we need to keep the same sense of humor with regard to our own quarrels about God. We too are trying to limit what cannot be limited, to confine in words that which cannot be confined.

नाहं प्रकाशः सर्वस्य योगमायासमावृतः ।
मूढो ऽयं नाभिजानाति लोको मामजमव्ययम् ॥७-२५॥

25. Few see through my veil of Māyā; not knowing that I am without birth and changeless, the world is deluded.

The ice show we took our nieces to see recently is a good example of how Māyā works. Just before the show started, the stadium was plunged into darkness. After a fanfare of trumpets, lights of blue, gold, and rose began to play on the ice rink, and one by one, graceful figures in beautiful costumes came gliding onto the ice. Usually our finances give us the privilege of watching shows like this from afar, and distance makes the view even more enchanting. From our position the skaters were incredibly graceful, showing skill which must have taken years to develop. The costumes, the tinted lights, the makeup which must have taken an hour to apply, all made everyone appear breathtakingly beautiful. It was only after Māyā's show was over and the skaters had removed their makeup and shed their costumes for street clothes that I could see their real beauty, which came not from these external trappings but from the Lord of Love within us all.

Imagine watching an ice show for so long that you forget when you came in. It would never occur to you that there was a world outside, or that there was something much more real than greasepaint and tinted lights. The stadium would be your universe. Doesn't Hamlet say, "I could be bounded in a nutshell and count myself a king of infinite space"? You would spend your life studying the performances and analyzing the costumes, and if someone were to suggest that you turn in your ticket and get your money back you would object, "What are you talking about? This is the only show in town."

In a great leap of insight, the Hindu scriptures will tell us that all this world of separateness and change is Māyā, from the farthest galaxy to the body itself. Everything that is prakriti is Māyā, which means everything that is subject to change – not only matter, but mind and ego as well. Even the passage of time has no reality apart from the mind. Vast and varied as this universe is, it is only the surface of reality. It is real, just as a dream is real to the dreamer, but like a dream it is a lower level of reality out of which we can awaken.

We are so captivated by the promises of this dream that we do not want to wake up; in fact, we cannot even imagine what waking up would be like. All our attention is on the dream. But the mystics of all religions assure us that as our longing for fulfillment becomes more and more acute, and our dreams become more and more stale, we will begin to struggle to wake up into the state of joy. This is the touch of grace. As Sri Ramakrishna says, once the Divine Mother casts a glance at you out of the corner of her lovely eyes, the blandishments of Māyā will begin to fade. And when you finally awaken, you will rub your eyes in wonder that you ever could have been taken in by this dream of separate existence.

The wonder of this awakening can never be expressed in words, but it can be glimpsed in some of the marvelous stories we have in the Hindu tradition. One of these stories is about a famous sage named Nārada. Nārada was deeply devoted to Sri Krishna, and there are many stories told in the scriptures about their adventures together. One day, it is said, Nārada was taking a walk with Sri Krishna. The Lord was very pleased with his devotee and told him to ask for a boon, anything he might desire. Now, Nārada was already illumined. He had no personal desires worth speaking of, so he had to think some time before he could come up with an answer. Finally he remembered something even he had never understood, for all the breadth and depth of his spiritual experience. "Lord," he said, "explain to me how you have become the cosmos, from the smallest atom to the greatest star. Tell me how in every being you hide yourself in countless forms, so that people never see that beneath all life there is only One. Show me how you hide yourself as many; tell me the secret of your Māyā."

Sri Krishna smiled and did not answer immediately, for the secret of

Māyā is the final riddle of existence. But he had to say something; after all, he had given his word. "All right, Nārada," he said. "But first, I am very thirsty; will you please bring me a glass of water?"

The sun was burning fiercely in the tropical sky, but Nārada ignored the heat and immediately set off for the nearest house to fetch some water. It took some time, for the village across the rice fields that had seemed so near proved to be a much longer walk than he had guessed. The sun went down, and his feet grew tired; he began to think he might as well ask for *two* glasses of water, and drink the second one himself.

At last, very tired and thirsty, Nārada reached the village and knocked at the door of the very first house he saw. Who should open the door but a breathtakingly beautiful girl, who looked at him with such lovely dark eyes that he forgot all about his thirst. Nārada did not know what to say. He hemmed and hawed, and all the time he was hemming and hawing she just stood there with a gentle smile, looking at him with those eyes. Finally he blurted out, "Will you marry me?"

They got married and settled down, and Nārada was very happy. They had children, then some more children, and the children all graduated from school and got jobs in the village and settled down. Gradually, one by one, their children too got married and had children of their own. The years flew by. Nārada became the patriarch of a great dynasty; everything he turned his hand to prospered, and his family became a hundred strong, until their fields stretched for miles around.

Then, one day, a terrible flood overcame the village. It swept away cottages, it swept away cattle and human beings, and it devastated the land. Before his eyes, everyone in his family was drowned except Nārada, who was overwhelmed by grief. In a matter of hours, everything he had built up around him over the years – wife, family, home and lands – had been wiped out. With nowhere else to turn he cried out from the depths of his heart, "Help me, Lord!"

Immediately, as if a veil were lifted from his eyes, Nārada saw Sri Krishna standing before him with the peacock feather dancing in his hair and a playful smile on his lips, looking just as he had so many years before. "Nārada," Sri Krishna asked gently, "where is my glass of water?"

Then Nārada remembered, and he fell at the feet of the Lord. In one tremendous insight he had seen the nature of Sri Krishna's divine play.

वेदाहं समतीतानि वर्तमानानि चार्जुन ।
भविष्याणि च भूतानि मां तु वेद न कश्चन ॥७-२६॥

26. I know everything about the past, the present, and the future, Arjuna; but there is no one who knows me completely.

Until the end of the nineteenth century, I think, astronomers took it for granted that the Milky Way galaxy was the whole of the universe. Any student who questioned that would have been failed on the spot. Now, less than three quarters of a century later, we know that there are a billion galaxies within the limits of the observable universe alone. Our own sun used to be the featured player in the drama of astronomy, everybody taking orders from him, everybody dependent on him; now he is just another extra. It's like taking Hamlet and giving him a job holding a spear in the wings; if he doesn't want to come, there are lots of others the Lord can call. When the first quasar was discovered, a lot of prestigious astronomers got together and agreed that it was just another star within our galaxy. It took only a few years for these same men and women to realize that this was actually something a million million times brighter than our sun, and so far removed from our galaxy that our imagination fails to grasp it. This is the nature of scientific knowledge: it grows through trial and error, and it is always capable of growing more; there is no end to it.

Scientific knowledge, in other words, is confined to the everchanging realm of prakriti. Its mode of knowing is the intellect, which can only proceed by dividing something further; that is why intellectual inquiry can never satisfy us with a last word. In Spinoza's language, this is all knowledge of the surface world. It can tell us a lot about the ripples, but it can never see below the surface to the vast ocean in which all these ripples are held together in one whole. That's why I'm so fond of that image of Sri Krishna wearing the galaxies in a garland about his neck. Until recently, astronomers have been studying one bead in this necklace. Now we have discovered there are two beads, and everyone is very excited: remember, each of these is a little cosmos much vaster than we can comprehend. Who knows? At the end of the century we may have even found a few beads more. But the mystics, though they may be deeply impressed by the beauty of all these worlds, understand that this is a necklace that simply has no end. They are not satisfied with two or three beads; they want to realize the Wearer.

The only way to understand creation is to know the Creator: after all, he wrote all the rules, which is just another way of saying he is the source, the underlying unity, from which all the laws of nature derive. As the Upanishads say, "What is that One by knowing which all other things are known?" This knowledge is jnāna, knowledge of the unity of life, whose laws never need to be revised. Astronomy textbooks have to be rewritten every few years; sometimes they are outdated while they are on the press. But a scripture like the Bhagavad Gita, or the Sermon on the Mount, or the Dhammapada of the Buddha can never become dated. The values these scriptures teach – patience, for example – are as valuable now as they were five thousand years ago. And five thousand years from now, when we may be transporting ourselves to other solar systems and eating algae in undersea restaurants with mermaids to serve us and Neptune at the till, we will still need patience in order to be at peace.

इच्छाद्वेषसमुत्थेन द्वंद्वमोहेन भारत ।
सर्वभूतानि संमोहं सर्गे यान्ति परंतप ॥७-२७॥

27. Delusion arises from the duality of
attraction and aversion, O Bhārata; every
creature is deluded by these from birth.

The Compassionate Buddha had a rather mischievous saying: "Not to have that which we want is sorrow; to have that which we do not want is sorrow." We have conditioned our nervous systems to one-way traffic only – away from what we dislike towards what we like. This is all right as long as everything is going our way, but unfortunately, all too often things are going someone else's way instead. Then it's as if everybody in town has decided to stage a motor parade down our one-way street the wrong way. The nervous system screams in protest, which it lets us hear about in all kinds of ways: tension, headaches, asthma, peptic ulcer, numbness in the toes. Most of us respond to this by putting up bigger and bigger one-way signs: "Stop! Do not enter! Go back! This means *you*." The Buddha would say, this isn't going to work; life *is* two-way traffic, and there isn't any way to change it. Instead of trying to make life fit us, it makes more sense to accommodate our roads to traffic in both directions. Then if things go our way, of course we will be pleased, but if things don't go our way we will be just as even-tempered and enthusiastic as before. For a long time in meditation this is what most of us are doing: reconditioning the nervous system to accept two-way traffic.

The Katha Upanishad gives us two words that shed light on this reconditioning: *preya* and *shreya*. Preya is what is pleasant now, though in the long run it leads to insecurity and distress. Shreya is what is permanently beneficial, though it sometimes seems unpleasant at first. We are so poorly educated in the art of living that we prefer temporary satisfaction, even though it may lead to permanent loss, to the adventure of bearing a temporary displeasure that leads to permanent fulfillment.

We have to make this choice between preya and shreya continually every day. When we see a chocolate éclair in the bakery window, for example, the immediate appeal of it is so great that before we know it we have gone into the bakery, eaten one or two, and bought a dozen to take home. It never occurs to us that we have a choice. There is a chocolate éclair in the window; we *like* chocolate éclairs; therefore we must go in and eat one. For two minutes of satisfaction we eat something that gives us cavities and puts on fat. But just as we have developed a taste for wrong food, so with a little effort we can develop a taste for food that is nutritious. I remember trying chocolate candy for the first time when I was a teenager in India; it took several tries before I could develop a taste for it. We may not be mad about whole-grain bread or green salads, but by cultivating a taste for food that is healthy and learning to prepare it with a creative flair, we can soon become as enthusiastic about fresh garden vegetables as we are about chocolate éclairs.

Like our habits of likes and dislikes in eating, tension too develops only with sustained practice. This is particularly true in personal relationships. The collision of likes and dislikes is greatest in situations where we have to work closely with other people. After all, they have likes and dislikes too, and theirs are not likely to be the same as ours. So one of the most effective ways of reducing tension is to learn to work harmoniously even with people who do not do things our way. In our ashram family all of us were raised in different homes, but we have all learned the skill of working together harmoniously. At first it was far from easy. In the kitchen, for example, one person liked to keep the salt near the stove, another used to put it in a cupboard; then the first would search through the cupboards to find the salt and put it back near the stove. In every little detail, agitation can creep in. Even the way food is served can be a source of irritation. The clever voice of the ego ventriloquist is constantly whispering inside, "I don't like this; that's not the right way." When this goes on inside us for many years, our nerves gradually get more and more tense until at last we cannot bear to live with others; we have to live alone.

It is by reversing this process of estrangement and doing what adds to the joy of others that we release ourselves little by little from the tyranny of likes and dislikes. For example, in taking a job we can look for something that benefits others instead of something that happens to pay very well or offers an office overlooking San Francisco Bay. At home we can learn to enjoy our partner's Waldorf salad even though we can't stand walnuts, or join in our children's four-square game now and then, or look for projects like a backyard vegetable garden which the whole family can enjoy together. When we begin looking upon everything as an opportunity to draw closer to others, the days of the ego are numbered.

येषां त्वन्तगतं पापं जनानां पुण्यकर्मणाम् ।
ते द्वंद्वमोहनिर्मुक्ता भजन्ते मां दृढव्रताः ॥७-२८॥

28. But those who have freed themselves from all wrongdoing are firmly established in worship of me. Their actions are pure, and they are free from the delusion caused by the pairs of opposites.

Dvandva, the 'pairs of opposites' – happiness and sorrow, good and bad, pleasure and pain, and all the rest – are the very texture of Māyā. Self-will thrives on these dualities, especially likes and dislikes; they are the ego's way of self-expression. In every country and every community, no matter whether rich or poor, there is a rare type of person who from birth has very little self-will, who can forbear and forgive very easily. People like this are like freestone peaches; you have only to open them up and the seed of self-will falls out easily. The vast majority of us, however, are cling-peach types. With cling peaches, the seed seems glued to the rest of the peach. Not only does it not fall out easily; you have to put in a lot of effort prying all around it with a sharp knife in order to pull the seed out and throw it away. The knife the Lord gives each of us to perform this operation of ego-extraction is double-edged; it has patience on one side and suffering on the other. Unfortunately, we have no choice but to use this knife as long as we cling to our likes and dislikes. But, Sri Ramakrishna would say, we don't have to go on clinging forever. No one is making us cling but ourselves, and it is up to us to let go.

The more you learn to change your likes and dislikes at will, the more clearly you will be able to see the core of purity and selflessness that is the real Self in everyone. This is seldom easy. Some people *are* a little more irritating and self-willed than others; there is no doubt about it. But instead of criticizing such people, which only makes their alienation worse, you can focus all your attention on what is best in them. This is one of the most practical skills I have learned from my grandmother, and it can be tremendously effective in helping those around you. It is something like turning a flashlight on a particular spot. I don't diffuse my attention to take in both positive and negative behavior; I keep concentrating on what is kind, what is generous, what is selfless, and the amazing response is that this kind of support draws out and strengthens these very qualities. Not only that, as they become more secure, such people begin to spread this consideration to their other relationships too.

My grandmother had a very pungent phrase for difficult people: "A lash in the eye." We all know from experience how an eyelash in the eye can be so irritating that we just cannot think about anything else. That is exactly how difficult people affect those around them. But for the mystics, this lash in the eye is an opportunity for learning the skills in life that matter most: patience, forgiveness, and freedom from likes and dislikes. They will go and put their arm around someone who has been a thorn in their flesh and say with gratitude, "Without you, how could I ever have learned to be patient? How could I have learned to forgive?"

जरामरणमोक्षाय मामाश्रित्य यतन्ति ये ।
ते ब्रह्म तद्विदुः कृत्स्नमध्यात्मं कर्म चाखिलम् ॥७-२९॥

29. Those who take refuge in me, striving for liberation from old age and death, come to know Brahman, the Self, and the nature of all action.

Growing up close to my grandmother, I had the blessing of hearing early in life the tremendous truth that you and I are not this finite, mortal body but an eternal, immortal force. As a child I used to run home from school every afternoon to be with my grandmother, and every afternoon I would find her standing by the front gate waiting for me. Eagerly I would tell her everything that had happened that day – what I had learned in school, what the teacher had said, what had happened on the playing field. One day, though, I came walking slowly up the road with a cloud of gloom over my face. "What's the matter?" my grandmother asked. "Bad news, Granny," I said. "Today in geography our teacher told us that compared to the sun, we are just insignificant bits of dust." She laughed. "This sun will burn out," she replied, "but you and I will never come to an end."

This is true of every one of us. You and I were never born; therefore we will never die. We are not limited to this physical body; our real Self is divine. Compared with this Self, our sun is just a youngster. Astronomers tell us that it was born perhaps five billion years ago, long after countless millions of similar stars had come, blazed out their lives, and passed away; and, like them, in a few more billion years it will exhaust itself and die. Everything in the created world is part of this continuous process of birth and change and death. But this will in no way affect the Self, the eternal witness within your body and mine.

In the climax of meditation called samādhi we rise above physical consciousness completely, once and for all, to realize that this body is only an instrument which has been given us to use for the benefit of all. In these violent times, each one of us has a crucial role to play in reversing the destructive trends we see around us. Here Mahatma Gandhi gives a personal example we can all follow. So influential was his daily life that Nehru said of him, "Where he sat became a temple; where he trod was holy ground." We too can learn to make our contribution wherever we go by living not for our personal satisfaction but for the welfare of all – as the Buddha would say, *bahujanahitāya, bahujanasukhāya,* 'for the welfare of the many, for the happiness of the many.'

साधिभूताधिदैवं मां साधियज्ञं च ये विदुः ।
प्रयाणकाले ऽपि च मां ते विदुर्युक्तचेतसः ॥७-३०॥

30. Those who see me ruling the cosmos, who see me
in the adhibhūta, the adhidaiva, and the adhiyajna,
are conscious of me even at the time of death.

In this verse Sri Krishna uses three rather technical terms from the Upanishads. Arjuna is not familiar with these terms; he is a man of action, not a philosopher, and in the next chapter he will ask Sri Krishna to explain this verse. Here, however, he is completely absorbed in what the Lord is telling him about the time of death.

When we take to the spiritual life and begin to practice meditation, we come to see into the heart of life, and our awareness of unity in the world around us deepens immensely. Finally, we come to see the presence of the Lord everywhere: in the sky, in the sun and moon, in animals and birds, and of course in the "human face divine." For the God-conscious person, the wind sighing in the trees whispers of God; the waves sweeping across the beach sing the mantram. Everything is pervaded by the presence of the Lord.

When the mind is permeated like this with consciousness of God, there is no rupture in consciousness at the time of death. My grandmother sowed the seed of this awareness in me while I was still a child. Every morning she would go to our ancestral temple to worship Lord Shiva. On returning home she always placed a flower from the temple behind my ear with this simple blessing: "May you be like Mārkandeya." In the Hindu scriptures, Mārkandeya is an illumined teenager whose parents had prayed for a son who would be completely devoted to Lord Shiva. Their prayer was granted, but with the sad condition that the boy would die on his sixteenth birthday. As a baby, Mārkandeya's first words were, "Shiva, Shiva," and his love for the Lord grew daily until it filled his consciousness.

Finally, however, the day of his sixteenth birthday dawned. His parents, overcome by grief, came to him and told him that Yama, the King of Death, would claim him that very day. When he heard this, Mārkandeya sat down in deep meditation and became united with Shiva, who is known as the Conqueror of Death. When Yama appeared to claim his victim, from the depths of Mārkandeya's meditation Lord Shiva arose to protect his young devotee. Placing one hand on Mārkandeya's head in infinite love, and with the other pointing his trident at the King of Death, Lord Shiva said, "Don't you know that anyone who takes refuge at my feet has gone beyond your power? Mārkandeya has now become immortal through my grace." This is the secret of going beyond death, on which Sri Krishna will elaborate in the following chapter.

ज्ञानविज्ञानयोगो नाम सप्तमोऽध्यायः ॥ ७ ॥

CHAPTER EIGHT

The Eternal Godhead

अर्जुन उवाच ।
किं तद्ब्रह्म किमध्यात्मं किं कर्म पुरुषोत्तम ।
अधिभूतं च किं प्रोक्तमधिदैवं किमुच्यते ॥८-१॥
अधियज्ञः कथं को ऽत्र देहे ऽस्मिन्मधुसूदन ।
प्रयाणकाले च कथं ज्ञेयो ऽसि नियतात्मभिः ॥८-२॥
श्रीभगवानुवाच ।
अक्षरं ब्रह्म परमं स्वभावो ऽध्यात्ममुच्यते ।
भूतभावोद्भवकरो विसर्गः कर्मसंज्ञितः ॥८-३॥
अधिभूतं क्षरो भावः पुरुषश्चाधिदैवतम् ।
अधियज्ञो ऽहमेवात्र देहे देहभृतां वर ॥८-४॥

ARJUNA:

1. O Krishna, what is Brahman, and what is the nature of action? What is the adhyātma, the adhibhūta, the adhidaiva?
2. What is the adhiyajna, the supreme sacrifice, and how is it to be offered? How are the self-controlled united with you at the time of death?

SRI KRISHNA:

3. My highest nature, the imperishable Brahman, gives every creature its existence and lives in every creature as the adhyātma. My action is creation and the bringing forth of creatures.

4. The adhibhūta is the perishable body; the adhidaiva is Purusha, eternal spirit. The adhiyajna, the supreme sacrifice, is made to me as the Lord within you.

This chapter begins like a seminar. Sri Krishna has just told Arjuna how to go beyond death, but he is teasing him by using words which Arjuna does not understand. So Arjuna keeps asking, "What does this mean? What about that?" Then he hesitates, his face full of doubt. There is still one more question. He has saved it until last because it bothers him most. Now his tone changes, and he asks in simple, direct words the searching question that has troubled thoughtful people in all religions. "At the time of the great change called death, how can I remember you in the depths of my consciousness? How can I become united with you and go beyond death?" The answer to this question is the theme of chapter eight.

The Chāndogya Upanishad, one of the oldest of the Sanskrit scriptures, tells us about a young man named Shvetaketu who has just returned home from the ancient Indian equivalent of our University of California. Having completed his formal education, Shvetaketu now wants to learn how to live, and he asks his father to teach him the secret of Brahman. In reply, his father gives him one of the greatest spiritual formulas anywhere in mystical literature: *Tat tvam asi*, 'That thou art': Brahman, the supreme Reality, and Ātman, our real Self, are one and the same.

This is a very difficult concept to understand, but the Upanishads bring it out with a vivid image. They say that this very Brahman, who is beyond all change and limitation, has brought all things into existence as a spider spins her web out of herself. It is not so much a process of creation as of emanation. A spider doesn't need to go out to a yarn shop and buy fine silk thread for her web; she has everything she needs right within her. Similarly, the creative power of the Godhead, Māyā, spins out the cosmos so that a little bit of the Godhead is present everywhere. Sri Ramakrishna will say that these two – Brahman and Māyā, the Godhead and the power that creates and dissolves Its creation – are inseparable, like fire and its power to burn. We cannot imagine fire without the power to burn, or the burning power of fire without the fire itself. Similarly, Sri Krishna is reminding us, it is just as absurd to talk about the cosmos as separate from the Lord, who is present everywhere and in every being.

In living creatures, this divine presence is called *adhyātma*, the Ātman or Self. *Adhibhūta* refers to the countless seemingly separate houses in which this Self dwells, of which our own body is one. This house is constantly changing. Only a while ago we were toddlers, as sweet and angelic as any baby we see today. Just look at your old baby pictures and you cannot help wondering what happened to that wide-eyed child of not too many years ago. With the passage of time the body inevitably undergoes certain natural changes, the last of which is death. The dweller within the body, however, is unaffected by these changes.

The implication is that the body is only a powerful tool which the Lord lends us for this life. He trusts us to look after this tool, and to recycle it when our time is up; but we are not it, and it is not ours to do with as we like. Just as there are specific steps to follow in caring for more conventional power tools like ripsaws or hedge clippers, there are specific steps we should take to keep our body healthy, too. We should eat nourishing food, get plenty of vigorous exercise every day and our full quota of sleep every night, and find time for wholesome recreation with our family. We don't have to fall for the belief that good food can be had only in gourmet restaurants; we can prepare good-tasting, nutritious meals at home and share them with family and friends. We don't have to go to an expensive health club for exercise; a good, brisk walk is excellent exercise at any age. All these things help to keep the body strong and the nervous system resilient, which are particularly important in the practice of meditation.

Adhidaiva refers to the Lord as the Inner Controller in all. It doesn't apply only to human beings; it means that the Lord is present as the Operator in all the natural forces around us. In the sun he generates heat and light; in the tree he makes new branches grow and blossom. The force of gravitation, the energy transformations in a cell, the beating of our hearts all take place under his direction, not from without but from within.

The next term, *adhiyajna*, refers to Him to whom any real sacrifice in life is made. It is a rather subtle concept. Whenever we give up something for the sake of others – a movie we want to see, a vacation we want to take, the money we'd like to spend on ourselves – it is really an offering, not so much to others as to our real Self. It is not that others do not benefit from these things; they do. But it is we who benefit most, because it is we who grow.

All spiritual progress requires the sacrifice of self-will, not so much in one grand gesture as in a thousand and one little acts of thoughtfulness during the day. The responsibility for making this sacrifice rests squarely on each one of us; no one can do it for us. Spiritual teachers are like signposts pointing the way to immortality, but it is we who must make the journey. This is quite reasonable. After all, when we pass a signpost on the freeway, we don't expect it to get into the driver's seat and do the driving while we lie down in the back to take a nap. Similarly, we cannot expect other people to pick us up and carry us along the spiritual path. It is up to us to meditate regularly and with sustained enthusiasm, and to reduce our separateness from others in every way we can.

Since most of us have rather large amounts of self-will, we cannot expect to get rid of it overnight. Those who are terribly eager may expect to put all their self-will and selfishness in one big truck and cart it all to the dump. Unfortunately, there is no truck big enough, and even if there were we would not have the strength to get all our self-will into it. The safest and simplest method for people like us is to cart off a little bit of selfishness every day, day after day, year after year, until one day we find to our great surprise that all our separateness has been removed. Then the compulsive identification with body and mind will be completely broken, and death will be no more a change than taking off a jacket, hanging it up, and going home. The Sufi mystic al-Ghazzali puts this beautifully in a poem composed while he was dying:

When my friends weep over my dead body,
Ask them, Do you mistake him to be this?
Tell them I swear in the name of the Lord
That this dead body is not I. It was
My dress when I lived on earth; I wore it
During my stay there.

अन्तकाले च मामेव स्मरन्मुक्त्वा कलेवरम् ।
यः प्रयाति स मद्भावं याति नास्त्यत्र संशयः ॥८-५॥
यं यं वापि स्मरन्भावं त्यजत्यन्ते कलेवरम् ।
तं तमेवैति कौन्तेय सदा तद्भावभावितः ॥८-६॥

5. Those who remember me at the time of death will come to me. Do not doubt this.
6. Whatever occupies the mind at the time of death determines the destination of the dying.

These verses are a quiet statement of a powerful spiritual law. Whatever we think about most, whatever we labor for most, whatever we desire most, that will be the content of our consciousness at the time of death. When we think about something constantly, it sinks deep into our consciousness, and when the time for death comes we will be able to think of nothing else. The Hindu and Buddhist mystics say that at that time the powerful desires in our deeper consciousness will explode like a depth charge, sending us into the next life.

There is a great deal of interest in reincarnation in the West today. Almost every week it seems I get mail announcing some workshop in rebirth, in which people talk about who they were in previous lives. I usually ask, "Don't they want to know who they are in *this* life?" It's a much more pressing question. But I must admit that reincarnation, as it is presented in the Sanskrit scriptures, offers a powerful explanation of how we shape our lives by our deep desires.

The Upanishads throw light on reincarnation in a very scientific way. Psychologists will tell us that in sleep we pass in and out of the state of dreaming and the deep, restful state of dreamless sleep. In the Upanishads, these levels of awareness – waking, dreaming, and dreamless sleep – are said to be only different orders of reality. In dreaming sleep, they tell us, consciousness is withdrawn from the body and the senses, and we live completely in the world of the mind. It's not a particularly restful state, as all of us can testify, and these sleep researchers can show us all kinds of diagrams to show that the mind factory is really working overtime during these hours of dreaming. But in dreamless sleep, consciousness is withdrawn from the mind as well, and we rest in the lap of the Self. In this state, we are completely unconscious; the ego is completely asleep. Here the Upanishads ask a very penetrating question: where is your personality when this takes place? You are not aware of any desires, any fears, so at that time you *have* no desires or fears. Yet they are all there latent in the room of the mind, waiting for you to come back in and pick them up again when you wake up into the dreaming or waking state.

In a flash of insight, the Upanishads tell us that this is just what happens between death and life. When we die, consciousness is withdrawn from the body just as it is in dreamless sleep, and just as all our desires and fears wait for us to reclaim them and live them out again in a dream-body, they wait until they can take form again in another physical body and another life. In both cases, it is the restless desire for personal satisfaction that draws us back into separate existence.

This is difficult to grasp at first, but all of us can understand that when we think about something constantly, when we desire something deeply, we are training our minds to be focused on this even at the hour of death. Our deepest desires at the moment of death sum up this life and determine the context for the next. The consequences of this are tremendous: what we do each day shapes our destiny. We do not suddenly wake up one morning free from the lurid dream of separateness; unitary consciousness is the result of long years of trying to act, speak, and think for the welfare of all. The choices we make throughout life have a powerful, cumulative effect. The other day I saw a sign in a restaurant which read, "You are what you eat." How simple life would be if this were true! We could all be living in health and security simply by eating three good meals a day. Unfortunately, however, we are *not* what we eat; our body is. When the Compassionate Buddha gave us the Dhammapada, he did not begin by saying, "All that we are is the result of what we have eaten"; he said, "All that we are is the result of what we have thought."

In other words, it is the little choices we make every day that determine what we become. Life is the sum of all these small thoughts and actions. One of the many reasons I admire Mahatma Gandhi is that he could give his complete attention to the smallest problems of daily living as well as the immense problems presented by India's struggle for independence. Day in and day out, in even the smallest details, he did everything possible to realize the unity of life. This kind of determination was characteristic of Gandhi. From his early days as a student in London he refused to be overwhelmed by anything. When he was in London and could not find any vegetarian restaurants, he started cooking in his room. His specialty was carrot soup, but it is said that those who dropped in at his place at dinnertime never did so again. Then, when he was a lawyer in South Africa and the white barber refused to cut his hair, he did not become angry or try to get back at the man; he went out and bought a pair of scissors and cut his hair himself. The day after this historic haircut, when he went to court as usual, his fellow barristers teasingly asked him if the mice had been nibbling at his hair. Gandhi didn't mind; he just didn't like to depend on anyone, or to throw up his hands and say, "There is nothing I can do."

Meister Eckhart tells us, "Those who have God in mind, simply and solely God, in all things, carry God with them into all their works and into all places, and God alone does all their works." Those who use every minute of their lives to serve the Lord in those around them, as Gandhi did, carry God with them wherever they go. When the assassin's bullet took his life, the only word that escaped Gandhi's lips was his mantram, *Rāma*. He had made his life a continuous effort to remember the Lord, so he felt no hatred at the moment of death; his mind had no thought of anything but the Lord. Similarly, Sri Krishna promises each of us, "If at the time of death your heart is filled with love for me, if your consciousness is permeated with love for me, then you will come to me. Of this there can be no doubt." Men and women of God all over the world have corroborated this countless times. They have imbued their consciousness with such depth of love that at the time of death they are able to maintain continuing awareness of God. Their bodies do suffer, because the body is subject to the stress of pain, but inside there is continuing awareness which neither physical pain nor emotional suffering can disturb.

तस्मात्सर्वेषु कालेषु मामनुस्मर युध्य च ।
मय्यर्पितमनोबुद्धिर्मामेवैष्यस्यसंशयः ॥८-७॥

7. Therefore, remember me at all times and fight on. With your heart and mind intent on me, you will surely come to me.

If shraddhā is the key to destiny, meditation is the key to shraddhā. Here it helps greatly to remember that the Gita is no pastoral discourse; it is set in the middle of a battlefield, with elephants trumpeting and swords flashing and conchs calling the regiments to battle all around. If the Gita were written today there would be bombers overhead and tanks rolling over the ground while Sri Krishna tells Arjuna how to go beyond death. The point is that if we really want to live – not just driven by negative conditioning, but in complete mastery of ourselves – then we have to be prepared to fight. This is the grimmest battle any human being can face, and it has to be faced every day, day in and day out, until victory is won.

It isn't possible even to dream how terrible this fight is until we get below the surface level of consciousness and begin to see the forces ranged against us. Even then, for a long time we do not guess their real strength; all we see is the front lines. First there is the infantry, which is fear – all kinds of fears, most of which we are not even acquainted with. We may not think we have much fear to reckon with, but it is as deep as our separateness, which cuts deep into the consciousness of every one of us. Then there is the cavalry, which is anger. If you can imagine the effect that cavalry and chariots had when they suddenly made their appearance in some of the great civilizations of the ancient world, you will see how apt a comparison this is; a cavalry attack is much more ferocious than infantry and much more difficult to conquer. But the real backbone of the army in ancient India was the elephantry. Throughout India's long history there have been many occasions when another country would try to plunder our rich material resources. But when these invading armies would look up and see huge armored elephants coming down on them by the hundreds, sometimes by the thousands, they would be panic-stricken. The elephantry is self-will, and it is a thousand times more fierce than anger and fear. All this is what we have to overcome in order to be masters of ourselves, and those who have won this battle, even giants like the Compassionate Buddha, will tell us that nothing on earth is more difficult, more precious, or more exhilarating than this victory.

This fight goes on twenty-four hours a day; even at night there are going to be skirmishes. The alarm goes off in the morning and the fight is on: to get up or not to get up? Years of conditioning are whispering to you to doze on a few minutes more; it's the distant thunder of the cannon on the battlefield. No mystic has ever denied that at a time like this, especially when it's cold outside, it's very pleasant to turn up your electric blanket and go back to sleep. All they will say is, You're going to lose the fight. Here I can offer a simple and very effective tactic: don't stay there to weigh the pros and cons; throw off the blankets and jump out of bed. It will be a little difficult, but after a few days you will realize that the first skirmish of the war is over and you have won. It's a very good feeling, because this isn't a war in the grand old Clausewitz style. It's all guerilla warfare, and every skirmish counts.

So you jump out of bed, and the same instant you've won one encounter, you're in the middle of another one. Even once you're out of bed, the prospect of sitting down to meditate isn't exactly inviting. After all, the newspaper is waiting at your door; you can always sit in a beanbag chair with a cup of coffee and read the news instead. Nobody will say this isn't more pleasant than meditation. A beanbag chair may not do much for your spine, but at least it doesn't take much effort to sit in it; journalism may not be particularly nonviolent these days, but it *is* stirring. Here it is that you don't even give the beanbag chair a glance, let alone the paper; you go straight to your meditation room, sit down quietly, and start trying to meditate.

But the fight has only begun. It's not as if you left the battlefield with the beanbag chair; the battlefield is right inside you. You're sitting quietly in meditation, trying to keep your mind on the Prayer of St. Francis, and after a few minutes you find you're a little drowsier than you suspected. It's very difficult to fight when you're getting sleepy in meditation. For one thing, if your meditation is going well, it may not be normal sleep that's coming on. It may be what the Sanskrit scriptures call *yoganidrā,* the wave of oblivion that comes over the mind when you try to stay conscious beneath the conscious level. In yoganidrā there's not much motivation to fight; there's not much will. But there is no choice; you have to fight. Otherwise you cannot go forward. And when someone asks me, "What do I do when I don't have much motivation?" I just say, "You *make* it much – by trying." There is no other way. This is a problem that will keep coming up in meditation for many, many years, and if you don't begin to fight it now you will find it almost impossible to take on the fight later on. The point is not ever to yield, to say, "There is nothing I can do." As my grandmother used to say, there is always something you can do. If you yield, you have lost the fight; but if you do not yield, you are beginning to win.

Then you finish meditation, and after all these conflicts, all you want to do is take it out on the refrigerator. It's an opportunity again; it's another skirmish. Instead of tucking into things to which you have been conditioned – say, a few pieces of nice, light bread that weakens the body in twelve ways, loaded with butter and jam – get out the whole wheat bread. After two pieces of toast there's a foray by a third, but you fight it off. As you get to be a seasoned fighter, even your hand will get accustomed to fighting. Instead of reaching automatically for the coffee it will say, "Coffee, you're no friend of mine; all you give me is caffeine."

Do you see why I say that there's no boredom in life once you take to meditation? You can't get bored in the middle of a battle; you've got to be alert all the time just to save your skin.

It's like this all day long. You go to work and immediately the ego says, "What's the least I can give here and the most I can get?" It's bad for work; it's bad for you; it's bad for everybody. So there is fighting again – you have to try to give as much as you can. At lunchtime you can sit around and join in some gossip, or you can take a fast walk repeating the mantram. And when you go home, you bring the battlefield with you even in the car; if you can keep calm, everybody in the cars around you will be a little safer.

By the end of a day like this, if you've really been giving your best, there is every reason to want a chance to come home, put your feet up, and hang up your sādhana until the next morning. It's a very reasonable request. The problem is, your opponent wouldn't even dream of fighting by the rules. In his book, any minute is right for a sneak attack. Things haven't been going so smoothly at home either. The children have had a bad day, the cat is missing, the dryer is broken; there are all kinds of problems. The natural reaction is to say, "I've had my share of problems already," and to take it out on the first person who comes to greet you. Of course, you have had your share of problems; no one is denying that. But the cat and the dryer have sprung this sneak attack, and the only choice is whether you're going to win or lose.

There is a thrilling kind of satisfaction in this. You step out of the car into no-man's-land and little Susie comes up to tell you that George has broken your new hi-fi. That's all; no "Hello, daddy," just this news about George. It takes real stamina to say at a time like this, "Oh, sure, let's see if we can fix it. After all, hi-fi's aren't eternal." It may be a hi-fi or a tennis racket or a sewing machine or anything else that is your favorite; the point is, you can come back even to an upset home and immediately set to work at bringing peace into it again. Nothing in the world can give more satisfaction than this, and nothing can make you more precious to those around you. Everyone in the family will be looking forward to your return. Even your neighbors will be watching over the fence and saying, "There goes someone who really deserves a peace prize." They don't know that you're still fighting.

There's no end to this fight, and there is no end to the satisfaction it can bring, because there is always more you can give. Instead of rushing through dinner to go bowling, you can stay and listen with genuine interest to Susie's rambling account of what happened to her at school. That's what really makes a meal satisfying, not just the food. And after dinner, when you just want to go off to your room to watch the late show or plow on through *The Decline and Fall of the Roman Empire,* you can drop in at your neighbor's, where things have been getting a little strained, and say, "I've got the evening free; why don't your children come out with ours for ice cream so that you two can have a little time to yourselves?" You're not only fighting your own battles then; your example is making it a little easier for others to fight too, and helping to build up a neighborhood where there is solidarity and trust.

If you have been fighting like this all day and really giving it your best, it will be a great solace to go to bed at night. No waterbed in the world can ever give the kind of rest that comes when you have been trying your hardest all day to lead the spiritual life. Then, after your evening meditation, when you lie down, close your eyes, and give all your mind to the mantram, it is very much like dropping off to sleep in the arms of the Lord. When you fall asleep in the mantram it will go on in your consciousness throughout the night, nursing the wounds of the day and strengthening your spirit for the fight that will come the next day. You know now that you are fighting for the Lord, and He will give you all the health and strength and endurance you need until finally the battle is won, and you come – as this verse promises – to be united with Him forever.

अभ्यासयोगयुक्तेन चेतसा नान्यगामिना ।
परमं पुरुषं दिव्यं याति पार्थानुचिन्तयन् ॥८-८॥

8. When you make your mind one-pointed on the Lord through the regular practice of meditation, you will find the supreme glory of the Self.

A clever verse from ancient India describes the mind as a restless monkey that is stung by a scorpion, drunk, and possessed by a demon, all at the same time. We are all proud owners of this monkey, which gives us a clue as to why it is so incredibly difficult to bring our mind under control. Yet control it we must if we are to go beyond the conditioning of the mind.

The symbol of the monkey is easily understood in a country like India, where monkeys run about as freely as cats and dogs in the United States. Often in India you will see little monkeys trained to perform and entertain. My wife and I once saw a little one that had been taught to act just like a reluctant child on the way to school. He dragged his feet, kicked at pebbles, and kept looking back over his shoulder and watching the birds in the trees just as any schoolboy would. Then, on the way home, he jumped and ran cheerfully. Now, this restless creature did not learn schoolboy gestures overnight; his master trained him over a period of time. Similarly, we do not still our minds in a week or even a year; it takes a long, long period of steady, enthusiastic effort. We should never be impressed by anyone who claims to give us complete control over the conscious, preconscious, and unconscious levels of the mind in a four-week seminar. But even if it takes a lifetime to attain this state, it is worth all our time and attention.

It always amazes me to see the kind of skills people spend their time perfecting. We know of one boy who delivers his newspapers from a precarious perch atop his unicycle. On college campuses you will find a lot of students who have managed to embroider a whole garden of exquisite flowers on their blue jeans. These are all skills which demand a great deal of concentration to master, and whenever I see anyone with the capacity to excel in his or her chosen field, whether it is sculpture or gymnastics or jumping motorcycles over the Grand Canyon, I know that if that person would only take to meditation, he or she could really go far.

One of the signs of this capacity for concentration is that you will not get distracted when you are talking with someone; all your concentration will be on that person. This is an art which all of us can cultivate; it will help our meditation and our personal relationships too. There is a story about Samuel Taylor Coleridge, the English poet, that illustrates this point. Coleridge was an enthusiastic talker, full of ideas and theories. One day, it is said, he saw his friend Charles Lamb on his way to his London office and went up to him, saying, "Lamb, stop a minute; I've a new theory of literary criticism. Wouldn't you like to hear it?"

Lamb said, "Sorry, old chap, but I've an appointment at the office." "Let me give you just a few minutes' summary, then," said Coleridge. And he started on the theory that underlies the *Biographia Literaria*.

Now, just as Coleridge had developed a talent for talking, Lamb had developed a talent for escaping from long-winded conversations. So Coleridge, knowing Lamb's ways, grabbed hold of his friend's coat button to keep him from getting away. Minutes passed, an hour passed, and Coleridge went on and on; he had closed his eyes in concentration and was well into his exposition, secure in his hold on Charles Lamb's coat button. But he had underestimated his friend's resourcefulness. Lamb had pulled out a pair of pocket scissors, quietly clipped the button from his coat, and slipped away to get to his appointment.

Hours passed, and Lamb, who was a very busy man, went about his business in the City and forgot about his long-winded friend completely. But on his way home late in the afternoon, to his amazement, there was Coleridge, still hanging on to his button and holding forth on literary theory. It may be an exaggerated story, but it illustrates the concentration of genius. If only Coleridge had taken to meditation instead of drugs for inspiration, he could have gone very far on the spiritual path.

कविं पुराणमनुशासितारम्
अणोरणीयांसमनुस्मरेद्यः ।
सर्वस्य धातारमचिन्त्यरूपम्
आदित्यवर्णं तमसः परस्तात् ॥८-९॥
प्रयाणकाले मनसाचलेन
भक्त्या युक्तो योगबलेन चैव ।
भ्रुवोर्मध्ये प्राणमावेश्य सम्यक्
स तं परं पुरुषमुपैति दिव्यम् ॥८-१०॥

9–10. The Lord is the Supreme Poet, the First Cause, the Sovereign Ruler, subtler than the tiniest particle, the support of all, inconceivable, bright as the sun, beyond the darkness of Māyā. Remembering him in this way at the time of death, through devotion and the power of meditation, with your mind completely stilled and your concentration fixed in the center of spiritual awareness, you will realize the Lord of Love.

The Supreme Poet is at work wherever we look; we can see his touch in the beauty of the sky, in the vast oceans and the rivers, in the mountains and forests, in all the creatures who live on the earth. Even our careless habits, which have covered the earth with a blight of pollution, cannot obscure the infinite beauty of the Lord reflected in every blade of grass, every drop of water. Look at even that humblest of flowers, the dandelion, the plague of gardeners and a nightmare to anyone who wants a perfect carpet of green for their front lawn. How beautiful even this little yellow flower is! Look at any leaf and you can see the miracle of life, the perfect pattern created by the Supreme Poet. The German mystic Nicholas of Cusa looks at a simple nut and sees in it the creative force of the Lord; in one little nut lies the potentiality of thousands of trees to come.

In the Upanishads the source of all this creativity is called "the uncaused Cause." If some scientist were to decide that the ultimate constituents of the universe are protons, I would ask, "Who put those protons there?" If an astronomer tries to tell me that the cosmos was born from a black hole, I would still want to know, "Who bored that black hole?" This line of questioning has no end within the world of cause and effect; we can always ask where that primordial particle or black hole came from. But this infinite regression of questions comes to a halt where the Lord is concerned. If you ask Sri Krishna who created him, he will say, "Me. I put myself here." In mysticism everywhere the Lord is called the Self-created, the First Cause, which means that everything else, including you and me, is an effect.

All this is not just beautiful poetry; it has a terribly practical point to it. In this verse and those which follow, Sri Krishna is telling Arjuna in very precise terms how to maintain unbroken awareness through the cataclysmic changes we call death. It is important to realize that whether we prepare for it or not, death will come to us all. As the Katha Upanishad tells us, the body is like a city with eleven gates, and just as historical cities change, grow old, and eventually become archeological relics, the body too is bound to come to an end. Yet, as all the world's great scriptures assure us, we do not have to die when the body dies. If we have trained our consciousness over the years to be united with the Lord, we shall be able to guard ourselves against the rupture in consciousness that takes place for almost all human beings when the body is shed.

The key to this almost unimaginable achievement is devotion. It is all very well to talk about the Ultimate Reality, the Great Void, but we cannot love a Void, and I doubt very much if ordinary people like us would find much about the Void to remember as we entered the moment of death. Here it is that we need the Lord in the aspect we can love and understand – the Supreme Poet, the sustainer and protector of all, from whom we came into existence and to whom we shall return. For this, we need a divine ideal like Sri Krishna, Jesus the Christ, the Compassionate Buddha, or the Divine Mother, a divine incarnation in which the supreme Godhead assumes a human form. We have only to look at the picture of Jesus holding a lamb or reassuring the children of Galilee for our hearts to go out to him. We have only to see one of those South Asian statues of the Buddha seated in meditation, full of compassion and tenderness, for us to want to become like him. The great incarnations come to live among us, to talk and laugh and weep like us, so that we can love them more than we love ourselves. When we can love like this, it will be impossible for all our love not to flow to the Lord at the hour of our death. Absorbed in him completely, secure in the realization that we are neither body nor mind, we can shed the body as naturally as a dead leaf falls from a tree.

When we are setting out on this final journey, there should be nothing in our knapsack. We cannot afford to have a lot of things on our backs, like the hitchhikers we see on University Avenue all loaded down with transistor radios and guitars and camping gear. Similarly, on the last journey there should not be a movement in the mind. Every attachment, every desire, every resentment must be left behind, which means that the mind must be completely stilled. When there are no lingering desires and thoughts to tie us to the body, we can keep our minds absorbed in the Lord without any trace of reservation. This is the theme of the verses which are to come.

यदक्षरं वेदविदो वदन्ति
विशन्ति यद्यतयो वीतरागाः ।
यदिच्छन्तो ब्रह्मचर्यं चरन्ति
तत्ते पदं संग्रहेण प्रवक्ष्ये ॥८-११॥

11. I will briefly tell you of the eternal state all scriptures affirm, which can be entered only by those who are self-controlled. Those who are selfless in their daily lives and free from selfish attachments attain this supreme goal.

In a village in India it is impossible to be ignorant of death. Everyone knows everyone else, everyone's life is connected with the lives of everyone else, and it is not uncommon to hear that someone you saw only the other day, or with whom you played, or whose mango trees you used to climb, has passed from this life completely. It is a continual reminder of the transiency of all life. This kind of thing happened many times while I was growing up, and often people on their deathbed would send for my grandmother to come sit with them and hold their hand and ease their hearts a little in going through the agony with which most people face death. I don't think any of them had much idea of my granny's real stature, but everyone was aware that she was a great source of strength, and in moments like those all you had to do was look into her eyes to glimpse the great truth all scriptures tell us – that we are not the body, we are imperishable spirit, and death is no more than a change of rooms.

Even when I was a little boy, my grandmother would insist that I come with her on these deathbed vigils. It used to horrify everyone in my family, for no one, certainly not I, ever had any idea of why she should want to take an impressionable child to scene after scene of agony. But no one would argue with my granny. She was a very loving but a very determined spiritual teacher, and many years later I came to see that all those scenes of death and dying planted deep in my consciousness the fervent desire to go beyond death once and for all. The suffering I witnessed at those scenes still haunts me. There is no isolation from the dramas of birth and death as there often is in this country; life ebbed out in the presence of family and friends, and their grief used to add to the agony of the dying, which often went on for hours and sometimes even days.

Once, I remember, I took courage and asked my grandmother why there had to be such suffering. Granny didn't have much of a way with words; she taught me by how she lived. So she didn't quote the Gita at me; she just asked me to sit down in a chair and hold on to the arms with all my strength. Then she tried to pull me out of the chair. I was a rather strong fellow, and I held on for all I was worth; but she was stronger, and with one painful wrench she had me up on my feet. "That hurt, Granny," I said. "Now sit down again, Little Lamp," she told me, "but this time don't hold on." I sat down again, and she reached down and lifted me gently into her arms.

This is the secret of facing death. As long as there is something we want to get out of life before we go – a little more money, a little more pleasure, a chance to get in a parting dig at someone we think has hurt us – there will be a terrible struggle with death when it comes. As long as we think we are the body, we will fight tooth and nail to hold on to the body when death comes to wrench it away. The tragedy, of course, is that death *is* going to take it anyway; it was never ours to begin with. So the great mystics all tell us, "Give it away now and be free." Give up all these selfish attachments; then, when death does come, we can give him what is his without a shadow of regret, and keep for ourselves what is ours, which is love of the Lord. There is great artistry in this; that is why it appeals to me so deeply. Death comes and growls something about how our time has come and we just say, "Don't growl; I'm ready to come on my own." Then we stand up gracefully, take off the jacket that is the body, place it carefully in Death's arms and go on home.

सर्वद्वाराणि संयम्य मनो हृदि निरुध्य च ।
मूर्ध्न्याधायात्मनः प्राणमास्थितो योगधारणाम् ॥८-१२॥
ओमित्येकाक्षरं ब्रह्म व्याहरन्मामनुस्मरन् ।
यः प्रयाति त्यजन्देहं स याति परमां गतिम् ॥८-१३॥

12–13. Remembering me at the time of death, close down the doors of the senses and place the mind in the heart. Then, while absorbed in meditation, focus all energy upwards to the head. Repeating in this state the divine name, the syllable Om that represents the changeless Brahman, you will attain the supreme goal.

A decade or so ago there seemed to be a veiled conspiracy to pretend that death did not exist. Now it is just the opposite. Courses on death are given on university campuses; books on death are prominent in every bookstore. Yet, though most people will now admit "Oh, yes, we know we have to die; everyone has to die sometime," I have met very, very few people – even including those with terminal illnesses – who really believed it. The proof is that if you *really* believe you're going to die, you will do something about it. That is where the Gita comes in.

Some of the books on death we see in stores go so far as to recommend shedding the body in a state of mind where the senses are satiated. This seems to be the modern way – to hope to die with the senses all aroused. The Gita suggests a far different approach. It is not much help to die in a state of sense-pleasure – say, after having eaten a gourmet meal. The ultimate goal is to be able to shed the body without any rupture in consciousness at all, and for this we must be prepared to train ourselves for decades.

These two Gita verses follow closely the very precise description of the death process given in the Upanishads. First, the Upanishads say, the vitality of the senses is withdrawn into the mind. Then the mind, along with the life-force, descends into the heart, into the realms of deeper consciousness. Finally the Self, accompanied by mental impressions, departs from the body, following one of the tracks leading from the heart. In the case of the man or woman of God, the Self is said to depart upward through the crown of the head.

At the hour of death, the doors of the senses are completely closed. If we are to maintain awareness of the Self at that time, nothing can be allowed to take away from the complete concentration within. There is no hearing, no seeing, and there should be no desire to see or hear. Everything must be centered on the Self. For most of us, however, the onset of death precipitates a terrible longing for sensory experience and a feeling of agonized deprivation in the mind. That is when the real agony of death begins. All the attachments we have formed, all the virulent self-will we have cultivated, tie us down in the mind completely so that we cannot break loose. Yama, the King of Death, must tear us away. If I may use a grim image, this tearing away is like being thrown through the windshield in an automobile accident. It is horrible to be thrown through the windshield, but it is much worse to be thrown through the rigid barrier of self-will and selfish attachments when our body is wrenched away in death. This is the agonizing horror of death, even beyond the physical level.

I am not at all against alleviating the physical pain of death through the wise use of drugs, but these cannot relieve this kind of pain in the mind. The only way to be able to still the mind at the time of death is to train it from now on to be filled with love of the Lord, whom we must see in every creature around us. Then at death there is nothing in the heart but love of the Lord. There is no personal attachment or self-will; there is no conflict, no anger, no fear. The body may suffer, but there is no suffering in consciousness, for the mind is full only of the mantram or holy name.

One of the secrets of the Gita is how to use the mantram at the time of death. When vitality has been withdrawn into the mind and the mind into the heart, you have gone beyond the mind; therefore, you have gone beyond memory. This is a terribly practical point. You will not be able to remember the inspirational passage at that time. But when the mantram has become *ajapajapam*, when it repeats itself without any conscious effort, you do not need memory; you do not need coherence or connections between words. You do not have to remember to repeat the mantram; it will go on of itself.

There is a beautiful verse from the Mundaka Upanishad that describes ajapajapam:

> Take the great bow of the sacred scriptures,
> Place on it the arrow of devotion;
> Then draw the bowstring of meditation
> And aim at the target, the Lord of Love.
> The mantram is the bow, the aspirant
> Is the arrow, and the Lord the target.
> Now draw the bowstring of meditation,
> And hitting the target be one with him.

For the great mystics, the mantram has taken root and become established in their consciousness; the holy name echoes continuously in the depths of the heart. In sickness and in health, in favorable circumstances and in times of turmoil, the mantram continues to fill the heart and mind. When this happens, we are so established in

God-consciousness that death loses its terror. At the time we shed the body there will be no break in consciousness, for we have become continuously aware of the Lord who dwells within.

The mantram mentioned in these verses is *Om,* which is not really an external sound. It is an internal sound, which may occasionally be heard in very deep meditation. The Sanskrit scriptures call it "the unstruck sound"; in Zen it is alluded to as the "sound of one hand clapping." The most ancient of all the mantrams in the Hindu tradition, *Om* is considered to be the fundamental vibration which pervades the cosmos. So *Om* is not just an idle sound, but a powerful spiritual formula. For the mystics, this sound may come and go in their consciousness. But at the time of death, when they have trained their consciousness to be completely filled with the love of the Lord, *Om* is the sound that will reverberate in their hearts, drowning all mortal noises.

अनन्यचेताः सततं यो मां स्मरति नित्यशः ।
तस्याहं सुलभः पार्थ नित्ययुक्तस्य योगिनः ॥८-१४॥

14. I am easily attained by the person who always remembers me and is attached to nothing else. Such a person is a true yogi, Arjuna.

Our home on the Blue Mountain in South India was near the road to town, and every Saturday during the summer holidays the local tribal people used to go by our house on their way to the race track. They were a lively group when they passed our place in the morning. Somehow fifty of them could squeeze into a bus intended for thirty; they didn't mind having to stand the whole way with someone's elbow in their ribs, because they were having such a good time speculating on how much money they were going to win at the races. But in the evening it was a different story. The same bus would return shrouded in silence. My mother used to stand at the gate and watch them go by, and being a tender-hearted woman, she felt sorry to see them going home so depressed after all that cheering and singing in the morning.

This is the story of us all. We are conditioned to believe that we only have to pursue our pleasure, to pick up whatever profit we can and put it in our wallet; but the pleasure is never quite what we had hoped, and our wallet is sometimes snatched away in the bargain. In his mercy the Lord allows us a margin for experimentation, but after a while he expects us to get the point – that we cannot find fulfillment in making money or in stimulating the senses. Life on the sensory level is fraught with such frustration and anger that once we begin to make some progress on the spiritual path we can only ask, "How can people enjoy this kind of life?" We have only to look around us to see how much suffering there is in living for oneself – thinking about money and material possessions, comparing oneself with others, competing against even one's nearest and dearest. To the mystic, this is not living at all, and in an earlier verse in the Gita Sri Krishna says, "What most people call day is the night of ignorance to the sage."

In the deepest stages of meditation, when concentration has become complete, we go beyond the attraction of the sense-world once and for all. In this state, consciousness is withdrawn completely from fleeting pleasures and personal possessions, and all sense of separateness goes. All our vitality is consolidated within us, and the doors of the senses, which are usually in one position only – open to all incoming traffic – now swing completely shut. Consciousness has been withdrawn into the mind and the mind into the Self, just as at the moment of death. The all-important difference is that in meditation this is something we learn to do intentionally, over a period of many years of spiritual practice, so that instead of blacking out, our consciousness is intensely awake and filled with peace. In death all our selfish attachments are torn from us, but in the climax of meditation they have been thrown away of our own free will. Afterwards, when we return to the world of the senses, we are free to enjoy whatever is in harmony with the welfare of all, but we can never again be misled by anything life has to offer. We have already died to our little self to come to life in the Ātman, our real Self. So a great mystic like St. Paul will say, "I have already died to my little 'I'; how can I die again? *Not I, not I, but Christ liveth in me.*"

In every tradition there is a rare man or woman who embodies this ideal, so perfectly symbolized by the Compassionate Buddha, Jesus the Christ, and Sri Krishna, or by the Virgin Mary in the Catholic tradition and the Divine Mother in Hinduism. If you want to see beauty in its most radiant form, look at men and women who are trying to be like these, whose daily life reflects the divine presence. The other day, seeing a particularly striking statue of the Compassionate Buddha seated in meditation, I could not help thinking with humility but with great love: "I will do anything to be like him! I do not care about what others think of me, about what image I project; I just want to be like the Buddha."

मामुपेत्य पुनर्जन्म दुःखालयमशाश्वतम् ।
नाप्नुवन्ति महात्मानः संसिद्धिं परमां गताः ॥८-१५॥
आ ब्रह्मभुवनाल्लोकाः पुनरावर्तिनोऽर्जुन ।
मामुपेत्य तु कौन्तेय पुनर्जन्म न विद्यते ॥८-१६॥

15. Great souls make their lives perfect and discover me; they are freed from mortality and the suffering of this separate existence.
16. Every creature in the universe is subject to rebirth, Arjuna, except the one who is united with me.

In the early days of the Blue Mountain Center I once gave a series of talks on meditation to a group of hard-headed Kaiser businessmen, who followed most of what I had to say with attentiveness and appreciation. Once, however, I happened to refer casually to the Hindu and Buddhist concept of reincarnation. After the talk one of these men came up, took me aside, and said very persuasively: "You've been so rational all this time; you haven't said anything that we can't accept, even with all our scientific training. Why do you have to start dragging in these esoteric theories?"

Though reincarnation is emphasized in these verses, Sri Krishna is not going to require us to pass an exam on the theory of rebirth in order to attain the goal of life. There is no necessary connection between the practice of meditation and belief in reincarnation. We can believe in many births and still lead an unspiritual life, just as we can believe in only one birth and still lead a selfless life. But there is no contradiction at all between the theory of reincarnation and the theory of evolution. Both mystic and scientist agree on the stages through which life evolved; the mystic is only adding that there is another level than that on which the physical drama of existence is played out. In a crude form, each of us recapitulates these stages of evolution in the mother's womb, from the simplest organism – the single cell – up to the human being. To make this concept a little more personal, I like to imagine the dog-lover as once having been a little pup playing with a shoe, and when I come across someone who is especially partial to cats, I tell them they were once curled up by the fireside themselves, purring contentedly. The Sufi mystic Jalalu'l-Din Rumi expresses this universal evolution eloquently:

> I came forth from the Unmanifested
> And pitched my tent in the forest of life.
> I was a mineral, then vegetable,
> Then became an animal. I evolved
> Into a man, and in the company
> Of good people I wandered round and round
> The house of prayer. At last I chose the road
> That leads to Him, and became a servant
> At His gate. No longer were He and I
> Separate, for I was lost in Him.

Twelve years ago I had the pleasure of meeting Dr. Evans-Wentz, one of the world's foremost authorities on Tibetan mysticism. According to Evans-Wentz, the Tibetan contribution to the theory of reincarnation is vividly picturesque. Like the ancient Hindu sages, the Tibetan mystics say that we really have two bodies: the physical body, *sthūlasharīra,* and the subtle body, *sūkshmasharīra*. The subtle body, which consists of our thoughts and emotional tendencies, is immaterial, nonphysical. This is why we find it difficult to believe it exists, and go through life thinking of ourselves as being so many inches tall and weighing so many pounds. But within this physical sheath there is a subtle body too, which has an ego so many units broad, a lot of samskāras – what you call "hang-ups" – a subtle mass of tamas or inertia, some rajas or energy, and a little sattva or serenity.

At the time of death, this subtle body and the physical body part company. The physical body is shed and resolved back into its constituents of calcium, phosphorus, and other elements, while we go in our subtle body to a kind of prenatal waiting room which the Tibetan mystics call Bardo, the 'in-between state.' These mystics say that we often have to wait in Bardo for a long while before the proper situation for our next birth becomes available. The Upanishads tell us penetratingly that there is some similarity between this state and the state of dreamless sleep between two periods of waking. It can be a source of great consolation to those who are facing death. In deep dreamless sleep, the Upanishads add, our problems all disappear for the time being; we are not conscious of either the body or the mind. But when it comes time to wake up, don't we still wake up the same person, into a world that is changed only by a short passage of time? It is the same in Bardo. At the moment of death, consciousness is withdrawn from the physical body, and we get a long period of rest and recuperation. Then, when we are ready, we wake up again into the physical context to give it one more try.

The other day I went with my wife to a large drop-in clinic in Oakland for our annual physical examinations. One of the first tests they always give you is to see how long you can wait. Finally I presented my card, and they decided that I was who it said I was. It can take some time, because the only proof I have of my identity is not the kind that clerks are prepared to accept. Then they took me into another room, took away my clothes, and gave me a white paper gown to wear while I went from room to room to wait for test after test.

Bardo is very much like that. You have to stand in a queue to register; then you show your identification card to the receptionist and she tells you to sit in the waiting room until she calls your name. There's always a certain amount of waiting, because it's not easy for the administration to find the right constellation of circumstances for you. If you haven't been very kind to your parents in this life, you have to be born into a home where you will have rebellious children – which actually is not too difficult to find. If you haven't been very considerate to your wife, you have to be born into a context where you will have an irate husband, which also is not too difficult to find. And if you have been a very poor neighbor, walling yourself off and ignoring those around you, you have to be placed in a neighborhood where people will look right through you and not even remember your name. It's like that even down to your dog or cat; you have to have the right dog or cat in your home, too. Everything must be perfect for your future growth. When these circumstances are put together, among the millions of possible homes there is only one into which you can be born that is just right.

In this verse, Sri Krishna says that until we become united with the Lord, all of us have to keep coming back into our old context, exactly where we left off at the time of death. It is a brilliant theory, because it places the responsibility for our life in our own hands. If we can lead a selfless life, contributing to our family and community, then we will have made a better life for ourselves in our next birth. On the other hand, if we lead a selfish life marked by lack of love and respect for others, we are setting the stage for unfavorable circumstances the next time around. You and I are responsible for the situation in which we find ourselves, and there is no point in blaming our parents or our partner or our children for it. Instead we can take our life in our own hands, practice meditation, learn to reduce our selfishness, and create a better life now as well as for the next time around.

In other words, whatever context we find ourselves in is a suitable one in which to overcome our problems and grow to our full height. We tend to look upon the *other* home as peaceful, the other couple as perfect, the other parent-child relationship as ideal, but this is not very likely. Whenever she heard someone talking like this, my grandmother used to remark pungently, "The jasmine in your neighbor's garden always smells sweeter." Most of us, if I may say so, have nice parents, and most of us have good friends and children. Naturally they all have certain liabilities as well as assets; this is part of the human condition. If our parents were completely perfect, they would not be here; according to the theory of reincarnation, they would have passed the parent test in the school of life *summa cum laude*. The very fact that we have come into this life shows we have some imperfections to correct. The mystics are loving realists. They don't say, "Let me see your angel's wings"; they remind us that we all make mistakes in life, and that without making a reasonable amount of mistakes, most of us cannot learn to improve. So none of us need be depressed about our past or present; on the path of meditation, even past mistakes can be made into powerful assets if we have learned something by making them.

To put it in simple terms, life is a kind of school where we keep coming back until we realize the unity of life. Only then can we graduate. Suicide, according to this theory, is the worst crime we can commit against ourselves. Both the Hindu and Buddhist scriptures agree that those who commit suicide when they find themselves in an extremely difficult situation will be born again and again into a similar web of circumstances until they learn to improve that situation. Even in this life, the purpose of difficult situations is to get us to master something in ourselves, and until we do this by facing such situations squarely, they will come to confront us again and again, more complicated and more distressing each time around. No matter what circumstances we find ourselves in, however distressing they may be, the Lord expects us to try to reduce our selfishness and forget ourselves in contributing to the welfare of those around us. He does not promise any easy way out of our problems, but he does tell us that by eliminating our separateness we can be united with him and see him dwelling in the hearts of everyone, even our enemies. Then we shall have attained the goal of life and need not enter the cycle of birth and death again.

There is a powerful story about Arjuna's oldest brother Yudhishthira, who is a remarkable character in Hindu spiritual lore. One of his many names is Ajātashatru, 'he who has no enemies.' When he is banned from his kingdom with his brothers, Yudhishthira goes to live as an exile in the forest for thirteen years. During this time he is visited by sages who come to cheer him up and bring news of his kingdom and countrymen. One such sage, curious about his epithet, asked him, Sir, how can you claim to have no enemies when you have been driven from your kingdom and subjected to more difficulties than ten men put together? Yudhishthira replied, "It's true that I have been exiled for many years from those I love, but I don't think of my usurpers as enemies. I'm still prepared to serve them in any way that contributes to the welfare of all. They may call me their enemy, but as far as I am concerned, they are my friends." He had learned to see the Lord in every living creature, even in those who attacked and cheated him. This is the lesson which we are all born to learn, and the scriptures go on to say that Yudhishthira was not born again, but was reunited at the time of his death with the Divine Ground of all existence.

सहस्रयुगपर्यन्तमहर्यद्ब्रह्मणो विदुः ।
रात्रिं युगसहस्रान्तां ते ऽहोरात्रविदो जनाः ॥८-१७॥
अव्यक्ताद्व्यक्तयः सर्वाः प्रभवन्त्यहरागमे ।
रात्र्यागमे प्रलीयन्ते तत्रैवाव्यक्तसंज्ञके ॥८-१८॥
भूतग्रामः स एवायं भूत्वा भूत्वा प्रलीयते ।
रात्र्यागमे ऽवशः पार्थ प्रभवत्यहरागमे ॥८-१९॥

17. Those who understand the cosmic laws know that the day of Brahmā ends after a thousand yugas and the night of Brahmā ends after a thousand yugas.
18. When the day of Brahmā dawns, forms are brought forth from the Unmanifest; when the night of Brahmā comes, these forms merge in the Formless again.
19. This multitude of beings is created and destroyed again and again in the succeeding days and nights of Brahmā.

Hindu cosmology divides the history of the earth into four periods or ages called *yugas*. In *satya yuga,* the Age of Truth, right after creation, everybody put the welfare of the whole first, and there was a real kingdom of heaven on earth. This period is traditionally represented by a bull standing firmly on all four legs – steady, balanced, and secure. Gradually, however, selfishness crept into our desires. Pleasure and profit became more important, robbing mankind of support. In this period, *tretā yuga,* the bull loses one of its legs and begins to wobble. He is still able to balance, but not quite so steadily. Then, as self-will increases, the poor bull loses another leg, leaving him with one in front and one in back – a very precarious position, as you'll see if you can get a bull to demonstrate it for you. This third age, called *dvāpara yuga,* is characterized by a half-for-me, half-for-others attitude. You never know when someone is going to pursue his personal pleasure and when he is going to contribute to the happiness of the whole. Finally, the bull loses its third leg, which marks the beginning of our age, *kali yuga.* It is a very factual name for our era, because *kali* here means anger and violence, qualities which have come almost to dominate our times.

These four yugas taken together constitute one great yuga, or a yuga of the gods. One thousand such great yugas make up what is called a *kalpa,* which Sri Krishna here tells us is a day of Brahmā, the Creator. It's a very personal conception. The Lord wakes up and the world of name and form comes into play, very much as it does when we wake up out of deep sleep. Creation starts; matter and energy, time and space, all come into existence; the great chain of evolution begins. There are even some calculations made by the sages of ancient India as to how long all this should take; according to them, one day of Brahmā is 4320 million years.

But, the Hindu scriptures tell us, after a while the Lord becomes tired of all this cosmic play and wants to take a nap. When you or I take a nap there is no awareness of the world outside us; it drops out of our consciousness completely. So here the Lord curls up on his endless serpent Ananta, and the whole of creation, which the Sanskrit scriptures tell us is just a thought in the consciousness of the Lord, is withdrawn into a state of latency, with no more reality than the tree which will sprout from a seed. This state of primordial equilibrium is the night of Brahmā, in which everything is dissolved and all creation returns to the Unmanifest.

Recently I have been dipping into a few books on astronomy, because it fascinates me to see how easily the two major theories of cosmology are accommodated in the Gita. One of these is called the evolutionary or "Big Bang" theory; the other is the steady-state theory. Supposedly they represent opposite camps, but in the light of the Gita they become different aspects of one and the same truth. It's like picking up a cosmic kaleidoscope: turn it to the left, look inside, and the universe was created and will someday be dissolved; turn it to the right and look again, and the universe has neither beginning nor end. In meditation we gain a higher mode of knowing which enables us to look behind this kaleidoscope and see the Lord at his divine play, making beautiful patterns with galaxies and quasars, gathering the pieces back into his hands, and then spreading them out again into another magnificent pattern, another universe.

The Big Bang theory is similar in many ways to the insights we find in the Sanskrit scriptures. The first modern statement of this theory came from a Belgian priest, Abbé Georges Henri Lemaître, who conjectured that the universe began at a specific point in time, at least ten billion years ago. At that time it was an incomprehensibly dense mass which was equal to the mass of the universe today. All matter that ever existed was stuffed into what Lemaître called a "primeval atom" or "cosmic egg" – a term, by the way, which closely translates the Sanskrit term *brahmānda*. In one of his most pregnant statements, Lemaître suggests that in this primordial state there was not even time or space. Then the cosmic egg exploded, sending matter and energy outward in every direction. I can imagine the Lord jiggling the kaleidoscope ten or twelve thousand million years ago to make the universe start expanding, as it still is today.

When Lemaître formulated his theory he thought that the universe would come to an end someday, since no new matter was being created. But astronomers after him decided that there were some other alternatives. "After the universe explodes," they asked themselves, "mightn't the gravitational attraction of all this matter gradually slow its expansion to a halt? Eventually all the galaxies would start drifting in towards the center again until finally all matter would rush into a single point, forming a new cosmic atom. Then it would explode again, starting the universe once more." This theory of the oscillating universe, as it is called, is so close to the presentation of the Gita that I can almost see Sri Krishna smiling to himself and saying, "These fellows are beginning to catch on to my game." Just as we have day followed by night, then day again, month after month, year after year, so too the day of Brahmā follows the night of Brahmā over and over again without end. In India you often find the Lord represented as a mischievous little boy, and I can imagine little Krishna here chewing bubble gum, blowing the bubble of the cosmos out of his mouth, and then sucking it back in again, over and over.

The other camp of astronomers, the steady-state adherents, has had a good look through the cosmic kaleidoscope too. According to them, there was no specific beginning to the universe. It did not decide to start itself up at 12:30 on a Friday afternoon billions and billions of years ago; it has always existed and it always will exist, without beginning, without end. Not only that, it is continuously coming into being, because new matter is always being created as the universe expands. It sounds surprising, but as one astronomer points out – from the other camp – whether we talk about Big Bang or steady state, matter has to come into existence somehow, and it is no more unlikely for it to come little by little than in one big explosion.

One gifted proponent of the steady-state theory, Sir Fred Hoyle, is a particular favorite of mine, because he is capable of great insight and yet uses language that any of us can understand. I had an opportunity to attend one of his lectures on the Berkeley campus; before the talk I was sitting right behind him and was delighted to see the friendly way he greeted everyone, from the professor emeritus to the young graduate student. He was completely at home with his subject and made a number of very penetrating remarks, some of which had a creative touch that reminded me of the Gita. Of course Sir Fred was not able to refer to the supreme goal of life, which is usually considered out of bounds for astronomers, so his lecture ended on a note of pessimism. But a few of his more positive remarks can help us understand the cosmology of the Gita.

Hoyle's position is that all matter has a beginning, but the universe itself has neither beginning nor end. It is far greater than all these separate bits of matter of which it is composed. He also pointed out that the universe is everywhere. Substitute the word *Lord* for *universe* and you have the Gita; as Sri Krishna says earlier, the universe exists in him, so he is everywhere. Then, in a flash of insight, Hoyle suggests that there is a creative principle at work throughout the universe. Just as there is a nuclear field binding together atomic nuclei and a gravitational field binding together the stars and galaxies, so we can speak of a field of creation from which all matter comes. This creative source is similar to what the mystics call the Divine Ground underlying all that exists. An imaginative scientist tells us that matter comes forth from and returns to a creative field of forces; the mystic tells us that all creation comes forth from and returns to the Divine Ground of existence. It is a superb instance of how the principles of science converge on spiritual truths.

Recent evidence has led Hoyle to modify his position somewhat in an even more suggestive theory. In this new view, the mass of an object is not something independent of its environment; it is a function of the "mass field" of the universe as a whole. It's not just Hoyle's idea; other great scientists, including Einstein, have believed that the properties of the universe at any place are affected by the rest of the whole. Among other things, this means that mass can vary from place to place and from time to time. With rigorous mathematics, Hoyle points out that instead of talking about squeezing the whole mass of the universe into an infinitesimal point, we can talk just as precisely about a universe that has always been the same size, in which the total mass "cancels out" from time to time. The Big Bang still occurs, but it's not really a creation out of nothing; the universe as a whole was never created and will never be destroyed.

Examples like this are helpful in bridging the chasm of

misunderstanding that has developed between science and the spiritual tradition. The reason for this misunderstanding is not in scientific or spiritual principles, but in not knowing how to use the contributions of science to interpret the insights of the mystics. In samādhi we develop the higher mode of knowing called *turīya,* which is a kind of intuitive leap beyond the intellect to a unified state of consciousness in which knower and known become one. In this state there is no Sir Fred Hoyle searching the universe with his powerful instruments; Hoyle and the universe are one. Then we get a glimpse of the Lord of the immense, starry heavens at work, boring black holes, twirling Milky Ways, and setting the universe in motion as effortlessly as a college student sends a Frisbee spinning through the air.

परस्तस्मात्तु भावो ऽन्यो ऽव्यक्तो ऽव्यक्तात्सनातनः ।
यः स सर्वेषु भूतेषु नश्यत्सु न विनश्यति ॥८-२०॥

20. Beyond this formless state there is another,
unmanifested Reality, which is eternal and is
not dissolved when the cosmos is destroyed.

When the universe is withdrawn into the Lord at the end of a kalpa, there is no more earth, no more sea, no more galaxies, no more life; everything is dissolved back into the formless state. But Sri Krishna says, "I will still be there, for I am eternal." It is a quiet way of telling us that we are immortal too. When the sun has burnt itself out, when the galaxy has disappeared into a black hole, Sri Krishna says, "I will still be here, and so will you, for I am your deepest Self." In the Katha Upanishad we have the same declaration in beautifully exalted words:

The supreme Self is beyond name and form,
Beyond the senses, inexhaustible,
Without beginning, without end, beyond
Time, space, and causality, eternal,
Immutable. They who realize the Self
Are forever free from the jaws of death.

Do you see the prize that is being offered us by the Lord? It is inconceivable, beyond the grasp of the most brilliant intellect or the most fertile imagination. It is so great that no price would be too high to pay for it; compared to this supreme goal, any material comforts or honors the world can offer seem utterly insignificant.

In other words, the mystics all say, if you want illumination, do not ask about the price. Do not complain, do not begrudge what the Lord takes from you; when you begin to see this wisdom and love within you, nothing else will seem worthwhile. Illumination is only for those who are prepared to pay the highest price, who will never haggle. When we have difficulties with the palate, when we cannot get up early for meditation, we are haggling. When we act self-willed, we are trying to bargain with the Lord, which means we can only lose.

अव्यक्तो ऽक्षर इत्युक्तस्तमाहुः परमां गतिम् ।
यं प्राप्य न निवर्तन्ते तद्धाम परमं मम ॥८-२१॥

21. Those who have realized the supreme goal of life know that I am unmanifested and unchanging. Having come home to me, they are never separate again.

Whether we were born and raised in America or Europe, in Africa or Asia, none of these places is our real home. We are all transients on earth, and to most sensitive people there comes now and then a strange feeling of homesickness for our permanent home, which Sri Krishna calls here *mama dhāma,* the land of abiding joy and security within us. The main reason for restlessness, for the recurring impulse to travel, is this desire to find our real home. If we go to Iceland to find peace of mind, or try to escape to the "land of the kangaroo," as the travel advertisements put it, what we are looking for will only slip through our fingers. We will come back tired and frustrated, and those of us who are sensitive will confess that what we really want is something that the world of change and limitation can never give us.

In meditation we travel inwards, beyond the frontiers of time and space, to discover our true home. This is a journey to the land of light.

To visit this land we do not have to reserve tickets or get a passport or a visa; all we need to do is throw away our biggest piece of luggage, the ego. If we can extinguish our selfishness, if we can put an end to our self-will and separateness, then wherever we go, whether it is Iceland or Australia, we will find ourselves in the kingdom of heaven.

In describing our true nature, Sri Krishna uses the word *akshara*, 'that which does not age, decay, or die.' Our real Self can never die, but it is the nature of the body to change continuously until it comes to the last great change that is death. My mother, who lives with us as an important member of our spiritual family, has a special way of remembering this fact. When she came to stay with us in this country, she brought with her from India a supply of ashes. The customs official must have been a little puzzled; probably he could not have guessed their grim purpose. Every morning she puts a mark on her forehead with these ashes to remind everyone, including herself, that someday this is what our bodies will become. There is a very practical purpose behind many of these Hindu customs, and often it is to help us remember that the purpose of life is to learn to go beyond death. Every mystic worth his or her mantram will tell us not to waste a single day, not to postpone the practice of meditation even a single morning, but to start living today in such a way that we will be able to transcend the body when death takes place.

I remember once reading a story about a man who kept putting off taking to the spiritual life in order to have just a little more pleasure, or one more windfall of profit. Again and again he vowed that next week, or next month, or next year, he would change his life. Then one night he had a terrible dream: he dreamed he was about to die. There was no chance now to change his direction; time had passed him by, and all the plans he had had for making a new start in life could never be. It was a terrifying experience, and as he struggled to wake up and shake it off he vowed passionately not to put off the practice of meditation a single morning more. But when he tried to sit up, he could not make his body obey him. Then, wide awake at last, he realized that the dream was true.

We cannot afford to put off changing our habits, even for what appear to be very good reasons. If we are not in the best physical condition, meditation will improve our health. If we have emotional problems, either with others or with ourselves, in meditation we will be able to get beneath these problems at their source. Any difficulty, any problem can be an incentive for practicing meditation. No matter how many drawbacks we may have, no matter how many mistakes we may have made, the Lord will accept us joyfully. This is why in Hinduism he is called Mitra, our truest friend.

पुरुषः स परः पार्थ भक्त्या लभ्यस्त्वनन्यया ।
यस्यान्तःस्थानि भूतानि येन सर्वमिदं ततम् ॥८-२२॥

22. This supreme Reality which pervades all existence, the true Self of all creatures, may be realized through undivided love.

This one short sentence gives away the secret of the spiritual life. The medieval Cloud of Unknowing says in very similar words: "By love may He be gotten and holden, by thought never." The supreme Reality cannot be attained by any amount of reasoning, for He is one and indivisible, beyond all duality. But by loving Him "with all our heart, and all our soul, and all our strength," we can come to live in Him completely and go beyond death here and now. And St. John of the Cross gives us the reason: we do not live in what we think; we live in what we love.

There is nothing abstract about this kind of love, nothing philosophical. Loving the Lord means loving those around us, in each of whom he is present as the innermost Self. The chief thing is somehow to increase our capacity to love. Here, at the beginning, everyone has the same question: how? I imagine people have been asking this question for as long as there have been spiritual teachers on earth. And the answer has been the same all along, in every spiritual tradition. There is a charming story about St. Francis of Sales, a very practical spiritual teacher in sixteenth-century France, that puts it beautifully. One of his disciples, a young bishop of the church, asked Francis how to attain perfection.

Francis's answer was straight from his Master: "Love the Lord with all your heart, and your neighbor more than yourself."

These were scarcely new words to the bishop, and he was a little frustrated by them. "I don't want to know what perfection is," he objected; "I want to know how to attain it."

"Oh," said Francis. "Then you must love the Lord with all your heart, and your neighbor as yourself."

And that was all the bishop could get out of his friend, though he kept on asking several times more. Finally, seeing his frustration, Francis explained with words we can all remember: "Many people have asked me for a secret way to perfection, but there is no secret except undivided love of God, and the only way to gain that love is by loving. You learn to speak by speaking, to study by studying, to run by running, to work by working; in just the same way, you learn to love by loving."

Love grows by practice; there is no other way. Whenever you forgo something you want to do in order to give your time and help to those around you, you are increasing your capacity to love. Naturally, at the beginning, there will be reservations in your heart: "All right, we'll go to the opera – but I still want to go to *Gone With the Wind!*" That is the time to ignore your reservations, put on a smile, and repeat the mantram instead. As you begin to forget yourself and see how much your partner is enjoying the opera, or how much your little girl is enjoying her fourth performance of *Alice in Wonderland*, your reservations will fade away. St. Teresa of Ávila says beautifully, "*Amor saca amor*": love draws out love. By putting the people around you first, you *are* loving more, not only them but the Lord himself, in whom they and you are one.

यत्र काले त्वनावृत्तिमावृत्तिं चैव योगिनः ।
प्रयाता यान्ति तं कालं वक्ष्यामि भरतर्षभ ॥८-२३॥
अग्निर्ज्योतिरहः शुक्लः षण्मासा उत्तरायणम् ।
तत्र प्रयाता गच्छन्ति ब्रह्म ब्रह्मविदो जनाः ॥८-२४॥
धूमो रात्रिस्तथा कृष्णः षण्मासा दक्षिणायनम् ।
तत्र चान्द्रमसं ज्योतिर्योगी प्राप्य निवर्तते ॥८-२५॥

23. There are two paths, Arjuna, which the soul may follow at the time of death. One leads to rebirth and the other to liberation.
24. The northern path, the path of light, of fire, of day, of the bright fortnight, leads selfless souls to the supreme goal.
25. The southern path, the path of smoke, of night, of the dark fortnight, leads the others to the light of the moon and to rebirth.

These three verses borrow symbolic language from the Upanishads to describe two paths which the soul travels after death. The meaning of these verses is rather obscure, and scholars have had some difficulty in interpreting these two paths. One is called *uttarāyana*, 'the northern path,' and the other is *dakshināyana*, 'the southern path.' The usual interpretation is that the northern path is a reference to the six months during which the sun appears to move across the northern hemisphere of the sky, and the southern path is a reference to the six months of the sun's southern passage. This is the literal explanation, but for me it is much more practical to interpret these paths in terms of the destiny we choose for ourselves.

Every one of us – rich or poor, educated or not so well educated – has to choose continually between what leads to personal, private satisfaction and what leads to the welfare of the whole. But while most of us can appreciate the ideal of living for others, we still do not know how to translate this ideal into our own lives. As long as we are self-centered, we are not even likely to see what is in another's best interest, and often we make the wrong choices unwittingly. Our problem has a very simple diagnosis: clouded vision. We have cataracts of self-will that keep us from seeing life as it really is. Even with the best of intentions we may do things that disrupt personal relationships, and then we give up and retire into our own seemingly safe pursuits. But clouded vision is not an incurable disease. It is possible for us to clear our eyes, and as we do so, we will be able to distinguish more and more surely these paths of light and darkness.

When I was growing up in my village, I heard from my grandmother many stories that help to explain difficult verses like these in the Bhagavad Gita. One story, from the *Mahābhārata*, was of a patriarch called Bhīshma. Bhīshma was a splendid spiritual teacher, but unfortunately he was a teacher to the Kauravas, the forces of darkness, and though he tried to win them away from violence, they would not listen to him. Unable to understand his teaching, they ignored his warnings and went to war against Arjuna and his brothers at Kurukshetra, the very battle in which the dialogue of the Gita unfolds. Bhīshma was mortally wounded in this battle. Pierced by many arrows, he lay in agony for fifty-eight days – "on a bed of arrows," as the epic poet says. Despite this terrible suffering, however, he kept his body alive through a great effort of will until the sun had crossed the equinox from the southern hemisphere to the northern, so that he could shed his body during the northern path of the sun, the time considered auspicious for death according to ancient Hindu tradition. He was prepared to suffer any amount of pain in order to attain the path of the sun, the path of light and unity.

My grandmother never read a book on the Gita, but all these things were a natural part of her daily life. She was a simple Hindu woman with complete, unshakable faith in Sri Krishna's message, and for her, to believe something was to live in accord with it. When she was stricken with a fatal illness at the age of seventy-seven, which is a ripe old age in India, it was the dark period of the sun's path, the six months of dakshināyana. In spite of our doctor's prediction that her death was imminent, my grandmother, who had utter faith in Sri Krishna, bravely kept her body functioning until the period of uttarāyana came. Her deep faith in the Lord enabled her to wait until the remaining months of the southern path were finished. Then, as soon as uttarāyana began and the sun entered its northern path, she gave up her body. It showed us all that anyone with great love for the Lord, who lives not for herself but for the welfare of those around her, has a deeper will to sustain her and support her.

We, too, should count no cost too high for attaining the realization of God. When we start training our senses, most of us who have not had any experience of this discipline suffer acutely. But we should cheerfully put up with any feelings of deprivation, for the time will come when training the senses is a source not of suffering but of joy.

In this verse, uttarāyana is called the path of light; dakshināyana is the path of darkness. Those who let their senses run amuck, who follow the call of self-will, are traveling on the dark path. Often such people quickly lose their vitality and fall victim to sickness; and in the latter part of life they find themselves left in the worst state any human being can endure – having all the strong desires they had when young but no capacity to indulge them; having fierce self-will and no one left near them on whom it can be imposed. Feeling life to be desolate, they wait for death to come and relieve them of their burden. That is the path of darkness. There are millions of people treading this path because they cannot bear to pay the price of suffering that comes in changing habits; they cannot face the suffering that comes in reducing self-will. This is the price that is asked. If we remember this interpretation of the path of light and the path of darkness, these three verses can provide deep motivation for the practice of meditation.

शुक्लकृष्णे गती ह्येते जगतः शाश्वते मते ।
एकया यात्यनावृत्तिमन्ययावर्तते पुनः ॥८-२६॥

26. These two paths, the light and the dark, are said to be eternal, leading some to liberation and others to rebirth.

In the Hindu scriptures, there are said to be seven realms of consciousness, each of which is associated with a particular center along the spinal column. In most human beings, who have not made a disciplined effort to arouse spiritual awareness, the evolutionary energy called *kundalinī* circulates among the three lowest centers. These are the centers of physical consciousness, connected with the functions of the body. It is when kundalinī rises to the higher levels of consciousness, the fourth center and beyond, that you begin to see the light spoken of in this verse.

Along with this vision of light comes a greater capacity to see life clearly, because every experience in the depths of meditation has its effect on daily life. This is the test of any so-called spiritual experience: does it have a beneficial effect on your conduct and character? If at any time, especially during meditation or at night, you experience a vision of light or have some similar experience, the following day there must be an immediate benefit. Old inhibitions will have fallen away; a long-standing conflict in personal relationships may be resolved; you will have a much clearer perception of the unity of life. This is the test. If such changes do not take place, I would say your experience has not been a valid one. But if these changes do occur, then there is no mistaking your progress.

When you have been leading an ordinary life for many years, for a long time you will have no perception of the light within. If you manage to rouse kundalinī to the fourth center, there will seem to be only a few dim rays of light. Actually, the mystics say, the room is full of light; it is only that you haven't yet learned to see inside. As Cardinal Newman puts it, you are still "blinded by the garish day." You cannot yet see clearly, but you are beginning to make out the outline of things. You now have a consuming enthusiasm for meditation, and you are beginning to perceive the unity underlying life. It is not enough now to be concerned for your family's welfare alone; you must expand your love to a much wider circle. You cannot help grieving when a child in Africa is hungry, and you feel a sense of loss even at the death of the smallest creature – not out of sentimental attachment, but out of a deep awareness of unity.

Slowly, as kundalinī begins to travel upwards towards the fifth center, at the level of the throat, you begin to see more and more clearly. At last, after many long years of intense spiritual struggle, kundalinī reaches the center between the eyebrows, the center of Krishna-consciousness or Christ-consciousness. Then you see quite clearly. As St. Paul tells us in those wonderful lines from Corinthians, "Now we see as through a glass darkly; but then we shall see face to face." The Hindu scriptures call this state *savikalpa samādhi,* a state of deep concentration in which we have the vision of our chosen spiritual ideal. After that we will see the Lord present everywhere, which means we can never bring ourselves to harm any living creature.

When, in a few very rare men and women, kundalinī finally rises to the seventh center, there is nothing but light, a light that can never be seen by physical eyes. This is the complete unitive state, called *nirvikalpa samādhi.* The light is so bright it is like the direct light of the sun, which we cannot bear to look at lest our eyes be burned or our vision lost forever. This is why it is so important on the spiritual path for us to strengthen our will, train our senses, and master our passions; otherwise we cannot bear to look at even a small ray of this light, let alone the dazzling radiance of samādhi. Only the rare person who has prepared himself or herself over many decades or many lives can withstand this stupendous experience, which is the goal of spiritual evolution.

This ascent through the seven centers of consciousness is the bright path, the path of the sun, which is also called *devayāna,* 'the path of the gods,' 'the divine path.' It is this path we set out on when we make the choice to practice meditation and turn our backs on petty, personal pursuits. The Mundaka Upanishad describes very precisely those who travel by this path to reach the supreme state:

> But those who are pure in heart, who practice
> Meditation and conquer their senses
> And passions, shall attain the eternal Self,
> The source of all light and source of all life.

On the other side is the dark path, the path of the moon. The moon has no light of its own; it has only borrowed light. When they stood on the moon, our astronauts said, the earth looked beautiful but the moon was cold and bleak, completely devoid of life, altogether unlike the shimmering image we have of it in earthly skies. In the Gita, the path of the moon symbolizes the path of greater and greater darkness. To me this refers not to astrological phenomena but to successive stages in life. When we dwell on ourselves, indulge ourselves more and more – eating what is not nourishing, eating too much, growing addicted to alcohol or to drugs – in the long run, as Jesus says, the whole body becomes filled with darkness. Health goes, and health is the light of the body, the very basis of beauty. Those who do not have the will to control their senses soon lose not only their health but their physical beauty, too.

Look at those who pursue the life of pleasure – people who are often envied for their wealth or youth, as in the song my friend Jeff sings, "If I had his money, I would do things my way." The Gita would say, "If you had his money and did things your way, you would probably just fall sick." In our twenties, we can get away temporarily with quite a lot – if we want evidence of the mercy of the Lord, all we have to do is look at our past and see what we have got away with. But we are not going to be in our twenties for the rest of our lives. Finally, as the Buddhist scriptures are so fond of telling us, we must all grow old. Then, after the ebullience and vitality of youth have passed, we may well be left feeling rootless, without any direction in life at all. We can still be vitally alive even in our last years, but not when we use our body for pleasure or cling to it for security. Then the body will lose its strength far more quickly than is necessary.

The more self-willed we are, the more darkness there will be inside. Always in the dark, we will always be insecure, not knowing how to relate to people or how to be at home with others. Not knowing how to love or how to be loved: that is the path of darkness. Just as in meditation we go from light to more light and finally to light that is infinite, so in living a selfish life we go from darkness to increasing darkness – not only on the physical level, but on the emotional level also.

As self-will increases, rigidity increases too. Rigid people cannot change habits; they have to have their way always. Most tragically, they cannot even understand how other people can have different ways and different conditioning. Without this understanding, how can they be patient? After thirty, it becomes increasingly difficult for the impatient person to learn patience, increasingly difficult for almost all of us to change our ways. There is no statement more poignant to me than an older person saying, "I can't change." I hear this often, and not only from older people, either. I always reply that everybody can change. It is going to be more and more difficult as we grow set in our ways, but no matter how long we may have spent on the path of darkness, we can always cross over to the path of light.

नैते सृती पार्थ जानन्योगी मुह्यति कश्चन ।
तस्मात्सर्वेषु कालेषु योगयुक्तो भवार्जुन ॥८-२७॥

27. Once you have known these two paths, Arjuna, you can never be deluded again. But to attain this knowledge, your perseverance must be unfailing.

In Sanskrit the delusion of separateness, symbolized by the path of darkness, is called *līlā,* the play of the Lord. It's not a play that takes place somewhere off Broadway; the entire universe is līlā, and it is the Lord, simultaneously wearing countless billions of masks, who plays all the parts.

The tragic part of this play is that all of us have forgotten that we are in costume. We have been playing our little drama for so many billions of years that we have forgotten who we really are. Little by little we have become completely entangled in the part we are playing. This is the delusion of Māyā. It is only when our ego is dissolved and our self-will extinguished that we make the remarkable discovery that we, along with everybody else, have been participating in a cosmic theatrical production, sometimes playing our role well and sometimes botching our lines completely.

Some time ago, for example, we saw Richard Burton and Elizabeth

Taylor in a film version of *The Taming of the Shrew.* Both of them played their parts with enthusiasm, and I greatly enjoyed the crucial scene when Petruchio finally bends a bedraggled Kate to his self-will:

> "Kate, I say it is the moon that shines."
> "I *know* it is the moon."
> "Nay, then, you lie; it is the blessed sun."
> "Then, God be blessed, it *is* the blessed sun."

It was all very convincingly done. But I couldn't help wondering what would happen if Richard Burton kept on thinking he was Petruchio after the scene was shot and they both went home; I don't think he would have got so far. Yet that is just what we do in life; we forget all about our costumes and makeup and keep on acting the same old part twenty-four hours a day.

Tragically, the drama we are acting out isn't always a comedy; all too often it's more like *Othello* or *King Lear.* Try watching *Othello* with real detachment; then, when Othello is raving in jealousy, you'll want to climb up on the stage, tap him on the shoulder, and say, "That's just a *handkerchief* you're getting so excited about; you can get four of them for a dollar at Penney's. It's your imagination that is driving you into a frenzy." Even in life, that is all that is behind most of our misunderstandings. At breakfast our husband or wife makes some innocent remark that we don't appreciate and in a few minutes, because of what we imagine he or she was saying, both of us are so agitated that we cannot even finish our toast. Do you see the absurdity of it? We are getting indigestion not over what was said or even what was meant, but over our *idea* of what the other person really meant. That is why the Buddha says so penetratingly, "The problem is not with the other person; the problem is with your mind." When our mind is calm we can see clearly, and we can act all our parts in life with consummate artistry. This is a very refreshing change of perspective. I think it was Noel Coward who was asked for the secret of good acting. He replied, "Speak your lines clearly and don't bump into people." When all is said and done, when you can get through life without bumping into people, you have managed a great deal.

Once I began to see through this game of līlā, I used to go into my classroom very much as if I were going onto the stage. I would put on my professorial robes, put on a suitably intellectual look, and say, "Now you're Eknath Easwaran the professor of English," and I would go into my classes and give them all a really good show. Not only that, I used to do all the paperwork in just the same spirit. But when the last class was over and it was time to go home, I would hang up my professorial role right there with the robes, and step into my next role like one of those quick-change artists you see in the circus. There is a lot of satisfaction in this, and once you master it you have gone a long way towards mastering the art of living.

वेदेषु यज्ञेषु तपःसु चैव
दानेषु यत्पुण्यफलं प्रदिष्टम् ।
अत्येति तत्सर्वमिदं विदित्वा
योगी परं स्थानमुपैति चाद्यम् ॥८-२८॥

28. There is merit in studying the scriptures,
in selfless service, in giving of oneself, and
in going against self-will, but the practice of
meditation carries you beyond all these to
the supreme abode of the Lord of Love.

Meditation is the very basis of the spiritual life. It is meditation that enables us to understand the teachings of the mystics and apply them in our daily life; it is meditation that gives us the immense power to stay patient and forgiving when all our conditioning is crying out for an eye or a tooth. There is nothing exciting about meditation, nothing glamorous, and I have never presented it as anything but a lot of hard, hard work. But when the alarm goes off in the morning, even in the dead of winter when the bed is warm and the blankets don't want to let them go, my friends get up for their meditation with eagerness and enthusiasm every day, rain or shine, well or not so well, because they know now from their own experience that meditation is the key to the art of living. This is the theme of the next chapter.

अक्षरब्रह्मयोगो नामाष्टमोऽध्यायः ॥ ८ ॥

CHAPTER NINE

The Royal Path

श्रीभगवानुवाच ।
इदं तु ते गुह्यतमं प्रवक्ष्याम्यनसूयवे ।
ज्ञानं विज्ञानसहितं यज्ज्ञात्वा मोक्ष्यसे ऽशुभात् ॥९-१॥

SRI KRISHNA:

1. Because of your faith, I shall tell you the most profound of secrets: obtaining both jnāna and vijnāna, you will be free from all evil.

A few years ago, at a Halloween party we gave for the children at our āshram, my two nieces Meera and Geetha made me up to look like a maharaja. It didn't take much in the way of props; most of the disguise was a silk sari tied into a turban, with a fancy crest which my wife had picked up for ten cents in some bargain basement. When I went to show my mother – who still hasn't figured out what Halloween is all about – I asked her playfully, "Well, do I look like a maharaja?" With great love in her eyes she answered simply, "You *are* a maharaja." It wasn't just figurative language. *Rāja* means king, and rāja yoga is meditation, the 'royal path,' because by mastering meditation we become masters of our lives.

This chapter opens with the same theme with which we opened this volume: jnāna and vijnāna. These are the fruits of meditation. Jnāna is knowledge – not of the natural world, but of the unity of life. Vijnāna is the artful capacity to apply this knowledge to the problems of daily living. Sri Ramakrishna says that intellectual knowledge is like knowing that you can get a fire from two sticks; jnāna is actually making the fire. But vijnāna is cooking rice on the fire, eating it, and being strengthened by its nourishment.

In other words, jnāna and vijnāna together make up the art of living. This art is not a luxury; it is a dire necessity. Not long before he died, Arnold Toynbee, one of the most perceptive historians of any age, observed with deceptive simplicity that the main reason our civilization has made so much progress in science and technology is that a lot of people have applied themselves to science and technology. That's all; there is no inherent reason. We have applied ourselves to the "arts" of war, so now we can kill everyone on earth several times over. We can manipulate genes; we can transplant vital organs from one body to another; we can send coded messages into outer space so that anyone out there receiving these messages will be intrigued about who we are. We can do all these things because a lot of people have tried to do such things, over a period of time. And Toynbee adds, if we remain ignorant of the meaning of our lives, if we can't even live in peace together as individuals or as nations, it is only because we have been writing all our entries on the other side of the ledger.

There is no need to get despondent over this; it is only a matter of lack of balance. There is nothing wrong with science or technology. The problem is simply that they cannot give themselves a sense of direction. No amount of studying the physical world can ever give us knowledge of spiritual values. It is we human beings who must give direction to what we investigate, what we invent, what we apply; otherwise we are racing along at an impressive rate with no one at the wheel. If we want to change the situation in which we find ourselves today, Toynbee is telling us, we have to get behind the wheel. If we gave even a little of the attention we now give science to what Sri Krishna calls here *brahmavidyā,* the 'supreme science' of Self-knowledge, most of the problems that threaten our world could be banished once and for all.

Here it is interesting to look at a current area of investigation in the neurosciences, the divided brain. The two sides of the brain seem to have very different functions. The left half, which is highly analytical, tends to dominate personality; it specializes in intellectual skills like speaking, writing, reasoning, and mathematics. This is the half with which researchers feel most comfortable: they at least understand what it is good for, even if they don't know how it does what it does or why. But the right half of the brain is much more of a mystery, because its contribution is not to intellectual capacities but to ill-defined realms like creativity, intuition, and the appreciation of beauty. However, though we do not know much about how the brain functions in these areas, or what else the right half of the brain does which we haven't yet discovered, virtually everyone agrees that you can't get along well in life with half a brain. If you have spent all your life putting muscles on the left side of the brain, you may be able to eat and sleep and work crossword puzzles and carry on an intelligent conversation, but to be a whole person you need to develop the right side of the brain as well.

This is what happens in the practice of meditation. Meditation *is* the integration of consciousness, and one of the many physiological developments that take place naturally as our meditation deepens is that all the activities of the brain begin to come into balance. In some of the Sanskrit scriptures these developments are said to take place with the rise of kundalinī, or evolutionary energy, through the spinal column towards the brain. When, after many years of sincere effort in meditation, kundalinī finally reaches the crown of the head, the billions of cells in the brain all burst into integrated activity. This is samādhi, the stupendous climax of meditation, and it brings about a complete transformation of personality. Afterwards there is a never-ending flow of creative power for solving the problems around us, and the immense endurance not to rest until a lasting solution can be found.

To take just one example of this approach, look at the problem of violence. From international organizations down to local communities, everyone is concerned about the spread of violence, but it never seems to occur to anyone that this is a problem that can actually be solved. Everywhere the assumption seems to be, "We just have to learn to live with it." In my language, that means we will only learn to die with it. To prevent robbery and assault, we are told to put more locks on our doors, to train our dogs to bite even worse than they bark, to install burglar alarms that will upset the whole neighborhood, and to carry harmful chemicals in our pockets or purses for spraying would-be attackers. All these are just palliatives; they do not touch the causes of violence at all. I am not denying that there are some first-aid measures, such as gun control legislation, that should be put into effect as soon as possible. But the root cause of violence is separateness, and until we do something about separateness, violence is going to increase unchecked no matter what else we do.

Here the solution of the mystics is daring in its simplicity: we can show, through our own example, how to build rich, steadfast personal relationships everywhere we go. After all, this is what gives life meaning: not money, or prestige, or power, or even pleasure, but plenty of deep relationships that cannot be shaken by any change in fortune. If you think it is farfetched, just try it. Start with your home and begin to rebuild your neighborhood. Get to know your neighbors; make your home the center of your life. Don't go to some other neighborhood every night for entertainment or sit alone with the television; go out for walks with your friends, share your porch with your neighbors on summer evenings, do things with your children and the children of those around you. It is when all the houses on your block are separate Bastilles of loneliness – or worse, just empty shells – that a neighborhood begins to be plagued by violence. When you live in a community of trust, full of friendly relationships and human activity, problems like violence will not arise at all. Not only that, they will be replaced by a way of life that is so much more satisfying that people will look back on these days of separateness and fear as a nightmare from which they have awakened into day.

राजविद्या राजगुह्यं पवित्रमिदमुत्तमम् ।
प्रत्यक्षावगमं धर्म्यं सुसुखं कर्तुमव्ययम् ॥९-२॥

2. This royal knowledge, this royal secret, is the greatest purifier. Supreme and imperishable, it is a joy to seek and can be directly experienced.

Many years ago I was taken to the library of someone who had collected almost all the books ever published on meditation in any language. I had never seen so many books on meditation in my life, and I told my host, "You must meditate regularly."

He coughed apologetically. "Actually," he explained, "what with all these books to study, I don't have time for meditation." Then he asked politely, "You must be familiar with most of these titles?"

I, too, coughed apologetically. "No," I said, "I don't have time to read many books on meditation. I use the time to meditate."

It is not enough to read about meditation, or talk about meditation, or do research on meditation; if you want Self-realization, you have to learn to meditate. And there is only one way to learn to meditate – through trying to meditate. Wasn't there someone who said he would never get into water unless he had learned to swim?

Meditation is often presented as a pleasant experience in which you hear birds singing and see flowers blooming while you float along in a wonderland. Actually, floating in a wonderland is just the opposite of meditation. In order to learn to meditate, you have to put in a great deal of work. For a month or two the person who has just taken to meditation will tell you all about how grand it is. But it is only fair to point out that, once you really get started, this initial surge of enthusiasm is going to wane. To guard against such ups and downs, I would make several suggestions.

First, it is very helpful to meditate with others. A group of friends meditating along the same lines can meditate together and draw support from one another. As Jesus says, "Where two or three are gathered together in my name, I am present in the midst of them." It is especially helpful if husband and wife can meditate together, even if it takes some rearranging of schedules. Any family in which both partners meditate is blessed, and children growing up in such a household will have a legacy of security on which they can draw throughout their lives.

Second, be very regular about your meditation. There is a saying in India that if you miss meditation just one morning, it takes seven mornings to make it up. You can see that if you miss seven mornings, you have a big job on your hands. So please do not ever skip your meditation, no matter what the temptation. If you are ill, or if you are feeling exceptionally well and think you don't need any meditation that day, that is just the time you should meditate. The ego is such a clever customer that it waits for the slightest opportunity to regain any territory it may have lost.

You can make time for meditation anywhere. I have sometimes had to meditate on the train or even in the faculty lounge, and on board ship on my way to this country I used to have my meditation on the sports deck, which is a remarkably quiet place early in the morning when the games enthusiasts are still asleep. If you can always meditate at the same time of day, too, you will find that helps a great deal. The mind becomes used to behaving itself when the time for meditation comes around. If you are still asleep, it will start to nag at you and say, "It's six o'clock; if you don't get up now you're not going to have time for breakfast," and when you sit down to meditate, the mind will gradually resign itself to a little discipline for half an hour.

Third, it is very important to practice the disciplines related to meditation, such as repeating the mantram and putting the welfare of those around us first. These are elaborated on in the Introduction in my eight-point program for spiritual living. Meditation taps a source of tremendous power, and the other seven points in this program play a vital role in harnessing this power so that it can be used wisely for the benefit of all.

Fourth, check all your living habits very carefully – your food, your sleep, your exercise, everything. To make steady progress in meditation, you need to be as careful as an athlete during training – eating only good, nourishing food in appropriate quantities, getting the amount of sleep you need rather than more or less, and getting plenty of physical exercise. Meditation is turning inwards, and it needs to be balanced by plenty of physical activity. This body of ours is meant for motion, and one of the best ways to see that it gets it is by walking whenever you get the chance: to work, to the post office, before breakfast, after dinner. A long, fast walk is not only excellent exercise; it is relaxing and invigorating, especially when it is combined with the mantram. For those who are young, hard physical work is good too, especially when it is at something that benefits those around you.

Finally, I would emphasize the need to be with people and to contribute to life around you. When you are meditating regularly, you need the counterpoise of being with family and friends. As you begin to taste the security and joy within, you may develop the tendency to bask in this inward state. From my own experience, I would say that this is just the time to turn your attention outwards. Unless we maintain close relationships with those around us, there is the danger of getting caught inside, locked within the lonely prison of the ego. To learn to live in harmony with others, to feel at home with everyone, we need the close ties of a wide circle of family and friends. None of us can afford to retire into ourselves and do our own thing if we want to become aware of the unity of life.

After singing the praises of meditation, I would like to give a few precautions now concerning its practice. For one, make sure that you are concentrating fully on the words of the inspirational passage and not letting them slip away from your grasp as meditation deepens. Following the passage is rather like flying a kite, carefully letting the string pass through your fingers as you watch the kite become just a speck in the sky. If you do not pay enough attention to the string, which is the passage, it will slip from your grasp and you will lose the kite, which is concentration. So if you find stray words, or odd sounds, or lights and colors trying to coax your attention away, please ignore them and give your attention more and more to the words of the inspirational piece. It is important, right from the first days of meditation, to develop the habit of not letting distractions get the better of you.

Of course, the mind is going to wander somewhat in spite of your best efforts. The one thing necessary is to keep bringing the mind back whenever distractions disturb you. As St. Francis of Sales points out, "And even if you did nothing during the whole of your hour but bring your heart back and place it again in our Lord's presence, though it went away every time you brought it back, your hour would be very well employed." After many years, your concentration is going to take you into the depths of the unconscious mind. What you will be attempting to do then is to enter the unconscious while remaining completely conscious. At that time, even if you can remain awake in this uncharted area, you will not know how to walk. That is where the inspirational passage serves as a lifeline, helping you travel the vast realms of the unconscious in security. There are certain areas in the mind which resemble an Alice's Wonderland of fears and fancies, but as long as you keep the words of the passage as your lifeline, you will be able to discriminate between the facts and fictions of the unconscious.

Another common problem to guard against is sleep in meditation. Sleepiness is bound to come as your meditation progresses, so it is good to prepare for it now. As concentration deepens, the neuromuscular system relaxes. One sign of relaxation is a very happy look on the face; then, the next thing you know, your head may be on your chest. Often people are not aware that they have gone to sleep in meditation, and sometimes they continue in this state for as much as fifteen minutes. To avoid this, draw yourself away from your back support into a firm, erect posture the moment you feel sleepy. If that isn't enough, open your eyes and repeat your mantram – *Jesus, Jesus, Jesus* or *Rāma, Rāma, Rāma*. But when you do this, do not let your eyes wander; your mind will wander as well. Choose some spot in front of you that helps to focus your attention – it might be a picture of Sri Krishna, or Jesus, or the Compassionate Buddha – and let your eyes rest on that while you repeat your mantram. After a while the wave of sleep will pass, and you can close your eyes again and continue with the words of the passage.

It is important to keep on memorizing new passages for use in meditation; then the words will always be fresh with meaning. The Prayer of St. Francis of Assisi is a beautiful one, but if you try using nothing else for several months, it will become so familiar that the mind will not be sufficiently challenged and may move through the words mechanically. There is a wide range of inspirational passages from the world's great spiritual traditions, some of which I have mentioned in the Introduction to this volume.

In India we have a peculiar yellow fruit called the amla which is a great favorite with children. When I first bit into an amla, I thought there must be some mistake; it was so sour that I wanted to spit it out. But my grandmother told me to keep chewing. I made a wry face but kept on chewing, and slowly it began to get sweeter. Finally it became so sweet that I asked if she had any more. Meditation is like this amla fruit. At first it is not exactly pleasant, but if you stick with it and never let anything come in the way, the time for meditation will become the most precious part of the day.

अश्रद्दधानाः पुरुषा धर्मस्यास्य परंतप ।
अप्राप्य मां निवर्तन्ते मृत्युसंसारवर्त्मनि ॥९-३॥

3. But those who have no faith in the supreme law of life do not find me, O scorcher of the foe; they return to the world, passing from death to death.

The word used for faith here is *shraddhā* – literally, 'that which is placed in the heart.' Shraddhā is what we believe will bring us the fulfillment that all of us are seeking – not what we think will bring us fulfillment, but what we really believe in our heart of hearts. In this sense, everyone has faith in something. Just look at people who are devoted to skiing, who love the challenge of hurtling down precipitous slopes at top speed on two little pieces of fiberglass. These are people with a tremendous amount of energy and enthusiasm and nothing to do with it. They need an outlet for all this energy, so they jump at the most difficult challenge they can find. But no less tremendous than their energy is their faith – that skiing has the power to make them happy. All of us have our own equivalent of skiing, whatever we think will bring us lasting joy. The tragedy is that wherever this faith is in something outside us – money, or drugs, or personal pleasure, or the thrill of the dangerous and the unknown – it is inescapable that someday we are going to be let down. So the Buddha warns pointedly, "Don't ever put your faith in what is changing; it *has* to fail you in time."

One of the most tragic examples of misplaced shraddhā is substance abuse. A CBS documentary in 1986 reported that 60 percent of the world's illegal drugs are used in the United States, reflecting the frightening rise in cocaine addiction. But alcoholism may still be the country's biggest drug problem. Over twelve million Americans have symptoms of alcoholism, and more than 57 percent of adult Americans report that they are "current users." The human being has to put faith in something, and these are cases where shraddhā has got locked in a bottle or a packet of powder. It is especially tragic with young people, most of whom, I feel, turn to drugs when they look around them and find no channels where the natural idealism of youth can flow. We should never look down on such people. All of us are searching restlessly for fulfillment, usually in the wrong places, and the thirst for spirits, as William James said, is really a spiritual thirst for the living waters of life.

The Gita takes an extremely positive approach towards this problem. It says that even though our faith may not be in something that is particularly relevant to living, the very fact that we are capable of such faith means that there is hope. Once our faith is changed, we can become as enthusiastic a spiritual aspirant as we were a skier or world traveler. For the skiers, all I have to tell them is, "Your kind of skiing isn't worthy of such faith. How would you like the challenge of skiing *up* the slope?" This is meditation: no chair lift, no towline, no source of momentum at all. You must ski uphill, against all that is easy, against every impulse that says, "Go your own way; do your own thing." Anyone who can respond to a challenge like this has the capacity to transform shraddhā, and when shraddhā is transformed, the alcoholic may emerge a stronger person than the teetotaler, because he or she has access to tremendous drives which now can be brought under control.

मया ततमिदं सर्वं जगदव्यक्तमूर्तिना ।
मत्स्थानि सर्वभूतानि न चाहं तेष्ववस्थितः ॥९-४॥
न च मत्स्थानि भूतानि पश्य मे योगमैश्वरम् ।
भूतभृन्न च भूतस्थो ममात्मा भूतभावनः ॥९-५॥
यथाकाशस्थितो नित्यं वायुः सर्वत्रगो महान् ।
तथा सर्वाणि भूतानि मत्स्थानीत्युपधारय ॥९-६॥

4. I pervade the entire universe in my unmanifested form. All creatures find their existence in me, but I am not limited by them.
5–6. Behold my divine mystery! These creatures do not really dwell in me, and though I bring them forth and support them, I am not confined within them; they move in me as the winds move in every direction in space.

This is a paradox which lies at the very heart of the mystical experience. The Lord is present in every living creature, in every atom, yet he is in no way limited by any of these forms. In the climax of meditation, when we have the tremendous experience of union with the Lord, we too will be lost in wonder that he whom the galaxies cannot contain, whom the entire cosmos cannot contain, is contained in your heart and mine.

This is the mystery of Māyā. How is it that this hand of mine appears solid and brown? Physicists would tell me it is not solid and brown at all, but a pattern of countless tiny nodes of energy, like the swirl of winds in the air. If I see it as having a fixed shape and color and call it my hand, that is just because of the inherent limitations in my perception. In other words, its shape and other characteristics are not in the world outside me; they are in the very fabric of thinking and perceiving. In the great leap of insight that comes in samādhi, the mystics tell us that all this world of names and forms is nothing but the Lord. As Shankara says so beautifully, "Names and forms are like gold bangles and bracelets; the Lord is like the gold."

Towards the end of *The Tempest*, Shakespeare uses the language of great poetry to convey a similar idea:

> Our revels now are ended. These our actors,
> As I foretold you, were but spirits, and
> Are melted into air, into thin air.
> And, like the baseless fabric of this vision,
> The cloud-capped towers, the gorgeous palaces,
> The solemn temples, the great globe itself –
> Yea, all which it inherit – shall dissolve
> And, like this insubstantial pageant faded,
> Leave not a rack behind. We are such stuff
> As dreams are made on, and our little life
> Is rounded with a sleep.

Aldous Huxley, who was associated for many years with Swami Prabhavananda in this country, commented: "Prospero is here enunciating the doctrine of Māyā. The world is an illusion, but it is an illusion which we must take seriously, because it is real as far as it goes, and in those aspects of the reality which we are capable of apprehending. Our business is to wake up. . . . We must continually be on our watch for ways in which to enlarge our consciousness. We must not attempt to live outside the world, which is given us, but we must somehow learn how to transform it and transfigure it. . . . One must find a way of being in this world while not being of it. One must find a way of living in time without being completely swallowed up in time."

Sometimes, to remind him that he is not the body, I tease my friend Jim by telling him there is no Jim there at all; it is only an energy process walking down the road. The truth is that until I have the direct experience that he is really the Ātman and the body I see is just Māyā, there is a Jim there. As long as we live in Māyā, we have to treat these names and forms as real. But we should never forget, even for an instant, that under all these disguises there is no one but the Lord.

सर्वभूतानि कौन्तेय प्रकृतिं यान्ति मामिकाम् ।
कल्पक्षये पुनस्तानि कल्पादौ विसृजाम्यहम् ॥९-७॥
प्रकृतिं स्वामवष्टभ्य विसृजामि पुनः पुनः ।
भूतग्राममिमं कृत्स्नमवशं प्रकृतेर्वशात् ॥९-८॥
न च मां तानि कर्माणि निबध्नन्ति धनंजय ।
उदासीनवदासीनमसक्तं तेषु कर्मसु ॥९-९॥

7. At the end of the age these creatures return to unmanifested matter; at the beginning of the next cycle I send them forth again.
8. Again and again I bring forth these myriad forms and subject them to the laws of prakriti.
9. None of these actions bind me, Arjuna; I am unattached to them, so they do not disturb my nature.

According to the Hindu scriptures, the universe is created and dissolved over and over again. In the interregnum, everything in the universe rests in a primordial state without any differentiation, without time or space. But in the instant of creation this equilibrium is disturbed, setting loose the long chain of action and reaction in which all the elements and forces of the universe become manifested.

The personal aspect of this is that in each of these cycles, the whole of creation is said to be evolving towards the unity of life. When, after billions of years, we come into the human context, the Hindu scriptures say we must come back over and over again until we learn to go beyond the biological conditioning of animal life and realize that beneath all these forms of creation, we are all one in the Lord.

In other words, according to this view, all of us are going to be saved. Sooner or later, even if we do everything possible to put it off for billions of years, every one of us must reach the highest state of consciousness. If we drag our heels, the very painfulness of our mistakes and our separateness will slowly force us to change our ways. That is what evolution means on the human level. Just as a species blindly evolves certain characteristics by exposure to the world around it, we are constantly shaping ourselves by the consequences of everything we do. This is the law of karma, which states unequivocally that any suffering we cause to other people *must* come back to us. It is an inescapable consequence of the fact that all of us are one. That is why it grieves me so deeply to see anybody treating another person harshly; it's like hitting yourself with your own hand.

In the traditional classification, there are three types of karma. The first may be called "cash" karma, because it is all over with immediately. John hits Joe, and Jim hits John; there is no suspense, and John's karma comes to a fast end. The second kind is more painful; it is the consequences we reap from past actions. "Others fear what will happen tomorrow," says the Sufi mystic Ansari of Herat; "I fear what happened yesterday." The Compassionate Buddha describes this kind of karma as an arrow we have already shot: it is on its way, and the best we can do is accept the suffering that comes from it and learn from that suffering not to shoot that arrow again.

The third type of karma is that which we are about to create right now, in the immediate present. This is karma over which we have some control. If we can't do anything about the arrows we have shot in the past, we can at least refrain from shooting more arrows in the future. Often we find ourselves in a situation where our passions have been roused, our anger is ready to burst, and all we can think of is retaliation. The arrow rests on the bowstring and the bow is drawn, ready to shoot. But, says the Buddha, we do not need to let the arrow go; the choice is up to us. That is the time to repeat the mantram, relax our hold, and put the arrow safely away.

Here it is that the Hindu mystics make a really daring proposal. We do not need to let ourselves be buffeted towards the Lord by our own karma over millions and millions of years; we can take our evolution into our own hands. That is precisely what meditation is for, and great mystics like Sri Ramakrishna or St. Catherine of Siena are really pioneers in consciousness who have gone millions of years beyond us in human evolution. Patanjali, the great teacher of rāja yoga in ancient

India, tells us that any of us can make this great leap; the capacity is within us all. We are all born with enough vital energy for the journey, and a little extra to play around with while we get used to the car. The choice is ours what we do with this energy. Some of my friends tell me that in their earlier days, they used to leave their house in Berkeley early Monday morning fully intending to drive straight to New York City. They would stop at the grocery store for some orange juice, then go to a friend's house and listen to a record or two, then remember to get some incense on Telegraph Avenue, and by the time it was nightfall they would still not have got out of town. But there are some people – St. Francis of Assisi, Mahatma Gandhi – who want so badly to get where they are going that they don't spend any time on side trips. They put all their energy into the practice of the spiritual life and do everything they can to learn not to repeat the mistakes that all of us make. Every one of us can choose to do this, and the harder we try, the farther we will go.

In the Sanskrit scriptures there is a vivid dramatization of this immense leap across evolution into the unitive state. The story is about Mārkandeya, the boy whose devotion to Lord Shiva rescued him from death in his sixteenth year. In this story, with all the daring of a teenager, he asks Sri Krishna to explain to him the secret of Māyā. It's a question which allows for some rather imaginative answers. As soon as the words are out of the boy's mouth the Lord disappears, and in one great roar all the seven seas rush in around Mārkandeya and rise up to the clouds in flood, the way they did in Genesis before the world was made. Everything is engulfed in the waters, not only the earth but the sun and all the starry firmament. And Mārkandeya, the boy who had gone beyond death, floats on these cosmic waters for billions of years, evolving from lifeless matter up the long ladder of animate existence.

Suddenly he bursts into the human context. Life after life of selfish existence passes; he begins to shed all his selfishness and develops great devotion to the Lord. Then he sees in the distance a wonderful little baby, dark like the monsoon cloud, lying on a banyan leaf on that endless expanse of water. In a flash of recognition, Mārkandeya recognizes the baby Krishna, playing on the waters just as any other baby does, with one of his toes tucked into his little rosebud of a mouth.

A thrill of unutterable joy runs through Mārkandeya at the thought of lifting and cradling in his arms this divine infant, whose playfield is the universe. But all these eons have been just one gentle breathing out of the baby Krishna, one day of Brahmā; now he begins to breathe in again, and Mārkandeya is sucked inside through that tiny mouth into the body of the Lord, where he sees in wonderment all the galaxies of the universe suspended in the cosmic night. Outside there is again nothing but the primeval waters; matter and energy, time and space, everything is inside while creation rests.

The experience must have lasted for billions of years. Then baby Krishna breathes out again. Mārkandeya is thrown out, and he is so overcome that he embraces little baby Krishna in adoration and tries to find words to express his gratitude for this vision of the Lord's Māyā. But the baby disappears in his arms, and Mārkandeya finds himself back in his own āshram seated in meditation. It's a magnificent rendering of what can happen in samādhi, when we see that all the vast sweep of evolution is only the play of the Lord.

मयाध्यक्षेण प्रकृतिः सूयते सचराचरम् ।
हेतुनानेन कौन्तेय जगद्विपरिवर्तते ॥९-१०॥

10. Under my watchful eye the laws of nature take their course. Thus is the world set in motion; thus the animate and the inanimate are created.

I remember an article in *Scientific American* entitled "Why Doesn't the Stomach Digest Itself?" It is a rather practical question. How is it that the stomach, which secretes hydrochloric acid able to dissolve metal, does not harm itself? What protects it from the corrosiveness of its own chemistry?

Scientific research gives us extensive information on the physiology of the body, but it cannot help us know who is closer to us than this body of ours. Although we spend millions of dollars on coronary care units, we do not know who is in our heart of hearts. Textbooks now have precise illustrations of the lens of the eye and the cochlea buried in the inner ear, but no book can show us who it is that sees, who it is that hears.

Everywhere we look we see evidence of the miracle of life. On the beach where we took our walk this morning, I was watching a little creature of which I'm very fond, the sandpiper. It waited for a wave to break, and when the water was about to reach its toes it ran off so fast that I could hardly see its legs. Where does it get the power to run? Science can describe its legs – the angle at which they move, their velocity, the condition of the sand, the wind's resistance – but the power that enables the tiny sandpiper to outrun the tide is the power of God.

In the operations of the body, in the movements of the stars, every expression of energy in the universe is the power of the Lord. When the sun converts hydrogen into helium, the energy released is the power of the Lord, just as is the energy released in your body in the process of digestion. It is all the same energy; that is what the unity of life means. The Lord *is* the power of the universe, and the Law governing all laws. This doesn't mean that the laws of motion or thermodynamics are incorrect; these laws are only aspects of the law of unity which supports all existence.

One of the key phrases in this verse is *jagad viparivartate,* 'the universe turning around.' When the universe began to evolve, the Sanskrit scriptures say, the power behind that evolution was the creative aspect of the Lord. From that dynamic imbalance, the interplay of all the forces of nature began, never to cease until they are withdrawn again into the Lord at the end of the age. It's as if the cosmos is an immense globe like those globes of the world that children are so fond of spinning. The Lord gives this globe one big slap from inside and it goes on spinning for billions on billions of years.

In the Hindu tradition, this idea that the Lord is the source of all law is conveyed in all sorts of stories, many of which I heard often from my grandmother. One of these stories is from the *Mahābhārata,* in which this dialogue of the Bhagavad Gita takes place. Arjuna's enemy, Karna, had taken a vow to kill him in battle. Karna was an exceedingly skillful warrior and was armed with supernatural weapons, but as the battle raged, even though Arjuna was losing ground, his charioteer, Sri Krishna, seemed in no hurry to come to his aid. Then, just as Karna aimed the fatal arrow at Arjuna's head, Sri Krishna caused the earth to sink beneath their chariot. The arrow passed overhead, leaving Arjuna unharmed. My granny told me stories like this in a very matter-of-fact manner, because to her it seemed obvious that he who made the whole cosmos could tell the earth to sink for his devotee's protection. To her there was no conflict here with the laws of nature; the lower laws of physical phenomena had simply been superseded by a higher law for the time being.

There is another story about the great mystic Shankara, whose mother was an ardent devotee of the Lord. Every morning she used to walk several miles to the river for her bath and then to the temple for her daily worship. One day she fell during this journey, and her friends had to carry her home. Shankara, who was a teenager at the time, was grief-stricken. He took the Lord severely to task for not taking better care of his mother. After all, his mother was going to the temple to worship the Lord; shouldn't He protect her? It is said that the Lord murmured something about being distracted by the problems of the world and promised to make amends for this lapse. Then he told the river to flow closer to Shankara's home. To this day geologists speculate about the peculiar changes in the course of this river. There may be numerous other explanations, which I do not deny in the least, but they do not conflict with the capacity of the Lord to effect any number of wonders from within the forces of his creation.

Nothing can take place without the power of the Lord. Sri Ramakrishna used to say that the Divine Mother even hears the footfall of the ant. Ever since I read this I cannot look at an ant without imagining the Lord listening to the *thud, thud, thud* of its tiny feet. Jesus gives us the same truth when he says, "Not a sparrow falls without the will of the Father." Just imagine the supreme master of the cosmos keeping track of all the sparrows in his huge map room. His eyes are everywhere; he sees everything and hears everything because he is everything. If his secretary reports a comet is creating a bit of trouble, he says, "Straighten it out." Astronomers on earth, watching this comet, may gather from all over the world for a conference on its idiosyncrasies, but no conference can ever reveal who set the comet in motion. We can study the physics, the chemistry, the biology of our small corner of the universe, but only through the practice of meditation will we be able to meet the Supervisor.

अवजानन्ति मां मूढा मानुषीं तनुमाश्रितम् ।
परं भावमजानन्तो मम भूतमहेश्वरम् ॥९-११॥
मोघाशा मोघकर्माणो मोघज्ञाना विचेतसः ।
राक्षसीमासुरीं चैव प्रकृतिं मोहिनीं श्रिताः ॥९-१२॥

11. The immature do not look beyond physical appearances to see my true nature as the Lord of all creation.
12. The knowledge of such deluded people is fraught with disaster, and their work and hopes are all in vain.

To help us change our direction in life, Sri Krishna occasionally uses some rather strong language. The word he uses in these two verses is *mūdha*, 'slow-witted.' Anyone who cannot see below the surface of life, who believes only in what can be touched and measured, Sri Krishna says, simply is not thinking intelligently. When we think there is no more to life than physical objects and sensations, when we identify ourselves completely with the body and deny that there is any unifying principle in life, everything we do will be futile; there will be no fulfillment in life at all. That is the nature of the physical world: everything in it is limited; everything is fleeting. Not only that, Sri Krishna warns us, this is not something that affects us alone. There can be great danger in living on the surface of life, because there will always be this blindness about the welfare of the whole. Even with the best of intentions, people with this kind of shallow vision can be led into activities that really endanger life around them.

To take just one example, look at the people who think that by producing more and more and consuming more and more, we will eventually reach the land where all troubles end. The phrase Sri Krishna uses for this self-centered way of life is quite contemporary: *moghāshā moghakarmāno,* 'with vain hopes, and with work in vain.' Those who go on producing for the sake of profit, who continue to consume for the sake of pleasure, will end in futility and frustration. Many of our business empires and technological exploits, built on the idea of unlimited material progress, are now facing the fact that the earth's resources are very limited indeed. To the mystic, the real problem is not with our resources; it is what we are trying to do with those resources that is futile.

As we are forced to give up some of these activities, we make a marvelous discovery that the mystics have been trying to tell us about all along: a simple life can be a joyful life. By "simple life" I do not mean a romantic return to a rustic state. Nor is simplicity something we must just put up with because we are running out of energy. The simple life is much more creative and practical than most of us imagine. It is a life that values human qualities, one that is rich in lasting relationships with family and friends and community.

Most people do not have time to get to know their neighbors, or listen to what their children have to say, or be sensitive to the needs of their friends. They are too busy traveling between their city condominium and their country cabin. They have to work additional hours to buy two cars; then they need separate kitchens, separate bank accounts, separate televisions, separate sets of silverware, separate everything, all because they cannot live in harmony. Finally, they lose the capacity to exercise choice over their lives; the living room must be redecorated again and last year's car has to be traded in for a new model. Before they know it, life has become incredibly complicated – and far from satisfying.

Simple living can be beautiful, right down to the smallest details. Some of the Japanese homes I have been in are remarkably beautiful with just a few well thought-out touches. On the other hand, I have also been in elaborate homes where I had to watch every move for fear of knocking an antique off its pedestal. Unfortunately, the more possessions we accumulate, the more we are possessed by them. It is only after we begin to taste the joy of simple living that we realize that these accessories can actually stand between us and our fulfillment.

Our modern way of life seems to be making us busier and busier about less and less. This is the vain superficiality Sri Krishna is warning us against. The more we divide our interests, our allegiances, our activities, the less time we have for living. The simple life doesn't mean a drab routine; it means giving our time and attention to what is most important. For parents, it means having time and energy to devote to their children – and no matter what the latest psychological theory may tell us, our children can never grow to their fullest without continual support from the parents, particularly the mother. For friends, simplicity means taking the time to deepen a relationship, and remaining loyal in times of trouble. To remain loyal even when someone is causing us a great deal of trouble, we must know that person very well, well enough to warn our friend when he or she is about to make a mistake. Such relationships take time. We cannot get to know someone intimately in a day or establish a lasting relationship during a weekend conference. If we spend eight hours a day at our job, an hour or so at a bar after work, and the evening watching television, where is the time for cultivating close friendships? But if we simplify our lives, we shall find plenty of time and energy to be together with our circle of family and friends. These are discoveries all of us can make.

महात्मानस्तु मां पार्थ दैवीं प्रकृतिमाश्रिताः ।
भजन्त्यनन्यमनसो ज्ञात्वा भूतादिमव्ययम् ॥९-१३॥

13. But truly great souls seek my divine nature.
They worship me with a one-pointed mind, having
realized that I am the eternal source of all.

The vast majority of people have many-pointed minds. Just go to a large department store on the day after Christmas; everyone's attention is divided between the sale tables, an old acquaintance, a crying child, and the exchange of unwanted gifts. When a person's eyes are darting in every direction like this, it's not only a sign of restless eyes; it's a sign of a restless mind as well. Once this kind of distraction becomes a habit, nothing in life can hold our interest. We take up bowling, but after a week or two we become bored; we decide to master classical guitar, or pick up a little French, or learn to skin dive, but very soon we will want to do something new. But as Ecclesiastes says, "There is nothing new under the sun." There is a limit to the new things we can do in this world, and the more restlessly we search for novelty, the less likely we are to be successful at anything we take up.

The key to this problem is not more new things but better concentration. Boredom and fulfillment have nothing to do with the world outside us. When we can give our attention to it, the classical guitar seems fascinating; when we cannot give our attention to it, it seems dull. The guitar itself is neither fascinating nor dull; all the interest is in the attention we can bring to bear on it. If we can learn to make the mind one-pointed, we will be interested and effective in everything we do.

When I was a little boy, I saw an experiment by one of our science teachers which illustrates the power of concentration. Without giving us a clue as to what he was going to do, he picked up a lens, put a lot of paper underneath, and let the rays of the tropical sun pour through the lens. We watched quizzically for a minute, totally unprepared for the climax. For a while nothing happened at all. Then there was a thin little curl of smoke, and all of a sudden the paper burst into flames. We thought it was some kind of magic. But our teacher explained that there was no magic at all; the heat that had been diffused had been brought together to bear on one point through the lens.

This is more or less what we do in the practice of meditation. Most of the time, the capacities of our mind are wasted in innumerable little cravings for things which do our bodies no good, our minds no good, and no one else any good either. Ordinarily we have no way of harnessing these little cravings; that is why most of us are not as effective as we could be, do not have particularly secure relationships, and are not able to make the contribution to life that we would like. So the question is, how do we make the mind converge? And the answer is, through the practice of meditation.

In meditation, when you go as slowly as you can through a passage like the Prayer of St. Francis without letting distractions creep in between the words, you are learning to focus your attention completely on one train of thought. Gradually your whole thinking process will become slowed down, which releases a great deal of tension and removes a great deal of conflict. It takes many years to achieve this kind of mastery of the mind, but finally, when your consciousness is unified completely, you will be able to keep your mind calm, clear, and concentrated even in the most agitating circumstances.

Slowing down thoughts is one of the most effective methods for changing negative habits of thinking. As long as the mind is working furiously, it's not possible to stop it; it's not even possible to make a turn. But when you are able to see thoughts going by in single file, you can recognize them and say, "Hey, you're no friend!" You can choose not even to say hello to a negative thought, and its power to agitate you will be completely lost. This is how we learn not to identify ourselves with our thoughts, which means we have the power to pick and choose which thoughts to think.

To do this requires more than just the practice of meditation; we also need to cultivate a one-pointed mind throughout the day. There is a great deal of energy dissipated when we do or think several things at once. To be insecure, for example, consumes a lot of energy. You can't simply sit back and say, "Now I'll be insecure"; you have to put in a lot of time comparing people, thinking about what others did to you to foil your plans, and dwelling on how much you are to be pitied. All this requires a lot of energy. Last evening we had a fire in our fireplace, and to keep the fire going for about one hour we had to pile on a big stack of firewood and keep on piling on more. If it had been really cold and we had had to keep that fire for many more hours, we wouldn't have had any firewood left at all. That is how insecurity works; you have to go on feeding it constantly, and there is no energy left for anything else.

Later, my friend Rick – who probably learned about fires when he was living in the jungles of Paraguay – explained to me that we had built the fire wrong and used the wrong kind of wood. So tonight he got us a good, heavy log, one that burns slowly and puts out a lot of heat, and if we hadn't finally put it out it would still be burning now. Instead of piles and piles of wood, all we needed was that one log. There is a good deal of potential energy in a log like that, but it's all very carefully conserved. Only a little of the wood needs to be consumed to give light and heat to all. It is the same with vital energy. When you scatter your attention everywhere, you really get drained – if you want proof of it, just spend a day window-shopping and see how you feel when you get home. But when you can work slowly, with complete concentration, at one thing at a time, very little energy is consumed. At the end of the day there will still be a lot of firewood left, which is what unshakable security means.

सततं कीर्तयन्तो मां यतन्तश्च दृढव्रताः ।
नमस्यन्तश्च मां भक्त्या नित्ययुक्ता उपासते ॥९-१४॥

14. Constantly striving, they make firm their resolve. They worship me without wavering and, full of devotion, sing of my divine glory.

Pelagius has a strong but very practical aphorism on the spiritual life: If you don't want to fall back, you have to keep running forward. If that is what is required just to keep standing still, you can imagine what is called for to make real progress. To go as far as you can in meditation, you need to be striving every minute. Every morning you renew your commitment to the spiritual life.

From my own experience, I would say that the problems get tougher the farther one proceeds along this path. Palate problems – which seem to be omnipresent in the beginning – are, after all, not so serious, because you can always refrain from eating. If you don't pick up your fork and put food in your mouth, no one is likely to do it for you. If you are tempted to overeat, you can always run out of the house and go for a fast walk. Similarly, if you feel yourself drawn to a rock concert, you can give your money away instead; if you don't have money with you, there's not much danger of getting past the box office. In other words, these are not serious temptations because they are external. That is the positive, practical side of Jesus' words when he prays, "Lead us not into temptation": do not put yourself in situations where your will may break down; do not go in and ask for trouble.

So physical indulgence is not a very grave problem. The real problems come in the deeper stages of meditation. Then you are no longer on the surface level of consciousness, and you begin to see the roots of your problems, which go deep. On the surface you see only innumerable little weeds, which you think can simply be pulled up and thrown out. But as your meditation deepens you will see that what you thought were twenty weeds have actually only ten roots. Then, deeper still, you see that these seemingly ten roots are actually ten shoots off five stout stems, each of which is so strong that you scarcely know how to get at it. At last you get to the taproot, which is self-will. Then the going really gets rough. After this long journey you realize that you have only been trekking across the prison of the ego. There are no doors, no windows, no exits of any kind. Imagine finding yourself in a room where there is no door, where you cannot even move or turn around. What effort do you make against a blank, seamless wall? That is the problem.

These problems in the deeper stages of meditation are gigantic simply because they are not outside you any more; they are inside. When they come, you cannot help fighting; there is nowhere to go. You cannot say, "Don't look at me; I'm a lover, not a fighter. Let me know when it's all over." When you come face to face with the ego in the basement of consciousness, you have to do something about it. Every morning in your meditation for a long, long time you will have to fight this battle with the ego, which will call for every ounce of endurance you can muster and a little more. But every defeat only strengthens your resolve.

I saw this kind of fierce resolution the other day in a film of two fellows climbing a sheer rock wall in Yosemite. They had all sorts of climbing gear, but what is more important, they had commitment. As the commentator said, what is essential is to decide to leave the ground;

after that, it is just a matter of going on. The beginner may look at the steep face of Washington's Column and say, "I'd better think twice about this; a fall from there is going to be *bad*." But these young men were dedicated climbers; they made the initial decision and then never even once thought of turning back.

These climbers were following a system of cracks up the cliff, pounding pitons into the cracks and then hanging their ropes from these pitons and slowly pulling themselves up a little higher. Everything went well until they got halfway up the face of the peak. Then the crack system stopped, and above them stretched a sheer, unclimbable rock wall with not even the tiniest crack into which to pound a piton to go higher. At that point most people would shrug, give up, and go back down to Glacier Restaurant to console themselves with a big dinner. But these two fellows had set their hearts on the top, and nothing could make them quit. The sheer impossibility of their situation only deepened their resourcefulness. One of them started swinging like a pendulum from one ledge to another, looking for a new crack system. Finally he found one, and while I watched amazed they picked up their climb from this new point and made it to the top of the peak.

In meditation too we need this kind of tenacity, the capacity to keep on climbing when the going gets rough. More than once, as we continue to climb, we will reach a point when the crack system ends. This is an inescapable part of the spiritual ascent, and it will test our dedication to the fullest. Then it is that instead of getting anxious or depressed, we renew our resolve and give everything we can to find some way to go farther. Our responsibility is only to give our very best; the outcome we leave to the Lord. When he sees that our sense of dedication is strong enough to withstand the rigors of the climb ahead, a little door will open in our consciousness and give us access to the deeper resources we need to continue climbing.

There is a beautiful story in this connection about St. Teresa of Ávila, the great Christian mystic of sixteenth-century Spain. Teresa spent decades founding convents throughout Spain, traveling long distances over terrible roads in every kind of weather. In most places she had to work with people who were adamantly opposed to her order. Often she was ill and physically exhausted, but her determination and enthusiasm never wavered. Then, towards the end of her life, she was struck in an epidemic of influenza. After that she never recovered her physical strength. But in the dead of winter the call came from her superior to inaugurate a new convent at Burgos. Teresa hesitated; after all, she was very ill. But the Lord, she said, reproved her: "I am the true warmth. What is there to be afraid of?"

As Teresa and her companions set out in their mule-drawn carts, sky and earth seemed fused in one torrential stream of water. The carts became so mired that the nuns had to wade much of the distance in their sandals. Teresa was shaking from head to foot from the exposure and her illness, but she was determined to obey the Lord and him alone.

Next day, the river Arlanzón had to be crossed. When they reached what had been the bank, all they saw was an enormous sheet of water. All the bridges had been carried away by the flood and there was only a makeshift footbridge, which was so narrow that at the slightest movement of the current, carts, mules, and nuns would roll right into the raging flood. Teresa's carriage moved forward first. Those who were still on the bank saw it swerve and stop, then begin to tip as if to fall into the torrent below. Teresa jumped out and hurt herself. While the river raged just below her feet, she stood clinging to the cart. "Lord," she exclaimed, "amid so many ills why do you add this to all the rest?"

In the depths of her consciousness she heard a voice reply: "Don't be upset, Teresita; that is how I treat my friends."

"O my Lord!" Teresa replied, as only his beloved handmaiden could. "No wonder you have so few of them!"

The Lord must not have been displeased with this answer, for the whole caravan reached the far bank unharmed.

Of course, Teresa was a great saint, so the Lord made great demands on her. But he tempers the wind to the shorn lamb, and all he asks of little people like you and me is that we remember him constantly in all the small daily encounters in our family and our community. For most of us, that is quite challenge enough.

ज्ञानयज्ञेन चाप्यन्ये यजन्तो मामुपासते ।
एकत्वेन पृथक्त्वेन बहुधा विश्वतोमुखम् ॥९-१५॥

15. Others follow the path of jnāna, spiritual wisdom: they see that where there is One, that One is me; where there are two, they both are me; they see my face everywhere.

This verse has puzzled those who look for a hidden meaning. Actually it is a simple account of what happens in the climax of meditation, when we realize that all creation is one in the Lord. Then, though we still see beauty in all the abounding variety of life, we will always be aware that underlying this variety there is only the Lord, who the Sufis say beautifully is "the face behind all faces." This is the hallmark of the mystical experience everywhere. In Jewish mysticism there is a charming anecdote about a Hasidic master who had to put on his glasses in order to remember that people around him saw things as separate, for otherwise he saw everyone and everything as One. And the Shvetāshvatara Upanishad says:

The Lord dwells in the womb of the cosmos,
The creator who is in all creatures.
He is that which is born and to be born;
His face is everywhere.

In the Krishna tradition, there is a little story I like very much which illustrates this vision of unity. Once again, it is a story about Nārada, a sage who was deeply devoted to Sri Krishna. On this occasion, Nārada asked the Lord to tell him the deepest truth of the spiritual life. Sri Krishna has a rather playful way of answering these questions, and this time he just smiled mischievously and disappeared, leaving Nārada standing bewildered in the bustling street of a village he had never seen before. Nārada was not one to be at a loss, but even he didn't know what to do. Was he still in heaven, or was he back on earth? He waited and waited for Sri Krishna to reappear, but there was no sign of him anywhere.

Finally, Nārada began to get hungry. In India it has been a tradition for thousands of years for householders to give food to wandering spiritual aspirants; it is a great blessing for the householder and the whole family. So Nārada took out his wooden bowl and went up to the nearest house to ask for a little food. But when the door opened Nārada gave a start, for the woman who answered had Sri Krishna's eyes. Not only that, as she handed back the bowl, he was sure she gave him just the hint of a wink before she disappeared into the shadows of the house again and closed the door.

A little bewildered, Nārada went on to the next house, where a whole family was just sitting down to dinner. This time there was no wink from the lady of the house, but a little boy with those same eyes ran over to greet him and said a little too mischievously, "Sir, have you ever seen Sri Krishna? Can you sing us some of his praises?" It was like that in every house. In one place it was an infant, in another a teenager, in a third the grandmother, but in every family Nārada visited, one of the family was the Lord. At last he realized that for all the differences in age and appearance, there was no one in that village except the Lord, and in that instant of realization the village disappeared and Nārada was back with Sri Krishna again in the heavenly realm of Vaikuntha.

अहं क्रतुरहं यज्ञः स्वधाहमहमौषधम् ।
मन्त्रो ऽहमहमेवाज्यमहमग्निरहं हुतम् ॥९-१६॥

16. I am the ritual and the sacrifice; I am true medicine and the mantram; I am the offering and the fire which consumes it, and he to whom it is offered.

This verse and those that follow serve as a prelude to chapter ten, in which the Lord will describe the endless glory of his attributes. Here the Lord is drawing his illustrations from parts of ancient Vedic ritual, but when he talks about sacrifice, he means the sacrifice of our self-will.

When I want to see how well someone is doing in meditation, I don't ask if he or she is seeing visions or hearing voices; I look to see how easily that person can go against his or her self-will. This is the way to make progress on the spiritual path, and in this verse the Lord is reminding us that whenever we turn our backs on ourselves in order to move closer to him, it is he within us who is prompting us to make the offering.

The dynamics of this process are quite interesting. Breaking through to a deeper level of consciousness in meditation is very much like trying to open a door which keeps banging shut. You just cannot keep it open; every time you open it a crack, the handle slips out of your hands and the door slams shut. At the beginning this is only frustrating, but eventually it becomes quite tantalizing. The more you are able to peek through the door, the more your concentration is drawn to what is on the other side. It is as if the Lord is standing on the other side of the door, opening it a little until you can almost see in and then quickly closing it again. Finally you decide you are going to keep that door open, come what may. You will get up from meditation with the door haunting your memory; you will go through the day without being able to get it out of your mind. This is a very hopeful sign, because it means that even in your unconscious you are working on ways to get your foot in the door.

In general, there are two ways you can strengthen yourself to solve problems like this, which are bound to come as your meditation deepens. The first is to look for an opportunity to defy your self-will. When you begin to get the motivation, you will find hundreds of opportunities for this every day. Wherever there are likes and dislikes, wherever there is friction in personal relationships, that is an opportunity for going against self-will.

The second very powerful ploy for getting through that door into deeper consciousness is to defy a strong desire. It may be for cigarettes, or for alcohol, or for some selfish activity that benefits no one – whatever it is, large or small, power is locked up in that desire. When you come to an obstacle in meditation and find that you cannot break through, you will discover the important connection between desire and will.

Desire *is* will. Every strong desire has a great deal of will locked up in it; the problem is that usually we do not have any control over it. This is what happens in compulsive desires, the biggest and most powerful of which is sex. Every time you turn against a strong desire, it immediately strengthens the will. Often you can see the results the very next time you sit down for meditation. Whenever you can do this you will find your physical and emotional health improving, your relationships deepening, and your energy increasing. These are signs that you are going forward.

If the desire is particularly strong – something to which you have been conditioned over a period of several years – you can think of it as a continual source of power. Every time that desire comes up and you defy it, there is power generated. Once you get a taste of this and you really want to make progress in your meditation, you won't just wait for a strong selfish desire to start to pick you up; you will go around ferreting out all sorts of little cravings everywhere.

This desire to go against desires is the surest sign of grace. To give you an idea of how far it can go, the moment a desire rises in my mind and starts to tell me what to do, my immediate response is to defy it. Then I have to step in, tap myself on the shoulder, and remind myself that after all, it is time for dinner, and there is nothing wrong with a moderate helping of spinach crepes. It is a wonderful state to be in, because it means I am always master in my own little house of the mind.

When you keep on digging away at a powerful desire over a period of years, the great day will come when you can get underneath it and pluck it out at the root. Then it is like opening a perpetual spring of power; where that desire used to be, there is now continuous access to the vitality it used to consume. You will see the effects of a breakthrough like this in every aspect of daily living. Your patience will be greater; your relationships and security will deepen; even your body will be bathed in the restorative waters of this spring. One of the surest signs that you have changed to a deeper level in meditation is that some emotional or physical problem that had been bothering you for years – a digestive problem, or asthma, or chronic headache, or high blood pressure – will begin to disappear. So Sri Krishna says, "I am *aushadham,* your best medicine"; the more you draw on him, the more he will heal, not from without but from within.

In making this sacrifice of self-will, the mantram can be a tremendously effective ally. Unlike meditation, the mantram does not call for strenuous discipline; anyone can repeat a mantram and benefit from it. We are all familiar with the power of words, if only through the effect advertisements have on what we do and even what we think. Millions of people, for example, know that smoking causes cancer; we have irrefutable evidence of this today. Yet the number of people who smoke is on the increase. To see why, we have only to look at the billboards and magazine advertisements all around us; the advertiser's words go right into our consciousness. But just as Madison Avenue's words work to condition our desires, the holy name from any of the world's great religious traditions can free us from this conditioning. All we have to do is keep on repeating the mantram in our minds whenever a desire threatens to make us do what it says.

It sounds too simple, but just try it and see how powerful the mantram can be. The next time you are angry or afraid, go out for a long, fast walk repeating the mantram. Do not take your anger out on others, but use this strong emotion to drive the mantram deep into your consciousness. You don't need to wait for a chance to exit gracefully, either; just take to the nearest door. When you return, the transformation in your consciousness will more than make up for any toes you might have stepped on on your way out.

Similarly, when you have a compulsive urge to eat something or do something – especially if it is not good for you – go for a long walk repeating the mantram. In an hour's time, the urge will pass away. When the urge is upon you, you feel like you must yield or explode. All your concentration is on the cigarette you must smoke or the hot fudge sundae you must eat. But if you can switch your concentration over to the holy name, you will forget the cigarette or the sundae completely. Sometimes, of course, the mantram is like a car that hasn't been driven for a long, long time; when you try to start it up, at first it only groans and growls. But all you need do is just keep trying – once it gets going, the mantram will run smoothly.

पिताहमस्य जगतो माता धाता पितामहः ।
वेद्यं पवित्रमोंकार ऋक्साम यजुरेव च ॥९-१७॥

17. I am the father and mother of this universe, and its grandfather too; I am its entire support. I am the sum of all knowledge, the purifier, and the syllable Om; I am the sacred scriptures, the Rik, Yajur, and Sāma Vedas.

When parents in an Indian village want their sons or daughters to go to college, which is beyond the means even of most middle-class people, they look for a college in a place where they have relatives. Then their children can stay right in the relatives' home. This is not looked upon as an imposition; it is something that everybody does, and if your sister leaves her son with you for four years while he studies engineering, you can always console yourself that when the fellow grows up and gets a job, others will billet their sons or daughters on him. But an even more important reason than saving money is that with this arrangement there is the same family atmosphere, and if your son comes back a little late one night, he will be taken to task just as if he were at home.

In this verse, the Lord is assuring us in his own very personal way that he is responsible for us completely. No matter how old we are, no matter where we stray, we can count on his support. The other side of this, which he is too tactful to mention outright, is that he is not going to let us get away with a single, solitary thing. He will keep on taking us to task, severely if the situation demands, until we are prepared to be selfless always.

This verse personifies the nature of reality with the Hindu flair for the dramatic, but we find the same basic insight in modern science. The language is quite different – instead of the Lord we have a unifying force of nature – but the truth is the same; the Lord *is* the unity of life, the Divine Ground in which all forces in the cosmos cohere. The same laws govern the universe everywhere. The elements here are the same as those in the farthest reaches of the universe, and so are the forms of energy. So Sri Krishna says, "I am the sum of knowledge: knowing me, you know that which supports all things." It is the language of Spinoza also. And the Chāndogya Upanishad explains beautifully: "As by knowing one lump of clay we come to know all things made of clay – that they differ only in name and form, while the stuff of which all are made is clay – so through that spiritual wisdom, dear one, we come to know that all life is one."

गतिर्भर्ता प्रभुः साक्षी निवासः शरणं सुहृत् ।
प्रभवः प्रलयः स्थानं निधानं बीजमव्ययम् ॥९-१८॥

18. I am the goal of life, the Lord and support of all, the inner witness, the abode of all. I am the only refuge, the one true friend; I am the beginning and end of creation, and the receptacle for the eternal seed.

The Lord is everything for us. When we become God-conscious, all our needs are met; all our deepest desires are fulfilled. Sri Krishna says, "I am the supreme goal of life, your sole support; you have no other master than me. I am the eternal witness within you, your true home, your only refuge; when everyone else deserts you, I am still your friend." Jesus puts it in very simple words: "Follow me; I am the way, the truth, and the life."

In a beautiful little poem, St. Teresa of Ávila tells of the deep security that comes when we find our refuge in the Lord:

Let nothing upset you;
Let nothing frighten you.
Everything is changing;
God alone is changeless.
Patience attains the goal.
Who has God lacks nothing;
God alone fills all her needs.

Let nothing upset you. That is the first result of this realization: you become unupsettable. It means that none of your energy will be wasted, and you will have a long life with abounding energy to carry on the work of the Lord. *Let nothing frighten you.* There is going to be tragedy in life for everyone – loss of money, loss of face, loss of loved ones, and finally loss of everything on earth. You may grieve, but you never get oppressed by any loss, because through the deprivation you can see the Lord present always.

Everything is changing. The more experience I have of life, the more I appreciate the stark grandeur of this line. The other day I received a letter from India telling me that somebody I knew, somebody I loved, somebody I used to work with is now no more. When we move into the second half of life, this is the news that will come to us more and more often. The Katha Upanishad exclaims hauntingly, "Like corn, a man ripens and falls": everything is changing, and everything that changes is going to pass away. *God alone is changeless:* turn to him, love him with all your heart, and you will be secure always; you will find fulfillment everywhere you go.

Patience attains the goal. The logic is as ruthless as the words are beautiful. No matter how difficult a situation is, no matter how difficult another person is, everything and everyone must yield to patience, which outlasts all obstacles. In the heart of every storm in life there is always this unchanging center which is the Lord, and when you can bear with those who rage against you and keep your trust in them, you are helping them to trust and respond to their real Self. If you can only be patient and remember these lines of Teresa's – "everything is changing; God alone is changeless" – those who oppose you, those who differ from you, those who make life impossible for you will *have* to respond; it is only a matter of time.

Who has God lacks nothing. That's why everybody throws away their defenses before a person who has realized God. Such people do not lack anything at all, so they have nothing to try to get from anyone. They live for our benefit, not for their own. You can take what you like from them; they will still be full. They can give anything away; they will still be full. You can give them any kind of trouble; they will still be full. As Teresa concludes beautifully, *God alone fills all their needs.*

तपाम्यहमहं वर्षं निगृह्णाम्युत्सृजामि च ।
अमृतं चैव मृत्युश्च सदसच्चाहमर्जुन ॥९-१९॥

19. I am heat and light; I give and withhold the rain. I am immortality and I am death; I am what is and what is not.

Working through the forces of nature, the Lord gives life with one hand and takes it away with the other. Not only is he the force sustaining life; he is the force behind change and death as well, and the power which we harness to go beyond death to immortality. Therefore, as Swami Vivekananda is said to have remarked, if we can understand the meaning of death, we will understand the meaning of life. In Somerset Maugham's powerful novel *The Razor's Edge*, a young American, Larry, who is the hero of the story, sees one of his friends lying dead on the battlefield. With consummate skill, Maugham conveys in one short sentence the profound shock in Larry's consciousness: "The dead look so dead when they are dead." All of us can benefit from this rather grim reminder and put all our effort into going beyond death here and now.

In the Upanishads there is a profound statement that whatever is in the outside world is within our consciousness also. Many of the forces Sri Krishna talks about in verses like these apply not only to the natural world but to events we experience as our meditation deepens. When the Lord says he is heat and light, for example, he is not just referring to the sun. The mystics of all traditions describe the blazing effulgence that can take place in the final stages of meditation. If you are meditating sincerely and systematically, the time may come when you experience a sudden, dazzling flash of light in the head. It will be so intense that you might even open your eyes thinking that the sun is rising, only to discover that it is still the small hours of the night. Such flashes give a glimpse of the radiance that is within us. When at last our self-will has been removed, the Lord can show us his divine glory, which the Gita will tell us is like the splendor of a thousand suns rising at the same time. It is no wonder the man or woman who has become united with the Lord is radiant with lasting joy.

For the great majority of us, this experience would be quite overwhelming if it came on all at once, so the Lord in his mercy spreads out our spiritual development over many years. The Indian mystics are fond of drawing a comparison with the Hindu wedding processions that are a common sight in the villages. When a wedding is about to take place in a Punjabi village, the villagers can hear the band playing long before they see anything. Then the first part of the wedding party, the men bearing banners and presents, comes into view. When the villager hears the music and sees the banners and gift-bearers approaching, he calls to his friends, "There's a wedding coming!" They stop their work to watch the procession, but for a long time they still do not see the bride or the bridegroom. Instead, the father-in-law comes by with great majesty, dominating the scene with his measured stride. Then comes the horse on which the bridegroom rides, covered with garlands. You can see the horse but not the bridegroom; all that is visible is a giant bouquet, behind which, if you look closely, you may see an arm or a bit of an ear. Finally, the wedding party reaches the bride's home. The bridegroom gets down from the horse, the flowers are taken away, and the bridegroom and bride stand before us together at last.

It is very much like this on the spiritual path too. You do not see the Lord right away, but in the later stages of meditation there will be a number of signs that he is on the way. My suggestion is not to look for these signs. When you keep waiting for something to happen in meditation, you are actually keeping yourself from going deeper, and anything you experience is not likely to be valid. If you are waiting for a deep-hued monsoon cloud, the symbol of Sri Krishna, to float across your mind's eye, you may find yourself thinking in meditation: "'Lord, make me an instrument of thy peace' . . . *Where is that cloud?*" When this happens, you are no longer meditating. So do not pay undue attention to anything you experience in meditation. If the experience is genuine, it will bear fruit in your life the very same day, whether you dwell on it or not. But if you allow yourself to get excited over it, a depression will come in its wake and your progress will be impeded.

Then the Lord says, "I give and withhold the rain." St. Teresa of Ávila describes the soul as a garden which must be watered by meditation, which she calls interior prayer, until the Lord gives it the rain of grace.

> It seems to me that our garden can be watered in four ways: by taking the water from a well, which is hard work; or by a water wheel and buckets, when the water is drawn by a windlass (I have sometimes drawn water in this way; it is less work and yields more); or by a stream, which waters the ground much better, for it saturates it more thoroughly and there is no need to water so often, so that the gardener's work is much less; or by heavy rain, when the Lord waters it with no labor of ours, a way infinitely better than any of the others.

For a long time, meditation is like drawing water from a very deep well. The well in my ancestral home in Kerala is about a hundred feet deep, and during the summer, when the sun is scorching the plains of India, people who draw water from the well have to use almost the full hundred feet of rope to lower the bucket down into the water. Often in a very poor village the bucket will have leaks, so that by the time it reaches the top, even after all their struggle, they have only half a bucketful to take home. This is how it is when we start meditation; our bucket will have quite a few leaks. We will meditate with great concentration and finally succeed in filling the bucket with the soothing waters of forgiveness, but then the leaks – impatience, irritation, resentment, indolence begin to sap our will until we wonder sometimes if our bucket is anything more than a lot of holes put together. We may even have struggled a great deal to bring the bucket up, only to find that there is no water in it at all. On days like that we are tempted to say, "There just isn't any water in the well." "Oh, no," Teresa would answer, "there is a lot of water in the well; you just need to plug up the holes." There is no beginner's luck in meditation. In the beginning it is only hard work and more hard work, because we can rely only on ourselves.

After some years of leading the spiritual life and practicing meditation, our awareness becomes deeper. Now, Teresa says, meditation is more like drawing water with the help of a Persian wheel – a large wheel with many buckets hung around the rim, each of which scoops up water as the wheel goes around. It is a marvelous image, which St. Teresa draws not from books but from the things she observed around Ávila. In this second stage of spiritual living, you still have to do a lot of hard work, but instead of having one old, leaky bucket you now have many good buckets. Now you are able to water the garden more abundantly with less effort, and the peace obtained in meditation is not drained away by the little anxieties and resentments of the day.

In the third stage, Teresa tells us, we see a little brook making a channel into our field, as if to say, "Just keep your bucket in a corner and let me do the watering." The effort needed to keep the mind still in meditation is becoming less and less, and the waters of selflessness now flow continuously. St. Teresa says of this state: "The Lord is now pleased to help the gardener, so that he may almost be said to be the gardener himself, for it is he who does everything." When we are able to forget our own needs in trying to solve the problems that threaten us all, the Lord is beginning to act through us. He is the Operator, and we become the instruments of his peace. Finally, Teresa says, the grace of the Lord descends in a shower, bathing the garden constantly in a gentle rain.

त्रैविद्या मां सोमपाः पूतपापा
यज्ञैरिष्ट्वा स्वर्गतिं प्रार्थयन्ते ।
ते पुण्यमासाद्य सुरेन्द्रलोकम्
अश्नन्ति दिव्यान्दिवि देवभोगान् ॥९-२०॥

ते तं भुक्त्वा स्वर्गलोकं विशालं
क्षीणे पुण्ये मर्त्यलोकं विशन्ति ।
एवं त्रयीधर्ममनुप्रपन्ना
गतागतं कामकामा लभन्ते ॥९-२१॥

20–21. Those who follow the rituals given in the Vedas, who offer sacrifices and take soma, free themselves from evil and attain the vast heaven of the gods. There they enjoy celestial pleasures. When they have enjoyed these fully, their merit is exhausted and they return to this land of death. Thus observing Vedic rituals but caught in an endless chain of desires, they come and go.

According to the traditional interpretation, people who take to the spiritual path to gain worldly ends, for the sake of their own private happiness, go after death to a heavenly realm where the satisfactions they have been searching for will be multiplied many times. Eventually, however, these pleasures will be exhausted. The grand time will come to an end, and they will return to good old terra firma to learn to make wiser choices the next time around.

There is another, more practical way these verses can be interpreted to apply to daily living. When you practice meditation for the sake of some private, personal goal, without training the senses and putting other people first, it can be a tremendously dangerous combination. The deeper resources in your consciousness are beginning to flow into your hands, giving you the capacity to fulfill some of your deepest desires, but you have no control over what these desires are. You may be able to amass an immense amount of money, acquire great prestige, even live a very long life, but there will be no more direction to your life than before. It's all quite possible; in fact, I have known some people whose lives illustrate these verses perfectly. Instead of going to the orthodox Hindu heaven of the gods to have a grand time, they go to Acapulco or the south of France to live their life in just the way they like. It's not necessarily unaesthetic; after all, these are people with highly refined desires and all the means with which to satisfy them. They have their meditation every morning by the Mediterranean, go for a brisk swim in some secluded cove, and then have a good, nourishing breakfast in the finest restaurant around. For entertainment they don't sit and watch *The Godfather*; they fly to London for the new opening of *King Lear* or spend a week or two in Salzburg for a Mozart festival. And wherever they go, people get interested in them. Photographers like to take pictures of them for the weeklies; journalists gather to ask them all kinds of questions because the answers are always interesting. And they derive great pleasure from all of this; it is the fulfillment of their dreams.

But then, the next verse says, look at where all this leads. *Kshīne punye martyalokam vishanti:* after a while, all these things begin to tire you. *Kshīne* means 'worn out,' exhausted; the Sanskrit word for tuberculosis comes from the same root. All this adulation becomes a nuisance; the questions and the questioners become a bore. You get tired of the Mediterranean and try the Caribbean for a season, but it's the same old crystal blue water, the same questions from the press, the same kind of company as you left behind. What has happened is that you have become tired of pleasure, but you don't understand that; you think you have become tired of Nice and Cannes. So you start growing a beard, wearing dark glasses, registering in hotels under a false name; and instead of luxurious restaurants, you begin to frequent little out-of-the-way places where the furniture is deliberately mismatched and the food is served in handmade bowls. Everything that used to please you now begins to irritate you – the radical becomes a reactionary, the reactionary becomes radical, the profligate becomes more puritanical than a Puritan. Such people have simply grown tired of living for themselves, and all this time has been misspent as far as the spiritual life is concerned. As this verse reminds us, they will have to return to the "land of mortals" – the everyday world – and try again to live in harmony with others and contribute to the welfare and happiness of those around them.

Meditation is a tremendously powerful discipline, and there can be real danger if it is misused for selfish ends. I get frightened sometimes at the literature I receive by mail: learn to meditate and you will be able to influence people; learn to meditate and you will be able to get whatever you want. There will always come a time when these powers will turn against you. That is the theme of Marlowe's *Faustus*, and at the end of the play, when Faustus is faced with destruction of his own making, he cries out in haunting lines:

> Mountains and hills, come, come and fall on me . . .
> O soul, be changed to little water drops
> And fall into the ocean, never to be found!

There is no place to hide when the powers you have developed and misused turn against you. To take an extreme example, even the story of Hitler may be interpreted in this way. Not too long ago I saw a powerful film in which Sir Alec Guinness, a very accomplished actor, brought Hitler to life as a maniac with tremendous power to influence the will and lives of other people. In the end the same destructive forces he had created turned against him and his party and tore them to pieces. It is for our own protection that most of us will not be able to make real progress in meditation unless we are trying sincerely to train our senses and to put the happiness of all those around us first. But if we are giving our very best to all the disciplines of the spiritual path, our progress will be swift and safe.

अनन्याश्चिन्तयन्तो मां ये जनाः पर्युपासते ।
तेषां नित्याभियुक्तानां योगक्षेमं वहाम्यहम् ॥९-२२॥

22. Those who worship me and meditate on me constantly, without any thought for their own welfare, I will provide for all their needs.

Many years ago, when we started the work of the Blue Mountain Center of Meditation in Berkeley, we had hardly any money and not many dedicated friends to help us. I used to do part of the grocery shopping and the gardening; Christine was receptionist, accountant, secretary, editor of our newsletter, cook, chauffeur, you name it. Most people looked upon the whole thing as a foolhardy venture. My friends asked me, "How much money do you have in the bank?" They always looked a little depressed when I would tell them I didn't have a bank account. "Without substantial financial support," they warned me sincerely, "by yourselves, you cannot build any organization in this country."

"Exactly," I replied. "We are not building it by ourselves."

"Then you must have a sponsor?"

"Yes, the very best."

"Who? The Ford Foundation? Rockefeller?"

"Better than that: Sri Krishna."

Usually there would be a stunned silence; they seemed unwilling to credit the Lord with solvency. But I wasn't joking at all; I had the promissory note right in this verse. When we devote ourselves wholeheartedly to the spiritual life, without any reservation for ourselves, Sri Krishna says, *Yogakshemam vahāmyaham:* "Not only am I entirely responsible for your spiritual progress; I am also responsible for paying your bills."

No mystic from any spiritual tradition East or West has ever found this guarantee to fail. In the early years of the Center, I remember, at a time when things were looking particularly thin, we looked in our donation bowl after the evening's class and found a bill so large that I don't think I had ever seen a picture of that particular president before. It kept the wolf from our door for several weeks. Even Christine was a little surprised, but I have to say that I was not; I had already learned that I could trust the Lord to keep his word. On another occasion that same year we opened the bowl and found nothing but a big sheaf of Blue Chip stamps. We went out and bought seven folding chairs to use in our meditation classes, and now when I see those same chairs being used in our āshram and look around to see how much the Center has grown, it always makes me remember the promise of this verse.

ये ऽप्यन्यदेवता भक्ता यजन्ते श्रद्धयान्विताः ।
ते ऽपि मामेव कौन्तेय यजन्त्यविधिपूर्वकम् ॥९-२३॥
अहं हि सर्वयज्ञानां भोक्ता च प्रभुरेव च ।
न तु मामभिजानन्ति तत्त्वेनातश्च्यवन्ति ते ॥९-२४॥

23. Those who worship other gods with
faith and devotion will also come to
me, Arjuna, but by other paths.
24. I am the object of all worship, and every act
of selfless service is done for me. But those who
fail to realize my true nature must be reborn.

When we were living on the Blue Mountain, my wife and I met an American spiritual aspirant who had come to India after World War II. He had grown up in a Christian family and graduated from Harvard, but when he began to feel a great need for a deeper purpose in life he went to an āshram in India, presided over by an orthodox Hindu teacher from Bengal. He lived with his teacher and practiced meditation for twelve years, which is the traditional period of sādhana. I remember him telling us in amazement, "Here I travel all the way from Boston to Bengal, where they worship Mother Kālī and Lord Shiva; I practice meditation with a Hindu teacher and use a Hindu mantram, and who should reveal himself in the depths of my consciousness? Not Sri Krishna, not Lord Shiva, but Jesus the Christ."

In our case, too, there is no need to debate the pros and cons of various incarnations. We can leave the choice in the capable hands of the Lord. One person may be meditating on the Christ, another on the Buddha, a third on Sri Krishna, but the names do not make the slightest difference. If we are meditating sincerely and regularly and trying our best to eliminate self-will, all of us are going to be united with the Lord one day. When we call upon Jesus or the Buddha, we are calling on Sri Krishna too; when we call upon Sri Krishna, we are calling equally upon the Christ, or Allah. When I was teaching at the university, I had a student whose name was Shivarāmakrishna – his father hadn't wanted to take any chances when he named him, so he just covered all the bases with one name. I used to tell him, "Wherever heaven is, you'll find your way to it; at least one of those names is sure to open the right door."

Though you may not be greatly drawn towards any particular incarnation when you start meditating, gradually the time will come when you will have such longing for the Lord that you will feel the need for a divine ideal of your own – an *ishtadevatā,* as it is called in Sanskrit. Often, however, you may not know which incarnation is most suitable for you. You feel drawn to "gentle Jesus, meek and mild"; then you have a look at the Buddha, full of compassion for everything that lives, and you feel torn between the Buddha and the Christ. In such cases, it is good to leave the decision to the Lord. He – or she – will come to you in whatever form fulfills your deepest needs. At the appropriate point on the spiritual path, it is not unlikely that in a dream you will see a great incarnation or hear his or her name. You may see Jesus carrying a lamb, or you may hear resonating in your consciousness the mantram associated with the Compassionate Buddha, *Om mani padme hum.* Then there will be a tremendous response in the depths of your heart that will leave no doubt in your mind.

यान्ति देवव्रता देवान्पितृन्यान्ति पितृव्रताः ।
भूतानि यान्ति भूतेज्या यान्ति मद्याजिनो ऽपि माम् ॥९-२५॥

25. *Those who worship the devas will go to the realm of the devas; those who worship their ancestors will be united with them after death. Those who worship phantoms will become like phantoms; but my devotees will come to me.*

The key to this verse is that we become what we meditate upon. If we meditate for the sake of solving a particular physical problem, often that problem will be solved. If we meditate for the sake of solving some emotional problem, that too can be solved, if we are sincere and systematic in our practice. "But," Sri Krishna says, "if you meditate on me, you will go beyond all your problems." As Jesus reassures us, "Seek ye first the kingdom of heaven and everything else will be added unto you."

This is practical advice. We cannot find joy by solving a physical problem if we still have a lot of emotional difficulties. If we go to heaven's gate, St. Peter will say, "Your cholesterol level is less than 220; your blood pressure is 120 over 70; you don't have any cavities. But what a lot of fear, anger, and greed you have! Sorry, old chap, can't admit you this time. Come back again when you've learned a little patience." Similarly, after we have made our fortune, St. Peter will still say, "You've shown a lot of enterprise and enthusiasm, but we don't need money up here. Why don't you use it to work for a worthy cause, and then come and see me?" But if we seek first the kingdom of heaven, all our other needs will be provided for as well.

The Hindu tradition has a genius for dramatizing the desires which shape our lives. In the *Rāmāyana*, for example, the demon king Rāvana is the perfect symbol of selfish power. Rāvana has a brother named Kumbhakarna, the personification of indolence and apathy, who sleeps for six months of every year. When we sit back and fail to contribute to life, this verse reminds us, we are worshiping Kumbhakarna. When we live for ourselves, we are praying to Rāvana to take us to his kingdom and make us his servants forever. In other words, it is we who choose the kingdom to which we go, even in this life, by our choice of what to desire. If we want to go to the kingdom of heaven, it is only appropriate that we not walk in the other direction.

Similarly, Sri Krishna warns, there are those who let their desires entangle them in the past. Ancestor worship is not an exotic custom, confined to communities which have yet to enter the modern age. Visit the home of an established family and look at the gallery of paintings and photographs on the walls. Your host or hostess will gladly give you a guided tour. "Here is my great-great-grandfather, who founded our town; here is my great-aunt Agatha, who dined at Buckingham Palace." It is true that our great-great-grandparents may have had many qualities worth emulating – for one, they had a simpler way of life, from which we can learn a great deal. But we have to use our discrimination and select from the past only what is most helpful for today's world.

I understand there is a special society of people in this country who want to live as they did prior to Independence, in the days of the British Empire. The tragedy of such people is that often their wishes come true. They can come to live completely in the past, which means that in the present they are no more than ghosts. It is very much the same with people who pretend to be others. Whenever my wife and I take a walk in Berkeley or San Francisco, we see people who are pretending to be their favorite movie star or tennis champion or rock musician. Once we went to a restaurant where the waitress was trying to be like Shirley MacLaine. I was tempted to tell her I was Walter Matthau. By trying to be someone else, these people have no life of their own. They, too, become ghosts.

In another sense, this "world of spirits" Sri Krishna mentions here refers to the vast continents of fear, anger, and greed within our consciousness. The more we dwell on any negative emotion, the deeper we wander into its uncharted domain. For example, most of us are prone to all manner of fears, from loss of life to loss of hair. When we look in the classified pages to see how we can have hair grafted, or spend hours training our hair to cover a little bald spot, the motivation is really fear. As more and more hairs continue to fall out, our sense of security goes with them, for the more we dwell on a fear, even a little fear, the bigger it becomes. So in my case, when it began to look as if my head was going to become quite bald, I remember saying in the spirit of true renunciation, "All right, let it all go." Time may have diminished my hair since then, but it has not diminished me. My niece Meera, who likes everything about me, even goes so far as to say admiringly, "Uncle, what beautiful hair you have!"

When we are meditating, instead of welcoming fear by giving him attention, we can politely tell him to leave. If our meditation is going well, he will slink out muttering, "Sorry; I must have the wrong address." Fear wants us to worry about him. He will tempt us to study his genealogy from the time of William the Conqueror, and by the time we have finished discussing his life history he will have drawn us into his realm and shut the door behind us. Many people live in this world of fear, in which they are upset by continual anxieties. They are prone to a number of psychosomatic ailments which can lead to serious diseases, and they suffer from estrangement in their personal relationships because they are suspicious even of those they want to love. Such people can benefit greatly from meditation. Fear is concentration of which we are not the masters; it is a way of dwelling compulsively on ourselves. In meditation we gain the capacity to withdraw our attention from our problems and concentrate on the needs of those around us. When we do this, we find ourselves really coming to life in the present while our fears simply fade away.

पत्रं पुष्पं फलं तोयं यो मे भक्त्या प्रयच्छति ।
तदहं भक्त्युपहृतमश्नामि प्रयतात्मनः ॥९-२६॥

26. Whatever I am offered in devotion
with a pure heart – a leaf, a flower,
fruit, or water – I accept with joy.

Now we are entering the climax of this chapter. In some of the most beautiful language in the Gita, the Lord is inspiring us to make everything an offering to him. Leaves, flowers, fruit, and water are often used for ritual worship in India. In one widely used ritual, the worshiper stands before the divine image and repeats the names of the Lord, offering a flower petal at the deity's feet with each name. Sri Ramakrishna used to worship the Divine Mother in this fashion, but with a divinely peculiar twist of his own. He would close his eyes and begin repeating the beautiful names of the Divine Mother, but soon, completely absorbed in her, he would lose all outer consciousness and begin throwing the lotus petals on his own head rather than towards the image. Such was his devotion to the Divine Mother that he had become united with her.

The practical approach to this verse is to look upon everything that we do, no matter how seemingly insignificant, as a gift to the Lord. If we hoe the garden carefully so that our family can have fresh vegetables for dinner, that is an offering to the Lord. If we work a little more than is expected of us at something that benefits others, that too is an offering to the Lord. Everywhere, in every detail of daily living, it is not a question of quantity or expense that makes our offering acceptable; it is cheerfulness, enthusiasm, and the capacity to forget ourselves completely in helping those around us. The verse that follows will go into some of the ways in which this offering can be made.

यत्करोषि यदश्नासि यज्जुहोषि ददासि यत् ।
यत्तपस्यसि कौन्तेय तत्कुरुष्व मदर्पणम् ॥९-२७॥

27. Whatever you do, make it an offering to me – the food you eat, the sacrifices you make, the help you give, even your suffering.

Every term in this verse has a practical application in our daily living. The first is *yat karoshi:* "Whatever you do, make it an offering to the Lord." Instead of doing what pleases you, what you are accustomed to, what feels right to you, try to do something that benefits someone else instead. It may be distressing at first, but if you are making your best effort, the Lord will accept your offering. The proof of it comes in your daily living. The Lord isn't sitting at an altar somewhere and accepting what we offer him; he is right inside, and when we do something that pleases him it means that there is tension released at a very deep level throughout the body and mind.

Then the Lord says, *Yad ashnāsi:* "Whatever you eat, make it an offering to me." Considering the wealth of this country, it has always surprised me how poorly many Americans eat. Some of my friends were telling me the other day that it is not uncommon for people to have only a cup of coffee and a roll for breakfast, often topped off with a cigarette. Over the years such inadequate food habits contribute to very poor health – and in the case of mothers-to-be, the damage is not only to them but to their unborn children, too. Some advertisers no longer even bother to call what they are marketing "food"; they just say "products." When we sit down to dinner, most of us don't want to eat products; we want food – and tasty, nourishing food at that. It is so easy to cultivate a little backyard garden and have fresh fruits and vegetables for lunch or dinner. Even if there is no more than a window box or a small plot by the back door, we can still grow a few vegetables. We don't need to resign ourselves to food that has become stale or polluted with chemicals, or to products that have no food value at all.

In Sanskrit, however, "eating" refers to more than food. The Gita means whatever we consume, not only through our mouths but through our eyes, ears, and skin. Just watch children with their eyes glued to the television: they are having a big meal, often full of sex and violence. Since the average American household watches television an astonishing seven hours a day – one hour more than in 1977 – these "TV dinners" are rather large. At best, like junk food, they displace real nutrition: the human interactions by which a child learns to love, understand, feel, and give. At worst they spoon in the lowest possible image of the human being. "You are what you think," the Buddha warns. We all have a responsibility not to support any media production that fills our minds with junk thoughts and images.

Next Sri Krishna tells us, *Yaj juhoshi:* "Whatever you offer in renunciation, make that an offering to me." This is hard-hitting advice. He is not asking us to renounce our antique almirah or our tickets to the World Series; the sacrifice the Lord wants us to make is our self-will. It is not ideological differences that cause family conflicts or lead to clashes between man and woman; it is self-will. Reducing self-will is a terribly painful renunciation to make, because the ego will try every trick in the book to undermine our efforts. Fortunately, every one of us has a defiant streak that can enable us to turn against our self-will and overcome it. Eventually there is a tremendous sense of exhilaration in this, because it frees us from the conflicts which make life so miserable for us today.

The practical question is how to make this offering of self-will. I would suggest starting on a very small scale. Just as the mountain climber does not begin with Mount Everest, you cannot get rid of all your self-will immediately. You start with little things. When you go out to dinner with a friend, instead of choosing carefully just what you like, have what the other person is having instead. It might be your favorite, but more likely it will be something you would just as soon pass over.

That is the time to smile and eat. It is especially good if husband and wife can do this, for then there is the motivation to learn to like what the person you love likes. In such cases you cannot help moving closer to each other, for you will have got a little of your self-will out of the way. If you can even ask for seconds, you can mark that day on your calendar; the ego has started to pack its bags.

Then Sri Krishna says, *Dadāsi yat:* "Whatever you give, make it an offering to me." The finest gifts we can give are forgiveness and patience. We can't give anyone joy or security by increasing her bank account or adding to his collection of vintage wines. The only thing these gifts will increase is the gross national product, and after some experience of life we should be able to see that there is no connection between the gross national product and real security. In the spiritual lore of India there is a story that the Lord whispered only one word in our ears when he sent us into the world: "Give." Give freely of your time, your talent, your resources; give without asking for anything in return. This is the secret of living in joy and security. The moment you expect reward or recognition, you are making a contract.

Even parents and children suffer from this contract relationship. While I was teaching at the university in India I met some parents with good intentions who wanted to make their boy or girl into the scientist or musician they had never been. I used to be very close to most of my students, and they didn't mind confiding in me that their real talent lay in some other field. Parents can help their children tremendously by avoiding this "I gave this to you, therefore you do that for me" approach, encouraging them instead to follow their own star.

My grandmother, who did not know how to read or write, showed great wisdom in what she expected of me. I remember how she responded to my downfall in mathematics. I was in high school and had just been introduced to the world of Shakespeare, which was so glorious to me that my mind was full of Capulets and Montagues, of Falstaff and Prince Hal. I forgot all about my mathematics class, and when my mathematics test came, I didn't do very well. As I came home from school, my friends teased me with, "How could this possibly have happened to you?" My family was even less understanding. Only my grandmother remained unperturbed; she did not say a word about it.

That night I made up my mind to go to the top of the class in mathematics, just to please my grandmother. Her attitude of not losing faith in me gave me such motivation that I took to Euclid like a blood brother and did extremely well. Immediately, most of my family wanted me to become an engineer. I tried to tell them that I had no deep commitment to Pythagoras or Euclid, that my heart was given to literature, but the elder members of my family simply told me, "Nonsense. You've done very well in mathematics. India needs engineers and pays them well, too, so you should become an engineer." They had picked out the engineering college and even the courses I should take. My grandmother did not get drawn into this debate, but when I was leaving for college she gave me her support in a way I shall always be grateful for: "Follow your own star." It was the soundest educational advice she could have given. After all, if I had become an engineer I don't think I would have been too eager to cross a bridge of my own design.

Finally Sri Krishna says, *Yat tapasyasi:* "Whatever you suffer, make it an offering to me." This is the crux of sādhana. It is not easy to forgive someone who is bristling with hostility. It is not a simple thing to help someone who irritates you and frustrates your attempts to mend an estranged relationship. Until we learn these skills, there can be a lot of anguish in going against our self-will when everything within us is crying out to let it have its way. But if we are to make progress on the spiritual path, we have no choice but to face this suffering and grow.

To use the language of the Compassionate Buddha, we all suffer from ourselves. Most of us are inclined to lay the blame for our problems at our parents' or our partner's doorstep, but the culprit is not 'he' or 'she'; it is 'me.' The day we can tell ourselves honestly, "You created this mess all by yourself; now you can get yourself out all by yourself", we have become strong enough to pull ourselves out.

शुभाशुभफलैरेवं मोक्ष्यसे कर्मबन्धनैः ।
संन्यासयोगयुक्तात्मा विमुक्तो मामुपैष्यसि ॥९-२८॥

28. In this way you will be freed from the bondage of karma, and from its results both pleasant and painful. Then, with your heart free, you will come to me.

All of us have had moments of regret when we look back upon the past – particularly upon our early days, when we were ignorant of the pitfalls of life and simply did not know which was the way to fulfillment. But on the spiritual path it is essential not to look back either in sorrow or in anger. Here the Gita can console and strengthen us, because it takes into account how easy it is for us to make mistakes. Instead of condemning us or criticizing us, the Gita shows us how we can correct those mistakes through the practice of meditation.

When we suffer from guilt about the past, it is very much like a record player when the needle gets stuck. We are playing our favorite song, "I should have known better," and it keeps on repeating, "I should have known better, I should have known better . . ." The same thought goes round and round, and every time it goes round the groove becomes deeper. At times like these we forget that there is any other song in our repertoire. But there is a breathtakingly simple solution to this problem: all we need to do is reach out, lift up the needle, and move it to a new song.

This is what we do in meditation, when we recall our mental energy from dwelling on our thoughts. It is not the mistakes we have made that torment us; it is our dwelling on those mistakes. All this obsessive repetition charges them with power, and just as a demolition unit can go into a building and defuse a bomb, in practicing meditation we can defuse a memory of its power to hold our attention and agitate us. When thoughts of the past are coming up – as they will for almost all of us – what I would suggest is, don't pay any attention to them, and don't let anyone else talk to you about them either. It is very much like dealing with a distraction in meditation: you don't fight it directly; you simply withdraw your attention from the distraction by giving more concentration to the words of the passage. Here, instead of dwelling on your mistake and talking it over with all your friends, go for a long, fast walk repeating your mantram. You will find that this is all it takes to change the needle to a new, positive line of thinking.

But it's not enough if we simply repeat the mantram; we need to keep from putting the needle on that same old groove again. When we ask the Lord to forgive us, most people look upon it as a passive prayer: "Lord, forgive us, please." If we are going to keep on committing mistakes and saying, "Lord, forgive us, please," our whole life will be spent between erring and repenting, erring and repenting. From the little I know of Sri Krishna, he will say, "What about tomorrow?" He *will* forgive us; there is no end to his mercy. But as one physician used to say, "The Lord may forgive us our mistakes, but our nervous system will not." Every time we repeat a mistake, every time we dig the groove a little deeper, we are making it more difficult for our nervous system to change.

In my interpretation, therefore, forgiveness means learning to draw upon the deeper powers in our consciousness and change the wrong ways of thinking that have conditioned us to make these mistakes. No matter what we may have done in the past, it is always possible for us to change. That is why the mystics say that the Lord's forgiveness is always held out for us to take. But the choice to reach out and take it is left to us.

Most people in the modern world object strongly to the concept of divine punishment, because they think it means there is somebody in outer space meting out sentences with a firm hand. So instead of talking about sin and punishment, I prefer to talk about mistakes and consequences. It is the same thing; the only difference is in the language. Here the Compassionate Buddha's approach is very easy to understand. He would say when we are angry, we are punishing ourselves; anger is its own punishment. On the physical level, for example, when we are angry our respiration changes, and in the long run this may lead to asthma. Our digestion is affected, and after many years of this we can develop serious digestive problems. Even dandruff is like that. Dandruff is not inflicted by God; it is a light sentence which we impose on ourselves. When we have been eating wrong food, or smoking, or not getting enough exercise, we are working hard at giving ourselves a really stiff punishment, and the way to ask the Lord for forgiveness is to draw on the power released in meditation to give up smoking and change our wrong habits of eating and behaving so as to have a peaceful heart.

If you want to see the miracle of the Lord's forgiveness, you have only to look at how complete this change can be. To give you just one example, I have had friends who have given up alcohol after many years of heavy use, and I have been overwhelmed at the mercy of the Lord when I see how swiftly they can learn to relate to people well and overcome many of their physical disabilities after all those years of abuse. Even though we may have serious problems, none of us need throw up our hands in despair and say we can never stand straight again. Whatever the mistakes of our past are, however much they may have affected our body and mind, there is such resilience in our consciousness that by changing our ways, all of us can release ourselves in a large measure from the consequences of our past.

समो ऽहं सर्वभूतेषु न मे द्वेष्यो ऽस्ति न प्रियः ।
ये भजन्ति तु मां भक्त्या मयि ते तेषु चाप्यहम् ॥९-२९॥

29. I look upon all creatures equally; none are less dear to me and none more dear. But those who worship me with all their heart live in me, and I come to life in them.

This verse is simple but very deep in its significance. In sweet words, the Lord tells Arjuna: "I have no favorites; race or sex, place of birth or social status make no difference to me. All that is important is that your life be devoted to me."

Arjuna looks at Sri Krishna quizzically. "Then why is it," he asks, "that you often say of a particular devotee *sa ca me priyah,* 'I am wildly in love with him, head over heels in love with her'?" So the Lord explains gently the relationship he has with those who are completely devoted to him. "Those who meditate on me with all their heart, who try to see me in every creature, live in my love and security completely." Then he adds, "I who am infinite, whom all the galaxies cannot contain, I live in such people too."

When we begin to realize the magnitude of this statement, we shall have profound veneration for our real Self, the divine spark within us. The Compassionate Buddha calls this body of ours a frail clay pot. Who can fathom the wonder of the Lord of the cosmos taking up residence in this brittle little vessel? The Hindu greeting *namas te* expresses this reverence for the Lord of Love, who dwells within each one of us. It means "I bow unto you" – not unto Jonathan Swift or Tom Jones, but to Him who is seated within Jonathan Swift, Tom Jones, and you and me.

अपि चेत्सुदुराचारो भजते मामनन्यभाक् ।
साधुरेव स मन्तव्यः सम्यग्व्यवसितो हि सः ॥९-३०॥
क्षिप्रं भवति धर्मात्मा शश्वच्छान्तिं निगच्छति ।
कौन्तेय प्रतिजानीहि न मे भक्तः प्रणश्यति ॥९-३१॥

30–31. Even a sinner becomes holy when he or she takes refuge in me alone. In a short time that person is completely dedicated to the spiritual life and attains to boundless peace. Never forget this, Kaunteya: no one who is devoted to me will ever come to harm.

These beautiful verses have been a source of consolation to millions of men and women down the ages, for they remind us that no matter what our past is like, even what our present is like, none of us is ever lost in the eyes of the Lord. All of us are only frail human beings – "born to trouble," as the Bible puts it, "as the sparks fly upward" – and all of us have committed mistakes in the past, mostly in our ignorance of the unity of life. That is human conditioning, which every one of us shares. But just as it is our nature to be liable to these mistakes, all of us have the inborn capacity – which is never lost – of erasing this futile writing on the wall which we ourselves have done through many years of wrong living.

When we really understand the implications of this approach, so loving and yet so practical, we will never again be oppressed by the burden of the past. During the many years in which I have been teaching meditation in this country, I have come into intimate contact with hundreds of thoughtful people, young and old, some of whom have led lives of no earthly benefit to anyone, not even themselves. It always touches me deeply to hear such people confide how lonely they have made themselves, how estranged from the loving support of those around them, how despairing of any chance to change. I do not pretend that their past has been flawless; I do not ask about their past at all. Instead, I remind them that no amount of mistakes can ever banish the Lord of Love from our hearts. He is always there, and because he is always there, we always have the choice to turn our backs on the past completely and learn to live in peace with ourselves and in harmony with those around us.

In other words, as Jesus puts it so tenderly, all of us are children of God, and however misguided our conduct may be, a loving father – or, as we would say in India, a loving mother – does not disavow his or her children. That is the deep appeal of Jesus' parable of the prodigal son. Here is a young man who has received his full legacy from his father and gone away to squander it all in riotous living, painting the towns red from one end of Judea to the other. Naturally, as the wheel of his deeds begins to turn against him, he eventually finds himself alone and friendless, utterly without resources, without even the means to feed himself. Then he understands the enormity of what he has done, and stricken with grief, he decides to return to his father's house – not for a second legacy, but merely to work for his father as a servant rather than starve in a foreign land. And it is a very moving scene when Jesus tells us that the father, in the joy of seeing his son again, runs out to meet him on the road, and embraces him, and returns the young man to his full legacy with great love and ceremony, saying in words that we can remember always: "This my son was dead, and is alive again; he was lost, and now he is found."

There is no question here of the nature of our mistakes. In every country, in every tradition, the annals of mysticism are filled with stories of men and women whose errors in life may have been much worse than ours, but who have managed to reverse their lives completely once they glimpse this birthright of forgiveness within us all. Sometimes it is those with the greatest capacity for doing harm to themselves and others who become tremendous channels for good, for when it is harnessed, all their aggression, all their militancy, all their destructiveness can enable them to go very far on the spiritual path. I think it is St. Teresa who says beautifully that the sun of God's love is always shining, and though we may have kept the curtains drawn for a whole lifetime, filling our hearts with darkness, once we reach out and open the curtains there is no darkness so deep that it will not be dispelled by the brightness of that light.

But it is not enough to say that we are all children of the Lord; we have to learn to act as children of the Lord. In my ancestral home in India, when the younger girls were just learning to cook on our wood stoves, they would sometimes spill a little curry or burn a little rice, and their mothers or aunts would sometimes criticize them for being all thumbs. On such occasions, my grandmother would always say for the benefit of both generations, "In order to learn to cook, you have to burn a little and spill a little." But then she used to add to the girls, "But if you never do anything but burn and spill, you will never learn to cook." It is very much the same in our lives too. I have great sympathy for people when they come and tell me of the mistakes they have committed, because I know how easy it is for all of us to make such mistakes ourselves. But where I get bewildered is when they go on committing those same mistakes without doing their best not ever to commit them again.

All of us, as human beings, have the marvelous capacity to relearn all our patterns of living, to change every liability into a strength. I am always amazed at how quickly this transformation can take place. Here is someone who has been eating unhealthy food for years, and in a few months he is able to change his habits completely. There is someone who has been suffering from terrible bouts of anger, and after a few years of meditation she has already begun to change anger into compassion and hatred into love. Even if we have been in the slough of despond for fifty years, we need not work fifty years to get out of it.

This is divine mercy. Even though we may have been very selfish, even if we have developed all kinds of unpleasant habits over the years, such as smoking, or drinking, or always brooding on ourselves, Sri Krishna says, *Kshipram bhavati dharmātmā:* we swiftly become the soul of goodness, often even stronger in body and mind than we were before these negative habits began to drain us of our strength.

As our spiritual awareness deepens and we begin to see ourselves more clearly, there will be times when past mistakes will swim into our vision and do their best to consume us in guilt or regret. At such times, it is essential to repeat the mantram and turn all our attention outwards, away from ourselves. Analyzing our mistakes and dwelling on how to repay them is of no earthly benefit at all. But here I can offer one consoling application of the law of karma. If, when you were in Milwaukee, you happened to say something insulting about your girlfriend's dog, it is not necessary to go to Milwaukee and find your old girlfriend or her dog to make amends. Every dog you treat with kindness will be a proxy for that dog. If you have treated a particular person badly, even if you can no longer win that person's forgiveness, you can still win the forgiveness of yourself, of the Lord of Love within, by bearing with everyone who treats you badly and doing your best never to treat anyone else badly again. This is the tremendous practical implication of St. Francis's words, "It is in pardoning that we are pardoned." Whatever we have done, we can always make amends for it without ever looking backwards in guilt or sorrow.

Here the question I like to hear is, How do we do this? We are convinced of the folly of looking backwards, of analyzing our weaknesses or our guilt; now how do we go about changing ourselves so that all of these habits can be unlearned? This is the purpose of meditation and its allied disciplines, which gradually give us the wisdom to see what changes to make in ourselves and the will and skillfulness to translate these changes into our daily lives.

First there is the physical level, which is very much the level of the body and the senses. As the Buddha would say, we are not punished for our sins, we are punished *by* our sins, and I think that many of the serious diseases which have become so widespread today – heart disease, hypertension, digestive and breathing disorders, even many kinds of cancer – are influenced by things like poor diet and smoking and environmental pollution, which are entirely within our means to avoid. Even if our problems are not of this kind, a healthy body and a relaxed, resilient nervous system are essential if we are to overcome the emotional problems to which all of us are subject in some measure.

So the first step we must take once we take to meditation is to change our way of living. To begin with, our attitude towards food begins to change. Instead of eating what benefits only the palate, what appeals to our taste, we begin to eat what benefits the body. Then our whole attitude towards exercise begins to change. Where we used to drive to the corner to post a letter, we now begin to walk everywhere – after breakfast, during our morning break, every time we get a chance. Walking briskly while repeating the mantram is excellent exercise; it can go a long way towards releasing tension, and as one doctor I was reading says, virtually every muscle in the body is utilized except the jaws. And whenever we get some free time – a day off, or a weekend, or a summer vacation – instead of doing something that pleases no one but ourselves, we can give our time and our energy to people or worthwhile organizations who are in need. All these are changes we can make in our external lives which strengthen us immensely to turn our backs upon the past.

But external changes like these are only the beginning. On the emotional side, even those with strong, healthy bodies, who lead very temperate lives, are not immune to the restlessness, the loneliness, the insecurity that we see all around us today. Here, meditation and the allied disciplines can give us such peace of mind that negative states such as insecurity and depression can be banished from our lives forever. This takes more time than physical changes, but it is within the reach of every one of us. Then, when we can make these changes, the Lord says, *Shashvacchāntim nigacchati:* in a very short time our hearts will be at peace, and we will live at peace not only with others but with ourselves.

Arjuna is overwhelmed by these statements, because he sees in this promise of Self-realization how infinite is the mercy of the Lord.

Arjuna's mother is Kuntī, and this mighty warrior has become so like a little child in his gratitude and his love that Sri Krishna calls him by a very tender name: *Kaunteya,* 'Kuntī's child.' He says, *Kaunteya, pratijānīhi:* "Always remember" – when the senses get turbulent, when the ego becomes rebellious, when the world threatens to overpower you – *na me bhaktah pranashyati:* "those who are devoted to me, who meditate on me, will never come to harm." It is a promise which has been verified by so many mystics that we can trust it as an eternal spiritual law.

मां हि पार्थ व्यपाश्रित्य ये ऽपि स्युः पापयोनयः ।
स्त्रियो वैश्यास्तथा शूद्रास्ते ऽपि यान्ति परां गतिम् ॥९-३२॥
किं पुनर्ब्राह्मणाः पुण्या भक्ता राजर्षयस्तथा ।
अनित्यमसुखं लोकमिमं प्राप्य भजस्व माम् ॥९-३३॥

32. All those who take refuge in me, whatever
their birth, race, or sex, will attain the
supreme goal; this realization can be attained
even by those whom society scorns.
33. Kings and sages too seek this goal with devotion.
Therefore, having been born in this transient
and forlorn world, give all your love to me.

No matter who we are or what our past, every one of us can become aware of our real Self, the Ātman, which is beyond any barrier life can erect – nationality, race, sex, social status, anything.

In India, there is a story about a poor peasant boy who came from one of the so-called lower castes. This boy was a great lover of Lord Shiva, always repeating Shiva's name and meditating on him. So when it came time for the annual festival to celebrate the glory of Shiva, this boy desperately wanted to go. But all his days were committed to working in the rice fields of his landlord, whose permission he had to obtain before he could go. The landlord was a very wealthy man but not a very spiritual one, and he just laughed at the boy's request: "Imagine you wanting to go to the Shiva festival, which is usually attended by brahmins! What do you know about the scriptures?"

The boy replied, "I don't know anything about the scriptures. I can't even read or write. But I have such love in my heart for Shiva that even the sound of his name thrills me."

"That's all very well," said the landlord, "but the rice fields are ready for harvesting and I need you here." Then he added in an unkind joke, "Have the harvest completely finished by tomorrow morning, and I will give you permission to go."

Now, normally a rice harvest takes many days of backbreaking labor, and there was no way in which even a small part of this work could be done overnight. But the boy was undaunted, for his landlord had given him an opportunity that a boy of his caste would ordinarily never get. He went home, sat in his hut in deep meditation, and asked Lord Shiva from the very depths of his heart: "I have such a good landlord; he has promised to let me go to your temple and celebrate your glory if I can harvest all the rice from the fields by tomorrow morning. Help me, O Shiva, so that I may go to your festival." Then, after he had laid his prayer at the feet of the Lord, the boy was so full of faith that without any doubts troubling him further, he lay down and fell asleep.

Early the next morning an excited crowd of villagers gathered outside his hut. Not only had the fields been completely harvested; the rice bundles were neatly tied and arranged on the bullock carts, ready to go. Everybody was crying, "Miracle! Miracle!" Even the landlord was profoundly moved. He asked the boy to forgive him and to explain how this miracle had been performed. The boy replied in utter guilelessness: "What is there so miraculous about it? I love Shiva, and he is the Lord of the universe. I just told him I had a little job to do before I could go to his celebration." This is the faith that harvests rice fields and moves mountains, and it may be attained by any of us, no matter what our birth or background or social status.

Today, however, most of us find it so easy to support the underdog that I would like to say a good word in favor of the upper dog, too. Just because someone is cultured, or wealthy, or has led a good life, he or she is not barred from going far on the spiritual path. In my experience, those who have undergone all the discipline it takes to become scholars, doctors, engineers, lawyers, artists, and scientists can take to meditation very easily. All they have to do is take the energy, concentration, and effort they used to achieve excellence in their field and turn it towards the supreme goal of life. Wherever you find people who can concentrate with absorption, you have found promising potential spiritual aspirants. Once they understand how to harness their capacities through the practice of meditation, such people can grow to great spiritual heights.

मन्मना भव मद्भक्तो मद्याजी मां नमस्कुरु ।
मामेवैष्यसि युक्त्वैवमात्मानं मत्परायणः ॥९-३४॥

34. Fill your mind with me; serve me; worship me always. Seeking me in your heart, you will at last be united with me.

This is the refrain of the entire Bhagavad Gita. The Lord sums up the supreme secret of the spiritual life in one word, *manmanā*: "Let your mind be filled with me." Let your heart dwell only on the Lord and let nothing else distract you. In your dreams, see the Lord; in your sleep, hear his voice. Under no circumstances must you ever forget him. In the deeper stages of meditation, the Lord will put you to some simple tests to see if you have unified your consciousness in him. He may strike a great blow at you, and when your whole being is agitated he will say, "Now let me see you meditate." It is a stiff, honest test. The mind may rise in tides of turmoil and object, "How can I meditate when you have struck at me like this? I'm completely stunned." If that is so, you haven't passed the test. But if you have been meditating steadily and enthusiastically over a long period of time, your mind will remain centered on the Lord no matter what blows life deals you. Whatever reverses come your way, your heart will always be filled with love. Then the Lord will say, "You pass." When he says that, all your problems pass, too.

Under no circumstances should we forget that the Lord alone is worthy of our deepest love. We should never sacrifice our meditation for the sake of any other interest. When we base our life on meditation, our health, our security, our intellectual and creative capacities *have* to improve; there is no other alternative. If we try in this way to fill our hearts with love for him, we will be united with him without any doubt at all.

राजविद्याराजगुह्ययोगो नाम नवमोऽध्यायः ॥ ९ ॥

CHAPTER TEN

Divine Splendor

श्रीभगवानुवाच ।
भूय एव महाबाहो श्रृणु मे परमं वचः ।
यत्ते ऽहं प्रीयमाणाय वक्ष्यामि हितकाम्यया ॥ १०-१ ॥
न मे विदुः सुरगणाः प्रभवं न महर्षयः ।
अहमादिर्हि देवानां महर्षीणां च सर्वशः ॥ १०-२ ।
यो मामजमनादिं च वेत्ति लोकमहेश्वरम् ।
असंमूढः स मर्त्येषु सर्वपापैः प्रमुच्यते ॥ १०-३ ॥

SRI KRISHNA:

1. Listen further, Arjuna, to my supreme teaching, which gives you such joy. Desiring your welfare, O great-armed warrior, I will tell you more.
2. Neither gods nor sages know my origin, for I am the source from which the gods and sages come.
3. Whoever knows me as the Lord of all creation, without birth or beginning, knows the truth and frees himself from all evil.

When I was a boy, growing up in village India, I used to belong to the Boy Scouts. We were very much like Boy Scouts everywhere: we had the same khaki shorts and shirts, and a little patrol ribbon – ours was an elephant – and even a tenderfoot badge. The only difference was that the official uniform included a green turban.

Not far from our village there was a dense forest, and one of the things we used to do as Boy Scouts was tracking. We would divide into two groups and then one group would go hide in the forest, leaving all sorts of clues about where they had gone – tearing off one leaf and placing it next to another, breaking a twig in a particular way, things like that. Then the rest of us, after a decent wait, had to go through the forest very observantly and try to find and interpret all these little signs. We would roam around in our khaki shorts and our green turbans, peering closely at everything, and now and then someone would spot something out of the ordinary and exclaim, "Aha! That's not nature; that's some Boy Scout!" I wasn't very good at this game, but fortunately there were others who were quite skillful and we always worked as a team. At last, after we had found several of these signs, one of these more skillful chaps would look up into a tree, squint his eyes, and say, "Hey, that's not a monkey; that's our Scout leader!"

This is what the Lord has done; he has strewn little signs of his presence throughout the universe, and the person who is very observant, who is very spiritual, will always see these signs and recognize where the Lord is to be found. Most of us see these signs but pass over them; we do not recognize them for what they are. But as our eyes begin to clear through the practice of meditation, when we see someone being extremely patient, someone who can listen quietly to criticism without retaliating or losing his temper, we will think, "Aha! That's not my friend Richard; that is the Lord in Richard."

Richard may leave broken twigs of patience, torn leaves of kindness, but the men and women who have realized God leave big signposts of His presence everywhere they go. There is a marvelous story about a man looking for the Buddha the way one follows the tracks of an animal in the jungle. He went around asking people everywhere, and whenever he found a person whose life had been transformed he would exclaim to himself, "Those are the tracks of a really big elephant!"

This chapter is rather like a divine tracking manual, in which Sri Krishna tells Arjuna a few of his favorite signs. Though the Lord is present everywhere, the expression of his presence varies throughout the infinite variety of his creation. Wherever perfection is approached, his glory is revealed a little more – among people, among trees, among stars, in all the qualities of life. As the Persian mystic Jamī writes:

> To display His eternal attributes
> In their inexhaustible variety,
> The Lord made the green fields of time and space
> And the living garden of the cosmos,
> So that each branch, leaf, and fruit reveal
> His innumerable glories.

बुद्धिर्ज्ञानमसंमोहः क्षमा सत्यं दमः शमः ।
सुखं दुःखं भवो ऽभावो भयं चाभयमेव च ॥१०-४॥

अहिंसा समता तुष्टिस्तपो दानं यशो ऽयशः ।
भवन्ति भावा भूतानां मत्त एव पृथग्विधाः ॥१०-५॥

4–5. The different qualities found in living creatures have their source in me: discrimination, wisdom, understanding, forgiveness, truth, self-control, and peace of mind; the dualities of pleasure and pain, birth and death, honor and dishonor; nonviolence, charity, equanimity, contentment, and perseverance in spiritual disciplines.

All the faculties of life have their origin in the Lord: not only pleasure but pain too, not only honor but dishonor too. It is not that the Lord is capricious or unloving; these are distinctions that we make ourselves. Once we make ourselves whole, we see everything as whole, which is what it means to see the Lord everywhere. But until then, as long as there is division in our minds, everything is split into two: good and bad, right and wrong, pleasant and unpleasant, friend and foe.

There is a story by Edgar Allan Poe called "The Purloined Letter" in which a certain cabinet minister steals a letter and then threatens to blackmail its owner. The Paris police almost take the man's apartment apart looking for the letter – inside the vases, up the chimneys, behind the walls, everywhere they can think of – but none of them is able to find even a clue. Only the amateur detective Dupin is able to guess where it is: in the most obvious place possible, lying on the man's desk in front of everyone's eyes.

This is what the mind has done to us. The Lord is all around us, but we cannot see him as long as we have to depend on the mind, which has an unfortunate obsession with cutting everything up into two. It is pointless to blame the mind for this; it cannot help itself. Do you remember Charlie Chaplin in *Modern Times?* He plays a worker on an assembly line, whose sole job all day long is to take his wrench and tighten one particular bolt a quarter turn. After a day of this, doing the same thing over and over again, even on his way home he walks along tightening everything a quarter turn. This is how the mind is. It has its tool chest of saws for every possible purpose, and every time it runs into something – objects, ideas, perceptions, people – it pulls out a hacksaw or a pocket chain saw and saws that thing into two. That is all that is required; we cannot see the unity of life anywhere.

In practice, all that this collection of saws amounts to is likes and dislikes. As your meditation deepens and you begin to see the ways of your mind more clearly, you will notice that there is a constant chorus of likes and dislikes going on inside. Usually we are not aware of this chorus because it goes on beneath the surface of consciousness. But if we could listen in on a little of what literary critics call the "stream of consciousness" – really it is more a stream of unconsciousness – we would be embarrassed to see how petty this chorus can be. Just watch your mind when you respond to a person; what is it you are really responding to? "I don't like his walk; it looks too pompous. I don't like her voice; it grates on my nerves." What about your walk? What about your voice? Once, when I was responsible for recording something for All India Radio, I played back one of the programs for a student to hear. She listened to it all with a rather pained expression, and afterwards she commented, "That's a really unpleasant voice. I don't like it." The voice was her own; she hadn't recognized it at all.

As long as the mind feels compelled to keep us posted on its opinions like this, consciousness has to be divided, which means that we are going to be tormented by vacillation and lapses in everything: in our loyalty, in our patience, in our security, in our capacity to see clearly and make wise decisions anywhere in daily living. All the qualities in this verse have a role to play in helping us see through this fog of separateness, called *moha* in Sanskrit. *Moha* literally means 'delusion.' *Sammoha* is 'super-delusion,' and the word used here is *asammoha,* 'without any trace of delusion,' which means complete awareness of the unity of life. I have translated *asammoha* as wisdom because in its practical application, it means that you will never be deluded by anything the world has to offer – money, pleasure, power, prestige, anything.

Sammoha is the distorting medium of self-will through which all of us perceive life. Self-willed people go around in this kind of ego-fog always; that is why they are constantly bumping into people and running down blind alleys. Everything is distorted: friends appear menacing, harmful activities promise fulfillment, and the road to happiness that looks so shimmering in the fog turns out to be the road to the dump. As your vision begins to clear through the practice of meditation, you really have to rub your eyes. It will scarcely seem like the same world, and yet nothing will have changed except your way of seeing.

One of the most practical ways I know for clearing our eyes of this fog of suspicion and self-will is *kshamā*. Kshamā is not only forgiveness, it is patience, forbearance, and understanding too, all wrapped into one. No matter how much we feel we have been wronged, no matter how much we feel others may not appreciate us, we should learn to be patient and to forgive – not only because it helps those around us, but because it helps us to free ourselves from the pall of suspicion and resentment. Gradually, as our eyes become clearer, this can save us a good deal of embarrassment. Because of the distorting mirror of self-will, most of us are liable to complain at some time or other: "Why is so-and-so always rude to me? I said hello to her this morning and she didn't even answer." It is only when we learn that she had received bad news that morning, or was up all night with her baby, that we realize we had not been wronged at all. It was only because we were so wrapped up in ourselves that we took her silence personally.

Bearing with people, especially those who really do cause us problems, is the essence of forgiveness. It is not particularly helpful to do this with a feeling of martyrdom, either; we need to bear with people cheerfully. But this does not mean making ourselves into a doormat. Letting people take undue advantage of us is not helpful for them any more than it is for us. Instead, we can learn to bear with them and at the same time improve the situation with their help.

When it is necessary to show our love by expressing disapproval, we should learn to disagree constructively. Sri Ramakrishna advises us to hiss gently when necessary, but not to bite. This is particularly applicable in relationships with children, who can be ingenious at needling us to see how far they can go. What they are trying to say is, "Hiss at us so we'll know when to stop." I saw the value of a well-timed hiss when I was out for a walk with our dog Muka, who tries to play with every creature he sees. He found a snake in the garden and offered to play with it. The snake was doing whatever snakes do early in the morning, and when Muka tried to get it to play there was a sharp *hsss!* and Muka came hopping out of the grass like a jackrabbit.

The secret of seeing through sammoha is in not dwelling on ourselves. The more we think about what *we* enjoy and don't enjoy, what *we* want and don't want, the more we are going to be caught in this net of separateness, cut off from others and from ourselves. So Sri Krishna says, *Tushti:* "Be content with what life sends you." Don't be a beggar, sitting with your little tin cup and begging of life, "Please give me a few cents of pleasure, or at least don't give me any pain." Don't ask always what you can get from life, but *dānam:* ask what you can give. Stand up to your full height and give freely to those around you – your time, your resources, your talents, your extra clothes or vegetables from your garden, whatever you have. It doesn't matter whether the gift is simple or modest; what matters is that it be given freely, wholeheartedly, without any reservations, without even the left hand knowing what the right hand is doing. You are not wealthy simply because you have a lot, you are wealthy when you have given a lot away; and the more you give, the more you will have to give – not in money, but in the richness of your life.

It is not enough in life to do no harm; we should be able to contribute to life wherever we go. In the Hindu tradition we have a story about a man who was the perfect model of respectability, who always did what the letter of the law demanded of him. He never offended anybody or injured anybody; he always kept up with the Ramaswamis, and when he was called on to give a speech he always had a grand audience, because he used to tell them just what they wanted to hear. When the time came for this man to pay his final bill, he was taken before Chitragupta, a kind of cosmic auditor in the Hindu scriptures. Chitragupta looked up the man's record and there it was, not a single entry on the debit page. Chitragupta was really impressed, because even in the case of the great mystics there are debit entries, sometimes rather a lot of them. "Wow!" he said. "I've never seen anyone like you." Then he turned to the credit page and stared in astonishment, because that page was completely blank too. Chitragupta just stood there and scratched his head; he didn't know what to do. The man had never let anybody down, never helped anybody; never offended anybody, never loved anybody – he couldn't be sent to heaven, but on the other hand he couldn't be sent anywhere else either.

Finally Chitragupta took the chap to Brahmā, the god of creation in the Hindu Trinity. "You made this guy," he said; "what shall I do with him?" Brahmā looked at the statute books and couldn't find anything to cover the case, so he said, "Send him over to Krishna." And Sri Krishna said, "The buck stops here." He examined the record very carefully and there, almost illegible, was an ancient credit entry: "Gave two cents to a beggar at the age of six." "There," Sri Krishna said; "return his two cents and send him back to try again."

महर्षयः सप्त पूर्वे चत्वारो मनवस्तथा ।
मद्भावा मानसा जाता येषां लोक इमाः प्रजाः ॥ १०-६ ॥

6. The seven great sages and the four ancient ancestors
were born from my mind and received my power.
From them came all the creatures of this world.

The Hindu tradition has a gift for personalizing the forces of nature and of the mind, and to me these seven great sages and the four ancient ancestors of all living creatures represent the laws by which the universe and life evolved. As ruler of the cosmos, the Lord delegates his duties to specific powers. These are not just the laws of the physical world. In Hindu and Buddhist thought, there is no real distinction between the world outside us and the world of thoughts and feelings within, and the same unity that keeps the outer world running smoothly governs the world within us too.

Whenever we try to harm each other we are violating this law of unity. Today it should be clear to any sensitive man or woman that when we inflict suffering on others, we only destroy ourselves. Our world today is like a jet airliner without a pilot, in which most people are so busy trying to save their own seats that they can't be bothered to think about the plane. We are prepared to fight all the other passengers and even to rip our seat out of the floor if that is what it takes to have it all to ourselves.

All of us can play an important part in the conquest of violence by throwing our full weight behind peaceful, effective programs for eliminating the situations from which violence arises. But most important, we need to do everything we can to remove every trace of hostility and resentment in ourselves. The violence that is flaring up all around us on our streets and on our campuses is not so much the result of social conditions as the inevitable expression of the hostility in our hearts. Hostility is one of the most infectious diseases I know of, and whenever we indulge in a violent act or even in hostile words or expressions, we are passing this disease on to those around us.

To take just one example, look at what can happen in even a little family quarrel. When we quarrel at home, it is not just a domestic problem; we are contributing to turmoil everywhere. Suppose Tom Jones gets up on the wrong side of the bed, sits down at the breakfast table, and dares Amelia to tell him where she ever learned to make coffee. Amelia, being upsettable, gets upset. Tom goes off to work in a black cloud, and just to make sure that his day will be irritating, he keeps on rehearsing what he's going to tell Amelia when he gets home. And

Amelia, who is doing the same thing, is still so upset two hours later that she makes an unkind remark to the clerk in the store, who takes it out on the next ten customers.

These are small things, but over the day, day after day, they all add up. In the language of Hindu psychology, all these little moments of irritation and resentment build up into a samskāra, which means that they become a habitual response to everything around us. When a samskāra like this becomes deeply ingrained, almost anything can trigger a hostile reaction, often without any rhyme or reason. You have only to pick up the morning paper to see how commonplace this kind of reaction has become. That is why it is so important for all of us to learn to respond to hostility with patience and good will, and never to say or do anything that adds to this chain reaction of anger.

This applies not only to our words and actions; it applies even to the look on our face. It is said that the English satirist Jonathan Swift enjoyed his pessimism so much that he used to wear mourning on his birthday and go around with a scowl. Probably he thought it was no one's business but his own. But depression is everybody's business. In my teaching days in India, when I would remind a student that he was looking a little gloomy, he would object, "But sir, it's *my* face." I would reply, "Yes, but it's we who have to look at it." Not even the look on our face is our own business; all these things affect the people around us.

एतां विभूतिं योगं च मम यो वेत्ति तत्त्वतः ।
सो ऽविकम्पेन योगेन युज्यते नात्र संशयः ॥ १०-७॥
अहं सर्वस्य प्रभवो मत्तः सर्वं प्रवर्तते ।
इति मत्वा भजन्ते मां बुधा भावसमन्विताः ॥ १०-८॥
मच्चित्ता मद्गतप्राणा बोधयन्तः परस्परम् ।
कथयन्तश्च मां नित्यं तुष्यन्ति च रमन्ति च ॥ १०-९॥

7. Whoever understands my power and the mystery of my manifestations comes without doubt to be united with me.

> *8. I am the source from which all creatures evolve.*
> *The wise remember this and worship me with loving devotion.*
> *9. Their thoughts are all absorbed in me, and all their vitality flows to me. Seeing me in one another, talking about me always, they are happy and fulfilled.*

In Sanskrit there is a vivid name for the Lord, *Prānadā,* 'he who gives us *prāna.*' Prāna is energy, power, in the most basic sense of the word. All forms of energy in the universe are only different manifestations of prāna, which is one and indivisible. It is by prāna that the sun burns, the clouds rain, and the wind blows; it is by prāna that cells reproduce, the eyes see, the mind thinks, and the heart loves. Physicists throw light on this when they say that behind all matter is a field of energy, a unified field of forces. The language is different, but the idea they are expressing is the same: it is all the same prāna, whether we class its action as physical, mental, emotional, or spiritual.

The practical application of this is that it is the Lord, Prānadā, who gives us this prāna. As the Prashna Upanishad tells us, "Prāna is born of the Self. As a person casts a shadow, the Self casts prāna into the body at the time of birth." Therefore, the mystics ask, where do we get the idea that anything can be ours? We hang on dearly to our car, our savings, our stereo tape deck, yet not even the life in our bodies is ours; everything belongs to the Lord. So a great mystic like Shankara will tell the Lord, "What is there to renounce in this world? There is nothing here that I can call my own; everything is already yours."

Do you see the humor of this? It is as if I were to go up to my friend Jeff and say, "Jeff, I renounce your guitar once and for all." He would say, "What do you mean? It doesn't belong to you, it belongs to me." So where is the difficulty in renouncing it? Whatever we give up on the spiritual path, this is all it amounts to: we are simply letting the Lord know we understand that everything has always been his.

As we come to realize this on a deeper and deeper level – not intellectually, but in our hearts, so that it is reflected in our daily living – a great deal of the tension in our lives will begin to dissolve. When we want to have something that cannot be ours, we are putting ourselves on the horns of an impossible dilemma, and naturally there is tension below the surface level of our consciousness. This kind of constant tension wastes a good deal of prāna. It is very much like leaving the lights of your car on all night: when you get up in the morning, you find your battery is dead. That is what is happening when we go through life always feeling a little under par, a little unequal to what the day may bring; prāna is continuously draining out in the basement of our consciousness.

In deep meditation, however, we learn to get hold of the switches of our prāna, which means getting control of our desires. Only then do we have the choice to turn the switch off and conserve the energy it would drain. Whenever we can do this, the results are immediate; the entire nervous system relaxes a little, and the very next day the battery will have more power. Eventually we get our hands on the master switch of the whole circuit, which is sex. It is a very satisfying state of affairs. If we choose to, we can close the switch and all our vital capacity will be at our disposal. But we can also choose to leave the switch off, which is like pulling the plugs of all the appliances in the house. There is no outflow of prāna anywhere, which means that every part of the body is at rest.

Then, as this verse puts it, all our prāna is flowing to the Lord, who is within. The immense security of this state cannot be described; it has to be experienced to be understood. You know from your own experience that there is no limit to the power of the Lord within you, so there is no limit to your love or your capacity for service. The Hindu scriptures describe this state as *pūrnatā* – complete fullness, in which nothing can ever be lacking. There is no better example of the Lord's sense of humor: in giving up what was never ours to begin with, we are filled with everything; all our deep desires are fulfilled.

तेषां सततयुक्तानां भजतां प्रीतिपूर्वकम् ।
ददामि बुद्धियोगं तं येन मामुपयान्ति ते ॥१०-१०॥
तेषामेवानुकम्पार्थमहमज्ञानजं तमः ।
नाशयाम्यात्मभावस्थो ज्ञानदीपेन भास्वता ॥१०-११॥

10. To those steadfast in love and service I give spiritual wisdom, so that they may come to me.
11. Out of compassion I destroy the darkness of their ignorance. From within them I light the lamp of wisdom and dispel all darkness from their lives.

With infinite tenderness, the Lord lets it dawn on us only gradually that we are not separate, that we belong entirely to him. If this realization were to come overnight, ordinary people like you and me would not be able to withstand it; it would be more than our nervous systems could bear. That is why the Lord is so gentle with us; he spreads the transformation from separateness to unity out over many years so that all these changes in the mind and body can take place gradually, often at such a deep level that we are not even aware they are taking place until we look back and remember how we were some years before.

I like to illustrate this gradual ascent to unity with the trip up to my home high on the Blue Mountain in South India. The scorching heat of the Indian summer begins early in March, and in the old days, when I was a professor in Central India, I used to count the days until summer vacation when I could leave the crowded cities and the hot, dusty air of the plains behind me. On the very same evening of the last working day I would be on the train for Madras, and we used to pull into Madras Central Station twenty-four hours later just in time to catch the Blue Mountain Express. It was a long, hot, tiring journey, and it was a very satisfying moment when I could open my eyes after the morning's meditation and see the Blue Mountain beckoning on the horizon as we reached Coimbatore.

But even though there would be just fifty miles more to go, the journey would be far from over. At Coimbatore I had to leave the train and get onto a bus, and for a long, long time the bus would make its way slowly along the twenty-five mile road to Mettupalayam at the foot of the Blue Mountain. If you don't know the road and close your eyes, it's easy to imagine that you're climbing. But all you have to do is open your eyes and look out the window at the cars and roadside merchants and bullock carts to see that you are still very much on the plains. It is a dull, dreary journey, with nothing to recommend it except that it has to be put behind you. The real climb is yet to begin.

Then, as the bus begins to climb, the scenery changes, and the road becomes beautiful. First you see areca nut palms, swaying gracefully in the wind, and then the dense forests of the foothills, full of wild animals like tigers and elephants. Then, as the bus climbs above three thousand feet, there are rich coffee plantations and terraced tea gardens, dotted with silver firs whose leaves sparkle in the sun. And there was a particular point where I used to feel the cool, invigorating air of the mountains. It was almost as if I could draw a line where that change would occur. The hot, dry, dusty air of the plains would suddenly leave us, and my whole body and mind would drink in the cool, bracing air of the hills.

It is very much like that on the path of meditation. For a long, long time you are on level ground. You *are* traveling forward, but it's still on level ground; the air is still dry and dusty, and you get gas fumes occasionally. But all this time, though you may think that you are getting nowhere, you are building up momentum for the climb ahead. It is only after you have been very diligent about your meditation, after you have been very loyal in keeping your eyes always on the goal and very resolute in observing the disciplines of the spiritual life, that the scenery will begin to change. But change it surely will, and these changes will be reflected in every aspect of your daily living. It is a sure sign that you are entering the foothills and beginning to leave the plains behind. At work, you may find that you can get along with someone who always seemed to specialize in rubbing you the wrong way. When you go into a bookstore, instead of looking for books on literary criticism or getting glued to a sensational novel, you will begin to ask if there is a new edition of the Bhagavad Gita or an anthology of mystical poetry. And instead of going to restaurants where food lacking in nutritional value is served at outrageous prices, you will find yourself looking for vegetarian restaurants where the food is nutritious and the prices are within range.

At first your family may look askance at the way your life is changing, and your friends may raise their eyebrows at your flagging interest in old pursuits. If you don't have a certain amount of detachment from your opinions, this criticism may be difficult to take. At home in Berkeley you may be calm and true to your convictions, but as you walk slowly up the driveway to your parents' home, your security begins to waver. Then the door opens and the head of the household greets you with, "What's this I hear about meditation?" All security vanishes. You become either apologetic or defensive, state your case too vehemently, and find yourself in a very difficult position. But as you begin to gain security, you will be able to answer gently but firmly, "Yes, I'm trying to live a spiritual life, and I think it will benefit all of you, too." They may never have heard of the Bhagavad Gita; they may give an embarrassed cough and say, "That's not the life for us"; but they will begin to respect your efforts. After a while, when they see that you can be secure in the face of opposition and ridicule, that you can be true to your convictions and still keep your sense of humor, their critical remarks will change. Your father will tell your mother, "I never thought he had this in him"; your mother may even begin to tell her friends, "We might be able to take a leaf from her book."

During this first half of the ascent we have to travel under our own power. We have to make all the decisions ourselves; we have to strengthen our will and turn our backs on all sorts of temptations. It is only after this first part of the climb has been accomplished, after we have prepared ourselves, that we find the air becoming fresh and exhilarating. Then, slowly, during the second half of the ascent, we begin to realize that there is an inner power not our own which is drawing us forward. It is almost like reaching five thousand feet and then looking down from a narrow path to see how awesome the precipice is; one slip could plunge us to disaster. It makes us realize how miraculously we have been protected by the Lord all along the path. And though we can see the sheer, rocky peaks rising above us, we come to have a quiet faith that the same grace that has brought us this far will give us the support and inspiration we need for making the most difficult, most dangerous part of the climb which lies ahead.

Finally, at the very end of the spiritual ascent, we will reach a point beyond which we cannot go by our own effort. Though we must do everything we can to purify ourselves completely, the great mystics all testify, it is not possible for a human being to be finally united with the Lord by any amount of willing; it is up to the Lord to draw us to him if and when he chooses. This is a period of joyful agony, of watching and waiting as a bride waits for her bridegroom, for as Jesus says, the Lord will come as unexpectedly as a thief in the night. But finally, when we least expect it, the auspicious moment of union comes. Then, the Hindu mystics say, it is as if a lamp is lit in a temple which has been dark for many years: one minute the room is full of darkness; the next minute every corner is ablaze with light.

अर्जुन उवाच ।
परं ब्रह्म परं धाम पवित्रं परमं भवान् ।
पुरुषं शाश्वतं दिव्यमादिदेवमजं विभुम् ॥१०-१२॥
आहुस्त्वामृषयः सर्वे देवर्षिर्नारदस्तथा ।
असितो देवलो व्यासः स्वयं चैव ब्रवीषि मे ॥१०-१३॥

ARJUNA:

12–13. All the great sages and seers – Nārada, Asita, Devala, and Vyāsa, too – have called you the supreme Brahman, the highest abode, the supreme purifier, the self-luminous, eternal spirit, first among the gods, unborn and infinite. Now you have declared these things to me yourself.

Arjuna's words here emphasize the unity of all religions. All the great spiritual teachers speak of the same Reality and inspire us to strive for the same supreme goal. All have come to tell us of the divine spark within us. But for some curious reason, it is very difficult for us to accept our divine nature. This has always puzzled me. We pay money for books about how destructive we are; we stand in queues to buy magazines that emphasize our capacity for making trouble; we go to encounter groups where we agitate each other over our weaknesses. Then, when Jesus comes to tell us that the kingdom of heaven is within us, we say, "There must be some mistake." It is to convince us that our real Self is always pure and eternal that men and women of God keep arising among us and repeating the good news, that the source of all joy and security is right within.

सर्वमेतदृतं मन्ये यन्मां वदसि केशव ।
न हि ते भगवन्व्यक्तिं विदुर्देवा न दानवाः ॥१०-१४॥
स्वयमेवात्मनात्मानं वेत्थ त्वं पुरुषोत्तम ।
भूतभावन भूतेश देवदेव जगत्पते ॥१०-१५॥

14. Now, O Keshava, I believe that everything you have told me is divine truth. O Lord, neither gods nor demons know your real nature.
15. Indeed, you alone know yourself, O supreme spirit. You are the source of creation and the master of every creature, God of gods, the Lord of the universe.

Arjuna confides in Sri Krishna, "Every word that you say goes right to my heart. How can I ever think of knowing you completely?" This is one of the deepest questions asked in the scriptures. How can we talk about knowing God, write about God, speak about God, become an authority on God, if God is without name and form? The Hindu sages tell us that all we can hope to become is the dust of his lotus feet; Christian mystics will say all we can hope to do is touch the hem of God's garment.

The Lord is everywhere; there is nowhere that he is not. We can never know him through our physical senses, but for the man or woman of God, he is more real than any object of the senses can be. When

St. Francis of Assisi says he sees Jesus, we should not think he is talking figuratively just because he saw what others did not. Similarly, when St. Teresa of Ávila says, "His Majesty told me so," she is not referring to something she heard from King Philip; she *did* hear her King, but not with the outer ear. Sri Ramakrishna, who worshiped God as the Divine Mother, would sometimes break off in the middle of a sentence and tell his disciples, "Shh! Mother is coming; I can hear her anklets jingling." This is not hearing in the way we hear the jingling of coins or the tinkling of glasses; the Divine Mother is so real to him that he hears her in the very depths of his consciousness.

In his trenchant way, Meister Eckhart says that people think they can see God the way they see a cow. Actually, Eckhart tells us, we see God with the same eye with which he sees us. It is an image which I enjoy very much. Imagine peeking through a keyhole and discovering you are looking right into the eye of the Lord! We cannot know God in the usual way of knowing, the way we know the phenomenal world. He is the Ātman, the divine Self within us, and it is by identifying ourselves with this Self that we realize the Lord.

वक्तुमर्हस्यशेषेण दिव्या ह्यात्मविभूतयः ।
याभिर्विभूतिभिर्लोकानिमांस्त्वं व्याप्य तिष्ठसि ॥१०-१६॥
कथं विद्यामहं योगिंस्त्वां सदा परिचिन्तयन् ।
केषु केषु च भावेषु चिन्त्योऽसि भगवन्मया ॥१०-१७॥

16. Tell me all your divine attributes, leaving nothing unsaid. Tell me of the glories with which you fill the cosmos.
17. O Krishna, you are the supreme master of yoga. Tell me how I should meditate to gain constant awareness of you. In what things and in what ways may I meditate on you?

Arjuna is asking how he can become aware of the Lord always, in everything he does and in everyone around him. In meditation when we are concentrating completely on a passage like the Prayer of St. Francis – "It is in giving that we receive; it is in pardoning that we are pardoned" – we *are* meditating on the Lord; forgiving and giving freely are among the ways in which the Lord manifests himself in human beings. But it is not enough to meditate on him like this for an hour or so a day. We must learn to meditate on him always, which means bringing these qualities to life in our thought and action and learning to see the divinity that is within those around us too. This is not something sentimental, something we can do by sending cards saying "The Lord lives in you." We learn to see the Lord in those around us by *trying* to see the Lord in those around us. It is essentially a matter of practice, of constantly reminding ourselves over and over again throughout the day.

This is exactly what we are doing when we repeat the mantram, which is the name of the Lord. For those who have difficulty in remembering to repeat the mantram, I sometimes suggest putting a discreet little sign – "Repeat the Mantram" – wherever they are likely to see it frequently. Or, if they have a flair for the artistic and don't want to raise unnecessary questions from friends and coworkers, they can always write their mantram out in some original and decorative way – say, in the shape of an elephant, because an elephant never forgets. The point is somehow to remember the mantram; how we remember it is a matter in which there is considerable room for imagination.

The mind has a tremendous natural capacity to dwell on things, and in repeating the mantram we are channeling this capacity to train the mind to dwell constantly on the Lord. It is the same capacity, only we are giving it a different focus. There is a little story in the Hasidic tradition of Judaism in which a man asks his *zaddik* or spiritual teacher, "Do you mean we should remember the Lord even in the give-and-take of business?" "Yes, of course," the rabbi replies. "If we can remember business matters in the hour of prayer, shouldn't we be able to remember God in the transactions of our business?"

Finally, when we become established in the Lord, we shall see his glory everywhere, wherever there is beauty or excellence in the world around us. If I may say so, due entirely to the grace of my spiritual teacher, my grandmother, this is how I see life today. When I see the first green shoots pushing up through the ground after a rain, or our dog Muka running on the beach, or a mother being very patient with her child, it is the Lord I see as the essence, the inner Ruler in us all. Once we learn to see the world like this, there will be no need for external reminders; we will not forget even for a moment that everything in the world is sustained by the power of the Lord.

विस्तरेणात्मनो योगं विभूतिं च जनार्दन ।
भूयः कथय तृप्तिर्हि शृण्वतो नास्ति मे ऽमृतम् ॥ १०-१८ ॥

18. O Krishna, you who intoxicate people with love for you, tell me in detail your attributes and your powers; I can never tire of hearing your immortal words.

When you live in a royal palace, Sri Ramakrishna says, even if you are not exactly in the royal family, a little of the royalty rubs off on you as well. In India, even if a man is only the tenth footman in a royal palace, everybody thinks of him as a glamorous figure – his address is the royal palace. Even here it is like that; there is glamor in being a member of the White House staff, even if all you do all day is pluck out dandelions on the President's lawn. You still work at the White House, and sometimes you even get to go inside; you may have caught a glimpse of the President's little girl and perhaps even have picked up her pen and returned it to her when she was on her way to school. It's true that the Joint Chiefs of Staff won't even look at you, but when you go home everyone will listen with bated breath about how you picked up Amy's pen.

That is what is happening in this verse too. There is a little of the Lord's infinite glory present in all of us, and the deeper we go in our meditation, the more this glory will shine forth in our daily living. That is why, when we really begin to be serious about the practice of meditation, we never become tired of hearing about the glory of God from someone who is speaking from personal experience. Like Arjuna, the more we hear, the more we want to hear, because every word inspires us to reveal more of this divinity that is within us all.

श्रीभगवानुवाच ।
हन्त ते कथयिष्यामि दिव्या ह्यात्मविभूतयः ।
प्राधान्यतः कुरुश्रेष्ठ नास्त्यन्तो विस्तरस्य मे ॥ १०-१९ ॥

SRI KRISHNA:

19. All right, Arjuna, I will tell you of my divine powers. I will mention only the most glorious; there is no end to them.

In response to Arjuna's eager request, Sri Krishna begins to describe the glory that lies within all of us. It is a reminder that there is no limit to the power we can draw on for selfless work through the practice of meditation. Compared to the state we can reach, the condition we are living in today is really a dream. In the verses that follow, the Lord will be giving us a glimpse of what the world looks like to the person who is awake.

अहमात्मा गुडाकेश सर्वभूताशयस्थितः ।
अहमादिश्च मध्यं च भूतानामन्त एव च ॥ १०-२० ॥

20. I am the true Self in the heart of every creature, Arjuna, and the beginning, middle, and end of their existence.

In no other language with which I am acquainted is there a term for our real nature so precise as this word *Ātman*. All it means is 'the Self' – not the little self, the changing, self-centered personality with which most of us identify ourselves, but the higher Self, our real, changeless personality, which we discover in the very depths of our consciousness.

One of the most consoling implications of this is that no matter what mistakes we may have committed in the past, no matter what liabilities we are oppressed by in the present, our real Self can never be tarnished; the core of our personality is always pure, always loving, always wise. In both East and West, the mystics illustrate this by drawing a comparison with the sun. Even when it is completely hidden by the clouds, even when we close our eyes to it, the sun is always blazing away with the same radiance. Similarly, even if we have done our best for many years to cover up the splendor of the Ātman, it is still there, as radiant as ever, in our heart of hearts. We don't have to make ourselves loving or patient or forgiving; we have only to remove from our superficial personality everything hostile, everything impatient, everything resentful. When all these coverings are removed, the beauty of the Ātman will shine forth unimpeded.

The Hindu scriptures describe this discovery in wonderfully simple stories. One of these is about a prince who is kidnapped by a band of robbers when he is very young. He forgets all about the lap of luxury, about palaces and culture, even about his mother and father; he just grows up as a bandit, learning to master the bow and arrow and ambush passersby and disappear into the woods without being seen. And for twenty years, this is the only life he knows.

Then one day the king's spiritual teacher happens by. Many years have passed; the little child is a grown man now, rough and cocksure, looking for all the world like anything but a king's son. But the spiritual teacher looks at him closely: beneath his violent manners, this young bandit has the king's features, the queen's eyes, even a hint of regal bearing. The teacher recognizes him as the king's son, and with great love in his heart he goes up to him, embraces him, and calls him "your royal highness."

The bandit is outraged. "What do you mean? I'm not your royal highness or anybody else's; I'm a bandit, and everybody in this kingdom is afraid of me."

But the teacher's faith is unshaken. Instead of being repulsed by this young man's bad manners, he puts his arm about him and begins to tell him stories about his childhood – how his father used to carry him on his shoulders, how his mother used to sing him to sleep with the mantram, how life used to be in the palace. And gradually the prince begins to remember. "Go on, go on!" The spiritual teacher continues his stories, and finally, in the depths of his consciousness, the young man's memory clears. He draws himself up straight, his eyes are bright and steady; he has become a different man. "Now I recall," he says slowly, as if awakening from a dream. "I'm not really a bandit at all. I'm not bad, I'm not violent; I simply forgot who I was." He throws his arms about his teacher. "You're my greatest friend," he exclaims; "you helped me to remember who I am!" And truly a prince now, he goes home to his father, the king.

आदित्यानामहं विष्णुर्ज्योतिषां रविरंशुमान् ।
मरीचिर्मरुतामस्मि नक्षत्राणामहं शशी ॥ १०-२१ ॥

21. Among the shining gods I am Vishnu; of luminaries I am the sun; among the storm gods I am Marici, and in the night sky I am the moon.

From the earliest times, men and women must have wondered about the sun, the moon, and the stars in the heavens, the forces governing the storms and the cycles of light and darkness. Even those of us who are not astronomically inclined must have had moments when we asked the sun, "What are you doing there?" or the stars, "Are you friendly with one another?" Now, in this century, astronomy has developed high-powered instruments for looking beyond the galaxy we live in to probe a universe much vaster and more wonderful than we had ever imagined – a universe in which there are billions of other galaxies, each with millions of solar systems, all held together in the embrace of a unifying force.

To me, this unifying force is the infinite love of the Lord, operating on the physical level. Just as all of us are one, so all things in the created universe are one in the Lord. That is why he is called Vishnu, 'he who is everywhere.' When the Lord puts his arms around creation so that it can work in harmony, this is love on a cosmic scale. Just as people live together as a family fostering each other's welfare and happiness, so the cosmos is a family in which every member is related. If even a distant planet like Neptune or Pluto were removed from the solar system, life here on earth would be a little different for us all. There is no possibility of anything in the universe – a sun, a star, or you and me – existing separately. Each part derives its significance from the whole, which is what the mystics call the indivisible unity underlying all life.

When Sri Krishna says he is the sun, this can be interpreted with both scientific precision and spiritual wisdom. The sun is the source of heat and light, both of which are necessary for life on earth. We can ask ourselves, "How has it been possible for the sun to give out this heat and light continuously for more than six thousand million years"? The astronomer and the physicist account for this heat in terms of hydrogen being converted into helium. With a dramatic touch they compare the sun to a hydrogen bomb exploding continuously for millions of years, and they add that it takes twenty million years for this energy to reach the sun's surface from its center, where the temperature is thirteen million degrees. But they cannot tell us why this process goes on or who is responsible for it. For this we have to draw upon the wisdom of spiritual insight.

I like to imagine Sri Krishna standing quietly in the center of the sun in an incomprehensible whirlwind of heat and light, playing on his magic flute. On a hot summer afternoon, when the temperature in our city goes up to ninety-five, my friends come home exhausted and consume gallons of iced lemonade. Now imagine the Lord, whom we are calling Sri Krishna, standing comfortably in the midst of thirteen million degrees and playing on his flute. If he were to play a little louder the temperature of the sun would go up, affecting life on earth; even a small rise in the earth's temperature and we could not survive. And if the Lord should allow his hidden melody to become a little softer, the temperature of the sun would fall, again making life on earth impossible. The question that any scientist would ask is, "How is it that this thirteen million degrees at the center of the sun gives the perfect temperature for life on earth?" It cannot be dismissed as an accident. According to the Gita, the sun has an inner law – or, to be more personal, an inner ruler – which maintains a perfect balance of energy, pressure, and temperature. This balance is an expression of the divine unity of existence, which keeps all the local forces working together so that the unity of the solar system may be maintained.

वेदानां सामवेदो ऽस्मि देवानामस्मि वासवः ।
इन्द्रियाणां मनश्चास्मि भूतानामस्मि चेतना ॥१०-२२॥

22. Among the scriptures I am the Sāma Veda, and among the lesser gods I am Indra. Among the senses I am the mind, and in living beings I am consciousness.

The Vedas are the sacred scriptures of Hinduism. They are four in number – Rig, Sāma, Yajur, and Atharva – and together they form the source of India's perennial philosophy, which extends in an unbroken tradition over more than five thousand years. *Veda* comes from the Sanskrit root *vid,* 'to know,' and the Vedas teach the only essential knowledge, which is to know who we are. Socrates gives us the same injunction: *Gnōthi seauton,* 'Know thyself'; that is the beginning and end of wisdom. For this kind of knowledge we need to practice meditation, which gradually awakens a transcendental mode of knowing latent in all of us.

When I talk about a "transcendental mode of knowing," people sometimes raise their eyebrows. It is beyond the range of their experience, so they have no way of judging it. In answer, I sometimes tell them about a cat we had staying with us when we returned to the United States from India. Woosh was a very sophisticated cat. Not only was she widely traveled, she had a special diet, an elaborately decorated scratching post, and all sorts of toys for recreation. But I am sure that if we could have asked her what she thought the highest faculty of knowing was, she would have answered, "Instinct." In her next incarnation, if she were to become a human being, she would probably tell us it was reason; but as long as she is a cat, instinct is the highest mode of knowing open to her. Similarly, just as human beings develop reason, which is an evolutionary step beyond instinct, so the mystics develop a higher mode of knowing with which they see life whole.

The second line of this verse deals with the mind and consciousness.

The mind – *manas* in Sanskrit – not only records the perceptions of the other senses, it can re-experience a perception even though nothing is immediately perceived by the senses. There is an important connection here with desire, for sense desires, especially obsessive desires, thrive on this faculty of recollection. Even if we are miles away from a pizza, when we remember one and want it we can easily recall just how it looks and tastes. If we are a little compulsive about eating, we may even dwell on all the pizza perceptions of our past experience. In doing this, of course, we are only deepening our pizza samskāra, our pizza obsession, making it harder to resist eating *two* pizzas the next time we get a chance. The Gita would ask, where is the freedom in this? In terms of the damage we do our will, the difference between the pizza we dwell on and the pizza we eat is mainly a matter of calories – and even that difference disappears when, after dwelling on pizza for so long, we overeat the next time we get a chance. So the mind is by far the most important and powerful of the senses, and we can master the senses only through the mind.

Most of us have let the mind go unattended for such a long time that cultivating it requires full-time effort. I was admiring our vegetable garden this weekend and was pleased to see that the tomatoes and corn were doing very well. Then I noticed another crop which was really flourishing. I didn't recognize that particular variety of greens, so I asked my friend Sarah about it. She explained, "Those are the weeds." This is very much the usual state of the mind. If there were an exhibit of mind-weeds, most of us could enter some rather fascinating crops.

Anger is one of the worst of these weeds; it spreads over every inch of ground and keeps other plants from growing. But all negative states of mind – fear, hostility, jealousy, depression – make it difficult for useful plants like kindness and consideration to grow. It is not a question of our soil being infertile; it is that very few try to get rid of the weeds. There are even people who admire these weeds, who talk about weeds of anger and fear as though they were lilies and lotuses. Unfortunately, when we talk about our problems, write about them, think about them as we fall asleep, we are driving them deeper into consciousness. After a while the roots may go so deep that we cannot pull them out. So instead of dwelling on the negative aspects of the mind, let us turn our attention to the positive side and make the mind a beautiful garden. By practicing meditation regularly and repeating the mantram whenever a weed tries to send out a new shoot, we can trim back our negative tendencies and eventually weed them out of the mind forever.

In Hindu psychology, it is important to remember that the mind is not thought of as being conscious any more than a television set is, or the engine of a car. Just as the body is the external instrument we use, the mind is the internal instrument; it reflects consciousness, but it is not conscious itself. So Sri Krishna adds that he is not only the mind; he is consciousness itself in every living creature. If you go to a potter's stall in an Indian bazaar, you will see all types of pots, tall and short, stout and slender. But the tall pot does not contain a different kind of air than the short pot; all of them are filled with the same air. Similarly, though each of us is quite different in appearance, underneath all these variations we are all one. Inside each of us is the same pure, undifferentiated consciousness, the Ātman, the same in you as it is in me.

रुद्राणां शंकरश्चास्मि वित्तेशो यक्षरक्षसाम् ।
वसूनां पावकश्चास्मि मेरुः शिखरिणामहम् ॥१०-२३॥

23. *I am Rudra and I am Shankara. Among the spirits of the natural world I am Kubera, god of wealth, and Pāvaka, the purifying fire; among mountains I am Meru.*

Shankara means 'he who brings about our lasting welfare'; *Rudra* means 'he who makes us grieve.' Both are traditional names of the Lord of Love, and in the one short phrase with which this verse opens, Sri Krishna is giving us one of the deepest secrets of life: often the grace of the Lord comes to us in the form of sorrow.

One of the most distressing facts of life is that most of us do not learn without a certain measure of suffering. The question we must ask is whether we prefer to be stunted or to suffer some distress and grow up. Suffering in life comes as an enemy only when we do not know how to receive it as a friend. We can either benefit from suffering to improve our health and security, or we can become frustrated and embittered because we cannot change our ways of living under the impact of pain.

Several days ago I went with a friend to a restaurant just to see what people are eating. It was one of the better restaurants in the area, yet these educated, cultured people were eating the worst possible kind of food. It always amazes me on such occasions to realize how strong the human system is. It is a wonder that our bodies continue to function; it is only the mercy of the Lord that prevents us from causing ourselves more physical problems than we do. If you want to see how perfect the nervous system can be, look at a sleeping infant, as relaxed as a cat curled up in the sun. Yet thirty-five years or so later, many of us have managed to throw a big spanner into the machinery of the body. Tension, high blood pressure, chronic headaches, and peptic ulcers don't arise overnight; these are problems we slowly develop by making ill-considered decisions day after day, year after year.

Suffering is like the red signboard on the freeway: "Go Back; You're Going the Wrong Way." The first time I saw this sign I thought the freeway designers had borrowed a slogan from the Gita; it has the practical touch of Sri Krishna. First the Lord puts up a little sign saying "Pain Ahead," but we continue on our way. Then he puts up another, bigger sign, "Turmoil Coming," but still we don't pay attention. Finally he sets an enormous blockade. Most of us do not know how to respond, and instead of putting on the brakes we step on the gas. Then we wonder why we crash.

The mature person responds to Sri Krishna's first signboard. As soon as there is even a little suffering, physical or mental, he starts looking around to see how to improve his ways of thinking and behaving. Often, of course, this presents a practical difficulty. When we have become addicted to wrong habits over a period of time, it is terribly difficult to change them. I have known people who want to give up smoking, drinking, or drugging, but who do not have the will to carry out their desire. Here it is that meditation comes into play. Almost all my friends who meditate regularly have been enabled to give up such addictions, for meditation gives us the will and wisdom to go against our previous conditioning.

This same capacity to change habits can be applied to the way we use our natural resources. The serious problem of pollution in our air, lakes, rivers, and oceans is just as much a source of suffering as physiological disorders, and it too is a warning: we have mercilessly exploited the environment and will have to change in order to survive. The ocean, for example, is not just something that stands between us and Paris or Tahiti; it is an underwater world where four-fifths of the creatures of earth live. In these vast depths there are gorges deeper than the Grand Canyon, peaks higher than Mount Everest, and great plains which stretch for hundreds of miles. All life depends ultimately on our oceans, yet the amount of oil, sewage, and industrial effluent that we are pouring into them threatens to turn this vast, teeming world into a wasteland. This is a flashing red warning signal telling us to reassess our way of living and simplify our needs so as to reduce the demands we make on the precious resources of the earth.

In spite of what the popular media may tell us, we should not pretend that there is no pain at the core of life. Whether in Africa or America, whether poor or prosperous, people are suffering everywhere; that is the nature of life. Even if we live in the midst of plenty, we do not say goodbye to pain. As our spiritual awareness deepens, we will find it impossible to go after our personal pleasure or profit when there is so much suffering to alleviate in the world around us. I often describe the mystics as hard-nosed. It is they who really know the facts of life; most of us live in a private fantasy land where we think that if we keep up an appearance of prosperity, everything is all right. We have only to open our eyes to see that behind this facade, there is sorrow all around us – not just on the grand scale of war and poverty, but in millions on millions of anonymous, private lives. The more we close our eyes to this suffering, the more we shall have to suffer ourselves, for the simple reason that this is what it takes to rouse us out of our complacency and make us go to the help of those around us.

So the Lord adds that he is Pāvaka, the fire that purifies. A few years ago on a trip to Yosemite we stopped to visit an abandoned mining town, where we saw an exhibit about how gold is purified. It is a good analogy for what happens on the spiritual path, where the Lord comes with his fire, hammer, and anvil to burn away our selfishness and forge us into shape. The immature person takes one look and says, “Thank you very much, but I'd rather stay covered with this crusty ego.” But the person who can go far will ask the Lord, “Put me on the anvil and use your heaviest hammer; I want to be freed from this ego-crust once and for all.” When a person is able to say this, he or she has outgrown the need for suffering. The Lord may lift his hammer, but it does not fall. Instead he throws it aside and embraces that person in loving arms.

पुरोधसां च मुख्यं मां विद्धि पार्थ बृहस्पतिम् ।
सेनानीनामहं स्कन्दः सरसामस्मि सागरः ॥ १०-२४ ॥

24. Among spiritual teachers I am Brihaspati,
and among military leaders I am Skanda.
Among bodies of water I am the ocean.

Brihaspati is often mentioned in the Hindu scriptures as a tremendous spiritual teacher. It is not possible for the vast majority of us to approach the stature of such a teacher, but it is important to recognize that all of us, whether we like it or not, are in the role of teacher to those around us every waking hour of the day. This is especially clear in our relationships with children. Anyone who spends much time with children knows that they do not do what we ask them to do but what they see us doing. Education is based on a breathtakingly simple proposition: we teach by what we are. It is easy to buy a book on patience and security and give it to our children, but if we are impatient ourselves, no amount of reading will teach them to be otherwise. If we want our children to be patient, secure, and selfless, we have to give them an example of these qualities in our personal life.

This is a continuous struggle, so Sri Krishna adds that he is not only the ideal teacher, he is the ideal warrior too. Skanda is an invincible general in the scriptures who destroyed the forces of evil. It is a reminder to all of us that even the most aggressive temperament can be harnessed in this struggle to become commanders of ourselves.

Kālidāsa, one of India's greatest poets, has written a long epic poem relating the story of Skanda's birth, youth, and victory over the demon Tāraka, who symbolizes tyranny and evil. Tāraka was so powerful that all the gods had been defeated by him in battle over and over again. They had even had to vacate their homes because heaven itself was not safe against his rage. Only a son born of the great god Shiva could have the power to destroy this demon, so the gods went to this eternal bachelor and begged him to bring forth a son. Kālidāsa's poem tells how Pārvatī, Himālaya's daughter, after failing to attract Shiva by her unequalled beauty, finally wins his love by taking to the spiritual life. They are married, and Skanda is born to destroy Tāraka and his demon armies. It is a beautiful story, because Skanda is born not of physical passion but of Shiva's self-control. That is why he has the power to defeat Tāraka and rescue the cosmos from its misery.

Next Sri Krishna says he is the ocean. When the Lord is represented as sleeping on the cosmic ocean, it is not just the sea outside; he is also reclining on the sea inside. In one sense this is consciousness, but even on the physical level it can be illustrated as well. The same type of salt solution that was in the sea eons ago, bathing and nourishing the first cells when life began, is in our body fluids today. The oceans cover seventy percent of the earth's surface, and this same kind of fluid makes up almost seventy percent of the human body. It is not too far-fetched to say that we have a little of the sea flowing in all of us, giving sustenance to the millions of cells which compose our bodies.

The noted marine biologist and explorer Jacques Cousteau remarked that the ocean has become a universal sewer where all pollution ends up, so much so that a swimmer can contract an infection from just one swim in some of our more contaminated seas. Just as the sea outside is becoming polluted, the environment inside us suffers from pollution, too – the constant pollution of anger, fear, and greed, all of which we can clean up through the practice of meditation.

महर्षीणां भृगुरहं गिरामस्म्येकमक्षरम् ।
यज्ञानां जपयज्ञो ऽस्मि स्थावराणां हिमालयः ॥ १०-२५ ॥

25. Among the great seers I am Bhrigu, and among words, the syllable Om; I am the repetition of the holy name, and among mountains I am the Himālayas.

Bhrigu is associated with one of the most beautiful stories I know of about the infinite mercy of the Lord. According to this story, there was once a thriving āshram in ancient India where men and women worshiping the Lord in different forms – Shiva, Rāma, Krishna, the Divine Mother – all lived and meditated together in harmony, each respecting the other's chosen way. Then one day Nārada happened to stop by. This Nārada appears in many of our stories. He was a great devotee of Sri Krishna, and spent much of his time traveling around from one holy place to another, where he showed a certain gift for stirring up spiritual controversy. So at this āshram Nārada asked mischievously, "Do you all worship the Lord in different forms?"

"Yes," one of the members of the āshram said, "the Lord takes on different forms to meet the needs of his devotees. Knowing that, we find it easy to meditate together and respect each other's spiritual ideal."

"That's very good," Nārada agreed. "But one of those ideals must be best, don't you think? Which do you think it is?" Then, while the members of the āshram began to talk over this idea, Nārada quietly slipped out and went on his way.

A month or so later, when Nārada returned, the āshram was in a hubbub. Cliques had formed, and some people wouldn't even talk to each other. Everyone was convinced that his or her approach to God was best. Some said that Shiva was the perfect embodiment of the Lord;

others said Krishna; others said it was Rāma or the Divine Mother. "This is silly," Nārada said. "Why don't you go find out?"

"I'll go," volunteered Bhrigu, who loved the Lord with all his heart. "I'll test Sri Krishna's love myself; then you'll see why I say that there is no limit to his forgiveness." Bhrigu went up to Sri Krishna, who was sleeping with his head on the lap of his consort, Lakshmī, and while the rest of the āshram looked on in horror he kicked the Lord on the chest. Everyone was terrified; they expected Bhrigu to be burned up on the spot. But Sri Krishna simply opened his eyes and immediately saw into Bhrigu's heart. "It takes great faith to subject me to a test like that," he said tenderly, "but now everyone has seen that there is no limit to my forgiveness. This mark your foot has left on my chest will be my adornment, *srīvatsa;* I will wear it always." It is a beautiful illustration of why Sri Krishna is called Kshamāsāgara, the ocean of *kshamā* – forgiveness, patience, and compassion all in one.

"Among words," this verse continues, "I am *Om,* and the repetition of the holy name." It is so easy to repeat the mantram or holy name that at first most of us cannot believe that it is charged with the power of the Lord. Only after we use it for a while do we begin to see that repeating the mantram is not just a mechanical exercise; it is a direct line to the Lord within – as I like to put it, "calling the Lord collect." We don't make any promises; all we do is repeat the mantram when we are agitated – angry, or afraid, or speeded up, or caught in worries or regrets – and the Lord opens a little door to the reserves of our deeper consciousness.

In college I used to be very interested in public speaking; it is an interest which still serves me well today. Whenever there was a talk being given I used to go to hear it, no matter what the subject, just to study the presentation and the delivery and all the little tricks of the trade. The principal of the school, whom I admired greatly, saw my enthusiasm and encouraged me in all this, and whenever there was an opportunity to speak or to debate I used to volunteer to go and represent our school. But no matter how often I spoke before an audience, the period of waiting to be called to the podium always turned my knees to rubber and my stomach upside down. It didn't matter how many times I had faced an audience before; I was always afraid that when my name was called I would trip on the stairs or open my mouth and find that no words would come out.

When I confessed this to my granny, she had a very simple piece of advice: not to go over my notes, not to try to size up my audience, just to repeat the mantram. It was so simple that I didn't put much faith in it, but because of my love for her I promised to give it a try. The next time I had to face an audience I sat quietly awaiting my turn and repeating *Rāma, Rāma, Rāma* – and every now and then I would slip in, "I hope it works." After a while it became "*Rāma, Rāma, Rāma* . . . I think it works!" And now, on the basis of many years of experience, I can assure you with complete certitude, I *know* it works. At first it may just be a first-aid measure, but after many years, together with meditation, the mantram can enable us to transform our consciousness and rise to our full stature.

Most of us do not even suspect the height to which we can rise through the practice of meditation. On the walls of the Capitol in Sacramento is a line of poetry which I like very much: "Give me men to match my mountains." It makes me proud to remember that in India, where we have the highest and most majestic mountains in the world, there has been an unbroken tradition of spiritual giants, men and women of such tremendous stature that they tower as high above you and me as the Himālayas above the plains below. That is why the last line of this verse sounds so sweet to me. To my partial eyes, I don't think there is any symbol of spiritual awareness more beautiful than the Himālayas, the 'home of perpetual snow,' higher than which no human being can climb.

Here Sri Krishna is reminding us that there are Himālayan ranges inside us, too: the Himālayas of consciousness. When you begin meditating you enter the foothills, and as your meditation deepens, you climb higher and higher. Finally you reach the top of one of the lower peaks. But there is no time to sit down and congratulate yourself; another peak is already beckoning to you, saying, "Come and conquer *me.*" This is the challenge of meditation. Your legs are aching and your oxygen supply is exhausted. You have been waiting for the chance to sit down for a rest, but you just cannot be satisfied with anything less than the highest. So you start climbing again, hoping there will be a chance to build a little shack when you get to the top. But no sooner do you reach the summit than you see an even more magnificent mountain ahead of you. Then you realize that you have only been warming up; the real challenges are just beginning.

This is putting restlessness to work. Show me someone who is restless and I can help that person harness his or her restlessness in climbing the vast Himālayan ranges of consciousness, where the peaks never end. Even if, after years and years of climbing, you finally reach Mount Krishna, or Mount Christ, or Mount Buddha, you will see that there is no way to conquer these heights in the span of one human life; and even if it were possible to stand at the summit of these vast peaks, you would still be standing only at the foot of the highest of all mountains, Mount Brahman, lost completely beyond the universe.

अश्वत्थः सर्ववृक्षाणां देवर्षीणां च नारदः ।
गन्धर्वाणां चित्ररथः सिद्धानां कपिलो मुनिः ॥१०-२६॥

26. Among trees I am the ashvattha, and among the gandharvas I am Chitraratha. Among divine seers I am Nārada, and among sages I am Kapila.

The ashvattha is the holy fig tree, important in both Hindu and Buddhist traditions. This tree, which lives for a very long time, is the basis for the image of the Tree of Eternity in the Upanishads – the cosmic tree with its root above, in God, and its branches here below on earth. You and I are its fruits; we are here on earth to satisfy the hunger of those around us.

This tree suffers if even the smallest leaves are injured. It is as if the leaves of a magnolia tree were to divide themselves into north and south and then wage war over the trunk; the whole lovely tree would soon die. This is the absurd situation we create between individuals, communities, races, and nations, when we forget that we are all part of one whole, the beautiful Tree of Life.

In the next epithet Sri Krishna tells Arjuna that he is Chitraratha, the leader of the gandharvas. The gandharvas are a little like angels in the Hindu scriptures. Just as in Judaism and Christianity you have cherubim and seraphim and other orders of the heavenly hosts, so in Hinduism we have gandharvas, devas, and other beings inhabiting the realms beyond earth. In particular, the gandharvas are cosmic musicians, and are responsible for what Shakespeare called the "music of the spheres." The scriptures tell us there is music everywhere if we have ears to hear it. In the language of mysticism, every star is singing; throughout the universe there is a symphony. There is music even in the subtlest of cosmic radiation, to which scientists listen with delicate instruments; there is music even in the sap running through the trunk and branches of a tree. Thomas Huxley tells us that the wonderful noonday silence of a tropical forest is after all due only to the dullness of our own hearing, and could our ears catch the murmur of the tiny maelstroms as they whirl about in innumerable myriads of living cells which constitute each tree, we should be stunned as by the roar of a great city. This is not a mystic speaking; it is a great biologist, using the language of mysticism to describe a biological phenomenon. Everywhere the Lord is singing his divine melody, only we are unable to hear it with our small, sensuous ears.

In the Sanskrit scriptures, Nārada is not just a celestial figure; he is an illumined sage of divine stature, a fervent devotee of Sri Krishna who often acts as intermediary between the heavenly realms and the world of human beings. Usually he is portrayed as floating in space playing on his vīnā and singing the praise of the Lord, and in many Hindu religious plays he is given a part even when he is not essential to the action, just because he is such a familiar symbol of devotion. Something of a spiritual correspondent, he is always carrying news from one āshram to another, motivating aspirants to greater effort by remarks like, "Yes, you're doing well enough; you're not falling asleep in meditation. But do you know that in the āshram I just visited, two people attained illumination last week?"

Nārada had immense wisdom, but being a member of the monastic order he was under the impression that householders like you and me are not capable of much progress on the spiritual path. Sri Krishna has a soft spot in his heart for householders, and one day, it is said, he got the opportunity to correct Nārada's perspective. The two were walking together in heaven, and Nārada was taking advantage of his love for the Lord to ask him all kinds of questions. "Lord," he asked finally, "why do you like these householders so much? They're not very regular in their practice. One minute they're enthusiastic and resolve to be very spiritual, and the next minute they've forgotten all about it."

Sri Krishna had a way of not answering Nārada's questions directly. This time he said, "Look, Nārada, here's a little oil lamp. Why don't you carry it around this temple three times; then I'll answer your question. But don't let the flame go out."

The Lord gave Nārada the lamp, and Nārada lit it and went outside. As soon as he was out of the door, the Lord called Marut, the wind, and said, "Now blow for all you're worth!" Marut blew up a real typhoon, and then he called in his relatives to help him make it a hurricane. Nārada was hard put. The north wind was blowing and the south wind was blowing, and there he was with this little oil lamp which he couldn't let go out. But being a divine sage, he wasn't completely without resources. He held the lamp close and huddled over it to shield it from the wind, and somehow or other he managed to get around the temple three times with the flame still flickering. When he finally got back to Sri Krishna he was a little disheveled but still undaunted. "Well, Lord," he said breathlessly, "here is the lamp."

Sri Krishna smiled. "Tell me, Nārada," he said. "You're always singing my praises and repeating the mantram. While you were going around the temple just now, how many times did you remember to repeat my name?"

Nārada hemmed and hawed. "With all this wind blowing, the north wind and the south wind . . . actually, Lord, I'm afraid I didn't remember you even once."

"You see, Nārada," Sri Krishna said, "these householders have so many problems – television, and the generation gap, and Madison Avenue to contend with; the wind is blowing against them all the time. If they are able to remember me only a little part of the day, I am very pleased." It is a good story to remember whenever we find it difficult to remain calm and patient in all the storms of daily living.

Then, among sages, the Lord says he is Kapila, a spiritual teacher in ancient India whose stature was so tremendous that he was content to remain unknown. We know virtually nothing about his life. He was not interested in whether those who came after him would remember his vital statistics; he wanted only that we follow his teachings. If we could have interviewed Kapila he would have said, "Why do you want to know when I was born? How will knowing my height and weight help you realize the unity of life? None of this is relevant to going beyond suffering." All Kapila's greatness is inferred from the legacy he left behind him, which has influenced virtually every spiritual tradition in India since his time. Patanjali, who wrote the classic Indian text on meditation, follows Kapila's *sānkhya* philosophy and may have been one of his direct disciples, and the Bhagavad Gita, the Katha Upanishad, and the teachings of the Compassionate Buddha himself all show the strong stamp of the sānkhya outlook. An old Sanskrit saying testifies to the immense effectiveness of these teachings: "There is no knowledge like sānkhya, no power like yoga." Sānkhya, the philosophical aspect, gives us a systematic diagnosis of our human predicament; yoga – raja yoga or meditation – gives us the cure.

In this verse Kapila is called *muni*, 'the silent one.' What is meant here is not silence of the tongue but silence of the ego. For the sages who have forever silenced their self-will, this is a perfect name. After many years of meditation, when you have risen above body consciousness and your ego has been dissolved, you will have gone beyond the words of the inspirational passage. Then you will find yourself on the very seabed of consciousness, where everything is still. This stillness is the greatest source of joy, for the cacophony of self-will is the cause of all our suffering in life. The mind is completely still, so there can be no anger, no greed, and no fear.

उच्चैःश्रवसमश्वानां विद्धि माममृतोद्भवम् ।
ऐरावतं गजेन्द्राणां नराणां च नराधिपम् ॥ १०-२७॥

27. I was born from the nectar of immortality
as the primordial horse and as Indra's noble
elephant. Among men, I am the king.

This verse refers to the story in the Hindu tradition about the churning of the cosmic ocean to bring forth life as we know it. The story is a little reminiscent of the passage in Genesis which describes how the spirit of God moved upon the waters of life. According to the Hindu scriptures, before creation there was only a vast ocean of undifferentiated consciousness. Then the gods of light, representing the forces of selflessness and goodness, and the demons of darkness, representing the forces of selfishness and violence, took the head and the tail of the serpent king, Vāsuki, and began churning the cosmic ocean in order to obtain the nectar of immortality. Out of this churning, life as we know it began to evolve, and many creatures sprang forth.

In its practical application, the churning of the cosmic ocean is the churning of primordial, undifferentiated consciousness, and the creatures that come forth are the mighty forces released from the unconscious during meditation. The Lord brings out these forces within us so that we can work as his instruments, adding to human welfare and to world peace. Those who work for the welfare of the whole are leaders among men, which is the meaning of "king" in this verse. This is leadership based on love and service; it is leadership that is granted rather than taken for oneself. When we give up our private interests like this for the sake of serving others, two divine qualities are released which are essential to effective, selfless leadership. The elephant of Indra, king of the gods, is the perfect symbol of power; Indra's white horse, called the king of horses, symbolizes the gracefulness that comes when immense power is combined with complete self-control.

During the churning of the cosmic ocean, before these precious gifts emerged, all the poison of selfishness and separateness came to the surface. This poison threatened all life, and no one, neither gods nor demons, knew how to get rid of it. Then Lord Shiva said, "Let me drink it myself, to save the world from its own selfishness." He took the concentrated poison and drank it, but his queen, Pārvatī, was so anguished at the sight that she put her hands around his neck to keep the poison from going down his throat. So one of the most loving names for Shiva is Nīlakantha, from *nīla,* 'blue,' and *kantha,* 'throat': 'he whose neck turned blue' when he drank the poison of the world to save all creation. This is what true leadership means: even if there is sorrow and suffering, it is our privilege to take it on ourselves rather than let others become victims. When we choose to suffer for others rather than let our family, our country, or our world suffer, we become a little like Nīlakantha.

Finally, after the poison, out of the cosmic ocean came the nectar of immortality called *amrita. Mrita* is cognate with the word *mortal,* and amrita is that which makes us immortal. This was the ambrosia the gods and demons were hoping to find by churning the sea with the serpent Vāsuki. The nectar of immortality is what all of us are seeking, and we will find it eventually if we are vigilant in practicing meditation. In meditation we dive into the sea of the mind, where we learn how to transform all our poisonous, negative tendencies into selfless qualities. When at last we rid our hearts and minds of all fear, anger, and greed, the nectar of immortality will emerge. It is a symbolic way of saying that we rise above physical consciousness to realize that we are a permanent force for the welfare of all.

आयुधानामहं वज्रं धेनूनामस्मि कामधुक् ।
प्रजनश्चास्मि कन्दर्पः सर्पाणामस्मि वासुकिः ॥१०-२८॥

28. Among weapons I am the thunderbolt. I am Kāmadhuk, the cow which fulfills all desires; I am Kandarpa, the power of sex, and Vāsuki, the king of snakes.

Here Sri Krishna uses *vajra,* the thunderbolt, as a symbol of the power of selflessness, which cannot be broken by any other power on earth. In the Vedas, Indra, leader of the gods, carries the thunderbolt as his weapon; it is with the thunderbolt that he slays the cosmic demon. The story of how this weapon was made is a marvelous one. The gods were terribly distressed at the strength of the forces of violence in the world, so they went to Indra and asked him to conquer this violence and separateness. His strange reply was, "I must first have an invincible weapon, which can be made only from the bones of a sage who is pure and perfect."

The devas searched far and wide for such a sage. They told many spiritual aspirants of their plight. "Oh, yes," the aspirants would say, "we would like to help you out. What can we do?" The unexpected answer was, "Give us your bones." As it turned out, the aspirants preferred having their bones inside them instead, and so the search went on.

Finally the devas came to Dadhīci, a simple, sweet figure who had come to identify himself so completely with all life that everyone's suffering was his own. The devas confessed, "We are at the end of our tether. Violence is rising high on all sides, and we haven't been able to get the weapon we need to stop it, for it can be fashioned only from the bones of a sage who is pure and perfect."

"If you will accept it," Dadhīci reassured them, "my body is yours. You don't have to look any further." He sat down in meditation, united himself with the Lord, and shed his body so it could be used for the happiness of mankind.

This capacity to do anything to relieve the suffering of others is a sign of invincible power. We usually misuse the word *power* to mean the capacity to destroy another country, or race, or fellow creature. This is not power; this is a liability. Power rises from within us. The power that we have to forget ourselves, to subordinate ourselves to the welfare of the whole, is the only power that is real. As long as we have the desire and the resoluteness to contribute to life, we need not be diffident about our efforts to solve the problems that face us. The Lord tells us in this verse that he is Kāmadhuk, the wish-fulfilling cow. This mythical cow satisfies desires that are for the general welfare, but if there is any personal taint in our wish, she will not grant it.

Because I come from India, people used to ask me if I consider cows sacred. I used to tell them, "Of course I do – and tigers, buffaloes, beavers, and Chihuahuas, too. All animals are sacred to me." We are learning more and more about the nutritional advantages of vegetarianism, but I would say the more important point about not eating meat is that it makes for sound spiritual living, because it affirms the unity of life. In India, where we have a tradition of vegetarianism stretching back thousands of years, we have a loving, protective feeling for most of our animals. In my ancestral home, for example, my grandmother used to give our cows beautiful Sanskrit names. When visitors came to our home and my grandmother gave them the news, she would always include the latest about the cows, who were just like members of the family to her. "Shanti is not doing very well today," she would say. "Shoba's calf is eating better now." My mother kept cows, too. One of them grew to a ripe old age and developed rheumatism, and my mother used to tell her friends with wry humor, "Both of us are rheumatic." Once someone suggested she sell the cow. Her answer was perfect: "That's like asking my son to sell me." The cow had served us well, giving us milk, yogurt, and butter for many years. Out of simple gratitude my mother wanted her to live her last years in comfort.

Kandarpa and *Vāsuki* are references to the power of sex. Vāsuki is the serpent who was used in churning the cosmic ocean, but it is also a symbol of kundalinī. And *Kandarpa* is one of the names for Kāma, who is the Cupid of Sanskrit literature. These are ways of saying that the Lord is the power of sex, because sex holds the key to life. One of

Kāma's many names is *Pancashara*, 'he who has five arrows in his quiver,' each tipped with the flowers of spring. On college campuses it is easy to see Kāma busy at work. He pulls out his first arrow, which has ten flower-power, and quite a few students fall; one shot and they are down. But there are some who say, "I've got to work hard and get into medical school; I haven't got time for archery." For them, Kāma pulls out a second arrow with twenty flower-power and down they go; medical school is forgotten. Then there is the postdoctoral research fellow, who thinks he is flowerproof. For him Kāma pulls out the third arrow, and he falls victim to its thirty flower-power. So far, the man or woman who is self-controlled most of the time has managed to escape. But spiritual aspirants too can have moments when their vigilance nods, when Kāma can claim them with the fourth or forty flower-power arrow. Finally comes the person who is almost invincible, who has gone some distance on the spiritual path. Kāma waits patiently for a long time, until just the right moment comes. Then he quickly uses his fifth and last arrow, against which no one can be completely safe.

I would say, beware of the first arrow. The minute you see it coming, repeat your mantram and leave the scene. Here Jesus gives us simple, sound advice: "Lead us not into temptation, but deliver us from evil." Given the constant drone of the mass media, most of us have become so susceptible to Kāma's arrows that we need to be particularly careful about not putting ourselves in situations where we are likely to be swept away. Our most effective protection against turmoil is to not base our relationships on sex. Whenever a man and a woman put each other's welfare first, romance will never come to an end; they will fall more deeply in love every day.

अनन्तश्चास्मि नागानां वरुणो यादसामहम् ।
पितॄणामर्यमा चास्मि यमः संयमतामहम् ॥ १०-२९ ॥

29. I am Ananta, the cosmic serpent, and Varuna, the god of water; I am Aryaman, the noble ancestor of mankind. Among the forces which control the universe, I am Yama, the god of death.

Ananta is the endless serpent on which the Lord, in the form of Vishnu, is said to sleep. This cosmic serpent, as we saw in the previous verse, is also a symbol for the evolutionary energy called kundalinī. Just as we need gasoline to drive our car, so we need the power of sex to rouse kundalinī up the spinal column to the highest center of consciousness in the head. If we want to evolve to the highest level possible, this is the power we must use. Fortunately, there is no limit to this energy once we have begun to put it to spiritual use; that is why it is called *ananta*, 'without end.'

Aryaman, another figure from Hindu mythology, is the symbol of all that is noble in our ancestry. This is a reminder that we owe a great debt to those who have gone before us – our parents, our grandparents, our teachers, and everyone else who has helped make us what we are today. You can imagine your grandfather looking out of your eyes, because it is his tendencies that you have inherited. Sometimes I tease my young friends by saying that when we add twenty-five years to them, we get their mother or father. It works the other way, also: the next time you see a mother and daughter together, try subtracting twenty-five years from the mother and you will have the daughter. It is a very fine compliment to tell a daughter that she looks just like her mother, or a son that he is like his father. Whatever inadequacies our parents may have, they brought us into this world and therefore deserve our complete respect. Once, I remember, we took my grandmother to a big store in a nearby town. She looked around carefully, and when we were leaving we asked her, "Well, Granny, what do you think of this store?" "You can get everything you need here," she replied, "except the love of your father and mother."

Finally, the Lord makes a strong remark: "Among the forces which control the universe, I am Yama," the King of Death. Yama is a rather frightening figure in the Sanskrit scriptures, but he can be a good teacher to those who want to receive his message. In the Katha Upanishad, the daring teenager Nachiketa goes straight to Yama to learn how to go beyond death. "You're the King of Death," he tells him; "who could have a better teacher than you?" When we face the implications of death squarely, it can give us all the motivation we need to take to meditation and learn to overcome our identification with the body once and for all.

Today, when life is so cheap and violence surrounds us, the theme of conquering death is particularly relevant. It is all too easy to resign ourselves to the constant threat to life and accept without question half-remedies which only feed the fires of violence. Take the problem of holdups, which are rapidly becoming commonplace. It is no answer to carry a gun; that only endangers our own life and the lives of innocent people around us. For a lasting solution we have to help our society change its values, and the best place to begin is for all of us to stop playing up money and material possessions. It is much more difficult to do this than to arm ourselves, but no other solution goes to the heart of the problem. When we are constantly being goaded to buy more, to own more, to measure everything in dollars, it is only a matter of time before we think we can't be happy without a new sports car or Tiffany diamonds or a trip to Acapulco. Our cupidity is inflated in even the smallest matters. When I first came to this country, I was amazed to see how gas stations compete with each other. I thought they would be offering better gasoline or better service; instead they offer you a drinking glass or a can of nuts. My first response was, "Are we supposed to put these in our tank?" Even the strongest person can be affected by this incessant appeal to get, get, get, even if it is things we do not need or really want.

To help our society free itself from this deadly conditioning, we need to show that what makes life worth living is not money but personal relationships. We don't do this by talking about it; we do it primarily by our own example. In their hearts, I think everybody knows that money and possessions can satisfy only for a short, short time. The problem is that most people do not have a clear, appealing alternative. But the person with a rich family life and deep, lasting relationships, who is always interested in other people and is not easily shaken by their ups and downs, is a reminder of the real meaning of life wherever he or she goes.

All of us can make of our lives this kind of shining example. Instead of spending our time making extra money, we can spend time with our family and friends, rediscovering the joy of being together. We can simplify our lives so we do not need that second sports car, and instead of taking to the road every weekend or sitting in front of the television, we can start some community project like a vegetable garden with our neighbors. Turning off the television to work with family and friends like this is not a sacrifice; the relationships it enriches will be a source of lasting satisfaction.

Another source of violence is the constant emphasis placed on sex. Now, for example, it is dangerous for college and university women to walk alone in the evening even on campus. You and I can counteract this source of violence in many different ways – by not buying magazines or books that play up sex, by writing to newspapers and television stations when their programs are objectionable, by not giving box-office support to movies which exploit sex. More than that, we need to show in our own lives that rich, lasting, fulfilling relationships between two people *are* possible when there is complete loyalty and mutual respect. Sex can have a beautiful place in such relationships, but if loyalty is absent, if sex is made the basis of the relationship and both parties are content to go their own ways, tragedy is going to follow for everyone concerned.

प्रह्लादश्चास्मि दैत्यानां कालः कलयतामहम् ।
मृगाणां च मृगेन्द्रो ऽहं वैनतेयश्च पक्षिणाम् ॥ १०-३० ॥

30. Among animals I am the lion; among birds, the eagle. I am Prahlāda, born among the demons, and of all that measures, I am time.

Some of the greatest characters in the Hindu scriptures are teenagers, and one of them is Prahlāda, who had boundless devotion to the Lord. The example of Prahlāda, Mahatma Gandhi tells us, was one of his earliest inspirations as a child. Born into a demonic society full of disharmony and violence, Prahlāda steadfastly kept his eyes on the divine unity of life. In spite of his family's objections, in the face of all sorts of obstacles and trials, he remained unswerving in his devotion to the Lord of Love. Throughout India he is deeply loved as a model of bhakti yoga, the path of love and devotion.

Then Sri Krishna quietly slips in one of the most powerful statements in this chapter: "I am time." It has far-reaching implications, for our inability to see below the surface of life is closely tied to our preoccupation with time. Almost everything we do is under pressure of time. The constant emphasis is on hurry, hurry, hurry, and our greatest praise goes not to those who can do something better but to those who can do it faster. Just see the absurdity of this speed mania. Yesterday somebody was telling me about a camera that can develop film in ten seconds instead of sixty seconds. My comment was, "What am I to do with the fifty seconds I have saved?"

Instead of trying to do things faster and faster, it is more effective to work at a steady pace with complete concentration. The person who does things very fast usually does a shoddy job. At my university in India, I often saw students go into the examination hall, dash off their answers, and leave, saying, "We finished the whole thing in an hour's time." To be accurate, they ruined the whole thing in an hour's time. An experienced observer can spot the good student easily: it is the person who studies the question first and tries to understand exactly what the examiner is asking. The student who is in a hurry, who begins writing immediately, often gives the examiner stone instead of bread.

When we work under the constant pressure of time, traveling as fast as we can and eating on the run, we are making our nervous system tenser and tenser. Eventually it simply goes out of control. When you see people being rude or thoughtless to those around them, it can help to remember that they may not really be unkind; their nervous systems may simply have been pushed beyond the limit. Instead of adding to their burden by giving tit for tat, we can help such people by being patient and courteous ourselves and by helping them to slow down.

Gradually, as we learn to slow down the mind through the practice of meditation, we begin to free ourselves from any compulsion of time. But we do not do this by throwing our watches away. Living in the midst of the world, I am always very particular about being on time, because being late affects not only us but everyone around us too. Being late makes for greater hurry and greater tension for everyone involved, and it tends to accumulate throughout the day. So even when I go out to a film or a play I like to arrive half an hour or so early, so that there is plenty of time to find a parking place, get the tickets, and find good seats without stepping on people's toes. This is the way to become master of time and gradually slow down the furious pace of living.

पवनः पवतामस्मि रामः शस्त्रभृतामहम् ।
झषाणां मकरश्चास्मि स्रोतसामस्मि जाह्नवी ॥ १०-३१ ॥

31. Among purifying forces I am the wind, and among warriors I am Rāma. Among water creatures I am the crocodile, and among rivers I am the Ganges.

The wind is a powerful purifier; without the wind to keep impurities from accumulating, our atmosphere could not continue to sustain life. On more than one occasion now, the Bay Area has been so stifled with smog that children have been asked not to run or play for fear that they might breathe too much of this deleterious air. Then a strong wind blows in from the ocean, and on the following morning the sky is blue and the hills stand out clearly, glad to be clothed in the clean air again. In tropical countries like India, when there is no wind, the air can become so still it is suffocating, and many people sleep outdoors under the stars to catch any gentle breeze that blows.

In most ancient cultures the wind is deified as a divine power, endowed with tremendous capacity for both evil and good. My friend Bron has been telling me about the chinook, which is a hot wind you have only in America, east of the Rocky Mountains. What is surprising is that it makes its appearance in winter. One March day in Montana, it raised the temperature thirty-one degrees in just three minutes. In the dead frost of winter, the chinook can come down from the mountains like a corps of angels to rescue herds of cattle from death by freezing and starvation. Another interesting wind I've been reading about, the harmetan, has earned the title of "doctor." It blows from the hot, dry Sahara to the humid coast of Africa. Following the professional services of Dr. Harmetan, ague disappears, the pangs of arthritis are relieved, and everyone is invigorated. But it is not only extraordinary winds like these that purify; even a gentle breeze does its part to keep our air circulating so that impurities don't accumulate. The whole globe is enveloped in a mantle of giant wind systems, all kept in constant motion by the immense power of the sun. One scientist has calculated that the energy driving these systems is equal to that of seven million atomic bombs. All this is part of the continuous miracle which sustains life.

In this verse, Sri Krishna is reminding us that the same power for purification which is found in the wind is found in you and me. Any person whose life benefits others is a purifier. In contrast, those who spread anger and fear, who pursue their own interests at the expense of others, are like smog; they afflict people wherever they go. Look at their homes and you will see how the eyes of their families smart, how their hearts burn with the selfishness that hangs in the air. Unfortunately, each one of us today is polluted with the smog of self-will to some degree. But through the practice of meditation we can learn the science of purification. This is simply another way of describing the skill for transforming hatred into love, resentment into compassion, and fear into fearlessness that comes with sustained practice of meditation. The person who has this inner fortitude, whose spirit cannot be broken by any adverse circumstances, is a purifier.

Then the Lord says, "I am Rāma." Rāma is the hero of the Indian epic the *Rāmāyana*. Like Sri Krishna, he is a divine incarnation of the spiritual power of Vishnu, the Preserver in the Hindu Trinity. Vishnu came down to earth many times to save humanity from danger, and he came as Sri Rāma before his incarnation as Sri Krishna.

Rāma is deeply loved in India because he represents the perfect son, the perfect husband, and the perfect king. His wife, Sītā, is equally cherished as the perfect wife and mother. Rāma and Sītā were always deeply devoted to each other, and were loyal through all sorts of trials.

In the *Rāmāyana,* the story of these trials takes on deep spiritual significance. There, as Sri Ramakrishna used to say, Rāma represents the Lord, and Sītā the human soul. Rāma is so loyal to his father that to fulfill a rash promise his father made, he gives up his kingdom and goes into exile in the forest for fourteen years. Of her own accord, Sītā goes with him, giving up all the comforts of the court in order to be with the one she loves. During their exile, Sītā is abducted by a demon king called Rāvana, the embodiment of the ego. At the end of many trials, Rāma succeeds in slaying Rāvana and is reunited with Sītā. This mortal combat between Rāma and Rāvana, like the battle which is the backdrop for the Bhagavad Gita, is the struggle between the selfless and selfish urges within all of us, and the reunion of Sītā and Rāma represents the unitive experience which is the supreme goal of life.

This story of Rāma and Sītā is known all over India. In countless homes, especially in the villages, it is read and told over and over again, because it conveys spiritual values in a vivid way that even children can appreciate and absorb. Mahatma Gandhi was especially fond of the *Rāmāyana,* for his mantram was the name of Rāma, who is the perfect embodiment of one who never swerves from truth. After many years of conscious effort, Gandhi made *Rāma* an integral part of his consciousness. Then, when the assassin's bullets struck him at point-blank range, he was able to greet his attacker with *Rāma* on his lips and infinite compassion in his heart.

Among creatures that live in the water, Sri Krishna says he is the crocodile. We saw some crocodiles in the aquarium the other day, and what impressed me most about them was their almost impenetrable armor. This is the kind of armor we have to develop in order to withstand the onslaught of life. To meet every challenge as it comes, we cannot allow vacillations in fortune and fame to affect us. One well-known film star has confessed that he chose to go into films to gain as much attention as possible, thinking that he would find security. It was the one thing he did not find. Security is armor which we must learn to put on *inside* of us; we cannot get it anywhere outside. Every time we are patient in the face of agitation, every time we return forbearance for resentment, we strengthen this armor and deepen our security.

The final epithet has profound mystical significance, for the Ganges, the sacred river of India, is a symbol of the life-force contained in sex. In sex lies the secret of life itself. That is why I always repeat that sex can have a beautiful place in a relationship where there is complete love and loyalty. In meditation we gradually gain control over this deep drive, so that instead of being its victim, subject to every whim of desire, we become its master. Then sex becomes a source of tremendous creative power which draws people together in the unity that underlies us all.

सर्गाणामादिरन्तश्च मध्यं चैवाहमर्जुन ।
अध्यात्मविद्या विद्यानां वादः प्रवदतामहम् ॥ १०-३२ ॥

32. I am the beginning, middle, and end of creation. Of all the sciences I am the science of Self-knowledge, and I am reason in those who debate.

Patanjali, the great teacher of meditation in ancient India, tells us to take to the spiritual life so that we may realize who we are. To me, this is real education – not education for degrees but education for living, which is a perfect description of meditation. Meditation enables us to find, right in the context of our daily lives, the answer to that most important question, "Who am I?" We may know all about wines, or skiing, or even English literature, but until we learn who we really are, nothing else we learn or do can ever give us fulfillment, security, or peace of mind. The Lord is asking us here, "Before you try to learn everything else, why don't you give half an hour every morning to learning about yourself?"

In this verse Sri Krishna does not try to impress us with terms like "transcendental wisdom" or "the clear light within"; he uses simple, chaste language: "I am reason." Sometimes when I hear people discussing the possibility of intelligent life on other planets, I am inclined to ask, "Is there intelligent life on earth?" Far from expecting an age of mysticism, I hope only for an age of reason, which is noticeably absent in most of our activities today. For example, how can we live in harmony with our family and friends if we persist in returning anger for anger? How can we bring about lasting peace by adding to the probability of nuclear holocaust? To live in the midst of conflict with peace in our hearts, transforming those around us through patience and forgiveness, requires enormous internal strength, which is gradually developed through the practice of meditation.

अक्षराणामकारो ऽस्मि द्वंद्वः सामासिकस्य च ।
अहमेवाक्षयः कालो धाताहं विश्वतोमुखः ॥ १०-३३ ॥

33. Among letters I am A; among grammatical compounds I am the dvandva. I am infinite time, and the sustainer whose face is seen everywhere.

In many alphabets, including Sanskrit, *A* is the first letter; when the Lord says that among letters he is *A*, it is a grammatical reminder that he is the origin of all life. As Jesus says, "I am the alpha and the omega"; we come from him and we return to him. We may be born into the world through our parents, but our real origin is divine.

Dvandva is another reference to grammar. Sanskrit authors were fond of making big words by running smaller words together, sometimes so many of them that they wander off onto the next page like a snake. The most democratic of these compounds are called *dvandvas;* usually all their smaller words have equal value. But there may be another reason why Sri Krishna singles out the dvandva here. Sanskrit scriptures are full of dvandvas or opposites to describe life on the physical level: *sukhaduhkha,* 'pleasure and pain'; *labhālabha,* 'profit and loss'; *jayājaya,* 'victory and defeat.' Duality is the very nature of the world of change, and if we are to live in freedom we have to learn to dispel this fog called *dvandvamoha,* the delusion of separateness which keeps us from seeing that life is one.

In the last verse but two, the Lord told us he was time the measurer; now he says that he is infinite time as well. This is the eternal present, which we sometimes glimpse in the deeper stages of meditation when all awareness of the world of change has been withdrawn. Then we begin to understand just how relative time is. The passage of time has no reality of its own; it is very much a part of the functioning of the mind.

All of us are familiar with this. When we are absorbed in something we like very much, hours can pass before we know it, but when we are doing something we dislike intensely, every little second seems to drag on endlessly. Patanjali would say that this has nothing to do with the world outside us; it is a matter of the mind being concentrated. When we are doing something we like, all our attention is on the present; when we have to do something we dislike, the mind is always wriggling out into the past, or the future, or its own little world of might-have-been.

In this connection, there is a good story about Dr. Albert Einstein – probably apocryphal, as a great many of these stories are – which tells how this delightful man of genius had to sit through a talk which seemed to have no direction and no end. Einstein was a very patient man, but after some time of this he began to shift uneasily from side to side and look down at his hands. Finally he leaned over and whispered to a friend sitting next to him, "I have discovered only relativity; this fellow has discovered eternity."

The practical application here is that eternity is within the reach of every one of us. By gradually learning to still the mind through the practice of meditation, we can learn to live in the Eternal Now. Then we can enjoy not only what we like, but what we dislike as well. More than that, as we begin to live more and more in the present, we make the exhilarating discovery that past and future exist only in our minds. It is a tremendous realization, for it means that we are released from any burden of guilt about the past and any anxiety about the future. We think that past and future are real because we keep brooding over what we have done and what others have done to us, what we will do and what others will do to us. But it is not past and future that are real; it is our brooding on the past and the future that is real. If we could withdraw our attention from these will-o'-the-wisps, many of our problems would simply dissolve.

Many years ago I stayed at the home of an hospitable woman in the Bay Area who happened to believe in ghosts. Her home had a beautiful view which took in a cemetery nearby, and though she was very fond of me, nothing I could say could convince her that ghosts from that cemetery did not pay her visits at unlikely times. So one day I announced casually that I was going for a walk in the cemetery to meet one of these ghosts myself. When I returned she was wringing her hands. "Did you see any ghosts?" she asked anxiously.

"Oh, yes," I said. "Three."

"What did you do?"

"I told them you were too nice a woman to be living in fear all the time, and that they should go away and leave you alone."

"And what did they say?"

"They said, 'We can't. As long as she believes in us, we *have* to stay.'"

She stared at me for a second and then laughed out loud. Because of her affection for me those simple words had gone in deeply, and after that she was never afraid of ghosts again.

Whenever we worry about something in the past or the future, what we are doing is setting up our own little haunted house and peopling it with our own special ghosts – Aunt Agatha, looking the way she did when she scolded us at the dinner table twenty-five years ago, or our little boy disguised as Marion Brando in *On the Waterfront.* To banish these ghosts, all we need to do is stop thinking about them. They will never bother us again, because they were never there at all.

As we learn to disentangle ourselves from past and future and bring our consciousness to rest in the present, we enter into eternity. The Compassionate Buddha gives us the key to understanding how this happens in his doctrine of momentariness, called *kshanikavāda,* which tells us that there is no inherent connection between one moment and the next. Every moment is unique and discrete. When our concentration is complete, we rest like a king in the present, not concerned with what happened in the past, not anxious over what might happen in the future. Completely absorbed in the present, we are able to give our best concentration to everyone we deal with and everything we do.

The last epithet, *Vishvatomukha,* means 'he whose face is everywhere.' Nicholas of Cusa says that in every face there is the face of the Lord, hidden behind a veil. This divine face can be seen only when we enter into what Nicholas calls "mystic silence," which is what samādhi may be said to be.

मृत्युः सर्वहरश्चाहमुद्भवश्च भविष्यताम् ।
कीर्तिः श्रीर्वाक्च नारीणां स्मृतिर्मेधा धृतिः क्षमा ॥ १०-३४॥

34. I am death, which overcomes all, and the source of all beings still to be born. I am the feminine qualities: fame, beauty, perfect speech, memory, intelligence, loyalty, and forgiveness.

Over and over in these chapters the Lord is driving home to us that he is not only life and love, he is also death – *mrityuh sarvaharah,* by whom all of us one day are going to be struck down. No good spiritual teacher will fail to drive this into our consciousness, for once it penetrates our hearts we will give everything to the practice of the spiritual life; we will not let a day pass without doing our very best to surpass our efforts of the day before. The conquest of death is such an immense achievement that a lifetime is not too long for it, and when we let even a single day slip by, we are letting life itself slip through our fingers.

In the Hindu and Buddhist traditions we say that even a lifetime is not enough; all of us have been working towards this conquest for many lives. To me, the argument for reincarnation was summed up pithily by one of our children: "I don't want to be dead *always*". The Lord of Love, by whatever name we call him, is not likely to keep us dead forever. Each time around we have the opportunity to conquer death, and each time most of us decide that we have other things to do instead. The Lord waits patiently while we experiment for a number of years, but finally, if we have still not learned that the purpose of life is to go beyond death, he comes to take us back for "R and R," rest and recuperation. Then, when the right circumstances develop for us to take up where we left off, he gives us a strong, new body and sends us forth to try again.

All this is very much like a loving father, but in many parts of India – particularly Bengal, where Sri Ramakrishna was born – we don't talk about God as our Father but as our Mother. I think it is a particularly appropriate perspective for this verse, for the selfless love of a mother for her child is the perfect symbol for the love the Lord has for every one of us. Just as we have been born on earth to our earthly mother, all of us are children of the Divine Mother. In the Krishna tradition, one of the names of the Lord is *Hiranyagarbha,* the 'womb of the cosmos.' She is the Source from which the universe was born, and the Upanishads, echoed by some theories in contemporary astronomy, tell us that when her creation becomes so vast that it threatens to disperse itself forever, she gathers the galaxies and all their creatures into herself to be born again. In the beautiful words of Christian mysticism, we all come from God, abide in God, and return to God, who is the Divine Mother of us all.

Sri Ramakrishna used to say frequently that we should look on all women as the embodiment of the Divine Mother. What he meant is that the qualities which make for a perfect woman are the qualities which make for a deeply spiritual person. This is the sense of Sri Krishna's reference to "feminine qualities" in this verse: it does not apply only to women; it applies equally to men. In the totally integrated person, man or woman, there is a part that is masculine and a part that is feminine. In the Hindu tradition this is represented by a glorious image called Ardhanārīshvara – one half thoroughly masculine, the other utterly feminine, united in one person. It is unrealistic to deny that there are masculine qualities, just as it is unrealistic to deny that there are feminine qualities. There are both, and each is meant to be completed by the other. Gandhi was like that; there was never more of a soldier than Gandhiji when he was fighting for truth, and no one more tender when he was nursing the sick or comforting a little child. Here all that is best in man and all that is best in woman have come together. There is no contradiction in this, no discrimination, no competition; there is only completion. It is not only women who love such a man, and not only men who love such a woman; everyone loves the person who has realized the unity in which man and woman are one.

As a boy, growing up under the guidance of my mother and my grandmother, I absorbed this attitude naturally at an early age. The family tradition in which I grew up in the state of Kerala is like no other culture with which I am acquainted. It is a matrilineal tradition, highly civilized, in which women have had equal rights with men for centuries. One of the practical consequences of this is that while most boys and girls in India grow up almost in different worlds, I spent my first sixteen years under the roof of a large joint family in close daily contact with girls as well as boys, women as well as men. It still impresses me to remember how the ideals of that tradition were passed on to all of us by the quiet example of our women. Even when I was very young, I used to admire how girls no older than I was could put others first and win people over by their patient example with a grace that most of us boys never managed to achieve at any age, even when we tried. My grandmother was the perfect flower of that tradition, and it was from her that I learned how perfectly the qualities mentioned here apply to either sex.

Some of these qualities deserve special attention, because they have no precise English equivalents. *Sri,* 'beauty,' has nothing to do with superficial attractiveness; it refers to the inner radiance that shines in the eyes of those who are selfless. I have never seen anyone so beautiful with *sri* as my grandmother, even in the twilight of her life. My granny was not given to praising people easily, and she always took a deep interest in the women who married into our ancestral family because of its ancient matriarchal heritage. There were not many brides who could meet her expectations of what a woman should be, but when she saw one who did, she would say with quiet approval, "That girl has *sri* in her face." No one could have asked for higher praise.

Dhriti, 'loyalty,' is a precious quality that we have almost lost sight of today. In relationships between two people, especially where sex is concerned, I think loyalty is considered old-fashioned, even unrealistic. Yet without loyalty, it simply is not possible to love.

When I first came to this country, everybody was talking about freedom. The idea was that if you came together freely, you were always free to walk out; this was supposed to be a complete safeguard against unhappy relationships. When my friends would talk this way I used to answer, "Oh, yes, you *are* free to walk out of such a relationship. There is no obligation; there are no bonds; there are not even any ties. But what happens if you go on doing this is that you never acquire the capacity to love."

Loyalty is the quintessence of love. When two people tell each other, "As long as you do what I like, I'll stay with you, but as soon as you start doing things I don't like, I'm packing my bags" – to me that is not love; that's indifference. Loving somebody means that even when they trouble you, you don't let yourself be shaken; even when they are harsh to you, you don't move away; even when they make a mistake that hurts you, you don't go off and make the same kind of mistake to hurt them. All of us are so liable to human error that unless we have some capacity to bear with the errors of others, we will not be able to maintain a lasting relationship with anybody, which is the tragic situation that many people find themselves in today.

I am not idealizing intimate relationships when I talk like this. Despite what the media tell us, there is nothing easy about learning to love. It takes a lot of hard work, and if you want a relationship to get deeper and deeper with the passage of time, you will go on strengthening it all your life. Naturally there are going to be differences between you and your partner; that is the nature of life. Even identical twins have differences of opinion, and they come from the same combinations of genes and the very same background; why should two people from, say, New York City and Paris, Texas, expect life together to be smooth sailing? Even on the honeymoon there are going to be difficulties, and all too often one party is going to write home after the first week and say, "I never thought it would be like this!" You open Pandora's box expecting a lot of doves and out come a couple of bats instead. Here it is the mystics who are the real romantics, because they are the most practical. They won't get upset or despondent; they will say, "The doves are there; they're simply lying low. Why don't we get to work and clean out these bats?" This is the approach I learned from my grandmother, which I try to apply in everything: never to dwell on the negative, but always to respect the potential in other people and help them to realize that potential through your support.

To do this we need *kshamā* – forgiveness, patience, the capacity to forbear. Kshamā is so important that I look upon it as another aspect of yoga. In the last chapter we discussed rāja yoga, the royal path of meditation; here we can introduce kshamā yoga, the path of patience and forgiveness, which will come into its real beauty in the climax of this volume in chapter twelve. It is a path that is suited to people in all walks of life, from all religious backgrounds.

Poets like to write about love, popular singers like to glorify love, but nobody ever bothers to sing the praise of patience. Yet in order to love others you must have tremendous patience, to bear with them come what may. None of us are born with this capacity, but all of us can develop it through practice. In a situation where there is a lot of friction, where others differ from you and everything seems to be going wrong, don't move away; move closer. It will be difficult, especially at the beginning. You may have to grit your teeth, you may have to bite your lip to keep from saying what is in your mind; and then of course you need to smile too, which doesn't add up to an especially pretty picture. It is a demanding art to do this gracefully, but I can give you an image from which you can draw consolation.

On the Blue Mountain in South India we had a little garden with a number of peach, pear, apple, and cherimoya trees. These trees had never been pruned; they had been allowed to grow in any direction they liked, and the garden was so small that they were all crowded close together. Their branches were tangled, fresh growth was choked by the snarl of dead limbs, and it was impossible for them to bear good fruit. It took a lot of work to prune that garden, and when we were done the trees looked denuded. All the dead branches had been cut away and nothing new had begun to grow. It was only when spring came that I was convinced that the pruning hadn't been a mistake, when I saw those trees all gracefully wearing their fresh leaves and decked with blossoms.

When we have free-roaming, unpruned self-will like this, when we've been letting our likes and dislikes run rampant for twenty or thirty years, the process of pruning can be quite painful. Not only that, we will not always be at our best. Sometimes we may be able to forbear gracefully, but there are going to be times when our smile looks like a grimace or we have to rush out the door repeating the mantram. This is the pruning period, when life can look pretty drab; the dead branches of our old habits will be lying all around us and the new leaves will not yet have begun to grow. But for all of us, if we keep at our pruning carefully, the spring is bound to come. There will still be gardening to do, but when we see our new ways blossoming and the good fruit we have begun to bear for others, this pruning of self-will will be a source of lasting satisfaction.

बृहत्साम तथा साम्नां गायत्री छन्दसामहम् ।
मासानां मार्गशीर्षो ऽहमृतूनां कुसुमाकरः ॥१०-३५॥

35. I am the Sāma Veda and the Gāyatrī. Among the months I am Mārgashīrsha, and among seasons I am spring, the season of flowers.

The Sāma Veda, one of the oldest of the Hindu scriptures, is so sonorous that it used to be sung. But no human recitation can compare with the beauty of such a passage in deep meditation, when concentration on the words is complete and each word reverberates through consciousness with unearthly beauty. The joy of this experience is so great that nothing the senses can offer is even worthy of comparison.

The Gāyatrī is a mantram from the Rig Veda, the earliest of the Hindu scriptures; it has been used throughout India for thousands of years. I interpret the word *gāyatrī* to mean 'that which protects the reciter against all harm.' The most enthusiastic Gāyatrī recitation I ever heard in India was not by any Indian, but by a Swiss friend with a good ear for music who used to recite it very much in a Wagnerian manner. But to reap the benefits of a mantram, you do not need to appreciate music or even be able to carry a tune. The Lord isn't going to listen to your recitation and say, "No, no, Roberta, let me hear that A again." All he is interested in is that we repeat the mantram whenever possible, with sincerity, concentration, and love.

Among months the Lord is Mārgashīrsha, the first month of the Hindu year. It is as if Sri Krishna is asking us to make a New Year's resolution to remember him in those around us throughout the year. Then he adds that among seasons he is the springtime, because all over the world spring is the season of birth, beauty, and joy. The birth that is meant here is the birth of the Lord in our hearts, which in the language of all the great religions is called our second birth, in which we wake up into eternal life.

द्यूतं छलयतामस्मि तेजस्तेजस्विनामहम् ।
जयो ऽस्मि व्यवसायो ऽस्मि सत्त्वं सत्त्ववतामहम् ॥ १०-३६ ॥

36. I am the gambling of the gambler and the radiance in all that shines. I am effort; I am victory; and I am the quality of sattva.

Some years ago I was in a bus depot and happened to hear the conversation of some people waiting for the bus to Reno. Everyone seemed to have their own foolproof system for blackjack, worked out through long research. Not only that, each person I listened to was absolutely convinced that their system could never fail. Even if the last time around they had lost their shirt and their T-shirt too, their faith was not affected. "Something was wrong with that dealer, or the angle of the table," they would say. "Or maybe the stars were all wrong. But this time my turn is going to come, and I'm going to double the stakes." As far as I could make out, they all had the same system: the more you lose, the more you double the stakes. Then, when you finally win, your losses are made up.

Now, according to the Gita, gamblers are not merely trying to win a game or break the bank; they are looking for the source of lasting satisfaction, which is the Lord. This is the compassionate view, which looks into the gambler's heart. People don't go to Las Vegas or Monte Carlo to make money or even to enjoy the thrill of winning; they go in search of the joy and security that can only be found within. It is very much like the man in one of my niece's favorite riddles. She takes delight in posing riddles for me, which I am seldom able to answer, and this time she asked: "Why was a man looking under the streetlight for the quarter he lost at the other end of the block?" The answer is really to the point: "Because there was more light there." This is very much our predicament. We are all looking for fulfillment in life, but most people are looking in places where they can never find what they are looking for, because the source of fulfillment is not outside us but within. We can render a real service to people like this by showing them that the thrill of winning can only be lasting when it comes from winning mastery of ourselves.

Next the Lord praises *vyavasāya,* 'effort.' Whenever you find the capacity to work enthusiastically for a selfless cause, the Lord is present, right in the effort itself. This does not include erratic effort, where we get up early and work nonstop until midnight, then go to sleep and do not wake up for two days. One of my schoolmates in high school actually did this; he went to sleep on Monday and woke up on Wednesday. We were all amazed. He couldn't understand why we were doing geography that day instead of history, because he didn't realize he had slept through an entire day. Such people do things on a heroic scale at the outset; then, when enthusiasm wanes and boredom sets in, they want something else to hold their fleeting interest. But there is a rare person who becomes more enterprising and resourceful with every difficulty that comes his or her way. Such people achieve success in any walk of life, and once they begin to harness their enthusiasm to achieve a selfless goal, they can really go far. So Sri Krishna adds here, *Jayo 'smi:* 'I am victory.' Mahatma Gandhi, one of the most inspiring examples of spiritual transformation I know of in this century, tells us out of his own experience: "Any man or woman can achieve what I have if he or she would make the same effort and cultivate the same hope and faith." And then he adds magnificently, "Full effort is full victory."

When you are really making your best effort on the spiritual path, there is a slow but tremendously potent rise of the spiritual energy called kundalinī. To an experienced eye, the marks of this rise are unmistakable. There is such drive, such resoluteness, such an indomitable will to achieve the goal of life no matter what stands in the way, that the mystics of both East and West use the image of fire to describe their personal experience of this power. To those around them, it is almost like seeing a human missile; every ounce of fuel is channeled into this tremendous attempt to reach an almost unreachable goal.

But finally, after samādhi is achieved, everything is transformed. Those who have become established in this state are so tranquil, so deceptively serene, that we might make the mistake of assuming that all their power has been consumed. It has not: it has become almost limitless, but now it is completely under control. It is like getting a second engine: you may have a Model T body, but now you get a Ferrari engine; just a touch of the accelerator and in seconds you can be at top speed. And then, the Hindu scriptures say, kundalinī is no longer fire; it is light. Going up, when all you can manage is to keep it under control, kundalinī is fire; but when it comes down again, to bathe all the centers of consciousness and release their deepest resources, it comes down as light. This divine radiance is called *tejas* in Sanskrit, and Sri Krishna is telling us here that this same light is within everyone, and it is the same radiance in the sun, in the stars, as in us all. Kabir says:

The moon shines in my body,
But my blind eyes cannot see it;
The moon is within me,
And so is the sun.

वृष्णीनां वासुदेवो ऽस्मि पाण्डवानां धनंजयः ।
मुनीनामप्यहं व्यासः कवीनामुशना कविः ॥१०-३७॥

37. Among the Vrishnis I am Krishna, and among the Pāndavas I am Arjuna. Among sages I am Vyāsa, and among poets, Ushanas.

The references to Sri Krishna in this verse reveal a wealth of meanings. First and foremost, Sri Krishna is the eternal, immutable, infinite Reality whom we call God – the source of all joy, all security, all beauty, and all wisdom, present in the depths of our consciousness. But in another aspect, the historical aspect, Sri Krishna is a divine incarnation who was born on earth. He was a member of the Vrishni clan; he played as a child, grew to be a handsome young man, and went through all the stages of human life.

These two – the eternal Godhead and the divine incarnation – are different aspects of the same supreme Reality. Similarly, the Compassionate Buddha was born a prince of Kapilavastu and grew to be a young man with a lovely wife and child; we know of his struggle to find the answer to the meaning of life. The life of Jesus the Christ is familiar to all of us too; we know of his birth in Bethlehem and his death on the cross. There is no contradiction between the historical aspect of the Lord and the supreme Reality, which was never born and will never die. All these incarnations are simply different manifestations of the same Reality. In the next chapter, Sri Krishna, the perfect divine incarnation, will give us a glimpse of his immortal, omnipresent nature. Then, after revealing his cosmic form, the Lord will once again assume his role in the human drama as Arjuna's guide and companion.

When my wife and I were in India we had to make a choice between going to the Taj Mahal and going to Vrindāvana, the historical birthplace of Sri Krishna. We still have not seen the Taj Mahal. Instead we took the evening train to Vrindāvana, and as it was a slow-moving train, we were able to watch leisurely all the timeless scenes of village India as we passed by. It was dusk, the "hour of cow dust," when the cows come home from the pasture raising dust with their hooves, and the scene around us immediately brought to mind the stories of Sri Krishna as an irresistible young cowherd. Vrindāvana is the perfect setting for these stories, with the river Yamuna winding round the village and Mount Govārdhana standing as a nearby sentinel.

Some of the most delightful episodes in Sri Krishna's life take place on this mountain. According to one legend, Indra wanted to test Sri Krishna to see if he was really a divine incarnation or just an imposter. So Indra, god of storms, told the rain, "Send down a deluge on Vrindāvana, and we'll see what this Krishna can do." Torrential rains poured down, and the whole village was in danger of being swept away. When Sri Krishna's friends begged him to protect them from the flood, he smiled, picked up Mount Govārdhana just as we would pick up a push-button umbrella, and held it up above the village to protect everyone from the rain. So one of the names for the Lord is Giridhara Gopāla, "he who holds the mountain as an umbrella to shelter all those who seek his refuge." It is a simple way of saying that we do not need to be afraid of any challenge when we seek the Lord's help.

In another story, Brahmā, god of creation, stole the calves and cowherds of Vrindāvana and hid them in a mountain cave. As the sun was setting, Sri Krishna went to look for his friends but could not find them. The families of these cowherds were eagerly waiting for their children to return home, and Sri Krishna couldn't bear to think how much they would worry if their children were late. So through the great power of his Māyā, he made himself appear as the missing cowherds, cows, and calves. Everyone apparently went home as usual, only this time there was unusually great joy in each home. The parents found their sons so perfect that they could not understand how they could ever have yelled at them, and their cows that night were such gentle creatures that no one wanted to part from them again. Nobody guessed that this was the perfection of the Lord appearing in the form of their sons and their cattle.

When Sri Krishna says, "Among Pāndavas I am Arjuna," Arjuna must be melting in ecstasy. He has given all his heart to Sri Krishna; he has eyes only for him; he has no thought other than of him. Because every corner of his consciousness is filled with love for the Lord, Sri Krishna says, "I am in him always, and he is united with me."

Then the Lord says that of sages he is Vyāsa. Vyāsa was not only a great sage but a great poet as well – in fact, he is the author of the *Mahābhārata* itself, the epic in which the Gita is the crowning jewel. So the Lord says that he is also Ushanas, the poet of poets. It is to remind us that if we have artistic talent, whether for poetry, painting, speaking, dancing, or music, we should use it in the service of the Lord to bring deeper awareness of the unity of life. Kālidāsa, another of the giants of Indian literature, wrote in one of his early epics: "I am like a little pygmy trying to pluck a fruit from a tall tree; I have no gift for poetry. How I would love to be a poet so I could sing the praise of the Lord!" According to legend, his desire was so deep and so selfless that the Divine Mother, called Kālī, appeared to him and wrote on his tongue the mantram *Om*. He took the name Kālidāsa, 'the servant of Kālī,' and became a genius in Sanskrit poetry and drama, using all his creative capacity to sing the praise of the Lord.

दण्डो दमयतामस्मि नीतिरस्मि जिगीषताम् ।
मौनं चैवास्मि गुह्यानां ज्ञानं ज्ञानवतामहम् ॥ १०-३८ ॥

38. I am the scepter which metes out punishment, and the art of statesmanship in those who lead. I am the silence of the unknown and the wisdom of the wise.

The Lord is not only the lawgiver; he is the law and that which enforces the law as well. *Danda* – 'scepter' or 'stick' – is a strong term in Sanskrit, implying punishment, penalty, or consequences. Since many people have some resistance to words like sin and atonement, I usually substitute terms like mistakes and consequences. This leaves no room for misunderstanding. For example, if we overeat, it is not a law passed by Congress that gives us dyspepsia. "He or she who overeats will suffer stomachache for three days, or three nights, or both" is not a law on the statute books; it is a law written within every cell of our body. This is the principle of mistakes and consequences, which we can ignore only at our peril.

Once our eyes begin to open, we shall see this principle working behind the scenes in all sorts of situations. Take vacations, for example. I have been looking at the advertisements for cruises in *The New York Times*. Much of the emphasis is not on seeing new lands or learning new languages, but on eating. One ad boasts, "We never give you the same menu twice during our world tour." Another describes the ship's twenty-two kitchens and one hundred eighty one cooks, and tries to entice the reader by saying, "We serve four gourmet meals daily, and you can come to the dining room anytime for a snack." If we were to go on a tour like that we would probably need to be met by an ambulance, and our friends would not be able to recognize us at all. "That's not my friend Jimmy," they would say; "that's some fat fellow." For some, it would take a month in the hospital to repair the damage of this overeating and underexercising. Overeating has obvious consequences – overweight, gastrointestinal problems, probably high blood cholesterol, and an increased likelihood of heart attacks, to name just a few – which eventually force us to correct our unhealthy living habits. The beauty of the Gita's approach is that it makes health our birthright, no less than security and joy. But in order to claim this birthright, we have to learn to make wise choices.

Then Sri Krishna says that in leaders he is statesmanship. This is statesmanship of an unusually high order, the mark of which is the capacity to return good will for ill will and nonviolent resistance for violence. Unfortunately, many of us have been conditioned to look upon violence as a way of solving problems. But one of the laws of life is that hatred can never cease through hatred. As the Buddha tells us, hatred ceases only through love. We cannot break this law; we can only break ourselves against it by not observing it in all our relationships. When, against the background of evolution, we come into the human context, the law of the jungle is superseded by the law of unity, which Jesus phrased perfectly: "Bless them that curse you, and do good to them that hate you."

It is not difficult to understand what happens when we violate this law, which applies from the individual level to the international. No matter what the situation, violence will never cease when met with violence. World War I, for example, was supposedly fought to bring lasting peace. But the Treaty of Versailles which ended it, far from healing the wounds of conflict, broke the spirit of Germany and paved the way for World War II. In those days there were very few who could see the futility of seeking peace through war. Now most thoughtful people are beginning to agree that the world is one, that all life is one, and that a war anywhere on this planet threatens the welfare of us all.

यच्चापि सर्वभूतानां बीजं तदहमर्जुन ।
न तदस्ति विना यत्स्यान्मया भूतं चराचरम् ॥ १०-३९ ॥

39. My seed can be found in every creature,
Arjuna, for without me nothing can
exist, neither animate nor inanimate.

Recently I have been reading a little of Spinoza, a mystic of the seventeenth century who was as unorthodox in the eyes of his Jewish community as Meister Eckhart was to the Christians of medieval Germany. Some of the things Spinoza says I like very much; they have the ring of personal experience, and they should appeal to any good scientist even if he or she professes not to believe in God. Spinoza calls God by a very surprising name: Substance. It is a very apt choice of words – *sub-stance,* "that on which everything in the universe stands." It is very much the same language that Eckhart uses when he talks about the Divine Ground of existence. The Lord is substance, the only reality; everything else is shadow. Here, because Arjuna is not very philosophically inclined, Sri Krishna puts it more personally: "Without me," he says, "nothing else could exist, because I am present everywhere."

"As the idea of a circle is to all circles," Spinoza says, "so is God to the universe." If I want my friend Jeff, who is an architect, to build a complex of buildings where we can carry on our work, I don't let him start with a few bricks and some old recycled boards and just let everything grow like Topsy; I ask him to put every detail into one coherent plan. It may take longer, but at least that way I know that we won't end up with two false ceilings and a door opening onto the wall of the building next door. It is very much the same with the Lord. He has the blueprint for his creation worked out so that every detail follows from some previous detail, and when the time comes he just gives the word and the universe unfolds in all its endless diversity.

In some traditions this is the language that is used, where the Lord is the Architect, or the Designer, or the cosmic Watchmaker. In the Hindu tradition, however, we prefer to talk not about plans but about seeds. That is why Sri Krishna says here, "My seed can be found in every creature": just as in the unseen genetics of one tiny seed there is the potential for countless full-grown trees, the whole of creation is implicit in the Lord of Love.

नान्तो ऽस्ति मम दिव्यानां विभूतीनां परंतप ।
एष तूद्देशतः प्रोक्तो विभूतेर्विस्तरो मया ॥ १०-४० ॥
यद्यद्विभूतिमत्सत्त्वं श्रीमदूर्जितमेव वा ।
तत्तदेवावगच्छ त्वं मम तेजोंशसंभवम् ॥ १०-४१ ॥

40. But there is no end to my divine attributes, Arjuna;
these I have mentioned are only a few.
41. Wherever you find strength, or beauty, or
spiritual power, you may be sure that these
have sprung from a spark of my essence.

With these verses Sri Krishna gives the message of this whole chapter: wherever we see selflessness or forgiveness, wherever we see someone choosing to suffer rather than bring suffering to others, we can be sure that the Lord is present there. To see God, we do not need to look for some physical or psychical manifestation. Patience and forgiveness are not just moral qualities, but forces for unity that are latent within us all.

Like physical forces, these spiritual forces are universal. It is not only human beings that respond to patience, to forgiveness; animals respond too. Among the legends that surround St. Francis, there is a wonderful story about a fierce wolf who had been troubling the town of Gubbio until finally he was captured by the townsfolk. In their fear, the people of Gubbio wanted to put an end to the wolf's life. But St. Francis, aware of his unity with the wolf as only a child of God can be, went up to this fierce, frightened animal and scolded him just as he would an erring disciple. Francis was so full of love for all creation that not even a wild animal could see in him anything to fear, and the wolf lowered his head and listened humbly while the friar scolded him. After that he was a model of good behavior, and soon the entire town came to love him.

अथ वा बहुनैतेन किं ज्ञातेन तवार्जुन ।
विष्टभ्याहमिदं कृत्स्नमेकांशेन स्थितो जगत् ॥ १०-४२ ॥

42. *But of what use is it to you to know all this, Arjuna? Just remember that I am, and that I support the entire cosmos with only a fragment of my being.*

Out of his love for Arjuna, Sri Krishna has patiently listed some of the ways his presence is manifested throughout creation. Using the example of ancient sages and modern householders, of mythological creatures and even grammatical compounds, the Lord has told us that he is in every creature and in every activity. In whatever reveals perfection, beauty, and awareness of unity, he is present. But now, having played the part of the professor and satisfied Arjuna's desire for knowledge, Sri Krishna warns him not to get lost in endless lists and categories. It is enough if we know that the Lord exists, and that his unifying force holds together the billions of galaxies throughout the cosmos with their countless forms of life. In the next chapter Arjuna will beg his friend to show him this infinite, universal form.

विभूतियोगो नाम दशमोऽध्यायः ॥ १० ॥

CHAPTER ELEVEN

The Cosmic Vision

अर्जुन उवाच ।
मदनुग्रहाय परमं गुह्यमध्यात्मसंज्ञितम् ।
यत्त्वयोक्तं वचस्तेन मोहो ऽयं विगतो मम ॥ ११-१ ॥
भवाप्ययौ हि भूतानां श्रुतौ विस्तरशो मया ।
त्वत्तः कमलपत्राक्ष माहात्म्यमपि चाव्ययम् ॥ ११-२ ॥
एवमेतद्यथात्थ त्वमात्मानं परमेश्वर ।
द्रष्टुमिच्छामि ते रूपमैश्वरं पुरुषोत्तम ॥ ११-३ ॥
मन्यसे यदि तच्छक्यं मया द्रष्टुमिति प्रभो ।
योगेश्वर ततो मे त्वं दर्शयात्मानमव्ययम् ॥ ११-४ ॥

ARJUNA:

1. Out of compassion you have taught me the supreme mystery of life. Through your words my delusion is gone.
2. You have explained the origin and end of every creature, O lotus-eyed one, and told me of your own supreme, limitless existence.
3. You have told me about your infinite glory, O Lord. Now I long to see you as the supreme Ruler of all creation.
4. O Krishna, if you think my love is strong enough to absorb the glory of this vision, show me your immortal Self.

Swami Vivekananda, one of the foremost disciples of Sri Ramakrishna, used to say that religion *is* realization of God; nothing less can satisfy us. As a teenager, then called Narendra, he had struggled with all sorts of doubts. Like many young people today, he was tormented by questions about the meaning of life. He searched the worlds of literature and philosophy, but nowhere could he find an answer that satisfied him. Then he turned to highly regarded spiritual teachers, and to each he posed the same blunt question: "Have you seen God?" Always the reply was no.

Finally he heard of a saint who lived quietly at a little temple of the Divine Mother outside Calcutta. Narendra found his way there and went straight up to this little man to ask the same burning question he had asked all the others: "Have you seen God?"

Ramakrishna smiled. "Of course," he said. "I see God more clearly than I see you now. You I see only with my physical eyes, but God I see with every cell of my being."

This quiet authority, which can come only from experiential knowledge, is the unmistakable stamp of the vision of God. After becoming established in this vision, the God-conscious person may seem to be quite ordinary, but under this surface appearance he or she is no longer a separate, fragmented creature but part of the irresistible love force that we call God.

After years of enthusiastic effort, the Lord may reveal himself to us too in some small measure. Then we shall see into the very heart of life. This vision may last for only a moment or two, but it leaves behind an unforgettable awareness of the living presence of the Lord. Afterwards, no matter what their color or background or political persuasion, we see everyone as this divine force. It is because we do not have this immense frame of reference that little pleasures get amplified out of all proportion. Once we have tasted the joy of this experience, the ordinary pleasures of life become insipid in comparison. All our desires will be unified around one great desire to recapture this experience, and we will cry, like David, "As the hart panteth after the water brooks, so panteth my soul after thee, O Lord."

When this great longing comes to us, the Divine Fisherman has got his hook into us forever. Isn't it Eckhart who says that the more we thrash about, the deeper the hook enters? We may try to run away, to do everything we can think of to get free; but finally, when we get a glimpse of who it is who has caught us, we realize what a blessing it is to be caught so firmly by the Lord.

श्रीभगवानुवाच ।
पश्य मे पार्थ रूपाणि शतशोऽथ सहस्रशः ।
नानाविधानि दिव्यानि नानावर्णाकृतीनि च ॥११-५॥
पश्यादित्यान्वसून्रुद्रानश्विनौ मरुतस्तथा ।
बहून्यदृष्टपूर्वाणि पश्याश्चर्याणि भारत ॥११-६॥
इहैकस्थं जगत्कृत्स्नं पश्याद्य सचराचरम् ।
मम देहे गुडाकेश यच्चान्यद्द्रष्टुमिच्छसि ॥११-७॥

SRI KRISHNA:

5. Behold, Arjuna, a million divine forms, with an infinite variety of color and shape.
6–7. Behold the gods of the natural world, O Bhārata, and many more wonders never revealed before; behold the entire cosmos turning within my body. These are the things you desired to see.

Now Sri Krishna is beginning to reveal his universal, cosmic form, in one of the most magnificent portraits of the Lord I have seen anywhere in mystical literature.

In the Upanishads, the body is picturesquely called a little city, whose ruler is the Self. Recently I have been looking into quite a few books about the body, the immune system and the senses and all the mechanisms of health and disease, and the more I read, the more apt this image seems. If we could see life as a bacterium might, the body would be as busy as Bombay or New York City. It is a world of its own, so vast that learned societies of bacteria could study it and publish papers on its workings for generations and never suspect either the existence of the Ruler or of anything more vast outside.

In a breathtaking leap of spiritual insight, the Hindu scriptures go on to say that just as this body is only the city we live in during our life on earth, so the whole universe is no more than the body of the Lord. This is the cosmic vision that Arjuna is entering now. It is a beautiful image. When the Lord goes out into the world, he dresses as Sri Krishna, or the Buddha, or Jesus the Christ, and goes about looking just like one of us. But when he goes back home after a hard day's work, he takes off these forms and wears all the galaxies of the universe as casual garlands about his neck. That is why Sri Krishna is always represented as dark blue in color; it is to remind us that his body is really the infinite vastness of space and time.

To get some idea of the scale of this vision, look at the sheer vastness of the universe. Even at one hundred eighty-six thousand miles per second, it takes four years for light to reach us from the nearest star. Our own galaxy is more than one hundred thousand light-years across, and yet it is only an infinitesimal part of the universe. How long does it take for light to traverse the universe – assuming that it is possible at all? We can get some dim idea if we remember that some of the stars we see at night may have ceased to exist thousands of years before the light from them reaches our eyes. In looking outward into the depths of space, astronomers remind us, we are also looking backwards into the depths of time, and the light we see from faint stars on a clear night may have set out on its journey before there were human beings on earth to see.

On this cosmic scale, the stars that seem to us to be eternal are not much more long-lived than fireflies on a summer evening. Like all created things, they too have a beginning and an end. Born out of great clouds of dust and gas, they pour out energy over a few billion years and die, often in the fierce throes of a chain of explosions from whose remains new stars will someday be born. This drama has been going on throughout the vast universe for billions of years, and will go on for billions of years more; and the Sanskrit scriptures, echoed by many modern astronomers, remind us that even this is but a single act in the Lord's drama. Before and after the universe we live in, there stretch an infinitude of universes equally vast in space and time. As one Indian mystic wrote:

Let the Himālayas themselves become
The black pigment from which to make the ink,
And the ocean the bowl to contain it;
Let the whole universe serve as parchment,
And the celestial kalpa tree as pen;
Let this pen be held by Sarasvatī,
Goddess of wisdom, and let her write on
Through all eternity: she will not reach,
O Lord of Love, the end of your glory,
Nor find a limit to your dazzling splendor.

न तु मां शक्यसे द्रष्टुमनेनैव स्वचक्षुषा ।
दिव्यं ददामि ते चक्षुः पश्य मे योगमैश्वरम् ॥११-८॥

8. But these things cannot be seen with your physical eyes; therefore I give you spiritual vision to perceive my form as the Lord of creation.

Our eyes, like our other senses, are meant for registering changes in the world outside us. They are fine for letting us know when the traffic light turns red or when it is time to get up in the morning, but when it comes to going beyond change they are completely helpless. That is why in meditation we learn to withdraw all the senses gradually from the world of change. In deep meditation, when concentration on the inspirational passage is almost complete, we do not hear the cars on the road outside or the planes overhead; all our consciousness is withdrawn from the senses in a state of intense awareness within.

When we achieve this kind of concentration, we begin to discover that there is no real barrier between the world outside us and the world within the mind. As one British philosopher has put it, "outside" and "inside" are distinctions that we make mostly out of convenience; in both kinds of experience, outer and inner, what we are really perceiving is the contents and the impressions of our own mind. In other words, we see things not as they are but as we are. As long as our eye is multiple, as Jesus puts it, we see everyone around us as separate, and we cannot help trying to manipulate them when they do not behave the way we think they should. But when our consciousness becomes unified through the practice of meditation, we no longer see a world of separate fragments; we see all creation as one indivisible whole.

"Some people," Sri Ramakrishna said, "think that God cannot be seen. Who sees whom? Is God outside you, that you can see him with your eyes? One sees only one's Self." The vision Arjuna is about to have, in which all of space and time is comprehended in the body of the Lord, is not something he will see outside himself; it is something he will experience in the very depths of his consciousness.

संजय उवाच ।
एवमुक्त्वा ततो राजन्महायोगेश्वरो हरिः ।
दर्शयामास पार्थाय परमं रूपमैश्वरम् ॥ ११-९ ॥
अनेकवक्त्रनयनमनेकाद्भुतदर्शनम् ।
अनेकदिव्याभरणं दिव्यानेकोद्यतायुधम् ॥ ११-१० ॥
दिव्यमाल्याम्बरधरं दिव्यगन्धानुलेपनम् ।
सर्वाश्चर्यमयं देवमनन्तं विश्वतोमुखम् ॥ ११-११ ॥

SANJAYA:

9. Having spoken these words, Hari, the master of yoga, revealed himself to Arjuna as the supreme Lord.
10. He appeared with an infinite number of faces, ornamented by heavenly jewels, displaying unending miracles and the countless weapons of his power.
11. Clothed in celestial garments and covered with garlands, sweet-smelling with heavenly fragrances, he showed himself as the infinite Lord, the source of all wonders, whose face is everywhere.

In this supreme vision the Lord reveals himself as having an infinite number of faces, and Arjuna sees the Lord in every face, in every creature. It can fill us with awe to realize that in our parents, our partner, our children, and our friends it is the Lord who is looking into our eyes, listening to us, responding to us. This is why we can learn to love the Lord while living in the midst of family and friends. Once the barrier of self-will falls in any of our close relationships, we will find the One – whether we call him the Christ, Sri Krishna, the Buddha, or Allah – in everyone around us.

Here the Lord appears to Arjuna as the source of miracles, not the least of which is the gift of life itself. Our every breath, our every heartbeat is a miracle; so are the wind blowing in the trees and the sun shining in the sky. We do not have to search the universe for miracles; they occur morning, noon, and night every day of our lives, only our eyes are not open to them. If we were in tune with this continuous miracle of life, we would put an immediate end to conflict – whether in our homes, between races, or among nations. We could not rest in peace until every creature was free from exploitation and violence and the threat of nuclear holocaust. As Mahatma Gandhi put it, "There can be no happiness for any of us until happiness has been had for all."

दिवि सूर्यसहस्रस्य भवेद्युगपदुत्थिता ।
यदि भाः सदृशी सा स्याद्भासस्तस्य महात्मनः ॥ ११-१२ ।

12. If a thousand suns were to rise in the heavens
at the same time, the blaze of their light would
resemble a little the supreme splendor of the Lord.

You and I cannot look directly at the sun without damage to our eyes; its power is so immense that a minute fraction of the energy it radiates into space, diffused over ninety-three million miles and tempered by our atmosphere, is enough to sustain all life on this planet. Now we are asked to imagine a thousand of these suns rising at the same time in the depths of Arjuna's consciousness; his whole being is flooded with light. The intellect lies helpless, unable to grasp the immensity of this splendor; even the imagination swoons. "When the soul looks upon this Divine Sun," St. Teresa says, "the brightness dazzles it . . . . And very often it remains completely blind, absorbed, amazed, and dazzled by all the wonders it sees."

Yet even this is still poetry, still understatement. The Lord is the source of all light; every sun, every luminous nebula in the cosmos is just a bead in his necklace. There are quasars, we are told, a million million times as bright as our own sun. The universe is filled with light; it pulsates with the power of the Lord.

The greatest wonder is that this tremendous radiance reflected throughout the cosmos shines within us too. As our spiritual awareness grows, as our separateness goes and our ego dissolves, we will experience a tremendous effulgence spreading throughout our consciousness, which no experience of the senses can ever help us comprehend. But Jesus gives the perfect description: "Thy whole body shall be full of light."

तत्रैकस्थं जगत्कृत्स्नं प्रविभक्तमनेकधा ।
अपश्यद्देवदेवस्य शरीरे पाण्डवस्तदा ॥ ११-१३ ॥

13. There, within the body of the Lord, Arjuna saw all the manifold forms in the universe united as one.

Here we have a glimpse of the mystery of the universe, which fills both mystic and scientist with awe. I get spellbound when I read about some of the discoveries in astronomy and atomic physics and realize that all this is just an infinitesimal part of the glory of the Lord. Even professional astronomers admit that the mind reels before some of these discoveries; the intellect cannot grasp their implications. We cannot even look at our own sun, and here are quasars that are millions of times brighter than our sun. We are told there are neutron stars in the universe where matter is so dense that a tablespoon of it is conjectured to weigh forty trillion tons. When matter gets this dense, the force of gravity is so immense at the core that the star is liable to collapse internally from its own weight, and millions and millions of tons of matter just disappear into a "black hole" in space – a bottomless hole with zero volume. You and I ask, "What kind of a hole is that?

Where did all that matter go?" And the astronomers can only shrug; they just don't know.

Now, in wonder, Arjuna sees that this whole vast universe of incessant change is all one in the Lord. The Gita will express this oneness in the language of poetry, drawing on all sorts of images from Hindu mythology. But the discoveries of science throw light on Arjuna's experience of unity too. Biologists tell us that every living thing, from a simple virus to a human being, has essentially the same DNA. It is a very personal tie that binds us to the beasts of the field and the birds of the air; even the plankton in the ocean are our kith and kin. But the unity extends deeper still, for the elements of life are the very same elements that are found throughout the universe, created in the depths of stars and strewn through space in the explosions of stellar death.

In the language of modern physics, the fabric of space and time, matter and energy, is continuous throughout the universe, from the nucleus of an atom to the farthest galaxy. To a great physicist like Albert Einstein, all forms of matter and energy are interrelated, and every point in the universe – say, an electron in one of the atoms of my hand – is affected by the rest of the universe as a whole. If we could see life at the subatomic level, the material objects we cling to for security would dissolve into patterns of energy, and the universe would be nothing but a sea of light. It is a precise description, but it is the language of Sri Ramakrishna too. On this level, we are at the very threshold of matter. The atomic particles of our everyday world are not fixed or solid; they come and go in and out of existence in the smallest fraction of a second. It is as if the Lord is teasing us in this subatomic world by playing a game of hide-and-seek. He comes and goes so quickly that we can never be sure where he is; no sooner do we think we have caught him than he slips away.

The deeper we probe into the nature of the universe, whether it is the vastness of space or the infinitesimal world within the atom, the more we shall see the glory of the Lord revealed. When I look at pictures taken through an electron microscope or the telescope at Mount Palomar, I don't see only beautiful, abstract patterns; I see illustrations for the Gita, showing the myriad forms of creation flowing from the Lord. Even the Andromeda galaxy and I have a common bond. In microcosm and macrocosm, the Lord holds all together in his embrace.

ततः स विस्मयाविष्टो हृष्टरोमा धनंजयः ।
प्रणम्य शिरसा देवं कृताञ्जलिरभाषत ॥ ११-१४॥
अर्जुन उवाच ।
पश्यामि देवांस्तव देव देहे
सर्वांस्तथा भूतविशेषसंघान् ।
ब्रह्माणमीशं कमलासनस्थम्
ऋषींश्च सर्वानुरगांश्च दिव्यान् ॥ ११-१५॥

14. Filled with amazement, his hair standing on end with joy, Arjuna bowed before the Lord with folded palms and spoke these words.

ARJUNA:

15. O Lord, I see within your body all the gods and every kind of living creature. I see Brahmā, the Creator, seated on a lotus; I see the ancient sages and the celestial serpents.

Once, it is said, the women of baby Krishna's village came running to tell his foster mother, Yashodā, that her little boy had been eating sand. Baby Krishna denied everything, but his mother saw the look in his eyes and caught hold of his chin to try to see for herself. Krishna obligingly opened his little mouth wide. There, within that little rosebud of a mouth, Yashodā saw the vast starry sky with its innumerable worlds, and all the creatures that had ever lived and would ever be born. It must have lasted only for a moment, but Yashodā was overcome with fear and wonder, for this was the child she had been scolding and treating like her own.

This is the vision that Arjuna is entering now, which is beyond anything that words can express. Some of the greatest figures in the world's spiritual traditions have been left speechless by the vision of God. Moses, it is said, returned silent from his encounter on Sinai, though his face was ablaze with the glory of the Lord. St. Paul lay paralyzed for three days and three nights after his vision of light on the road to Damascus. Pascal, a brilliant mathematician and writer, could only set down fragments: "*Certitude, certitude; sentiment, joie, paix*" – certitude, emotion, joy, peace. And St. Thomas Aquinas, the architect of Catholic theology, said simply after his experience, "All that I have written is no more than straw." Even the theories of modern physics become poetic when they try to describe the unity of life, and though their images may be more sophisticated than the sages and celestial serpents of this verse, I wonder if they have any more capacity to inform our deeper understanding.

But even if this vision of unity cannot be conveyed through words or pictures, it can be communicated in more subtle ways. It is said that of all the ways of giving spiritual instruction, the highest and most effective is through the living, personal example of an illumined teacher. Such people express the awareness of unity in everything they do, and through a kind of spiritual osmosis, those who love their teacher deeply can absorb this awareness and slowly learn to put it into practice in their own lives. That is why it is said that spiritual awareness is not so much taught as caught. I learned this from my grandmother, who is one of the most accomplished spiritual teachers I have seen or even read about in the annals of mysticism. She scarcely ever spoke about these things, but she was so skillful in conveying her awareness that it was not until much later, when I finally turned to meditation, that I realized that she had been my spiritual teacher all along. Most people have to find a teacher. I was literally born into my teacher's arms, and even now it fills me with wonder to see how every day I become a little more like her, trying in a small way to live out the awareness of unity which she, in her infinite love for me, implanted in my heart when I was growing up.

अनेकबाहूदरवक्त्रनेत्रं
पश्यामि त्वां सर्वतोऽनन्तरूपम् ।
नान्तं न मध्यं न पुनस्तवादिं
पश्यामि विश्वेश्वर विश्वरूप ॥ ११-१६ ॥

16. I see infinite mouths and arms, stomachs and eyes, and you are embodied in them all. I see you everywhere, without beginning, middle, or end. You are the Lord of all creation.

In Sanskrit, one of the names of the Lord is Vishnu, 'he who is everywhere.' Vishnu has a thousand names, which comprise all together one of the most sonorous of Sanskrit poems, and almost every name is to remind us of the all-embracing, all-pervading presence of the Lord.

It is said that when the suffering of Mother Earth became too great for her to bear, she came to Vishnu, the Lord of Love, and begged him to incarnate himself in a human body to lead humanity back to the unity of life. That is the story behind baby Krishna's birth, and just as with Jesus and the Compassionate Buddha, there are a number of stories surrounding this event which every Hindu knows from childhood, which help convey in simple language what it means for the Lord to be born among us in human form.

According to the Hindu tradition in Kerala, a baby is not given a name until it is a year old. Then there is a big feast to which all the friends and relatives of the family come to celebrate his or her birth when the name is given. Now, when baby Krishna was born, very much as with the baby Jesus, there was a prophecy that caused the king of the realm to want to take his life. But his parents managed to spirit the baby away to foster parents in the country almost as soon as he was born, and so it is in their home that the naming day celebration takes place. As is traditional, his foster parents, Yashodā and Nanda, invite a great sage named Garga to give their new child his name. Neither Yashodā nor Nanda nor anyone else in the village knows little Krishna's real nature, but Garga has only to see the baby to realize that he has been asked to give a name to the Lord Himself. He falls to his knees to worship the newborn child, and then he asks the foster mother and father, "What name can I give to a little boy who already has a thousand names?"

It is a beautiful way of reminding us that the Lord is in everyone, that all of our names are his names. It isn't just a thousand names; that is the poetic way of saying it. He has billions of names, for he is within the heart of everyone on earth. The infinite numbers of arms and eyes in Arjuna's vision are not the product of an artist's imagination; in the depths of his consciousness, Arjuna is seeing the Lord of the universe simultaneously wearing the countless masks of all his creation. Ramdas, who is one of the most practical and inspiring mystics of this century, tells us:

> Whenever we see any form, we must see not only the external form, but also the indwelling Reality. This is the true vision which liberates us from the sense of diversity and makes us realize the oneness of all existence. This is the message of the rishis. It is not merely in particular holy places and solitudes that we should have this vision, but even in the marketplace and the bazaar we should be able to maintain the consciousness of unity in diversity. We must feel the divine presence always about us.

किरीटिनं गदिनं चक्रिणं च
तेजोराशिं सर्वतो दीप्तिमन्तम् ।
पश्यामि त्वां दुर्निरीक्ष्यं समन्ताद्
दीप्तानलार्कद्युतिमप्रमेयम् ॥ ११-१७॥

17. You wear a crown and carry a mace and disk. Your radiance is blinding and immeasurable; it fills the universe with light like the fiery sun blazing in every direction.

Even Emily Post would appreciate the way the orthodox Hindu worships the sun; it is a very personal way of saying thank you to him who makes it possible for us to live, to work and play, to go to school, or even to make money. For us he is not just the sun; he is *Divākara*, "Mr. Daymaker." We draw our light from him, we draw our heat from him, we get our food from him; all life depends on the continuous miracle of the sun.

Here again, the astrophysicists can help us understand the dimensions of this miracle. Every second of every day for fifteen billion years, they say, 657 million metric tons of solar hydrogen are converted into 652.5 million metric tons of helium through a process of nuclear fusion – the same basic transformation as in the hydrogen bomb. The heckler will say, "Wait a minute; what happened to that other four and a half million tons of hydrogen?" And Mr. Daymaker replies, "That is what gets converted to energy; otherwise my solar furnace can't give you any heat or light. $E=mc^2$, you know; you can look it up in my file." The accounting is perfect. Everything is taken care of; there is no wastage. In all these millions, even an ounce is taken into account. That's how I understand those simple words, "He's got the whole world in his hands." He has his eye not only on these millions of tons of hydrogen; he has his eye even on the little micrograms. In Hinduism this is the aspect of the Lord that is called Chitragupta, the "cosmic accountant," where the Lord himself does his own auditing. Sri Krishna is very thrifty; everything must balance. In accounting circles in India there used to be a joke about an auditor looking over some particularly complicated account books where the entry was often GOK – "God only knows." It is like that. At the end of every day he tells the sun, "What about this, *hmm*? Four and a half million. Account for it." And then, smiling to himself, he writes, "GOK."

In other words, there is nothing superfluous in life. Everything is perfectly dovetailed into a delicate balance of matter and energy that extends throughout the universe, and which is just right for maintaining life here on earth. We look at the sun and take all this for granted; we forget the immensity of this miracle that makes life possible. It is not simply a matter of liberating an incomprehensible amount of energy every second; all this has to be tempered to our needs. The amount of energy released at the core of the sun is so vast that if it were released at the surface, there would be a wave of death that would spread throughout the solar system, destroying all life in its wake. Sir James Jeans, the British astronomer, writes that if we could take a bit of the sun no bigger than a pinhead and bring it here to earth, its heat could kill a person standing ninety-four miles away. To keep things from getting too hot for us, the Lord makes a very clever arrangement. The rays created at the core of the sun, astrophysicists tell us, are softened on their journey to the surface by atoms which play no part in the fusion process. They are the sidewalk superintendents who stand around and make comments; their job is to modulate the gamma rays until they leave the sun at just the right temperature to make life possible on earth.

When astronomers see all this, they too may feel a sense of awe at how delicately everything is balanced. But where the astronomer sees the laws of thermodynamics, the mystic sees the all-pervasive love of the Lord. The mystical poet William Blake declared: "I look through the eye, not with it. When the sun rises, I do not see a round disk of fire somewhat like a guinea; O no, no, I see an innumerable company of the heavenly host crying, *Holy, holy, holy*".

There is no contradiction at all between Blake's vision and the scientist's. When I say that even the miracle of the sun is an expression of the Lord's love, it is not that I think there is someone waving his flute and saying, "Let these hydrogen nuclei fuse and become one!" The Lord is there in the nucleus of each atom, and the laws by which these transformations of matter and energy come about simply express the unity of his creation. If a star could talk, it wouldn't write poetry about love; it would sing the praises of gravitation. Romantic young stars just a hundred thousand years old or so would be yearning to lose themselves in the immense attraction of a black hole. For them, the unity of life expresses itself in forces like these; for us, it expresses itself in love. The language is different, but the unity is the same.

त्वमक्षरं परमं वेदितव्यं
त्वमस्य विश्वस्य परं निधानम् ।
त्वमव्ययः शाश्वतधर्मगोप्ता
सनातनस्त्वं पुरुषो मतो मे ॥११-१८॥
अनादिमध्यान्तमनन्तवीर्यम्
अनन्तबाहुं शशिसूर्यनेत्रम् ।
पश्यामि त्वां दीप्तहुताशवक्त्रं
स्वतेजसा विश्वमिदं तपन्तम् ॥११-१९॥
द्यावापृथिव्योरिदमन्तरं हि
व्याप्तं त्वयैकेन दिशश्च सर्वाः ।
दृष्ट्वाद्भुतं रूपमिदं तवोग्रं
लोकत्रयं प्रव्यथितं महात्मन् ॥११-२०॥
अमी हि त्वा सुरसंघा विशन्ति
केचिद्भीताः प्राञ्जलयो गृणन्ति ।
स्वस्तीत्युक्त्वा महर्षिसिद्धसंघाः
स्तुवन्ति त्वां स्तुतिभिः पुष्कलाभिः ॥११-२१॥

18. You are the supreme, changeless Reality, the only thing to be known. You are the refuge of all creation, the immortal spirit, the eternal guardian and support of all.

19. You are without beginning, middle, or end; you touch everything with your infinite power. The sun and moon are your eyes, and your mouth is fire; your radiance warms the entire cosmos.

20. O Lord, your presence fills the heavens and the earth and reaches into every corner of the universe. I see the three worlds trembling before this vision of your wonderful and terrible form.

21. The gods enter your being, some calling out and greeting you in fear. Great saints sing your glory, praying, "May all be well!"

Arjuna tells us over and over again how he is overcome with wonder at this revelation of the infinite power of the Lord. Scientists sometimes are suspicious when they hear all this ascribed to the power of God, but this is simply because they do not understand what the word *God* means to those who have realized him. All of us in the modern world have been conditioned to look upon God as something outside us, something other than us; even in our wildest dreams it is not possible to suspect that he is our real Self. This is the core of the mystical experience, and nowhere has it been more beautifully expressed than in the Sufi tradition, where these great Muslim mystics will say that he whom the vast heavens cannot contain is contained within your heart and mine.

In other words, there is no conflict between the vision of a great scientist and the experience of a great mystic, as we can see in the work of a scientist like Einstein who has access to a higher mode of knowing than the intellect. One such figure in modern astronomy is Abbé Georges Lemaître, a Catholic priest from Belgium, who hit upon a theory about the origin of the universe that shows not only brilliant intellect but the intuition of genius as well. Lemaître suggested that the cosmos was originally packed into an incomprehensibly dense primeval atom, a kind of "cosmic egg" in which there is neither time nor space – perhaps the way matter in a neutron star becomes so dense that it collapses into a black hole, pulling space and time in after it. It is very much the language of the ancient Hindu scriptures, which talk about *Hiranyagarbha* or *Brahmānda*, the 'egg of Brahman,' the germ out of which the cosmos grew. According to Lemaître, this cosmic egg exploded to become our universe, and it is still expanding from the force of this explosion.

Now, the question naturally arises, "What made this primeval egg explode?" The scientist, of course, looks for some cause other than the egg, some external force which struck a big blow at this egg and made it explode. But the mystic will say that the power of the Lord is right there in the egg itself – just as it is within everything, from the hydrogen nuclei in the core of the sun to the seed that will grow into a giant tree. When I look at an acorn, though I don't know much about botany, I know that the power of the Lord is contained in that little seed. That power shows itself not in making a tree appear out of nowhere, but in the seed transforming itself and bursting open to send out a slender shoot that pushes its way upwards to grow into a sturdy tree. Everywhere in that tree there is the expression of the power of the Lord – in the growing branch, in the leaves making food with the energy of the sunlight, in the sap running through every growing part.

Gandhi once said that we may look upon God as *dharma,* the Eternal Law – very much as a scientist would – or as *dharmakartri,* the Lawmaker. Because of our intellectual orientation, many of us today have no trouble accepting it when a mystic like the Buddha talks about an unchanging Law that underlies all existence. It is when we talk about a Lawgiver that many people have reservations. Yet either way, it is the same Reality. Sri Ramakrishna goes straight to the heart of the matter by saying God is both personal and impersonal; the Law and the Lawgiver are two aspects of one supreme Godhead. All laws derive from the same unity of life. The laws of physics or chemistry all express various aspects of the unity underlying the world of change, and though the wording of physical laws will vary as our understanding grows, it is the same unity that is behind both physical and spiritual laws.

In other words, the universe is one. There cannot be a number of unrelated laws; the result would be chaos. If there were no underlying unity in life, there could be no order; we could never know what to expect. We could plant an acorn and poison oak might grow; why not? We could throw a tennis ball into the air and it might never come down. There are laws everywhere, in all the phenomena of existence. The mystic would say that all these laws come from the same source, express the same unity. The law of gravity comes from the same source as the principle of Archimedes; Boyle's Law – it used to plague me as a student – comes from the same source as the law of relativity. How could it be otherwise? One of the most fervent hopes of Einstein was to find an overriding law of nature in which all the laws of matter and energy would be unified. This is very much the driving question in some of the ancient Hindu scriptures, too: "What is That by knowing which all other things may be known?" In samādhi we have direct knowledge of this unity, which is both the source of all laws and the Lawgiver as well.

रुद्रादित्या वसवो ये च साध्या
 विश्वे ऽश्विनौ मरुतश्चोष्मपाश्च ।
गन्धर्वयक्षासुरसिद्धसंघा
 वीक्षन्ते त्वा विस्मिताश्चैव सर्वे ॥११-२२॥
रूपं महत्ते बहुवक्त्रनेत्रं
 महाबाहो बहुबाहूरुपादम् ।
बहूदरं बहुदंष्ट्राकरालं
 दृष्ट्वा लोकाः प्रव्यथितास्तथाहम् ॥११-२३॥
नभःस्पृशं दीप्तमनेकवर्णं
 व्यात्ताननं दीप्तविशालनेत्रम् ।
दृष्ट्वा हि त्वां प्रव्यथितान्तरात्मा
 धृतिं न विन्दामि शमं च विष्णो ॥११-२४॥
दंष्ट्राकरालानि च ते मुखानि
 दृष्ट्वैव कालानलसंनिभानि ।
दिशो न जाने न लभे च शर्म
 प्रसीद देवेश जगन्निवास ॥११-२५॥

22. The multitudes of demigods and demons
are all overwhelmed by the sight of you.
23. O Lord, at the sight of your mighty arms, the
multitude of your eyes and mouths, your arms
and legs, your stomachs and your fearful teeth,
I and the entire universe shake in terror.
24. O Vishnu, I can see your eyes shining; your mouths
are open, you glitter in an array of colors, and your
body touches the sky. I look at you and my heart
trembles; I have lost all courage and all peace of mind.

> *25. When I see your mouths with their fearful teeth burning like the fires at the end of time, I forget where I am and I have no place to go. O Lord, you are the support of the universe; have mercy on me!*

Arjuna has been overcome with awe at the splendor of the Lord; now he describes with horror the grim aspect of the Lord as the destroyer, the power which brings phenomenal existence to an end, whether it is a microbe, a person, or a star. If it is a microbe, the end may come after a few hours; if it is a star, it may not come for billions of years; but sooner or later, as the Buddha puts it, all that has been put together must one day be dissolved.

The Hindu scriptures make this point by drawing a comparison to the monsoon moth, whose life span is only about two and a half hours. After the torrential monsoon rains in South India, thousands of these moths fill the air. They come like the locusts in the biblical plague; you cannot even yawn without running the risk of getting one in your mouth. For just a short while they are everywhere; and then, suddenly, they are gone. Their lives are spent in just a fraction of a day. And the scriptures say, look at the concept these moths must have of time. They don't want a calendar on their wall; they will say, "What's the use? What is this 'month'? We don't believe there *is* a month; life is exhausted in two and a half hours. Give us a calendar for just two and a half hours; give us a watch for one hundred and fifty minutes to last us from birth to death." Every little second would count terribly; every millionth part of a second would be precious to that moth. If we were to try to tell these creatures that a human being lives hundreds of thousands of times longer, they would not even be able to grasp the scope of it. And yet – it is a very grim reminder – our own lives are compared to the lives of these monsoon moths, who come and go in a matter of hours.

At the other end of the scale, there is our own sun – 'Mr. Daymaker.' He was born about six billion years ago, and – poor fellow – he will probably go the way of all suns after about ten billion years of age. Among the galaxies they would all say, "What a premature death; the fellow didn't last long. Here yesterday and gone tomorrow." It is like the day of Brahman and the night of Brahman, measured in units of a million million years. We cannot even grasp these things; for us the universe is eternal. But it is just a difference in scale. Just as fifty years from now not many of us are going to be playing baseball or mowing the front lawn, so after a few more billion years the sun will lose its rugged, youthful vitality. Already our Mr. Sun is middle-aged, and gradually, with the passage of time, he will become a solar Falstaff, big and lethargic. He may pretend to be the same boisterous fellow as before, but we would know otherwise. The fire at his core, his *prāna* or life-breath, now about fifteen million degrees Kelvin, will slowly burn lower and lower, and as his temperature drops, life on earth will become impossible. Then he will shrink into what astronomers call a white dwarf, and finally, when his life span of ten billion years is over, he will no longer be a sun; he will be just a lifeless body no larger than the earth, another dead shell floating in space. One astronomer even says that the phenomenon of the black hole is very much like a giant star digging its own grave, falling in, and pulling the grave after it. It is a terrifying picture. According to the Gita, even the universe itself will come to an end. Estimates of its life span begin at forty billion years and go up from there, but eventually Sri Krishna will come as death and say, "Even for you, time is up."

The wonder of this is that you and I can break out of this terrible cycle to which even the galaxies are subject; you and I can conquer death. This is the promise of all the great religions. We all accept death as inevitable, but there have been spiritual geniuses in every age who dared to challenge death and emerged victorious. Mohammed tells us the secret of this victory in four simple words: "Die before you die." In the Hindu tradition we have a saying that just as a robber does not kill someone who carries no precious gems or gold, death cannot destroy those who no longer wear the jewels of their selfish desires. We go through life decked with such desires: "I must eat this food, wear that dress, travel to this country, own that kind of car." It is these unfulfilled cravings that tie us to our physical and mental condition. Then, when the great robber Death sees us, he cries out, "Here is a rich person. So many desires for me to rob!" If we can learn through the practice of meditation to remove all our selfish desires, we will have cut through the obsessive identification with the body once and for all. After that, though our body will come to an end in the course of time, there will be no rupture in consciousness at the time of death. Instead there will be an unbroken awareness of our real Self, the Lord of Love, who cannot be affected even by the last great change called death.

अमी च त्वां धृतराष्ट्रस्य पुत्राः
सर्वे सहैवावनिपालसंघैः ।
भीष्मो द्रोणः सूतपुत्रस्तथासौ
सहास्मदीयैरपि योधमुख्यैः ॥११-२६॥
वक्त्राणि ते त्वरमाणा विशन्ति
दंष्ट्राकरालानि भयानकानि ।
केचिद्विलग्ना दशनान्तरेषु
संदृश्यन्ते चूर्णितैरुत्तमाङ्गैः ॥११-२७॥
यथा नदीनां बहवोऽम्बुवेगाः
समुद्रमेवाभिमुखा द्रवन्ति ।
तथा तवामी नरलोकवीरा
विशन्ति वक्त्राण्यभिविज्वलन्ति ॥११-२८॥
यथा प्रदीप्तं ज्वलनं पतंगा
विशन्ति नाशाय समृद्धवेगाः ।
तथैव नाशाय विशन्ति लोकास्
तवापि वक्त्राणि समृद्धवेगाः ॥११-२९॥
लेलिह्यसे ग्रसमानः समन्ताल्
लोकान्समग्रान्वदनैर्ज्वलद्भिः ।
तेजोभिरापूर्य जगत्समग्रं
भासस्तवोग्राः प्रतपन्ति विष्णो ॥११-३०॥

> *26–27. I see all the sons of Dhritarāshtra; I see Bhīshma, Drona, and Karna; I see our warriors and all the kings who are here to fight. All are rushing into your awful jaws; I see some of them crushed by your teeth.*
> *28–29. As rivers flow into the ocean, all the warriors of this world are passing into your fiery jaws; all creatures rush to their destruction like moths into a flame.*
> *30. You lap the worlds into your burning mouths and swallow them. Filled with your terrible radiance, O Vishnu, the whole of creation bursts into flames.*

This is the Lord in his most terrifying form, the personification of death. To those who follow the voice of self-will, who pursue their personal pleasure and profit at the expense of their family and friends, their community and their world, death often comes in the awful form of violence.

Because of years of conditioning, particularly by the mass media, most of us have become caught in a way of life that increases separateness fiercely. Now we find it difficult even to see the connection between our egocentric lives and the violence which threatens us today. But on every level, from international warfare to domestic quarrels, to ignore our unity is to invite social chaos and destruction. Even the ideological differences between two superpowers, for example, sustain the interest in armaments around the globe. We have become so accustomed to discussions of nuclear warfare and its threat to destroy the earth that we hardly raise an eyebrow when we read that there are enough nuclear weapons on alert around the world to kill each person on earth twelve times or more.

In 1960, in constant 1983 dollars, world military expenditures were 344 billion. By 1986 they were approaching 900 billion – $1.7 million dollars every minute. This much buying means a lot of selling, and the big arms sellers are still the United States and the Soviet Union, who hold roughly half of this highly profitable market. Some of the biggest customers, ironically, are the developing countries, who now account for one fifth of the world's arms expenditures. Since 1963, almost half of this trade has come from the United States and its NATO allies; another third came from the Soviet Union. We seldom think how we cripple these emerging nations by encouraging them to buy weapons. But the money they spend on guns means less food, less housing, and poorer medical attention for people who lack these essentials of life.

When we pursue this trade in armaments, profitable though it may be, the Gita reminds us grimly that we are courting death. This courtship embraces more than the immediate buyer and seller. It includes the manufacturers and intermediaries and even those of us who fail to raise a voice of protest. The reminder is not pleasant, but the Gita has to shock us into seeing the tragic connection between the petty pursuits we follow with such narrow vision and the death and violence that torment our world today.

Fortunately, we have good reason to believe that even problems like the nuclear arms race can be solved if we set our minds to the task. On December 8, 1987, President Reagan and General Secretary Gorbachev signed the first nuclear arms reduction agreement in history – only a first step, yet a "truly momentous development," as President Rajiv Gandhi of India acclaimed, for it "vividly demonstrated that given the necessary political will," obstacles to peace can be overcome. But we should not expect governments to provide that will. We, the people, must insist on it ourselves.

Violence, of course, is not just an international problem. We Americans kill our own family and friends more frequently than do citizens of any other civilized nation. In the drawers, closets, and glove compartments of the United States are over sixty million handguns – part of an arsenal of private weapons that amounts to nearly two hundred million firearms. People use these guns because they are available. Nearly three out of four murders committed in this country are "crimes of passion": that is, the killing of a family member or a friend in the blind heat of anger, often simply because a weapon was at hand. On the average, 69 persons were murdered by handguns every day in 1980; and in 1981, when President Reagan was shot, one handgun was sold every twelve seconds in the year. Yet we still can't make up our minds to effect some simple measure to control this gun menace.

This kind of insensitivity to violence will plunge not only you and me into suffering, but our children and grandchildren as well. The Gita compares this to the life of a moth which rushes into a flame. Look at the monsoon moths I mentioned in the preceding verses: only two and a half hours to live, and even that is too long for them; they rush to their extinction in the very first fire they see. After the monsoon rains in Kerala, when the evening sky is so full of those moths that you cannot eat or sleep in peace, people light huge bonfires, and it is a terrifying sight to see thousands on thousands of these creatures throwing themselves into the flames to die. Now, in the depths of his consciousness, Arjuna sees all the warriors who are with him on the battlefield, uncles and cousins, friends and enemies, throwing themselves like moths into the jaws of death.

The more we build our civilization on selfishness and separateness, the Gita is telling us, the more we live like these monsoon moths. When we go on pursuing pleasure and prestige and power, we become blind and deaf to everything around us. Then we forget that the stream of life runs out quickly, as a rain-swollen river runs out to sea. This is why the great spiritual teachers of all religions tell us not to postpone the spiritual life for even one day; every day lost is one we cannot regain. We are moving closer to death with every moment that passes, and once this realization penetrates our hearts, we will begin doing everything we can to go beyond death here and now.

आख्याहि मे को भवानुग्ररूपो
नमोऽस्तु ते देववर प्रसीद ।
विज्ञातुमिच्छामि भवन्तमाद्यं
न हि प्रजानामि तव प्रवृत्तिम् ॥ ११-३१ ॥

31. Tell me who you are, O Lord of terrible form.
I bow before you; have mercy! I want to know
who you are, you who existed before all creation.
Your nature and workings confound me.

Arjuna is shaken to the depths of his being by this vision of the destructive power of the Lord. Just like you and me, he stammers, "I don't understand; you are the Lord of Love, but all I see now is a terrifying vision of birth and death, suffering and destruction. Have mercy upon me." He has glimpsed the central truth of existence – all life, from the simple virus to the vast galaxy, is marching from birth to death, to birth and death, again and again.

Death is not an event which takes place on a particular day in a particular place. It is a process that starts the day we are conceived in our mother's womb, and every moment that passes brings us that much closer to the day this body will be taken away from us. Even within us the cells of the body are dying every second; it is only the limits of our vision that keep us from seeing that the body we identify with is in a constant state of change. That is why the Book of Common Prayer tells us in haunting words, "In the midst of life we are in death." We can escape this process only when we cure ourselves of the fatal disease of ignorance which makes us identify with the body.

In other words, as Sri Ramakrishna puts it, life is a hospital; the Lord has sent us here so that we may cure ourselves of separateness and become whole. When we encounter violence and hostility, we have an opportunity to improve our condition by remaining steadfast and secure. Unfortunately, we all too often worsen things by retaliating; then we suffer a relapse and have to be readmitted to intensive care. But finally, once we have suffered enough, we realize that retaliation only spreads the highly communicable disease of self-will to everyone around us.

The Compassionate Buddha's Four Noble Truths are a perfect diagnosis of our sickness by a supreme physician. After a careful examination the Buddha gives us the First Noble Truth, that we are seriously ill. Then he gives us the Second Noble Truth, that the cause of the disease is the fierce thirst of self-will. It is a worldwide epidemic, and no one has any immunity against it. At this point, thoroughly shaken, we ask, "What are my chances, doctor? Please give me a straight answer; I can take it." And the Buddha, full of mercy, gives us the Third Noble Truth: "The prognosis is very bright, if you will follow this eight-course treatment." The Fourth Noble Truth is the Buddha's prescription for a complete cure, the Noble Eightfold Path: right knowledge, right purpose, right speech, right conduct, right occupation, right effort, right attention, and right meditation. It is a prescription we can follow right in our own home, by practicing meditation, turning our attention away from personal desires, and trying constantly to serve the welfare of everyone around us.

श्रीभगवानुवाच ।
कालो ऽस्मि लोकक्षयकृत्प्रवृद्धो
लोकान्समाहर्तुमिह प्रवृत्तः ।
ऋते ऽपि त्वा न भविष्यन्ति सर्वे
ये ऽवस्थिताः प्रत्यनीकेषु योधाः ॥ ११-३२ ॥

SRI KRISHNA:

32. I am time, the destroyer of all; I have come to consume the world. Even without your participation, all the warriors gathered here will die.

These are words that have made the Gita known the world over. It was this verse that came to Robert Oppenheimer's mind as he watched the first atomic bomb explode across the desert sky. The devastating word used here is *kāla,* which has a double-edged meaning – 'time' and 'death.' Time *is* death; time is separateness. Its all-devouring jaws are following us always, closer than our shadow. As we grow older and our family and friends begin to pass away, we see how relentlessly time is pursuing all of us; every death should remind us of the imminence of our own. People with whom we played and laughed – they are no more. Great figures who have walked across the stage of life – they are no more. Dynasties and empires have returned to dust. It is only because of the mercy of the Lord that you and I survive each day. Those who are sensitive to this have tremendous motivation to take to the spiritual path and slay this monster of time and death.

Arjuna's experience in this verse is not poetic fancy. It is a realistic vision of what time means, which in a smaller way can come to anyone. A friend of mine in India, a great devotee of Krishna, was once in the midst of a group of people who had gathered on a religious holiday to sing songs in praise of the Lord. At such times her intense devotion used to bring on a deeper state of consciousness. Something must have triggered such a change, because she suddenly looked around in horror; before her eyes, the people there turned into bare skeletons.

The vision lasted several moments. It terrified her so deeply that it haunted her for years. When she confided it to me, she called it the most dreadful thing she had ever experienced. I replied, "It's probably the greatest thing you could have experienced. Instead of blocking it out, try to remember it always." Her whole attitude was changed; instead of a curse, she began to understand it as a blessing.

This is the same service my grandmother rendered me. Even when I was a boy, just entering my teens, she knew how to open a little window in my consciousness and tell me, "Look carefully. If you can see far enough you'll see Yama waiting for you, just as he is waiting for us all." I have to admit that I did not appreciate this at the time. I could not understand why I, among all the children I knew, should be singled out to be made aware of this dreadful destiny. And Granny seldom tried to explain herself; she planted the seeds of this awareness without ever using words. Though all my cousins were shielded from such experiences, she loved me so passionately that she opened that window onto death for me again and again. More than anything else, she wanted me to understand that nothing is more important than remembering death – not to live in fear, but to make it our first priority to go beyond time and death here and now.

Even now I marvel at the artistry of her teaching. Whenever someone died in our large ancestral family, relatives and friends would gather around a central courtyard in my ancestral home where the grim ceremonies of a funeral are performed. Most of the other boys and girls would not be present on such occasions. But my grandmother insisted that I stand right in front and watch carefully what was taking place. The body was bathed and taken from the courtyard, and as it was carried away a heartbreaking chorus of hundreds of voices would break out in lamentation. Often it was old people crying, but when it was children my heart would almost stop beating at the sound. Then Granny would tell my uncle, “Now take him to the funeral pyre.” I didn’t know or guess that this was what great love means. All I knew was that I had to go and stand in the southern courtyard while the body was lowered onto the pyre, to watch the most harrowing scenes I have witnessed in my life.

This fate is waiting for everyone. “I am time, the destroyer of all; I have come to consume the world.” For most of us these are only words; for my friend they suddenly became a vivid, shattering experience, burned like Arjuna’s into her memory. Far from morbid, I think nothing could be more positive. It is no blessing to be able to forget death, to pretend it does not exist, while we go on playing with the froth and foam of life. It can be the greatest of blessings to remember that every moment is precious, and a lifetime not too long.

My mother is in her late eighties now, a ripe age by any standard. She came to live with us at Ramagiri the same summer we moved in, when work on the first chapter of this book had just begun. Now, in the eleventh chapter, I open the door to her bedroom every morning and stand for a few minutes to watch her sleeping. So much love floods my heart, and so much sorrow. In her younger days she was lissome and graceful, the most beautiful woman in our village. On the Blue Mountain, even in her sixties, she used to walk four, five, six miles a day. Now she can barely walk, scarcely get up or drink her tea. Often it is a great effort for her simply to open her eyes to see that I am there.

If you and I have the good fortune to move so close to ninety, this is the state our bodies are likely to be in too. It is love that makes me say this. It is love that makes me remind myself and those around me to keep this verse in mind every day; it will give a clear goal in every activity, bring complete dedication, strengthen you greatly in the hour of temptation. In my own sādhana, whenever I was tempted by some strong physical urge, the recollection of my granny’s teaching would suddenly well up in my consciousness. I would see death standing by my side, and that temptation would turn to ashes. Similarly, when you feel angry, jealous, hostile, or depressed, remember; this is waiting for us all. There is no time to quarrel, no time to feel resentful or estranged. There is no time to waste on the pursuit of selfish pleasures that are over almost before they begin. Time runs out so soon! In our twenties and thirties we have ample margin to play with the toys life has to offer. But we should find out soon how fleeting they are, no more permanent than writing on water; for the tides of time can ebb away before we know.

Not long ago my mother was reminding me of one of my great-uncles, a contemporary of my granny. I stood in awe of him as a child because of his immense physical strength and courage. His mother was like that too, and when she shed her body at a very advanced age there was an elaborate funeral, lasting by Kerala tradition for fifteen days. On the fourteenth day the ashes were taken from the funeral pyre and carried to a river about six miles from my village to be immersed. We had a huge procession, including caparisoned elephants. And on the way back this great-uncle of mine, physically so strong, had a heart attack and passed away on the spot.

We couldn't believe it. He had seemed indestructible to us. Here we had just finished fifteen days of mourning, and now there was another fifteen. It made me understand that even when we are healthy and strong and vigorous, in the prime of our lives, death can come at any moment. A venerable monastic friend of mine on the Blue Mountain used to say, "Don't ever put things off until tomorrow. How do you know you will be here tomorrow?" It was not rhetoric for him. It was a simple awareness that we live from moment to moment by God's grace, and that none of us knows when Yama will come to cut the thread of our lives.

"This life of separateness," says the Compassionate Buddha, "may be compared to a dream, a phantasm, a bubble, a shadow, a drop of dew, a flash of lightning." It is good to bear in mind how evanescent life is so that we do not postpone the voyage across this sea of separate existence called *samsāra* in Sanskrit, the ceaseless process of birth and death.

तस्मात्त्वमुत्तिष्ठ यशो लभस्व
जित्वा शत्रून्भुङ्क्ष्व राज्यं समृद्धम् ।
मयैवैते निहताः पूर्वमेव
निमित्तमात्रं भव सव्यसाचिन् ॥ ११-३३ ॥
द्रोणं च भीष्मं च जयद्रथं च
कर्णं तथान्यानपि योधवीरान् ।
मया हतांस्त्वं जहि मा व्यथिष्ठा
युध्यस्व जेतासि रणे सपत्नान् ॥ ११-३४ ॥

33. Therefore arise, Arjuna; conquer your enemies and enjoy the glory of sovereignty. I have already slain all these warriors; you will only be my instrument.
34. Bhīshma, Drona, Jayadratha, Karna, and many others are already slain. Kill those whom I have killed. Do not be afraid. Fight in the battle and you will conquer your enemies.

In the *Mahābhārata,* the epic in which the Gita appears, Karna, Jayadratha, Bhīshma, and Drona are famous heroes among the forces ranged against Arjuna. For you and me, these forces are the forces of darkness, destructive powers which we can observe in our own lives. These particular warriors are mentioned because they were supposed to be invincible; yet, as the Lord reassures Arjuna, even the most destructive forces of violence can be brought to an end, because they violate the unity of life.

None of us, therefore, can consider himself exempt from the responsibility of joining battle against these forces. I have always had a great deal of reverence for Mahatma Gandhi because of the way he chose to take upon himself this gravest of responsibilities. Gandhi taught us that evil has no existence of its own; it is when we connive at evil that it exists. When we all withdraw our support from the powers of destruction, we discover that they are an enemy which has already been slain. This is the principle of *satyāgraha,* 'clinging to truth,' which is very inadequately translated as "nonviolent resistance."

Gandhi's discovery of satyāgraha took place when he was still a young, ineffectual lawyer in South Africa, when he was thrown out of a train at night in the high mountain town of Maritzburg because of his brown skin. This must have happened to hundreds before him, but in Gandhi's case it released a tremendous force within him; it whispered in his ear that he could draw upon his deepest resources, through the grace of the Lord, to bring this conflict between races to an end. Many years later, when he was asked what was the most creative experience of his life, Gandhi told the story of that night he spent shivering in the cold of the Maritzburg station, when he dedicated his life to eradicating the barriers which human selfishness has built up.

Gandhi was thrown into prison many times, but he was such a cheerful prisoner that he won the love and affection even of his jailers. While in prison in South Africa he made a pair of sandals especially for General Smuts, the man whose duty it was to oppose him in his struggle for justice. Later General Smuts returned the sandals as a gesture of friendship, saying, "I am not worthy to stand in the shoes of so great a man." Incidents like these, which became commonplace in Gandhi's life, showed us that there is no one who cannot respond to the person who is not trying to manipulate others for his own prestige, profit, or power. When we are with such a person all our defenses are lowered; we relax and begin to trust him, and gradually we too develop the conviction that goodness cannot fail to win and evil cannot fail to lose.

संजय उवाच ।
एतच्छ्रुत्वा वचनं केशवस्य
कृताञ्जलिर्वेपमानः किरीटी ।
नमस्कृत्वा भूय एवाह कृष्णं
सगद्गदं भीतभीतः प्रणम्य ॥ ११-३५॥
अर्जुन उवाच ।
स्थाने हृषीकेश तव प्रकीर्त्या
जगत्प्रहृष्यत्यनुरज्यते च ।
रक्षांसि भीतानि दिशो द्रवन्ति
सर्वे नमस्यन्ति च सिद्धसंघाः ॥ ११-३६॥
कस्माच्च ते न नमेरन्महात्मन्
गरीयसे ब्रह्मणो ऽप्यादिकर्त्रे ।
अनन्त देवेश जगन्निवास
त्वमक्षरं सदसत्तत्परं यत् ॥ ११-३७॥
त्वमादिदेवः पुरुषः पुराणस्
त्वमस्य विश्वस्य परं निधानम् ।
वेत्तासि वेद्यं च परं च धाम
त्वया ततं विश्वमनन्तरूप ॥ ११-३८॥

SANJAYA:

35. Having heard these words, Arjuna trembled in fear. With joined palms he bowed before Krishna and addressed him stammering.

ARJUNA:

36. O Krishna, it is right that the world delights and rejoices in your praise, that all the saints and sages bow down to you and all evil flees before you to the far corners of the universe.
37. How could they not worship you, O Lord? You are the eternal spirit, who existed before Brahmā the Creator and who will never cease to be. Lord

of the gods, you are the abode of the universe.
Changeless, you are what is and what is not, and
beyond the duality of existence and nonexistence.
38. You are the first among the gods, the timeless spirit,
the resting place of all beings. You are the knower
and the thing which is known. You are the home of
all; with your infinite form you pervade the cosmos.

In his joy, Arjuna tells Sri Krishna that he sees the entire cosmos rejoicing in the sovereignty of the Lord. "You are the refuge of all creatures," he says; "all beings in the universe can find their rest only in you. You are everything that has been and will ever be, and the beginning and end of all creation." This is the experience attained by men and women of God in every age and every tradition who have dared to tread the razor-edged path that leads from death to immortality. Saints and sages like Sri Ramakrishna or Shankara, St. Teresa of Ávila or Jalalu'l-Din Rumi, the Ba'al Shem Tov or Jacob Boehme, all use very similar words to tell what they have experienced with every cell of their being. The Italian mystic Jacapone da Todi says:

> The doors are flung open. United with the Lord, it possesses everything that is in him; it feels that which it never felt; it sees that which it never saw; it has that which it never thought could be; it tastes that which it never tasted. Being freed from itself, it now has attained perfection.

It is such a thrilling vision that even hearing about it makes us long for it. When we meet somebody who has actually been granted this awareness, our longing becomes intense; we light our torch from such a person, for he or she is burning with love for the Lord.

वायुर्यमोऽग्निर्वरुणः शशाङ्कः
प्रजापतिस्त्वं प्रपितामहश्च ।
नमो नमस्तेऽस्तु सहस्रकृत्वः
पुनश्च भूयोऽपि नमो नमस्ते ॥११-३९॥

39. You are Vāyu, god of wind, Yama, god of death, Agni, god of fire, and Varuna, god of water. You are the moon and the creator Prajāpati, and the great grandfather of all creatures. I bow before you and salute you again and again.

Arjuna is prostrating himself at the feet of Sri Krishna, whom he now sees everywhere, in everyone. His voice is trembling in awe as he tells the Lord: "You are the whole cosmos, yet you are beyond it; you are in my grandparents and my parents; you are in every creature and in all the forces of nature." Not only is the Lord in you and me, he is in the air, in the seas and rivers, in the life-giving power of heat and light and all the other forces of the universe. Existence is an unbroken continuum; only the scale of its parts is different. That is why we suffer so when we damage or exploit anything in nature. As John Muir, the great naturalist, observed, "When one tugs at a single thing in nature, he finds it attached to the rest of the world."

Thomas Vaughan, the English mystic, tells us simply: "Have thy heart in heaven and thy hands upon the earth. Ascend in piety and descend in charity. For this is the nature of Light and the way of the children of it." There is much the same image in Jewish mysticism, in which the life of the man or woman of God is said to be a ladder between heaven and earth. In all creatures, the God-conscious person sees the presence of the Lord.

Only when we become insensitive to this unity of life do we take the lives of other creatures wantonly. This is not only in matters like hunting and fishing; often we do not pay attention even to the needs of our pets. People take along a dog to entertain them during their summer vacation and then abandon it when they go back home, or think nothing of locking up a cat for life within an apartment in the city. Instead of denouncing such people, which will only alienate them, we can show persuasively how animals need to look to us as their protectors. My young friend Josh once went about this in a very winning manner. When he was in the third grade, his Boy Scout troop was planning a program for Thanksgiving. Josh championed the cause of the turkey.

Then someone suggested that they represent the Pilgrim Fathers fishing. The other boys thought this was a harmless pastime, but Josh got up and bravely said, "Fish are God's creatures, too." It speaks very highly of his friends that they could appreciate his point of view, and the Pilgrim Fathers were finally represented as gathering nuts – which, after all, are an excellent source of protein.

नमः पुरस्तादथ पृष्ठतस्ते
नमो ऽस्तु ते सर्वत एव सर्व ।
अनन्तवीर्यामितविक्रमस्त्वं
सर्वं समाप्नोषि ततो ऽसि सर्वः ॥ ११-४० ॥

40. You are behind me and in front of me; I bow to you on every side. Your power is immeasurable. You pervade everything; you are everything.

In Hindu society there is an age-old custom which prescribes the direction in which a person should lie when sleeping. One of the many names for the Lord is Dakshināmurtī, 'he who faces south,' and in this tradition it is considered improper to lie with one's feet towards the north, because that is the abode of the Lord.

Now, some centuries ago in the state of Tamil Nadu there was a great woman mystic named Āndāl, who once had to spend the night in the home of some orthodox devotees. When the woman of the house came to wake her up, she found her guest lying in the wrong direction. The woman was shocked and confused; she didn't know whether to call this great saint's attention to her mistake or not. But Āndāl, seeing her confusion, explained gently: "In what direction shall I point my feet that they not point towards the Lord? If I point them to the north, that is his home, but if I point them to the south, is he not there also? It is the same with east and west. I would sleep standing on my head rather than displease him, but he is above and beneath us also. Where shall I place my feet that they will not point towards the Lord?" It is the same language as in the Koran, in a verse which was a favorite of Mahatma Gandhi's: "Unto Allah belong the East and the West; wherever you turn, there is Allah's countenance."

In the climax of meditation called samādhi, when the mind becomes still and the ego is silenced, we shall see the Lord everywhere around us, enthroned in the heart of every creature. In the Hindu tradition we have countless stories to help us understand this experience. One such story is about Hanumān, an extraordinary monkey who is mentioned in the Hindu scriptures to remind us that the Lord dwells not only in human beings but in monkeys too. Hanumān is completely devoted to Rāma, an incarnation of the Lord. He has to undergo all sorts of trials which test and reveal his love for Rāma. Once, sent on a dangerous mission by Rāma, he is captured and taken before Rāvana, the ten-headed demon who personifies the ego in all its multiplicity. Rāvana's courtiers gather to humiliate Hanumān, but the monkey's devotion to Rāma is so great that he remains undaunted. Personally, he tells the assembly, he doesn't mind being relegated to a seat on the floor, but as Rāma's representative he deserves to sit in a chair. The only response he gets is laughter. But Hanumān prays to Rāma to save his representative from this humiliation, and his faith is so complete that the Lord is able to make his tail longer and longer, until finally it coils up into a tail-throne on which Hanumān sits high above the courtiers.

Rāvana is terribly impressed by Hanumān's devotion to Rāma. To test him further, the demon king takes a pearl necklace from his neck and offers it to Hanumān to try to buy his allegiance. But the monkey only bites one or two pearls and then throws the necklace out the window. The courtiers are outraged, but Hanumān's indifference only makes Rāvana more intrigued. He asks his prisoner, "Don't you know that necklace was worth a king's ransom?"

Hanumān replies, "For me everything is worthless if it doesn't enshrine the Lord. I bit the pearls and saw that the Lord was not there."

Rāvana asks, "Then just where is the Lord?" And Hanumān, in answer, rips open his chest and reveals his heart where Rāma is enshrined in all his splendor. It is a simple story, but it shows in a very vivid way the capacity of all of us to enter into the depths of our consciousness and see there the source of all joy and all security who is the Lord.

सखेति मत्वा प्रसभं यदुक्तं
हे कृष्ण हे यादव हे सखेति ।
अजानता महिमानं तवेदं
मया प्रमादात्प्रणयेन वापि ॥ ११-४१ ॥
यच्चावहासार्थमसत्कृतो ऽसि
विहारशय्यासनभोजनेषु ।
एको ऽथ वाप्यच्युत तत्समक्षं
तत्क्षामये त्वामहमप्रमेयम् ॥ ११-४२ ॥

41–42. Sometimes, because we were friends, I rashly said, "Oh, Krishna!" "Say, friend!" These things I said casually, openly. Whatever I said lightly – whether we were playing or resting, alone or in company, sitting together or eating – if it was disrespectful, forgive me for it, O Krishna. I did not know the greatness of your nature, unchanging and imperishable.

Now comes a moment of great tenderness, when Arjuna begs Sri Krishna to forgive him for forgetting his friend's divine nature. How perfectly Arjuna represents us, for the instances he mentions in daily living are the very ones in which we too forget that the Lord is within us all. As Jesus says, "Truly I say unto you, as you did it unto one of the least of these, you did it unto me."

As the supreme source of love, the Lord would never have us beg, "Will you kindly consider my application for forgiveness and arrive at an early decision?" Real love knows no reservations or contracts. Most of us may not find it too difficult to ask the Lord for unreserved forgiveness, but we usually find it hard to forgive others when they have offended us. For me this is the perfect test of love: can I forget my own hurt feelings and ensure their welfare, no matter how he or she has treated me? If I can, my love for that person is secure. My friend, or partner, or son, or daughter will be so certain of my desire to do what is best for them that even if I do something wrong, they will not hold it against me; they will know that I am incapable of doing anything to harm them. This trust is the basis of perfect relationships anywhere, particularly between man and woman.

The marvel of forgiveness is this: when we can completely forgive someone the tantrum they threw this afternoon, loving them even a little more because we see they really need our support, we are at the same time beginning to forgive ourselves for every tantrum we have ever thrown at others. You can see how practical a step it is to take. All those other people may long since have forgotten what we did and said – maybe some of them didn't really care much in the first place. But deep in our own minds, every single storm has left its mark. Every storm has burst a little hole in consciousness through which angry thoughts, angry words, and angry acts gradually seep into our daily life. In this sacred act of forgiveness we are mending thousands of these little holes. It relieves us of part of the tremendous burden that all of us carry within, healing our consciousness and taking the pressure of anxiety off our mind and our nervous system. And it makes us much less likely to get provoked the next time someone rubs us the wrong way. This is the miracle forgiveness works.

St. Francis of Assisi will say that when we have lost this capacity to forgive, we have lost the greatest source of joy in life. Once, in wintertime, it is said that Francis and his disciple Brother Leo were making an arduous journey on foot through the cold, snowy countryside of Italy. They had been walking along in silence for some time – probably repeating their mantram – when Brother Leo turned to St. Francis and asked him, "How can we find perfect joy?"

Francis stopped for a moment and then replied, "Brother Leo, even if all our friars were perfect in their holiness and could work all kinds of miracles for others, we still would not have perfect joy."

He turned to walk on, and Brother Leo ran after him. "Then what is perfect joy?"

St. Francis stopped again. "Even if we knew all the languages of men and of angels, if we could speak with the birds of the air and the beasts of the field and know all the secrets of nature, we still would not have perfect joy."

He started to go on again, but Brother Leo caught at his sleeve. "Then, Father Francis, what is perfect joy?"

"Even if we could cure all the ills on the face of the earth, we would still not have found perfect joy."

Now all Brother Leo's enthusiasm was aroused. "Then please, Father Francis," he pleaded, "what is the secret of perfect joy?"

"Brother Leo," St. Francis asked, "aren't you cold and tired and hungry from our day's walk through the snow? Well, suppose we now go to that monastery across the field and tell the gatekeeper how weary and cold we are, and he calls us tramps and thieves, and beats us with his stick, and throws us out into the winter night and slams the gate in our faces. Then, Brother Leo, if we can say with love in our hearts, 'Bless you in the name of Jesus,' then we shall have found perfect joy."

Most of us, of course, do not have to forgive on such a grand scale, but all of us have little resentments which we can forgive every day. Often these resentments are buried so deep in consciousness that we are not aware of the extent to which they undermine our security, drain our vitality, and interfere with our personal relationships. Here it is not very effective to analyze the wrongs we have suffered and then forgive them one by one. If I may say so, often the "wrongs" are not wrongs at all; it is only that our self-will has been violated, not infrequently because we failed to understand what the other person did or said. Instead, it is much more effective not to dwell on the past at all. Whenever a little thought arises and wants to talk over something in the past, don't talk to that thought, don't argue with it; simply repeat the mantram. This is really what forgiveness means, because when we can withdraw our attention completely from the past, it is not possible to be resentful; it is not possible to be oppressed by either past wrongs or past mistakes. All our attention is in the present, which means that every moment is fresh, every relationship is fresh, and there is no possibility of staleness or boredom.

पितासि लोकस्य चराचरस्य
त्वमस्य पूज्यश्च गुरुर्गरीयान् ।
न त्वत्समो ऽस्त्यभ्यधिकः कुतो ऽन्यो
लोकत्रये ऽप्यप्रतिमप्रभाव ॥ ११-४३ ॥
तस्मात्प्रणम्य प्रणिधाय कायं
प्रसादये त्वामहमीशमीड्यम् ।
पितेव पुत्रस्य सखेव सख्युः
प्रियः प्रियायार्हसि देव सोढुम् ॥ ११-४४ ॥

43. You are the father of the universe, of the animate and the inanimate; you are the object of all worship, greater than the great. There is none to equal you in the three worlds. Who can match your power?
44. O gracious Lord, I prostrate myself before you and salute you. As a father forgives his son, or a friend a friend, or a lover his beloved, so should you forgive me.

In the simple, sweet words of a child, Arjuna goes on asking the Lord to forgive his lapses: "You are my father; doesn't a father forgive his child when he makes a mistake?" It is a beautiful example of the parent-child relationship which each of us can have with the Lord.

Sometimes – especially when the neighbors are saying "Report him to the police" or "Did you hear what your daughter did?" – parents become insecure and confused. They weigh the pros and cons of the situation and ask themselves, "Does this deserve forgiveness? Are there special grounds here for giving them a second chance?" Driving bargains like this does not result in forgiveness. No child should have to wonder what the chances are that we will forgive them. If there is love in our relationship, our son or daughter will be able to come and say, "I've made a lot of mistakes, but I know you love me so much that you'll keep me from getting into this trouble again."

My granny had a unique gift for standing by people when they got themselves in trouble and at the same time teaching them not to get into that trouble again. One of my cousins was much more daring than the rest of us – and who doesn't have a cousin like that? He was always finding situations to put us into where his daring would show itself. Now, all of us used to play soccer until late in the afternoon, and after the game we liked nothing better than to run to the river for a swim. But by the time we started for home it would already be dusk, and dusk is the time when all kinds of snakes love to come out and take their walks. The raised paths between the paddy fields used to be crawling with them. In the fading light it was very difficult to distinguish snake from grass from stick, and without knowing you could easily step on one of these creatures and be bitten before you had a chance to jump. Not only that, some of these snakes are poisonous. Yet this daring cousin of mine loved to lead us home at dusk along these paths, knowing full well we were frightened out of our little wits.

My grandmother had warned me many times of the extreme danger of doing this, and she had told me repeatedly to come home before dark. Her warnings, unfortunately, fell on deaf ears; I continued to follow after the others. But one evening after our swim, just as we got to a part of the path where snakes loved to make their home, whom should we come upon but my granny, standing there barefoot by the side of the path just waiting for me. There was no telling how long she had been standing there, and from her expression I understood that she was prepared to wait there for me every night if necessary. She didn't need to say a word. I was cured. I never came home after dark that way again.

अदृष्टपूर्वं हृषितो ऽस्मि दृष्ट्वा
भयेन च प्रव्यथितं मनो मे ।
तदेव मे दर्शय देव रूपं
प्रसीद देवेश जगन्निवास ॥ ११-४५ ॥
किरीटिनं गदिनं चक्रहस्तम्
इच्छामि त्वां द्रष्टुमहं तथैव ।
तेनैव रूपेण चतुर्भुजेन
सहस्रबाहो भव विश्वमूर्ते ॥ ११-४६ ॥

45. I rejoice in seeing you as you have never been seen before, yet I am filled with fear by this vision of you as the abode of the universe. Please let me see you again as the shining God of gods.
46. Though you are the embodiment of all creation, let me see you again not with a thousand arms but with four, carrying the mace and disk and wearing a crown.

The Bible tells us, "Fear of the Lord is the beginning of wisdom." The image of the Lord with thousands of arms, the embodiment of all creation, can fill us with awe when we realize that it means he is everywhere; there is no way we can escape from him. He is in our parents, our children, our husband or wife or boyfriend or girlfriend, even in our dog or cat. It means that whatever we do, wherever we go, we need to be very vigilant about not causing distress to any other creature, because the eyes of the Lord are always right there watching us.

Even when we are alone, we haven't succeeded in escaping those watchful eyes, because the Lord is within us too. As the Upanishads put it, he is our real Self. Even when our little self is sleeping, the Seeing Eye is watching all our thoughts not because he is a busybody, but because he is everywhere and never sleeps. This is the aspect of the Lord which the Sanskrit scriptures call Sākshī, the Internal Witness. The traditional derivation of this word is from *sa,* 'with', and *akshi,* 'eye.' *Sākshī* is 'he who is all eyes,' sitting right inside us and everyone else, impartially taking note of everything we say and do and even what we think.

I remember how awestruck I was when I began to grasp the implications of this. As a schoolboy I was under the impression that God was floating about in space, issuing mandates and expecting us to carry them out. Most of us boys reassured ourselves that the Lord's secret service agents were not too efficient, that he would never know about many of the things we did. When we were up to something that he would not have been too pleased about, we would say, "Why bother him with these details?"

Then, one day, a few of us boys got together and made a pact under a particular mango tree to rob a neighbor's mango grove. It wasn't a very malicious plan; we were young, we were all fond of mangoes, and it seemed to us that our neighbor had many more of them than he would ever be able to use. But since we knew he would probably not agree with this conclusion, we all took a solemn oath not to reveal our plans to anyone, and not to speak to anyone among us who let our secret out.

Somehow my granny managed to find out about all this before I even reached home. When she met me at the gate she asked, "Little Lamp, is there any particularly significant event in which you took part today?"

"Not to the best of my knowledge, Granny."

"Did you happen to see anyone under the mango tree this afternoon?"

"Well, we did walk home that way."

"What happened, Little Lamp?"

Silence.

"Who was with you?"

More silence.

Then she said, "It doesn't matter if you conceal something from me, or your mother, or your aunt and uncle. But there is somebody inside you who is watching everything you do, and who hears everything that you say and think."

Hearing this from her lips made it official. You may be able to hide from your neighbor or keep your dog from following you to the library, but how do you hide from someone who is watching everything you do from the inside? I felt I couldn't do anything without the divine snooper finding out. After that, whenever I was with one of my friends who was prone to mischief, I could always hear her saying, "There's somebody watching. There's somebody listening." If he would wink for just a split second, we could get away with something that he wouldn't like to see. If he would doze off for a moment, we could make a remark without his knowledge. But he is there all the time, and we have no choice but to act in such a way as to win his quiet little nod of approval from within.

Once we begin to realize this, we become extremely alert about everything we say and do. But this does not mean we should always be listening to our own thoughts or thinking about what we are going to do next – quite the opposite. Instead of brooding on ourselves, which is what listening to our thoughts means, we become acutely aware of how the things we think and say and do may affect others. After all, the same Self that is watching us from within is watching in the other person too. If a chance remark of ours happens to hurt someone else, it is not enough to say, "I didn't mean any harm." We should be so fearful of hurting people that even if a clever remark is rushing off our tongue, we can stop it at the gate and take a look at it from the other person's point of view. If it is beneficial – which is not usually the case with clever remarks – we can stamp its visa and let it out. But if there is any chance that the remark will be misunderstood, we should be able to swallow our cleverness and say something else instead. It is better to say something banal but harmless than to be clever at someone else's expense. If worst comes to worst, we can always write the remark down and send it to the *Reader's Digest*; they may publish it and send us five dollars.

In this connection, there is an Arabic proverb that has appealed to me for its practicality. The tongue, the Arabs say, should have three gatekeepers. When words arise, the first gatekeeper asks, "Is this true?" That stops a lot of traffic immediately. But if the words get past the first gatekeeper, there is a second who asks, "Is it kind?" And for those words that qualify here too, the last gatekeeper asks: "Is it necessary?"

Most of us, if these gatekeepers were awake, would find very little to say. Here I think it is necessary to make exceptions in the interests of good company and let the third gatekeeper look the other way now and then. After all, a certain amount of pleasant conversation, when we are sincerely interested in the other person and what he or she has to say, is part of the artistry of living. If we go through life mum as a clam, it doesn't contribute much towards seeing the Lord in those around us. But where the first two gatekeepers are concerned, I think it is very important to keep them alert always – not indulging in gossip of any kind, not speaking ill of anyone, and especially not taking part in arguments or acrimonious discussions, which only agitate everyone involved. If we can learn to be watchful like this about what we say as well as what we do, we are well on the way towards identifying ourselves with our true Self within.

श्रीभगवानुवाच ।
मया प्रसन्नेन तवार्जुनेदं
रूपं परं दर्शितमात्मयोगात् ।
तेजोमयं विश्वमनन्तमाद्यं
यन्मे त्वदन्येन न दृष्टपूर्वम् ॥११-४७॥
न वेदयज्ञाध्ययनैर्न दानैर्
न च क्रियाभिर्न तपोभिरुग्रैः ।
एवंरूपः शक्य अहं नृलोके
द्रष्टुं त्वदन्येन कुरुप्रवीर ॥११-४८॥

SRI KRISHNA:

47. Arjuna, through my grace you have been united with me and received this vision of my radiant, universal form, without beginning or end, which no one else has ever seen.
48. Not by knowledge, nor service, nor charity, nor rituals, nor even by severe asceticism has any other mortal seen what you have seen, O heroic Arjuna.

If we ask any mystic in any of the great religious traditions how the vision of God comes about, they will all give us the same reply: it is not because we are worthy of it, but because the Lord is so merciful. All that we can do is to make our best effort to purify our minds and hearts through the practice of meditation and its allied disciplines. Finally we will reach a point where we can go no further, where we have done everything we can to remove the last impediments of the ego which stand between us and the Lord. Then, with faith that wells up from the very depths of consciousness, we say to the Lord, "It doesn't matter if I don't have a glimpse of you. I want only to love you with all my heart; I expect nothing in return." Rabia, a tremendous woman of God in the Sufi tradition, exclaims:

> Lord, if I love you out of fear of hell,
> Throw me into hell.
> If I love you for the sake of heaven,
> Close its gates to me.
> But if I love you for the sake of loving you,
> Do not deny yourself to me!

When we can say this to the Lord with complete love – whether we call him Sri Krishna or Allah, the Divine Mother or the Buddha or Jesus the Christ – it is only a matter of time before we will be united with him in the form we cherish most. Anyone who has reached this state *is* God-conscious.

In all the annals of mysticism. East and West, there is no finer inspiration than the unanimous testimony to this miracle of grace. *The Imitation of Christ* overflows with it:

> O Lord, how entirely needful is thy grace for me, to begin any good work, to go on with it, and to accomplish it. For without that grace I can do nothing; but in thee I can do all things when thy grace doth strengthen me.

St. Teresa of Ávila puts it in wonderfully practical terms:

> However much we may practice meditation, however much we violate our self-will, however many tears of devotion we

shed, we cannot produce this blessing; it is given only to whom God wills to give it. We are His; may He lead us along whatever way He pleases.

And the Sufi mystic Jalalu'l-Din Rumi sums it up beautifully:

It is not we who shoot the arrow; we are only the bow. The archer is the Lord.

मा ते व्यथा मा च विमूढभावो
दृष्ट्वा रूपं घोरमीदृङ्ममेदम् ।
व्यपेतभीः प्रीतमनाः पुनस्त्वं
तदेव मे रूपमिदं प्रपश्य ॥ ११-४९ ॥

49. Do not be troubled; do not fear my terrible form. Let your heart be satisfied and your fears dispelled in looking at me as I was before.

The Lord is not only love, he is also terror. In the Hindu tradition, this other face of the Lord is expressed by the law of karma, and we can see the fearful effects of its workings all around us today. In the twentieth century, we are reaping all that we have sown. The wars which this century has seen, which have cost so many millions of lives and brought so much sorrow and destruction, have not been inflicted upon us by anybody from outside. The destructive forces in life are not only outside us; they are within us too, in the very depths of our consciousness. All of us are involved in the fearful course our world is taking today. That is why I say so often that just to live is to be responsible – not only for what we do, but for what we fail to do.

To take just one example, there is a saying in my mother tongue that it takes two to get married and two to quarrel. It takes two to trade arms also. If the United States is exporting eight billion dollars worth of armaments, then other countries are importing eight billion dollars worth of arms from us – which means a lot of people who are involved in manufacturing, trading, transporting, stockpiling, and deploying

American instruments of war. Every American shares responsibility for this deadly trade. I am not saying that other nations do not share this responsibility; they do. But I live in this country, not in France or the Soviet Union, and I believe it is the stronger party who must take the first step. As our awareness of the unity of life deepens, we see more and more how far-reaching are the consequences of all our actions. You or I may not have put a gun in an angry man's hand, but if we are involved in the manufacture or sale of guns, if we fail to oppose these arms deals or to support gun control legislation, we are implicitly involved when any gun is used.

But there is a very positive aspect to the law of karma too. Just as it is we who have got ourselves into this situation, it is still within our reach to pull ourselves out again. Even though the debit side of our ledger may be red with entries, with scarcely a mark on the credit side at all, there is no need to be despondent. All that is necessary is to stop making entries on the debit side and throw ourselves heart and soul into adding entries to our credit. In this verse, Sri Krishna is reassuring Arjuna by telling him not to be oppressed by the destructive forces he has seen, but to devote his life to revealing the Lord of Love in his own life.

One of the most practical aspects of this is that it does not matter if the entries are large. Most of us do not have occasion to make large sacrifices, and if we wait for the opportunity to make a really big entry on the credit side, we may still be waiting when the cosmic auditor decides to close the books. What is important is to begin where we are and do the best we can. Even on the international level, we do not need to be in a position of fame or power in order to begin making a contribution to world peace. Often I think the world's problems can be solved more effectively by many little people acting together than by presidents or parliaments or corporations.

To begin with, we can begin to make our opinions heard. There is no need to worry about how many people will listen. If our words are true, they have to have an effect; it is only a matter of time. Remember Lincoln's words about government by the people and for the people?

They still hold true today. Everyone from Capitol Hill to our local community center is interested in a calm, thoughtful, practical presentation. We can all write letters, and we can talk with our friends and neighbors and encourage them to write letters too. Those with speaking talent can address groups in their communities, and anyone with a flair for writing can put together an article for a magazine or take advantage of one of our biggest forums, the Letters to the Editor page of local and national newspapers. When friends get together for bridge or bowling they can give part of their time for letter-writing; it can be every bit as enjoyable.

Then, second, we can refuse to be a party to violence in any way, no matter how indirect. Many industries and occupations, for example, are involved in the making of arms; many others are involved in their development and sale. If even a small proportion of us withdraw our support from this machinery of violence, these problems could be brought under control.

संजय उवाच ।
इत्यर्जुनं वासुदेवस्तथोक्त्वा
स्वकं रूपं दर्शयामास भूयः ।
आश्वासयामास च भीतमेनं
भूत्वा पुनः सौम्यवपुर्महात्मा ॥ ११-५० ॥
अर्जुन उवाच ।
दृष्ट्वेदं मानुषं रूपं तव सौम्यं जनार्दन ।
इदानीमस्मि संवृत्तः सचेताः प्रकृतिं गतः ॥ ११-५१ ॥

SANJAYA:

50. Having spoken these words, the Lord once again assumed the gentle form of Krishna and consoled his devotee, who had been so afraid.

ARJUNA:

51. O Janārdana, having seen your gentle human form my mind is again composed.

In a moment of infinite tenderness, the Lord reveals to Arjuna that He who contains all the galaxies is still none other than Sri Krishna, his beloved companion and guide. Arjuna breathes a sigh of relief, and in his joy he calls Sri Krishna by a very sweet name: Janārdana, 'he who intoxicates people.' Most of us think that intoxication is something that comes through drugs or drinking, but these changes in consciousness are artificial. They are prompted by external circumstances, and when the circumstances change, we are left wide open to depression. The joy Arjuna experiences, the joy of being united with the Lord, is permanent.

After attaining this state of union the mystic lives in the continuous presence of God, seeing and serving him in all around. John Woolman, the American Quaker, describes in memorable words how this awareness came to him:

> I saw a mass of matter of a dull, gloomy color between the North and the East, and was informed that this mass was human beings, in as great misery as they could be and live; and that I was mixed up with them and henceforth I must not consider myself as a distinct or separate being.

Woolman's life reminds us that when, by the grace of the Lord, we attain this state of illumination, we cannot just tear up our identification cards, sit back, and put our feet up on our desks. The Lord saves his most difficult work for those who have become united with him. It is true that the person who has reached the summit of human consciousness wants nothing more of life than to remain on the spiritual Himālayas, and may be tempted to stay there for eternity. But there are rare men and women who attain these heights and look back upon the plains of the earth to see millions of us crawling through life like ants. They want to live on this Mount Everest of bliss, but every time they close their eyes to the misery below, something in them says, "How can I bask in this happiness when my brothers and sisters are trapped in suffering?" Fortunately for us, these mystics have learned how to make the arduous journey back into the world of change and multiplicity, so that they can show us how we too can put an end to sorrow.

It is said that even the Compassionate Buddha, on the night of his enlightenment, faced this temptation to withdraw from life and its misery. Māra, the tempter, had tried every trick in his book to prevent the Buddha from attaining illumination. Finally, having realized that he could not distract him with sensual temptations, Māra tried a clever psychological ploy. "Blessed One," he said, "I admit that you have found the perfect joy of nirvāna. Why not remain in this state of bliss, instead of going back to a world of selfishness and suffering? When you go back, who is going to understand you? Who is going to strive as you have striven?" It is a heartbreaking question, which comes to every mystic who attains the vision of God. But after a long pause the Compassionate Buddha replied with infinite resolution, "Perhaps there will be a few to listen to me, and believe in me, and follow what I say."

This is all the man or woman of God expects. They do not hope for a meditation revolution sweeping from Alaska to the tip of Chile; when just one person attains Self-realization, the whole world benefits. As the Hindu mystics say, "When the lotus blooms, the bees come looking for it." When the love of God blossoms in anyone's heart, people will be drawn there, for everyone is looking for the permanent joy and security such a person offers.

The trip down from the spiritual summit is fraught with difficulties, for it involves learning how to be in the midst of the world without being of it. In order to reach people and touch their hearts, you must live among them and participate fully in life, yet remain aware every instant of the Lord within you and within all those around you. This is why spiritual living is so challenging. But when the going is rough, you have only to open your heart to be strengthened by the melody of Sri Krishna's flute or the tender image of Jesus. Even though the world outside may be overcast by a pall of violence and suffering, the temple within remains lit in radiance always.

श्रीभगवानुवाच ।
सुदुर्दर्शमिदं रूपं दृष्टवानसि यन्मम ।
देवा अप्यस्य रूपस्य नित्यं दर्शनकाङ्क्षिणः ॥११-५२॥

नाहं वेदैर्न तपसा न दानेन न चेज्यया ।
शक्य एवंविधो द्रष्टुं दृष्टवानसि मां यथा ॥११-५३॥
भक्त्या त्वनन्यया शक्य अहमेवंविधोऽर्जुन ।
ज्ञातुं द्रष्टुं च तत्त्वेन प्रवेष्टुं च परंतप ॥११-५४॥

SRI KRISHNA:

52. It is extremely difficult to obtain the vision you have had; even the gods are always longing to see me in this aspect.
53. Neither knowledge, nor austerity, nor charity, nor sacrifice can bring the vision you have seen.
54. But through unfailing devotion, Arjuna, you can know me, and see me, and attain union with me.

As Jesus reminds us, it is only the pure in heart who see God. It is only the pure in heart who are capable of complete faith, which is what it takes to see the Lord everywhere around us always.

In the Hindu tradition we have beautiful stories showing the power of such faith, which is often dramatized as characteristic of a simple child. One of these stories is about a boy named Haridās, whose mother was a great devotee of Gopāla, the youthful Krishna. Every day Haridās had to walk to school through a forest inhabited by all kinds of wild animals. The journey frightened him so much that he asked his mother what to do. "Don't be afraid, Hari," she replied. "You have a big brother, Gopāla, who lives in the forest. All you have to do when you pass that way is call his name and he will come and escort you to school."

Haridās had never heard about this older brother before, but he believed his mother's words completely. The next time he entered the woods he called out, "Gopāla! Gopāla!" At first no one appeared, but the boy's faith was so great that he just went on calling and calling. After a while, out from behind a tree stepped a handsome young man in a yellow silk dhoti, wearing a peacock feather jauntily in his rich black hair. "What's all the shouting about?" he teased. The two became good friends, and from that day on Krishna appeared every time the boy called, and went with him as far as the edge of the forest. Haridās was never afraid in the woods again.

One day, however, the boy came walking home from school very slowly, with his head drooping. "There's a feast tomorrow," he told his mother, "and the teacher asked us all to bring something to eat. But we're so poor that I don't think I'll have anything to take."

But Hari's mother was unperturbed. "Don't worry," she said; "just ask your brother tomorrow for some yogurt for you to take."

The next day Hari arrived at school with a little bowl of yogurt, and when they all sat down to eat, Hari's yogurt was passed around with all the other dishes. It was just a small bowl, and there should have been scarcely enough for three or four. But no matter how much was taken from it, the bowl was never empty.

Naturally, the teacher became quite interested in this phenomenon. "Hari," he asked, "where did you get this bottomless bowl?"

"From my older brother, Gopāla, who lives in the woods."

"But you don't have an older brother," his teacher objected. "Come on, now, tell me the truth."

But Hari, of course, only stuck to his story.

Finally the teacher decided to accompany the boy home that afternoon and meet this mysterious "older brother" Gopāla, who handed out miraculous, unending bowls of food. But in his heart he still thought the boy was lying. They reached the woods and Hari called out, "Gopāla! Gopāla!" Sure enough, Krishna appeared around the bend of the path, looking quite natty in his silk dhoti and peacock feather. Hari waved and cried, "Hi, Gopāl!" Then he turned to his teacher and said, "See, *there* is my older brother. Now will you please excuse me so I can run home to tell my mother about the feast?" And without waiting for a reply, he hurried off into the forest. But the schoolteacher was left standing there feeling rather ridiculous, because he could not see anyone at all.

It is a simple story, but it illustrates the power of complete faith. When we come to have this kind of unquestioning trust in the Lord within us, without any kind of selfish reservation for ourselves, there is no end to the inner resources that will flow into our lives.

Most of us, of course, do not begin the spiritual life with this kind of devotion. But love for the Lord is not something that descends miraculously from the skies; it can be fostered and deepened immensely through our own effort. At present, very little of our love is likely to be flowing to the Lord. Most of it is flowing to all sorts of other things down other channels towards money, or pleasure, or a new sports car or quadraphonic stereo set. In some cases, our vital capacity has been flowing down these channels for so long that they have been cut very deep. Then, when the time comes to dam them up and divert the love in them to flow towards the Lord, we feel we are standing there throwing pebbles into the Grand Canyon.

Here it is necessary not to become depressed by the immensity of the task, but just keep on throwing in the pebbles. They may not seem like much, but after a while they all add up. Take the problem of overeating. A handful of Brazil nuts may be a small thing, and no one would deny that once in a while they are not likely to do anyone any harm. But every time we pass up a snack, our will becomes a little stronger; we have thrown one more rock into the canyon. After a while, when we learn to do this freely, every rock we throw in will precipitate an avalanche, and soon – often before we even realize it – the Grand Canyon of that particular craving may be completely filled.

But there is another very practical suggestion I can make here. It *is* necessary to dam up the old channels down which our love is flowing, but if we do nothing but block the flow, there is always the danger that the dam may break or the water may overflow. So instead of giving all our attention to the rather negative work of throwing rocks, we can do our best throughout the day to dig a new channel straight to the Lord in those around us – by being patient, by being loyal, by always keeping our eyes on their welfare rather than our own. For a long, long time this new channel may seem terribly dry, but if we just keep digging, it will soon begin to drain off a little of the love that is now flowing down other channels. Finally it will become so deep that all our desires will be unified in a vast flood of love for the Lord.

मत्कर्मकृन्मत्परमो मद्भक्तः सङ्गवर्जितः ।
निर्वैरः सर्वभूतेषु यः स मामेति पाण्डव ॥११-५५॥

55. Whoever makes me the supreme goal of all
his work and acts without selfish attachment,
who devotes himself to me completely and is free
from ill will for any creature, enters into me.

For a few great men and women of God, who are capable of total devotion to a divine incarnation, seeing God may mean an actual vision. In the Christian tradition, for example, St. Francis of Assisi was blessed with visions of Jesus the Christ, and in India Sri Ramakrishna saw the Lord as the Divine Mother. But while the idea of seeing visions and hearing angelic voices may capture our imagination, I would like to present a much more practical interpretation of what it means to see God. As Sri Krishna tells us in these magnificent verses, the man or woman who performs all actions as an offering to the Lord, without a trace of selfish attachment or ill will, is aware of the Lord always. In our own age, Mahatma Gandhi is a perfect example of what this kind of awareness means. With his characteristic candor, Gandhi once said that he had seen no lights, heard no voices, and witnessed no visions. But Gandhi was nonetheless a man of immense spiritual awareness. He was able to work tirelessly for the welfare of all those around him not just of those who were for him, but of those who were opposed to him also without any thought of his own comfort or prestige, disarming his opposition not through force but through the power of his love.

This is the vision of the Lord which we can cultivate everywhere, all the time. Whenever we are able to forget our own petty satisfactions in working for the welfare of the whole, whether it is for our family, our community, or our world, we are becoming a little more aware of the Lord. Whenever we are able to remember that what hurts us hurts others too, and are able to refrain from unkind words and deeds and even thoughts, we are becoming a little more aware of the Lord.

Whenever we are able to respond patiently and positively to others even if they are hostile to us or rub us the wrong way, we are becoming a little more aware of the Lord. So when Sri Krishna tells us about devotion, he doesn't mean a private relationship between us and the Lord; he means the whole of our relationships with every living creature.

When you are always aware of the unity of life, you see the Lord in every living creature. Then you welcome every opportunity to serve others, and you become incapable of doing anything at their expense. To put it more personally, you see everyone as dear to you; every child is your child, and every dog is your dog. I don't think anyone has ever put it more beautifully than the Compassionate Buddha, when he tells us that we should love and protect every man, every woman, every child, every creature on earth, the way a mother loves and protects her only child.

In this final verse of chapter eleven, the Lord gives us his promise that if we devote ourselves to him completely – whether we call him Krishna or Christ, the Buddha or Allah or the Divine Mother – we will be united with him without fail, entering into his wholeness to become one with the indivisible unity he has revealed. As Jesus says, "I am the true vine, and my Father is the husbandman. Abide in me, and I in you. As the branch cannot bear fruit of itself, except it abide in the vine, no more can ye except ye abide in me."

If we keep our eyes on this supreme goal all the time, our life will be full of meaning; every decision we make will be significant to the whole. Every morning we will renew our decision not to live for ourselves but to do what adds to the welfare of everyone, and once we have learned to make this decision we can live in any country or any society and give a good account of our lives. Of course, everyone does not make the same kind of contribution. Some are doctors or nurses, some are teachers, some are mothers or fathers. But whatever our place in life, each of us has a contribution to make that can be made by no one else. Each of us can learn to apply the changeless values of selfless living to his or her own life, and because the Lord dwells in every one of us, none of us need ever be diffident about our capacity to leave the world a little better than we found it.

There is a story from the folklore of India that illustrates this point effectively. On the first day of the sun's creation, people expected to see it shining in the sky forever. No one knew that the sun had to dip into the water in the evening for a twelve-hour bath so that it could rise refreshed in the morning. So on the first evening of creation, everyone was terrified to see the sun about to set and the darkness beginning to spread across the world. They didn't know what to do. Then one little person stood up and said, "I'll light a candle." Someone else added, "I will too." Here, there, everywhere, millions of people started lighting candles, and soon the whole world was filled with light again.

This simple little story shows the importance of every person on earth, no matter how insignificant our lives may appear to be. Ordinary though we may be on the surface, within the heart of each of us lie tremendous capacities for love and service, and if we can keep our eyes always on the Lord of Love, there is no problem on earth too dire for ordinary people like you and me to solve.

विश्वरूपदर्शनयोगो नामैकादशोऽध्यायः ॥ ११ ॥

CHAPTER TWELVE

The Way of Love

अर्जुन उवाच ।
एवं सततयुक्ता ये भक्तास्त्वां पर्युपासते ।
ये चाप्यक्षरमव्यक्तं तेषां के योगवित्तमाः ॥ १२-१ ॥

ARJUNA:

1. Of those who love you as the Lord of Love,
ever present in all, and those who seek you
as the nameless, formless Reality, which way
is sure and swift, love or knowledge?

Arjuna has just been granted the vision of the Lord's universal form. Now, overwhelmed by love for Sri Krishna, he is ready to do anything to be united with him forever.

This intense longing is the keynote of any genuine mystical experience, and we hear it echoed in the writings of the men and women of God in all ages and all traditions. In Hinduism it is beautifully expressed in a scene between Sri Krishna and the lovely village girl named Rādhā. Rādhā is passionately in love with Sri Krishna, and her intense passion represents the heart's longing for union with the Lord.

The scene opens with Rādhā entering the glade where she and Sri Krishna had often wandered lost in love. Now he has gone, and tormented, she searches everywhere for him until finally all her other desires are consumed in the intensity of her love.

Then, from far off, she hears the haunting notes of Sri Krishna's flute. Slowly the music comes closer. At last she sees him, and Rādhā is transported with joy. But only for a moment: just as quickly as he came, her

Beloved disappears again, leaving her alone once more in the renewed anguish of desolation.

In the Western tradition, St. Teresa of Ávila uses almost the same image to explain her own experience:

> We can compare this kind of union to a tryst, because it is over in the very shortest time. All giving and taking have now come to an end, and in a secret way the soul sees who this Spouse is that she is to take. By means of the senses and faculties she could not understand in a thousand years what she understands in this way in the briefest space of time. But in that one short visit her Spouse, being who he is, leaves her worthier than before to join hands with him in union; and the soul, for her part, becomes so fired with love that she will do anything not to thwart this divine betrothal.

It is to deepen our love, to unify our desires, that the Lord gives us this fleeting taste of the joy of union. Once we taste this joy, all we want is to be permanently aware of him in everyone, everywhere, every minute. And here Arjuna, fresh from his experience of unity, asks a very practical question: "How can I best attain this state, through knowledge or through love?" It is a question with far-reaching implications, because it involves a very basic issue: what are we, as human beings, and what can we become?

This is not just a philosophical issue; it affects every aspect of our lives. Our upbringing, our relationships, our attitudes towards the environment, our physical and emotional well-being are all conditioned by the assumption that the basis of human personality is physical. In scientific language, personality is a product of our genetic makeup, shaped in part by the environment we encounter as we grow up. Deep in our consciousness, whether we think about it or not, this is the picture to which all of us subscribe: our character has already been determined, and we have no choice but to accept ourselves the way we are.

This belief has tragic consequences; it limits our outlook everywhere to the lowest common factor of existence. As William James says, it is like having the whole human body at our disposal and going through life moving only our little finger. We don't even suspect that there *is* a body; we think this one little finger is all we have.

Here I like to remember the example of Albert Einstein, whose theories revolutionized the physical sciences. When he was asked how he discovered relativity, Einstein replied simply, "By questioning an established axiom." In the same way, this chapter of the Gita is going to question our concept of the human personality, and therefore the basis of our civilization.

The challenge is simple: *we* are not what our genes are; the body is. We are what we think. Conditioned behavior may be dictated by our genetic makeup, but when we get below the surface level of consciousness and get hold of the thinking process itself, we can go beyond conditioning and change our personality completely.

Up to now, in previous chapters, I have been trying to show that there is no conflict between scientific knowledge and spiritual wisdom. There can be no conflict, because any investigation of nature *is* an inquiry into the unity of life. There is no better example than Einstein's theories of relativity, which – to use the words of C. P. Snow – "quietly amalgamated space, time, and matter" in the search for the underlying unity of nature. But no matter how far its investigations proceed, science can never go beyond the physical world of finite objects and passing events, which is just the surface of reality. As Spinoza puts it, "The finite rests upon the bosom of the Infinite."

This applies not only to the world of space and time, matter and energy; it is equally true of the human personality. There too, with our physical orientation, we see only the surface and mistake it for reality. But unfortunately, very few of the important problems in life – those which threaten our health, our happiness, our relationships, our very survival – can ever be solved on the physical level. More than that, when we try to apply a physical solution we are all too likely to make such problems more acute, because we are usually dealing not with the cause but with the symptoms.

The other day, for example, I was reading about how physicians sometimes deal with compulsive overeating by making a surgical detour around some of the organs of digestion. The underlying assumption is that there is nothing else that can be done. From the mystic's perspective, there is always something more that can be done – in this case, actually to go beneath the surface of consciousness and undo the compulsion to overeat. But even to understand that this is possible, we need a wholly different concept of human nature. To use Spinoza's image, the biochemical level is only the surface of personality. Our real Self, the Ātman, is at the very core of consciousness; and if we can get below the surface, we can change our personality at will.

This is in full accord with the principles of genetics; it is simply a larger picture. Recently I saw a physiology textbook that compared the genetic code to a movie film, unrolling through our lives with every interior event predetermined. The rationale is that brain neurons, like other cells, have their special properties coded by our genes. From this, many scientists conclude that the patterns of thought and personality are written into our genetic code. As long as we identify ourselves with the body and are subject to biological conditioning, this may be valid. But to repeat, we are *not* what our DNA is. Genetics may limit how tall we can be, but it can't limit the stature to which we can grow spiritually. If we can change our way of thinking, many processes of the brain can be modified – not only the production of the behavior-related neurotransmitters and hormones, but perhaps even which portions of the DNA are expressed in certain cells. It is as if each DNA molecule had a secret key of its own: "You can change the expression of these genes through the practice of meditation."

If our lives were on film, the genes would only be stagehands; the ego is the director. The mind and senses get the supporting roles, and thousands of distractions run about as extras to make up for the lack of plot. This is the first reel, and if we could see it clearly, most of us would walk out.

In meditation, however, we get hold of the camera and turn the directing over to the Ātman. The supporting cast is the same, the makeup artist and set designer are the same, but we get a new script and a new star. Even biologically, it means that we have become a different person: the genetic material is the same, but the person is wholly transformed. In the language of mysticism both East and West, we have been born again. As Eckhart says, "The old man is dead and the new man is born; the pauper is dead and the prince is born."

श्रीभगवानुवाच ।
मय्यावेश्य मनो ये मां नित्ययुक्ता उपासते ।
श्रद्धया परयोपेतास्ते मे युक्ततमा मताः ॥ १२-२ ॥

SRI KRISHNA:

2. For those who set their hearts on me and
worship me with unfailing devotion and faith,
the way of love leads sure and swift to me.

In India there is a story about a villager who wanted to learn to meditate. For several weeks, following his teacher's instructions, he repeated the mantram *Om* and tried to fix his mind on the formless Absolute. But his mind did nothing but wander. Finally he went back to his teacher and complained, "Sir, I just can't keep my mind on the Absolute. I don't know what it's like."

The teacher got the hint and decided to take a more practical approach. "All right," he said, "what is it that appeals to you most deeply?"

With some embarrassment the villager replied, "My cow."

"Very well," said the teacher, "go and meditate on your cow." That is one of the skills of a good spiritual teacher; he always knows how to begin where you are.

A few days later the teacher decided to look in on his new student. To his surprise, the man hadn't come out of his meditation room for three days. His teacher pounded on the door. "Open up!" he commanded. "What are you doing in there?"

There came a faint answer, a little like a bellow: "Meditating."

"Come out at once," the teacher repeated. "I have some instructions to give you about moderation."

"Sir," came the reply, "I *can't* come out. My horns are too big to fit through the door."

This is the basis of meditation: we become what we meditate on.

Whatever we constantly dwell on shapes our desires, our decisions, and finally our destiny. And the mystics of both East and West draw the same conclusion: then we become what we love.

In this sense, every one of us has been meditating for a long time. The problem is that we have no control over what we meditate on. To take a negative example, look at what happens over a period of years to people whose love has been captured by money. At first they may show only a tendency to be greedy. But if they dwell on making money, that desire starts to condition their ways of thinking. Making a profit comes easily to such people, for the simple reason that they don't really see anything else. As the Buddha would remind us, we don't see with our eyes. We see with our mind, and here the mind is always thinking about money. If they see a redwood grove, they think, "That's a dollar a board foot!" If they see the Grand Canyon, they want to dam it up and turn it into a resort. And the tragedy is this: after many years, they won't be able to think of anything else. They will be so preoccupied with profit that they won't be aware of the needs of family or friends or society. They may even be willing to work at jobs that are harmful to others, such as manufacturing cigarettes or armaments, just to make a few more dollars. In a sense, it is no longer realistic to expect them to be otherwise; they just can't *see* any other way. This is the immense power of thoughts, which few of us even suspect.

But all this has a positive side too. Just as we stunt ourselves by dwelling on some private, personal satisfaction, we can grow to our full stature by giving our love to an ideal that embodies the perfection of human nature.

The annals of mysticism are full of examples of this, but I know of none more appealing, more human, than that of St. Francis of Assisi. He was born into a well-to-do merchant family, and though he must have been a sweet-tempered young man, his mind seems to have been full of no more than poetry and music and the romance of the Crusades. But when his heart turned to Jesus, his desire to become like Him was so passionate that it transformed and transfigured him completely. As G. K. Chesterton has said, if you find the Jesus of the Gospels unapproachable, if you find it hard to believe that the Sermon on the Mount can actually be practiced by a human being, you have only to look at Francis, the perfect image of his Master.

If this is difficult to understand, it is because most of us have no idea of what love really means. Look at how the word *love* is used today, not only in the mass media but by some of the most respected people in every profession. It shows how unreal our world has become; everything is a matter of biology. If someone says, "Two people are embracing each other; they are making love," we consider that an intelligent statement. But if I were to see someone being patient in the face of provocation and say, "*That* person is making love," people would think it was a quaint example of a professor from India mixing up his English idioms. How thoroughly we have turned life upside down! What is untrue is universally accepted, and what is true cannot even be understood.

When I first came to this country, I gave a talk on the spiritual life to a group of teenage girls. In those days practically no one had heard of meditation, so I centered my remarks around something in which girls of that age are always interested: personal relationships. The young president of the club listened very carefully, and when I had finished she said, "You have used the word *love* a lot, but not the way we are used to hearing it. Will you please tell us what love means to you?"

I like that kind of direct question very much, and I told her: "When I say I love a person, it means only one thing: that person's happiness, that person's welfare, means more to me than my own."

She looked around at the others. "Well, girls," she confessed, "I guess that means none of us has ever been in love."

It was a thoughtful observation, for this is a concept of love that does not even occur to most of us today. To the mystics, love has very little to do with sentimental or physical attraction. I don't think anyone has described it better than St. Paul:

> Love suffereth long, and is kind; love envieth not; love vaunteth not itself, is not puffed up, doth not behave itself unseemly, seeketh not its own, is not easily provoked, thinketh no evil;

rejoiceth not in iniquity, but rejoiceth in the truth; beareth all things, believeth all things, hopeth all things, endureth all things. Love never faileth. . . .

Now, in the traditional interpretation, the message of this chapter of the Gita is to love the Lord. But I don't think it is any exaggeration to say that the meaning is simply to love. The reason is simple: even to love another person completely, consciousness has to be united.

Look at the universality of mystical language East and West. In Hinduism, the relationship between God and creation is said to be *advaita,* 'not two'. In Christianity, all mystics would concur with St. Paul's eloquent exclamation: "Not I, not I, but Christ liveth in me." In other words, lover and Beloved are one. And if we can cast our eyes to the summit of human nature, isn't it the same even between individuals? "Here are my duties, here are yours. This is the boundary line. If you stay on your side, I'll respect you; but if you cross over, you're an invader." Wherever people go their separate ways like this, there can be no love; there is scarcely a relationship. The very nature of love is not to have qualifications or reservations at all.

When I talk like this people sometimes object, "I've never spent a day like that, much less a lifetime! If that's what love means, I don't think I'm capable of it." I have never accepted this statement from anybody. Every one of us can learn to love. Naturally, we all start with imperfections: self-will, self-centeredness, demands and opinions of our own. But there is no need to throw up our hands as so many are doing today and say, "Let us be separate *and* have a relationship;" it is not possible to do both. Instead, we start where we are – somewhat selfish, somewhat self-willed – but with a deep desire to relate lovingly to each other, to move closer and closer together. It requires a lot of stamina and many years of hard work, and there will be anguish in it as well as joy. But immediate consolation: we don't have to wait until our love is perfect to reap the benefits of it. Even with a little progress, everyone benefits – not only those we live with, but ourselves as well.

This is what the Gita means by the way of love. It can be practiced in all relationships, but a loving relationship between man and woman provides a particularly good context. There the desire for union is already present. It needs only to be nurtured, so that every day you love each other a little more.

The Sufis have a vivid image to illustrate this, which I can elaborate from my own experience. In some parts of Muslim society, it is still not uncommon to see women wearing the veil. I first saw this at close quarters when I was teaching on a campus in Central India, where the women students would sometimes sit together behind a common veil on one side of the room. This veil aroused great curiosity: all the boys wanted to see who was behind it. You could hear the girls' bangles jingling and now and then a soft ripple of laughter, and none of my best quotes from Shakespeare could compete with those delicate sounds.

At first the veil looked quite opaque. But as I looked with more concentration, I began to make out silhouettes behind it. Then I could see some of the features, and finally, as I learned what to look for, I was able to recognize the faces on the other side.

This is what happens in personal relationships on the way of love. At first there is just an opaque curtain between us and the one we love. The Lord *is* there, but we cannot see him – in fact, at the beginning we scarcely know what to look for. Gradually, however, our concentration deepens. Now we sense that there really is someone behind the curtain, and every once in a while we glimpse a silhouette. As vision becomes clearer, we seem to see the beautiful eyes of Sri Krishna or Jesus or the Divine Mother behind our partner's eyes – and the more we see, the deeper is our desire to see more.

In the end, all our other desires merge in the immense longing to have no barrier between us and our real Beloved. Only one veil remains, and it is so thin that every morning we go to meditation knowing that this may be the day that we are united with the Lord at last. We may wait like this for years, but finally, without warning, the veil falls at last. Then, in the rapturous language of St. John of the Cross, we merge in the Beloved and are transformed: "*Amado con amada, amada en el amado transformada.*"

Most of us think of love as a one-to-one relationship, which is all it can be on the physical level. But there is no limit to our capacity to love. We can never be satisfied by loving just one person here, another there. Our need is to love completely, universally, without any reservations – in other words, to become love itself. It can take our breath away to glimpse the vastness of such love, which Dostoevsky describes beautifully in *The Brothers Karamazov:*

> Love all that has been created by God, both the whole and every grain of sand. Love every leaf and every ray of light. Love the beasts and the birds, love the plants, love every separate fragment. If you love each separate fragment, you will understand the mystery of the whole resting in God. When you perceive this, your understanding of this mystery will grow from day to day until you come to love the whole world with a love that includes everything and excludes nothing.

This is what it means to realize the unity of life, and in these troubled times, when turmoil has invaded our society, our homes, and even our hearts, I don't think there is any more precious attainment. That is why this chapter of the Gita is so acutely relevant today. As one Hasidic rabbi put it, the community of the living is the carriage of the Lord. Where there is so little love that the carriage is torn asunder, we must love more, and the less love there is around us, the more we need to love to make up the lack.

A man once came to Rabbi Israel Ba'al Shem and said, "My son is estranged from God; what shall I do?" The Ba'al Shem replied simply, "Love him more." This was my granny's approach to every problem, and I know of no more effective or artistic or satisfying way to realize the unity of life in the world today. It is an approach to life in which everything blossoms, everything comes to fruition. As Sri Krishna will go on to explain, Arjuna's question about love and knowledge is really unnecessary. Where there is love, everything follows. To love *is* to know, *is* to act; all other paths to the Lord are united in the way of love.

ये त्वक्षरमनिर्देश्यमव्यक्तं पर्युपासते ।
सर्वत्रगमचिन्त्यं च कूटस्थमचलं ध्रुवम् ॥ १२-३ ॥
संनियम्येन्द्रियग्रामं सर्वत्र समबुद्धयः ।
ते प्राप्नुवन्ति मामेव सर्वभूतहिते रताः ॥ १२-४ ॥

3–4. As for those who seek the transcendental Reality, without name, without form, contemplating the Unmanifested, beyond the reach of thought and of feeling, with their senses subdued and mind serene and striving for the good of all beings – they too will verily come unto me.

This is the other concept of God: not a personal ideal that can be loved, but the formless, impersonal Ground of existence. It is an idea that many people subscribe to intellectually today, in the belief that faith in a personal God is either superstition or intellectual weakness. But jnāna yoga, the 'way of knowledge,' has nothing to do with the intellect. The intellect can operate only in a world of duality, where there is subject and object, knower and known. Here we must soar beyond all divisions into a realm of absolute unity, where the separate personality merges completely in this formless, infinite Reality and all distinction between knower and known disappears. In this supreme state, called *nirvikalpa samādhi* in Sanskrit, there is no one present to take notes. Sri Ramakrishna used to tell about a doll made of salt who went to measure the depth of the ocean. As soon as she waded into the water, she dissolved – and then, Ramakrishna asks, who was left to tell of the ocean's vastness?

In this realm all trace of distinction disappears, so it is not surprising that we find mystics of all epochs and all traditions struggling to describe their experience in nearly identical language. Meister Eckhart in thirteenth-century Germany and Shankara in eighth-century India often sound interchangeable; and Dionysius the Areopagite, probably a Christian monk writing at the end of the fifth century, uses terms reminiscent of this very verse:

> Then, beyond all distinction between knower and known, . . . the aspirant becomes merged in the nameless, formless Reality, wholly absorbed in That which is beyond all things and in nothing else. . . . Having stilled his intellect and his mind, he is united by his highest faculty with That which is beyond all knowing.

To the intellect, which *has* to classify, the different traditional approaches to God – called, in Hinduism, jnāna, bhakti, karma, and rāja – are watertight compartments. But in fact, these are not separate paths. They are different aspects of the same spiritual experience, which flow together in life and practice.

To see this, all we have to do is look at those men and women who have followed the path of knowledge – not at their philosophy, but at their lives. Historians, for example, like to remember Shankara as a towering intellectual, the architect of an imposing philosophical structure that expounds his direct experience of the transcendent, impersonal Brahman, "One without a second." But this same uncompromising nondualist was also an ardent lover of the personal God who poured out his devotion to Shiva and the Divine Mother in magnificent poetry, sometimes as a simple child of the Lord:

> You are the Mother of the universe;
> Why should I wonder at your love for me?
> Even if his faults cannot be counted,
> A mother never abandons her child.

Shankara died at the age of thirty-two, but in that short lifetime he traveled all over India, tirelessly revitalizing its spiritual heritage – founding monastic orders, establishing monasteries, teaching successors, and leaving behind a great body of writing to pass on the fruit of his spiritual experience. In such a life, love, selfless service, and spiritual wisdom all fuse; each path comes to perfection in the same soul.

In the language of Hinduism this underlying Reality, called Brahman, is said to be *advaita,* 'not two.' It cannot be described, because there is nothing from which It can be distinguished. It is "what is and what is not," from which, as Shankara says, both "words and thought recoil." Still, to inspire us, the first part of these verses tries to convey a little of the stark majesty of this infinite, eternal Reality. *Aksharam:* it is inexhaustible, imperishable, without either beginning or end. *Anirdeshyam:* we cannot point to it or define it, because it is neither outside nor inside; subject and object are one. *Avyaktam:* it is unmanifest; it cannot be seen. Who could be the seer? Yet, *sarvatragam:* it is everywhere; it is Existence itself. And finally, *acalam:* unshakable, beyond all change.

These are inspiring words, because as the Upanishads say, "*Tat tvam asi*:" this is our real nature. We were never born; we shall never die. But at the same time, it gives us some idea of the awesome challenges of jnāna yoga, which I do not hesitate to say is beyond the capacity of all but a handful of people in any age. It is all very well to go about saying, "I am not my body, I am not my mind," but for most of us, how much effect would this have on consciousness? We would still get angry, still harbor resentments, still be subject to doubt and vacillation. As long as it is only an intellectual effort, this sort of exercise has nothing to do with jnāna. In fact, there is a danger to it. Far from shrinking the ego, it can actually swell it and make us more acutely aware of ourselves.

In the second half of these verses we get the qualifications we need to practice jnāna yoga. They are really stiff. *Samniyamy 'endriyagrāmam:* first, there has to be complete self-control. There should be no clamor from the senses at all, and if they do happen to ask for something that is not beneficial, we should be able to withdraw our desires without a hint of protest. *Sarvatra samabuddhayah:* no likes and dislikes, no personal entanglement in the world of sense objects. Friend and enemy should be equally respected. *Sarvabhūtahite ratāh:* our only joy should be in serving the welfare of others, without any thought of our own individual satisfaction. To me, it is all very much like the escape clauses you find in small print on the back of a contract: "If you can practice this yoga, you don't need it; if you need it, you won't be able to practice it."

In this connection, Sri Ramakrishna tells a story about the *gopīs* or cowherd girls who were Sri Krishna's companions in Vrindāvana. In these stories the gopīs represent all of us, the aspiring human soul; and they are passionately in love with Sri Krishna, the Lord of Love.

One day, Ramakrishna says, a jnāna yogi came to Vrindāvana. Seeing that the gopīs were completely devoted to an incarnation of God, the man began to teach them about Brahman, eternal and immutable. One by one, the girls fell asleep. When they woke up again they explained gently, "Holy one, we don't understand any of this. All we know about is our Krishna, whom we can see and enjoy and love."

Ask any young man whether he would rather have a date with Miss Principle of Femininity or with his girlfriend. Miss Femininity is perfect, but she is also formless – in fact, she doesn't have any attributes at all. If I know anything about men, that chap will tell you candidly to keep your Miss Perfection for yourself; he would rather go out with the girl he loves. She may have freckles and an unpredictable temper, but she has a hand he can hold, eyes he can gaze into, and a smile that lightens his heart. And Sri Krishna says now gently, though we may pride ourselves on our intellect, it is the same with us. With our physical conditioning, how is it possible for people like us to aspire to disembodied consciousness? It is not enough that the Ātman be eternal and immutable; it must also be packaged attractively in a human form. This is the miracle of divine incarnation, and when the Lord comes to life like this in a human being, it can capture our imagination and unify our dedication completely. St. Bernard gives the same explanation within the Catholic tradition: "The main reason for the invisible God incarnating himself physically in the midst of human beings was to lead them who can only love physically to the healthy love of his physical appearance, and then, little by little, to spiritual love."

क्लेशो ऽधिकतरस्तेषामव्यक्तासक्तचेतसाम् ।
अव्यक्ता हि गतिर्दुःखं देहवद्भिरवाप्यते ॥ १२-५ ॥

5. Yet hazardous and slow is the path to the Unrevealed, difficult for physical creatures to tread.

A few centuries ago, a mystic from Kerala summarized the problem of jnāna yoga perfectly: "Jnāna is for those whose senses have come under control."

That is the rub. For those who meet the qualifications – giants like Meister Eckhart, Shankara, or Anandamayi Ma – jnāna yoga is a perfectly adequate way to Self-realization. These are people who are already free from the clamor of the senses, so they scarcely identify with their bodies at all. But if you believe in your heart that you are essentially physical, Sri Krishna says dryly, you are going to find this path very tough going.

Unfortunately, there are very few in the world today who do not fall into this category. Virtually all of us believe that we are the body, and if you doubt it, all you have to do is look around and ask a very simple question: how do we spend our time? When we want to celebrate, do we meditate or do we eat? When we get a vacation, what do we choose to do? What are the usual themes in the books and magazines we read, the songs we listen to, the movies and television shows we watch? We may protest, "This is the age of science. The path of knowledge *has* to be right for us." But Sri Krishna would only smile. "Do your senses listen to you? If they do, you might be on the right track. But if they do not, you'd better consider the way of love instead."

This is not a comment on the effectiveness of jnāna yoga. It is a comment on the physical conditioning with which all of us have grown up. Ours *is* a physically-oriented world, so we should not be embarrassed to discover that we have learned to look on life with wholly physical eyes. But it is equally important to understand that we need not resign ourselves to this conditioning. We can change our thinking completely – and if we do not, we will find it very difficult to maintain any lasting relationship with those around us. The fiercer our physical conditioning is, the more separate we will feel, and the more we will be prey to all the problems of a divided mind: vacillation, depression, jealousy, and alienation. These problems *can* be solved, but not on the physical level where they arise. We need access to much deeper levels of consciousness.

Take, for example, a Don Juan who is all involved in a "meaningful relationship" with a young lady named Dulcinea. Juan is a very passionate fellow and intensely jealous. His mother will tell you that is his nature; he cannot change. Unfortunately, since Dulcinea is attractive, Juan's life is an agony of suspicion. The minute she is out of his sight he can't concentrate on anything, he can't enjoy anything, he can't stop worrying about what she is doing.

Now, according to one school of thought, if Don Juan can exchange his Dulcinea for a Juanita, as loyal as she is lovely, this uncertainty can be dispelled. "Change the environment, change the response" – isn't it axiomatic? But unfortunately, as most of us know from our own experience, this simply doesn't work. Juan has a jealous mind. He *has* to be jealous of somebody, and if Dulcinea is not around, he will be jealous of her maid. The problem is not with Dulcinea or Juanita or anything else in the outside world; the problem is the uncertainty in the mind of Don Juan. As long as he is living on the physical level, he cannot help being possessive. But it *is* possible for Juan to overcome his jealousy: not by reasoning with it, not by suppressing it, not by taking security hormones, but by learning to be master of his mind. When that is done, all insecurity goes – not only insecurity over Dulcinea, but insecurity over anything. Then he can take Dulcinea out to the Alhambra café, where her former boyfriend plays flamenco, and not be apprehensive at all. His face may look the same, his fingerprints may be the same, but Dulcinea will testify that he has become a different person.

Unless we can get beneath the physical level of consciousness, however, the conditioning of this level cannot be undone. Abraham Maslow, I think, says that if the only tool you have is a hammer, you treat every problem as if it were a nail. That is what we do when we try to deal with human problems from within a physical orientation. All we can look for is physical solutions, which cannot be effective because the problems are not physical in origin. Worse, such attempts can have dangerous consequences.

Recently, for example, I have been reading about the biochemical approach to personality. It is a fascinating area for research. Just as in our galaxy there are about one hundred billion stars, there is a galaxy within us too: the ten billion cells of the human brain. When Galileo is looking through his telescope at the stars, he is seeing them through those stars inside. And just as the Milky Way contains all kinds of little worlds, each seemingly self-contained but part of an integral whole, there are biochemical island-worlds within the galaxy of the brain – the cerebral cortex, the hippocampus, the thalamus, the amygdala – each with its histories of growth and commerce in which whole dynasties of proteins rise and fall.

This is not merely figurative language. I'm trying to show not only the fascination, but also the unity of these realms. Just as it is all one universe, for all those billions of apparently separate stars, it is all one head. It sounds elementary, but look at current research. Scientists have managed to probe into the molecules in the cells of the brain and are able to trace neurotransmitters like dopamine and serotonin which seem to trigger changes in mood. It is an amazing achievement. But when they suggest that by manipulating neurotransmitters we can help the brain to achieve its maximum potential, we have to raise our eyebrows. The brain is not conscious; it is an instrument of consciousness. When consciousness is changed, of course there will be correlated changes in brain biochemistry and in behavior. But by changing brain biochemistry, we can never change consciousness itself. All we can do is suppress particular symptoms, which is like trying to solve an electrical problem in a car by removing the little red light on the dash.

To take a particular example, neuroscientists tell us that there is an "appestat" in the hypothalamus that tells us when to eat or drink. When we feel hungry, we *have* to eat. Sometimes, in fact, even when we don't feel hungry we have to eat. The appestat has gone off, the juices are flowing, and even if the refrigerator has been locked up we will find some way to get inside. In other words, we have very little choice.

Now, as long as we are completely identified with the body this is an accurate picture, and all of us know people who are victims of compulsive eating. But in meditation, we can learn to reset the appestat – not to turn our backs on it or stifle it, but to change our appetite at will. In fact, for those who are meditating, the problem of overeating is one of the easiest problems to solve. It means that even the hypothalamus can be put in its place.

Now take another very practical application: hyperactivity. Researchers have learned that certain drugs can have a quieting effect on children whose learning problems have been ascribed to their "hyperactive" behavior. These are children with uncontrollable energy – which, from the biochemical perspective, is a serious liability. To me, however, this kind of behavior is often the expression of tremendous vital capacity which is crying out to be harnessed. Often such children have the potential for great achievements, and quieting their behavior with drugs, while it may be necessary in extreme cases, is going to suppress their capacity for achievement as well as their capacity for running amuck. It is the same capacity: that is the key. The capacity to cause trouble is the capacity to solve the problem of causing trouble – just as the capacity to be selfish is the capacity to become loving. In sedation, what happens is that the medication blunts the cutting edge of consciousness. After some time of this, we don't even have the blade of consciousness any more; we have only the handle. This is the danger of manipulation on the physical level. There may be a temporary relief of symptoms, but there is often a worsening of the problem.

The real issue with manipulating personality like this is the damage to human growth. In all these so-called solutions on the physical or chemical level, the will is forgotten or even undermined – and without the will there is no capacity for choice, no capacity for growth, no capacity for love. That is what physical conditioning leads to when it is taken to extremes. To overcome this conditioning we need to get to a deeper level of consciousness, where we can deepen our will and make the choices which enable us to grow.

ये तु सर्वाणि कर्माणि मयि संन्यस्य मत्पराः ।
अनन्येनैव योगेन मां ध्यायन्त उपासते ॥ १२-६ ॥
तेषामहं समुद्धर्ता मृत्युसंसारसागरात् ।
भवामि नचिरात्पार्थ मय्यावेशितचेतसाम् ॥ १२-७ ॥

6–7. But they for whom I am the supreme goal, who do all work renouncing self for me and meditate on me with single-hearted devotion – these will I swiftly rescue from the fragment's cycle of birth and death to fullness of eternal life in me.

When my wife and I were living on the Blue Mountain, we had a visit from a young American who had been living in India as a spiritual aspirant for a number of years. He was dressed just like a traditional Indian *sādhu,* but when he spoke, his English still had its old Harvard accent.

We talked about the spiritual life for some time, and when evening came he offered to come with us to our little meditation center and give the inspirational talk. Our group consisted mostly of simple villagers, and I was afraid his words might be too sophisticated. But there was no cause for worry. He spoke their native Tamil without stumbling, and the story he told was one that anyone could understand.

"Look," he said, stretching out his hands with open palms. "Sri Krishna is saying to every one of us, 'Here, I have a very special gift for you – the gift of immortality. Won't you reach out and take it?'

"'Thank you,' we say, 'but can't you see? Our hands are full of these sweet mangoes.'

"Sri Krishna smiles. 'Let go of the mangoes,' he explains patiently. 'Then your hands will be free.'

"'But Lord,' we protest, 'we *like* mangoes. Why don't you give us your present first? Then we promise we'll throw away the mangoes.'"

This is the essential conflict in every human heart. Part of us wants to reach out for the highest, part cannot let go of our little personal desires. Consciousness is split in two – between our higher and our lower natures, between the selfless and the selfish. And the Lord says simply, "Make yourselves whole." *Matparāh:* "Make me your only goal." Don't do anything just to please yourself; don't do anything just to please Tom, Dick, and Harry. Everything should be for the sake of the Lord, the Self, in you and in those around you.

In this – and here the mystics of all traditions are unanimous – there is no room for doubts or reservations. The other day I read a remark that the Ten Commandments are rapidly becoming the Five Suggestions. This is the contemporary approach: we just don't like to be told what to do. So why not have Moses say, "Here are Five Suggestions for your careful consideration, for those who have the time?" But Sri Krishna says, *Sarvāni karmāni:* "No exceptions. Give me everything: not only the big things, even the trifles." Moses and Jesus use the same language: "Thou shalt love the Lord with *all* thy heart and all thy spirit and all thy strength."

For the most part, this is not something we do on the surface level of awareness. We need to get into the very depths of our personality, where the fierce desires for personal satisfaction arise. Meditation enables us to enter these levels, but meditation by itself is not enough. Once we break through the surface of consciousness, we come to places where we can neither go forward nor withdraw. We see the doors to deeper awareness there in front of us, but we don't know how to open them. At such times, no amount of exertion on our part is going to make it through those doors. It takes both hands, and one hand is still hanging on to something personal, something private, that we don't want to leave behind. Until we let go, we are saying in effect, "Yes, Lord, I *would* like to go forward – just as long as I can stay here too."

No one has described this more vividly than Augustine. At the time of which he is writing, in his *Confessions,* Augustine is thirty-one. The storm within him has been going on for over twelve years. Now it is almost resolved, but he does not realize it: on the surface of personality, the conflict has grown so fierce that he feels torn in two. "I was bound," he exclaims –

> not by another man's chains, but by my own iron self-will. My capacity to desire was in enemy hands, and he had made a chain of it to hold me down. For a will that is bent awry becomes selfish desire, desire yielded to becomes habit, and habit not resisted becomes compulsion. With these links joined one to the other . . . a hard, hard servitude had me in its grip. The new will being born in me . . . was not yet strong enough to overcome the old will that had been strengthened by so much use. Thus two wills warred against each other within me – one old, one new; one physical, the other spiritual – and in their conflict they wasted my spirit.

Then, with penetrating insight, he gives us the clue to victory:

> I was in both camps, but there was a little more of me on the side I approved than on the side I disapproved . . . for it had become more a matter of unwillingly experiencing [my desires] than of doing something that I actively wanted. . . .
>
> It was I who willed and I who was unwilling: it was *I*. I did not wholly will; I was not wholly unwilling. Therefore I strove with myself and was distracted by myself. . . .

The analysis is perfect. It is not two selves in conflict; it is one self – sometimes on one side, sometimes on the other. And to win, all we have to do is put more and more of ourselves in the other camp. Every time we withdraw our desires from some self-centered activity, a little more of us has defected from the side of darkness to join the side of light.

The dynamics are simple; but to do this, especially at the deeper levels of personality, is terribly, terribly hard. For a long time we cannot even see our choices clearly; we cannot bring our will to bear. In the latter stages of spiritual development, even the greatest mystics have cried out from the depths of their heart when they see how far off the goal is and how frail their strength, how limited their capacity. As Augustine says, it is like trying to wake up out of the seductive torpor of a dream – knowing it is time to wake up, longing to see, but unwilling to open our eyes.

If we could watch our dreams, we would see that there is no freedom in the unconscious; our dream actions are all compulsive. And Augustine says, it is the same in waking life: our will is not our own.

> By this time I was certain that it would be better to give myself to Your grace than to yield to my own desires. But though the former appealed to me and convinced me intellectually, the latter still ruled my wishes and bound me. I was still stuck for an answer to Him who said, *Wake up, sleeper, and rise from the dead, and the Christ will give you light.*

In these verses Sri Krishna is answering a practical, penetrating question: when we are immersed in this dream, how is it possible to wake up simply by willing it? We may see our choices clearly enough on the surface, but deep in the unconscious our will is fast asleep, and we want to go on dreaming. Here knowledge is not enough. "We require," says St. John of the Cross, "a more ardent fire and a nobler love" – something that means more to us than the petty, passing satisfactions of the senses; something we desire so deeply that we are willing, in the end, to give up every self-centered attachment to obtain it. This is the supreme purpose of an incarnation of God: to draw us forward with such "burning fervor," as St. John says, that when the time comes to leave some personal desire behind us, we let go so eagerly that we do not even look back.

The French mystic Blaise Pascal brings this out beautifully in a little note he wrote towards the end of his life, after an experience of the unitive state. His language bears the unmistakable stamp of personal experience. For about two hours, it seems, his individual personality has been consumed in the intense fire of union with the Lord. Then the fire subsides; the experience comes to an end. But the proof of its reality is that now he is prepared to pay any price for making that experience permanent.

He puts it very movingly: "*Mon Dieu me quitterez vous?*" My Lord, are you going to leave me? You come and fill my heart with joy and then you abandon me; what kind of cruelty is that? "*Que je n'en sois pas séparé éternellement*": shall we then be separated forever? I know

now what it is like to be united with you, and I cannot bear to be separate again. How can I possess this joy forever? . . . And then he answers himself with words that could have come right out of the Upanishads: "*Renonciation totale et douce*"; renunciation, complete and sweet. When we finally want to be united with the Lord more than anything else, there is no longer any bitterness in giving up our attachments. It is sweet – not because there is no pain in it, but because it takes us closer to the object of our love. The Sufi epigram is perfect: "When the heart grieves over what it has lost, the spirit rejoices over what it has found."

In the final stages of meditation we need such dedication, such total trust, to let go, that in my own small experience I have no doubt I would have found it impossible without the all-consuming love I developed for Sri Krishna. I was not born with this kind of love. I learned it, through the long, hard process of withdrawing all my personal desires from every selfish channel and redirecting them to flow towards Sri Krishna. In every tradition, we have the testimony of men and women who have learned to do this and crossed the chasm of separateness into the unitive state. And Augustine's words can strengthen all of us when he exhorts himself, "Can you not do what these men and women have done? Or could they have done it by themselves, without the Lord their God? . . . Cast yourself upon him and do not be afraid; he will not draw away and let you fall."

This is not blind faith. It is tested continually as spiritual experience deepens, and those who have made their faith unshakable – great saints like Sri Ramakrishna, Francis of Assisi, Teresa of Ávila – tell us pointedly from their own experience that Jesus the Christ or the Divine Mother is much more real than we are. Physical reality is superficial: it is all a matter of physics and chemistry, a world of constant change. And the mystics say with one voice, "That alone is real which never changes." The body will perish, the universe itself is transient; but the Self in each of us will never pass away.

With infinite tenderness, Sri Krishna is leading us in these verses to the theme of death and immortality. As long as we hold on to the passing pleasures of the physical world, we cannot avoid the suffering that overtakes the body in the course of time. In the first half of life, we have a certain margin for learning this – a certain amount of time to assess the value of physical satisfactions and weigh what they promise against what they actually give. But as we grow older, if we fail to assess wisely, life is not going to ask us if we are ready to give up our attachments. It is going to take them from us, and in that taking is most of the suffering of old age and death.

Here, I think, my granny was at her best. "Little Lamp," she used to ask, "don't you have a sense of self-respect? Why do you have to be forced to make choices that you can make voluntarily? Don't let life back you into a corner and rob you. Give these things up now, when you are strong; that is the way to be free." On the spiritual path we let go of all our selfish attachments little by little, according to our capacity – not under duress, but of our own free will – until finally we no longer need to hang on to anything else for support. To be forced to surrender is bitter. But to give up something for one we love, though at first it may seem a cup of sorrow, is found at last to be immortal wine.

"*Wake up, sleeper, and rise from the dead, and the Christ will give you light.*" This is the promise of all the great religions: when we unify our consciousness completely, we pass beyond the reach of change and death into eternity. East and West, the language is the same. "Wake up!" says the Compassionate Buddha. "It is time to wake up. You are strong and young in heart; why do you waver?" The alarm is ringing, and no one can sleep forever; it doesn't behoove us to pull the blankets over our heads. And when we're awake, all we can do for a while is rub our eyes. What once seemed day is now the night of ignorance. We have been living in our sleep, and now, as St. Teresa says, we live in "the light that knows no night," in a day that never ends.

मय्येव मन आधत्स्व मयि बुद्धिं निवेशय ।
निवसिष्यसि मय्येव अत ऊर्ध्वं न संशयः ॥ १२-८ ॥

8. Still your mind in me, still yourself in me,
and without doubt you will be united with
me, Lord of Love, dwelling in your heart.

In my classes in India, I had two brothers who were excellent soccer players. They knew each other so well that they seemed to communicate at another level of consciousness; they played as one man.

Once, after a particularly good game, I suggested, "Look, why don't you use that same concentration in my class? That's all you need to get an A."

They just laughed. "To tell the truth," one replied, "we don't know how we do these things. We don't even think about it. Our feet do everything; we just watch."

Ask any champion athlete. With some self-knowledge, he or she will tell you the same thing: "When we're playing, our mind doesn't play a part." If the mind does step in, the consequences can be disastrous. You worry about losing; you remember something your boyfriend said or a remark some newscaster made about your game. Concentration goes, and you begin to make mistakes. I think any good athlete will understand and agree when I say that if you reason while you're playing, you're lost. You can't afford to stand there deciding what to do: "Shall I kick it or head it – or try to dribble? And if I decide to kick, where shall I kick it?" By the time you have made up your mind, you will be in the middle of the next play.

All of us understand this when it comes to physical skills, but when you talk about having a still mind in life, people think you mean becoming a zombie. It is quite the opposite. Just as an athlete comes to life on the playing field when he or she can play without thinking, we come to our full stature as human beings only when the mind becomes still. The reason is simple: the only source of mental agitation is the ego. A still mind means a still ego – and when the ego is still we can see clearly, we are free from compulsions, and there are no barriers to interfere with our personal relationships.

I have said this many times, but here let us look at the dynamics of self-will and love. The more self-will we have, the harder it is to love. So in order to love, we have to reduce self-will – and if we are not reducing self-will, no matter what else we are doing, we are not learning to love. If you look at the rest of the verses in this chapter, you will see that they all have one unifying theme: making the mind steady, especially in relationships, by rising above self-will.

The less self-willed we are, the more detached we become – not from others, but from ourselves. You can see the mechanics of it. Without detachment from yourself, you get easily caught up in your own reactions. Then it is easy to become jealous, or to lose interest in a person, or to become resentful when you don't get your own way. On the other hand, the more detached you are from yourself, the easier it is to remember the needs of others, without which you cannot love.

Most of the time we can think of the mind as a see-saw, constantly going up when things are the way we like and down when they are not. And gradually, as self-will subsides and detachment rises, this see-saw motion becomes less and less erratic. When motion ceases completely, the mind is still. There is no self-will, no separateness, no sense of compulsion. We live in unity always, and the natural expression of unity is love – not just love for one person or another, but love for all people, all life. This is our native state. It is not necessary to acquire anything to become loving: when all self-will is removed from the personality, what is left *is* love.

This is an inspiring picture, but more than that, it can be practiced – by all of us, even those whose minds are far from calm. For one, "Still your mind in me." In practice, the meaning is simple: if you want to rest your mind in the Lord, the Self, don't try to rest it on the ego. In other words, don't brood on yourself. This kind of brooding can come up in many ways. It may be self-righteous reflection on the past: "Why doesn't so-and-so behave the way I want?" It may be a fear of what somebody will say, or a bewitching memory, or a fantasy of MGM Studios calling on the phone, or a thousand and one other things. The content of these thoughts varies endlessly, but the focus is always the same: *I, I, I.* Whenever you dwell on yourself like this, you are trying to rest your mind on the ego. And the answer is quite straightforward: the minute you catch yourself doing this, start repeating the mantram.

In the beginning, it will take some time to recognize these thoughts for what they are. As detachment increases, however, you discover that there are only a few basic themes, with innumerable variations. One of the most popular themes with everybody is "I Don't Like It." Whether the "it" is breakfast cereal or the way your friend laughs, the emphasis is always on the "I." So as soon as you catch yourself thinking "I don't like this" – or especially "I don't like you" – don't stop to ask whether the opinion is legitimate or not; just repeat the mantram. Gradually, as you become more vigilant, the mantram will come to your rescue more quickly and more often.

There was a good illustration of this the other day in our back yard. Our nonviolent ways must have given us a reputation in animal circles, because we have attracted a number of gophers who are completely unintimidated by our presence. If they put their heads up and see me standing nearby, they don't hesitate; they come right up and go about eating whatever they like. But when they pop their heads out of the ground and see that our cat Charles is around, Charles has only to give one little smile and the gophers disappear.

That is how the mantram should be. In the early days, a self-centered thought will come up and nibble away at our attention until it is full. Then, after retiring for a nap, it comes back out of its hole again for more nibbling, all in its own sweet time. That is what agitation is: a thought burrowing in and out of consciousness as it likes, eating whatever it wants. But once we remember to bring the mantram on the scene, the thought will disappear. As we become more alert, the gap between the gopher popping up and Charles smiling – between the thought and the mantram – will narrow, until the response is immediate. That is a very promising state, because it means that soon all our negative thoughts will go looking for quieter turf.

Next, "Still yourself in me." The word used here is *buddhi:* the intellect, discrimination. Not only the mind, but the intellect too has to rest completely in the Lord. Otherwise there is still the possibility of turmoil. This doesn't mean that the intellect should be put to sleep forever. But to function well, it needs to rest securely under the direction of the Self. Its job is to make discriminating judgments: "What are the implications of this particular action? What will follow if I do this or do not do that?" To do this, it needs an overriding goal against which to compare and evaluate. Without a goal, on its own, it is liable to stay in its own little closet splitting hairs while the mind makes all the decisions, mostly on the basis of "I like this" and "I don't like that." So "still your intellect in me" means to look at life not from the narrow perspective of the ego, but from the perspective of the Ātman. In practical terms, don't judge things only by your own interests; look at the needs of the whole.

People sometimes ask me, "How can we know what the perspective of the Ātman is? Let alone identify with it, we don't even know where to look." It's a fair question: after all, most of us seldom look at life from any perspective other than our own. Here there are a number of questions you can ask. For one, whenever you are about to do something – or are already in the middle of doing something – that you like very much or that is getting your mind all excited, ask yourself, "Whom will this really benefit?" You may get some rather partial testimony from the ego: it's all for the other person's benefit in the long run, simply a coincidence that it's what you really want too, and so on. But that is the purpose of the intellect, to be a good judge – listen very carefully, ask penetrating and embarrassing questions, and finally render a sternly worded judgment: "This doesn't benefit anybody, not even yourself."

This isn't to say that you shouldn't care about your own personal benefit. But don't go *exclusively* after your personal benefit. Keep the needs of the whole in view; then your own needs are included automatically. When you can do this always, continuously, you won't even have to think about personal needs; they are taken for granted in the overall picture.

Second, take a long view of everything. The ego is short-sighted. It can't see past the end of its nose, because it is all caught up in what it can get for itself right now. But the Ātman is detached, which means that it can look far down the chain of cause and effect to see the long-term result of every action – not only the result on the doer, but on others too.

Once we get past our early twenties, for example, I think most of us will have burned our fingers enough to draw the conclusion that if we see a flame, we can be reasonably certain that it will burn. Especially where pleasure is concerned, it can be very helpful to ask simply: "What does this promise and what has it actually delivered, to the best of my knowledge?" You can make a ledger and draw your own balance: "One German chocolate cake. Promise: gourmet ecstasy. Delivered: fifteen minutes of sweetness, stomachache, surrealistic dreams, and two pounds of extra weight." It can help, even with a powerful desire like sex. But it's not enough simply to analyze on the surface. You have to look deep within yourself and take a long view to see the total picture: what it promised and what it actually gave, not simply the next day but two years, ten years later.

Third, remember the injunction of the previous verse: *Matparāh*, "Make me your only goal." Everything can be referred to that. "Will this deepen my meditation, improve my concentration, make my mind more even, make me less self-centered?" If it will, I will do it; if it won't, I will not. "Will this divide my attention, isolate me from others, make me more speeded up, activate an old memory or desire?" If it will, I won't do it, no matter how pleasant or how innocent it may seem. Keep the words of the Katha Upanishad always in mind: "What is pleasant is one thing; what is wise is another. The first leads to sorrow, though pleasant at the time. The latter, though at first unpleasant, leads to lasting joy."

Then, more subtly, don't allow yourself to be caught in anything. The moment you get caught in a particular activity, detachment goes. Worse, you are that much more cut off from the whole. One small part of life becomes blown up out of proportion, and all the rest shrinks into the background without your even realizing it. It is not possible to see this clearly without an overriding goal, but when you have such a goal, you can measure all your priorities against it.

Look, for example, at the question of physical fitness. Currently everyone seems to be running – not just jogging, but running for several miles every day. Not long ago there was a cross-city competition announced in San Francisco, a distance of some seven and a half miles, and almost fourteen thousand people showed up to take part. Now, I am all for physical fitness; who isn't? It is important for everyone, and it is especially important for those who are meditating seriously. But after all is said and done, running can be only a part of the spiritual life. If this is forgotten, there is the danger of filling your life with running – at the expense of meditation.

Let me make myself clear: I am all for running. But I would apply the same criterion to it as to every other human endeavor: "How much does this help me to realize the goal of life?" That is the measure of its value and the index of its priority.

"Still yourself in me." Next to the entrance to a bridge in San Francisco there used to be a sign with a short message from an Indian mystic of this century, Meher Baba: "Do your best. Don't worry. Be happy." I suppose many of the businessmen crossing that bridge at rush hour thought Meher Baba was playing Pollyanna. He was not; he was being supremely practical. Worry is usually no more than self-will in one of its more subtle disguises: everything is either "Am I up to this?" or "Is so-and-so going to manage to do this the way I want?" When you really *are* doing your best – in your meditation, in the other spiritual disciplines, at work, at home – there is no attention left over for worrying. Then you are beginning to rest yourself in the Lord, the Ātman, at the very core of your being.

All this can be effectively practiced in personal relationships, which is the central theme of this chapter. Wherever there is agitation in a relationship – vacillation, estrangement, doubt, reservation – the capacity to love is divided; love is not yet complete. "How much did you do for me today? How much did you put into the emotional till? Six cents? I'm going to count. If it is six cents, I'll give you six cents back. But if it's five, I'm not going to give you more than five." This is what we are accustomed to call love, even in some of the great romantic affairs of literature and history. But the mystics say, "That's not love; that's a commercial contract." It divides two people, and it divides consciousness. If you want to love, all these reservations have to go.

When your mind is still always – twenty-four hours a day, seven days a week, not only in waking life, but even in your dreams – then, says Sri Krishna, "You will live in me continuously, absorbed in me, beyond any shadow of a doubt." It is a state that is almost impossible to describe in words, but there are certain signs. For one, your awareness of the

Lord will be unbroken. In a sense you will be meditating wherever you go, even if you are at your office or caught in the downtown shopping. Brother Lawrence's words are perfect:

> The time of business does not with me differ from the time of prayer, and in the noise and clatter of my kitchen, while several persons are at the same time calling for different things, I possess God in as great tranquility as if I were upon my knees at the blessed sacrament.

To put it another way, the well of your love will be always full and always flowing. It will be natural for you to love; it will be impossible for you *not* to love. You won't have to stop to think about how to respond to others. You will respond naturally, spontaneously, however is most appropriate for that person's long-term welfare. And in your personal relationships there will be no conflict, no doubts, no reservations, no irritation. You will not need to prompt or force your love, and you will need no reason for loving or trusting or forgiving. As St. Bernard says, love is its own reason: "Love seeks no cause beyond itself and no fruit; it is its own fruit, its own enjoyment. I love because I love; I love in order that I may love."

अथ चित्तं समाधातुं न शक्नोषि मयि स्थिरम् ।
अभ्यासयोगेन ततो मामिच्छाप्तुं धनंजय ॥ १२-९ ॥

9. If you cannot still your mind in me, learn to do so through the regular practice of meditation.

Here I imagine Arjuna, so much like us, complaining, "I'd like to still my mind, but it just keeps jumping around. Don't you know some shortcut?"

Sri Krishna says, "Of course. I'll give you a way that has worked for spiritual aspirants all over the world."

Arjuna, expecting some great secret, leans forward eagerly. And Sri Krishna whispers in his ear: "*Try* – and keep on trying until you succeed."

It sounds hard – it *is* hard – but there is no other way. Nothing about meditation is easy; nothing takes place overnight. Even a giant like the Buddha is said to have taken seven years to attain nirvāna – and if someone of his stature requires seven years, I think it is only reasonable for people like you and me to be patient with ourselves and admit that even a lifetime would not be too long for this stupendous achievement.

Recently I read an advertisement for an "enlightenment workshop" that promised illumination in a weekend. Being taken in by claims like these is like thinking you can put on a pair of toe shoes and make a guest appearance with the Bolshoi Ballet without any practice or preparation. I saw some sequences from Bolshoi performances in a film the other day, with shots of great dancers like Rudolf Nureyev and Margot Fonteyn. When Nureyev took one of his famous leaps, he seemed to be suspended in midair. It looked so effortless that I could almost imagine myself out there on the stage, making wonderful leaps and breathtaking glissades. But the shots of the training that young dancers receive at the Bolshoi School brought me back to earth. What torture! Standing at the practice bar all day long, kicking your legs up while the ballet master stands there like a galley slave driver counting "One, two, three! One, two, three!" It wasn't anybody's idea of effortless grace; it was just hard work.

That training, I understand, goes on for ten years or more. Often it starts at a very tender age. And once you make your professional debut, the work only becomes more arduous. Nureyev doesn't say, "I don't feel like it today." Whether he feels like it or not, he goes to the bar and practices – four, five, six hours every day. As I watched, I understood: this is the secret of excellence in anything. Spontaneity, effortless grace, comes only after years of practice. Dancers like Nureyev and Fonteyn *are* gifted, but the gift is not gracefulness; it is dedication.

Now, meditation is training the mind, which in many ways is like training the body. When you start jogging or doing sit-ups, at first you hear nothing from the muscles but complaints. It isn't because they are being overused, but because they have never been used. Similarly, when you try to concentrate in meditation, there are going to be taut tendons in your mind. If you are impatient and start trying to be patient, your mind is going to ache all over; by the end of the day it will be begging you to stop. But I have never seen anybody who sincerely wanted better health say, "My tendons ache today, so I'm not going to run. I'm going to stay here in bed and give them a rest." Everybody knows that you just keep on running; soon the muscles become stronger and stop complaining. That is how it is with meditation. You keep working at it every day with the same enthusiasm and determination I saw in the faces of those students at the Bolshoi. There is no easy way.

Now, I have to confess that I have developed a rather personal interpretation of these verses. If you look at the text of this verse and the two that follow, it is quite explicit: "If you cannot still your mind, learn to meditate; if you can't meditate, serve me in those around you," and so on. But when it comes to something as important as Self-realization, I am the kind of person who won't leave any stone unturned. Even if it is only a little pebble, I have to turn it over. If I am going to devote so many years of my life to extinguishing the ego, I want to make sure it is extinguished once and for all. So even if Sri Krishna himself assures me that meditation, for example, is enough by itself, I will still say, "Excuse me, Lord. It may be enough for the Compassionate Buddha, but a little person like me can't afford to take chances. I'm going to do everything I possibly can: meditate *and* put others first *and* learn to be detached from the results of action, all together." It is a very practical attitude, which I must have absorbed from my grandmother's example: there is always something more that you can do.

Let me illustrate from my own life how I began to apply this. When I started meditating, just like every beginning meditator, by the end of an arduous day I would have used up most of the power that had been released in my morning meditation. But for some time, it never occurred to me that I could meditate again in the evening. I had a very full work load, and often, even when the day was over, I would go back to campus again after dinner to attend faculty meetings or other college functions and try to make a contribution there. So naturally, when I did have a little time to myself in the evening, I liked to relax: read some of my favorite authors, listen to classical music or the All India news, attend a play or lecture.

Then I began to realize that there was more I could do about my meditation, and immediately my priorities underwent a change. To begin with, I told All India Radio it would have to miss me, and I began to meditate regularly every evening too. I didn't understand it at first, but I was beginning to make my day whole, which meant that I was making my consciousness whole as well. Now instead of a sometimes slender thread connecting one morning's meditation with the next, there was a thread connecting morning and evening – and then a new thread connecting evening with the following morning. I could see the benefit almost immediately – not only in my morning meditation, but in the quality of my life during the day. And to strengthen that new thread, instead of falling asleep in a Dickens novel or in classical Indian music, I started to read the great classics of world mysticism, beginning with the *Gospel of Sri Ramakrishna*. It wasn't always easy, because I enjoyed literature and music very much. But soon I discovered that though my liking for these was still present, I got much more from the words of a great saint like Ramakrishna – simple, powerful, profound words, which went straight to my heart. It wasn't long before I was looking forward to my reading and my meditation every evening. After that, even if a favorite play came to campus, unless there was a matinee I would just tell my friends, "I'm sorry, I have some other engagement."

That gave me the key: put meditation first. Make it the first priority; everything else can be second. Nothing important will ever suffer by this. And once I realized that, I began putting it into practice everywhere. I even used to meditate at noon when I could – right in the faculty room, seated quietly in a chair with my eyes closed, so that people must have thought I had been up all night reading Shakespeare and now was catching forty winks. I wasn't; I was practicing the refrain of the Bhagavad Gita: *Matparāh*, "Make me your only goal." In ways like this I discovered that everybody has time for meditation, and every day is full of odds and ends of time that can be used for spiritual growth.

The key word in this verse is *abhyāsa,* 'practice': trying to keep the mind focused on a single point by bringing it back gently but firmly whenever it strays. I have translated *abhyāsa* here as "the practice of meditation." But after some experience, I began to see that *abhyāsa* is essentially a matter of training attention. It throws light on every minute of daily living, because it means we don't need to confine our practice to a half hour or so in the morning and evening. We can train our attention wherever we are, whatever we are doing. The dynamics are twofold: we unify consciousness by making the mind one-pointed, and by keeping it focused on what we choose, we keep it from dwelling on itself.

In practical terms, this means gaining control over the thinking process itself. When we can finally put our attention wherever we choose, we can think whatever we choose. The implications are tremendous: we can *become* whatever we choose. As Ruysbroeck put it, we can be as holy as we want to be – or as secure, or as loving.

Eventually – this is the ideal to be aimed at – the mind should not wander at all. Only then can it become still. When the mind wanders, consciousness is divided; attention is weaving all over the road. Everybody knows what it is like to share the highway with a bad driver. He is driving along in the lane next to you and suddenly, without warning, he wanders into your lane. Perhaps his eye has been caught by a sign, perhaps he has remembered an errand; his mind may even be in a different county. Then, with equal abruptness, he realizes what he has done and overreacts – first with the brake, then with the accelerator – and darts back into his own lane.

If we could only see it, everything in life suffers like this when attention wanders. A mind that darts from subject to subject is out of control, and the person who responds to it weaves through life oblivious to others, running into difficult situations and colliding with other people. But the mind that is steady stays in its own lane. It cannot be swept away by an impulsive desire or fear, and because it stays completely in the present, it cannot be haunted by an unpleasant memory or by anxiety about the future. Most of our problems in life are caused by the mind weaving out of the here-and-now into a Never-Never Land of what was, or might be, or might have been, and that is why I have come to the conclusion that there is no skill more worth learning than the art of directing attention as we choose.

In principle, the practice of this is simple: when the mind wanders, bring it back to what it should be doing. The problem arises when the distraction is not stray but compulsive: resentment, irritation, apprehension, craving. The power of such thoughts is that they are egocentric. There is nothing the ego likes to do more than to think about itself, and when a self-centered thought comes up, everything in our conditioning screams, "Hey, look at that! Pay attention to that!"

Here again, our greatest ally is the mantram. Whenever a selfish thought comes up, repeat the mantram. When the mantram takes hold, the connection between the thought and your attention is broken. A compulsive thought, whether it is anger or depression or a powerful sense-craving, does not really have any power of its own. Thoughts, in this sense, are very much the same; none of them has any more muscle than the others. All the power is in the attention we give – and when we can withdraw our attention, the thought or desire will be helpless to compel us into action.

Now, attention is very much like a searchlight, which is mounted in such a way that it can be trained on any subject freely. When we are caught up in ourselves – in other words, when attention becomes compulsive – this searchlight has become stuck. After many years of this, it is hard to believe that the light *can* turn: we think, in other words, that that compulsion has become a permanent part of our personality. But gradually, all of us can learn to work our attention loose. Once we do this, we can redirect our attention freely.

This can be practiced. For one, try to work cheerfully at jobs you dislike. It has nothing to do with the job; you are freeing your attention. Second, whatever you do, give it your best concentration – and, when necessary, learn to drop what you are doing and shift your attention immediately to something else. When you leave your office, for example, leave your work there too. Don't bring it home in a briefcase or, just as bad, in your mind. And finally, the moment you take up something that does not require attention – doing the dishes, for example – start repeating the mantram. All this is the spiritual equivalent of those kicking exercises in the Bolshoi School. By practicing these things, anybody can learn to direct attention freely. And when you can do this, you will never again direct it at yourself: not only because it brings such suffering, but because the ego, by its very nature, is such a crashing bore.

I like to illustrate all this by comparing the mind to a theater. Thoughts are the actors, and getting into the unconscious, if you like, is like going backstage into the green room, where everybody is getting made up. Anger is there putting on his long fangs, fear is rattling his chains, jealousy is admiring herself in the mirror and smearing on green mascara. And attention is the audience.

Now, these actors are like actors everywhere: they thrive on a responsive audience. When jealousy comes out on stage and we sit forward on our seats, all eyes, she really puts on a show – if you want to see how much of a show, look at what happens in *Othello*. But on the other hand, what happens if nobody comes to see the performance? No actor likes to play to an empty house. If they're real professionals they might give their best for a couple of nights, but after that they're bound to get a little slack. Jealousy doesn't bother with her makeup any more; who's going to admire it? Anger throws away his fangs, fear puts away his chains; whom can they impress? And finally, the whole cast gives it up as a bad job and goes out for a midnight cup of hot chocolate.

In other words, when you can direct attention, problems will never be compulsive again. I wish I could convey what freedom this brings. No matter how severe the problem, how painful the experience, how powerful the craving, you will be able to go to your meditation room and get up again after an hour or so with all sense of oppression gone and your mind refreshed. That is the beginning of freedom in life. There may still be shackles on your hands, but now you know from your own experience that though it may take a long time and a lot of effort, every one of them can be removed through the practice of meditation and the allied disciplines.

अभ्यासे ऽप्यसमर्थो ऽसि मत्कर्मपरमो भव ।
मदर्थमपि कर्माणि कुर्वन्सिद्धिमवाप्स्यसि ॥ १२-१० ॥

10. If you lack the will for such self-discipline,
engage yourself in selfless service of all around you,
for selfless service can lead you at last to me.

Here again, my application of this verse is personal but practical. Even in the early days, I have to confess, my capacity for concentrating in meditation was rather good. If I had taken this verse literally, I could easily have concluded that these words were not addressed to me. Instead, I tried to practice this verse too. It helped my meditation greatly, and that is why today I never talk only about meditation; I always say "meditation *and* the allied disciplines." Meditation is essential, but for the vast majority of us today, meditation by itself is not enough. The task of training the mind is so difficult that we need the support of a comprehensive program of spiritual disciplines which work together to strengthen each other.

Again, let me illustrate this from my own experience. When I began meditating morning and night, I could have been excused if I had decided not to try to squeeze any more into my day. But as I said, I don't like to leave any stone unturned. So when I saw an occasion when I could be of help to someone around me – by taking time to be with a student, for example, when he was in the hospital – I took a close look at my schedule and told myself, "Well, you don't have to go to that movie on Saturday. You don't have to attend this concert on Friday night." I don't say that there wasn't a pang or two, especially when I had to miss an event I had been looking forward to. But the rewards more than made up for any momentary sense of loss. For one, my meditation deepened. Often I would notice the difference the very next morning. But more than that, there was a fierce joy in turning my back on myself to help people. I know that in a sense I was not doing it for them personally; I was doing it for the Lord in them.

Gradually, I began to understand that "serve me in all around you" didn't mean merely reading to the sick or feeding the poor. It meant, in the simple words my grandmother used, putting other people first. Once my eyes were opened, I didn't need special occasions to practice this. There were opportunities every day – on a busy day, many times every hour. And the dynamics of it is this: whenever you are mindful of somebody else's needs, you forget yourself. Forget yourself completely, and you are united with the Lord.

The more I read in world mysticism, the more I appreciate the penetrating practicality of this approach. When all is said and done, I doubt very much if any of us in the modern world is able to extinguish the fierce fire of self-will without the benefit of personal relationships. In many traditions, the approach is what has been called the Via Negativa: you try to destroy the ego by a direct assault. It has worked for many great mystics, but for most of us, there is no motivation that we can grasp – and where there *is* motivation, the mechanisms are absent, for it is almost impossible to forget yourself when you are living in a world of one. But in a close relationship between man and woman, parent and child, or friend and friend, it *is* natural to want to put the other person first at least part of the time. I don't say it is easy. But it *is* natural and fulfilling, because the desire for unity is already there. You have something in common with the other person, so you can identify with him and find joy in contributing to his welfare. This is the Via Affirmativa, the positive way, to emphasize not what is lost but what is gained.

There are some important things to remember when trying to put this into practice. To begin with, putting other people first does not mean saying yes to everything they say and do. I repeat this often, because it has a vital place in love. In fact, saying yes to everything can be the opposite of love, because it is not always in the other person's real interests. To love, we have to learn the art of saying no tenderly but resolutely when those we love are about to do something that can only bring them sorrow.

Most of us fall short of this, even in our most intimate relationships. Often instead of saying no we remark casually, "When you have time, will you turn this suggestion over in your mind?" Or we write a little note: "This passage from Corinthians may be of interest to you." This is called dropping a tactful hint, but unfortunately nobody notices these hints and nobody picks them up.

To me vague remarks like this show lack of love, because they are made out of fear of how the other person might respond. If someone we love is about to do something harmful to himself or others, we should have the security to say, "Even if you don't speak to me for a month I'm going to stand in your way, lovingly but firmly, until you change your mind." At the time it may be a source of irritation. But after that person has a chance to cool off, he will know he has a friend who really cares about his lasting welfare.

This doesn't apply only to relationships between man and woman. It can be practiced everywhere: between friends, between parents and children, even between doctors and their patients. I learned this in my early days as a college teacher. Boys and girls used to come to our town fresh with the simplicity of Indian village ways, and sometimes, after a little exposure, they would get caught in activities that could only bring them sorrow in the long run. Some of my colleagues insisted that it was not my responsibility to intrude into my students' lives. "You're not their father," they said. "You're here to teach them Shakespeare and syntax." For a while I accepted this as the voice of experience. But I had a deep love for those students, and in turn they came to love me and trust me. It hurt me to see them hurt, and quite naturally, without doubt or vacillation, when I saw that they were about to get into trouble I would take them out for a walk, talk to them, and help them to see more clearly the consequences of what they were about to do. It wasn't always easy for them to accept this kind of loving criticism, but I don't think any of my relationships suffered. On the contrary, my students and their families came to appreciate me for it. "He's not just trying to please us," they would say. "He really cares what happens."

People sometimes ask me, "How can we tell how to put somebody else first?" I don't think there is any special secret to this. The same answer is given in all the world's great religions, but I especially like the phrasing of the Compassionate Buddha: "Remember – what hurts you, hurts others too. What irritates you, irritates others too." To take just a few examples, people may differ in their preferences for salad dressing, but nobody likes a joke at his expense. No one likes to be talked about behind her back. No one likes to be ignored when he says hello, or to be talked down to, or to be interrupted in what she is saying or doing. Everybody is hurt by rudeness, irritated by an angry word, agitated by being rushed or pressured. One Western mystic sums it up in a simple phrase: "Be kind, be kind, be kind." That is the sum and substance of putting others first.

What keeps us from doing this? In one word: *samskāras*. Put simply, a samskāra is a compulsion, a rigid, automatic response to life which we think of as a permanent part of someone's character. But the samskāra itself is not rigid; it is a process. A samskāra is nothing more than a thought repeated over and over a thousand times, leading to words repeated a thousand times, resulting in action repeated a thousand times. People with an anger samskāra, for example, are prone to anger over anything. Their behavior has very little to do with external events; by conditioning, anger has simply become the way their mind responds to life. By thinking angry thoughts, saying unkind things, and finally indulging in hostile behavior, they have made themselves an angry person. A kind of neurological shortcut has been dug in their mind, down which consciousness flows automatically to the same conditioned response.

What we call personality is nothing more than a collection of samskāras. In other words, we are what our samskāras are. It is a revealing but hopeful analysis. On the one hand, it means that there is very little freedom in what we do or even when we think. But on the other hand, it means that personality is not really rigid; it too is a process. Though we think of ourselves as always the same, we are remaking ourselves every moment by what we think, just as every tissue in the body is in a constant state of repair and change.

Usually, because of our samskāras, we go on repairing the same old shaky structure. But actually, every thought is an opportunity for choice. Just as a samskāra is built up through repeated thought and word and action, it can be unbuilt through repeated thought and word and action of the opposite kind.

Now see what this means in practice. If someone provokes you and you respond with anger, you are actually making your anger samskāra stronger. Even if you avoid that person afterwards, you are making the samskāra stronger. It will be that much more disruptive in all your relationships in the future, and that much more difficult to overcome. But look at the mystic's attitude: when you feel angry towards someone, that is all the more reason to be kind. It's not simply being kind to that particular person. You're being even kinder to yourself, because you are undoing a compulsion, taking one more step towards being free.

There is a particularly vivid way to illustrate this. Until we are free from our compulsions, we are like hand puppets; the samskāras are the puppeteers. We may think we choose to get angry – I have actually had somebody tell me this. But more accurately, the anger samskāra is doing everything: putting its fingers up into our arms and head – say, where the amygdala is – and making us throw crockery about, slam the door, and use words that are anything but kind. It is an apt illustration, because it is the nervous system itself that has been conditioned. But it can be deconditioned, and when it is, we are free.

The deconditioning process is straightforward enough: when a samskāra comes up, don't act on it. When it tries to tell you what to do, say no. Repeat the mantram, go out for a long, brisk walk if possible, and throw yourself into hard, concentrated work, preferably for the benefit of someone other than yourself. When you can shift your attention to your work or to the mantram, you have shifted it away from the samskāra. Immediately the samskāra is weakened a little, and the will to resist is strengthened.

Conversely – this can provide motivation – if you do act on the samskāra it is strengthened, and you have struck a blow at your own will. To put it another way, you can't choose not to fight. When you act on a samskāra, you *have* joined the battle. The trouble is, you have joined the wrong side.

If you really want to land a blow at a samskāra, go against it. Do just the opposite of what it says. It is a daring approach which appeals to me very much. If somebody has been unkind to you, go out of your way to be kind to him. It can require a lot of endurance simply to be patient with such a person, but I'm talking about more than endurance now; I'm talking about daring. Try it: there is an exhilaration in it, and a special delight in seeing the other person rub his eyes in disbelief. "I was just rude to that chap, and now he's being thoughtful. Is he out of his mind?" Few people can go so far, but there is the same keynote in those marvelous words of Jesus: "If someone takes your coat, give him your cloak as well; if he makes you go a mile with him, go with him two."

Samskāras go deep into consciousness, and the will and intellect usually operate only on the surface. We may say in all sincerity, "I'll never get angry again!" But the samskāra asks smugly, "Says who?" We don't even see these forces lurking in the unconscious, and if we do get a glimpse of them, we don't recognize them for what they are. It is only below the surface of consciousness in meditation that we begin to encounter samskāras without their makeup on. For a long time, vision is blurred in those depths. But when you get close to a samskāra in meditation, there are certain external signs.

For one, there is a period of expectancy. You are about to get into trouble, about to repeat some conditioned pattern of behavior which you will later regret, and your subconscious is on the lookout for an opportunity. Second, concentration will be more difficult. Your attention will be scattered; it will be hard to keep your mind on a job, and you will find all sorts of excuses for putting off jobs that you don't want to do. And in meditation, it will be especially difficult to keep your mind on the passage. Attention will wander, and if you are not vigilant you may follow a distraction for a long time or even fall asleep.

Like road signs, all these signs have an explicit meaning: "Go Slow. Drive Carefully. Samskāras At Work." That is the time to be especially vigilant about all your spiritual disciplines. Be regular in meditation, use the mantram as much as possible, and work hard during the day, giving everything your one-pointed attention and enthusiasm. Be careful not to get speeded up or to allow your senses too much license. And especially, don't get caught in brooding on yourself. When you do that, you are inviting the samskāra to come in and stay as long as it likes.

Undoing a samskāra is the most challenging battle a human being can face. If you have been impatient for many years, for example, learning patience can be excruciating. At the end of the day, if you've really been trying hard, every cell in your nervous system will be crying out for rest. Samskāras can erupt anywhere, everywhere, and they don't pay attention to the rules of Queensberry. They'll hit you from behind, below the belt, in your sleep; they'll gang up on you; it's all open street fighting. The fight can be terribly dispiriting, especially when you get below the surface level and see how powerful these forces really are. But there is a positive side too: this is the opportunity you have been waiting for. Every time you come face to face with a samskāra, it is an opportunity to change yourself. The reversal in outlook is revolutionary. When you're tired, when people are provoking you, when your patience has worn thin and your morale is turning blue at the edges, you can rub your hands together with anticipation: you're in the ring at last, and the bell is about to go off. Previously you might have said, "I don't want to go home now. The minute I walk through the door, I know I'm going to blow up." Instead of going home, you'd be off to Sonoma Joe's for a few rounds of bitter ale. But now you say, "Sure – one partner, two children; three people to irritate me. That's just the odds: three chances to learn to be more patient. Even if I miss one, I'm sure to have another."

The samskāra may knock you around a few times, but as long as you keep on fighting like this, you're training. Your muscles are getting stronger, and the samskāra, though it may not look any weaker at first, is taking the beating of its life. You are beginning to change your personality, and though the bigger samskāras are going to be in the ring for a good, long time, every round of the fight is bringing you closer to your goal.

अथैतदप्यशक्तो ऽसि कर्तुं मद्योगमाश्रितः ।
सर्वकर्मफलत्यागं ततः कुरु यतात्मवान् ॥ १२-११ ॥

11. If you are unable to do even this, surrender yourself to me in love, receiving success and failure with equal calmness as granted by me.

This verse, which sounds so simple, is probably one of the hardest verses in the Gita to put into practice. If it seems easy to follow, it is because the idea of surrender has been so often misinterpreted. Surrender has nothing to do with doing nothing – and as for "just letting things flow," that is a state that is achieved only after years of almost superhuman effort. The Gita is essentially a call to action. But it is a call to *selfless* action, that is, action without any selfish attachment to the results. In other words, it is not action or effort that we must surrender; it is self-will – and this is something that is terribly difficult to do. You must do your best constantly, yet never allow yourself to become involved in whether things work out the way you want.

It takes many years of practice to learn this skill, but once you have it, as Gandhi says, you will never lose your nerve. All sense of inadequacy goes – in fact, the question of "Am I equal to this job?" cannot even arise. It is enough that the job needs to be done, and that you are doing your absolute best to do it. Then, no matter how stiff the challenges or how bleak the prospects, you can throw yourself into selfless action without conflict or diffidence or fatigue.

This is an elusive concept, and sometimes people ask me incredulously, "You mean you're not interested in the results of what you do?" Of course I am interested. I doubt that there is anybody more interested in his work than I am, because I know how much people can benefit from what we are doing at the Blue Mountain Center of Meditation. But after many years of practice, I have learned to do my best and then not worry about whether things will work out my way.

Worrying about results not only makes us less effective, it is futile. By our very nature we see only a small part of the total picture, and we make our plans on an appropriately narrow and egocentric scale. The result is usually about D minus, barely passing – unless, of course, somebody else is trying to get things *his* way too, in which case everybody runs the risk of getting an F. But when we learn simply to do our best and leave the question of success or failure to the Lord, the result can really be spectacular. Where we had something barely passing in mind, the Lord turns up with results that rate an A.

One of the most moving episodes in the *Rāmāyana* illustrates this vividly. In just twenty-four hours, young Prince Rāma's life is turned upside down. He goes to sleep expecting on the following day to be crowned heir to his father's kingdom; the whole city is celebrating. But he wakes up to find that his stepmother has turned against him, and instead of receiving his birthright, he is sent into exile in a forest for fourteen years. Rāma's brother Lakshmana wants to take matters into his own hands. But Rāma pacifies him with a very simple question. "Lakshmana," he asks, "haven't you ever planned something down to the last detail – done everything you could to make sure nothing goes wrong – and then had the whole affair turn out completely differently? Doesn't that show you that there is a power in the universe that encompasses us all, that it is not possible to ordain our lives the way we will?"

If we could but stand back from our lives and take a much longer view, even the smallest events would be seen to fit into a vast picture in which, as Jesus says, every hair of our heads is numbered. There is no contradiction between this idea and free will. The power Rāma speaks of is the law of karma: we are shaping our lives continuously by what we think and say and do. To Lakshmana, Rāma's banishment seems nothing less than a disaster. But it is all part of a much larger drama. Many years earlier, by accident, Rāma's father killed the son of an old sage. When Rāma is banished, King Dashāratha loses *his* son: and that same exile, which seems so cruel, is actually the door through which Rāma enters into his own glorious destiny. Shakespeare's words go deeper than he may have known: "There's a divinity that shapes our ends, rough-hew them how we will."

If I may say so, the Lord is a very thorough teacher. When necessary, he will see to it that those who love him are tested from every quarter – as my granny would say, not any more severely than they can bear, but never any less severely either. For most of us, there is no other way to learn to remove the last vestige of selfish attachment from our work. When you are taking refuge under one corner and it caves in, you can always hide under another. If all four corners fall in, you can at least stand in the center. But when you are standing in the center, about to breathe a sigh of relief, and the roof falls in, you have nowhere left to look for help but inwards. And the amazing thing is that when you trust in this completely – *and* do your best – help always comes. It may not be in the way you expect it, it will not be at the time you expect it, but it *will* come; of that there is no doubt.

In a small way, this is the history of our own meditation center too. There were times in the early days when we faced nothing but obstacles – not only relevant obstacles, the kind one expects at the outset of spiritual work, but sometimes unnecessary, even silly difficulties too, which I think the Lord must have placed before us only out of a Puckish sense of humor. At such times, I kept on reminding myself that it was not *my* work. From the assurances in the Gita, I knew that all I had to do was empty myself of all self-will and put myself in the hands of the Lord – how he used my life after that was not for me to worry over. And today, after many years of practicing this, I do not get upset over anything where the work of our Center is concerned. I have no doubt now that work that is free from all self-seeking *has* to prosper in the long run – though it calls for resourcefulness, discrimination, and a lot of dedicated effort.

This is not blind faith; it is acquired after many years of trial. When I first took to meditation, though I had the example of my granny to guide me, I had no experience of these truths myself. As my meditation deepened, I had to face some difficult decisions about the conduct of my life. At such times, I usually made the best choice I knew how, even when it was not particularly pleasant – and, like most ordinary people, I sometimes made wrong decisions that carried painful consequences.

But after a while I began to notice that even when the decision was not the wisest, if I had really done my best in deciding, the painful consequences would not be too painful. Either I would surmount the difficulty through some turn of events, or the difficulty would prove to be an opportunity. It was not at all clear at the time, but now I can look back and see that all these difficulties were training me to do my best and leave the rest to the Lord. When you do this, you can be sure that things will work out for the best of all concerned. "After all," Sri Krishna asks simply, "don't you trust me? I who am responsible for the rhythms of the galaxies, if you are really trying to serve me, don't you think I can be trusted to give you all that you need for spiritual growth?"

श्रेयो हि ज्ञानमभ्यासाज्ज्ञानाद्ध्यानं विशिष्यते ।
ध्यानात्कर्मफलत्यागस्त्यागाच्छान्तिरनन्तरम् ॥१२-१२॥

12. Better indeed is knowledge than mechanical practice. Better than knowledge is meditation. But better still is surrender in love, because there follows immediate peace.

This beautiful verse wraps up the four which precede it. On the intellectual level, it may seem obscure. But after some years of practicing these disciplines, the meaning becomes clear if we remember that here, words like "knowledge" and "surrender" are not watertight categories. After all, where there is knowledge of the unity of life, there *is* love. Where there is love, there is a direct apprehension of unity. And unless the mind is stilled through meditation, it is not accurate to talk about either transcendental knowledge or love. All these are categories of the intellect, which cannot help dividing. But in practice they flow together, which is why I have no hesitation about recommending the approach I have found effective in my own life: to practice all of them together.

"Better indeed is knowledge than mechanical practice." This is not to deprecate mechanical practice: after all, at the beginning, the practice of any spiritual discipline is bound to be mechanical. If somebody comes to me and asks, "You want me to repeat the mantram *mechanically*?" I say simply, "Of course." How else can we repeat it at the start? To be able to repeat the mantram with devotion, self-will has to be very small. But – and this is the very heart of this chapter of the Gita – devotion can grow. We begin repeating the mantram with as much enthusiasm as we can, whenever we can, and after a lot of practice, it slowly begins to penetrate to a deeper level of consciousness.

Similarly with meditation. At the beginning, though it should never be mechanical, meditation is only on the surface. It takes a lot of regular, enthusiastic work to break through the surface and open up a channel into our deeper consciousness.

Gradually, however, as we practice these disciplines, insight grows. We begin to see that living for ourselves has certain inescapable consequences for which we hadn't bargained: alienation, loneliness, deteriorating relationships, a sense of desolation. The more we grab for our own happiness, the faster it recedes. And conversely, we discover that when we go after the happiness of others, relationships improve, depression disappears, and it is easier to face the challenges of life with resourcefulness and peace of mind. This is the advent of jnāna. We are beginning to see beneath the surface of life, through the bewitching illusion of separateness called Māyā, and everything benefits from it: meditation, relationships, security, love.

But understanding life is not enough. These insights need to be practiced. And for translating insight into daily living, we need meditation – not meditation on the surface now, but one-pointed concentration that drives spiritual ideals deep into consciousness and releases the power to act selflessly during the day.

As we practice this, the barrier of the ego is lowered and love grows. We ask less and less "What can I get?" and more and more "What can I give?" At last, after many years, if our practice of these disciplines has been sincere and systematic, we may reach a stage when we can truly say "I love." All barriers are gone; every trace of self-seeking has been removed. We no longer want anything only for ourselves; we live in all. Then, and only then, the heart is flooded with utter peace – the "peace that passeth understanding." The ego has been stilled forever, so there can be no more turmoil in the mind, no more vacillation, no more depression. It is not a temporary experience; every corner of the personality is bathed in peace that cannot be taken away. Jesus says, "Peace I leave with you; my peace I give unto you: not as the world giveth, give I unto you." And St. Catherine of Genoa explains out of the fullness of her own experience:

> . . . when the soul is naughted and transformed, then of herself she neither works nor speaks nor wills, nor feels nor hears nor understands; neither has she of herself the feeling of outward or inward, where she may move. And in all things it is God who rules and guides her, without the mediation of any creature. And the state of this soul is then a feeling of such utter peace and tranquility that it seems to her that her heart, and her bodily being, and all both within and without, is immersed in an ocean of utmost peace. . . . And she is so full of peace that though she press her flesh, her nerves, her bones, no other thing comes forth from them than peace.

अद्वेष्टा सर्वभूतानां मैत्रः करुण एव च ।
निर्ममो निरहंकारः समदुःखसुखः क्षमी ॥ १२-१३ ॥
संतुष्टः सततं योगी यतात्मा दृढनिश्चयः ।
मय्यर्पितमनोबुद्धिर्यो मद्भक्तः स मे प्रियः ॥ १२-१४ ॥

13–14. That one I love who is incapable of ill will and returns love for hatred. Living beyond the reach of 'I and mine,' and of pleasure and pain, full of mercy, contented, self-controlled, firm in faith, with all his heart and all his mind given to me – with such a one I am in love.

Now we are entering one of the most beautiful, precise, and practical descriptions of the man or woman of God that I have seen. The purpose of such descriptions is not merely to inspire us, but to show us our real evolutionary potential: what kind of person you and I can actually become, in a marvelous transformation, through the practice of meditation and the allied disciplines.

In a sense, the words of an inspirational passage like this are not just words. They are more like depth charges, which are set to go off when they reach a certain level of consciousness. In meditation, by the concentration we give, we drive each word deep into consciousness so that it can release its potential. But when these words explode, instead of causing damage, they heal. Internal conflicts are resolved, doubts and reservations fall away, and we get the certitude that we are equal to challenges from which we used to run away.

This does not happen overnight, and like most people who are meditating sincerely, I used to wonder at times if this explosion was ever going to take place in my own consciousness. After all, I reasoned, the words of the Gita are thousands of years old; even the best of ammunition can fizzle after the passage of time. But I went on giving my best every day, and eventually I reached a stage in meditation where I could almost feel these words trembling deep in my consciousness, ready to go off. I didn't know what was happening, but for a long time there was a strange air of expectancy. Then, one by one, each word released its potential, and I realized that the passage had become an integral part of my consciousness.

When translated literally, many of the words in these two verses sound negative: "without ill will for any creature, without any sense of *I* or *mine*." But in this case, what is a negative construction in grammar has a wholly positive meaning in life. By *not* acting selfishly, speaking harshly, thinking negatively, we finally arrive at our native state, which is love itself.

In other words, this transformation does not take place by meditation alone. Meditation gives the power, but we then have to draw on this power to check every self-willed impulse during the day. Unless there are changes in our day-to-day behavior, even if they are modest and slow, we cannot talk about the transformation of personality.

You can see that this puts personal relationships in a wholly different light. From the spiritual perspective, if we are resentful towards a particular person, it is a much more serious problem than just one impaired relationship. That resentment is preventing us from attaining our native state. These verses do lead to deeper relationships, but their real purpose is much more: to enable us, *through* personal relationships, to realize the unity of life. If only in terms of our own spiritual progress, we need to learn to relate with kindness and consideration not only to a little clique of people whom we happen to like, but to everybody: at home, at work, in the store, on the bus, wherever we are.

It is easy to write this, or to read it and nod approval. But to practice it, day in and day out, is a constant battle. The other day an acquaintance was telling me he had been a soldier for twenty-five years. I wanted to reply, "Me, too." The person who tries to live in accord with verses like these has been drafted into the toughest battle that life has to offer, and sent to the front lines without even a drop of rum.

Sometimes, riding my bicycle home from the university after a day of crossfire between department difficulties and student problems and all the university red tape, I used to think with a sigh of the spiritual aspirants in their caves on the Himālayas, watching the deer come to drink at a nearby brook and listening to the wind in the trees. I wouldn't really have traded places with them, because it is only the rarest of individuals in any age who can extinguish self-will in the solitude of a cave. But there is nothing easy about realizing the Lord in the midst of society either. From first to last, it is a battle – and in a sense, every word in these verses is a battle strategy.

The very first phrase gives the key to all the others: *Adveshtā sarvabhūtānām*, 'incapable of ill will towards any creature.' Look at the daring of these two simple words! It is not enough not to express ill will; we must become incapable of it. Who even considers it possible today? Ill will is probably the most insidious enemy anyone could face. It doesn't conquer us overnight, so that we wake up the next day with a different personality. It infiltrates consciousness with a few well-trained paratroopers: dislikes, resentments, petty, personal grudges. Paratroopers, as you know, wear camouflage, and the moment they land, they pretend they are part of the shrubbery. That is exactly what resentment does. It has all kinds of disguises, such as rationalization and righteous indignation. And like a good commando, it doesn't stay hiding in the bushes; it immediately tries to occupy the strategic centers of the mind. Judgment is one of the first to fall, and once judgment has been occupied by resentment, we do not see things as they are. We feel threatened where there is no danger, and where there *is* danger we don't see anything at all. After some time of this, the final occupation is easy. We welcome the enemy forces as liberators, and our loyal friends – equanimity, unselfishness, good will, trust – we treat with suspicion as traitors.

Even at this stage, I would say, it is possible to resist and win. But any strategist from Hannibal to Ho Chi Minh will say that if you intend to drive an enemy out, the least you can do is not first invite him in. In other words, don't wait until the mind is teeming with invading resentments. As soon as you see a hostile thought, shoot it down with the mantram. It doesn't matter if the thought seems justified or not; that is part of the camouflage. Don't stop to ask questions; don't wait for it to land and give you a password – shoot. At the beginning there may be a number of wild shots, but keep repeating the mantram until the thought drops out of sight. After a while, with a lot of practice, you will be able to pick off an invading resentment with just one shot.

At the heart of problems like this is our compulsive attachment to two narrow concepts: *I* and *mine*. This is the ego's vocabulary. It goes around with a little mental stamp like those you pick up in a stationer's, stamping everything and everybody it fancies: *Mine, Mine, Mine*. What it really means is *Me, Me, Me*.

Look at how people identify with their cars, or their clothes, or even their hair styles. I have a close friend, for example, who is devoted to her Volkswagen "bug." If I compliment her on it, she is pleased; if I tell her what Ralph Nader says about VWs, she feels insulted. Where is the connection? *She* is not a bug.

Or take the way some people feel about their hair. If you make a remark about my hair – or lack of it – my hair might have reason to bristle, but why should I? I am not my hair; and if I start identifying with my hair, or with anything else external, my ego would swell to such a size that it couldn't help bumping into other egos and taking offense.

This can be extended even to opinions, which is where many difficulties in personal relationships arise. Most of us identify ourselves with our opinions. Then, when we are contradicted, we take it personally and get upset. If we could look at ourselves with some detachment, we would see how absurd this is. There is scarcely any more connection between me and my opinions than there is between me and my car, and once we realize this at a deeper level of consciousness, most of the resentment in differences of opinion disappears.

This kind of detachment does not come easily, but it can be cultivated. Again, it may be helpful if I illustrate from my own life. In my earlier days – to change a few names – if Henry Ford, say, objected to my opinions on history and told me point-blank, "History is bunk," I used to get upset. After a few times, I would begin to think of Henry Ford not as the man who made Detroit, but as the man with irritating views on history. In other words, I began to make a simple, common, but disastrous equation: "Henry Ford *is* the opinion that history is bunk." Once the equation is drawn, it follows that if you dislike the idea, you have to dislike Henry Ford: and that is exactly what I used to do, except, of course, that I am using Mr. Ford here only as an illustration. After a while I would even block out his name; I would think, "Oh, you know, what's-his-name: the man who thinks history is bunk."

Now, I am not denying that there are people who are disagreeable about their opinions. There are such people in every walk of life, and it is only normal to avoid them. But the Gita is not talking about being normal; it is talking about living in freedom. And when I began to understand this, I said to myself, "Why not try sitting back from your opinions with a little detachment? After all, it doesn't mean you have to give up your opinions. You don't have to agree that history is bunk in order to like Henry Ford." The real issue is not opinions at all; it is how to lower the barrier of self-will that keeps us from relating freely to everyone.

My desire to learn this was so great that if no one was around to contradict me, I used to seek out somebody whose ideas made my hair stand on end and say, "Hello, Henry, why don't you explain to me your views on history?" And instead of arguing, I would sit and listen carefully and draw him out with the utmost courtesy. It had several surprising consequences. For one, I discovered I didn't really mind the man after all. In fact, once I got my prejudices out of the way, I began to like him, simply as a human being. Second – which I hadn't expected – I began to understand his point of view. I didn't always agree with it, but I began to understand it: and that enabled me to listen with real interest, because it helped me to understand my own position better too. And third, even more unexpected, he began to listen with respect to me.

In other words, there is nothing wrong with disagreement. In fact, where relationships are concerned, it is a necessary part of love to disagree when the other person is about to do something he or she will later regret. What upsets us in such situations is simply lack of detachment: we don't know how to disagree with complete respect.

Though I have been in this country for many years now, there are still many American expressions that I don't understand. I remember trying to explain about meditation to a young fellow in Berkeley who kept shaking his head and saying, "Man, I just don't hear you." In all innocence, I started over again a little louder. Finally it dawned on me what he really meant: "I just don't *want* to hear you. I don't like what you're saying, so I'm going to plug my ears until you're finished."

This is what most of us do when there is disagreement. We carry around a pair of earplugs, and the minute somebody starts saying something we don't like, we stuff them in our ears until he or she is through. Watch with some detachment the next time you find yourself quarreling with someone you love. It won't look like a melodrama. A detached reviewer would write, "First-rate comedy! Two people trying to reach an understanding by not listening to each other." One is saying, "What did you do the other day when I said such-and-such?" And the other replies, "What about you?" Can you imagine anything more comical? They are not trying to settle their differences; they are trying to make sure that they will never forget them.

If we could ask the mind on such occasions why it doesn't listen, it would answer candidly, "Why should I? I already know I'm right." We may not put it into words, but the other person gets the message: "You're not worth listening to." It is this lack of respect that offends people in an argument, much more than any difference of opinion.

But respect can be learned – again, by acting as if we had respect. And one of the most effective ways to do this is simply to listen with complete attention, even if we don't care for what the other person is saying. Try it and see: the action is very much like that of a classical drama. For a while there is the "rising action," just as I used to draw it for my students on the blackboard. The other person's temper keeps going up, language becomes more and more vivid; everything is heading for a climax. But then comes the denouement. The other person begins to quiet down: his voice becomes gentler, his language kinder, all because you have not retaliated or lost your respect for him.

When detachment has deepened considerably, you can actually see the mental states behind a person's behavior. It is an extraordinary leap in human perception. Just as a physician makes a diagnosis from X-rays of a patient's lungs, you gain the capacity to read a kind of X-ray of a person's mind and understand why he or she is behaving in a particular way. When this comes with detachment, you stop judging others. Then you can begin uprooting ill will not only from your words and behavior, but from your very thoughts.

Fortunately, this capacity does not ordinarily come without considerable detachment from oneself. The reason is simple: without detachment, there is too much of the ego in the way for vision to be clear. It is a precious safety clause, because sometimes even behind pleasant words, the mental state is anything but pleasant. But when you look at a person's behavior with detachment, it's almost like seeing the inner mechanisms of a clock. Most of us, when we have a problem with an alarm clock, don't throw it out the window. We turn it around and try to find out what has gone wrong. Here it is much the same. You still see the face of the clock – the dial, the hands, the pendulum swinging back and forth, the little bird sticking out its beak at you and saying "Cuckoo!" But now, instead of taking all this personally and getting angry, you can look behind the face to the mechanisms inside and see what has gone wrong. It releases great compassion, for as Voltaire says, "To understand all is to forgive all."

The words Sri Krishna uses here are among the most beautiful in the Sanskrit language. *Karuna*: there is a continous flow of love and sympathy, which comes when you see yourself in all and all in you. *Kshamī:* 'full of mercy,' ready to forgive everybody no matter who they are or what they may have done. This is much more than simply shaking hands and saying, "I forgive you." Real forgiveness flows automatically, and with it comes the desire and the capacity to move closer to those who offend you, and to help. *Maitrah:* this is real friendship, where you never withdraw your respect, never retaliate, but always see the best in people and help them to live up to the highest of which they are capable. Then, says Sri Krishna, "*Yo madbhaktah sa me priyah.*" This *is* loving the Lord; and when we try to live like this, we not only benefit those around us, we are helping to unite ourselves with the Lord once and for all.

यस्मान्नोद्विजते लोको लोकान्नोद्विजते च यः ।
हर्षामर्षभयोद्वेगैर्मुक्तो यः स च मे प्रियः ॥१२-१५॥

15. *Not agitating the world or by it agitated, he stands above the sway of elation, competition, and fear, accepting life, good and bad, as it comes.*

"Wherever you go," my granny used to tell me, "you are going to encounter ups and downs – pleasure and pain, fortune and misfortune, people who like you and people who don't care for you at all." The nature of life *is* up today and down tomorrow, and the Gita says simply, let it go up and down; you don't have to go up and down with it.

Recently there has been a lot of popular interest in "biorhythms." According to the current theory, each of us has built-in cycles of emotional ups and downs. For two weeks I can be cheerful, but then for the next two weeks I have to go into a slump. If I'm irritable in those two weeks, I'm sorry, but I *have* to be irritable; that's just the way my cycles go.

The idea, of course, is that if you can plot all these cycles, you can pursue your goals when you're at your best and stay at home in bed when you are not. Unfortunately, the demands of life pay very little attention to anybody's cycles. If they did, I doubt that we would ever learn to grow up, which in the Gita means being at our best always – loving when life is for us, equally loving when life is against us. This is just the opposite of a colorless existence. It means going beyond the conditioned cycles of elation and depression to live in an abiding sense of joy.

Most of us do not think of elation as a problem. After all, doesn't everybody like to be on cloud number nine? I agree: if we could stay on cloud number nine, life might be very pleasant. But as all of us know, the cloud eventually evaporates. Then we not only come abruptly back to earth, we usually burrow right into its depths and hide – that is, we go into a depression.

In other words, the problem with elation is depression. "What goes up must come down" is true of moods as well as of Newton's apple. Elation and depression are inseparable aspects of the same phenomenon, the erratic swinging of the mind: up with what it likes, down with what it doesn't like. Because of our conditioning, we like to make a distinction: when the mind swings up, we say that the swinging is pleasant; when the mind swings down, we say it's unpleasant. But a good spiritual scientist like the Buddha would say, "No. Swinging is swinging." In both elation and depression the mind is in agitated motion, and if we let it get agitated over what it likes, it will stay agitated when it encounters – as it must – something it does not like. The agitation is the same; the focus of attention has simply changed.

This is an important point, because depression today has become literally epidemic. By more than a few doctors' appraisal it is the most serious mental health problem in this country, the condition most frequently encountered in a doctor's office today. Perhaps as many as twenty million people a year suffer from depression acutely enough to require medical attention, and no one can guess at how many more cases have not been recognized and counted.

In an important sense, however, depression is not a medical problem. There are drug approaches that can be effective first aid, but they do not get at the mechanisms of depression; they only affect its symptoms. When Dr. Paul Dudley White, the distinguished American heart specialist, was asked what he considered the best treatment for heart disease, he answered simply, "Prevention." That is the best treatment for depression too, and it is entirely possible. Until we understand the connection between excitement and depression, we are not likely to be able to keep depression from recurring. But once we understand the mechanisms of the mind, the picture becomes very reassuring: no matter how severely we may have been subject to depression in the past, we need never be depressed again.

There are a number of ways to illustrate how excitement and depression work. One way that throws light on the role of the senses here is to think of the senses as windows. In my old state of Kerala, houses are mostly one-story buildings with large wooden windows, which open out onto verandas when weather is pleasant and which close securely during heavy rains or the oppressive heat of the afternoon. Windows made from good wood can function well for centuries, but those made from cheap wood pose a constant problem: after a little exposure to tropical heat and monsoon storms, they warp. Then they open only with difficulty, and there is always the danger of forcing them open so wide that they get stuck and can't be closed again. When that happens, you are at the mercy of all kinds of weather – until finally a good strong storm comes along and slams the windows stuck with a vengeance. After that, you can't easily get them open again. One minute you're wide open to the world, everything outside is blown right in; the next minute you're sealed inside.

The senses behave in a very similar way. They are windows into the mind, meant to open smoothly when we are interacting with the outside world and to close securely when they are not in use. But in a person who gets easily excited, the windows of the senses are not just opened gently. They are thrown open as far as they can go, because of the intense desire to take in all the stimulation of the outside world.

We are not usually aware of this when it happens, because all our attention is turned outwards; there is no attention left for reflection and self-knowledge. But what happens is that the senses are thrown open with such force that they get stuck that way, leaving us completely at the mercy of the weather. We take in everything without discrimination; and just as we tried to take in what we thought was pleasant, we have to take in what is unpleasant too.

Then, eventually, there comes a storm. Something unpleasant comes along and slams the senses closed with a bang, locking us inside. That is depression.

What follows then is really tragic: we cannot help brooding on ourselves. In a mechanical sense, the senses continue to receive impressions – sights, sounds, and so on – but attention has turned completely inwards. If you look at a depressed person's eyes, you will see a little sign: "Closed. Nobody Home." There *is* somebody home, but he or she isn't answering any calls. You can take him to a movie and he won't respond; you can talk to her and she may not even hear: their attention is all caught inside, in brooding on themselves. There is even a characteristic expression, like the look on the face of somebody listening to the hi fi with a big set of earphones, slumped down in a chair all absorbed in a world of his own. But depression is listening to an "in-fi": the ears are covered to the outside world, and the person is hearing nothing, listening to nothing, except his or her own thoughts. And the tragedy is that the program is never positive. Everything is in negative mode: "Nobody likes me, I don't like anybody, I can't stand myself."

In personal relationships, the tragedy is at its worst. In a sense, while we are in a depression, we are not aware of any relationship with those around us – which means, among other things, that we are cut off from the major source of joy and meaning in life. To relate to people, attention has to flow outwards to them, so that we can identify with them and include them in our world. But if the windows of the senses are closed, there is no connection with others at all. We can be in the midst of a jolly crowd and still feel utterly alone.

There is an interesting comparison here with meditation. There too the senses are closed down, and the mind is trained upon itself. But in meditation, this is done freely. You choose a time and place for going inwards, and coax the eyes and ears and other senses to sit still while your higher mind takes a close look at your lower mind and concludes, with compassion, "What a clown!" All this is done in free choice, and after meditation you can turn your attention outwards again with the same freedom. But in depression, when the senses are slammed shut without your consent and the mind is turned in on itself compulsively, what happens is not a matter for joking. Everything is distorted, the way it is in a house of mirrors. Your partner looks as big as an elephant, you look like a little mouse; one side of you seems twisted and deformed. Smiles look like grimaces, and every gesture is threatening. If the bout of depression is prolonged, or if such bouts come frequently, you can even come to think that's how you and those around you really are.

Here, as usual, the approach of the Gita is very practical. Don't expect such people to be able to love, to be steadfast or patient or to work consistently at their jobs; show them how to get the windows open. Once that has been accomplished, you can teach them how to open and close their senses gently and with discrimination, so that they can guard themselves against depression coming again.

Essentially, the biochemical approach to depression is to force the windows open again, very much in the way in which they were slammed shut – that is, involuntarily. This approach can save lives, but it cannot do much to change the habit of oscillation in the mind. This is the real problem, and unless this habit is changed, depression is bound to recur. But to change the habit, we have to learn to open and close the windows of the senses for ourselves.

There are innumerable ways to do this, but here let me suggest just a few that are most effective in first aid. For one, don't isolate yourself; be with people. When you are in a depression, all your conditioning is crying out for you to lock yourself in your room, put on your headphones, and brood over how depressed you are. This may be natural, but it is probably the worst thing you could do. To open the sense-windows you need to come out, be with people, and give them your full attention. It is especially good if you can throw yourself into hard, selfless work with other people. Activity, especially hard physical activity, helps to keep your mind off yourself. And don't act depressed; act normal. Your mind may complain about the company – "a lot of crashing bores" – but you can still pretend to be interested. You don't have to talk, but you can at least listen with interest – and smile, even if you have to pull the corners of your mouth up with your fingers. *You* know you're really depressed, other people may know it too, but what does it matter? By acting normal you are becoming normal, freeing your attention from where it has been compulsively caught. The moment will come when you forget that you are acting. Then you are not acting any longer; the depression has lost its hold on you.

In all these approaches, the key is the same. A depressed person has lost the capacity to direct his attention. To get out of a depression, it is necessary to go against your conditioning and turn attention outwards again. When you can keep attention focused outwards, depression is gone; the windows are open again.

But there is another way to look on the mechanics of depression, and that is in terms of vital capacity: in Sanskrit, *prāna*. This is an extremely useful approach, because it connects directly with the cause of depression: excitement.

For purposes of this discussion, prāna is very much like gas in a car. It is the energy of life, not only on the physical level but on the emotional level as well. Now, in terms of energy, being excited consumes a lot of gas. It shows in many ways. There are people who, as soon as they get excited about something, begin to talk and talk. Excitement means that the mind is a bit out of control, and the lack of control overflows into their speech. Other people simply get speeded up, trying to fit more and more into their day, their sentences, even their thoughts. All this burns a lot of fuel, not only on the physical level but on the emotional level as well. If you could monitor your body when you're excited, you would see all sorts of signs that energy is being burned excessively. The heart beats faster, muscles become tense, breathing is rapid and irregular. It is like punching holes in your gas tank: in all these ways, vitality is draining out. That is why excitable people often feel harassed and tired as the day wears on, always busy but accomplishing comparatively little.

Then, after prāna drops to a certain level, the capacity for excitement drops too. We may still be in the same surroundings – on the same cruise, with the same people, visiting the same Caribbean island – but what seemed so exciting earlier now seems dull or irritating. This is depression. We have opened the petcock on our gas tank, and after a while we find that there is no more fuel with which to generate attention. In general, unless we can reverse the conditioning of depression, it takes as long for the tank to fill up again as it took to drain it through our excitement.

Actually, to me, this is a precious safety mechanism. The conditioning of excitement is so powerful that without some kind of cut-off, most of us would go on getting excited and drain a lifetime of prāna before it occurred to us that we were throwing away our capacity to live. In this sense it is possible to think of depression as a friend, very much like indigestion. Without indigestion, many of us would overeat until it was difficult to reverse the damage. Similarly, depression is a friend that is sending us an urgent reminder, special delivery: "You haven't been using your senses very well; you haven't been taking care of your mind. No more prāna until you give your mind and body a rest." It isn't pleasant, but depression gives a kind of recuperative period in which the senses close down so that our tank can fill up again.

One of the clearest illustrations of this is that in severe depression, sexual desire is often absent. There is a direct connection, because there is no more powerful stimulus to excitement than sex – not simply sex on the physical level but especially in the mind, where the desire arises. Dwelling on sex, anticipating it, longing for it, all takes up a lot of prāna. Then the tank is depleted, and when sexual desire is absent for a while in depression, we are getting a little breathing spell in which to consolidate vitality again and to learn to protect ourselves against undue excitement in the future.

But let me be clear on this point: it is not sexual desire that is the problem. It is elation, the mind going out of control. Prāna is drained by any kind of excitement, and today, everything is supposed to be exciting: vacations, restaurants, music, cars, even breakfast cereals and lipstick. There is a general attitude of seeking excitement that is in the air, and to me it bodes very ill for our civilization if we do not learn how to change. Where people are looking for excitement everywhere, epidemic depression *has* to follow: and as I said earlier, this is what we are beginning to see today.

Recently, for example, I saw a newspaper story about what was billed as one of the most exciting events of the season: a "Look Like Greta Garbo" party. Imagine – five hundred women paying a small fortune to come to a party all looking alike, not only in their costumes but in their wigs, their accents, even their gestures. There must have been weeks of feverish anticipation, planning, rehearsing, fantasizing, talking, dwelling on the pleasure that party would bring. With the Gita's perspective, I had only to read that article to know that before long the offices of practitioners all over that city would be full of five hundred look-alike depressives.

Ultimately, it is not overindulging the senses that is the problem in depression; it is indulging our self-will. Whenever we dwell on ourselves – rehearsing pleasure, replaying the past, worrying about getting our way – we are indulging self-will. And the result, as far as vitality goes, is like letting your car sit in the garage all night with the engine idling: you go out in the morning and find that there is no more gas.

The critical message here is that all this can be prevented – by not wasting prāna. Depression, put simply, is an energy crisis. With conservation there is no crisis. Your tank is always full, so there is always plenty of vitality with which to weather life's ups and downs. In terms of the mind, there is no more erratic motion; the waves of agitation have been stilled. The exhilaration of this state is conveyed in precise, simple language by St. Teresa of Ávila in one of her rare little poems, stamped with her own experience:

Her heart is full of joy with love,
For in the Lord her mind is stilled.
Having renounced all selfish attachments,
She draws abiding strength from the One within.
She lives not for herself, but lives
To serve the Lord of Love in all,
And swims across the sea of life
Breasting its rough waves joyfully.

अनपेक्षः शुचिर्दक्ष उदासीनो गतव्यथः ।
सर्वारम्भपरित्यागी यो मद्भक्तः स मे प्रियः ॥१२-१६॥

16. He is pure, efficient, detached, ready to meet every demand I make on him as a humble instrument of my work.

I once knew a chap who was an expert at card games, who had a quiet way of making the most of every hand. "A good player," he explained, "can't afford to depend on chance. He's got to be able to play whatever he's dealt." Then he would add, with understandable pride, "Let anybody you like set up the cards – some good, all bad, I don't care. At the end of the evening, I'll still come out on top."

He was talking about cards, but I was thinking, "That's the way to live in freedom too." The word the Gita uses here is *anapekshah*, for which "detached" is a very pale translation. Literally, *anapekshah* means 'without expectations.' It sounds negative, even passive, but it is just the opposite. *Anapekshah* means always ready for the unexpected – in other words, ready for anything. It is a very daring attitude, because it means telling life, "I'm not concerned with what you send me. Good or bad, pleasant or unpleasant, it doesn't matter; I can make the best of whatever comes."

The opposite of this is not preparedness; it is rigidity. Most of us are subject to this, and it comes to the surface when we have to deal with unexpected problems. From what I have seen of life, problems are a repertory theater. We may see all sorts of characters, but only a very few problems are playing all the roles. Self-will, of course, is one of the most versatile. Now, give us a problem that we recognize – dressed in a particular costume, cast in a particular role, appearing at a particular place and time – and we know how to deal with it. But the moment the same problem appears in a way we do not expect – say, wearing a false moustache and a fez – we go to pieces. The mind looks through its catalog and throws up its hands: "Boss, this isn't supposed to happen! I don't know what to do."

In other words, to live without expectations is the secret of freedom, especially in personal relationships. There is a song from *My Fair Lady* in which Rex Harrison sings in exasperation:

> Why can't a woman be more like a man? . . .
> Why can't a woman be like *me*?

It did not surprise me to learn that this was a very popular song. In every emotional relationship, even if we don't know how to put it into words, each of us has a rigid set of expectations which require the other person to act and think in a particular way. Interestingly enough, it is not *that* person's way; it is our own. Then, when he or she acts differently, we get surprised and feel irritated or disappointed. If we could see behind the scenes, in the mind, this sort of encounter would make a rather good comedy. Here I am, relating not to you but to my idea of you, and I get irritated because you insist on acting your own way instead!

In the end, this is the basis of most difficulties in personal relationships. It is really no more than stimulus and response. If you behave the way I expect, the way I want, I'll be kind. If you behave otherwise,

I'll act otherwise too: rude or irritated or disappointed or depressed, depending on my personality, but always something in reaction to you. It means, very simply, that none of us has much freedom; our behavior is dependent on what other people say and do.

When I first began to observe this in myself, I was astonished. Imagine going through life with handcuffs on and thinking that you're free! Being a college professor, I had always assumed that my intellect did a rather good job. But when I saw that my behavior was nothing but stimulus and response, I looked my intellect in the face and it hung its head. "Look at you," I said, "so well trained, so clever! How is it that you couldn't see that my daily living isn't being done by me but by Tom and Dick and Harry?" It was a shocking discovery, but on the other hand, it was a hopeful one. With that discovery came a deep desire for freedom to take my life away from that dubious trio and bring it into my own hands.

There is a simple but effective way to do this: give your best everywhere, without reference to anybody else. It frees you from all the vagaries of stimulus and response. On the one hand, by using verses like these in meditation, you set yourself very high standards of conduct – perhaps the highest that can be imagined. Then you try to apply these standards to everything you do and say and even think throughout the day, without being swayed by anybody else's reaction. If things go your way, you can give your best; if they don't go your way, you can still give your best. All the choices are yours.

In practice, this means that we become the same person always. Most of us *think* we are the same always, but if we could make objective observations at certain critical times of the day, we would have to conclude that the similarities are on the surface. A mother may say of her pediatrician, "Oh, Dr. Jekyll! He's always so kind, never loses his temper with little Jamie." But ask his wife or his medical assistant; they may tell you a very different story. "Come see the doctor at home; he's a regular Mr. Hyde." It's like people being meticulous about how they look when they go out, but going about unshaven or with their hair up in curlers when they're at home. To me, it's a curious reversal of perspective. I don't want to be at my best only with the mail carrier or the checkout clerk; I want to be at my best always, with everyone, beginning with those who are nearest and dearest.

Now, I will be the first to admit that this takes a lot of endurance. When you start giving another person your best, especially in an emotionally entangled relationship, he may not notice it for weeks. This kind of indifference can really sting. You want to go up to him, tap him on the shoulder, and say, "Hello, George, I've just been kind to you." George would say, "Oh, thank you, I didn't even know it" – not because he was trying to be rude, but because he was preoccupied with himself. To be patient and go on giving your best, you can't have expectations about how other people are going to respond. You can't afford to ask, "Does he *like* me? I've been putting him first for two whole weeks, and I don't think he even cares." What does it matter? If you go on putting him first, never mind that he benefits from it too; you're growing.

Especially in a loving relationship, this question of "Does my partner love me in return?" should not be asked at all. Give the person you love your very best and don't ask about the response. It frees you in your relationship, but more than that, it strengthens the other person. In one-to-one relationships, most of us tend to lean on each other. If one person wobbles, the other person wobbles too, and sometimes even falls. When you are always at your best, you become a real source of strength to those around you. No matter how much they may vacillate, they know they can always lean on you and trust you to stand firm.

If it takes patience to do this in even the best of relationships, it requires real courage in the face of hostile opposition. Here I can make some practical suggestions. For one, concentrate on your own personal conduct. Don't allow your attention to wander to how rude the other person is; concentrate on not being rude yourself. It is terribly difficult, but it frees you to choose your response.

In a sense, this is like the attitude a good athlete has in competition. When the going gets rough, there are some players who get rattled and lose their capacity to concentrate on their own game. I have seen a well-known tennis champion lose to a chap who didn't have half his skill, simply because he lost his concentration whenever his challenger got ahead. But there are other players who are at their best when they're behind. They don't start thinking about the other player and get all rattled. They dig in and concentrate even harder on their own game, and some of the most brilliant tennis I have seen comes when a fellow like Bjorn Borg fights his way out of a hole against heavy odds to win.

Another suggestion I can offer that used to help me greatly when I caught on to it is this: in an emotionally charged situation, when you find it difficult to concentrate on giving the other person your best, pretend you're an actor on the stage. Play the role of someone who is detached – and give your best to your performance.

Let me give a personal example. In earlier years, as a professor, I often had to attend faculty meetings, where sparks can really fly. Naturally, when the issue was important to me, I used to express my opinion at those meetings – and as often as not, somebody who felt just as strongly about the opposite view would stand up and take to pieces everything I had said. Certain people did this with such regularity that the minute they stood up, my adrenal glands would start working overtime, simply because I was about to be contradicted.

Then I began to pretend that instead of *being* a professor, I was playing the part of a professor: using learned, professorial words, striking certain intellectual attitudes, but all as if it were a role in an off-Broadway performance. If somebody contradicted me, my mind could just sit back and watch; it was all part of the play. I even came to enjoy practicing, and when my opinions came under fire, I would pretend to be Laurence Olivier: take my time to reply, bring the fire of righteous indignation into my eyes, and then state my position in forceful but courteous Victorian English.

Remarkably enough, my colleagues seemed to appreciate this too. Two or three even went so far as to say, "You know, you've really been making a contribution to these meetings." After all, I felt the same responsibilities, held the same educational concerns; I was simply learning to hold my opinions without rancor in the face of opposition. And where I used to go home after a heated meeting feeling irritated, I now felt like a critic going home after a show. "*Much Ado About Nothing* again – same cast, modern dress. But not a bad performance from E. E."

People sometimes object, "Isn't this being hypocritical?" Not at all. If anything is hypocritical, it is being angry, behaving rudely, using words that are calculated to hurt another person. Any kind of negative behavior is untrue to our real Self, and when we try to play the role of someone who is kind, we are really learning to be ourselves. There is no need to be afraid of past performances. After all, some of Hollywood's best known "good guys" aren't always such good guys off the screen. Similarly, no matter what you have been like, you can always play a better part, which you will gradually assimilate.

When we quarrel, when we act resentful, that too is a play. It seems natural only because we have rehearsed it so many times. In acting with respect towards others, we are still taking part in the same play, but we have chosen a different role.

Naturally, it is difficult to remember this in the heat of the moment, let alone to do it. Even good actors sometimes forget their lines, drop out of character for a moment, and whisper, "What do I say next?" You can do the same – repeat the mantram and recall these beautiful verses, which meditation will drive deep into your heart: "Pure, efficient, detached, ready to meet every demand I make on him as a humble instrument of my work." And then go back to the play. You may not feel the epitome of compassion, but I promise you, you can learn to play the part to perfection.

The marvel of this is that the more often you practice it, the more easily the lines and actions come. After a while they become an integral part of your consciousness. Some time ago in India there was a play about a great saint which must have been performed all over the country for a number of years. The actor who played the title role, by his own account, was not at all saintly when he took the job. But after so many years of speaking those inspired lines, taken mostly from the saint's own words, and acting like a saint night after night, the man's consciousness began to change. He began to want to *be* a saint. Finally, after the run of the play was over, he gave up acting and devoted himself entirely to the spiritual life.

Ultimately, to give up expectations is to lay aside all the absurd impositions of self-will. Then there is nothing that you require of life; all you want is to give. You have thrown away your defenses: they serve no purpose, for there is nothing that life can take from you. As the Upanishads put it, you are always full – "Take away from fullness and it is still full, give to fullness and it is still full." And the rest of us, in the presence of such a person, lay down all our defenses too.

Some time ago I took my wife and some friends to see the film version of *Camelot.* One of the younger members of the party was just entering the age when the promises of romance seem eternal, so after the film I asked her what she thought of all those knights.

"Oh," she said, "they must have had a very thrilling life. But imagine having to carry around those silly shields!"

Unfortunately, it's not only in Camelot that people carry shields. Virtually all of us labor under defenses that are much more rigid and cumbersome: our expectations. Whenever we feel challenged, we shove these shields up in front of us – and then, when we have trouble relating to others, we complain about bad communication! Even when two people say they are in love with each other, though each may be trying to embrace with one arm, the other arm is still holding on to the same old shield, ready to bring it up again the moment he or she feels a little insecure.

How much vitality is wasted in life by carrying around these shields! They don't even protect us; and as far as relationships go, they constitute most of our problems. And the Gita says simply, "Throw all your shields away." Then you have both arms free to embrace with – in the end, to embrace all life. When you can really embrace with both your arms, the message is clear to anyone: "There is nothing I want from you; all I want is to give." This is what all of us are looking for: not only to receive such love but to offer it, freely and consistently, so that our lives will be cherished by everyone around us.

यो न हृष्यति न द्वेष्टि न शोचति न काङ्क्षति ।
शुभाशुभपरित्यागी भक्तिमान्यः स मे प्रियः ॥१२-१७॥

17. He is dear to me who runs not after the pleasant or away from the painful, grieves not over the past, lusts not today, but lets things come and go as they happen.

A friend of mine once asked her eight-year-old son what he wanted for Christmas. She was expecting him to say a bicycle or some Beatles records, or perhaps an electric guitar. His answer took her completely by surprise: "A pair of handcuffs."

When we go through life running after what we like and away from what we dislike, this is just what we are asking for: handcuffs to inhibit every chance of relating to others in freedom. I have met people who were as proud of their handcuffs as that eight-year-old boy. "I'm a man of strong opinions," they say. "I'm a woman who knows what she likes. I'm spontaneous; I'm free." But someone like St. Francis just gives them a curious smile. "Free, is it? What are those things on your wrists?"

With rare exceptions like St. Francis, this is the conditioning that all of us share: to run after the pleasant and to avoid the unpleasant. It is the old story of stimulus and response. The other day I was reading that certain microorganisms, which ordinarily go about in random motion, become intentional when particular substances are introduced into their environment. If the substance is pleasant, they move towards it; if it is obnoxious, they move away. I said to myself, "How human!" But there is a crucial difference between us and the rest of creation. All of us, as human beings, have the capacity to decondition ourselves, to train the mind to make the choices that take us beyond conditioned behavior.

The villain here is not actually the mind; it is the ego. The ego has an obsession with taking everything personally. It can't let anything go by without putting in its opinion: "I like this, I don't like that." We may not be aware of it; but if we could listen in on our thoughts, this is the incessant refrain behind all our experience.

When I was living in Oakland I used to go for long walks around the park, and on Sunday afternoons during the summer I would encounter a band concert. After a while, I began to take my walks at a different hour. It wasn't that I didn't like the music. What I objected to was that there wasn't any choice about listening to it; wherever you went, you had to be accompanied by John Philip Sousa.

That is the way the ego is. He has a large repertoire of songs and dances, but they all have the same chorus: "I like this, I don't like that." Isn't there a famous choir in which all the singers are boys? Here all the voices are our *samskāras,* our compulsions. They take every part from soprano to bass, and if they are sometimes squeaky or raucous, they make up for it in enthusiasm. They're willing to practice seven days a week, twenty-four hours a day, as long as we're willing to listen. And the ego is the conductor, standing there with his baton and making sure that everybody comes in on cue.

It is absurd how flimsy likes and dislikes can be. Often, when we meet someone, all it takes to set us off is one little personal characteristic – his nose, her voice, the way he laughs, the way she shows her teeth. Immediately the chorus will set in. And the ego is a good conductor. He doesn't have to saw the air; he just lifts his baton and cocks his eyebrows and everybody starts right up: "I don't like it, I don't like it, I don't like it!"

It is pointless to blame the ego for this; it is his nature. If the ego had to declare his identity going through customs, he would say proudly, "I'm a conductor." And if the officials asked, "Is there anybody accompanying you?" I am sure that he would trot out his whole band. "Come on up, boys!" And they would start up right there in the customs shed: "I like this, I don't like that." That is the ego's show, and to paraphrase the Compassionate Buddha, if we hire the ego, we hire the show too.

To put it into practical language, underneath all our liking and disliking is one and the same samskāra. A samskāra, remember, is a habit of mind that operates independently of external circumstances. I sometimes compare it to a searchlight: once a searchlight is on, it *has* to shine, no matter where it is pointing. In this case, we may think we have all sorts of unrelated likes and dislikes – peppermint chip ice cream, hang gliding, names that begin with *A* – but underneath all of them is the same old samskāra: "I like this, I don't like that."

To take an example, look at procrastination. "I don't like" puts on a fancy costume and calls itself "I have postponed." The disguise can be quite elaborate: "I have all this urgent work to do," "My other responsibilities just don't leave me time," "I still haven't cleaned out the garage." There may be all sorts of complicating reasons, but underneath, it is often no more than "This isn't pleasant, so I'm not about to do it." That is why Jesus says so often, "Forthwith." If something needs to be done, do it now, without even asking whether it is pleasant or unpleasant. Then you are undoing the samskāra, getting rid of your handcuffs.

Now, for a bigger surprise, look at vacillation. Who would think that there is a connection between finding it difficult to make decisions and not being able to love? But as we begin to see the mental states behind behavior, it becomes clear that vacillation has very little to do with external circumstances. The mind has simply learned to wobble, and it will wobble back and forth over anything whenever its security is upset.

There is a good word for vacillation in Sanskrit: *cancala*. It almost sounds like the bangles on a dancer's ankles, and in Sanskrit poetry, a girl with dancing eyes is called *cancalākshī:* 'she whose pupils are always darting back and forth.' In the days of classical Indian drama, this was considered a rare attribute. But I see eyes like this every time I go into a supermarket – trying to decide whether to get mint toothpaste or regular, weighing the pros and cons of two brands of soap, wondering whether herbal essence or musk best suits their personalities. People of both sexes are subject to this. They may think they are making independent decisions, but underneath, they are asking the same question over and over again: *Do I like this?* It can lead to taking half an hour to decide what kind of toothbrush to buy. "Do I like this? It says it's soft, but there are only two rows of bristles. Or do I like this? It has three rows, but there's no recommendation by the ADA." We aren't satisfied any more with liking one thing and sticking to it; we have to keep asking about it more and more often, so that our attention is dancing all over the store.

Now, here is the Gita's revelation: this has very little to do with shopping. It is a habit of mind, and the person who has trouble making decisions in any part of life is going to have trouble making decisions everywhere. In the end, that person will vacillate even in personal relationships. The underlying question is still the same: *Do I like this?* "Do I like him or don't I? He has a nice nose, and I think he likes me, but sometimes I don't care for the way he walks." When we think this way, every time the other person does something we don't like we stagger a little in our stance. Then he staggers too – we're uncertain, so he's uncertain. It can come to such a state that neither person is able to stand firm; and when that happens in a relationship, life can really be miserable.

That is how far this samskāra can go: in the end, "I don't like" becomes "I can't love." This is why I put so much emphasis on going against likes and dislikes in little things like food. It has really very little to do with food; you're working on the samskāra. Enjoying something nourishing which you detest – say, broccoli – may not seem like much of a challenge. But when you learn to eat without rigid attachments, you are really undoing the conditioning of liking and disliking in everything, opening up the handcuffs that keep you from being free.

The problem here, the Gita says, is that our relationships are upside down. We try to build relationships on what is pleasing to us, on physical or emotional attraction. But if there is anything sure about physical attraction, it is that it *has* to change. We cannot build on it; its very nature is to come and go. To build on a firm foundation, we have to stop asking this question of "What do I like?" and ask only, "What can I give?"

Physical attraction, in other words, is a sensation – here one minute, gone the next. Love is a relationship. It *is* pleasant to be with someone who is physically attractive, but how long can you enjoy an aquiline nose? How long can you thrill to the timbre of a voice when it doesn't say what you like? It's very much like eating: no matter how much you are attracted to chocolate pie, there is a limit to how much you can enjoy. Beyond that limit, if somebody merely mentions chocolate, your stomach stages a revolt.

That is the most tragic truth about the satisfactions of the senses: they cannot last. It is their nature to come and go, and when the initial attraction begins to wane, the very things that seemed so pleasant now begin to irritate you. He had such a nice sense of humor when you first met; how is it that his jokes seem corny now? Her smile used to dazzle you; why does she now seem to be all teeth? The wave of passion has risen, now it has to fall: that is all. Pleasure cannot last, any more than the tide can rise without falling again. If you want to build a relationship, don't build it on what changes. Build it on what endures, where the question "Do I like this?" doesn't even arise. Then there is joy in everything, because there is joy in the relationship itself – in ups *and* downs, through the pleasant and the unpleasant, in sickness and in health.

In Sanskrit, physical attraction is called *kāma:* selfish desire, in which I ask only what pleasure I will receive. It is a tremendous force, as we can see from the lives of those with strong passions who are hurled in and out of relationships even against their will. But *kāma* can be transformed – not negated or repressed, but made a matter of free choice, by gradually changing the focus from *me, me, me* to *you, you, you.* Then we say in Sanskrit, *kāma* becomes *prema:* pure love, where my attention is not on my own pleasure but on the happiness and welfare of those around me.

One of the difficulties in talking about this is that our English word "love" has become almost impossible to use. We talk about a mother's love for her children and mean one thing; we talk about "making love" and mean another. We even talk about loving cheesecake, and we use the phrase "falling in love" as if it were something that could happen every day, like falling into a manhole. Is it so easy to fall in love? We have to learn to love, and it takes a lot of time and a lot of effort.

Listen to our popular songs; look at our magazines and newspapers. When they say "I love you," that's not what I hear; I hear "I love me." If we could listen in on a marriage proposal with the ears of St. Francis, this is what we would hear. The man gets down on bended knee and says, "Sibyl dear, I love me; will you marry me?" Isn't it an accurate translation? *You'll make me happy, so won't you marry me?* And Sibyl, who is nobody's fool, says, "I love me too – and you'll make *me* happy. So I will."

To be honest, there is a little undertone of this in the relationships of almost all of us. There is no need to be ashamed of it: this is how we have been conditioned, to put ourselves first at least some of the time. But where I like to place emphasis is on the fact that all of us can change. Every relationship begins like this to some extent: some passionate *I love you's* and some undertones of *I love me*. But if you want your relationship to blossom, you won't dwell on each other's weaknesses; you'll set to work to correct them and really learn how to love.

I wish I could convey what unending artistry there is in this challenge – artistry and satisfaction and lasting joy. Every day we should be able to love more than the day before. Otherwise there is no growth, which means that things are getting pretty dull. Every day the same old story, "I love you with all my heart?" It may be enough for the romance magazines, but it's not enough for a mystic.

Look at our travel ads – "Experience the Bahamas." How gullible we can be! They show us a couple of swaying palms, some azure waters lapping at white sands, and then they ask innocently, "Wouldn't you like to sit beneath these coconut palms and fall in love?" I come from Kerala, the "land of the coconut palm," and you can take it from me: never try to pursue your dreams beneath a coconut tree. Coconuts have a way of falling on romantic heads, and even the smallest nut, if it drops from a height of fifty feet, can put an end to your romance before it starts. What do swaying palms and azure waters have to do with love? Love doesn't need an exotic setting; it can flourish in the kitchen, in the garden, wherever two people are putting each other first.

If you want to know what love is, look at a woman who knows how to be patient when her husband is irritated. Instead of fanning his mood, she strengthens him by bearing with him until his mind quiets down. In my book, that woman is a great lover. Or look at a man who comes home after work instead of going to a bar, who plays with his children even though he's tired, stays and talks with his wife while they do the dishes instead of flopping down in front of the TV. He is a great lover, even if you never see his name on the Hollywood marquees.

When you live with a person like this, the time will come when you find it impossible even to think a harsh thought about each other. You may not completely understand each other, you may not always see eye to eye, but each of you will know without doubt that the other's loyalty will never waver. When this happens, you are no longer living in Berkeley or San Francisco. It is paradise, "Jerusalem's green land," right here on earth. There may be differences on the surface, but underneath the surface there is only pure, selfless love.

Two people like this are no longer two; they are one. When things are sunny, you may not notice how their relationship shines. But wait until the storms begin to blow outside, when everything is going wrong: you will see unfailing support between them, unfaltering loyalty, tenderness that never ends. "Call it not love that changes": it is wise advice. This is the pinnacle of love, and nothing less can ever satisfy us.

समः शत्रौ च मित्रे च तथा मानावमानयोः ।
शीतोष्णसुखदुःखेषु समः सङ्गविवर्जितः ॥ १२-१८ ॥
तुल्यनिन्दास्तुतिर्मौनी संतुष्टो येन केन चित् ।
अनिकेतः स्थिरमतिर्भक्तिमान्मे प्रियो नरः ॥ १२-१९ ॥

18–19. Who serves both friend and foe with equal love, not buoyed up by praise or cast down by blame, alike in heat and cold, pleasure and pain, free from selfish attachments and self-will, ever full, in harmony everywhere, firm in faith – such a one is dear to me.

I don't think anyone illustrates these verses better than Gandhiji, for whom love and selfless action were one. "I don't want to be at home only with my friends," he said; "I want to be at home with my enemies too." It wasn't a manner of speaking; he lived it out through forty years of solid opposition.

The other day I saw some newsreel footage of Gandhi with a prominent political figure who opposed him so relentlessly that people said he had a problem for every solution Gandhi offered. These scenes were shot in 1944, when the two leaders met for a series of talks in which literally millions of lives were hanging in the balance. It took my breath away to see Gandhi treating his opponent with the affection one shows an intimate friend. At the beginning of each day's discussions the man's face would be a mask of hostility; at the end of the day both men would come out together smiling and joking. Then by the next morning the man would have frozen over again, and Gandhi would start all over with the same cheerful patience, trying to find some common ground.

That is how the mystic approaches conflict, and it pulls the rug out from under all the traditional theories. There is a lot being written these days about conflict resolution, which I am glad to see. But no matter what you read, they will always say in effect, "This is how you deal with your opponent." Gandhi, St. Francis, St. Teresa, would all say, "No. The moment you start thinking about the other person as an opponent, you make it impossible to find a solution." There are no opponents in a disagreement; there are simply two people facing a common problem. In other words, they are not in opposite camps. They are in the same camp: the real opponent is the problem.

To apply this, you have to set aside the question of who is to blame. We have a saying in my mother tongue: "It takes two to get married and two to quarrel." No matter what the circumstances, neither person bears sole responsibility for a quarrel. It is an encouraging outlook, because if both are responsible, both together can find a solution – not merely a compromise, but a way actually to resolve the quarrel peacefully.

To do this, however, it is necessary to listen – and listen with respect. Don't be afraid if the other person is angry. An angry person is blind. He is so absorbed in his own point of view that he cannot see what is happening around him, including what is happening to himself. We don't get angry with those who are blind; we help them: after all, unless they have taught themselves to be extraordinarily sensitive with their other faculties, blind people can bump into things and hurt themselves and others. That is just how an angry person is; and when we have to face such people, we need to listen with patience and respect and help them not to rush off blindly into a lamp post. Whether the other person is polite or not, the objective is still the same: how can we find the common point of view?

Here the mystics ask a simple but subtle question: how can you end a quarrel if you do not even hear what the quarrel is about? How can you solve a problem with two sides if you never hear what the other side is? More than that, if you can't listen to the other person with detachment, you will not have the detachment to understand your own position objectively either. It's not just one side of the problem you can't see; it's both. So listen with respect: it may hurt you, it may irritate you, but it is a healing process.

Gradually, if you can bear with this, you will find that you are no longer thinking about "my point of view" and "your point of view." Instead you say, "There is a point of view that is common to you *and* me, which we can discover together." Once you can do this, the quarrel is over. You may not have arrived at a solution – usually, in fact, there is a lot of hard work left to do. But the quarrel itself is over, because now you know that there are two of you playing on the same side against the problem.

Not long ago I was watching the Brazilian athlete Pelé play his last game of soccer. He is retiring now at the peak of his career, one of the best soccer players the world has seen, and in this last game he was playing with the New York Cosmos against a team for which he had scored his most memorable goals: Santos of Brazil. For the first half of the game, Pelé played his best for the Cosmos. But the second half had a brilliant touch: he joined his opponents and played his best for *them*. This is what we should do in a disagreement: play halftime for the other side, halftime for our own. It is not a question of sacrificing principles; this is the only way to see the whole.

If we could only see the game more clearly – and the results were not so tragic – the spectacle of a quarrel would make us laugh. When we played soccer in my village, one of my cousins used to get so excited that he would shoot the ball into his own goal. We used to say, "Never mind the other side; watch out for Mandan". But when two people quarrel, that's just what they are doing – scoring against their own side. Whatever the disagreement, *we* are the Home Team, the Cosmos – all of us. Our problems, whether personal or national or environmental, are the Visitors. And the mystics say simply, "Support your team. *There* is the opponent, down at the other end of the field. Unite against the problem; don't go scrapping among yourselves."

Otherwise, if I may say so, there are no winners in this game. Once we divide against ourselves, whether at home or between races or nations, there can only be losers. On the other hand, there is no disagreement so serious that it cannot be set right if both sides can join hands and work hard for a common solution. It is not at all easy, and the results will not be immediate. But wherever there is hatred, complete love can be established; wherever there is conflict, complete unity can be established. The choice is up to us.

Jesus puts it perfectly: *Love your enemies.* You will never see any loftier words, but never any more practical either, for he is telling us how to rise to our highest stature. Look at the sun, he says; does it shine only on those it likes? It shines on all, it gives to all; and we should learn to love the way the sun shines, without favor or interruption. *Bless them that curse you; do good to them that hate you.* In time they may learn to love you, but that is not the point. What we are called on to do is to be at our best always.

There is room for great artistry in this – especially when it is not on a grand scale, as it was for Gandhi, but in the everyday life of home and work. Here, I think, there is no better example than St. Thérèse of Lisieux:

> In our community there is a Sister who has a talent for displeasing me in everything – her ways, her words, her character seem to me *very* disagreeable. However, she is a holy Sister whom the good Lord must find quite agreeable. So, not wanting to give in

> to the natural antipathy I was feeling, I told myself that charity must consist not in sentiments but in action. Then I applied myself to do for this Sister just what I would do for the person I love most. . . . I tried to render her every possible service, and when I was tempted to answer her in a disagreeable way, I contented myself with giving her my friendliest smile and tried to change the subject. . . . As she was absolutely ignorant of how I felt for her, . . . she told me one day with a contented air, almost in these very words: "Would you tell me, Sister Thérèse, what attracts you so much towards me? Each time you see me I see you smiling." Ah! What attracts me is Jesus, hidden in the depths of her soul – Jesus who makes sweet that which is most bitter. ... I answered that I was smiling because I was pleased to see her. (Of course, I didn't add that it was from the spiritual point of view!)

In a small way, this is something that every sincere spiritual aspirant must go through in order to learn to love. In my own life, I too had to deal with people who disliked me – and I have to confess, I did not care for them either. But as meditation deepened, I began to understand: *that* was the challenge of it. As Jesus asks, "Where is the achievement in loving those who like you? Anybody can do that." If you're daring, it is a challenge that can appeal deeply. After all, if you really want to play championship tennis, you won't want to play against people like me. You'll say, "Put me across the net from Chris Evert or Jimmy Connors. Even if I lose, the game is going to be worthwhile."

Once I got that perspective, I really joined battle with my likes and dislikes where relationships were concerned. If there was someone I had always avoided, who always avoided me, I gritted my teeth and began to try to win him over. The first few times, my knees were shaking as if somebody had given me a pair of boxing gloves and put me in the ring with Muhammad Ali. And sometimes, at the beginning, I *was* knocked down. But I wasn't depressed: even if I hadn't laid a glove on my samskāra, I had made it through the first round. That itself was a triumph and a revelation. I wanted to cheer, to pat my mind on the back and say, "Never mind about winning or losing. At least we know that now we can make a fight of it; we don't have to give up and be knocked out by the very first blow." I felt as if all my chains had been broken, and if I had been the uninhibited kind, I would have got up and danced like Zorba the Greek. And after that, if a desire to retaliate or speak harshly came up, I would fight it with all I had.

It hurt. After all, I was a professor of the English language. I knew how to use words, I had a large vocabulary at my disposal, and sometimes all sorts of choice remarks would rush to my tongue and pile up behind my teeth, clamoring to get out. But no matter how much pain it caused, I wouldn't speak until I could make my point in calm, courteous language that would not hurt the person who had hurt me.

Sometimes, after a lot of patient effort, I was successful in winning over such people. But sometimes, though I tried my level best, I was not. It was terribly disheartening. At times I was tempted to ask myself, "Wasn't all that effort wasted? All that time you spent with that person, listening to him, walking with him, playing tennis with him, when you could have been reading the Gita?" But then I looked again. I hadn't lost a thing – and I had made myself so secure that I could flourish in any relationship and never be let down.

Be ye therefore perfect, Jesus says, *even as thy Father in heaven.* That *is* the goal, nothing less. Why ask if it is possible? It doesn't matter; we can always move towards perfection. In India – I imagine the same is true all over the world – children like to measure their height each year with a little mark on a wall. We can do the same: take a few minutes to take stock of our day and see how we can improve. Don't psychologize or dwell on major failures. Two or three minutes morning or evening should be enough to take a bird's-eye view of landmark events and look for ways in which you can do better on the next day. When you came to breakfast, were you a little abrupt? Did you get caught up in a silent dialogue with your oatmeal? Make a point of being especially attentive the following day. Was there somebody at work to whom – perhaps unintentionally – you gave a cold shoulder? Next day make it warm.

That is all – little things. Life consists of these little things, and it is by putting other people first every day in a thousand little acts of kindness that we make ourselves perfect in love.

There are people, I am told, who examine their faces every evening for signs of advancing age. I would say, don't look for crow's-feet on the surface; turn the mirror inwards. Take a detached look, shake your finger at the mirror, and tell yourself, "Watch out! You think you did pretty well today – but tomorrow I'm going to be even more patient; I'm going to love even more."

If you want to love with all your heart, this is the key: don't ever ask how much you can get. Ask how much you can give. It is applicable everywhere. Last week I saw a very accomplished actor, Paul Scofield, in a film of one of Shakespeare's finest plays: *King Lear.* The tragedy is relentless; and when you watch it from the perspective of the scriptures, it can tear your heart to hear old Lear, in the twilight of his life, trying to bolster himself with attestations of his daughters' love: "Regan, how much do you love me? Goneril, how much do you love me?" For me, I had only to hear those lines to foresee that terrible moment when Lear cries out to the gathering storm,

> You see me here, you gods, a poor old man,
> As full of grief as age. . . .

I am no longer an English professor; my whole life is devoted to teaching meditation. But if I could make a sally back into the world of letters, I could write a very different version of that play. I wouldn't write a tragedy. Lear would learn to change his whole way of thinking: it would all be "Goneril, how much can I love you? Regan, how can I love you more?" And at the end of the play, instead of huddling on the moors all buffeted by the winter weather, he would stand erect and tell the sky, "Look upon a man as full of love as he is of age." *That* is King Lear; the other was a pauper. It can be true of all of us: the power to rewrite is in our hands.

"If you want to know how good a person is," the mystics say, "ask how much that person loves." It is a perfect epigram, but I like to turn it around. If you want to test the depth of someone's love, look at how kind he is, how patient she is – not when things are going smoothly, but in their hours of trial. A ship isn't tested in a harbor; it's tested on the high seas. There are great scientists, artists, philosophers, soldiers, who function well enough when life is with them but go to pieces when the storms begin to blow. And the mystics say, "Set aside the goal of life, set aside meditation; what good is a ship that's only seaworthy in port?" Look at the daring of a great lover like Gandhiji or St. Teresa. When somebody opposes them, instead of running away, they move closer; when someone is angry with them, they try all the harder to be kind.

Love "has no errors," says William Law, "for all errors are the want of love." When we have problems in our relationships, it is not that love has failed; these are defects in our ability to love. In our contemporary climate of separateness, it has become almost impossible for a man and woman to remain together for more than a short period of time. But to throw up our hands and say that love won't work, that lasting relationships are no longer possible, simply betrays our ignorance of what love means.

I read a lot these days about the decline in literacy. But when it comes to love, virtually all of us are illiterates. It is not a condemnation. When you were two, did you know how to read? And even when you began to learn, wasn't it mostly things like "See Spot run"? There is no need to be embarrassed about it; that is how all of us began. To read a writer like Shakespeare with real understanding takes most of us twenty years – and even then we may not be able to follow the simple words of John of the Cross when he soars into realms where we have never been. It is the same with love. At the outset, it is wise to admit freely that this is an art that we do not know. But we can put ourselves to school; and if we are willing to put in at least the time it takes to understand Shakespeare, all of us can become perfect in love.

When two people love each other, there is one sure sign: they want to lose themselves in their unity. The words are simple; but the more you reflect on them and try to practice them, the more you will see how profound a concept this is, how difficult to practice. It is just the opposite of what we hear around us: "Maintain your individuality, maintain your own little separate personality, and then try to get along together as best you can." In the Gita's terms, this is the denial of love. Each person is drawing a little circle around himself or herself and saying, "I will function freely in my circle; you can function freely in yours." The circles do not even overlap, which means that there is no real relationship between those people at all.

This is how we begin. Most of us, if we could see objectively, stand inside virtually separate circles, which we ourselves have drawn. That is what self-will does; and to move closer, we need to reduce self-will. It is difficult, distressing, even dangerous; that is its challenge. But gradually, as self-will decreases, the circles you and your partner have drawn around yourselves move closer together, until at last they touch.

After that, the work is equally strenuous. Now you try to make the circles overlap, so that each intersects a little arc. During eight hours together, you try to preserve at least one hour when there is no acrimony, no competition, no selfishness. For the other seven hours, your mind may have been complaining bitterly. It's quite all right: there is now an arc in common. There are still vast areas that need to come together, but you can concentrate on that little area of unity and say, "Yes, it *is* possible. Even if it takes years, these circles can become one."

If we could but see it, there are not many separate circles; there is only one. All have the same center and the same radius; nobody's area is different from anybody else's. You may have been born in Rhodesia and your partner in Rhode Island – two different environments, different languages, different cultures – but there is not the slightest difference between the Self in you and the Self in him or her. This is the realization that comes in samādhi. All circles merge, and afterwards you don't see separate circles at all. Love is playing like a perpetual fountain in your heart: love not for only one person but for all people, all creatures, all forms of life.

The closer two people grow, the deeper is the longing to become closer still. But nothing short of absolute unity is going to fulfill the deep, driving need in the heart of every one of us to be one and indivisible. Even in the most passionate Romeo-and-Juliet relationship there will always be a void, a hunger that can be satisfied only for a short while. Pick up the paper almost any morning and you will find somebody complaining that this satisfaction has come to an end. "We're together all week long; I need a vacation from him." "She's always there when I come home; I need one evening a week all to myself." I read recently about two people trying to preserve their relationship by seeing each other only on weekends. I wanted to ask, "What relationship is there to preserve?" If the object is to keep life from becoming humdrum, why not just have a breathless encounter once a year when your paths cross in the air terminal at St. Paul?

When two people really love each other, they will want to be together always. It is one of the surest tests of love. It doesn't mean becoming dependent on each other, or sitting together on a love seat writing sonnets. It means working together in a selfless cause, merging two lives into a single, beneficial force. When you have a relationship like that, even a hundred years together would not satisfy you. If you can be satisfied by anything that is limited, your love is not complete. When your two circles come together you will cry, with the daring of the mystic, "Let there be no separation."

In the spiritual tradition of India, we have a story that illustrates this beautifully. There was a girl who was born of highly spiritual parents. She went to school, where she had many friends among the other girls; and gradually, as they reached the age for marriage, she began to come home with wonderful news. "Mummy," she would say, "Nalini is going to get married! You know Nalini, the one who wears jasmine in her hair. She is going to get married, and her mother is getting her a beautiful new sari, and she'll be exchanging garlands and wearing new jewelry . . ."

And her mother, who knew how to read the mixed look of joy and longing in her daughter's eyes, would smile and say, "Be happy for her."

This happened many times, year after year, until at last our little girl had grown well into her teens. Finally, on the day of her graduation, she came home crying as if her heart would break. "Mummy," she said, "all the girls in my class are married now! I saw their faces shining at the wedding, and now I don't see them any more. Their lives are joyful – and look at me; I don't think I'm going to be married at all."

The mother, who was a woman of great spiritual stature, did not try to answer immediately. She took her daughter into the meditation room, sat down with her, and taught her how to meditate. Then she explained, "These marriages you have seen were good; but in life, the sunshine is always mixed with shadow. There are days that are sweet, but there are also days that are bitter: and after this play of light and shadow, sweet and bitter, has gone on for many years, time itself is going to bring the relationship to an end."

"Is there no marriage that is perfect?" the daughter asked. "Is there no relationship that lasts, that has no end?"

"There is," her mother said. "It *is* possible to love for ever; but it is terribly, terribly hard."

"That's what I want," the girl pleaded. "That is what I have been longing for all these years, and to love like that, I am prepared to give up everything else."

"Then give all your love, your heart, your time, your life, to serve the Lord of Love. Offer him everything: 'whatever you do, whatever you give, whatever you enjoy, even what you suffer'; do it only for him. Make your whole life a gift to him, and you will be united with him by a love that time can never bring to an end." She looks at her daughter, so eager and so strong, and asks: "Are you able to do all this?"

And the girl, now gone far beyond her years, answers simply, "I am." Like the other great teenagers of the Hindu scriptures – Nachiketa, Mārkandeya – she devotes herself completely to the overriding goal of going beyond change and death. And the story tells beautifully – almost in the same language that Catholic mystics use – that at last, in the supreme experience of samādhi, Sri Krishna comes to her in the depths of her consciousness and takes her as his eternal bride. "*Amado con amada,*" writes John of the Cross, "*Amada en el amado transformada*" – lover with the Beloved, united, transfigured, transformed.

ये तु धर्म्यामृतमिदं यथोक्तं पर्युपासते ।
श्रद्दधाना मत्परमा भक्तास्ते ऽतीव मे प्रियाः ॥ १२-२० ॥

20. But even dearer are the devotees who
seek me in faith and love as life's goal.
They go beyond death to eternal life.

In the Rig Veda, one of the most ancient of the Hindu scriptures, there is a prayer that must still find a response in every heart:

Lead me from the unreal to the real,
Lead me from darkness to light,
Lead me from death to immortality.

This is the central theme of mysticism in all religions: the quest for deathlessness, for everlasting life.

Until I took to the practice of meditation, it never occurred to me that immortality could be any more than a figure of speech – a rhetorical device that can strengthen and inspire us, but nothing that could be literally true. It was only by observing my granny's attitude towards death that I began to understand that the quest for deathlessness was real – a living search that any person with drive and enthusiasm could undertake, not after death but in this very life. In both East and West there have been rare men and women who have been enabled through spiritual disciplines to transcend the conditioning of time, place, and the physical body. For people like this, there *is* no death. The body dies, of course; but there is no interruption of consciousness when the body falls away, because their identification with the body has already been severed.

In deep meditation, when consciousness is withdrawn from the body and senses, there actually come a few moments when you go beyond the body. The five buttons of the body-jacket – the senses – are undone, and for a short while you are able to slip your arms out, hang up your jacket in the meditation room, and rest in your real nature. That is a taste of immortality right on earth, and there is such joy in it, such a deep sense of peacefulness and rest, that afterwards you will be willing to give everything to extend those moments into the full twenty-four hours of the day.

Once that is done, the ties of identification with the body are severed once and for all. You know at the deepest level that you are not the body but the Self, and when death comes, it is simply a matter of hanging up this particular jacket for the last time. As al-Ghazzali asks, where is the cause for grief in this? Is consciousness ruptured when you take off your shirt at night?

There are no words to describe this state, but the mystics of all religions say quietly, "It's like waking up." Before the realization of God, we are living in our sleep – dreaming that we are separate fragments of life, small enough to be satisfied with wisps of experience that come and go. Aren't the experiences of a dream real while we are dreaming? In a vivid dream, there is at best only a hazy memory of another state of consciousness to which we can wake up. Yet when we *do* wake up again, the dream falls away. And the mystics ask a very simple question: when you have been dreaming that you are Marco Polo, ranging all over the world into distant lands, and you wake up, are you a different person? Do you grieve that Marco Polo is gone? He isn't gone: you were dreaming that you were he; now you wake up, the dream is forgotten, and you remember who you really are.

In the Katha Upanishad, there is a daring teenager named Nachiketa who goes straight to the King of Death for the secret of immortality. "I have heard," he tells Death, "from the illumined sages that there is a kingdom where you never come, where one lives free from death in everlasting joy." There *is* such a kingdom, but it is not outside us. In the early part of our lives, most of us are off on an external journey, looking for Shangri-la in the lands of the senses. But to those who are sensitive, there comes more and more insistently a sense of homesickness, of being wanderers on the earth; and finally there comes a point where we throw aside all the travel brochures of the sense-world and turn inwards to find our real home. Then the quest for deathlessness begins in earnest.

This is a demanding, arduous, challenging journey. As meditation deepens and we get beneath the surface level, we see a wholly different world within us: the world of the unconscious, as vast as the world outside us, without boundaries in time or space. Gerard Manley Hopkins gives a glimpse of these realms in a tortuous poem:

> O the mind, mind has mountains; cliffs of fall
> Frightful, sheer, no-man-fathomed. Hold them cheap
> May who ne'er hung there. . . .

To those who live on the surface of life, the dangers of this world seem "cheap," insignificant. But once we glimpse the scope of the unconscious, it can take our breath away. Hopkins is not exercising poetic license; these mountains and cliffs and gorges are as real as those beneath the surface of the sea. To make a journey like this, it is not enough to have courage and determination. We should also have some idea of where we are going.

I saw an intriguing book title the other day: *If You Don't Know Where You're Going, You'll Probably End Up Somewhere Else.* We are already somewhere else; our need now is to get back home. If you have a goal in life, it is like a polestar: you can guide your whole journey by it. You may have taken detours, but if you keep your eyes on the goal, you will always be able to know when you are off course and what to do to get back again. Without a goal there can only be wandering; with a goal you can never get lost. And Sri Krishna says here, *Matparamā:* "Don't settle for anything outside you; make me your only goal."

A few weeks ago my little friend Rāma received a picture puzzle of an elephant, and last night I came into the living room and found pieces strewn all over the floor. I grew up among elephants, so I thought I would be able to recognize an elephant from any conceivable angle. But no amount of looking at those pieces enabled me to distinguish head from tail. Then Rāma showed me the picture on the box. After that, even though it might take a long time and a lot of trial and error, I knew I would be able to make those pieces into an elephant if I tried.

This is what we do in meditation. I would suggest memorizing this chapter of the Gita, "The Way of Love," and using it regularly in meditation; there is no more inspiring portrait by which to arrange the pieces of our lives. As you travel deeper into consciousness, these verses will shape your daily living; even in your sleep you will want to realize them. "Free from selfish attachments and self-will, ever full, in harmony everywhere . . ." At the beginning they are only inspiring words, describing someone like Mahatma Gandhi or St. Teresa. But after many years of meditation and the allied disciplines, when this ideal has been completely integrated into your consciousness, it will be in a small way a portrait of yourself: not the little self with which you identified when you began this journey, but a person who has been transformed, reborn, remade in the image of this all-consuming ideal.

In the final stages of this journey, it is necessary to use all kinds of contradictions to describe what is happening within you. Everything is coming together, your desires are almost unified; and when you sit down for meditation, you drop like a plummet into the very depths of consciousness. In some strange way, you expect without expecting. You wait impatiently, yet you are prepared to wait a hundred years. Every day you give your very best in your meditation, your work, your personal relationships, so that nothing will delay this tremendous climax. And in the evening too you stay vigilant, keeping the mantram going ceaselessly; for as Jesus warns, "Ye know not what hour thy Lord may come"; he may come like a thief in the night. In these final stages there can be deep experiences in your sleep, experiences which are preparing the way for samādhi. You may hear the mantram reverberating through your consciousness, or the words of a passage you have been using in meditation. You may see one of the great spiritual figures you love deeply, or even have a vision of Jesus or Sri Krishna or the Compassionate Buddha. It is like the curtain trying to go up on a play you have been waiting for all your life. You can see the feet of the stagehands, you know that the sets are being moved into place, but that is all; and it so inflames your eagerness that you exclaim, like India's great saint and poet Mīra,

Oh, how I long to see my Lord!
At dawn I search for Him
Every day in my meditation;
I cannot sleep until my eyes behold Him.
Ages have I been separated from you, Beloved!
When will you come?

This is not the experience of a few days. It can go on for months, even years, and it is the most deliciously difficult time in sādhana. No mystic would ever be spared that agony. There is such joy in it that the Sufis ask, how much more joy must there be in the final union, when all separateness comes to an end? Then, says Abu Said in rapture, "I am lover, Beloved, and love in one; beauty and mirror and the eyes that see." Jāfar exclaims:

I have joined my heart to Thee: all that exists art Thou.
O Lord, beloved of my heart, Thou art the home of all;
Where indeed is the heart in which Thou dost not dwell?. . .
From earth below to the highest heaven, from heaven
  to deepest earth,
I see Thee wherever I look: all that exists art Thou.

When we are united with the Lord, every created thing, from the farthest star to the atoms in our bodies, is our kith and kin. Remember William Blake looking at the sun and seeing a choir of angels singing *holy, holy, holy*? The whole of creation is singing; if we cannot hear it, it is simply because we are asleep.

When I was growing up at the feet of my grandmother, though I loved her passionately, I understood very little of her perspective. My attention was elsewhere, on Shakespeare and Dickens and the "Ode to a Nightingale"; I couldn't hear what her life was proclaiming every instant – in the simple words of St. Angela, almost the same as those of the Gita, "the whole world is full of God."

There is no barrier between us and this realization except self-will. That is all that keeps us thinking that we are separate from the whole. The more we love, the less our self-will – and the less subject we are to time and death. All of us have moments when we forget ourselves in helping others. In those moments of self-forgetfulness, we step out of ourselves: we really cease, if only for an instant, to be a separate person. Those are moments of immortality, right on earth. Stretch them out until they fill the day and you will no longer be living in yourself alone; you will live in everyone. And St. John of the Cross reminds us, "We live in what we love." If you love the Lord in all, if you *live* in the Lord in all, what is there to die when the body dies?

On her deathbed, St. Thérèse of Lisieux was asked what she thought heaven would be like. Thérèse replied in her gentle way that she couldn't imagine it would be so very different. "Oh, I know I'll *see* God. But as for being in his presence, I couldn't be more so there than I am here."

Perfect words. When the little prison of the ego has been left behind, there is no longer any real difference between "there" and "here." We no longer live in a separate body, a separate little personality. As Shankara says, the whole universe is our home.

Sri Sarada Devi, mourning for Sri Ramakrishna on the evening after he died, heard him ask in the depths of her consciousness: "Am I dead, that you are acting like a widow? I have only moved from one room to another." And the Compassionate Buddha, in one of the most magnificent passages in mystical literature anywhere, chooses almost the same image:

> In vain have I gone around these countless cycles of birth and death, looking for the builder of this house. How wearisome is the suffering of being born again and again! But now I have seen you, housebuilder; you shall not build this house of separateness again. The rafters are broken, the ridgepole has been destroyed: I have gone beyond all selfish craving; I have attained nirvāna, in which all sorrows end.

भक्तियोगो नाम द्वादशोऽध्यायः ॥ १२ ॥

PASSAGE FOR MEDITATION

The Way of Love

ARJUNA:

Of those who love you as the Lord of Love,
Ever present in all, and those who seek you
As the nameless, formless Reality,
Which way is sure and swift, love or knowledge?

SRI KRISHNA:

For those who set their hearts on me
And worship me with unfailing devotion and faith,
The way of love leads sure and swift to me.

Those who seek the transcendental Reality,
Unmanifested, without name or form,
Beyond the reach of feeling and of thought,
With their senses subdued and mind serene
And striving for the good of all beings,
They too will verily come unto me.

Yet hazardous
And slow is the path to the Unrevealed,
Difficult for physical man to tread.
But they for whom I am the goal supreme,
Who do all work renouncing self for me
And meditate on me with single-hearted
Devotion, these will I swiftly rescue
From the fragment's cycle of birth and death
To fullness of eternal life in me.

Still your mind in me, still yourself in me,
And without doubt you shall be united with me,
Lord of Love, dwelling in your heart.
But if you cannot still your mind in me,
Learn to do so through the practice of meditation.
If you lack the will for such self-discipline,
Engage yourself in selfless service of all around you,
For selfless service can lead you at last to me.
If you are unable to do even this,
Surrender yourself to me in love,
Receiving success and failure with equal calmness
As granted by me.

Better indeed is knowledge than mechanical practice.
Better than knowledge is meditation.
But better still is surrender in love,
Because there follows immediate peace.

That one I love who is incapable of ill will,
And returns love for hatred.
Living beyond the reach of I and mine
And of pleasure and pain, full of mercy,
Contented, self-controlled, firm in faith,
With all their heart and all their mind given to me –
With such as these I am in love.

Not agitating the world or by it agitated,
They stand above the sway of elation,
Competition, and fear, accepting life
Good and bad as it comes. They are pure,
Efficient, detached, ready to meet every demand
I make on them as a humble instrument of my work.

They are dear to me who run not after the pleasant
Or away from the painful, grieve not
Over the past, lust not today,
But let things come and go as they happen.

Who serve both friend and foe with equal love,
Not buoyed up by praise or cast down by blame,
Alike in heat and cold, pleasure and pain,
Free from selfish attachments and self-will,
Ever full, in harmony everywhere,
Firm in faith – such as these are dear to me.

But dearest to me are those who seek me
In faith and love as life's eternal goal.
They go beyond death to immortality.

Glossary & Guide to Sanskrit Pronunciation

GUIDE TO THE PRONUNCIATION OF SANSKRIT WORDS

Consonants. Consonants are generally pronounced as in English, but there are some differences. Sanskrit has many so-called aspirated consonants, that is, consonants pronounced with a slight *h* sound. For example, the consonant *ph* is pronounced as English *p* followed by an *h* as in ha*ph*azard. The *bh* is as in a*bh*or. The aspirated consonants are *kh, gh, ch, jh, th, dh, ph, bh.*

c as in *ch*urch	*g* as in *g*old
h as in *h*ome	*j* as in *J*une

The other consonants are approximately as in English.

Vowels. Every Sanskrit vowel has two forms, one short and one long. The long form is pronounced twice as long as the short. In the English transliteration the long vowels are marked with a bar (¯). The diphthongs – *e, ai, o, au* – are also pronounced twice as long as the short vowels. Thus, in the words *nīla* 'blue' and *gopa* 'cowherd,' the first syllable is held twice as long as the second.

a as in *u*p	*ri* as in w*ri*tten
ā as in f*a*ther	*e* as in th*ey*
i as in g*i*ve	*ai* as in *ai*sle
ī as in s*ee*	*o* as in g*o*
u as in p*u*t	*au* as in c*ow*
ū as in r*u*le	

SPELLING OF SANSKRIT WORDS

To simplify the spelling of Sanskrit words we have used a minimum of diacritical marks, retaining only the long mark (¯) for the long vowels and omitting the other diacritics which are sometimes used in rendering Sanskrit words into English.

abhyāsa Regular practice.

adhyāropa [or *adhyāsa*] Shankara's theory of superimposition; the process of ascribing the qualities of one thing to something else of a different nature.

advaita ['not two'] Having no duality; the supreme Reality, which is the One without a second. The word *advaita* is especially used in Vedānta philosophy, which stresses the unity of the Self (Ātman) and Brahman.

ajapajapam The holy name (*mantram*) repeating itself in the consciousness of the devotee without effort on his part.

akshara The eternal; the syllable *Om*.

Ananta The cosmic serpent on which Vishnu reclines in rest.

Ardhanārīshvara "The Lord who is half female (and half male)," name of a form of Shiva.

Arjuna One of the five Pāndava brothers, and an important figure in Indian epic and legend. He is Sri Krishna's beloved disciple and friend in the Bhagavad Gita.

āshram [Skt. *āshrama*, from *shram* 'to exert oneself'] A spiritual community, where meditation and spiritual disciplines are practiced.

Ātman 'The Self'; the innermost soul in every creature, which is divine.

avatāra [*ava* 'down'; *tri* 'to cross'] The descent of God to earth; the incarnation of the Lord on earth; the birth of the Lord, of divine consciousness, in the heart of man.

Bardo [Tibetan *bar* 'between'; *do* 'two'] In Tibetan mysticism, the state between two lives in which the soul awaits a proper body and context for rebirth.

Bhagavad Gītā [*Bhagavat* 'Lord'; *gītā* 'song'] "The Song of the Lord," name of a Hindu scripture which contains the instructions of Sri Krishna.

bhakti [*bhaj* 'to serve, worship, love'] Devotion, worship, love.

bhakti yoga The Way of Love.

Bhārata India; a native of India; a descendant of King Bharata.

Bhīshma A revered elder of the Kaurava dynasty who allows himself to be killed by Arjuna in the *Mahābhārata* battle.

Brahmā The god of creation. Brahmā, the Creator, Vishnu, the Preserver, and Shiva, the Dissolver, make up the Hindu Trinity. *Brahmā,* a word with masculine gender, should not be confused with *Brahman,* which has neuter gender. (See next entry.)

Brahman The supreme Reality underlying all life, the Divine Ground of existence, the impersonal Godhead.

Brahmānda "The egg of Brahman," the primordial atom from which the cosmos evolves.

Brahmavidyā The science of knowing Brahman.

Buddha [from *budh* 'to wake up'] "The Awakened One." An enlightened being; the title given to the sage Siddhārtha Gautama Shākyamuni after he obtained complete illumination. The Buddha lived and taught in North India during the sixth century B.C.

buddhi Understanding, intelligence; correct view, idea, purpose.
deva A divine being, a god.
Dhammapada [Pāli, from Skt. *Dharmapada*] An important early Buddhist scripture.
dhārana The first stage in meditation.
dharma Law, duty; the universal Law which holds all life together in unity.
dhyāna Meditation; specifically, in Patanjali's yoga, the second stage in meditation.
dvāpara yuga See *yuga*.
Ganges [Skt. *gangā*] A great river of northern India, looked upon as a sacred symbol.
Gītā "The Song," a shorter title for the Bhagavad Gita.
gopī Cowherd girl, milkmaid, especially the companions of Krishna as a young man in Vrindāvana.
guna Quality; specifically, the three qualities which make up the phenomenal world: *sattva*, law; *rajas*, energy; and *tamas*, inertia.
Hanumān The monkey devotee of Rāma.
Hari [*hri* 'to steal'] "He who has stolen our hearts," name of Vishnu or Krishna.
Himālaya [*hima* 'snow'; *ālaya* 'abode'] The great mountain range which stretches across the northern border of India, important in mythology as the home of Shiva and other gods.
jnāna [*jnā* 'to know'] Wisdom; higher knowledge derived from spiritual disciplines.
jnāna yoga The Way of Wisdom.
Kālī "The dark one," name of the Divine Mother as the consort of Shiva.
Kālidāsa "Servant of *Kālī*," name of a celebrated poet of ancient India.
Kali yuga See *yuga*.
kalpa A period in cosmic time equaling one day of Brahmā or 1,000 "great yugas" – a total of 4,320 million years. See also *yuga*.
kalpa tree A wish-fulfilling tree said to grow in paradise.
Kāma Selfish desire, greed; sexual desire, sometimes personified as Kāmadeva, "god of desire."
karma [*kri* 'to do'] Action; former actions which will lead to certain results in a cause and effect relationship.
karma yoga The Way of Action; the path of selfless service.
Kauravas "The sons of Kuru," usually referring to Duryodhana and his brothers, who are the enemies of the Pāndava brothers.
Keshava "He who has long, beautiful hair," name of Krishna.
Krishna ['black'; or from krish 'to draw,' 'to attract to oneself'] "The Dark One" or "He who draws us to Himself," name of an incarnation of Vishnu. Krishna was born in response to Mother Earth's plea to Vishnu to save her from the evils threatening her. Many stories are told of his childhood in a small, simple village, and he is often worshipped in the form of a

child. As a young man he was adored by all the village girls, especially Rādhā, and their romance symbolizes the lover – Beloved relationship which the devotee may have with the Lord. Later on Krishna became the friend and advisor of the Pāndava brothers, especially Arjuna, to whom he reveals the teachings of the Bhagavad Gita. He is the Lord of Love who dwells in the hearts of all.

kundalinī "The serpent power," spiritual or evolutionary energy.

līlā Game; the divine play of the Lord disguising himself as many.

Mahābhārata Name of a great epic composed from two to three thousand years ago, traditionally attributed to the sage Vyāsa. It relates the conflict between the descendants of Pāndu (the forces of light) and those of Dhritarāshtra (the forces of darkness).

mahātma "Great soul."

manas The mind; specifically, the faculty which registers and stores sensory impressions.

mantram [or *mantra*] A holy name or phrase; a spiritual formula.

Māra "The Striker"; in Buddhism, the Tempter, the Evil One who tries to prevent the Buddha's enlightenment.

Māyā Illusion; appearance, as contrasted with Reality; the creative power of the Lord.

muni A sage.

Nārada The divine musician and sage who is a devotee of Sri Krishna.

nirvāna [*nir* 'out'; *vāna* 'to blow'] Complete extinction of self-will and separateness; realization of the unity of all life.

nirvikalpa samādhi A state of spiritual awareness in which there is no perception of duality, of inside or outside, of subject and object; merger in the impersonal Godhead.

Om [or *Aum*] The cosmic sound, which can be heard in deep meditation; the Holy Word, taught in the Upanishads, which signifies Brahman, the Divine Ground of existence.

Pāndavas "The sons of Pāndu," a collective name for Arjuna and his four brothers, Yudhishthira, Bhīma, Nakula, and Sahadeva.

Patanjali The author of the *Yogasūtras,* a concise description of the way to Self-realization through meditation. He lived around the second century B.C., and his method is sometimes referred to as *rāja yoga.*

prakriti The basic energy from which the mental and physical worlds take shape; nature.

prāna Breath; vital force.

prema Intense divine love.

preya (opposite of *shreya*) That which seems pleasing to the senses; passing pleasure.

Purusha ['person'] The inner soul, the spiritual core of man. In the Gita, the terms *Ātman* and *Purusha* are virtually interchangeable.

Rādhā The milkmaid who is Sri Krishna's beloved while he sojourns in Vrindāvana. She represents the human soul seeking the divine Beloved.
rāja yoga The Royal Path; the path of meditation taught especially by Patanjali in the *Yogasūtras*.
rajas Passion, energy; the second of the three qualities (*gunas*).
Rāma [from *ram* 'to rejoice'] The Lord of Joy; the principle of joy within.
sādhana A body of disciplines or way of life which leads to the supreme goal of Self-realization.
sādhu A holy man, sage.
samādhi Union with the Lord; a state of intense concentration in which consciousness is completely unified.
samsāra The world of flux; the round of birth, decay, death, and rebirth.
samskāra A personality trait conditioned over many lives or one life: a mental and behavioral pattern; a latency or tendency within the mind which will manifest itself if given the proper environment and stimulus.
Sanjaya The sage who divinely perceives the narrative of the Gita and reports it to the blind king Dhritarāshtra.
Sānkhya One of the six branches of traditional Hindu philosophy. Sānkhya seeks to liberate the individual *Purusha* (spirit) from *prakriti* (mind and matter) through the knowledge of the ultimate separation of these two realities.
sattva Goodness, purity, law; the highest of the three qualities (*gunas*).
satyāgraha [*satya* 'truth'; *āgraha* 'grasping'] Gandhi's term for a moral struggle as opposed to a violent opposition.
satya yuga See *yuga*.
savikalpa samādhi [*sa-vikalpa* 'having distinctions' or 'admitting separateness'] Samādhi in which some duality of subject and object remains, the devotee being absorbed in his meditation upon the Lord without becoming completely one with Him; union with the personal God.
Shankara "Bringing about eternal welfare," name of Shiva. Also name of a Hindu saint of the sixth or seventh century A.D., born in Kerala, who is the author of many devotional hymns and philosophical works, including a commentary on the Gita. He is the leading teacher of the doctrine of nondualism or Advaita Vedānta.
Shiva Third in the Hindu Trinity; he who destroys the ego and conquers death.
shraddhā Faith
shreya The Good, that which is permanently beneficial.
Sītā The wife of Rāma and the ideal for womanly love and loyalty.
soma A drink used in Vedic ritual in ancient India; the drink of the gods.
Srī [pronounced *shrī*] A title of respect originally meaning "Lord" or "holy"; in modern India, simply a respectful form of address.
sthūlasharīra The physical body.
sūkshmasharīra The subtle body, made up of *samskāras*.

tamas Inertia, ignorance; the lowest of the three qualities or gunas.
tanhā [Prākrit, from Skt. *trishnā* 'thirst'] The thirst for selfish satisfaction, the craving of the senses and the ego.
tapas Austerity, control of the senses; the spiritual power acquired through self-control.
Tat tvam asi "That thou art." Quoted from a verse in the Chāndogya Upanishad: "That subtle essence which is the Self of this entire world, That is the Real, That is the Self, That thou art."
tejas Brightness; spiritual energy and power.
tretā yuga See *yuga*.
turīya "The Fourth," the highest state of consciousness, union with Brahman. The other three states are waking, dreaming, and dreamless sleep.
Upanishads Ancient mystical documents found at the end of each of the four Vedas.
Vaikuntha Vishnu's heavenly realm.
Veda [*vid* 'to know'] "Knowledge"; the name of the most ancient Sanskrit scriptures. Orthodox Hindus regard them as the direct revelation of truth from God to the first sages.
vīnā An ancient South Indian stringed instrument used in classical music.
Vishnu Second in the Hindu Trinity; the Preserver who incarnates himself in age after age for the establishment of dharma and for the welfare of all creatures.
Vrindāvana Name of a village on the Yamunā River where the historic Krishna spent his youth as a cowherd, befriending the local cowherds and milkmaids. Today it is an important place of pilgrimage.
yoga [from *yuj* 'to unite'] Union with the Lord, realization of the unity of all life; a path or discipline which leads to such a state of total integration or unity.
yogī A man who practices spiritual disciplines.
Yudhishthira Arjuna's elder brother, who is famous for his adherence to dharma at all times.
yuga An age, eon. In Hindu cosmology there are four yugas, representing a steady deterioration in the state of the world from age to age. Satya yuga is the age of perfection, followed by tretā yuga. The incarnation of Sri Krishna is said to mark the end of the third yuga, dvāpara. We are living in the fourth and final yuga, kali, in which the decline of creation reaches its lowest point. Together the four yugas equal a *mahayuga* ('great yuga') or *kalpa,* a period of 4,320,000 years. One thousand *mahayugas* equals one day of Brahmā. At the end of one such day the cosmos is recalled into the Lord, and for an equal period – one night of Brahmā – there is a cosmic rest. At the dawn of the next day of Brahmā, the whole process of creation begins anew.

Index

END

Blue Mountain Center of Meditation

The Blue Mountain Center of Meditation publishes Eknath Easwaran's books, videos, and audio recordings, and offers retreats and online programs on his eight-point program of passage meditation.

For more information and resources, please visit: www.bmcm.org

The Blue Mountain Center of Meditation
Box 256, Tomales, California 94971 USA
Telephone: +1 707 878 2369
Toll-free in the US: 800 475 2369
Email: info@bmcm.org

The Bhagavad Gita

for Daily Living

VOLUME III: TO LOVE IS TO KNOW ME

SECOND EDITION

भक्त्या मामभिजानाति यावान्यश्चास्मि तत्त्वतः । ततो मां तत्त्वतो ज्ञात्वा विशते तदनन्तरम् ॥ १८-५५ ॥
सर्वकर्माण्यपि सदा कुर्वाणो मद्व्यपाश्रयः । मत्प्रसादादवाप्नोति शाश्वतं पदमव्ययम् ॥ १८-५६ ॥

To love is to know me: thus one shares in my glory and enters into my boundless being. All his acts are performed in my service, and through my grace he wins eternal life.

— BHAGAVAD GITA 18:55–56

The Bhagavad Gita

for Daily Living

VOLUME III: TO LOVE IS TO KNOW ME

SECOND EDITION

EKNATH EASWARAN

JAICO PUBLISHING HOUSE

Ahmedabad Bangalore Chennai
Delhi Hyderabad Kolkata Mumbai

Published by Jaico Publishing House
A-2 Jash Chambers, 7-A Sir Phirozshah Mehta Road
Fort, Mumbai - 400 001
jaicopub@jaicobooks.com
www.jaicobooks.com

Published in arrangement with
Nilgiri Press
P.O. Box 256, Tomales, California 94971
www.easwaran.org

To be sold only in India, Bangladesh, Bhutan,
Pakistan, Nepal, Sri Lanka and the Maldives.

THE BHAGAVAD GITA FOR DAILY LIVING
Volume III:
To Love Is to Know Me
ISBN 978-93-91019-83-9
(Set of 3 Volumes)

First Jaico Impression: 1997
First Jaico Impression (Second Edition): 2021
Third Jaico Impression: 2025

Printed by
Nutech Print Services - India, New Delhi

To my Teacher

EKNATH CHIPPU KUNCHI AMMAL

my Grandmother & my Playmate

Table of Contents

INTRODUCTION

A Higher Image

One of the first lessons I learned in geography was that the earth is round. Our little village in South India had been left out of the march of modern civilization, and most of us hadn't heard this terrible news. Even my teacher was a little diffident in presenting it to us. "You may not believe this," he began, "and if you don't, I sympathize completely. But this is what they gave me to understand when I did my teacher's training in Madras."

When I went home that afternoon, my granny was waiting for me as always by the front gate, ready with her usual greeting: "Well, Little Lamp, what did you learn in school today?" Somehow this was never an automatic question; each time it was fresh and her interest genuine.

"Brace yourself, Granny," I said. "You may not believe this, and if you don't, I sympathize completely. But today my teacher told us that the earth is really round." Shattering the illusions of a granny's lifetime.

Not a hair fell out of place. "What does it matter?" she asked. "You can be selfless whether the earth is round or square or triangular."

That took some wind out of my sails. But there was still my mother; she was much easier to surprise. I marched over and said, "Guess what we learned today."

"I can't," she said. "You tell me."

"The earth is round!"

She fell into a paroxysm of laughter which still rings in my ears. She never let me forget that moment, and I don't think she ever believed me either. Now and then, when I would leave in the morning for school, she would send me off with "Goodbye – and don't slip off!" Even after I became a university professor, which is a very prestigious position in India, she used to introduce me to a new friend by saying proudly, "This is my son, who is Chairman of the Department of English. He writes for the *Times of India* and delivers talks over All India Radio." Then she would add, "But he still thinks the earth is round!"

I used to try to reason with her. "This isn't just some theory, Mother," I'd say. "It has been proved over and over again." Her point was inarguable: for her, a flat earth worked. "When I go to the temple," she'd say, "I don't roll off. When you go to school, you don't slide down the sides. It looks flat; why should I change my mind?"

Once I saw the practicality of this point of view, I ceased trying to convince her. In fact, when I reached this country I was impressed to learn that there is a Flat Earth Society with many members who probably function in life quite adequately. As long as you keep within a certain sphere of activity, believing that the earth is flat is a harmless piece of ignorance which interferes very little with daily living.

Virtually all of us, however, are subject to a much more pervasive kind of ignorance which affects every detail of our lives: we believe that we are wholly physical creatures, who can be satisfied in wholly physical ways. This belief has profound practical implications. On the individual level, it means we believe that if we can give a person the capacity to satisfy physical needs and desires, he or she will be happy. Technology will be able to solve our health problems and provide material comfort for everyone. It will also be able to solve our mental problems, since personality and behavior are determined by our chemistry. Progress is measured in terms of material growth, value in terms of material assets. Even a person's work is evaluated as a commodity. Finally, there is nothing like a moral order, only the principles of natural selection; so our only rational guide for action is self-interest.

The great religions of the world have always taught that there is more to the human being than the body: an essential core of personality that is not physical but spirit, divine. Yet at the very deepest levels of thinking, almost all of us identify with the physical body: "When my body dies," we say, "*I* die." All our responses to life are conditioned by this belief. In a sense, of course, this is simply the human condition. But today, I think, the physical approach to life has become a kind of epidemic in modern industrial civilization, East as well as West. Never in history, to my knowledge, has a civilization reflected a lower image of the human being: a physical, chemical organism with no motivation higher than self-interest, no aspirations that cannot be fulfilled on the physical level.

Sometimes I hear the same argument that my mother used to give to support her belief that the earth is flat: "Well, whatever you may say, this physical image *works*. It's true that I think of myself as just a physical creature, but I've done all right. I haven't fulfilled all my desires, but I've gained some of what I wanted out of life. With just a little more, I'd call myself happy. And in terms of human progress, it seems to me that the more we've concentrated on the physical level of life, the better things have been for everyone: more prosperity, more comforts, more leisure time, better health, more variety of things to do and have and enjoy."

I never try to argue with this at all. In small situations where there is no great challenge, you *can* squeak by in life with such a limited self-image, just as you can get to the store and back without believing that the earth is round. Unfortunately, however, "small situations" are becoming fewer and fewer: in today's troubled world, it is a major challenge simply to raise a family or to keep personal relationships intact. Individually and globally, I would say, this business of looking on the human being as no more than physical is leading us into disaster.

Let me give two or three examples; there are many more in the chapters which follow.

For one, I have just finished reading a well-written article in a popular magazine on brain research. Neuroscientists now have the technology to study brain activity at the molecular level, and they feel they are on the threshold of the human personality, the "last frontier." "Can you believe," the writer asks, "that the seat of the human personality is a three-pound glob of matter with the consistency of Jello?" I replied frankly, "No, I can't." To me, looking for personality in the brain is like taking apart a light bulb to learn about electricity. The brain is a physical organ; personality is a force – or, more precisely, a complex of forces, as the Gita will explain in the next chapter. The brain is necessary for the expression of these forces in a human being, and this has certain chemical consequences. But to confuse the consequences with the cause is not only superficial, it leads to dangerous conclusions as well.

I was quite interested in the details of this research. The brain, researchers now estimate, consists of perhaps a hundred billion neurons, each as complex as a little computer. During recent decades, with dedicated study and the help of sophisticated technology, they have isolated and identified more than a dozen neurotransmitters – chemicals produced in the brain which transmit electric signals, and therefore information, from neuron to neuron. Recently they have learned to map the myriad folds of this three-pound glob without invasive surgery. On this map researchers hope to locate the seat of various human characteristics, so they can locate, for example, the area of the brain that lights up when we feel jealous. If they can then synthesize a chemical block for the neurotransmitter involved, they say, and get it to the proper site in the brain, no one need be plagued by jealousy again.

Now, I am not saying this won't work. In fact, I suspect it will prove possible to control many human emotions in this way, at least for a short period of time. But in the long run, when the audit takes place, the price to be paid will be terrible. Jealousy, to continue the same example, arises from insecurity. The more insecure your mind is, the more jealous you are likely to be of anything and anyone. Jealousy is a terrible state; it can gnaw at your mind day and night, distort your judgment, wither your love. If a chemical solution to this becomes available, there will be many, many insecure people to provide a ready market.

Now I would like you to imagine the results. One of your co-workers draws a lot of praise and you get jealous: you want to be praised for a good job too, and after all you deserve it more than he did. When you can't shake all these thoughts off, you take a couple of pills. Then you can go up to your colleague, smile at him, talk to him cheerfully, and not care whether he has done well or not – or, probably, whether you can improve your own performance either. The next time this happens, you know what to do: take a couple more pills right away, so those gnawing self-doubts don't even start. I am not saying this is impossible chemically, but over a period of time you will become so insecure that you will not be able to function anywhere. You will not be able to face any challenge; you will doubt yourself in everything you do. This kind of result is the inescapable consequence of applying physical solutions to problems of the mind.

For another example on the individual level, look at personal relationships, particularly those between man and woman. Very often I hear today, "We're in love! Our chemistry is just right." I want to say, "How tragic!" That is not love; it is physical attraction. Love is a relationship; sex is a sensation, and sensations are terribly short-lived. If a relationship is based on physical attraction, it cannot last: not because of any moral judgment against it, but because that is the nature of physical phenomena. Just as in the war this country turned out "ninety-day wonders," our modern civilization is full of ninety-day relationships. We have come to accept this as the nature of love, simply because our image of the human being reduces everything to sensations and biological urges.

Third – on a much larger scale now – with this image, it is almost axiomatic that progress consists in multiplying material possessions and increasing physical comforts. We are physical creatures, so we can be satisfied with physical things. It follows that the more we can have, the happier we will be; the more a nation can produce, the better a place it will be in which to live. Today, I believe, we stand at a crisis in one of the greatest experiments in history. Believing that the human being is physical, we have by some three centuries of concentrated effort developed the technology to do what we like in the physical world. We have an unprecedented capacity to pursue material goals and produce material goods to satisfy every desire. If the physical image of the human being is accurate, we in the United States must be living in the Golden Age. Never have we had it so good. To begin with, we have so many things we can buy. The average man or woman can go into a supermarket or department store and find a variety of things to eat and own that a monarch of earlier times would envy. And we have such a wealth of ways to entertain ourselves. Whatever our means, almost all of us can watch TV as much as we like, go to movies, play video games, or listen to concert-quality music in our bedroom. Almost everyone who wants to own a car can do so, though admittedly it is more and more costly to drive anywhere. We have more leisure time than ever, and more sophisticated health care; we have a vast array of products available for easing the aches, pains, effort, tedium, and depression of daily living.

I won't ask you to look at the evidence of today's paper, from the front-page news through the entertainment section to the want ads and personals at the end. Just ask yourself, "*Is* this the Golden Age? Am *I*, Jonathan Doe, as happy as a human being can be?" As far as I can remember, I have never heard anyone claim that we have reached the pinnacle of progress. If you ask your neighbor, he is likely to object, "Are you kidding? Sure, I've got a good job and a car and a nice house with decent plumbing. But every year my paycheck buys us less. Every year my government spends billions of dollars it hasn't got to pile up weapons it can't use because they're too terrible – and then it keeps talking about ways to use them, even if it means the rest of us might be destroyed. I can't walk at night in my own neighborhood without wishing I had a police escort. My children are afraid to go to school, and so are their teachers: they're not even trying to teach any more; they're just trying to stay alive until they can retire. But we're luckier than most. Our family is still together. Most of our friends have given up on marriage now; their kids come home every day to an empty house. Seems like everybody is out for number one, angry with the world."

If we were merely physical creatures, all our material benefits should add up to happiness. If getting were the highest human motivation, all of us should be in seventh heaven. It is precisely because we are *not* merely physical creatures that these things are not enough to satisfy us: that, in fact, they only seem to make us hungrier for a life of lasting value. In the Bible's phrase, we are "sick unto death" of living on the physical level alone. In this country particularly, where we have had ample opportunity to evaluate the benefits of modern civilization, I think many, many people now feel in their hearts a deep desire for a more meaningful way of life.

From the spiritual perspective, this acute dissatisfaction with physical living is a very positive sign. If we have been measuring human existence by its shallowest measure, the Gita would say, it is good to feel "sick unto death." It would be terrible if we felt satisfied. The fact that we do not, that we are suffering with the consequences of our present values, gives hope that we can change direction and reclaim our spiritual dimension.

Here we encounter one of the dominant themes in this volume of the Gita: the law of karma. Put briefly, *karma* means consequences: all the effects that follow from our actions, words, and ways of thinking. Consequences, the Gita would say, are contained in an action the way a tree is implicit in a seed. If you plant an apple seed with the intent of getting apples, you don't simply get apples; you get the whole tree. Our modern civilization, in its desire for certain material fruits, has got the whole tree: a few good apples, many that are sour, and a lot of unexpected branches, all the effects that follow from the values of a wholly physical view of the human being and the world.

When you eat sour apples, you get a stomachache. As my grandmother used to tell me, this is proof that the Lord loves us. If your stomach didn't complain, you might eat half a dozen sour apples and never know what damage was being done inside. That is the purpose of karma too: when we violate spiritual laws, the consequences are painful, and that very pain serves as a reminder that something is wrong with our way of living. The longer we go on making the same mistakes, the more consequences accumulate and the more painful the suffering.

Karma is sometimes looked upon as a punitive force: if you do something wrong, you will be punished for it, as if by some cosmic Lawgiver out beyond Uranus. I do not share this view at all. Karma is consequences that we bring upon ourselves; and to me the law of karma is very much a corrective, guiding force, the "healing hand of God." Pain is not always an enemy; it can be an invaluable friend. When we are acting foolishly, thinking selfishly, making decisions that are at the expense of other people or other creatures, straying into illness, alienation, loneliness, or despair, it is good to feel anguished. In this sense, many of the problems that threaten us on a global level today – poverty, war, the arms race, our poisoned environment, the breakdown of the family, violence in our streets and homes, even the failure of the industrial economic order to provide for human needs – all these can be seen as the healing hand of life, telling us like the warning sign on the freeways: "Go back. You're going the wrong way."

The Gita, I like to repeat, is not a book of commandments but a book of choices. In this volume it tells us that we have two paths in life: one takes the highest view of the human being, as an essentially spiritual being; the other takes the lowest, as a physical creature governed by the biological drives of survival and self-gratification. Each of us, as individuals, has the choice between these two paths every day – the Gita would say many times each day, and it will illustrate how and when. But on a much greater scale, it is no exaggeration to say that we face this choice as a race today, at a particularly critical period in history. It is time to evaluate this immense gamble on physical living, on which we have staked so much of our material and human resources for the last three hundred years. And if we do not feel satisfied with what we have gained, we must choose a higher image of the human being to aspire to; the lower image will be proven worse than useless.

Like all the other great scriptures of the world, the Gita gives us such a higher image. It tells us unequivocally that we are not merely physical creatures; our innermost Self is divine. More than that, it tells clearly and in detail what we need to do to realize this divine image in our everyday lives – in our work, our relationships, our motivation, our health, our economic and social values, even our recreation. This has profound implications. It means that the Gita can be treated as a manual not only for the spiritual life but for what philosophers call the good life: life as it is worth living, in fulfillment, health, vitality, joy, and the abiding awareness that every day you live you have made the world a little better. This does not require that we become saints, but merely that we begin trying to live in accord with the highest image of ourselves. In the same way, on a much larger scale, the Gita shows how all the grave problems of our globe can be solved by basing our scientific, political, and economic decisions on this higher image of humanity. This is not impossible or impractical, as I hope to illustrate in this volume. All it requires is the same dedication we have given to physical achievements in this age of material progress, which is coming to a close.

Many years ago, when I first began teaching meditation in this country, I had many beatniks in my classes in San Francisco. They were a very earnest lot. I knew they were interested in Buddhism, particularly in Zen, so in my first talk I used the Buddha's word to refer to the goal of life: nirvāna. I didn't realize that the word was even more misunderstood than *karma*. After my talk, two or three fellows came up and said, "You know, we don't *want* nirvāna. We don't want extinction. We *like* to live."

I said, "Well, do you want real health? Not just to be free from disease, but to be full of vitality and resilience?"

"Sure," they said.

"Do you want your relationships to be deep and lasting? When something goes wrong in a relationship, would you like the quiet assurance of knowing you have the knowledge and the skill to set it right?"

"That sounds very good."

"Would you like the springs of creativity to flow continuously, instead of having to wait weeks or months for inspiration to decide to strike?" Some of them were artists or writers; they liked that idea very much.

"Wouldn't you like to know that you are equal to any challenge life can deal you? To enjoy life every moment, its downs and ups alike, knowing you have something to offer in every situation? Wouldn't you like to be whole in body, mind, and spirit?"

"Of course!"

"Well," I said, "nirvāna is all those things."

"In that case," they replied, "we *do* want nirvāna." For nirvāna is not the extinction of personality, as is often thought; it is Self-realization: the fulfillment of all that is highest in our nature.

Everyone, the Gita would say, is seeking this in some measure. Even if we do not want to dedicate ourselves to the spiritual life, all of us want the benefits of a life based on spiritual values. We want health, vitality, wisdom, courage, clear-headedness, the capacity to love and to draw love; we want a world at peace, free from fear, where everyone can earn an honest living with work of dignity and value. In other words, because the human being *is* more than physical, every human problem has a spiritual solution.

It follows that the Gita is not just for spiritual aspirants. It is a handbook for anybody in politics or education or medicine or the home or any other field who is dissatisfied with the kind of life that is offered to us today and wants to make it a little better. I have tried to address this volume of the Gita to all such people. They may come to it with no interest whatever in meditation or spiritual living; that is quite all right. They can see from these pages how great is our need for a higher image of the human being, and how practical are the Gita's suggestions for realizing it. If they then go on to try to translate these suggestions into their lives and work and thought, they will discover for themselves how essential meditation and its allied disciplines are.

For the transformation to a higher image cannot be accomplished easily. It goes against the full current of contemporary conditioning, and to swim against that current requires tremendous effort, endurance, faith, and a clear, constant vision of the goal – in a word, access to deep inner resources. So far as I know, this access can be gained only through the practice of meditation.

Since *meditation* can refer to so many practices today, I think it will be helpful to summarize the eight-point program for spiritual living which I have found effective in my own life. These steps are elaborated more fully in my book *Passage Meditation*.

THE EIGHT-POINT PROGRAM

1. *Meditation on a Passage.* The heart of this program is meditation: half an hour every morning, as early as is convenient. Do not increase this period; if you want to meditate more, have half an hour in the evening also, preferably at the very end of the day.

Set aside a room in your home to be used only for meditation and spiritual reading. After a while that room will become associated with meditation in your mind, so that simply entering it will have a calming effect. If you cannot spare a room, have a particular corner. Whichever you choose, keep your meditation place clean, well ventilated, and reasonably austere.

Sit in a straight-backed chair or on the floor and gently close your eyes. If you sit on the floor, you may need to support your back lightly against a wall. You should be comfortable enough to forget your body, but not so comfortable that you become drowsy.

Whatever position you choose, be sure to keep your head, neck, and spinal column erect in a straight line. As concentration deepens, the nervous system relaxes and you may begin to fall asleep. It is important to resist this tendency right from the beginning, by drawing yourself up and away from your back support until the wave of sleep has passed.

Once you have closed your eyes, begin to go *slowly,* in your mind, through one of the passages from the scriptures or the great mystics which I recommend for use in meditation. I usually recommend learning first the Prayer of St. Francis of Assisi:

Lord, make me an instrument of thy peace.
Where there is hatred, let me sow love;
Where there is injury, pardon;
Where there is doubt, faith;
Where there is despair, hope;
Where there is darkness, light;
Where there is sadness, joy.

O Divine Master, grant that I may not so much seek
To be consoled as to console,
To be understood as to understand,
To be loved as to love;
For it is in giving that we receive,
It is in pardoning that we are pardoned,
It is in dying [to self] that we are born to eternal life.

Do not follow any association of ideas or try to think about the passage. If you are giving your attention to each word, the meaning cannot help sinking in. When distractions come, do not resist them, but give more attention to the words of the passage. If your mind strays from the passage entirely, bring it back gently to the beginning and start again.

When you reach the end of the passage, you may use it again as necessary to complete your period of meditation until you have memorized others. It is helpful to have a wide variety of passages for meditation, drawn from the world's major traditions. Each passage should be positive and practical, drawn from a major scripture or from a mystic of the highest stature. Passages from the Gita which are perfect for meditation will be found at the end of each volume of this commentary. In addition, I heartily recommend the Lord's Prayer, the Twenty-third Psalm, the Beatitudes, St. Paul's *Epistle on Love* (1 Corinthians 13), and the first and last chapters of the Dhammapada of the Buddha. These and many other beautiful passages can be found in my collection *God Makes the Rivers to Flow.*

The secret of meditation is simple: we become what we meditate on. When you use the Prayer of St. Francis every day in meditation, you are driving the words deep into your consciousness. Eventually they become an integral part of your personality, which means they will find constant expression in what you do, what you say, and what you think.

2. *Repetition of a Mantram.* A mantram is a powerful spiritual formula which, when repeated silently in the mind, has the capacity to transform consciousness. There is nothing magical about this. It is simply a matter of practice, as all of us can verify for ourselves.

Every religious tradition has a mantram, often more than one. For Christians the name of Jesus itself is a powerful mantram; Catholics also use *Hail Mary* or *Ave Maria*. Jews may use *Barukh attah Adonai,* 'Blessed art thou, O Lord,' or the Hasidic formula *Ribono shel olam,* 'Lord of the universe.' Muslims repeat the name of Allah or *Allahu akbar,* 'God is great.' Probably the oldest Buddhist mantram is *Om mani padme hum,* referring to the 'jewel in the lotus of the heart.' In Hinduism, among many choices, I recommend *Rāma, Rāma, Rāma,* which was Mahatma Gandhi's mantram, or the longer mantram I received from my own spiritual teacher, my grandmother:

Hare Rāma Hare Rāma
Rāma Rāma Hare Hare
Hare Krishna Hare Krishna
Krishna Krishna Hare Hare

Select a mantram that appeals to you deeply. In many traditions, it is customary to take the mantram used by your spiritual teacher. Then, once you have chosen, do not change your mantram. Otherwise, as Sri Ramakrishna puts it, you will be like a person digging shallow holes in many places; you will never go deep enough to find water.

Repeat your mantram silently whenever you get the chance: while walking, while waiting, while doing mechanical chores like washing dishes, and especially when you are falling asleep. You will find that this is not mindless repetition; the mantram will help to keep you relaxed and alert. Whenever you are angry or afraid, nervous or worried or resentful, repeat the mantram until the agitation subsides. The mantram works to steady the mind, and all these emotions are power running against you which the mantram can harness and put to work.

3. *Slowing Down.* Hurry makes for tension, insecurity, inefficiency, and superficial living. To guard against hurrying through the day, start the day early and simplify your life so that you do not try to fill your time

with more than you can do. When you find yourself beginning to speed up, repeat your mantram to help you slow down.

It is important here not to confuse slowness with sloth, which breeds carelessness, procrastination, and general inefficiency. In slowing down we should attend meticulously to details, giving our very best even to the smallest undertaking.

4. *One-Pointed Attention.* Doing more than one thing at a time divides attention and fragments consciousness. When we read and eat at the same time, for example, part of our mind is on what we are reading and part on what we are eating; we are not getting the most from either activity. Similarly, when talking with someone, give him or her your full attention. These are little things, but all together they help to unify consciousness and deepen concentration.

Everything we do should be worthy of our full attention. When the mind is one-pointed it will be secure, free from tension, and capable of the concentration that is the mark of genius in any field.

5. *Training the Senses.* In the food we eat, the books and magazines we read, the movies we see, all of us are subject to the dictatorship of rigid likes and dislikes. To free ourselves from this conditioning, we need to learn to change our likes and dislikes freely when it is in the best interests of those around us or ourselves. We should choose what we eat by what our body needs, for example, rather than by what the taste buds demand. Similarly, the mind eats too, through the senses. In this age of mass media, we need to be very discriminating in what we read and what we go to see for entertainment; for we become in part what our senses take in.

6. *Putting Others First.* Dwelling on ourselves builds a wall between ourselves and others. Those who keep thinking about *their* needs, *their* wants, *their* plans, *their* ideas cannot help becoming lonely and insecure. The simple but effective technique I recommend is to learn to put other people first – beginning within the circle of your family and friends, where there is already a basis of love on which to build. When husband and wife try to put each other first, for example, they are not only moving closer to each other, they are also removing the barriers of their ego-prison, which deepens their relationships with everyone else as well.

7. *Spiritual Fellowship*. The Sanskrit word for this is *satsang*, 'association with those who are spiritually oriented.' When we are trying to change our life, we need the support of others with the same goal. If you have friends who are meditating along the lines suggested here, you can get together regularly to share a meal, meditate, and perhaps read and discuss this commentary on the Gita. Share your times of entertainment too; relaxation is an important part of spiritual living. Who has ever seen a mystic with a sour face?

8. *Spiritual Reading*. We are so immersed these days in what the mass media offer that it is very helpful to give half an hour or so each day to reading the scriptures and the writings of the great mystics of all religions. Just before bedtime, after evening meditation, is a particularly good time, because the thoughts you fall asleep in will be with you throughout the night.

By practicing this eight-point program sincerely and systematically, as I can testify from my own small personal experience, it is possible for every one of us to realize the supreme goal of life. Even a little such practice, the Gita says, begins to transform our personality, leading to profoundly beneficial changes in ourselves and in the world around us.

The Bhagavad Gita for Daily Living, Volume 3

CHAPTER THIRTEEN

The Field of Karma

श्रीभगवानुवाच ।
इदं शरीरं कौन्तेय क्षेत्रमित्यभिधीयते ।
एतद्यो वेत्ति तं प्राहुः क्षेत्रज्ञ इति तद्विदः ॥१३-१॥

SRI KRISHNA

1. The body is called a field, Arjuna. Only those who know they are not this field can be said to know the field truly.

Many years ago I remember traveling north by train to Simla, once the summer seat of British government in India. We had not been long out of Delhi when suddenly I became aware of a chatter of conversation around me. The man beside me seemed particularly voluble. I asked him if something had happened. "Kurukshetra!" he replied. "The next stop is Kurukshetra!"

I could understand the excitement. Kurukshetra, "the field of the Kurus," is the setting for the climactic battle of the *Mahābhārata*, the vastest epic in any world literature, on which virtually every Hindu child in India is raised. Its characters, removed from us in time by perhaps three thousand years, are as familiar to us as our relatives. The temper of the story is utterly contemporary; I can imagine it unfolding in the nuclear age as easily as in the dawn of Indian history.

Everyone in our car got down from the train to wander for a few minutes on the now peaceful field. Thousands of years ago this was Armageddon. The air rang with the conch-horns and shouts of battle for eighteen days. Great phalanxes shaped like eagles and fish and the crescent moon surged back and forth in search of victory, until in the end almost every warrior in the land lay slain.

"Imagine!" my companion said to me in awe. "Bhīshma and Drona commanded their armies here. Arjuna rode here, with Sri Krishna himself as his charioteer. Where you're standing now – who knows? – Arjuna may have sat, his bow and arrows on the ground, while Krishna gave him the words of the Bhagavad Gita."

I agreed. But already I had begun to understand that the battle in which the Gita is set is not merely an historical event. The real battlefield the Gita talks about is this body and personality, where there rages an unceasing battle between the forces of selflessness and selfishness, of light and darkness, love and hatred, unity and separateness, harmony and violence. The ringing words with which the Gita opens – "Tell me what took place at Kurukshetra, the field of the Kurus, the field of dharma" – apply to us; the dialogue of the Gita takes place on this field within us, in every one of us, in every age.

In other words, when Sri Krishna compares the body to a field in this verse, he is talking about more than the physical frame. "Body" refers to the whole separate person with which we identify ourselves: in Western terms, not only body but personality. To call this a battlefield is vivid language indeed. It means that from the physical level – for example, in our health – down to the depths of the unconscious, we live in the cross fire of two opposing forces, what is selfish in us and what is selfless.

This is the war within, but it has spread increasingly to outer war all around us. There are enough nuclear weapons in national arsenals to destroy not just a battlefield in ancient India but life on earth, and not in eighteen days but in eighteen minutes. As many as a dozen countries are riven with cruel civil wars; yet Belfast even in the midst of conflict was less dangerous to live in than Detroit in times of so-called peace. Similarly, many families are private battlefields, whose conflicts spill over into our relationships, our work, our politics, and even our entertainment. All this is the net effect of the turmoil in our minds, the decisions and desires of millions of little people like you and me who together shape the world. That is why the Gita maintains that no matter how violent the times outside us, the real war is always the war within – the only war in which victory can bring real peace.

But we can also think of body and mind as a different kind of field, much less martial.

In India we have a story about a man who was asked his occupation. The man replied, "Farmer."

"You don't look like a farmer," he was told. "How much land do you have?"

"Five and a half feet."

There was a loud laugh. "How much can you raise in five and a half feet of land?"

"This is very special soil," the man replied. "This body is my field. My thoughts and actions are the seeds, and karma, good and bad, is the harvest."

The Gita is using the same image. Body and personality, it says, are very much like a farmer's field. In the soil of the mind we sow thoughts: desires, hopes, fears, resentments, and so on. There they take root and grow – into habits, attitudes, personality traits, patterns of responding to the world around us. And these finally bear fruit on the physical level, particularly in our health. That is the meaning of the much misunderstood word *karma,* which this whole volume will explore.

Sri Krishna begins by pointing out that we are not the field we till. Put that way, it sounds absurdly simple. Yet if someone asks us who we are, most of us point to our bodies. "This is me – five foot eight, one hundred thirty pounds, brown skin, not very luxuriant hair on the head." Sri Krishna would object, "That's not you. That's your field, your little garden. You are the gardener." To me this is a most comfortable way of looking on my body: a handkerchief kitchen garden, just the right size for my needs and abilities. I can appreciate other people's gardens, but I like mine as it is; what would I do with someone else's? So I take very good care of my body-garden: but I never believe that this is who I am.

I have a friend, Steve, with a talent for gardening. Every day after work in spring and summer he takes his children out to their large backyard to plant vegetables and flowers, and he lets them do a lot of the planning. The last time I visited, I saw none of the straight rows and tidy signs of a conventional grown up garden. Instead I found all kinds of twisted paths – Beet Boulevard, Carrot Corners, Artichoke Alley – making leafy, colorful designs through the yard. By August the garden was as lush and dense as the jungle in India near which I grew up. I was unable to locate anything there. But the children knew just where to find the reddest tomatoes and the sweetest snap peas, and just where to hide too. Their teepee of scarlet runner beans was so thick that all four could huddle inside without a grown-up ever seeing them.

Steve knows that garden too. With a taste he can tell if the soil lacks anything. He knows the nuances of sunlight, temperature, runoff, and mineral content from place to place, and how each plant affects the others around it. He and the children are able to bring me gifts of their finest produce all summer long.

But imagine what would happen if Steve believed he is his garden. I don't think he would know that plot of land at all. He wouldn't like being dug into and turned over with a spade; and as a result, the soil wouldn't get cultivated. He would object strenuously to people planting vegetables in him that he did not like. If somebody criticized his soil, he would take it personally and feel people were insulting *him*. And suppose he didn't enjoy children poking their fingers into him? All in all, that garden would do rather poorly. There would be no way for Steve to stand outside himself and see the garden objectively, no way to evaluate what it needed and what would do it harm.

Each of us goes through the day making a very similar mistake. We believe we are the body; we believe we are our mind. The consequences are disastrous. To the extent that we identify ourselves with the body, we are constrained to define happiness by what the body and senses find pleasant. It is a definition that excludes a good deal of life, especially as the body grows older. We might eat too much, or eat what is not healthful, simply for the sake of taste. We might smoke, drink, or take drugs because we find the sensations stimulating; we might fail to get enough exercise because inertia seems more pleasant than activity. Or we might spend all our time thinking about the body, trying to reform our complexion with queen bee preparations or to improve the definition of our biceps, as if who we are depended on how we look. All this can only make us more insecure. The body *has* to age and change and die. When we think that is all we are, the passage of time becomes a terrible burden.

In other words, unless you know that you are not this garden of body and mind, how can you cultivate it? You can have very little control. That is the essential message of this verse. But there is a deeper implication that should be spelled out too: that body and mind are not separate, but two aspects of the same field. The medical implications alone are far-reaching enough to shatter our conventional ideas of health and aging.

With all the progress of science over the last two centuries, modern civilization has reached a stage where almost all of us believe there is nothing more to life than the physical, biochemical level. Even thought is currently held to be reducible to electrophysiological events. This is the lowest possible view we can take of life, particularly of the human being. It is like thinking there is nothing to your garden except its harvests: no soil, no seeds, no nutrients, not even any roots. Plants simply adhere somehow to the surface of the earth, no one knows how, and we get good or bad harvests by chance. Our knowledge of the physical world amounts to the discovery that apple trees, to a statistically reliable degree, can be counted on to produce apples rather than pears or any other fruit; that is all.

Now, this is useful information, I agree. But a botanist would not be impressed. "If you think that's useful," she might say, "let me tell you about seeds and soil. Those little black things inside the apple are seeds. If you plant them in the right kind of soil and take care of them, you'll get more apples – every time." Imagine the significance of this kind of knowledge if you had never known about seeds! You would realize that you had never scratched the surface of gardening. It is the same with the garden of body and mind, which are as intimately connected as fruit and seed. When you see the way thoughts and desires grow into hard, physical conditions, and how surely a certain kind of thought leads to a certain kind of action, you will feel you have scarcely scratched the surface of life.

Our prehistoric ancestors, I imagine, might not know about anything but harvests. They like apples and know how to pick them, but they might not know there is any relationship between seeds and plants: after all, these look utterly different. And they might not know there is any relationship between the apple they eat and the soil, rain, sunlight, and so on by which it grew. They have all kinds of seeds lying around – apples, thistles, pigweed, pansies – but these are so tiny, so insignificant, that they don't pay any attention to them. If the apple seeds lie on clay and the thistle seeds in well-drained humus, what does it matter?

The person who thinks there is no more to a human being than the physical body is in a very similar situation. What does it matter to his body, his health, what thoughts he thinks? He thinks what he likes, waters his thoughts with a lot of attention, and after many years – for thoughts do grow slowly – he begins to suffer a few physical ailments, which look no more like a thought than an oak tree looks like an acorn.

"All that we are," the Buddha says, "is the result of what we have thought." He means even physically, as I can try to illustrate. Suppose a person is habitually resentful: that is, he frequently responds to unfavorable circumstances by thinking resentful thoughts about the people involved. Many unfavorable consequences follow from this, but here I want to look only at those that affect bodily health. Those thoughts are seeds; if he keeps on sowing them, and particularly if he keeps on watering and feeding them with his attention by brooding over them, they have to begin to germinate. All this takes place in the soil of the mind, out of sight. But after a while, if favorable conditions persist, those seeds of resentment sprout. In the language of medicine, the physiological correlates of resentment – stomach tension, elevated blood pressure, and so on – become a habitual conditioned response, which any adverse circumstance can trigger.

This response can be unlearned, just as it was learned; the garden of resentment can still be weeded and new seeds planted. But if it is not weeded, after many years there will be a harvest of ill health. Physiologically, the body will be living in a state of almost continual readiness for defense – a grossly exaggerated response, granted, but that is the only way the body knows how to respond. Its resources for dealing with stress will be mobilized day and night, like the National Guard in a state of emergency, as we can tell from the signs and symptoms that may come: high blood pressure, chronic stomach tension, digestive problems, migraines, irritability, perhaps a low resistance to common ailments like colds and flu. All this takes a severe toll on the body's resources for good health. For various reasons, including genetic factors, the final breakdown will differ from person to person. One might develop arthritis; another, a gastric disorder. But whatever the ailment, it is the fruit and harvest of a mental state, the seeds of resentful thinking.

Ironically, such people often respond even to these physical problems with resentment. Life, they say, has dealt them one more unfair blow. That is how entrenched the mental habit has become: resentment has taken over the whole field. And so, tragically, the harvest of ill health goes on reseeding the mind.

For a more cheerful picture, look at patience. Isn't there a flower called *impatiens,* which they say anyone can grow anywhere? Anyone can grow patience too, though it's not yet one of the twenty favorite houseplants of the mind. And it is a highly medicinal herb. Imagine the same people going through life with a garden full of patience instead of resentment. The same events that once provoked a stress response would be met with calmness, detachment, even a sympathetic respect. Those people are likely to live longer and feel better than if they lived in chronic resentment: good health is the body reaping the harvest of right thinking.

As long as we identify with the "field" – the physical, chemical organism that is the body – glands and hormones dictate our lives. Many people today believe in astrology, but almost everyone believes in hormonology. "I was born under the sign of Adrenaline," they say. "He was born under the Gonads, with Thymus rising." The lives of those who identify completely with the body *are* dictated by their chemistry; the Gita would not disagree. When life is reduced to biological functions, it says, what else can you expect? But those who break through this identification can undo this tyranny. They can rise above and eventually transform their chemistry; for the chemistry of our living follows rather than dictates the responses of our mind.

This breakthrough culminates a complete remaking of personality. Over and over again I hear talk about alternative lifestyles. Change your clothes, talk differently, grow a mustache or paint your eyelids mauve, and you have changed your life. This simply doesn't follow. But there is a way to change your life, and that is to change your ways of thinking.

When Michael down the street ceases to think of himself as his body, he is no longer Michael – at least, not the same Michael with whom you went to school. That was the old Michael, the pauper, as Meister Eckhart would say. This is the new man, a prince of peace.

This transformation is not all peaches and cream. There is a terrifying aspect to it. When mystics speak of the death of the old man, the pauper, the ego, this death is not at all symbolic. It is very real. The ego *is* done away with, or nearly so, and it does not appreciate the process either; it suffers. But even while it suffers we can experience the fierce joy of knowing that beneath the surface, a radiant new personality is being born.

क्षेत्रज्ञं चापि मां विद्धि सर्वक्षेत्रेषु भारत ।
क्षेत्रक्षेत्रज्ञयोर्ज्ञानं यत्तज्ज्ञानं मतं मम ॥ १३-२ ॥

2. *I am the Knower of the field in everyone, Arjuna.*
To know the field and its Knower is true knowledge.

If you think you are your field, there is no way to imagine a cultivator. Seeds, you say, come by chance; nobody plants them. Similarly, harvests are good or bad by chance. If you get a good crop – health, some happiness, a loving family, a few trustworthy friends – you say, "Well, fortune's been good to me." And if you get a few shrivelled ears of corn and a lot of weeds, that too has no connection with what you have done. You say what gardeners always say: "Fortune's been bad to me. Unseasonal frosts. Not enough rain. Too much rain. Right amount of rain, but at the wrong time." The Gita would correct this kind of talk gently but firmly: "*You* are responsible for what you grow and reap. Nobody else. If you let things go to seed, you can't expect a rose garden."

When you leave a field to itself, of course, it quickly reverts to weeds. Whatever grows best there takes over and crowds out everything else. The same thing happens to an untended personality: that is, to the ego. You can look on the ego as an abandoned lot of weedy samskāras. There are flowers there too, but they run a constant battle for survival against the thistles and dandelions and crabgrass.

Let's slip into Alice's Wonderland for a moment. We have been asking what it would be like if Steve believed he was his garden; now let me ask what would happen if the garden thought it was Steve.

Imagine that you have been visiting the children in their garden and have fallen asleep in the sun after a glass of Steve's dandelion wine. When you wake up you find that the garden has become a jungle, with immense stalks and flowers that tower over your head and make soft rustling sounds like whispers as they move. And after a while you become aware that you have grown much, much smaller, and those whispers actually are speech. The plants in the garden have learned to exchange "information," rather like neurons in the brain, and they have learned to function together like a biological unit. The cabbages and carrots come and go, but the Garden goes on forever. It is the Garden that is alive. It is the Garden that has intelligence, that can speak and reason and savor immortality – at least, to hear the Garden tell about it. "I'm the greatest," it says modestly. "Tell me frankly, do you know of anything more wonderful?"

"Be serious," you say. "You're nothing but a lot of stems and seeds!"

Science fiction readers will be aware that this is a dangerous way to talk to an intelligent garden, especially if you happen to be in the middle of it. For this garden obviously has plenty of ego: in fact, as you will have guessed, it is the ego itself. "Better watch yourself," it warns. "You're on *my* turf now. If you argue with me, I may just swallow you up."

"Who made you?" you demand.

"Nobody," says the Garden. "I 'just growed.' I make myself."

Yet there are the telltale paths, which now look to you as big as superhighways: Artichoke Alley, Beet Boulevard, Carrot Corners, Rutabaga Row. You get bolder. "Garden," you ask, "can you grow what you like?"

The Garden hems and haws: it cannot. "I grow what's right," it says defensively. "I like whatever comes up."

"And what happens when the big freeze comes?"

"I do die back," the Garden admits. "But after a while, I grow and flourish again. My plants come and go, but I'm immortal."

You shake your head. "Garden," you say, "by yourself, you amount to nothing at all. You have a gardener that makes you what you are – chooses your seeds, plants and waters and feeds them, and makes all these paths. You can't do anything yourself. You have taken all the qualities of your gardener and claimed them for yourself."

That is just what the ego does, and very cleverly too. Nevertheless, it is only a field, an assemblage of parts, a process; it has no intelligence of its own. Only the Self can be said to know.

Interestingly, the word used for 'field' in these verses – *kshetra* – also means 'temple' in many modern Indian languages. Mystics often speak of the body as a temple, for the Lord dwells in each of us. The altar of this temple does not have to be built. Each of us has a sanctum sanctorum in the depths of consciousness, where the Self is present always. He is the Knower, our real Self, the same in all.

Overeating desecrates this temple. So does smoking, which is just the opposite of burning incense. Merely remembering that the body is the house of the Lord should help us to refrain from addictions, get regular exercise, eat good food in moderate quantities, and in general do everything we can to keep the body at its best.

Even here, however, we cannot forget the mind. It too is part of the temple, and if it is not kept calm and kind, no amount of physical care will keep the body free from disease. Insecurity, for example, lowers everybody's resistance, no matter how sound the body may be. As I write this, the country is dwelling on another attack of some exotic flu. "It's coming!" the papers announce. "Are you prepared?" And everyone asks, "Is it coming *here*? Am *I* prepared? Am I going to get it – have I got it already?" When you dwell on flu, the Gita would say, you become flu. Take care of yourself, live for others, and then do not worry. Your security and resistance will be high, and if the flu does bite, you will probably throw it off easily.

The body *is* a temple, agrees the German mystic Johannes Tauler: but before it can serve as one, he adds, we have to drive out the money changers and pigeon-sellers and other squatters who have taken it over for their own purposes. This is a dig at the ego, who has ensconced himself in our inner chambers. If the Lord is to be revealed in this temple, the impostor ego has to go.

Christmas is approaching now, so I took my mother to a department store where they were setting up a full-size Nativity scene in the display window. Hindus respond easily to the Divine Mother in every tradition, and the display appealed to my mother deeply. But one thing was still missing; the window dressers hadn't finished their job. "Son," she said, "I see the cradle. But where is the baby Jesus?"

All of us, Tauler would say, have the cradle ready and waiting in our hearts. But when we look inside we don't see anything but the ego, so immense that his arms and legs are sticking out through the slats. Fortunately we don't have to hunt for a Christ Child to put inside. All we have to do is slowly get the ego out; once we do that, we find the divine child is already there.

This is what St. Paul means when he says, "I was dead, and yet I live: yet not I, but Christ liveth in me." Paul, as you know, was no spiritual aspirant in the early days. He was a violent tentmaker named Saul, who I imagine used to beat his competitors with his tent poles. Whenever a customer came to him and said, "I can't stand that Jesus of Nazareth," Saul would exclaim, "I'll give you a discount!" Yet all this time a force from the very depths of his consciousness must have been working up to the surface, to burst like a bomb while Saul was traveling to Damascus. Then the rough, violent, virulent ego of Saul was thrown out with the vigor formerly shown only to Jesus's followers, leaving the tentmaker of Tarsus blind and paralyzed for three days and nights. When he opens his eyes again he is a new man, with all that destructive capacity changed to tenderness, love, and tireless energy for carrying the words of Jesus throughout the world. You and I need not be so dramatic, but when we are able to extinguish our self-will, there will be celebration everywhere: "Glory be to the newborn king!"

I mention St. Paul to show that this can come to anyone. The most seemingly unregenerate person in the world can change his thinking if he desires. When I was teaching English literature, I sometimes illustrated this lightheartedly with Macbeth, who as you know was not exactly a gentle man in a gentle world. Even Macbeth could have learned to meditate. It might not have made much of a play, but no one wants to live a tragedy. Fierce, violent, tormented Macbeth could have become secure. He could have told those witches, "Why are you trying so hard to stir up greedy ambition? Here's a mantram, *Jesus, Jesus, Jesus*; why don't you take that and sing it around the caldron all night instead?" Those witches are not outside, you know. There is real valor in turning your back on a whispering witch inside your mind – valor and freedom and joy.

The Gita is presenting here two levels of knowing. Knowledge of the field – the world of change, whether within or without – is called in

Sanskrit *apara,* "lower knowledge." This is not deprecation; when wisely guided, science and technology can contribute immensely to human welfare. *Para,* "higher knowledge," is called higher simply because it enables us to make wise choices, based on a sure understanding of the unity of life.

When my friend Steve analyzes his soil and measures the density of his earthworm population, that is *apara,* invaluable for getting a good harvest. But as we have seen, it is important also for him to know who he is: that he is not his soil, seeds, and harvest. That is *para,* direct knowledge of the knower.

Unlike lower or intellectual knowledge, spiritual wisdom has a direct connection with the will. I can illustrate with the example of a young lady I met when I first came to this country as a Fulbright scholar. I was then at my first American campus, where this woman was a graduate student. She was intelligent, attractive, and quite strong-willed. With all this went a fiery temper, but fire can be an asset on the spiritual path if you can learn to harness it.

It hurt me deeply to see that she was a chain smoker. The medical evidence against smoking had not yet accumulated, but even so I had some idea of how harmful the habit was, not only to the lungs but to the will. I knew she trusted me, and I knew too that she had daring and will to draw on. So one day I asked point-blank, "May I take advantage of our friendship to ask you a personal question? If you don't want to answer, I'll never ask it again."

She was intrigued. "Please do."

"Why do you smoke like that? It hurts me to know what damage it must be causing."

She got defensive for a moment and gave all kinds of intellectual answers. I listened to them all. Then I asked simply, "Don't you know that there is much more satisfaction in defying a compulsive desire than there is in yielding to it?"

She just stared. Then she broke into a smile, and I saw that my words had gone in. So far as I know, she never smoked another cigarette. With that instant of insight had come an immediate connection with the will.

This connection is a sure sign of *para,* spiritual wisdom. By contrast, I have seen a highly qualified physician studying X-rays of a cancer-ridden lung with a lighted cigarette in his hand. That is *apara:* the man knows, but there is no connection between what he knows and what he does.

St. Francis used to say, "Your knowledge is only as deep as your action" – that is, no deeper than your will. Ironically, because of this, higher knowledge can actually be much more practical than lower knowledge when it comes to what matters most in daily living, as the contrast between that physician and my graduate friend illustrates.

Often someone objects to me that spiritual wisdom leads to passivity. They may even point to India's present condition as an illustration, ignoring the fact that when India was much more firmly established in its spiritual heritage, it was one of the most prosperous and culturally advanced nations in the world. I would go to the extent of saying that India's recovery from the devastating effects of foreign rule has more to do with rediscovering its spiritual roots than with adopting modern technology. That was the source of Gandhiji's strength, and his greatest contribution to India was to awaken its hundreds of millions of common people to the power and dignity of these timeless spiritual values. Even in India, I think most people do not realize how much of this work was begun in the tremendous spiritual reawakening sparked by Sri Ramakrishna. To anyone with a sense of history who has looked over these events, there is no more convincing evidence of the power of spiritual values. They can transform a culture; today, with global interrelationships inescapable, they can change the basis of our civilization.

Spiritual wisdom cannot lead to passivity. It deepens our sensitivities and magnifies our capacity to battle with destructive forces without and within. We live in a world of unity, where all peoples on earth share a single condominium. One room may have tables and chairs, another may have mats and polished floors, but all the rooms are under one roof. If there is poverty in one room, everyone in the place will suffer, not merely in some vague moral way but economically. Similarly, if we set fire to one room, the whole building may burn down; this is what we do when we wage war. And if there is plague at the other end of the house, we can't just sit back and think, "It's only those people at the back; there's nothing to get alarmed about." Plague is infectious. It is only a matter of time before we too fall ill, and who is left then to play the doctor?

With modern technology, we – *Homo sapiens* – have reached a point in history when we have the capacity to embrace the whole globe in health, peace, and welfare. As never before, we have the choice of two paths: one leading to unprecedented, unwarranted sorrow, the other to unprecedented prosperity and happiness. Without spiritual wisdom, "lower knowledge" can destroy – I would go so far as to say that it *will* destroy, for it has no capacity to choose where to go. But with spiritual wisdom as well, we have the capacity to make a heaven on earth.

तत्क्षेत्रं यच्च यादृक्च यद्विकारि यतश्च यत् ।
स च यो यत्प्रभावश्च तत्समासेन मे शृणु ॥ १३-३ ॥

3. Listen and I will explain the nature of the field and how change takes place within it. I will also describe the Knower of the field and his power.

Most of us, I imagine, think of ourselves as standing in the midst of the world looking out. We see trees, cars, animals, and people as separate objects; and we see ourselves as separate from all of them: the seer, the knower, looking out of the body at the world we know.

Yet a physicist would remind us that the things we see "out there" are not really separate from each other. We perceive them as separate because of the limitations of our senses. If our eyes were sensitive to a much finer spectrum, we might see the world as an atomic physicist describes it: a continuous field of matter and energy.

Once, I remember, it was considered a tremendous breakthrough when scientists agreed that matter consisted of molecules. The atom became the "building block" of the universe, and it was then believed to be a solid little entity of its own. Yet soon it was accepted that these supposedly solid atoms were actually made up of a few much subtler particles and were mostly empty space. Not only that, the "particles" were so elusive that they sometimes masqueraded as radiant energy instead of matter. Now scientists are probing so deeply into the nucleus of the atom that it too has become a shadow, with such a bewildering array of constituent particles that I have given up trying to keep count.

This adds up to a very intangible version of physical reality. Nothing in it resembles a solid object in our usual sense of the word; everything is elusive and nothing is at rest. "The external world of physics," wrote Sir Arthur Eddington, "has thus become a world of shadows. In removing our illusions we remove the substance, for indeed we have seen that substance is one of the greatest of our illusions." If we perceive solidity and separateness only because our senses are so limited, where does this leave our idea that we are separate, physical creatures?

I have been reading about a proposal for a new supermicroscope that would enable us to see the atomic structure of almost any solid material. Imagine what it would be like if this were the range of our ordinary vision. The boundaries of objects would be no more substantial than shadows; we would see life on a kind of threshold between separateness and continuity. It would be a wondrous world. You could watch air and water moving in and out of molecules that made up leaves, roots, rocks, and skin. Perhaps you could even watch sunlight becoming food in the tiny factories of plants, and watch food broken down again to be assimilated into the body of a growing organism. When that body died, you would see its shadowy boundaries fade as chemical elements and energy flowed back into the world around it. From the point of view of life as a whole, it would be clear that that organism is part of an indivisible unity.

Let me go back to Steve's garden. Behind all the vegetables is the fence that marks the boundary where Steve's place stops and his neighbor's dairy farm begins. He thinks of that fenced-off area as separate, and this makes sense on a practical level. I feel sure that the dairyman next door, for example, does not think his fences are arbitrary; he probably paid a surveyor to be sure they are not six inches too far south. But to an earthworm, those fences make no difference at all. The worm is sublimely indifferent. It sees nothing separate about Steve's garden. The soil goes right on, and so does the worm. And it is not wrong. There *is* only one field. If Steve's neighbor uses chemical fertilizers, to take just one example, they are going to leach into Steve's garden and be fed to Steve's two children. Our body is like that: separate in some important ways, yet continuous with the rest of the ecosystem in other, more basic ways.

In a larger sense, then, when Sri Krishna talks about the "field" he means more than simply the body. The whole of the environment is one field, in which we sow our actions and reap their consequences. It sounds simple, but the implications are vast. It means, in part, that the consequences of every action can extend the full reach of the field.

Let me illustrate on the physical level first. I have been reading about what I am afraid will become an all too familiar kind of tragedy: the fate of Times Beach, Missouri. Much more will undoubtedly have been added to the story by the time you read this, but today it is still unraveling; the outcome is uncertain. This much is known: many years ago a trucker sprayed the roads of Times Beach with oil to keep the dust down. Years later, by accident, it was discovered that the oil was contaminated with dioxin, one of the deadliest chemicals known. In laboratory animals, at the lowest levels tested, dioxin causes birth defects, nervous disorders, cancer and other diseases, and even death. Concentrations in some Times Beach streets measured one hundred times those levels, and floods have washed dioxin-contaminated mud all through the town. How many children have played in it? How deep has the poison penetrated? Has it entered the water supply, the food chain? How can the poison be tracked down and disposed of safely? All these are consequences of many little decisions a decade ago: by the hauler who had trucks spray this and many other sites with dioxin-laced oil, by officials who ignored early warnings of contamination, by scientists who advised that dioxin probably degrades faster than it actually does. And the consequences are still spreading: genetic damage, for example, can be passed on to later generations.

This is just one incident. I have read that the government estimates there are at least fourteen thousand hazardous waste dumps in the United States. You can see how vast this web of consequences can be, not only in space but in time too.

In another recent accident, much smaller, the consequences were actually tracked down. Feed contaminated with PCBs – polychlorinated biphenyls – from a damaged transformer in a single plant spread to ten states. Incorporated in various food products, the poisons were found in seventeen states. Some of these products had gone to national suppliers that might have spread the contamination all over the country, even overseas. This kind of tragedy often results from a simple error made by a single person – perhaps only a trucker confusing poorly labeled containers. Yet look how far the consequences can reach! That is the unity of this field of karma: a seed sown in one corner can spread harvests of sorrow everywhere.

This unity is the source of a grim justice about karma which will be amply illustrated in the rest of this volume. The point of karma is to drive home to us that we cannot live for ourselves alone. We ourselves are going to reap what we sow, even if we only intend to sell the karma-crop to others. Again, I can illustrate from agriculture. A number of pesticides and herbicides that have been banned or severely regulated in the United States because of their toxicity have been sold in the rest of the world, generally to Third World countries, without any warning or regulation. But the hazards, it turns out, do not stay confined to those countries. Expensive pesticides are not generally used on crops grown for local consumption, where the market value is not high. They are characteristically saved for export crops – and so the poisonous residues often come full circle and return to consumers in the United States.

These are all essentially illustrations of the law of karma, which is so crucial a concept in this volume – and so misunderstood – that it needs a detailed explanation right at the outset. Literally, the Sanskrit *karma* means something that is done. Often it can be translated as 'deed' or 'action.' The law of karma states simply that every event is both a cause and an effect. Every act has consequences, which in turn have further consequences and so on; and every act, every karma, is also the consequence of some previous karma.

This will turn out to have the vastest possible implications. But let me begin with karma on the individual level, where it is simplest: the karma we sow and reap in our own little agricultural field of body and mind.

To most people who are familiar with the word, in India as well as in the West, *karma* refers to physical action. In this sense, the law of karma says that whatever you do will come back to you. If Joe hits John, and later Jack hits Joe, that is Joe's karma coming back to him. It sounds mysterious, even occult, because we do not see all the connections. But the connections are there, and the law of karma is no more occult than the law of gravitation.

Let me illustrate. In the example I just gave, where Joe hits John, the law of karma states that that blow has to have consequences. It cannot end with John getting a black eye. It makes an impression on John's consciousness – predictably, he gets angry – and it makes an impression, probably subtler, on Joe's consciousness as well. Let us trace it first through John. He might take his anger out on Joe then and there, simply by hitting him back: that is what I call "cash karma," where you do something and are repaid immediately. But for many reasons, John might not act on his anger until later, quite possibly in unrelated ways: he might explode at his wife, for example, or throw out the cat unceremoniously when it tangles with his legs.

Now, karma is rarely so simple; this is only for illustration. But what is clear is that John's anger will have repercussions throughout his relationships. Those repercussions will have repercussions – say, John's wife gets angry at Jack's, and she takes it out on Jack, who works with Joe; and the next time Joe irritates Jack, Jack lets him have it. Poor Joe, rubbing his chin, can't have the slightest idea that he is being repaid for hitting John. All he feels is anger at Jack: and so the chain of consequences continues, and Joe's karmic comeuppance becomes the seed of a new harvest.

We do not realize how far our lives reach, how many people are affected by our behavior and example. Once you begin to see this, you get some idea of how complex the web of karma actually is. No one has the omniscience to see this picture fully. But I hope you can see that the idea of a network of such connections is plausible and natural – so plausible, in fact, that even though we cannot see the connections, we can be sure that everything that happens to us, good and bad, originated once in something we did to someone else.

The implications of this are terribly practical: we ourselves are responsible for what happens to us, whether or not we can understand how. Therefore – here is the wonderful part – we can change what happens to us by changing ourselves; we can take our destiny into our own hands.

As I said, all this is karma on the physical level, which is how most people think of it. The view is accurate, but it is not complete: in fact, the physical side of karma is only the tip of an iceberg. To get an inkling of how far karma reaches, you have to look at the mind.

Let me go back for a moment to Joe and John. I said that when Joe hits John, there are several effects: one on John's face, one in John's consciousness, and one in the consciousness of Joe himself. To put it simply, by acting on his anger, Joe has made it easier to act on his anger again. He may think he has relieved some pressure, but he has actually made himself a little more angry than before, a little less patient, a little more likely to respond to problems with violence.

Everything we do, in other words, produces karma in the mind. This is not at all theoretical; it has very tangible consequences. For one, look at how Joe is changed by his actions – not from without, from within. Over the years, if he keeps giving in to anger, he will become more belligerent. He may find himself swinging his fists more and more often; and by some quirk of human nature, he will find himself more and more frequently in situations that prompt his anger. Sooner or later he will get into a fight where he is more than repaid in kind; that is one way in which his karma with John can come back to him.

Even more intriguing to me is the karma of our health. Again, let me illustrate one or two kinds of connection.

For one, the Buddha says that we are not punished for our anger; we are punished *by* our anger. In other words, anger is its own karma. Joe may think he feels better for having hit John, but a detached physician would not say so. He would observe all that happens in Joe's vital organs and nervous system while Joe is getting heated up – watch his blood pressure soar and his heart race, measure the adrenaline and other hormones dumped into the body, and so on – and conclude, "You're putting yourself under severe physiological stress!" To my eyes, a bout of anger is one thousandth of a heart attack. You pay for it on the spot; and if you go on getting angry, you go on paying for it too.

Suppose Joe's anger does become chronic. Even if Jack never gets back to hit him, Joe is hitting himself from inside. He comes to live in a world of constant stress, with his "fight or flight" mechanisms on duty around the clock. There is good evidence that this kind of stress can lead to heart disease, to psychosomatic ailments like migraine and ulcer, and even to cancer; these too are routes by which the karma of anger can be reaped.

Further, Joe's aggressiveness and irritability make him harder to live with. His relationships deteriorate. Perhaps his friends start to avoid him; perhaps his co-workers respond to him with increasing irritation and anger, all of which provokes him even more. Life in these circumstances can be miserable. Joe may punish himself further by drinking heavily or smoking more. He may look for relief in high-risk activities like skydiving, rock climbing, or stock car racing. All these provide more ways in which karma can be reaped, and there are many more ways also, which I do not want to go into here.

One more fascinating point about karma: you can see that even if Joe does not actually strike anybody, the karma of anger is still generated in the mind and body. To the extent he gets angry, his blood pressure will still shoot up, his stomach get tense, his heart race, and so on. Of course, the consequences are much more serious if you hit someone than if you do not! But the point is that thoughts have consequences too. They shape the way we see life, which in turn affects our health, our behavior, our choice of work and friends – in short, everything we do.

I hope you can see how logical the law of karma is, and why I say that karma in the mind is the most potent kind of all. It *is* more subtle than physical karma, but it is also much more powerful and longer-lived. That is why I like so much this figure of speech that the body and mind are like a field. A thought is like a seed: very tiny, but it can grow into a huge, powerful, wide-spreading tree. I have seen places where a tiny seed in a crack in a pavement grew into a tree that tore up the sidewalk; its roots spread beneath a house and threatened the concrete foundation. It is terribly difficult to remove such a tree. Similarly, it is terribly difficult to undo the effects of a lifetime of negative thinking, which can extend into many other people's lives.

I never like to talk about this without presenting the brighter side, which is very reassuring. You may have seen from all these examples how much in our karma depends on us: what we think, how we respond. The real source of karma is the mind, which means that all our unfavorable karma can be undone by changing the way we think. If someone gets angry with us and we respond with patience and compassion and the "soft reply that turneth away wrath," that too is karma – good karma. Everybody benefits. The karma of the person who got angry is mitigated, even physiologically: his nervous system is calmed, so his anger subsides; he will not go on to spread it to other people and create still more bad karma. And our own mind and body benefit too. Even if we had to grit our teeth for a while to keep back angry words, afterwards we will feel good inside. All our vital organs can relax, put their feet up on the desk, and say, "Good job!" We know we have helped the other person, and we have the quiet thrill of self-mastery too. In St. Francis's words, which appeal to me very deeply, we know we have been an instrument of peace.

ऋषिभिर्बहुधा गीतं छन्दोभिर्विविधैः पृथक् ।
ब्रह्मसूत्रपदैश्चैव हेतुमद्भिर्विनिश्चितैः ॥ १३-४ ॥

4. These truths have been sung by great sages in a variety of ways, and expounded in precise arguments concerning Brahman.

"As ye sow," said Jesus, "so shall ye reap." Perfect words. Everyone who heard them in those times, on the Mount in Galilee, must have grasped the connections immediately. Push a seed into the ground, take care of it, and it will grow – but not into any old thing; you get the crops you planted. When Jesus added, "Your actions are those seeds, and so are your thoughts," the farmers in the crowd must have gasped with insight.

Most of us in twentieth-century America do not live close to the earth, and Jesus' words are so familiar that we probably seldom stop to think of them. Yet the truth of those words still holds. We cannot breathe a sigh of relief and think, "He must have meant that in some particular context, for a particular audience in Biblical times on the shores of Galilee." They are as valid today as they were in Palestine two thousand years ago, and they will be just as valid in the ages to come. Still, to make them fresh again, spiritual teachers interpret the truths of the scriptures anew for us from age to age, depending on our needs, our conditioning, our culture, and the times in which we live.

When the Buddha wanted to talk about mastering the mind, he used all sorts of images that would be familiar to his village audiences. One was a thatched hut. "If you live in a hut with a poorly thatched roof," he asked, "doesn't rain get in? You get wet, feel miserable, maybe catch pneumonia. It is the same with the mind: if you don't patch all its leaks through the practice of meditation, passions seep in." After a while, you may develop some serious psychosomatic ailments.

The Buddha's thatched hut is a perfect image. But in today's civilization, where psychologizing is the order of the day, the idea may benefit from more development. First, consider the body as a cottage, the dwelling in which you live. This is not really a metaphor; in a sense, that is all the body is. But it's a living house: the kind of place you read about in science fiction, where the walls grow and toasters talk back and the television watches *you*. I'll have more to say about this process-house later on, because it becomes particularly fascinating when you get inside, within the mind. But let me start with the building itself, the actual physical body.

The cottage I live in at our āshram is made of wood. My body-cottage, according to the Upanishads, is made of food: spinach from our garden, *desem* bread made by Laurel, soymilk made by Sandra, even some cheese from our cow, Shobha. It looks like a solid structure, but its tissues and cells are in a state of constant change and repair.

The other day, when I was visiting San Francisco with a teenage friend, we passed a store window displaying a remarkable cottage made out of chocolates and sugar candy, visited by Santa Claus and "eight tiny reindeer." "Julia," I asked, "what do you think of that?"

"I'd like to eat the whole thing," she confided candidly.

"Wouldn't you like to live in a house like that?"

"Oh, no!" she giggled. "It'd be icky. Besides, what would you do when it rains?"

If we eat enough chocolate, we *will* live in a house like that. We may not be what we eat, but our bodies are. The body is continuously remaking itself – brick by brick, so to speak. If I eat chocolate all day, whenever my body asks for a brick I am handing it a bonbon and saying, "Here, use this instead," If I end up living in extra adipose tissue, I cannot blame the landlord; no one but me has done the construction. We cannot afford to choose building materials on the basis of whether or not they titillate the taste buds; the foods we eat should be those that make for a strong, healthy body.

But there is much more to the house than this. It has an interior too, with many levels: senses, mind, intellect, and so on. A thatched hut is not complex enough for our times, for it cannot illustrate the fascinating workings of the mind. In this post-Freudian age, we live in highly elaborate mansions like the Victorian homes I saw the other day in a fashionable section of San Francisco. Most of us spend a good deal of time taking care of our exteriors, which does make for an attractive appearance. But I know many people who have never been inside their own houses. They may not even know they have a door. They camp in the patio, and when life sends a storm they just get wet. This distresses me deeply. Every one of us has a home in which to take shelter, and interior shelter is vitally necessary for our health, our security, and our relationships. Yet every message we get today says, "There is nothing inside. You're only the body. Getting wet and catching pneumonia is part of life."

The whole reason I like this simile of Victorian houses is that it allows for the endless complexities of the mind. Some years ago, when I was visiting in San Jose, I remember encountering a house with a fascinating story behind it: the so-called Winchester Mystery House. Mrs. Winchester, it seems, was a woman of occult leanings who has been told by someone else of occult leanings that she would not die until the renovation of her house was completed. Mrs. Winchester put two and two together and decided she would go on renovating forever.

I have to admit that I never went into the house; the privilege currently costs four or five dollars. But I have it on good authority that the interior is bewildering. A lot of the construction went on with no rationale except to keep on going. There are rooms that Mrs. Winchester probably never saw, doors that open onto walls, staircases that lead nowhere – she was, the guidebooks say, very fond of stairs. And probably there are the sliding bookcase panels and trapdoors and hidden chambers which a good mystery mansion ought to provide. You could easily get lost in a house like that and never find your way out. In a sense that is what happened to Mrs. Winchester, who became more and more absorbed in the idea that she was her house; when it ended, she was bound to end too. I don't know how it came about, but I suppose for some reason building had to cease: at any rate Mrs. Winchester did finally shed her body, though at a ripe old age.

That is how I would present the mind today. It has endless passageways and chambers, closets and vestibules, big bay windows that look out on scenes you never see from the street. It has several stories too – emotions, intellect, and so on – each of which literally recedes forever. You can never get to the back of any flat in the mind.

Just as there are people who never go inside, there are others who venture in and get caught in this fascinating labyrinth. They may lose all capacity to come out again and relate to other people. To function harmoniously in life, it is necessary to be able to come and go freely: that is, to turn outward in selfless action when necessary, and to turn inward regularly in meditation to restore our security, vitality, and will. And it is not enough merely to go inside. Many people who thirst for an interior life do manage to get into the vestibule; but once they get in, they do not know how to explore. They look around, see four walls and a velvet chair and the mailboxes where the senses drop their mail, and they conclude, "Well, this is all there is." There is much, much more, but you have to know where to look, what to look for, and how to open the doors and climb the stairs. All that is what you learn in meditation if you have the guidance of a good, experienced, loving teacher.

I once gave a talk on the house of the mind in which the ego lived in a penthouse suite, presiding over a private fantasy world and looking somewhat like Orson Welles in *Jane Eyre*. But instead of his mad wife being hidden in a locked garret, the prisoner is the Self, the rightful heir. All in all, I thought it would make a good radio drama.

Here, however, I want to look further into the other extreme of the house, the basement. Actually, the house of the mind has several basements, each of which would give psychologists material for a lifetime. Freud barely glimpsed two or three of these levels, and his discoveries literally revolutionized the way people conceive of themselves today. It gives a clue to how much might be changed if we knew how to get into these areas consciously and transform whatever we find.

As I write this there is a good deal of public interest in dungeons, mostly in computer games. You enter an abandoned house, find a trapdoor in the floor, and make your way down into the dark, there to find various treasures in endless chambers. The mind is somewhat like that. After some years of meditation you manage to get into the basement, just beneath the surface level of awareness. In this basement you make some important discoveries, the first of which is the light switch. It might sound trivial, but even to turn on the lights in this dark chamber is a tremendous achievement. Then you can look around and find some important clues to some of the problems that have been plaguing your daily behavior – sources of problems in personal relationships, for example, of which you might have been unaware.

Even on this level there is plenty to deal with. But the mystics say, "Look deeper! You've barely begun." Many passageways lead away from this basement to other rooms and levels, most of which do not need to be explored. As I said, there is a dark fascination about the unconscious that can lure away an aspirant who does not constantly keep his eyes on the supreme goal. For no other reason I can think of except my granny's grace, I passed straight through one level to the next without even looking to left or right. I was aware at crucial junctures that there were things to look at, but I had only one purpose in mind: how to reach the deepest level of the unconscious as quickly as possible, so that I could bring up to the surface treasures from which everyone around me could benefit.

The unconscious mind has many of these subterranean levels. Most remain unknown, though we may slip in unawares now and then – usually in dreams – and catch a glimpse of realms so unfamiliar that we shake our heads afterwards and wonder, "Now where did *that* come from?" As we go deeper, these levels are more and more alike from person to person. But of course we have no way of knowing this at first. We must not only learn to remain conscious in the unconscious, but to navigate these strange chambers as confidently as if we were in our own kitchen.

In many of these chambers we make some fascinating discoveries. If I remember accurately, I believe that archaeologists excavating some ancient cities once came across huge urns where seeds had been stored. Although they had been sealed away underground for thousands of years, once the seeds were exposed to the proper conditions they germinated and grew. Similarly, in the basements of consciousness we can find great urns of karma seeds, *karmabīja,* stored away waiting for the proper time and conditions for sprouting. We have been accumulating these seed treasuries for a rather awesome time: the whole of evolution.

At the upper levels, where they are readily accessible, are the seeds of individual karma – when John hit Joe, for example. But at deeper levels we find seeds from a common store: *yugakarma*, the collective karma of our times. Just our being in this same century together, the Hindu and Buddhist sages say, shows that we have some very basic karma in common – karma which our century provides the perfect climate for ripening. There is no hit-and-miss in karma. Our times, our country, our parents, our social situation all provide the conditions we need to grow, which we ourselves have selected from the seed catalogs of past thought and action.

At the deepest level of the unconscious, we find ourselves in a vast chamber which seems to have no walls anywhere. This is an extraordinary place, which literally seems to go on forever. The other basement levels have been individual, belonging to your house alone. But this chamber is universal. We could call it collective unconsciousness, for it belongs to everybody. But the Buddhist mystics have a more suggestive name: *karmabījālaya,* "storehouse consciousness." Everybody's basements open onto this one vast room, where the karma-seeds of universal samskāras are stored. Some are evolutionary heritages from our animal origins, like anger, greed, lust, and fear: millions on millions of seeds, stored there in huge containers. We get seed deliveries from this basement every day, and usually we carry the packages right out to the back yard for planting. We may think emotions like anger are provoked by someone or something in particular, but everybody gets these seeds.

When you can enter and move about consciously on these levels, you can draw daily on a limitless source of love, wisdom, strength, and inspiration. Words and actions from this depth have tremendous power to reach and help and inspire other people, for they come up from a level that is common to all.

There is much, much more to this subject than I can get into here. The unconscious alone would require volumes. But I hope I have said enough to show why I feel the mind warrants so much attention and illustration. The psychology of the Gita is profound, and a good deal of commentary based on personal experience is necessary to draw out its practical applications. That is why Sri Krishna says the scriptures keep drawing fresh commentaries. Yet at the same time, we should never forget that all great scriptures and mystics speak essentially the same language and deliver the same message. The experience of mysticism and the dynamics of sādhana are everywhere the same.

महाभूतान्यहंकारो बुद्धिरव्यक्तमेव च ।
इन्द्रियाणि दशैकं च पञ्च चेन्द्रियगोचराः ॥१३-५॥

5. *The field, Arjuna, is made up of the following: five essences of perception and their corresponding five elements; five sense organs and the five organs of action; the three components of the mind, manas, buddhi, and ahamkāra; and mahat, the undifferentiated stuff from which all these evolved.*

I learned to drive in Berkeley about two decades ago: rather late by American standards, but then I learned to ride an elephant as a boy, which most Americans still haven't mastered. I finished the course, too, though I have to admit that out of respect for life I rarely drive. My driving teacher was excellent. He must have taught Berkeley professors before, for he was very good at explaining.

For a long time I had trouble changing gears. He began by trying to tell me just what was happening inside. "This stick is connected to a gear called a spider gear," he said, drawing deft, vague lines on the back of an envelope. "When the stick is here, so the gear's not touching any other gear, you're in neutral. But over here are four other gears –"

"Excuse me," I said. "Do I really need to know this in order to drive?"

"No," he admitted. "You can learn what to do with your hands without ever knowing what's going on beneath the surface. But some people learn more easily if they understand a little theory too."

"Please proceed," I said. "If what you say can be applied, I'll try to follow."

In verses like these, Sri Krishna too seems to be getting a little more technical than practical sense demands. We should bear with him, for these "twenty-four cosmic principles" are the components of a fascinating description of the universe with very practical applications. In

Hindu philosophy this theory is called *sānkhya,* which literally means counting or listing; *yoga,* or meditation, is its corresponding practice. Sānkhya and yoga are traditionally taught together, for they support each other: understanding helps your meditation, and meditation provides the experience that makes the theory real. Particularly after some years of sādhana, these ancient theories can throw a good deal of light on yoga or meditation and difficulties thrown up by the mind.

I know of no English words to use for most of these twenty-four constituents. It is misleading even to use approximations because they bring in all kinds of associations from Western philosophy, which has a wholly different orientation. Behind all the categories and philosophy of sānkhya lies a powerful, practical assumption: it is not trying to describe physical reality; it is trying to analyze the mind, for the sole purpose of unraveling our true identity. So sānkhya does not begin with the so-called material universe as something different and separate from the mind that perceives it. It does not talk about sense objects outside us and senses within and then try to get the two together. It says, This is one world of experience. Sense objects and senses are not separate; they are two aspects of the same event. Mind, energy, and matter are a continuum, and the material universe is not described as it might be in itself, but as it presents itself to the human mind.

Let me illustrate. This morning I had a fresh mango for breakfast: a large, beautiful, fragrant one which had been allowed to ripen until just the right moment, when the skin was luminous with reds and oranges. You can see that I like mangos. I must have eaten thousands of them when I was growing up, and I probably know most varieties intimately by their colors, shapes, flavors, fragrance, and feel.

Sānkhya would say that this mango I appreciated so much does not exist in the world outside – at least, not with the qualities I ascribed to it. The mango-in-itself, for example, is not red and orange; these are categories of an eye and nervous system that can deal only with a narrow range of radiant energy. Our dog Muka would not see a luscious red and orange mango. He would see some gray mass with no distinguishing features, much less interesting to him than a piece of buttered toast. But my mind takes in messages from five senses and fits them into a precise mango-form in consciousness, and that form – nothing outside – is what I experience. Not that there is no "real" mango! But what I experience, the objects of my sense perception and my "knowing," are in consciousness, nowhere else. A brilliant neuroscientist I was reading recently says something similar in contemporary language. We never really encounter the world, he says: because of the mediation of our senses, all we can experience is our own nervous system.

When the Gita says the physical world is made up of five "material elements," then, it is talking about the world *as we perceive it* through our senses. That is, the furniture of this world is not material; it is in the mind. In this sense, "physical objects" require a mental component also: five "essences" of perception, each corresponding to one of the five senses. From these five *tanmātras* derive, on the one hand, the five sense organs; on the other hand, the five material elements. You can see that the number five and the correspondences of sānkhya are not arbitrary, but reflect the ways we have of sorting information supplied to the brain in electrochemical code.

Four of these elements have names similar to those from ancient philosophy in the West – earth, air, fire, and water. It is not impossible, in fact, that the Greeks got this terminology from Indian philosophy. But if we remember that we are talking about principles of perception rather than "earth-stuff," "fire-stuff," and so on, it should become clear that this is not an antiquated theory left behind by the progress of physical science. It is quite sophisticated and accommodates contemporary physical thought rather well, for it assumes that in the act of knowing, the knower cannot be separated from what is known. *Tejas*, for example, is not really 'fire' but something more like 'brightness' or 'brilliance of light.' It is a quality of perception, dominant in the mind-form we make and call a fire.

The fifth gross element is *ākāsha*, which is sometimes translated as 'ether.' This word too has misleading associations from the history of science, where it referred to an elusive physical medium. Since nobody likes to talk about ether after Einstein, I prefer not to translate but to keep *ākāsha*. Physicists today tell us that matter and energy cannot be thought of outside a field of space and time – a kind of frame of reference which has no substance, yet is "shaped" by the objects and forces in it. Ākāsha is like that; it is the frame of reference needed to describe the physical universe.

Senses and sense objects, then, are intimately related. There is a causal connection, for example, between the things we see and the physical organ of seeing, the eye and its related branches of the nervous system: both depend on the underlying form in the mind that conditions how we perceive light. The objects we see are shaped, so to say, by the *way* we see. So senses and sense objects "make sense" only together. Yoga psychology explains that is why there is such a strong pull between senses and the sense objects that complement them – and why indulging the senses only makes this conditioned pull stronger.

On the other hand, the Gita says earlier, this pull has nothing to do with us – the Self, the knower. It is an interaction between elements of the field, very much like a magnetic pull between two objects. *We* are not involved. Unless we confuse ourselves with the field, we can sit back and observe these interactions without jumping in and getting all entangled. When I look at my Prince Alfonso mango, it is natural for my senses to respond; that is their nature. But I should be able to stand aside and watch this interaction with some detachment, the way people sometimes stand and watch while movers unload a van. In that way I can enjoy what my senses report, but I always have the freedom to tell my hand, "No more. We've eaten enough for one meal; let's save this one for tomorrow."

Sānkhya's twenty-four elements are parts of a vast saga: the evolution of unitary consciousness into the countless forms of sensory experience. This is analogous to the evolution of the physical universe from the Big Bang. Working backward, most cosmologists agree that the universe must have expanded from an incredibly hot, supercondensed "primeval atom" consisting almost entirely of energy. At the zero instant just before creation, we would have to conjecture a state in which all the matter and energy in the universe were condensed into a single point, a kind of universe-seed before time and space were born. That is applying words where they cannot go. Yet I cannot help feeling amused when I read such accounts, when science is led beyond the reach of language. When mystics talk this way, scientists pull out their hair or shrug it off as poetry.

In this model, the equilibrium of this pure, undifferentiated point of energy must have been disturbed, for the early universe exploded with an incredible release of radiation. Within four minutes, it had expanded and cooled enough for neutron clusters to survive, but it would be more than half a million years before these nuclei could begin to form the simplest of the elements we know today. Then, John Gribbin writes, "the entire universe resembled the surface of the sun. It was hot, opaque, and filled with a yellow light. As matter and energy decoupled, it suddenly became transparent," marking the ascendancy of matter over energy. Ever since, the cosmos has continued these trends, expanding and evolving toward increasing diversity in its forms.

The description of sānkhya runs parallel to this, but it begins not with energy but with consciousness. Its purpose is to show how the diverse forms we perceive in the physical universe evolved out of unitary consciousness. Following that thread, we can retrace this evolution and discover the unity that is the divine ground of existence.

I have six-year-old friends whose current hero is Johnny Appleseed. When they eat an apple now, they save the seeds: someday, they threaten, they will run away from home and plant them too. I looked at one little seed through their eyes. Who would believe a tree could come from something so tiny? Where could it come from? Yet plant it, water it, and watch: from the air, water, soil, and sunlight it somehow makes tree-stuff to do different jobs in different places, so that this becomes part of a root and that of a leaf; and it grows and becomes huge. How? How does something vast, complex, and alive grow from something tiny and inert? How does it know how to repair itself? Why doesn't it end up with some of its roots in the air? I know that biologists have good answers to these questions, but they remain good questions, no less wonderful if we understand enough to explain.

Here is an apple seed, tiny and inert yet full of potential, with an interior blueprint that can prompt it to sprout a root and a couple of leaves, diversify itself, and explode into a living tree. And here is a universe-seed without dimensions, yet with an implicit blueprint of laws by which energy evolves into stars, plankton, and human beings. Our cosmos too, sānkhya says, is a tree: the Tree of Life, "with its branches below, on earth" – on the sensory level of experience – "and its taproot above," in the undifferentiated consciousness called *mahat*. Like the conjectured seed-state of the cosmos, mahat is vast, for it contains in potential the entire universe. Yet it too is dimensionless and beyond time, for time and space, matter and energy, are still undifferentiated in this primal state.

And here too, it is said, equilibrium was disturbed and differentiation began. From mahat, step by step, the phenomenal world evolved in all its complex forms and forces, very much the way a huge tree emerges from a seed and bears fruit. First come *ahamkāra,* the principle of separateness, and *buddhi,* the faculty that separates, distinguishes, analyzes, and differentiates. From these evolve mind, senses, and the ingredients of the perceptual world.

This derivation can get terribly complicated, and the complications have no practical value. But the rough outlines of this process of evolution can be verified if you like in deeper meditation. The stages of this evolution, as I said, are levels of consciousness – from unity to diversity, from subtle to gross. In an individual, we might call them levels of personality. There is a level on which we are physical creatures; this is the level at which we are most separate. But it is only the surface. Beneath the physical universe are deeper and deeper strata of consciousness, until we reach a realm so deep that nothing individual can be found. The whole thrust of sense-oriented living is to keep us on the visible surface of life, with the rest of our personality in the dark. In meditation, however, we learn to turn inwards and retrace the steps that led to our identifying ourselves as a separate, physical creature. We get deeper and deeper into the mind until finally, in the very depths, we find our source in pure, unitary awareness.

"After a certain state of development," I read one biologist saying yesterday, "further progress in the life sciences requires breaking a system down to the molecular level." That is not the bottom floor of life. Even the atomic level is not the bottom floor. There is a level, as the Upanishads say, that is "subtler than the subtlest": consciousness itself. Only when you enter into the "dark waters" of pure, unitary consciousness, where there is neither name nor form, can you really understand how the mind and senses function, or even why the physical organism has evolved the way it has.

The end of evolution is to lead us back to the divinity that is our source. Meister Eckhart has a remarkable saying: "Whether you like it or not, whether you know it or not, secretly Nature seeks and hunts and tries to ferret out the track in which God may be found." The whole purpose of every experience, every human activity, every faculty, is to turn us inward and lead us back to our divine source. See the compassion of this view! Every person looking for something in the outside world, it says – pleasure, power, profit, prestige – is really looking for God. All the traits we develop, even those that seem negative, have a positive purpose: to enable us to fight this "war within" in the depths of the unconscious and discover who we are.

I don't know if I have managed to convey the vastness of this: it means that sādhana is really the culmination of evolution. When you undertake this battle, the negative forces that you are striving to transform are part of everybody's human heritage from our animal past, "red in tooth and claw." That is why the mystics say that everyone who takes to the spiritual life does so on behalf of all humanity. And every victory won is a victory for all; for it shows what is possible, what is our highest nature. Gandhi said, "I believe that if one man gains spiritually the whole world gains with him, and if one man falls, the whole world falls to that extent." And he added, "I do not help opponents without at the same time helping myself and my co-workers."

इच्छा द्वेषः सुखं दुःखं संघातश्चेतना धृतिः ।
एतत्क्षेत्रं समासेन सविकारमुदाहृतम् ॥ १३-६ ॥

6. In this field arise desire and aversion, pleasure and pain, the body, intelligence, and will.

In the last verse, Sri Krishna gave the ingredients of the phenomenal world. Now he gives the recipe for blending these ingredients into a person. The body is part of this recipe, but you will notice that it is a relatively minor part. Most of what a person is belongs to the "world within": what we loosely call the mind. Yet within or without, the point is that all these ingredients are part of the same phenomenal world: that is, part of a continuously changing process, with which we have only a passing relationship.

Let me begin to illustrate with my body. It seems solid and warm and brown, yet my medical friends tell me it is constantly changing. In some sense, these are the same hands that I have always had; yet the skin is different, the muscles are different, even the bone tissue has changed. While I am sitting here, my hand is busily engaged in an immense kind of interior urban renewal project of which I am not aware. At the same time my hand remains a hand, and it remains *my* hand. The tissues do not decide to turn it into a flipper or something else instead, although each cell has that capability.

My whole body is like that. It is not the body I had twenty years ago, yet it also is not a different body; it is very much mine. In other words, the body is not so much a thing as a process. The realization subtracts considerably from personal vanity. You can be proud, I suppose, of having an aquiline nose, but who can feel proud of an aquiline process?

To add further insult, this process is mostly space. There is very little solid matter to it; most of the body is space. I read somewhere that if you could get rid of all the excess space somehow, you could fit yourself into a peanut shell. This is fascinating, if not exactly flattering. It makes us see that the space is as important as the material substance, which is why ākāsha is considered one of the elements. But how much self-importance can we feel about a thing that is mostly air?

If we could really absorb this idea, it would probably be quite unsettling. Romance might be difficult to maintain. What would Romeo think of a Juliet that was mostly not there? Would he fall in love with a process – something he could tuck into a peanut? Māyā cannot tolerate this kind of perception, so she draws a veil over it. One of the delightful contraries of human nature is that no matter how many times Romeo tells himself "just a peanut, just a peanut," his heart will still race and his blood pressure rise when he holds Juliet's hand; it will feel very solid indeed.

This is already dizzying, but we can take it further. Look at the mind. Every day you wake up the same person. Why? What makes you the same? You probably feel different: yesterday, perhaps, you felt on top of the world; this morning you have a chip on your shoulder. "Wait till after breakfast," you say. "I'm not myself till I get something in my stomach." And it is true that after a good meal, your personality may be different. All of us are like that: at different times and with different people, we are different too. At work we might be considered sweet; at home, a self-centered grouch – two separate personalities. Our moods shift and flicker, even in those who are emotionally stable. Similarly, our desires change. When you were two, you might have wanted to be a garbage collector and drive a big, noisy truck around at five in the morning; probably now you have something else in mind. And opinions change. I know a number of people who used to be radically liberal, but who today are bastions of conservative thought. Change is the nature of the mind.

Philosophers have observed this flux of thoughts and sensations in themselves and asked, "Then where am *I*?" The parts do not add up to who we are. They don't really add up to anything; they just flow by, "signifying nothing." The mind too is a process, and its contents so transient that if we reflect on it, we feel relieved to think there is enough of us to fit into a peanut after all.

Just as to the physicist, the physical world dissolves into a sea of subatomic particles and energy, the mind dissolves into a river of impressions and thoughts. Yet through all this change, there *is* something that is the same person from day to day, moment to moment. The mind-process is repetitive. It could think anything, but in fact it keeps throwing out the same old thoughts over and over. Just as the tissues in my hand keep remaking the same hand, though never *quite* the same, so the mind keeps remaking the same old mind – at least, until we learn to change it in meditation. Nothing in the stuff of the mind is solid, fixed, tangible in any way. All that we have to cling to as "real" is the patterns of remaking – the dominant traits, obsessions, and "hang-ups" of our personality, called in Sanskrit *samskāras*.

All this adds up to a very shaky self-image for the ego. It loves to take center stage, yet when the spotlights come on, we can scarcely see anyone there. Here is a haphazard bundle of desires, predilections, resentments, insecurities, tied together with some random associations. What can hold this bundle together? When you take it up in your hands, it all falls apart. It is no wonder that when we identify with it, we feel insecure down to our toes. Anything can threaten this shadow house of cards. As a result, much of the string with which the ego tries to hold itself together is made out of defenses.

Just as the mind's flow of thoughts makes sense only by reference to the ego, nothing holds the ego together except by reference to the Self. Only because there is an underlying Self can the ego usurp its place and put on all its qualities. This is a rather pathetic spectacle. The ego wants to be everything the Self is. It puts on the Self's evening jacket and Brooks Brothers tie and expects – demands – to be intelligent and creative and loved and even immortal, just like the Self. But some small part is never fooled. It goes to admire itself in the mirror and finds no reflection, nothing solid, nothing to last from moment to moment. All this fills the ego with insecurity and fear, which can only be erased from our consciousness by the discovery of who we really are.

In calling this whole process a field, Sri Krishna has hit on terminology that is remarkably apt for our modern way of thinking. We speak now of matter and energy as being grosser and subtler aspects of a physical field of forces – an idea which, though now presented on prime time television and taught in high schools, was considered preposterous and occult within my memory. It is good to remember this, because it reminds us how readily our ideas of reality can be enlarged. That is exactly what the Gita is implying. This concept of a field of forces, it says, needs to embrace a still subtler realm than nuclear energy: the forces of the mind.

This is not rhetoric. We cannot see a physical force like electricity; we can only know its effects. It is the same with the forces of personality too. When you look at a magnet, for example, you see only a simple bar of iron. But if you put the bar into a lot of iron filings, they jump into position along the magnetic lines of force. Then you can actually see the lines; you can see the shape of the field.

In the same way, you can learn to see what I might call the shape of personality by knowing how to observe its effects. The most obvious portrait is the physical body itself. On the atomic level, I read one biologist saying, the body could be described as a complex bundle of energy. What we ordinarily call our body is the "solid" part of this bundle, the aspect that is perceptible to the senses. In the same way, the Hindu and Buddhist scriptures go one step further: the physical body, they say, is the solid part of personality, shaped over many years by our ways of thinking. This is not as occult as it might sound. These scriptures are trying to remind us how much of our physical health, for example, has been determined by the decisions of lifestyle and behavior we have made from childhood on: what we have been eating (and how often), how we work, how we respond to life's give and take, how we spend our leisure time. All these make an immense impact on health status; and all, as this verse reminds us, are essentially a matter of our personal likes and dislikes, our will, and the deep, driving desires that motivate our lives. This does not deny the obvious importance of genetic factors. But in many cases, what our genetics contribute are *propensities*. A slow metabolism, for example, may mean we are liable to put on weight easily, but it does not condemn us to be overweight. It is our desires and behavior – the thousand and one little choices we make throughout each day – that actualize these tendencies and turn latent factors into real conditions.

But there is much more to the field of forces that is the mind, as we can see by its effects on others.

Once in a museum in San Francisco I saw a very powerful electromagnet. Two large poles as high as my waist were standing about a foot apart, bent towards each other at the top like two crooked fingers. When you passed your hand between them, you felt absolutely nothing. But it was a different story when the current was switched on. Then, when you tossed a handful of filings between the poles, the filings leaped into the lines of force and froze into a rigid bridge. You could push it and even rest your hand on it; though nothing seemed to be holding those tiny filings together, the bridge would remain intact. That is how real an invisible field can be; it literally molds and shapes the space around it.

A person can be like that too. Don't we say, "She has a strong personality"? Like a magnet, personality creates a field of forces around itself wherever it goes, for better or for worse. That is why a person may attract certain types and repel certain others. Interestingly enough, we do not necessarily attract those whom we would like to attract, or repel those we want to avoid. On the contrary. If I may mix metaphors somewhat, we often attract those with whom we can sow and reap our karma. A person who is always resentful may actually draw to him people and situations that provoke resentment.

Given fertile circumstances, the field of forces thrown up by such a person can reach far beyond the realm of personal contact. In the Invocation to the Gita, Duryodhana, the ruler who masses the powers of darkness in the *Mahābhārata*, is referred to vividly as a vicious whirlpool in the river of life. I don't know if you have seen a whirlpool; when

I was a boy we encountered them sometimes while swimming in the river, particularly during the monsoon rains. It was a terrifying sight to see those swift, dark, powerful swirls that could reach out across the river like an invisible arm beneath the surface of the water and draw a huge branch helplessly into its mouth. Duryodhana was just like that; his obsessive resentment and swollen ego drew the world around him into a vortex of destruction. I mention him not for any literary reason; to those who have read the life of Hitler and traced the resentments that came to dominate his life, the parallel is striking.

This image of a field of forces illustrates vividly the interconnectedness of our lives and the potential reach of our thought and actions. Just as you cannot separate an eddy from the rest of the river, the field of forces that is each of us cannot be considered limited to the physical body in which we live. The interplay of these eddies – the millions of little desires and actions of ordinary people like you and me – can create a whirlpool whose sweep reaches around the globe.

For illustration, I have been reflecting on some of the effects of one very common, innocent desire – the craving for high-beef living. I am not talking about meat-eating, either, but simply of the craving to eat a particular kind of meat out of all proportion to any physiological need or purpose – beef, beef, beef every day, often twice a day, so that it becomes not food but some kind of symbol. This has nothing to do with a normal diet, meat-based or not. It is an obsession, a desire fanned out of control; and whenever a desire gets fanned out of control in a society, there is a lot of money to be made. When these two, obsessive desire and greed, get together, you can expect a web of ill effects to spread.

As I understand it, the United States did not become a nation of what Russell Baker calls "beefaholics" until about World War II. But after the war, beef – particularly steak – came to stand for American affluence and a superior way of life. By the mid-fifties, the desire to share in this way of life had been fanned into a billion-dollar appetite. When I came to this country, the climate was saturated with beef ideals: Big Macs and Whoppers every day for lunch; steaks every evening, if possible, for dinner; barbecues in the patio when you wanted to entertain. I don't think many people could imagine an American Way of Life without steak and hamburger.

Since then, following the flow of prosperity, the hamburger habit has spread around the globe: to Western Europe, to Japan, to the wealthy elite of Latin America.

Now see how far the ramifications can spread, along chains of cause and effect that no one would suspect. This desire for beef, for example, is one of the biggest causes of deforestation in Latin America, which in turn has effects that threaten the future of our whole planet.

Let me focus on Brazil, where about half of the Amazon basin – one million acres, an area roughly the size of California – was opened to foreigners in the nineteen-seventies, with generous financial incentives for those who invested in the country's booming cattle business.

Because of the methods used for clearing land for grazing, however, cattle ranching is generally considered to be the most ecologically destructive of all tropical activities. "Ranchers" in the Amazon – often not individuals but corporations, including multinationals – carve their spreads out of virgin rain forest. Tractors shear vegetation off the thin layer of topsoil, and vast areas are cleared with herbicides like Agent Orange. The debris that remains, and the wildlife, are then burned. Three to five years later, soil fertility declines, grasses become less nutritious, poisonous weeds start poking up, and the range has to be abandoned; the cycle is repeated at a new forest site.

"So what?" investors argued. "There's still plenty of forest untouched. We can't afford to let millions of acres lie idle just because some bleeding hearts think wilderness is wonderful." The government of Brazil agreed; it liked the flood of finance capital.

But other floods came too. By December 1980, an article in Science had reported that "the height of the annual flood crest of the Amazon has increased markedly in the last decade" because of "rapid ravages of deforestation. . . . Perhaps a fifth or a fourth of the Amazon forest has already been cut, and the rate of forest destruction is accelerating." Higher floods meant a massive, irreversible loss of topsoil – and the loss of topsoil, together with the loss of transpired moisture from one-fifth less forest, pointed to a drop in rainfall that "might eventually convert much of now-forested Amazonia to near desert."

Reports of the repercussions kept coming in, pointing to an ever larger picture. Destruction of the forests threatened food sources throughout South America – even, it turned out, on the other side of the globe. Already enough forest had been destroyed to alter global weather patterns, causing monsoons to dump their rain at sea instead of on the parched fields of India, Burma, and Southeast Asia. Who would think cattle ranching in Brazil could contribute to drought, famine, and flooding twelve thousand miles away?

Within a few years, scientists were convening to discuss what threatened to become an unprecedented ecological disaster. "Rain forests are being destroyed faster than any other natural commodity," the Institute for Food and Development Policy observed in 1987. "If the present rate of destruction continues, in seventy-five years they will disappear entirely." Brazil, which contains nearly one third of the world's tropical forest, "has the dubious distinction of destroying more rain forest per year than any other country: over 3.6 million acres."

At stake, biologists realized, is a truly global resource. Although rain forests make up less than one twelfth of the earth's land surface, they are necessary for life as we know it. Besides their effects on food sources around the world, they have been called "the lungs of mother Earth" because they filter and cycle out pollutants like ozone and carbon dioxide, returning to the atmosphere vast quantities of oxygen and water. These processes, in turn, help temper the greenhouse effect: the overall warming of the globe, heightened by industrial pollution, which threatens to shift climate as drastically as the Ice Age. The Amazon forests, mysterious and misunderstood, have been helping all along to protect us from the effects of rampant industrialization.

Finally, rain forests are home to at least half of the earth's species. No one really knows the long-term consequences of destroying a gene pool like that, but at the very least we know we would lose an unimaginably rich source of new food crops and medicines. Only a fraction of these species has been studied, yet that fraction – barely tapped – includes four thousand species of edible fruits and vegetables, ninety-nine percent of which are still undeveloped, and at least one fourth of the ingredients for prescription drugs now on the market. The October 3, 1988, issue of *Science* put this kind of destruction in its proper perspective:

> With the forests vanished or largely disrupted, up to half the

> world's species of animals, plants, and insects would disappear too. . . . According to David Raup, of the University of Chicago, a figure of 50% extinction would be closely comparable with the mass extinction of 65 million years ago, during which dinosaurs finally disappeared together with 60 to 80% of the rest of the world's species.

At this scale, one tragic consequence often goes unnoticed. I learned about it years ago in a piece in the *New Yorker* about a remarkable man named Robin Hanbury-Tenison and a small organization called Survival International, which is trying to prevent the extinction of whole tribes of human beings. Hanbury-Tenison got his start, it seems, reading an article in the London *Times* Sunday Magazine entitled "Genocide": not something about Nazi Germany, but about the Amazon Indians. Perhaps six million Indians lived in Brazil in 1500, when Cabral came. Today the count is just five percent of that figure, and declining to extinction. During this century, an average of at least one tribe per year has disappeared – cynically and systematically removed to make room for the expanding demands of cattle ranchers, prospectors, road builders, real estate developers, and others at the leading edge of advancing civilization. To me, it is an all too familiar example of the mental state to which any kind of exploitation of the earth has to lead.

I have been tracing the effects of one relatively innocent desire: let us say, the simple desire to eat something we have been taught is good for us and which shows that we have "arrived." In anybody, this is not a strong desire; rather a small one. Yet it is widespread, it goes unquestioned, and therefore there is money to be made from it. Those who can make that money fan the desire, particularly with very effective advertising, playing on our natural aspirations: to nourish ourselves, to give our children the best we can afford, to enjoy the fruits of our hard-earned prosperity. Then with corporate growth come truly big ways to make money, and the capital to finance immense, global efforts. Whole countries, measuring economic progress by gross national product, get involved at this stage, turning over precious resources to feed the habits of the well-to-do rather than the needs of their own people. And so it spreads. By this time the "desire" may be just a habit, well under the advertiser's control. We need to be careful of every desire, even those that are small. Even a little desire puts a handle on us, which anybody can reach out and grasp and use.

अमानित्वमदम्भित्वमहिंसा क्षान्तिरार्जवम् ।
आचार्योपासनं शौचं स्थैर्यमात्मविनिग्रहः ॥ १३-७॥

7. Those with true knowledge are free from pride and the desire for ostentation. They are gentle, forgiving, upright, and pure, devoted to their spiritual teacher, filled with inner strength, and self-controlled.

This verse and the four which follow give a telling portrait of those who live in detachment, who have realized they are neither body nor mind.

There are portraits like this in every tradition. The words may differ, but the character portrayed is the same. I don't think you will ever find the Buddha saying that arrogance is the mark of wisdom. Nowhere will you hear Jesus say, "Blessed are those who are proud." The qualities mentioned in these five verses are signs of true spiritual wisdom. They shine forth wherever a man or woman attains Self-realization, independent of time, place, and culture.

But this is more than a catalog of inspiring virtues. We can think of it also as a seed catalog: each of the qualities mentioned is one we can cultivate to gain detachment. In other words, they are both fruit and seed. If we plant them and nurture them, they will thrive until they fill the field of the mind, yielding harvests that enrich us throughout our lives.

Such virtues are not unrelated. To my eyes this verse has a single theme beneath the surface, and that is forgiveness. The man or woman who knows how to forgive – not merely with the lips, but from the heart – can work in harmony everywhere without any fear. The secret is simple: a small ego. All the virtues of detachment come from that.

First comes humility, Sri Krishna says – literally, the absence of pride. For some reason I could never understand, pride is often taken as a sign of strength and humility as weakness. But anyone can see how pride weakens; for pride means rigidity. It is not different values or opinions that keep people from mending rifts in personal relationships; it is just plain pride. Neither party wants to take the first step. Those who are secure and strong can turn their backs on their pride and take not only the first step toward reconciliation but the second and third, and as many more as may be necessary.

There is a direct connection here with *ahimsā*, 'nonviolence.' Ahimsā means much more than refraining from harmful acts; it is essentially a mental state. You have made your mind free from anger – or, more practically, you have learned how to transform anger into kindness and compassion.

Ahimsā is our natural state, and it is very fertile soil. You don't have to plant kindness in it; kind words and actions come forth naturally. But the field is choked by self-will – all the selfish, self-centered behavior that comes when we think of ourselves as separate creatures. As self-will is weeded out, security and fulfillment grow – not as a reward from some external power, but as the natural fruit of your mental state of kindness. On the other hand, by the same law, if you sow the dragon's teeth of discord, you will reap a harvest of discord. Isn't it Jason who faced the consequences of this kind of gardening? Where each tooth fell into the soil, an army sprang up to fight. This may be fanciful, but it is not an inaccurate way of describing the violence we read about in the papers almost every day.

Violent attitudes spread like a chain reaction. The other day I was standing with a friend watching our dog Muka watch a neighbor's cat. The cat, in turn, was watching a flock of birds. For a moment the scene was tranquil. Then the cat, being a cat, suddenly leaped at the birds. Almost at the same moment Muka, being a dog, leaped after the cat. And my friend leaped after Muka. That is exactly what happens in human affairs too. If someone is rude at work, we take it out on our partner at home, and he or she spreads irritation to everyone the next day. It happens not only with individuals; you can see nations behaving to each other the same way.

Many years ago I remember a man on television demonstrating a chain reaction. He stood in a room filled with mouse traps, each of which would release two table tennis balls when sprung. At the blackboard he explained a little about uranium atoms being split by one neutron and releasing two. Then, without warning, he casually tossed a single table tennis ball into the traps. There was a *snap*, then a couple of other *snaps*, and in an instant, with a rattle like hail, the whole room was pelted with balls.

Without exaggeration, our globe is like that today. One person in a chronic state of anger spreads anger everywhere. When many people live in this state, continually on the edge of resentment, frustration, and hostility, the harvest is violence everywhere – in our hearts, our homes, our streets and cities, between estranged races, factions, and nations.

Detachment can break this chain reaction. A cat is conditioned to leap on birds; it has no choice. Muka, being a dog, is conditioned to chase cats. But you and I are human; we have the capacity to choose our response. We can snap the chain of stimulus and response behavior by meeting resentment with patience, hatred with kindness, and fear with trust, in a sustained, consistent endeavor to stanch the spread of violence that threatens us all.

Through meditation, as our minds become calmer and self-will fades, detachment comes and our vision clears. Only then can we see that most of the obstacles to forgiving others do not arise from ideological or philosophical differences. Put plainly, obstacles arise because we want to impose our way, our self-will, on others, and they want to impose their self-will on us. Seeing this clearly goes a long way toward releasing forgiveness; as Voltaire said, "To understand all is to forgive all." But something more than clear seeing is required, and that is the will. It takes a good deal of inner strength to remain calm and compassionate in the face of fierce opposition, never losing your balance or resorting to harsh language. But when you can do this, a kind of miracle takes place which all of us can verify. The other person becomes calmer, his eyes clear a little too; soon communication is established once again.

There is a cult of anger in our modern civilization, often propagated in the name of better communication. But anger only disrupts communication. It widens any gap between people, destroys relationships, says without needing any words, "You don't matter to me. You're not worthy of my respect." The only way to communicate is to be patient and sympathetic, even when it hurts. It *will* hurt; it will try your resources to the limit. That's why the spiritual life is so difficult. But the more you give, the more it will enlarge your capacity to go on giving. "To those that have," Jesus says, "more shall be given." Then he adds, somewhat mischievously, "And to those that lack, even the little they have shall be taken away." If a Philistine should complain, "Rabbi, that's not fair!" Jesus would probably smile and ask, "What's unfair? The choice is up to you."

There is only one way to learn this, and that is in the normal give-and-take of personal relationships. People who are close to us may sometimes provoke us, just as we may provoke them; that is the natural state of emotional relations in every country in the world. When two people – particularly man and woman – have gone to different schools, grown up in different backgrounds, developed different ways of working, playing, eating, speaking, and thinking, we should be deeply impressed if they do not quarrel sometimes. All these differences provide opportunities for practicing patience, forgiveness, and respect, which are not going to be learned in any other way.

Forgiveness is important in every relationship, but it is essential in love. When two people love each other deeply, if one makes a mistake, the other doesn't lose respect or say, "I'm going to do that too; then we'll be even." That is the time to stand by the person you love and offer support: not conniving at the mistake, but helping that person to overcome it and grow. This is a great art. It cannot be done in judgment or condescension, which means we have to get the ego very much out of the way. Most of us are not able to draw on a deeper will and a higher wisdom to do this; therefore our relations go wrong and we run away. There is no reason to bemoan this. I have made many mistakes in my ignorance, and so has everybody else I know. But from now onwards, by building our lives on meditation, we can learn to stand firm in situations where we used to crumble, stand loving and respectful when we used to get resentful, hostile, or vindictive.

We need not expect perfection. Robert Browning says in a magnificent simile that it is enough just to draw one small arc; the Lord will complete the circle. He will take into account the times in which we live – horrible times; just look at any paper to see: money and sex played up constantly, meaningless violence all over the globe. He will make allowances for our country, our culture, our physical and intellectual limitations, and then he will say, "Just do your best to forget yourself in the interests of those around you. Aim always for the welfare of the whole. If you can do that much, you will be a tremendous force for unity, harmony, and peace."

The Lord of Love is infinite compassion, infinitely forgiving. We receive this compassion to the extent that we show compassion to those around us. There is nothing otherworldly about this. When I forgive someone, the inner world of the mind is so real to me that I can almost see my tensions dissolving, which is a tonic to my nervous system and to every vital organ in the body. In orthodox language, that is the Lord forgiving me. Just as anger can cause severe physical problems, forgiveness can heal – not only emotional ailments, but even physical ones that have their origins in emotional disturbances.

The other day as we tried to leave a parking garage near the Berkeley campus I noticed a lot of spikes protruding from the asphalt, leveled at the car like lances in some medieval fortress. The sign warned, "Do Not Enter. Severe Tire Damage May Result." From the looks of those spikes, I would say that was putting it mildly; our tires would probably have come out looking like ravioli. There is a sign like this inside us too: "Don't Be Selfish. Severe Damage May Result – Spiritual, Emotional, Physical." When Jesus or Sri Krishna tells us not to retaliate or resort to unkind words, these are not copybook maxims intended only for Sunday pulpits. They are living laws. The more we indulge in unkind thinking, speaking, and behaving, the more damage we do ourselves. When you forgive, on the other hand – particularly when you forgive wrongs you have suffered in emotionally charged relationships – you are doing much more than repairing those relationships; you are discharging pent-up resentments and hostilities which are often responsible for severe physical problems. People used to ask me, "Does it help others if I pray for them?" I replied, "I don't know how much it helps others, but it certainly will help you."

This, Sri Krishna says, is right knowing: seeing the Lord in all, despite any differences that seem to separate us. The only way to know God is to try as hard as we can to become like him. To know Jesus, we have to try in all humility to be like Jesus, who forgave even from the cross. He gave us his life as a personal example of how to live – wisely, compassionately, for the benefit of all. Of all the ways to honor him, perhaps the most fitting is to give ourselves as gifts to him in return, so that in all our relationships we can show the spirit of utter forgiveness which made him say, "Father, forgive them, for they know not what they do."

इन्द्रियार्थेषु वैराग्यमनहंकार एव च ।
जन्ममृत्युजराव्याधिदुःखदोषानुदर्शनम् ॥ १३-८ ॥

8. Detached from sense objects and self-will, they have learned the painful lesson of separate birth and suffering, old age, disease, and death.

Sri Krishna is continuing his portrait of the man or woman who lives in detachment.

This verse emphasizes what I call the mechanical side of personality, for our body and mind are instruments which we use in life. The discovery that we are not our machinery frees this machinery to function smoothly, which is a state of optimum physical and mental health. Even more wonderfully, we learn that it is only this machinery that suffers, decays, grows ill, and dies. We, the operator, are immortal.

It is not too difficult intellectually to see the body as an instrument: a sophisticated, powerful vehicle which we use to get around with, just as we use a car or train or plane. When I want to go to San Francisco, I travel in our Volvo; the trip takes about an hour. In just the same way, if I had more time I could go in this subcompact car I call my body. That is very much the way I look on my physical frame: it is not I; it is the vehicle with which I get through life in time and space.

But here the confusion arises. We can point to our car and say, "That is the vehicle in which I came here." But we cannot point to the body and say, "This too is the vehicle in which I came here." If we could say this truly, we would have no difficulty in returning this vehicle to the rental agency after a hundred years. But we have identified ourselves with this particular car. Through a monstrous error called simply *avidyā*, 'ignorance,' in Sanskrit, we have come to believe that we are the body, subject to birth and therefore to death. In the Judeo-Christian tradition this is "the Fall" – the fall from the divine state in which we knew that we are not the body but a beneficial force, beyond division, beyond death. When we regain that state, we live again in paradise right here on earth.

I have a friend who is ardently devoted to Volkswagens. I point to my body and tell her, "You have a red VW bug; this is a brown one. It's a rent-a-car: get it here, leave it there." If I take good care of it – give it regular checkups, lubes, check the oil and tires – it should be good for a hundred years of service. And it is just the right size. Tibetan mystics say that between lives we line up in Bardo, the "in-between state," and wait for a car that is just right for our needs and personality. So this little brown car is perfect for me. I don't feel any jealousy over big luxury vehicles that take up so much parking space and drink a lot of gas. I have a car with minimum gasoline consumption and maximum maneuverability, and its engine is as powerful as a Ferrari's.

This kind of attitude brings detachment in how we regard the body we have. People without this detachment are highly body-conscious: in their clothes, their food, their pleasures, in everything physical. They have no choice where the clamor of the senses is concerned; if the senses want something, all they know is how to yield. Detachment from the body means the capacity to tell your taste buds, "That's not what my body needs! That's what Madison Avenue is telling you to buy. It may look good, but it's made for shelf life; it's not going to help *your* life at all." Only when we have the choice to say no if necessary to physical demands are we able to give the body the care it needs to make it healthy, resilient, and beautiful.

Athletes understand this. When a great gymnast has her eyes on an Olympic gold medal, she takes care of her body the way a race driver takes care of his car. Everyone understands the reason, too: after all, if you had a chance at an Olympic decoration, would you feel tempted by a pizza? What amazes me is that when it comes to a much longer lasting award – vibrant health and a long, full life – people object, "It's not worth it. Beer and pizza are what make life worth living." The Gita makes this distinction between the operator and the machine for one purpose: to show us that we do not have to obey the machine we operate; the machine should obey us.

To the extent we *do* take care of our car, most of us devote our time to the body – painting the chassis, fixing the windshield wipers, installing an eight-track sound system or a three-tone horn. These things *are* important; we certainly need a horn at times. But by spending our time and energy on the body, we have forgotten that there is an engine: the mind.

Many years ago, when I was still new to this country, a friend took me out to see his new car. "Look!" he said proudly. "I want to show you a mechanical miracle. They've finally developed a car that doesn't need an engine." He opened the hood with a flourish. Sure enough, I didn't see anything except some old rags and a little roll of tools. Only later did he confess that with this particular car, the engine was in the back.

That is how most of us think of ourselves. The body doesn't need an engine; it just goes. No wonder the engine is often in the worst condition possible! It has never been looked at; only by the mercy of the Lord does it function well enough to get us through the day without major mishaps. Therefore, the Gita tells us, work on your engine first: your ways of thinking, your emotional responses, your love, your will. If you have a powerful engine, it doesn't really matter if you don't have a horn. It doesn't even matter much if you don't have sides for your car: after all, jeeps don't have sides and people are able to drive them. Work on the engine; that's what you cannot do without. Work on your mind. After you have brought it up to specifications and tuned it to perfection, if you still have time, you can get a hula doll to hang in the rear window. Before that, Sri Krishna says drily, it's a little premature.

One of the greatest misunderstandings of modern science is that if we study the brain, we will understand the mind. "Despite massive research," a recent article reports, "neuroscientists say they still cannot answer the age-old question, 'Is the material body really the seat of consciousness?' Although there is a feeling of imminent breakthrough, such scientists have still to find the point in the brain where perception occurs – where nerve endings become music, or vision." And that is perception, which is only the tip of consciousness. "As a matter of fact," this writer adds, "the whole concept of consciousness has become even more uncertain." This is unavoidable, because of the way the question is asked. When you base all your study of something on the assumption that it is something else, "more uncertain" is all it can become.

"Looking at the human brain as some sort of intricate computer," says a specialist at Massachusetts Institute of Technology, "scientists confronted a system so vast and awe-inspiring that it makes all else simple to the point of triviality." That is how wonderfully complex the brain is; yet at the same time, it is nothing more than a computer, which is to say a machine. We can put it on the workbench and study it all we like; even if we succeed in duplicating some of its functions, we will learn nothing about the operator of the computer, who is seated beneath the bench waiting for us to get around to him.

Many years ago I went to a computer exhibition in Oakland. There were computers all around, their beady eyes blinking, going *beep, beep, beep*. After a few minutes a man came up to me. Seeing that I came from another country, he asked, "Do you know what these are?"

Out of politeness I said, "Please tell me."

"They are computers," he said with evident satisfaction. "Do you know what they can do?"

I said, "Please tell me."

"They can do *everything* you can do."

I just laughed. "Oh, no. They don't know how to meditate!"

The point may have been lost on him; I don't think he knew what meditation is, so probably he didn't feel any sense of loss. If he could have shown me a computer as sophisticated as the human brain, he would probably have felt very proud. But however complicated it may be, we can never make a computer that can do what every human being can, by virtue of being human: go beyond words, thought, and sensory experience into a higher realm of knowing, where awareness cannot be broken even by death. The reason is simple: the computer has no Ātman. It is just machinery; nothing can make it more than that. The terror some people feel of the machine, of computers and the like becoming a kind of Frankenstein, is a terror not fully warranted; machines will never be able to "take over" anything in the sense of coming alive. But on the other hand, the sublime confidence that machines will someday solve all our problems, elevate our consciousness, and enable us all to fulfill life's purpose is just as exaggerated and much more dangerous.

"This erring race of human beings," Sri Aurobindo writes, "dream always of perfecting their environment by the machinery of government and society. But it is only by the perfection of the soul within that the outer environment can be perfected. 'What thou art within, that outside thee thou shalt enjoy.' No machinery can rescue you from the law of your own being." And he concludes: "What then shall be our ideal? Unity for the human race by an inner oneness, . . . the pouring of the power of the spirit into the physical and mental instrument, so that we shall exceed our present state as much as this exceeds the animal state from which science tells us we have issued." Aurobindo is not talking from book knowledge, though he was a great scholar. Statements like these are stamped with the vision that comes from personal experience.

As detachment deepens, health improves. It is amazing to see how easily we can change physical habits: eat better food, get more exercise, sleep better. But more important, we get peace of mind, without which no amount of food and exercise can guarantee good health.

In most of the books on health that I see, the mind is hardly emphasized. Current research into heart disease or cancer, for example, emphasizes only external factors such as dietary fats, smoking, or high blood pressure. Very few are even asking about internal factors, the influence of the mind; and when they do ask, given the physical orientation of our times, they scarcely know what to look for. I am certainly not minimizing the importance of external factors. But I think the damage that anger can do to the circulatory system, to take just one example, may be much greater than the harm ascribed to cholesterol. Hostility, depression, fear, and greed – not just for money but for power or pleasure – all threaten our health as surely as junk food or sedentary living. I once read about someone who devoured a bag of potato chips with every meal. I doubt his body appreciated it. But if you can be kind all day, even with three bags of chips you may be better off than someone with an exemplary diet who seethes with resentment inside.

Coffee's adverse effects, for example, prompted me long ago to switch to a rare cup of decaf. But when people start telling me about the evils of caffeine, I sometimes try to restore a sense of proportion. "Mind you," I say, "I'm not disagreeing. But what you really ought to worry about is anger. If you can give that up, you can take a cup of coffee in your stride." The worst threats to health come from the Big Four: anger, fear, greed, and self-will. It is these we should focus on, for they sabotage our health, our security, and our capacity to love.

When you do not identify with your body, it is much less likely to be ravaged by disease. It doesn't even feel easily the ravages of time. Gandhi was an outstanding example of this. So was the Compassionate Buddha, who was magnificently fit into his seventies. The chronicles and art of southern Asia, where Buddhism is oldest, depict him as tall, strong, and vibrantly alive – clad only in an ochre robe, owning nothing but a begging bowl, but every inch the king that he was born.

After all is said and done, the passage of time is going to affect all of us physically. But it is the obsessive identification with the body that really leaves it prey to the ravages of time. Will Rogers, I think, used to say that when he saw a pretty girl, he had to remind himself that in twenty years she was going to look five years older. That can be true of spiritual aspirants too. When you are meditating, though twenty years pass, the body may show the effects of only five.

I am not speaking here about events after samādhi, which may well seem remote. Even before this, you enter a stage where you are not conscious of the body during meditation. In the later stages of sādhana you may slip into this state involuntarily while you are asleep at night. If this happens, don't jump out of bed; repeat your mantram for a few minutes and then get up slowly. The experience is exhilarating. After your first taste of it, you look on your body completely differently from the way you did before. You can develop a very affectionate relationship with it, as I have, but you no longer ascribe any personal significance to the body as the seat of satisfaction. And there is no more question of resisting temptations or cravings; the question no longer applies. Temptations and cravings belong in one world; you now live in another.

असक्तिरनभिष्वङ्गः पुत्रदारगृहादिषु ।
नित्यं च समचित्तत्वमिष्टानिष्टोपपत्तिषु ॥ १३-९ ॥

9. Free from selfish attachment, they do not get compulsively wrapped up even in home and family. They are even-minded through good fortune and bad.

Now we come explicitly to personal relationships: the perfect context for learning detachment, and for reaping its benefits too.

Once I went up to a three-year-old friend and said politely, "Good morning, Laurie. How are you today?"

"You'd better keep away from me," she said. "I haven't had my nap."

In fact, I was especially nice to her that day. I complimented her on her hair, her dress, even her appetite. No wise man wants to provoke a three-year-old, you know. But everything I said only got a nod.

With three-year-olds you can give a certain margin for this kind of behavior, especially if you are playing the role of uncle. But for grownups to act this way is quite another matter. I can't imagine an adult saying, "I only got four hours of sleep last night, so don't say anything I don't like," or "I'm hungry now, so I can't possibly see anybody's point of view except my own. Talk to me after I've eaten." Yet that is how many of us behave, at least at times, though we seldom put it into words. Just the other day I read about certain political negotiations being conducted after a fine meal, on the grounds that wining and dining "makes for communication."

When you know you are not your mind but the person who operates it, you get a good deal of detachment from your moods. If your mind is having trouble, the problem is mechanical; it can be solved. If someone contradicts you, even if you haven't slept very well or have a little headache, you may experience some irritation, but that will not affect your attitude of love and respect for others. You can imagine the beneficial effect on your relationships!

Getting detached from emotional states is one aspect of learning that you are not your mind. Another aspect is learning that you are not your opinions either. This is detachment from another mental instrument: the so-called higher mind, *buddhi* in Sanskrit, which corresponds roughly to the intellect.

We live in such a pseudo-intellectual climate today that this kind of detachment is hard to achieve. Most of us identify ourselves completely with our opinions. Even on university campuses – perhaps especially on university campuses – I have met very few intellectuals who could look at their opinions with cool detachment and say when necessary, "Oh, no, this isn't so good. Let me throw it away." Usually, instead of "This isn't good," we say "This is mine. Therefore, how can I throw it away?" Look at the logic! When we actually discover that we are not the intellect – not merely believe, but actually experience it at a deep level of awareness – we can listen to opposing opinions with great interest and a quiet sense of security. If we find that someone else's opinion is better than ours, even if we have held onto ours for twenty-five years, we can say cheerfully, "Where's the waste basket? I'll throw out my opinion and keep yours."

In the latter stages of meditation we come to look on the mind as an instrument not unlike a vacuum cleaner: it makes a lot of noise, but it can do a good job. I saw one of our little boys using a vacuum cleaner the other day; he had managed somehow to attach the hose to the wrong end, and it was blowing dust and paper all over the place. That is how we usually use the mind, to blow our likes and dislikes over everyone who comes by. But properly used, the mind can suck up all this litter and remove it. That is meditation: using the mind to clean up the mind; or, more precisely, using the higher mind to clean up the lower mind.

From my personal experience, I can give a very effective technique for learning detachment from moods and opinions: work on reducing your likes and dislikes, not only in personal relationships but in everything. They may be very well rationalized, but virtually every pet like or dislike is the ego indulging in what it likes to consider creative self-expression.

The sānkhya account of how the mind works can throw light on this kind of ego-art. In Sanskrit the stuff of consciousness is called *chitta*. We can think of it as amorphous mind-clay – unbroken, undifferentiated, without shape, contour, or size. By our thinking, we make this clay into anything we perceive, anything we dream, anything we imagine: trees, birds, dolls, people, even mental states like anger, sympathy, or regret. But through constant repetition of the same compulsive thoughts, we make our chitta into a Madame Tussaud's wax museum. Everybody in our personal world is represented there in some detail, depending on how close they are to us: parents, partner, children, Aunt Josie, the office staff, even our dog. Interestingly enough, the Aunt Josie in chitta may have little to do with anybody outside. This is a figure we have made ourselves, the Aunt Josie that *we* see. When we quarrel with her, we go back into our museum and add a fang. "I make 'em the way I see 'em," the mind explains. Sri Krishna would shake his head. "No, you see them the way you have made them." Everything we perceive, everything we experience, is through these chitta-models of consciousness. They condition how we see life; therefore they govern how we respond.

When anger, fear, or greed molds this clay into rigid shapes, it is very difficult to break the mold. "I know my faults," people sometimes say pathetically. "I know I'm not easy to live with. But I can't change." Everybody can change; that is the miracle of meditation. All the rigid pots and pans of chitta that we have been throwing at people in consciousness can be reduced to fresh, pliable clay again. Then chitta is plastic and responsive. We can make new things, beautiful things – forgiveness, patience, goodwill, fearlessness, anything we choose. The skill is the same. But formerly it was destructive forces that shaped consciousness; now creative forces make forms that are beneficial, not only for us but for others too.

Most mental turmoil, in fact, can be traced to trivial likes and dislikes that have been magnified by self-will: put bluntly, "I want this and I can't have it" or "I don't like this and I can't get rid of it." We don't have to put up with this; that is the whole point of having what Sri Krishna calls an "even mind." We can learn to hold our likes and dislikes lightly, and when we do, most of the difficulties in personal relationships evaporate.

Try this with jobs and responsibilities – the nagging little things you have to do but just don't want to. It's a rare spirit that can say, "I loathe this job – so let me at it!" For most of us, the voice of self-will has only to say, "Listen, count me out of this one. I can't stand licking stamps, and besides, I don't want to work next to Mabel." We say obligingly, "All right, you're excused." Self-will grows fatter and bolder. Next time it doesn't bother with formalities. It just says, "*Mabel*. Remember?" We say, "Excused." And finally it grows arrogant and tells us point-blank, "Forget it!"

If we give in to self-will like this in every little like and dislike, we get rigid. When we find ourselves in a situation where we have to yield to the needs of others, self-will complains up and down the nervous system. "I can't yield! I'm made of one bone; I can't bend." At the outset the protest may be only in the mind, but the mind has channels; as they get deeper, they dig into the body. Self-willed people are subject to all kinds of emotional and physical problems like allergy and migraine. When their self-will is thwarted and they cannot freely express their likes and dislikes, their breathing gets irregular, blood pressure climbs, the pulse races, the immune system is depressed. As Dr. Hans Selye observes, "Stress leads to distress" – first in the mind; then, if we don't reverse it, in chronic physical ailments that make us miserable while they shorten our lives.

Fortunately, the distress of self-will can be completely avoided by reducing likes and dislikes. Whenever somebody benefits from it, go against your likes and dislikes, especially in relationships. If you dislike Mabel so intensely that you go in the other direction when you see her, make yourself look her in the eye; make yourself smile. After two or three tries, it won't even be forced. You are stretching your compulsions, beginning to make them looser, more elastic. It is painful, it is difficult, but the benefits are tremendous. Your nervous system becomes sound and resilient, your vitality and resistance immense. If things don't turn out as you expected, you won't get depressed or irritable; if everything goes your way, you won't lose your equilibrium. Your castle in the air may be blown to bits; if others benefit, you will not care; you may not even notice.

मयि चानन्ययोगेन भक्तिरव्यभिचारिणी ।
विविक्तदेशसेवित्वमरतिर्जनसंसदि ॥१३-१०॥
अध्यात्मज्ञाननित्यत्वं तत्त्वज्ञानार्थदर्शनम् ।
एतज्ज्ञानमिति प्रोक्तमज्ञानं यदतो ऽन्यथा ॥१३-११॥

10. Their devotion to me is undivided. Enjoying solitude and not following the crowd, they seek only me.
11. This is true knowledge, to seek the Self as the true end of wisdom always. To seek anything else is ignorance.

Like the preceding verses, these two describe both a means to detachment and its end.

Once we have realized experientially that the Lord dwells in us as our real Self, we see clearly that everything else in life is transitory. We are here on earth to serve; nothing can attract us again into any kind of selfish attachment. People sometimes ask me, "Don't you ever feel tempted?" I reply, "By what?" When you know in every cell that you have the source of joy within you, where is the temptation in a chocolate truffle? It is not that I do not enjoy truffles, but compared with the joy of Self-realization, even the most sublime sensory satisfaction cannot be taken seriously.

Of course, this is the fruit of samādhi. The path of sādhana itself is full of temptations, and though they become fewer as we progress, they also grow immensely more compelling as our desires become unified. Right from the outset, therefore, it is important to do everything we can to make Self-realization our primary goal. The transformation of personality is so difficult that to accomplish it we cannot afford to dedicate ourselves to other objectives and try to practice sādhana on the side.

This does not mean we should have no other activities. In Sanskrit the earth is called *karmabhūmi*, which has a double-edged meaning: *karma* is work, but *karma* is also karma. This earth is the world of work, and the world of work is the world of karma. Harmonious work with other people is a vital part of spiritual living. It is indispensable. If we do not live and work with other human beings who differ from us, how can we undo the karma of our previous difficulties and mistakes? If we don't participate in life, particularly when it gets challenging, how are we going to learn to face challenges with courage, patience, courtesy, and unfailing respect? All this is part of what it means to see the Lord in all, which is the purpose of our being here on earth.

In the early days, however, this often means a change in some of our familiar activities. Several old acquaintances will gradually fade from our circle. Someone once asked Somerset Maugham, "Should auld acquaintance be forgot?" Maugham replied drily, "Sometimes." To rebuild our lives, we have to change our associations and our ways of living. This is painful at first. But afterwards, when we return to our old friends, it will not be a case of the blind leading the blind; we will be a beacon in their lives.

In many parts of India, horse-drawn carriages are still a common sight. Usually the owner puts blinders on his horses, so they won't be distracted by sights around them on the busy streets. Spiritual aspirants have blinders too. One is detachment, not identifying with the body, senses, and mind. The other is discrimination, constantly reminding yourself of the supreme goal in the midst of every activity. Without a goal, drawn here and there by the attachments of the senses, we become like horses without blinders on a busy street, willing to go in any direction, confused by what we see and hear.

In this connection we should remember to be on our guard against the influence of mass movements, which can sweep even the most sincere men and women off their feet. We need to be extremely vigilant too about the influence of the media, not only in the early days of sādhana but all along. I cannot emphasize this too strongly; it is one of the obstacles that spiritual aspirants in earlier times and less technological cultures did not have to face. Most of us have very little idea how easily the words and images of television, film, and popular music drop into the depths of the mind. On a seed catalog the other day I saw a confident guarantee: "Our seeds *grow*!" Let me assure you, media seeds grow too, as you will verify for yourselves in the later stages of meditation, when you get into the unconscious and look around. By that time every media-weed will have to be removed, which is a monumental task.

I can illustrate sādhana with different kinds of trains, based on my experience in India. Most of us begin meditation as passenger trains. We set out from Madras Central Station, say, bound for the Himālayas, over two thousand miles away. But a passenger train has to stop at every little station along the way. People have to get down or climb aboard, and every station has vendors with tasty wares to sample before the train moves on again. Similarly, there are aspirants who like to settle all their affairs before taking to meditation. Once they get started, they have to get down at every station and explore its possibilities before they move ahead again. When the sun goes down at the end of the day they are still in some rural station, hundreds of miles from their goal. Finally it has grown dark, and they have run out of time.

Like the passenger train, this kind of aspirant *will* reach his destination someday. But such an approach requires many lifetimes. Even if we are on the track and moving forward resolutely, all of us have a long way to go. The latter stages of the journey are a steep, arduous climb. Under such conditions, the human being simply does not have enough fuel in one lifetime to explore every byway that presents itself and still make it to the goal. If we had a thousand years to live, there might be no harm in this. We could play game after game in life, doing all the little things that appeal to us, and still have time left for realizing the goal of life. But a hundred years would not be too long, and most of us have but a fraction of that time before vitality and resolution begin to wane. We do not have time to dally with wayside distractions. "The affairs of the world will go on forever," says the Tibetan mystic Milarepa. "Do not delay the practice of meditation."

By contrast, there is the express. When I was teaching in India, the Grand Trunk Express used to leave Madras Central in the morning and go straight to Nagpur, at the heart of the Indian subcontinent, almost a thousand miles away. It did stop, but only at a few of the most important junctions. Even in those days the passenger bound for Simla, on the lower slopes of the Himālayas, could take express connections from Madras Central and reach his destination in two or three days. That is the second kind of spiritual aspirant, which all of us can become. Such a person may have made a lot of mistakes. His home town may still be talking about the trouble he caused. But when he takes to meditation and puts all his heart into practicing spiritual disciplines, he goes like an arrow to the goal.

ज्ञेयं यत्तत्प्रवक्ष्यामि यज्ज्ञात्वामृतमश्नुते ।
अनादिमत्परं ब्रह्म न सत्तन्नासदुच्यते ॥ १३-१२ ॥

12. I will tell you of the wisdom that leads to immortality: the beginningless Brahman, which can be called neither being nor nonbeing.

The whole point of spiritual wisdom is to go beyond death. It *is* possible. It can be done, and it has been done, by cutting the nexus of identification with the body.

"When a person dies," Nachiketa asks the King of Death in the Katha

Upanishad, "there arises one question." All of us must have asked this question at some time or other, when we have seen someone dying or been robbed of someone we loved: *Where did he go? Where did she go?* Nachiketa continues, "Some say he still exists somewhere. Others say, 'Absurd. He's just disappeared; there's an end to it.' Teach me the truth, O Lord of Death; I want to know for certain."

I have friends, three fellows, who live in a geodesic dome, an apt symbol of the earth. They go out to work every day, and in the evening they come back to their dome. Imagine if one evening they came home and decided never to leave again. Someone brings them groceries and collects the garbage, but they never see who; they take it for granted. And after a while, their memory of the city grows dim. They forget their cars, for they never drive. They forget that there are roads leading to farther cities full of other people. Eventually they forget even the fields and pine trees beyond their windows, they become so preoccupied with the things inside: their books and records and old *National Geographics*, faded photographs and clippings from the newspaper, the patterns made by the stains from leaky plumbing, the drama of spiders on the ceiling. If you could ask them questions about San Francisco, they would shake their heads; the city would seem like something from a dream. "I don't know," they would answer. "I don't remember." After some years they would say in bemusement, "I doubt if it exists." Finally they would conclude, "It does *not* exist. San Francisco is unreal. What is the evidence that there is an outside world at all?"

How have we forgotten where we came from, "trailing clouds of glory"? How have we forgotten we are all one, come from the same divine source, to whom we shall return? We have simply become preoccupied. Over a long, long period of dwelling on ourselves, thinking only about our own private pursuits and basking in our separateness, we don't remember any of this; worse, we deny it. Those who subscribe to the biological school of thinking answer Nachiketa's question with, "It's over. When a person dies, that's the end." The King of Death says simply, "Not at all." When my friends ask what is the evidence for an outside world, I might reply, "Just open the door! Go outside, look around for yourselves, and tell me what you see." It is no answer for them to object,

"I don't want to open the door. Why should I? There's nothing there." If they do go out, they rediscover the world. If, through meditation, we step outside our egocentric personality, we rediscover who we are: part of the eternal, immortal Reality that we call God.

सर्वतःपाणिपादं तत्सर्वतोक्षिशिरोमुखम् ।
सर्वतःश्रुतिमल्लोके सर्वमावृत्य तिष्ठति ॥ १३-१३ ॥
सर्वेन्द्रियगुणाभासं सर्वेन्द्रियविवर्जितम् ।
असक्तं सर्वभृच्चैव निर्गुणं गुणभोक्तृ च ॥ १३-१४ ॥
बहिरन्तश्च भूतानामचरं चरमेव च ।
सूक्ष्मत्वात्तदविज्ञेयं दूरस्थं चान्तिके च तत् ॥ १३-१५ ॥

13. It dwells in all, in every hand and foot and head,
in every mouth and eye and ear in the universe.
14. Without senses itself, it shines through
the functioning of the senses. Completely
independent, it supports all things. Beyond
the gunas, it enjoys their play.
15. It is both near and far, both within and
without every creature; it moves and is unmoving.
In its subtlety it is beyond comprehension.

Our two dogs sit outside my door every morning, waiting to see me and to have their breakfast snack. When I come out after my morning meditation, I don't just see dogs; I see the Lord wearing two rather curious costumes. This is the best I can do to put the experience into words, but it is not metaphor; that is what I actually see. When I watch them playing with a stick, I see Sri Krishna playing – a small part of the eternal game that Sanskrit calls *līlā,* the play of life. The whole of creation is this divine game, in which the Lord plays all the roles: our dogs chasing sticks, the children who throw them; our neighbors, each with their different goals; the lilac outside my window that explodes in bloom every spring. "Look around," the mystics say. "The world is full of God."

In this vision you can see life struggling upward in evolution, like a plant reaching toward light. The field of the created world is full of these sunflower-creatures, all growing toward God. Our dog Muka, when he sees me after meditation, actually tries to talk to me in human sounds; one of them almost sounds like *Om*. To me he is saying, "I want so much to be human!" He wants to be like us, and if we meditate, he wants to learn to do so too. That is the force that drives evolution, reaching up through Muka for the goal. With that kind of unified desire, I like to think, he *will* manage to be born into an āshram as a human being the next time around. The whole of life is moving like this toward the source from which it sprang.

It is impossible to have this vision except through the grace of the Lord. As Sri Ramakrishna puts it, the Divine Mother must say, "Let Brian have this vision." She gives him a sidelong glance from those beautiful eyes and touches a desire deep, deep in his heart, deeper than all worldly desires. In the heart of every one of us this desire is lying latent, a seed of divinity waiting for its spring. After that, even if Brian tries to cling to selfish pursuits or to hold himself back in any way, her power will draw him forward – sometimes by deepening desire, sometimes by the heightened suffering that comes when you happen to forget your overriding goal. Every person who has attained the supreme vision will attest to the power of this grace, which will come to everyone who longs for it with an undivided heart and mind.

अविभक्तं च भूतेषु विभक्तमिव च स्थितम् ।
भूतभर्तृ च तज्ज्ञेयं ग्रसिष्णु प्रभविष्णु च ॥ १३-१६ ॥
ज्योतिषामपि तज्ज्योतिस्तमसः परमुच्यते ।
ज्ञानं ज्ञेयं ज्ञानगम्यं हृदि सर्वस्य विष्ठितम् ॥ १३-१७ ॥

16. It is indivisible, yet appears divided in separate creatures. It is to be known as the creator, the preserver, and the destroyer.
17. Dwelling in every heart, it is beyond darkness. It is called the light of lights, the object and goal of knowledge, and knowledge itself.

Again and again the Gita tells us that the Self is light, the very source of light. This is not merely metaphor, as can be experienced in the deeper stages of meditation. But until that experience, these words are very difficult to understand.

The Buddha might explain by saying that until we realize the Self, we *are* living in darkness, actually dreaming that we are the body. This is good scientific language. Even physiologically, there is much less difference than we like to think between the dream experience in sleep and the Māyā-dream we experience while we are awake. The Buddha would go so far as to say that most of us pass through life like sleepwalkers – coming and going on cue, reading our lines, yet no more aware of our actions than someone in a dream.

"Preposterous!" we want to say. "Don't I see? Don't I hear? The sun is shining, the birds are singing, the neighbors are quarreling downstairs; I'm not aware of any of these things while I'm asleep." But might not a sleeper say the same? After all, we see and hear not with our eyes and ears but with our mind. As long as we are asleep, the things we see and hear in dreams *are* real. Watch a dog dreaming: you can see its ears move and its nose twitch, and you know he is seeing and smelling – sensing a dream cat, made out of mind-stuff and memories, while his body slumbers. Our dog Muka runs on the beach in his sleep; you can see his paws trying to trot. Similarly, when you dream that something is attacking you, your heart races and adrenaline surges in your body just as if the attack were real.

"All right," we say, "but look at the sequence of events in dreams. One minute you're on a train in Canada at the age of five; the next minute you're paddling around in the Dead Sea wearing a fez. There's no logic in a dream world. You don't have any control over what happens."

But is our waking world so rational? One minute you're talking amiably with a friend; the next minute, for no reason you can follow, she says something unimportant and you explode. You find yourself being kind to people in the office and short-tempered with those you love. All of us are familiar with this kind of bewildering behavior in ourselves, and to someone who is truly awake – say, the Compassionate Buddha – it looks no more logical than a dream. In both waking and dreaming, we experience with the same mind through the same conditioning. Our waking responses are not always more rational than our dream responses; they are simply better disguised by the conscious mind.

To be able to say we are awake, the Buddha would say, we must be able to turn our attention freely, at will, wherever we choose. It is as simple as that; yet nothing in the world is more difficult to do.

Imagine that you are seated in your room, trying to concentrate on the report you have to present in tomorrow's meeting, when some word reminds you of college days. In a moment you have left your study. Your eyes do not see the pictures on the wall; your ears do not hear the noise on the street. You are back in Berkeley, wandering at midnight on Telegraph Avenue, recapturing dubious memories. This happens to all of us, much more often than we realize. Most of us can come back again with some effort, though usually only after the mind has finished exploring – in other words, when the mind gives us its permission. But some people actually lose the ability to come back. They keep wandering off to the same place in their mind so long that for practical purposes they actually live in the past. Their thoughts claim them; their memories oppress them. Such people *are* asleep, the Buddha would say. They are dreaming.

I have chosen an extreme example, but this is what a wandering mind means. When your mind is wandering from subject to subject, from memory to memory, from desire to desire, you say, "This is rational thinking. Continuous thought." "You are asleep," the Buddha would correct, "and you are having a series of dreams. The main difference with ordinary nighttime dreaming is that you can articulate some thoughts and make certain automatic responses." These are not trivial differences, but they are differences of degree, not of kind. To say you are awake – the literal meaning of the word *buddha* – you have to be able to put the car of your mind in one lane and drive it straight to where you want to go, without weaving in and out of anybody else's lane.

The consequences of this are enormous. If you are driving in only one lane, no anger can come to you. To get angry, your mind has to change lanes. To get greedy or jealous, your mind has to change lanes. This is a very compassionate view of human nature. If someone makes a mistake in a dream, who will hold it against him? It was a dream mistake, made with dream people: creations of the mind. Similarly, isn't it rather unfair to condemn people who do not have control over their thinking process? Isn't it rather unloving to condemn them? They have never learned to drive.

Quite a few people, though they admired and respected me, used to get terribly upset by the idea that we are living in our sleep once they saw the personal implications. "You sit laughing with the rest of us," one good friend told me, "and then suddenly you say something like this. It goes into my heart like an arrow and comes out on the other side."

Mostly this was in reference to sex, which is where many human beings naturally have their greatest vested interest in body-consciousness. "This is the highest summit of reality for me," this friend told me candidly. "If sexual experience isn't real, what is?"

I could tell from the way he was looking at me that he was expecting one of those arrows. So I just asked a simple question. "Do you have sexual dreams?"

"Of course."

"Do you experience pleasure in them?"

"Of course."

"Do you remember the experience afterwards?"

I did not have to say anything more; the arrow had gone in. For a thoughtful person, this observation is enough to prompt reflection on the permanence and validity of sensory experience. Later I came across a quotation from Havelock Ellis, the psychologist who spent so much of his life studying human sexuality. "Dreams are real as long as they last," he said. "Can we say more of life?"

Even when the body is sleeping, all of us experience dreams that are very similar to the experiences of waking life, complete with sensory content and even physiological reactions. This has profound significance. Even if physical consciousness is absent, mental activity continues and our identity remains intact, showing that body-consciousness is not a necessary criterion of life.

The Gita is not saying that life on the physical level is unreal. It says simply that the waking state is not the highest level of reality. Just because you are making a bit of money and have had a couple of meals, you cannot say you are awake. All too often this is a kind of automatic activity on a relative level of reality, very much like dreams.

At this level, all sense experience has a kind of magnetic attraction.

The moment the senses pull, we follow. In dreams, we know, we have very little say in what happens; we speak and act out of some kind of hidden compulsion. More often than not, we do the same during the day, with one important difference: in the waking state, if we can but exercise it, we do have a choice. Once we begin to exercise this choice by resisting the compulsive pull of the senses, we begin to wake up. I wish I could convey the joy that comes about then! You will be awake every moment, able to yield to a sensory desire when you approve of it and to say no to it effortlessly when you do not.

In the early days of meditation this is not at all effortless; often you will have to draw on the will to say no, and the mind will scarcely let you hear the end of it. But in the end this becomes as natural as walking or breathing. "My hand obeys me instantly," St. Augustine complained. "Why doesn't my mind?" Just as we train our hands to reach and hold through a million acts of self-control, usually when we are toddlers, we can train the mind to obey us gracefully and agreeably. This freedom defines the waking state. All that we lose by waking up is bondage.

इति क्षेत्रं तथा ज्ञानं ज्ञेयं चोक्तं समासतः ।
मद्भक्त एतद्विज्ञाय मद्भावायोपपद्यते ॥ १३-१८ ॥
प्रकृतिं पुरुषं चैव विद्ध्यनादी उभावपि ।
विकारांश्च गुणांश्चैव विद्धि प्रकृतिसंभवान् ॥ १३-१९ ॥

18. I have revealed to you the nature of the field and the meaning and object of true knowledge. Those who are devoted to me, realizing these, are united with me.
19. Know that prakriti and Purusha are both without beginning, and that from prakriti come the gunas and all that changes.

Three terms are introduced here that are basic in sānkhya philosophy. *Prakriti* is the field in its largest sense: energy, matter, and mind. The physical universe can be derived from energy, though strictly speaking we never encounter this energy as such. Similarly, sānkhya derives not only matter but the components of the mind from a kind of primordial energy-stuff, which is not knowable by the senses but is the substance of all the objects and events we experience. In my earlier account of the twenty-four "cosmic principles" of the field, prakriti is the first principle, the original undifferentiated stuff from which the perceptible universe evolved.

Purusha, which literally means 'person,' is the Knower of the field. Everything that can be an object of knowledge is prakriti; Purusha is the only knower. It is the Ātman, the Self.

Guna, the third term, has a very important place in this volume. According to sānkhya, the evolution of consciousness begins when prakriti differentiates itself into three basic states or qualities of energy. These are the gunas. Every state of matter and mind is a combination of these three: *tamas,* inertia, *rajas,* activity, and *sattva,* harmony or equilibrium. These are only rough translations, for the gunas have no equivalent in any other philosophy I know.

In high school we learned about three states of matter: solid, liquid, and gas. The gunas can be presented similarly. Tamas is frozen energy, the resistance of inertia. A block of ice has a good deal of energy in the chemical bonds that hold it together, but the energy is locked up, bound up, rigid. When the ice melts, some of that energy is released as the water flows; rajas, activity, predominates. We know what power a swollen river has; that is an expression of rajas. And sattva can be compared with steam when its power is harnessed.

Alternatively, in terms of the mind, we can think of the gunas as different levels of consciousness – say, from basement to upper story. Tamas, the lowest, is the vast unconscious. Most basements I have seen are piled with belongings: furniture, boxes, appliances, old books and magazines, and an incredible variety of odds and ends. The unconscious is like that: chaos, a dumping ground for eons of accumulated mental states. There is great power in the unconscious, but it is covered up and inaccessible to the will.

Rajas is the ground floor, the ordinary mind that races along desiring, worrying, resenting, scheming, competing, frustrating and getting frustrated. Rajas is power released, but uncontrolled and egocentric.

Sattva, finally, is the so-called higher mind – detached, unruffled, self-controlled. This is not a state of repressive regulation, but the natural harmony that comes with unity of purpose, character, and desire. Negative states of mind do still come up, but you do not have to act on them.

This forms the basis of the most compassionate account of human nature I have come across in any philosophy or psychology, East or West. It not only describes differences in character; it tells what the forces of personality are, so we can reshape ourselves after a higher ideal.

The rest of this volume will develop this theory, beginning with the next chapter; but I can give a preview here. In its natural state, consciousness is a continuous flow of awareness. But through the distorting action of the gunas, we have fallen from this native state into fragmented, divided, sometimes stagnant awareness. In this sense we can think of the gunas as spectacles, trifocals, through which we look at life. They are fragmented, so we see things as separate wherever we look: separate selves, antagonistic interests, conflicts within ourselves.

Evolution, according to the Gita, is a painfully slow return to our native state: pure, unbroken awareness. First we have to transform tamas into rajas – apathy and insensitiveness into energetic, enthusiastic activity. But the energy of rajas is self-centered and dispersed. It must be transformed into sattva, so that all this passionate energy is channeled into selfless action. There is great happiness in this state, which is marked by a calm mind, abundant vitality, and the concentration of genius. But even this is not the end. As long as we are wearing these spectacles of the mind, we cannot help seeing ourselves and the rest of life as fragments. The goal of evolution and of meditation is to take these spectacles off in samādhi: that is, to still the mind. Then we rest in pure, unitary consciousness, which is a state of permanent joy. Those who go beyond the gunas see no separateness anywhere; they see themselves reflected in everybody, and everybody reflected in themselves. This is seeing life as it is, indivisible and whole.

I think it is Ruysbroeck who says that we behold what we are, and we are what we behold. We see through the glasses of the mind. When you are divided, you cannot help seeing everybody as separate. When you are whole, you see the same divinity in your heart and the heart of every other creature.

कार्यकारणकर्तृत्वे हेतुः प्रकृतिरुच्यते ।
पुरुषः सुखदुःखानां भोक्तृत्वे हेतुरुच्यते ॥१३-२०॥
पुरुषः प्रकृतिस्थो हि भुङ्क्ते प्रकृतिजान्गुणान् ।
कारणं गुणसङ्गोऽस्य सदसद्योनिजन्मसु ॥१३-२१॥

20. Prakriti is said to be the agent, instrument, and effect of every action, but it is Purusha that experiences pleasure and pain.
21. Purusha, resting in prakriti, enjoys the play of the gunas born of prakriti. But attachment to the gunas leads Purusha to be born for good or evil.

These are very difficult concepts to understand, because we identify so thoroughly with the field of matter and the mind. The Gita reminds us over and over that actions occur only within the field; thoughts take place only in the field; they interact and have consequences only in the field. Yet the field itself is inert. There is no consciousness in this field of matter and mind, which means that the mind does not really enjoy anything of itself; the intellect cannot really analyze; the senses cannot experience. Only the Self, pure consciousness, the same in all, can be said to see, enjoy, and understand.

All this is just philosophy until you begin to see the practical consequences, which are really shattering; they can turn our world upside down. To take one illustration, a good friend gave us a can of maple syrup this Christmas and our children have been making good use of it. I was watching them enjoy it with pancakes the other morning and reflecting on this nearly universal appeal of sugar. How many people, I wondered, would understand if I said that sugar is not *pleasant*; it is simply *sweet*? The words are clear, but the meaning is so deep to grasp. Pleasure is not pleasant. It is "apleasant": neither pleasant nor unpleasant, simply a sensation.

You can see this in many everyday experiences, but even if you make the observation, it is terribly difficult to generalize it and draw practical conclusions. Many experiences in sports, for example, I would find terribly unpleasant; yet a participant may enjoy them. I can think of few things less pleasant than bouncing along on the back of a horse, yet if I were to say that in riding circles, people would scarcely know what I mean. The sensations are the same, but the interpretations are worlds apart. I say, "Horseback riding is unpleasant." They say, "Oh, no, it is very pleasant!" Neither is right; it is apleasant.

It is the same with food. I know people who enjoy strong, bitter coffee. Millions find beer pleasant; millions would say the same about whiskey, which is even more bitter and burns all the way down. Indian gourmets like spices so hot that if you are not used to them, you feel that your mouth is on fire. And so on; we are all familiar with such differences. But we do not draw the conclusion: that the liking or disliking lies entirely in the mind.

Now take it one step further: an emotional experience is neither pleasant nor unpleasant. It is just an emotional experience, simply a mental state. You can watch it take place and then shake it off; the memory will remain without any emotional surcharge, which means that nothing can trigger that memory later and cause it to explode into words or action. This is what detachment means.

Incidentally, my friends – particularly parents – sometimes ask me how children get this kind of conditioning about food. Actually, a certain amount of this kind of experience seems to be necessary in life. That is why I don't object to children having sweets within reason now and then, so long as they get plenty of good-tasting, nutritious food at meals and so long as taste is not presented as an end in itself. As far as I can remember, I enjoyed my food as a child primarily because it was prepared by people I loved deeply. Tastes are learned, and there is no motivation like love.

In this connection, I don't think I have ever met anyone so free from the conditioning of the palate as my mother. Granny, you know, enjoyed good food. She never thought about it until it was time for her to eat, and while she was eating, it got her full attention. But to my mother, food really was apleasant. She was neither for it nor against it; eating was simply something one did, like washing dishes. This is a very rare capacity, which I am glad to say I did not inherit; I take after Granny. But my mother's detachment played a part in my spiritual education too.

She was an excellent cook. She used to prepare delicacies for me and then sit by my side in the Indian manner while I ate them, and I could never understand why she didn't feel any desire for them at all. What she enjoyed was my enjoyment. This, I am pleased to say, is a capacity I did acquire. Today, after long years of practice in detachment, I don't have any palate cravings, which means I can enjoy good food much more than any gourmet. Even when I take teenage friends out for ice cream or chocolate cake, I enjoy it more than they do; my enjoyment is multiplied by theirs, which I literally share.

उपद्रष्टानुमन्ता च भर्ता भोक्ता महेश्वरः ।
परमात्मेति चाप्युक्तो देहे ऽस्मिन्पुरुषः परः ॥ १३-२२ ॥
य एवं वेत्ति पुरुषं प्रकृतिं च गुणैः सह ।
सर्वथा वर्तमानो ऽपि न स भूयो ऽभिजायते ॥ १३-२३ ॥

22. *Within the body the supreme Purusha*
is called the witness, approver, supporter,
enjoyer, the supreme Lord, the highest Self.
23. *Whoever realizes the true nature of Purusha,*
prakriti, and the gunas, whatever path he or
she may follow, is not born separate again.

When I was on my way to this country via Europe over twenty years ago, I remember with what great interest I stood at the railing of our P&O vessel as it rounded the Arabian peninsula and entered the Gulf of Aden. I had many Muslim friends in India, several of whom were scholars and poets steeped in Arabic and Persian literature. From them I had intimate exposure to Muslim culture. All this made it a very personal experience for me to see the barren deserts of Arabia rise ahead of us and to reflect on their legacy to India and the world.

Most of all I remember the long passage through the Red Sea. I had never thought of it as being so large; I had thought we might pass through in a day and night at most, yet it took three. The air was warm and humid, and the waters unruffled by any breeze. The passengers were so wrung out by the heat and humidity that the ship soon seemed deserted above decks. I thought of myself as the Ancient Mariner, "alone on a painted sea." It was much too stuffy to sleep in our cramped, crowded cabin. When the purser wasn't looking, I took my bedding out on deck and watched for hours with quiet fascination while the mountains slipped by beneath the stars.

One night, I remember, I suddenly caught sight of pillars of fire rising against the dark shapes of the Arabian peninsula – an alarming, awesome sight, as if the land were licking the sky with tongues of flame. Was that the way the Prophet describes hell? Had Armageddon come?

A sailor laughed. "No," he said, "it's just the refineries."

When you know you are the Self, in a sense you pass through the turmoil of life with the same sense of detachment I remember from those nights on deck, watching deserts and refineries slip by without a sound. An unknown medieval German mystic wrote, "Nothing burns in hell except self-will." There is the desert of alienation, the flames of suffering and sorrow; yet you know you are not the refineries; you are not on fire yourself. You watch in peace. Life is not an empty illusion then, but full of meaning. Even when you pass through sorrow, you know that there is an eternal backdrop to all tragedy, an end to sorrow, and you get unending joy in knowing how to help and relieve the suffering of those who suffer around you. In the midst of activity, your heart and mind remain at peace.

Part of this peace comes because the vast burden of the past slips from your shoulders entirely, the way the mountains of the Arabian shore slipped by and disappeared: they were real, yet no more real to me than shadows. When we believe we are the body, separate from everybody else, all of us make mistakes. We can cause a lot of trouble to ourselves and others just because of the way we see. But when we see clearly who we are, all these mistakes no longer burden us. They belong to someone else, someone in the past, and the past is gone. People sometimes asked Mahatma Gandhi why he did a particular thing or said a particular thing when he was, say, twenty-two. Gandhi would reply simply, "That is how I saw life then. I see more clearly now."

Once you attain the Self, the scriptures say, you are not born again as a separate creature. This is not an easy statement to understand. In one school of Hindu and Buddhist thought, it is taken literally: you are not born again, full stop; you are out of the game. I am glad to say that I belong to the other school, in which I have good reason to believe. According to this view, though not born again as a separate personality entangled in the net of life, the man or woman who attains Self-realization may return to life again and again in order to help others and alleviate their sorrow.

Even having this perspective can help immensely in facing death, which is not an end but an open door. When I was a boy, I remember my granny once called me to the shed where one of our cows was dying. The cow raised her head a little to gaze at me, and I saw in her eyes the same fear, the same uncertainty, that I had seen in the eyes of relatives lying and waiting for death to come. They seemed to say, *What is happening? What comes next – or is everything over at last?* When you remove that uncertainty – not at a superficial level, but in the depths of the mind – the fear of death is gone. In every tradition the great mystics tell us quietly, "We are not afraid of death. We *know*."

When you go to sleep, you know that you will wake up. If you did not know, you would be terrified. That is the Buddha's approach. He would simply ask us, "Didn't you go to sleep last night? When you woke up, was it the same you? While you were asleep, wasn't there a period when you weren't aware of yourself as a separate individual?" It is the same with death, if we could only see. The body dies, being made of matter, but the Self can pass through this great change as quietly as my P&O vessel passed through the Red Sea.

I have had the privilege of being with many people at their hour of death, sitting by their side, holding their hand and repeating my mantram, helping them to understand that death is not the end but a chance to rest before a fresh beginning. One man several years ago responded as sweetly as a little girl. The others who were with him had gone out, but I remained for a few more minutes. "Is there any personal question you'd like to ask me?" I asked.

"Yes," he smiled. "Only one: after I shed this body, will I see you again?"

I just said, "That depends on you. If you deeply desire that we not be separated, sure, we *will* be together again."

When you love your teacher deeply, the scriptures say, that love becomes a bond that death cannot sever. And in the bodhisattva tradition, those who attain Self-realization love all of creation so deeply that they return to this life again and again to alleviate sorrow and help the rest of us realize the goal of life. "As long as a single creature is suffering," the Buddha said, "I shall not make the final crossing into nirvāna."

ध्यानेनात्मनि पश्यन्ति के चिदात्मानमात्मना ।
अन्ये सांख्येन योगेन कर्मयोगेन चापरे ॥ १३-२४॥
अन्ये त्वेवमजानन्तः श्रुत्वान्येभ्य उपासते ।
ते ऽपि चातितरन्त्येव मृत्युं श्रुतिपरायणाः ॥ १३-२५॥

24. Some realize the Self within them through the practice of meditation, some by the path of wisdom, and others by selfless service.
25. Others may not know these paths; but hearing and following the instructions of an illumined teacher, they too go beyond death.

In the Hindu tradition, there are four kinds of yoga or ways to God: *jnāna yoga,* the path of wisdom, *karma yoga,* the path of selfless service, *rāja yoga,* the path of meditation, and *bhakti yoga,* the way of love. If you look at the lives of those in India who have realized the Lord, you will generally find that they emphasize one of these aspects of sādhana over the others, according to their temperament and the needs of the times. But you will also see that none of these excludes the others, and that all have an important place in sādhana.

A luminous representative of jnāna yoga in recent times is Sri Ramana Maharshi, one of the most outstanding spiritual figures of any age, who lived in relative obscurity in South India until the nineteen-fifties. For karma yoga, the path of selfless service, you could not ask for a better example than Mahatma Gandhi. And for bhakti yoga, the way of love so well represented in the Christian tradition, I always draw on the life of Sri Ramakrishna, a perfect lover of God. But for those who consider these three yogas as watertight compartments, I like to point to a fourth shining example, my own spiritual teacher. Granny was not at all intellectual. If someone had tried to convince her that she could have her choice of wisdom, love, or selfless service, but not all three together, she would have found the idea absurd. Wisdom and service flow naturally from love, and all three are released through meditation and its allied disciplines. So where Gandhi says, for example, that the Gita is a manual for karma yoga, selfless action, I would add without contradiction that it is equally a manual for the way of love as embodied by my granny. As Sri Aurobindo says, all life is yoga. All the paths mentioned in the Gita are blended when we base our lives on meditation and work hard in loving, selfless activity during the day.

The word *yoga* itself contains the clue to this. Patanjali gives us the essence of it in a famous definition: "Yoga means stilling all waves of thought in the mind." By this definition, any set of disciplines that stills the mind is yoga, and this excludes some activities that are called yoga and includes spiritual disciplines from other, non-Indian traditions. What the Gita calls yoga is central to mystical experience everywhere.

यावत्संजायते किंचित्सत्त्वं स्थावरजङ्गमम् ।
क्षेत्रक्षेत्रज्ञसंयोगात्तद्विद्धि भरतर्षभ ॥ १३-२६ ॥

26. Whatever exists, Arjuna, animate or inanimate, is born through the union of the field and its Knower.

Hinduism represents the Godhead and its creative power as Shiva and Shakti. Shiva, the eternal masculine principle, is always united with Shakti, the eternal feminine. *Shakti* literally means power, strength, energy; in this unique tradition, strength is represented as a woman. Shiva is the changeless, Shakti the dynamic. Thus Shakti is prakriti – the whole field of creation, both mind and matter, and the forces by which it is shaped. Every woman embodies Shakti, which means that in spiritual terms the woman can make a much more important contribution to the world than can the man. One selfless woman can enable everyone around her to grow. On the other hand, an insecure and self-willed woman can impede everyone else's growth; so this is an awesome responsibility. Following my granny, I treat every woman with great love and respect because this is her potential; this tremendous power is what every woman represents.

For creation to take place, according to this tradition, Shiva and Shakti have to unite. From this union the world and all beings are born. Kālidasā, whom I would call one of the greatest poets and dramatists in the world, begins his epic *Raghuvamsha* with an invocation to Shiva and Shakti: "I meditate on the parents of the world, who are united like a word and its meaning." You cannot separate a word from its meaning; it would no longer be a word. Similarly, the world makes no sense apart from God, who is Mother and Father in one.

समं सर्वेषु भूतेषु तिष्ठन्तं परमेश्वरम् ।
विनश्यत्स्वविनश्यन्तं यः पश्यति स पश्यति ॥१३-२७॥
समं पश्यन्हि सर्वत्र समवस्थितमीश्वरम् ।
न हिनस्त्यात्मनात्मानं ततो याति परां गतिम् ॥१३-२८॥

27. He alone sees truly who sees the Lord
the same in every creature, who sees the
Deathless in the hearts of all that die.
28. Seeing the same Lord everywhere, he does not harm
himself or others. Thus he attains the supreme goal.

I remember a film in which there was a violent forest fire. Where it spread across the meadow, each blade of grass seemed to be made of flame; when the fire reached the woods, it leaped up to take the shape of trees. Each branch seemed to consist not of wood but of flame. While the trees stood, each tree of fire stood; when a tree fell, you saw a tree of fire lying on the ground, its branches glowing orange and gold.

Fire neither stands nor lies, of course; it takes the shape of the object it consumes. The Self does the same. The Katha Upanishad says,

As the same fire assumes different shapes
When it consumes objects differing in shape,
The one Self takes the shape of every creature
In whom it is present.
As the same air assumes different shapes
When it enters objects differing in shape,
The one Self takes the shape of every creature
In whom it is present.

This is not merely philosophy. I remember reading some comments by Jean Mayer, one of the world's foremost nutritionists, written after he attended the World Food Conference of 1974 in Rome. I respect his observations greatly, not merely because he knows his field but because his concern gives him wide, sympathetic vision. While the representative from Bangladesh was speaking to the conference about the imminent threat of starvation in his country, Dr. Mayer remarked, very few people were present in the hall. Most of the delegates were at a cocktail party, drinking alcohol made from grain – that is, from food. By his calculations, the quantity of grain converted to alcoholic beverages might have fed twenty million people. And he asked, Who at this conference on world hunger even saw the connection?

People sometimes object, "What does it matter? The alcohol has been made; why shouldn't we drink it?" The answer is that if we do not drink it, it will not be made. We have a choice, Dr. Mayer points out: there is a connection between a habit which benefits no one (except, of course, the industry) and the hunger of millions.

The intellect can see this, but it is the heart that enables the intellect to understand and empowers the will to act. A sensitive person, after grasping this connection, will not be able to lift a highball without seeing the eyes of a hungry child over the rim of the glass.

There is another common objection: "Even if I do give up drinking, so what? They're not going to give the grain I save to the poor. They'll make gasohol with it, or burn it to keep prices up, or fatten animals in feedlots with it." In the short run, there is truth to these objections; withdrawing our personal support of a particular industry is only the beginning. But withdrawing support is essential. The Gita is talking about a whole view. We have choices everywhere; one by one, we need to open them.

This is not a matter of the intellect, though a clear intellect can help. It comes from a change in consciousness, in which we gradually learn to see the Lord in all and to act and live accordingly.

Dr. Mayer observed that at that time the nations of the world, including many developing nations facing starvation, were spending almost a billion dollars every day on armaments. (In the 1990s the figure has been running almost two and a half billion dollars a day.) If a fraction of that money could be rechanneled into the development of local resources for self-sufficiency, the world food problem could be completely solved.

Look only at the arms industry; you will see what incredible things can be achieved in a few decades when some of the best talent in science and engineering and finance concentrates on a single area. If the same energy and imagination were brought to bear on getting food to those who need it, not only in the poorer countries but in countries like the United States too, starvation could be eradicated from the globe within a generation. It is not that the problems are so large, but that people's interests, self-interests, and attention are drawn to other things.

In an article contributed to the *Encyclopaedia Britannica Book of the Year for 1975*, Prime Minister of India Indira Gandhi wrote:

> No country can afford to take a narrow view of its own interests, since it has to live in a world that is closely interlinked. The richer regions cannot abdicate their concern. Prosperity for some cannot be enjoyed in the midst of poverty for most. It is not military confrontation alone that imperils world peace; disparity is an equal danger.

And she concludes: "The quest for an egalitarian society is not merely humanitarian. It is a practical necessity if the world order is to survive. . . . Unless the minds of people are remolded, infused with comprehension of and compassion for the suffering of the many, progress itself will be unreal."

Again, this is not rhetoric. The United States is the wealthiest nation the world has seen; yet programs and support for children, for the poor, and for social problems are being cut while weapons spending and the public debt soar. Literally millions of children and old people now live in such poverty that they do not get enough to eat. I wish I were exaggerating, but the reality is even more tragic than I care to paint it. All this is because we do not put people first, but greed. Not only the poor but the middle class too are beginning to pay the price of a material kind of "progress" that ignores the welfare of individuals.

A few months after that World Food Conference, a perceptive piece by James Reston appeared in the *New York Times*. He too was pointing out that times are changing fast for people in the developing countries, who are no longer likely to sit quiet and watch in resignation while developed countries maintain a standard of living that is excessive and wasteful, which exploits the raw materials and cheap labor of the poor. We have entered an era of international terrorism, Reston says, when even a small group can lay hands on nuclear materials and hold a nation to ransom or precipitate a war. By the end of this century, if trends continue, enough fissionable material will be in transport at any given time to make twenty thousand nuclear bombs. "The truth," as Fred C. Icklé said, "is that we are basically defenseless" – not only against this sensitive situation, but against an organized nuclear attack. All this massive expenditure on deterrents and detection systems has essentially come to nothing – except, of course, that it has left us more vulnerable to attack by enemies whom we should never have made our enemies in the first place. The law of compassion and unity cannot be violated without consequences.

There is only one basis on which we can live together, and that is to trust one another, considering the needs of the whole planet and subjecting ourselves cheerfully to small deprivations when necessary to serve those needs. This is not at all a negative note. Very little has been done along these lines. Very little has been done to make people understand that there is great joy in living like this, using all our personal resources in concerted, dedicated action to banish the threat of the suicide of the earth.

प्रकृत्यैव च कर्माणि क्रियमाणानि सर्वशः ।
यः पश्यति तथात्मानमकर्तारं स पश्यति ॥१३-२९॥
यदा भूतपृथग्भावमेकस्थमनुपश्यति ।
तत एव च विस्तारं ब्रह्म संपद्यते तदा ॥१३-३०॥

29. They alone see truly who see that all actions are performed by prakriti, while the Self remains unmoved.
30. When they see the variety of creation rooted in that unity and growing out of it, they attain fulfillment in Brahman.

When I was a boy I remember being fascinated by the novels of Alexander Dumas the younger, particularly *The Man in the Iron Mask*. So far as I know, it has never been decided for certain who the real man in the iron mask was. History simply records a poor chap who was held as a state prisoner by Louis XIV for over forty years and finally died in the Bastille, his identity still a mystery. But Dumas' theory made a great story: the mysterious stranger is King Louis' twin brother, involved in a plot to impersonate and imprison the king himself.

This makes a good allegory too. Each of us, the Gita would say, goes through life in an iron mask, riveted on so securely that over the years – or, from the Hindu and Buddhist perspective, over many, many lives – we forget we have a face. We think the mask is who we are, and of course so does everybody else. But beneath this mask is the king, our real Self.

This mask is our separate personality, and what makes it interesting is that it is not material. To be more accurate, Hindu psychology might say we are wearing two masks, one inside the other and fitted to it perfectly. The outer mask is the physical body; the inner is called in Sanskrit *sūkshmasharīra,* the 'subtle body' – that is, the mind, intellect, and ego. Both are made of prakriti, created out of our obsessive identification with the body and mind. The wearer is Purusha, the Self.

Between these two masks there is a quiet correspondence, which has many ramifications for physical health. Put simply, the body can be said to mirror or materialize the more rigid conditions of personality. In many cases, disease processes in the body may be said to correspond to and develop out of compulsive ways of thinking.

This is not so occult as it might sound. For one thing, compulsive ways of thinking lead eventually to compulsive habits of behavior, which have consequences in the body. Chronically high blood pressure associated with some kinds of aggressive personality is a familiar example. But there is a deeper side too. The subtle body, as I said earlier, is a highly complex field of forces – anger, fear, desires, and so on – all consisting of prāna. The same prāna that is the vital energy for bodily organs and systems, including the brain, is the prāna that makes up the mind. If thought-patterns grow rigid and compulsive, parts of the body cannot help being deprived of prāna, of vital energy. Over the years this can lead to serious disabilities.

Of course, this is a highly simplified picture. Personality is complex, and each individual comprises many physical and mental factors that come together in the development of illness. Still, there is increasing evidence to indicate that especially the so-called degenerative diseases – cardiovascular disease, arthritis, even cancer – may have their origin in this kind of pattern. That is why I like the prescient advice Sir William Osier used to give other physicians: "Ask not what kind of disease a patient has, but what kind of patient has the disease."

Hindu and Buddhist mystics would say that we have been at work fashioning this subtle-body mask for many lives. Every thought, every feeling, every act, every choice, shapes the mask further. I find this a very fair, sensible exposition. Whenever we dwell on a selfish thought – or, for that matter, whenever we act on an unselfish one – we are shaping tremendous forces in consciousness into molds of selfishness or unselfishness.

At first we make just a temporary kind of mask: grease paint, putty, a false mustache. You can clean yourself up in a few minutes if you choose. This is the natural state of the subtle body: elastic, pliable, spontaneous, with no rigid shape of its own. But the mind's natural tendency, perversely, is not to stay in its natural state. It likes to think and think and think, to desire and desire and desire; and as it goes on thinking and desiring, it becomes more self-centered and more rigid. Finally we have a real iron mask, riveted on seemingly forever – so long that we believe it is part of us, our real personality. Fortunately, this mask can be taken off; that is the whole purpose of meditation and its allied disciplines. And when the mask is off, we see ourselves as we really are: pure, complete, inseparable from the rest of life.

अनादित्वान्निर्गुणत्वात्परमात्मायमव्ययः ।
शरीरस्थो ऽपि कौन्तेय न करोति न लिप्यते ॥ १३-३१ ॥
यथा सर्वगतं सौक्ष्म्यादाकाशं नोपलिप्यते ।
सर्वत्रावस्थितो देहे तथात्मा नोपलिप्यते ॥ १३-३२ ॥
यथा प्रकाशयत्येकः कृत्स्नं लोकमिमं रविः ।
क्षेत्रं क्षेत्री तथा कृत्स्नं प्रकाशयति भारत ॥ १३-३३ ॥
क्षेत्रक्षेत्रज्ञयोरेवमन्तरं ज्ञानचक्षुषा ।
भूतप्रकृतिमोक्षं च ये विदुर्यान्ति ते परम् ॥ १३-३४ ॥

31. This supreme Self is without a beginning, undifferentiated, deathless. Though it dwells in the body, Arjuna, it neither acts nor is touched by action.
32. As ākāsha pervades the cosmos but remains unstained, the Self can never be tainted though it dwells in every creature.
33. As the sun lights up the world, the Self dwelling in the field is the source of all light in the field.
34. Those who, with the eye of wisdom, distinguish the field from its Knower and the way to freedom from the bondage of prakriti, attain the supreme goal.

Movies were rare while I was growing up in India. Our little village was not much exposed to the routes of world trade, and we had no theaters or auditoriums. But once in a while some enterprising individual would come by with a truck, a projector, a gas-powered generator, and an ancient print of a Hollywood film. We would set up the projector in a tent, and almost everybody in the village would assemble at nightfall to watch. It was all terribly new, and people in my village in those days were quite unsophisticated. Many had never even gone as far away as the neighboring town. So when we watched these films, most of us did not have a clear idea of what it was we were seeing. On the one hand, we knew it was not a live performance; nobody felt any reluctance about translating out loud or offering an unsolicited explanation of the action for the benefit of those who would listen. But the images had such power that we forgot ourselves. It all seemed so real! The screen would show a thief sneaking up on his sleeping victim, and while we watched we would hold our breath like children. Then suddenly one of my uncles would shout to the sleeper, "Wake up! He's got a knife!"

It is interesting to look back on those days now, because we have become so accustomed to the illusions of film that we forget just how powerful they are. They hold us "spellbound in darkness," as Pauline Kael says, in a kind of willing suspension of the world in which we really live. Life – the world of separate existence – does the same. In fact, movies make a good illustration of how the illusion of separateness works.

The other day Christine and I went again to see *Gone With the Wind*. For an instant at the start the screen was still a screen, filled with dazzling white light. Then suddenly it became a window, losing all dimension of its own, as we lost ourselves in the Deep South of another century. Without counting the extras, we must have watched dozens of characters come and go at various times. For a while the screen would be full of Clark Gable, then of Vivien Leigh; then both would disappear and the window would fill with horses and soldiers and the noise of battle. But when it was over, all the images vanished and the screen was again a screen: flat, white, and unaffected.

My uncle in the village might have wondered. The pictures seemed so real, but nothing had been painted on the screen. The film never touched it. The passion, the warfare, the terrible flames as Dixie burned – none of this had left a trace. And all those characters that looked so different were made by the same light. Imagine, the light that brought Clark Gable to life also shone through Vivien Leigh! Similarly, we look at each other at work or in the supermarket and wonder, "They look so different. They act so different. I would never wear a dress like that, answer my boss that way, buy that brand of macaroni. How *can* we be the same underneath?" But just as the projector's light creates separate characters, the Gita says, the light of the Self shining through the field creates the illusion of separate individual selves.

We should not press this too far, for I do not want to give the impression that *we* are illusions. But our separateness is an illusion, and everything about us from body to personality depends for its reality on the Self shining through us. When a movie stops and the projector is turned off, even the most colorful character vanishes. There was nothing on the screen; it was the film that seemed to stain it with color and characters alike. Similarly, the Katha Upanishad asks, when the Self leaves the body, what remains? Nothing but inert matter. Life, light, intelligence, awareness, all come from the Self.

One theater in San Francisco, I notice, has been showing a highly popular disaster movie for the last several weeks. Now it is showing Richard Attenborough's splendid film *Gandhi*. The first, I would say, gave us the lowest possible image of the human being: violent, self-centered, motivated by fear and sexual desire. *Gandhi* shows us the highest possible image of the human being, an ordinary little man who transformed himself and uplifted us all by basing his life on love, truth, and nonviolence.

Of course, I was very pleased to see the theater make this change. I know the whole city benefited. Yet it made no difference to the screen which film was projected on it. You can show violence on it and it will not be harmed; you can show a fire and it will not be burned. Similarly, Sri Krishna reminds us, the Self remains untouched through all our thoughts and actions.

When we truly understand this, it can lift from our shoulders the whole weight of past mistakes. We are not our body; we are not our mind. The body is matter; of its very nature, it has made mistakes in the material world. The mind, of its very nature, has made mistakes. These are interactions in the field: the karma of the body, the karma of the mind. But *we,* the Self, are not stained or diminished by those mistakes. All human beings, no matter what we may have done, have this core of purity and perfection in the depths of personality. Therefore, whatever our drawbacks and past errors, every stain on our personality can be wiped clean, leaving no trace behind.

क्षेत्रक्षेत्रज्ञविभागयोगो नाम त्रयोदशोऽध्यायः ॥ १३ ॥

CHAPTER FOURTEEN

The Forces of Evolution

श्रीभगवानुवाच ।
परं भूयः प्रवक्ष्यामि ज्ञानानां ज्ञानमुत्तमम् ।
यज्ज्ञात्वा मुनयः सर्वे परां सिद्धिमितो गताः ॥ १४-१ ॥
इदं ज्ञानमुपाश्रित्य मम साधर्म्यमागताः ।
सर्गे ऽपि नोपजायन्ते प्रलये न व्यथन्ति च ॥ १४-२ ॥

SRI KRISHNA:

1. Let me tell you more about the wisdom that transcends all knowledge, through which the saints and sages have attained perfection.

2. Those who rely on this wisdom will be united with me. For them there is neither rebirth nor fear of death.

The distinction here is between what the Upanishads call *para* and *apara*: intellectual knowledge on the one hand, spiritual wisdom on the other. The purpose of intellectual knowledge is simply to know more, which can be useful. But the supreme purpose of spiritual wisdom is to take us beyond death.

The more we identify with the body, the more terrible death is. I can explain this in two ways. First, when we identify people in physical terms – when we love them, for example, because of certain physical characteristics they may have – we feel we are losing them when our physical awareness begins to dim at the time of death. The anguish of separation can be unbearable. Knowing that we are about to be deprived of those physical personifications, we may go to pieces.

Second, death wrenches your own body away. If you believe you are the body, this is fraught with fear. You cling to your body with all you have, at the very moments when it is failing and full of pain. Physically oriented people suffer dreadfully at death, not only on the conscious level but even after their awareness has been withdrawn into the unconscious in the final phase of dying, simply because of this agonizing inability to let go. Even when the body lies motionless, a sensitive eye can sometimes see this dreadful struggle, sure to be lost, still going on in consciousness.

I mention these aspects of death for one reason only: to inspire you to break through this wrong identification with the body and to build your relationships with other people more and more on the spiritual level. It may take years, but as relationships become more spiritual and less physical, especially between man and woman, you cannot help discovering the unity between you and those you love. After that, there is no parting. It is not possible to understand this on the physical plane, but two people who do not want to be separated under any circumstances can be so completely united that death cannot part them at all.

मम योनिर्महद्ब्रह्म तस्मिन्गर्भं दधाम्यहम् ।
संभवः सर्वभूतानां ततो भवति भारत ॥ १४-३ ॥
सर्वयोनिषु कौन्तेय मूर्तयः संभवन्ति याः ।
तासां ब्रह्म महद्योनिरहं बीजप्रदः पिता ॥ १४-४ ॥

3. My womb is prakriti; in that I place the seed. Thus all created things are born.
4. Everything born, Arjuna, comes from the womb of prakriti, and I am the seed-giving father.

Last night I watched a documentary on the Pacific salmon, done so beautifully that I found myself identifying with these valiant creatures as they made their way through the cycles of their lives. Spawned high in the mountains, they grow to about six inches in the bright, clear, secluded headwaters of a river. But then something prompts them to follow the current down to the sea, a wholly different environment. The water is dark and briny instead of clear. In place of seclusion, they find a realm that teems with other creatures which they have to learn to eat, ignore, or fear – a realm that must seem almost unlimited in its breadth and depth. Waves roil its surface, and below the surface great currents sweep the length of continents. As I watched, I remembered the Gita's term for life as we know it: *samsāra-sāgara,* the sea of birth and death.

Here the salmon spends its days, adapting to its new environment completely. It even changes its appearance, much the way I used to see students do when they got away from home and came to the university at Berkeley. To all appearances it is a saltwater creature forever. But abruptly, for no apparent reason, a kind of alarm goes off inside. *It is time,* the alarm says, *time to return,* time to retrace its course.

The rest of the story is thrilling to see. Following that inaudible call, the salmon finds the mouth of a river – often the same river down which it came – and begins to fight its way against the current, back to the quiet waters where it was spawned. There seems nothing natural about this, certainly nothing easy. The little creature has to fight for every foot of the way. Somehow it almost seems to gain energy as it struggles along, so that by the time it reaches the fierce currents of the mountain heights it is leaping like a flame of prāna. As I watched, there seemed to be nothing in it but pure energy, no desire except the overwhelming, overriding, exhilarating determination to reach its goal. "That *is* the battle," I said to myself. The words of the Gita's invocation came to my mind: this was *rananadī,* the river of battle, the river of life.

Then, finally, it was over. Somehow the little creature made it up the last waterfall, over the last rocky plunge of white water, into the quiet of a mountain lake. There it spent its remaining hours in the bright solitude of its birth, spawning the eggs of a new generation.

For some, I was pleased to learn, even this is not the end. Certain species spawn and then return to the sea, only to fight their way upstream again when the time comes, perhaps three or four times more. They come back again and again. Perhaps they remember the headwaters when they reach the sea again, and can assure the others that life has a source and the battle to return to it can be won.

In one hour, that show managed to capture the full lifespan of a Pacific salmon. If it could be spread out over five billion years or so, you would have the story of evolution from the Hindu and Buddhist perspective. Against the vast backdrop of reincarnation the individual creature, called *jīva* in Sanskrit, emanates from God, ascends the ladder of biological evolution, and finally enters the human context, where it begins the long struggle to return to its divine source.

सत्त्वं रजस्तम इति गुणाः प्रकृतिसंभवाः ।
निबध्नन्ति महाबाहो देहे देहिनमव्ययम् ॥ १४-५ ॥

5. It is the three gunas born of prakriti – sattva, rajas, and tamas – that bind the immortal Self to the body.

From its divine source, according to the scriptures, life evolves through the differentiating power of three forces. This theory of the three *gunas*, as they are called, is one of the most important concepts in the Gita. The gunas are the very fabric of prakriti. All that exists in the realms of matter, energy, and the mind can be described in terms of these three principles, forces, or qualities, which unfortunately have no equivalent names in English. Roughly *sattva* stands for law, harmony, balance, *rajas* for energy, and *tamas* for inertia. In personal terms, sattva can be looked upon as the door into the kingdom of joy and security that is our source, our home. Rajas then is the force we can harness to take us there; unharnessed, however, it takes us everywhere else. And tamas is the obstacle that blocks our way.

Before the universe came into existence, the Hindu scriptures explain, there was undifferentiated consciousness, the indivisible unity called God. In mythology he is represented as Vishnu, 'he who is everywhere,' resting on the endless serpent Ananta in the midst of the cosmic sea. As long as consciousness remained unitary, any kind of separateness was impossible. But then, in the language of Genesis, "The Spirit of God moved upon the face of the waters." The Lord began to meditate on himself. Consciousness began to divide, so to speak, at the behest of the Lord, in accordance with three principles: inertia, force, and law. From these three, matter and energy were born. These are the gunas, the stuff of the phenomenal universe. In Hindu mysticism, strictly speaking, there is no creation; there is emanation. As a spider weaves a web out of herself, the Upanishads say, the Lord weaves the web of the universe out of himself; and the threads are the three gunas.

In human beings, after millions and millions of years of evolution, sattva, rajas, and tamas are found in differing proportions. One person is full of energy; another is the victim of inertia. A third, much rarer, is calm, resourceful, and secure. In each a particular guna predominates, representing different stages of personal growth.

Yet at the same time, all three gunas are present in each of us. Their interplay is the dynamics of personality. The same person will have times when he is bursting with energy – particularly when he has to do something he likes – and times when inertia descends and paralyzes his will, usually when he is faced with something he does *not* like. The person is the same; he is simply experiencing the play of the gunas, though without his knowledge or control.

Sometimes this interplay is a function of time and energy. In the morning you may be full of life and vitality, able to get all kinds of things done "first things first." But by afternoon, particularly after lunch, you may drag around accomplishing nothing. A detached observer might almost say these are two different individuals, so differently does the personality respond. And there is a third individual in us at rarer moments too. In everyone, simply by virtue of our being human, sattva is present also: kindness, security, equability, self-restraint. These qualities may be latent, but their mere possibility means that to some extent we have evolved. We have used the force called rajas to overcome the obstacle called tamas, and then brought the energy of rajas under selfless control.

The concept of the gunas provides the most penetrating analysis of personality differences that I have found anywhere. But it does much more: it also tells us how our character can be changed. Its descriptions are not passive. The Gita tells us what the forces of personality are, so that we can reshape ourselves after a higher ideal.

None of us, in other words, is cast in a rigid mold that limits our capacity to grow. We can change ourselves completely if we really want to. But we must have a strong enough desire to change the direction of our lives, to swim against the current of our conditioning. First we have to transform tamas into rajas – apathy into energetic, enthusiastic effort. This is the purpose of rajas: we have passions like anger, fear, and greed so that we can harness them all into the immense drive that is required to overcome the inertia of physical living. This is the power that will take us to the goal.

But that is far from enough. We then have to transform rajas into sattva, channel all that passionate energy into selfless action. And finally, if we want to cut ourselves free from all conditioning, we have to go beyond the gunas completely.

All three gunas evolve from the same source: prāna. Just as potential energy can be transformed into kinetic energy and harnessed for power, tamas can be changed into rajas and rajas into sattva. Tamas is frozen power. It has been kept in the refrigerator so long that it has become a block of ice. It just sits there, hoping someone will come along and pour ginger ale over its head. But a block of ice can be melted, and tamas melted is rajas, a powerful, flowing river. It can move things, overcome obstacles, get from one place to another. But it can also flood and rage, causing great destruction. And sattva is steam, harnessed to drive engines and turbines. The simile is apt. The energy of sattva and rajas *is* present in tamas, only it is locked up, potential. The more tamas is heated, the more power is released.

As tamas melts, a tremendous stream of energy pours into our lives. This gives a precise test of how meditation is going: if you find yourself postponing urgent projects, it means your meditation can be improved. When you are meditating it is extremely important to be active, both physically and intellectually, in ways that benefit family and society. Hard, active work harnesses the energy released when tamas is transformed into rajas.

Selfless action, says Teresa of Ávila, "is the end and aim of prayer. Works are the best proof that the favors we receive have come from God." Another simple, practical test: how *well* are we working – hard, with concentration, selflessly, for the welfare of all? Hard work by itself is not enough. That is rajas, whose signal danger lies in slowly inveigling us to do jobs just because we like them, even when they are neither necessary nor beneficial. I see a lot of rajas running amuck today, doing the most useless, futile, often harmful things on the face of the earth.

Yet restlessness is not at all a bad quality. Compared with stick-in-the-mudness, which is another name for tamas, it is a definite improvement.

Restlessness to me is a clear signal: "Learn to meditate. You are ready to turn inwards." People who feel restless usually misunderstand the signal and start running from state to state, country to country, job to job, deal to deal. This is just wasting the power that is rising. When you feel consumed by restlessness, you want to ship out on a tramp steamer, drive your van around the world, plunge into pleasure, turn the financial world upside down, perform all kinds of fantastic feats which appear adventurous to you but benefit nobody except your own ego. That is the time to take to meditation. When the energy of these activities is collected and harnessed in sattva, we are at the door to the kingdom of heaven within.

तत्र सत्त्वं निर्मलत्वात्प्रकाशकमनामयम् ।
सुखसङ्गेन बध्नाति ज्ञानसङ्गेन चानघ ॥ १४-६ ॥

6. Sattva – pure, luminous, and free from sorrow – binds us to happiness and wisdom.

Sattva, rajas, and tamas can be looked on as three stages in individual evolution. Those who are easily overcome by inertia, who procrastinate, who feel they have very little energy and cannot bring themselves to do anything worthwhile in life, whose actions say, "I don't care; what does it matter?" – these are people in whom tamas is predominant. Those who have plenty of energy for compulsive activities, who are always "on the go" but with no particular direction, who have tempestuous passions but not the will to govern them, are people in whom rajas is predominant. And those who give their time and energy freely to help others, who are "slow to wrath" and quick to forgive, have attained sattva. They have released the energy latent in every human being and learned to harness it for the welfare of all.

Sattva and tamas may both appear quiet, even easygoing. But there is a world of difference between the two. Tamas is torpid; a really tamasic person can scarcely get up from his chair except to go to bed. The sattvic person is as full of energy as a Ferrari, but all his energy is conserved. He is not interested in being one of the ten most rajasic persons of the year; he knows when and how to spend his energy.

"So do I," Tamas objects. "When I think something needs to be done,

I do it. But usually," he adds candidly, "it doesn't need to be done. Wait and see; that's my motto. Things usually work out by themselves if you leave them alone."

Sattva does not get upset easily, and the result is a tremendous accumulation of energy. He has a normal prāna income and a modest amount in his checking account, but behind all that is an immense amount in liquid, leveraged investments. In an emergency, he can move thousands into checking at a moment's notice. Rajas, by comparison, keeps everything in checking. He has a big handful of credit cards which he uses freely; he enjoys living "close to the wire." His assets are large, but so are his expenditures. As he moves into the second half of life, he may find he is spending more than he has, paying more and more frequent charges for overdrafts. And Tamas just loses money. When the normal bills of life arrive, he puts them on his desk. He does mean to get to them, but each day there is too much else to think about; they pile up; they get lost. It isn't only outward activity that spends prāna; dwelling on yourself is a terribly extravagant expenditure. Tamas goes about from day to day worrying about himself, brooding on his problems and desires, and while he does so, the bills pile up. "Fantasizing about vacation, 20 pranadollars. Self-pity, 75. Rehashing what to say to boss, 100. Total June resentments, 477.95." No wonder he gets tired!

Our local utilities company has put up signs by the side of the road, reminding us how to save energy: "Don't do this. Turn off that." We can conserve prāna immensely through an equally simple process: by turning off attention from ourselves and switching it to the needs of others. Just turning attention away from ourselves – say, by repeating the mantram when you start to dwell on some personal problem – saves a good deal of expense. But switching attention to others actually builds up savings. That is the source of Sattva's fortune. St. Francis's line, "It is in giving that we receive," is literally true. If you give ten pranadollars to your partner, the Lord adds twenty to your account in savings. You can test it and see. You can also test the corollary: "It is in grabbing that we debilitate ourselves." Not only do we not get; we lose what little we have.

We can also compare in terms of the will. Tamas simply doesn't have any. It is a simple, accurate definition. He can't attend to the job at hand because he doesn't have the will. You can tell him over and over again the consequences of procrastination; he won't hear. Tamas keeps his ears open, but his mind is closed with the wax of inertia.

Rajas, of course, has much more drive, more passion. But his will is still rather small – unless, of course, it is compulsively harnessed by a compelling desire. This combination of strong desire and weak will gets Rajas into a lot of trouble. The one thing I can say in favor of Tamas is that he is immune to temptation, for the simple reason that there is no energy to be tempted with. If you take the world's finest chocolate cake and hold it in front of a pillar, the pillar will not feel tempted in the slightest. It is the same with Tamas. He loves to overeat, but he can't be tempted to exert himself even for the sake of self-indulgence. Tamasic people can pass themselves off as statues. Set them in some situation and come back a couple of years later; they will still be standing in the same old place, surveying the scene with blank hauteur. Similarly, tamasic people cannot get angry. It is not that they are forgiving; their desires are so feeble that if you thwart them, they shrug it off. What does it matter? And they cannot get greedy – not because they are detached, but because they have no capacity to feel or desire. They cannot love; they can't even have a passing fancy. Imagine how terrible it would be not even to have a passing fancy! If Tamas sees an ad for a three-week cruise to the Bahamas or a lavishly appointed new Mercedes, he can't even say, "Wouldn't I like to have that!" All he can respond with is, "Who cares?"

There is no sensitiveness in tamas, no awareness. Swami Vivekananda used to say that it is much better to be greedy than not to be capable of greed, better to feel angry than not to be able to feel angry, better to live a little than to sit there dead. This remark can help all of us in our moments of tamas. It is much better to move than to sit; even if you go in the wrong direction, at least you are going somewhere. When you're moving, you can always change direction.

Unlike those who are tamasic, rajasic people get angry easily; they don't have to take lessons. They find it natural to feel resentful, to crave things, to insist on their own way. It is no challenge for them to feel sustained hostility; they have a good memory, very well maintained. You may say, "What a negative state!" True, but at least rajas has possibilities. When you send a Christmas card to a resentful person, you can always write, "To a potentially ideal companion." Power is present; therefore, so is the capacity to change.

Tamas, by comparison, is a damp squib. Swami Vivekananda compares tamas with a sodden log: you can light match after match and never get a fire. All you do is waste the matches. Rajas is like Georgia fatwood; just show him the matchbox and he blazes. His volatility may be dangerous, but at least Rajas is active; he has power.

Rajas likes to be active. In fact, he can't be anything else. If he has to wait for a bus, he doesn't know what to do, so he lights a cigarette or practices cracking his knuckles. He can't simply sit and watch a movie; he has to keep his hands and mouth busy with a carton of popcorn and a soft drink. If the action is too slow, he gets up and walks out. When he's driving he plays the radio to relieve his restlessness, beating time with his fingers on the steering wheel and switching from station to station. At a stop light he pulls out the newspaper or dictates a letter. And at night, of course, his mind keeps on racing. His work and problems nag him into tossing and turning, follow him into his sleep. If he tries to count sheep, they *baa* derisively or turn into bulls and bears.

Tamas, on the other hand, would rather walk than run. Jogging around the block is his idea of torture. If you warn him about fatty arteries, he'll say, "I'll take my chances." The heart attack hasn't come yet, so he can't imagine it. Why exert any effort for something you can't imagine? Tamas would rather sit than walk, and the sticker on his car admits, "I'd rather be lying down." Unlike Rajas, he doesn't have any trouble sleeping. Unconsciousness is his specialty. But his mind keeps churning all the same. He may not do anything physically, but Tamas never really rests. In the dark recesses of his mind – which means, in most of it – the Midnight Rocky Horror Show is going around the clock.

Only Sattva knows how to rest. He works hard when work is to be done, but his mind is free from turmoil. It doesn't get worn down. And when the time comes to relax – to go to a movie with his family, to play tennis, to linger after dinner for good conversation with friends – he doesn't stuff unfinished business into a corner of his mind so he can peek at it when somebody else is talking. He leaves his work at the office, physically and mentally too. Wherever he goes he is all there, one hundred percent. He falls asleep easily, and his sleep rejuvenates. During the day he may get as much done as two or three of the rest of us. His secret is detachment: he doesn't get personally entangled in his work. He does his best, then doesn't worry; he leaves the results to the Lord.

I like to illustrate this with the example of a good actor. A few years ago I went to see Sir Michael Redgrave and others read some of my favorite pieces from English literature. They took first a scene from *Pickwick Papers* – that curious episode where Mr. Tupman succumbs to romance – and for a while, just for that scene, Sir Michael and his supporting actress actually became Tupman and Miss Wardle. Then they did a scene from Wilde's *The Importance of Being Earnest,* and everything changed. They spoke so differently, behaved so differently, that I thought they were different people altogether. For a poem of John Donne's they changed roles again; then again for Shakespeare, again for Shaw. Yet through all those roles, it was the same Sir Michael Redgrave. We never forgot that; therein lay half the artistry. More important, Sir Michael never forgot it either.

Sattva is like that. He knows who he is, so he doesn't confuse himself with the roles he plays. If he is a doctor, when he goes to his clinic in the morning he becomes a doctor – puts on a white coat and an expression of infallibility. This is part of his profession; it inspires confidence in his patients. But at the same time, he never forgets that this is Mr. Sattva playing the role of doctor. When he goes home, he leaves his infallibility at the clinic with his lab coat; it is not so welcome elsewhere. At home he has other roles: loving partner to his wife, loving father to his children.

Dr. Rajas forgets. He knows the textbooks backward and forward, but he is so caught up in himself that he gets emotionally entangled with his patients and their problems. When he goes home he is still the doctor, worrying about whether he will be able to do anything about Susie Smith's depressions and save Sam Bass from alcoholism. He scarcely sees his children or his wife. Interestingly enough, when he goes back to the clinic, the same preoccupation is going to keep him from giving his full attention to the next day's patients. He will still be carrying the burden of the past as if it were all his own. It doesn't help Susie Smith, and it doesn't help anybody else either.

This lack of detachment is the main source of professional burnout.

Recently I read a thick book on this subject, full of charts and case histories. I don't think it occurred to the author that a good professional need never burn out if he or she can learn to be detached.

It is the same for a teacher. Here I can speak from personal experience. The college professor is not really a professor; he is just a nice fellow, handy at home, normal, regular. But when he steps onto the campus, a pall of profundity descends on him. He goes into the library stacks and brings out the biggest books he can find. When he lectures, with his notes and diagrams and slides and prepared jokes, he speaks with an air of learned authority. But after he leaves campus, when he goes to look over the drugstore paperback collection, he is no longer the professor. He is Mr. Middle America, looking for something new in science fiction or the latest advice on inflationary investments.

Sattva plays each role with detachment. When she is a wife, she plays that role perfectly. With her children, she plays the perfect mother. At work she is the perfect doctor, teacher, accountant, programmer, clerk. After a lot of practice this becomes natural and spontaneous, as it must have been for Sir Michael Redgrave. You never forget you are really the Self, with many parts to play in life which require your best effort if those around you are to benefit.

Each guna has its characteristic problems. Tamas is full of fear. He doesn't necessarily run from his own shadow; he may never think of himself as fearful. But fear comes in countless disguises. Tamas worries, though it seldom leads to action. He is anxious about the economy and the latest strain of flu. He wonders what people think of him, whether they like him, whether they will respond the way he expects. Often too he responds only to fear, which is not the most elevating kind of motivation.

Rajas, on the other hand, has two ways of responding: anger and greed. He cannot choose, but at least there is some variety. Rajas has possibilities; he can learn to change.

And Rajas has some will: not much, it is true, but at least he has something to work on. The problems arise because his desires are compulsive. In rajas, will and desire are like a little boy with his daddy. Desire strides along, and little Will can't keep up. But Daddy Desire doesn't wait; he's too impatient. "Got to learn to keep up," he says. "Step along!" Usually Will does not step along. He lags farther and farther behind, and wherever the will lags behind desire, there is trouble. You become a victim of your desires. You have no freedom of choice; you are driven. You may even become obsessed. When you can't stop thinking about something, some thing or person you want, when you can't switch your mind off it or drop that desire at will, the will is lagging so far behind that it is helpless.

When a desire is that strong, it can split your consciousness until the desire is satisfied. On the job, over dinner, at the movies, behind the wheel, in your sleep, whatever else you may be trying to think about, some part of your mind will be on that desire. You can't concentrate, can't do a good job at work, can't keep your attention on those you love – all because the will is weak.

Fortunately, meditation can give the will walking lessons. I don't know how you go about this here, but in India mothers often use a simple kind of three-wheel walker when a child is ready to learn. The child holds on to the handles; when the device rolls forward a little, he takes a few faltering steps to keep his balance. He totters over to his mother in this way and gets an orange. Then one day the walker mysteriously disappears. "Never mind," his mother says. "Step over here and get your orange anyway." The child tries, falters, takes a step or two, then a third. "You're doing very well," she encourages. "Try another step!" When he finally reaches the orange, he falls over his mother in relief. But he has walked. Soon he will be running around and playing soccer; she won't be able to keep him home.

That is exactly how we teach the will too. We start with food – not eating between meals, turning down foods that are not good for the body, eating less sugar and fat and more fresh vegetables. This is not only good nutrition; you are teaching the will to walk.

You don't train the senses just for the sake of training the senses. The point is to get at the will, which is difficult to reach in any other way. I see ads in the magazines promising, "Make it a pleasure to quit smoking! Take our ten-day Caribbean cruise. When you come back, you'll think 'Lucky Strike' has something to do with bowling." Promises like these are fairy tales by which we shouldn't be fooled. Similarly, you don't strengthen the will just to get what you want or have your way. The purpose of a strong will is to free you from the compulsions of rajas, so that your passions can be harnessed for the welfare of all.

By training the senses, Rajas develops a stronger and stronger will. Gradually he is turning into Sattva, who has a will like Mr. America. The sattvic will has to spend a lot on clothing; he has so much muscle that he would burst the seams of an ordinary sports jacket. But he doesn't have much work to do. If a desire comes that Sattva doesn't approve of, the will just flexes his biceps; desire gulps and disappears. The only desire that can challenge the sattvic will is sex. Then the will meets a foeman worthy of his steel, and the real battle of sādhana begins. It goes on for a long, long time.

There is no need to feel embarrassed or despondent about this. Sex is the strongest desire we have, the highest physical satisfaction life offers. That is precisely why it contains such a tremendous amount of power. Strong sexual desires means a lot of gas in your tank. You don't want to throw the tank away; the choice we all face is simply, Shall I be victim of this desire or master? When sex is mastered, it leads to tremendous power and a magnetic personality. The power in that desire becomes *kundalinī*, the energy we draw on to elevate our consciousness and go forward on the path of evolution. So much power is caught up in sexual desire that once it comes under control, it can lead even an ordinary person like you or me to great heights of spiritual wisdom and selfless action.

In sattva the will becomes so tremendous that even sex comes under its governance. Then, the Gita says, the heart becomes pure. As Jesus says, none but the pure in heart shall see God. It is to purify the heart of all selfish passions that we make the will immeasurably strong.

रजो रागात्मकं विद्धि तृष्णासङ्गसमुद्भवम् ।
तन्निबध्नाति कौन्तेय कर्मसङ्गेन देहिनम् ॥ १४-७॥

7. Rajas is passion, breeding selfish desire and attachment. These bind the Self to compulsive action.

Rajas binds us, ties us up, throws us into prison. Why? Because everything in this state is tainted with selfish attachment – "I, me, mine." This is Rajas's fatal flaw. He does represent a higher state than tamas; he has at least some sensitiveness with all that passion and energy. But everything is selfishly directed. "Sure, I'm sensitive," Rajas says. "I'm a very sensitive guy – sensitive to Number One. I'm really aware of what I want." Rajas knows what he wants, and he is going to get it come what may. If he hurts somebody in the process, it doesn't matter. If it means spoiling the landscape, "Well, we have to put up with it," say Rajas. "That's the price of progress." If it fuels an arms race, "Well, that's the risk we have to take."

Take smog. The curious thing to me about the smog issue is that antismog devices and so on are just tinkering with the problem. The cause of smog is not in the materials or the furnace or the engine; it is within you and me. In biology the human being is characterized as *Homo sapiens,* "the thinking member of the family." This is an unwarranted tribute. I think it was Bergson who said that a better name for the species would be *Homo faber,* "he who makes things." "I *have* to make things," Rajas says. "What else would I do with myself? I'm going to make products all over the place, as many as I can. Then I'm going to get everybody to want them, even if they don't know what to do with them." If something can be made, we have to make it – highways, cities, cars, games, toothbrushes, airplanes, bombs.

There is some satisfaction in making things; I do not deny it. But that very satisfaction is what binds us. While Rajas is making something, he gets caught in it. He climbs inside his product or project and seals himself in, and afterwards he is as deaf and blind as Tamas to the cries for help from the community outside.

Walk down Main Street, or through the malls of any shopping center. Look in the windows of the stores. How many of the things you see are necessary? How many are truly beneficial? If we rule out everything that is neither, things that were made because *Homo faber* fever has got us, the whole shopping center could probably be reduced to a single store.

As consumers, you and I have a close connection with this phenomenon. It is we who buy. When we go on acquiring new cars, new clothes, new appliances, when they are not really necessary, we are contributing to pollution. I am not pleading for poverty, merely for simplicity. The simple life is beautiful, artistic. A life that is cluttered with things we do not need, even if they are objects of art, is a life cluttered with attachments.

When my wife and I were living in Oakland, I remember looking out the window one morning to see a huge moving van pulling in down the block. "They're coming all the way from New Jersey!" our neighbors told me. Sure enough, World Movers announced on the side of the van that they would take you anywhere. I watched with great interest to see what kind of furniture and *objets d'art* were worth the cost and care of being transported three thousand miles.

The doors opened, and out came a stream of stuff you could have picked up at Goodwill – armchairs, bedsteads, lamps, chaise longues, gilt-framed paintings of seascapes and sunsets, and boxes on boxes of old *National Geographics*, stamp and button collections, figurines, coat hangers, and recipe cards. They could have left it all in Camden, picked up what they needed in Oakland, and never known the difference. But human beings get attached, and once attached we are bound. We carry everything around with us, without noticing the burden of our attachments to things and to the past.

Please don't rush out at this point, call Goodwill Industries, and say, "I've got a houseful. Come and take it all." The point is not to get attached to things. Even if you have the world's finest collection of Ming vases or Moghul miniatures, which are undeniably beautiful, please do not get attached to them. If you do, you cannot really even appreciate them.

We can get selfishly attached to people too. I always stress the word *selfish* here, because the words *attachment* and *detachment* are so easily misunderstood. Unselfish attachment is pure love. You have no thought of your own pleasure or gain; your only interest is the other person's welfare. But selfish attachment prevents love. Unselfish attachment deepens a relationship; selfish attachment disrupts it. As with things, once you get selfishly attached you are no longer free. You cannot see the other person's needs – in fact, you cannot see your own real needs either. To love completely, every taint of wanting to possess other people or to affix that stamp "Mine, Do Not Touch" has to go.

All of us have a certain desire to grab and to be grabbed; this is the human condition. So while we are young, the Lord gives us a margin for experimentation in order to learn that grabbing fulfills no one. At first everything seems perfect – that is one of the marks of selfish attachment. But then the sky begins to change. A little cloud "no larger than a man's hand" appears – some slight difference in how the toast should be served, or whether it should be whole wheat toast or rye. The two of you agree to disagree. But the cloud spreads to the coffee. Rajas wants dark roast, full of caffeine, to get him off to an unnecessarily fast start on an enterprising day. Mrs. Rajas wants decaf; she is speeded up already. The cloud no bigger than a man's hand is now the size of a man's head.

Then Mr. Rajas comes home for lunch. Mrs. Rajas embraces him warmly. "I've been waiting fifteen minutes for you, dear."

"Come on," says Rajas. "It's only five by my watch. Besides, do you remember how long I had to wait for you last month at the Dairy Queen?"

"Don't bring up the past, dear. Try to live in the present. Besides, that wasn't the Dairy Queen. You're thinking of Foster's Freeze."

Little by little. This is what happens in selfish attachment; it turns against itself. After a while comes one of the most painful ironies of what we call love today: the very thing that attracted you to the other person now becomes irritating. Her nose, as perfect as Cleopatra's, promised such delight; after a while, when the delight doesn't come regularly, you feel chafed just to look at it. He had the voice of your dreams; when those dreams don't materialize, the same voice starts to rasp at your nerves. This is what relationships are like in rajas, particularly today. But they do not have to deteriorate like this; and if they have deteriorated, they can be rebuilt by transforming rajas into sattva.

I was reading the other day about lichens, which shows how far afield my reading goes. I am always looking for ways to illustrate the changeless laws of life, and even lichens provide grist for my mill. My mind occasionally complains about this. "You're a man of letters," it tells me. "Why don't you dip into a good play once in a while, instead of reading about borderline organisms?" But I read to get material, and these lichens provided a very interesting illustration. They can thrive in environments where no other plant can, and scientists have always wondered why and how. The answer, it seems, is that a lichen is actually two organisms, an alga and a fungus, each supporting the other. Their metabolisms are different, their views are different, their temperaments are different. But one provides food and the other provides water and support, so that together they become a unity which can face great environmental stress and thrive.

This is what man and woman can do. They are made to complete each other, not only in marriage but in every relationship. If they support each other they can forge an unbreakable unity that no outside stress can tear asunder. In this atmosphere romance flourishes.

Where there is competition, on the other hand, there is neither romance nor love. Not even synthetic romance can subsist in that soil. Where competition rages, only death can flourish. One of the great tragedies of our modern life is the constant attempt, sometimes in the very name of romance, to play man and woman against each other in every field of life. I see it daily in books, in films, on television, on campuses, in homes; I hear it in popular songs. All of us can bend our will to prevent this tragedy by emphasizing the unity between man and woman in everything we do.

तमस्त्वज्ञानजं विद्धि मोहनं सर्वदेहिनाम् ।
प्रमादालस्यनिद्राभिस्तन्निबध्नाति भारत ॥ १४-८ ॥

8. Tamas, born of ignorance, deludes all creatures through heedlessness, indolence, and sleep.

Up until now Sri Krishna has only given what in India we call trailers about tamas – what you call previews. "Next verse, coming to this theater, one of the most interesting characters in the cosmos! With all his cohorts – heedlessness, indolence, vacillation, disloyalty, and stupor." A most motley crew. Everyone finds it entertaining to see a motley crew, so we may find Tamas dominating this volume the way Satan dominates *Paradise Lost.*

In this verse Sri Krishna lists some telltale signs of tamas. First is *pramāda,* 'lack of earnestness.' This is a fatal weakness. People who are not earnest do not go very far. They get diverted; their attention is drawn away by a few playthings of life. To those who *are* earnest, Patanjali says, success has to come. They have, keep, and continually deepen the capacity to follow one supreme goal without ever giving up or wandering. Spiritual teachers in India often wait a few years before accepting a student completely, watching closely to be sure he or she is capable of sustained effort. To do otherwise would not be a wise use of a teacher's time and energy, for this is the most precious gift any human being can give or receive.

Second is *ālasya,* for which the nearest English equivalent I know is 'indolence.' *Ālasya* means partly negative euphoria, partly positive inertia. You bask in your laziness. Even when you are simply walking along, you show you are not alert; your eyes are open, but nobody is home. Half your mind is thinking about what took place yesterday; the other half is on tomorrow. Naturally your body slows down. Your steps slow, your head droops; if you are sitting, you slump – which, incidentally, is hard not only on the will but on the spine, particularly for a meditator.

Last, Sri Krishna says, tamas ties us to *nidrā,* 'sleep.' This is not legitimate sleep, "that knits up the ravelled sleeve of care." It is a torpor in which we try to take refuge. When a problem comes knocking on the door, you go looking for your blanket. This is one of the commonest responses to problems. Suddenly you can scarcely keep your eyes open. You may be watching a movie, in a meeting, at the dinner table; it does not matter. Something reminds you of a problem left unsolved, a task left undone. You feel drowsy, you yawn, your attention wanders, and the next thing you know you are asleep.

This happens often in the classroom, of course. Hasn't someone defined a professor as a person who talks in other people's sleep? One fellow in my freshman class in India used to sit right in the front row, and while I was pouring out the wealth of my love of life and literature, his eyes would glaze over and slowly roll upward until nothing showed but unnerving white orbs. Then his chin would hit his chest. I once took the liberty of asking him to tell me exactly what he saw at a time like that. His answers were worthy of a Gothic novel. "For a while you look like a ghost," he said. "Then you become a kind of vapor. After that, you vanish into thin air."

When you have burdensome emotional problems, it is not really sleep that comes at times like this. Clouds of the unconscious rise and overpower you. Even if you try to wake yourself up, you cannot. It can happen at work, or in the company of particular people, or behind the steering wheel; it can happen anywhere. At such times, even if you try your level best to break out of that bout of unconsciousness, you will not be able to.

No amount of clenching your fists and sticking out your jaw is going to help. These are all physical attempts, and what is happening is not physical at all. That is where you need the mantram. You fight it out by clinging to the holy name, which St. Bernard called "the energizing Word."

Tamas's motto is "I Don't Care." He wears it on his coat of arms, beneath a rusty helmet and two turtles dormant. "I don't care what happens to other people," he says. "What does it matter? I don't even care what happens to me." Quite a lot of people today are victims of this what-does-it-matter attitude. The Gita would say these are people who are hardly alive. They might as well be made of stone. It is the nature of a stone to say, "I'm not going to move. Even if a fire comes, I'm just going to sit here. Let it burn all around me, even if it burns me up." In the same way, insensitivity is characteristic of tamas. I see it everywhere today. How many seem unaware of the dangers that confront us all! War, violence, hunger here as well as abroad, the breakdown of the family, a poisonous environment – insensitivity to others on a massive, staggering scale. These are fires that threaten to consume us all. It does not require much imagination to see the flames on the horizon; every newspaper brings reports.

Psychologists and sociologists say there is no motivation to do anything about these problems. That is another characteristic of Tamas; he just cannot get motivation. About the only thing he responds to is fear. Similarly, to be stuck in a groove is part of tamas. Many people like the safety of a groove, where nothing can happen to them. They don't have to do anything; they can just coast along, never seeing the world. Grooves, I would point out, do not usually touch. A man and woman may live in the same house, speak to each other at mealtimes morning and evening, raise children together, and never see each other. He is in his groove; she is in her own.

Change, therefore, is a particular fear of tamas. When we have to face a challenge or our life undergoes some alteration, many of us respond with tamas. Yet change is the texture of life. The Buddha reminds us that everything is change; nothing ever stays the same. We should be able to adapt effortlessly, yet still keep our center within ourselves. But Tamas, when change or challenge comes, simply says, "I can't. I can't change. I'm rigid; I can't bend or yield. I can only break."

The other day a friend's little boy showed me a Japanese doll weighted in a fascinating way. Push it and it yields without resistance; yet the minute you take your hand away, the doll jumps up again. That is how we should be. When circumstances overpower us, we may have to yield gracefully. But as soon as the burden of circumstance is off our backs, we should spring up again with even greater resilience.

Tamas, by contrast, lies down and stays down. Often you don't even have to push him; lying down is a state he finds natural and comfortable. "I give up" comes easily to his lips.

I used to see such people sometimes in my meditation classes. The first day they are full of enthusiasm. "I'm all set," they tell me. "I've got a new pillow to sit on and a special meditation robe. I know this is right for me. Everything *feels* so right." The next morning they sit down, close their eyes, and the monkey that is the mind goes berserk.

Isn't it an English author who says that the first time he sat down for meditation, a curtain went up on the theater of his mind? Books he had read poured into his consciousness. He started planning a novel with complicated subplots; the characters pushed and shoved themselves into his mind in a riot, all trying to capture his interest at once. Suddenly he realized his half hour of meditation must have been over long ago. He opened his eyes and looked at his watch: five minutes had gone by.

That is the pandemonium that erupts when we try to train the mind, and it is too much for Tamas. He takes his meditation pillow to the flea market. "Sell this on consignment," he tells the girl at the first booth, "and take anything you can get for it. I've had it; I'm giving up."

Tamas literally means darkness. Tamas can't see. He gropes in darkness throughout his life, stumbles around, bumps into things, falls down. He doesn't see war brewing, doesn't notice that he can't breathe the air, isn't aware when violence dominates his streets; his eyes are closed. The word "sleep" in this verse is especially interesting. Tamas may be able to walk about or get himself into a restaurant, but he is not really awake. He is walking in his sleep, which is a fascinating phenomenon. I remember reading about a whole family addicted to this nocturnal habit. They would get up in the middle of the night, go to the kitchen, and have a midnight snack together. Then the next morning everybody would say, "Who did all this?" It's not so different from what you and I do. Compared to the awareness we are capable of, most of us go through life having midnight snacks in our sleep.

Some years ago, when we took our nieces to the ice show, I saw a robot skating on the ice. A girl dressed in gauze and glitter was skating around beside him with some kind of electronic monitor in her hand, calling out commands as if to a little friend. "Turn, Robbie!" Robbie did a clumsy pirouette. "Run!" Robbie ran. "Open your mouth!" Robbie cranked open his jaws. This is what happens in tamas. The ego sits inside with a transistorized walkie-talkie through which he issues orders, and we obey. This is not living, the Buddha says, it's sleeping: being pushed and pulled about by selfish cravings which do no good to anybody, even us.

Sluggishness is one of the main characteristics of tamas. We find it difficult to think, to feel, to move, to get exercise, to get up from the TV to change the channel; naturally we find it difficult to resist evil and contribute something of value to the world. Tamasic people often put on weight easily. Their minds are heavy, so the body says, "Let me catch up!"

To strike a lighter note – which I always try to do with tamas, because its implications are so grim – I remember a piece of graffiti on a wall in Berkeley that makes a good epitaph for Tamas: "All I need is beer and weed." I wanted to add, "To go to seed." That is the song Tamas sings.

To release yourself from tamas, the first step is physical. You will be feeling listless, oppressed, weighted down by inertia; you won't want to do anything at all. You may feel persecuted: "Why shouldn't I be allowed to sit around if I feel like it?" You may feel you are not in the best condition physically, with aches and pains that nobody understands except yourself. But the worst thing you can do in tamas is rest. Rest is what you have been getting all along; what is required is the elimination of rest. Superficial physical symptoms may come by way of protest: a dull, throbbing headache, nerves on edge, no circulation in your legs, a head as heavy as your heart. Lying down and doing nothing only makes these conditions worse. Get up and go for a walk – and walk fast, repeating the mantram, even if you don't feel equal to it. Try to walk a little faster than you can. After ten minutes or so you will find yourself breaking through that physical lethargy. Don't stop then! Keep walking.

Or say you have a report to turn in – at your office, on your campus, wherever. And tamas strikes. You have managed to sharpen some pencils and bring them to the desk. You stack some supporting documents on the corner. But then all you can do is sit and stare. A fresh, blank pad of yellow paper stares up at you, waiting for the first words of inspiration. It has been waiting a long time. But the report is due tomorrow, and finally something has to be done.

You feel sure you haven't mastered the subject. Perhaps you are one of those people who will not write anything until they know all the facts that have been written about that subject in the world. Here "perfectionist" just means "procrastinator." There is nothing wrong with striving for perfection, but if you wait for perfection to come before you act, you are going to wait a long, long time.

Here I used to tell my students something I learned from personal experience: start writing with whatever knowledge you have. After all, you are not expected to make an original contribution. And do not worry about style. I know people who will not put a word onto paper, even if no one will see it except themselves, unless it is exactly the right word in exactly the right place. Sometimes you can sit for a couple of hours this way without writing a sentence. Style can wait; the important thing is to get started and keep moving. You can always polish and rewrite later.

That is the first step: physical activity. You just get the pencil moving; what you write doesn't matter. Gradually tamas will begin to melt, as rajas begins to get its teeth into the job. An idea creeps in, then another. They seem to contradict each other, but you write them down. And then you see a possible connection. You test it; you test again. After a while you realize that an hour has gone by. When somebody comes by to remind you of your coffee break, you say, "I'll take it later. Let me get this down first, while it's fresh."

By starting with physical measures – simply getting the pencil to move across the paper – you have begun to get tamas to melt, prāna to flow. Now you can work directly on your concentration. Try to give your attention completely to what you are doing. Tamas scatters attention everywhere, anywhere but on the job at hand. When it strikes, your mind will wander all over the map. This lack of attention is what makes a job dull – which, of course, means that it holds your attention even less. The worst thing to do in such circumstances is to drop that job; this only adds to the problem. Whenever you find a job uninteresting, the answer is to give it more attention. If you find your mind wandering, concentrate more. Bring your mind back just as you do in meditation; that is where this skill is learned. At first it will seem painful, but after a while it becomes natural and rewarding.

Meditation enables us to direct attention at will. I carry a powerful little penlight in my shirt pocket; in the evening I can take it out, push the button, and train the light where I like. That is how the will should work: it should be "ever ready." Most of us have a will that is never ready, for the simple reason that we leave it on in our pocket where it can't do any good. When we take it out and try to flash it on something, nothing happens.

When the will has been trained, we can give full attention to the job at hand. This is genius. Those who have trained their will from top to bottom can give their complete attention to any problem. They don't ask "Do I like this?" or "What's in it for me?" If it helps to solve a problem like pollution or violence, they can absorb themselves in it so completely that they are no longer aware of their private personality. In this kind of work, tension and frustration disappear.

सत्त्वं सुखे सञ्जयति रजः कर्मणि भारत ।
ज्ञानमावृत्य तु तमः प्रमादे सञ्जयत्युत ॥ १४-९ ॥

9. Sattva binds us to happiness; rajas binds us to action. Tamas, distorting our understanding, binds us to delusion.

Most of our responses are compulsive. They are not really responses; they are reactions. If money comes near, most of us immediately feel attracted, even without our knowledge. Pleasure is an even more universal magnet. It draws everybody, rich and poor alike. We may say, "I can take it or let it alone." But the magnet would have a different view.

When we start meditating, if pleasure starts to draw us and we feel ourselves slipping closer without meaning to, we find we can draw back.

The magnet naturally feels annoyed. "This isn't cricket," Pleasure says. "You *have* to respond to me. That's what life's all about, isn't it? Look around. Do you see anybody else running away? Everybody likes me; I'm everybody's friend." But someone like St. Francis would reply, "I'm not subject to the law of attraction and repulsion any longer. I go where I choose, not where you draw me."

It takes a long, long time in meditation to discover that what we call free decisions, made calmly and objectively without any trace of outside influence, are actually reactions that could not have turned out any other way. They are not decisions; they are deep desires. We get these independent decisions from a slot, like stamps from a stamp machine; we have no say in them at all. That is why one word for Self-realization in Hinduism is *moksha,* liberation, from the root *muc,* 'to release': meditation frees us from compulsions.

The tamasic person, overcome with inertia, wakes up and thinks, "I don't feel so good. I have decided to spend the day in bed." Old Tamas splits his sides laughing. "I just push this guy back with one finger," he says, "and he gives up. He might as well be tied to his bed with ropes." If you tell that person he has no freedom, he won't believe you. "What do you mean? Look, I can lift my arm. I can move my legs. I can roll over. Sure, I'm free."

We ask, "Then why don't you get up?"

"I could get up if I wanted to. I've *decided* to stay in bed."

Another person comes to work and announces, "I've decided to go to Las Vegas this weekend!" It is Rajas's turn to laugh. "This lady is so restless I can make her go anywhere," he says. "If there were a casino on the North Pole where she thought she could break the bank, she would go there." These are compulsive forces. They bind us to action because they bind us to a particular outlook, or *shraddhā* in Sanskrit: the firm, fixed, unquestioned belief that something *out there* will make us happy. This belief is not peculiar to modern times. Pleasure hunters have been around since the dawn of history. Virtually everybody hunts pleasure, at least for a while, yet no one manages to find it for very long.

Most of us go on thinking that sensory satisfaction *is* out there somewhere; we have just been missing it. Only a few have enough self-knowledge to conclude, "It's not here. I have to look inside." That is the transition to sattva, the state of maturity, where we gain some capacity to make real decisions.

The word "maturity" is bandied about so miserably that we often forget what it means. The song today is "Go After What You Like." In my ears this translates into "Be As Immature As You Can." Maturity demands detachment. Immature people are acutely attached to themselves – their desires, their opinions, their way of doing things, their view of others. Mature people can stand back from their own likes and dislikes and go against them easily, without resentment, when it benefits other people.

"Sattva," says Sri Krishna, "binds us to happiness." This is a subtle point: we can be bound to happiness too. It means that when you reach the state of sattva, you will not be content with any worldly satisfaction. A few minutes of pleasure, an hour or two of most refined aesthetic satisfaction, will not be enough. You will demand a state of fulfillment that lasts always. This is the immense desire that impels us beyond sattva, beyond all the gunas, into full freedom and joy.

I was perhaps ten or eleven, I remember, when I was introduced to the beauty of English literature. I couldn't believe there were such beautiful stories, such interesting people; here was a whole world I had never thought about. My high school library was just one big shelf behind the headmaster's desk. He loved literature, so he was quite selective about lending these books to those who could really get absorbed in them. English novels can be big, you know – particularly those of Charles Dickens, whom I liked very much – and English was a very difficult language for us. So my reading went slowly. The novels went on and on, and I was captivated with every page. As I got toward the end, I used to feel a little sad that the story would soon be over. I would close the book and keep it aside for a while, just to try to make it last. My young niece Meera used to do the same thing when Christine gave her a bar of Cadbury's chocolate: open it up, give it one lick, then hold it for a long time before licking it again. This is all right for children, but for you and me to lick at a bar of pleasure and then try to keep it around for another lick is not worthy of an adult.

When newcomers come to my talks on meditation, one of the simple ways I observe them is to see how easily they get dissatisfied with temporary satisfactions. Anybody quickly discontented with passing pleasure has good possibilities for spiritual awareness. Such a person has outgrown the toys of life. Many of the people I see around me today are like this. They may still be playing games with their clothes or hair style, but once they encounter the spiritual life as it should be presented – difficult, challenging, demanding a deep commitment to the goal – they can respond and go very far.

"Rajas," Sri Krishna continues, "binds us to action." When you are seething with rajas, you will be doing a hundred things and never concentrating on one of them. You will always be active, always restless.

Today on the way home I saw a big garbage truck with a sign at the back: "Frequent Stops." This is a good reminder for rajasic people. The garbage truck stops everywhere. It opens up with a loud noise, picks up a lot of stuff, and dumps it in; then it goes a few more feet and does the same thing all over again. Those who get caught in pleasure and reckless activities are like this. They go in some store and spend a while there, then into another store to do the same – from tavern to tavern, game to game, country to country. Life is lost like this, often in the name of change. "I need a change," we say. Change is the last thing we need; we have very little else. Our deep need is for something that abides.

Compulsive action is often responsible for tension and alienation. Those who are constantly trying to make more money, for example, will not have time to be aware of the needs at home. They will not be able to enjoy their family; they will not even be able to enjoy a vacation.

The slogan of rajas is "The end justifies the means." Actually it is not even a slogan; it is an axiom. Rajas thinks only about ends. The one criterion he applies to the means to an end is, Will it work? This is not only immoral, it is futile. One of the most fundamental spiritual laws is that only right means can produce right ends. War cannot produce peace; only peace can produce peace. War produces only more war. Greed cannot produce satisfaction; it can only produce more greed. Competition cannot lead to anybody's long-term welfare; it can only increase separateness.

Means and ends, Gandhi said, are one and the same. When you are using right means to bring understanding and unity to your home, you do not even have to ask, "Am I succeeding?" The question is not relevant. As Gandhi says, "Full effort is full victory." Similarly, all that you and

I have to do is give our very best to the solution of terrible problems like violence. We can use our time, energy, and resources to support causes like our own Blue Mountain Center of Meditation, which in the Buddha's words are doing the highest work by driving out anger, fear, and greed. All we have to ask is, "Am I doing my best – every day, every way I can?"

"Tamas," the verse concludes, "binds us to delusion." Literally, it smothers wisdom, wraps it up in a dense blanket of ignorance and sits on top to make sure no awareness escapes. The lowest kind of human being is the one who is overcome by tamas, who cannot and will not act because he or she does not care.

When we have to do something we don't like, Tamas overtakes us, ties us up, and throws us into the trunk of his car. We might as well be paralyzed. We can't act; we can't feel; we become utterly insensitive, utterly unaware of the suffering our attitude causes others. It is not that we want them to suffer; we are simply unaware of anything except ourselves. Many acts of infidelity or disloyalty are committed in bouts of tamas, when we don't understand what loyalty means and cannot imagine that acts have consequences.

In this state, if we see someone being exploited – some person, group, race, or nation – we feel neither sympathy nor anger. We cannot act to relieve distress; suffering and injustice scarcely make an impression on our consciousness. We are in the trunk, and there is no one behind the wheel to feel or act. It is a tragic situation. Many people today seem unaware of the suffering in which so much of the world lives, simply because they are insensitive to anything other than themselves.

Some time ago I opened the morning paper and learned that the mayor of San Francisco had been shot to death right in his office by a former city councilman. The assassin felt he had been treated unfairly, so he went and got a gun. I expected the city to be so shocked, so concerned, that everybody would demand stricter handgun laws to try to keep this kind of crime from going on and on. Instead there was mourning for a day, a statement or two, and then the tragedy was forgotten again – as it was for President and Senator Kennedy, for Dr. Martin Luther King, Jr., for over seven thousand others every year, men, women, and children, shot to death often by one of their own family or friends when anger raged out of control. The tragedy makes no impact. Life goes on as usual. That is tamas: business as usual. There is no capacity to understand that this is writing on the wall for all of us, demanding selfless, nonviolent action to set it right.

All of us, Sri Krishna says, are obliged to contribute to life. That is the sole purpose for our being here. Those who are so caught up in themselves that they do not care what happens to others, who cannot see consequences past their own nose, have pulled the covers of tamas over their heads and are trying to pretend to life that they are not there. Circumstances can treat such people very roughly. Yet even this kind of person can throw off the pall of tamas through the practice of meditation.

रजस्तमश्चाभिभूय सत्त्वं भवति भारत ।
रजः सत्त्वं तमश्चैव तमः सत्त्वं रजस्तथा ॥ १४-१० ॥

10. Sattva predominates when rajas and tamas are transformed. Rajas prevails when sattva is weak and tamas overcome. Tamas prevails when rajas and sattva are dormant.

No one could want to live under the sway of rajas or tamas. But most human beings do. Why, in spite of good intentions, are we unable to remove the mental blocks that bar our way to selfless action? Why do we get caught so easily in self-centered activities, even some that are detrimental?

This is the human dilemma. Sometimes when we have a job to do, we feel paralyzed. We cannot bring ourselves to look at the job and if we do, we feel so inadequate that we say, "I can't do it! Better get somebody else." Yet when something we like comes, we can do it with energy and gusto. There may not even be any profit in it; it may actually bring us or others harm – the next day, some months later, or in the next generation. It does not matter. We get so absorbed that we never notice how time flies, and we neglect duties that have to be attended to even if they are unpleasant. Either way we fill our time but miss the point of life.

This simple verse gives a great secret: to live in sattva, get control over rajas and tamas. Keep rajas in rein and don't even let tamas out of the barn. When any two gunas languish the other will flourish, for these are the whole fabric of life.

You can watch this interplay yourself. You may read the Gita on Monday and feel inspired. The words touch you deeply; you immediately want to change your life and pursue its supreme goal. The next morning you get up early, have a good meditation, a sattvic breakfast, work with concentration at your job, speak kindly, return courtesy for unkindness. If you start feeling lethargic, you go for a fast walk repeating the mantram or turn to some job you have been putting off. If you start speeding up, you repeat the mantram and slow down. If you find yourself caught in some third-priority item because you enjoy it, you have the will and discrimination to drop it and turn to item number one. In all these ways you are withdrawing attention from rajas and tamas, and sattva flourishes – till the middle of the week.

By then, despite your intentions, the will is beginning to flag. Inspiration has lost its edge. And the pace of the week has quickened at work. Deadlines loom, people make demands; the old habit of speed starts to draw you in again, perhaps without your realizing it. You try to fit more things in, and begin snapping at people if they get in your way. Perhaps by Thursday you are taking work home, thinking about it at dinner, cancelling that date with your partner so you can finish the week's report by Friday. Sattva is neglected; rajas dominates the scene.

Saturday morning you crash. You can't get out of bed; it feels so cozy, and you're enjoying your dream. When you finally sit down for meditation, you fall asleep again. "Better relax this weekend," you say. "I've had a hard week." You treat yourself to a heavy breakfast and take your coffee cup out to the yard, where you can sit in the sun and plan a few improvements.

And Sunday morning you don't know what is wrong. You're not really in pain, but things just don't feel right. Your throat feels a little raspy and you're drained of energy. "Probably some virus," you say. "I'd better not inflict myself on others today. I'll meditate here in bed. Honey, will you call the church and tell them we can't make it to the work party this afternoon?" There is an old paperback on exorcism lying around. You start to leaf through it. A page catches your eye. . . .

Maintaining sattva in the teeth of rajas requires a fight that goes on for a long, long time. But most important, don't let yourself fall into tamas. When sattva is about to collapse, give it all your support. It will be excruciating, but you can develop your will only by exercising it; there is no other way.

सर्वद्वारेषु देहेऽस्मिन्प्रकाश उपजायते ।
ज्ञानं यदा तदा विद्याद्विवृद्धं सत्त्वमित्युत ॥ १४-११ ॥

11. When sattva predominates, the light of
wisdom shines through every gate of the body.

This is the Upanishadic image of the body as the kind of city people had in ancient and medieval times, with a wall all around and gateways for traffic in and out. The body's gates, of course, are the senses. Sri Krishna is reminding us that there is a mayor inside, looking out through these gates. If the city is in order, the gatekeepers obey when the mayor says, "Let this fellow in; keep that one out." That is sattva. But in the city of Rajas the gatekeepers do their own thing, and in the city of Tamas they are fast asleep. In either case there is trouble.

To take a simple example, I still remember the time a particularly explicit horror movie came to our little city of Petaluma. Grown men and women stood in line to pay through the nose just to get sick in the stomach. That was the attraction. In one theater in San Francisco, I read, a lady went into convulsions right in the aisle.

I saw couples in that line, waiting to get in. I could imagine the scene at the box office window. "Here's my Juliet," Romeo says. "I love her so much I want to give her convulsions."

The eyes and ears are gateways to the mind. When we watch a movie like this, we are trucking everything we see and hear right inside, where the untrained mind can have a heyday with it.

The Self, the scriptures tell us, is light itself. We do not suspect this when we keep trucking in garbage, of course. Tamas is a blackout; rajas is a city riot. But in sattva, the city is peaceful. Your heart is full, rich, loving, and wise, so the splendor within shines forth freely.

लोभः प्रवृत्तिरारम्भः कर्मणामशमः स्पृहा ।
रजस्येतानि जायन्ते विवृद्धे भरतर्षभ ॥ १४-१२ ॥

12. When rajas predominates, a person runs about pursuing selfish and greedy ends, driven by restlessness and desire.

What prevents the light of the Self from shining through? What keeps us from having tender, lasting relationships? It is rajas, Sri Krishna explains, and the first sign of rajas is greed.

Rajas is full of passion, but passion that is unharnessed. It cannot help erupting in anger, fear, and greed. Wherever he goes, Rajas is always thinking, "What can I get out of this?" If he sees a beautiful landscape, he subdivides it and puts up tract houses. If he sees a dense forest, he wants to raze it and sell the lumber. If he sees a school of trout shimmering in a stream, his first thought is to get his fishing gear. This way of thinking is depleting our world today. Gandhi said, "There is enough on earth for every man's need, but not enough for every man's greed." In India, against the background of a poverty-stricken subcontinent, he went so far as to say that if you had one button more than necessary, you were a thief; that button was at somebody else's expense. In our affluent society, of course, it is not necessary to go so far. Everyone should be able to live at a reasonable level of comfort. But it is still good to simplify our lives and not spend time and energy acquiring things that add to pollution or deplete the resources of the world.

Greediness is a fierce, tenacious glue. It can stick a human being to anything on earth, without his even being aware that he is stuck.

Take the automobile. I have to be careful here, because misunderstanding comes so easily. I am not at all against automobiles; they perform a very useful function. But when we get greedy about what automobiles can do for us, we get glued to them. We cannot do without them. We change our way of living for them, rearrange our cities for them, do everything we can to accommodate more and more of them at higher and higher speeds. Nothing is without problems, and cars are naturally no exception. But when we get glued, we can no longer ask, "Is this still worth the cost? Do we have to have more cars every year? Do we have to keep building faster roads just because cars can go faster?" The cost includes pollution and suffering. Automobiles kill almost fifty thousand people in this country every year, and the long-term toll of pollution on our air, water, and food is incalculable.

Sometimes I see a country's progress toward civilization measured in terms of how many automobiles it has. Why not measure in terms of bananas? There is as much connection. We have become so attached to cars that we cannot imagine civilization without them. Automobiles *are* useful, but they have nothing to do with being civilized.

California, the papers say, is expecting to have its twenty millionth motor vehicle on the highways before long. We could observe that day as a day of mourning. When I drive to San Francisco I am always struck by how many cars cruise by with only one passenger; I would estimate at least seventy-five percent. By what standard do we "need" millions of cars to get the same number of people to work at the same hours in the same places?

On the positive side, I feel heartened to learn that car pools are slowly growing in popularity. People are increasingly willing to wait five or ten minutes for a neighbor in order to reduce pollution and congestion.

When rajas prevails, Sri Krishna says, *pravrittir ārambhah*: we take up all kinds of activities. Rajas makes big plans, then drains all his prāna in excitement. When he starts to act on those plans, he often runs out of steam. It is the nature of excitement that it cannot last. It has to die down, and when it does, the same project you began with such enthusiasm looks utterly boring. It is full of dull, drab details that you had not foreseen. And you give up. The project has not changed, but prāna is gone. When we say something is interesting, it is not that the project is full of some substance called "interestingness" that sticks us to it until it oozes away. *We* are full of prāna, the fuel of attention; that is what makes it interesting. Rajas takes the prāna and runs. Then Tamas comes in and says, "The place is mine!"

People who are prone to excitement, the Gita says, will find it difficult to achieve anything worthwhile in life. They do not have the sustained capacity to carry through. Sri Krishna takes a long view here. Many people – this country has an abundance of them – have enough prāna for decades of excited, enthusiastic activity. But activity, the Gita says, is not achievement. It is not enough to rush about beginning a lot of things or keeping busy. Even without reference to spiritual goals, a well-spent life is one that rounds out what it has begun. The life of a great artist or scientist is usually shaped by a single desire, carried through to the very end. Without this capacity to carry through, we scatter our lives. Like seeds broadcast on an uncultivated field, our activities do not bear fruit.

Restless activity is a hallmark of our age. It is not a wholly negative quality. I would say it is a signal bell, announcing readiness for the practice of meditation. When we feel restless, power is rising. We should never waste this power by running from place to place, flying from continent to continent, doing dangerous things just because they are dangerous or new things just because they are new.

With their immense energy and restlessness, young people sometimes get caught in daring activities – hang gliding, surfing, mountaineering, solo flying – simply because nothing else demands enough of them. They don't find much challenge in making money or getting ahead in the world, and they don't feel inclined to do what the rest of the world is doing. Sometimes they cause a lot of trouble to themselves and others, all because power is rising and they don't know what to do with it. They are ready for meditation.

The Meditation Aptitude Test has two questions: One, have you got a lot of energy? Two, are you so restless that nothing satisfies you? If the answer to both is yes, you are admitted to the class. This is a fertile combination. With immense restlessness and immense energy you can go very far, because this is the gas with which a human being travels.

I believe I am one of the few spiritual teachers who will come out and say that there is nothing wrong with desire. Desire is power, and power is neither good nor bad. What *is* good or bad is the use to which we put it.

All of us believe that a strong desire leaves us only two alternatives: yield to it or be repressed. Give in to it and be happy; repress it and suffer a host of horrible consequences we associate vaguely with Sigmund Freud. The Gita says there is a third alternative. When a fierce desire surges up until your mind feels as if it is going to burst, your heart is racing, your glands are working overtime, everything in you is clamoring for that desire to be fulfilled, Sri Krishna asks quietly, "Have you got daring?" You say, "Talk to me later." He says, "Anybody can give in to pleasure. Where's the challenge in that? If you're tough, defy it." This is power rising. Don't explode it all over the road; and don't just sit there in the lot and race your engine till you are out of gas, which is repression. Get behind the wheel and use that energy to take you fast and far to a selfless goal. That is what I mean by transforming a desire.

People with strong desires can go very far on the path of meditation. When I meet people with a passion for making money I say, "Come learn to meditate." All they have to do is get their hook out of money and get it into meditation. There is a technique for this. It is the same for sex or any other dominant passion; every desire can be harnessed to a spiritual goal.

अप्रकाशो ऽप्रवृत्तिश्च प्रमादो मोह एव च ।
तमस्येतानि जायन्ते विवृद्धे कुरुनन्दन ॥ १४-१३ ॥

13. When tamas is dominant a person lives in darkness – slothful, confused, and easily infatuated.

Now Tamas gets his turn again, which he always finds gratifying. Rajas, of course, he considers a bore. "Krishna," he says, "talk about *me*."

"First," Sri Krishna replies, "you're *aprakāsha*." *Prakāsha* is brightness: a glowing skin, luminous eyes, a vibrant voice, the whole body shining with pent-up selfless energy. Such a person is utterly alive, certain that he or she can face any emergency squarely. *Aprakāsha,* which describes Tamas, is just the opposite. His eyes are dull, almost glazed; he can scarcely keep them open. No amount of Lustre Tone or vitamin E can make glazed eyes glow. When the lamp of love is lit inside, on the other hand, even your skin has to show it.

Even physically, tamas makes us ugly. If we have a good bone structure and don't eat too much candy, we may be able to hide the worst physical effects of tamas while we are in our teens and twenties. After that, however, every body begins to wear, and I think every sensitive person is aware of the dullness that comes to the skin and eyes and mouth of someone who is aware of nothing but his own pleasure.

Second is *apravritti,* 'utterly inactive.' If you ask Tamas why he never contributes to anybody else's welfare, he replies candidly, "Why should

I? I don't do anything even for my own welfare." Tamas is a very impartial fellow: no work for anyone.

Interestingly enough, this is untenable. When Dr. Selye says that work is a biological necessity, that is another way of saying that no one can be one hundred percent tamasic. This is an encouraging comment. When his personal likes are roused, even the most tamasic person you can find will spend hours rearranging his record collection, playing cards, or clipping magazines. If he has something that appeals to his self-will, he may get so entangled that he forgets about dinner, which for Tamas is saying a good deal. All of us, in other words, have the capacity for working hard. All we need do is release that capacity and then harness it by gaining detachment from ourselves.

Third is *pramāda,* 'lacking in earnestness' without zeal or gusto. Everybody, I think, appreciates a person who is full of enthusiasm, intense both in attitude and in action. People like that are good material for spiritual living. Tamas, again, is the opposite. If he takes up art, he doesn't get past smearing large areas with color; he likes whatever goes onto the canvas. If he takes up gardening, he usually gets bogged down after the planting plan is finished, when the time comes to dig.

Fortunately, earnestness can be cultivated. Those who are not born earnest can become earnest. I admire a person who is earnest, but I have a special admiration for the lethargic person who has *made* himself earnest.

Last comes *moha,* 'infatuation.' Tamas gets easily infatuated, because he has very little discrimination. Any little thing can put its hook in him. He sees a teenager playing "Space Invaders" in a video parlor and immediately he gets fascinated; he will stay the rest of the afternoon putting in quarters and getting overcome by electronic extraterrestrials. When he sees his first electronic game watch, video recorder, food processor, or home computer, he has to have one.

Everybody knows how easy it is to get caught like this. The trend today is almost universal. A few years ago, I remember, San Francisco proudly hosted the First International Exhibition of Erotic Art. (I don't believe there was a second.) Cultured, well-educated men and women flocked to it, to show they had cast off the fetters of our Victorian past. Another show that lingers in my memory was an exhibition of coffins.

One was made in the shape of a Mercedes Benz; the entrance, so to say, was through the trunk. I have seen exhibitions of embroidered jeans, museum collections of corkscrews, beer cans, bread sculpture, candy wrappers, and buttons. These are not the work of unintelligent people; this is what happens to any human being when moha settles like a fog.

Moha is what advertisements exploit. Rajas is the ad agency and the client, but Tamas is the prime consumer. Label something "More" and he will buy it, even if it may kill him. Or don't promise anything at all. Show him a lissome blonde beside a babbling brook in a verdant field and say, "Wide-open flavor!" He won't even ask, "What's the connection?" As Emerson says, he loves to be deceived. Rajas asks, "Don't you want to be *alive* with pleasure?" Tamas says, "Sure. Do I have to do anything?" "Just buy this and put it in your mouth." Sattva would object, "The least you could do is show him the other side. 'Alive with pleasure', dying with pain."

Tamas gets caught in doing little things that benefit nobody. Then, as he dwells on them, these trivial activities begin to look *big*. He holds them closer than the nose on his face, so that they fill his field of vision. It sounds like a harmless case of myopia, but I think no state of mind is more tragic. When you get caught in doing your own pleasant little thing, even if it is not harmful in itself, a voice inside starts saying, "I don't care. I don't care what happens to anybody else, even to myself. What does it matter as long as I can keep on doing what I like?"

Sattva advises, "Move back a little." As we gain detachment, life falls into perspective. Games and hobbies appear trivial then against a world backdrop, where the lives of millions of people can be improved, even if only a little, by how we live and what we do.

यदा सत्त्वे प्रवृद्धे तु प्रलयं याति देहभृत् ।
तदोत्तमविदां लोकानमलान्प्रतिपद्यते ॥ १४-१४॥
रजसि प्रलयं गत्वा कर्मसङ्गिषु जायते ।
तथा प्रलीनस्तमसि मूढयोनिषु जायते ॥ १४-१५॥

14. Those dying in the state of sattva
attain the pure worlds of the wise.

15. Those dying in rajas are reborn among people driven by work. But those who die in tamas are conceived in the wombs of the ignorant.

If the Lord lives in all of us, why are our lives so different? Why are many in such great misery and so few truly happy? Why do some succeed, find what they seek, yet die unfulfilled? Why do some attain fulfillment and others neither seek nor question?

Every sensitive human being asks these questions. I have never seen such a well-reasoned, sympathetic, or hopeful answer as in this chapter of the Gita, which lays the responsibility for our lives at our own doorstep, yet gives us full hope for changing ourselves completely.

Behind these two verses stands the immense backdrop of reincarnation. But the application of Sri Krishna's words is easiest to understand if we think in terms of this life only. Every day – the Buddha would say every instant – we are shaping our lives by how we think, speak, and act. If we lead a selfless life, we become secure and spread security to others. If we lead selfish lives, caring only about ourselves, we make ourselves insecure, rigid, self-willed, and alienated. We cannot blame God for this, nor Providence, Nature, society, or the times. The first act of adult growth is to say, "I did this to myself. Nothing brought me to this unpleasant situation except my own foolish choices. Therefore I can also get myself out, by making my own wise choices."

Scrooge, in *A Christmas Carol,* goes to bed an utterly selfish man. That night the ghost of old Marley, his former business partner, comes to visit him, rattling his chains. "Made every link myself," says Marley, "with every loan, every deal, every greedy thought. You have made a chain like this too, Ebenezer." Scrooge is terrified. The very next day he changes all his responses from selfish to selfless; he becomes a different man.

Why can't *we* change ourselves overnight? We get up in the morning and decide to do everything right – to be kind, detached, patient, and sattvic. But then the momentum of the day picks us up, and before we know it we have blown up at our partner or snapped at the children. By the end of the day we are all too clearly the same old person. What happens?

Samskāras are forces. When we go to sleep, the Upanishads say, these forces do not simply disappear. The dreaming state, in fact, is a Free Play Day. Unhampered by time or space, our samskāras get to run around and do whatever they like, acting out our favorite fantasies and fears. In dreamless sleep, however, they go backstage and sleep it off. Then it is that we truly rest. In this state, the Upanishads say, a king is not a king nor a pauper poor; there is neither old nor young, male nor female, sensation, sickness, nor sorrow. If we could wake up in that state, we could make choices free from any past conditioning. But we are unconscious in that state. After a while the samskāras start to wake up again, dragging us back to the waking state to take up all our desires and fears and aspirations just where we left off the day before – the same person, yet a little different too.

Similarly, the Upanishads say, samskāras do not vanish when we die. I know of no explanation more sensible, more down-to-earth. Just as we enter dreamless sleep every night, yet pick up every morning where we left off, so we pick up at birth where we left off the previous life, to continue working out the same samskāras.

That is why Hindu and Buddhist mystics lay so much importance on the state of consciousness we are in at the moment of death. Against this background, your life and mine this time around are entirely the result of the innumerable good and bad choices we made in previous lives. There is no such thing as an accident, the Hindu and Buddhist sages say. As Jesus puts it, "Not a sparrow shall fall without thy Father."

When I first came to this country, I was introduced to the "layaway plan." I don't believe I had even heard the phrase before. I was waiting in a big department store, looking at something expensive and useless which I could use as an example in my meditation classes, when the saleslady came up. "Wouldn't you like to buy this?" she asked. "It's marked down to sixty dollars."

I laughed. "I have only six dollars," I said, to be polite.

"That's all right," she said cheerfully. "That's enough for the first payment. We'll lay it away for you while you come and pay six dollars every month. Before the year is over, it's yours!"

I was impressed. "May I take it with me?"

"Oh, no! This is layaway. We keep it here on the shelf until you've paid for it."

I told the lady I would keep my six dollars too.

Karma is layaway on a cosmic scale. In every life we have done certain selfless things, helped a few people, served a few worthy causes; so we have a small packet of good karma, kept carefully in a pigeonhole with our name on it. When we die, according to the Tibetan mystics, we get a waiting period for rest and recuperation in which we are expected to look over our previous life to see what mistakes we have committed, so we can avoid committing them again – a little like our friend Scrooge. Then we claim our packets of karma, good and bad, and look for a suitable context – country, race, parents, environment – in which to try again.

When I explained this to a friend, she objected, "I don't know if I agree with that. If I had had a choice, I wouldn't have chosen to be born in Queens. Why wouldn't everybody pick rich parents and be born with a silver spoon?"

"That is the rub," I said. "You don't get a choice that way. You have already made your choice, by all the things you said and thought and did in the life before." After we die, all this information is fed into a cosmic computer which would be a hobbyist's dream. It has unlimited memory, and it never crashes or loses any of its data. It takes in all the particulars, looks over the available openings, and matches your karma with the karma of parents, cousins, neighbors, city, nation, and epoch. You are born to a family with similar or complementary samskāras so that you can work out your own samskāras; and you are born into times that will allow those samskāras to come to fruition. Your samskāras will lead you to behave a certain way in school, to go out with particular kinds of friends, to choose the right kind of partner for getting the kind of children you need in order for you to grow. If you were difficult as a child, you have to have a difficult child the next time around; how else could you learn? If you have been a good husband, you may get a context in which you have a good husband, so you can learn to be a good wife.

When this is understood, reincarnation ceases to be a mysterious product of the Eastern imagination and becomes a cogent, compassionate explanation of our lives and times. It offers meaning, and it offers hope. It means that we have selected everything ourselves, not so much consciously as by our desires. The appeal is simple. Life is an educational process, a kind of school, with all the responsibility of making progress left to us. Whatever situation we are in is the perfect context for us to learn to face a problem in ourselves. When we learn to face a problem squarely, the Hindu mystics say, that particular situation will not recur. There is no need to learn the lesson again.

But here let me again sound a note of caution. In India we seldom talk about reincarnation because everybody believes in it. In the West, however, the topic seems exotic, so people sometimes get caught up in it. I still receive invitations to attend workshops on reincarnation or to give a talk on who I was in some previous life. I want to reply, "I am much more concerned with who I am in this life." If the theory of reincarnation helps you to understand how to face difficult situations with patience and compassion, well and good. Beyond that, I would not advise getting intellectually caught up in it. All kinds of fruitless speculation can result.

Against this background, these esoteric-seeming verses make good common sense. Let me take up the second one first, because I like to end with the silver lining.

When a person dies in a mood of tamas, Sri Krishna says, he is born in a family full of tamas. I find this very reasonable. He has to learn to transform tamas; until he does so on his own, he cannot graduate to the next grade. So this hypothetical fellow is born into a family where everybody is inert. The father has no job, the mother overeats; every member of the family has the brakes on. They don't have much will, can't bring themselves to act, like to postpone everything. He will fit that family perfectly, because he is coming in with his brakes on too.

In India we have an official on the public roads called the brake inspector. He has only one job – to stop any car, any bus, any truck he chooses and say, "Let me see your brakes." He is not interested in any other aspect of the car; he just wants to see if the brakes work.

Tamas's brakes work fine; that is the problem. In those who do not have much will, who cannot bring themselves to act, who like to postpone everything, the brakes are permanently set. There is nothing wrong with the car. It is still in decent shape, and there is plenty of gas in the tank. The tamasic person cannot come into this life and complain, "I've got a lemon. Take it back and give me a better vehicle." All that has happened is that the hand brake is on. I don't have to tell you what kind of wear and tear results from this; that is what happens with tamas too. But there is no irremediable problem; we just have to release the brake and move our foot over onto the accelerator. Then the tamasic person can shoot forward like a Ferrari.

To continue this automobile language – which used to be as difficult for me as Sanskrit – one difficulty in tamas may be that the battery is dead. The car is in good condition, you have enough gas, but there is no power for getting the car started. I asked Christine what you do in such a situation. She said, "You call the auto club." The person comes, jump-starts your car, and then drives off with a cheery smile. That is what a spiritual teacher can do. There are certain situations in which the will is paralyzed; we feel unable to move a muscle. Then the teacher can connect the cables, tell you to stay behind the wheel, and start you off his own battery with his support, love, and continuing inspiration.

I am assured that this kind of thing is a free service of the auto club, but as you say in this country, there is no such thing as a free lunch. The same is true in sādhana. If we get a start from our teacher, he expects us to make the best of it – to keep on driving, recharge the battery, and head straight for our destination. If we pull off to the side of the road again, switch off the engine, and put our feet up, the battery will go dead again, and the dispatcher may not consider the second call as urgent an emergency.

If we find ourselves in a family which is ignorant of the unity of life, lacking both energy and initiative, that is all the more reason why we should release the brakes in our own lives. When others in our family see this, they may be motivated to learn to do it too. In many families I have seen, after watching John or Josie meditate for a few years, somebody thoughtful will ask casually, "How do you do this Indian thing?"

Similarly, when a person full of rajas dies, he or she is born in a car that has no brakes. Tamas keeps his foot on the brake and leaves the hand brake on too; Rajas doesn't have either. His transmission is automatic, and the only pedal on his floor is an accelerator.

When he was ten or so, my friend Josh had a kind of car he had made himself. It consisted of a platform with an uncomfortable seat, on which he had mounted four undersize wheels. Everything about that vehicle was primitive except those wheels. "Josh," I said, "How do you steer?"

"Simple," he said. "If you want to turn, you pull on this rope." It was fastened to the front axle at both ends; he hauled on it as he would reins on an ox.

"And where are the brakes?"

"It doesn't have any," Josh said cheerfully.

"What do you do if you have to stop?"

"You drag your feet."

Rajasic people are born into a car like Josh's. They have to keep going from morning to night, often doing things that help nobody including themselves. They can get caught in anything. Whatever they take up becomes an obsession; a casual hobby becomes a full-time occupation. I saw this many times when I was a professor, though it is by no means confined to campuses. Somebody writes a paper and gets praised for his understanding of punctuation; after a while he is working on his dissertation, "The History of the Comma Down the Ages." He *does* care about what happens in the rest of the world, at least to some extent. He feels regret when he reads that there is famine in the Sahel, or that one out of four in his generation will probably die of cancer from environmental causes. But these are vague issues to him, beyond anything he can do. The size of his universe is measured by just one question: "Comma or semicolon?"

The person who dies full of rajas, Krishna says, is born in a home where everybody is busy from morning till evening. Everybody in the family is making something, whether it is money or mischief; nobody has enough time to sit still and cultivate the garden inside, or observe himself or others. This kind of stillness can be healing. It makes us more sensitive, gives us an opportunity to see life whole. But the rajasic family has no time for reflection, and the rajasic child born into such a family rubs his hands together and says, "Perfect! This is the place for me." It is: perfect for getting more rajasic, but also perfect for suffering the consequences of rajas and learning to transform it, which is a service to the whole family.

Finally we reach the silver lining of these verses: the man or woman who has cultivated selflessness and learned to live for others becomes full of sattva. When they die, Sri Krishna says, such people are born into a selfless family. The father forgets himself easily in the welfare of his wife and children; the mother is a shining example of strength and tenderness, who can hold her family together when all the storms of life are blowing. The child born into such a family grows up strong, secure, and selfless. That is the climate in which he is born; that is the air she breathes. There is no contradiction between this and modern psychology. Such people take easily to the practice of meditation, sometimes very early in life. When they are earnest, they find a guide who will love them, cherish them, and show them how to overcome the conditioning of all the gunas and set their course for the supreme goal of life.

This is how I would account for someone like Thérèse of Lisieux, who when she was still a child could say with utter honesty, "There is only one desire in all my heart, and that is to become a great saint." She swept toward her goal so swiftly, with such single-minded purpose, that in the language of Hinduism we would have to say that she merely picked up in this life where she left off in the last. By the time of her death, barely twenty-four years later, she had attained such stature that Pope Pius X called her "the greatest saint of modern times."

The "other Teresa," Teresa of Ávila, tells us that she took twenty years to unify her desires. I would say that is one reason she became such an excellent teacher; she understood deeply the conflicts most of us face, and she knew from her own experience exactly how to deal with them. To me she is one of the most magnificent examples of womanhood in the world, as beautiful as she was spiritual. She had an unerring gift for selecting young girls of great spiritual promise, some even in their teens, to follow her way of life. According to the Hindu and Buddhist tradition, these are girls who have come into this life ready to take to spiritual disciplines. They responded to Teresa enormously. The Gita would say they must have been born into sixteenth-century Spain just to come into the orbit of this great saint, the perfect spiritual teacher for their needs.

कर्मणः सुकृतस्याहुः सात्त्विकं निर्मलं फलम् ।
रजसस्तु फलं दुःखमज्ञानं तमसः फलम् ॥ १४-१६ ॥

16. The fruit of sattva is a pure heart.
The fruit of rajas is suffering. The fruit of
tamas is ignorance and insensitivity.

Sattva breeds kind actions, and the fruit of kindness is a pure heart: no malice, no hatred, no ill feeling, no compulsive desire to cling to or manipulate anybody else. The sattvic person is kind to everybody, regardless of how he or she is treated in return. This kind of attitude purifies consciousness, because it is the same in all circumstances; there is no room in it for resentment, hostility, or fear. We can purify our hearts like this by moving closer when there are differences between us and others. Moving away from difficult people serves no purpose at all; it neither heals the breach nor helps either party.

Understanding, insight, wisdom, proceed from sattva and sattva alone. Rajas can pursue a subject as long as it likes; it may ferret out a great deal of detail, but it cannot penetrate the inner whole in which the details cohere. If you are full of rajas, you can study religion for twenty years and still not understand those simple statements of Jesus or the Buddha, which men and women of no scholarly standing have grasped with the heart for hundreds of years after they were spoken.

Sattva sees into the core of life, into its unity; its understanding leads to deeper understanding. Rajas, intent on finding more and more, only succeeds in becoming more and more confused by what it finds. Every mental state, Sri Krishna explains, bears fruit of the same kind.

Rajasas tu phalam duhkham: wherever actions are restless or greedy, motivated by one's own self-interest, the immediate results may be pleasant, but the long-term result is suffering and sorrow. Sales people in the tobacco industry may make a good deal of money, enough to buy a lot of things for themselves and their families. They may never even question where the money comes from, never make the connection between the product they sell and the hundreds of thousands who die of lung cancer, heart attack, stroke, and emphysema every year in the United States alone. But whether they notice or not, the fruit of their work is sorrow: sorrow for others, sorrow eventually for themselves. Every state of mind has consequences, not only in behavior but in the mind itself. Just as the kindness of sattva is its own reward, the restless, burning desire of rajas is its own punishment. It is a painful truth, but most of us need this kind of suffering to teach us the consequences of living for ourselves alone. If we do not learn this lesson, as the preceding verse points out, we have to go back to the same classroom the next time around, to reap the fruit of our present state of mind.

Ajnānam tamasah phalam: those who are full of tamas, who are content to do as little as possible in a halfhearted sort of way, also reap the fruit of their own state of mind: they do not grow. Unable to settle their debt of karma, they manage only to add to it. Insensitive to anything outside themselves, they move from darkness into greater darkness.

Unhappiness, as someone has observed, is not the worst thing in life. The worst that can befall us is insensitivity. In our pleasure-oriented world, unhappiness is looked upon as something frightful. In my opinion it is much better to be unhappy and grow up than never to grow up at all. If we are sincere about leading the spiritual life, we should not be afraid to be unhappy if it enables us to become more sensitive to the needs of others. But the tamasic person, easily contented with what life has to offer, cannot take anything but pleasure. He or she is at the mercy of whatever life sends.

सत्त्वात्संजायते ज्ञानं रजसो लोभ एव च ।
प्रमादमोहौ तमसो भवतो ऽज्ञानमेव च ॥ १४-१७॥

17. From sattva comes understanding; from rajas, greed. But the outcome of tamas is confusion, infatuation, and ignorance.

Once again, let me start with tamas. *Pramādamohau* is a potent combination: Confusion and Infatuation, Inc. They have combined their fortunes, and Tamas owns most of the stock. In an utter lack of proportion, he gives his energy to little things, to foolish, trifling activities, for one compelling reason: he likes them. They give him pleasure, enhance his sense of self-importance, and generally swell his ego. Tamas may be no intellectual, but he reads a lot of books, billions of dollars worth every year. Yet even publishers admit that most of these works need never have seen the light of day. I am not thinking merely of mass-market "escape literature" either. Many of these books are written by gifted writers, whose praises are sung in reviewers' columns and the halls of great universities. But the authors are so caught in "doing their own thing" that they do not have the freedom to ask themselves what the effect of their books will be.

A few years ago, to take just one example, you could find a particular sex manual stacked in high piles in bookstore windows everywhere. It sold millions of copies; I believe it was even recommended reading for some college courses. The author is an honest professional with sound credentials. I feel sure he wrote his book with good intentions. But he is so entangled in his subject that he cannot see the results. He cannot see what that book will do to the millions of people who read it avidly and put its advice into practice, whose lives are so drab that they will jump at any avenue that promises some pleasure.

The theme of that book was simple: Put yourself first and everybody else last. Anybody who takes such advice seriously is going to become more lonely, more estranged, and more frustrated with every year. When we get caught in the sensory game, there *is* some satisfaction at the outset; no one would deny that. But gradually we get sucked in and entangled. Then we are in a compulsion. It is no longer a matter of choosing to go after a particular sensation; we are being driven to it.

This book calls itself something like a "gourmet guide to loving." It sounds tantalizing. How easy, how pleasant, to love! I can understand anybody in these sensation-saturated times being attracted by these words and experimenting for themselves. But in a short, short time it is no longer experimentation; we have no choice. Anybody with some detachment can see how soon this kind of advice breaks up relationships. You find yourself going from one partner to another, then to another, for shorter and shorter periods of satisfaction. If I wrote the blurb for that book it would be, "A gourmet guide to disrupted relations." Instead of joy, I would talk about "the sorrow of separateness." That is what it leads to. One side of the coin is the promise of joy; the other is the fact of loneliness and despair. The Gita says simply, "Make your choice." Choose which you prefer. But if you find yourself living in increasing dissatisfaction, don't blame it on God or society or the times we live in. Sex has a beautiful place in a completely loyal, loving relationship between two people, but where there is neither loyalty nor faith nor honor nor tenderness, sex is a terrible, disruptive force.

Ignorance is the hallmark of Tamas, just as wisdom is the hallmark of Sattva. If Tamas's eye falls on a book that says, "Do this; you'll like it," he immediately takes it up. He doesn't even ask about the logic or the consequences.

Greed has subtler forms too. Going after "our own thing" is usually just being greedy: "I don't care if this benefits anybody, even myself. I'm going to do it because I want to!" I have seen people standing in line all day because they wanted to hear the Rolling Stones in concert – in a theater in one of the most depressed areas of San Francisco. If a little of that day, that endurance, that desire, went into improving the neighborhood, what could not be done?

Every negative quality, Sri Ramakrishna says, can be turned into positive. "You say you're greedy?" he asks. "Why not be *really* greedy? Instead of wanting things just for yourself, want them for everybody. Don't settle for anything less." We should not be content with getting the best just for ourselves. Why not go after the best for everybody? If we give it the same time and energy we give to our personal interests, we can make a real difference in people's lives. So if you meet a greedy person, congratulate him. If he can turn his greed to human welfare, it will be a tremendous motivating force. The greed will still be there, but harnessed and mastered. The same is true of anger and fear; they are power that can be transformed. When Mahatma Gandhi's secretary, Mahadev Desai, was asked where Gandhi got all his power, Desai replied in effect, "He has forged all human passions – fear, anger, lust, greed – into one selfless, irresistible passion for the welfare of all."

A theater in Berkeley recently offered an intriguing bill: *Tarzan and Jane* and *Planet of the Apes*. The marquee said, "Go ape!" I saw quite a few students standing in the queue, waiting to pay three dollars for this privilege. I don't know exactly what it means to "go ape," but I wanted to protest, "This is backwards! Go human; don't go ape." Being resentful, hostile, or vindictive is going backwards in evolution. Two tigers fighting is all right; that is their nature. It may be natural for animals to be red in tooth and claw, but you and I have forfeited that. If we wanted to be hostile, the Hindu mystics say, we should have told the Lord, "I still have a few violent hang-ups to work out. If you don't mind, I prefer to stay in the jungle a couple of centuries more."

ऊर्ध्वं गच्छन्ति सत्त्वस्था मध्ये तिष्ठन्ति राजसाः ।
जघन्यगुणवृत्तस्था अधो गच्छन्ति तामसाः ॥ १४-१८॥

18. Those who live in sattva go upwards, those in rajas remain where they are. But those immersed in tamas sink downwards through their own inertia.

Near my village when I was growing up was a *sadhu* or holy man with an unusual way of teaching. In the morning Mad Nārāyana, as he was called, would go to the foot of a hill nearby and start rolling a huge rock up the slope. It was terribly hard work, especially in the heat of the Indian sun. People came to stand around and watch while he struggled.

Finally, toward the end of the day, he had the rock at the top. Then he motioned his audience to move away a safe distance, and with one hand he gave the rock a push. It rumbled down the slope, bouncing from spot to spot as it gathered speed, until it reached the bottom and crashed against a tree. All the while Mad Nārāyana watched and laughed. "It's so hard to go uphill," he explained. "But to go downhill you don't have to do anything at all!"

It took a long time before I understood the profundity of this simple teaching. It *is* hard to go uphill in life. You have to struggle for every inch, and you can't afford to stop and rest; if you do, the weight of your load will begin to slide you back again. But anybody can go downhill. It takes no effort. You don't have to make any decisions, resist any impulses, deny yourself any desires. You just do whatever you like, and it is automatic: down you go.

This is the dynamics of will and desire. Tamas, the abyss of unconsciousness, is like the trunk of our car, where Will and Desire have been locked up trussed and chloroformed. Tamasic people have neither will nor desire, which is a deceptive state. They may look serene, tranquil, established in peace of mind. Worse, they may think of themselves in just such terms: relaxed, easygoing, easy to deal with, "just an ordinary man." As

Gandhi said, this is the tranquility of the graveyard, where nobody moves, nobody talks, nobody lives – in other words, just the opposite of sattva.

But gradually desire and will begin to help each other untie the ropes. They are still in the trunk, but once an arm gets free here and a leg there, a feeble desire begins to stir. You tell yourself, "I think I wouldn't mind a little coffee." It's not much, but that is all you can muster; most of your capacity for desire is still tied up. With effort you manage to reach the stove, put the water on, and get some instant coffee powder into a paper cup. The result is nothing a connoisseur would recognize, but it is stimulating. As you drink it, desire wakes up a little more. Your mind has made a subtle connection: "Physical effort can lead to satisfaction." The development of rajas has begun.

Now, Desire is a smart chap. Once he and Will are out of the trunk of the car, he wants to keep control. So he tells Will, "Now that I got us out, why don't we go for a ride? You don't have to do anything. Sit in the back seat; there is a blanket you can curl up in if you like, and safety belts to keep you from getting up. I'll get behind the wheel."

Will has just been rescued from utter immobility; he scarcely has enough power to move. "Good idea," he tells himself. "Desire certainly is an obliging friend. Those are wise words of help." "All right," he says aloud. "You do the driving. I'll sit back here, make myself comfortable, and offer a few suggestions from time to time" – to which, in the tradition of back seat driving, nobody is expected to pay attention.

Now Will and Desire enter a kind of Laurel and Hardy phase. Desire is Oliver Hardy; Will is Stan Laurel. Everything is "Stan, do this" and "Of course, Ollie; you're so right." For Desire is now behind the wheel, and the first thing he does is start making the rounds of those restaurants that offer drab food at exorbitant rates. "Where are we going?" Will wants to know. "I don't have much money, Des, and I know who's going to get the bill. I don't like paying through the nose to put that kind of stuff into my mouth." But Desire is getting stronger and stronger. The greed for food, for the stimulating titillation of the taste buds, has grown fiercer. "Hey, Will, keep quiet!" he says. "I know what's good for you." He looks so convincing – you remember Oliver Hardy, with those big, strong shoulders and that little hat? – that Will says meekly, "You must be right."

At this stage Will is a harmless, accommodating fellow. But as the calories and cholesterol go on and on, he finally has to protest. "Des," he complains, "I'm sick of all these restaurants!"

"You make me tired," says Desire. He has grown loud and aggressive through self-indulgence. "I do all this driving for you, and what do you do? Nothing but sleep on the back seat and complain." He shoves Will down and drives on.

When they stop for gas, there is a sale on cigarettes. "Try this," says Desire. "It'll make you feel *cool*. Alive with pleasure. You've come a long way, Baby. Don't you owe it to yourself?" Poor Will believes all this; he still hasn't grown.

Soon the trunk in which they used to be tied up is full of discount cigarettes and throwaway cans of wine. Desire is no fool. He knows that nothing strikes at the will like a compulsive habit. As long as he can keep Will incapacitated in the back seat, Desire can stay behind the wheel to do as he likes.

Unfortunately, Desire doesn't really know what he likes. He is bursting with energy; he clamors for challenges, the bigger the better; but he has no idea of where he wants to go. He drives to Hollywood, then Disneyland, then Las Vegas; finally they manage to cross the Mexican border. By the time they come back, there is heroin in the hubcaps and hashish under the hood. Desire swells with pride. "Got past everybody!" he says. "What an achievement!" There is always satisfaction in a job well done, even if the energy is wasted in a wrong direction.

Actually, this is a state of tremendous potential. Rajasic people are full of energy; when they take to meditation, all that restless energy and the desire for challenges gradually come under control. After a while they clean out the trunk; those articles are not being used any longer. They ask themselves, "Why did I put this there, anyway? Why did I put all that stuff in the hubcaps and under the hood? Let it all go." That is sattva; you are in control.

In sattva, Will and Desire are driving in a dual-control car, like the kind in which I took my driving lessons. Desire is still behind the wheel, but Will is the driving instructor, behind the other set of controls. As long as we are motivated by right desires – for the welfare of the whole family, the whole community, the whole of life – Will sits back and enjoys the ride. But the moment Desire starts to take a selfish turn, Will grabs the master control wheel, touches his foot to the brake, and says sharply, "That's no way to drive!"

In the early days of this, of course, Desire will thump on the steering wheel and cry. "I'm going to call the Highway Patrol!" Will just says, "I *am* the Highway Patrol. You haven't got anyone else to call. I'm the instructor, the police, everything." After a while Desire realizes that Will is his friend and protector, who has kept him from disaster again and again.

You do not lose your desires in sattva; not at all. All your right desires become immense. But the will is always in control. Those in rajas are content just to drive around, always trying to see what is on the other side of the mountain. When night falls they are still driving aimlessly. The gas tank is almost empty, the tires are worn to the cords, yet they haven't got anywhere. And tamas, of course, can't even find his keys. He has an engine, but he can't use it; all he can do is roll downhill. "But those in sattva go upward," Sri Krishna says simply: upward toward the summit of consciousness, against the pull of gravity. You're not in an old Morris Minor any more. You're in a Ferrari, surging with power, taking the hairpin bends effortlessly.

नान्यं गुणेभ्यः कर्तारं यदा द्रष्टानुपश्यति ।
गुणेभ्यश्च परं वेत्ति मद्भावं सो ऽधिगच्छति ॥ १४-१९ ॥
गुणानेतानतीत्य त्रीन्देही देहसमुद्भवान् ।
जन्ममृत्युजरादुःखैर्विमुक्तो ऽमृतमश्नुते ॥ १४-२० ॥

19. The wise see clearly that all action is a product
of the gunas. Knowing that which is above
the gunas, they enter into union with me.
20. Going beyond the three gunas which form the
body, they leave behind the cycle of birth and death,
decrepitude and sorrow, and attain to immortality.

Everything with which we are familiar – things, thoughts, actions, personality – is woven from the gunas. When Sri Krishna talks about going beyond all this, it almost sounds like going beyond the human condition altogether. I would say rather that it is going beyond human *conditioning* – the obsessive belief that we are the body and mind.

When we rise above this conditioning completely, we are no longer just a person. We become a permanent, beneficial force released into the stream of life forever. The Buddha is such a force; he can never die. As long as even one creature is bound, as he himself said, he cannot die. When we learn to live as the Buddha lived – "for the welfare of all, for the joy of all" – this force is released in our own lives. Then the Buddha, the Christ, comes to life in us.

When I came back from India to Berkeley in the early sixties, I found an amazing number of people who believed this force could be released by chemical means. Leading figures spoke persuasively about "chemical grace," and millions of people who wanted access to some higher level of reality were exploring the whole smorgasbord of psychoactive drugs. This is the sort of thing that happens when you believe you are physical; it is just another side of the belief that you can solve a personal problem with a pill.

I have been watching with fascination a new doctrine: electronic grace. (It is very much the same.) We are fascinated by computer technology and laser magic, and we believe there is nothing more to personality than chemistry and physics; why not produce spiritual awareness, love, insight, imagination, through cerebral engineering?

Perhaps – who knows? – technology will find some way to analyze brain waves so accurately that we will be able to identify waves of patience and impatience, sympathy and resentment, and so on. Engineers may be able to invent electronic controls to carry in your pocket, so that when your partner is making you lose your temper you can set the indicator on Patience, sit back, and listen with a calm mind. They may even find a transformer for likes and dislikes, so that when you sit down for dinner and see something you detest, you can switch over your brain waves and enjoy it. I am not saying this sort of thing cannot be done. But at what expense? The human being would cease to be a human being. We would lose our sensitiveness, our originality, our tenderness, our creativity, all because we never developed the capacity to use our will. Without the will we have no freedom, and without freedom of choice we become machines. That is the theme of Huxley's *Brave*

New World, and I think it tells us why the increase of impersonality we see today has been accompanied by an increasing loss of sensitiveness.

I have seen claims, for example, that "illumination tanks" can bring about the integration of consciousness. You sit inside with light and sound and so on all cut off, and you stay there till you are illumined. This is picking up the stick by the wrong end. It is true that to enter a higher level of consciousness, you have to be able to leave the world of sensory awareness behind. The crucial difference is that in sensory deprivation, some external agent deprives the senses of their stimuli. In such cases, consciousness is not withdrawn from the senses. They are still full of prāna, which means that the eye is still clamoring to see, the ear to hear, and so on. As a result, they may see and hear what is not there. In meditation, however, consciousness is withdrawn from all the senses by the will. All desires to see, hear, taste, touch, and smell are withdrawn into an immense desire to turn inward toward the Self. The power of these desires is harnessed by the will, which grows huge and strong like Jack's beanstalk. When the will is that strong, the power of your desires is at your disposal.

When you can withdraw power from your senses at will, you go through life with such economy of personal energy that you scarcely feel stress at all. The Gita calls this "action in inaction." There is no tension, no friction, no effort. You have gone beyond the gunas, beyond all human conditioning.

अर्जुन उवाच ।
कैर्लिङ्गैस्त्रीन्गुणानेतानतीतो भवति प्रभो ।
किमाचारः कथं चैतांस्त्रीन्गुणानतिवर्तते ॥ १४-२१ ॥

ARJUNA:

21. What are the characteristics of those who have gone beyond the gunas, O Lord? How do they act? How have they passed beyond the gunas' hold?

When a man or woman is completely evolved, what happens? What does it mean to be completely integrated in character, conduct, and consciousness?

It is those who attain this state who show us what life really means. It is a mistake to think of Sri Ramakrishna, St. Teresa, St. Francis, or Mahatma Gandhi as consisting of body and mind. Their lives reveal the transformation from a separate personality into a universal beneficial force. These are not petty individual personalities from a particular period. St. Francis is much more alive today than most of the population of the world. We should not think of him in terms of a limited period of time – sixty or seventy years – or a circumscribed place. When a person is obsessively identified with a particular body and mental state, his influence is extremely limited; it cannot last long. But when we go beyond the gunas, we are no longer limited by time, place, and circumstance. We become a lasting beneficial force, as the immense power of the Self is released through us into the stream of life.

This force is called *kundalinī* or evolutionary energy in Sanskrit, and it is present in every one of us. No one should say "*I* can't make myself a beneficial force!" The force is already there. But we are spellbound by what Hindu mystics call Māyā, the potent hypnotism of the senses and self-will. We cannot suspect even for an instant that in this fragile, limited frame of body, mind, and intellect a virtually limitless spiritual power is compressed a million times, waiting to be released.

In my early days in this country people used to ask me, "Isn't meditation simply self-hypnosis?" It is just the opposite: meditation is self-*de*hypnosis. I saw an ad recently that said, "Learn to hypnotize your friends!" This is carrying coals to Newcastle. Continual, constant hypnosis is the human condition; we live in a hypnotized world. Sri Ramakrishna, I believe, compares it to a puppet show. If we could interview Punch of "Punch and Judy," he would tell us, "Sure, we're free! I can hit Judy; she can throw a pot at me. Isn't that what free choice means?" But those of us outside the puppet theater can see a fellow with red hair standing in the back and pulling the strings.

In our case, Sri Ramakrishna says, *we* are Punch or Judy. The puppeteer is the ego, pulling strings from inside. A little tug and we flare up. Afterwards we say, "I *chose* to get angry." I have actually heard people say this. Or perhaps the strings go slack and we fall into tamas. We say, "This is a personal choice I have made. I want to be lethargic. I like to feel dull." The Buddha would smile gently at this kind of talk. "When someone is angry with you," he would say, "if you can remain calm, compassionate, and respectful, *then* you can call yourself free." You will have broken loose from the puppeteer's strings. After that the ego can tug at them as long as he likes; it will not govern your responses.

श्रीभगवानुवाच ।
प्रकाशं च प्रवृत्तिं च मोहमेव च पाण्डव ।
न द्वेष्टि संप्रवृत्तानि न निवृत्तानि काङ्क्षति ॥ १४-२२ ॥
उदासीनवदासीनो गुणैर्यो न विचाल्यते ।
गुणा वर्तन्त इत्येव यो ऽवतिष्ठति नेङ्गते ॥ १४-२३ ॥

SRI KRISHNA:

22. They are unmoved by the harmony of sattva, the activity of rajas, or the delusion of tamas. They feel no aversion when these forces are active, nor do they crave for them when these forces subside.

23. They remain detached, undisturbed by the actions of the gunas. Knowing that it is the gunas which act, they abide within themselves and do not vacillate.

In practical language, those who transcend the gunas go beyond likes and dislikes.

This may sound like a trivial, even undesirable achievement. "Do you want me not to like or dislike *any*thing?" people sometimes ask. "I might as well not be living!" In fact, life as we usually live it does mean mostly liking this and disliking that, liking him, disliking her. But this is what makes us the puppets of our circumstances. When you are subject to likes and dislikes, you are standing on the street with an old tin can and begging of life, "Please treat me kindly. I can't walk; I can scarcely stand. Look at my tin can and drop in a few crumbs of pleasure as you pass." Most of us, I feel sure, would much prefer my granny's attitude. "Little Lamp," she used to tell me, "you just tell life, 'I don't care what you bring me; I'll make the best of it. I'm prepared for anything.'"

It *is* pleasant when life gives us something we like. That is what the mind lives for. When things go our way, the mind gets all excited. It calls its friends, talks incessantly, and runs around trying to do twelve things at once. "If only things could be like this always!" it says. "Wouldn't that be heaven?" But of course, things are not like that always. After a while, life perversely goes against us. Things happen that we do *not* like, often without warning. And the mind has run out of steam. For the time being, its vitality and vivacity have been spent. All it can do is lie down with a couple of aspirin and a cold washcloth over its eyes and wonder, "Why does this have to happen to me?"

Most of us, I think, believe this is all life has to offer: some precious periods of excitement and ebullience, when we are full of *joie de vivre*; some stretches of depression; and in between, our normal state – not bad, not good, a little irritable, but civil enough as long as nobody crosses us.

"It does not have to happen to you," Sri Krishna explains. "You don't ever have to feel depressed again. But you have to stop tying your moods to circumstances. Stop getting excited over what you like; then you won't get depressed by what you don't like."

Virtually all of us get excited easily. Nobody can escape this pressure today. The mass media promise us excitement from everything on the face of the earth: movies, news programs, holidays, hair sprays, investments, toothpaste, towels. Is it any wonder that when these promises go unfulfilled, we live on the edge of frustration and depression? Millions of men and women in this country suffer from serious depression every year. In addition, since negative states inhibit the immune system, I would say depression is a hidden causal factor in billions of cases of colds, flu, migraine, dyspepsia, herpes, allergies, and asthma. And then there is the dull, minimal, just-able-to-cope state that the vast majority of us have come to regard as normal, which I would classify as subclinical depression. All in all, perhaps one quarter of the people in this country walk about in a chronic state of resentment or depression because life is not giving them what they think it promises – blaming the mango tree, my grandmother would say, because it can't give coconuts.

If you don't want to get depressed, Sri Krishna says, the first thing is not to get into situations where you know you get excited. This requires some self-knowledge, and a good deal of vigilance. If, in spite of doing your best to avoid such situations, you find yourself caught and your mind beginning to race out of control, start repeating the mantram.

The mantram is a stabilizer, the kind that enables ships to steer through rough seas and keep on an even keel. On my way to this country from India I traveled as far as Marseilles on an old P&O vessel that had no such device. When the monsoon burst on the way to Aden, one moment we would see only sky, the next moment only water. The ship pitched and rolled like that for two or three days, and virtually everybody got seasick, including most of the crew. It was a British vessel out of Australia, with some real empire builders on it. That is when I discovered that empire builders are human too. After a while they were asking for a brown bag and rushing to the rail with the rest. It brought home to me the unity of life.

The first day of this I managed to avoid asking for a paper bag. On the second morning, however, I woke up with my mind thinking, "Boss, this is it! I've gone as far as I can go." My stomach felt terribly sick. Although I am not easily subject to nausea, my first thought was to get a bag like everybody else and spend the rest of the day at the rail looking down at the water.

Instead, without my even thinking about it, the mantram came to my rescue. I was determined to let nothing come in the way of my meditation. I went to a corner, sat down for meditation, and in a few minutes I had gone so deep that I had left my body behind. A couple of hours later I got up feeling terribly hungry. The ship was still pitching about. I walked into the breakfast room and sat down in solitary dignity, the monarch of all I surveyed. The purser couldn't believe his eyes. He was a hard-boiled type, but he was so intrigued that he came over and asked, "What kind of tablets do you use?"

That is the power of the mind. When it is calm, the body stays calm; when it gets excited, the body too is thrown into turmoil. So whenever your mind starts surging up and down like that P&O liner, repeat the mantram. Then the mind becomes more like the majestic *Queen Elizabeth,* on which I crossed the Atlantic a week or two later. We slid through rough seas with quiet, steady grace. When I asked the captain why, he replied, "This ship has stabilizers. She's not afraid of any storm."

समदुःखसुखः स्वस्थः समलोष्टाश्मकाञ्चनः ।
तुल्यप्रियाप्रियो धीरस्तुल्यनिन्दात्मसंस्तुतिः ॥१४-२४॥

24. Established within themselves, they are equal in pleasure and pain, praise and blame, kindness and unkindness. Clay or a rock are the same to them as gold.

Many years ago, a little fellow about four or five years old who was staying in our household came up and tried to sit on Christine's lap. She said, "I'm sorry; I'm typing an article for the *Little Lamp*. Can you find somebody else for now?" He came to me, but I said, "I'm writing an article for the *Little Lamp*. Can you find somebody else?" He went to sit on Mary's lap, but Mary was busy folding the current *Little Lamp*. Finally he said in exasperation, "Then I'm going to sit on my own lap!"

That was a profound remark. *Svasthah,* which I have translated as 'established within themselves,' means literally something like 'self-standing' or 'self-seated' The only lap on which you can sit comfortably is your own. If you try to sit on somebody else's, you can feel secure only as long as that person remains seated; if he or she stands up, you get dumped onto the floor. If you learn to sit on your own lap, you rest there always. You are not dependent on anything external – the prime rate, the praise of your employer, the moods of your partner, the performance of your car.

Yesterday Christine and I went downtown to get a library card. She had a card in her name which she had lost, though I hinted that if it had been entrusted to me, I would have taken good care of it. When she said she had lost it, I was almost tempted to say, "What did I tell you?" But like a gentleman, I refrained.

We walked up together to the librarian, who explained that due to some technical difficulty a new card could not be issued to her just then. "But," she said brightly, "your husband could take out one in his own name."

I stood before her and gave the usual information: name, address, and so forth. Then she wanted a telephone number. "I don't have a telephone," I said.

"That's all right," she said. "Can you establish your identity?"

"I can," I said confidently. "That is my profession."

She waited, but I failed to produce anything tangible. Finally she asked, "Do you have a driver's license?"

"No," I said.

"Don't you drive?"

"I do. I mean, I know how to drive. But I have too much respect for the public interest."

She stared. "Do you have any credit cards?"

"As a matter of fact," I said, "we did get a credit card in the mail some months ago. We had great difficulty destroying it. We couldn't tear it, we couldn't cut it, we couldn't burn it. I think we may have buried it. You see," I added, seeing her expression, "I like to pay cash for things. I don't like being in debt."

"That's very admirable," she said. "But I need something that tells me who you are. You must have some letter sent to you by somebody? Some card?"

That made a connection. "Yes," I said, "I do have a card." I owned the only membership card that the Blue Mountain Center of Meditation ever issued, and it was right in my wallet. "I happen to be the first member," I explained with a touch of pride. I opened my wallet, and out fell Christine's library card.

Sri Krishna is trying to tell us, "You already have your card. You don't have to get another one. If you can get into your wallet, deep in that inside pocket you have forgotten, you will find the source of security and joy."

मानावमानयोस्तुल्यस्तुल्यो मित्रारिपक्षयोः ।
सर्वारम्भपरित्यागी गुणातीतः स उच्यते ॥१४-२५॥

25. *Alike in honor and dishonor, alike to friend*
and foe, they have given up every selfish pursuit.
Such are those who have gone beyond the gunas.

These are astonishing statements, which deserve careful reading and reflection. *Gunātīta* means literally someone who has gone beyond human limitations. He or she has transcended the barriers of separateness and self-will, which are the greatest scourge of this century. Only by rising above these states do we enter our true nature, which is to love, to forgive, to heal.

"Alike to friend and foe" has nothing to do with being indifferent. Sri Krishna is talking about good will, patience, forgiveness, understanding – not only to those we like or when it is convenient, but to everyone always. These are not moral maxims. When St. Francis says "It is in pardoning that we are pardoned," he is giving us a truth on which our very survival may depend.

For example, although most people buy handguns to make themselves feel safer, merely having a gun often heightens the sense of insecurity and suspicion. You start looking on everyone not as a friend but as a potential threat. Your guard is up everywhere. You are prepared to defend yourself against anyone, and you know that "the best defense is a good first strike." Someone seems to be following you, he does something suspicious, and you shoot. If you get in a quarrel, your gun is handy. It has been estimated that 65 percent of all homicides are committed in a spasm of anger, jealousy, or fear, with handguns purchased for "self-defense." Ironically, the same guns place the owners in greater danger too. It makes them aggressive, even cocksure, so that they are almost looking for trouble. Rather than deter assault and robbery, it seems to invite assailants to use a gun themselves. But guns are only the instrument. Suspicion and separateness pull the trigger.

The situation is the same between nations. Historians look back at the beginning of this century and see how clearly the seeds of World War II were sown in the fear, hatred, suspicion, resentment, and retaliation that accompanied World War I. Similarly, well before World War II was over, the Allied powers had begun among themselves a suicidal race for military supremacy that might well have ended in World War III. And in the last analysis, the atomic bombs dropped on Hiroshima and Nagasaki seem to have been significantly motivated by a desire to "get even" for Pearl Harbor, as well as to impress on the Russians the kind of power we had and were willing to use. Violence breeds violence, resentment breeds retaliation, hostility perpetuates hostility – on a vaster and vaster scale, for higher and higher stakes. With nuclear weapons now in the hands of at least nine nations, each with its own alliances and desired spheres of influence, war between two countries might precipitate not only world war but worldwide disaster. Even scientists who worked on the first atomic bombs say today that they were not aware of what these weapons can do. They are not alluding merely to the deaths of twenty or a hundred million people in one or two nations. They are speaking of the effects of a nuclear exchange on the air, water, soil, vegetation, radiation levels, and species survival all over the globe. Now more than ever it should be clear that we live in "one world or none." When two countries fight, even if they are not superpowers, the war involves much more than those two countries. The whole unity of life is violated.

मां च यो ऽव्यभिचारेण भक्तियोगेन सेवते ।
स गुणान्समतीत्यैतान्ब्रह्मभूयाय कल्पते ॥ १४-२६ ॥

26. By serving me with steadfast love, a
man or woman goes beyond the gunas.
Such a one is fit to know Brahman.

Sri Krishna uses a strong word here, *avyabhicāra,* for which "steadfast" is a pallid translation. The opposite is *vyabhicārinī* – a prostitute, who tries to please many people. Those who give away their love and loyalty in many directions, the Gita says, can never reach life's goal. This is not a penalty enacted by an outside power. When we scatter our love, consciousness is dispersed; how can we expect it to be whole?

For many years, sādhana means learning the skills by which we can unify desires. Gradually we subordinate everything else to the attainment of life's supreme goal. Personal activities, attitudes, conditioning, prejudices, predilections, everything has to take second place. There is pain in this and a tremendous amount of self-denial from the flouting of self-will. The supreme quality here is endurance – the capacity to go on whatever the odds, to grow in determination as the challenges grow greater.

This requires tremendous discipline. Excellence in anything requires discipline; even to play marbles you have to practice, and here we are talking about the highest state of evolution. I was reading an interview with Nureyev, one of the greatest male ballet dancers in history.

Ask him if he found it easy to scale the pinnacle of his art! All you and I see on the stage is spectacular, graceful, apparently effortless movement. Backstage, Nureyev says, it is a bloodbath. Margot Fonteyn uses equally strong language: if we only knew the torture a dancer imposes on herself to achieve that effortless grace, she says, we would feel we were watching a bullfight.

The Gita talks the same way. Sri Krishna reminds us, "This is a battle." If you want to live at the summit of life, free from conditioning from the surface of consciousness clear to the basement, you have to fight for every inch of progress. It is not enough merely to transform rajas into sattva, which is a tremendous achievement in itself. Even in sattva thinking is conditioned, although your motives are pure. To be free you have to go beyond the gunas completely – beyond time, space, and circumstance, where the mind is completely stilled and the ego disappears.

To understand what this means, we need the personal testimony of men and women who have succeeded in this immense endeavor. Recently I have been reading the life of St. Teresa of Ávila, a remarkably modern woman of great spiritual genius who sanctified medieval Europe. She grew up with every possible advantage a girl in that age and place could have: she was cultured, talented, attractive, and high-spirited, with a bright intellect and a strong will that in those days did not always work to her advantage. Yet she was so highly evolved that nothing fleeting could satisfy her. Even as a girl she could say passionately, "I want something that lasts forever!" This is the mark of mystical genius: not to be satisfied with something you can get today and lose tomorrow, but to demand a legacy that will be yours always.

This woman who was to become one of the world's greatest mystics went through twenty years of doubt and struggle, torn between the pull of the world and the pull of God. When someone talks about attaining illumination overnight, I always want to reply, "Teresa took twenty years. Do you really think people like you and me should be able to do it in less?" Her words can inspire all of us, for everyone begins with doubts and conflicts and is likely to feel disheartened:

> On the one hand I felt the call of God; on the other, I continued to follow the world. All the things of God gave me great pleasure,

> but I was held captive by those of the world. I might have been said to be trying to reconcile these two extremes, to bring contraries together: the spiritual life on the one hand and worldly satisfactions, pleasures, and pastimes on the other.

When you have doubts about your capacity for spiritual progress, which is only natural, it is good not to feel despondent, dispirited, or defeatist. That is the prerogative of tamas. Instead please remember St. Teresa and act as if you had no doubts at all. Keep on striving, keep on trying, and if you fall, pick yourself up. But never give up the struggle. This is all we are expected to do. Little people like us are likely to be haunted by doubts and conflicts for a long, long time.

Teresa was about forty-five when she became established in God. In Hindu mysticism this supreme state is called *sahaja samādhi,* 'samādhi that never leaves you.' Waking or sleeping, your awareness of the unity of life is not broken even for an instant. Then you have gone beyond the gunas once and for all.

ब्रह्मणो हि प्रतिष्ठाहममृतस्याव्ययस्य च ।
शाश्वतस्य च धर्मस्य सुखस्यैकान्तिकस्य च ॥ १४-२७॥

27. For I am the support of Brahman, the eternal, the unchanging, the deathless, the everlasting dharma, the source of all joy.

In this final verse, Sri Krishna is reminding us gently of the close connection between the gunas, time, and death. One of the pathetic characteristics of modern civilization is to try to cling to time as it rushes past, almost begging time to stop. We want to continue to be what we are now. We don't want to be subjected to the ruthless physical changes that are an inescapable part of life. The deep-seated insecurity that results is what comes from a physical approach to life. As we grow older it leads to all kinds of problems, physical, emotional, and psychosomatic. None of our affluence or technology has been able to guard us against this nagging fear of inadequacy in the face of time's advance, which haunts millions of lives today.

Nothing we do can prevent the body from growing older from the day that we were born. In the grim language of mysticism, our death began the moment we were conceived. When my mother dips her finger in ashes every morning to put a white mark on her forehead, it is to remind her and those around her that the nature of the body is to change, up to the last change we call death. Anybody who tries to stand on what is changing, who tries to cling to things that are slipping away, cannot help getting more desperate and insecure.

"When you live for the whole of life," Sri Krishna says, "your state of consciousness will be mine" – that is, unfathomable love, which brings the unshakable security of knowing that every moment your life counts. In this state you are much more than a single, separate person. You become a permanent force that is released wherever you go, to ameliorate the terrible conditions which threaten the world today. Your life is an investment for every creature. No bear market can threaten this investment. It increases through good fortune and bad, and nobody has to buy shares to get the dividends; they are distributed to all. You are *avyaya*, inexhaustible: the more you give, the more you receive in patience, endurance, security, resilience, and love.

गुणत्रयविभागयोगो नाम चतुर्दशोऽध्यायः ॥ १४ ॥

CHAPTER FIFTEEN

The Supreme Self

श्रीभगवानुवाच ।
ऊर्ध्वमूलमधःशाखमश्वत्थं प्राहुरव्ययम् ।
छन्दांसि यस्य पर्णानि यस्तं वेद स वेदवित् ॥ १५-१ ॥

SRI KRISHNA:

1. Sages speak of the immutable ashvattha tree, the Tree of Life, with its taproot above and its branches below. On this tree grow the scriptures; seeing their source, one knows their essence.

This image of the Tree of Life is one of the most magnificent in the Gita. Most of this tree is not physical. The whole phenomenal universe – matter, energy, and mind – is only its canopy of leaves. This is all we can see. But each leaf grows from a twig, which grows from a branch, which in turn grows from a vast trunk. And supporting the trunk and all its leaves and twigs and branches, completely hidden, is the taproot, extending deep into pure being. Farthest from the root is the world of multiplicity and change: countless little leaves. But the taproot of this tree is the Lord, the eternal, changeless Self.

The application of this tremendous image is personal and practical. As long as we live on the surface of life, we believe we are separate, individual leaves. We lead private lives that bear no relation to the rest of the tree, even though when we are cut off from that tree we have no life. Look at the problems that face the world today because of this crude superstition that we are separate. We have violence in our streets and homes because individuals value no one's welfare but their own. We have poverty and war around the globe because nations and corporations pursue private ends without regard to the cost to others. Most poignantly of all, we see men, women, and even children cutting themselves off from others around them so they can pursue what they want without hindrance. When we are driven by self-will like this, we cannot imagine we are forfeiting the whole of life for the little leaf we call our individual personality. So when you get up in the morning, while you are at work, before going to bed, or whenever you feel ruled by private passions, remind yourself of this magnificent simile, which asks us to claim the whole Tree of Life and not be content with being one passing leaf.

अधश्चोर्ध्वं प्रसृतास्तस्य शाखा
गुणप्रवृद्धा विषयप्रवालाः ।
अधश्च मूलान्यनुसंततानि
कर्मानुबन्धीनि मनुष्यलोके ॥ १५-२ ॥

2. Nourished by the gunas, the limbs of this tree spread above and below. Sense objects grow on the limbs as buds; the roots hanging down bind us to action in this world.

The Tree of Life, called *ashvattha* in the Hindu scriptures, is traditionally considered to be one of the giant fig trees found in southern Asia. A great deal has been written on the question of proper botanical classification: is this *Ficus bengalensis,* the banyan tree, or *Ficus religiosa,* the sacred pipal or bo tree, under which the Buddha attained illumination?

Shankara, who often drives Western scholars to exasperated footnotes, does not seem to care about this question. Instead he goes to the heart of the matter with a touch of imaginative etymology. *Ashvattha,* he says, can be derived from three little words: *a* 'without,' *shva* 'tomorrow,' and *stha* 'standing.' This is the tree of what will not be here tomorrow: in other words, of all created things. The universe today is not what it will be tomorrow; it changes even from instant to instant. Your body today is not what it was yesterday, and tomorrow it will not be what it is today. Every tissue is changing, even the bones. After some decades, the body will not be around at all.

Trees like the pipal and banyan are extremely long-lived. In an ancient temple compound, where you can see one still growing and spreading while the stones around it are cracked and worn with age, you feel that its roots must reach into the beginning of time. These species of *Ficus* also have another characteristic alluded to in this verse: what botanists call aerial roots. In some cases the seeds germinate not in the earth but high in some other tree (such as a palm) where they have been deposited by birds and monkeys. From there they send out long shoots that twine around the trunk of the mother tree until they reach the ground. Then they burrow in and become true roots.

The senses, Sri Krishna says, are like these aerial roots. When we yield to the clamor of the senses we are pushing consciousness out into sensory offshoots, making them longer and longer. Finally they reach the ground and burrow in, rooting us in the world of change. This is what the media promise us: the senses will supply everything we desire of life. "Indulge your senses," they say. "Don't be afraid to build your life on pleasure. If it feels good, do it!" By the time a person in this country reaches the age of twenty, he or she may have received this message a million times – from television and the movies, from magazines, newspapers, and books, and of course from the daily example of other people. With this kind of brainwashing, is it any wonder that our lives are as shaky as leaves?

The more we try to put our senses out to enjoy the world, the more we are sticking out our necks. I may be mixing metaphors, but this is an apt expression. People who are highly taste-oriented, for example, are extruding their palate farther and farther and farther. Obsessed with food, always thinking about what to eat and when and where and how often, they squeeze all their consciousness into their taste buds; they are feeling the world through the palate.

You will find such people very physically oriented – which means, among other things, that they get easily upset. Since they do not have much security within themselves, they try to correct their upsets by getting something from the pharmacy or the refrigerator and putting it into their mouths. Overeating is one of the most familiar illustrations of how consciousness can be concentrated on a particular sense organ, which really leaves it out on a limb. That is why Gandhi said the control of the palate is such a valuable aid to controlling the mind. If you can withdraw consciousness at will from the sense of taste, your mind will be much less upsettable.

The same can happen with any other sense. Children who grow up watching TV four, five, or six hours a day are squeezing much of their consciousness into their eyes. Those who listen for hours on end to quadraphonic sound are putting consciousness in their ears. In this way, consciousness is a little like toothpaste: it is easy to squeeze it out, but excruciatingly difficult to get it back into the tube again. When consciousness has been extruded into the senses, not much is available where it is needed – for concentration, security, sensitiveness, self-reliance, and imagination.

We should be able to withdraw consciousness from the senses at will, the Gita says, as easily as a tortoise withdraws its limbs into its shell. When we see a lot of goodies displayed in a bakery window and the palate is clamoring for us to move closer and glue our eyes to the glass, we should be able to say "Withdraw!" and recall consciousness back from the palate into the core of our being. The sense organs – taste buds, nerves, and so on – will be physically the same, but consciousness will not be present to activate them. Later, when we approve – say, when faced with a nutritious, tasty meal – we can send consciousness back out to the senses and enjoy our food.

All the senses can be trained this way. You are not forcing them inside or putting them in jail to punish them for their excesses. You are telling them, "When the sun is shining and it's good to play, come on out; make hay. But when the weather gets cloudy, come in and take shelter."

This means a tremendous consolidation of energy. Prāna ebbs out through the senses; that is why people who overindulge their senses often feel tired and inadequate. Their resistance is low, the will is weak, and judgment gets clouded just when it is needed most. When you can regulate your senses, you can enjoy everything beneficial and still protect your mind and body against the ravages of undue indulgence.

I see advertisements for vacation cruises that proclaim, "Our dining room is always open!" After breakfast you're not locked out until noon;

you can come for a snack, come again for lunch, and still return for high tea before dinner. The variety of dishes is endless. And when you're not dining, you can float in the pool with a cocktail: the drinks are free, so you can drink as much as you like. Then at night there are parties, movies, and gaming tables going until dawn; you never have to sleep. Now and then you get a day in a duty-free port, where you can pick up a few expensive items you don't need. When the cruise is over, I imagine, they even have a fleet of ambulances waiting to take you to intensive care. This kind of indulgence leaves us vulnerable to every wind that blows.

When the senses come under control, prāna is consolidated in the will. I like to repeat that what matters in life is not so much IQ as WQ, "will quotient." There is no harm in having a high IQ, but it is not of much value in helping you deal with anger or fear. I have known gifted people with high IQs who were utterly unable to tackle their fears and conflicts. No amount of talking or reasoning could help; they had to deepen their will by digging through stratum after stratum of consciousness. When the will gets deep enough you can reach down into your unconscious, pick up a fear, and throw it out. After that, if you encounter a big fear again in your digging operation, you know you will be able to deal with it. Then that fear can no longer make you afraid.

It is the same with anger. Angry people are usually quite self-willed. They don't have the strength to be patient or turn back harsh words because self-will eats away the will. If you want to transform anger and harness it, you have to strengthen the will.

When you have some detachment, the will becomes a kind of emotional barometer. You can use it to tell when storms are coming, probably more accurately than your local weatherman can predict rain. You go to your willometer in the morning, tap it a couple of times, and ask, "What's the weather going to be like today?" If you did your best yesterday to control your senses and reduce self-will, your will *has* to be stronger. Then it doesn't much matter what external events come your way; the day is going to be clear for you.

Trying to talk out anger and fear has become so commonplace today that I never mind repeating the Gita's very practical advice. Instead of analyzing your fears and resentments – putting them under a microscope, scrutinizing them from different angles, classifying them, talking about them, reading books about them – work on strengthening your will. Brooding over these problems only makes them more obsessive. But as the will gets taller, emotional problems like fear, anger, and greed get smaller. When you have a strong will, if you feel lethargic, you can flex its muscles and watch your lethargy disappear. If you feel diffident, flexing the will brings self-confidence. A strong will can transform fear into fearlessness, anger into sympathy, resentment into compassion, hatred into love.

The intimate relationship between senses and sense objects is a recurring theme in the Gita. Just as aerial roots reach out for the ground to dig themselves in, the senses reach out to root themselves in objects of sensory experience. There is nothing wrong with this. It is the nature of senses to grasp, and there is nothing immoral about the force of their attraction, any more than there is about physical forces like magnetism or nuclear binding energy. Forces are not wrong; it is the use to which we put them that can be wrong.

In meditation, we learn to withdraw and consolidate prāna from the senses back to its source. This takes years to learn. At first, though we are trying to give our attention completely to the passage on which we are meditating, we hear everything that goes on outside us. The reason is that consciousness is still in the ear, waiting to catch sounds. But as you learn to sink deep into yourself, you withdraw consciousness slowly from the ear. The organ still functions, but no hearing takes place. It is the same with the other senses too. St. Teresa of Ávila relates that she was so absorbed in prayer one evening that the candle she was holding burned down to her fingers without her being aware of the pain.

When we are pleasure-oriented, on the other hand – as our whole modern civilization is – consciousness is always looking for sense-stimulation. Some part of the mind is constantly watching for pleasant experiences on the surface level of life. Consciousness is out on the patio with binoculars, searching for sensations like a bird-watcher. The patio is the skin: most sensory stimulation is only skin deep. When we live in a world of skin-deep pleasures, they seem to be fabulously sweet, incredibly intense. Only when we leave the patio to retire deep into what Teresa calls the "interior castle" do we get a real standard of comparison. Once we discover the riches of this inner realm, we laugh at ourselves for sitting in the patio and gloating over some third-class mail from the senses.

न रूपमस्येह तथोपलभ्यते
नान्तो न चादिर्न च संप्रतिष्ठा ।
अश्वत्थमेनं सुविरूढमूलम्
असङ्गशस्त्रेण दृढेन छित्त्वा ॥ १५-३ ॥
ततः पदं तत्परिमार्गितव्यं
यस्मिन्गाता न निवर्तन्ति भूयः ।
तमेव चाद्यं पुरुषं प्रपद्ये
यतः प्रवृत्तिः प्रसृता पुराणी ॥ १५-४ ॥

3–4. The true form of this tree – its essence, beginning, and end – is not perceived on this earth. Cut down this strong-rooted tree with the sharp axe of detachment; then find the path which does not come back again. Seek That, the First Cause, from which the universe came long ago.

Most of the Tree of Life, we should remember, lies in the world within. Sri Krishna is telling us to get beneath the surface and trace our way back to our source.

One school of thought speaks of this Tree as an illusion, because separateness is an illusion. But I would say each leaf is precious. Each individual creature deserves our respect, love, and protection. So instead of talking about cutting down trees, I would rather talk about digging to the root, deep in the soil of consciousness.

Meditation is the tool for digging. I don't know if you have ever had to dig up an old, established tree; when the surface of the ground is knotted with thick, hardened roots, it can be painfully difficult to break through. Similarly, for many years in meditation we have to dig hard to break through the crusted strata of samskāras we have accumulated over the years – or, from the Hindu and Buddhist perspective, over many lives. To do this, we have to keep a sharp edge on our meditation. Like any tool, it must be kept in good condition. If it is not used for a week, even for a day, it will get rusty.

Sometimes the surface level of consciousness is soft loam, easy digging for the first twelve inches or so. You are still on the surface, but because the blade of your shovel is turning over soil you say, "This is easy! Isn't meditation great?" Then you strike something hard and impenetrable. Your hands sting from the shock, and your arms ache. That is the first stratum of bedrock – a dense, rock-hard layer of tamas, sheer resistance.

One of the most common signs of hitting this layer is that you find yourself overcome by waves of sleep in meditation. It is very much like your shovel striking a rock. You are saying, in effect, "My shovel is getting blunted, and my arms are tired. Why not stop digging and have a snooze?" It is extremely important not to yield to this inclination, right from the first days of meditation. These are problems that continue for years. We have a lot of strata to dig through, and those who do not learn to deal with sleep in the early stages have a terribly difficult time later on.

When you have learned to dig effectively, you strike through this bedrock of resistance and change your level of consciousness. This has to be done under the skilled, personal guidance of your teacher. You can no longer afford to be self-willed or to be a victim of your senses. If you haven't reduced your self-will and trained your senses and passions well, on a deeper level of awareness you will encounter serious difficulties in daily living. That is why I always tell those around me not to increase their period of meditation without meeting the basic requirements. They should be getting enough exercise, nourishing food, and adequate sleep, and they should be careful not to isolate themselves from the give-and-take of life, which is essential for reducing self-will.

The signs that you have changed a level of consciousness are utterly practical: better health, more energy, better control over your cravings, less self-will, and more of the joy that comes from drawing nearer to the unity of life. Unless these tests are satisfied, I say over and over again, please don't go by anything you see or hear in meditation, any sensation you experience, any "vision" or dream. All these have very little relevance to daily living. Do you have more patience and security? Do you find it easier to get along with difficult people? Can you turn your back on your own likes and dislikes when necessary, to contribute to the welfare of those around you? If you can, you have changed your level of consciousness. If you cannot, the chances are that you are not yet ready to change.

Sri Ramakrishna, I believe, describes the role the gunas play in this. Sattva, rajas, and tamas all have to come on stage; otherwise life's drama cannot be enacted. Tamas, he says, is the rock of resistance. This is a reassuring description: without a rock, how can you develop your digging arm? Rajas, of course, is hard, energetic, sustained digging. And sattva is the mastery that comes when you have overcome tamas deep in consciousness and are making steady progress.

निर्मानमोहा जितसङ्गदोषा
अध्यात्मनित्या विनिवृत्तकामाः ।
द्वंद्वैर्विमुक्ताः सुखदुःखसंज्ञैर्
गच्छन्त्यमूढाः पदमव्ययं तत् ॥ १५-५ ॥

5. Not deluded by pride, free from selfish attachment and selfish desire, beyond the duality of pleasure and pain, ever aware of the Self, the wise go forward to that eternal goal.

Self-will is responsible for most of our spiritual problems, many of our emotional problems, and even some of our physical problems too. Broken relationships, disloyalties, and disruptions in spiritual progress can generally be traced to self-will. Everyone who wants to attain the supreme state, Sri Krishna says, must fight self-will until victory is won. It is a long, hard, uphill battle.

One very helpful strategy is to remember the needs of the whole always. Don't ever go just by what appeals to you or what you find pleasing; that is the way to separateness. Go against your likes and dislikes whenever it is in the interests of all, and then continue to go against them resolutely until victory is won.

This can't be done just from ten to twelve on Sundays. We have to go on fighting all the time, everywhere. Most of us have two personalities, the public and the private, which makes for tension, conflict, and vacillation. When you learn to fight self-will continuously, this deep division heals. Public and private personalities merge, until you are the same in all circumstances and all roles.

Selfish desires need a lot of attention. They are not very hardy; unless their needs are met precisely, they cannot last long. If we do not water and fertilize them regularly – thinking about them, dreaming about them, planning, wishing, fantasizing over them – they will wither and die. To get plants to thrive, I understand, it is considered helpful to talk to them in soothing, friendly tones. Selfish desires thrive on talk too; the more we talk about them, the stronger they get. So whenever you feel driven by a compulsive, selfish desire, throw yourself into work for others. It can starve the desire away, at least for the time being.

In the way we work, the way we eat, even the way we play, we can always do what is in the interests of the whole. For a long time, of course, this cuts across our likes and dislikes. But even then we reap benefits. The more likes and dislikes we have, the more physical and psychosomatic problems we are likely to develop; worst of all, the more turmoil we will feel inside. People with strong likes and dislikes go about with a little sign that says, "Upset me." Everywhere they go, they meet a lot of other people wearing the same sign who are only too happy to oblige. Those who are free from likes and dislikes, on the other hand, are full of security. They function in freedom wherever they go. Once you reach this state, Sri Krishna says, you will live there always. You will never fall back into insecurity, turmoil, or disloyalty.

न तद्भासयते सूर्यो न शशाङ्को न पावकः ।
यद्गत्वा न निवर्तन्ते तद्धाम परमं मम ॥ १५-६ ॥

6. Neither the sun nor the moon nor fire can add to that light. This is my supreme abode, and those who enter there do not return to separate, selfish existence.

The Self is the source of light. When you attain it, as Sri Ramakrishna says, you feel like a fish swimming in a sea of light. Everything separate disappears, everything that is dark with ignorance.

We are so used to this darkness that we mistake it for reality. We cannot recognize light because we believe the darkness *is* light. This makes for a very upside-down world. People who exploit separateness are called successful; those who make war are immortalized in bronze or marble. This is living in pitch darkness, Sri Krishna says, and calling the darkness day. Those who really see are those who forget themselves completely in living for the welfare of all.

St. Teresa of Ávila refers to the various levels of consciousness as different mansions in the interior castle of the soul. When you go from one floor to the next, there are sudden experiences of blinding light. This seems to be a characteristic phenomenon in the deeper stages of meditation. You are so completely absorbed in going through the words of the inspirational passage that your mind is completely one-pointed; not a single ray of your mental energy is flickering. As the Gita says, your mind is as steady as the flame of a lamp that is kept in a windless place. Then you are ready for the tremendous experience of dazzling, radiant light that St. Augustine describes so vividly:

> I entered into the secret closet of my soul, led by Thee,... and beheld with the mysterious eye of my soul the Light that never changes, above the eye of my soul, above my intelligence. It was not the common light which all embodied creatures can see; nor was it the same kind but greater, as if the light of day were to grow brighter and brighter and flood all space. This light was none of that, but something other, altogether different.... He who knoweth truth knoweth that light: and who knoweth it, knoweth eternity. Love knoweth it.

Not only dazzling light but limitless love floods your heart, the infinite compassion that Buddhism calls *mahākarunā,* which embraces all life. The Franciscan mystic Jacapone da Todi says,

> Love above all language,
> Goodness unimagined,
> Light without measure
> Shines in my heart!

"Love above all language": your heart is flooded with love; it bursts its barriers. The dam of separateness breaks, and a great sea of love surges up from inside – "goodness unimagined," love for all creatures, all individuals, all countries, even those who may have offended or wronged you. And "light without measure": even the sun blazing in the sky, the source of all physical radiance, borrows the effulgent light from your heart and mine. To understand this is to realize the immense glory of being human.

ममैवांशो जीवलोके जीवभूतः सनातनः ।
मनःषष्ठानीन्द्रियाणि प्रकृतिस्थानि कर्षति ॥ १५-७॥
शरीरं यदवाप्नोति यच्चाप्युत्क्रामतीश्वरः ।
गृहीत्वैतानि संयाति वायुर्गन्धानिवाशयात् ॥ १५-८॥

7. An eternal part of me enters into the world at birth, assuming a body and mind made of prakriti.
8. When the divine Self enters and leaves a body, it takes along its samskāras as the wind carries a scent from place to place.

In the long drawn-out drama that is sādhana there are three actors. One is the Self, the changeless Ātman, pure Being. This shining Self is within all, yet it cannot shine forth because of the mask of negative qualities and self-will that we call personality. This is the second actor, called *jīva* in Sanskrit – the separate, individual ego with which we identify ourselves. And third is Māyā, the compulsive sense of separateness: as Evelyn Underhill puts it, the "web of illusion, here thick, here thin, [which] hems in, confuses, and allures" us in our evolution toward Self-realization.

Part of Māyā's power comes from the fierce clamor of the senses. This is an inheritance we have received from the animals, a natural part of our evolutionary heritage. Its power is especially poignant in personal relationships; for as everyone who has been through the experience knows, any relationship based on physical attraction *has* to end in heartbreak. It is not merely that the relationship comes to an end so soon; physical desire sets up such fierce expectations, and the disillusion that follows can last so long that some people never recover from it. All this is the work and delusion of Māyā. Even today, when I see a movie depicting scenes of entanglement and sorrow, I breathe a fervent prayer from the bottom of my heart to Krishna, the same prayer that Sri Ramakrishna used to repeat over and over: "May I never fall under the spell of Māyā again!"

In the terms of classical mysticism, only one of these three actors, the Self, can be called real. Yet to the extent that we identify ourselves with the jīva, our ever-changing personality, we live as well in the "unreal" world of change, bound to it by self-will and the fierce, compulsive play of the senses. The farther we progress spiritually, the more we become aware of the gulf that yawns between these two worlds: the one of sheer physical existence, the other of pure spiritual being. Yet eventually – this is the marvel of samādhi – a bridge is built between the two. Then, as Sri Aurobindo says, the divine invades the physical world; even in physical things we see the radiance of the Lord.

"In every creature," Sri Krishna says, "a little part of me is present." Those are very personal words that go right into my heart. Not only human beings but even the lowest creature has a spark of divinity within, infinitesimal but inalienable. It is this tiny part, he tells Arjuna, that travels through time in the process of reincarnation. The life-line of the jīva runs back five billion years or more; in five billion years, I could say, the amoeba has become me. This is perfectly compatible with biological evolution. But spiritual evolution does not consider this blind growth; it would not even call it arbitrary. We play a part in our own evolution; that is the vital difference. The other influencing factors – time, circumstance, and so on – are still present, but we hold the key in every life. "All that we are," the Buddha says, "is the result of what we have thought." And not merely the result: the word he uses is *manomāyā*. This jīva is actually 'made of the mind' that we have used for many, many lives. There is no reference here to any external or supernatural power. My growth is entirely in my hands; your growth is entirely in yours. The continuous improvement we are able to make in the quality of our thinking is what decides our lives.

Not only that, this is what decides even the kind of body we have. According to the Gita, I have worked on my body for many lives. There is a quiet correspondence between the kind of body I have and the kind of mind I have. Just in the course of one life it is not difficult to see how the way we think shapes the way we eat, work, sleep, and exercise; how it determines the risks we take, the occupations we enter, the places we live in, the people we live with, and the way we respond to stress. All of these have an obvious bearing on our physical well-being. Now, says the Gita, extend the same influence over many lives: just as in this life we develop the health and physical condition that our thinking warrants, we enter the next life with the right kind of body to pick up where we left off.

There are many, many factors in this, as I shall attempt to illustrate. Personality is not at all a simple picture. So I would not recommend that anyone try to analyze why he or she has a particular kind of body or wonder how some physical liability can be traced to a past life. It is enough to understand that there is a connection, and that whatever our physical condition, we can rest assured it is the right one for working out our samskāras and going forward on the spiritual path.

In the same way that each jīva shapes the body by its thinking, each of us lives in a personal world very much of his or her own making. We experience the world as we are; we respond to it as we are; we are continuously reshaping it according to how we are. That is what the Christian mystics mean when they say, "My sin is stamped upon my universe." But the Hindu mystic would say, "My goodness is stamped upon my universe." Both statements are true: one simply takes the perspective of the jīva, while the other looks at the world through the shining Self.

The divine fragment called the Ātman is the same in all people, all races, all creatures. This is not theory; that is how you actually see life after the Self is realized. The other day a kid was born prematurely to one of our angora goats, and a friend took a picture of me holding the tiny, fragile creature in my arms. When I saw the photograph I said, "That's not just a guy and a goat." I was not looking at myself; I saw the Ātman, realized in me through billions of years of evolution and still latent in little Gautami, the goat, to be revealed in her after perhaps millions of years of evolution more. In that picture Gautami and I are gazing into each other's eyes. She is marveling, "I'm going to look like you someday!" And I am smiling back: "Well, millions of years ago I looked like you." That awareness fills my heart with joy and releases an immense desire to save the lives of all these creatures, knowing they are not merely my kith and kin but the same spark as you and I.

This divine fragment travels through time from stage to stage in evolution, revealing a little more of its divinity at every stage. Our dog Muka, for example, shows more of the spark than a tiger does; our cow Shobha shows more than a panther. Even in the human context this development continues. People who are terribly violent may look like human beings, but they still live largely in the animal world. Similarly, though someone who has extinguished self-will may look like the rest of us, he or she is no longer in the animal world at all. Such a person, Sri Krishna says, "lives in me" – in the state of Krishna-consciousness, Christ-consciousness, from which there is no fall.

As the jīva travels through time, it picks up a samskāra in every stage of evolution. Our dog Muka is adding a samskāra to his jīva-nature, and so are his canine friends Hebbles and Ganesha – three very different dogs. The black cat who lives in our greenhouse, whom the children call Luther Purrbank, is developing a samskāra of his own: he still claws the hand that feeds, and I have very little doubt that he will continue to do so when he becomes a human being. Every creature adds a samskāra of its own, a tiny seed of a samskāra in every life. And, these verses explain in thrilling poetry, the jīva blows through time like a wind, starting five billion years ago as a little breeze and growing stronger and stronger, blowing through the phenomenal world to its end. When a spring breeze blows through a garden, it picks up fragrances from the roses and nasturtiums and sweet peas so that though the flowers remain, their essences are carried on. In much the same way, this jīva-wind picks up samskāras in every life. That is how the immaterial karmic legacy of each of us is carried on: not in the body, not physically or chemically, but by this wind of prāna.

And from life to life the samskāras become heavier, more complicated. Good and bad, kind and unkind, selfish and selfless, mingle into a complex perfume that we call personality. Against the background of millions of lives, this makes for highly elaborate combinations. One person's greed, another's anger, may be a million years old. But no one is all greed or anger. Each of us has redeeming qualities too: a bit of love, a little forgiveness, a touch of sympathy to offset our jealousy. That is what makes the human personality such an elaborate, complicated affair.

This verse adds a subtle but very interesting touch: it is not only the samskāras of the mind that are carried along like this, but also those of the senses. The mind is called the "sixth sense" here because there is such a close relationship between it and the other five members of the sense family. Each sense can have its own samskāras, carried on from life to life, and these sense-samskāras have a telling effect on health.

Modern medicine, for all its triumphs, has one serious limitation: it looks for a cause of illness in something outside us. This approach is valid on the physical level, but it is incomplete; therefore it is inadequate. Of course external circumstances or agents can cause sickness. But there is also a mental factor, not only in so-called psychosomatic ailments but in every case of illness, because of the effect the mind and senses have on the immune system. So when the Buddha says, "All that we are is the result of what we have thought," it includes our illnesses; it includes our general health.

The Gita, I would say, goes a step further than the world of medicine today. It takes in not only the physical body but also what spiritual psychology calls the mental or subtle body, which is closely linked to the physical organism by a very quiet correspondence. In this view, for an illness to develop, bacteria or bacilli are not enough; you must also have developed a susceptibility to that illness. How is it that of ten people who are exposed to the same bacillus, nine may succumb and one escape? Some say chance, others luck. Most physicians would offer the explanation that there are innumerable differences in individual physiology and genetic makeup, including resistance to disease, but this is still on the physical level and only begs the question. The explanation I would give in the light of verses like these is that the immune system is not just a physiological or biochemical network; there is a corresponding mental network also. Resistance is not merely physical, and among all the myriad factors it involves, I would give the mind primary importance.

There is scope for a whole volume on this subject, and someday I hope to write one; the ramifications for the healing professions are tremendous. Here let me just touch on a few aspects, to give some idea of the depth of application these verses offer.

First and foremost, I would say that if you want the highest resistance to illness of any kind, then a deep desire to live for others is a tremendous immunological force. The same is true for resistance to the ravages of time. From my own experience, as well as from the towering example of my grandmother, I can testify that the vast majority of problems associated with old age – problems with vitality, memory, attention, endurance, resilience – need never arise at all.

Every older person, even those who do not meditate, can draw inspiration from my small example. I have probably ten times the vitality I had when I was thirty, and perhaps a hundred times the capacity to contribute to life. I may not be able to run the way I did then, but my judgment is sounder, my understanding is deeper, and my endurance is greater; I can work long hours without tension or fatigue.

If you lead the kind of life many older people do, of course, the problems of senility are inevitable. Living for oneself, indulging the senses, having no overriding goal, all make tremendous demands on prāna, and in the latter part of life we do not have prāna to lose. But if you have an overwhelming desire to contribute to the welfare of others, if your heart is full of love for all, Sri Krishna promises that he will magnify all your faculties – your memory, your creativity, your energy, your resources, your capacity to draw people and win their love and respect and help them to change their lives. All this happens naturally when prāna is conserved.

This desire to live for all can extend to the roots of your being. Psychologists talk about the importance of the will to live, but that generally means no more than the will to live for oneself. It can go no deeper than the ego, beneath which lie vast worlds of consciousness. Because we see only the surface of personality, we cannot understand how shallow the ego's will to live often is. But the will to live for the whole of life, because it goes so deep, preserves and strengthens us down to the core of our being.

Second, and closely related, is what happens to the immune system when your heart is flooded with love. I am not thinking of love for one person here and another there, no matter how deep or genuine. I mean love universal, continuous, "love without an object." It expresses itself in countless little choices you make throughout the day, all of which have a direct bearing on physical health.

I can give my own example again. When you haven't been able to sleep for two or three nights, as everyone knows, the adverse effects can be terribly debilitating – not only physically, but mentally and intellectually as well. It is only natural at such times, especially for those who are older, to want to sleep on until the sun is high in the sky and then go and sit in the patio over a cup of tea. This is the body's legitimate response, dictated by certain physical principles. But the body also responds to spiritual principles – because, among other things, they dictate the flow of prāna, on which the body draws for energy. Depression, for example, inhibits the immune system because it drains prāna. In the same way, I would say, the capacity to love others more than yourself floods the immune system with prāna, strengthening it immeasurably.

I get very little sleep, often only three to four hours a night; I have not had more for many years. This is one of the developments that can take place after samādhi: once you wake up in the depths of the unconscious, you feel a very deep-seated reluctance to abandon, even for a few moments, the continuous awareness of God. I have actually had to teach myself to fall asleep again, and I feel rather pleased with myself when I manage to drift off in the mantram in the early hours of the morning. This kind of pattern produces a good deal of physiological stress, and once I do fall asleep, my body's natural need is to go on sleeping late into the morning. Instead I get up early for meditation and then go to the beach for a long, fast walk. Ask yourself if this is the natural response to a sleepless night! Northern California beaches are cold and foggy in the morning; I do not go for pleasure. I go for exercise, so that my body will stay healthy and strong for many years more – not to enjoy life longer but to continue the work of our meditation center, which stands to benefit millions. That is the motivation. I come back from the beach with a ravenous appetite and have a really good breakfast to see me through another long day of work.

All this is to illustrate how even physical faculties can be invigorated and physical limits extended by the immense desire to live for others. This is not at all like driving oneself for personal gain, which takes a terrible toll on the body. Though I have maintained this pattern for years, day in and day out, I do not feel fatigued by it; I thrive on it. So I have no hesitation in saying that none of the problems associated with advancing age are necessary. Not only that, you can look forward to doing much better in the second half of your life than you did during the first.

Sickness, I said earlier, is caused by an external agent with the cooperation of an internal agent, the mind. The link is the immune system, through which resistance to disease is lowered or enhanced. To connect this with this verse I have to bring in the law of karma to some extent; for Sri Krishna says that from one life to another, it is not only the samskāras of the mind that are carried along but also the samskāras of the individual senses. This is a subtle distinction, but it means that samskāras which begin in the mind gradually become more physical, until they begin to invade the body through the senses. This is the first stage of disordered health.

A samskāra of pleasure, for example, can become particularized through constant overindulgence in eating – and not only eating, but reading about food, talking about food, cooking, observing, thinking, tasting, imagining; in short, through dwelling constantly on the pleasures of the palate. Over years, over lifetimes, what began as a mental habit takes over the sense of taste and becomes a physiological compulsion with very real physical problems. I don't like to sound occult, but when you know this is a person's mental state you can actually anticipate the kind of problems he will have in the next life. You can list them for him, *a, b, c.*

The implication is acutely practical: because such problems are not caused only by something outside us, they cannot be cured only by something from outside us. I wonder how much drugs can cure an illness, however much they may help with symptoms. To solve even a physical problem you have to get inside the mind, which is the purpose of meditation and the mantram.

Take the most pronounced characteristic of our contemporary society, rage. You can take a person who is full of rage and almost predict the kind of physical and emotional problems he will have the next time around. There is nothing particularly occult about this. When a person comes into life with certain pronounced proclivities, he will find himself drawn into situations that provoke those proclivities. Without realizing it, an angry person will seek out circumstances that enrage him; he will get into situations that make him more hostile or resentful. These are the natural consequences of an anger samskāra, and their purpose, if I may so call it, is to teach us to change our way of thinking.

If we do not learn, however, the samskāra gradually invades the body. This can happen in many ways, depending on the individual. We have to remember that each of us comprises countless samskāras, which can reinforce or counter each other in patterns as complex as those of the ripples that dapple a lake. One angry person, for example, may develop peptic ulcer; another, some pulmonary disorder: anger changes the breathing rhythm, and chronic anger can lead to chronically disordered breathing. This process continues over many lives, but you can see it develop even in the span of a single lifetime. In any case, once the condition is established, that person comes into life with a tendency to serious breathing problems. As soon as he finds himself in contexts that provoke him – an angry home, an angry teacher, angry classmates, an angry partner – the physical problem erupts.

The positive side is this: Meditation, as I can testify from helping thousands of people, can help you use the same situations, formerly detrimental, to *improve* your health and state of mind. The same circumstances that once would have wrecked your health can actually be used to rescue it. That is why I say when someone is angry with you, put up with it cheerfully; return good will and do not withdraw your support. It will help that person, but it will help you even more, by helping to solve your physical and emotional problems too.

This is tough, I agree. But isn't surgery tough? That is the way the Buddha talked; he always called a spade a spade. Surgery is a frightful procedure. It amazes me to see how willingly people in this country submit to it. Instead of getting myself into an untenable health problem and then paying through the nose to go through the trauma and indignities of surgery, I much prefer to take my health into my own hands.

You do not have to attain samādhi to do this, but you do have to change not only your lifestyle but your thoughtstyle. Then, as meditation deepens and you can repeat your mantram from a deeper level of awareness, prāna is gradually withdrawn from sense-samskāras and consolidated as vitality, resilience, and resistance to stress and disease.

श्रोत्रं चक्षुः स्पर्शनं च रसनं घ्राणमेव च ।
अधिष्ठाय मनश्चायं विषयानुपसेवते ॥ १५-९ ॥

9. Using the mind, ears, eyes, nose, and the senses of taste and touch, the Self enjoys sense objects.

In Sanskrit the stuff of the mind is called *chitta,* which you can think of as a peculiarly elastic modeling clay. Chitta is pure, shapeless consciousness, which takes the form of individual containers like you and me. It flows out through the senses, following desire; it goes where our attention goes. When you are listening to your favorite rock group in quadraphonic sound, chitta runs out of the mind and into the ear. Then it is difficult to get it back in again. This is prāna that is flowing out, vital energy that is lost. That is why people who get conditioned to loud, agitating music usually find their security falling and their restlessness swelling past endurance.

The other day I went into a record store in Berkeley while Christine was shopping across the street. Loud rock music was playing as I went in, and everybody in the store – customers and staff alike – was doing a kind of St. Vitus's dance in time to the beat. I just stood and watched; I couldn't believe my eyes. Imagine doing this every day! When you subject yourself to this kind of music regularly for a couple of years, this is how you are going to be inside. Not only your limbs but your nervous system will jerk and bob about everywhere you go, even during your sleep. Your body may not be bobbing, but the movement has got into the mind. When the mind is dancing to St. Vitus's tune, it is in a constant state of excitement or depression, a condition that has become endemic today.

As the mind travels further and further from the center like this, the lines of communication with the Self become overextended. We need fresh supplies of security, energy, judgment, willpower, but the supply lines are broken; we cannot get in touch with the center of our being. Depression or despair may set in; discrimination, sound judgment, is exhausted. We may set off in pursuit of anything that promises satisfaction, whatever the cost, though our vital capacity for enjoying anything has already been drained. Like a ship that has lost its anchor, we are at the mercy of any storm that comes.

In reaching out through the senses, we travel far away from the indivisible unity of life at the center of our being. To get back, we have to rise above everything that is separate in us: our physical urges, our emotional cravings for aggrandizement, our compulsive imposition of self-will on all around us. These are powerful forces that fling consciousness away from its center. If we are to turn and travel inward, each of these forces has to be harnessed.

To do this, it helps a good deal to look on everybody else as an extension of ourselves and on ourselves as an extension of everyone else. When we are physically oriented, we think we stop with the outermost layer of our skin. Inside that boundary is home territory. There I have to consider my comforts and conveniences, my pleasure and profit, because this is home. After all, if you don't take care of your own home, who will? But beyond that, we don't care what happens. "That's not my problem," we say. "It's Bob's. That's *his* home, not mine."

Those who live for physical satisfaction are driven by this sense of otherness, which cannot help leading to alienation. They become estranged from others because they are estranged from themselves. But if you can break through the surface stratum of consciousness, you will find the gap of separateness becoming narrower and narrower. You get a sense of nearness to people. Where formerly you saw a chasm between you and your partner, now you see only a little creek; with practice, you can jump right over.

How close can you move to your partner, your boyfriend or girlfriend, when some disagreement is pushing you apart? How easily can you yield your own opinions for the sake of the relationship? How gracefully can you go against your own self-will? When someone you love is going off in a wrong direction, can you correct that person with respect and sympathy, even if it means some temporary agitation? If you can do these things, you are making excellent progress. These are the arts of love, which have been completely forgotten in the modern world.

As long as you are self-willed, you will find a long distance between you and those around you, even your boyfriend or girlfriend. No matter how much you try to be together, you will not be able to lessen this distance until you raise the banner of revolt against your own ego. If you want to assess your meditation, take your tape measure out every

New Year's Day and measure the distance between you and your family. Our natural tendency is to think of ourselves as the center and others on the circumference. Instead, think of yourself as the circumference; the rest of life is the center. Every year we should be able to move closer to the center. The marks are more patience, deeper understanding, greater security when things do not go our way.

To draw closer to others, you have to rebel against yourself. Often you will have to hurt your own private feelings so that others can benefit. "Thy will be done," Jesus says, not "my will be done." Thy will is unity; my will is separateness. It is so terribly difficult to practice this that most people do not try; those who do try often do not persist. But if you have the inner toughness this fierce fight requires, you will find you need less and less tape to measure the gap between you and others. Finally you discover you are at the center, no longer separate from the whole. Then you can throw the tape away.

उत्क्रामन्तं स्थितं वापि भुञ्जानं वा गुणान्वितम् ।
विमूढा नानुपश्यन्ति पश्यन्ति ज्ञानचक्षुषः ॥ १५-१० ॥

10. The deluded do not see the Self when it leaves the body or when it dwells within it. They do not see the Self enjoying sense objects or acting through the gunas. But they who have the eye of wisdom see.

Until the mind is stilled it is not possible for any human being, however gifted, to see the unity underlying life. The mind is not equipped to see unity. It is meant to register change on the surface of life, and to that which does not change, which has no parts, it is simply blind.

In the Buddha's presentation, the mind is not a thing or a state; it is a process. James Joyce and Virginia Woolf might have been interested to learn that the idea of a stream of consciousness was well worked out in Buddhist circles twenty-five hundred years ago. According to the theory of *kshanikavāda,* each thought is born and dies every moment. There is no connection between one thought and the next and the next; each is separate from the others, like frames on a movie film. And just as in a movie, what makes things look connected is the speed at which these separate thought-frames move by.

Some time ago a filmmaker friend brought home a print of an old Humphrey Bogart movie. For almost two hours we watched a lot of fast, furious action. Afterwards, before it was rewound, I went to look at the film. Terry obligingly unrolled a few yards at the end and brought out his little magnifying glass. There was no action at all. We saw a lot of shots of someone standing with his hand up, then out; then some other chap is leaning precariously backward. But no blow takes place. You see this, then you see that, and you put two and two together and say, "Ah! He hit him. Hit him again, Bogie!"

This is what happens in the mind. A fast mind means a lot of thoughts crowding through, trying to get by at once. Each is separate, but they are all crowded so close that they are like a row of dominoes. You knock over the first thought – "She is looking at me with the corner of her mouth turned up" – and all the rest fall over in an instant, until the last thought topples off the edge of the table and you conclude that she is smirking because of that one stupid remark you made at Henry's two weeks ago. "What a small mind she must have," you say, "to go on acting amused because of something that happened two weeks ago! What about all those stupid things *she* said?"

This absurd process is the ego – *ahamkāra* in Sanskrit, that which makes us feel separate. This is the film that is always going on in the theater of consciousness, even while we sleep. When we slow it down through meditation, the day comes when we can see for ourselves that every thought is separate. Where formerly thoughts were crowding and jostling each other like rush-hour commuters on the downtown subway, you begin to separate them. I remember a cartoon in an English magazine showing a team of American football players bent over in a huddle. A goat on the sidelines, taking this as a personal invitation, was lowering its head to charge. This is what you do in meditation; you start butting clinging thoughts apart. Finally you slow the thinking process to such an extent that each thought comes freely, without dragging any others along with it. Then your responses are free; conditioned thinking becomes a thing of the past.

When thoughts are crowded close together, it is very difficult to get free from the tyranny of thinking. We are helpless, particularly in the peculiar instance of circular thinking, in which the same old thought goes round and round: "I hate her, I hate her, I hate her, I hate her." That is all anger is, the same compulsive thought over and over. Most of us do not know what to do with this. If it gets particularly oppressive – usually as we are tossing and turning in bed – we may exclaim to ourselves, "If only I could stop thinking!" But we do not know how.

This kind of obsession is like a scratched record. The needle has got stuck, and all the mind can do is repeat the same thought over and over. Yesterday a friend was playing a Beatles song that made no sense to me at all. John Lennon, I believe, was singing, "I am the egg man, I am the walrus . . ." "Very good," I said to myself, "this is a song about the unity of life." Then he went on, "I am the walrus, the walrus, the walrus, the walrus."

"Julia," I said, "why does he go on like this? Can't he think of anything else?"

Julia just laughed. "The needle's stuck," she explained. "Doesn't it sound funny?"

When the mind gets stuck, it makes very little sense to wail to yourself, "Why does it do this to me? Can't it think of anything better?" Once you can elbow your thoughts apart, you can lift the needle when it is between two thoughts and place it a groove or two ahead, where the whole thinking process can pick up as if nothing had happened. This is a truly amazing accomplishment. Most of us know that when we get angry, resentful, afraid, or agitated, although we may have honorary degrees or be the union's toughest negotiator, we cannot do this one little thing: put out a finger, lift the needle, and make the song move on. That is what meditation can do.

The more self-willed we are, the closer thoughts get to each other. Self-willed thoughts are a gregarious, pushy lot; they like to put their arms around their buddies, climb on each other's shoulders, and generally make themselves at home. But as self-will subsides, thoughts become as orderly as if they were on parade. In a marching band, aren't you supposed to keep a precise distance from the person in front? Your thoughts will become like that; they keep a certain distance. If someone offends you, it will not provoke a resentful response. You may feel a little displeased, but you can drop your displeasure immediately.

यतन्तो योगिनश्चैनं पश्यन्त्यात्मन्यवस्थितम् ।
यतन्तो ऽप्यकृतात्मानो नैनं पश्यन्त्यचेतसः ॥ १५-११ ॥

11. Those who strive resolutely on the path of yoga see the Self within. The thoughtless, who strive intermittently, do not.

One of the reasons Sri Krishna gives for people being self-willed, separate, and selfish is laziness. It's a simple but penetrating diagnosis. They are not prepared to make the effort of reducing self-will, even if they would like to be secure. They are not willing to work on their consciousness to try to remove what is negative. They follow the path of least resistance; wherever self-will flows, they follow. As a result they often end up becoming automata, without any life to their credit.

People like this remind me of the trucks I see sometimes taking a big mobile home along the freeway. They have red warning flags sticking out on both sides, front and back, and big signs that warn, "Wide Load." Everybody on the road moves over as far as possible, because they know there is no arguing with this fellow; he will just get into your lane.

Self-willed people are very much like this. You may not have meant any offense, but their nerves are so raw that they will take offense. You may have meant only a slight joke; all you expected was a laugh. But they go home, dwell on it, and come back the next day with that remark inflated into a big problem.

This is what happens when you dwell on yourself: you take a limp little balloon of a problem, keep on blowing it up, and make it huge. It is helpful to remember that the personal problems we talk over with confidants, write up in our journals, brood over, and dream about are not as big as they seem. We have inflated them by thinking about them for hours, until they become huge. We may not be able to see the red flags or read those warning words, "Wide Load"; but others know, and avoid us when they see us coming.

Many, many people today who are intellectually gifted, materially prosperous, personally attractive, culturally advanced, have been hypnotized by separateness and inflated by their own importance. Whatever their gifts, Sri Krishna says, they cannot see unity. Therefore, their opinion or contribution cannot be of permanent benefit to humanity.

यदादित्यगतं तेजो जगद्भासयते ऽखिलम् ।
यच्चन्द्रमसि यच्चाग्नौ तत्तेजो विद्धि मामकम् ॥ १५-१२ ॥

12. The brightness of the sun, which lights up the world, the brightness of the moon and of fire – these are mine.

Yesterday Christine and I went to the Hyatt Regency hotel in San Francisco, which has achieved notoriety for its unusual architecture. I always appreciate a good view, and I wanted to visit the revolving penthouse restaurant from which you can look out over the whole city.

We entered the Regency's portals and went straight to the top, the Equinox. I felt like a wide-eyed boy set down on another planet. A nice server came and showed us to a plush corner with huge windows and mirrors on all sides, where she promised we would be able to get a good view.

Then the usual restaurant topic of vegetarian food came up. This can lead to highly philosophical discussions about what comes with what and how it is prepared, whether fish and birds can count as vegetables, and other botanical and ontological topics. At the end of all this the server said, "I'll bring you a special chef's salad." That suited me perfectly. "There's no need to hurry on," I assured Christine. "Why don't we sit here until we've seen the whole city pass by?"

Out of the window we could see the ships coming and going in San Francisco Bay. While we worked our way through the salad, the Bay slipped out of sight and more and more of the city swung into view. "Look at that!" I said to Christine after a while. "You can see Coit Tower."

Christine laughed. "That's not really Coit Tower," she said.

"Of course it is," I said. Everybody in the Bay Area knows Coit Tower; it looks like a giant fire hose nozzle.

"You're looking at its reflection," said Christine.

She was right. I realized suddenly that I had been looking in the wrong direction, gazing into one of the full-height mirrors with which our booth was paneled. How much of what I had been watching had been real? I couldn't tell what was window and what was mirror.

"There," I said, pointing in another direction. "Isn't that the Equitable Insurance building?" Another landmark; I recognized the parking lot.

Christine looked closely. "That's not a window either," she decided. "In fact, I think it's not just a reflection; it's a reflection of a reflection."

I lost all confidence in my vision. Only when we escaped from the Equinox and got back to Union Square did I feel I knew where I was and what I was seeing.

Shankara compares the whole phenomenal world to a city seen in a mirror. This is not a poetic fancy. When we look at people as physical entities, talk to them and deal with them and try to possess or manipulate them as if they were physical entities, we are dealing with reflections of our own mind-making. Just like Coit Tower, they *do* seem real. Until Christine pointed out that I was looking in a mirror, I would have sworn that I was looking at the real Coit Tower. Even then, in order to understand that this was only a reflection, I needed to be able to compare it with something real. In the Equinox I could do that simply by looking in a different direction. But in life, if you want to see what is real, you have to get below the surface level of consciousness.

This illusion can lead to painful comments on relationships, particularly the romantic. "Making love," for example, has no necessary connection with love. I would say this is "making physical relationships" – making reflections of reflections of love. Love means affirming the unity between two people; indulging in physical relationships for physical satisfaction is denying that unity. Anyone who has tried to build a relationship on sexual attraction knows how fleeting it is, how soon satiation and irritation come.

We have a story in India about a courtesan who was notoriously fond of money. One evening a rich man came to her salon and happened to see her standing before a mirror. The image was so voluptuously beautiful that he went and gallantly kissed the reflection. Immediately she said, "That will be one hundred rupees."

This was a resourceful chap. He took out a hundred rupees, held it up, and gestured toward its reflection in the mirror. "You may collect that," he said.

It is tragic, but in personal relationships we are often dealing with a reflection. Trying to possess somebody is trying to possess a reflection; it cannot be done. Imagine Romeo seeing Juliet's reflection and carrying away the mirror! That is just what physically oriented people do when they try to possess, manipulate, and enjoy. Sooner or later this is accompanied by negative reflections of reflections: doubt, jealousy, insecurity, alienation, frustration, anger, depression. Love never asks "What can I get from this person?" It asks only, "What can I give?" That is the way to go beyond reflections to the real person.

After we finished our salad at the Equinox and paid the bill, we didn't know how to get out. We wandered around the periphery looking for one of those glowing exit signs, but all we could see in that eerie half-darkness was windows, mirrors, and red plush. Finally we asked our server for help. "You just walk out," she said. We had been looking for some special exit, but right in front of us was a gap through which we could pass from the Equinox back to the everyday reality of San Francisco.

"Don't wait for signs," Jesus says. Right where we are standing we can find the exit from the world of separateness and enter into the world of unity. All we have to do is turn our backs, to the best of our ability, on our private needs, demands, and self-indulgences.

Otherwise, the Gita says, the world we live in will become darker and darker. Living in separateness means being dominated by private urges, trying to have our own way and do only what we like, unable to see what cries out to be done for the welfare of the world around us. When this darkness becomes deep enough, we can't see which direction to go; we will always be losing our way, never coming out at all. When we decide to say no to private, personal urges, we start to enter a world of light where the path is clear. We know where we are going, and we can travel safely and surely.

गामाविश्य च भूतानि धारयाम्यहमोजसा ।
पुष्णामि चौषधीः सर्वाः सोमो भूत्वा रसात्मकः ॥१५-१३॥
अहं वैश्वानरो भूत्वा प्राणिनां देहमाश्रितः ।
प्राणापानसमायुक्तः पचाम्यन्नं चतुर्विधम् ॥१५-१४॥

13. With a drop of my energy I enter the earth and support all creatures. Through the moon, the vessel of life-giving fluid, I nourish all plants.
14. I enter each living creature and dwell within as the life-giving breath. I am the fire in the stomach which digests all food.

These verses again refer to prāna, the primordial energy underlying all the forms of matter and energy with which we are familiar. The universe hums with prāna, and its forces and processes can be described as the flow of prāna. The Upanishads say that prāna streams from the sun and flows into plants to be stored, to be released later in human beings and animals when the plants are eaten, to power the work of the body, senses, and mind. No biologist would find this inaccurate; it is a poetic description of what the life sciences would call "energy flows in an ecosystem." I have seen textbooks refer to the oxidation of food as "the fire of digestion," which echoes the Gita almost word for word.

We can also think of prāna as flowing through time, powering the growth of the Tree of Life since the universe began. It is the energy of evolution, pushing its way through root, trunk, and branch to feed each individual leaf. And when a man or woman nears the end of the evolutionary journey and takes to meditation, this immense power bursts into new levels of activity.

I can illustrate this with an incident that occurred yesterday evening while we drove across the Richmond Bridge. Suddenly the roadway began vibrating wildly. I thought to myself, "Well, the earthquake has finally arrived." Every few years, you know, papers and magazines in California start carrying fresh predictions that this is the year in which the San Andreas Fault is finally going to allow half the state to slide into the sea. But as it turned out, this was no quake. A huge ship was passing beneath the bridge, unseen in the gathering darkness and the fog. Its horn went off just as we reached the central pier, shaking the car with its blast.

That is how it feels when a long-standing samskāra comes to the surface from the depths of the unconscious. You have to face it and do battle with it, which brings upheavals on every level of personality, physical, emotional, intellectual, and spiritual. We have to be prepared to change with these impacts and develop new ways of living – more aware of the unity of life, less and less aware of the fragmented personality we once were.

This tremendous adjustment is accomplished through the energy these verses call *ojas*. The word has several implications. Partly *ojas* means the will, running all through the conscious mind to the very depths of the unconscious. Partly it means the prompt obedience of the senses, body, mind, and intellect to the slightest signal of the Ātman. Few of us have ever experienced this. Our usual state of personality is a free-for-all, where senses, feelings, judgment, and so on behave like those electric bumper cars at county fairs, skittering about colliding with each other. When this erratic activity subsides, there is a great consolidation of vital energy that flows into your life like a steady stream.

Ojas is prāna in the intense, superconcentrated form called *kundalinī*. All of us have a vast reservoir of this vital energy, which is the power that impels the individual creature through higher and higher states of evolution. In those who are selfish, kundalinī is hardly used. They do not need it; they are living just for themselves. To get along on the surface level of life, we need just one candlepower of kundalinī. But we have much vaster capabilities, merely by virtue of being human. As we begin to economize our extravagant expenditure or sense-energy, kundalinī gradually rises. Every time we defy a strong sensory urge, a little more of its power is available to us.

On the other hand, indulging a powerful desire like sex for the purpose of sensory satisfaction prevents kundalinī from rising. There is a vitally close connection between kundalinī and sex, and though we are not asked to become ascetics on the spiritual path, it is essential to get hold of this vast source of power and bring it under our control. I always have to repeat that this does not mean the faculty of sex is lost. It means simply that you have a choice in when and how it is expressed – which very few of us ordinary human beings can honestly say we have.

When sexual passions are fanned into flame, how difficult it is to understand that we are not our desires! Once we are caught in the fire, we have no freedom. The push is so fierce that we feel we have to succumb. At such times we are not using our desires; our desires are using us. All the Gita is saying is that we should not serve them; they should serve us. When sexual desire is mastered, it floods the body with the invigorating energy of kundalinī and strengthens the will until it cannot be broken by any tragedy, calamity, or danger.

सर्वस्य चाहं हृदि संनिविष्टो
मत्तः स्मृतिर्ज्ञानमपोहनं च ।
वेदैश्च सर्वैरहमेव वेद्यो
वेदान्तकृद्वेदविदेव चाहम् ॥ १५-१५ ॥

15. *Entering into every heart, I give the power to remember and understand; it is I again who take that power away. All the scriptures lead to me; I am their author and their wisdom.*

Sri Krishna is continuing the same theme: that everywhere in the universe he is prāna.

When Einstein discovered that matter and energy are interchangeable and began looking for a unified field theory, he may have had a concept like prāna in mind. But prāna not only underlies matter and energy on the physical level; it is also the power supplying the world within. If there is potential energy in a body at rest, imagine the energy in a strong desire or in compulsive anger! One fixed desire can launch a man or woman through thirty years or more of sustained, energetic action; it can overpower a continent, free a nation, transform a technology, eradicate a disease. All that power is prāna. We have ample evidence of the immense energy in the nucleus of an atom, but when I say that there is as much energy in a thought, people think I am being poetic. As an acorn gathers prāna and explodes into an oak tree, thoughts explode into action. If the thought is big enough it can work on for decades, draw in thousands of lives, change the course of history.

Dr. Hans Selye discovered that a laboratory rat can adapt to cold and other kinds of physiologic stress until it can not only survive but thrive under conditions where an unadjusted rat will perish. If the rat gets enough food to meet its body's energy needs, it should be able to continue in this state indefinitely. Yet, curiously, there comes a point at which something "gives out." After that, this well-fed rat will die if it is exposed to even moderate stress. Selye asks properly, What is lacking? Some other kind of energy, he concludes: some inner reservoir of vitality that stress has finally drained. He calls it "adaptation energy." I would call it prāna.

Dr. Barbara Brown, a physiologist in biofeedback research, made some related observations. She came to the conclusion that vital energy – she calls it "nervous energy" – is leaking out from us into the environment all the time. I differ with some of her conclusions, but I admire her originality of mind, and I found this an amazingly perceptive observation. This energy too I would call prāna. Dr. Brown says she does not know how prāna leaks out, of course; the loss is not physical, though it has physical effects. And she does not know how to stop it. But the Gita and the Upanishads would explain that whenever we desire something through the senses for their satisfaction, prāna ebbs out. Not only the physical act of satisfying a desire, but the desire itself depletes our vital energy.

This leakage means loss of vitality, of will, of the capacity to adapt to and thrive under the normal stress of life. To prevent this, it is absolutely essential to be able to close and open the sluice gates of the senses at will. This means developing the inner equipment and the skill to release prāna whenever you have a giant job to undertake for the welfare of all – as did, say, Mahatma Gandhi, St. Francis of Assisi, St. Teresa of Ávila – and to withhold prāna when some private, personal yearning is clamoring to be fulfilled. This magnificent capacity can strengthen the will immeasurably and make the body healthy, strong, beautiful, and vital.

Ultimately it is in the depths of meditation that prāna is dammed until our reservoir of vitality is full. For prāna is not lost only through the senses. It is drained whenever the mind is scattered and divided, pulled in all directions by different thoughts – which, for most of us, is most of the time.

Conflict, for example, is a prime drain on prāna. Most conflicts arise because a selfless thought and a selfish thought want to occupy the same place in the mind. Often the selfish thought comes in first; when the right thought opens the door, there is Mr. Wrong with his feet up on the table. "This is *my* mind," he says. "Nobody was at the door, and I got here first." He doesn't want to go, so naturally a tussle ensues.

Much of our prāna is wasted not in making decisions but in the conflict we go through before we make decisions. We put ourselves on both sides, as Augustine says, and then we fight it out. Whichever side wins, we lose the prāna. We enter a dark arena to fight with the wrong thought, and after a while we discover we are pummeling Mr. Right by mistake. "Excuse *me*!" says Right. "I thought you were on my side." "Right you are," we confess. "Where's Wrong?" We go back to hitting the wrong thought for a while, and then somehow we switch sides again; and so it goes, back and forth, through the day and into the night. The next morning we are exhausted, and the problem is no closer to being resolved. "Arjuna," Sri Krishna asks, "where is the need for all this? Why not just post someone at the door? If the right thought knocks, let it in. If the wrong thought knocks, tell it to leave." When conflicts disappear, we get a tremendous accumulation of energy.

The next great consumer of prāna is worry. Worry means that prāna is leaking out through a thousand little wormholes. Most worms I have seen are small. Worries, similarly, may not be big thoughts, but a thousand of them means a lot of prāna lost. When a person generally feels unequal to challenges or tries to avoid personal problems, the reason is often this constant leakage of vitality through worry.

Some people cannot help worrying. You give them a job like opening an umbrella and they immediately start thinking, "Suppose it doesn't open? Suppose I get wet and catch a cold?" It is better to try to do a job, even if it turns out wrong, than to keep worrying about it and putting it off. "If I do this, there's going to be this trouble; if I do that, there will be that trouble." Do it and get into trouble if necessary; then you will at least know how to do it better the next time.

The cure here is "The early mantram gets the worry." Worry only enervates; it serves no purpose. If you can learn to peck up worry-worms with the mantram, you will have so much energy that you will never feel unequal no matter how big the challenge. You will have energy and time to offer even after your regular duties are done: time to do more, to give more, to live more.

A third waster of prāna, perhaps the biggest, is depression. Your doctor will tell you that most people today accept depression as a condition of life, largely because they think it is biologically unavoidable. We live; therefore we get depressed. Most of us have even lost the capacity to question this. We say, "Well, we just have to learn to live with it."

Again, this is because no one is watching the door of the mind. When excitement arrives, blowing its trumpet and trying to knock the door down, we say, "Whoopee! Somebody's brought me some joy; bring it right in!" We get so excited that we can't sleep, we can't stop talking; the mind is in overdrive twenty-four hours a day. In short, we fling the door of the mind open wide, all because we're so anxious to be pleased. And while we're entertaining Pleasure, her twin, Depression, slips in. You can't keep her out, because you're holding the door open to every thought you can get in. But you don't notice Depression till a few days later, when you come home and find, instead of your dream date, a little note taped onto the door: "Thanks for a lovely time – someday we'll have to do it again. Last night's lasagna is in the fridge. I asked my sister to keep you company." There is Depression, looking up at you with sunken eyes; she hasn't even got enough prāna for a smile.

Sri Krishna always gives Arjuna free choice. "You can go after pleasure if you like," he says. "But if you do, you have to accept depression too." Arjuna doesn't say anything, but his eyes ask, "What's the alternative?" So Sri Krishna adds, "Control your mind." When Excitement knocks and wants to move in, just say, "Why don't you try next door?" Then you can entertain angels. For when excitement and depression vanish, the state of mind that remains is joy. You have freed yourself from conflict, anxiety, anger, and fear; sorrow will come no more.

द्वाविमौ पुरुषौ लोके क्षरश्चाक्षर एव च ।
क्षरः सर्वाणि भूतानि कूटस्थोऽक्षर उच्यते ॥ १५-१६ ॥

16. In this world there are two orders of being, the perishable, separate creature and the changeless spirit.

I have been reading a thoughtful book, *Mankind and Mother Earth,* in which Arnold Toynbee refers to the human being as a "psychosomatic organism" – part *psyche,* spiritual; part *soma,* physical – who lives necessarily in two realms. "In the biosphere," he says, we act "within a world that is material and finite." That is precisely the language of this verse. *Kshara* means limited, exhaustible, perishable, finite. The term has become particularly poignant. Until recently, most of us believed that the biosphere was inexhaustible; we could do what we liked with its resources. Today we know that everything in our physical environment is limited: food, trees, minerals, soil, even water and air.

"On this plane of human activity," Toynbee continues,

> Man's objective, ever since he became conscious, has been to make himself master of his nonhuman environment, and in our own day he has come within sight of success in this endeavor – possibly to his own undoing.

This is a simple point, but it is often ignored. No matter what technological miracles we achieve, Toynbee says, we can never separate ourselves from the rest of the biosphere. We are a part of this "nature" that we want to master.

But our "other home, the spiritual world, is also an integral part of total reality," says Toynbee:

> it differs from the biosphere in being both nonmaterial and infinite; and in his life in the spiritual world, Man finds that his mission is to seek, not for material mastery over his nonhuman environment, but for a spiritual mastery over himself.

Our nature is infinite. Therefore, the Upanishads say, nothing less than infinitude can ever satisfy us. If we forget that our real home is the world of the spirit, imperishable and changeless, we will go on trying to mine, refine, extract, harvest, and manufacture an infinite number and variety of things out of an acutely limited world.

The very air we breathe is exhaustible. Berkeley used to scorn Los Angeles for its smog, yet already clean air in the Bay Area is the exception rather than the rule. Last week children in San Francisco were asked not to run and play outside because the air was so thick with smog – smog caused by greed. If we loved our children as we profess to, we should remember that the air is limited, exhaustible, a perishable member of the family of life. Treat it gently, the Gita says; treat it with care. Don't blow fumes into the air or dump poisons into the rivers and oceans just to make more money; and don't fan overconsumption by buying more and more things you do not need. It is not only manufacturers who carry the responsibility for pollution. Insofar as we tell them, "Produce all you want! We'll buy whatever you make," the rest of us are responsible too.

In economics it is considered imprudent to live off your capital; in fact, in times of inflation it is imprudent even to live off your interest. We have been spending the stuff of the world wantonly, as if it were profligate interest on some eternal trust. Instead it is apparent that this is irreplaceable capital.

This is the first point made by the perceptive economist E. F. Schumacher in his brilliant little classic, *Small Is Beautiful.* I like the subtitle very much: *Economics As If People Mattered.* Schumacher, who has absorbed a great deal from Gandhi and the Buddha, questions all the assumptions of modern economics, and he does so in language that is simple, persuasive, practical, and profound. Other economists probably find this exasperating, but he is not writing for other economists. He is writing for people like you and me, who he feels can make a difference. "A businessman," Schumacher says,

> would not consider a firm to have solved its problems of production and to have achieved viability if he saw that it was rapidly consuming its capital. How, then, could we overlook this vital fact when it comes to that very big firm, the economy of Spaceship Earth and, in particular, the economies of its rich passengers? . . .

> Look at the figures that are being put forward under the heading 'World Fuel Requirements in the Year 2000.' If we are now using something like 7000 million tons of coal equivalent, the need in twenty-eight years' time will be three times as large – around 20,000 million tons! . . .
>
> What is so special about the year 2000? What about the year 2028, when little children running about today will be planning for their retirement? Another trebling by then? All these questions and answers are seen to be absurd the moment we realize that we are dealing with capital and not with income: fossil fuels are not made by men; they cannot be recycled. Once they are gone, they are gone forever.

Then he comes to the essential conflict:

> An attitude to life which seeks fulfillment in the single-minded pursuit of wealth – in short, materialism – does not fit into this world, because it contains within itself no limiting principle, while the environment in which it is placed is strictly limited.

Thus even a great economist is led to the theme of this chapter: our isolation from the Tree of Life. We do not think of ourselves as part of nature, Schumacher says, "but as an outside force destined to dominate and conquer it. [Man] even talks of a battle with nature, forgetting that if he won the battle he would find himself on the losing side." That is what separateness does, and in this "outside force" we can recognize our old friend rajas. As Barry Commoner reminds us, technology has become such a terrible threat not because it has failed but because it has been so successful. It has succeeded so tremendously that since 1945 we have witnessed more technological progress, if that is the term I want, than in all the preceding years of human history; and the consequences of this progress threaten to close the pages of human history.

"Man," Toynbee points out, "is the first species of living being in our biosphere that has acquired the power to wreck the biosphere and, in wrecking it, to liquidate himself . . . . [He] is an integral part of the biosphere, and if the biosphere were to be made uninhabitable, Man, as well as all other species, would become extinct." It is good to remember that this is not rhetoric but a literal possibility, fraught with suffering drawn out over generations on a scale this tormented world has never seen before.

उत्तमः पुरुषस्त्वन्यः परमात्मेत्युदाहृतः ।
यो लोकत्रयमाविश्य बिभर्त्यव्यय ईश्वरः ॥ १५-१७॥
यस्मात्क्षरमतीतो ऽहमक्षरादपि चोत्तमः ।
अतो ऽस्मि लोके वेदे च प्रथितः पुरुषोत्तमः ॥ १५-१८॥
यो मामेवमसंमूढो जानाति पुरुषोत्तमम् ।
स सर्वविद्भजति मां सर्वभावेन भारत ॥ १५-१९॥

17. But beyond these there is another, the supreme Self, the eternal Lord, who enters into the entire cosmos and supports it from within.
18. I am that supreme Self, praised by the scriptures as beyond the changing and the changeless.
19. Those who see in me that supreme Self see truly. They have found the source of all wisdom, Arjuna, and they worship me with all their heart.

"Supreme Self" here is *Purushottama,* after which the chapter is named – the highest ideal we can have.

Even without talking about spiritual values, it can be said that most of the meaninglessness in modern life comes from our having no ultimate purpose, no overriding goal. The strongest argument I can offer against personal pleasure and profit is that they cannot function as a goal. And without a comprehensive purpose, events cannot make sense to us; incidents cannot be related to a whole. We don't have a framework for making wise choices. That is why every one of us has a crying need for the highest ideal, on which we can keep our eyes always. Whenever we wander, we can still find our way back. All of us, being human, are likely to make mistakes in life. But when we have a great purpose that transcends passing, personal satisfactions, a goal that rises high above the horizon like the polestar, we need not get lost and wander in the maze of our mistakes. By keeping our eyes on this shining ideal, we can retrace our steps, correct our error, and continue to pursue our journey until we reach the goal.

The pursuit of wealth is often placed before us as a goal. Most of us know people who launched some enterprise with the best of intentions and then slowly got possessed by the profit motive, losing all vision of life. There is nothing wrong with a fair profit on a beneficial product or service. But without a higher goal, there is no point of reference to warn you when the profit motive begins to lead you into activities and ways of living that can wreck your life or the lives of others.

Every country today has examples of how the compulsive desire for profit has driven people to make things that ruin human health. Many of the handguns used in violent crimes in this country are assembled here from parts made in Germany, so that manufacturers in both countries can realize their profits without actually violating the law. Drugs prohibited in the United States because they may cause cancer or birth defects are pushed shamelessly in Third World countries where regulations are lax or nonexistent. And there is probably no growth industry so bullish this century as that of munitions, where companies from a handful of countries – led, I am sorry to say, by the United States and a few other developed countries – thrive on the business of pumping lethal hardware into any nation that will buy, washing their hands of any consequences. The list could be multiplied dozens of times without effort, so commonplace has "business as usual" become today. Once you see this, you rule out the giants of business and finance as ideals to be followed.

Similarly, in almost every country, personalities from sports and entertainment are held up as ideals. People want to look like them, talk like them, live like them, though they may be far from happy. Sports, movies, and the like do have a place; all of us need some time for exercise and relaxation. But if you do not have any higher purpose, you can end up setting your goal in life on perfecting your tennis strokes or cutting down your time on the mile. We must have an ideal. If we do not have anything big enough, we clutch at whatever is available: football players, race drivers, rock singers, movie stars.

All the great religions give us a supreme goal that brings out what is best in us from the very depths of consciousness. Jesus or Sri Krishna or the Compassionate Buddha is placed before us as an ideal for one reason: so that insofar as is in our capacity, we may gradually become like these luminous figures in our lives and hearts.

Toward the end of his life, St. Francis of Assisi asked his companions to stay behind while he went up into the wild, secluded heights of La Verna for solitary prayer. After some thirty days and nights, just before sunrise, he entered a state of deep ecstasy – what the Hindu mystics would call samādhi, union with the Christ within. In that supreme state he prayed fervently for two favors: "The first, that I may, as far as it is possible, feel in my soul and in my body the suffering which thou, O gentle Jesus, sustained in thy bitter passion; and the second, that as far as it is possible I may receive in my heart the overflowing love that moved thee to suffer so much for us." So complete was his identification with the Christ, the chronicles say, that he experienced both: the unutterable joy of complete love and the other side of that love, the cruelty of the wounds which Jesus suffered on the cross.

This complete identification is the meaning of samādhi. Those who attain it feel the joys and sorrows of others exactly as they would their own. They suffer and rejoice with all. The rest of us – less evolved, more self-centered, more separate – are scarcely aware of the full extent of suffering around us. The more separate we feel, the easier it is to forget about others' troubles, ignore the tragedies that surround us all, and bury ourselves in the pursuit of personal satisfactions.

The more you grow in selflessness, the more deeply you will feel the sorrow that throbs at the heart of life. But this is not a paralyzing sentimentality. Wherever you see suffering, you will have to do something to relieve it. You will never throw up your hands at the magnitude of a problem and say, "There's nothing I can do. The world is going to pieces; let it go." Your deep identification with all of life will release the resources to go to the causes of sorrow and devote your life to alleviating it.

इति गुह्यतमं शास्त्रमिदमुक्तं मयानघ ।
एतद्बुद्ध्वा बुद्धिमान्स्यात्कृतकृत्यश्च भारत ॥ १५-२० ॥

20. I have shared this profound truth with you, Arjuna. Those who understand it will attain wisdom; they will have done that which has to be done.

This simple phrase was a favorite of the Buddha's too: "That which was to be done has been done." No grand poetry, no trumpets, no philosophy; just a quiet statement that life's supreme purpose, the goal of millions of years of evolution, has been attained.

The implication is sobering: until we reach this state, nothing has been done. If you come and tell Sri Krishna that you have won the Irish Sweepstakes, climbed Annapurna without a sherpa, become the first woman to venture beyond Mars, he would say, "That isn't what has to be done. You haven't accomplished what you are here for."

Once you have done what has to be done, you have no interest in making money; therefore you do not exploit others or pollute the environment. Greed has left you, and so have anger and fear. You are no longer interested in your personal pleasure, so you are not capable of selfish attachment. You see life clearly, and you will not do things simply because they please you. There is nothing more you can want from life, nothing more that life can offer you except the opportunity to give.

पुरुषोत्तमयोगो नाम पञ्चदशोऽध्यायः ॥ १५ ॥

CHAPTER SIXTEEN

Two Paths

श्रीभगवानुवाच ।
अभयं सत्त्वसंशुद्धिर्ज्ञानयोगव्यवस्थितिः ।
दानं दमश्च यज्ञश्च स्वाध्यायस्तप आर्जवम् ॥ १६-१ ॥
अहिंसा सत्यमक्रोधस्त्यागः शान्तिरपैशुनम् ।
दया भूतेष्वलोलुप्त्वं मार्दवं ह्रीरचापलम् ॥ १६-२ ॥
तेजः क्षमा धृतिः शौचमद्रोहो नातिमानिता ।
भवन्ति संपदं दैवीमभिजातस्य भारत ॥ १६-३ ॥

SRI KRISHNA:

1–3. Be fearless and pure; never waver in your determination or your dedication to the spiritual life. Give of yourself freely. Be self-controlled, sincere, truthful, loving, and full of the desire to serve. Realize the truth of the scriptures; learn to be detached from material things and to take joy in renunciation. Do not get angry or harm any living creature, but be compassionate and gentle; show good will to all. Put others first and yourself last. All these, Arjuna, will reveal your real nature, which is divine.

Some time ago I was reminded of this chapter when I picked up the morning paper and exclaimed to Christine, "This layout artist must have been reading the Gita!" There, facing each other on inside pages, were stories illustrating the two paths between which the Gita says each of us has to choose continually: an upward path that leads to abiding joy, a downward path that leads to increasing sorrow.

The left-hand page was an interview with a man offering advice on how to come out "on top" in the economic, social, and ecological disaster that he says is sure to come. Without reading more than the opening sentence, I knew which path he represented and where it had to lead. Because of its very premise – how to grab, not how to give – the advice he offers cannot lead anywhere but down.

He started with some grim forecasts: an economic collapse, acute food and energy shortages, rioting and pillage in the cities until production could be restored. Against the backdrop of ecological hazards and the likelihood of nuclear war, it did not make an attractive picture of the future – particularly, I thought, if you went on to follow his advice about how to face all these calamities. By the time I finished, I felt I was back in the Stone Age, defending myself with rocks against neighbors who wanted to steal my spark plugs and cans of tomato soup.

It was a great relief to look on to the next page and find it entirely devoted to the upward path, the way of love. The layout was dominated by photographs and eyewitness accounts of the arrival in Oslo of Mother Teresa of Calcutta, come to receive the Nobel Prize for peace. To me this was one of the most promising events of the year. As you know, the prize doesn't often go to a real peacemaker, and here it was being presented to someone who had never addressed herself to war directly but had simply gone about trying to help the poor. There was a charming photo of her with the children of Oslo, presenting her with a gift that must have meant more to her than the one she had come to collect: a "Poor People's Nobel Prize" of money collected from grassroots supporters. And there were stories about her childhood, her work, and her reception in Oslo, where she won my heart by asking the Nobel Committee to forgo the usual banquet in her honor and give the money to the poor instead.

Mother Teresa is one of those beacon figures who represent what the Gita calls here "the path that leads to the divine." Her life provides a very personal illustration of how the qualities in these verses gradually purify personality, allowing the divinity within us to shine through.

Mother Teresa was not born in India but in Yugoslavia. She went to India at the age of eighteen as a missionary, and took her vows as Sister Agnes to become a teacher in a girls' school in Calcutta. She must have been an excellent teacher; even now she confesses, "I love teaching most of all." If she had continued in that profession, doing what she loved, the world would rightly have considered her a success.

Instead something happened to change her life completely. At the age of about thirty-five, I believe – well into her vocation – she was traveling northward to Darjeeling, seven thousand feet above sea level in the Himālayas. The route passes through some of the most spectacular scenery in the world, vistas of such beauty that the cities and problems of humanity seem as distant as a dream. But for Sister Agnes, a bomb burst in consciousness that must have been ticking away for more than a decade. "In that train," she recalls simply, "I heard the call to give up all and follow Him into the slums to serve Him among the poorest of the poor."

Calcutta in those days was "the second city of the British Empire," an enclave of British power and a center of Indian culture. St. Mary's School for Girls was a tranquil, well-kept, secluded place, with beautiful gardens and bright, responsive students from the aristocratic families of Bengal. Leaving her school, Mother Teresa has said, was harder even than leaving her home. St. Mary's must have held for her the fulfillment of most human desires: beauty, companionship, comfort, security, the rewarding awareness of success in a selfless profession. She left it all without hesitation to join the homeless who lived in the streets and slums outside the school walls – with one rough, white cotton habit draped like a sari, a few rupees, and no plan but to follow her call. It was not an impulsive act; she was careful first to get some training in medical care. For the rest, however, she proceeded just as St. Francis had at a similar stage in his life: step by step, by helping the first person she encountered, then the next, then the next.

Today, like Francis, Mother Teresa has an order of spiritual descendents that ministers to the poor and dispossessed around the globe. Millions, I feel sure, revere her as a saint. Yet to me, what is most memorable in her story is that like the rest of us, she was not born a saint. Step by step, over decades, by making selfless choices that any man or woman can make, she ascended what the Gita calls the bright path that leads toward divinity. We do not start life with virtues perfected; no one does. We simply do our best to practice them, and as we practice they get stronger.

There were portrait photos on each of these two pages: one of the doomsday counselor, the other of Mother Teresa. The first showed a solid, honest man in his forties, confident, energetic, and self-reliant. You could see from the look in his eyes and the set of his jaw that he was sure of his ability to take care of himself and his family come what may. I guessed that he set high standards for himself, and expected others to measure up to them too. It was difficult to imagine him defending spark plugs against marauding neighbors. Yet if I were a gambler, I would bet any odds that at least in the physical sense, this man and his family would survive the future whatever it brought. He would pay the cost without even being aware of how high a price this kind of survival exacts.

How different to look at Mother Teresa's face, shining from the opposite page! Small, frail-looking, but suffused with vitality, she wore her body as casually as she wore that white cotton sari; like Gandhi, she scarcely seemed aware of it. And in every photograph – with children in Oslo, with dignitaries, with the poor again in Calcutta – you could see how her smile and her deep, dancing eyes lit the faces of those around her. She would not survive whatever the future might bring; she would thrive. The more life tried to take, the more she would give. No one seeing her would ever question if she were happy. From their faces you could see where each path leads.

दम्भो दर्पो ऽतिमानश्च क्रोधः पारुष्यमेव च ।
अज्ञानं चाभिजातस्य पार्थ संपदमासुरीम् ॥ १६-४ ॥

4. Other qualities, Arjuna, make a person more and more inhuman: hypocrisy, arrogance, conceit, anger, cruelty, ignorance of the unity of life.

I wish I could go on about Mother Teresa, but it is Sri Krishna's unpleasant duty in this chapter to show Arjuna the dark alternative. It is a grim picture, but sooner or later every spiritual teacher finds it necessary to say clearly what will happen if the teachings of the scriptures are not followed. It puts life in proper perspective for us and gives us motivation.

In Sanskrit the two paths of this chapter are named after the states of consciousness to which they lead. *Daivī,* 'divine,' comes from the word *deva,* which literally means a god. The root sense implies something shining, effulgent, full of light. And *āsurī* comes from *asura,* which means a demon. In Hindu mythology the devas are the forces of light; the asuras, their perpetual enemies, are the forces of darkness. These forces interplay throughout history, and from time to time, when the powers of darkness become so strong that they threaten to overwhelm the earth with suffering, the Lord is born as a savior to rally the powers of goodness and restore dharma, the unity of life. In the *Mahābhārata* he has come as Sri Krishna, and we should picture him now speaking these words to Arjuna as they stand by their chariot between the vast armies of light and darkness, waiting for the outbreak of war on the Armageddon of their world.

This is history from a spiritual perspective, and it is not at all inaccurate. Yet at the same time, we should keep reminding ourselves that these are essentially forces within each of us. Self-will does wreak havoc on a global scale, but every disaster we face today – war, violence, starvation, cruelty, terrorism, ecological suicide – has not only been "born in the minds of men" but fostered there, nurtured, and unleashed in the world.

By folk etymology the devas are also called *suras*, as if *asura* meant 'not sura' the way *ahimsā* means 'nonviolence'. Scholars may not agree with the derivation, but it makes a practical point: without what is *sura,* divine, what is left is demonic. If you want to make yourself into a demon, you don't have to take a correspondence course or buy expensive paraphernalia. All you have to do is never do what a deva does. You won't achieve success overnight, of course. To become a real king of demons, you have to allow your personality to deteriorate for a long period of time. It happens so slowly, so naturally, that you may not notice the change from day to day. But as old Mad Nārāyana used to show us, it's as easy as rolling downhill. Before you know it, you're at the bottom.

In the previous verse Sri Krishna listed many qualities that make personality more divine. Imagine that you had a roommate who never practiced any of these: not somebody evil, but simply a person who always took the course of least resistance. He would have no control over his thoughts, words, acts, or passions, but would be vacillating and self-centered twenty-four hours a day. He would never tell the truth, and he would have an awful capacity to hold a grudge. He would be anxious, arrogant, lazy, greedy, and bad-tempered. You would say, "Not exactly heaven!" That is what "demonic" means.

No one, I would venture to say, is born an out-and-out, incorrigible demon. Because the Ātman is present in each of us, each has the innate capacity to make choices that benefit others instead of only ourselves. Personality is a process: we make ourselves more and more demonic, or more and more divine, with our own thoughts, words, and actions. Very simply, the qualities Sri Krishna lists here are moods and attitudes that worsen us. Almost everybody suffers from them at some time or other. But if we indulge them and go on indulging them, we deteriorate – physically, emotionally, and spiritually.

Self-will is the proper name of this affliction, and it is worse than any of the killing and crippling diseases we know of today because it brings distress not only to us but to everybody around us. The main reason we cannot see it as a disease is that there is such a lapse in time between cause and effect. The course the Black Plague took was clear enough; a person might cough two or three times in the morning and be dead by the next day. But in the case of self-will, you cough and think it's just pollen in the air. The adverse effects are too subtle to be recognized, too apparently unrelated, too far down the line of cause and effect.

Even physical ailments can be like this: a person exposed to radiation may not show signs of cancer for twenty or thirty years. Similarly, we may notice that our relationships are growing rocky, or that we can't find a job we like, or that our allergies are worse or our blood pressure dangerously high, without ever suspecting that all these can be traced to inflated self-will. We watch our neighbors arm themselves in fear, read in the papers about the breakdown of the family, suffer through erratic cycles of inflation and recession, bleed the economy bankrupt amassing weapons we can never afford to use, and send our children into war without ever reflecting that all these happen because of self-will raging on a national, even global scale. It spreads like the most virulent disease. Unless it is fought, selfishness deepens in us, spreads, reinforces selfishness in others. We support it with the votes we cast (or do not cast), the purchases and investments we make, the silent consent we give to the operations of our governments and businesses and institutions.

Let's look again at the doomsday advisor I mentioned. How could the path he had chosen lead anywhere but down? Once we accept the idea that what is most important is to look out for ourselves, the rest follows so naturally that we scarcely notice where it leads.

He began very reasonably. Since food shortages are almost certain, he advised, "stock up as much food as you can. If your cellar or attic will hold it, a twelve-month supply is not too much." This made sense enough from his perspective. But I couldn't help thinking how different my own response would be, drawing on the examples of my granny and Mahatma Gandhi. If I were told that food was going to be in short supply, my first thought would be, "What can I do without that I don't need? Is there anything that I would actually benefit from giving up?" Most of us, according to nutritionists, would thrive if we ate less. Not only that, in terms of our national health, millions of dollars could be saved in medical bills. It amazed me to see this man talking about stockpiling cigarettes, beer, wine, or your favorite candy bars – let alone, if worst came to worst, actually sitting around and enjoying such things while hungry neighbors roamed in search of food.

My second thought would be, "How much food can I grow myself?" You can see my granny's emphasis: always on self-reliance and turning obstacles into opportunities. Why go to the supermarket and spend your remaining currency on cans and packages of the same old stuff, just because it has a shelf life of twenty-four months? You can grow your own vegetables and even a number of fruits in many interesting places besides back yards and front lawns. Containers can go anywhere there is some sun: in patios, on doorsteps and rooftops, in windowsills and window boxes, suspended from eaves. Community vegetable gardens are blooming now in formerly vacant city lots. These are appealing, strengthening, sattvic solutions. Instead of subtracting from the food supply, they add to it. Instead of aggravating adversity, they actually improve the quality of life.

The next suggestion for survival follows from the first. Start hoarding other physical necessities: automobile parts, soap, razor blades, deodorant, paper towels, anything you do not want to do without. If you believe that life is not worth living without paper towels or that you can't be happy without a car, this too is reasonable advice. Once you have achieved a lifestyle you like, perhaps anything is worse than changing it. On the other hand, we should look at the price. The consequences *may* be worse after all; and as far as answers to deprivation go, our lives might benefit from simplification.

Third, this expert advises, buy gold. Buy silver. No matter what happens to the economy, he reasons, you should always be able to get enough canned vegetables and spark plugs for a Krugerrand. A good part of your savings should be in bullion, perhaps even in a foreign bank; but you should also keep a bag or so of silver dollars and a number of small gold coins for emergency spending, preferably hidden somewhere that no one else in your family knows about. It is not that you should mistrust your partner, but the less everyone knows, the safer your treasure is – and, he adds, the better everybody else will sleep.

Of course, it would not be prudent to invest everything you own in precious metals. So this chap advises diversifying somewhat. For one, he says, you should "own real wealth": that is, material goods. Even gold and silver are substitutes, he points out. "Wealth" is *things*, items that you can either use yourself or barter. The idea is simple: as much as possible, convert all your paper assets to material ones. So when you go out to purchase a year's supply of paper towels, you can add to your shopping list an imaginative selection of products you think you and your neighbors are likely to value most in an emergency. His suggestions were revealing: lumber, tools, candy bars, soft drinks, toilet paper . . . "Why," he demands, "should you be forced to abandon your chosen lifestyle just because your government can't pay its bills?"

The other alternative took me completely by surprise. "A reasonable portion of your assets," he said, "should be in things of lasting value – in the timeless treasures that have held their worth through decades, even centuries, of boom and bust, war and peace, depression and prosperity." "Ah," I thought to myself; "he is finally getting to spiritual values." I read on in increasing disbelief: "For example, great masters. Antiques. Collector's coins. Stamps. Comic books. Things that only go up in price because enough people always want them."

Then came the inevitable last step. Doesn't Jesus say, "Where your treasure is, there your heart is also"? It is not enough to stock up on the material "necessities" of your chosen lifestyle and all the things required to support it. You should be prepared to defend it – yourself, your family, your food, your gold, your auto parts – against anyone who might come seeking help or shelter. Without any wrong intentions, without any desire for animosity, that is where the path has to lead. "I don't want war," Bismarck is said to have remarked. "I just want victory." We say, "I just want to get what I want."

Sri Krishna will show all this to Arjuna – all the consequences, from individual to global, of a life based on self-seeking. "If that is the kind of life you want to lead," he will say, "no one can stop you. But don't talk about love; this way leads to hatred. Don't talk about peace; this way only leads to violence and war." And Arjuna will shake his head and say simply, "I don't want it."

दैवी संपद्विमोक्षाय निबन्धायासुरी मता ।
मा शुचः संपदं दैवीमभिजातो ऽसि पाण्डव ॥ १६-५ ॥

5. The divine qualities lead to freedom; the demonic, to bondage. But do not grieve, Arjuna; you were born with divine attributes.

My doomsday expert liked to think of himself as a self-reliant, self-made man. Among personal values, one of his highest was freedom. How surprised he would be, I thought, if he could hear the Gita's evaluation. Sri Krishna would not call such a person free at all. "You're a slave to your desires," he would explain. "You can't change when circumstances demand it; all you can do is hang on tighter." After all, what could be less free than feeling compelled to shoot another human being because you think he is after your canned goods and gold coins?

In fairness, Sri Krishna would add, very few of us can call ourselves free. Our responses are conditioned; we don't really have that much say in what we do. By contrast, it is easy to see how Mother Teresa radiates freedom. Whatever life brings her, she is always free to give.

What is important here is the mental state, for that is what colors our actions. It is very likely, for example, that our financial friend will never shoot anyone. He says sincerely that he never wants to. Yet the fact that he is willing to recommend it tells us something about the mental state behind everything else he does and recommends. The mental state is the seed; the fruit, Sri Krishna says, is bondage – bondage to the consequences of our values.

In the mid-seventies, after acute famine had flared up in many parts of the world, a prominent California biologist showed us the global version of this protect-your-gold-and-spark-plugs mentality. The term he used, *triage,* originated in the trenches of World War I, when medical personnel had to sort the wounded into categories so that they could decide whom to help first. One category was those who did not require immediate attention. They could hold on until the medics had taken care of soldiers in the second category: those who would probably live if given immediate care, but who otherwise would die. And the last was those who would probably die anyway, though perhaps later, even if they received first aid. The medics had to decide, "These people are going to die, and nothing can be done about it. All we can do is not listen to their cries, turn our eyes away, and hope that they die quickly."

Triage is still a part of military and emergency vocabulary; you see it in articles on "surviving" a nuclear war. But in the seventies it became fashionable in some circles to use the term in a new context: as a way of allocating food in times of famine. The argument was that there are certain countries facing famine which may be able to "pull out of it" and be of service to us later for political, economic, or military reasons. To those countries it makes sense to give food aid. But there are also countries that we decide are hopeless, not capable of solving their own problems; these we should allow to starve.

Perhaps because he is a biologist, this man takes a singularly biological view of the poor. Often, he says, they show so little self-restraint that they overreach the capacity of the land to sustain them. Then they run out of food. Countries with many such people, he says, are "basket cases" – another terrible term from war. For such countries we need an "adjusted ethics of survival dominated by unsqueamish self-interest" – a very interesting assemblage of words, for which I think you could find a good, blunt Anglo-Saxon translation. The term he coined is "lifeboat ethics." The rich nations, he says, are like lifeboats. Prosperous peoples in the developed countries look around from these lifeboats and see people from poorer nations drowning, calling out for help. If we keep taking all these people in, he says, our boat will sink. Therefore it is best for us as well as for them if they drown as quickly as they can; otherwise everybody will die.

A good student of logic should have no trouble in reducing this argument to pieces, beginning with the central metaphor. But it is not really a logical argument. It expresses an attitude, a mental state of fear and possessiveness very much like that of our survivalist friend: "I've got what I want, I deserve it, and nobody's going to take it away from me." The only way to dissuade people from this point of view is to allay their fears on the one hand and to open their sensitivity on the other. For the first, some facts and observations can help.

In their excellent and hopeful book *Food First,* Frances Moore Lappé and Joseph Collins quote from *Road to Survival,* in which one William Vogt wrote about a populous Asian country that it "quite literally cannot feed more people." He predicted, "Millions are going to die. There can be no way out. These men and women, boys and girls, must starve as tragic sacrifices, on the twin altars of uncontrolled reproduction and uncontrolled abuse of the land and resources." Most of us have heard similar words about many countries in Asia, Africa, and Latin America. They must be true, we feel. The graphs show population soaring, and we know food supply is limited by the amount of land.

Yet Mr. Vogt's words, so obviously true, were written about China in 1948. I am not at all advocating that any nation follow the Chinese example, but it does show how misleading it can be to pronounce a country hopeless and then turn away to allow its people to die.

In Mr. Vogt's day, when someone wanted to talk about basket case nations, nine times out of ten it was China and India that came up first. Today it is often Bangladesh, one of the areas of South Asia that was longest under colonial rule. Yet a report to Congress stated that Bangladesh is rich enough in agricultural resources "not only to be self-sufficient in food, but a food exporter, even with its rapidly increasing population size." Lappé and Collins go so far as to say that no country they investigated is a basket case; every country has the capacity to feed itself.

Agricultural experts say this planet can produce enough food without any kind of agricultural miracle. Put simply, the problems are not physical or geographic but economic. Food raised by the poor in poor countries is predominantly raised for and sold to rich countries, which can pay much higher prices for it. But the profits go to landowners and middlemen. The poor stay poor, and they have to buy their food at prices bid up beyond their reach by the demand of the world's well-to-do. This is a profitable arrangement for middlemen, but it guarantees poverty for the poor around the world. Those who can buy, eat; those who cannot buy, starve.

The main reason why there is starvation in parts of Asia, Africa, and South America is that these places have been reduced to poverty by centuries of exploitation. The material resources and labor of these continents produced a good deal of the prosperity that "developed" many of the developed nations, as any close student of history can testify. It is largely because of this kind of exploitation that one-sixth of the world lives in affluence while five-sixths are poor. If the United States has a lot of food at its end of the lifeboat, we should remember that much of it was raised by those we see appealing for help in the sea around us.

"Lifeboat ethics" has been called "deathboat ethics." Perhaps more to the point, someone has remarked that instead of a lifeboat, this biologist is talking about a luxury liner. In any case, the whole earth is a kind of lifeboat: "Spaceship Earth."

Here, I think, the metaphor becomes a little embarrassing to the developed nations. If, to simplify the picture, we say there are a hundred people on this lifeboat – representing all the peoples of the earth – then twenty seated at the stern have five-sixths of the provisions. To make the picture worse, a good deal of this has been taken from the eighty men, women, and children who remain. The "haves" complain that there are too many poor to feed; and by continuing to take what they want from the stores, they are ensuring that anyone "extra" is pushed out into the sea. The world's poor haven't jumped out of the boat. They have been conquered, colonized, and bled of their mineral wealth and their labor, and in many ways they are still being so treated today. The least we in the developed nations can do is help them back into the boat.

I am not saying that food aid will solve these problems, or that it is a solution for the developed nations to feed the rest of the world. In fact, I believe it is essential – and quite possible – for every nation to develop the capacity to feed itself. But I *am* saying that when people are starving, you share what you have; that is a simple matter of love.

Some months ago I saw a very moving performance of *The Diary of Anne Frank*, done by the Berkeley Repertory Theater. Towards the end, Anne and her family, her father's friend's family, and an utter stranger have been hiding together in a garret for well over a year, in constant fear of being discovered by the Nazis. Food has become terribly difficult to get, and the refugees in the garret are dependent on what can be smuggled in. After months of getting by like this, they discover that it is not rats that have been gnawing at their meagre stores; Mr. Frank's friend has been stealing food for himself while the others sleep. No one is more shocked and repelled than Mrs. Frank. "You've been stealing from the *children*," she cries, "while you could hear your own son crying in his sleep from hunger!" When the children are our own, or in our own house, most of us find it easy to identify with them. Would we ignore them if we could not see their faces or hear their cries?

By contrast, I read a story the other day from Mother Teresa that moved me deeply – partly because it comes from Calcutta, where the differences between Hindus and Muslims have been exploited to the point of terrible violence. "Some weeks back," Mother Teresa says,

> I heard there was a family who had not eaten for some days – a Hindu family – so I took some rice and I went to the family. Before I knew where I was, the mother of the family had divided the rice into two, and she took the other half to the next-door neighbors, who happened to be a Muslim family. Then I asked her: "How much will all of you have to share? There are ten of you with that bit of rice." The mother replied: "They have not eaten either."

I began by talking about freedom. Who shall we say is free, the woman who gives like this or the man who feels so terribly compelled to take? Behind all the sophisticated language of "lifeboat ethics" are the same primitive feelings that make for bondage: insecurity, possessiveness, fear.

You can see the same lack of freedom on an international scale in the web of dependencies that bind the rich and powerful nations to the small. The rich and powerful find it humiliating to discover this, and sometimes they resort to violence to "show who is boss." But the fact remains. United States foreign policy, for example, is not made in freedom. It could be debated how much freedom the most powerful nation on earth actually has. Our policy decisions are usually reflexes, determined by what some other country does. Because of our dependence on certain minerals and the strategic balance of power, we have felt compelled to prop up illegitimate, repressive regimes, sometimes to the cost of billions of dollars and thousands of lives in war. Presidents and other leaders have repeatedly declared their willingness to go to war with some vastly weaker nation on the other side of the world to ensure that we keep getting "our" oil. And it is not only oil: many strategic minerals are supplied primarily by small, undemocratically governed nations whose leaders can dictate their terms to the industrialized giants. Our national response is the same as for doomsday: buy and hoard, and be prepared to go to war if necessary to keep the stockpiles from being used.

This is the kind of world that self-interest leads to – the only kind of world self-interest *can* lead to. The virus, Sri Krishna warns, is in all of us. Unless it is resisted, self-will can so invade the personality that an apparently good person – or nation – becomes an instrument of suffering for many others.

द्वौ भूतसर्गौ लोकेऽस्मिन्दैव आसुर एव च ।
दैवो विस्तरशः प्रोक्त आसुरं पार्थ मे शृणु ॥ १६-६ ॥

6. Some people have divine tendencies, others demonic. I have described the divine at length, Arjuna; now listen while I describe the demonic.

Almost every day, a physician friend tells me, she sees a patient who smokes. "I have to tell them they're bucking the odds," she says. "The scientific consensus is that smoking kills more than a third of a million Americans every year. But people can't identify with statistics. They just say, 'I know that, doc. But I've tried to quit and I can't.'"

"What do you say then?" I asked.

"It depends on the person. I never try to scare anybody. But if they have some imagination, and especially if they are still young, I try to bridge the gap in time that they can't bridge. I want them to look thirty years down the road and give the future a fair chance.

"When I see them, they're in their twenties or thirties. They're still active, nothing but a little cough; they think they'll feel like that forever. I try to help them feel what it's like to wheeze with every breath. I describe the panic that comes when you just can't get enough oxygen. I show them what happens inside their lungs and blood vessels. I try to turn the statistics into something real. Then I say, 'At the roulette table, you at least get to see what you stand to win or lose. Don't you want to see what you're gambling against here? If you lose, you get emphysema, lung disease, or stroke. If you win, you get a pack of cigarettes a day. Now you choose.'"

When we persist in a wrong course of action, a good physician has to tell us the consequences. She knows the laws of physiology, and she has seen perhaps hundreds of cases like ours. She may not be able to predict with total accuracy – there are many imponderables – but she knows vividly the sequence of cause and effect in the human body. To us it is only a vague possibility. But to her it is so real that if she sees a disease in its early stages, she already sees its end.

In the same way Sri Krishna, noting the signs and symptoms of our times, has to describe what will be the outcome if we do not change our ways. It is not too late to turn back. But the mental states of fatal illness – greed, separateness, and anger – are present in our times, and unless they are eradicated, their consequences are inexorable. Here the theme of karma that runs through this volume finds its most explicit statement. We need not dwell on it, but at the same time we need to know what selfish thinking has to lead to if it goes unchecked, no matter how pleasant or harmless it may seem at first.

प्रवृत्तिं च निवृत्तिं च जना न विदुरासुराः ।
न शौचं नापि चाचारो न सत्यं तेषु विद्यते ॥ १६-७ ॥
असत्यमप्रतिष्ठं ते जगदाहुरनीश्वरम् ।
अपरस्परसंभूतं किमन्यत्कामहैतुकम् ॥ १६-८ ॥

एतां दृष्टिमवष्टभ्य नष्टात्मानो ऽल्पबुद्धयः ।
प्रभवन्त्युग्रकर्माणः क्षयाय जगतो ऽहिताः ॥ १६-९ ॥

7. The demonic do things they should avoid
and avoid the things they should do. They have
no sense of uprightness, purity, or truth.
8. "There is no God," they say, "no truth,
no spiritual law, no moral order. The basis
of life is sex; what else can it be?"
9. Holding such distorted views, possessing scant
discrimination, they become enemies of the
world, causing suffering and destruction.

"There is no God, no truth, no moral order; the basis of life is sex." The words sound so contemporary that it is hard to believe these are opinions expressed thousands of years ago. You could go to the newsstand of any supermarket and find the same argument repeated over and over. It says simply that there is no unity in life, no underlying order, nothing but the events that we can apprehend through the five senses: in short, nothing to life but the physical level.

Once someone is said to have complained to G. K. Chesterton, "The trouble today is that people don't have anything to believe in."

"Not quite," Chesterton replied. "The trouble is that because they have nothing to believe in, they'll believe in anything."

That is a very penetrating remark. How many of the problems we face as a society are the result of people just believing in anything that comes along? This is one of the characteristics of Tamas. If someone on television or in the popular magazines tells him "Do this; you'll like it," he will go out and do it, so long as everybody else is doing it and it doesn't require too much effort.

When you don't have a reference point to refer to, Sri Krishna says here, you do what you should not do and you don't do what you should. This is a classic definition of confusion. The capacity to know what should be done and what should not be done is called *viveka,* discrimination, and it is one of life's most precious secrets. My granny used to be fond of a Sanskrit proverb, which unfortunately we gave her numerous opportunities to quote: *Avivekam param āpadām padam,* "Lack of discrimination is the source of the greatest danger." When discrimination goes, there is no reason *not* to do anything. If you look around, you will see intelligent, educated, cultured people throwing their energy and resources into enterprises that help nobody – enterprises, as this verse says, that even end in widespread harm.

Here we find ourselves in an age of unprecedented technological development, yet much of our mastery over nature has gone to find ways to hide or postpone the natural consequences of doing what we want. As a result, it becomes easier and easier to believe there *are* no consequences. You can do what you like and never pay for it.

This is not merely an individual weakness. We may deprecate people who go on buying and buying on credit cards without ever asking the price, but from the point of view of ecology, for example, modern industry and agriculture are continually mortgaging the future to pay for the profits of the present. "Buy now and pay later" has become "Buy now and refinance later," so you never have to pay at all.

Yet there are consequences, even if the asuric mind manages to hide them from its view. You may buy whatever you like with your credit cards in March, but in April or May the bills start rolling in. You have to start paying something – at first perhaps just the finance charge, but sooner or later the principal. We can always try to circumvent physical consequences by more technology, but what we really ought to worry about, the Gita says, are the consequences for the mind.

I would like to write a story in which science had come up with pills that could eliminate the physical consequences of our behavior entirely, so that every day you could indulge yourself however you liked without any ill effects. You could eat as much as you liked and not gain an ounce. You could drink as much as you liked and never get sick or face another "morning after." You could party all night and still be fresh the next day. And so on; each of us can supply our own favorite details. Doesn't it sound wonderful?

The Gita would object, "It sounds horrible!" Even if nothing untoward took place on the physical level, what would happen to the will? Not many people value the will these days; it's slightly out of fashion. But imagine going through life with a will like limp spaghetti: you couldn't say no to anything. If a foot-high challenge came out from behind a bush, you would lie down and say, "I've got a headache. I can't go on." And you would be so insecure that if someone said anything critical, you might go to pieces or carry a grudge against that person for years. We don't usually see the connection with the will in such situations, but that is what willpower means: a mind that does what you say.

Now we can trace the thread running through these verses. When you can't say no to anything, as this verse says, you end up "doing things that you ought to avoid and avoiding things that you ought to do" – eventually, though it pains me to say it, "without any sense of uprightness, purity, or truth."

Sex makes a good example here, not only because it is emphasized in the verses but because it is such a popular focus for our attention. "The basis of life is sex," the asuric mind proclaims. "What else can it be?" Most people might not agree so openly, but how do we live? What do we value most, to judge from our magazines, our movies, our books, our songs, our advertisements, our choice of words, our idea of a "good time"?

I dislike being a wet blanket, but the long-term consequences of this trend are ghastly. Rajas looks at sex and finds it grand. Naturally he proceeds to do with it what he tries to do with everything: maximize it. "If a little is the greatest thing on earth," he reasons, "more must be better."

But the corollary of "More is better" is "Anything goes." Once you accept the premise that life is physical, there is no basis for judgment. There is no one to explain that the real damage is done to the mind. Children who are continually exposed to sex in the media are particularly susceptible. By the time they reach adolescence, their minds and senses are going to be completely out of control; they will be at life's mercy before their adult lives have truly begun. Their minds will be full of anger and frustration, and putting themselves first will have become a constant, conditioned habit. What will support them during the fierce buffeting of the teenage years? What will they have to build a lasting relationship on? Even setting aside the questions of love and loyalty, they won't have the will to face any kind of challenge. Life treats such people mercilessly. No parents want this for their children; it is just the opposite of love.

I am not talking about right or wrong now; but simply in medical terms, look at where all this leads. What is at stake is prāna, which is life itself. In younger years we are allotted enough prāna to experiment with pleasure and discover what it can deliver; but we are expected to learn, not to go on performing the same old experiment over and over and over. For overindulgence drains prāna, and prāna is the very energy of life. Loss of sexual capacity in later years may be the body's compassionate way of saying, "Let's start to conserve! I'm running low on gas."

It grieves me deeply to read that patients recovering from serious ailments – especially those who are older – are sometimes given hormones or other drugs to whip an exhausted body into action to satisfy the mind's desires. That is just the opposite of therapy. The body needs rest so that all available prāna can be marshalled in the processes of healing. Instead, the pleasure centers open the prāna petcocks and drain the day's tank almost dry. From the body's point of view, it seems so unfair: the mind demands the pleasure, but the body pays all the bills.

The other day I saw some of our āshram children playing in the sandbox with their toys: a couple of dump trucks, some blocks and wooden animals, a few big spoons and cans for digging. "They can go on like that forever," one of the mothers told me happily. "From one fantasy to another to another." That is fine for toddlers – but even then, not forever. Imagine their parents playing there instead! Two computer experts, a professor, and a physician, pushing sand around with old tin cans and bursting into tears when one person's road construction project destroys another's farm. There is a time for toys, the mystics say, and a time to grow up. From this perspective, nothing is more tragic than to see men and women in the last stages of their lives doing everything they can to become like teenagers again.

In a sense even this is not an end; for though the body dies, the samskāras of desire carry over to our next life. I still remember vividly a friend in the twilight of his life recalling his teenage years and saying plaintively, "How I wish I could live through all those experiences again!" I don't think I have ever felt a deeper stab of sorrow; for these last deep desires sum up our lives. That wish was like getting through second grade and then saying at the end, "That was fun! I'm going to go back and do it all again."

"Life is not worth living without pleasure." The logic is relentless: when your very capacity for sensory pleasure runs out, why go on living? What does life hold? Some years ago I remember reading that a distinguished philosopher and his wife swallowed overdoses of sleeping pills in order to avoid the prospect of a "useless old age." The assumption is that life is physical; we are the body. Old age is "useless" only if you are living for yourself, in which case any age could be called useless. If you live for giving, you can go on making a vital contribution to the rest of life right up to your last day in this body. Even if you are confined to a wheelchair, you will be able to inspire, support, and strengthen many people who come in contact with you.

काममाश्रित्य दुष्पूरं दम्भमानमदान्विताः ।
मोहाद्गृहीत्वासद्ग्राहान्प्रवर्तन्ते ऽशुचिव्रताः ॥१६-१०॥

10. Hypocritical, proud, and arrogant,
living in delusion and clinging to deluded
ideas, insatiable in their desires, they pursue
unhesitatingly their own selfish ends.

The other day I saw a book on economics with an intriguing title: *Greed Is Not Enough*. This is true of most demonic activities also. Asuric Enterprises, as we might call it, is a joint venture of two partners. Rajas, "Mr. Greed," is the senior, but Tamas is almost as important. His role is generally to be insensitive, but he also knows how to vacillate, postpone, prevaricate, refuse to change his mind, and simply do nothing when necessary, all of which provides Rajas with the support he needs to do his work. Rajas doesn't understand this; he likes to think of himself as independent. But if he were capable of some self-knowledge, he would see that he is utterly dependent on Tamas for support.

Tamas clings to the status quo; he doesn't like to "make waves." But Rajas thrives on crisis. Where times are turbulent or technology is in flux, he knows there are markets to be cornered, power to consolidate, profits to be made. In fairness, this is not simply a matter of greed. Rajas just likes to keep busy. He can't possibly sit still when opportunity is knocking, even if he is already juggling more opportunities than he can handle. His style is to keep moving, even if he isn't sure where he is going, while Tamas sits in back and writes memos to cover his tracks.

Thoreau, I think, had a good remark to make on this subject. "It's not enough if you are busy," he said. "The question is, What are you busy about?" This is a terribly practical question. You may remember my quoting a Sanskrit proverb that was often on my granny's lips: "Lack of discrimination is the source of the greatest danger." I don't think this is exaggeration at all. If you look around, you will see that most of the dangers that threaten us today are not the result of wickedness. I would say they are the result of intelligent, educated, well-intentioned men and women running as fast as they can after what they want, never caring to slow down, look around, and ask where they are going.

Rajas has a good reason for this: if you stop to look around, he would say, you may not like what you see. Worse, you may try to reason, by which time the opportunity – whatever it is – will have passed. If problems arise, Asuric Enterprises has two ways of dealing with them: Rajas likes to push them aside and keep on going; Tamas prefers to ignore them and hope they will go away.

I can give you one example that is highly relevant today: the way we pursued nuclear power. This is what you might call a national obsession: a very large number of individuals compulsively caught in the same idea. It illustrates very well the power of a particular mental state – part rajasic, part tamasic – to acquire a life of its own, regardless of facts or circumstances.

In the forties and fifties, crowning a century of breakthroughs, nuclear technology must have looked like the grandest of them all. It offered two heady promises: unlimited energy and perpetual peace.

The very idea raised Rajas to poetic heights. "For the first time in history," he liked to say, "man has released power that did not come from the sun!" Perhaps – Rajas tends to get easily inebriated by breakthroughs – perhaps soon we wouldn't even *need* the sun. We knew how to grow vegetables in water with the help of lights; we were making "food" out of chemical constituents and planning space colonies with their own water and air. Now that we could turn matter into energy, what could we not do? "In a decade or so," Rajas proclaimed proudly, "energy will be so cheap that you'll have to give it away."

The other promise was the Bomb. The irony was fascinating: here was the most terrible weapon ever discovered, and just because it was so terrible it could be the instrument of world peace! It was a military dream come true, the secret weapon that nobody else seemed likely to get. In our enemies' hands it could hold the world hostage; in ours, it could enforce peace and democratic principles around the globe.

This was a package too good to pass up, and as this verse suggests, we bought it without hesitating – that is, without ever asking about the consequences. We knew virtually nothing about atomic energy except that its potential for energy release – constructive or destructive – was staggering beyond imagination. Many nuclear scientists say they felt like the Sorcerer's Apprentice, letting loose unknown, supernormal forces without any hope of turning back. Sheer common sense would object, "Let's go slowly and be sure where we are going." Yet from the first, Asuric Enterprises scarcely questioned anything. It was obsessed by a Big Idea.

In my high school physics class, I remember our teacher explaining about inertia. "It doesn't just mean sitting and doing nothing," our teacher said. "A body at rest tends to remain at rest and a body in motion tends to remain in motion, unless acted on by some outside force." As an illustration he might have used the rock that Mad Nārāyana used to roll down the hill outside our village, which had tremendous inertia. You could deflect it only at great risk, and you could stop it only by absorbing all that energy, which usually meant a crash.

Ideas are similar. I like to say that thoughts are things – in fact, in some ways, they are more "thingy" than material things. A rolling idea can have tremendous inertia. It is hard to stop, hard to deflect; often it even goes unquestioned. That is the power of tamas.

"We've got a tiger by the tail," Rajas liked to say about nuclear power. "We've *got* to go forward, whatever it costs." Without going into details, I want to look at some of those costs. Two or three I find particularly moving, for the karma of this Big Idea has led to widespread sorrow.

Here we encounter one of the truly dark corners in the asuric mind. By the time the Bomb was developed, Tamas was already on the stage. Even in wartime, a certain measure of insensitivity is required to destroy a city of civilians, but I do not want to dwell on that; the decision-makers must have felt they were saving thousands of American lives. What I find more astonishing, because the callousness is so calculated, is what happened after the war. Tamas is not very discriminating; his job is to be insensitive. He begins by being insensitive to enemy lives, but he quickly goes on to show the same insensitivity to those he is supposed to protect.

The first to experience this were U.S. soldiers, from whom I have been reading some moving personal accounts. Just forty-five days after Nagasaki was bombed, Marines and Seabees were sent in to clean up without any word about radiation hazards. "We didn't want to worry anybody," Rajas explained. "We had every reason to believe that after the fallout subsided, there was no danger from radioactivity." (The scientists who visited these areas must not have been told this, for they wore protective suits.) For weeks these men were billeted near ground zero, around which the wind must have strewn radioactive dust and particles for miles. They drank the same water as the survivors, ate locally grown food, breathed the same dust-laden air. Today, thirty years later, they are dying of the same kinds of cancer.

"I don't hold a grudge against my government for sending us in like that," one man said in effect. "They had their reasons for not telling us, and anyway I was a soldier; it was my job to take risks for my country. What makes me so bitter is that now that we are sick or dying, our country won't acknowledge any responsibility." The official position is the same today as it was then: "There was no danger from radiation in Hiroshima and Nagasaki after the first five days."

There is an important reason for this kind of prevarication, which is part of the mental state involved. In the official view, we had the Bomb and therefore had to use it; and that had certain implications too. Like it or not, we had to develop a nuclear arsenal. We had to prepare citizens to accept and deal with the possibility of nuclear attack. And we had to develop nuclear energy. Therefore, in asuric reasoning, it was "counterproductive" to question the Bomb and its consequences, whatever facts might come to light. To worry people or to admit how little we knew was dangerous. It might mean we could not proceed, and that would be playing into enemy hands – for although we were at peace, all this was pursued as a continuation of war.

The Bomb aside, there remains the complete lack of caution in how we pursued nuclear energy for utilities. It looked so wonderful then! "Makes itself," Rajas liked to say. "Breeds its own fuel. What more can you ask? Power too cheap to meter." Surely it is fair to ask by now, too cheap for whom? It is not cheap in human health; it is terrifyingly expensive. According to articles I saw some months ago in the *Wall Street Journal,* it is not even cheap in money. Fortunes have been poured into nuclear plants, though no doubt it could have cost much less if we hadn't begun to require safe construction. But even from the earliest days, nuclear power was so fraught with unknowns and potential hazards that no one would invest in it unless the government agreed to underwrite it; no insurance company would touch it.

Much more significant are the human costs. Another example is the uranium miners. Uranium is expensive, but fortunately it was discovered in the United States – on the supposedly worthless lands that had been given (if I may use that word) to Native American tribes when the rest of their lands were engulfed by the spread of Western civilization. I don't know if anyone was embarrassed to discover that something valuable had been given away. In any case, the Bureau of Indian Affairs – created ostensibly to protect Native American interests – persuaded them not only to lease their lands for uranium mining but to do the actual mining themselves. Nobody warned them about radioactivity; they might not have wanted to proceed with the deal.

A Public Health Service director has since called those mines "radiation chambers," with "one hundred times the levels of radioactivity allowed today." Millions of tons of exposed radioactive waste – "tailings" – have been piled near people's homes. "Much of the land where our people have lived for thousands of years," one Native American spokesman says, "is now poisoned by radioactivity – and will remain poisoned for many thousands of years." This applies not only to the water and air, but even to many homes made from local building materials.

Finally, in spite of the incredible ingenuity that has gone into nuclear power development – and it has drawn some of the best scientific and engineering talent in several countries – we still don't have the slightest idea of what to do with nuclear waste. To me that is like admitting that on a proposed trip from San Francisco to New York, we haven't yet left the garage.

Some months ago we had a big holiday dinner at our āshram, which meant several people working in the kitchen at once to prepare a gracious quantity of food. Suppose you showed up to help and were told, "Sorry, we don't have a garbage can. Why don't you put the garbage in the back seat of your car and figure out what to do with it later?" You say, "At least you can give me a plastic bag!" "We haven't got plastic bags," Laurel says, "but maybe you can fit it into these grocery bags. If you line them with waxed paper, they won't start to leak for three or four hours." Pretty soon, of course, they will fall apart. But why talk about such things now? You've got to get dinner on the table. Lug the garbage out, stuff it in the car, and enjoy your feast. Maybe you'll pass a dump on the way home. If not, well, half of it will decompose every twenty years . . . .

That is exactly what we have done about nuclear waste – except, of course, that we are talking not about messy potato peelings but about substances like plutonium, which is fatally toxic in microscopic amounts and has a half-life of twenty-five thousand years. We haven't the slightest idea of what to do with the stuff, and it is one of the most poisonous substances known. Yet we are so greedy to proceed with our wonderful new discoveries that we just bury what we can't deal with and hope we won't be around when it starts to poison the rivers and soil where our children's food is grown – or, worse, the oceans that sustain the world.

"Just do it," says Rajas, "and then we'll see. Technology will improve. If we can't come up with anything better, we can always toss it into outer space. A few hundred garbage cans of radioactive waste hurtling around in a billion billion cubic miles of nothingness, what can they harm?" It is not only lack of love and logic, it is such a fatal paralysis of imagination. We had the same idea about the oceans and air just a few decades ago, and now we are surprised when a school is closed because of poisonous air, or when we read that lead from industrial emissions is accumulating in the trenches of the deep ocean floor.

"Well, what do you know?" Rajas muses. "Who could have predicted things like that?" Perhaps no one, but we could at least learn from such unexpected outcomes that we live in a complex world in which there is no such thing as "out of sight, out of mind." There is already more radioactive waste than we can hide; it is leaking from its containers, poisoning livestock and people, and altering our genetic material, not to mention providing enough weapons-grade plutonium to put a nuclear weapon in the hands of every terrorist group and small-time dictator in the world; yet still we want our energy so badly that we keep on producing more of this stuff and talk about sending our garbage to Alpha Centauri. It makes one wonder. Cross the seas, fly in the air, burrow into the ground, the Buddha says; you will not be able to hide from the law of karma.

चिन्तामपरिमेयां च प्रलयान्तामुपाश्रिताः ।
कामोपभोगपरमा एतावदिति निश्चिताः ॥१६-११॥

11. Although burdened with fears that end only with death, they still maintain with complete assurance, "Gratification of lust is the highest that life can offer."

In Hindu psychology, the forces of self-will are often grouped under three big categories: lust, anger, and fear, all of which are closely related. These three are the source of most personal problems, for they are working away almost incessantly in the deeper regions of the mind.

I have written predominantly about lust and anger for what I might call first-aid reasons: these are the forces that cause the most direct damage to others, and they are rampant today. But here I would like to give due attention to fear, which this verse connects subtly to the lust for selfish satisfaction.

"Lust" here, I should point out, is not just sexual desire. It can be any kind of fierce craving for personal satisfaction. There is lust for money, of course, and lust for any kind of pleasure; sex is merely the most acute. Lust for power is one of the most furious of lusts. So here I will be talking about no particular passion, but simply lust in general.

I sometimes see recruitment posters that say, "The Marines are looking for a few good men." General Lust, by contrast, is not particular about who fills his army. Any obsessive, personal, self-centered desire can qualify. The recruitment application asks only one question: "Are you willing to let other people get in the way of your fulfillment?" If the answer is a resounding no, that desire is in.

General Lust is tough – at least, in his own eyes. He knows what he wants, and he gets what he goes after. He has tattoos on his arms, smokes cigarettes without filters, and wouldn't dream of letting some namby-pamby speed limit law keep him from driving the way he likes. I saw a book of jokes on the best-seller list the other day: *Real Men Don't Eat Quiche.* General Lust doesn't even want to know how "quiche" is pronounced. He would be furious if he understood what Sri Krishna is hinting in this verse: that in every selfish desire is hidden a corresponding fear. That is part of the karma of lust; and as usual with karma, it is not some separate punishment. If lust is one side of a coin, fear and anger are imprinted on the other side, inseparable.

Fear is a whole world of its own within the mind. Most of us never see this world with our conscious eye, though it prompts much of our waking thought and action. I think it is Carl Jung who says that in the depths of the unconscious of every human being lies the fear of death and dissolution – the fear that we may cease to exist as a separate, personal creature. This is the root of all other fears. In a sense, every human being lives in a world of fear of which we are not aware. That is our protection. If we were to become consciously aware of all the great fears that lurk in the unconscious, life would become impossible. It is a merciful amnesia that we do not remember these fears. We may not even suspect that they lurk within us, far below the threshold of consciousness. To an experienced eye, however, the signs are clear. Wherever people overreact in anger, or get agitated easily, or are excessively rigid when they cannot have their way, there is a good chance that fear is pulling the strings from deep within. Almost every kind of insecurity or anxiety fits the Gita's definition of fear.

In his *Century of Verses on Renunciation,* the great Indian poet Bhartrihari wrote a stanza of epigrams on fear. The first line sets the keynote: "In the pleasures of the senses lurks the fear of decay." The poet is playing off two rhyming words: *bhoga,* which means sensual enjoyment, and *roga,* one of the sights that impelled the Buddha to seek Self-realization: disease, decrepitude, dissolution, decay.

We need a good deal of detachment to understand the depth of Bhartrihari's statement. It can be taken at several levels, on each of which the consequences are subtler. The simplest is that of physical consequences, which the modern mind finds repellent and vaguely medieval: if you indulge in such and such a pleasure, you'll be punished for it. Today we do not believe in being punished, and many of the efforts of modern science have been to find ways to avoid the physical consequences of sensual indulgence.

Perhaps the most obvious example is overeating. All thinking people, though they may not put it into words, are aware that if they go on eating more than they need, they are going to put on weight. Today even corporation executives are mindful of this, for obesity is more than an aesthetic flaw; it is a health hazard. Too much body fat aggravates heart trouble, high blood pressure, diabetes, and other ailments, and in addition it adds to the risk of smoking – all of which doctors and the popular media are making widely known.

Wherever there is any understanding of this, overeating carries a slight but nagging fear. Even while you are eating your second helping of french fries or chocolate cake and thinking, "This is really good!" there is a little voice inside, barely audible, saying, "It's *not* so good. You're asking for trouble." We have learned to stifle this voice, even ignore it with a show of bravado. "Who cares? I'm not that fat, and I can still take it or leave it." Even so, the Gita says, we have planted another tiny seed of fear beneath the surface of consciousness: the fear that we have added a little more weight not only to the body, but to the unknown burdens of the future.

This is even more clear with addictive habits like smoking, drinking, and drugging. I have never deprecated people who are caught in these habits, because I know how easy it is to get caught. Today a boy or girl can be an alcoholic even before getting into high school. Many children smoke by then, and probably most have at least sampled drugs. There must be very few today who think these activities do not have dangerous consequences. They just don't care. Often they feel they have very little to live for, which is a tragic state. In any case they are young; they like to "live dangerously." Consequences are far down the road, and words like *cancer* and *emphysema* convey only vague conditions. Yet as many smokers have confided in me, the fear *is* there. Even while they are inhaling, a little part of their consciousness is thinking about cancer.

This kind of fear has a useful function. It can act as a brake, keeping us from overindulging our senses or getting caught in addictive habits, both of which drain prāna terribly. When you cannot see the connection between sensory pleasure and prāna, the Lord says, how can you be expected to act on it? So to try to keep us from wasting our prāna as fast as possible, life provides these fearful physical consequences, which anyone should be able to see.

In other words, if you are going to smoke, it is good not to be fearless about it. You can use that fear; you can capitalize on it, by drawing from it more will and more resolution. To be fearless about the risk of cancer, the Buddha would say, is not a sign of a strong character but the sign of a thick head. The Buddha was not one to mince words; some chapters of his Dhammapada are just as fierce as this chapter of the Gita.

Most of us, however, do not regard adverse physical consequences as a blessing. Here we are, trying to enjoy ourselves, and once we cross a certain line the pleasures start coming hand in hand with problems. The universal human response, the gift of rajas, is straightforward: find some way to get around the problems, so we can go on doing what we like. *Homo sapiens* has probably been doing this since the dawn of civilization, but it is only in the age of rajas, the age of science, that we developed the amazing technological capacity to suppress any physical consequence we choose.

Vast industries are built on this idea, which can be called the Free Lunch promise. "Every pleasure," it maintains, "can be safely indulged indefinitely. Adverse consequences are incidental. Being physical, they can be physically prevented, just like the causes of a disease. All that is necessary is to find the chemical or mechanical means." This was widely held and hailed when I arrived in this country, and it opened my eyes to technological progress. Why not eat too much when you can avoid stomachache and heartburn by dropping a couple of fizzing tablets into a glass of water? Why not have a few extra "meaningful relationships" when there's the Pill? Why be afraid of burning yourself out in pursuit of pleasure when you can get a new face for the price of a new car? "For every fear we have a cure": that is the motto of Asuric Labs.

Of course, Asuric has had its problems. The fizzing tablets don't keep you from getting fat, and that new face may cost you your health. And there is good evidence now that the Pill, which is used by millions of women in the world today, is a causal factor in thromboembolic diseases and, in some, heart attacks. The Gita would ask, How do you expect to get rid of consequences? It has never been done; it can never be done. If you block one effect, another will occur; if you block them both, you will get a third. As the Buddha says, nowhere in the universe can you hide from karma, for the simple reason that action and consequences are one.

Nonetheless, the search goes on. There is money in it, and if someone invents a better diet pill or contraceptive, the world will happily beat a path to his front door. As long as we can even hope for such a breakthrough, fear is held at bay.

Trying to avoid consequences like this reminds me of a scene I once saw at the beach, when our children were trying to dam a little river that flows through the dunes into the sea. They managed to block the channel, but the water wouldn't obey. It forced its way through the dam, and when those holes were plugged, it flowed over the top. When the children made the dam higher, the water burst around at the end.

That is how the law of karma works too. If the effects of an action are blocked in one direction, they have to find expression somewhere else. This is not a moral principle; it is simply cause and effect.

Rajas pursues consequence-blockers like a beaver racing against time. If an unwanted consequence bursts through here, he patches it; when another erupts over there, he patches that too. Like the Corps of Engineers, he believes perfection is just a patch away. If you suggest to him that it may not be possible to create a dam without adverse consequences, he would find the suggestion foolish, irresponsible, and vaguely immoral, as if you were pleading a case for evil.

Adverse consequences include physical illness, because body and mind are part of a whole. In every human being, there is a deep-seated sense of disquiet provoked when we ignore this fabric of responsibilities and think and act just for ourselves. We *know*, deep down, that we are not separate from the rest of life, but the primordial urges of the unconscious – the pleasure principle, the sex drive, the instinct for self-aggrandizement – pull us in a different direction. Freud is not wrong when he says we have stuffed these dark forces into the basement of consciousness and slammed the door tight. But repressed urges don't lie around meekly. They hold mass meetings, pass resolutions, go on strike, hold demonstrations that have to be suppressed with the mental equivalent of tear gas. This round-the-clock control is a constant drain of prāna. And since prāna is the energy for every function of life, low prāna means less vitality, more frequent depression, less ability to cope with stress, lower resistance to disease.

This model may have important implications for health. Emotional factors may well inhibit the immune system: negative mental states like depression, for example, seem associated with susceptibility to illness. I suggest that not only negative emotional states, but any chronic drain on prāna – including excessive indulgence of the senses – weakens the immune system, leaving it more vulnerable to infection. If true, one promising corollary of this hypothesis is that activities which conserve prāna – training the mind, training the senses – should enhance our capacity to heal ourselves and resist disease.

Up to this point we have been looking only at physical consequences. Yet this is only the surface. There are more subtle consequences which take place in the mind, and the fear of these goes deeper even than the fear of disease.

This level is much more elusive and difficult to talk about, but we have some clues in everyday experience. I think it is Art Hoppe who remarked that someday they will invent a pill to take away every consequence of our actions except guilt. "Guilt" is not a word that I like to use, because there is nothing positive about it. But when we do something selfish, the Gita would say, even if no harmful physical consequences follow that we can see, there will always be a quiet witness inside to observe and comment, "Shabby, shabby, shabby." This is a good sign. The observer is the Self, who is sometimes referred to in yoga psychology as the Inner Witness of all action. The Self is never involved in our behavior, good or bad, or in its consequences, because the Self is not at all physical. But this dry comment of "shabby, shabby, shabby" is its way of reminding our "lower mind" – our emotions, feelings, and senses – that it has not been acting in harmony with the unity of life.

Most of us today never hear this verbalized, as people used to in simpler times. Instead we feel vaguely divided within ourselves – a little uncertain of ourselves, a little anxious, unself-confident, insecure. That is the beginning of fear. If I had to put it into words, I would say it is something like the fear that our behavior is moving us farther and farther from our real Self – in a word, the fear of alienation. The more we indulge a selfish desire, the deeper this fear becomes. In people who are compulsively self-indulgent, the results can be terribly debilitating. Such people can get caught in a vicious circle of behavior: they have a low self-image, expect very little of themselves; so they act the way they believe themselves to be – say, raid the refrigerator on a midnight binge – and plunge their self-esteem even lower.

Fear of being caught in these negative forces goes very deep in us, because without meditation most people feel they are being swept away by a power beyond their understanding or control. Meditation offers great hope to such people, for we can learn to transform these forces completely.

Subtlest of all is the deep, nagging fear that the pleasure in which we are indulging cannot last. Until we have made some progress in meditation, I think it is asking too much of even a good intellect to grasp this. The intellect will object, as my beatnik friends used to, "I don't buy that." And even when it does buy, the mind – our feelings – will balk. "You and your theories," it will say. "To say I suffer from anxiety when I enjoy some private pleasure is absurd." Yet deep down – "on the gut level," as my medical friends say – every one of us knows this fear. The evidence is simple: if we were not afraid, we would not have to clutch at pleasure and try to make it last.

Ultimately, this is the fear of the final deprivation. Death in Sanskrit is called *Antaka,* 'he who puts an end to everything.' This fear is lurking in the depths of the consciousness of every human being – written there, as the Hindu and Buddhist mystics would say, over and over and over through countless lives. Death in the West has been called "the great unknown." The Gita would not agree with this; you can't really fear what you don't know. Each of us does know in the depths of the unconscious what death is like, because each of us has experienced it many times. Even a tiny creature, when it dies, suffers the agony that a human being suffers. Because of this, yoga psychology maintains, every attempt to grasp at some outside support – pleasure, power, prestige, possessions – is prompted at the deepest level by the fear of death. On the downward path, this fear swells until it becomes obsessive. But it can be healed through meditation and the allied disciplines, and the relief from insecurity this brings is one of the great benefits of spiritual living.

आशापाशशतैर्बद्धाः कामक्रोधपरायणाः ।
ईहन्ते कामभोगार्थमन्यायेनार्थसंचयान् ॥ १६-१२ ॥

12. Bound on all sides by scheming and anxiety, driven by anger and greed, they amass by any means they can a hoard of money for the satisfaction of their cravings.

Some years ago I saw a very entertaining movie, *The Treasure of the Sierra Madre.* Humphrey Bogart plays the part of Fred C. Dodds, a man down on his luck in the Mexican port city of Tampico. He and a friend meet up with an old prospector, played by Walter Huston, who knows the gold country of Mexico like the back of his hand. Interestingly enough, though he has spent the greater part of his life prospecting, Walter Huston is rather detached about gold. Bogart feels detached too. "What's gold going to do to change a guy?" he asks. "A guy's a guy, whether money comes to him or not." Walter Huston smiles back knowingly. "You don't know gold," he says.

The three go prospecting together, and after a long while they discover a rich vein. They are hard workers, and they dig and carry for all they're worth. All three are equal partners. But slowly the consciousness of Bogart and his friends is changing, and presently, when a stranger is discovered following them, a very interesting discussion takes place: shall they kill him, or shall they not? Bogart, you know, is a "right guy," and right guys don't kill out of greed: if the man wants to dig too, there is plenty of gold to go around. But the question has been raised, and both men know now in their hearts that there are circumstances under which they would have gone ahead.

Gradually Bogart becomes more entangled. An idea takes hold of him: if the others were gone, the gold would all be his. He projects this idea onto his friend also – "he must be thinking the same thing" – and grows increasingly suspicious. Finally, convinced that the other man wants to kill him for his share, Bogart kills his partner, takes the gold, and runs away.

In the end nobody gets the gold. Poor Fred C. Dodds loses his life, and all the gold dust he and his partners had accumulated is caught up in a sandstorm and dispersed in every direction, hopelessly mixed with sand. Even Hollywood appreciates the law of karma.

"Money can't do anything to a guy," said Fred C. Dodds. "A guy's a guy, whether money comes to him or not." This same "right guy" becomes suspicious, starts to distrust his friends, and ends up murderous, without even realizing what has happened. In a smaller way, this can happen to almost anyone. You don't have to look to movies or history for examples; just look in the daily paper, talk to people around you. You will see how many relationships have been disrupted by the love of money: how many marriages it has broken up, how many friendships embittered, how many families torn in two. Beyond that, on a vaster scale, I can only suggest some of the costs the profit motive exacts from many millions of workers and consumers around the world. We have no idea, I think, of how powerful and how destructive a force the lust for money can be; it can soak up our capacity for sensitivity so insidiously that we do not even see it happening.

Many people would reject categorically the idea that they love money. "I like what it can buy," they might say. "I like to be able to buy whatever I want; who doesn't? But 'love'? Oh, no." This is sincere enough as far as the surface level of awareness goes. But the test of what we love is what we think about, what consumes our attention through most of the day. By this test, it must be admitted, money is one of the top two objects of devotion in the modern world.

When we give our love to money – think about it, read about it, worry over it, measure people and activities by it, give it our attention, our time, our energy – we are helping to spread an epidemic of misery. "Money" here means not only currency but any kind of wealth in the economic sense: the obsession with accumulating material possessions is the same bacillus.

This is not just a moral issue. I am trying to focus on the consequences of greed, not merely on how it deprives other people but on the corrosive effect it has on those it infects. Little by little, the desire to have what we play up everywhere as "the good things of life" – cars, clothes, jewelry, expensive vacations, home entertainment equipment, the million and one ridiculous, costly, useless insignia of excess wealth – can consume so much of consciousness that a father doesn't realize he has neglected to love his children, a wife her husband, a grown-up son his parents.

Let's start with the children. I was shocked to hear a friend say the other day that many young couples think of children as an economic liability. All they do is cost money! One recent magazine article estimated it takes almost one hundred and fifty thousand dollars to raise a child in an average family through the first eighteen years of life. I would question those figures; but in any case, these young couples see that children are going to take a lot of money out of their paychecks for a couple of decades, and they conclude, "Why not spend it on ourselves instead?"

The tragedy is that this realization often comes only after a child is born. Then the child grows up unwanted, a constant burden and irritation to one parent or to both. Many of the million of America's children who run away from home every year must be in this category. Often they say they would return if even a little love awaited them. The homes they leave are often literally empty, with the parents (or parent) away at work during the day and away for entertainment in the evening. Frequently they are escaping from serious abuse or criminal neglect. Frustration in such a family is high. A parent with an unwanted child and strong selfish desires is going to be frustrated often, as the child demands time, costs money, encumbers personal pursuits like recreation or a career, or simply gets in the way. I don't want to go into the details of the kind of treatment that results; it can be terrible and even fatal. Child abuse cases number in the millions, increasing every year, and that is only what is reported; many, many incidents never come to light. I vividly remember one journalist asking a runaway boy why he was living in the streets. "Mister," the boy said, "if you lived with my mother and father, you'd run away too."

Parents today are "putting their own needs ahead of those of their children," a university psychologist said recently. "My concern is that if they don't feel cared about, then they can't ever care about anybody else – or about themselves." They grow up angry, rigid, and unresponsive to those around them – including, of course, their own parents and their own children, if they have any. That is where the law of karma comes in.

It has been many months since Christine and I went to San Francisco. I still think of it as "Baghdad by the Bay," but much of the beauty is gone; it saddens me deeply to see how much this city of St. Francis has ceased to care about its people. Within a block or two of Union Square, I read, thousands of America's grandparents are living alone in poverty and fear. Some have a room in a tawdry hotel, where friends who have worked with these people say they may not have adequate clothing for the cold, or furniture, or sheets and towels, or even food and heat. Soup lines feed some eight to ten thousand people, most of them elderly; for many, it is said, that is the only meal they will get that day. Literally thousands of others do not even have a room; they carry their worldly belongings in a shopping bag and sleep in parks and lobbies and theaters, in constant fear of robbery and attack. Can so many be without families to take them in and help take care of them, even if it means some hardship? The city seems full now of runaway young people and abandoned aged, many of them living in literal starvation and despair; and I am told the same is true in almost every big city in the United States today.

I am glad to say that San Francisco is trying to provide housing for its homeless. I deeply hope other cities will do the same. But these are first-aid solutions. In a country like ours, where national wealth is so high, no one should have to spend the last years of life in such terrible poverty. It is our privilege to help care for those whose income is inadequate, and on a larger scale, the karma for putting desires and careers ahead of the welfare of others is a dog-eat-dog society in which no one should want to live.

Similarly, millions of elderly Americans live in nursing facilities. They may be physically cared for, in the sense of having food to eat and a bed under a roof in which to sleep, but often they have been virtually abandoned by those they love. Their children may send cards on Mother's Day and candy at Christmas, but by their actions they are sending a different message: "We're too busy. We have our own lives to lead. You had your chance to make money and enjoy life; now we're having ours." Tragically, they are probably teaching that attitude to their own children; they may go on to become the abandoned aged of tomorrow.

The reverse can happen too. Many people are entering retirement age with the values of the "me generation": they have money, their children are grown, and they are ready to put themselves first for the rest of their "golden years." Their watchword, I'm told, is "I've paid my dues." Whatever happens to the rest of society is no longer their concern. They are not interested in paying taxes for child-related programs, even schools; they don't want to be bothered with all the troubles that children and teenagers cause; they choose a carefree lifestyle with the intention of avoiding as much of life's difficulties and challenges as possible. An article in the *Saturday Review,* I think, pointed out the central irony: such people are behaving like children again. At a period in life when, with their experience and financial freedom, they could be doing great things to benefit the rest of life, they want to throw all this away and live only for fun. Most of them, I imagine, will tell you candidly that they are not living in fun; they are dying of boredom. As Dr. Selye says, work is a biological necessity. I would add, a spiritual necessity too. We *need* to work, need to give, need to love; otherwise, at any age, we wither and die.

Throughout these verses I am trying to emphasize that greed is a process, the slow corrosion of personality. It can take over our lives quietly, little by little, so that we never feel different from one day to the next; yet like Scrooge in *A Christmas Carol,* we may be appalled toward the end of our lives to see what we have become. But the positive side, as I keep emphasizing, is that because it is a process we can arrest it, turn around, and go the other way. These verses, though grim, are not intended to condemn anyone. They are meant to help us see what tangled jungles of selfishness can grow when common, ordinary self-will is allowed to flourish, so that we remember to weed out self-will every day.

इदमद्य मया लब्धमिदं प्राप्स्ये मनोरथम् ।
इदमस्तीदमपि मे भविष्यति पुनर्धनम् ॥ १६-१३ ॥

13. "I got this today," they say; "tomorrow I shall get that. This wealth is mine, and that will be mine too."

On the highway between my home and Berkeley is a billboard advertising a particular variety of noxious weed. It makes no appeal to logic or taste or sensory satisfaction; it simply touts the brand name: "More."

Whenever I pass I think to myself, "That ad sums up our epoch." The civilization ushered in by the Industrial Revolution, in whose crises we are caught today, has been called the Age of Progress and the Age of Science; I would call it simply the Age of More. The word has two aspects here. The first is *There is always more of everything;* the second, *The more you have, the happier you will be.*

Several years ago I remember reading about a survey done over a wide base of salaries and occupations. One response caught my attention: almost everyone said they would be satisfied if they just had a hundred dollars a month more. The interesting thing was that it didn't seem to matter how much a person was getting; everyone wanted just a little bit more.

That is the human condition. The very nature of the mind is to desire, to desire, to desire; if desires could be satisfied once and for all, the mind would be out of a job. "Today I got this; tomorrow I'm going to get that": the words must have sounded contemporary even in the Stone Age, when the first caveman stepped out of his cave. But through most of history, the vast majority of human beings had narrow limits on what desires they could actually satisfy. The Industrial Revolution changed that, at least for some parts of the world, ushering in what the mystics might call the most potentially explosive epoch in history: an age when, to all appearances, any material desire can be satisfied. This is a terribly dangerous state of affairs; for as Schumacher points out, desires are infinite but material things are limited. There is only so much of everything to go around, and we have so cleverly magnified our means of getting and producing that it is now possible for human greed to despoil an entire planet and impoverish the lives of billions of people.

Recently I read an article celebrating the Great Exhibition of 1851 in London, the world's first industrial fair. The British Empire was at its zenith then, and the exhibit hall that journalists called the Crystal Palace was full of promise: the new engines and inventions of the Industrial Revolution; vast material wealth taken from places like India and China; the world's first display of consumer products. Science was conquering nature, medicine was conquering disease, Europe was conquering Asia and Africa. To those who visited the exhibition, two things must have seemed clear: that there was plenty of the earth's bounty for everyone, and that everything necessary for human happiness could be brought within reach through modern science, commerce, and industry.

There are still a good many people who believe this today, more than a century later. The difference is that it is no longer Great Britain which embodies the promise of prosperity. The ideal worshipped by most of the rest of the globe is the American Dream, which a European economic leader captured in four simple watchwords: "More, bigger, faster, richer."

How vast this promise must have looked in London in 1851! Every door was labeled "More": more lands to discover, more knowledge to acquire, more things to invent, more resources, more markets, more products. Wealth was everywhere, and you could not only pursue and get it but thereby be a benefactor of society. The history of those times is an epic story of Rajas Unbound, freed from every physical limitation – in a word, the story of greed. If you ask historians what made the miraculous progress of modern civilization possible, they will answer something like, "Coal. Iron. The concentration of capital. The rationalization of science." There is truth in all these, but I would answer on another level: "Desire." Behind all the seminal developments of the nineteenth century, you can trace the deep, driving desire for more, more, more. The Age of Progress made a science of greed. We have perfected that science, and now we are beginning to reap the karma.

Look at some examples, which I hope will provide a global perspective for these verses. Sri Krishna is trying to show what the result is when we allow the desire for profit to grow until it breaks out of every natural restraint, so that it is free to do what it likes. There are many sides to this, but here I want to look simply at greed on the largest scale.

It is an axiom of modern business that there is always more money to be made. The polite word for this is "growth." Not only should your bank account always be growing, the rate at which it grows should always be growing too. No matter how much you made last year, this year you should be able to make more.

Where is this growth to come from? The answer is one of the great discoveries of the Age of Rajas: unlimited growth comes from unlimited consumption – more energy, more materials, more capital, more labor. The more you consume, the faster you can grow.

"Progress," in this view, depends on resources being cheap and inexhaustible. Rajas's natural movement is expansive: use up what is cheapest and closest; then, when local resources run out – or get too expensive, which is the same in effect – you look farther afield. Today, of course, we can envision a time when "farther afield" no longer exists, though Asuric Enterprises still talks blithely of mining other planets. We know too that even before a resource runs out, it may simply become too expensive. But at the dawn of the Age of Rajas no one guessed this. Somewhere in the world there was always more to take. Who could consume all of the mineral wealth, the agricultural potential, the cheap labor of the vast continents that lay waiting, perhaps two thirds of the globe?

Thus in need of materials and markets, Asuric Enterprises rushed into the business of empire-building, which is the inevitable end of greed.

Last week I saw a movie version of one of my favorite plays by Bernard Shaw: *Caesar and Cleopatra,* starring Claude Rains and Vivien Leigh. The play was written around the turn of the century, when the British Empire seemed at the height of its power, and Shaw added a biting prologue about imperialism which the movie left out. The Egyptian god Ra comes out onto a dark stage, wearing his hawk's head, and scornfully tells his English audience how empires grow, whether British or Roman:

> Then the old Rome . . . robbed their own poor until they became great masters of that art, and knew by what laws it could be made to appear seemly and honest. And when they had squeezed their own poor dry, they robbed the poor of other lands, and added those lands to Rome until there came a new Rome, rich and huge. And I, Ra, laughed; for the minds of the Romans remained the same size, whilst their dominion spread over the earth.

As an Irishman, Shaw had reason to feel familiar with this process. The English, like the Romans, began at home. When I was in school in India, I remember reading about the terrible Irish potato famine as seen through English eyes. Our books had columns of figures that showed the Irish population shooting upwards, clearly out of control. They were too poor, we were taught, to raise anything except potatoes. But the land ran out – "too many people, too little land," a classic case of Malthusian overpopulation. (We Indians were to consider ourselves warned.) In 1845 the potato blight attacked and destroyed the one food crop of the Irish poor. Within five years at least a million Irish men, women, and children died of starvation; the actual number may be more than a million and a half. Another million or so others escaped to

North America in such terrible destitution that they died in the thousands on ship and shore.

What Shaw knew about this was something we were not taught in our English schools: that Ireland was as much a colony of England as India was. We never thought of this in India, you know. Ireland was part of the British Isles to us, and an Irishman was indistinguishable from an Englishman. So I was surprised to learn later that Ireland was colonized very much the way India was – in fact, the relationship was cemented through military force during the reign of Queen Elizabeth, at roughly the same time that the British East India Company was establishing itself in India.

The parallels continue, beginning with control of land. In Ireland, after a terrible attempt at simply liquidating the population, the Irish were driven off and disenfranchised and their land given to landlords and settlers supplied by England. The English landlords – who, understandably, found it safer as well as more pleasant to live in England and were therefore not in close touch with affairs on their estates – grew not what would feed Ireland but what could produce the greatest profit in England; those profits (and the high rents) were the reason they were in Ireland at all. Just as a gardener might set aside a particular plot for raising tomatoes, Ireland became an agricultural backyard for industrial England.

Over the same period, except for the manufacture of linen in what is now Northern Ireland, Irish industries were undermined and destroyed, creating a huge population of unemployed, landless poor. The English did not need industrial competition. They preferred to take out cheap raw materials and sell back finished goods, which was a highly effective way of making money. This remarkably profitable relationship is the essence of colonialism everywhere. It is the ultimate refinement of the profit motive.

One problem in Ireland was that Irish peasants, who numbered in the millions, did not constitute much of a market. They could not afford to buy back food they grew for others; the price was determined by what could be paid in England. Millions, in fact, could literally not afford anything; they lived in a subsistence economy. With no occupation open to them in Ireland except sharecropping, they had theoretically four alternatives: they could provide cheap labor for industries in England, join the English army, emigrate in destitution, or starve. Most were willing to pay almost anything to rent a piece of some absent landlord's land and till it for his profit. Demand kept rents exorbitant, and demand was forced higher by the fact that to keep surplus commodities from pushing prices down, a good deal of arable land – at least two and a half million acres, according to one English historian – was simply held idle. Nothing was grown on it; no herds were grazed.

The result was that Irish food, insofar as it came back to Ireland at all, fed those who were well-to-do. The poor ate potatoes, the best crop they could raise on a tiny plot of ground. The rest of the land, and all their labor, went to raise grain and other commodities to pay the rent.

In brief, there were not too many Irish for Irish land to support. There was plenty of land, and it supported English landlords bountifully. While perhaps two million Irish starved during the "Great Hunger," ample quantities of meat and grain went on being shipped across the channel for sale in English markets. One contemporary English observer wrote that every ship sailing in with relief grain was sure to meet six ships sailing out with food for England.

As Shaw suggested, the English no sooner began to work this system out at home than they exported it – notably (and most profitably) to India, the "brightest jewel in the British Imperial crown." What happened in Ireland happened in India too, and on a much vaster scale. I should add that the same exploitation took place all over what is now called the Third World, not only at the hands of England but of many other European powers. But India makes a very good example, and one I can write about from personal experience.

Westerners are often surprised when I remind them that ancient India was the United States of the world. It had tremendous wealth and thriving village industries, and in medicine, astronomy, mathematics, and technology India was teacher to the rest of the world. Precisely because of that wealth the country was invaded again and again, some twenty times in its recorded history.

Last to come were the British. Counting from the 1750s, when the

English East India Company began to establish a dominant military presence in Bengal, for almost two centuries India's material resources and labor were systematically drained for British profits, first for enterprising individuals, later for the Crown. And those profits were enormous. "Possibly since the world began," wrote the American historian Brooke Adams, "no investment has ever yielded the profit reaped from the Indian plunder."

This is a very important connection, and one of the great ironies of modern progress: the material development of the West was paid for largely by its colonies in the South and East. In particular, the explosive growth of Britain's industrialization – some fifty years ahead of her competitors – was directly financed by the wealth that poured in from India. One cartoon in an English magazine summed up the relationship very well: the Empire was portrayed as a huge cow with her udder in England, methodically eating up India.

The methods employed for this incredible venture were essentially the same as in Ireland, only more systematic, more sophisticated, and applied on a much vaster scale. Briefly, the English took control of the land and destroyed domestic industries, creating a landless, impoverished work force numbering eventually in hundreds of millions. The colonial government and its beneficiaries could pay minimally for materials and labor while charging impossibly high taxes and rents. On top of everything else, India paid the costs of being looted, up to the point of paying all the expenses of supplying Indian soldiers to die in British wars. This too became a standard feature of colonial rule everywhere.

"Well, so what?" says Rajas. "This is over and done with. Colonialism is dead, and no one mourns it. Why drag in the past?" Because it is not over and done with. I am bringing up the past to write about the present. The idea of systematically developing – or "underdeveloping" – poorer countries as a cheap source of resources and a huge market for finished goods is very much alive. So are the techniques of controlling land and its use, and the basic skill of draining capital. The ways in which global corporations control their land, labor, and sources of materials in the Third World are generally very similar to those developed by the English, French, Dutch, and other colonial powers in those same countries. Huge businesses have taken the place of colonial governments, but the relationships remain the same.

So the colonial inheritance is very much alive. Just last week I was reminded of the specter of bountiful harvests of wheat being shipped out of a starving Ireland when I saw an article describing the tragic famines in the Sahel area of Africa, on the edge of the Sahara. The Sahel is one of the places you see photographed most often when papers, magazines, and television want to show what they call "the face of famine." For years the area experienced severe droughts in which hundreds of thousands of people died. Yet while food aid was being shipped in during the drought, record harvests of food from the same region were being shipped out: peanuts, cotton, vegetables, and beef, the cash commodities that have taken the best agricultural land since the days when the Sahel became a colony of France. The main difference between now and colonial times seems to be that instead of the French government, it is large corporations – mostly French – which profit. Those who starve may not find the distinction of much interest.

In this sense, colonialism is not so much a relationship between two countries as it is an attitude of exploitation. The essence of colonialism is the control of one country's resources – not necessarily its other affairs – by and for some other power, rather than for its own people. It is no longer fashionable for one nation to colonize another, but there are more subtle and effective ways to make money than through outright physical possession. So today we have economic and military colonies: instead of the British Empire in India, for example, an Asuric Fruit Empire in Central America. To me the differences do not seem particularly great. Peasants in Haiti, Mexico, or Bangladesh may not care much who owns their crops. What matters is that they are not theirs, and that they have no control over what they raise, how much they can sell it for, or how they spend the little they can earn.

When Asuric Enterprises comes before the court of karma, it will have some answering to do. We can expect it to ask for rewards rather than punishment, for it claims nothing less than to have financed the progress of modern civilization. Without the free pursuit of profit, according to Rajas, we would still be living in mud huts and dependent